Comparative Politics Today
A WORLD VIEW

Contributors

OLADIMEJI ABORISADE
Obafemi Awolowo University, Nigeria

HOUCHANG E. CHEHABI
Boston University

WAYNE A. CORNELIUS
University of California, San Diego

RUSSELL J. DALTON
University of California, Irvine

FRANCES HAGOPIAN
Harvard University

ARANG KESHAVARZIAN
New York University

THAD KOUSSER
University of California, San Diego

A. CARL LEVAN
American University

MELANIE MANION
University of Wisconsin, Madison

SUBRATA K. MITRA
Universitat Heidelberg, Germany

G. BINGHAM POWELL, JR.
University of Rochester

TIMOTHY J. POWER
St. Anthony's College, Oxford

AUSTIN RANNEY
Late, University of California, Berkeley

THOMAS F. REMINGTON
Emory University

RICHARD ROSE
University of Strathclyde Glasgow

FRANCES ROSENBLUTH
Yale University

MARTIN A. SCHAIN
New York University

KAARE W. STRØM
University of California, San Diego

MICHAEL F. THIES
University of California, Los Angeles

JEFFREY A. WELDON
Instituto Tecnologico Autónomo de Mexico

Comparative Politics Today
A WORLD VIEW

ELEVENTH EDITION

G. Bingham Powell, Jr.
University of Rochester

Russell J. Dalton
University of California, Irvine

Kaare W. Strøm
University of California, San Diego

PEARSON

Boston   Columbus   Indianapolis   New York   San Francisco   Upper Saddle River
Amsterdam   Cape Town   Dubai   London   Madrid   Milan   Munich   Paris   Montréal   Toronto
Delhi   Mexico City   São Paulo   Sydney   Hong Kong   Seoul   Singapore   Taipei   Tokyo

Editorial Director: Dickson Musslewhite
Publisher: Charlyce Jones Owen
Program Manager: LeeAnn Doherty
Editorial Assistant: Maureen Diana
Director of Media and Assessment: Brian Hyland
Media Production Manager: Peggy Bliss
Media Project Manager: Claudine Bellanton
Marketing Manager: Wendy Gordon
Project Manager: Mirella Signoretto
Project Coordination, Text Design, and Electronic Page Makeup: PreMediaGlobal
Senior Project Manager, PreMediaGlobal: Melissa Sacco
Cover Design Manager: Jayne Conte
Cover Designer: Suzanne Behnke
Procurement Manager: Mary Fischer
Procurement Specialist: Mary Ann Gloriande
Printer and Bindery: Courier, Kendalville
Cover Printer: Phoenix Color/Hagerstown

For permission to use copyrighted material, grateful acknowledgment is made to the copyright holders on pp. 726–730, which are hereby made part of this copyright page.

Library of Congress Cataloging-in-Publication Data

Comparative politics today: a world view / edited by G. Bingham Powell, Russell J. Dalton, Kaare W. Strøm—
   Eleventh edition.
    p. cm
   ISBN-13: 978-0-13-380772-1 (alk. paper)
   ISBN-10: 0-13-380772-X (alk. paper)
   1. Comparative government.   I. Powell, G. Bingham.   II. Dalton, Russell J.   III. Strøm, Kaare.
   JF51.C62 2014
   320.3—dc23

                                                                    2013046431

2 3 4 5 6 7 8 9 10

ISBN-10: 0-13-380772-X
ISBN-13: 978-0-13-380772-1

The editors of the eleventh edition of
Comparative Politics Today wish to dedicate this edition to
Richard Rose, whose chapter on Britain (or England)
has been an important part of every edition of
CPT for 40 years.

Brief Contents

Detailed Contents

CHAPTER 19

Politics in the United States   678
by *Thad Kousser and Austin Ranney*

A Guide to Comparing Nations

This analytic index provides a guide to where specific themes are addressed in each chapter.

Topics	Chapters 1–7	Britain	France	Germany	Japan	Russia
History	28–29	152–156	197–198	247–252	298–300	340–344
Social Conditions	3–11	158–159	196–199	252–255	300–301, 308–309	350–352
Executive	109–116	161–166	227–229	257–258	302–304	344–346
Parliament	106–109	166–169	229–232	256–257	301–302	346–349
Judiciary	103–105	169–170	232–233	259–260	305	349–350
Provincial Government	102	156–158, 184–185	233–235	255–256	304–305	350–354
Political Culture	39–47	170–172	200–204	260–264	305–309	354–357
Political Socialization	47–52	172–174	204–208	264–266	309–311	357–358
Participation/Recruitment	56–60	174–176	208–210	266–269	311–312	358–361
Interest Groups	60–72	176–179	210–214	269–272	321–323	361–366
Parties and Elections	78–90	179–183	215–227	272–280	313–321	366–372
Policy Process	96–119	183–188	227–233	280–284	323–326	344–349
Outputs and Outcomes	122–145	188–189	235–238	284–289	326–332	372–379
International Relations	14–15, 143–145	189–191	238–240	289–290	326–328	379–380

China	Mexico	Brazil	Iran	India	Nigeria	United States
387–392	435–443	486–488	536–542	587–591	633–636	682–684
392	469–471	490–492	538, 572	591–595	636–642	685–687
393–394	456–458	493	544	596–599	656	714–715
395–396	452–456	493–494	544–547	599–602	656–657	689–690
396–397	472–474	494–495	545–546	602–603	657	690–691
425–426	451–452	492–493		604–605	653–656	688–689
405–407	443–445	495–499	553–557	613–615	642–647	691–693
403–404	445–448	499–500	557–561		647–650	693–694
400–402, 407–412	448–450, 458–460	500–504	561–562	615–616, 616–617	659–660, 650–652	695–697, 697–699
412–414	460–461	504–508	562–566	605–608	657–659	699–704
393–403	461–468	508–516	547–553	608–612	660–665	704–710
414–419	455	516–518	566–569	600–602	654, 656	712–715
419–425	469–475	518–524	569–573	617–625	666–671	715–719
426–427	475–477	525–526	573–576	621–622	671–673	680–682

A Brief Guide to Analyzing Visuals

We are used to thinking about reading written texts critically—for example, reading a textbook carefully for information, sometimes highlighting or underlining as we go along—but we do not always think about "reading" visuals in this way. We should, because images and informational graphics can tell us a lot if we read and consider them carefully. Especially in the so-called information age, in which we are exposed to a constant stream of images on television and the Internet, it is important to be able to analyze and understand their meanings. This brief guide provides information about the types of visuals you will encounter in *Comparative Politics Today: A World View* and offers some questions to help you analyze everything from tables to charts and graphs to news photographs.

Tables

Tables are the least "visual" of the visuals we explore. They consist of textual information and/or numerical data arranged in columns and rows. Tables are frequently used when exact information is required and when orderly arrangement is necessary to locate and, in many cases, to compare the information. For example, Table 7.3 Health Outcomes makes data on the various measures of citizens' health in many nations organized and easy to compare. Here are a few questions to guide your analysis:

■ What is the purpose of this table? What information does it show? There is usually a title that offers a sense of the table's purpose.

TABLE 7.3
Health Outcomes
Government efforts can help combat the problems of low economic development for citizens' health.

Country	Physicians per 1,000 Citizens, 2011	Life Expectancy at Birth, 2011	Infant Mortality per 1,000 Live Births, 2011	Fertility Rate, 2012
Brazil	1.8	74	14	1.8
Britain	2.8	80	4	1.9
China	1.5	79	13	1.7
France	3.4	82	3	2.0
Germany	3.7	81	3	1.4
India	0.7	65	47	2.5
Iran	0.9	73	21	1.9
Japan	2.1	83	2	1.4
Mexico	2.0	75	13	2.2
Nigeria	0.4	53	78	6.0
Russia	4.3	69	10	1.5
United States	2.4	79	6	2.0

Source: World Health Organization (data downloaded June 9, 2013, from http://apps.who.int/gho/data).

- What information is provided in the column headings (the table's top row)? How are the rows labeled? Are there any clarifying notes at the bottom of the table?

- Is a time period indicated, such as July to December 2009? Or, are the data as of a specific date, such as January 1, 2010? Are the data shown at multiple intervals over a fixed period or at one particular point in time?

- If the table shows numerical data, what do these data represent? In what units? Dollars spent on social service programs? Percentage of voters who support the British Labour Party? Years of life expectancy?

- What is the source of the information presented in the table? Is it government information? Private polling information? A newspaper? A corporation? The United Nations? An individual? Is the source trustworthy? Current? Does the source have a vested interest in the data expressed in the table?

Charts and Graphs

Charts and graphs depict numerical data in visual forms. The most common kinds of graphs plot data in two dimensions along horizontal and vertical axes. Examples that you will encounter throughout this book are line graphs, pie charts, bar graphs, and timelines. These kinds of visuals emphasize data relationships: at a particular point in time, at regular intervals over a fixed period of time, or, sometimes, as parts of a whole. Line graphs show a progression, usually over time. (as in Figure 17.2 Chronology of Casualties: Kashmir 1988–2011.)

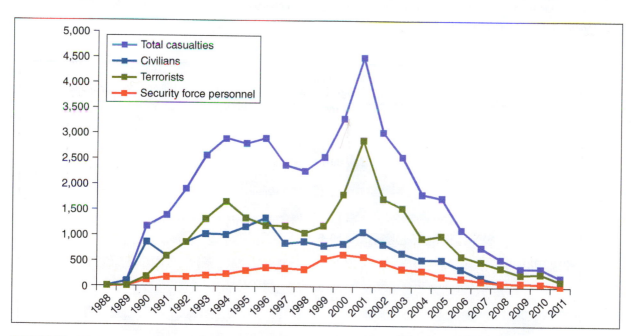

FIGURE 17.2
Chronology of Casualties: Kashmir (1988–2011)
Source: www.satp.org.

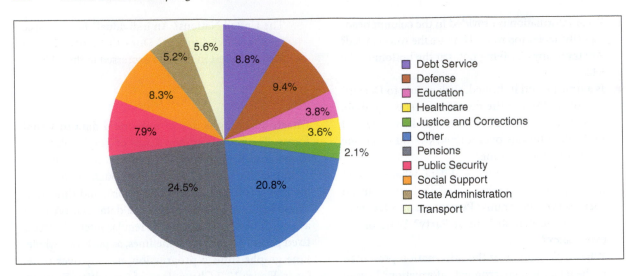

FIGURE 12.7

Russian State Budget Breakdown, 2013

Pensions take up a full quarter of the state budget, an expense that is likely to grow in coming years. It exceeds spending on education, health care, and assistance to the needy combined.

Source: Ministry of Finance website, www.minfin.ru

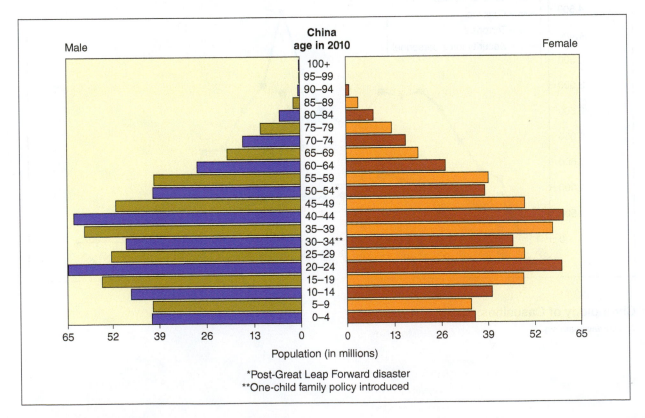

FIGURE 13.5

Population Structure, 2010 Midyear, by Age and Sex

Policies since the 1970s have reduced population growth in the world's most populous country.

Source: U.S. Census Bureau, International Data Base, www.census.gov/ipc/www/idb/country.php.

Pie charts (such as Figure 12.7, 2013 Russian Federal Budget) demonstrate how a whole (total government spending) is divided into its parts (different types of government programs). Bar graphs compare values across categories, showing how proportions are related to each other (as in Figure 13.5, showing the male and female populations in China by age bracket). Bar graphs can present data either horizontally or vertically. Timelines show events and changes over a defined period of time (such as the list of prime ministers of Britain in Figure 8.2). You will also encounter charts that map out processes and hierarchies throughout this book (as in the structure of the government of Nigeria shown in Figure 18.4).

Many of the same questions you ask about tables are also important when analyzing graphs and charts (see above). Here are more questions to help you:

- In the case of line and bar graphs, how are the axes labeled? Are symbols or colors used to represent different groups or units?
- Are the data shown at multiple intervals over a fixed period or at one particular point in time?
- If there are two or more sets of figures, what are the relationships among them?
- Is there distortion in the visual representation of the information? Are the intervals equal? Does the area shown distort the actual amount or the proportion? Distortion can lead you to draw an inaccurate conclusion on first sight, so it's important to look for it.

Maps

Maps of countries, regions, and the world are very often used in political analysis to illustrate demographic, social, economic, and political issues and trends. See, for example, Figure 16.1, Map of Iran's Ethnic Minorities.

Though tables and graphs might sometimes give more precise information, maps help us to understand, in a geographic context, data that are more difficult to express in words or numbers alone. Here are a few more questions to add to those in the above sections:

- What does the map key/legend show? What are the factors that the map is analyzing? Are symbols or colors used to differentiate sections of the map? Maps can express information on political boundaries, natural resources, ethnic groups, and many other topics, so it is important to know what exactly is being shown.

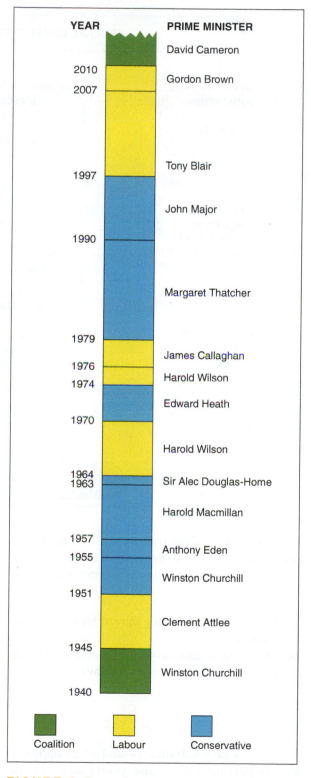

FIGURE 8.2

Long- and Short-Term Tenures at Downing Street
Prime Ministers and Governments since 1940.

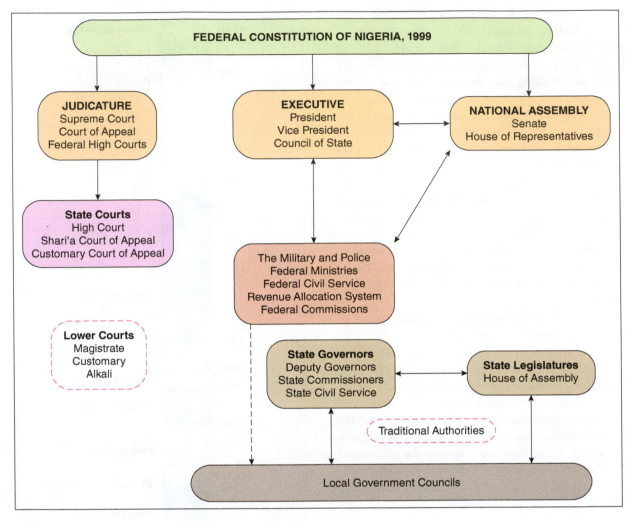

FIGURE 18.4

The Structure of Government under the 1999 Constitution

Nigeria has a presidential system with a bicameral legislature.

Source: Based on United Nations Development Program, Human Development Report 2009.

- What is the region being shown? How detailed is the map?
- Maps usually depict a specific point in time. What point in time is being shown on the map?

News Photographs

Photos can have a dramatic—and often immediate—impact on politics and government. Think about some photos that have political significance.

For example, do you remember the photos from the September 11, 2001, terrorist attacks? Visual images usually evoke a stronger emotional response than do written descriptions. For this reason, individuals and organizations have learned to use photographs to document events, make arguments, offer evidence, and even, in some cases, manipulate the viewer into having a particular response. The photo of a student protester confronting tanks in Tiananmen Square (page xix) captured the attention of the world and drew attention to the violent response of

Map of Iran's Ethnic Minorities

www.lib.utexas.edu/maps/middle_east_and_asia/iran_ethnoreligious_distribution_2009.jpg

Facing Down the Tanks in June 1989

In 1989, ordinary Chinese participated in the largest spontaneous protest movement the communists had ever faced. A lone protester shows defiance of regime violence in his intransigent confrontation with a Chinese tank.

Jeff Widener/AP Images

the Chinese government to the protesters. Here are a few questions to guide your analysis:

- When was the photograph taken? (If there is no date given for the photograph in its credit line or caption, you may be able to approximate the date according to the people or events depicted in the photo.)
- What is the subject of the photograph?
- Why was the photo taken?

- Is it spontaneous or posed? Did the subject know he or she was being photographed?
- Who was responsible for the photo (an individual, an agency, or an organization)? Can you discern the photographer's attitude toward the subject?
- Is there a caption? If so, what information does it provide? Does it identify the subject of the photo? Does it provide an interpretation of the subject?

Preface

We are glad to introduce this eleventh edition of *Comparative Politics Today: A World View*, which for the past three decades has been among the most influential textbooks in comparative politics. The world continues to grow more interdependent. Students are exposed to more cultures and communities; their lives and careers are affected by events around the world. An appreciation of comparative politics is becoming ever more essential. As a text, *Comparative Politics Today* is ideally suited for courses that combine a broad and comprehensive thematic overview with rich and high-quality country studies written by expert scholars in their respective fields.

The eleventh edition of *Comparative Politics Today* continues to teach students to understand politics through the conceptual system, process, and policy framework that Gabriel Almond introduced. The early editions of this book pioneered the teaching of systematic comparison of the political cultures, structures, processes, and policy performances of the world's political systems. Later editions have described how enormous changes—such as democratization and backsliding, the breakup of the Soviet empire, globalization, intensified threats from ethnic and religious conflict, and international economic recession—have shaped politics in many nations. Throughout, these editions build on the strong theoretical foundation that Almond constructed and apply his framework to the changing concerns of students of political science.

New to This Edition

There are many new features of this eleventh edition of *Comparative Politics Today*:

- A substantially revised set of theory chapters (1–7) introduces the key concepts and theories that are applied in the country studies. Data tables and references have been updated, with more of our countries systematically covered. A more extensive use of graphs and charts better illustrates relationships and enhances the text.

- Chapters 1, 3, and 7 provide more thorough discussion of globalization and its components and consequences. Chapters 1 and 2 have also been reorganized to create a more reader-friendly introduction.

- Chapter 7 introduces its concept of "political goods" with reference to the United Nations Millennium Goals and systematically treats policy goals and consequences, including welfare, fairness, liberty, and security outcomes. The chapter now includes a discussion of politicides, cases of extreme government abuses of their own populations.

- All chapters now include learning objectives keyed to the main chapter headings, as well as review questions designed to emphasize the key themes of each chapter.

- All of the country studies have undergone major revision and updating. A brief summary of the major changes includes:

  - Britain—The 2010 election produced Britain's first coalition government since World War II. The chapter describes how the coalition government of Conservatives and Liberal Democrats under the prime ministership of David Cameron has performed.

  - France—French voters rejected President Sakozy's bid for a second term in May 2012 and elected a self-confessed "normal" Socialist, François Hollande, as president. But even with a new legislative majority, Hollande's policy initiatives have had mixed successes.

  - Germany—In the recent 2013 election, voters strongly endorsed Angela Merkel's largely successful economic policies. But the FDP, her previous government partner, lost its legislative representation. A complex bargaining process eventually resulted in a grand coalition between the Merkel-led CDU/CSU and the SPD.

- Japan—The election of 2012, reinforced by the 2013 upper house election, returned the Liberal Democrats to government. The LDP prime minister, Shinzō Abe, has begun a dramatic reform program intended to revive the national economy.

- Russia—The 2012 election of Vladimir Putin to a third presidential term is covered, as well as the continuing slide toward autocracy and human rights abuses.

- China—China's Communist Party managed a successful transition to a "fifth generation" of leaders and was able to sustain continuing economic expansion and growing international economic influence, while still suppressing human rights and political challenges.

- Mexico—The 2012 election of President Enrique Peña Nieto brought the once-dominant PRI party back into power for the first time since Mexico's democratizing election of 2000. The chapter describes the new president's initiatives and efforts to deal with divided government in the context of an increasingly active citizenry using social media to hold politicians accountable.

- Brazil—Dilma Rousseff was elected president in 2011. She is continuing the economic and social programs of the Workers Party that began under the popular Lula administration.

- Iran—Hassan Rouhani's election as president in 2013 may mark a fundamental change in Iran's foreign and domestic policies—and a sharp break from Ahmadinejad's administration. Although he served in previous Iranian governments, Rouhani has expressed support for reform causes and has opened a dialogue with Western governments over their sanctions against Iran's nuclear program.

- India—India continues to face the dual challenges of deepening democracy and improving the economy in a global setting. The booming IT sector and some decline in militancy in Kashmir have created opportunities, but many obstacles remain.

- Nigeria—Nigeria continues its longest period of civilian rule under President Goodluck Jonathan, confirmed in a nationwide election in 2011. But intensified regional divisions, religious conflict, and massive corruption make governing difficult and democracy fragile.

- United States—President Barack Obama's re-election in 2012 is discussed, along with the continuing Republican control of the House of Representatives and the problems of policymaking under conditions of divided government and intense policy polarization between Democrats and Republicans.

With all these revisions and improvements, we hope and believe that this eleventh edition of *Comparative Politics Today: A World View* will serve students and instructors across the world better than ever.

Features

This newest edition begins by explaining why governments exist, what functions they serve, and how they create problems as well as solutions. The first chapter also introduces the three great challenges that face most states in the world today: building a common identity and sense of community, fostering economic and social development, and securing democracy, human rights, and civil liberties. Chapter 2 sketches the concepts needed to compare and explain politics in very different societies: political systems and their environments, structures and functions, and policy performance and its consequences. Jointly, these two chapters spell out the unique framework that this book employs.

Chapters 3 through 6 elaborate important political structures, functions, and processes. They discuss the causes and consequences of political cultures, interest groups, parties and other aggregation structures, constitutions, and key structures of policymaking. The unprecedented spread of democracy in recent decades is not only a development to celebrate but also a reason that issues of democratic representation, as discussed in Chapters 4 through 6, are increasingly relevant to an ever-larger share of the world's population. Growing prosperity in many parts of the world means that the challenges of development and public policy (Chapters 1 and 7) are changing. Chapter 7 compares the policies and their consequences in a framework consistent with the United Nations Millenium goals. These chapters give an unusually rich account of political processes in highly diverse environments. They provide theoretical foci and empirical benchmarks for the country chapters that follow.

While the global incidence and human costs of war have declined in recent years, conflicts still devastate or threaten communities in regions such as

Afghanistan, the Middle East in the aftermath of the Arab Spring, South Asia, Sudan, and other parts of Africa. Moreover, the world faces enormous challenges, new as well as old, in such areas as climate change, migration, globalization, epidemic disease, international terrorism, and nuclear proliferation. All these developments make it more important than ever to understand how political decisions are made and what their consequences might be, in the very different political systems that make up our political world. This edition, like the last, emphasizes democratization and globalization, particularly examining the international financial crisis of 2008–2011 and its continuing effects on rich as well as poor countries.

The bulk of the book, Chapters 8 through 19, presents systematic analyses of politics in twelve selected countries. In each case, the distinguished specialists who have contributed to this volume begin by discussing the current policy challenges facing citizens of that country and then provide a historical perspective on its development. Each chapter then uses the system, process, and policy framework to highlight the distinctive features of that country's politics. The most recent elections, leadership, and policy changes in each country are discussed. The systematic application of a consistent framework facilitates comparison among countries, and "A Guide to Comparing Nations" (pp. xii–xiii) helps students and instructors navigate such comparisons. The "Brief Guide to Analyzing Visuals" helps students understand and utilize the tables, graphs, maps, and photographs. The in-depth country studies in our book encompass all the major regions of the world, including five developed democratic countries (England, France, Germany, Japan, and the United States), six developing countries at various levels of democracy and dictatorship (Brazil, China, India, Iran, Mexico, and Nigeria), and Russia, with its fascinating blend of development and poverty, democracy and authoritarianism. The book thus includes most of the world's large and influential countries and illustrates a wide range of political possibilities, problems, and limitations.

Supplements

Pearson is pleased to offer several resources to qualified adopters of *Comparative Politics Today* and their students that will make teaching and learning from this book even more effective and enjoyable. Several of the supplements for this book are available at the Instructor Resource Center (IRC), an online site that allows instructors to quickly download book-specific supplements. Please visit the IRC welcome page at www.pearsonhighered.com/irc to register for access.

MyPoliSciLab This premium online learning companion features multimedia and interactive activities to help students connect concepts and current events. The book-specific assessment, video case studies, mapping exercises, comparative exercises, newsfeeds, current events quizzes, and politics blog encourage comprehension and critical thinking. With Grade Tracker, instructors can easily follow students' work on the site and their progress on each activity. Use ISBN 0-13-383338-0 to order MyPoliSciLab with this book. To learn more, please visit www.mypoliscilab.com or contact your Pearson representative.

Instructor's Manual/Test Bank This resource includes learning objectives, lecture outlines, multiple-choice questions, true/false questions, and essay questions for each chapter. Available for download only from the Pearson Instructor's Resource Center (IRC).

Pearson MyTest This powerful assessment generation program includes all of the items in the instructor's manual/test bank. Questions and tests can be easily created, customized, saved online, and then printed, allowing flexibility to manage assessments anytime and anywhere. To learn more, please visit www.mypearsontest.com or contact your Pearson representative.

PowerPoint Presentation Organized around a lecture outline, these multimedia presentations also include photos, figures, and tables from each chapter. Available for download only from the Pearson Instructor's Resource Center (IRC).

Atlas of World Issues (0-205-78020-2) From population and political systems to energy use and women's rights, the *Atlas of World Issues* features full-color thematic maps that examine the forces shaping the world. Featuring maps from the latest edition of *The Penguin State of the World Atlas*, this excerpt includes critical thinking exercises to promote a deeper understanding of how geography affects many global issues. To learn more, please contact your Pearson representative.

Goode's World Atlas (0-321-65200-2) First published by Rand McNally in 1923, *Goode's World Atlas* has set the standard for college reference atlases. It features hundreds of physical, political, and thematic maps as well as graphs, tables, and a pronouncing index. Available at a discount when packaged with *Comparative Politics Today*.

Acknowledgments

We are pleased to acknowledge the contributions of some of the many people who helped us prepare this eleventh edition of *Comparative Politics Today*.

We would like to thank the following individuals for their careful reviews and analyses of the book:

Luis F. Clemente, Ohio University
Howard Cody, University of Maine
Zachary Irwin, Pennsylvania State University
Erie Julie Van Dusky-Allen, Keuka College

Our co-authors wish to acknowledge their gratitude to a number of individuals who have contributed to their respective chapters. Kaare Strøm wishes to thank Lydia L. Lundgren for research assistance on several chapters. Frances Rosenbluth and Michael Thies thank Yui Margaret Komuro, Kota Matsui, and Evan Walker-Wells for research assistance on the Japan chapter. Subrata Mitra wishes to thank Lionel Koenig and Radu Carciumaru for assistance on the chapter on India. A. Carl LeVan thanks Peter Glover for research assistance with the Nigeria chapter. Thad Kousser thanks Mona Vakilifathi for research assistance with the U.S. chapter.

Our thanks also go to the editorial and production teams, at Pearson: Charlyce Jones Owen, Publisher; LeeAnn Doherty, Program Manager; Mirella Signoretto, Project Manager; Barbara Ryan, Permissions Project Manager; Annette Linder, Image Permissions Coordinator; and Maureen Diana, Editorial Assistant; and at PreMediaGlobal: Melissa Sacco, Senior Project Manager; and James Fourtney, Permissions Researcher.

G. Bingham Powell, Jr.
Russell J. Dalton
Kaare W. Strøm

CHAPTER 1

Challenge and Change in Comparative Politics

LEARNING OBJECTIVES

1.1 Briefly describe the public and authoritative aspects of political decisions.

1.2 Discuss the challenges of building a national identity for a nonhomogeneous population.

1.3 Explain the processes and challenges of economic development, giving specific examples from various countries.

1.4 Describe the characteristics of representative democracy and the connections between economic development and democratization.

1.5 Discuss the positive and negative effects of globalization.

1.6 List five ways in which a government can help its citizens.

1.7 List five ways in which a government can harm or hinder its citizens.

In the past few decades, the world has undergone a fundamental transformation that will affect the rest of our lives, especially for the young. One of the most dramatic changes was the Third Wave of democracy.[1] After forty years of Cold War conflict between East and West, and the dominance of autocratic governments in the Third World, the collapse of the Berlin Wall in 1989 expanded the new era of **democratization**, which had begun a decade earlier. The communist nations of Eastern Europe shed their autocratic regimes almost overnight, and developed into new and often vibrant democracies. Other nations in East Asia, Africa, and Latin America participated in this democratic transition, allowing hundreds of millions to enjoy democratic freedoms. Today, democracy has become the dominant method of organizing government, even if democratic development is still incomplete.

Behind this democratic transition has been a slow but relatively steady process of **socioeconomic modernization** in most regions of the globe. In the 1980s, a quarter of the world's population lived in absolute poverty, unable to meet everyday food and shelter needs and struggling with disease and the consequences of poverty. The number of people living in absolute poverty has dropped by nearly 1 percent a year since then, as the world's population has continued to grow.[2] In China alone, economic growth has taken 600 million people out of absolute poverty since 1981. In 2008, for the first time in history, less than half of the people in sub-Saharan Africa lived below the poverty line. Even in the advanced industrial democracies of Western Europe and North America, income levels and social conditions continued to improve compared to the 1950s and 1960s. The global recession of 2008 produced a partial retrenchment in socioeconomic conditions, but the world today is much richer and more socially secure than a generation or two ago.

This process of socioeconomic modernization has many consequences. Modernization has expanded the educational levels of the world's population, providing the skills and resources that lead to better occupations and hopefully to better citizens. In advanced industrial democracies, this has meant the expansion of university and graduate degrees; in the developing world, this has meant increasing rates of literacy and basic education. About 90 percent of the world's population is now literate.[3] The impact of modernization has especially transformed the conditions of women. In many developing nations, women were formerly second-class citizens, excluded from economic and political life. Literacy rates have increased the most for women, birth rates have fallen, and women's participation in the labor market in developing nations has expanded dramatically. In advanced industrial democracies, more women are being elected to governmental offices and taking high-ranking business jobs. Economic growth has also increased access to health care across the world, and contributed to dramatic progress in medical science. Among your own family, there are probably relatives who would have died in the 1950s and 1960s because necessary care was unavailable. And modernization has increased our access to information about the world and our lives. From the Nigerian taxi driver who watches the news on his cell phone to the Japanese college student who is connected 24-7, we live in a new information age. Often, social modernization is unsettling and evokes conflict, but the long-term benefits have improved the quality of life for most of the world's population. Moreover, these societal changes contribute to the expansion of democracy and citizen rights in both developed and developing societies.

The third force transforming contemporary societies is the rapid process of **globalization**, in which nations have become more open to and dependent on one another. Globalization has many faces. One is increasing trade in goods and services, which means that many of the products we buy are made in China and many of the telephone calls we make are answered in India. Outsourcing and loss of local jobs have been among the negative consequences of this aspect of globalization. Globalization has lowered the prices of many products and increased the richness of life. Globalization may also mean that citizens of all (or most) countries increasingly share common norms of an international system. But these effects have also created serious challenges for many states. Some, such as North Korea, Myanmar, and Iran, have sought to isolate themselves from its effects. Others have responded in a more accepting manner. Most of the industrialized countries of Europe have created a common market economy and a set of supranational political institutions embodied in the European Union.

What Is Comparative Politics?

1.1 Briefly describe the public and authoritative aspects of political decisions.

A key factor in these changes in the world today is the government system—which is the focus of this book. Governments, on their own or as representatives of their citizens, take policy actions that can foster or retard economic development. They are the primary guarantor of the rights and liberties of the citizens; sometimes they are the greatest threats to these liberties. They take actions that expand or retard the living conditions of their citizens. When nations must work together in the international system, governments attend international conferences and sign treaties. When states go to war, it is typically through the actions of a government or semigovernmental organization.

This book describes the variations in the governments and political systems that take these actions and make decisions affecting the nation. The actions of government constantly touch our lives. Our jobs are structured by government regulations, our homes are built to conform to government housing codes, public schools are funded and managed by the government, and we travel on roads maintained by the government and monitored by the police. Politics thus affects us in many important ways. Therefore, it is important to study how political decisions are made and what their consequences are.

Politics deals with human decisions, and political science is the study of such decisions. Yet not all decisions are political, and many of the social sciences study economic and social decisions that are of little interest to political science. Political scientists study decisions that are *public* and *authoritative*. The public sphere of politics deals with collective decisions that extend beyond the individual and private life, typically involving government action. Most of what happens within families, among friends, or in social groups belongs to the private sphere and is not controlled by the government. In totalitarian states, like East Germany before 1989 or North Korea today, the public sphere is very large and the private sphere is very limited. The state tries to dominate the life of its people, even intruding into family life. On the other hand, in some less developed nations, the private domain may almost crowd out the public one. Many people may be uninvolved in politics and are untouched by the decisions made in the nation's capital. Western democracies have a more balanced mix of private and public spheres. However, the boundaries between the two spheres are redrawn all the time and may be a matter of contention.

Political decisions are also authoritative. Authority means that formal power rests in individuals or groups whose decisions are expected to be carried out and respected. Governments and other authorities may use persuasion, inducements, or brute force to ensure compliance. For instance, a religious authority such as the pope has few coercive powers. He can persuade, but rarely compel, the Catholic Church's followers. In contrast, tax authorities, such as the U.S. Internal Revenue Service, can both exhort and compel people to follow their rules.

Thus, *politics* refers to activities associated with the control of public decisions among a given people and in a given territory, where this control may be backed up by authoritative means. Politics involves the crafting of these authoritative decisions—who gets to make them and for what purposes.

Our approach to studying the political process is based on two principles. The first was articulated by the late Seymour Martin Lipset, who frequently said that he who knows one country knows no country. Lipset's argument was that in order to understand any one nation and its government, we need to compare it to others to see what is truly distinctive or similar relative to other nations. For instance, all governments face the challenge of raising taxes; by comparing different tax systems across nations, we see the benefits and limits of various tax policies. We might think that the conditions in one nation are dependent on specific institutional arrangements or the nation's political history, but we can only determine this by comparing nations with different institutions or histories. The nature of good science, including political science, is comparison—and this book follows this premise by comparing a dozen nations of varying social and political conditions.

Our second principle is that to compare political systems and their governments, we need a conceptual framework that facilitates comparison of what are seemingly quite different elements. How does one compare, for example, the theocratic government of Iran with the centuries-old democracy in Britain, or the governing experience in Nigeria? Comparing apples and oranges is difficult, but it can be done. This book builds on a theoretical model that compares the governing process in its basic elements, connecting these elements together to describe the overall political process (see Chapter 2).[4]

We live in one of the most exciting times to study politics. The end of the Cold War created a new international order, although its shape is still uncertain. Democratic transitions in Latin America, Eastern Europe, East Asia, and Africa have transformed the world, although it is unclear how many of these new democracies will endure and what forms they might take. Throughout the world, globalization brings the citizens of different countries closer together and makes them more dependent on one another, for better or worse. Some of the issues that people in many societies confront—such as climate change and achieving international peace—are transnational and indeed global. Part of their solutions, we hope, lies in the political choices that people in different communities make about their collective future. In this book, we try to give you a sense of how governments and politics address these challenges.

Challenges: Building Community

1.2 Discuss the challenges of building a national identity for a nonhomogeneous population.

One of the first, perhaps the first, challenge that a new state faces is to build a national community. Most states do not have a homogeneous population, and instilling a sense of shared identity can be difficult to accomplish. Building a common identity and a sense of community is important because conflicts over national, ethnic, or religious identities can be explosive causes of political turmoil, as we have witnessed in Iraq, the former Yugoslavia, and the Sudan. It is difficult to advance socially, economically, or politically if the citizens of a region do not share some common bond and a commonly accepted set of goals.

While building community is a common challenge, some countries are in a much better situation than others. Japan, for example, has an ethnically homogeneous population, a common language, and a long national political history. Most Japanese share in the religions of Buddhism and Shintoism, and the country is separated by miles of ocean from its most important neighbors. Nigeria, in contrast, is an artificial creation of British colonial rule and has no common precolonial history. The population is sharply divided between Muslims and Christians; the Christians are divided equally into Catholics and Protestants. There are some 250 different ethnic groups in Nigeria, speaking various local languages in addition to English. Obviously, the challenges of building community are much greater in Nigeria than they are in Japan. The challenge of community building is most prominent in the developing world, where current political structures are relatively young, although even Europe faces challenges, as in Basque and Scottish autonomy movements.

Building a common sense of community is often described as part of a process of nation building. The word *nation* is frequently used interchangeably with the word *state*, as in the *United Nations*. Strictly speaking, however, we use the term **nation** to refer to a group of people with a common identity. That common identity may be built upon a common language, history, race, or culture, or simply upon the fact that these people have occupied the same territory. Nations may or may not have their own state or independent government. In some cases—such as Japan, France, or Sweden—there is a close correspondence between the memberships of the state and the nation. Most people who identify themselves as Japanese do in fact live in the state of Japan, and most people who live in Japan identify themselves as Japanese.

In other cases, states are *multinational*—consisting of a multitude of different nations. The Soviet Union, Yugoslavia, and the Sudan were multinational states that broke apart. Some nations are much larger than the corresponding states, such as Germany for most of its history or China. Other nations have split into two or more states for political reasons, such as Korea today and Germany between 1949 and 1990. Some groups with claims to be nations have no state at all, such as the Kurds, the Basques, and the Tamils.

Ethnicity

Ethnic groups are typically defined by common physical traits, languages, cultures, or history. Like nationality, **ethnicity** need not have any objective basis in genetics, culture, or history. German sociologist Max Weber defined ethnic groups as "those human groups that entertain a subjective belief in their common descent because of similarities of physical type or of customs or both, or because of memories of colonization and migration. . . . [I]t does not matter whether or not an objective blood relationship exists."[5] For example, the Serbs, Croats, and Muslim Bosnians may believe they are descended from different ancestors and hence are physically different as well. Over centuries, originally homogeneous populations may intermix with other populations, even though the culture may continue.

In many developing countries, the former colonial powers established boundaries that cut across ethnic lines. In 1947, the British withdrew from India and divided the subcontinent into a northern Muslim area—Pakistan—and a southern Hindu area—India. The most immediate consequence was a terrible civil conflict and "ethnoreligious" cleansing. There still are almost 100 million Muslims in India and serious religious tensions. Similarly, forty years ago, the Ibo ethnic group in Nigeria fought an unsuccessful separatist war against the rest of the country, resulting in the deaths of roughly a million people. The Tutsi and Hutu peoples of the small African state of Rwanda engaged in a civil war of extermination in the 1990s, with hundreds of thousands of people slaughtered and millions fleeing the country in fear of their lives.

The migration across state boundaries is another source of ethnic differentiation. The American descendants of formerly enslaved Africans are witnesses to the largest coercive labor migration in world history. In contrast, today, there are Indians, Bangladeshis, Egyptians, and Palestinians seeking better lives in the oil sheikhdoms around the Persian Gulf, Mexican and Caribbean migrant workers moving to the United States, and Turkish and North African migrants relocating to Europe. Two scholars refer to the contemporary world as living through an "Age of Migration" comparable in scale to that of the late nineteenth and early twentieth centuries.[6]

The later chapters of this book will focus on twelve states to illustrate the detailed working of the political process and how governments are structured to address the challenges they face. All twelve of these nations still include a significant ethnic or racial minority. For example, recent migration has made such previously homogeneous states as Britain, France, Japan, and Germany more multiethnic. Other countries, such as the United States, have long been multiethnic and have become even more so. India and Nigeria were multicultural regions that took on national form with colonization and decolonization. Russia reflects the diversity of

Globalization Takes Many Forms
German universities now have a diverse student body drawn from around the world.

historical empire building. Moreover, globalization and migration seem destined to increase the diversity of many societies worldwide.

Language

Another challenge in building community may be language differences. Language can be a source of identity that may overlap with ethnicity. There are approximately 5,000 different languages in use in the world today, and a much smaller number of language families. Most of these languages are spoken by relatively small tribal groups in the developing world. Only 200 languages have a million or more speakers, and only 8 may be classified as world languages.

English is the most truly international language. Close to one-third of the world's population lives in countries in which English is one of the official languages. Other international languages include Spanish, Arabic, Russian, Portuguese, French, and German. The language with the largest number of speakers, though in several varieties, is Chinese (with well over a billion speakers). The major languages with the greatest international spread are those of the former colonial powers—Great Britain, France, Spain, and Portugal.

Linguistic divisions can create particularly thorny political problems. Political systems can choose to ignore racial, ethnic, or religious differences among their citizens, but it is more difficult to function using several languages. Linguistic conflicts typically show up in controversies over educational policies, or over language use in the government. Occasionally, language regulation is more intrusive, as in Quebec, where English-only street signs are prohibited and large corporations are required to conduct their business in French.

Religious Differences and Fundamentalism

States also vary in their religious characteristics. In some—such as Israel, the Irish Republic, and Pakistan—religion is a basis of national identity for most of the population. Iran is a theocratic regime, in which religious authorities govern and religious law is part of the country's legal code. In other societies, such as Poland under communism, religion can be a rallying point for political movements. In many Latin American countries, the clergy have embraced a liberation theology that fosters advocacy of the poor and criticism of government brutality.

Christianity in its various forms is the largest and most widely spread religion in the world today. Roughly one-third of the world's population belongs to the Christian Church, which is divided into three major groups—Roman Catholics, Protestants (of many denominations), and Orthodox (e.g., Greek and Russian). Catholics are dominant in Europe and Latin America; there is a more equal distribution of Catholics and Protestants elsewhere. While the traditional Protestant denominations have declined in North America in the last decades, three forms of Protestantism—fundamentalist, Pentecostal, and evangelical—have increased there, and also, especially, in Latin America and Asia. The Muslims are the second largest religious group and the most rapidly growing religion. Between one-fourth and one-fifth of the world's population is Muslim, and it is concentrated in Asia and Africa. Islam has become revitalized in Central Asia, and Muslims have been particularly successful in missionary activities in sub-Saharan Africa.

Religion typically guides the social and political behavior of its supporters. This may lead one to be concerned about others, or become a source of intense disagreement with those who hold different beliefs. For instance, religious groups often battle over such issues as the rules of marriage and divorce, child rearing, sexual morality, abortion, the emancipation of women, and the regulation of religious observances. Religious communities often take a special interest in educational policies in order to transmit their ideas and ethics. On such issues, religious groups may clash with one another as well as with more secular groups.

Religious fundamentalism has emerged in some form in all major faiths, often in reaction to social modernization. While each religion disagrees over the interpretation of its sacred texts and values, fundamentalists believe in the absolute truth of their religion in relation to others. Some want political life to be organized according to their sacred texts and doctrines. The rise of fundamentalism has affected the entire world. For example, India has frequent confrontations between Hindus and Muslims; Nigeria sees conflict between Muslims and Christians.

Too often, religious fundamentalists employ violence to assert their positions. These acts of terrorism are intended to stagger the imagination, frighten, and weaken the will. The September 11, 2001, jihadist attacks on the World Trade Center and the Pentagon involved not only suicide pilot–hijackers but also aircraft filled with volatile fuel and innocent passengers converted into immense projectiles. These attacks were followed by jihadist assaults in Bali, Madrid, London, Riyadh, and other cities. Many nations worldwide now face the challenge of dealing with international terrorism by religious and other extremists.

Fostering Economic Development

 1.3 Explain the processes and challenges of economic development, giving specific examples from various countries.

The nation of Bhutan has a national goal to develop its level of Gross National Happiness (GNH). The Bhutanese idea is to measure social progress in terms of the quality of life in more holistic and psychological terms than the standard measures of economic well-being. Its Buddhist religious heritage has led to government programs and research to increase the happiness of the society, even though it is a low-income nation.

Bhutan is very unusual; people in most political systems want their government to foster social and economic development. Thus, economic and social development are important state goals. Economic development implies that people can enjoy new resources and opportunities, and that parents can expect their children to do at least as well as themselves. Many people expect government to improve their living conditions through economic growth, providing jobs, and raising income standards. The success of governments—both democratic and autocratic—is often measured in economic terms.

In affluent, advanced industrial societies, contemporary living standards provide for basic social needs (and much more) for most of the public. Indeed, the current political challenges in these nations often focus on problems resulting from the economic successes of the past, such as protecting environmental quality or managing the consequences of growth. New challenges to social welfare policies are emerging from the medical and social security costs of aging populations. For most of the world, however, substantial basic economic needs still exist, and governments focus on improving the socioeconomic conditions of the nation.

Over the past two to three decades, economic growth has transformed living conditions in many nations more than in any similar period in the past.

Construction in China
With the Chinese government encouraging economic growth and foreign investment, the Shanghai skyline is now a mix of high-rises and construction cranes.

The United Nations Development Program (UNDP) combines measures of economic well-being, life expectancy, and educational achievement into its Human Development Index (HDI).[7] The HDI shows dramatic improvements in life conditions in many regions of the world over the past three decades (see Figure 1.1). East Asia and South Asia have made substantial improvements since 1980. For instance, in 1975, South Korea and Taiwan had a standard of living close to many poor African nations, and they are now affluent societies. Even more striking is the change in the two largest nations in the world. China improved from a low HDI in 1975 (the same as Botswana or Swaziland) to a level that is close to Russia or Brazil by 2012; India followed a similar upward trajectory. These statistics represent improved living conditions for billions of people. Living conditions in sub-Saharan Africa have also recently begun to improve. Although severe economic problems remain, this development trend is improving the living conditions of hundreds of millions of people, freeing them from absolute hunger and poverty, and providing the resources so their lives can improve in other ways.

The process of economic development typically follows a common course. One element is a transformation of the structure of the labor force from an agrarian to an industrial and then an advanced industrial economy. The five advanced industrial countries in this book all have agricultural employment of less than 10 percent of the labor force. Poor countries, in contrast, often have more than two-thirds of their labor forces employed in agriculture. In addition, economic development is typically linked to urbanization as peasants leave their farms and move to the cities. In nations undergoing rapid economic development, such as China, urban migration creates new opportunities for the workers but also new economic and social policy challenges for the governments.

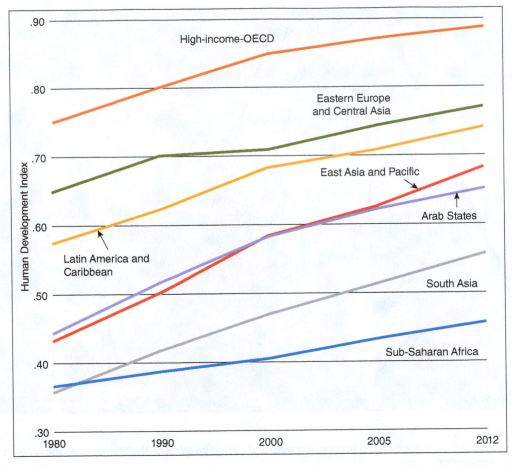

FIGURE 1.1

Changes in Human Development Index by Region

Source: United Nations Development Program, *Human Development Report 2013* (New York: United Nations, 2013).

Figure 1.2 presents the wide gap in living standards that still exists across the hundred largest nations in the world, and shows how levels of affluence affect basic social conditions. The horizontal axis in the figure aligns nations in terms of the **gross national income (GNI)** per capita, which is a measure of national affluence. The vertical axis displays average number of years of education for the population that is over fifteen years of age. The twelve core nations discussed in this book are highlighted in red.

Two things are obvious. Perhaps the most striking feature of this figure is the wide gap in living standards that still exists across nations worldwide, including eleven of the nations in this book. The level of affluence per capita is about twenty times higher in the Western advanced industrial democracies than in Nigeria.[8] Second, affluence is strongly related to the educational levels of a nation's people. The fit between

education and income is so strong that the United Nations combines these two items (and other statistics) to define the HDI.

Income levels and education are also related to other measures of social development. The countries with the fewest literate citizens also have the fewest radios and television sets—even though these devices do not require literacy. Economic development is also associated with better nutrition and medical care. In the economically advanced countries, fewer children die in infancy, the impact of disease is limited, and the resources exist to improve the quality of life in many ways. Improvements in living conditions have substantially increased life expectancy in many low-income nations, such as Mexico and China. However, the average life expectancy of a Nigerian is less than fifty years, it is sixty-three years for an Indian, and over eighty years for a Japanese. Material productivity,

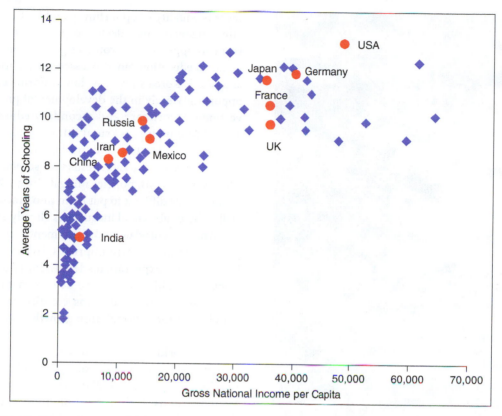

FIGURE 1.2

National Affluence and Schooling

Economic development improves the resources and opportunities of the public as seen in rising education levels.

Source: World Bank Indicators for 2011. Gross National Income is per capita based on purchasing power parity; years of schooling is for the population over age fifteen. Figure is based on 150 largest nations by population for which data are available.

education, exposure to communications media, and longer and healthier lives are closely interconnected.

Thus, low-income nations face the urgent issues of economic development: how to improve the immediate welfare of their citizens yet also invest for the future. Political leaders and celebrities, such as Bono and Angelina Jolie, have mobilized public awareness that these differences in living conditions are a global concern—for those living in the developing world, for the affluent nations and their citizens, and for international organizations such as the United Nations and the World Bank.

Problems of Economic Development

While economic development can be a partial solution to many of a country's needs, it can also create new challenges. Health, income, and opportunity are rarely evenly distributed within nations, and the unequal distribution of resources and opportunities can stimulate political conflict. A high national income may conceal significant poverty and lack of opportunities in some sectors of society. A high rate of national growth may benefit only particular regions or social groups, ignoring other parts of the population. Parts of the "inner cities" of the United States, the older parts of Delhi and Kolkata in India, remote and landlocked parts of many African states, many rural areas in China, and the arid northeast of Brazil all suffer from poverty and hopelessness, while other parts of these countries experience growth and improved welfare. Moreover, rapid economic development may increase such inequalities.

Generally speaking, economic development improves the equality of income, at least past a certain stage of economic growth. Wealthy nations like Japan, Germany, and France have relatively more egalitarian income distributions than middle- or low-income countries. Still, the wealthiest 10 percent in

Poverty in Third World Countries
Poverty in Third World countries is illustrated by this scene of a back street in Kolkata, India, where the poor make their beds in the streets. Similar scenes, though on a lesser scale, are to be encountered in modern American cities, where homeless people sleep on the sidewalks and in doorways.

Japan receive about the same total income as the poorest 40 percent receive. This is a large gap in life conditions between the rich and poor, but the gap is even wider in less affluent nations. In Mexico, a middle-income country, the ratio is closer to three to one; in Brazil it is more than five to one. The United States has higher inequality than Japan and the countries of Western Europe, but lower than most other countries. In Russia and other postcommunist societies, the development of new capitalist markets generated new income inequalities. Research suggests that a nation's political characteristics make a difference. India has consciously worked to narrow inequality, while inequality in China has steadily increased.

Various policies can mitigate the hardships economic inequality causes in developing societies. If there is equality of opportunity and high social mobility, inequality may decline over time and may not seem so oppressive to younger generations. Investments in education can also lessen inequality. Taiwan and South Korea show how land reforms equalized opportunity early in the developmental process. Investment in primary and secondary education, in agricultural inputs and rural infrastructure (principally roads and water), and in labor-intensive industries produced remarkable results for several decades. Thus, some growth policies mitigate inequalities, but it can be very difficult to put them into practice, especially where substantial inequalities already exist.

Another correlate of development is population growth. As health care improves, living standards increase, life expectancies lengthen, and populations grow. This is a positive development because it represents improved living conditions for these people, but rapid population growth also can pose new policy challenges. Some projections estimate that the world's population will increase to 7 billion by 2015, and poorer countries will see a more rapid rate of growth. In 2005, Hania Zlotnik of the United Nations (UN) population division estimated that "out of every 100 persons added to the [world's] population in the coming decade, 97 will live in developing countries."[9] Rapid economic growth in the developing world can create significant burdens for these nations.

These prospects have produced a development literature that mixes both light and heat. Economist Amartya Sen warns of a "danger that in the confrontation between apocalyptic pessimism on one hand, and a dismissive smugness, on the other, a genuine understanding of the nature of the population problem may be lost."[10] He points out that one of the first effects of "modernization" is to increase the population rapidly as new sanitation measures and modern pharmaceuticals reduce the death rate. As an economy develops, however, changing conditions tend to reduce fertility. With improved education (particularly of women), health, and welfare, the advantages of lower fertility become clear, and population growth rates decline.

Today, the native populations are decreasing in many affluent European nations because fertility rates are below levels necessary to sustain a constant population size. This pattern also seems to be occurring in parts of the developing world. Thus, annual population growth in the world has declined over the last two decades. The rate of population growth in India, for

Environmental Challenges
The world's increasing energy use is causing serious environmental challenges. The burning of fossil fuels—such as coal, oil, and gas—pollutes our air, water, and atmosphere, whereas nuclear power plants, such as this one in Northern Bohemia, pose the risk of nuclear radiation.

example, was 2.2 percent in the 1970s and has since declined. Latin America peaked at a higher rate and then came down sharply. Sub-Saharan Africa continues to experience relatively high birth rates.[11]

Economic growth can have other social costs. For instance, advanced industrial societies are dealing with the environmental costs of industrial development and a consumer society. Despoiled forests, depleted soils and fisheries, polluted air and water, nuclear waste, and endangered species now burden their legislative dockets. With increasing industrialization and urbanization in the developing world, many of these environmental problems could worsen. At the same time, some environmental problems are even more acute in less developed countries, where population growth and urbanization create shortages of clean air, clean water, and adequate sanitation.[12] And economic growth in a world based on a carbon economy has raised the new issue of global climate change that will impact the planet as a whole. Thus, economic development generally improves the living conditions of the public, but in the process, it produces new policy problems that governments must address.

Fostering Democracy, Human Rights, and Civil Liberties

1.4 Describe the characteristics of representative democracy and the connections between economic development and democratization.

Another major force transforming contemporary political systems is the democratization process, which includes the enhancement of **human rights** and the expansion of freedom. Democracy is the form of government to which most contemporary countries, more or less sincerely and successfully, aspire. A **democracy**, briefly defined, is a political system in which citizens enjoy a number of basic civil and political rights, and in which their most important political leaders are elected in free and fair elections and are accountable under a rule of law. Democracy literally means "government by the people."

In large political systems, such as contemporary states, democracy is achieved primarily through a process of citizen representation. Elections, competitive political parties, and representative assemblies make some degree of democracy—some degree of "government by the people"—possible. Representative democracy is not complete or ideal. But the more citizens are involved and the more influential their choices, the more democratic the system.

In contrast, **authoritarian** political systems lack one or several of democracy's defining features. Authoritarian states can take several forms (see Chapter 6). In **oligarchies**, literally "rule by the few," a small political elite withholds political rights from the majority of the population. South Africa until the abolition of apartheid in the early 1990s is a good example. Other authoritarian states, such as China or Zimbabwe, are party, military, or personal dictatorships. **Totalitarian systems**—such as Nazi Germany, the Soviet Union under Joseph Stalin, or North Korea today—are systems in which the government constricts the rights and privacy of its citizens in a particularly severe and intrusive manner.

As societies become more complex, richer, and more technologically advanced, the probability of public involvement and democratization increases. In the first half of the twentieth century, most Western states became democracies. After World War II, a second democratic wave—which lasted from 1943 until the early 1960s—saw both newly independent states (such as India and Nigeria) and defeated authoritarian powers (such as Germany and Japan) set up the formal institutions of democracy.[13]

Another round of democratic transitions began in 1974, involving Southern Europe, East Asia, Latin America, and a number of African states—the so-called "Third Wave" of democratization.[14] The most dramatic changes came in Central and Eastern Europe, where, in a few short years, the Soviet empire collapsed, and these countries rapidly converted to democracy; many joined the European Union. Similarly, much of Latin America has shifted from dictatorships (often military) to democracy. The end of the apartheid regime in South Africa was equally dramatic. Most recently, the Arab Spring has produced regime change in several North African nations, but the ultimate outcomes of these popular revolutions is still uncertain.

As a result of these three democratization waves, democracy has become a common goal of the global community (see Figure 1.3). In the 1970s, only a third of the world's independent countries had competitive party and electoral systems. Communist governments, other single-party governments, and other authoritarian regimes dominated the landscape. By 2013, almost two-thirds of states had a system of electoral democracy, and human rights and liberties were similarly spreading to more of the world's population.[15] The number of

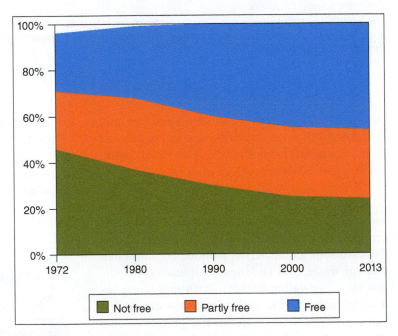

FIGURE 1.3

Growth in Free Governments over Time

The Free World has been growing.

Source: Freedom House, *Freedom in the World 2013* (www.freedomhouse.org). The figure displays the percentages for all states.

democracies has been stable over the past decade, with advances balanced by some backward movements.

This democratization process is broadly linked to the social modernization of nations.[16] Economic development transforms societies in ways that typically encourage democratization by creating autonomous political groups that demand political influence, expanding the political skills of the citizenry, and creating economic complexity that encourages systems of self-governance. Social modernization also transforms the political values and political culture of the public, which increases demands for a more participatory system (see Chapter 3). New democracies are much more likely to endure when founded in economically developed societies. Yet democracy typically does not come about overnight or as an immediate reaction to changing social conditions. It often takes time to establish

the conditions fostering democracy, create democratic institutions, and educate the public to comply with the rules of the democratic process.

Figure 1.4 illustrates the relationship between a nation's level of social modernization (the gross national income per capita on the horizontal axis) and the development of democracy (the World Bank's voice and accountability index on the vertical axis).[17] These two traits are strongly related. The figure shows that it can be especially difficult to consolidate democracy in less economically developed societies. In some developing nations, democratic processes fail to produce stable institutions and effective public policies and eventually give way to some form of authoritarianism. In Nigeria, for example, military coups overthrew democratically elected (but badly flawed) governments in 1966 and again in 1983, and redemocratization did not happen

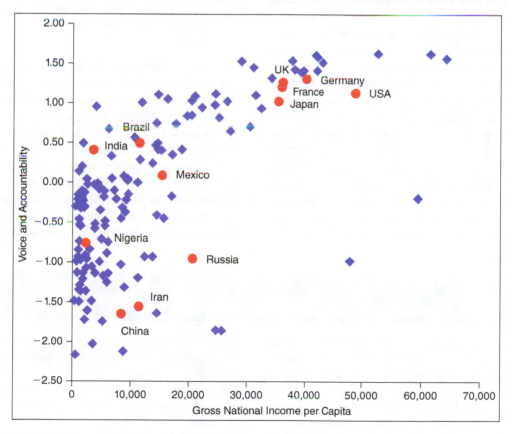

FIGURE 1.4

National Affluence and Democratic Development

Affluence increases the likelihood that a nation will have a more democratic political system, but this is not a perfect relationship.

Source: World Bank Indicators for 2011. Gross national income is per capita based on purchasing power parity; based on 150 largest nations by population for which data are available.

until 1999. Even today, democracy in Nigeria is limited. Nigeria is by no means unique. Transition can move in either direction, toward or away from democracy. Often the entrenched political class uses coercion or the threat of force to maintain their political control. For example, China has made major economic advances in recent years, but the regime limits those factors that might press for democratization and the expansion of citizen rights. And Russia has regressed democratically under Vladimir Putin's leadership. At the same time, India has been the counterexample by embracing democracy since gaining independence. So the relationship between social modernization and democracy is strong, but not total.

Democratization is also an ongoing process. Even when states adopt democratic institutions, there is no guarantee that they will grant human rights and civil liberties to all their people. In addition, the definition of appropriate rights and liberties evolves. Democracies have to balance between respecting the will of the majority and protecting the rights of the minority. Even when political rulers sincerely try to promote human rights and civil liberties (which is by no means always the case), they do not always agree on the nature of those rights.

A good example of the spread of rights and liberties—and cultural differences in the definition of rights—involves gender issues. Governments in Western industrial societies favor gender policies that guarantee equal access for women in society, the workplace, and politics. The UN and other international organizations are advocates of women's rights. But gender norms often vary across cultural zones. The UN's statistics indicate that many developing nations hesitate to grant equal rights to women, restricting their education and their involvement in the economy and politics.[18] Restrictions on women's rights are often stark in many Arab states, where they clash with social norms and religious beliefs. Ironically, improving the status of women is one of the most productive ways to develop a nation politically and economically (see Box 1.1), for example, by improving educational and health standards and stabilizing birth rates. In short, expanding human rights is an ongoing process in the world today, and there is much room for further progress.

The Contribution of Globalization

 Discuss the positive and negative effects of globalization.

Most social scientists agree that the globalization process is affecting both socioeconomic and political development—but they disagree on whether the consequences are positive or negative.[19] Discussions of globalization typically focus on the economic side. International trade of goods and services has increased, which has created massive investments in the economic infrastructure of developing nations. Product production shifts to where costs are lowest or production is most efficient. For example, Levi's jeans sold in the United States have been made in over a dozen different

---

nations in recent years, with only a single factory left in the United States. Products made in China may have been designed in California and use raw materials from Australia, memory chips from South Korea, and design elements patented in Europe. Then these products are shipped to a global customer base.

Some experts stress the positive economic effects of globalization. Globalization lowers the prices of many products, which benefits consumers in the nations that buy products from this international network. Access to new goods also expands choices. The production nations benefit from foreign direct investment and increased employment for their citizens. Indeed, the appeal of working in a factory for better wages is a magnet that draws millions to urban areas in developing nations. Consequently, a country's participation in the global economy is positively related to its levels of economic and democratic development.

At the same time, other experts point to the negative effects of globalization. Outsourcing and the loss of jobs hurt individuals, who often face unemployment as a result. A global economy exerts downward pressures on salaries in those parts of the economy that are part of the international system. There are repeated examples of companies exploiting workers in developing nations with sweatshop-like conditions.

Most discussions of globalization focus on its economic aspects, but it has important social and political effects as well.[20] Globalization promotes the diffusion of international norms as societies interact more and become more interdependent. For instance, greater participation in international trade and investment generates pressures to lessen economic corruption in developing nations. Globalization also appears to benefit the social and economic status of women, who gain rights and responsibilities that come from a developing nation's participation in international commerce and the social norms and equal rights values of the international system. Globalization has mixed effects, but in overall terms, it has positive benefits on the global economy and the spread of human rights, and those countries that shield themselves from fair trade generally suffer.

What Governments Do

1.6 List five ways in which a government can help its citizens.

A recent libertarian science fiction book begins with the scenario of a group of travelers landing at an airport after a long overseas flight. As they disembark from the plane, they notice that there are no police checking passports, no customs officers scanning baggage, and no officials applying immigration rules.[21] They have landed in a society without government, and the puzzle is what having no government would mean for the citizenry. The answer is: a great deal (see Box 1.2). As philosophers have pointed out, there are many reasons why people create governments and prefer to live under such a social order—in part because governments are important vehicles for addressing the challenges that face these societies.

BOX 1.2

U.S. Government's Top Ten List

Paul Light surveyed 450 historians and political scientists to assess the U.S. government's greatest achievements in the second half of the twentieth century. Their top ten list is as follows:

- Help rebuild Europe after World War II
- Expand the right to vote for minorities
- Promote equal access to public accommodations
- Reduce disease
- Reduce workplace discrimination
- Ensure safe food and drinking water
- Strengthen the nation's highway system
- Increase older Americans' access to health care
- Reduce the federal deficit
- Promote financial security in retirement

Several of these policy areas will be discussed in Chapter 7, but note that the first of these accomplishments had to do with the country's external environment: rebuilding Europe after World War II. Other achievements include important public goods (safe water, highways), as well as promoting fairness and building a social safety net.

Source: Paul Light, *Government's Greatest Achievements of the Past Half-Century* (Washington, DC: Brookings Institution, 2000) (www.brookings.edu/comm/reformwatch/rw02.pdf).

Community and Nation Building

As noted earlier, one of the first purposes of governments is to create and maintain a community in which people can feel safe and comfortable. Governments can help generate such communities in many different ways—for example, by teaching a common language, instilling common norms and values, creating common national myths and symbols, and supporting a national identity. However, sometimes such actions create controversy because there is disagreement about these norms and values.

Nation-building activities help instill common worldviews, values, and expectations. Using a concept discussed more in Chapter 3, governments can help create a shared **political culture**. The political culture defines the public's expectations about the political process and its role within the process. The more the political culture is shared, the easier it is to live in peaceful coexistence and engage in activities for mutual gain.

Security and Order

Many experts claim that only strong governments can make society safe for their inhabitants; providing security and law and order is one of the most essential tasks of government. Externally, security means protecting from attacks against the country. Armies, navies, and air forces typically perform this function. Internally, security means protecting against theft and violence by members of one's own society. In most societies, providing this protection is the police's function.

Providing security and order is a critical function of modern governments. While governments worldwide have privatized many of the services they once performed—for example, those involving post offices, railroads, and telecommunications—few, if any, have privatized their defense forces or police. This shows that security is one of the most essential roles of government. The jihadist terrorist attacks in New York City and Washington, D.C., on September 11, 2001, and subsequent attacks in London, Madrid, and elsewhere underscore the importance of security.

Protecting Rights

Thomas Jefferson reflected a larger reality when he wrote about the importance of "life, liberty and the pursuit of happiness" in the Declaration of Independence.

A prime goal of government is to protect social and political rights, such as freedom of speech and association, and protection against various forms of discrimination and harassment. Governments also play a key role in protecting the rights of religious, racial, and other social groups. Human development stresses the expansion of these rights and liberties, and governments play a key role in this process.

John Locke, an early political theorist, considered property rights to be another critical factor in developing a prosperous and lawful community. Without effective protection of property rights, people will not invest their goods or energies in productive processes. If you were an entrepreneur, would you invest your time in growing a business or expanding a farm if you didn't believe you were safe from someone (or the government) claiming the fruits of your labors? Unless property rights exist and contracts can be enforced, people will be hesitant to trade and invest. Anything beyond a subsistence economy requires effective property rights and contracts.

Many analysts argue that one of the most restrictive limitations on economic development in the Third World is the government's inability (or unwillingness) to guarantee such rights. Peasant families in many societies have lived for generations on a plot of land but cannot claim ownership, which erodes their incentive and opportunity to invest in the future.

Promoting Economic Efficiency and Growth

Economists have long debated the government's potential role in promoting economic development. Neoclassical economics shows that markets are efficient when property rights are protected, when competition is rigorous, and when information is freely available. When these conditions do not hold, however, markets may fail and the economy may suffer.[22]

Governments are especially important in providing **public goods**, such as clean air, a national defense, or disease prevention. Public goods mean that if one person enjoys them, they cannot be withheld from other members of the public. Consider clean air. In general terms, it is impossible to provide one person with clean air without also giving it to his or her neighbors. Moreover, my enjoyment of clean air does not mean that my neighbors have any less of it. Analysts often claim that because public goods are shared, and thus cannot be produced by individual action, only government can provide the right quantity of them.

Governments can also address the problems that arise when an economic activity has consequences that are not borne by the producer or the user. For instance, a company may produce environmental pollution if it ignores the environmental impact of its production methods. Polluting factories, waste dumps, prisons, and major highways can impose large costs on those who live near them. Governments can help protect people from such consequences or ensure that burdens are fairly shared.

Governments can also promote fair competition in economic markets. For example, governments can ensure that businesses follow minimum standards of worker protection and product liability. In other cases, the government may control potentially monopolistic companies to ensure that they do not abuse their market power. This happened in the nineteenth century with railroad monopolies, and more currently with technology monopolies such as Microsoft and Google. In these cases, the government acts as the policeman to prevent the economically powerful from unfairly exploiting their power.

Social Justice

Many people argue that governments should promote social justice by redistributing wealth and other resources among citizens, and that a just distribution of resources is necessary for effective citizenship and a prosperous economy.[23] In many countries, the distribution of income and property is highly uneven, and this is particularly troubling when there is little upward mobility or when inequalities tend to grow over time.

Government can redistribute resources from the better-off to the poor to lessen inequality and maximize a society's potential. Many private individuals, religious and charitable organizations, and foundations also do much to help the poor, but they generally do not have the capacity to tax the wealthy or expand social and educational programs to help the disadvantaged. Governments do, at least under some circumstances. Many tax and welfare policies redistribute income, although the degree of redistribution is often hotly disputed (see Chapter 7).

Some experts argue that governments should attempt to equalize the conditions of all citizens. Others prefer governments to redistribute enough to equalize opportunities, and then let individuals be responsible for their own fortunes. Yet people in most nations agree that governments should provide a social safety net and give their citizens opportunities to reach certain minimum standards of living.

Protecting the Weak

Governments should protect individuals and groups that are not able to speak for themselves. Groups such as the disabled, the very young, or future generations cannot effectively protect their own interests. Governments can protect future generations by, for example, preventing them from being saddled with economic debts or environmental degradation. In recent decades, governments have become much more involved in protecting groups that are politically weak or disenfranchised, such as children, the old, and the infirm or disabled, as well as nonhumans—from whales and birds to trees and other parts of our natural environment.

When Does Government Become the Problem?

 1.7 List five ways in which a government can harm or hinder its citizens.

Governments serve many political functions, yet their intervention is not always welcomed or beneficial. When and how government intervention is necessary and desirable are disputed issues in modern politics. During the twentieth century, the role of governments expanded enormously in most nations. At the same time, criticisms of many government policies have persisted and sometimes intensified. Such debate is directed at virtually all government activities, especially the economic role of government. Anarchism and libertarianism are two political and philosophical traditions that are critical of the role of modern governments. But they differ in their main concerns. Libertarians see the greatest problem of government as its encroachment on individual freedoms, whereas anarchists are concerned primarily with the threats that governments pose to social communities.

Destruction of Community

Some critics of government argue that it destroys natural communities. Government, they hold, implies power and inequality among human beings. Those who have power are corrupted, and those without it are degraded and alienated. For example, the philosopher Jean-Jacques Rousseau claimed that only people unfettered by government can form bonds that allow them to develop their full human potential. By imposing an order based on coercion, hierarchy, and the threat of force, governments destroy natural communities. The stronger government becomes, the greater the inequalities of power. Such arguments stimulated criticism of communism as limiting the potential and freedom of its citizens. Others argue that strong governments create a "client society," in which people learn to be subservient to authorities and to rely on governments to meet their needs.

Violations of Basic Rights

Just as governments can help establish many essential rights, they can also use their powers to violate these rights in the most serious manner. The potential abuses of government power illustrate a dilemma that troubled James Madison and other founders of the American Revolution: the challenge of creating a government strong enough to govern effectively but not so strong that it could destroy the rights of its citizens. They understood the irony that to protect individuals from each other, societies can create a government that has even more power to coerce the individual. Libertarians are especially concerned about the abuses and violations of basic freedoms that large governments may thus enable.

During the twentieth century, some governments violated basic human rights on a massive scale. Millions lost their lives to political persecution. Such horrors happened not only in Nazi extermination camps and during Stalin's Great Terror in the Soviet Union but also on a huge scale in China, Cambodia, and Rwanda. In other instances, governments stripped minority groups of their basic civil and human rights. Some governments did learn that with great power comes great responsibility.

Economic Inefficiency

Governments can help economies flourish, but they also can distort and restrict a state's economic potential. President Robert Mugabe, for instance, has destroyed the economy of Zimbabwe, which was once Africa's most prosperous state. Similar examples exist in many struggling economies. Economic problems may arise even if government officials do not actively abuse their power. Government regulation of the economy may distort the terms of trade and lower people's incentives to produce. Further inefficiencies may arise when governments actually own or manage important economic enterprises. This is particularly likely if the government holds a monopoly on an important good, since monopolies generally cause goods to be undersupplied and overpriced. Moreover, government industries may be especially prone to inefficiency and complacency compared to private firms. Such experiences have caused citizens in both developing and advanced industrial economies to worry about the potential negative economic effects of government policy.

Government for Private Gain

Society also may suffer if government officials make decisions to benefit themselves personally, or select policies to get themselves reelected regardless of whether those policies are best for the society. For instance, a local mayor plans an economic development project that will benefit his friends or supporters who own suitable land or who will supply contracts for the project. In another example, a government might enact a particularistic policy to advance its reelection, even though it recognizes the negative effects on the country as a whole. Such actions can impose large costs on society because policies are chosen for the private benefits they produce rather than for their social efficiency and because groups may expend great resources to control these spoils of government. These policies may turn into outright corruption when influence is traded for money or other advantage (see Box 1.3).

This kind of political exploitation is a particularly serious problem in poor societies. Holding political office is often an effective way to enrich oneself when political watchdogs such as courts and mass media are too weak to constrain government officials. Besides, many developing societies do not have strong social norms against using government for private gain. On the contrary, people often expect those in government to use their power to benefit themselves, their families, and their neighbors. Even in many advanced democratic societies, public officeholders are expected to appoint their supporters to ambassadorships and other public posts, although civil service rules may constrain such appointments. The temptations of office holding are

BOX 1.3   The Struggle Halting Corruption

What happens if politicians use their power in their own self-interest or to benefit individuals or groups that support them? One small example is the governor of an oil-producing region in Nigeria. Governor Diepreye Alamieyeseigha embezzled tens of millions of U.S. dollars in public funds and acquired real estate all over the world. Unfortunately for him, the London police found more than $1 million in cash at his home there. Dressed in drag, he escaped back to Nigeria. To his surprise, his state legislature impeached him, and in 2007,

Alamieyeseigha pleaded guilty to failing to declare his assets. He was sentenced to two years in prison but released the next day for time served. Then in March of 2013, his friend, the president, pardoned him. By some estimates, Africa loses up to a tenth of its national income to corruption that runs from the highest to the lowest levels of government and the economy.

Source: Adam Nossiter, "U.S. Embassy Criticizes Pardons in Nigerian Corruption Cases," *New York Times,* March 15, 2013.

---

great. Despite legal rules, press scrutiny, and citizen concerns, few governments anywhere finish their terms of office untainted by some corruption scandal. In Lord Acton's famous words, "Power tends to corrupt, and absolute power corrupts absolutely."

Vested Interests and Inertia

Government-created private gains are difficult to change or abolish once they have been established, because some people enjoy government jobs, contracts, or other favors. The larger the government and the more attractive the benefits it provides, the more likely it is that such vested interests will resist change (unless change means even larger benefits). Therefore, any government will foster officeholders and beneficiaries with an interest in maintaining or enlarging the government itself. Such groups may become a powerful force in favor of the status quo.

This situation makes it difficult to change government policies or make them more efficient. Once established, agencies and policies often live on far beyond their usefulness. For example, when the Spanish Armada threatened to invade England in 1588, the government established a military observation post at Land's End in southwest England. This observation post remained in place for four centuries! In the United States, the Rural Electrification Administration was created in 1935 to bring electricity to rural America. Although the country had long been electrified by then, the agency persisted for almost sixty years until it was finally merged into the Rural Utilities Service in 1994.

Such interests are particularly likely in political systems that are constructed to limit rapid political change. While the checks and balances in political systems such as in the United States are designed to safeguard individual rights, they may also protect the privileges of vested interests. Yet even political systems that contain far fewer such checks may exhibit an excess of political inertia. Britain is an excellent example. Until recently, the House of Lords represented the social groups that dominated British society before the Industrial Revolution more than 200 years ago (noblemen, bishops, and judges). Only in the last few years has Britain begun reforming the House of Lords to eliminate features that reflect Britain's feudal and preindustrial past.

Looking Forward

The last several decades have been a period of tremendous social, economic, and political change in the world. Economic development, improved living standards, the spread of human rights, and democratization have improved the life chances and life conditions of billions of individuals. In most of the world, the average child born today can look forward to a longer, better, and freer life than his or her parents—especially if that child is a girl.

At the same time, continuing social, economic, and political problems remain. Progress in one area can create new opportunities, but also new problems in another area. Economic development, for example, can sometimes stimulate ethnic strife and destabilize political institutions. Economic development can also disrupt social life. And the process of development has been uneven across and within nations. Many basic human needs still remain in too short supply.[24]

Even in the affluent democracies, as one set of policy issues is addressed, new issues come to the fore. Western democracies struggle to address issues of environmental quality, changing lifestyles, and the challenges of globalization. A more affluent and better-informed citizenry may also be less inclined to trust political parties, interest groups, parliaments, and political executives. Success in meeting these old and new challenges can improve the living conditions for the world's populations, decrease international conflict, and come closer to meeting the ideals of humankind.

Governments and politics have played a large role in human societies of the past. Some of their policies have greatly improved the quality of life of their citizens, while others have been disasters. Yet one way or another, governments and their activities are central to our political futures. Our goal in this book is to examine the ways in which citizens, policymakers, and governments address the policy challenges that face them today.

REVIEW QUESTIONS

■ What are the main challenges that countries face in building a political community?

■ What are the causes and consequences of economic development?

■ What are the causes and consequences of democratization?

■ How does globalization contribute to economic development and democratization?

■ What are the potential positive and negative outcomes of government activity?

KEY TERMS

authoritarian
democracy
democratization
ethnicity

globalization
gross national income (GNI)
human rights

nation
oligarchy
political culture
public goods

religious fundamentalism
socioeconomic modernization
totalitarian systems

SUGGESTED READINGS

Acemoglu, Daron, and James Robinson. *Why Nations Fail: The Origins of Power, Prosperity, and Poverty.* New York: Random House, 2012.

Bhagwati, Jagdish. *In Defense of Globalization.* Oxford: Oxford University Press, 2007.

Castles, Stephen, and Mark Miller. *The Age of Migration: International Population Movements in the Modern World,* 4th ed. New York: Guilford Press, 2009.

Horowitz, Donald. *Ethnic Groups in Conflict.* Berkeley: University of California Press, 1985.

Huntington, Samuel. *The Third Wave: Democratization in the Late Twentieth Century.* Norman: University of Oklahoma Press, 1991.

———. *The Clash of Civilizations and the Remaking of World Order.* New York: Simon & Schuster, 1996.

Lijphart, Arend. *Patterns of Democracy,* 2nd ed. New Haven, CT: Yale University Press, 2012.

Morris, Ian. *Why the West Rules—For Now: The Patterns of History, and What They Reveal About the Future.* New York: Farrar, Straus and Giroux, 2010.

Przeworski, Adam, Michael E. Alvarez, Jose Antonio Cheibub, and Fernando Limongi. *Democracy and Development: Political Institutions and Well-Being in the World 1950–1990.* New York: Cambridge University Press, 2000.

Sachs, Jeffrey. *The End of Poverty: Economic Possibilities for Our Time.* New York: Penguin, 2005.

Stiglitz, Joseph. *Globalization and Its Discontents.* New York: Norton, 2002.

———. *The Price of Inequality: How Today's Divided Society Endangers Our Future.* New York: Norton, 2012.

United Nations. *World Development Report.* New York: Oxford University Press, annual.

ENDNOTES

1. Samuel Huntington, *The Third Wave of Democracy* (Norman: University of Oklahoma Press, 1991).

2. "Global Poverty: A Fall to Cheer," *The Economist*, March 3, 2012.

3. Institute for Statistics, *Global Education Digest 2010: Comparing Education Statistics across the World* (Montreal, QC: UNESCO, 2010).

4. Gabriel Almond and G. Bingham Powell, *Comparative Politics: A Developmental Approach* (Glenview, IL: Scott-Foresman, 1978).

5. Max Weber, *Economy and Society,* ed. Guenther Roth and Claus Wittich (Berkeley: University of California Press, 1978), 389.

6. Stephen Castles and Mark Miller, *The Age of Migration: International Population Movements in the Modern World* (New York: Guilford, 1994).

7. United Nations Development Program, *Human Development Report 2013* (New York: United Nations, 2013) (http://hdr.undp.org/en/media/HDR_2013_EN_complete.pdf). See also www.undp.org for additional data and interactive presentations.

8. The per capita *gross national income (GNI)* (formerly gross national product [GNP]) is the sum of value added by all resident producers plus any product taxes (less subsidies) not included in the valuation of output plus net receipts of primary income (compensation of employees and property income) from abroad. Data are in current U.S. dollars. Rather than the traditional measures computed according to the exchange rates of the national currencies, the *purchasing power parity (PPP)* index takes into account differences in price levels from one country to another. Most analyses assume that the GNI/PPP statistics are more comparable measures of living conditions.

9. Hania Zlotnik, "Statement to the Thirty-Eighth Session of the Commission on Population and Development," April 4, 2005, .

10. Amartya Sen, "Population: Delusion and Reality," *New York Review of Books,* 22 September 1994.

11. United Nations, *Human Development Report 2013,* 22.

12. Yale Center for Environmental Law and Policy and Center for International Earth Science Information Network, "*Environmental Performance Index,*" http://epi.yale.edu/.

13. While many countries became formally democratic in these years, most of them quickly lapsed into authoritarianism. Many of these would-be democracies failed in their first

decade; another "reverse wave" in the 1960s and early 1970s swept away some older democracies (Chile, Greece, and Uruguay, for example) as well.

14. Huntington, *The Third Wave.*

15. Freedom House, *Freedom in the World 2013* (Washington, DC: Freedom House, 2013) (www.freedomhouse.org).

16. Christian Welzel, *Freedom Rising: Human Empowerment and the Quest for Emancipation* (Cambridge: Cambridge University Press, 2013); Adam Przeworski et al., *Democracy and Development: Political Institutions and Well-Being in the World 1950–1990* (New York: Cambridge University Press, 2000); and Seymour Martin Lipset, "Some Social Requisites of Democracy," *American Political Science Review 53* (September 1959): 69–105.

17. The outliers in the figure—those nations with high income but lower democracy scores—tend to be oil-producing states with high income per capita because of resource production but fewer of the social factors of modernization.

18. See United Nations, *Human Development Report 2013,* 156.

19. Joseph Stiglitz, *Globalization and Its Discontents* (New York: Norton, 2002); and Jagdish Bhagwati, *In Defense of Globalization* (Oxford: Oxford University Press, 2007).

20. Wayne Sandholtz and Kendall Stiles, *International Norms and Cycles of Change* (Oxford: Oxford University Press, 2008).

21. Martin Greenberg and Mark Tier, *Visions of Liberty* (New York: Baen Publishers, 2004).

22. See, for example, Douglas North, *Institutions, Institutional Change, and Economic Performance* (Cambridge: Cambridge University Press, 1990); Mancur Olson, "The New Institutional Economics: The Collective Choice Approach to Economic Development," in *Institutions and Economic Development, ed. C. Clague* (Baltimore: Johns Hopkins University Press, 1997); and S. Knack and P. Keefer, "Institutions and Economic Performance," *Economics and Politics 7* (1995): 207–29.

23. Joseph Stiglitz, *The Price of Inequality: How Today's Divided Society Endangers Our Future* (New York: Norton, 2012); and Kate Pickett and Richard Wilkinson, *The Spirit Level: Why Greater Equality Makes Societies Stronger* (New York: Bloomsbury Press, 2009).

24. Many of these issues are addressed by the United Nations Millennium Development Goals. Visit the UN website, http://www.un.org/millenniumgoals/.

CHAPTER 2

Comparing Political Systems

LEARNING OBJECTIVES

2.1 Explain the reasons for using the comparative method to study politics and the goals of description, explanation, and prediction.

2.2 Define the components of a political system and discuss the ways domestic and international environments can affect it.

2.3 List six types of political structures, and provide a few examples of how a similar structure functions differently in Britain than it does in China.

2.4 Discuss how the functions of Russia's political structures changed after the collapse of communism.

2.5 Describe the roles of conditions, policies, and outcomes in evaluating a political system.

Why We Compare

2.1 Explain the reasons for using the comparative method to study politics and the goals of description, explanation, and prediction.

The great French interpreter of American democracy, Alexis de Tocqueville, while traveling in America in the 1830s, wrote to a friend explaining how his own ideas about French institutions and culture entered into his writing of *Democracy in America*. Tocqueville wrote, "Although I very rarely spoke of France in my book, I did not write one page of it without having her, so to speak, before my eyes."[1] Tocqueville taught us that the only way we can fully understand our own political system is by comparing it to others. Comparing our experience with that of other countries deepens our understanding of our own politics and permits us to see a wider range of alternatives. It illuminates the virtues and shortcomings of our own political life. By taking us beyond our familiar arrangements and assumptions, comparative analysis helps expand our awareness of the potentials, for better or worse, of politics.

On the comparative method, Tocqueville offered this comment: "Without comparisons to make, the mind does not know how to proceed."[2] Tocqueville was telling us that comparison is fundamental to all human thought. It is the methodological core of the humanistic and scientific methods, including the scientific study of politics. Comparative analysis helps us develop and test explanations of how political processes work or when political change occurs. The goals of the comparative methods used by political scientists are similar to those used in more exact sciences such as physics. But political scientists often cannot design experiments, a major path to knowledge in many natural sciences. We cannot always control and manipulate political arrangements and observe the consequences. We are especially limited when dealing with large-scale events that drastically affect many people. For example, researchers cannot and would not want to start a war or a social revolution to study its effects.

We can, however, use the comparative method to describe the political events and institutions found

Aristotle's Library

There is historical evidence that Aristotle had accumulated a library of more than 150 studies of the political systems of the Mediterranean world of 400 to 300 BC. Many of these had probably been researched and written by his disciples.

While only the Athenian constitution survives from this library of Aristotelian polities, it is evident from the references to such studies that do survive that Aristotle was concerned with sampling the variety of political systems then in existence, including the "barbarian" countries, such as Libya, Etruria, and Rome: "[T]he references in ancient authorities give us the names of some 70 or more of the states described in the compilation of 'polities.' They range from Sinope, on the Black Sea, to Cyrene in North Africa; they extend from Marseilles in the Western Mediterranean to Crete, Rhodes, and Cyprus in the East. Aristotle thus included colonial constitutions as well as those of metropolitan states. His descriptions embraced states on the Aegean, Ionian, and Tyrrhenian Seas, and the three continents of Europe, Asia, and Africa."

Source: Ernest Barker, ed., *The Politics of Aristotle* (London: Oxford University Press, 1977), 386.

in different societies and to identify their causes and consequences. More than two thousand years ago, Aristotle in his *Politics* contrasted the economies and social structures of Greek city-states in an effort to determine how social and economic environments affected political institutions and policies (see Box 2.1). More contemporary political scientists also try to explain differences between the processes and performance of political systems. They compare two-party democracies with multiparty democracies, parliamentary with presidential regimes, poor countries with rich countries, and elections in new party systems with those in established democracies. These and many other comparisons have greatly enriched our understanding of politics.

a political event or institution well, we need to use words and phrases that our audience can understand clearly and in the same way, and which they can apply broadly. In order to describe politics, we thus need a set of concepts, a **conceptual framework**, which is clearly defined and well understood. In other words, we want our concepts to be **intersubjective** (understood and used in the same way by different subjects) and general. The easier our set of concepts is to understand, and the more broadly it can be applied, the more helpful it is to the study of politics. Conceptual frameworks are not generally right or wrong, but they may be more or less useful to the task at hand. The conceptual framework we use is described in more detail later in this chapter.

How We Compare

We study politics in several different ways: We describe it, we seek to explain it, and sometimes we try to predict it. These are all parts of the scientific process, though as we move from description to explanation and prediction, our task gets progressively harder. Each of these tasks may use the comparative method. The first stage in the study of politics is description. If we cannot describe a political process or event, we cannot really hope to understand or explain it, much less predict what might happen next or in similar situations.

Description may sound easy and straightforward enough, but often it is not. In order to describe

How We Explain and Predict

Once we are able to describe politics with the help of the conceptual framework that we choose, the next task is to explain it. Explanation typically means answering "why?" questions. More precisely, explaining political phenomena means identifying causal relationships among them, pointing out one phenomenon as the cause or consequence of another.[3] It is often important to be able to go beyond description to explanation. For example, we might be interested in the relationship between democracy and international peace (see Box 2.2). Description can tell us that in

BOX 2.2   Statistical Methods

A popular contemporary research program known as *democratic peace research* illustrates the pros and cons of statistical and case study research. International relations scholars studied the diplomatic history of the Cold War period and asked whether democratic countries are more peaceful in their foreign policy than authoritarian and nondemocratic ones. Many scholars took the statistical route. They counted each year of interaction between two states as one case. With roughly half a century of diplomatic history involving a state system of 100 countries or more, they had a very large number of cases, even after eliminating the irrelevant cases. Political scientists Andrew Bennett and Alexander George drew these conclusions after surveying the statistical research:

> Statistical methods achieved important advances on the issue of whether a nonspurious interdemocratic peace exists. A fairly strong though not unanimous consensus emerged that: (1) democracies are not less war-prone in general; (2) they have very rarely if ever fought one another; (3) this pattern of an interdemocratic peace applies to both war and conflicts short of war; (4) states in transition to democracy are more war-prone than established democracies; and (5) these correlations were not spuriously brought about by the most obvious alternative explanations.

Although much was learned from the statistical studies, they were not as successful at answering "why" questions. Case studies make clinical depth possible, revealing causal interconnections in individual cases. Careful repetition of these causal tracings from case to case strengthens confidence in these relationships. Thus, Bennett and George concluded that the best research strategy uses statistical and case study methods together, with each method having its own strengths.

Source: Andrew Bennett and Alexander George, "An Alliance of Statistical and Case Study Methods: Research on the Interdemocratic Peace," *Newsletter of the APSA Organized Section in Comparative Politics* 9, no. 1 (1998): 6.

---

the contemporary world, peace and democracy tend to go together. Democratic states are mostly (though not always) peaceful, and many peaceful states are democracies. But we do not fully understand why this is so. Are democratic states more peaceful because they are democratic, are they democratic because they are peaceful, or are they perhaps both peaceful and democratic because they are more prosperous than other states, or because they have market economies, or because their citizens have values (a political culture) that support both democracy and peace? A good explanation helps us find the right answer to such questions. Ideally, we want to put many political relationships in causal terms, so we can say that one political feature is the cause of another, and the latter is an effect of the former.

Theories are precisely formulated and well-supported statements about causal relationships among general political phenomena—for example, about the causes of democracy, war, election victories, or welfare policies. Theories need to be testable, and a good theory is one that holds up after continued tests, preferably after a series of concerted efforts to prove it wrong. **Hypotheses** are causal explanations

that have not yet been proven. In other words, they are candidate theories that have not yet been adequately tested or confirmed. Yet scientific theories are always tentative; they are subject to modification or falsification at any time as our knowledge improves. Theories are often modified and made more precise as we test them again and again with better and better data. A well-tested theory allows us to explain confidently what happens in specific cases or sets of cases—for example, that two countries have a peaceful relationship because they are democracies, or perhaps the other way around (see again Box 2.2).

Political scientists often develop theories as they seek to understand a puzzling case or an interesting difference between two or three political systems. For example, Tocqueville was intrigued by the fact that democracy was so widely supported in the United States, while it was fiercely contested in his native France. Researchers also often generate hypotheses about the causes and consequences of political change by comparing countries at different historical periods. In his other famous study, Tocqueville contributed to a general theory of revolution by comparing prerevolutionary and postrevolutionary France.[4] More recently,

Theda Skocpol based her explanation of the causes of revolution on a comparison of the "old regimes" of France, Russia, and China with their revolutionary and postrevolutionary regimes.[5]

But for an explanatory hypothesis to become a useful theory, we generally want it to explain not only the case(s) on which it was based but also other cases (revolutions, wars, elections, etc.) that fall into the same set. Hypotheses are therefore tested against many different kinds of political **data**. Researchers in political science distinguish between studies based on large numbers (large n) and small numbers (small n) of cases or observations. In large-n studies, particularly when the number of cases is beyond twenty or thirty, it is often possible and helpful to use statistical analysis. Such studies are usually referred to as *statistical studies*; small-n studies are usually called *case studies*. Many small-n studies examine only a single case, whereas others compare two or three or four (or occasionally more).

Statistical analysis enables us to consider possible alternative causes at the same time, accepting some and rejecting others. Large-n studies often have a sufficient number and variety of cases to enable the researcher to examine the relation among the variables associated with each case. **Variables** are the features in which our cases differ—for example, "religious heritage: Christian, Muslim, or Buddhist" or "rank in the United Nations quality of life index," or "income per capita." Large-n statistical studies thus allow us to be more certain and precise in our explanations. On the other hand, we need the depth that case studies provide. Small-n studies permit investigators to go deeply into a case, identify the particularities of it, get the clinical details, and examine each link in the causal process. They encourage us to formulate insightful hypotheses for statistical testing in the first place. They allow us to trace the nature of the cause-and-effect relations (sometimes called "causal mechanisms") better than large-n studies. In this manner, political scientists may come to know not only whether democracies are more peaceful than dictatorships but more precisely why democratic leaders behave in the way that they do. Most researchers recognize that these methods are complementary (see again Box 2.2).

The final and most challenging task in the scientific process is prediction. Prediction is testing hypotheses against data that were not known by the researchers who developed these explanations, often because the events had not yet happened. It is generally far more difficult to formulate predictions about events that have not yet happened than to explain events whose outcome we already know. This is both because we never know whether we have captured all the relevant factors that might affect the future and because the world itself may change as we try to understand it. Often, political actors learn from the mistakes of the past, so that the same patterns do not necessarily repeat themselves. Yet political scientists have made improvements in the act of prediction as well as in description and explanation. Many researchers have, for example, observed the close relationship between economic conditions and the results of U.S. presidential elections. When economic conditions are good (low inflation and unemployment, high growth), the candidate of the incumbent party tends to win; when times are bad, the opposition party tends to prevail. This theory is sufficiently strong that it allows researchers to make fairly precise and reliable predictions about the electoral result after observing economic conditions a few months before the election. Yet sometimes the predictions get it wrong, as they did in the 2000 presidential election, when most researchers predicted that Democratic candidate Al Gore would win handily. Such failed predictions imply the need to revise the theory to take additional factors into account. Successful predictions greatly increase our confidence in a theory, as well as being interesting for their own sake or to guide policy.

An example may suggest how you might go about theorizing in comparative politics, going beyond "just mastering the facts." It is well known that rich countries are more likely to be democracies than are poor countries; democracy and economic development are strongly associated. (See Figure 1.4. and the discussion of it.) But there are many possible reasons for this association. Some persons have suggested that this relationship comes about because democracy encourages education and economic development. Others have argued that as countries develop economically, their new middle classes or their emerging working classes are more likely to demand democratization. Yet others have seen that both democracy and economic development are commonly found in some regions of the world, such as Western Europe, while both tend to be scarce in the Middle East and Africa. This fact suggests that certain cultures may encourage or discourage both of them.

Yet the causal nature of this association is important, for reasons of both science and policy. Fostering economic development and securing democracy are two of the significant political challenges that we discussed in Chapter 1. Adam Przeworski and his associates examined democracies, nondemocracies, and transitions between them from 1950 until 1990.[6] From their statistical analysis, they concluded that the association between democracy and prosperity did not reflect regional histories or superior economic growth under democracy. Moreover, countries at any level of development seemed able to introduce democracy, although economically developed countries were somewhat more likely to do so. Instead, these researchers argued that the key to the relationship lies in the greater fragility of democracies in economically poor societies. Democracy can be introduced in poor societies, but it is often replaced by some kind of dictatorship. In rich countries, in contrast, democracy tends to survive once it begins. These democratic failures in poor countries produce a strong association between development and democracy. We still need to understand exactly why democracy is more precarious in less developed societies, but we are making progress in understanding the causal relationship between development and democracy.

Comparative analysis is a powerful and versatile tool. It enhances our ability to describe and understand political processes and political change in any country. The comparative approach also stimulates us to form general theories of political relationships. It encourages and enables us to test our political theories by confronting them with the experience of many institutions and settings.

Political Systems: Environment and Interdependence

 2.2 Define the components of a political system and discuss the ways domestic and international environments can affect it.

We began this book by discussing governments, but governments are only one part of a larger political system. Since the term **political system** is a main organizing concept of this book, it deserves a full explanation. A system by definition has two properties: (1) a set of interdependent parts and (2) boundaries for its environment.

A political system is a particular type of social system that is involved in the making of authoritative public decisions. Central elements of a political system are the institutions of **government**—such as legislatures, bureaucracies, and courts—that formulate and implement the collective goals of a society or of groups within it. The decisions of governments are normally backed up by legitimate coercion, and governments can thus typically compel their citizens to comply with their decisions. (We discuss legitimacy at greater length in Chapter 3.)

Political systems also include important parts of the society in which governments operate. For example, political organizations, such as political parties or interest groups, are part of the political system. Such organizations do not have coercive authority, except insofar as they control the government. Likewise, the mass media only indirectly affect elections, legislation, and law enforcement. A whole host of institutions—beginning with the family and including communities, churches, schools, corporations, foundations, and think tanks—influence political attitudes and public policy. The term *political system* refers to the whole collection of related, interacting institutions and agencies.

The political systems that we compare in this book are all independent states (we also more casually refer to them as *countries*). They represent some of the most politically important countries in the contemporary world. At the same time, they reflect the diversity of political systems that exist today. A state is a particular type of political system. It has sovereignty—independent legal authority over a population in a particular territory, based on the recognized right to self-determination. Sovereignty rests with those who have the ultimate right to make political decisions.

Figure 2.1 tells us that a political system exists in both an international environment and a domestic environment. It is molded by these environments, and it tries to mold them. The system receives **inputs** from these environments. Its policymakers attempt to shape them through its **outputs**. In the figure, which is quite schematic and simple, we use the United States as the central actor. We include other countries as our environmental examples—Russia, China, Britain, Germany, Japan, Mexico, and Iran.

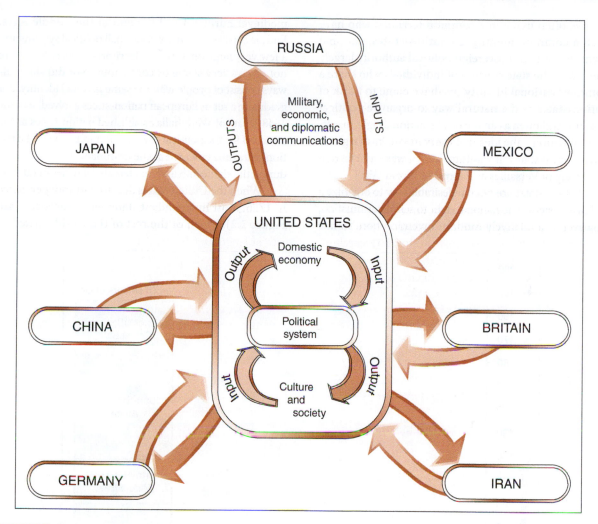

FIGURE 2.1

Political System and Its Environments

The political system of the United States interacts with domestic and international environments.

Exchanges among countries may vary in many ways. For example, they may be "dense" or "sparse." U.S.-Canadian relations exemplify the dense end of the continuum in that they affect many of the citizens of these countries in significant ways, while U.S.-Nepalese relations are far sparser.

Relationships among political systems may be of many different kinds. The United States has substantial trade relations with some countries and relatively little trade with others. Some countries have an excess of imports over exports, whereas others have an excess of exports over imports. Military exchanges and support with such countries as the NATO nations, Japan, South Korea, Israel, and Saudi Arabia have been of significant importance to the United States.

The interdependence of countries—the volume and value of imports and exports, transfers of capital, international communication, and the extent of foreign travel and immigration—has increased enormously in recent decades. This increase is often called **globalization**. We might represent this process as a thickening of the input and output arrows between the United States and other countries in Figure 2.1. Fluctuations in this flow of international transactions and traffic attributable to depression, inflation, protective tariffs, international terrorism, war, and the like may wreak havoc with the economies of the countries affected.

We often think of the world as a patchwork of states with sizable and contiguous territories, and a common identity shared by their citizens. A nation is a group of people, often living in a common territory, who have such a common identity. In **nation-states**, national identifications and sovereign political authority largely coincide—the state consists of individuals who share a common national identity. We have come to think of nation-states as the natural way to organize political systems, and often as an ideal. The national right to self-determination—the idea that every nation has a right to form its own state if it wants to do so—was enshrined in the Treaty of Versailles at the end of World War I.

Nation-states are often a desirable way to organize a political system. The national right to self-determination, however, is a relatively modern invention born in late medieval Europe. Until the end of the Middle Ages, Europe consisted of many very small political systems and a few very large ones, whose territorial possessions were not always very stable or contiguous. Nor did states always consist of people with the same national identity. But gradually, a set of European nation-states evolved, and the 1648 Treaty of Westphalia established nation-states as the standard for the political organization of Europe. The nation-state thus emerged as the dominant political system during the eighteenth and nineteenth centuries in Europe.

When the United States declared its independence in 1776, most independent states were European (see Figure 2.2). Much of the rest of the world existed as

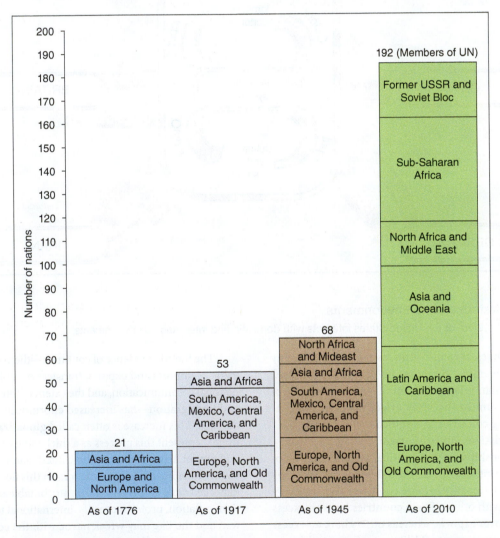

FIGURE 2.2

Formation of States since 1776

Most states emerged during the twentieth century.

Source: For Contemporary Members, Information Office, United Nations. Data to 1945 from Charles Taylor and Michael Hudson, *World Handbook of Political and Social Indicators* (New Haven, CT: Yale University Press, 1972), 26ff.

colonies to one of the European empires. In the nineteenth and early twentieth centuries, the number of states increased, principally in Latin America, where the Spanish and Portuguese empires broke up into twenty independent states. In Europe, newly independent countries emerged in the Balkans, Scandinavia, and the Low Countries.

Between the two world wars, new states came into being in North Africa and the Middle East, and Europe continued to fragment as the Russian and Austro-Hungarian empires broke up. After World War II, the development of new states took off, especially with the independence of India and Pakistan in 1947. By 2010, 126 new countries had joined the 68 states that existed in 1945. The largest group of new states is in sub-Saharan Africa. More than twenty new countries formed in the 1990s—mostly the successor states of the Soviet Union, Yugoslavia, and Czechoslovakia. Four states have joined the UN since 2000—most notably Switzerland, which until 2002 had stayed out because of its strict neutrality policy—but there have been few newly independent countries over the past decade.

The interaction of a political system with its domestic environment—the economic and social systems and the political culture of its citizens—is also depicted in Figure 2.1. Europe did not transform itself into distinct nation-states accidentally—indeed, the governments of the emerging nation-states had a great deal to do with it. In response to both internal and international pressures, they sought to instill a common national identity among the peoples they controlled. They did so, often heavy-handedly, by promoting a common language, a common educational system, and often a common religion. While this process of nation building was often harsh and conflictual, it produced a Europe in which the inhabitants of most states have a strong sense of community.

Many societies in the developing world today face similar challenges. Especially in Africa, the newly independent states that emerged in the 1950s and 1960s had very weak national identities. In many parts of Africa, large-scale national communities simply had not existed before these areas were colonized by Europeans and others. Even where such national identities did exist, they were rarely reflected in the boundaries that the colonial powers (such as Britain, France, and Portugal) drew between their possessions. After independence, many new states therefore faced huge nation-building tasks.

At the same time, in many countries, the globalization of the economy leads to demands from firms and workers in some industries for protection of their jobs. Natural disasters, such as the hurricane that devastated New Orleans in 2005, spur calls for the national government to lead reconstruction. Man-made disasters, such as the huge oil spill that contaminated the beaches of the Gulf of Mexico in 2010, also stimulate calls for government action to limit the environmental and economic damages and prevent future disasters. Local issues are seen as the responsibility of the entire country. People live longer. An aging population demands that governments do more to help with medical benefits. In input/output terms, socioeconomic changes transform the political demands of the electorate and the kinds of policies that it supports.

Thus, a new pattern of society results in different policy outputs: different kinds and levels of taxation, changes in regulatory patterns, and changes in welfare expenditures. The advantage of the system–environment approach is that it directs our attention to the **interdependence** of what happens between and within countries. It provides us with a vocabulary to describe, compare, and explain these interacting events.

If we are to make sound judgments in politics, we need to be able to place political systems in their domestic and international environments. We need to recognize how these environments both set limits on and provide opportunities for political choices. This approach keeps us from reaching quick and biased political judgments. If a country is poor in natural resources and lacks the capabilities necessary to exploit what it has, we cannot fault it for having a low industrial output or poor educational and social services. Each country chapter in the second half of this book begins by discussing the current policy challenges facing the country and its social and economic environment.

Political Systems: Structures and Functions

 2.3 List six types of political structures, and provide a few examples of how a similar structure functions differently in Britain than it does in China.

Governments do many things, from establishing and operating school systems, to maintaining public order, to fighting wars. In order to carry on these disparate activities, governments have specialized **structures**

(which we may also refer to as *institutions* or *agencies*), such as parliaments, bureaucracies, administrative agencies, and courts. These structures perform **functions**, which in turn enable the government to formulate, implement, and enforce its policies. The policies reflect the goals; the agencies provide the means to achieve them.

Figure 2.3 locates six types of political structures—political parties, interest groups, legislatures, executives, bureaucracies, and courts—within the political system. These are formal organizations engaged in political activities. They exist in most contemporary political systems. This list is not exhaustive. Some structures, such as ruling military councils or governing royal families, are found in only a few countries. Some, such as Iran's Council of Guardians, are unique to one country's political system.

We might think that if we understand how such structures work in one political system, we can apply this insight to any other system. Unfortunately, that is not always the case. The sixfold classification in Figure 2.3 will not carry us very far in comparing political systems with each other. The problem is that similar structures may have very different functions across political systems. For example, Britain and China have all six types of political structures. However, these institutions are organized differently in the two countries. More important, they function in dramatically different ways.

The political executive in Britain consists of the prime minister and the Cabinet, which includes the heads of major departments and agencies. These officials are usually selected from among the members of Parliament. There is a similar structure in China,

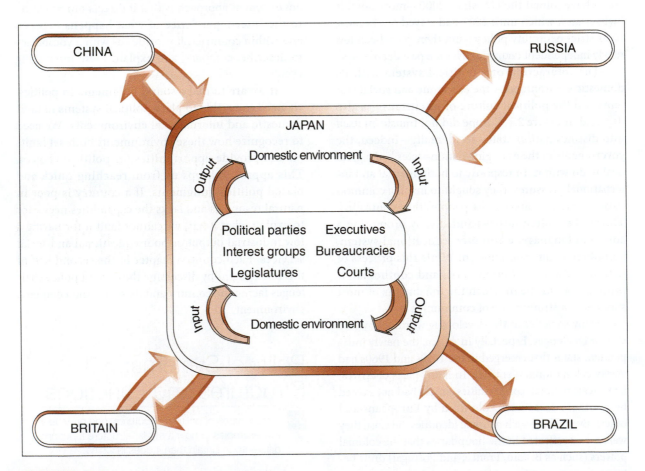

FIGURE 2.3

The Political System and Its Structures

Six types of political structures perform functions in the Japanese political system.

called the State Council, headed by a premier and consisting of the various ministers and ministerial commissions. But while the British prime minister and Cabinet have substantial policymaking power, the State Council in China is closely supervised by the general secretary of the Communist Party, the Politburo, and the Central Committee of the party, and has far less influence over public policy.

Both Britain and China have legislative bodies—the House of Commons in Britain and the National People's Congress in China. Their members debate and vote on prospective public policies. While the House of Commons is a key institution in the British policymaking process, the Chinese Congress meets for only brief periods, ratifying decisions made mainly by the Communist Party authorities. Usually, the Chinese delegates do not even consider alternative policies.

There are even larger differences between political parties in the two countries. Britain has a competitive party system. The members of the majority party in the House of Commons and the Cabinet are constantly confronted by an opposition party or parties, competing for public support. They look forward to the next election when they may unseat the incumbent majority, as happened in 1997, when the Labour Party replaced the Conservatives in government, and in 2010, when the Labour Party was in turn replaced by a coalition of Conservatives and Liberal Democrats. In China, the Communist Party controls the whole political process. There are no other political parties. The principal decisions are made within the Communist Party. The governmental agencies simply implement these policies.

Thus, an institution-by-institution comparison of British and Chinese politics that did not spell out the functions that the various agencies perform would not bring us far toward understanding the important differences in the politics of these two countries. Each country study in this book therefore includes a figure that shows how some of the major structures

select and control each other. Another figure illustrates how they fit into the policymaking process.

Figure 2.4 shows the functions of the political process that we can use to compare all political systems. The center of Figure 2.4 under the heading "**process functions**" lists the distinctive activities necessary for policy to be made and implemented in any kind of political system. (We discuss each concept in greater detail in Chapters 4, 5, and 6.) We call these *process functions* because they play a direct and necessary role in the process of making policy.

- **Interest articulation** involves individuals and groups expressing their needs and demands.
- **Interest aggregation** combines different demands into policy proposals backed by significant political resources.
- **Policymaking** is deciding which policy proposals become authoritative rules.
- **Policy implementation** is carrying out and enforcing public policies; **policy adjudication** is settling disputes about their application.

Before policy can be decided, some individuals and groups in the government or the society must decide what they want and hope to get from politics. The political process begins as these interests are expressed

Chinese National People's Congress
Delegates applaud below a screen that displays the very lopsided results of voting on the final day of the National People's Congress in Beijing's Great Hall of the People, March 16, 2007. This photo shows the importance of a structural-functional perspective, as votes in this "legislature" have little influence on policymaking. There is no real choice between alternatives.

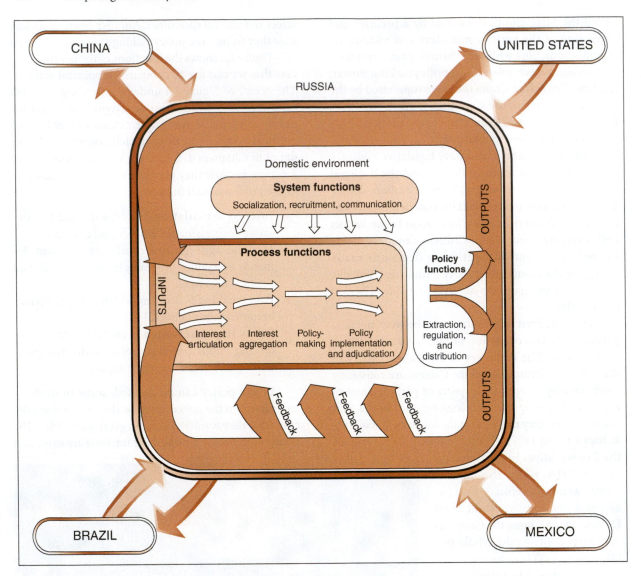

FIGURE 2.4

The Political System and Its Functions

System, process, and policy functions convert inputs into outputs.

or articulated. The many arrows on the left of the figure show these initial expressions. To be effective, however, these demands must be combined (aggregated) into policy alternatives—such as lower taxes or more social security benefits—for which substantial political support can be mobilized. Thus, the arrows on the left are consolidated as the process moves from interest articulation to interest aggregation. Governments then consider alternative policies and choose between them. Their policy decisions must then be

enforced and implemented, and if they are challenged, there must be some process of adjudication. Any policy may affect several different aspects of society, as reflected in the three arrows for the implementation phase.

These process functions are performed by such political structures as parties, legislatures, political executives, bureaucracies, and courts. The **structural-functional approach** stresses two points. One is that *in different countries, the same structure* *may perform different functions.* A second is that while a particular institution, such as a legislature, may specialize in a particular function, such as policymaking, *institutions often do not have a monopoly on any one function.* Presidents and governors may share in the policymaking function (and in the extreme case, each may be a veto power), as may the higher courts (especially in states that feature judicial review of statutes for their constitutionality).

The three functions listed at the top of Figure 2.4—socialization, recruitment, and communication—do not directly concern the making and implementation of public policy but are of fundamental importance to the political system. We refer to them as **system functions**. In the long run, they help determine whether the system will be maintained or changed. For example, will the military be able to maintain its dominance of policymaking, or will it be replaced by competitive parties and a legislature? Will a sense of national community persist, or will it be eroded by new experiences?

The arrows leading from these three functions to all parts of the political process suggest their crucial role in underpinning and permeating the political process.

- **Political socialization** involves families, schools, communications media, churches, and all the various political structures that develop, reinforce, and transform the political culture, the attitudes of political significance in the society (see Chapter 3).
- **Political recruitment** refers to the selection of people for political activity and government offices. In a democracy, competitive elections play a major role in political recruitment. In authoritarian systems, recruitment may be dominated by a single party, as in China, or by unelected religious leaders, as in Iran.
- **Political communication** refers to the flow of information through the society and the various structures that make up the political system. Gaining control over information is a key goal of most authoritarian rulers, as shown in the elaborate efforts of Chinese leaders to control content on the Internet.

Understanding the performance of the system functions is essential to understanding how political systems respond to the great contemporary challenges of building community, fostering economic development, and securing democracy that we discussed in Chapter 1.

The right side of Figure 2.4 illustrates the consequences of the policy process. The outputs are the ways in which policy decisions affect the society, the economy, and the culture. They include various forms of **extraction** of resources in the form of taxes and the like, **regulation** of behavior, and **distribution** of benefits and services to various groups in the population. The **outcomes** of all these political activities reflect the way the policies interact with the domestic and international environments. Sometimes, these outcomes are the desired results of public policies. But the complexities of policy and society sometimes result in unintended consequences. Among these may be new demands for legislation or administrative action, or increases or decreases in the support given to the political system and incumbent officeholders. We will return to the policy level after providing an example of a structural-functional comparison. The functional concepts shown in Figure 2.4 describe the activities carried out in any society regardless of how its political system is organized or what kinds of policies it produces. Using these functional categories, we can determine how institutions in different countries combine in making and implementing public policy.

An Illustrative Comparison: Regime Change in Russia

2.4 Discuss how the functions of Russia's political structures changed after the collapse of communism.

One way to better understand this framework is through a concrete example. Figures 2.5 and 2.6 offer a simplified graphic comparison of structures and functions in Russia before and after the breakdown of communist rule in the Soviet Union.[7] The figures use our comparative method to illustrate the way this political regime changed significantly in a short period of time. The point is to illustrate how we can use the tools of political analysis, rather than provide the details of the Russian case (which is discussed in depth in Chapter 12).

The figures depict the changes in the functioning of the major structures of the political system brought about by the collapse of communism. These include

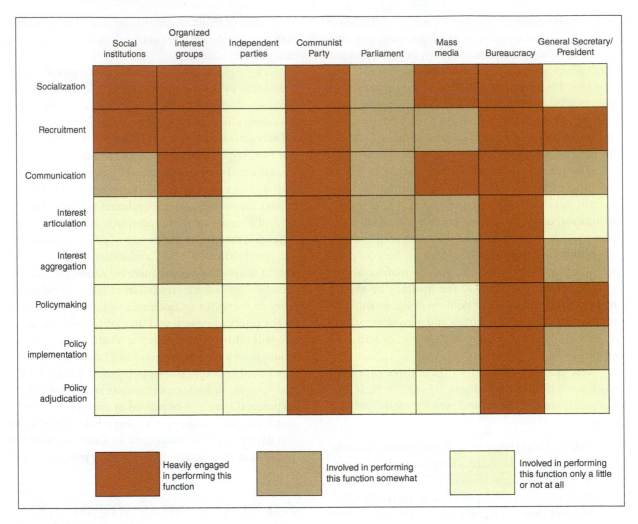

FIGURE 2.5

The Soviet Political System in 1985

The Communist Party and the state bureaucracy dominated all functions in the Soviet Union.

two revolutionary changes. One is the end of the single-party political system dominated by the Communist Party of the Soviet Union, which held together the vast, multinational Soviet state. The other is the dissolution of the Soviet Union itself into its fifteen member republics. As a result of these two remarkable events, Russia, the republic that was the core republic of the old union, became an independent noncommunist state.

Figure 2.5 therefore shows how the basic functions of the political system were performed in 1985, when the Soviet Union was a communist state. The Communist Party was the dominant political institution, overseeing schools and media, the arts and public organizations, the economy, and the courts through a massive state bureaucracy. For this reason, all the cells of the chart in the column marked "Communist Party" are shaded dark, as are the cells under the column marked "Bureaucracy." Although social institutions—such as the family, workplace, arts, and hobby groups—exercised some influence over such system-level functions as socialization, recruitment, and communication, it was the Communist Party and the state bureaucracy that dominated process-level functions. Under their tutelage, the mass media in 1985 were a key agent of communist political socialization and communication. Parliament was a compliant instrument for ratifying decisions made

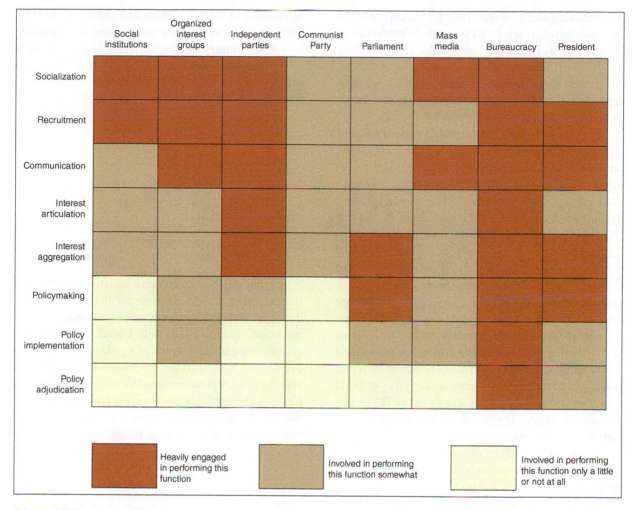

FIGURE 2.6

The Russian Political System in 2000

Many more structures played important roles in policymaking in Russia in 2000.

by the party and bureaucracy. By law, no parties other than the Communist Party were allowed. The only organized interest groups were those authorized by the party. The party's general secretary was the most powerful official in the country.

By 2000, the political system had undergone fundamental changes, as shown in Figure 2.6. Many more structures played a role in the political process, as is immediately evident by the larger number of cells that are heavily shaded. In particular, Parliament, independent political parties, and regional governments had all acquired important new policymaking powers. The freedom enjoyed by ordinary citizens to articulate their interests and to organize to advance them

had expanded enormously. The Communist Party, no longer an official or monopolistic party, had declined very substantially in power and was reduced to the role of an opposition party in the parliamentary game. The lighter shading for the Communist Party in Figure 2.6 shows its diminished influence. The state bureaucracy remained an important element in the political system, although adapting itself to the new trend of movement toward a market economy by adopting quasi-commercial forms.

The presidency has been a dominant policymaking institution in the new Russia, as shown in Figure 2.6. Parliament, although fairly representative of the diversity of opinion in the country, was frustrated in its policymaking and oversight roles by the inertia of the vast state bureaucracy, by its inability to compel compliance with its laws, by its weak links with the voters, and by the president's political power. Nevertheless, Parliament played a much greater role than before in aggregating interests and policymaking, as demonstrated by a comparison of Figures 2.5 and 2.6.

An updating of Figure 2.6 would show the eclipse of parties, Parliament, and the mass media by the president and the bureaucracy after 2000. This movement in a more authoritarian direction, although not back to communism, would be shown by fewer dark-shaded columns in the middle of the figure. These further developments are discussed in detail in Chapter 12.

These brief comparisons illustrate the use of the structural-functional approach. This approach enables us to examine how the same functions are performed in different countries, or in the same country at two different points in time. Similarly, we may examine changes in the functions performed by the same structures over time or across different political systems. In a country undergoing as rapid and dramatic a transition as Russia in the 1990s, this framework demonstrates substantial changes in the distribution of power.

Neither the analysis of structures nor that of functions is complete without the other. A structural analysis tells us the number of political parties, or the organization of the legislature. It describes how the executive branch, the courts, the bureaucracy, the mass media, interest groups, and other structures of a political system are set up and by what rules or standards they operate. A functional analysis tells us how these institutions and organizations interact to produce and implement policies. This kind of analysis is especially essential when we are comparing very different kinds of political systems.

The country-specific chapters in this book do not present formal structural-functional sketches like Figures 2.5 and 2.6. But at the core of each chapter is a set of discussions of these functions and the structures that perform them. We can see these in the section headings of the country studies and in the analytic guide at the beginning of this book. These tools make it possible to compare the workings of the very different political systems in this book.

The Policy Level: Performance, Outcome, and Evaluation

2.5 Describe the roles of conditions, policies, and outcomes in evaluating a political system.

Now, what differences do these variations in political structures and functions make for the citizens of the different states that we analyze? This question directs our attention to the **policy level** of the political system. We call the outputs of a political system—its extractions, distributions, regulations, and symbolic acts—its *policy performance*. We have to distinguish between these efforts, the things a government does, and the actual outcome of these efforts. Governments may spend equal amounts on education and health, or

Climbing the Wall

The wall dividing California and Mexico illustrates the input–output model of comparative politics. The two men are trying to escape from the poverty of the Mexican economy. The wall is part of the output of the American political system, intended to frustrate illegal immigrants. The two figures show that outputs do not necessarily produce the intended outcomes.

defense, but with different consequences. Government efficiency or corruption plays a role in the effectiveness of politics. But so do the underlying cultural, economic, and technological conditions.

Americans spend more per capita on education than any other people in the world. But their children perform worse in some subjects, such as mathematics, than do children in some other countries that spend substantially less. The United States spent enormous sums and many lives on the war in Vietnam in the 1960s and 1970s, as did the Soviet Union on its war in Afghanistan in the 1980s. Yet both countries were held at bay by far less well-equipped armed forces or guerrilla groups resolved to resist at all costs. Because of these costly failures, the United States and the Soviet Union were weakened internally. In the latter case, the costs of the war in Afghanistan contributed directly to the downfall of the communist regime. The outcome of public policy is thus never wholly in the hands of the people and their leaders. Legislatures may vote to wage a military conflict, but neither their votes nor the promises of political leaders can guarantee success. Conditions in the internal environment, conditions and events in the larger external world, and simple chance may frustrate the most thoughtfully crafted programs and plans. Each country study in this book concludes with a discussion of the country's performance, describing both policies and their outcomes.

Finally, we must step even further back to evaluate the politics of different systems. Evaluation is complex because people value different things and put different emphases on what they value. We will refer to the different conditions, outputs, and outcomes that people may value as political "goods." In Chapter 7, we outline a typology of various kinds of political goals and political goods. These include goods associated with the system level, such as the stability or adaptability of political institutions, and goods associated with the process level, such as citizen participation in politics. Finally, we consider and describe goods associated with the policy level, such as welfare, security, fairness, and liberty. To evaluate what a political system is doing, we assess performance and outcomes in each of these areas. We must also be aware of how these broad outcomes affect specific individuals and groups in the society, which may often be overlooked if we simply consider national averages.

A particularly important problem of evaluation concerns building for the future as well as living today. The people of poor countries wish to survive and alleviate the suffering of today but also to improve their children's lot for tomorrow. The people of all countries, but especially rich ones, must deal with the costs to their children of polluted and depleted natural resources as the result of the thoughtless environmental policies of the past.

REVIEW QUESTIONS

- How do the main elements in the environment of a political system affect the way it performs?
- Why are we unable to compare political systems simply by describing the different structures we find in them?

- What are the functions performed in all political systems as policies are made?
- What is the difference between outputs and outcomes of policy?
- How do we use theories to explain political events?

KEY TERMS

conceptual framework	functions	inputs	intersubjective
data	globalization	interdependence	nation-states
distribution	government	interest aggregation	outcomes
extraction	hypotheses	interest articulation	outputs

policy adjudication

policy implementation

policy level

policymaking

political communication

political recruitment

political socialization

political system

process functions

regulation

structural-functional
approach

structures

system functions

theories

variables

SUGGESTED READINGS

Boix, Charles, and Susan C. Stokes, eds. *Oxford Handbook of Comparative Politics*. New York: Oxford University Press, 2009.

Brady, Henry E., and David Collier. *Rethinking Social Inquiry: Diverse Tools, Shared Standards*. Lanham, MD: Rowman and Littlefield, 2004.

Collier, David. "The Comparative Method," in *Political Science: The State of the Discipline II*, ed. Ada W. Finifter, 105–19. Washington, DC: American Political Science Association, 1993.

Dogan, Mattei, and Dominique Pelassy. *How to Compare Nations: Strategies in Comparative Politics*. Chatham, NJ: Chatham House, 1990.

Goodin, Robert E. *The Oxford Handbook of Political Science*. New York: Oxford University Press, 2011.

King, Gary, Robert O. Keohane, and Sidney Verba. *Scientific Inference in Qualitative Research*. New York: Cambridge University Press, 1993.

Lichbach, Mark, and Alan Zuckerman. *Comparing Nations: Rationality, Culture, and Structure*. New York: Cambridge University Press, 1997.

Little, Daniel. *Varieties of Social Explanation: An Introduction to the Philosophy of Social Science*. Boulder, CO: Westview, 1991.

Przeworski, Adam, and Henry Teune. *The Logic of Comparative Social Inquiry*. New York: Wiley, 1970.

ENDNOTES

1. Alexis de Tocqueville to Louis de Kergolay, 18 October 1847, in *Alexis de Tocqueville: Selected Letters on Politics and Society*, ed. Roger Boesche (Berkeley: University of California Press, 1985), 191.

2. Alexis de Tocqueville to Ernest de Chabrol, 7 October 1831, in *Selected Letters*, 59.

3. For some related and alternative concepts of explanation, see Daniel Little, *Varieties of Social Explanation* (Boulder, CO: Westview, 1991).

4. Alexis de Tocqueville, *The Old Regime and the French Revolution*, trans. Stuart Gilbert (New York: Doubleday, 1955).

5. Theda Skocpol, *States and Social Revolutions* (New York: Cambridge University Press, 1979).

6. Adam Przeworski, Michael E. Alvarez, Jose Antonio Cheibub, and Fernando Limongi, *Democracy and Development: Political Institutions and Well-Being in the World, 1950–1990* (New York: Cambridge University Press, 2000).

7. Thomas Remington contributed to Figures 2.4 and 2.5 and the text of this section.

CHAPTER 3

Political Culture and Political Socialization

LEARNING OBJECTIVES

3.1 Describe the three levels of political culture and the factors that make them different.

3.2 List and describe the different sources of legitimacy for a political system.

3.3 Discuss how cultural norms and political institutions are interrelated.

3.4 Describe the agents of political socialization and their roles in forming political values.

3.5 List and describe three current forces that are affecting contemporary political cultures.

If you have ever traveled to a foreign country, you were probably surprised by how many of the normal things in your life were different there. The food was different, people wore different clothes, houses were constructed and furnished differently, and the pattern of social relations differed (for instance, whether people talked to strangers or stood in queues). You saw how social norms shape what people eat, how they dress, how they live, and maybe even on which side of the road they drive.

Similarly, each nation has its own political norms that influence how people think about and react to politics. To understand the political tendencies in a nation, one place to begin is with public attitudes toward politics and the citizen's role in the political system—what we call a nation's *political culture*. Americans' strong feelings of patriotism, the Japanese deference to political elites, and the French proclivity for protest all illustrate how cultural norms shape politics. The way political institutions function at least partially reflects the public's attitudes, norms, and expectations. Thus, the English use their constitutional arrangements to sustain their liberty, while the same institutions once allowed repression in South Africa and Northern Ireland.

When a new regime forms, a supportive public can help develop the new system, while the absence of public support may weaken the new system. The content of the political culture has been a very important aspect of the transitions to democracy in the past two decades, as new democracies needed to develop democratic orientations and behaviors among their citizens. It is hard to sustain democracy without a nation of democrats.

Chapter 1 stated that one main goal of any government, and a special challenge for a new government, is to create and maintain a political community. In part, this involves developing common structures and systems (such as a single economy), common political institutions, and common political processes. For the public, this involves developing common worldviews, values, and expectations that comprise the nation's political culture. Thus, studying political culture partially explains how a political community is created and sustained.

This chapter maps the important parts of political culture. We then discuss political socialization: how individuals form their political attitudes and thus how citizens collectively form their political culture. We conclude by describing the major trends in political culture in the world today.

Mapping the Three Levels of Political Culture

3.1 Describe the three levels of political culture and the factors that make them different.

A nation's **political culture** includes citizens' orientations at three levels: the political system, the political and policymaking process, and policy outputs and outcomes (Table 3.1). The *system* level is how people view the values and organizations that comprise the political system. Do people identify with the nation and accept the overall social system? The *process* level includes expectations of the political rules and decision-making methods, and individuals' relationship to the government. The *policy* level deals with the public's policy expectations for the government. What should the policy goals of government be, and how are they to be achieved?

The System Level

Orientations toward the political system are important because they tap basic attachments to the polity and the nation. It is difficult for any political system to endure if it lacks the support of its people.

Feelings of national pride are one example of these affective, emotional ties to a nation. National pride seems strongest in nations with long histories that emphasized feelings of patriotism—the United States is a prime example (see Figure 3.1). Such a common sense of identity and national history often binds people together in difficult political times. The figure shows that high levels of pride exist in nations with very different political and economic systems, such as Vietnam, Canada, Poland, and Turkey. Large majorities in most countries are proud of their nations. In contrast, national pride is low in Japan and Germany, two nations that have avoided nationalist sentiments in reaction to the World War II regimes and their excesses. And Russia's resurgence in the past decade substantially improved levels of national pride from earlier surveys in the late 1990s and early 2000s, while Moldova's continuing struggles since independence are signaled by the weak sense of national pride among its citizens.

Feelings of popular **legitimacy** are another basis for a stable political system. People may grant legitimacy to a government for different reasons.[1] In a traditional society, legitimacy may depend on the ruler's inheriting the throne or his/her commitment to religious customs. In a modern democracy, legitimacy may depend on the voters selecting elites in competitive elections and on the government's following constitutional procedures. Theocratic regimes, such as Iran, base their legitimacy on adherence to religious principles. In other political cultures, the leaders may claim legitimacy based on their special wisdom or ideology, which is typical for communist regimes or countries that emerged from national independence movements. Legitimacy presumes an agreement on the broad form of government for the political system and thus the standards of legitimacy: monarchical rule, a tribal system, a communist order, or a democratic system. Based on these different principles, people in widely differing political systems can still express support for their political systems because they are using different standards of legitimacy.[2]

Whether legitimacy is based on tradition, religion, elections, or ideology, these feelings reflect a basic understanding between citizens and political authorities. People obey the laws; in return, the government meets the obligations set by the terms of its legitimacy. As long as the government meets its obligations, the people are supposed to be supportive and act appropriately. If legitimacy is violated—the line of succession is broken, the constitution is subverted, or the ruling ideology is ignored—the government may experience resistance and perhaps rebellion. A political system and a government with high legitimacy are

TABLE 3.1
Political Culture
There are three levels of political culture, which tap different orientations toward politics.

Aspects of Political Culture	Examples
System	Pride in nation National identity Legitimacy of government
Process	Role of citizens Perceptions of political rights
Policy	Role of government Government policy priorities

100%	
	Canada
	Poland/Turkey
	India/Mexico/Spain
	Chile
	United States/Britain
	Iran/Nigeria
90%	Italy
	France
	Russia
	Brazil
	Netherlands
	Bulgaria
80%	
	China
	Germany
70%	
	Moldova
	Japan
60%	

FIGURE 3.1

Be Proud

Feelings of national pride vary across nations.

Source: Selected nations from the 2005–2008 *World Values Survey* and the 2000–2002 *World Values Survey* for Nigeria. Figure entries are the percentage "proud" and "very proud"; missing data are excluded from the calculation of percentages.

typically more effective in carrying out policies and are more likely to overcome hardships and reversals.

In systems with low legitimacy, people often resort to violence or extragovernmental actions to pursue their goals. Legitimacy is lacking where the public disputes the boundaries of the political system (as in Northern Ireland or Kashmir), rejects the current arrangements for recruiting leaders and making policies (as when Ukrainians took to the streets in 2004 to 2005, demanding new democratic elections), or loses confidence that the leaders are fulfilling their part of the political bargain (as when Egyptian protestors battled the government in 2011 and then again in 2013).

The Soviet Union disintegrated in the early 1990s because all three legitimacy problems appeared. After the communist ideology failed as a legitimizing force, there was little basis for a national political community without a common language or ethnicity. Similarly, the loss of confidence in the Communist Party as a political organization led many people to call for institutional reform. Finally, shortages of food and consumer goods caused people to lose faith in the government's short-term economic and political policies. Soviet president Mikhail Gorbachev failed in his efforts to deal with all three problems at the same time.

The Process Level

The second level of the political culture involves what people expect of the political process. Whether you are English or Nigerian, what do you think about the institutions of your political system and what is expected of you as a citizen?

One of the great advances in comparative politics research is the relatively recent expansion of our knowledge of the political culture in developing societies, and this has transformed our understanding of political culture on a global scale. Until then, researchers worried that the cultural bases of democracy were essentially limited to those nations that were already democratic, and thus the prospects for further democratization were limited.[3] Researchers reached this conclusion by assuming that economic development and affluence were prerequisites for democracy, and that authoritarian states persisted because people tolerated or even supported the government.

However, as public opinion surveys have become more common in developing nations, our images have changed. Cross-national studies of political culture document broad support for democratic principles and norms even in many autocratic nations.[4] Democratic norms emphasize the importance of a participatory process, majority rule and minority rights, and the values of political tolerance. Moreover, as more nations democratize and alternative regime forms lose their legitimacy, democratic norms have diffused to even more societies. Many nondemocratic forms of governance are no longer widely accepted. Communism still has strongholds in China and Cuba, for example, but it has lost its image as a progressive force for global change.

Consequently, current research finds that support for democracy is widespread in many developing nations in Africa, East Asia, and Latin America.[5] The World Values Survey asked respondents in more than sixty nations to state their approval of democracy and two nondemocratic regimes (military rule or rule by a strong leader). Figure 3.2 displays the percentage who prefer democracy, prefer either nondemocratic regime, or have mixed opinions across the nations discussed in this book.[6] In the established democracies, people express overwhelming support for democracy, but even here, some people are ambivalent about the regime form, and about a tenth actually prefer an authoritarian form of government. In the developing nations depicted in the figure, the picture is more mixed. Only a small percentage favor an authoritarian system over democracy, with the largest share of authoritarians in Russia (23 percent). However, a fair number of people in these developing nations rate democracy and authoritarianism equally. Among the seven developing nations in the figure, only in Nigeria and China do a majority clearly prefer democracy. It is not a positive sign for democracy in Brazil and Mexico, for example, when less than half of the public prefers democracy over autocracy. Democracy often receives plurality support in these developing nations, but there is a clear need to increase public support for democracy.

Furthermore, we should be cautious about taking support for democracy in a public opinion survey at full face value. Even if most people in the world today seem to favor a democratic political process, they differ in their understanding of how democracy actually functions. Expressions of support for liberty and tolerance in the abstract are easier than actually supporting these values when applied to your political opponents. Cultures also differ on how those principles should be applied. In some nations, the public states its support for equal rights for women, but then imposes Sharia restrictions on women. Even established democracies often strain to guarantee full democratic rights to groups that the majority dislikes. Still, the breadth of democratic aspirations is strikingly different than our images of developing nations in the past. These patterns seem to reaffirm Amartya Sen's claim that democracy is a basic human striving—something many scholars doubted a few short years ago.[7]

Another aspect of political culture is the individual's role in the political system. At one time, social scientists considered the population in developing nations as largely disinterested or even unaware

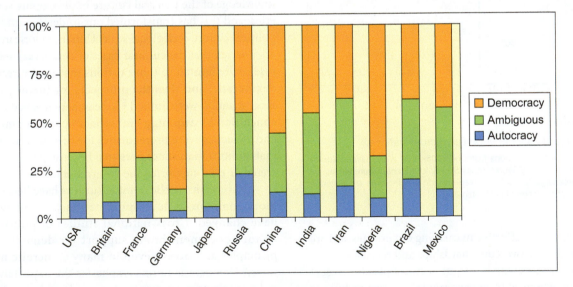

FIGURE 3.2

Democratic Aspirations

Support for democracy versus autocracy is widespread across regions.

Source: 2000–2002 *World Values Survey* and 2005–2008 *World Values Survey*. Respondents were asked about their support for either democracy or authoritarian system (either a nondemocratic leader or military regime); the ambiguous category is those who express equal approval for both.

BOX
3.1   A Small World

With a radio deep in a rural village, a person is abreast with a bomb blast in Bombay, and can follow a political crisis in Moscow. . . . People will take sides on issues far beyond their national borders. Whether the wife of dictator Ferdinand Marcos should be prosecuted or should be pardoned; whether the genocide in Rwanda could have been averted are issues which are enlivening beer-drinking discussions on a scale unprecedented in African history. . . . This knowledge revolution is making it difficult for African leaders to keep people ignorant of what they are entitled to or to stop them from demanding change and working for it. Hence there are shivers of change all over the continent.

Source: A Ugandan government official cited in Bruce Gilley, *The Right to Rule: How States Win and Lose Legitimacy* (New York: Columbia University Press, 2009), 78.

of politics because they were concerned with basic economic needs and lacked access to political information.[8] Again, this image has softened in recent years as research has documented considerable political interest even in unexpected places (see Box 3.1). The spread of democracy and the development of a global socioeconomic system connect an increasingly larger share of the world to domestic and international politics.

Still, actual participation in politics often involves resources, skills, and norms of active citizenship that are in short supply in many developing nations. Consequently, research finds that industrialization, urbanization, and improved living standards develop the cultural bases of active citizenship.[9] Exposure to modernity through work, education, and the media shapes an individual's personal experiences and sends messages about norms in other societies. It encourages citizen participation, a sense of individual equality, the desire for improved living standards and increased life expectancy, and government legitimacy based on policy performance. It also frequently disrupts familiar ways of life, traditional bases of legitimacy, and political arrangements that limit political engagement. In addition, the secularizing influences of science can alter economic and social systems, which then reshape the political culture. This modernization trend has powerful effects as it penetrates societies (or parts of societies).

Chapter 1 noted that this modernization process is spread unevenly across the globe. Recent economic growth in East Asia is transforming the political culture and political behavior in these nations. In contrast, modernization has proceeded more slowly and uncertainly in African and Arab nations.

Some political leaders in these nations even reject the principles of modernization as incongruent with their national values. However, there is persuasive evidence that where social and economic modernization occurs, it transforms the political culture to emphasize self-expression, participatory values, and autonomy.

The Policy Level

What is the appropriate role of government? If you ask political theorists, you get a wide range of answers—from the minimal state to the all-encompassing polity. And if you travel to other nations, you quickly realize that there is wide variation in how people answer this question.

Public opinions of what constitutes the good of society and the government's role in achieving accepted goals influence the policy activities of a country. Should government manage the economy, or should private property rights and market forces guide economic activity? Should the state intervene in addressing social and moral issues, or should it follow a minimalist strategy? The ongoing debates over "big government" versus "small government" in democratic states, and between socialist and market-based economies, reflect these different images of the scope of government.

We can illustrate differences in policy expectations with an opinion survey question that asks whether the government is responsible for providing for everyone versus individuals being responsible for providing for themselves (see Figure 3.3). The range in opinions is considerable; more than three-quarters of Russians believe government is responsible, compared with only two-fifths of

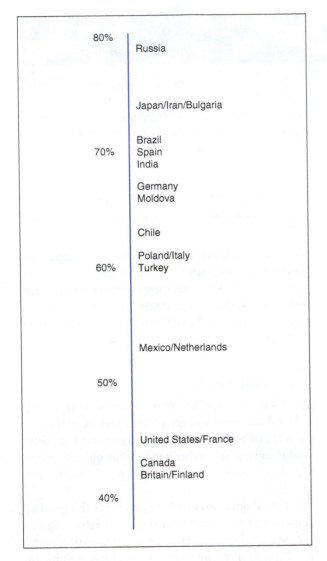

FIGURE 3.3

Who Is Responsible?

The belief that government is responsible for individuals' well-being.

Source: Selected nations from the 2005–2008 *World Values Survey*; missing data are excluded from the calculation of percentages.

Policy expectations also involve specific issue demands. Indeed, each country study in this book begins with a discussion of the policy challenges facing the nation and the public's issue concerns. This sets the agenda of politics that responsive governments should address.

Some policy goals, such as economic well-being, are valued by nearly everyone. Concern about other policy goals may vary widely across nations because of a nation's circumstances and because of cultural traditions. People in developing countries are more likely to focus on the government's provision of basic services to ensure public welfare. In advanced industrial societies, people are relatively more concerned with quality-of-life goals, such as preservation of nature and even government support for the arts.[11] One basic measure of a government's performance is its ability to meet the policy expectations of its citizens.

Another set of expectations involves the functioning of government. Some societies put more weight on the policy outputs of government, such as providing welfare and security. Other societies also emphasize how the process functions, which involves values such as the rule of law and procedural justice. Among Germans, for example, the rule of law is given great importance; in many developing nations, political relations are personally based and there is less willingness to rely on legalistic frameworks.

Consensual or Conflictual Political Cultures

Although political culture is a common characteristic of a nation, values and beliefs can vary within it. Political cultures may be consensual or conflictual on issues of public policy and, more fundamentally, on views of governmental and political arrangements. In some societies, people generally agree on the norms of political decision making and their policy expectations. In other societies—because of differences in histories, conditions, or identities—the people are sharply divided, often on both the legitimacy of the regime and solutions to major problems.[12]

When a country is deeply divided in its political values and these differences persist over time, distinctive **political subcultures** may develop. The people in these subcultures may have sharply different points of view on some critical political matters, such as the boundaries of the nation, the nature of the regime, or

Americans, Canadians, Britons, or the French. In general, people in developing nations and in the formerly communist nations of Eastern Europe are more supportive of a large government role—reflecting both their social condition and their past political ideologies. In some Western nations, traditions include a large role for the government. In general, however, support for government action generally decreases as national affluence increases.[10]

the correct ideology. They may affiliate with different political parties and interest groups, read different newspapers, and even have separate social clubs and sporting groups.

In some instances, historical or social factors generate different cultural trajectories. For instance, *ethnic*, *religious*, or *linguistic* identities in many parts of the world shape citizen values.[13] Moreover, as such groups increase their political skills and self-confidence, they may express their identities and demand equal treatment. In fact, the processes of globalization might actually heighten these cultural contrasts.[14] Where political subcultures coincide with ethnic, linguistic, or religious differences—as in Northern Ireland, Bosnia, and Lebanon—the divisions can be enduring and threatening. The breakup of Yugoslavia and the impulses toward autonomy and secession among ethnically distinct regions (such as in Scotland or separatist movements in Africa) all reflect the lasting power of language, culture, and historical memory to create and sustain the sense of ethnic and national identity. The exposure to values from other cultures also may intensify one's own self-image, which may increase cultural tensions. Although such exposure may eventually lead to greater tolerance, that outcome is not guaranteed.

Why Culture Matters

3.2 List and describe the different sources of legitimacy for a political system.

Political culture does not explain everything about politics. Even people with similar values and skills might behave differently from each other when they face different situations. Nor is political culture unchangeable. However, cultural norms typically change slowly and reflect stable values. Thus, political culture is important mainly because it encapsulates the history, traditions, and values of a society. To understand how most people in a nation think and act politically, we can begin by understanding their political culture. Political culture can create the common political community that is one goal of government.

In addition, the distribution of cultural patterns is typically related to the type of political process that citizens expect and support. This is the principle of **congruence theory**. For instance, support for a democratic system is typically higher in societies that have a more participatory political culture. Authoritarian states are more likely to endure where people lack the skills or motivations to participate and the state discourages their participation. These cultural norms represent the "rules of the game" for the political system, and the system works better when people accept these rules. Where political structures and political cultures are mutually reinforcing, a stable political system is likely to emerge.

We can illustrate the logic of congruence theory in terms of the relationship between political culture and the democratic development of a nation (Figure 3.4). The horizontal axis of the figure displays the public's adherence to "emancipative values" that emphasize the freedom of expression, tolerance, and personal autonomy, which in turn encourage citizens to become democratically engaged. Christian Welzel argues that these values reflect the democratic and participatory norms we

Cuba Si!
Cubans wave flags at a progovernment rally organized by the Castro government.

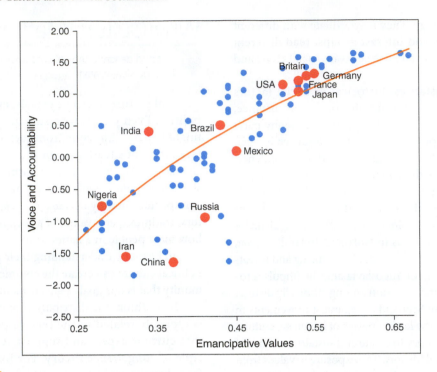

FIGURE 3.4

Culture Matters

The congruence of emancipative values and democratic development.

Source: Produced by the authors; emancipative values are measured using questions on support for freedom of expression and equality of opportunities asked in the 1999–2004 and 2005–2008 *World Values Survey*); the voice and equality index 2011 is from the World Bank Indicators database.

discussed earlier.[15] The vertical axis represents the democratic development of the nations based on the World Bank's 2011 voice and accountability index. Approximately 150 nations are plotted in the figure, with the nations from this book highlighted by red circles. You can see that citizen values and democratic development do overlap, albeit imperfectly. Nations low in emancipative values vary widely in their political structures because elites often run an authoritarian state, as in China; but some nations such as India or Mexico develop more democratic institutions. With growing public commitment to emancipative values, democratic institutions are also more strongly rooted.

Do democracies create a participatory democratic public, or does such a political culture lead to a democratic political system? It works both ways. For example, immediately after World War II, Germans were less supportive of democracy, but political institutions and political experiences transformed their culture over the next generation.[16] At the same time, democracy endured in Britain during the strains of the Great Depression and World War II, at least in part because the British public supported the democratic process. The important conclusion is that there is normally a relationship between political culture and political structures.

Beyond shaping the structure of the political system, a nation's political culture also influences the style of politics and the content of policymaking. We have stressed how the policy elements of a political culture can influence the content of policy. In addition, research suggests that cultural factors, such as social trust and engagement, influence the efficiency and effectiveness of government.[17]

Finally, culture can also divide nations and regions of the world. Samuel Huntington divided the world into different civilizations defined by their religious and cultural traditions.[18] He then predicted that these cultural differences will be a major source of international conflict in this century. While culture may have the power to divide, it also has the potential to build a common political community as people interact and learn which values they share.

Political Socialization

3.3 Discuss how cultural norms and political institutions are interrelated.

Political cultures are sustained or changed as people acquire their attitudes and values. **Political socialization** refers to the way in which political values are formed and political culture is transmitted from one generation to the next. Most children acquire their basic political values and behavior patterns by adolescence.[19] Some of these attitudes will evolve and change throughout their lives, while other attitudes will remain part of their political selves.

At any specific time, a person's political beliefs are a combination of various feelings and attitudes. At the deepest level, there are general identifications, such as nationalism, ethnic or class self-images, religious and ideological commitments, and a fundamental sense of rights and duties in the society. At the middle level, people develop attitudes toward politics and governmental institutions. Finally, there are more immediate views of current events, policies, issues, and personalities. All these attitudes can change, but those in the first level usually were acquired earliest, have been most frequently reinforced, and tend to be the most durable.

Three points about political socialization deserve mention. First, the socialization process can occur in different ways. **Direct socialization** involves an actor explicitly communicating information, values, or feelings toward politics. Examples of direct socialization include civics courses in the schools, public education programs of the government, and the political information campaigns of interest groups. Communist political systems also heavily use direct indoctrination programs (see Box 3.2). **Indirect socialization** occurs when political views are inadvertently molded by our experiences. For example, children normally learn important political values by observing the behavior of their parents, teachers, and friends. Or, people may learn by observing the political and social context that surrounds them, watching what governments do and how other citizens react.

Second, socialization is a lifelong process. Early family influences can create an individual's initial values, but subsequent life experiences—becoming involved in new social groups, moving from one part of the country to another, shifting up or down the social ladder, becoming a parent, finding or losing a job—may change one's political perspectives. More dramatic experiences—such as relocating to a new country or suffering through an economic depression or a war—can alter even basic political attitudes. Such events seem to have their greatest impact on young people, but people at any age are affected to some degree.

Third, patterns of socialization can unify or divide. Governments design public education systems, for instance, to create a single national political culture. Some events, such as international conflict or the death

---

BOX 3.2 Socializing Values

Communist East Germany had a special ceremony for eighth graders to mark their passage to adulthood. The heart of the ceremony was the endorsement of the following four pledges:

- As young citizens of our German Democratic Republic, are you prepared to work and fight loyally for the great and honorable goals of socialism, and to honor the revolutionary inheritance of the people?
- As sons and daughters of the worker-and-peasant state, are you prepared to pursue higher education, to cultivate your mind, to become a master of your trade, to learn permanently, and to use your knowledge to pursue our great humanist ideals?
- As honorable members of the socialist community, are you ready to cooperate as comrades, to respect and support each other, and to always merge the pursuit of your personal happiness with the happiness of all the people?
- As true patriots, are you ready to deepen the friendship with the Soviet Union, to strengthen our brotherhood with socialist countries, to struggle in the spirit of proletarian internationalism, to protect peace and to defend socialism against every imperialist aggression?

of a popular public figure, can affect nearly the entire nation similarly. In contrast, subcultures in a society can have their own distinctive patterns of socialization. Social groups that provide their members with their own newspapers, their own neighborhood groups, and perhaps their own schools can create distinctive subcultural attitudes. Distinct patterns of socialization can lead to a political gap among members of a nation.

Agents of Political Socialization

3.4 Describe the agents of political socialization and their roles in forming political values.

How do we learn our political attitudes? Individuals in all societies are affected by **agents of political socialization**: individuals, organizations, and institutions that influence political attitudes. Some, like civics courses in schools, are direct and deliberate sources of political learning. Others, like playgroups and work groups, affect political socialization indirectly.

The Family

What is your earliest political memory? It probably occurred when you were a child living with your parents. Most of us first learn about politics through our families. For instance, the family has distinctive influences on attitudes toward authority. Participation in family decision making can increase a child's sense of political competence, providing skills for political interaction and encouraging active participation in the political system as an adult. Similarly, unquestioning obedience to parental decisions may lead a child toward a more passive political role.

The family also shapes future political attitudes by defining a social position for the child: establishing ethnic, linguistic, class, and religious ties; affirming cultural values; and influencing job aspirations. For instance, in established democracies, many people inherit their party loyalties from their parents, as well as other social identities.

Social Groups and Identities

Our social characteristics also shape political orientations because our characteristics reflect different social needs, experiences, and social networks. For instance, your class or occupation can affect your life chances and political orientation. As one illustration, industrialization in Britain created a working class that lived in particular neighborhoods, worked at the same factories, and visited the same pubs. This working class developed its own forms of speech, dress, recreation, and entertainment, as well as its own social organizations (such as social clubs, trade unions, and political parties). In addition, labor unions provide an organizational base for informing their members on the politics of the day. Similarly, the life experience of the rural peasantry in many less developed nations is radically different from that of urban dwellers. Often, these social divisions are politically relevant; identifying yourself as a member of the working class or the peasantry leads to ties to groups representing these interests and distinct political views about what actions the government should take.

The religions of the world are also carriers of cultural and moral values, which often have political implications. The great religious leaders have seen themselves as teachers, and their followers have usually attempted to shape the socialization of children through schooling, preaching, and religious services. In most nations, there are formal ties between the dominant religion and the government. In these instances, religious values and public policy often overlap. Catholic nations, for instance, are less likely to have liberal abortion policies, just as Islamic governments enforce strict moral codes. Religious affiliations are often important sources of partisan preferences and can guide people in making other political choices.

Where churches teach values that may be at odds with the controlling political system, the struggle over socialization can be intense. These tensions can take a wide variety of forms: the clash between secular and religious roles in the French educational system, the efforts of American fundamentalists to bridge the separation of church and state, or the conflict between Islamic fundamentalists and secular governments in Tunisia and Egypt. In such cases, religious groups may oppose the policies of the state, or even the state itself.[20]

In addition, gender shapes social experiences and life chances, and, in many nations, provides cues about issue interests and political roles. Gender differences in politics have narrowed in many industrial nations, although they persist in many less developed nations.[21] The modern women's movement encourages women to become politically active and change social cues about how women should relate to politics. The lessening of gender differences in self-images, in parental roles, and in relation to the economy and the political system is affecting patterns of political recruitment, political participation, and public policy. Especially in the developing world, the changing role of women may have profound influences in modernizing the society and changing political values.[22]

Social identities are also often linked to membership in a racial or ethnic group. Whether it is an African American in the United States, an ethnic Pakistani living in London, or an Asian businessperson in South Africa, their distinctiveness partially defines their social and political identity. Ethnically and racially oriented groups provide social cues and information for members of these communities. In many instances, their identity creates a social network of interactions and life experiences that shape their values, while specific groups represent their interests in the political process and provide a network for political socialization and education.

Schools

Schools are often an important agent of political socialization. They educate children about politics and their role in the process, and provide them with information on political institutions and relationships. Schools can shape attitudes about the political system, the rules of the political game, the appropriate role of the citizen, and expectations about the government. Schools typically reinforce attachments to the political system and reinforce common symbols, such as the flag and Pledge of Allegiance, that encourage emotional attachments to the system.

When a new nation comes into being, or a revolutionary regime comes to power in an old nation, it usually turns to the schools as a means to supplant "outdated" values and symbols with ones more congruent with the new ideology.

In some nations, educational systems do not provide unifying political socialization but send starkly different messages to different groups. For instance, some Muslim nations segregate girls and boys within the school system. Even if educational experiences are intended to be equal, segregation creates different experiences and expectations. Moreover, the content of education often differs between boys and girls. Perhaps the worst example occurred under the Taliban in Afghanistan, where, for several years, young girls were prohibited from attending school. Such treatment of young girls severely limits their life chances, and ensures that they will have restricted roles in society and the economy—which was the intent of the Taliban system. The current Afghanistan government reversed this policy and included girls in the education system, but this is still resisted in parts of the nation.

Education also affects people's political skills and resources. Educated people are more aware of the impact of government on their lives and pay more attention to politics.[23] The better educated have mental skills that improve their ability to manage the world of politics. They also have more information about political processes and participate in a wider range of political activities.

Peer Groups

Peer groups include childhood playgroups, friendship cliques, school and college fraternities, small work groups, and other groups in which members share close personal ties. They can be as varied as a group of Russian mothers who meet regularly at the park, a street gang in Brazil, or a group of Wall Street executives who are members of a health club.

A peer group socializes its members by encouraging them to share the attitudes or behavior common to the group. Individuals often adopt their peers' views because they like or respect them or defer to the group's collective wisdom. Similarly, a person may become engaged in politics because close friends do so. One example of peer networks is the international youth culture symbolized by rock music, T-shirts, and blue jeans (and often more liberal political values). Some observers claim that it played a major role in the failure of communist officials to mold Soviet and Eastern European youth to the "socialist personality" that was the Marxist–Leninist ideal. Likewise, the "skinhead" groups that have sprouted up among lower-class youth in many Western countries have adopted political views that are reinforced by peer interactions.

Interest Groups

Interest groups, economic groups, and similar organizations can shape political attitudes. In most industrial countries, the rise of trade unions transformed the political culture and politics, created new political parties, and ushered in new social benefit programs. Today, unions typically are active participants in the political process and try to persuade their members on political matters. Other professional associations—such as groups of peasants and farmers, manufacturers, wholesalers and retailers, medical societies, and lawyers—also regularly influence political attitudes in modern and modernizing societies. These groups ensure the loyalty of their members by defending their economic and professional interests. They can also provide valuable political cues to nonmembers, who might identify with a group's interests or political ideology. For instance, when a group that you like (or dislike) publicly supports a policy, it gives you information on the likely content of the policy.

The groups that define a civil society are also potential agents of socialization. These groups might include ethnic organizations, fraternal associations, civic associations (such as parent–teacher associations), and policy groups (such as taxpayers' associations, women's groups, and environmental groups). Such groups provide valuable political cues to their members and try to reinforce distinct social and political orientations. They also provide settings to learn about how making political choices in small groups can be extended to politics.

In democracies, we think about interest groups as expressing the values of their members. But in authoritarian states, they can also be vehicles for the government to propagandize group members. For instance, Vietnam has an active network of social groups that socialize individuals into the norms of the communist regime, while civil society groups in the United States are treated as democracy-building organizations.

Political Parties

Political parties normally play an important role in political socialization in democratic and nondemocratic systems (also see Chapter 5). In democratic systems,

Meet the Press
European leaders President Grybauskaite of Lithuania, President Hollande of France, and Chancellor Merkel of Germany meet with the press at the 2013 EU Summit.

political parties try to shape issue preferences, arouse the apathetic, and find new issues to mobilize support. Party representatives provide the public with a steady flow of information on the issues of the day. Party organizations regularly contact voters to advocate their positions. In addition, every few years, an election enables parties to present their accomplishments and discuss the nation's political future. Elections can serve as national civics lessons, and the political parties are the teachers.

Partisan socialization also can be a divisive force. In their efforts to gain support, party leaders may appeal to class, language, religious, and ethnic divisions and make citizens more aware of these differences. The Labour and Conservative parties in Britain, for example, use class cues to attract supporters. Similarly, the Congress Party in India tries to develop a national program and appeal, but other parties emphasize the ethnic and religious divisions. Leaders of preindustrial nations often oppose competitive parties because they fear such divisions. Although this is sometimes a sincere concern, it is also self-serving for government leaders, and is increasingly difficult to justify against contemporary demands for multiparty systems.

Authoritarian governments often use a single party to inculcate common attitudes of national unity, support for the government, and ideological agreement. The combination of a single party and controlled mass media is potent: The media present a single point of view, and the party activities reinforce that perspective by directly involving the citizen. In a closed environment, single-party governments can be very effective agents of socialization.

Mass Media

The mass media—newspapers, radio, television, and magazines—are actively socializing attitudes and opinions in nations around the globe. The mass media are typically the prime source of information on the politics of the day. There is virtually no place so remote that people lack the means to be informed about events elsewhere—in affluent nations, the public is wired to the Internet; satellite dishes sprout from houses in Iran; and inexpensive radios (or even smartphones) are omnipresent even in Third World communities outside of urban centers.

There is one thing that most people in the world have in common: We sit before our televisions to learn about the world. Television can have a powerful cognitive and emotional impact on large public audiences by enlisting the senses of both sight and sound. Watching events on television—such as the broadcasts of government affairs or the civil war in Syria—gives a reality to the news. Seeing the world directly can shape political attitudes.

Today, the Internet provides another powerful source of news for those with access to it.[24] The Web provides unprecedented access to information on a global scale, especially in developing nations with limited traditions of a free press. One can hardly travel to any city in the world and not see Internet cafés or WiFi access. At the same time, the Internet empowers individuals to connect to others and to develop social and political networks. This may be why autocratic governments struggle to restrict unfettered access to the Internet (see Box 3.3).

BOX 3.3 The Great Firewall of China

The People's Republic of China has the largest number of Internet users of any nation in the world, and this fact has government officials worried. Chinese "netizens" find themselves surfing in the shadow of the world's most sophisticated censorship machine. A large Internet police force monitors websites and e-mails. On a technical level, the gateways that connect China to the global Internet filter traffic coming into and going out of the country. Even the Internet cafés are now highly regulated and state-licensed, and all are equipped with standard surveillance systems. Google was one of the Western companies that initially provided keyword-blocking technology to prevent access to offending sites. Pornography was banned, but also searches for the word "democracy" or "Tiananmen Square." After struggling with censorship requirements, Google redirected Chinese searchers through its Hong Kong servers. But China continues to restrict Internet access through Chinese-based search engines.

Access to information thus becomes an important political commodity in the contemporary world. Western democracies put a premium on freedom of the media, even if they frequently complain about what the media reports. In many European nations, the government still manages some television and radio stations because it views the media as a public service. Autocratic governments typically seek to control the media and what they can report, as well as the public's access to information. Social media provide a method for antigovernment protestors to communicate and organize in Egypt, and, when similar protests appeared in other authoritarian states, the government quickly closed down Internet access. In the contemporary world of Internet and satellite broadcasting, it is becoming increasingly difficult for governments to control the spread of information.

Direct Contact with the Government

In modern societies, the wide scope of governmental activities brings people into frequent contact with various bureaucratic agencies. Surveys of Americans find that about a third have contacted a government official in the preceding year, and online interactions with government are increasing dramatically.[25] Citizens contact a wide range of government offices, from federal officials to state and local governments to school boards and the police. In addition, the government touches our lives in a myriad of other ways, from running the public schools to providing retirement checks to providing social services. The degree of government intervention in daily life, and hence the necessity for contact with government, varies greatly across nations as a function of the political system and the role of government in the society.

These personal experiences are powerful agents of socialization, strengthening or undercutting the images presented by other agents. Does the government send retirement checks on time? Do city officials respond to citizen complaints? Are the schools teaching children effectively? Do unemployment offices help people find jobs? Are the highways well maintained? These are very direct sources of information on how well the government functions. No matter how positive the view of the political system that people have learned as children, citizens who face a different reality in everyday life are likely to change their early-learned views. Indeed, the contradictions

between ideology and reality proved to be one of the weaknesses of the communist systems in Eastern Europe.

In summary, the country-specific chapters in this book examine the patterns of political socialization for several reasons. The sources of political socialization often determine the content of what is learned about politics. If people learn about new events from their friends at church, they may hear different information than people who rely on the workplace or the television for information. The role of these different socialization agents and the content of their political messages also vary systematically across nations. In addition, the ability of a nation to recreate its political culture in successive generations is an important factor in perpetuating the political system. Finally, cultures change when new elements are added to the process of political learning. Thus, socialization provides the feedback mechanism that enables a political culture to endure or change.

Trends Shaping Contemporary Political Cultures

3.5 List and describe three current forces that are affecting contemporary political cultures.

A political culture exists uniquely in its own time and place. Citizens' attitudes are shaped by personal experiences and by the agents of political socialization. Yet in any historical period, there may be trends that change the culture in many nations. The major social trends of our time reflect both general societal developments and specific historic events.

For the past two decades, a major new development is the trend toward democracy in Eastern Europe, East Asia, and other parts of the developing world. This **democratization** trend reflects long-term responses to modernity as well as immediate reactions to current events. Modernization gradually eroded the legitimacy of nondemocratic ideologies, while the development of citizens' skills and political resources made claims to greater participation in policymaking (at least indirectly) more plausible. Thus, many studies of political culture in Eastern Europe and the former Soviet Union uncovered surprising popular support for democratic norms and processes as the new democratic system formed.[26]

Ironically, as democracy has begun taking root in Eastern Europe, citizens in many Western democracies are increasingly skeptical about politicians and political institutions. In 1964, three-quarters of Americans said they trusted the government; in 2012, less than a fifth of the public say as much—and the malaise is spreading to Western Europe and Japan.[27] At the same time, public support for democratic norms and values has strengthened over time in most Western democracies. Thus, these publics are critical of politicians and political parties when they fall short of these democratic ideals. Although this cynicism is a strain on democratic politicians, it presses democracy to continue to improve and adapt, which is ultimately democracy's greatest strength.

Another recent major trend affecting political cultures is a shift toward **marketization**—that is, an increased public acceptance of free markets and private profit incentives, rather than a government-managed economy. One example of this movement appeared in many Western European nations and the United States beginning in the 1980s, where economies had experienced serious problems of inefficiency and economic stagnation. Margaret Thatcher in Britain and Ronald Reagan in the United States rode to power on waves of public support for reducing the scale of government. Public opinion surveys show that many people in these nations feel that government should not be responsible for individual well-being (see again Figure 3.3).

Just as Western Europeans began to question the government's role in the economy, the political changes in Eastern Europe and the Soviet Union reinforced this trend toward marketization. The command economies of Eastern Europe were almost exclusively controlled by state corporations and government agencies. The government set both wages and prices and directed the economy. The collapse of these systems raised new questions about public support for marketization. Surveys generally find that Eastern Europeans support a capitalist market system and the public policies that would support such an economic system.[28]

Globalization is another trend affecting political cultures of many nations. Increasing international trade and international interactions tend to diffuse the values of the overall international system. Thus, as developing nations become more engaged in the global economy and global international system, the development of certain norms—such as human rights, gender equality, and democratic values—increases.[29] People in developing nations also learn about the broader opportunities existing in other nations, which can spur cultural change as well as economic change. Thus, although globalization has been a deeply divisive political issue for the past decade in many nations, the Pew Global Values Survey found broad support for globalization among citizens worldwide—especially in developing nations where it is seen as improving living standards and life chances.[30]

Clearly, political culture is not a static phenomenon, so our understanding of political culture must be dynamic. It must encompass how the agents of political socialization communicate and interpret historic events and traditional values. It must juxtapose these factors with the exposure of citizens and leaders to new experiences and new ideas. But it is important to understand the political culture of a nation, because these cultural factors influence how citizens act, how the political process functions, and what policy goals the government pursues.

REVIEW QUESTIONS

- What are the three key elements of a political culture?
- Why does political culture matter?
- Why is the process of political socialization important?

- What are the main agents of political socialization? List the possible agents of socialization, and then compare their relative importance across two different nations included in this book.
- What are the major trends in cultural change in the contemporary world?

KEY TERMS

agents of political
    socialization
congruence theory

democratization
direct socialization
globalization

indirect socialization
legitimacy
marketization

political culture
political socialization
political subcultures

SUGGESTED READINGS

Almond, Gabriel A., and Sidney Verba. *The Civic Culture.* Princeton, NJ: Princeton University Press, 1963.

———, eds. *The Civic Culture Revisited.* Boston: Little Brown, 1980.

Booth, John, and Mitchell A. Seligson. *The Legitimacy Puzzle in Latin America: Political Support and Democracy in Eight Nations.* New York: Cambridge University Press, 2009.

Bratton, Michael, Robert Mattes, and E. Gyimah-Boadi. *Public Opinion, Democracy, and Market Reform in Africa.* Cambridge: Cambridge University Press, 2004.

Dalton, Russell, and Christian Welzel, eds. *The Civic Culture Transformed: From Allegiant to Assertive Citizens.* Cambridge: Cambridge University Press, 2014.

Gilley, Bruce. *The Right to Rule: How States Win and Lose Legitimacy.* New York: Columbia University Press, 2009.

Horowitz, Donald. *Ethnic Groups in Conflict.* Berkeley: University of California Press, 2000.

Huntington, Samuel. *The Clash of Civilizations and the Remaking of World Order.* New York: Simon & Schuster, 1996.

Inglehart, Ronald, and Pippa Norris. *Sacred and Secular: Religion and Politics Worldwide*, 2nd ed. Cambridge: Cambridge University Press, 2011.

Inglehart, Ronald, and Christian Welzel. *Modernization, Cultural Change, and Democracy: The Human Development Sequence.* New York: Cambridge University Press, 2005.

Inkeles, Alex, and David H. Smith. *Becoming Modern.* Cambridge, MA: Harvard University Press, 1974.

Jennings, M. Kent. "Political Socialization," in *Oxford Handbook of Political Behavior*, ed. Russell Dalton and Hans-Dieter Klingemann, 29–44. Oxford: Oxford University Press, 2007.

Klingemann, Hans Dieter, Dieter Fuchs, and Jan Zielonka, eds. *Democracy and Political Culture in Eastern Europe.* London: Routledge, 2006.

Norris, Pippa, ed. *Critical Citizens: Global Support for Democratic Government.* Oxford: Oxford University Press, 1999.

Norris, Pippa, and Ronald Inglehart. *Rising Tide: Gender Equality and Cultural Change around the World.* New York: Cambridge University Press, 2003.

———. *Cosmopolitan Communications: Cultural Diversity in a Globalized World.* New York: Cambridge University Press, 2009.

Putnam, Robert. *The Beliefs of Politicians.* New Haven, CT: Yale University Press, 1973.

———. *Making Democracy Work: Civic Traditions in Modern Italy.* Princeton, NJ: Princeton University Press, 1993.

Rose, Richard, Christian Haerpfer, and William Mishler. *Testing the Churchill Hypothesis: Democracy and Its Alternatives in Post-Communist Societies.* Baltimore, MD: Johns Hopkins University Press, 2000.

Welzel, Christian. *Freedom Rising: Human Empowerment and the Quest for Emancipation.* Cambridge: Cambridge University Press, 2013.

ENDNOTES

1. This concept of legitimacy and its bases in different societies draws on the work of Max Weber. See, for example, Max Weber, *Basic Concepts in Sociology*, trans. H. P. Secher (New York: Citadel Press, 1964), chaps. 5–7.

2. Bruce Gilley, *The Right to Rule: How States Win and Lose Legitimacy* (New York: Columbia University Press, 2009).

3. Samuel Huntington, "Will More Countries Become Democratic?" *Political Science Quarterly* 99 (Summer 1984): 193–218.

4. Christian Welzel, *Freedom Rising: Human Empowerment and the Quest for Emancipation* (Cambridge: Cambridge University Press, 2013); and Russell Dalton and Christian Welzel, eds., *The Civic Culture Transformed: From Allegiant to Assertive Citizens* (Cambridge: Cambridge University Press, 2014).

5. Ronald Inglehart and Christian Welzel, *Modernization, Cultural Change, and Democracy* (Cambridge: Cambridge University Press, 2005); Russell Dalton and Doh Chull Shin, eds., *Citizens, Democracy, and Markets around the Pacific Rim* (Oxford: Oxford University Press, 2006); and Michael Bratton, Robert Mattes, and E. Gyimah-Boadi, *Public Opinion, Democracy, and Market Reform in Africa* (Cambridge: Cambridge University Press, 2004).

6. For the list of nations in the World Values Survey, see the project website: www.worldvaluessurvey.org.

7. Amartya Sen, *Development as Freedom* (New York: Knopf, 1999).

8. In prior editions, we discussed the differences between parochial, subject, and participatory roles, and the concentration of parochials in less developed nations. Current research leads us to consider this categorization as too stark, as technological and communications changes have spread political information and interest on a broad global scale.

9. Welzel, *Freedom Rising.*

10. Ronald Inglehart, *Modernization and Postmodernization* (Princeton, NJ: Princeton University Press, 1997), chaps. 6 and 7.

11. Ronald Inglehart, *Culture Shift in Advanced Industrial Societies* (Princeton, NJ: Princeton University Press, 1990).

12. Even within established Western democracies, there are internal differences in the appropriate role of government, the role of the citizen, and the perceived goals of government. See Ole Borre and Elinor Scarbrough, eds., *The Scope of Government* (Oxford: Oxford University Press, 1995).

13. W. Kymlicka and N. Wayne, eds., *Citizenship in Divided Societies* (Oxford: Oxford University Press, 2000); and Donald Horowitz, *Ethnic Groups in Conflict* (Berkeley: University of California Press, 2000).

14. Amy Chua, *World on Fire: How Exporting Free Market Democracy Breeds Ethnic Hatred and Global Instability* (New York: Doubleday, 2003).

15. See Welzel, *Freedom Rising.*

16. Kendall Baker, Russell Dalton, and Kai Hildebrandt, *Germany Transformed* (Cambridge, MA: Harvard University Press, 1981).

17. Robert Putnam, *Making Democracy Work: Civic Traditions in Modern Italy* (Princeton, NJ: Princeton University Press, 1993); and Robert Putnam, *Bowling Alone: The Collapse and Revival of American Community* (New York: Simon & Schuster, 2000).

18. Samuel P. Huntington, *The Clash of Civilizations and the Remaking of World Order* (New York: Simon & Schuster, 1996.

19. See Gabriel A. Almond and Sidney Verba, *The Civic Culture* (Princeton, NJ: Princeton University Press, 1963), chap. 12; and M. Kent Jennings, Klaus R. Allerbeck, and Leopold Rosenmayr, "Generations and Families," in Samuel H. Barnes et al., *Political Action* (Beverly Hills, CA: Sage, 1979), 485–522.

20. Such fundamentalism is often a defensive reaction against the spread of scientific views of nature and human behavior, and the libertarian values and attitudes that accompany these views. The influence of fundamentalism has been most visible not only in Muslim countries but also in Christian countries. Broadly speaking, fundamentalism seeks to raise conservative social, moral, and religious issues to the top of the contemporary policy agenda.

21. Pippa Norris and Ronald Inglehart, *Rising Tide: Gender Equality and Cultural Change around the World* (New York: Cambridge University Press, 2003).

22. Martha Nussbaum and Jonathan Glover, eds., *Women, Culture, and Development* (New York: Oxford University Press, 1995).

23. For example, see Sidney Verba, Norman H. Nie, and Jae-on Kim, *Participation and Political Equality* (New York: Cambridge University Press, 1978); and Pippa Norris, *Democratic Phoenix: Reinventing Political Activism* (New York: Cambridge University Press, 2003).

24. Pippa Norris and Ronald Inglehart, *Cosmopolitan Communications: Cultural Diversity in a Globalized World* (New York: Cambridge University Press, 2009).

25. Aaron Smith, Kay Lehman Schlozman, Sidney Verba, and Henry Brady, "The Internet and Civic Engagement," Pew Internet and American Life Project (Washington, DC: Pew Research Center, September 2009) (www.pewinternet.org).

26. Richard Rose, Christian Haerpfer, and William Mishler, *Testing the Churchill Hypothesis: Democracy and Its Alternatives in Post-Communist Societies* (Baltimore, MD: Johns Hopkins University Press, 2000).

27. Pippa Norris, *Critical Citizens: Global Support for Democratic Government* (Oxford: Oxford University Press, 1999); and Russell Dalton, *Democratic Challenges, Democratic Choices: The Erosion of Political Support in Advanced Industrial Democracies* (Oxford: Oxford University Press, 2004).

28. See William Zimmerman, *The Russian People and Foreign Policy: Russian Elite and Mass Perspectives* (Princeton, NJ: Princeton University Press, 2002), chap. 2; and Raymond Duch, "Tolerating Economic Reform," *American Political Science Review* 87 (1993): 590–608. Russian support for marketization noticeably lags behind that of most Eastern Europeans.

29. Wayne Sandholtz and Mark Gray, "International Integration and National Corruption," *International Organization* 57 (Autumn 2003): 761–800; and Mark Gray, Miki Kittilson, and Wayne Sandholtz, "Women and Globalization: A Study of 180 Countries, 1975–2000," *International Organization* 60 (Spring 2006): 293–333.

30. Pew Global Attitudes Project, *Views of a Changing World, June 2003* (Washington, DC: Pew Research Center, 2003), 71–81 (http://pewglobal.org/reports/display.php?ReportID=185).

CHAPTER 4

Interest Articulation

LEARNING OBJECTIVES

4.1 Define interest articulation, and provide some examples of interest articulation in different societies.

4.2 Explain three ways in which individuals can participate in the political system.

4.3 List four types of interest groups and give examples.

4.4 Describe the characteristics and benefits of a civil society.

4.5 Identify and describe the three main types of interest group systems, and give examples of nations where each is prevalent.

4.6 Compare and contrast legitimate and coercive channels of political access.

4.7 Describe the factors that contribute to the creation of interest groups.

Suppose an unjust or unfair law was being passed by the government—what could you do to express your dissatisfaction and try to stop the legislation? Or suppose you see a need that the government is not addressing—what could you do to encourage government action? These are the questions that we often face as citizens. What choices do we have for making our interests and needs known to policymakers?

People and social groups have some way to express their needs and demands to their government in almost every political system. This process, known as **interest articulation**, can take many forms. For example, a person might contact a city council member, or, in a more traditional system, he or she might meet with the village head or tribal chieftain. Or a group of people might work together on a common concern. In large, established political systems, formal interest groups are a primary means of promoting political interests.

As societies become internally more complex and the scope of government activity increases, the quantity and variety of ways to articulate public interests grow proportionally. People work together to address local and national needs, ranging from providing clean water in a village to passing national clean water standards. Social movements involve the public in issues as diverse as protecting the rights of indigenous people in the Amazon and debating nuclear power. Formally organized interest groups develop to represent labor, farmers, businesses, and other social interests. Large numbers of interest groups work in capitals like London, Washington, D.C., and Tokyo. Today, Internet chat rooms and blogging provide another forum for expression. In countries with powerful local governments, interest groups are active at the provincial or local level as well.

This chapter considers the multiple ways in which people can express their interests in contemporary political systems. First, we discuss the means of interest articulation that are available to individuals. Then, we describe how formal interest groups and associations provide another means of interest articulation. For example, in most countries that allow them, labor unions, manufacturers' associations, farm groups, and associations of doctors, lawyers, engineers, and teachers represent these interests. In the end, most political systems have many different forms of interest articulation to determine what the public and social groups want from their government.

Citizen Action

4.1 Define interest articulation, and provide some examples of interest articulation in different societies.

One aspect of interest articulation involves what you might do as an individual citizen. People can make requests and demands for policies in various ways (Table 4.1).[1] Each of these forms of action has different characteristics, as described in the table. The most common form of citizen participation is voting in an election. When elections are free, meaningful, and accessible, they enable people to express their interests and to make a collective choice about the government's past progress and the future policies for the nation. Although elections select political elites, they often are a blunt policy tool because they involve many different issues; moreover, between elections, officeholders may stray from the voters' preferences. Of course, resident noncitizens are not eligible to vote in most countries. As immigration has increased in many countries that are more prosperous or stable than their neighbors, the accessibility and obligations of obtaining citizenship have become important issues. Noncitizens are affected by government policies but have fewer avenues to try to influence them.

People can also work with others in their community to address common needs, as when parents work to better the local schools or residents express their worries about traffic in their community. These activities are typically very policy focused and exert direct pressure on decision makers. Such group activity exists in both democratic and authoritarian systems, although nondemocracies may limit the methods of expression to those that do not openly confront authorities.

Some interest articulation involves direct contact with government, such as writing a letter or sending an e-mail to an elected official or to a government bureaucracy (see Box 4.1). Some direct contact involves personal issues, such as when a veteran writes to his legislator for help in getting benefits approved, or when a homeowner asks the council member to ensure that the streets in her neighborhood are snowplowed regularly. These forms of personal contact are common across political systems, including the authoritarian ones. Other direct contact involves broader political issues facing the government, such as campaigns to support or block new legislation. Direct contact on policy issues occurs primarily in democratic systems, where citizen input is broadly encouraged. However, even in autocratic nations, the public often finds ways to petition the government on policy matters.[2]

The expression of interests also may involve **protests** or other forms of contentious action. A spontaneous protest over police harassment by outraged ghetto dwellers, the public protests that overthrew the communist governments of Eastern Europe, and the environmental actions of Greenpeace are all examples

TABLE 4.1
Articulating Interests
The forms of political participation vary in their scope and pressure on elites.

Form	Scope of Interests	Degree of Pressure on Elites
Voting, participation in elections	Broad, collective decision on government leaders and their programs	Modest pressure, but not policy-focused
Informal group	Collective action focused on a common interest	High pressure
Direct contact on personal matter	Normally deals with specific, personal problem	Low pressure
Direct contact on policy issue	Action on a government policy	Modest pressure
Protest activity	Highly expressive support for specific interests	High pressure
Political consumerism	Focused on specific issues, activities	High pressure

---

BOX 4.1   The *Shangfang* System

In 1949, the communist government in China created the *Shangfang* system, which allows individuals to petition the government formally to intervene on their behalf. This system was intended as a safety valve to allow disgruntled individuals to express their grievances, and as a method for the state to mobilize expression of support from the populace. The petitioners typically are concerned about personal problems or local issues, and this system allows them to bypass unresponsive local officials and petition Beijing. Sometimes, they even travel to the capital to present their petition in person. The use of Shangfang has ebbed and flowed over time, but it illustrates how even authoritarian governments seek input from their citizens. Experts estimate that the government in Beijing receives more than 10 million petitions, ranging from a complaint over an eviction notice to protests about the effects of the Three Gorges Dam. However, only a minuscule fraction of these petitions receive a government response, and, sometimes, local officials retaliate against the people who petitioned to a higher authority instead of coming to them.

---

of how protest articulates policy interests. Protests and other direct actions tend to be high-pressure activities that can both mobilize the public and directly pressure elites; these activities can also be very focused in their policy content.

Participation studies have found that political consumerism—buying or boycotting a product for political reasons—is another active form of participation, at least in Western democracies.[3] Such participation allows individuals to protest the activities of a firm that pollutes or has unfair labor practices. For example, organized boycotts against child labor practices have affected the sales and public images of many clothing manufacturers, and led to new public policies. Such efforts are very focused. If they become politically visible, they can have broader policy effects as well.

In summary, people can take many routes to express their interests, and each of these routes has particular characteristics associated with it.

How Citizens Participate

 Explain three ways in which individuals can participate in the political system.

The amount of citizen political participation varies widely according to the type of activity and the type of political system. Table 4.2 shows examples of the types of participation in several of the nations examined in this book.

The most frequent forms of political participation revolve around elections: turning out to vote, trying to convince others how to vote, or working with political parties. Because elections are the most common form of public involvement in the political process, they are important forms of interest articulation. During elections, people speak their minds on current issues, attend meetings, contribute to campaigns, express their opinions to pollsters, and ultimately cast their ballots. At the same time, elections perform many other functions: aggregating political interests, recruiting political elites, and even socializing political values and preferences through the campaign process (see Chapter 2).

Among the democracies, the United States has rather low levels of national voting participation: Both Western Europeans (with their long democratic experience) and several new democracies vote more frequently than Americans. Brazil, like a few other countries, has compulsory voting and achieves participation rates over 80 percent. However, as the table shows, Americans' low level of election turnout does not simply reflect apathy. Americans are relatively interested in politics and participate in other ways beyond elections. They also have more frequent election opportunities than citizens in most countries.

Public efforts to express political interests and influence public policy extend beyond elections. Grassroots politics—people working together to address a common problem—is a very direct method for articulating political interests and attempting to influence policy. Alexis de Tocqueville considered such

TABLE 4.2
How Are We Active?
People engage in a variety of political activities (percentage).

Type of Participation	Britain	Brazil	China	France	Germany	India	Iran	Japan	Mexico	Nigeria	Russia	United States
Voter turnout in most recent national elections	61	81	—	71	65	56	62	63	65	48	63	54
Interested in politics	44	49	65	38	62	44	46	64	34	—	39	59
Belong to environmental group	16	7	10	15	5	—	10	5	13	—	5	16
Signed a petition	68	56	6	67	50	29	—	60	21	—	8	70
Joined in a boycott	17	8	3	14	9	15	—	7	3	—	3	20
Participated in lawful protest demonstration	17	18	—	38	31	19	—	10	16	—	16	15

Sources: Election turnout data is percent of voting age public for most recent national legislative election from the International Institute for Elections and Democracy, downloaded from www.idea.org; 2005–2008 World Values Survey for other statistics. Some of the participation questions were not asked in each survey, and these missing items are noted by a dash in the table.

grassroots community action to be the foundation of democracy in America. Today, such activities are often identified with middle-class participation in affluent societies—such as parent–teacher association groups, community associations, and public interest groups—but group activity occurs in almost any nation.[4] Indian villagers working together to develop rural electricity and indigenous people protecting their land rights are other examples of community action. Table 4.2 presents membership in an environmental group as one example of public interest group activity. About a sixth of the public in the United States, Britain, and France belong to an environmental group, but such citizen action is lower in less developed nations and new democracies.

Perhaps the most expressive and visible form of citizen action involves contentious actions, such as signing a petition, joining a boycott, or participating in protests. For instance, many environmentalists believe that direct actions—hanging an environmental banner from a polluting smokestack, staging a mass demonstration outside parliament, or boycotting polluters—effectively generate media attention and

public interest in their cause. Political protests arise for quite different reasons. On the one hand, protest and direct action are often used by individuals and groups that feel they lack access to legitimate political channels. The mass demonstrations in Eastern Europe in the late 1980s and the public protests of the Arab Spring illustrate protests as the last resort of the disadvantaged. On the other hand, peaceful protests are also increasingly used by the young and better-educated citizens in Western democracies. To many democratic citizens, protest is the continuation of "normal" politics by other means.

The majority of the public in most Western democracies say they have signed a petition, although such open disagreement with government policy is more limited in new democracies and autocratic states (see Table 4.2). (However, petitions have a long tradition in some dictatorships; see Box 4.1.) In addition, about a sixth of the Western public say they have joined in a boycott or participated in a lawful protest. Protest activities are nearly as frequent in some developing democracies, such as Mexico and Brazil. The autocratic trends in Russia are now suppressing popular dissent (see Chapter 12). Indeed, protest generally increases with democratization, as governments become more tolerant of dissent and the rights of dissenters are protected.[5]

France is a nation where protests have become part of the tradition of politics. In the late 1960s, the French government nearly collapsed as a result of protests that began when university students stimulated a mass movement against the government. More recently, new policies to raise the retirement age to 62 generated massive protests in 2010, including "Project Escargot," in which truckers intentionally slowed traffic on the highways. In a typical year, Paris might experience protests by students, shopkeepers, farmers, homemakers, government employees, environmentalists, women's groups, and a host of other interest groups. Protest is almost a national political sport in France. We see in Table 4.2 that far more French citizens (38 percent) report having participated in lawful protest demonstrations than the citizens of any of the other countries discussed in this book.

Citizen participation also reflects the political context. In nations with active political parties and competitive elections, many people participate in the electoral process. In nations where such activities are limited, people may turn to group-based activity or protest in order to express their preferences, but it is more likely that they are politically inactive. As we noted in Chapter 3, a participatory political culture is often a by-product of political modernization.

Cross-national research shows that better-educated and higher social status individuals are more likely to use the various opportunities for participation. These individuals tend to develop attitudes that encourage participation, such as feelings of efficacy and a sense of civic duty.[6] They also possess the personal resources and skills that are useful in becoming politically active when duty calls or a need arises. Skill and confidence are especially important for demanding activities, such as organizing new groups or becoming a leader in an organization. This inequality in participation is less for easier activities, such as voting. The tendency for the better-off to be politically active is more evident in societies (such as the United States) with weak party organizations, weak working-class groups (such as labor unions), and less party attention to lower-class interests. In nations with stronger working-class parties and labor unions, organizational networks encourage the participation of less affluent citizens.

Participation patterns are important for several reasons. For citizens to influence government policy, they first need to articulate their interests to the government. A wider choice of activities presumably increases the citizens' ability to express their interests and be heard. Moreover, the forms of action differ in their policy content and political pressure (see again Table 4.1). Finally, people differ in their level of political activity and the ways in which they participate. These differences in voice likely affect policy outputs if the government responds to public pressures. In other words, those who are more active in articulating their interests are more likely to have their interests addressed by policymakers, often at the expense of the less involved.

Interest Groups

4.3 List four types of interest groups and give examples.

Interest articulation can also occur through the actions of groups that represent a set of people. In addition, interest groups can participate in the political process, serving on government advisory bodies and testifying at parliamentary hearings. Interest groups vary in structure, style, financing, and support base, and these differences may influence a nation's politics, its economics, and its social life. We begin by defining four types of interest groups: anomic, nonassociational, institutional, and associational.

Anomic Groups

Anomic groups are groups that suddenly form when many individuals react to an event that stimulates frustration, disappointment, or other strong emotions. They are flash affairs, rising and subsiding suddenly. Without previous organization or planning, frustrated people may suddenly take to the streets to vent their anger as news of a government action touches deep emotions or as a rumor of new injustice sweeps the community. The widespread use of cell phones and access to the Internet and social media have greatly facilitated the ability of individuals to gather and coordinate their actions in response to events. This technology has played an important role in the events of the Arab Spring in 2011 and afterward. Their actions may lead to violence, although not necessarily. Particularly where organized groups are absent or where they have failed to get adequate political representation, smoldering discontent may be sparked by an incident or by the emergence of a leader. It may then suddenly explode in relatively unpredictable and uncontrollable ways.

Some political systems, including both developed and developing nations, report a rather high frequency of violent and spontaneous anomic behavior.[7] Anger over the assassination of a popular political leader or another catastrophic event can also stimulate public outbursts. For instance, relatively spontaneous public demonstrations often occur when one nation takes a hostile action toward another nation. Wildcat strikes (spontaneous strike actions by local workers, not organized actions by national unions), long a feature of the British trade union scene, also occur frequently in other European countries and have started to emerge in China.

Sometimes, anomic groups are a subset of individuals drawn from a larger social grouping, such as a racial or ethnic group. For instance, in 1992, some residents in minority neighborhoods of Los Angeles rioted and looted following the acquittal of police officers accused of excessive violence in the beating of an African American suspect. Similarly, in 2005 to 2006, protests broke out in many Muslim countries over the depiction of Mohammed in the Western press, producing deaths and mass violence. We treat these as anomic group actions because there is no structure or planning to the event, and the people involved disperse after the protest ends.

We must be cautious, however, about calling something an anomic political behavior when it really is the result of detailed planning by organized groups. For instance, the demonstrations against the G8 summit in Genoa in 2001, and similar "Stop G8" protests subsequently, including the "Carnival Against Capitalism" in London in 2013, owed much to indignation but little to spontaneity (see Box 4.2).

Nonassociational Groups

Unlike anomic groups, **nonassociational groups** are based on common interests and identities of ethnicity, region, religion, occupation, or perhaps kinship. Because of these ties, nonassociational groups have more continuity than anomic groups. But nonassociational groups rarely are well organized, and their activity is episodic. Subgroups within a large nonassociational group (such as an ethnic minority or workers) may act as an anomic group, as in the 1992 Los Angeles riots, the 2005 Paris immigrant riots, and the Middle East protests against the Danish cartoons of Mohammed in 2006. Throughout the world, ethnicity and religion, like occupation, are powerful identities that can stimulate collective activity.

Two kinds of nonassociational groups are especially interesting. One is a large group that is not formally organized, although its members may perceive common interests. Many ethnic, regional, and occupational groups fit into this category. It can be very difficult to organize such groups because, although members share a common problem, no one

---

BOX 4.2   Attacks on Globalization

In July 2001, tens of thousands of protestors arrived in Genoa, Italy, to demonstrate at the G8 Summit Meeting. Hundreds of different groups came to protest at the meetings, and several of the more radical groups engaged in running battles with the police. Many of the most violent clashes involve the "Black Block." The Block comprises several loosely organized anarchist and radical groups, wearing trademark black clothing, black hoods, and gas masks. Confrontations with police often appeared choreographed in advance, coordinated by cell phones, and videotaped by sympathetic

activists—and subsequently distributed on the Internet. Many other protest groups in Genoa were worried that the radical anarchist goals of the Block detracted attention from their policy concerns about the economic and social impacts of globalization. Similar violent actions occurred during protests at the G8 summits in Germany in 2007, Switzerland in 2009, and London and Belfast in 2013. The violence perpetrated by some groups overshadowed both the elected politicians at these summits and the policy goals of the nonviolent groups.

makes the effort to organize other members because the individual costs outweigh the individual benefits. This is commonly known as the **collective action problem**.[8] If large collective benefits—for example, ending discriminatory legislation or cleaning up water pollution—are achieved, they are shared even by those who did not work, the so-called "free riders." This pattern of people waiting for the rewards without sharing the cost or risk of action affects other types of groups as well. For instance, students who might benefit from lower tuition fees are typically underrepresented because they lack effective organizations to articulate their interests. Understanding the collective action problem helps us to see why some groups (including governments and revolutionary challengers) become organized and others do not, and under what circumstances the barriers to collective action are overcome.

A second type of nonassociational group is the small community group or ethnic subgroup whose members know each other personally. A small, face-to-face group has some important advantages and may be highly effective in some political situations. If its members are well connected or its goals are unpopular or illegal, the group may remain informal or even inconspicuous. Such groups may take various actions, such as engaging in work stoppages, circulating student petitions to demand better support and training, requesting that a bureaucrat continue a grain tariff to benefit landowners, or asking a tax collector for favored treatment to benefit relatives. As the last example suggests, personal interest articulation may often have more legitimacy and perpetuate itself by invoking group or personal ties.

Institutional Groups

Institutional groups are based in formal organizations that have other political or social functions in addition to interest articulation. Business corporations, political parties, legislatures, armies, bureaucracies, and churches often have separate political groups with special responsibility for representing a group's interests. Either as corporate bodies or as smaller groups within these bodies (legislative blocs, officer cliques, groups in the clergy, or ideological factions in parties and bureaucracies), institutional groups claim to express the interests of their members. The influence of these interest groups is usually drawn from the strength of

their primary organizational base—for instance, the size of their membership or their income. A group based on a governmental institution has direct access to policymakers.

In industrial democracies, bureaucratic and corporate interests use their resources and special information to affect policy. In the United States, for instance, the military industrial complex includes the U.S. Department of Defense and defense industries that support military expenditures. Similarly, the farm lobby and the U.S. Department of Agriculture together often advocate agricultural policies. In most societies, government bureaucracies do not simply react to pressures from the outside; they also can act as independent forces of interest representation.

Nonpolitical institutional groups can also participate in the political process. In Italy, for example, the Roman Catholic Church has exerted significant influence on the government. In electoral politics, the Church used to ask Catholics to vote against the communists. Less overtly, the Church has members of the clergy call on officeholders to express opinions on matters of concern to the Church. In Islamic countries, fundamentalist clergy pursue a similar role, prescribing what morals public policy should follow, actively lobbying governmental officials, and sometimes participating in the governing process.

In authoritarian regimes, which prohibit or at least control explicitly political groups, institutional groups can still play a large role. Educational officials, party officials, jurists, factory managers, officers in the military services, and government bodies representing other social units had significant roles in interest articulation in communist regimes. In preindustrial societies, which usually have fewer associational groups (with limited popular support), military groups, corporations, party factions, and bureaucrats often play prominent political roles. Even where the military does not seize power directly, the possibility of such action often forces close government attention to military requests.

Associational Groups

Associational groups are formed explicitly to represent the interests of a particular group, such as trade unions, chambers of commerce, manufacturers' associations, and ethnic associations. These organizations have procedures for formulating interests

Taking to the Streets
Pakistanis in Karachi, Pakistan, protest publication in Europe of offensive cartoons depicting Mohammed.

belief in a political ideology or a policy goal.[9] The environmental movement, many women's groups, human rights organizations, anti-immigration associations, and other civic groups illustrate this kind of associational group. In Nigeria, the Transition Monitoring Group pushed for electoral reform and organized to monitor polling stations against electoral fraud during Nigeria's transition to democracy. In some of these issue groups, the members may seldom interact directly and may not even share common social characteristics (such as employment or ethnicity), but are bound together by their support of a political organization, such as Greenpeace, Amnesty International, or the National Rifle Association in the United States. On the organizational side, many of these groups have fluid and dynamic organizations, with frequent turnover in both leadership and membership. On the tactical side, they use a wide range of approaches, often discounting the value of partisan campaigning and conventional lobbying in favor of unconventional protests and direct actions.

Civic associations represent another way for citizens to articulate their policy goals by supporting groups that advocate their preferred policy positions. Such groups have proliferated in most advanced industrial democracies in the past generation, and they are now spreading to the developing world.

In summary, a social interest can manifest itself in many different groups. We can illustrate this point with examples of different groups that might involve members of the working class:

Anomic group: a spontaneous group of working-class individuals living in the same neighborhood

Nonassociational group: the working class as a collective

Institutional group: the labor department within the government

Associational group: an association of labor unions

Distinguishing among the types of groups is important for several reasons. The nature of a group typically reflects the resources it can mobilize to support its

and demands, and they usually employ a full-time professional staff. These groups are often very active in representing their members' interests in the policy process. For instance, in recurring debates about health care in the United States, there is an enormous mobilization of pressure groups and lobbyists—from representatives of doctors and health insurance organizations to consumer groups and the American Association of Retired Persons (AARP)—seeking to influence legislation.

Associational interest groups—where they are allowed to flourish—affect the development of other types of groups. Their organizational base gives them an advantage over nonassociational groups, and their tactics and goals are often recognized as legitimate in society. Labor unions, for example, are often central political actors, because they represent the mass of the working class; in the same way, business associations often speak for the corporate interests of the nation. Associations of professionals, such as the British, American, and Nigerian medical associations, or the Nigerian Union of Journalists, attempt to shape public policies that affect the interests of those in their respective professions.

A special subset of associational groups consists of citizens who are united not by a common economic or individual self-interest but by a common

Labor Organizations Press for Workers' Interests
In a speech before the International Labour Organization in June 2012, newly freed democracy activist and now member of parliament Aung San Suu Kyi praises the ILO and urges their continuing efforts on behalf of workers' rights in Myanmar.

political efforts. Perhaps one of the most important resources is an institutional structure that will sustain political efforts until the government responds to the group's interests. The nature of a group also may signify the tactics it uses to gain political access. Finally, since the articulation of interest is the first step in policy influence, the nature of groups suggests which types of interests are more likely to get a hearing in the political system and which interests may be underrepresented.

Civil Society

 Describe the characteristics and benefits of a civil society.

Political analysts have devoted increasing attention to whether an extensive network of interest groups and public participation in these groups creates a **civil society**—a society in which people are involved in social and political interactions free of state control or regulation. Community groups, voluntary associations, and even religious groups—as well as access to free communication and information through the mass media and the Internet—are important parts of a civil society.[10] Participation in civil society groups can socialize individuals into the political skills and cooperative relations that are part of a well-functioning society. People learn how to organize,

express their interests, and work with others to achieve common goals. They also learn that the political process itself is as important as the immediate results. Thus, a system of active associational groups can lessen the development of anomic or nonassociational activity. Group activity can help citizens to develop and clarify their own preferences, provide important information about political events, and articulate the interests of citizens more clearly and precisely than parties and elections.[11] Thus, an active public involved in various interest groups provides a fertile ground for the development of democratic politics.

As political and economic conditions become interdependent across nations, there is also increasing attention directed toward the development of a global civil society. Individuals and groups in one nation are connected to groups with similar concerns in other nations, and jointly reinforce their individual efforts. Environmental groups in the Western democracies, for example, assist environmental groups in developing nations with the expertise and organizational resources to address the issues facing their countries. National groups meet at international conferences and policy forums, and the network of social relations, as well as Internet connections, extends across national borders.[12] This is another sign of how the international context of domestic politics is growing worldwide.

One problem facing newly democratizing nations is how to build a rich associational group life in societies where the government had suppressed or controlled organized groups.[13] The Communist Party and the government bureaucracy dominated the nations of Eastern Europe for over forty years and prevented autonomous action. The process of building new, independent associational groups to articulate the interests of different citizens is under way and will be important to the democratic process. Similarly, if democratization is to succeed, many less economically developed nations need to create a civil society of associational groups to involve citizens in the political process and represent their interests.

Interest Group Systems

4.5 Identify and describe the three main types of interest group systems, and give examples of nations where each is prevalent.

The relationship between interest groups and government policymaking institutions is another important feature of the political process. Different types of connections create different interest group systems. All modern societies have large numbers of interest groups, but their relationships with government can follow different models. Interest group systems are classified into three major groupings: pluralist, democratic corporatist, and controlled.[14]

Pluralist Interest Group Systems

Pluralist interest group systems have several features involving both how interests are organized and how they participate in the political process:

- Multiple groups may represent a single societal interest.
- Group membership is voluntary and limited.
- Groups often have a loose or decentralized organizational structure.
- There is a clear separation between interest groups and the government.

For instance, not only are there different groups for different social sectors (such as labor, business, and professional interests) but there may be many labor unions or business associations within each sector. These groups compete among themselves for membership and influence, and all simultaneously press their demands on the government. The United States and France are the best-known examples of strongly pluralist interest group systems. Figure 4.1 shows their low levels of union membership, around 10 percent of the workforce. Canada and New Zealand are also cited as examples of pluralist interest group systems. Despite its greater labor union membership (see Figure 4.1) and somewhat greater coordination of economic associations, Britain tends to fall on the pluralist side in most analyses of policymaking. Japan has a more mixed system, with a small role for organized labor.

Democratic Corporatist Interest Group Systems

Democratic **corporatist interest group systems** are characterized by a much more organized representation of interests:

- A single peak association normally represents each societal interest.
- Membership in the peak association is often compulsory and nearly universal.
- Peak associations are centrally organized and direct the actions of their members.
- Groups are often systematically involved in making and implementing policy.

For instance, in a democratic corporatist system, there may be a single peak association that represents all the major industrial interests; a pluralist system may have several different business groups that act autonomously. In addition, in a democratic corporatist system, peak associations are centrally organized, while groups in a pluralist system typically have decentralized organizational structures. The most thoroughly corporatist of the democratic interest group systems are in Austria, Finland, Norway, and Sweden. The Nordic nations are characterized by very high levels of union membership, around 65 percent of the employed population, which is more than double the highest memberships in Figure 4.1, based on

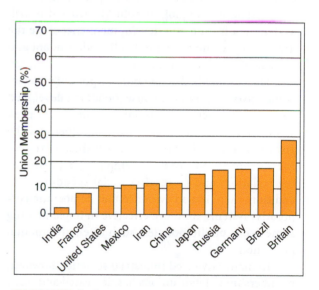

FIGURE 4.1

Union Membership

Labor union density varies widely across nations, but the role of unions varies even more.

Source: International Labour Organization, *International Statistical Inquiry into Trade Union Density and Collective Bargaining Coverage 2008–2009* (www.ilo.org). The figure plots union membership as a percentage of employed population. For China, Iran, and Russia, ILO data are missing and the figure is the percentage of respondents who mentioned being a member of a labor union in the 2005–2008 World Values Surveys.

the same data source. Moreover, these nations, like Austria, have highly centralized and united labor movements.

Equally important, interest groups such as labor unions in these systems often regularly and legitimately work with government agencies and/or political parties as partners in negotiating solutions to policy problems. For instance, German labor unions have formal membership on many government commissions, have special access to policy administration, and are very influential through informal channels of influence. Thus, despite an average level of union membership, Germany is a close fit to the democratic corporatist model (see Chapter 10).

Mexico and Brazil are examples of another form of corporatist politics. Union membership is modest in Mexico, although higher in Brazil (see again Figure 4.1). However, the trade unions and peasant associations in both countries were organized by the state during authoritarian regimes and remain closely tied to political parties or religious interests. Usually these groups mobilize support for the political parties or social institutions that dominate them, and they are closely tied to the state when their party is in power. This system is changing in both Mexico and Brazil, as democratization and development encourage the unions to become more politically independent and influential (see Chapters 14 and 15).

The best-studied democratic corporatist arrangements involve economic consequences in developed societies. Democracies with business and labor peak associations that negotiate with each other and the government have had better records than more pluralist countries in sustaining employment, restraining inflation, and increasing social spending.[15] In addition, there is also evidence that democratic corporatist systems are more effective in implementing some other public policies, such as environmental protection.[16]

In many advanced industrial societies, however, membership in labor unions has decreased and some bargaining patterns have become less centralized. Countries that have relied on democratic corporatist patterns have adapted this system to these new settings and applied corporatism in new ways.[17] In contrast, several nations in Eastern Europe are attempting to develop more democratic corporatist structures to nurture interest group politics, but the system of autonomous interest groups remains underdeveloped.

The experience with democratic corporatist models in developing nations is even more varied.[18] The very low level of union membership in India shown in Figure 4.1 illustrates a pattern common in many developing democracies. Interest groups, such as unions, are often not well developed and have a limited mass membership. They are participants in the political process, but without the mass membership or formal access that gives labor unions influence in established Western democracies of either the pluralist or corporatist model.

Controlled Interest Group Systems

Finally, **controlled interest group systems** follow a different pattern:

- There is a single group for each social sector.
- Membership is often compulsory.
- Each group is normally hierarchically organized.
- Groups are controlled by the government or its agents in order to mobilize support for government policy.

The last point is the most important: Groups exist to facilitate government control of society. The best examples are the traditional communist systems in which the party penetrates all levels of society and controls all the permitted associational groups. For instance, Figure 4.1 shows that 12 percent of the adult citizens of China belong to a union.[19] As discussed in Chapter 13, unions and other interest associations in China are subordinated to the Communist Party, and they are only rarely permitted to articulate the interests of their members. Russia once followed this communist model, and the unions still have substantial memberships as a result of this experience. Chapter 12, on Russia, discusses how the unions are struggling to gain autonomy from the state and play an influential role in the postcommunist system. But they have made limited progress. And the Putin regime has taken steps to control autonomous interest articulation.

These nations limit interest articulation to leaders who can use their positions in major political institutions as a base for expressing their demands. Numerous institutional interest groups can emerge in these societies, especially from parts of the party and bureaucracy, such as the military, as well as informal nonassociational groups.

Access to the Influential

4.6 Compare and contrast legitimate and coercive channels of political access.

To be effective, interest groups must reach key policymakers through **channels of political access**. Otherwise, groups may express their members' interests yet fail to have an impact on policymakers. Political systems vary in the ways they respond to political interests. Interest groups vary in the tactics they use to gain access. Group tactics are partially shaped by the structure of policymaking, as well as by their own values and preferences.

There is a significant distinction between legitimate and constitutional channels of access (such as the mass media, parties, and legislatures) and illegitimate, coercive access channels. By legitimate, we mean informal and formal channels that people and policymakers consider appropriate for the type of political system in which they live. (See the discussion of legitimacy of the political system itself in Chapter 3.) These two channels reflect the types of resources that groups can use to influence elites as well as the group's perceptions of which tactics will be most successful. Groups with substantial resources—money, members, or status—typically have an easier time working through legitimate constitutional channels. Groups with limited resources or legitimacy may feel they must act through coercive channels because they are not accepted by the political system. In democracies, groups tend toward legitimate channels because the system expects and allows group activity. In contrast, nondemocratic systems typically limit legitimate access, which might stimulate illegitimate or coercive activities.

Legitimate Access Channels

The legitimate channels of access can take many forms, and these often exist in both democratic and nondemocratic systems. For instance, personal connections are an important means of reaching political elites in all societies—the use of family, school, local, or other social ties. An excellent example is the information network among the British elite based on old school ties originating at Eton, Harrow, or other "public" schools, or at Oxford and Cambridge universities. Similarly, many alumni of the University of Tokyo

Law School hold top positions among the Japanese political and bureaucratic elites who interact because of these personal ties. Although personal connections are commonly used by nonassociational groups representing family or regional interests, they serve other groups as well. In modern nations, personal connections are usually cultivated with special care. In Washington, D.C., the business of advising interest groups and individuals on access to politicians is an increasingly lucrative profession (and increasingly a target of government regulation and potential corruption). These activities are often carried out by former officeholders, who use their personal governmental contacts for their lobbyist clients.

The **mass media**—television, radio, newspapers, and magazines—are important access channels in democratic societies. The mass media and the Internet can mobilize support for interest group efforts, leading to donations of time and money, and encouraging sympathizers to support the group. Many interest groups hire public relations specialists, purchase direct advertising, and seek favorable attention in the media. Interest groups encourage media reports on their needs as well as coverage of their policy views. When a cause receives national media attention, the message to policymakers carries added weight if politicians know that millions of voters are interested in the issue. Moreover, groups believe that in an open society, "objective" news coverage has more credibility than sponsored messages.

The potential power of the media could be seen when the communist governments in Eastern Europe loosened control over the media in the late 1980s. This action gave a huge boost to democracy movements. For instance, when asked what caused the democratic revolution in Poland in the 1990s, Lech Walesa pointed to a television and said, "That did." Media reports on the failures in communist government policy and the contrasting lifestyles in the West undermined the legitimacy of the regimes. As democratic protests spread across Eastern Europe, stories of successful protests in other parts of the country, or in other countries, enhanced the confidence of demonstrators. Citizen protests encouraged by mass media reports helped convince the ruling groups that their support had vanished.

Political parties are another important access point. Democratic political parties often rely on interest groups for financial and voter support, and act as representatives of these interests within government. In a nation like Germany, the various parts of the party organization, particularly parliamentary committees, are important channels for transmitting demands to the cabinet and the party in power. In some cases, other factors limit the parties' role as interest representatives. For instance, highly ideological parties, such as most communist parties, are more likely to control affiliated interest groups than to communicate the interest groups' demands. Decentralized party organizations, like those in the United States, may be less helpful than individual legislators in providing access.

Legislatures are a common target of interest group activities (see Box 4.3). Standard lobbying tactics include making appearances before legislative committees and providing information to individual legislators. In the United States, political action committees raise campaign contributions for individual members of Congress and usually receive some political attention in exchange. In parliamentary systems, the strong party discipline in the legislature often lessens the importance of individual members of Parliament (MPs) as access channels.[20] In contrast, in the United States, the combination of loose party discipline and a decentralized legislative system makes the individual members of Congress major targets of group efforts.

Government bureaucracies are another major access point in most political systems. Contacts with the bureaucratic agencies may be particularly important where the bureaucracy has policymaking authority or where interests are narrow and directly involve few citizens. A bureaucrat sympathetic to a group may try to respond to its demands by exercising administrative discretion without leaving bureaucratic channels. A government official may also give public consideration to an issue or frame an issue in a way that receives a sympathetic hearing by policymakers. The bureaucracy may be an especially important access point in nondemocratic systems because other legitimate channels of citizen access do not exist.

Government officials may consider protest demonstrations, strikes, and other forms of dramatic and direct pressure on government to be either legitimate or illegitimate tactics, depending on the political system. Protests may be either spontaneous actions of an anomic group or a planned use of unconventional channels by an organized group. In democratic societies, demonstrations often mobilize popular support—or electoral support—or media attention for the group's cause. On a regular basis, the Mall in Washington, D.C., and similar locations in other national capitals host groups protesting a wide variety of policy issues. Protests can supplement other channels, especially in gaining the attention of the mass media and social media. Thus, we find doctors in New Delhi, farmers in Japan, and "gray panthers" (the elderly) in Germany using a tactic that once was limited to the poor and minorities.[21] In nondemocratic societies, such demonstrations are more hazardous and often represent more extreme dissatisfaction that cannot find voice through conventional channels of access.

BOX 4.3   Lobbying Behind the Scenes

British beer companies use a variety of means to support their industry. For example, the industry contributed funds to Labour MPs who recently voted for longer opening hours for British pubs. They also provide travel support for MPs who are favorable to the industry. A group of MPs who support the industry formed the All-Party Parliamentary Beer Group (APBG). The group's announced goal is "to promote the wholesomeness and enjoyment of beer and the unique role of the pub in UK society." The parliamentary group campaigned to have beer taxes reduced, conducted hearings on whether the government overregulates British pubs, and supported the extension of pub hours. The group hosts a series of functions at Westminster, giving industry chiefs the opportunity to meet MPs and showcase their products. The parliamentary group also selects a "beer drinker of the year," who receives an award at their annual dinner. The parliamentary group receives direct financial support from breweries, and the secretary for the group is paid by the alcohol industry.

Visit the APBG website: www.publications.parliament.uk/pa/cm/cmallparty/register/beer.htm.

Vote by Vote
Protesters hold a massive demonstration in front of Mexico's electoral court to demand a ballot-by-ballot recount of the disputed 2006 presidential election.

Coercive Access Channels and Tactics

Most scholars see the level of collective violence as closely associated with the character of a society and the circumstances in the nation. In his studies of civil strife, Ted Robert Gurr argued that feelings of relative deprivation motivate people to act aggressively.[22] These feelings can stimulate frustration, discontent, and anger—which may then lead to violence. People also may turn to violence if they believe it is justified and will lead to success. If they think that their government is illegitimate and that the cause of their discontent is justified, they will more readily turn to political violence. To this end, it is the responsibility of the government and its institutions to provide peaceful alternatives to violence as a means of change.

This general description of political violence should not overlook the differences among the types of violent political activities. A riot, for example, involves the spontaneous expression of collective anger and dissatisfaction by individuals. (Some people may also join for fun and profit as police are overwhelmed and order breaks down.) Though riots were long dismissed as aberrant and irrational action by social riffraff, modern studies have shown that rioters vary greatly in their motivation, behavior, and social background.[23] Most riots seem to follow some fairly clearcut patterns, such as confining destruction or violence to particular areas or targets. Relative deprivation appears to be a major cause of riots, but the release of the frustrations is not as aimless as is often supposed.

For instance, the 2005 riots in Paris were triggered by the accidental deaths of two teenagers, but most analysts see their deaths as only a proximate cause, a "spark" that ignited already volatile factors. Gangs of minority youth burned thousands of automobiles, damaged shops, and attacked police who attempted to quell the violence. The French president and then the Parliament declared a state of emergency in reaction to the violent protests, establishing a curfew and limiting civil liberties. Even though much of the mayhem seemed poorly related to effective political action, it was a cry for attention. Youth from immigrant families had high levels of unemployment and felt that social and economic discrimination was limiting their life chances. Even in a democracy, the government sometimes overlooks the needs of its own citizens and allows such frustrations to explode into violence.

While deprivation may help fuel the discontent, strikes and obstructions are typically carried out by well-organized associational or institutional groups. For instance, a long series of violent protests against globalization involves highly organized activities among some of the more radical groups participating in the protests (see again Box 4.2).

Historically, labor unions used the general strike to pressure the government or employers on fundamental issues. The influence of strikes and obstructions has varied, however, depending on the legitimacy of the government and coercive pressure from other groups. A general strike after vote fraud in the 2004 Ukrainian elections produced a transition to a new democratic government, but student-inspired boycotts in Korea in the 1980s had only a modest impact on the government. Most spectacularly, the strikes, obstructions, and demonstrations in Eastern Europe in 1989 and 1990, like the earlier people's power movement in the Philippines, had massive success against regimes that had lost legitimacy.

Finally, radical groups sometimes use **political terror tactics**—including deliberate assassination, armed attacks on other groups or government officials, and mass bloodshed. The assassinations and bombings in Northern Ireland, the suicide bombings by Palestinians in Israel, and the attacks of jihadist terrorists in New York City, Madrid, London, Bali, and other cities demonstrate the use of such tactics. The use of terrorism typically reflects the desire of some group to change the rules of the political game or to destroy a political system rather than to gain political access.

The use of political terror is more often likely to produce negative consequences rather than construct positive policy change. Massive deadly violence may destroy a democratic regime, leading to curtailment of civil rights or even military intervention when many people and leaders feel that any alternative is preferable to more violence. For example, democratically elected governments justified their suppression of democratic institutions in Peru in 1992 and India in 1975 (see Chapter 17) in response to the violent actions of terrorists. An authoritarian, repressive response often promises quick results against terrorists; however, small-group terrorism usually fails when confronted by united democratic leadership.[24] In a democratic society, violence often forfeits the sympathy that a group needs if its cause is to receive a responsive hearing. The current conflict between the West and jihadist terrorists has renewed the debate on how democratic governments should balance the need for security against the preservation of civil liberties.

Groups and Channels

In order to understand the formation of policies, we need to know which groups articulate interests, their policy preferences, and the channels of influence they use. Table 4.3 gives examples of legitimate and coercive interest articulation for different types of interest groups. Each case provides an example of the differences in legitimate access channels, from informal meetings by Mexican business leaders lobbying their government to Greenpeace testifying before European Parliament committees. Similarly, coercive acts range from spontaneous outbursts by anomic groups to Al Qaeda using terror bombings against the Western democracies. This framework also helps us to think about how a single interest group might pursue its goals through multiple channels, including protests, representation by institutional groups, and lobbying by associational groups. For instance, honeybee farmers in the United States have lobbied their representatives in Congress to maintain federal price supports, and they also use their allies in the U.S. Department of Agriculture to support their position (will honeybee protests be next?). This table presents examples from many nations in order to suggest the varied possibilities that exist in each nation.

TABLE 4.3
Examples of Interest Articulation
Interest groups can use either legitimate or coercive channels of action.

Types of Interest Groups	Channel of Action	
	Legitimate Channel	**Coercive Channel**
Anomic groups	Chinese workers stage impromptu strikes for better pay and working conditions	Iranians attack Danish embassy to protest cartoons depicting Mohammed
Nonassociational groups	Mexican business leaders discuss taxes with president	Minorities in France riot in 2005 over their social conditions
Institutional groups	U.S. Department of Agriculture advocates subsidies for honey production	Egyptian army in 2011 supports movement to overthrow dictatorship
Associational groups	Greenpeace lobbies the European Parliament to ban genetically modified foods	Al Qaeda launches terrorist attacks on U.S. embassies and World Trade Center

Interest Group Development

4.7   Describe the factors that contribute to the creation of interest groups.

One consequence of modernization is a widespread belief that the conditions of life can be altered through human action. Modernization normally involves education, urbanization, rapid growth in public communication, and improvement in the physical conditions of life. These changes are closely related to increases in political awareness, participation, and feelings of political competence. Such participant attitudes encourage more diverse and citizen-based interest articulation.

At the same time, modernization produces an increasing diversity of life conditions and a specialization of labor as people work in many types of jobs—a process that leads to the formation of large numbers of special interests. The interdependence of modern life, the exposure provided by mass communications, and a larger policy role of government further multiply political interests that are organized into different interest groups. Globalization processes have also increased the interactions between interest groups across nations, or between domestic groups and international actors.[25] Thus, the diversity of interest groups and their activities is another by-product of modernization.

Successful democratic development leads to the emergence of complex interest group systems that express the needs of groups and individuals in the society. Yet this process is by no means automatic. The Internet, social media, and the spread of cell phones have facilitated coordination. But the problems of organizing large groups for collective action are huge. Societies vary widely in the extent to which people engage in associational activity. The level of trust shared among members of a society is one factor influencing social group participation.[26] The resources and societal support available for collective action is another factor. Modernization may weaken traditional structures in some societies and then fail to develop effective associational groups in their place because of restrictive social attitudes. A nation's ability to achieve either stability or democracy will be hindered as a result.

In other cases, authoritarian parties and bureaucracies may control associational groups and choke off the channels of political access. For nearly half a century, the communist governments of Eastern Europe suppressed autonomous interest groups. China today devotes much energy to attempting to control use of the Internet (Chapter 13). Eventually, the processes of economic modernization should pressure these systems to allow more open organization and expression of political interests.

The development of organized interest groups should not, however, lead us to conclude that every group has equal standing. Using the American experience as an example, the articulation of interests is frequently biased toward the goals of the better-off, who are also often better organized.[27] It is frequently pointed out that the AARP is a highly effective group that is not counterbalanced by a "Young Taxpayers Group," and that the traditional labor–management competition leaves consumers underrepresented. Small groups also find it easier to organize on behalf of their goals.

We might test the breadth of citizen representation by evaluating systems in terms of their inclusiveness: What proportion of the population is represented to what degree in national level politics? South Africa under apartheid illustrates the extreme case where the majority was prevented outright from forming associational groups. In the Third World, competing interests in the capital rarely involve the interests of rural peasants; peasant organizations are sometimes brutally suppressed, while urban middle- and upper-class groups can petition authorities. It is no coincidence that the bias in group inclusion appears greatest where the gaps in income and education are widest. As noted above, pushed to the extreme, those excluded from the process may engage in anomic activity or resort to violence.[28] Even in less extreme cases, the presence of different levels of political awareness means that every interest group system is somewhat biased. Democratization involves not only the provision of competitive elections but also the reduction of the bias in interest representation.

Another challenge faces the patterns of interest articulation and representation in advanced industrial democracies. There are claims that participation in associational groups is decreasing in the United States and perhaps in other established democracies.[29] For instance, memberships in labor unions and formal church engagement have steadily trended downward in most Western democracies over the past several decades. Some scholars argue that this trend represents a growing social isolation in developed nations, as people forsake social and political involvement for the comfort of a favorite chair and a favorite television program. However, other researchers argue that we are witnessing a change in how citizens organize and express their interests, such as through public interest groups, the Internet, and blogging.[30] Even in nations such as India and China, millions of people are now using the Internet to learn about politics and how they can articulate their interests.

What can be said for certain is that democratic politics rests on a participatory public that uses individual and group methods to express and represent its interests. Thus, developing an active social and political life is an important standard for measuring the political development of a nation.

REVIEW QUESTIONS

- How do the different forms of citizen action vary in their potential influence on policymakers?
- What are the main types of interest groups?
- How does a "civil society" differ from a noncivil society?
- What are the key differences among pluralist, neocorporatist, and controlled interest group systems?

- What are the consequences when an interest group works through legitimate channels of influence rather than coercive channels?
- If you studied interest articulation patterns in one of the nations discussed in this book, could you build a table (like Table 4.3) showing examples of the types of groups and the channels they used?

KEY TERMS

anomic groups
associational groups
channels of political access
civil society

collective action problem
controlled interest group systems
corporatist interest group systems

institutional groups
interest articulation
mass media
nonassociational groups

pluralist interest group systems
political terror tactics
protests

SUGGESTED READINGS

Dahl, Robert A. *Polyarchy: Participation and Opposition.* New Haven, CT: Yale University Press, 1971.

———. *Democracy and Its Critics.* New Haven, CT: Yale University Press, 1989.

Dalton, Russell J. *Citizen Politics: Public Opinion and Political Parties in Advanced Industrial Democracies,* 6th ed. Washington, DC: CQ Press, 2013.

Hirschman, Albert. *Exit, Voice, and Loyalty.* Cambridge, MA: Harvard University Press, 1970.

Howard, Marc Morjé. *The Weakness of Civil Society in Post-Communist Europe.* New York: Cambridge University Press, 2003.

Maloney, William, and Jan Van Deth. *Civil Society and Activism in Europe: Contextualizing Engagement and Political Orientations.* London: Routledge, 2010.

Norris, Pippa. *Democratic Phoenix: Reinventing Political Activism.* New York: Cambridge University Press, 2003.

Olson, Mancur. *The Logic of Collective Action.* Cambridge, MA: Harvard University Press, 1965.

Paxton, Pamela, and M. Hughes. *Women, Politics and Power: A Global Perspective.* London: Pine Forge Press, 2007.

Putnam, Robert D. *Bowling Alone: The Collapse and Revival of American Community.* New York: Simon & Schuster, 2000.

———, ed. *Democracies in Flux: The Evolution of Social Capital in Contemporary Society.* Oxford: Oxford University Press, 2002.

Rootes, Christopher. *Environmental Protest in Western Europe.* Oxford: Oxford University Press, 2007.

Schlozman, Kay Lehman, Sidney Verba, and Henry Brady. *The Unheavenly Chorus: Unequal Political Voice and the Broken Promise of American Democracy.* Princeton, NJ: Princeton University Press, 2012.

Shi, Tianjian. *Political Participation in Beijing.* Cambridge, MA: Harvard University Press, 1997.

Tarrow, Sidney. *The New Transnational Activism*. New York: Cambridge University Press, 2005.

———. *Power in Movement: Social Movements and Contentious Politics*, 2nd ed. New York: Cambridge University Press, 1998.

Thomas, Clive. *Political Parties and Interest Groups: Shaping Democratic Governance*. Boulder, CO: Lynn Rienner, 2001.

Verba, Sidney, Norman H. Nie, and Jae-on Kim. *Participation and Political Equality*. Cambridge: Cambridge University Press, 1978.

Welzel, Christian. *Freedom Rising: Human Empowerment and the Quest for Emancipation*. Cambridge: Cambridge University Press, 2014.

Zurn, Michael, and Gregor Walter, eds. *Globalizing Interests: Pressure Groups and Denationalization*. Albany: State University of New York Press, 2005.

ENDNOTES

1. This framework draws on Sidney Verba, Norman N. Nie, and Jae-on Kim, *Participation and Political Equality* (New York: Cambridge University Press, 1978), chap. 2.

2. See, for example, the range of activities of Beijing residents described in Tianjin Shi, *Political Participation in Beijing* (Cambridge, MA: Harvard University Press, 1997).

3. Michele Micheletti, Andreas Follesdal, and Dietlind Stolle, *Politics, Products, and Markets: Exploring Political Consumerism Past and Present* (Piscataway, NJ: Transaction Publishers, 2003).

4. Pippa Norris, *Democratic Phoenix: Reinventing Political Activism* (New York: Cambridge University Press, 2003); and Verba, Nie, and Kim, *Participation and Political Equality*.

5. Russell Dalton, Alix van Sickle, and Steve Weldon, "The Individual–Institutional Nexus of Protest Behavior," *British Journal of Political Science* 40 (2010): 51–73.

6. See Verba, Nie, and Kim, *Participation and Political Equality*; and Norris, *Democratic Phoenix*.

7. See the evidence in J. Craig Jenkins and Kurt Schock, "Political Process, International Dependence, and Mass Political Conflict: A Global Analysis of Protest and Rebellion, 1973–1978," *International Journal of Sociology* 33 (2004): 41–63.

8. Studies of these problems were stimulated by the now-classic work of Mancur Olson, *The Logic of Collective Action* (Cambridge, MA: Harvard University Press, 1965). See also Mark Lichbach, *The Rebel's Dilemma* (Ann Arbor: University of Michigan Press, 1994).

9. Christopher Rootes, *Environmental Protest in Western Europe* (Oxford: Oxford University Press, 2007); Amrita Basu, ed., *The Challenges of Local Feminism: Women's Movements in Global Perspective* (Boulder, CO: Westview, 1995); and Pamela Paxton and M. Hughes, *Women, Politics and Power: A Global Perspective* (London: Pine Forge Press, 2007).

10. Jean Cohen and A. Arato, *Civil Society and Political Theory* (Cambridge: Massachusetts Institute of Technology Press, 1992); and M. Walzer, ed., *Toward a Global Civil Society* (Oxford: Berghahn Books, 1995).

11. See Table 4.1; John Pierce et al., *Citizens, Political Communication, and Interest Groups: Environmental Organizations in Canada and the United States* (Westport, CT: Praeger, 1992).

12. Sidney Tarrow, *The New Transnational Activism* (New York: Cambridge University Press, 2005); and Margaret Keck and Kathryn Sikkink, *Activists beyond Borders: Advocacy Networks in International Politics* (Ithaca, NY: Cornell University Press, 1998).

13. Marc Morjé Howard, *The Weakness of Civil Society in Post-Communist Europe* (New York: Cambridge University Press, 2003); and Russell Dalton, "Civil Society, Social Capital and Democracy," in *Citizens, Democracy, and Markets around the Pacific Rim*, ed. Russell Dalton and Doh Chull Shin (Oxford: Oxford University Press, 2006).

14. Philippe Schmitter, "Interest Intermediation and Regime Governability," in *Organizing Interests in Western Europe*, ed. Suzanne Berger (New York: Cambridge University Press, 1981), chap. 12; and Arend Lijphart, *Patterns of Democracy* (New Haven: Yale University Press, 2012), 162–70.

15. On the relative success of the corporatist systems in economic performance, see Miriam Golden, "The Dynamics of Trade Unionism and National Economic Performance," *American Political Science Review* 87, no. 2 (June 1993): 439–54; and Arend Lijphart, Ronald Rogowski, and R. Kent Weaver, "Separation of Powers and Cleavage Management," in *Do Institutions Matter? Government Capabilities in the United States and Abroad*, ed. R. Kent Weaver and Bert A. Rockman (Washington, DC: Brookings Institution, 1993), 302–44.

16. Lyle Scruggs, "Institutions and Environmental Performance in Seventeen Western Democracies," *British Journal of Political Science* 29 (1999): 1–31.

17. Oscar Molina and Martin Rhodes, "Corporatism: The Past, Present and Future of a Concept," *Annual Review of Political Science* 2 (2002): 305–31.

18. Howard Wiarda, ed. *Authoritarianism and Corporatism in Latin America—Revisited* (Gainesville: University Press of Florida, 2004); and Julius E. Nyang'Oro and Timothy M. Shaw, *Corporatism in Africa: Comparative Analysis and Practice* (Boulder, CO: Westview Press, 1990).

19. We should also note that half of the Chinese population still live in rural areas and are not wage earners. On the varying memberships and roles of interest groups in Asian dictatorships and democracies, see Dalton, "Civil Society."

20. See the discussion of party cohesion in parliamentary systems in Chapter 6. Also see John M. Carey, *Legislative Voting and Accountability* (New York: Cambridge University Press, 2009).

21. Norris, *Democratic Phoenix*.

22. T. Robert Gurr, *Why Men Rebel* (Princeton, NJ: Princeton University Press, 1970).

23. See Pippa Norris, Stefaan Walgrave, and Peter van Aelst, "Does Protest Signify Disaffection? Demonstrators in a Postindustrial Democracy," in *Political Disaffection in Contemporary Democracies*, ed. Mariano Torcal and Jose

Ramón Montero (London: Routledge, 2006), 279–307. On the older tradition on riots, see the review by Anthony Oberschall, *Social Conflict and Social Movements* (Englewood Cliffs, NJ: Prentice-Hall, 1973), chap. 1.

24. On violence and democratic survival, see G. Bingham Powell, Jr., *Contemporary Democracies: Participation, Stability, and Violence* (Cambridge, MA: Harvard University Press, 1982), chap. 8; see also the contributions to Juan J. Linz and Alfred Stepan, eds., *The Breakdown of Democratic Regimes* (Baltimore: Johns Hopkins University Press, 1978).

25. Michal Zurn and Gregor Walter, eds., *Globalizing Interests: Pressure Groups and Denationalization* (Albany: State University of New York Press, 2005); and Keck and Sikkink, *Activists beyond Borders*.

26. Ronald Inglehart, *Culture Shift in Advanced Industrial Societies* (Princeton, NJ: Princeton University Press, 1990), 34–36.

27. Jeffrey M. Berry, *The Interest Group Society* (New York: Longman, 1997).

28. See Christian Houle, "Inequality and Democracy: Why Inequality Harms Consolidation but Does Not Affect Democratization," *World Politics* 61 (2009): 589–622.

29. Robert Putnam, *Bowling Alone: The Collapse and Revival of American Community* (New York: Simon & Schuster, 2000); and Robert Putnam, ed., *Democracies in Flux: The Evolution of Social Capital in Contemporary Society* (Oxford: Oxford University Press, 2002).

30. Cliff Zukin et al., *A New Engagement? Political Participation, Civic Life, and the Changing American Citizen* (New York: Oxford University Press, 2006); and Russell Dalton, *The Good Citizen* (Washington, DC: CQ Press, 2009), chap. 4.

CHAPTER 5

Interest Aggregation and Political Parties

LEARNING OBJECTIVES

5.1 Describe patron–client networks.

5.2 Explain how groups can act as interest aggregators.

5.3 Compare and contrast competitive and authoritarian party systems and their roles in interest aggregation.

5.4 Discuss the types of electoral systems and their relation to patterns of electoral competition.

5.5 Describe the features of different competitive party systems.

5.6 Compare and contrast exclusive and inclusive authoritarian party systems.

5.7 Describe the range of the military's role as an interest aggregator.

Many citizens want their governments to make decisions on the basis of a coherent policy program. For political decisions to be made this way, interests must not only be articulated but also packaged into alternative visions or programs. **Interest aggregation** is the process by which political demands are combined into policy programs. For example, when politicians make economic policy, they often have to balance farmers' desires for higher crop prices, consumers' preferences for lower prices and taxes, and environmentalists' concerns about water pollution and pesticides. Who prevails in such balancing acts depends in part on political institutions, which is the subject of Chapter 6. But interest aggregation depends also on political skills and resources, such as votes, campaign funds, political offices, media access, or even armed force.

How interests are aggregated is a key feature of politics. The aggregation process determines which interests are heard and who is allowed to participate. Interest aggregation can help create a balanced government program out of competing policy goals, but it can also generate a bundle of compromises that satisfy no one. How stable and effective governments are depends on their success in interest aggregation.

Interest aggregation can occur in many ways. An elected leader or military dictator may have a considerable personal impact. Yet large states usually develop more specialized organizations for aggregating interests. Political parties are just such organizations, and they aggregate interests in democratic, as well as in many nondemocratic, systems. Each party (or its candidates) promotes a set of policies and tries to build a coalition of support for this program. In democracies, two or more parties compete to gain support for their alternative policy programs. In autocracies, the ruling party or administration may try to mobilize citizens' support for its policies, but the process is frequently covert, controlled, and top-down rather than bottom-up. In other words, autocratic (authoritarian) parties mobilize interests to support the government rather than responding to demands by ordinary citizens or social interests.

It is important to remember that political parties may perform many functions other than interest aggregation and that interests may be aggregated by many different structures. For instance, parties frequently shape the political culture as they strive to build support for their programs and candidates.

Parties recruit voters and select candidates for office. They articulate interests of their own and transmit the demands of others. Governing parties are also involved in making public policy and overseeing its implementation and adjudication. Yet parties are particularly important structures of interest aggregation. In this chapter, we therefore devote special attention to the role of parties in interest aggregation, but we also compare parties to other structures that aggregate interests.

Personal Interest Aggregation

5.1 Describe patron–client networks.

One way to bring political interests together in policy-making is through personal connections. Virtually all societies feature **patron–client networks**—structures in which a central officeholder or authority figure, the *patron*, provides benefits (patronage) to *clients* in exchange for their loyalty and support. Such networks were the defining principle of feudalism. The king and his lords, the lord and his knights, the knight and his serfs and tenants—all were bound by ties of personal dependence and loyalty. The American political machines of Boss Tweed of New York or Richard Daley, Sr., of Chicago were similarly bound together by patronage and loyalty. Personal networks are not confined to relationships cemented by patronage only. The president of the United States, for instance, usually has a circle of personal confidants, a "brain trust" or "kitchen cabinet," bound to their chief by ideological and policy propensities as well as by ties of friendship.

The patron–client network is so common in politics that it resembles the cell in biology or the atom in physics—the primitive structure out of which larger and more complicated political structures are composed. Students of politics in all countries report such networks. When interest aggregation is performed mainly within patron–client networks, it is difficult to mobilize political resources behind unified policies of rapid social change. This is because political decisions depend on ever-shifting agreements among many factional leaders (patrons) who all want to benefit. Patron–client politics thus typically means a static political system with little policy innovation.

Contemporary research on patron–client relationships was pioneered in studies of Asian politics, where this structure runs through the political processes of countries such as the Philippines, Japan,

Elections and Protest

Elections can stir strong feelings of joy or disappointment. Here, French protesters demonstrate against the election of President Nicolas Sarkozy in May 2007. The placard translates as: "No to capitalism with a human face."

TABLE 5.1

Structures Performing Interest Aggregation in Selected Contemporary Nations
Parties are not alone.*

Country	Extensiveness of Interest Aggregation by Actor				
	Patron–Client Networks	**Associational Groups**	**Competitive Parties**	**Authoritarian Parties**	**Military Forces**
Brazil	Moderate	Moderate	Moderate	—	Low
Britain	Low	High	High	—	Low
China	Moderate	Low	—	High	High
France	Low	Moderate	High	—	Low
Germany	Low	High	High	—	Low
India	High	Moderate	Moderate	—	Low
Iran	High	Moderate	Low	—	Moderate
Japan	Moderate	High	High	—	Low
Mexico	Moderate	Moderate	Moderate	—	Low
Nigeria	High	Low	Moderate	—	Moderate
Russia	Moderate	Low	Moderate	—	Moderate
United States	Low	Moderate	High	—	Low

*Extensiveness of interest aggregation rated as low, moderate, or high. Rating refers to broad-level performance issue areas at different times. Blank (—) implies that such actors do not exist.

and India.[1] But parallels exist in Europe, the Middle East, Latin America, and most regions of the world. Patron–client relationships affect recruitment to political office, interest aggregation, policymaking, and policy implementation. Yet as Table 5.1 shows, patron–client networks are a particularly important means of aggregating political interests in poorer countries, often because patrons more reliably provide what ordinary citizens want than do the governments of those countries.

Institutional Interest Aggregation

5.2 Explain how groups can act as interest aggregators.

In developing societies, as citizens become aware of larger collective interests and have the resources and skills to work for them, personal networks tend to be regulated, limited, and incorporated within broader organizations. Interest groups with powerful resources can easily cross the subtle line between interest articulation and aggregation. Associational groups (see Chapter 4) often support political contenders such as political parties. But they can occasionally wield sufficient resources to become contenders in their own right. For instance, the political power of the labor unions within the British Labour Party historically rested on their ability to develop coherent policy positions and mobilize their members (who were typically also party members) to support those positions. As we discussed in Chapter 4, corporatist interest group systems empower both labor and business groups to become actively engaged in making economic policies. These arrangements include continuous political bargaining among organized labor, business interests, political parties, and government representatives. Such corporatist systems interconnect organizations that in other political systems play very different, often antagonistic, roles. Table 5.1 illustrates how associational groups tend to play a larger role in democracies that accept interest groups actively attempting to influence government policy, which is often where these groups have close ties with particular political parties.

Institutional groups, such as bureaucratic agencies and military factions, can also be important interest aggregators. Indeed, the bureaucracy performs this function in most societies. Although established primarily to implement public policy, the bureaucracy may negotiate with interest groups to identify their preferences or to mobilize their support. Government agencies may even be "captured" by interest groups and used to press their demands. Bureaucrats often cultivate client support networks to expand their organizations or to enhance their power. Military organizations, with their special control of physical force, can also be powerful interest aggregators. We will have more to say about their role later in this chapter.

Competitive Party Systems and Interest Aggregation

5.3 Compare and contrast competitive and authoritarian party systems and their roles in interest aggregation.

In many contemporary political systems, parties are the primary structures of interest aggregation. Political parties are *groups or organizations that seek to place candidates in office under their label.* In any given society, there may be one party, two parties, or as many as ten or twenty. We refer to the number of parties, and the relationships among them, as properties of the **party system**. A major distinction exists between **competitive party systems**, in which parties primarily try to build electoral support, and noncompetitive or **authoritarian party systems**, in which ruling parties do not have to worry about electoral competitors. This distinction does not depend on the closeness of electoral victory, or on the number of parties. It depends instead on the ability of political parties to form freely and compete for citizen support, and on whether this competition for citizen support is the key to gaining control of the government. Thus, a party system can be competitive even if one party wins an election resoundingly or even dominates several consecutive elections, as long as other parties are free to challenge its dominance at the polls.

The role of competitive parties in interest aggregation depends not only on the individual party but also on the structure of parties, electorates, electoral laws, and policymaking institutions. Typically, interest aggregation in a competitive party system occurs at several stages: within the individual parties, as the party chooses candidates and adopts policy proposals; through electoral competition; and after the election, through bargaining and coalition building with other parties in the legislature or executive.

Political parties have been around as long as there have been elections and representative assemblies, but modern democratic parties began developing in Europe and the Americas from about the mid-nineteenth century. They have since emerged in all societies that have adopted free and fair elections and democratic government. Parties differ in their purposes and organization. Some have elaborate policy platforms, whereas others are little more than vehicles for ambitious politicians to get elected (or even to enrich themselves). Some parties are highly structured mass organizations, whereas others are loose, *personalistic* groups dominated by their leaders (see Box 5.1).

The first parties were typically *internally created*; their founders were politicians who already held seats in the national assembly or other political offices. These parties were often committed to broad constitutional principles (such as republican government, universal suffrage, or separation of church and state), but, otherwise, they often had only loose policy programs and little organization outside the legislature. They often had colorful names that said little about their policies, such as Whigs and Tories in Britain, Whites ("Blancos") and Reds ("Colorados") in several Latin American countries, Hats and Caps in Sweden, or for that matter, Democrats and Republicans in the United States.

During the late nineteenth and early twentieth centuries, other types of parties emerged as the democratic countries industrialized and urbanized, and as an increasing number of adults gained the right to vote. The growth of the industrial working class led to the formation of socialist, social democratic, communist, and other workers' parties. Farming interests gained representation through agrarian parties, and other parties emerged to represent religious communities (such as Catholics or Hindus) or ethnic or linguistic minorities. In countries that were not independent, parties of national independence often became a dominant force. All of these parties were typically *externally created*—they first organized *outside* government and legislatures. They often had much stronger mass-membership organizations than their older competitors, and they often had (and continue to have) closer ties to specific interest groups. Thus, social democrats

BOX 5.1 Personalistic Parties

Political parties are typically formal organizations with officers, members, statutes, and official policy programs. Sometimes, however, parties can be much looser *personalistic* movements built around one political leader, or a small group of leaders. Personalistic parties are particularly common in new democracies. In Russia, for example, President Vladimir Putin (2000–2008 and 2012–) was able to form a party (United Russia) with a strong personal following. Even India and France have highly personalistic parties. In India, the Congress Party has been dominated by the families of its most important founders, Gandhi and Nehru. In France, most presidents have come out of the Gaullist movement, which has had many names but was dominated from the start by President Charles de Gaulle and later by some of his followers. Personalistic parties commonly do not have a very clear policy program. They are often susceptible to clientelistic politics and sometimes become vehicles for purely personal ambitions and rent-seeking.

Shmuel Flatto-Sharon offers an extreme example. Flatto-Sharon was a Polish-born businessman of Jewish background living in France. In 1977, he fled to Israel because the French authorities wanted to prosecute him for embezzling $60 million. To get immunity from prosecution and avoid extradition, he ran for election to the Knesset (the Israeli national assembly). He formed a party, which he ran as a one-man operation—it had no other candidates or officers. Flatto-Sharon refused to identify himself as left, right, or center. He appealed for Jewish solidarity, arguing that Israel should not allow him to be extradited. He also promised a free television set to all Israeli households (this was before television sets became inexpensive and commonplace) and subsidized apartments for young couples. And he promised to pay people who voted for him as "campaign workers." Remarkably, Flatto-Sharon won two parliamentary seats, even though, as his party's only candidate, he could not fill the second seat. In 1981, however, he lost his bid for reelection. He was later convicted of bribery for his vote-buying scheme and sent to jail in Israel, but was never extradited to France.

Some personalistic parties seem to have no other purpose than to make fun of politics and politicians. In Denmark, comedian Jacob Haugaard several times ran for office as a candidate for the Association of Deliberate Work Avoiders. In 1994, he won election to the Danish Parliament. His election platform included demands for disability pensions for people who lack a sense of humor, tailwinds on all Danish bike paths, more generous Christmas presents, more renaissance furniture at IKEA, and more whales in Danish waters. Haugaard also promised his voters free beer, and he used the public funds his party received from the Danish government to fulfill this campaign commitment (he bought beer and hot dogs for his supporters after the election).

---

and communists tend to have strong ties to labor unions, agrarian parties to farmers' organizations, and many Christian democratic parties (at least Catholic ones) to the Vatican and religious organizations.

Most of these parties still exist and continue to play a leading role. They have settled into stable *party families* of social democrats, conservatives, Christian democrats, liberals, nationalists, and others, which often maintain close contacts across national boundaries. The party systems of most established democracies show a great deal of stability, and many of the dominant parties of a hundred years ago are still the most important parties today. Yet two important new types of parties have emerged in the past several decades, particularly in advanced industrial countries. "New left" or "green" parties emerged in many countries in the 1960s and 1970s to champion international peace and disarmament, environmental protection, gender equality, and minority rights. They are often more supportive of alternative lifestyles than traditional working-class parties of the left (such as social democrats). The other important type of new party is the "populist right" party, such as the Forza Italia in Italy and the National Front in France. These parties tend to be critical of existing parties and political leaders, whom they see as elitist, corrupt, or out of touch. They are concerned with crime and security and favor strict law-and-order policies, but criticize what they see as "politically correct" government interventionism in other policy areas. They dislike the distortions that welfare states sometimes create, such as policies that make it unattractive to work and easy to live off welfare benefits (see Chapter 7). And they typically champion national sovereignty and citizenship rights and oppose large-scale immigration and international integration.

The party systems of most democratic countries reflect a mix of these various party families. But no two party systems are exactly alike, and not all party families are represented in all countries. The variations in party systems reflect differences in demographics, economic development, and political histories. They also depend on differences in electoral systems, as we will discuss below.

Elections

In democracies, political parties live and die by their performance in elections. The simple act of voting, and thereby supporting a political candidate, party, or policy proposal, is therefore one of the most consequential forms of political participation. Through voting, citizens collectively decide about their future leaders and public policies. And elections are one of the few devices through which diverse interests can be expressed equally and comprehensively.[2]

The simple act of voting can have profound implications for interest aggregation. Electoral outcomes directly or indirectly determine who manages the affairs of government and makes public policy, and parties generally fulfill their electoral promises when they gain control of government.[3] When leftist governments come to power in advanced industrial democracies, they tend to expand the size and ambitions of the government; conservative parties generally slow the growth of government programs and promote private enterprise. Parties that want radical change or have not recently been in office often find it difficult to implement their programs when they eventually come to power. When, for example, the German Greens came to power in 1998 as part of a coalition government, they had to modify their promise to shut down Germany's nuclear power plants immediately. Instead, they negotiated a phase-out over many years, and they had to accept German military involvement in the civil conflict in Kosovo, even though their program was critical of such military interventions. But, by and large, parties try hard to implement their programs, and citizens can therefore influence interest aggregation and policymaking through their role in elections.

When they aggregate interests and make policy, party leaders are often caught between the demands of their party activists and the voters. Party activists often want policies that are more radical than those that most voters prefer, and activists typically insist more vigorously that the party program should be implemented, whereas ordinary voters are often happier when governments compromise and listen to opinions outside their own parties. There is a broad and ongoing debate about the extent to which democracy requires political parties to be internally democratic (see Box 5.2). Advocates of participatory democracy strongly support this idea, as do parties such as the European Greens. On the other hand, the famous Austrian economist Joseph A. Schumpeter argued that vigorous competition *between* parties is what matters for a healthy democracy and that democracy *within* parties is irrelevant or even harmful.[4]

Elections often have other functions as well (see also Chapter 4). Autocrats often manipulate elections to legitimize their governments. Until 1990, voters in the Soviet Union were given only one candidate to vote for, and this person was always the nominee of the Communist Party. Voter participation was very high because the government pressured people to participate and express their symbolic support for the regime, not because the elections actually decided anything. Elections played a role in socializing and shaping citizens' attitudes but had little to do with interest articulation or aggregation.[5]

In most democracies, citizens can freely choose whether to vote. Yet some countries require citizens to vote, and impose penalties on those who do not. Voting choices reflect a mix of motivations.[6] Many citizens try to judge the parties' policy promises. For others, elections are a simple referendum on government performance. They vote to throw the rascals out if times are bad, and to reelect them if times are good. In other cases, elections can be dominated by the charisma of a strong leader or the incompetence of a weak one. In each case, however, elections aggregate these diverse concerns into a collective decision on the composition of the government.

Electoral Systems

The rules by which elections are conducted are among the most important structures that affect political parties. We refer to these rules as the **electoral system**. These rules determine who can vote, how to vote, and how votes are counted. The rules that determine how votes are

BOX 5.2	The Iron Law of Oligarchy

Can political parties be the main vehicles of democratic representation if they do not govern themselves democratically? This has been a main concern among students of modern political parties. In 1911, young German sociologist Robert Michels published a study of the German Socialist Party in which he formulated the **"iron law of oligarchy,"** which states that all organizations tend toward oligarchy (rule by the few) rather than democracy. "Who says organization says oligarchy," Michels famously observed. He identified several forces that push organizations such as political parties toward oligarchy. One is the need for specialization and differentiation that exists in all large, modern organizations. A second cause of oligarchy lies in the facts that most ordinary members do not have the time or resources to hold their leaders accountable and that they often crave strong leadership. A third reason is that parties foster leaders who live "off" politics rather than "for" politics. They exploit their leadership positions to advance their own ambitions for wealth or power, often to the detriment of their followers. (In contemporary terms, we would refer to such self-interested pursuit of power as *rent-seeking.*) Michels' study was particularly troubling because he found these tendencies even in a party, the German Socialist Party, with which he sympathized and that was considered particularly strongly committed to democratic ideals.

Source: Robert Michels, *Political Parties* (New York: Free Press, 1962).

converted into seats are especially important. The United States, Britain, and many countries influenced by Britain (such as India and Canada) are divided into a large number of election districts. In each district, the candidate who gains more votes than any other—a *plurality*—wins the election. This simple, **single-member district plurality (SMDP) election rule** is often called "first past the post," a horse-racing term, because the winner need only finish ahead of any of the others but need not win a majority of the votes. This system seems obvious and natural to Americans, but it is rarely used in continental Europe or in Latin America. Another version of single-member district elections is the **majority runoff** (or **double-ballot**) system used in France and in presidential elections in Russia. Under this system, voting happens in two stages, normally separated by a couple of weeks. In the first round, it takes a majority of all votes (50 percent + one vote) to win. To win, then, a candidate has to earn not just more votes than any other candidate but more votes than all other candidates combined. If there is no majority winner in the first round, only a smaller number of candidates (in French and Russian presidential elections, the top two) make it into the second round, in which whoever gets the largest number of votes (a plurality) is elected.

In contrast to the single-member district system, most democracies in Europe and Latin America use **proportional representation (PR)**. Under PR, the country is divided into a few large districts, which may elect as many as twenty or more members each. These districts are often the states or provinces that make up the country, such as the sixteen states of Germany. In the Netherlands and Israel, the entire country is a single electoral district that elects more than a hundred representatives, but these countries are the exceptions, and most PR systems are more like Germany. The parties offer lists of candidates for the slots in each district. The number of representatives that a party wins depends on the overall proportion of the votes it receives, though no system is perfectly proportional. A party receiving 10 percent of the vote would thus win roughly 10 percent of the legislative seats. Sometimes, parties must achieve a minimum threshold of votes, usually 3 to 5 percent nationally, to receive any seats at all. If so many parties compete that many of them fall below this threshold, many voters may be left unrepresented, as happened in Russia in 1995, when forty-three parties appeared on the ballot, and only seven of them won any seat in Parliament.

In order to compete effectively, parties must formulate appealing policy programs and nominate attractive candidates for office. A successful program must both spell out policy positions that are popular with the voters and satisfy demands within the party. Parties must also anticipate and try to counter the offerings of their competitors. Besides adopting programs and selecting candidates, parties also attempt to publicize them and mobilize electoral support through rallies, media advertising, door-to-door campaigning, and other activities. The procedures that parties use to develop their programs vary greatly from country to country and from party to party. In the United States, national party conventions held before each presidential election adopt a platform and select a slate of candidates, and thus formalize the party's positions. In other countries, parties have more regular congresses, and centralized party organizations issue party programs (also known as *platforms* or *manifestos*).[7]

Parties must also offer candidates for office. In the United States, voters directly select these candidates through **primary elections**. But primaries are an unusually open form of candidate selection. In most other countries with **single-member district (SMD)** elections, party officials select the candidates, either locally or nationally. In proportional representation elections, the party draws up a list of candidates for each district. In **closed-list PR systems**, the elected representatives are then simply drawn from the top of this list, in declining order, and ordinary voters have no say about their candidates. In **open-list PR systems**, in contrast, voters can give preference votes to individual candidates, and these votes determine which candidates will represent the party in that district.

Patterns of Electoral Competition

In democratic party systems, the electoral system is a major determinant of the patterns of electoral competition. Two famous political science theories help us understand this connection: Duverger's Law and Downs' median voter result. **Duverger's Law**, which is named after the French political scientist Maurice Duverger, is one of the best-known theories in political science.[8] It states that there is a systematic relationship between electoral systems and party systems, so that single-member district plurality election systems tend to create **two-party systems** in the legislature, while proportional representation electoral systems generate multiparty systems. Duverger identified two mechanisms that cause this regularity. He called them the *mechanical effect* and the *psychological effect*. The **mechanical effect** is a direct consequence of the way that different electoral systems convert votes into seats. In single-member district systems, parties get no representation unless they finish first in at least one district. Therefore, smaller parties that run second, third, or fourth across many districts receive little or no representation. In the 2010 election in Britain, for example, the Liberal Democratic Party (Britain's

third-largest party) received 23 percent of the votes but only 9 percent of the seats in the House of Commons. The **psychological effect** lies in the fact that both voters and candidates anticipate the mechanical effect. Therefore, voters do not throw their support behind "hopeless" parties and candidates. Instead, they may support their second-best (or even third-best) option in order to keep a party that they strongly dislike from winning. And knowing that the voters will not support them, minor party candidates are reluctant to run, and contributors think twice about supporting them. Giving your support to a party or candidate that is not your first choice in order to avoid an even worse outcome is known as **strategic voting**. Duverger argued that strategic voting tends to work to the advantage of parties that are already large and to the disadvantage of small ones. In U.S. elections, it has been fairly common for third-party candidates to run well in the polls until close to the election date, when voters realize that these candidates are not going to win. Their support then often declines rapidly.

Anthony Downs examined the effects of the number of parties on their policy positions. He developed a theory to show that when two parties compete along a single left–right (or other) policy dimension, they will tend to target centrist voters, or "converge." Downs assumed that parties are interested only in winning elections, and that all voters will choose the party that positions itself closest to their own policy preferences. He showed that under these conditions, the parties will moderate their policies so as to try to win the support of the median voter (the voter who is at the midpoint of the distribution of voters, with as many other voters to the right as to the left). Downs' contribution is known as the **median voter result** and applies to elections with two parties. Under these circumstances, parties have to try to win a majority, and therefore target the "center" of the electorate. PR systems tend to have many political parties, however, and none of them typically has much chance of winning a majority. On the other hand, parties can survive with much less support. Therefore, in multiparty systems, there is not the same centrist pull, and parties may instead spread themselves out across the policy spectrum.[9] The upside is that even voters who are not middle-of-the-road can find a party that voices their concerns. The downside is that more extremist parties can make for political instability.

Figure 5.1 offers a comparative "snapshot" of parties and voters in several democracies. It shows where

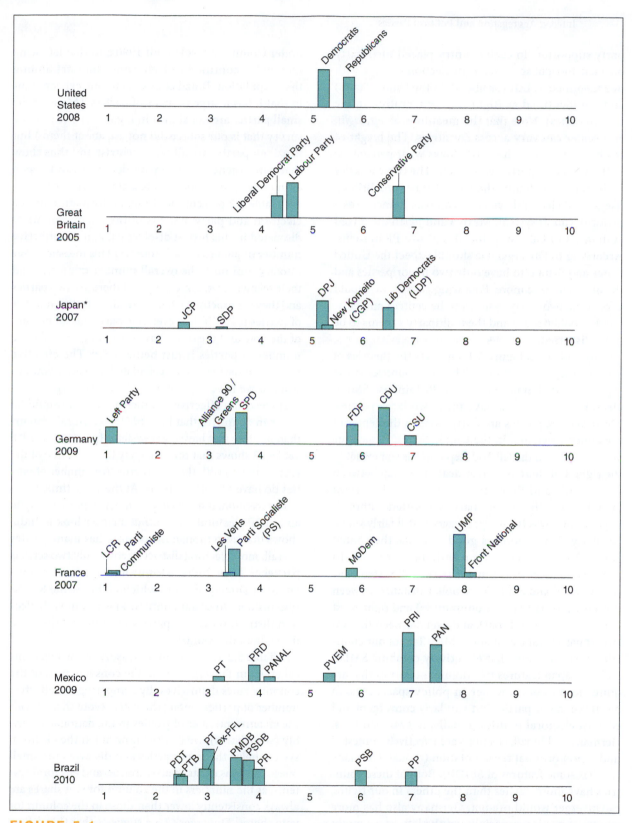

FIGURE 5.1
Placement of Parties on the Left–Right Scale and Their Voter Support in Elections

*Percent upper house

Source: The Comparative Study of Electoral Systems (www.cses.org), CSES Modules 2, 3; U.S. National Election Study 2008.

party supporters in each country placed their party on a left-to-right scale in recent election surveys, with one identified as Left (or liberal, in the United States) and ten identified as Right (or conservative, in the United States). Note that the meanings of *left*, *right*, and *center* can vary across countries. The height of the columns above the scale shows what percentage of the voters supported each party. The two countries at the top of the figure, the United States and Britain, use SMDP electoral systems, whereas France uses a majority runoff system, Mexico and Japan use mixed systems, and Germany and Brazil use PR systems. According to Duverger, we should expect the United States and Britain to have only two major parties and the others to have more. Following Downs, we should expect the two-party systems to be centrist and clustered in policy space and the multiparty systems to be more dispersed.

By and large, Figure 5.1 supports the theories of both Duverger and Downs. The two countries at the top, the United States and Great Britain, use SMDP electoral systems and have only two large parties. Moreover, the parties are fairly close to the center of the policy spectrum. In the United States, Democrats are somewhat to the left and Republicans somewhat to the right, but there is a great deal of overlap between Democratic and Republican voters. The left–right "gap" between the average party supporters, although larger than it was twenty years ago, is still fairly small. Similarly, Britain looks a good deal like the United States, but the parties are a little farther apart. In contrast, France, with a majority run-off system, has many parties and a very large policy distance between the left-most party (the Communists) and right-most party (the National Front), and even between the two largest parties (Socialist and UMP). Two of our countries have elections that effectively combine SMDP and PR. Japan features two dominant parties that are quite close to one another in policy space. Mexico has three major parties but similarly convergent and centrist electoral politics. Finally, in two countries, Germany and Brazil, elections are effectively contested under proportional representation (though Germany also has some features of SMDP). Both of these countries have more parties than the others in our figure, as Duverger would predict. Germany also has more extremist parties, especially on the left, as we might expect following Downs. However, this may also, in part, be a legacy of the fact that East Germany was

under Communist rule until 1990 and that left-wing ideologies continue to have some support among that population. Brazil conforms to our expectations in that it has a large number of parties. (Many of the small parties are not shown in Figure 5.1 because the survey that is our source did not ask about them.) But Brazilian parties are all fairly centrist and thus show that convergence or policy moderation can happen even under proportional representation elections.

Table 5.2 presents additional information on the electoral and party systems of the twelve countries discussed in this text. It displays data on the **effective number of parties** in each country. This measure takes into account both the overall number of parties and their relative sizes. For example, if there are two parties and they are exactly the same size, the effective number of parties is 2.0. If, however, one party has 80 percent of the vote and the other has 20 percent, the effective number of parties is just below 1.5.[10] The effective number of parties can be calculated for either votes or seats, as we have done in Table 5.2. If Duverger's Law is correct, the effective number of parties should be lower in countries that have SMDP electoral systems than in those that have other systems (particularly PR). Table 5.2 shows that this is largely true, as three of the four countries with the lowest effective number of parties do have SMDP elections. At the same time, India is an exception; it has a large number of parties despite an SMDP electoral system. But a closer look at India shows that even though the country has many parties overall, most electoral districts feature only two serious parties.[11] Thus, India helps us understand one limitation of Duverger's Law, which is that while SMDP systems tend to sustain only two parties in each election district, these two parties need not be the same throughout the country.

Table 5.2 also gives us a measure of the mechanical effect in Duverger's Law, the consequences of the counting rules themselves. By comparing the effective number of parties among the voters (vote shares) with the effective number of parties in the national assembly (seat shares), we can see how much the electoral system helps the large parties and disfavors the small ones. This bias exists in all countries and electoral systems, as the numbers in the column for seat shares are always consistently lower than those in the column for vote shares. Duverger's Law suggests that this difference should be greater in "first-past-the-post" (SMDP) systems than elsewhere.

TABLE 5.2
Elections and the Effective Number of Parties (Lower House of Legislature)
Rules matter.

Country	Electoral System	Effective Number of Parties—Vote Shares	Effective Number of Parties—Seat Shares	How Are Individual Candidates Selected?
Brazil	PR open list	11.21	10.36	Candidate preference vote
Britain	SMD Plurality	3.71[a]	2.57[a]	Nominated local constituency association
China	No contested elections	No contested elections	No contested elections	No contested elections
France	SMD majority runoff	5.27	2.83	Nominated by local constituency association
Germany	Mixed system: SMD plurality + PR closed list	5.58[b]	4.83[b]	National party and state party conventions
India	SMD plurality	7.74	5.01	Nominated by local constituency association
Iran	MMD majority runoff	No data	No data	Must be approved by Council of Guardians
Japan	Mixed system: SMD plurality + PR closed list	3.15[c]	2.10[c]	National Party
Mexico	Mixed system: SMD plurality + PR closed list	3.77	2.75	Nominated by local constituency association and national party
Nigeria	SMD plurality	2.62	2.34	Nominated by local constituency association
Russia	PR closed list	3.10	2.80	National party
United States	SMD plurality	2.15	1.97	Primary elections

Notes: Data from the most recent national elections, as of August 2, 2012. PR: proportional representation; MMD: multimember district; SMD: single-member district.

[a]Calculated on the basis of 649 out of 650 seats due to postponement of the 2010 poll in the constituency of Thirsk and Malton.

[b]Calculated with CDU and CSU as separate parties (see Chapter 10).

[c]Based on total votes and total seats.

Source: Arend Lijphart, *Patterns of Democracy: Government Forms and Performance in Thirty-Six Countries* (New Haven, CT: Yale University Press, 1999); www.ElectionGuide.org; www.Wikipedia.org.

Competitive Parties in Government

If a competitive party wins control of the legislature and the executive branch, it will (if unified) be able to pass and implement its policies. Sometimes, this control emerges directly from the electoral process, as a single party wins a majority of the vote. But, in many countries, the election laws help the largest party gain a governing majority even if it does not enjoy majority support among the voters. Thus, less than 50 percent of the vote may be converted into more than 50 percent of the legislative seats. Such "artificial" or "manufactured" legislative majorities have been the rule in countries with SMDP electoral systems, such as Britain.[12]

For example, from 1979 until 2010, either the Conservative Party or the Labour Party consistently won a majority of seats in the British House of Commons, even though neither party was ever supported by a majority of the voters in any of these elections. Margaret Thatcher's Conservative Party won a solid majority in the House of Commons in 1983 and 1987 with only about 42 percent of the vote. With almost exactly the same level of support, Tony Blair and the Labour Party won nearly two-thirds of the seats in 1997 and 2001. In 2005, Labour's share of the vote fell to about 35 percent, but the party still got a clear majority of the seats. In 2010, although they actually received a slightly larger share of the vote than Labour had in 2005, the Conservatives fell just short of a majority in the House of Commons. In all of these elections, the 25 to 35 percent of the voters that supported the smaller British parties received 10 percent or less of the parliamentary seats.

In other countries, multiparty elections do not yield single-party majorities, but party coalitions formed before the election may still offer the voters a direct choice of future governments. Before the election, a group of parties may join forces, agree to coordinate their election campaigns, or agree to govern together if they jointly win a parliamentary majority. When such coalitions form, as they have in many (but not all) elections in France and Germany, it is almost like a two-party system. Voters can clearly identify the potential governments and reward or punish the incumbents if they so choose. They thus have the ability to choose the direction of government policy through their party choice.

When elections do not create a majority party and there is no pre-electoral coalition, the political parties and their leaders must negotiate a new government after the election. This is common in many multiparty parliamentary systems, such as the Netherlands and Italy.[13] In these nations, interests are not aggregated through elections, because the election does not directly determine who governs. Instead, the aggregation of interests occurs in negotiations between different parties over control of the executive branch, most often after an election but also sometimes when an existing coalition breaks up (see also Chapter 6, specifically Figure 6.2).

The aggregation of interests at the executive rather than electoral level can have both costs and benefits. On the one hand, when elite party coalitions determine government policy, voters may feel that the government is not accountable to them, and because interest aggregation occurs among political elites, different elite coalitions can form on different issues. This can be confusing to citizens (and even informed observers). It may be difficult for voters to assign clear responsibility for government policy, and it may seem unfair that the electoral losers sometimes get to decide. This situation lessens the value of the vote as an instrument to shape future policy or to punish parties responsible for bad policy choices in the past.

On the other hand, there may be benefits for minority interests when all parties, not just the election winners, are represented in policymaking. All citizens hold minority opinions on some issues, and some are in the minority on many issues. If even minority representatives can influence policy between elections, they may feel that they have more political protection. Finally, even governments that win a majority of votes typically do not have majority support for all of their policy proposals. So there may be benefits for the nation as a whole when even the winners have to negotiate the different parts of their programs. Such bargaining may even increase the likelihood that policies reflect different majorities on different issues. When parties have to form government coalitions, the policies they adopt may therefore be more in line with what voters want. On the other hand, it becomes more difficult for the same voters to use their ballots to select the representatives they want or to "throw out the rascals."[14]

Cooperation and Conflict in Competitive Party Systems

Competitive party systems can be classified by the number of parties as well as by the patterns of competition or cooperation among them. **Majoritarian two-party systems** either are dominated by just two parties, as in the United States, or have two dominant parties and election laws that usually create legislative majorities for one of them, as in Britain. In **majority-coalition systems**, parties establish pre-electoral coalitions so that voters know which parties will attempt to work together to form a government. Germany and France have, in most elections, been in this category. Pure **multiparty systems** have election laws and party systems that virtually ensure that no single party wins a legislative majority, and have no tradition of pre-election coalitions. Interest aggregation then depends on a coalition of parties bargaining and coming to agreement after the election.

The degree of antagonism or polarization among the parties is another important party system characteristic. In a **consensual party system**, the parties commanding most of the legislative seats are not too far apart on policies and have a reasonable amount of trust in each other and in the political system. These are typically party systems like those shown toward the top of Figure 5.1. Bargaining may be intense, but it seldom threatens to break down into violence or civil war. In a **conflictual party system**, the legislature is dominated by parties that are far apart on issues or are antagonistic toward each other and the political system, such as the Russian party system in the 1990s. The risk of a serious confrontation may therefore be greater.

Some party systems have both consensual and conflictual features. In **consociational** (or **accommodative**) party systems, political leaders seek to bridge intense social divisions through power sharing, broad coalition governments, and decentralization of sensitive decisions to the separate social groups.[15] In this way, a consociational system can enable a deeply divided nation to find a way to peaceful democratic development. In Austria and Lebanon after World War II, mutually suspicious and hostile groups—the socialists and Catholics in Austria, and the Christians and Muslims in Lebanon—developed such consociational arrangements. Austria's accommodation occurred within a two-party system, and Lebanon's occurred among many small, personalistic religious parties. Austria's consociationalism was largely successful. After some twenty years of the consociational "Grand Coalition," in which both major parties held office together, these parties felt much less antagonistic and reverted to "normal" competition for office. The Lebanese experiment was less happy. After 1975, the country fell victim to civil war. South Africa also adopted consociational practices in its transition to democracy in the 1990s. Party leaders representing the white minority as well as different segments of the black majority negotiated power-sharing arrangements for a transitional period. The "Interim Constitution" guaranteed a share of power—cabinet posts—to all parties winning over 5 percent of the vote. Later, as democracy became more secure, South Africans abandoned this kind of power sharing.

Consociational practices thus offer deeply divided democracies hope but no guarantees of long-term stability. As Austria and South Africa show us, consociationalism may be especially suitable as a temporary solution after a period of intense conflict or turmoil. But consociationalism means that small groups of politicians make many important decisions behind closed doors. If these politicians are able to work together

more constructively than their respective supporters, consociationalism can be a happy solution. If, however, the politicians are intransigent or self-interested, consociationalism may fail.

The number of parties does not always tell us much about their degree of antagonism. The United States and Britain are relatively consensual majoritarian party systems. They are not perfect two-party systems, because minor parties exist in both countries, especially in Britain. In the United States, the degree of consensus changes from election to election because of the shifting programs of presidential candidates. Moreover, the looser cohesion of American parties and the frequency of divided government lead to postelection bargaining that is similar to consensual multiparty systems.

But not all majoritarian party systems are consensual. Austria between 1918 and 1934 was a conflictual majoritarian party system. Antagonism between the Socialist Party and the other parties was so intense that in the mid-1930s, it produced a brief civil war. The Austrian experience also illustrates how party systems can change. As we noted above, after World War II, the two major parties negotiated an elaborate coalition agreement of mutual power sharing—checks and balances—to contain the country's conflicts. In recent years, Ukraine has been another example of a conflictual majoritarian party system.

Multiparty systems tend to have larger policy differences between the parties, but such systems are not always conflictual. There are good examples of consensual multiparty systems in Scandinavia and the Netherlands, for example. On the other hand, France (1946–1958), Italy (1945–1992), and Weimar Germany (1919–1933) are historical examples of conflictual multiparty systems, which had powerful communist parties on the left and conservative or fascist movements on the right. Cabinets had to form out of centrist parties, which were themselves divided on many issues. This resulted in instability, poor government performance, and loss of citizen confidence in democracy. These factors contributed to the collapse of the French Fourth Republic in 1958, to government instability and citizen alienation from politics in Italy by the 1990s, and to the Nazi overthrow of democracy in Germany in the 1930s. New democracies, especially those divided by language or ethnicity, sometimes face similar challenges. Some of the new party systems in Central and Eastern Europe, such as

Hungary, have fallen into the pattern of conflictual, multiparty competition, but most of these former Communist countries have weathered the transition to democracy well.

Thus, although the number of parties affects political stability, the degree of antagonism among parties is more important. Two-party systems are stable and effective, but they may be dangerous if society is too deeply divided. Multiparty systems consisting of relatively moderate parties can often offer stability and fairly effective performance, especially if the parties are willing to commit themselves to pre-electoral coalitions. Multiparty systems without pre-electoral coalitions are more prone to ineffectiveness, but some have worked well over long periods. Where social groups and parties are highly antagonistic, however, collapse and civil war are ever-present possibilities, regardless of the number of parties. When crises develop, the most critical factor is typically how committed party leaders are to working together to defend democracy.[16]

Authoritarian Party Systems

 5.4 Discuss the types of electoral systems and their relation to patterns of electoral competition.

Authoritarian party systems can also aggregate interests. They develop policy proposals and mobilize support for them, but they do so in a completely different way from competitive party systems. In authoritarian party systems, aggregation takes place within the party or in interactions with business groups, unions, landowners, and institutional groups in the bureaucracy or military. Although there may be sham elections, the citizens have no real opportunity to shape aggregation by choosing between party alternatives.

Authoritarian party systems vary in the degree of top-down control within the party and the party's control over other groups in society. At one extreme is the **exclusive governing party**, which insists on almost total control over political resources. It recognizes no legitimate interest aggregation by groups outside the party. Nor does it permit any free activity, much less opposition, from interest groups, citizens, or other government agencies. In its most extreme form, sometimes called *totalitarianism*, it penetrates and tries to control the entire society through

policies developed at the top. Its policies are based on a political ideology, such as communism or national socialism (Nazism), that claims to identify the true interests of the citizens, regardless of what the citizens themselves believe.[17] At the other extreme is the **inclusive governing party**, which recognizes and accepts at least some other groups and organizations, but may repress those that it sees as serious challenges to its own control.

Exclusive Governing Parties

In a purely totalitarian society, there is only one party with total top-down control of society, and no autonomous opposition parties or interest groups. Totalitarian single-party systems can be impressive vehicles of political mobilization. A clear ideology provides legitimacy and coherence, and the party penetrates and organizes society in the name of that ideology and in accordance with its policies. Historically, most totalitarian governing parties have been communist or fascist, but there are also cases of more nationalistic parties, such as Saddam Hussein's Baath Party in Iraq. But totalitarianism is difficult to sustain. Although the ruling communist parties of the Soviet Union before 1985, of Eastern Europe before 1989, and of North Korea, Vietnam, and Cuba today resemble this model, few parties have long maintained such absolute control. China is an interesting mixed case. While the Chinese government has withdrawn from the direct administration of much of the economy, it does not recognize the legitimacy of any opposition groups. The ruling party permits, within bounds, some interest articulation by individuals, but not mass mobilization against government policy.[18]

Exclusive governing parties may experience more internal dissent than is commonly recognized. Within the party, groups may unite around their region or industry, or behind leaders of different policy factions. Beneath the supposedly united front, power struggles may erupt in times of crisis. Succession crises are particularly likely to generate such power struggles, as at the deaths of Stalin in the Soviet Union and Mao Zedong in China. Several times, the Chinese Communist Party has had to rely on the army, and even on coalitions of regional army commanders, to sustain its control.

Not all exclusive governing parties are totalitarian. Many leaders committed to massive social change—for example, national independence from colonialism—have used the exclusive governing party as a tool for mass mobilization. Yet it is difficult to build an exclusive governing party as an agent for social transformation. The seduction of power regularly leads to rent-seeking or other abuses of power that are not checked by competitive democratic politics and that may distort the original party objectives. The exclusive governing parties in some African states also had limited capacity to control society. Furthermore, the loss of confidence in Marxist–Leninist ideology and in the Soviet model led all eight of the African regimes that had once invoked it to abandon that approach by the early 1990s.

As exclusive governing parties age, many enter a stage in which they maintain control but place less emphasis on mobilization. Some, such as North Korea, may degenerate into vehicles for personal rule and exploitation by the ruler's family and supporters.[19] Finally, as shown by the collapse of communism in the former Soviet Union and Eastern Europe, if and when the party leaders lose faith in the unifying ideology, it is difficult to maintain party coherence.

Inclusive Governing Parties

Among the preindustrial countries, especially those with notable ethnic and tribal divisions, the more successful authoritarian parties have been *inclusive*. These systems recognize the autonomy of social, cultural, and economic groups and try to incorporate them or bargain with them rather than control and remake them. The more successful African one-party systems, such as in Kenya and Tanzania, have permitted aggregation around personalistic, factional, and ethnic groups within a decentralized party.

Inclusive party systems, such as in Mexico, have sometimes been labeled *authoritarian corporatist systems*. Like the democratic corporatist systems (see Chapter 4), some of these systems encourage the formation of large, organized interest groups that can bargain with each other and the state. Unlike the democratic corporatist systems, however, these authoritarian systems place no power directly in the hands of the people. Authoritarian corporatist systems suppress independent protest and political activity outside of official channels. The party leaders permit only limited autonomous demands within the ranks of the party and by groups associated with it.

The inclusive authoritarian systems may permit substantial amounts of autonomous interest aggregation, which may take many forms. The party typically tries to gather various social groups under the general party umbrella and negotiate with outside groups and institutions. Some inclusive parties have attempted aggressive social change. Others have primarily been arenas for interest aggregation. Many inclusive party governments permit other parties to offer candidates in elections, as long as these opposition candidates have no real chance of winning. Indeed, one interesting feature of politics since about the 1980s, along with the increasing number of liberal democracies, has been the growth of **electoral authoritarianism**. This is where there is a facade of democracy providing "some space for political opposition, independent media, and social organizations that do not seriously criticize or challenge the regime."[20] The Mexican Partido Revolucionario Institucional (PRI) was long a successful example of an inclusive governing party featuring electoral authoritarianism (see Box 5.3).

The fact that some inclusive authoritarian parties have been impressively durable does not necessarily mean that they are strong or successful. In many countries, these parties coexist in uneasy and unstable coalitions with the armed forces and the civilian bureaucracy. In some countries, the party has become window dressing for a military regime or personal tyranny. Seldom have these parties been able to solve the economic or ethnic problems that face their countries.

These inclusive parties were often created in a struggle against colonialism, and as colonialism becomes more distant, they may implode. As memories of the independence struggle fade and the leaders die off or retire, the ties of ideology and experience that hold these parties together weaken. These developments, in conjunction with the worldwide expansion of democracy, have caused the single-party model to lose legitimacy in many countries. In some cases (as in Tanzania), political leaders have adjusted by permitting real party competition. More frequently, they have resorted to electoral authoritarianism with varying degrees of manipulation to provide a veneer of domestic and international legitimacy. In more than a few cases, they have turned to naked coercion, with the military as the final arbiter.

BOX 5.3   Mexico's PRI

One of the oldest and most inclusive authoritarian parties is the Partido Revolucionario Institucional (PRI) in Mexico. For more than fifty years, the PRI dominated the political process and gave other parties no realistic chances of winning elections. The PRI attained this dominance after President Lázaro Cárdenas turned it into a "big-tent" coalition in the 1930s. It also carefully controlled the counting of the ballots. The PRI incorporated many social groups, with separate sectors for labor, agrarian, and middle-class interests. The party dealt with its opponents in carefully designed ways. While some political dissidents were harassed and suppressed, others were deliberately enticed into the party. The party also gave informal recognition to political factions grouped behind such figures as former presidents. Various Mexican leaders mobilized their factions within the PRI and in other important groups not directly affiliated with it, such as big-business interests. Bargaining was particularly important every six years when the party had to choose a new presidential nominee, since

the Mexican Constitution limits presidents to one term. This guaranteed some turnover of elites.

As a consequence of its elaborate schemes of governing, the PRI did not have to fear electoral competition, at least until the 1990s. Yet rising discontent made it increasingly difficult to aggregate interests through a single party. The urban and rural poor who had not shared in Mexico's growth joined with reformers to demand a more fully democratic system. An armed uprising of peasant guerrillas in early 1994 shocked the political establishment and led to promises of genuine democratic competition. Legislative elections in 1997 were more open than earlier contests, and ended the seventy-year rule of the PRI, which then lost the presidency to the National Action Party (PAN) in 2000. After that election, the PRI quickly diminished as a political force, and in 2006, its candidate ran a distant third in Mexico's presidential election. By 2012, however, the party had rebounded and recaptured the Mexican presidency (see Chapter 14).

The Military and Interest Aggregation

 5.5   Describe the features of different competitive party systems.

After independence, most Third World nations adopted at least formally democratic governments. But, in many countries, these civilian governments lacked effectiveness and authority, which often led to their breakdown and replacement by **military governments**. The military had instruments of force and organizational capacity, and in the absence of a strong constitutional tradition, it was an effective contender for power. Even under civilian rule, the military had substantial political influence and often constituted a significant power contender. In Brazil, for example, the military played a crucial role in interest aggregation, even under the civilian government prior to the coup of 1964. After that intervention, it was the dominant actor for the next twenty years. In many other countries, the military has long been a similarly important interest aggregator. Many Latin American countries had military governments on and off for

much of the twentieth century, and African countries such as Nigeria experienced a wave of military coups after their decolonization in the 1960s.

The military's virtual monopoly on coercive resources gives it great potential power. Thus, when aggregation fails in democratic or authoritarian party systems, the military may emerge by default as the only force able to maintain orderly government. The military may also intervene for more self-interested reasons, such as protecting its autonomy or budgets from civilian interference, and in many countries, military governments have served as a vehicle for ethnic politics.

About two-fifths of the world's nations have confronted military coup attempts at some time, and in about a third of the nations, these coups were at least partially successful in changing leaders or policy (see Box 5.4). Fewer than half of these coup attempts, however, focused on general political issues and public policy. Most coups seemed motivated by the professional interests of the military.

What happens after the military intervenes can vary. The soldiers may support the personal tyranny of a civilian president or a dominant party. Or, the armed forces may use their power to further institutional or

BOX 5.4   Trying to Make Democracy Work

Nigeria is in many ways typical of the rough road to democracy that many developing countries have traveled. After gaining its independence, Nigeria experienced brief periods of democratic government in the 1960s and again in the late 1970s. In both cases, the military quickly intervened and ousted governments that had become oppressive or ineffective. The military government responded to the global democratization wave of the early 1990s by introducing measured reforms leading up to a presidential election in 1993, but the military kept strict control of the electoral process and disqualified politicians who had held office under previous civilian regimes (because they were considered to be tainted by corruption). Voters were left with a choice of only two parties, both created by the government. Voting turnout was low because many voters became cynical about the process. These doubts were confirmed when the military annulled the presidential election even before the results had been announced, apparently because the

"wrong" candidate was winning. General Sani Abacha then launched a coup that banned all political activity, dissolved the legislature, dismissed the elected governments in Nigeria's thirty-six states, and thus ended Nigeria's cautious experiment with elections. In 1998, President Abacha suddenly died of a heart attack, and the reform process began anew. In spring 1999, a presidential election was held. The victor was a former army general and president (1976–1979), Olusegun Obasanjo, who went on to implement democratic reforms. He was reelected four years later and stepped down in 2007 after his second term. The new president who was chosen in the 2007 election later died in office and was replaced by his vice president, Goodluck Jonathan, who went on to win reelection in 2011. Thus, Nigeria has by now experienced its longest period of civilian government ever. But continuing ethnic and religious violence, corruption, and abuses of power have made Nigerian democracy fragile (see Chapter 18).

ideological objectives. Military rulers may try to create military and/or bureaucratic versions of authoritarian corporatism, linking organized groups and the state bureaucracy with the military as final arbiter. They may undertake "defensive" modernization in alliance with business groups or even more radical modernization. Most Latin American versions of authoritarian corporatism have relied on a strong military component rather than a dominant authoritarian party.

The major limitation of the military in interest aggregation is that it is not designed for that function. The military is primarily organized to have an efficient command structure. It is not set up to aggregate internal differences, to build compromise, to mobilize popular support, or even to communicate with social groups outside the command hierarchy. Nor do military regimes have the legitimacy in the international community that elections provide. Thus, the military lacks many of the advantages held by elected party leaders. These internal limitations may be less serious when the military is dealing with common grievances or responding to abuses of power by unpopular politicians. The same limitations become a major problem, however, when a military government needs to stake out its own course and mobilize support for it. For

these reasons, military governments frequently prove unstable and are often forced to share power with other institutions or simply to withdraw from politics.

Recent surveys show little popular support for military government anywhere in the world. Perhaps because most citizens do not consider authoritarian rule legitimate, the military throughout the world is now more likely to dominate from behind the scenes than through direct rule. In such important Latin American countries as Argentina, Brazil, Chile, and Uruguay, military regimes have been replaced by competitive party regimes. The same thing has happened in a number of African countries, including Nigeria (see Chapter 18).

Trends in Interest Aggregation

5.6 Compare and contrast exclusive and inclusive authoritarian party systems.

As we have previously noted, the democratic trend in the world gained momentum in the 1980s, when many Latin American countries democratized. This trend began accelerating in 1989 in Eastern Europe, with new pressures for democracy in the developing world also. By the late 1990s, for the first time in history, there were more free than unfree states in the world. The collapse of communism in Europe and elsewhere was in large part responsible, but the number of military dictatorships also declined. The declining acceptance of authoritarian governments, as well as the withdrawal of Soviet support, contributed to this trend, especially in Africa. Many African nations moved toward democracy and openness during the 1990s. Yet a few authoritarian exclusive governing parties are still around, such as in China and Cuba. Most of the remaining unfree states are in the Middle East, Central Asia, and Africa. Many African nations still feature some variety of the "electoral authoritarianism" discussed earlier, with severe constraints on civil freedom and electoral opposition. A few remain unabashed authoritarian systems (as in Zimbabwe) or are mired in deadly civil war (as in Sudan and Somalia).

We cannot assume that democratization will continue relentlessly. Democratically elected politicians who seem unable to cope with economic and social problems often lose their legitimacy. Such is now the challenge facing many developing countries, especially in Africa, where competitive party systems may exist but where citizens have very little trust in them and often consider them to be corrupt, and military coups continue to happen, as in Thailand and Fiji in 2006, in Niger in 2010, and in Egypt in 2013.

Significance of Interest Aggregation

 Describe the range of the military's role as an interest aggregator.

How interests are aggregated is an important determinant of what a country's government does for and to its citizens. Successful public policy depends on effective interest aggregation. Interest aggregation narrows policy options so that the desires and demands of citizens are converted into a few policy alternatives. Many possible policies are eliminated in the process. Those that remain typically have the backing of significant sectors of society.

In democratic countries, competitive party systems narrow down and combine policy preferences. Through elections, voters throw their support behind some of these parties and thus shape party representation in the legislature. Even at the legislative stage, further consolidation and coalition building take place. At some point, however, most policy options have been eliminated from consideration—either no party backed them or the parties supporting them fared badly in the elections.

In noncompetitive party systems, military governments, and monarchies, aggregation works differently, but with the similar effect of narrowing policy options. On some issues, aggregation virtually determines policy, as when a military government or a faction of an authoritarian party can decide the government's program. In other cases, the legislative assembly, military council, or party politburo may contain several factions that must negotiate over policy.

Politics shapes its environment as well as reflecting it. Interest aggregation often alters the political culture. That is one reason why politics is so fascinating. Well-organized and well-led political parties might, at least for a while, be able to dominate politics and limit the strength of extremist groups in the legislature. Conversely, well-organized extremists might be able to appeal to the fears, envies, and prejudices of some groups and get their support at the polls, thus gaining more legislative strength in an otherwise consensual country.

How successful interest aggregation is ultimately affects whether the government will be able to adapt and survive. Authoritarian interest aggregation tends to create political power structures that do not reflect popular opinion. In highly divided and conflict-ridden societies, rulers may portray such lack of representation as a virtue. Leaders of military coups often justify their overthrow of party governments by claiming to depolarize politics and rid the nation of conflict it cannot afford. Similarly, heads of authoritarian parties typically claim that their nation must concentrate all its energies and resources on common purposes and that party competition would be too polarizing.

In contrast, most proponents of democratic interest aggregation argue that the best way to accommodate conflicting interests lies in free and fair electoral competition, followed by negotiation

The Army Takes Power
Onlookers cheer as members of a military junta speak to supporters in Niamey, Niger, Saturday, February 20, 2010. Thousands of people rallied on the streets of Niger's capital in support of a military coup that ousted the West African nation's strongman president.

among those groups that gain the voters' favor. Democracy thus leads policymakers to act as the people wish. In a polarized political culture where democratic interest aggregation breeds division and uncertainty, the price for citizen control may seem to be high. As the frequent instability in authoritarian governments indicates, however, it may be easier to do away with the appearance of polarization than with the reality. Competing demands may find their way to the surface anyway, and the citizens may end up with neither freedom and participation nor stability.

REVIEW QUESTIONS

- What structures other than political parties aggregate interests?
- What is Duverger's Law? Which two effects does it imply?
- What is the median voter result, and why does it pertain only to two-party systems?
- What are the differences between totalitarian parties and other single-party systems?
- Why have many countries turned to military governments, and why are military governments often short-lived?

KEY TERMS

accommodative party systems

authoritarian party systems

closed-list PR systems

competitive party systems

conflictual party system

consensual party system

consociational

double-ballot

Duverger's Law

effective number of parties

electoral authoritarianism

electoral system

exclusive governing party

inclusive governing party

institutional groups

interest aggregation

iron law of oligarchy

majoritarian two-party systems

majority runoff elections

majority-coalition systems

mechanical effect

median voter result

military governments

multiparty systems

open-list PR systems

party system

patron–client networks

primary elections

proportional representation (PR)

psychological effect

single-member district (SMD)

single-member district plurality (SMDP) election rule

strategic voting

two-party systems

SUGGESTED READINGS

Bratton, Michael, and Nicolas van de Walle. *Democratic Experiments in Africa*. Cambridge: Cambridge University Press, 1997.

Cox, Gary W. *Making Votes Count: Strategic Coordination in the World's Electoral Systems*. Cambridge: Cambridge University Press, 1997.

Dalton, Russell J., and Martin P. Wattenberg. *Parties without Partisans: Political Change in Advanced Industrial Democracies*. New York: Oxford University Press, 2000.

Decalo, Samuel. *Coups and Army Rule in Africa,* 2nd ed. New Haven, CT: Yale University Press, 1990.

Downs, Anthony. *An Economic Theory of Democracy*. New York: Harper & Row, 1957.

Geddes, Barbara. "What Do We Know about Democratization after Twenty Years?" *Annual Reviews of Political Science* 2 (1999): 115–44.

Jackson, Robert H., and Carl G. Rosberg. *Personal Rule in Black Africa*. Berkeley: University of California Press, 1982.

Kitschelt, Herbert. *The Transformation of European Social Democracy*. New York: Cambridge University Press, 1994.

Laver, Michael, and Norman Schofield. *Multiparty Government.* New York: Oxford University Press, 1990.

Lijphart, Arend. *Electoral Systems and Party Systems*. New York: Oxford University Press, 1994.

———. *Patterns of Democracy: Government Forms and Performance in Thirty-Six Countries*. 2nd ed. New Haven, CT: Yale University Press, 2012.

Linz, Juan J. *Totalitarian and Authoritarian Regimes*. Baltimore: Johns Hopkins University Press, 2002.

Michels, Robert. *Political Parties*. New York: Free Press, 1962.

Powell, G. Bingham, Jr. *Contemporary Democracies: Participation, Stability, and Violence*. Cambridge, MA: Harvard University Press, 1982.

———. *Elections as Instruments of Democracy*. New Haven, CT: Yale University Press, 2000.

Riker, William H. *Liberalism against Populism*. San Francisco: W. H. Freeman, 1982.

Strøm, Kaare, Wolfgang C. Müller, and Torbjörn Bergman, eds. *Cabinets and Coalition Bargaining: The Democratic Life Cycle in Western Europe*. Oxford: Oxford University Press, 2008.

ENDNOTES

1. See, for example, Luis Roniger and Ayse Gunes-Ayata, eds., *Democracy, Clientelism, and Civil Society* (Boulder, CO: Lynne Rienner, 1994); S. Eisenstadt and L. Roniger, *Patrons, Clients, and Friends* (Cambridge: Cambridge University Press, 1984); Lucian W. Pye, *Asian Power and Politics* (Cambridge, MA: Harvard University Press, 1985); and Martin Shefter, "Patronage and Its Opponents," in *Political Parties and the State* (Princeton, NJ: Princeton University Press, 1994).

2. Unfortunately, elections cannot solve all the problems of aggregating interests fairly. For example, giving each citizen one vote does not take into account the varying intensities with which different people may hold their opinions. Moreover, economists and political scientists have found that when there are three or more alternatives in any decision, there is no fair way to aggregate votes to select a single, best outcome (a problem known as "Arrow's Paradox"). See Kenneth

Arrow, *Social Choice and Individual Values* (New Haven, CT: Yale University Press, 1951). For an accessible discussion of some political implications, see William H. Riker, *Liberalism against Populism* (San Francisco: W. H. Freeman, 1982); and Kenneth A. Shepsle, *Analyzing Politics: Rationality, Behavior, and Institutions*, 2nd ed. (New York: Norton, 2010).

3. For studies that show that parties tend to keep their promises, see Hans-Dieter Klingemann, Richard Hofferbert, and Ian Budge, eds., *Parties, Policy, and Democracy* (Boulder, CO: Westview, 1995); Richard Rose, *Do Parties Make a Difference?* (Chatham, NJ: Chatham House, 1984), chap. 5; and Russell J. Dalton, David M. Farrell, and Ian McAllister, *Political Parties and Democratic Linkage* (New York: Oxford University Press, 2011). On the other hand, democratic politicians do not always keep their promises, as Susan Stokes shows in her study of party promises and postelection switches in Latin America in the 1980s: Susan C. Stokes, *Mandates and Democracy: Neoliberalism by Surprise in Latin America* (New York: Cambridge University Press, 2001).

4. Joseph A. Schumpeter, *Capitalism, Socialism, and Democracy* (New York: Harper, 1943).

5. However, in China, semicompetitive elections for village leadership positions have in some areas brought the opinions of local leaders and ordinary citizens closer together. See Larry Diamond and Ramon H. Myers, eds., *Elections and Democracy in Greater China* (Oxford: Oxford University Press, 2001).

6. See Russell J. Dalton, *Citizen Politics: Public Opinion and Political Parties in Advanced Industrial Democracies*, 5th ed. (Washington, DC: Congressional Quarterly Press, 2008).

7. Ian Budge, David Robertson, and Derek Hearl, eds., *Ideology, Strategy, and Party Change: Spatial Analyses of Post-War Election Programmes in 19 Democracies* (New York: Cambridge University Press, 1987); and Richard Katz and Peter Mair, eds., *How Parties Organize: Change and Adaptation in Party Organizations in Western Democracies* (Thousand Oaks, CA: Sage, 1994).

8. Maurice Duverger, *Political Parties: Their Organization and Activity in the Modern State*, trans. Barbara and Robert North (New York: Wiley, 1963). See also Gary W. Cox, *Making Votes Count* (Cambridge: Cambridge University Press, 1997). For two recent discussions of Duverger's Law and the conditions under which it holds, see Robert Moser and Ethan Scheiner, *Electoral Systems and Political Context: How the Effects of Rule Vary across New and Established Democracies* (NY: Cambridge University Press, 2012); and Mala Htun and G. Bingham Powell, eds., *Political Science, Election Rules and Democratic Governance* (Washington, DC: American Political Science Association, 2013).

9. Anthony Downs, *An Economic Theory of Democracy* (New York: Harper & Row, 1957).

10. The effective number of parties is calculated as follows: First, calculate the proportion of seats (or votes) held by each party.

Square each of these proportions and then add them all up. Finally, divide 1 by the sum of all the squared proportions. See Markku Laakso and Rein Taagepera, "'Effective' Number of Parties: A Measure with Application to West Europe," *Comparative Political Studies* 12 (1979): 3–27.

11. Pradeep Chhibber and Kenneth Kollman, *The Formation of National Party Systems* (Princeton, NJ: Princeton University Press, 2004).

12. Douglas Rae, *The Political Consequences of Election Laws* (New Haven, CT: Yale University Press, 1967); and Arend Lijphart, *Electoral Systems and Party Systems: A Study of Twenty-Seven Democracies, 1945–1990* (Oxford: Oxford University Press, 1994).

13. On government coalitions, see especially Michael Laver and Norman Schofield, *Multiparty Government: The Politics of Coalition in Europe* (New York: Oxford University Press, 1990); and Kaare Strøm, Wolfgang C. Müller, and Torbjörn Bergman, eds., *Cabinets and Coalition Bargaining: The Democratic Life Cycle in Western Europe* (New York: Oxford University Press, 2008).

14. See G. Bingham Powell, Jr., *Elections as Instruments of Democracy* (New Haven, CT: Yale University Press, 2000), chaps. 5–10.

15. Arend Lijphart, *Democracy in Plural Societies* (New Haven, CT: Yale University Press, 1977); and Arend Lijphart, *Patterns of Democracy: Government Forms and Performance in Thirty-Six Countries,* 2nd ed. (New Haven, CT: Yale University Press, 2012).

16. Lijphart, *Patterns of Democracy*; G. Bingham Powell, Jr., *Contemporary Democracies: Participation, Stability, and Violence* (Cambridge, MA: Harvard University Press, 1982), chaps. 8 and 10; and Juan J. Linz and Alfred Stepan, eds., *The Breakdown of Democratic Regimes* (Baltimore: Johns Hopkins University Press, 1978).

17. Juan Linz, *Totalitarian and Authoritarian Regimes* (Boulder, CO: Lynne Rienner, 2000); and Amos Perlmutter, *Modern Authoritarianism: A Comparative Institutional Analysis* (New Haven, CT: Yale University Press, 1981), esp. 62–114.

18. Melanie Manion, "Politics in China," Chapter 13 of this text; for the earlier period, see, for example, Franz Schurman, *Ideology and Organization in Communist China* (Berkeley: University of California Press, 1966).

19. Juan Linz calls these "sultanistic" regimes; see his *Totalitarian and Authoritarian Regimes*, 151–57; Houchang Chehabi and Juan Linz, eds., *Sultanistic Regimes* (Baltimore: Johns Hopkins University Press, 1998); and Robert H. Jackson and Carl G. Rosberg, *Personal Rule in Black Africa* (Berkeley: University of California Press, 1982).

20. Larry Diamond, "Thinking about Hybrid Regimes," *Journal of Democracy* 13 (2002): 26; see also other articles in the same issue.

CHAPTER 6

Government and Policymaking

LEARNING OBJECTIVES

6.1 Describe the features of a constitution, focusing on decision rules, and explain why Britain is unusual.

6.2 Compare and contrast democratic and authoritarian systems.

6.3 Discuss the presidential and parliamentary forms of democratic government, using the United States and Britain, respectively, as examples.

6.4 Define confederal, federal, and unitary divisions of governmental power.

6.5 Discuss the role of the courts in overseeing democracies and give examples from several countries.

6.6 List three methods used to remove political leaders from office.

6.7 Describe the varied forms, functions, and compositions of government assemblies.

6.8 Discuss the ways chief executives are chosen, their powers, and the role played by cabinets.

6.9 Explain Max Weber's definition of a bureaucracy and describe the forms bureaucracies can take.

In a social science class, you might have discussed how to form a government in a new nation. This is a theoretical exercise, but, in fact, dozens of nations have created new governing systems in the past few decades. Decolonization meant that many newly independent states formed in the decades after World War II. More recently, the fall of Communist dictatorships in Europe and of military and other dictatorships in Latin America and East Asia have led to the formation of new democracies. Other nations have experienced major reforms in the institutions of government.

Such reforms of government institutions often cause major changes in the way policy is made. **Policymaking** is the pivotal stage in the political process, the point at which bills become law or rulers issue their edicts. To understand public policy in a particular political system, we must know how decisions are made. Where is power effectively located? What does it take to change public policy: a majority vote in the legislature or a decision by the president? Or is it a decree issued by the military

commanders or the party central committee? Or is it merely the whim of the personal dictator?

This chapter focuses on the various agencies within a government—such as legislatures, chief executives, bureaucracies, and courts—and how these agencies enact public policies. While parties, interest groups, and other actors may actively articulate and aggregate interests, government officials do most of the initiation and formulation of policy proposals. Interest group demands to give tax relief or to protect endangered species cannot succeed unless government officials transform them into policy. And before these policies become effective, they must be implemented by other officials.

Yet government action does not flow in one direction only. The interaction between government and citizens is a two-way process. It includes an upward flow of inputs and demands from citizens, as well as a downward flow of decisions from the government (refer back to Figure 2.3).

Constitutions and Decision Rules

6.1 Describe the features of a constitution, focusing on decision rules, and explain why Britain is unusual.

Policymaking processes are shaped by the constitutions under which they take place. A constitution establishes the basic rules of decision making, rights, and the distribution of authority in a political system. We sometimes use the term "constitution" to refer to a specific document laying out such principles—for example, the one adopted by the Founders of the United States in 1787. But a constitution need not be embodied in a single document. In fact, it rarely is. We should therefore think of a constitution as a set of rules and principles, whether it is a specific written document, a set of customs or practices, or, as is usually the case, both. Even a military or party dictatorship typically sets procedures for having decrees proposed, considered, and adopted.

Written constitutions are particularly important in political systems based on the *rule of law*. This means that government should take no action that has not been authorized by law and that citizens can be punished only for actions that violate the law. Under the rule of law, the constitution is the supreme body of laws.

A constitution thus contains a set of **decision rules**—the basic rules governing how decisions are made. Policymaking is the conversion of social interests and demands into authoritative public decisions. Constitutions establish the rules by which this happens. They confer the power to propose policies on specific groups or institutions. They may give others the right to amend, reject, or approve such proposals, or to implement, police, or adjudicate them.

Decision rules affect political activity because they determine what political resources help influence decisions and how to acquire and use these resources. For example, in a federal and decentralized system such as Germany, a pressure group may lobby both the legislative and the executive branches of government, and it may have to be active at both the state and the federal levels (and perhaps also in the European Union). Or, in countries where decisions are made by the commander of the armed forces or by the central committee of the ruling party, groups will need to influence these crucial policymakers.

Even in democracies, decision rules differ significantly from one political system to the next. Some decisions may be made by a chief executive, president, or prime minister, for example, acting alone. Other decisions may require broad majorities of elected representatives. The most inclusive voting rule is unanimity, which means that any one member can block any decision.

Both the government as a whole and its component agencies have decision rules, which may be simple or complex. For example, the U.S. Congress has many different decision rules that apply under various circumstances. Decision rules may be more or less formal and precise. Most legislatures have formal and precise decision rules, whereas cabinets at the head of the executive branch often have informal and flexible rules.

In most modern assemblies (legislatures), the voting rules are *egalitarian* so that each member has the same voting power—simply speaking, one person, one vote. That is hardly ever true in government departments (ministries), however, or in dictatorships. There, decision making is *hierarchical*. Everybody is supposed to defer to his or her superior. In a pure hierarchy, only the vote of the person at the very top counts. Hierarchical decision making makes it easy to respond quickly in an emergency, but few interests or ideas may be taken into account.

Even when decisions are made through equal voting, the inclusiveness of the decision rules still shapes the outcomes. Many institutions, such as the British House of Commons, mainly operate through simple majority voting: In a choice between two options, whichever option gets the larger number of votes wins. Other assemblies sometimes use more inclusive rules—such as "qualified" majorities of three-fifths, two-thirds, or even three-fourths—for particularly consequential decisions. Amending the U.S. Constitution, for example, or overriding a presidential veto, requires two-thirds majorities in both houses of Congress.

Different decision rules have different attractions. More inclusive rules—such as those that require the cooperation of several agencies or the support of over 50 percent of voters—can protect against hasty decisions. They can also prevent decisions that disadvantage large minorities (perhaps close to half) of the voters. At the same time, more inclusive rules can give a minority the power to block proposals that most citizens badly want. The more inclusive the voting rules are (as the decisive majority approaches unanimity), the less likely it is that any decision can be made at all. Less inclusive decision rules make it easier to make decisions, but the downside is that many interests may be ignored.

It is important that decision rules in a democracy be transparent and stable. If they are not, citizens will not know what to expect from government. That may erode political legitimacy and make people less willing to accept and support government actions. It may also lead to serious conflicts, and, ultimately, government may break down and issues may be decided by force. Thomas Jefferson suggested the importance of having predictable decision rules in his introduction to the first *Manual of the House of Representatives*: "A bad set of rules is better than no rules at all."

Making Constitutions

Making a constitution is a fundamental political act; it creates or transforms decision rules. Most current constitutions were formed as the result of some break, often violent, with the past—war, revolution, or rebellion against colonial rule. New decision rules were made to accommodate new internal or external powers. Thus, the defeated powers of World Wars I and II and their successor states all adopted new constitutions or had new constitutions imposed on them.

Britain is unusual in having not a formal written constitution but only a long-accepted and highly developed set of customs and conventions, buttressed by important ordinary statutes. This reflects the British record of gradual, incremental, and (on the whole) peaceful political change. Nevertheless, the major changes in British decision rules—such as the shift of power from the Crown to Parliament in the seventeenth century—followed periods of civil war or unrest.

Perhaps the most significant exception to the association between disruptive upheavals and constitution creation is the peaceful development over the last fifty years of the constitution of the European Union, whose growing powers are altering the decision rules affecting about 504 million Europeans in twenty-eight countries. While there has been no violence associated with the formation and growth of the EU, its origins lie in the bitter lessons of World Wars I and II, which devastated much of Europe.

The decades since World War II have seen much constitutional experimentation. Not only the defeated powers but many new states—such as India and Nigeria, which achieved independence with the breakup of colonial empires—introduced new political arrangements. Some developing nations, such as Nigeria, have subsequently changed their form of government several times. In the last two decades, the worldwide trend toward democracy, the end of the Cold War, and the dissolution of the Soviet Union produced a new round of constitutional design. The recent constitutional crafting in Eastern Europe, Russia, East Asia, and Africa has reignited old debates about the virtues and faults of different constitutional arrangements, or about the very wisdom of constitutional engineering.[1]

Democracy and Authoritarianism

 6.2 Compare and contrast democratic and authoritarian systems.

The most important distinction in policymaking is between democratic and authoritarian systems. **Democracy** means "government by the people." In small political systems, such as local communities, "the people" may share directly in debating, deciding, and implementing public policy. In large political systems, such as contemporary states, democracy must be achieved largely through indirect participation in policymaking. Policymaking power is delegated to officials chosen by the people.

Elections, competitive political parties, free mass media, and representative assemblies are political structures that make some degree of popular governance possible in large political systems. Competitive elections give citizens a chance to shape policy through their selection and rejection of key policymakers. Such indirect democracy is never complete or ideal. Moreover, the democratic opportunities in less economically developed societies are often meaningful to educated elites or to those living near the centers of government but less relevant to the average citizen in the countryside. The more citizens are involved and the more influential their choices, the more democratic the system.

We call nondemocratic political systems **authoritarian** or **autocratic**. There are many forms of authoritarianism. Authoritarian policymakers may be chosen by military councils, hereditary families, dominant political parties, or in other ways. Citizens are either ignored or pressed into symbolic assent to the government's choices.

The basic decision rules of political systems—both democratic and authoritarian—differ along three important dimensions:

1. The separation of powers among different branches of government.
2. The geographic distribution of authority between the central (national) government and lower levels, such as states, provinces, or municipalities.
3. Limitations on government authority.

We shall discuss these dimensions in order, beginning with the separation of authority between executive and legislative institutions.

Separation of Government Powers

 6.3 Discuss the presidential and parliamentary forms of democratic government, using the United States and Britain, respectively, as examples.

The theory of **separation of powers** between different institutions of government has a long and venerable history going back at least to the work of Locke and Montesquieu.[2] Separation of powers, they argued, prevents the injustices that might result from an unchecked executive or legislature. Madison and Hamilton elaborated this theory in *The Federalist*,[3] which described and defended the institutional arrangements proposed by the U.S. Constitutional Convention of 1787.

Political theorists often draw upon two successful historical cases of representative democracy—Britain and the United States—to create the "classic" separation of powers theory. This theory argues that there are essentially two forms of representative democratic government: the presidential and the parliamentary.

The **democratic presidential regime** provides two separate branches of government—the executive and the legislative—separately elected by the people (see Table 6.1, column 3). Each branch is elected for a fixed term, neither branch can unseat the other by ordinary means, and each has specific powers under the constitution. Ultimate power to make laws and approve budgets resides with the legislature. Different presidential regimes give their presidents various powers over government appointments and policymaking. For example, some presidents have the authority to

---

TABLE 6.1

Distinguishing Features of Parliamentary and Presidential Democracies

Parliamentary and presidential democracies differ in the selection and removal of the chief executive, as well as in the authority to legislate.

Distinguishing Features[a]	Parliamentary Democracies	Presidential Democracies
Title of chief executive	Prime minister (head of government)	President (head of state and government)
Selection of assembly	By citizens in competitive election	By citizens in competitive election
Selection of chief executive	By assembly after election or removal	By citizens in competitive election
Removal of chief executive before fixed term?	By assembly: (No) confidence vote	Fixed terms
Dismissal of assembly before fixed term?	Prime minister may call for early election[b]	Fixed terms
Authority to legislate	Assembly only	Assembly plus president (e.g., veto)
Party relations in assembly and executive	Same parties control both; cohesive party voting	Different party control possible; less cohesive party voting

[a]These define the pure parliamentary and presidential types; as discussed in the text, many constitutional systems, especially in Eastern Europe, "mix" the features of the two types.

[b]Some constitutional systems that are parliamentary in all other ways do not allow for early legislative elections. All parliamentary democracies provide for legislative elections after some maximum time (from three to five years) since the last election.

veto legislation or, under some conditions, to make policy by executive decree.[4] In the United States, both the legislature and executive (Congress and the presidency) have large and significant roles in policymaking. In some other democratic presidential systems, such as Brazil, the president may have such a variety of constitutional powers (including the power to make laws through "emergency" decrees) that he or she can overshadow the legislature. But policymaking still requires coordination between the separate institutions of executive and legislature.

Parliamentary regimes make the executive and legislative branches much more interdependent (see Table 6.1, column 2). First, only the legislative branch is directly elected. The prime minister and the cabinet (the collective leadership of the executive branch) emerge from the legislature. The cabinet is chaired by the prime minister, who is the head of government and selects the other cabinet members.[5] Typically, neither branch has a fixed term of office. Commonly, the legislature (the parliament) is elected for a maximum term of four or five years, but it can be dissolved, and new elections held, before that term is up. The cabinet can be voted out of office at any time by the legislative majority.

The critical feature that makes this possible is the **confidence relationship** between the prime minister and the parliamentary majority. In a parliamentary system, the prime minister and the cabinet must at all times enjoy the confidence of the parliamentary majority. Whenever a parliamentary majority, for whatever reason, adopts a motion expressing a lack of confidence in the prime minister, the latter and all the other cabinet members have to resign. At the same time, the prime minister typically has the power at any time to dissolve parliament (thus ending its term) and call new elections. The parliamentary majority's **dismissal power** and the prime minister's **dissolution power** make the two branches of government mutually interdependent. This structure induces agreement between them by forcing each branch to be acceptable to the other.

Prime ministers in parliamentary democracies therefore lead precarious political lives. Unlike presidents in presidential systems, prime ministers can be voted out of office at any time, and for any reason, by a parliamentary majority. There are two ways this can happen. First, parliament may pass a motion expressing a lack of confidence in the prime minister—a no-confidence motion. This is typically introduced by the parliamentary opposition in the hope of bringing down the prime minister. Second, parliament may defeat a motion expressing confidence in the prime minister—a confidence motion. Confidence motions are normally introduced by prime ministers themselves.

It might seem unlikely that prime ministers would ever introduce a confidence motion and thus put their political survival at risk. But, paradoxically, the confidence vote can be a powerful weapon in the hands of the prime minister. It is typically attached to a bill the prime minister favors but the parliamentary majority does not. By attaching a confidence motion to the bill, the prime minister forces the members of parliament to choose between passing the bill and removing the cabinet. This can be a particularly painful choice for dissident members of the prime minister's own party. If they vote for the bill, they may bring down their own government and perhaps immediately have to face the voters, too (see Box 6.1). Therefore, the power that a confidence motion places in the hands of the prime minister helps explain why party discipline tends to be stronger in parliamentary than in presidential systems.

Because of the mutual interdependence between the cabinet and the parliamentary majority, parliamentary democracies do not experience the **divided government** that is common under presidentialism. This is when the party that controls the presidency does not control the legislature. In parliamentary systems, the chief executive (prime minister and cabinet) instead becomes the agent of the parliamentary majority and depends on this majority for its political survival. In most parliamentary systems, the cabinet consists largely of members of parliament. Conflicts between parliament and the executive are less likely to occur than under presidentialism. The cabinet tends to dominate policymaking, and the legislature may be less influential than under a presidential constitution.

Not all democracies fit neatly into the presidential or parliamentary category. Some, such as France, are often characterized as mixed, or "**semipresidential**." In these types, the president and the legislature are separately elected (as in presidential systems), but the president also has the power to dissolve the legislature (as in parliamentary systems). In these systems, the president may appoint the cabinet (as under presidentialism), but subject to dismissal by the legislature

BOX 6.1　The Confidence Vote in Britain

British prime ministers can resort to the confidence motion in order to bring rebellious party members into line. Usually, the mere threat of a confidence motion is sufficient. But in 1993, Conservative prime minister John Major faced a parliamentary crisis over the ratification of the Maastricht Treaty, which expanded the powers of the European Union. Major had only a slim majority in the House of Commons. Many "eurosceptics" in his own party were opposed to the Maastricht Treaty. About twenty of these Conservative dissidents voted with the Opposition and helped defeat the Maastricht Treaty in the House of Commons.

Immediately after this embarrassing defeat, however, Major introduced a confidence motion on his Maastricht policy. He announced that if he lost this vote, he would dissolve the House of Commons and hold new elections. Many of the Conservative dissidents feared that their party would do poorly in such an election and that they might personally lose their seats. Major's confidence motion passed by a vote of 339 to 299, and the House of Commons approved the Maastricht Treaty.

(as under parliamentarism). A variety of arrangements exist for such shared control. Their consequences are often sharply affected by which party or coalition controls the presidency and legislature. Many of the constitutions of the newer democracies of Eastern Europe and Asia are of this mixed type.

Reading across Figure 6.1, we see political systems classified by the separation of policymaking powers between executive and legislative institutions, from concentrated to dispersed. The vertical dimension of the table shows geographic division of power, which is discussed in the next section. In authoritarian governments (on the left of the figure), executive, legislative, and judicial powers are typically concentrated. Two of the twelve countries discussed in this book—China and Iran—have authoritarian governments not chosen in competitive elections. (Iran, however, has an elected president with some influence, although subordinate to the Supreme Leader, as discussed in Chapter 16.) Britain, Germany, Japan, and India are parliamentary systems in which executive and legislative powers are concentrated in cabinets responsible to the popularly elected lower houses of parliament. At the extreme right of Figure 6.1 are pure presidential systems, such as Brazil, Mexico, Nigeria, and the United States. In between are mixed systems, such as France and Russia, although the latter has become increasingly authoritarian (see Chapter 12).

Many political theorists traditionally favored the British-style parliamentary system as the best form of representative democracy. This version of parliamentarism—which couples plurality (SMD) voting rules that usually create single-party majorities in parliament with a cabinet and prime minister responsible to parliament—can result in stable governments responsible to the public will. Parliamentarism coupled with proportional representation has historically seemed more crisis prone, as in Germany and France between the two world wars. Such crises occurred because large extremist political parties emerged and prevented the formation of stable cabinets of parties that were willing and able to work together. However, the Scandinavian countries demonstrate that parliamentary systems with proportional representation can be quite stable when the ideological conflict between the political parties remains moderate. Moreover, a single party that is able to form a dominant parliamentary majority in a divided society, as in Northern Ireland until 1998, can sometimes threaten minority groups and intensify conflict.[6] In comparison with both versions of parliamentary government, the U.S. presidential system is often criticized for periodically producing divided government, which could result in stalemate or "gridlock."

The third wave of democratization reopened these parliamentary/presidential debates. Advocates of proportional parliamentarism argue that it provides a consensual framework in which different economic, ethnic, and religious groups can find representation and negotiate their differences. Parliamentary systems also have the flexibility that makes it possible to change governments between regular election dates if the people or the legislators disapprove of the executive. Since many transitional democracies are deeply divided, a parliamentary, proportional representation system may be particularly suitable. Presidentialism seems more susceptible to political conflict and even democratic breakdown. This may be because under divided government, a confrontation between the two separately elected branches of government, both representing the people, can tear a political system apart. Or, a strong president can use executive powers to repress competition.

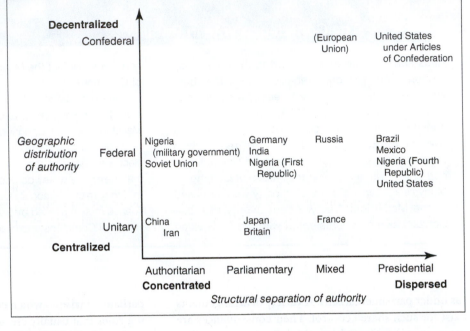

FIGURE 6.1
Division of Governmental Authority
Government authority may be divided along geographic or institutional dimensions, or both.

On the other hand, there are practical advantages of presidential systems with significant executive power, and they have proven popular across much of the world.[7] Even in the domain of the former British Empire (such as in Nigeria) and in most of Eastern Europe and the Soviet successor states, the constitutions provide for powerful presidents. Presidential regimes have dominated Latin America for more than a century. Some of the important attractions of presidentialism are that it offers citizens a more direct choice of their chief executive and that it puts more effective checks on the power of the legislative majority.

Geographic Distribution of Government Power

 Define confederal, federal, and unitary divisions of governmental power.

Another distinction between governmental structures lies in their geographic division of power: **confederal systems** at one extreme, **unitary systems** at the other extreme, and **federal systems**

in the middle (see the vertical dimension of Figure 6.1). The United States under the Articles of Confederation was confederal. Ultimate power rested with the states. The central government had authority over foreign affairs and defense but depended on the states for financial and other support. Under the Constitution of 1787, the U.S. government changed from confederal to federal, which is to say that both central and state governments were given separate spheres of authority and the means to implement their power. Today, the United States, Germany, Russia, India, Nigeria, Mexico, and Brazil are federal systems in which central and local units each have autonomy in certain public policy spheres. Britain, France, China, Japan, and Iran are unitary systems with power and authority concentrated in the central government. Regional and local units have only limited powers specifically delegated to them by the central government, which may change or withdraw these powers at will.

Most of the world's states are unitary. In fact, only eighteen states are federal, or fewer than one in ten. Although the federal states are relatively few in number, they tend to be large and politically important. Thus, federal states account for more than one-third of the world's population and 41 percent of its land area. In general, the larger and the more diverse a state is, the more likely it is to be federal.

Federalism has several attractive features. In culturally divided societies, it may help protect ethnic, linguistic, or religious minorities, particularly if they are geographically concentrated. It may serve as a check on overly ambitious rulers and thus protect markets and citizen freedoms. Moreover, federalism may allow subunits (such as states) to experiment with different policies. Governments may thus learn from the experiences of others. In addition, citizens may be free to "vote with their feet" and choose the local government and policy environment that best fit their preferences.

While federalism promotes choice and diversity, it does so at the expense of equality. Federalism allows local governments to pursue different policies. One implication is that citizens may get different treatments and benefits from different states or local governments. Unitary governments, on the other hand, may be in a better position to redistribute resources from richer regions to poorer regions, if that is desirable.

In comparing confederal, federal, and unitary systems, we must distinguish between formal and actual distributions of power. In unitary systems, in spite of the formal concentration of authority at the center, regional and local units may acquire power that the central government rarely challenges. And in federal systems, apparent regional autonomy may be undermined by centralized party control, as in the former Soviet Union, or by the fact that the bulk of government revenue runs through the central government, as in Nigeria (see Chapter 18). Mexico also illustrates the discrepancy between formal and actual federalism. Until recently, the governing PRI party centralized control in this formally federal system. Recent democratization, however, which has resulted in formerly opposition parties winning the presidency and many state governments, has produced some "real" Mexican federalism to go along with the formalities (see Chapter 14). Thus, the real differences between federal and unitary systems are not always what the formal constitutions would suggest.

Limitations on Government Power

 6.5 Discuss the role of the courts in overseeing democracies and give examples from several countries.

Unlike authoritarian regimes, democracies are characterized by some legal or customary limitation on the exercise of power. Systems in which the powers of government units are defined and limited by a written constitution, statutes, and custom are called **constitutional regimes**. Civil rights—such as the right to a fair trial and freedom to speak, petition, publish, and assemble—are protected against government interference except under specified circumstances.

The courts are crucial to the limitations on governmental power. As illustrated in Table 6.2, governments may be divided into those at one extreme in which the power to coerce citizens is relatively unlimited by the courts and those at the other extreme in which the courts protect the rights of citizens and ensure that other parts of the government exercise their powers properly. In the United States, Germany, and India, high courts have the power to rule that other units of government have exceeded their constitutional powers. This practice of **judicial review** exists to various degrees in about half of the world's

TABLE 6.2
Judicial Limitation of Governmental Authority
The power of judicial review of legislation is found in about half of the world's democracies, but it varies in effectiveness.

Unlimited		Limited
Nonindependent Courts	Independent Courts	Judicial Review
China	Britain	United States
Iran		India
Nigeria		Germany
		France
		Brazil
		Japan
		Russia

democracies. But judicial review is often weakened by the lack of independence of the judges or by their ineffectiveness in overcoming executive power.

Other constitutional regimes, such as Britain, have independent courts that protect persons against the improper implementation of laws and regulations, but that cannot legally overrule the assembly or the political executive. The citizens' substantive rights in these systems are protected by statute, custom, self-restraint, and political pressure—which are also essential to the effectiveness of courts, even under judicial review. In authoritarian systems, policymakers do not usually allow courts to constrain their use and abuse of power, even though brave judges occasionally attempt to rule against them.[8]

Arend Lijphart characterizes only four of the thirty-six democratic systems he examines as having "strong" judicial review, including Germany, India, and the United States.[9] The Supreme Court of India is most similar to the U.S. Supreme Court, having successfully declared many national laws and ordinances to be unconstitutional (see Chapter 17). The German Constitutional Court also significantly influences national and state policymaking through its rulings and through government's anticipation of those rulings.[10]

About a quarter of Lijphart's thirty-six democracies have at least medium-strength judicial review. In France and Brazil, new legislation may be challenged in court by opposition members of parliament even before it takes effect, a process called "abstract" judicial review. A little over half of the thirty-six democracies have "weak judicial review," with the powers of courts constrained by very limited constitutional authority (as in Ireland) or by judges who are not very independent because their careers depend so much on the governing parties (as in Japan). In the remaining democracies, courts enjoyed no power of judicial review of legislation, although they may still protect individuals from government abuse not specifically authorized by law (see again Table 6.2).[11]

Many of the new democracies of Eastern Europe proclaim judicial review in their constitutions, but it has proved harder to implement in practice. There have been striking successes in constraining governments in some countries, but failures in others. In Nigeria, the courts long retained a surprising degree of judicial independence under a succession of otherwise undemocratic military regimes. However, the courts were shown little respect under the Abacha military

dictatorship (1993–1998), which established special military tribunals to prosecute its perceived enemies. After Nigeria redemocratized in 1999, however, the courts gained new powers.

China, in contrast, after explicitly rejecting any limits on "mass justice" from the late 1950s to the 1970s, has gradually introduced a very limited "rule by law." One recent reason is Chinese participation in the global economic system, which requires a legal basis for trade and investment. Chinese rulers see this as a way to encourage stability and economic growth and control corruption. Yet the practice falls far short of the promise to limit government authority (see Chapter 13).

All written constitutions provide ways in which they can be amended. Most framers of constitutions recognize that basic decision rules must be adaptable, because of potential ambiguities, inefficiencies, changes in citizen values, or unforeseen circumstances. If amendments are too easy to make, they may jeopardize important constitutional protections. Therefore, many constitutions contain certain articles that may not be amended (for example, the provision in the U.S. Constitution granting each state equal representation in the Senate).

Amending procedures vary widely, ranging from the simple to the complex. Perhaps the simplest case is that of the United Kingdom, where the passage of an ordinary parliamentary statute by simple majority vote may alter the constitution. The U.S. Constitution has the most difficult formal procedure, requiring large majorities in both houses of Congress and ratification by three-fourths of the states. In some countries, such as Denmark, constitutional amendments must also be approved by a popular vote.

In summary, constitutions may concentrate or disperse government power along several dimensions.[12] There are necessary trade-offs involved in making such constitutional choices. Probably no one who favors democracy and individual liberties would argue for extreme centralization of power in an omnipotent dictator, as in Thomas Hobbes's *Leviathan* (see Chapter 1). However, constitutional democracies that concentrate power to a somewhat lesser degree, such as the British system, have some important advantages. Their governments tend to be effective and efficient, and by relying on majority rule, they tend to treat all citizens equally. No small group can hold up a decision favored by a solid majority. In contrast, constitutions that disperse power, as in more inclusive decision rules, have their own advantages. They are more likely to check potential abuses of power, such as the tyranny of a majority, and policies will tend to be more stable over time.

Checking the Top Policymakers

 6.6 List three methods used to remove political leaders from office.

One challenge of government is to control the top political leaders and prevent them from abusing their power. In many authoritarian systems, there is no legal and institutionalized way to remove the top political leaders if they become unpopular or commit atrocities. Moreover, authoritarian leaders can usually change or simply ignore the formal constitution when it suits them. Democracies have various procedures for keeping the leaders in check. In parliamentary systems, chief executives can be removed virtually at any time through a vote of no confidence if they lose the support of a parliamentary majority. In Germany, for example, Social Democratic Party chancellor Helmut Schmidt was ousted by Helmut Kohl of the Christian Democratic Party in October 1982.

Democratic presidential systems fall somewhere in between. Unlike prime ministers under parliamentary constitutions, presidents have fixed terms of office. Most presidential systems provide for the removal of presidents, but typically only if they are guilty of

serious crimes or other wrongdoing. This procedure is called **impeachment**. Impeachment typically involves three components: (1) impeachable offenses are usually identified as presenting unusual danger to the public good or safety, (2) the penalty is removal from office (sometimes with separate criminal penalties), and (3) impeachment cases are decided by the legislature but require more than ordinary majorities and may involve the judiciary in some way. The positive value of impeachment is that it provides a way of legally mobilizing political power against a threat to the constitutional or legal order. At the same time, the danger is that it can be used for mere partisan or personal goals.

In the U.S. system, impeachment procedures can be used against political incumbents, even the president (as in the cases of Presidents Nixon and Clinton), if their activities stray too far beyond legal bounds. No U.S. president has yet been convicted by the Senate and removed from office, although that fate has befallen other federal officials, such as judges. Impeachment is associated with constitutions having powerful presidencies with fixed terms of office, such as those in the United States, Brazil, South Korea, and the Philippines (see Box 6.2). Impeachment rules have also been adopted in the constitutions of semipresidential regimes, such as Russia, and even in purely parliamentary regimes.

Another method that can be used to remove unpopular officeholders, even if they are not guilty of major crimes, is the recall election, which is common in state constitutions in the United States, but which is rarely used for national executives around the world.

BOX 6.2   Impeachment in Latin America

Brazil, Mexico, and many other Latin American nations with strong presidents have impeachment rules and traditions. Many are modeled on the U.S. Constitution. In Mexico, the president, state governors, and federal judges are subject to impeachment. Brazil has an impeachment process similar to that of the United States, except that it takes a two-thirds vote in the lower house of the assembly to charge the president and other high civil officers with impeachable offenses. A two-thirds vote is also required in the Senate to convict. The clause was

invoked in 1992, when Brazil's president, Fernando Collor, was impeached on charges of large-scale corruption. He resigned before trial in the Senate. Impeachment procedures also forced presidents from office in Venezuela in 1993 and Paraguay in 1999. A slightly different procedure was used by the Congress in 1997 to declare the incumbent president of Ecuador mentally unfit.

Source: Anibal Perez-Linan, *Presidential Impeachment and the New Political Instability in Latin America* (New York: Cambridge University Press, 2007).

In the long run, the ultimate control of democratic order is periodic and competitive elections. This need to achieve and regularly renew their popular mandates is the fundamental device that leads politicians to respond to the needs and demands of citizens. Elections are deeply imperfect for this purpose. It may be difficult to tell when elected officials are incompetent, deceitful, or just unlucky. The complexities of policymaking may baffle the attempt of even trained observers to assign responsibility for successes or failures. The multiplicity of political issues may leave citizens torn between their candidate choices. Or, none of the choices may seem very palatable. Yet, deeply imperfect as they are, elections give every citizen some influence over the policymaking process. For this reason, we consider the competitive election to be the most significant democratic structure.

Assemblies

 Describe the varied forms, functions, and compositions of government assemblies.

Legislative **assemblies** have existed for thousands of years. Ancient Greece and Rome had them, for example. Indeed, the Roman Senate has given its name to modern assemblies in the United States and many other countries.

Almost all contemporary political systems have assemblies, variously called *senates, chambers, diets, houses,* and the like. Assemblies are also known as "legislatures" (regardless of what role they actually play in legislating) or as "parliaments" (mainly in parliamentary systems). Their formal approval is usually required for major public policies and especially for the making of laws and national budgets. They are generally elected by popular vote, and hence are at least formally accountable to the citizenry. Today, 186 countries have such governmental bodies. The almost universal adoption of legislative assemblies suggests that in the modern world, a legitimate government must formally include a representative popular component.

Assembly Structure

Assemblies vary in their size—from less than 100 to more than 1,000 members—and their organization. They may consist of one chamber (in which case they are called *unicameral*) or two chambers (*bicameral*). Most democracies, and some authoritarian systems, have bicameral (two-chamber) assemblies. Federal systems normally provide simultaneously for two forms of representation; often, representation in one chamber is based on population, and representation in the second chamber is based on geographic units. The bicameral German parliament grew out of both federalism and the desire to separate the power of the federal government. Even in unitary systems (such as France or Japan), **bicameralism** is common, but the purpose of the second chamber is to provide a check on policymaking rather than to represent subnational units.

In most bicameral systems, one chamber is dominant, and the second (such as the Russian Council of the Federation or the French Senate) has more limited powers often designed to protect regional interests. While representatives in the dominant chamber are popularly elected, those in the second chamber are sometimes chosen by the regional governments (as in Germany) or in other indirect ways. In most parliamentary systems, the prime minister is responsible only to the more popularly elected chamber, which therefore has a more important position in policymaking than the second chamber. (See the discussion of the vote-of-confidence procedure earlier in this chapter and in Box 6.1).

Assemblies also differ in their internal organization in ways that have major consequences for policymaking. There are two kinds of internal legislative organization: party groups and formal assembly subunits (presiding officers, committees, and the like). There is often an inverse relationship between the strength of parties and the strength of other subunits (such as committees): The stronger the parties are, the weaker the committees are, and vice versa. As in most parliamentary systems, British members of Parliament vote strictly along party lines much more consistently than members of the U.S. Congress. Because cabinets generally hold office only as long as they can command a parliamentary majority, deviating from the party line means risking the fall of the government and new elections. And the strength of party-line voting means that committees cannot easily foster compromises that cut across party lines.

In presidential systems, the president and the legislators are independently elected for fixed terms of office. Thus the fate of the executive is less directly tied up with voting on legislative measures. Moreover, the president and the legislative party leadership may offer conflicting messages to the president's party, leading to party divisions. For both reasons, party voting is less cohesive in presidential systems, depending also on whether the election rules foster competition within the parties.[13]

All assemblies have a committee structure—some organized arrangement that permits legislators to divide their labor and to specialize in particular issue areas. Without such committees, it would be impossible to handle the large flow of legislative business. However, the importance of committees varies.[14] In some legislatures—such as those in the United States, Japan, and Germany—committees are very influential. This is partially because they are highly specialized, have jurisdictions that match those of the executive departments, and have numerous staff resources. Strong committees tend to have a clear legislative division of labor that matches the executive branch, allowing for specialized oversight of executive activity, and they tend to be committees to which legislators get reappointed term after term, so that they can acquire a great deal of expertise. They are often arenas in which the opposition can be influential. British committees, by comparison, are much weaker, since they have small staffs, are dominated by the governing party, and get appointed for one bill at a time. Hence, they cannot accumulate expertise in a particular policy area.

Assembly Functions

Assembly members deliberate, debate, and vote on policies that come before them. Most important policies and rules must be considered and at least formally approved by these bodies before they have the force of law. Assemblies typically also control public-spending decisions; budgeting is one of their major functions. In addition, some assemblies have important appointment powers, and some may serve as a court of appeals. Although laws typically need assembly approval, in most countries, legislation is actually formulated elsewhere, usually by the political executive and the upper levels of the bureaucracy.

In its policymaking influence, the U.S. Congress, which plays a very active role in the formulation and enactment of legislation, is at one extreme. The other extreme is represented by the National People's Congress of the People's Republic of China, which meets infrequently and does little more than listen to statements by party leaders and rubber-stamp decisions made elsewhere. Roughly midway between the two is the House of Commons in Britain. There, legislative proposals are sometimes initiated or modified by ordinary members of Parliament, but public policy is usually initiated and proposed by members of the Cabinet (who are, to be sure, chosen from the members of the parliamentary body). The typical assembly provides a deliberating forum, formally enacts legislation, and sometimes amends it.

Assemblies are not only legislative bodies. All assemblies in democratic systems have an important relationship to legislation, but not necessarily a dominant role. Their political importance is based not just on this function but also on the great variety of other political functions they perform. Assemblies can play a major role in elite recruitment, especially in parliamentary systems, where prime ministers and cabinet members typically serve their apprenticeships in parliament. Legislative committee hearings and floor debates may be important sites for interest articulation and interest aggregation, especially if there is no cohesive majority party. Debates in assemblies can be a source of public information about politics and thus contribute to the socialization of citizens generally and elites in particular.

Representation: Mirroring and Representational Biases

Contemporary legislatures, especially in democratic systems, are valued particularly because they represent the citizens in the policymaking process. It is not obvious, however, what the ideal linkage between citizens and government officials should be. Some argue that government officials should mirror the characteristics of the citizens as far as possible. This principle, also known as **mirroring** or **descriptive representation**, is held to be particularly important with respect to potentially conflictual divisions (such as race, class, ethnicity, gender, language, and perhaps age).

The bad news is that political elites, even democratically elected members of legislatures, hardly ever mirror the citizens they represent on any of the standard social characteristics. Even in democracies such as Britain and France, political leaders tend to be of higher social status, unusually well educated, or upwardly mobile individuals from the lower classes. There are exceptions. In some countries, trade unions or leftist political parties have served as channels of political advancement for people with modest economic or educational backgrounds who have acquired political skills and experience by holding offices in working-class organizations. During the long political domination of the Norwegian Labor Party (1935–1981), none of its prime ministers had even completed secondary school. But these are rare and vanishing examples. In most contemporary states, the number of working-class people in high office is small and declining.

Women have traditionally been poorly represented in political leadership positions in most countries. However, the situation has changed significantly in the last thirty years.[15] In 1980, women held about 10 percent of the parliamentary seats around the world. By 2010, that figure had nearly doubled, to 19 percent. Women have also held the chief executive office in a growing number of countries (see Box 6.3). Angela Merkel, for example, became chancellor of Germany in 2005 and was reelected in 2009 and 2013 (see Chapter 10).

But women's advancement has been uneven.[16] In many Northern European countries, such as Sweden, by 2010, women accounted for 40 percent or more of the legislators and a similar proportion of cabinet members.

In Germany, Mexico, Britain, and China, women held over 20 percent of the legislative seats. But in Brazil and Nigeria, women still accounted for fewer than 10 percent. The proportion in Iran was only 3 percent.

Political elites also tend to be unrepresentative with respect to age. In many countries, legislators (much less chief executives) under age forty are a rarity, whereas a large proportion of leading politicians are past normal retirement age. In many countries, university graduates—and often lawyers and civil servants in particular—are vastly overrepresented, whereas ethnic, linguistic, and religious minorities are often underrepresented. Representational biases are thus numerous and pervasive. And while women's representation is increasing, class biases are getting worse.

However, descriptive representation is not the only concern in recruiting public officials. The limits of mirroring were inadvertently expressed by a U.S. senator. In defending a U.S. Supreme Court nominee who was accused of mediocrity, the senator lamely contended, "[E]ven if he were mediocre, there are a lot of mediocre judges and people and lawyers. They are entitled to a little representation, aren't they?"[17] Most people would probably not agree that government officials should mirror the general population in their

---

BOX 6.3 Women as Chief Executives

From about 1970 on, women have gained chief executive office in a growing number of countries. Interestingly, many of the early leaders were from Asian and Middle Eastern countries, where women's roles in public life traditionally have been limited. Sirimavo Bandaranaike of Sri Lanka (1960–1965 and 1970–1977), Indira Gandhi of India (1966–1977 and 1980–1984), and Golda Meir of Israel (1969–1974) were among the pioneers. In the 1980s and 1990s, women also came to power in the Philippines, Pakistan, Bangladesh, and again in Sri Lanka. In Burma, Nobel Peace Prize winner Aung San Suu Kyi won the election of 1990, but the military prevented her from taking office.

Women have recently made inroads in leadership positions in Europe and the Americas, though they are still few and far between in Africa. The first female leader in a major European country was Prime Minister Margaret Thatcher of Britain (1979–1990). Her strong

and decisive leadership made her one of Europe's most influential politicians in the 1980s. Women have come to power in other Western countries as well. Angela Merkel is now chancellor of Germany. In Norway, Gro Harlem Brundtland held the prime ministership for a total of about ten years between 1981 and 1996. In Latin America, female presidents have recently come to office in Argentina, Brazil, Chile, and Costa Rica.

The career paths of Asian women leaders have tended to differ from those elsewhere. Many of the former have come from prominent political families, such as the Gandhi family in India and the Bhuttos in Pakistan. In several cases, they have been the widows or daughters of important political leaders. In Europe and Latin America, women leaders are more likely to have made independent political careers, and they can rely on stronger women's interest groups.

abilities to do their jobs. Instead, we generally want political elites to be the best possible *agents* for their constituents. In this view, government officials should be selected for their ability to serve the interests of the citizens, whether they share the voters' background characteristics or not.

For politicians to be good agents, they need to have similar *preferences* to the citizens they represent *and* they need the appropriate *skills* to do their jobs. In democracies, political parties and elections are the most important mechanisms by which the preferences of citizens and the preferences (or at least commitments) of leaders are aligned.[18] As far as skills are concerned, political and governmental leadership—particularly in modern, technologically advanced societies—requires knowledge and skills that are hard to acquire except through education and training. Natural intelligence or experience may, to a limited degree, take the place of formal education.

Hence, it might be a good thing for government officials to be better informed, more intelligent, more experienced, and perhaps better educated than the people they serve. Just as medical patients tend to look for the most capable physician rather than the one who is most like them, one could argue that citizens should look for the best-qualified officeholder. In this view, selecting government officials, including representative policymakers, is like delegating to experts. It may be a hopeful sign that citizens in many modern democracies are increasingly willing to select leaders who do not share their background characteristics.

As in the case of so many other political choices, there is no obvious or perfect way to choose between mirroring and expert delegation. This is an old debate, and in many situations, it is necessary to make a trade-off between the two. Different offices may require different considerations. Most people would, for example, probably put a higher emphasis on mirroring in their local assembly than in a regulatory agency overseeing nuclear technology.

Political Executives

 Discuss the ways chief executives are chosen, their powers, and the role played by cabinets.

In modern states, the executive branch is by far the largest, the most complex, and typically the most powerful branch of government. It is not easy to describe executives in simple ways, but it is sensible to start at the top. Governments typically have one or two **chief executives**, officials who sit at the very top of the often colossal executive branch. Such executives have various names, titles, duties, and powers. They are called *presidents, prime ministers, chancellors, secretaries general*, or even *leader* (in Iran). There are even a few kings who still have genuine power. Titles may mislead us as to what functions these officials perform, but they tend to be the main formulators and executors of public policy.

Structure of the Chief Executive

Democratic governments typically have either a single chief executive (in presidential systems) or a split chief executive of two offices: a largely ceremonial head of state (who represents the nation on formal occasions) and a more powerful head of government (who determines public policies). Table 6.3 distinguishes among executives according to the bases of their power to affect policymaking. The left column represents the chief executives in authoritarian systems. The middle and right columns show the chief executives in democratic countries. The middle column shows executives whose power rests primarily on their partisan influence in the legislature, which is the case for the prime ministers in most parliamentary systems. The right column includes chief executives whose ability to influence legislation resides in powers directly granted them by the constitution, rather than partisan connection alone. Strong presidents may be able to veto legislation, for example, issue legal decrees, or introduce the budget. They usually have the power to appoint and dismiss members of the cabinet.

Reading down the table, we see the distinctions between executives with effective power over policy, purely ceremonial roles, or both effective and ceremonial power. Political executives are effective only if they have genuine discretion in the enactment and implementation of laws and regulations, in budgetary matters, or in important government appointments. Where they do not have these powers, they are symbolic or ceremonial. In presidential systems, the ceremonial and effective roles are almost always held by the same person, the president, as we see at the bottom of Table 6.3. In parliamentary democracies, and in some authoritarian systems, the two roles are separated between the "head of state," who is primarily a

TABLE 6.3
Bases of Legislative Power of Chief Executives
Chief executives vary in the effectiveness and in the bases of their legislative powers.

Authoritarian	Democratic: Partisan Influence	Democratic: Constitutional Powers
Effective		
General Secretary, China	British Prime Minister	
	French Prime Minister	
	German Chancellor	
	Indian Prime Minister	
	Japanese Prime Minister	
	(Russian Prime Minister)	
Ceremonial		
Chinese President		British Queen or King
		German President
		Indian President
		Japanese Emperor
Ceremonial and Effective		
Iranian Leader	French President	Brazilian President
		Mexican President
		Nigerian President
		Russian President
		U.S. President

ceremonial official, and a "head of government," who makes and implements the decisions. The British, German, Indian, and Japanese prime ministers appear in the second column at the top of the table, while their ceremonial counterparts appear at the center right.

These distinctions are not absolute. Even largely ceremonial presidents can exert important influence if the parties are divided or by exercising special constitutional powers (or both, as happened in India in the 1990s). Moreover, partisan influence in the legislature is useful even to the strongest democratic presidents. Still, it is usually easy to determine the primary sources of legislative power, even where the formal names may be misleading.

A few countries have both significant presidents and prime ministers. The balance of power between them depends on the constitutional powers of the president and on the partisan division in the legislature. The Russian constitution gives the president very great powers of veto and decree, which have

been expanded under recent authoritarian trends. The prime minister has been mostly just another administrator with little effective power, but this was very different when Vladimir Putin held the office between 2008 and 2012. In France, in contrast, the president's formal powers are much weaker; when his party does not control the legislature, it has elected a prime minister who has effectively dominated policymaking, greatly reducing the president's political influence.

In China, the chairman of the Communist Party is the most powerful political figure and the effective chief executive. The Chinese president is the head of state, which is a purely ceremonial role, without associated powers. However, in recent years, the same individual has held both offices, and also a key role as chairman of the party military commission. A separate premier, or head of government, is a largely administrative position.

Monarchies are much rarer at the beginning of the twenty-first century than they were at the beginning of the twentieth. Some monarchs, such as the king of Saudi Arabia and some other Arab monarchs, still exercise real power. Most contemporary monarchs, however, have little or no actual political influence. Monarchs like the British, Japanese, or Scandinavian royal families hold principally ceremonial and symbolic positions with limited political powers. They are living symbols of the state and nation and of its historical continuity. Britain's queen may bestow honors or appointments on the nobility with a stroke of her sword, but these appointments are effectively decided by the prime minister. The Japanese monarchy has also traditionally been dignified and exalted, and played an important role as a national symbol. In contrast, the Scandinavian monarchies are more humdrum. Because members of these royal families occasionally use humbler means of transportation, these dynasties are sometimes called "bicycle monarchies." In republican democracies with parliamentary systems, presidents perform the functions that fall to kings and queens in parliamentary monarchies. Thus, German presidents give speeches on important anniversaries and designate prime ministers after elections or when a government has resigned.

Separating the ceremonial executive from the effective executive has a number of advantages. The ceremonial executive symbolizes unity and continuity and can be above politics. The U.S. presidency, which combines both effective and ceremonial functions, runs the risk that the president will use his ceremonial and symbolic authority to enhance his political power or that his involvement in politics may make him a less effective symbolic or unifying figure.

Recruitment of Chief Executives

Historically, finding effective and legitimate ways to select the individuals to fill the top policymaking roles has been critical to political order and stability. "Recruitment structures" are the means by which nations choose their top policymakers and executives. Table 6.4 shows the recruitment structures in the countries discussed in this book.

Democracies regulate the potential conflict involved in leadership succession and confine it to the mobilization of votes instead of weapons. This is a major accomplishment that reduces the risk of

Chief Executives
NATO Secretary General Anders Fogh Rasmussen and U.S. Secretary of State John Kerry shake hands with the leaders of allied nations at a NATO summit.

TABLE 6.4
Recruitment of Chief Executive
Political parties of various kinds are involved in the recruitment of most chief executives.

Country	Chief Executive Structure	Recruitment Structures	How Often Has This Type of Government Survived Succession?[b]
Brazil	President	Party and voters	Often
Britain	Prime minister	Party, House of Commons, voters	Very often
China	Party secretary[a]	Party and military	Often
France	President/prime minister	Party, (Assembly) voters	Often
Germany	Chancellor	Party, Bundestag, voters	Often
India	Prime minister	Party, Lok Sabha, voters	Often (one interruption)
Iran	Leader	Religious elites	Once
Japan	Prime minister	Party, Diet, voters	Often
Mexico	President	Party and voters	Twice
Nigeria	President	Party and voters	Twice
Russia	President	Party, president, voters	Twice
United States	President	Party and voters	Very often

[a]"Party secretary" refers to that position or to a similar one as head of party in a communist regime.
[b]"Often" means that at least three successions have taken place under that type of government.

serious conflict. In presidential systems, parties select candidates for nomination, and the electorate chooses among them. Russia and France have directly elected presidents but also give an important role to the prime minister, who is appointed by the president but can be removed by the legislature. Mexico is now similar to other presidential systems. But for half a century, the PRI had such control over the electoral process that the voters merely ratified the party's presidential nominee. Until the 2000 election, many voters remained skeptical that a non-PRI president could really come to power.

In both presidential and parliamentary democracies, the tenure of the chief executive is limited, directly or indirectly. In the presidential system, this limitation is usually direct and explicit, in the form of fixed terms of office for the chief executive. In the parliamentary system, there is a maximum term for the parliament, which then indirectly also limits the life of the cabinet, since the prime minister is accountable to the new parliamentary majority and can be removed by it. The important role played by political parties illustrates the great need to mobilize broad political support behind the selection of chief executives. The frequent appearance of parties also reflects, no doubt,

the modern legitimacy of popular sovereignty: the promise that the rulers' actions will be in the interest of the ruled.

Table 6.4 also illustrates the role of the Communist Party and the military organizations in China and nonelected religious elites in Iran. Authoritarian systems rarely have effective procedures for leadership succession. The more power is concentrated at the top, the riskier it is to transfer it from one person to the next. Very often, authoritarian leaders do not dare to relinquish their power, and leadership succession occurs only when they die or are overthrown. In communist regimes, the Communist Party selects the general secretary (or equivalent), who is the controlling executive force. Individual succession is not a simple matter. These systems do not limit the terms of incumbents, who are difficult to oust once they have consolidated their supporters into key party positions. Nonetheless, they always have to be aware of the possibility of a party coup of the type that ousted Nikita Khrushchev from the Soviet leadership in 1964. As a system, however, the Soviet leadership structure seemed quite stable until the 1991 coup attempt against Mikhail Gorbachev, which marked the beginning of the end of the Soviet Union. After the collapse

Bicycle Royalty
Crown Princess Victoria, heir to the Swedish throne, illustrates why the Scandinavian and Low Country monarchies are commonly referred to as "bicycle monarchies."

of the Soviet Union, Russia managed its first democratic transition surprisingly smoothly, from Boris Yeltsin to his chosen successor, Vladimir Putin, who was elected president in 2000. Putin arranged a less democratic transition in 2008, when Dmitri Medvedev was elected president in an unfree election, and in 2012, when he (Putin) returned to the presidency (see Chapter 12).

The poorer nations show substantially less stability, and the regimes usually have had less experience at surviving succession crises.[19] Nigeria experienced a succession of military coups and governments from 1966 until 1979 and then introduced a competitive presidential system, which was overthrown by another military coup in 1983. The military rulers finally allowed a return to civilian rule in 1999, and Nigeria has since gone on to elect three successive civilian presidents.

Military governments, stable or unstable, have also been common in Latin America and the Middle East, although they are now more likely to work with other groups or from behind the scenes (see Chapter 5). The Chinese Communist Party has remained in power for fifty years but has suffered several periods of internal strife, and the army has been involved in recruitment at all levels. India's democracy has been an exception to the rule among poorer nations. The country has had a number of democratic successions, with a single interlude of authoritarian emergency rule in the 1970s.

The Cabinet

In many political systems, the **cabinet** is the most important collective decision-making body. Its power can be particularly great in parliamentary systems, where its formation is closely linked to selection of the prime minister. It typically contains the leaders (often called "ministers") of all the major departments (sometimes called "ministries") of the executive branch. The cabinet meets frequently, often several times per week. It is typically led by the head of government: the president in presidential systems and the prime minister in parliamentary ones. The leadership role of prime ministers varies. In some parliamentary systems, the prime minister is little more than "first among equals," especially in multiparty coalition governments. The prime minister then typically leads one of the coalition parties but has to negotiate with the leaders of the other parties in the coalition. In other parliamentary systems, such as Germany, the constitution confers much more authority on the chief executive.[20]

How is the cabinet selected? In presidential systems, selecting cabinet members is typically a presidential prerogative, though sometimes (as with the U.S. Senate) the legislature has the right to approve or reject the nominee. The president can typically also dismiss cabinet members at will, whereas the legislature's ability to do so is most often severely limited. In parliamentary systems, the process is very different, since the prime minister and the cabinet need to maintain the confidence of the parliamentary majority. Therefore, cabinet formation depends on the result of parliamentary elections and on the partisan make-up of parliament. Sometimes, the election directly determines who controls the majority and can therefore form the cabinet. Thus, in pure two-party systems, one party always receives a parliamentary majority. It can also happen in multiparty systems, whenever one party gets more seats than all its competitors combined. When one party controls a parliamentary majority, the party almost always forms a *majority single-party cabinet* by itself.

In most multiparty countries, the typical election result is that no party has a parliamentary majority by itself. The election laws play an important part in shaping legislative representation of the parties: As Duverger claimed, proportional representation tends to produce multiparty parliaments. The more parties there are, the less likely it is that one of them will have a majority on its own. Most commonly under such circumstances, several parties (two, three, or more) join forces and form a **coalition cabinet** in which they are all represented. Sometimes, parties anticipate this need to form coalitions before the election. They may make a formal agreement and inform the voters that they intend to govern together if they collectively get enough votes. The coalition parties may thus encourage their respective voters to support their partners' candidates where their own party's candidates seem weak. Many German and French governments have come to power in this fashion. (See especially the discussion of German coalitions in Chapter 10.) In such cases, the voters can have a direct voice in the choice of the cabinet and the direction of government policy, much as they do in two-party systems.

If no party or pre-election coalition wins control of the legislature through the election, parties may bargain after the election to form a new cabinet. In countries such as the Netherlands and Belgium, such bargaining has often taken months, or even a whole year. However, only a few days were needed to form a coalition government of the Conservatives and Liberal Democrats after the British election in 2010 (see Chapter 8).

In parliamentary systems, whether bargaining takes place before or after the elections, the parties typically have many options concerning the composition of the cabinet. Figure 6.2 illustrates these various possibilities. In some cases, a single party decides that it can form a **minority cabinet** alone, often because the other parties disagree too much among themselves to offer any alternative. With a minority government, however, the governing parties must continually bargain with other parties to get policies adopted and even to remain in office. In majority coalitions, bargaining occurs primarily among coalition partners represented in the cabinet. In both of these circumstances, the power of the prime minister may depend on the bargains he or she can strike with leaders of other parties.

These complications illustrate two of the problems of combining parliamentary government with electoral systems of proportional representation. Since PR elections rarely produce a single majority party, they do not give the voters a very clear choice over who will control the executive branch. Instead,

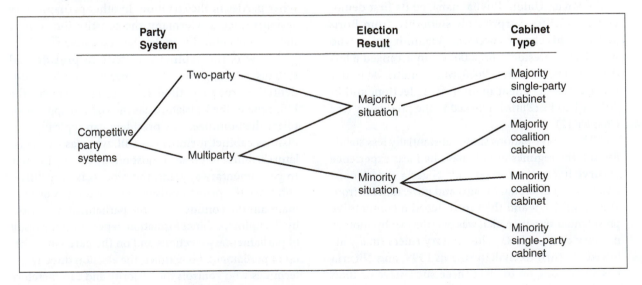

FIGURE 6.2

Cabinet Formation in Parliamentary Democracies

Party system and election results shape cabinet formation processes and outcomes.

the parties may determine this behind closed doors after the election. Sometimes, the results are paradoxical, as when parties that have just lost the election are able to negotiate their way into a governing coalition. The second problem is that multiparty cabinets are sometimes unstable. Italy, for example, has had, on average, more than one change of government per year since World War II. Yet such problems need not always emerge with parliamentarism and PR. In Germany, cabinets have been quite stable, and the voters have generally been given fairly clear options ahead of elections.

Functions of the Chief Executive

Typically, the chief executive is the most important structure in policymaking. The executive normally initiates new policies. Depending on the division of powers with the legislature and the partisan balance, the executive also has a substantial part in their adoption. In presidential systems, the president very often has veto powers. Thus, the chief executive typically has both the first and the last word in policymaking. In parliamentary systems, on the other hand, the chief executive is less likely to be able to exercise a veto.

The political executive also oversees policy implementation and can hold subordinate officials accountable for their performance. The chief executive also generally makes key foreign policy decisions and generates new political initiatives and programs. A bureaucracy without an effective executive tends to implement past policies rather than initiate new ones. Without politically motivated ministers, bureaucracies tend toward inertia.

The decision of a president, prime minister, cabinet, or central party committee to pursue a new foreign or domestic policy is usually accompanied by structural adaptations—the appointment of a vigorous minister, the establishment of a special cabinet committee, and the like. Where the political executive is weak and divided, as sometimes in Italy, this dynamic force is missing. Initiative then passes to the bureaucracy, legislative committees, and powerful interest groups—and general needs, interests, and problems

Pre-election Coalition in India
The government of India is headed by the United Progressive Alliance (UPA), a coalition formed by parties before the parliamentary election. The coalition is led by the Indian National Congress, whose president, Sonia Gandhi (shown here in the center of the photo, meeting with heads of other coalition partner parties), serves as the chairperson of the UPA.

may be neglected. In a separation-of-powers system, when the presidency and the congress are controlled by different parties, even a strong president may be hampered in carrying out an effective policy. And if the president is hamstrung, the assembly can rarely fill the gap.

Chief executives also perform important system functions. Studies of childhood socialization show that the first political role perceived by children tends to be the chief political executive—the president, prime minister, or king or queen. In early childhood, the tendency is to identify the top political executive as a parent figure. As the child matures, he or she begins to differentiate political from other roles, as well as to differentiate among various political roles (see Chapter 3). The conduct of the chief executive affects the trust and confidence that young people feel in the whole political system, and they carry that with them into adulthood. The role of the chief executive in appointing cabinet and other officials is obviously also important. The political executive also plays a central role in communication, in explaining and building support for new policies.

The Bureaucracy

 6.9 Explain Max Weber's definition of a bureaucracy and describe the forms bureaucracies can take.

Modern societies are dominated by large organizations, and this applies to governments as well. **Bureaucracies**, by which we mean all the members of the executive branch below the top executives, generally implement government policy. The size of government bureaucracies increased over the course of the twentieth century. This is partly due to the expanding policy responsibilities and efforts of governments. It may also be partly due to the tendency for government agencies, once they have been established, to seek growth for its own sake. In reaction to this tendency, and as part of the concern about government inefficiencies, there has been a recent movement in many advanced democracies to reduce government budgets and to downsize the bureaucracy (see Chapter 7).

Structure of the Bureaucracy

The most important officials in bureaucracies are the experienced and expert personnel of the top **civil service**. The British "government" consists of approximately 100 top executive positions of ministers, junior ministers, and parliamentary secretaries. This relatively small group of political policymakers oversees some 3,000 permanent members of the **higher civil service**. These civil servants spend their lives as an elite corps, moving about from ministry to ministry, watching governments come and go, and becoming increasingly important as policymakers as they rise in rank. Below the higher civil service is a huge body of more than half a million permanent public employees, ordinary civil servants, organized into about twenty government departments and a number of other agencies. The total number of British civil servants rose from 100,000 in 1900 to more than 700,000 in 1979; it declined under Conservative governments of the 1980s to 1990s and numbers about 500,000 today.

The importance of the permanent higher civil service is not unique to Britain. In France, too, the higher civil service is filled with powerful generalists who can bring long tenure, experience, and technical knowledge to their particular tasks. In the United States, many top positions in government agencies go to presidential appointees rather than to permanent civil servants, but there are permanent civil servants in the key positions just below the top appointees in all the cabinet departments. These people tend to be specialists—such as military officers, diplomats, doctors, scientists, economists, and engineers—who exert great influence on policy formulation and execution in their specialties. Below these specialists and administrators are the vast numbers of ordinary government employees—postal workers, teachers, welfare case agents, and so forth—who see that governmental policies are put into practice. In 2009, the United States had 21 million public employees of all kinds (federal, state, and local), or about 17 percent of the total labor force. In many European countries, that proportion is even higher, approaching a third of the labor force in Norway, Denmark, and Sweden.

Functions of the Bureaucracy

Bureaucracies have great significance in most contemporary societies. One reason is that the bureaucracy is almost alone in implementing and enforcing laws and regulations. In so doing, they may have quite a bit of discretion. Most modern legislation is general and can be effectively enforced only if administrative officials work out its details and implementation. Policy implementation and enforcement usually depend on bureaucrats' interpretations and on the spirit and effectiveness with which they put policies into practice. But the power of bureaucracies is not restricted to their implementation and enforcement of rules made by others. In Chapters 4 and 5, we discussed how bureaucratic agencies may articulate and aggregate interests. Departments such as those for agriculture, labor, defense, welfare, and education may be among the most important voices of interest groups. Moreover, administrative agencies in modern political systems do a great deal of adjudication. Tax authorities, for example, routinely determine whether citizens have faithfully reported their income and paid their taxes, and these authorities assess penalties accordingly. While citizens may in principle be able to appeal such rulings to the courts, relatively few actually do. Finally, political elites, whether executives or legislators, base many of their decisions on the information they obtain from the public administration. Similarly, interest groups, political parties, the business elites, and the public depend on such information.

Bureaucracy and Performance

We commonly use the term *bureaucracy* to refer to all systems of public administration. Strictly speaking, however, *bureaucracy* refers to a particular way of organizing such agencies. According to the classical German sociologist Max Weber, bureaucracies have the following features:

1. Decision making is based on fixed and official jurisdictions, rules, and regulations.
2. There are formal and specialized educational or training requirements for each position.
3. There is a hierarchical command structure: a firmly ordered system of superiors and subordinates, in which information flows upward and decisions flow downward.
4. Decisions are made on the basis of standard operating procedures, which include extensive written records.
5. Officials hold career positions, are appointed and promoted on the basis of merit, and have protection against political interference, notably in the form of permanent job tenure.[21]

No organization is perfectly bureaucratic in this sense, but professional armies come reasonably close, as do tax revenue departments.

These features of bureaucracies have a number of desirable effects. They promote competence, consistency, fair treatment, and freedom from political manipulation. Imagine what life would be like without bureaucracies. Before the advent of modern bureaucracy, public officials were often a sorry lot. Some of them inherited their jobs; others got them through family or political connections. Yet others bought their posts and used them to enrich themselves, gain social status, or both. They often used their powers arbitrarily, to favor friends and neighbors, and to the disadvantage of others. Many devoted little time to their duties. No wonder, then, that public officials were often incompetent, uninterested in their jobs, corrupt, or all of the above. Given the lack of rules and records, aggrieved citizens typically had few recourses.

Yet, the negative connotations of the word "bureaucracy" suggest that such organizations have liabilities as well. Bureaucratic organizations can become stodgy, rule-bound, inflexible, and insensitive to the needs of their clients. In many cases, bureaucrats have few incentives to be innovative and efficient or even to work very hard. Although bureaucracies are supposed to be politically and ideologically neutral, they are often influenced by the dominant ideologies of the time, have partisan propensities, or pursue institutional interests of their own.[22] Many citizens are exasperated with bureaucracy and its propensities for inefficiency and lack of responsiveness. This frustration is reflected in popular cynicism as well as in periodic attempts to reform government.

Modern authoritarian systems discovered that the bureaucracy was an essential tool of government control. Therefore, recruitment to the bureaucracy was part of a larger pattern of control. Bureaucratic selection in the former Soviet Union, as in China today, was controlled through a device called *nomenklatura*. Under this procedure, important positions were kept under the direct supervision of a party agency that had the final word on recruitment. Without the approval of the nomenklatura, you could not gain a high-ranking position in society. Moreover, the party offered inducements to control the behavior of the chosen officials. These inducements made it difficult for any but the topmost officials to have much freedom of action. Soviet leaders used normative incentives (such as appeals to party, ideology, and national idealism), financial incentives (such as better salaries, access to finer food and clothing, better housing, and freedom to travel), and coercive control (such as reporting by police, party, and bureaucrats). They used demotion or imprisonment, and even execution, as penalties. To avoid a coup by police or military forces, the varied layers of command and inducement structures were interwoven, so that no layer could act independently.

Among the forces that constrain bureaucracies are public opinion and the mass media, as well as interest groups of various kinds. In democracies, assemblies and courts also help control the bureaucracy. Legislative committee hearings or judicial investigations may bring bureaucratic performance into line with political desires. Sweden invented the **ombudsman** to prevent bureaucrats from doing injury or injustice to individuals.[23] This invention has been copied by other states, such as Britain and Germany. Ombudsmen investigate claims from citizens that they have suffered injury or damage as a result of government action. Ombudsmen typically have no power of their own but report to the legislature for remedial action. Their cases rarely lead to criminal conviction, but government officials often change their policies as a result of embarrassing publicity. Thus, ombudsmen offer a more expeditious and less costly procedure than court action.

Controls on civil servants tend to be less effective outside the advanced industrial democracies. Authoritarian systems lack many potential controls, such as effective elected political executives and legislators, independent courts, free mass media, and interest groups. Therefore, authoritarian regimes are particularly prone to bureaucratic inefficiency and inertia. Moreover, in many developing nations, the mass media are neither independent nor influential, few citizens participate in politics, and lower-level government employees are poorly trained and paid—all conditions that encourage bribery, extortion, and bureaucratic mismanagement.[24]

Successful democracy requires that public policies made by national assemblies and chief executives be implemented fairly and effectively; democracy depends on the rule of law. When rent-seeking politicians and parties demand kickbacks of public money from construction firms seeking public works contracts, the democratic process is subverted (see Chapter 1, specifically Box 1.3). Similarly, when tax officials and border authorities take bribes to overlook tax deficiencies and customs violations, democratic lawmaking is undermined. Citizens who must bribe teachers to get education for their children or health officials to get immunizations are deprived of the benefits of democratic public policies. Such practices, which we generically call **corruption** (abuses of political power for personal gain), are all too common in the poorer nations of the world.

Failure of the rule of law is difficult to study systematically, but surveys of how businesspeople, academics, and analysts perceive corruption in the public bureaucracies of different countries provide some comparative insight. These surveys have been combined into the Corruption Perceptions Index, which rates about 100 countries each year on a scale from 0 ("highly corrupt") to 10 ("highly clean"). Figure 6.3

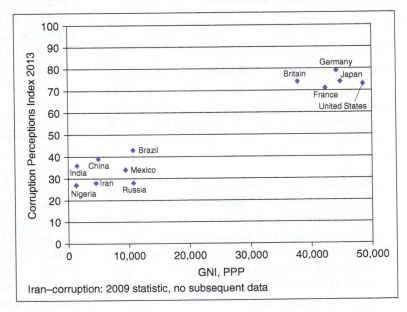

FIGURE 6.3

Perceived Corruption and Economic Development

Economic development encourages higher levels of perceived transparency.

Source: Economic development level from United Nations Development Program, *World Development* Report 2009, downloaded from www.undp.org, July 2010; Corruption Perceptions Index from Transparency International, downloaded from www.transparency.org on June 21, 2010.

shows, on the vertical dimension, the corruption ratings for the twelve countries studied in this book. All of these countries experience some levels of corruption. However, Figure 6.3 shows that corruption is very strongly associated with poverty and underdevelopment.[25] The affluent democracies in our comparisons—Britain, Germany, the United States, France, and Japan (despite notorious individual corruption cases in each)—rate in the top half of the scale. Developing countries such as Brazil, China, India, and Mexico are substantially more corrupt, with scores in the lower range of the scale. Nigeria, Russia, and Iran score even worse. Russia is notably more corrupt than we would expect from its middle-level income. Despite the theocratic nature of its regime, Iran is rated as one of the world's least transparent and most corrupt countries.

The ills of bureaucracy, including inefficiency and inertia, are pandemic. This is truly a dilemma, because we need the organization, division of labor, and professionalism that bureaucracy provides. Its pathologies can only be mitigated. The art of modern political leadership consists of defining and communicating appropriate goals and policies, as well as getting them implemented by a massive and complex bureaucracy—which makes it necessary to learn how and when to press and coerce it, reorganize it, reward it, teach it, or be taught by it.

In summary, the structure of government affects the political process and the strengths and weaknesses of the government. Some government structures are better at representing public preferences, while others are more effective in implementing policy. Some government structures allow for more debate and deliberation, while others are more decisive in making policy decisions. There is no perfect form of government, but there are clear differences that flow from the organization of the government in the types of interests that get represented, the methods of devising public policy, and the implementation of public policy.

REVIEW QUESTIONS

- What are the advantages of more inclusive decision rules in making policies? What are the disadvantages?
- Why is the confidence relationship so important in parliamentary democracies?
- In what different ways can policymaking power be dispersed and limited by constitutional arrangements?
- What are the advantages and disadvantages of assembly representation that mirrors the characteristics of citizens?
- How are cabinets formed after national elections in parliamentary systems?

KEY TERMS

assemblies
authoritarian regimes
bicameralism
bureaucracy
cabinet
chief executives
civil service
coalition cabinet
confederal system

confidence relationship
constitutional regimes
corruption
decision rules
democracy
democratic presidential
    regime
dismissal power
dissolution power

divided government
federal system
higher civil service
impeachment
judicial review
minority cabinet
mirroring (descriptive
    representation)
ombudsman

parliamentary regimes
policymaking
semipresidential
separation of powers
unitary system
women as chief executives

SUGGESTED READINGS

Carey, John M. *Legislative Voting and Accountability*. New York: Cambridge University Press, 2009.

Colomer, Josep M. *Political Institutions: Democracy and Social Choice*. New York: Oxford University Press, 2001.

Döring, Herbert, ed. *Parliaments and Majority Rule in Western Europe*. New York: St. Martin's Press, 1995.

Hicken, Allen. *Building Party Systems in Developing Democracies*. New York: Cambridge University Press, 2009.

Htun, Mala, et al. "Symposium: Between Science and Engineering: Reflections on the APSA Presidential Task Force on Political Science, Electoral Rules and Democratic Governance." *Perspectives on Politics* 11 (September 2013): 808–40.

Huber, John D. *Rationalizing Parliament*. Cambridge: Cambridge University Press, 1996.

Huber, John D., and Charles R. Shipan. *Deliberate Discretion? The Institutional Foundations of Bureaucratic Autonomy*. New York: Cambridge University Press, 2002.

Laver, Michael, and Norman Schofield. *Multiparty Government: The Politics of Coalition in Europe*. Ann Arbor: University of Michigan Press, 1998.

Lijphart, Arend. *Democracy in Plural Societies*. New Haven, CT: Yale University Press, 1977.

———. *Patterns of Democracy: Government Forms and Performance in Thirty-Six Countries*, 2nd ed. New Haven, CT: Yale University Press, 2012.

Linz, Juan, and Arturo Valenzuela, eds. *The Failure of Presidential Democracy: Comparative Perspectives*. Baltimore: Johns Hopkins University Press, 1994.

Mainwaring, Scott, and Matthew Shugart, eds. *Presidentialism and Democracy in Latin America*. New York: Cambridge University Press, 1997.

North, Douglass. *Institutions, Institutional Change, and Economic Performance*. Cambridge: Cambridge University Press, 1990.

Perez-Linan, Anibal. *Presidential Impeachment and the New Political Instability in Latin America*. New York: Cambridge University Press, 2007.

Powell, G. Bingham, Jr. *Contemporary Democracies: Participation, Stability, and Violence*. Cambridge, MA: Harvard University Press, 1982.

Secondat, Charles de, Baron de Montesquieu. *The Spirit of the Laws*. London: Hafner, 1960.

Shugart, Matthew, and John Carey. *Presidents and Assemblies: Constitutional Design and Electoral Dynamics*. Cambridge: Cambridge University Press, 1992.

Stone-Sweet, Alec. *Governing with Judges: Constitutional Politics in Europe*. Oxford: Oxford University Press, 2002.

Strøm, Kaare. *Minority Government and Majority Rule*. Cambridge: Cambridge University Press, 1990.

Tsebelis, George. *Veto Players: How Political Institutions Work*. Princeton, NJ: Princeton University Press, 2002.

Weber, Max. "Bureaucracy," in *From Max Weber*, ed. H. H. Gerth and C. Wright Mills. New York: Oxford University Press, 1976, 196–244.

ENDNOTES

1. For a skeptical view of constitutional design, see James G. March and Johan P. Olsen, *Rediscovering Institutions: The Organizational Basis of Politics* (New York: Free Press, 1989), 171–72. For a more sanguine argument, see Giovanni Sartori, *Comparative Constitutional Engineering* (New York: New York University Press, 1995).

2. John Locke, *Two Treatises of Government*, ed. Peter Laslett (Cambridge: Cambridge University Press, 1960); and Charles de Secondat, Baron de Montesquieu, *The Spirit of the Laws* (London: Hafner, 1960).

3. *The Federalist: A Commentary on the Constitution of the United States* (Washington, D.C.: National Home Library Foundation, 1937).

4. On presidential decree powers, see John M. Carey and Matthew S. Shugart, *Executive Decree Authority* (New York: Cambridge University Press, 1998); for more general discussions of presidential powers, see Matthew S. Shugart and John M. Carey, *Presidents and Assemblies: Constitutional Design and Electoral Dynamics* (Cambridge: Cambridge University Press, 1992); and Scott Mainwaring and Matthew S. Shugart,

eds., *Presidentialism and Democracy in Latin America* (New York: Cambridge University Press, 1997).

5. It is important to avoid confusion between the formal titles of government officials and the source of their selection and bases of their powers—which determine the type of political system. For example, Germany is a parliamentary system, whose executive is headed by a prime minister, although his official title is *chancellor*. The German head of state is a president, chosen by a federal convention, with little policymaking power. See also Table 6.3.

6. G. Bingham Powell, Jr., *Contemporary Democracies: Participation, Stability, and Violence* (Cambridge, MA: Harvard University Press, 1982); and Arend Lijphart, *Patterns of Democracy: Government Forms and Performance in Thirty-Six Countries*, 2nd ed. (New Haven, CT: Yale University Press, 2012). On Northern Ireland, see David McKittrick and David McVea, *Making Sense of the Troubles: The Story of the Conflict in Northern Ireland* (Chicago: Ivan R. Dee, 2002).

7. Donald Horowitz, "Comparing Democratic Systems," in *The Global Resurgence of Democracy*, ed. Larry Diamond and

Mark F. Plattner (Baltimore: Johns Hopkins University Press, 1993), 143–49. Also see Shugart and Carey, *Presidents and Assemblies*.

8. Gretchen Helmke and Frances Rosenbluth, "Regimes and the Rule of Law: Judicial Independence in Comparative Perspective," *Annual Review of Political Science* 12 (June 2009): 345–66.

9. Arend Lijphart, *Patterns of Democracy*, 215.

10. Georg Vanberg, *The Politics of Constitutional Review in Germany* (New York: Cambridge University Press, 2005). Also see Chapter 10.

11. Moreover, in Britain, as in France, Germany, and the twenty-four other members of the EU, the European Court of Justice provides some degree of judicial review to ensure that national laws and government activities are compatible with EU treaties and laws.

12. A major recent trend in the division and limitation of policy-making powers is the growth of independent central banks. Central banks, such as the Federal Reserve in the United States, regulate the supply of money and interest rates, as well as many financial transactions for government and society. In most countries, such bank policy was long controlled by the chief executive as part of the government bureaucracy. But in the last twenty years, many countries have given their central banks substantial independence and set for them the primary task of using monetary policy to maintain price stability and limit inflation. Such independence reassures investors, domestic and foreign, and seems to constrain inflation, but it limits the economic policy alternatives of the chief executive and cabinet.

13. John Carey, *Legislative Voting and Accountability* (New York: Cambridge University Press, 2009).

14. For a survey of parliamentary committees in Europe, see Ingvar Mattson and Kaare Strøm, "Parliamentary Committees," in *Parliaments and Majority Rule in Western Europe*, ed. Herbert Döring (New York: St. Martin's Press, 1995), 249–307.

15. For a discussion of the rapidly growing research on the effects of electoral rules, including the expanding use of gender quotas and PR elections, on the legislative representation of women and ethnic minorities, see Mona Lena Krook and Robert G. Moser, "Electoral Rules and Political Inclusion," *Perspectives on Politics* 11 (September, 2013), 814–18.

16. Data from the Inter-Parliamentary Union. Downloaded from www.ipu.org on June 21, 2010.

17. Senator Roman Hruska, quoted in *Time* magazine, March 30, 1970.

18. In multiparty systems, the process of building coalitions between executive and legislature also plays a role. See Gary Cox, *Making Votes Count* (New York: Cambridge University Press, 1997), chap. 12; and G. Bingham Powell, Jr., *Elections as Instruments of Democracy* (New Haven, CT: Yale University Press, 2000). A substantial body of political science research has begun to explore how such congruence between voters, legislatures, and governments is created or disrupted.

19. Adam Przeworski et al., *Democracy and Development: Political Institutions and Well-Being in the World, 1950–1990* (New York: Cambridge University Press, 2000).

20. See the relevant chapters in Michael Laver and Kenneth A. Shepsle, *Cabinet Ministers and Parliamentary Government* (New York: Cambridge University Press, 1994).

21. See the discussion in Julien Freund, *The Sociology of Max Weber* (New York: Random House, 1969), 234–35.

22. See Joel Aberbach, Robert D. Putnam, and Bert A. Rockman, *Bureaucrats and Politicians in Western Democracies* (Cambridge, MA: Harvard University Press, 1981).

23. See Christopher Ansell and Jane Gingrich, "Reforming the Administrative State," in *Democracy Transformed*, ed. Bruce Cain, Russell Dalton, and Susan Scarrow (Oxford: Oxford University Press, 2003), 164–90.

24. On the difficulties involved in reducing administrative corruption in developing countries, see Robert Klitgard, *Controlling Corruption* (Berkeley: University of California Press, 1989).

25. For a statistical analysis explaining scores on the Corruption Perceptions Index, see Daniel Treisman, "The Causes of Corruption: A Cross-National Study," *Journal of Public Economics* 76 (June 2000): 399–457, who suggests lower levels of economic development, shorter exposure to democracy, and federalism to be among the factors encouraging more perceived corruption. Also see Melanie Manion, *Corruption by Design: Building Clean Government in Mainland China and Hong Kong* (Cambridge, MA: Harvard University Press, 2004).

CHAPTER 7

Public Policy

LEARNING OBJECTIVES

7.1 Distinguish between system goods, process goods, and policy goods.

7.2 Define the four types of policy outputs and discuss how they are shaped by a nation's level of economic development.

7.3 Discuss the quality-of-life outcomes sought by domestic government policy, with examples from various countries.

7.4 Discuss the international economic and security issues addressed by government policies and explain how they are affected by globalization.

7.5 Provide examples of the trade-offs that may be necessary between desired policy outcomes.

Public policy consists of all the authoritative public decisions that governments make—the **policy outputs** of the political system. Policies or outputs are normally chosen for a purpose—they are meant to promote end results that we refer to as **policy outcomes.** Different policies may be more or less efficient ways to reach the outcomes that policymakers want. But the values and goals of policymakers and citizens affect their evaluation of the political outcomes they actually reach. Since politicians and citizens often disagree over **political goods** and values, it is important to keep these goals in mind when we study public policy.

Government and What It Does

7.1 Distinguish between system goods, process goods, and policy goods.

Governments do many things. A key point is that they provide a way to organize social forces to make authoritative judgments for the nation. These authoritative judgments involve public policies on how society, the economy, and our lives should function. Some things they do are timeless. In the days of the Roman Empire, defense against external and internal enemies was a major government responsibility. It continues to be so in most societies today. In other ways, governments today do things that were unthinkable in the past. For example, governments now regulate telecommunications and air traffic, policy areas that were unknown until the twentieth century.

Governments produce many goods and services, though exactly which ones varies a great deal from country to country. In most societies, governments provide law enforcement, roads, and postal services, and, in many countries, they do much more. In socialist states and some other authoritarian states, governments own and operate most major industries and produce everything from military equipment to such consumer goods as clothing and shoes. In a capitalist society, such as the United States, most consumer goods are produced in the private sector. In much of Europe, the governments have a larger role than in the United States, but far less than in a socialist system.

The range of government involvement varies not just among countries but also among different parts of the same country. For example, government agencies in the United States employ few of the people engaged in mining and manufacturing but a much larger proportion of those working for the utilities that supply gas, water, and electrical power. Yet there is no society in which the government produces no goods or services and, conversely, no state in which all industries are run by the government. Even in communist Cuba, part of the agricultural sector is private, as are many simple consumer services, such as babysitting.

Political Goals and Political Goods

To compare and evaluate public policy in different political systems, we need to consider the political goals that motivate different policies. As we discussed in Chapter 1, the policymakers in any political system may be self-interested, seeking benefits for themselves rather than development, or exploiting divisions rather than building community. But, particularly in democratic societies, politicians have incentives to pursue political goals that seek to satisfy the values and aspirations of the citizens. We refer to these as "political goods."

We can organize this framework of political goods around each of the three levels of analysis used in this book: system, process, and policy (see Table 7.1).

At the *system level*, a long tradition in political analysis emphasizes order, predictability, and stability. Citizens are most free and most able to act purposefully when their environment is stable, transparent, and predictable. We call these conditions *system goods*, since they reflect the functioning and effectiveness of the whole political system. While people generally want some measure of change and new opportunities, most prefer stability to abrupt and unforeseeable

---

TABLE 7.1
Political Goods
Difficult trade-offs, as well as constraints, may be involved in obtaining desirable goods.

Levels of Political Goods	Classes of Goods	Content and Examples
System level	System maintenance	The political system features regular, stable, and predictable decision-making processes.
	System adaptation	The political system is able to adapt to environmental change and challenges.
Process level	Participation in political inputs	The political system is open and responsive to many forms of political speech and action.
	Compliance and support	Citizens fulfill their obligations (e.g., military service and tax obligations) to the system and comply with public law and policy.
	Procedural justice	Legal and political procedures are orderly and fair (due process), and there is equality before the law.
	Effectiveness and efficiency	Political processes have their intended effects and are no more cumbersome, expensive, or intrusive than necessary.
Policy level	Welfare	Citizens have access to health care, learning, and economic and environmental goods, which the government seeks to distribute broadly.
	Security	The government provides safety of person and property, public order, and national security.
	Fairness	Government policy is not discriminatory and recognizes individuals from different ethnic, linguistic, or religious groups; both genders are respected; vulnerable or disadvantaged citizens are protected.
	Liberty	Citizens enjoy freedom from excessive regulation, protection of their privacy, and respect for their autonomy.

change. Political instability—constitutional break-downs, frequent leadership changes, riots, and the like—upsets most people's plans and can cost lives and cause material destruction. Creating and sustaining a compatible political community, whose members share many values and respect differences when they disagree, helps support political stability. System goods address the regularity and predictability with which political systems work, but also their ability to adapt to environmental challenges. Regularity and adaptability are typically somewhat in conflict.

Another category of goods is associated with the *political process*—citizen participation and free political competition. Democracy is good and authoritarianism is bad, according to this school of thought, because of the way citizens are treated in the process, and not because democracy might produce better economic or security results. Democratic procedures and various rights of due process, then, are process goods. Process goods include participation, compliance, and procedural justice. We value participation not merely as a means to responsive government, but for its own sake, since it enhances citizen competence and dignity. Procedural justice (trial by jury, *habeas corpus,* no cruel and unusual punishment, and fair and equal treatment) is another crucial process value, without which citizens would have much greater reasons to fear their governments. Procedural goods also

include effectiveness and efficiency. We prefer political processes that actually deliver the desired results. And, all else being equal, we especially prefer institutions that give us such outcomes at low cost and relatively quickly.

A third focus is on **policy goods**, such as economic welfare, quality of life, freedom, and personal security. Most people value policies that they view as improving their living conditions. Yet well-meaning people do not always agree on which of these policy goods are most important. Political philosophers have long debated the content and importance of policies in the public interest. In different cultures and times, these goods have given priority to different needs and aspirations. But over the past 200 years, a series of public documents, from the U.S. Declaration of Independence to the UN Millennium Development Goals, have expressed developing public support for expanded human rights. Box 7.1 shows the eight Millennium Development Goals that were officially supported by 189 nations at a summit in 2000. These were not meant to be all-inclusive, but they reflect a consensus on the meaning of improving the lives of citizens around the world. Eradicating extreme poverty, reducing mortality, combating disease, providing primary education, developing environmental sustainability, and promoting gender equality won this support and probably seem unobjectionable to most of us.

BOX 7.1   Millennium Development Goals

In 2000, the leaders of 147 nations and official representatives of many others attended the Millennium Summit at the United Nations Headquarters in New York City. At the end, 189 nations agreed to support the United Nations Millennium Declaration, which confirmed their intention to help the world's poorest nations improve the lives of their citizens by 2015. The Millennium Development Goals, a concrete series of targets, were derived from this declaration. Many other international organizations have also agreed to these goals. They include eight general goals and suggest specific indicators for monitoring progress in achieving them. The official list of Millennium Development Goals (MDGs) includes:

- Goal 1. Eradicate extreme poverty and hunger.
- Goal 2. Achieve universal primary education.
- Goal 3. Promote gender equality and empower women.
- Goal 4. Reduce child mortality.
- Goal 5. Improve maternal health.
- Goal 6. Combat HIV/AIDS, malaria, and other diseases.
- Goal 7. Ensure environmental sustainability.
- Goal 8. Develop a global partnership for development.

The Millennium Development Goals represent, at least in principle, a contemporary consensus on policy goals that could be considered policy goods.

Source: Adapted from http://mdgs.un.org/unsd/mdg/.

Although these eight goals were accepted by leaders of many nations, they conceal sharp differences—not only regarding their relative importance but in the way they affect other values. For example, at a follow-up summit in 2005, a substantial controversy erupted over their relationship to birth control policies and to national sovereignty. Yet these goals provide a starting point for identification of important policy goals that encompass our discussion in Chapters 1 and 2: the functions and purposes that governments serve and the challenges that confront them.

Even if we were to agree on the Millennium Development Goals, we would not necessarily know what weight to give to one goal when it conflicts with another, or what to do with policies that might help some groups at the expense of others. For example, how do we choose between enhancing one person's health care versus improving another person's educational opportunities? In such difficult cases, one criterion that most of us would agree upon is that government policy should be *fair*. The problem is that people often disagree over what is fair. In some situations, we believe that **fairness** requires all people to be treated equally (as when family members attempt to divide a tempting pie). In other situations, fairness demands that individuals be treated according to performance (as when grades are given in a college course). In yet other situations, fairness means that people are treated according to their needs (for example, in cases of medical treatment). Thus, fairness can imply *equal treatment* in some cases, *just desserts* (reward in proportion to merit or contribution) in others, and *treatment according to need* in yet others. Different value systems, such as ideologies or religious systems, may even define fairness differently. Many **public policies**—for example, pension systems such as social security in the United States—rely on some combination of these criteria. The debate over these various conceptions of fairness is never settled.

A final policy regarded highly in Table 7.1 is *freedom*. As anarchists, libertarians, and other government skeptics would remind us, public policies should promote and protect freedom and basic human and political rights. If two policies are equally efficient and fair, we would prefer the one that better respects the rights and liberties of citizens. But even citizens in democratic societies do not always choose freedom over other political goods. For example, freedom of speech is a constitutional guarantee, but many people want to prohibit speech that is insulting, blasphemous, or offensive.

Liberty is sometimes viewed only as freedom from governmental regulation and harassment. Yet even private individuals and organizations may violate the liberty and privacy of others. In such cases, government intervention may enhance liberty. Much legislation against racial segregation and discrimination generally has been impelled by this purpose. Liberty to act, organize, obtain information, and protest is an indispensable part of effective political participation. Nor is it irrelevant to social, political, and economic fairness. Prior to the breakdown of communism in Eastern Europe and the Soviet Union, it was a common view that these communist countries were trading liberty for equality. In contrast, capitalism was said to trade off equality for liberty. However, the collapse of communism uncovered the extent of corruption and privilege in communist societies. While they had surely traded off liberty for a basic security of employment, it was not clear that the communists had otherwise gained much in the way of equality.

Table 7.1 draws on our three-level analysis of political systems to present a checklist of political goods that are widely valued in contemporary societies. There is no simple way to say which value should prevail when they conflict. In fact, different preferences among such values as freedom, fairness, and efficiency set different cultures, parties, and political philosophies apart. One society or group of citizens may value fairness over liberty; another may make the opposite choice, as in Patrick Henry's famous exclamation, "Give me liberty or give me death!"

This chapter focuses on the third category in Table 7.1—policy goods. We first describe the varieties of activities that governments perform, such as extracting resources to support the government in the various means of providing policy goods. Then we focus on the four policy goods outlined in the table: welfare, security, fairness, and liberty.

Public Policy Outputs

 7.2 Define the four types of policy outputs and discuss how they are shaped by a nation's level of economic development.

One aspect of government is public policy outputs, or different instruments of policy. We can compare the actions that governments may take to accomplish their policy purposes under four types of policy outputs:

1. **Extraction** of resources—money, goods, persons, and services—from the domestic and international environments.
2. **Distribution**—of money, goods, and services—to citizens, residents, and clients of the state.
3. **Regulation** of human behavior—the use of compulsion and inducement to bring about desired behavior.
4. **Symbolic outputs**—used to exhort citizens to engage in desired forms of behavior, build community, or celebrate exemplary conduct (see Chapter 1).

Political systems have different policy action profiles. Some governments distribute a great deal of goods and services but regulate little. Elsewhere, the government may be heavily engaged in regulation but may rely on the private sector to produce most goods and services. In the next sections, we discuss these four types of policy outputs, beginning with extraction.

Extraction

Before governments can spend, they must have ways to collect money and other resources. All political systems *extract* resources from their environments and inhabitants. When societies go to war, for example, young people (typically men) may be called on to fight. Anthropologists estimate that in some hunter-gatherer societies, such obligations have been so onerous that about half of all males have died in warfare. (Thomas Hobbes would not have been surprised.) Such direct extraction of services is found in many modern states in the form of compulsory military service, jury duty, or compulsory labor imposed on those convicted of crimes.

The most common form of resource extraction is taxation. *Taxation* is the government's extraction of money or goods from members of a political system for which they receive no immediate or direct benefit. A related form of extraction is "social contribution," or "social insurance" revenues, which are typically held as special funds targeted

for social protection benefits, such as old age pensions (social security). Revenue policies are designed to meet many different objectives, which sometimes conflict. On the one hand, governments often want to collect as much revenue as possible to finance various public services. On the other hand, governments do not want to kill the goose that lays the golden egg. The more that governments tax their citizens, the less incentive people and businesses have to increase their income. If the tax burden becomes too great, they may try to evade taxes or even leave the country altogether.

Another common trade-off in extraction policies is between efficiency and equity. *Efficiency* means collecting the most revenue possible at the lowest cost. *Equity* means taxing so that no one is unfairly burdened, particularly those who have the least. In most societies, the tax and spending systems redistribute wealth in favor of the less well off. Therefore, income taxes are generally progressive, which means that citizens with greater incomes pay at higher rates than those who earn less. However, highly progressive taxes can reduce the incentives for high earners to work and invest, and thus lessen the incentives for economic growth. Therefore, such taxes are often inefficient.

Personal and corporate income taxes, property taxes, and taxes on capital gains are called **direct taxes**, since they are directly levied on persons and corporations. If you pay a tax bill at the end of the year, or have taxes withheld in your paycheck, you are paying

Protesting Taxes
French farmers protest taxes and a fall in agricultural prices by driving tractors through the Place de la République in Paris on April 27, 2010.

taxes directly. Payroll taxes tend to hit the middle class and those in the labor force, since the wealthy tend to get a larger share of their income from dividends, interest, and capital gains, and retirees get a larger share from pensions. High taxes on wages can also hurt employment or drive businesses into the "underground economy," in which they do not report their incomes or expenditures.

Indirect taxes include sales taxes, value-added taxes, excise taxes, and customs duties. These are commonly included in the prices of goods and services that consumers buy. The redistributive effects of indirect taxes depend on who pays them. Since the poor spend more of their income on food and clothing, sales (or value-added) taxes can be regressive (which means that the poor pay relatively more than the rich), so many nations have a lower tax rate on necessities. In contrast, indirect taxes on luxury goods may be progressive, since the poor rarely purchase luxury items like fine jewelry. Countries with weak administrative capacities often prefer indirect taxes. Particularly where financial record keeping is imprecise, indirect taxes are easier to collect. In addition, indirect taxes tend to rise with inflation or as the costs of products increase, which provides a natural source of increasing government revenue.

Besides redistribution and efficiency, tax policies often promote such values as charity, energy conservation, or home ownership. For example, many countries stimulate home ownership by making mortgage interest payments tax-deductible. Several European nations have a large gasoline tax to reduce energy consumption and encourage the sale of energy-efficient automobiles. In France, 70 percent of the cost of gasoline is for government taxes, which raises the price to about $8 a gallon.

Given the many difficult issues involving taxation, and the inevitable public resistance to high taxes, it might seem a blessing if a government could receive income windfalls from other sources. Countries with large reserves of oil or other valuable natural resources are often in this situation. Many oil-producing countries, such as Iran, Russia, and Nigeria, can tap their natural resource reserves and sell them at a large profit in the international market. Yet when the riches from easily obtained natural resources are a large share of a government's income, the consequences can be far from an unmitigated blessing. A large political science literature focuses on the potential problems of

so-called **rentier states**, which derive much of their revenue from selling oil and other natural resources.[1] This literature often refers to a "resource curse" impeding development and democracy when the economy is distorted by oil windfalls.

Why should oil or diamonds or copper constitute a "curse" when they can finance public policies without burdening citizens with taxes?[2] One explanation suggests that windfall resource profits can make governments independent from their citizens. As Samuel Huntington put it, "Oil revenues . . . reduce the need for the government to solicit the acquiescence of its subjects to taxation. The lower the level of taxation, the less reason for the public to demand representation."[3] If politicians do not feel such demands from their citizens, they may be less likely to behave accountably. Direct resource-based revenues also may enable authoritarian rulers to pay off citizens through patronage (e.g., subsidized goods, services, and loans) without yielding political power to them. Or, the easy money of the rentier state may be a tempting target for predatory authoritarians who use these funds to repress society while taking the profits for themselves. Although the resource curse is common wisdom in studies of less economically developed economies, the windfall income can soften the intensity of redistributive conflict in very unequal societies and have positive consequences for democracy.[4] Nor do such windfalls seem problematic in already economically developed democracies, such as Norway.

Figure 7.1 shows the general government revenues as a percentage of **gross domestic product (GDP)**, the total value of goods and services produced by a country's residents in a year. For the average country, about a quarter of the GDP is extracted by the government, but in some countries, the proportion is much higher. Most of the more developed democracies rely primarily on taxes and social contributions for government revenues. In Germany and France, the social contributions are nearly as large as the taxes.

Figure 7.1, however, shows that some governments also get substantial revenues from nontax and noncontribution sources (the top portion of the columns), such as administrative fees, rents, and income from business enterprises that they run. In Iran, a classic rentier state (see Chapter 16), nontax income is over two-thirds of the government's revenues. Russia is also rich in oil and other natural resources, and it relies heavily on nontax income. If we had data on Nigeria,

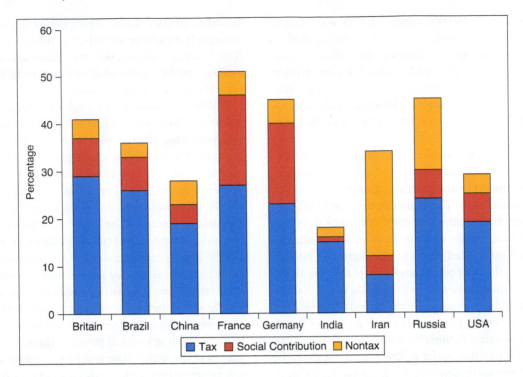

FIGURE 7.1

Government Revenue

In most countries, especially in democracies, taxes are the largest source of revenues.

Source: International Monetary Fund, downloaded from www.imfstatistics.org/GFS on November 21, 2013.

it would probably show a similar picture. China relies somewhat on nontax sources from government-owned enterprises, a carryover from its socialist past despite its marketization of much of the economy. Democracy has had a hard time in all these countries, although dependence on nontax revenues is not the only reason.

The tax profiles of different countries vary both in their overall tax burdens and in their reliance on different types of taxes. France has the highest tax rates overall among these countries, as it extracts more than 50 percent of its GDP in taxes, (a level similar to that in Sweden.) Germany and Russia are in the 45 percent range., while Britain is among the advanced industrial societies that collect about 40 percent of GDP, while the United States extracts only about 30 percent. The USA countries depends more on direct income taxes than on sales or consumption taxes. Brazil has a very substantial government sector for a middle income developing country, with revenue that is a third of GDP. The government revenue of India is only about 18 percent. For the states that are highly dependent on natural resource windfalls, these proportions can fluctuate sharply with the price of their export commodities, which can create additional problems for government and for development.

In the long run, governments cannot spend more money than they raise. If governments fail to balance their books and instead run budget deficits, they have to borrow money. This creates debt that future generations of taxpayers have to pay off. Even rich governments are notoriously bad at balancing their books, and many run budget deficits year after year. In 2004, nineteen of the twenty-eight (highly developed) Organization for Economic Co-operation and Development (OECD) countries ran budget deficits, and the average deficit was equal to 3.5 percent of GDP. The United States briefly balanced its budget in the late 1990s, but then slid back into fiscal imbalance. When Germany, France, and many other European countries decided to adopt a common currency, the euro, they also committed themselves to keeping their national deficits smaller than 3 percent of GDP. In practice, however, they have often broken that promise. Since the financial crisis of 2008–2009, most of these countries have borrowed massively to finance emergency spending to combat the worldwide recession, greatly increasing their national debts.

Recently, in some European countries, especially Greece, the combination of massive, long-standing deficits and the more recent pressures of the global financial crisis threatened the country's ability to meet its future financial obligations. Despite a large aid package promised by other euro countries in exchange for Greece's drastically cutting its spending, the debt crisis threatened the financial stability of all the European countries. The 2008–2009 economic crisis and its aftermath produced similar economic strains on the governments of many developing nations. It is a measure of the globalization of trade and financial capital flows that this economic crisis rapidly created difficult budgetary choices in countries throughout the world as economies contracted, unemployment rose, and revenues faltered.

Distributive Policy Profiles

Distributive policies include transfers of money, goods, services, honors, and opportunities to individuals and groups in the society. Distributive policies generally consume more government resources and employ more government officials than anything else that modern governments do. Distributive policies include support for infrastructure, agriculture, and various other industries, but the most common form of distributive policies are social welfare programs.

The first modern welfare state programs were introduced in Germany in the 1880s. In response to rapid industrialization and urbanization, the German government offered social insurance programs that protected workers against unemployment, accidents, sickness, and poverty during old age. During the twentieth century, and particularly from the Great Depression of the 1930s until the 1970s, most industrialized states adopted, and greatly expanded, such welfare state policies. Over time, welfare state policies expanded to include broader health care programs, disability benefits, public education, housing subsidies, child and childcare benefits, pensions, and other distributive policies.

As developing countries become wealthier, they also tend to spend more of their resources on welfare programs. In Mexico, for example, recent presidents have each launched major social welfare initiatives. In

Brazil, the *Bolsa Familia* program is the world's largest conditional cash transfer program and a flagship of the administrations of President Lula and President Rousseff. The program reaches a quarter of the Brazilian population and is especially targeted at eradicating hunger (see Chapter 15).

Welfare policies typically combine a social insurance system and a program of social redistribution. It is partly paternalistic (forcing people to put away money for their old age and potential illnesses) and part Robin Hood (taking from the rich and giving to the poor). The balance between these two functions depends on which programs a country emphasizes and how it finances them. Not all welfare programs are alike. Even among the advanced industrial countries, some welfare states are larger than others or offer different benefits. All the wealthier nations try to assist the aged, the disabled, and the unemployed. However, differences in expenditures reflect the priorities of citizens and their governments, social and economic conditions (such as a country's age distribution and unemployment levels), and historical experiences.[5] Countries that have more frequently elected social democratic governments generally have larger welfare states.

In countries with clientelist party systems, distributive benefits are frequently targeted to supporters of the governing party. Such party systems are particularly common in Africa and other parts of the less developed world. Many studies have shown the way government administrations have systematically distributed public employment and public spending programs to their clients. For example, Kramon and Posner examine distributive policy benefits in six African countries and show that, in most of them, when a president from a different ethnic group is elected, his coethnics tend to gain differential benefits from at least some government policies.[6]

Developed countries generally allocate the majority of their government expenditures to health, education, and social protection. France, Germany, and Japan spend about two-thirds of their budgets in these areas, compared with about one-half in the United States. The U.S. model stresses equality of opportunity through public education, making a greater and earlier effort in this area than did most European nations. Americans began spending on social protection programs later and still make less effort in these areas. This may reflect the U.S. heritage as a nation of immigrants, many of whom arrived poor and have been expected to prosper by their own efforts.

Sadly, the countries that need them most, such as India, have the least to spend on education and health. Figure 7.2 shows the relationship between economic development level and public health expenditures. As we see, public health expenditures in our developed countries, such as the United States, France, Germany, and Japan, are $2,500 to $4,000 per capita. In the poorest countries, health spending in absolute dollars is miniscule—around $50 per person in Nigeria and India. Although such spending has been increasing, the absolute levels are still very small. These spending numbers are generated in part by varying public policy efforts, as the poorer countries have much more constrained budgets. (Countries also prefer to rely on their private sector to varying degrees to finance health spending.) But they are shaped much more by the enormous variations in income between developing and advanced economies. Poor nations, with limited national income and many pressing demands, lack the resources for health, education, and social protection. Resources are scarce, and shorter life expectancies and high birth rates mean that there are comparatively few older people. Also, many people

live in rural areas, where unemployment is less easily observed and where the aged and the infirm typically receive some care through the extended family; these services go unreported in our statistics.

National security spending follows a different pattern. Particularly among less developed countries, spending varies as much with the international environment as with overall economic means. Some states that are locked in tense international confrontations make extraordinary defense efforts. India, Iran, and the United States spend more than 10 percent of their government outlays (2 to 5 percent of GDP) on defense. Because of its worldwide security commitments and large economy, the United States is by far the heaviest military spender in absolute terms.

Challenges to the Welfare State   Welfare states have many beneficial consequences. The Western European countries that pioneered these programs have virtually eradicated dire poverty, and they have created a much more "level playing field" for their citizens. Crime rates tend to be low in countries with extensive welfare states, and most of the programs are popular with ordinary citizens. Yet the welfare state is also expensive. As total government expenditures have grown

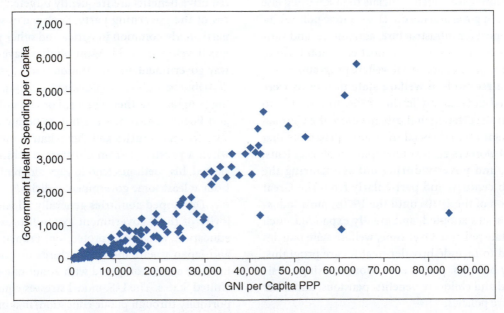

FIGURE 7.2

Economic Development and Government Health Spending

Government spending on health policies depends greatly on the country's level of economic development.

Source: World Bank, World Development Indicators, data downloaded from http://databank.worldbank.org/data on July 10, 2013.

to around half of GDP in many industrial democracies, this has created political opposition to high taxes and deficits. One of the most serious problems is the generational deficit that these policies are creating. Welfare programs are providing generous benefits, but the bill will eventually fall on future generations (your generation) to pay. At the same time that senior citizens qualify for greater pension benefits and health care costs are rising rapidly, the ranks of the elderly are swelling relative to those in the workforce. Thus, the ratio of those outside the workforce (because they are too young or too old) to those in the working-age population is increasing rapidly in Europe and Japan. A smaller number of working people in future years will have to pay higher taxes just to support existing health and welfare programs.[7]

In addition, some welfare state policies give citizens fewer incentives to work. Norway and Sweden are among the leading countries in the world in life expectancy and public health statistics. Yet workers in these countries are on sick leave about twice as often as workers elsewhere in Europe, and record numbers of these Scandinavians are on permanent disability pensions. This is partly because of generous sick leave benefits and partly because it is easy to qualify for disability benefits. But these policies are costly and reduce incentives to work.

These problems with the welfare state have stirred efforts to prevent further increases in spending

obligations (entitlements) and to contain the costs of those already in effect. Thus, the gradual expansion of welfare benefits that characterized most of the twentieth century in the developed countries can no longer be taken for granted.

Regulation

Regulation is the exercise of political control over the behavior of individuals and groups in the society. Most contemporary governments have a large regulatory role. Our civilization and amenities depend on regulation. Economic production and commerce, for example, rely on government regulation to establish and protect property rights and to enforce contracts. There need to be rules to keep traffic moving smoothly on the freeways, in the air, and on the airwaves. Citizens and consumers often demand protections against fraud, manipulation, and obnoxious externalities, such as toxic waste and pollution. Governments are increasingly involved in setting product standards, particularly for pharmaceuticals and food, to make sure that these products are safe. Governments also regulate to shield their citizens, and often particularly children and women, from physical and other abuse. However, regulation can create an opportunity for government officials to extract bribes from citizens (see Box 7.2).

In the developed democracies, government regulation has proliferated enormously over the last century. Industrialization and urbanization have caused problems in traffic, health, and public order. Industrial growth has also generated concerns about industrial safety, labor exploitation, and pollution. Moreover, the growth of science and the belief that humanity can harness and control nature have led to increased demands for government action. Globalization has created increased pressures to regulate the international flows of capital, trade, and people. Finally, changes in citizen values have led to demands for new kinds of regulation. Immigration policy, safety standards for offshore oil drilling, and banking regulation have become major policy disputes. At the same time, however, most Western societies have lessened their regulation of

Receiving Distributions
Indian school children are served government-sponsored free midday meals at a government primary school in Hyderabad, India, June 23, 2010.

BOX 7.2   Regulation and Development

In the advanced industrial countries of North America, Japan, and Western Europe, regulation has grown enormously along with their industrial and postindustrial economies. It is easy to think, therefore, that there is more regulation in wealthy countries than in poor ones. But this is not always true. In fact, low-income countries sometimes regulate more than rich ones. This is particularly true of regulations of business entry and competition. In many less developed countries, it is cumbersome and time-consuming, for example, to get the permits necessary to start a new business. Such regulations often mainly serve to create *rents* that government officials can exploit for their own benefit (see Chapter 1). They favor existing businesses by giving them monopolies or other protections. Many politicians expect the businesspeople who benefit from these regulations (often their family members, friends, or business associates) to show their gratitude through kickbacks and other favors. Or, business owners pay off politicians or civil servants to get around onerous regulations or to avoid long delays in handling their applications. Overregulation of this kind tends to hurt economic productivity and keep out foreign investment.

The Peruvian economist Hernando de Soto reports a sobering experience with abusive government regulation. As an experiment, he registered a small clothing factory in Lima, Peru, and decided in advance not to pay bribes. While he was waiting for his business to be registered, government officials asked him for bribes no fewer than ten times. Twice, he broke his own rule and paid the bribe so that he would not be forced to give up his experiment. After ten months, his factory was finally registered. In New York, a similar procedure takes four hours.

Source: World Bank, *World Development Report 2005: A Better Investment Climate for Everyone* (New York: Oxford University Press), chap. 5; and William Easterly, *The Elusive Quest for Growth: The Economists' Adventures and Misadventures in the Tropics* (Cambridge: Massachusetts Institute of Technology Press, 2001), 233.

birth control, abortion, divorce, blasphemy, obscenity, and sexual conduct.

Governments regulate the lives of their citizens in many ways. Although we often associate regulation with legal means, there are other ways to regulate. Governments may control behavior by offering material or financial inducements or by persuasion or moral exhortation. For example, many governments try to reduce tobacco use by a combination of methods: bans on smoking, tobacco sales, or advertising; sales ("sin") taxes; and information campaigns to convince people of the hazards of smoking.

Even though there are many similarities in regulative policies across the world, states still differ substantially in their policy profiles. Patterns of regulation vary not only with industrialization and urbanization but also with cultural and ideological values. For example, population control policies in China and Islamic dress code policies in Iran illustrate the varieties of ways in which governments can regulate their societies. Figure 7.3 shows the degree to which different countries try to control their economic markets. (This measure is intended to include "market-unfriendly" policies such as price controls or inadequate bank supervision, as well as excessive regulation of foreign trade and business development.) Although the capitalist democracies, such as Britain, the United States, Germany, France, and Japan at the bottom left of the figure, tend to be the friendliest to market competition (as well as a free press), the nondemocracies vary greatly in their government regulatory profiles. China is far more open than Iran, and, in these policies, rather similar to India. Public policy studies describe regulatory differences among political systems by asking what aspects of human behavior are regulated, what social groups are regulated, and what sanctions are used to pressure people to comply.

Although all modern states use sanctions, they vary in their goals and strategies. Yet one aspect of regulation is particularly important politically: government control over political participation and communication. Figure 7.3 also shows freedom of the press, which is heavily shaped by the legal and political environment. Recall from earlier chapters that democracy requires political competition. As we might expect, the authoritarian systems control the press much more severely than do their democratic counterparts. China, Iran, and Russia are ranked as "unfree" in their press freedom scores and have the highest regulatory levels, as we see at the top right of the figure. A recent Freedom House

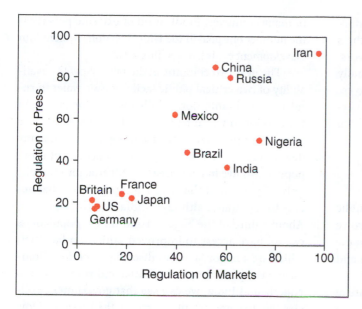

FIGURE 7.3

Controlling Markets and the Press

Governments vary in their use of regulatory policy to control the economy and communication.

Note: Market regulation is a World Bank measure of the "perceptions of the ability of the government to formulate and implement sound policies and regulations that permit and promote private sector development" (from http://info.worldbank .org/governance/wgi/pdf/rq.pdf). Shown on a 0-to-100 scale, where 100 is most regulated. Press freedom rating also on a 0-to-100 scale, where 100 is most controlled; data downloaded from www.freedomhouse.org on July 9, 2013.

study of Internet regulation in fifteen countries also showed the extensive efforts at controlling access and content of the Internet in China and Iran, while Brazil and Britain allowed their citizens relatively uncontrolled access. Authoritarian governments often suppress political competition by prohibiting party organization, voluntary associations, and political communication. All too often, they repress political opponents through imprisonment, disappearances, and torture. Studies of governmental repression have found that government abuses of physical integrity rights of citizens were best explained by nondemocratic political institutions and conditions of war and social disorder.[8] A lower level of economic development also is associated with a weaker human rights record.

Community Building and Symbolic Outputs

A fourth type of output is symbolic policies. Political leaders often appeal to the courage, wisdom, and magnanimity embodied in the nation's past, or appeal to

values and ideologies such as equality, liberty, community, democracy, communism, liberalism, or religious tradition. Or they promise future accomplishment and rewards. Political leaders appeal to such values for different reasons—for example, to win elections or to push their own pet projects. At the same time, many symbolic appeals and policies are trying to build community, such as by boosting people's national identity, civic pride, or trust in government.

Symbolic outputs also can enhance other aspects of performance: making people pay their taxes more readily and honestly; comply with the law more faithfully; or accept sacrifice, danger, and hardship. Such appeals may be especially important in times of crisis. Some of the most magnificent examples are the speeches of Pericles in the Athenian Assembly during the Peloponnesian War, Franklin D. Roosevelt in the depths of the Great Depression, or Winston Churchill during Britain's darkest hours in World War II. Symbolic policies are important even in less extreme circumstances. Public buildings, plazas, monuments, holiday parades, and civic and patriotic indoctrination in schools all attempt to contribute to a popular sense of governmental legitimacy and citizens' willingness to comply with public policy.

Domestic Policy Outcomes

 Discuss the quality-of-life outcomes sought by domestic government policy, with examples from various countries.

While we described different government policy outputs in the previous section, their consequences in providing actual policy goods are not always clear. How do extractive, distributive, regulative, and symbolic policies affect the lives of people? Unexpected economic, international, or social events may frustrate the purpose of political leaders. Thus, a tax rebate to stimulate the economy may be nullified by a rise in the price of oil. Increases in health expenditures may have no effect because of unexpected epidemics or rising health costs, or health services may not reach those most in need. Sometimes, policies have unintended and undesirable consequences, as when the introduction of benefits for troubled social groups leads others to simulate the same troubles to get the same favors. **Policy outcomes** represent the results that actually follow from government activity. Consequently, to estimate the effectiveness of public policy, we have to examine actual policy outcomes as well as governmental policies and their implementation.

Welfare Outcomes

We begin by comparing different measures of public welfare across our set of nations. Welfare can involve the living standards of the average citizen but also the other social conditions that affect quality of life and life chances.

The first column of Table 7.2 reports a measure of lack of economic well-being: the share of the population living on less than $2 per day. The severe problems of Nigeria and India are particularly notable: Over a quarter of those populations live on less than $2 a day. Yet these proportions have been reduced significantly, even in the last decade. Governments in most poor countries try to encourage economic development with the help of international organizations and donors. Although there is still far to go, notable growth has been achieved

in many countries. Eradication of extreme poverty is the number one goal in the United Nations Millennium Development goals list (see Box 7.1).

The next two columns in the table show the availability of two critical public facilities: safe water in rural areas and sanitation. While most of the people in the developed world have access to safe water, this is true for less than half of the rural populations of many developing countries. And, often, a majority of those populations live in rural areas. In Nigeria, for example, only 43 percent of the large rural population has access to safe water, although India fares much better. About a third of the Nigerian and Indian populations overall have access to improved sanitation facilities, which are a major factor in disease prevention. Comparing the performance in China and rural Brazil to Nigeria and India, we can see that government policies can, to some extent, overcome the barriers of low economic development.

The last column in Table 7.2 shows one of the negative outcomes of higher economic development: pollution. Carbon dioxide emissions per capita, which are a major contributor to air pollution and to global warming, are much higher in developed economies. The worst record is created by the most industrialized country, the United States, followed (distantly) by

TABLE 7.2
Welfare Outcomes
Economic development helps sustain basic material and health amenities, but also creates potential for environmental damages.

Country	Population below $2 per Day PPP (%), ca. 2010	Rural Population Access to Safe Water (%), 2010	Access to Sanitation (%) 2010	Carbon Dioxide Emissions, metric tons/capita, 2009
Brazil	5.4	85	79	1.9
Britain	—	100	100	7.7
China	9.1	85	64	5.8
France	—	100	100	5.6
Germany	—	100	100	9.0
India	24.5	90	34	1.7
Iran	—	92	100	8.2
Japan	—	100	100	8.6
Mexico	1.0	91	85	3.8
Nigeria	39.2	43	31	0.5
Russia	—	92	70	11.0
United States	—	94	100	17.3

Source: World Bank, *World Development Indicators* (data downloaded July 9, 2013, from http://databank.worldbank.org/data).

Russia, Japan, Germany, and Britain. Russia produces much higher emissions than we might expect for its development level. These countries have all introduced measures to regulate pollution, but they are lagging far behind need. Carbon dioxide emissions are not a problem so far in Nigeria, India, or Brazil. But China and Iran are closing in on the more industrialized countries. China's huge population and rapid growth make its pollution a serious threat to both its own population and the global population. Because of their dual needs for economic growth and pollution control, these countries face hard regulatory policy choices (see Chapter 13).

Health outcomes also figure largely in the Millennium Development Goals (Box 7.1). Table 7.3 shows that the average developed nation has about three physicians per 1,000 people, compared with 1.3 in the developing world. In Nigeria, there are only 0.4 doctors per 1,000 people. Nigeria has a high birthrate, but almost one out of ten infants fails to survive the first year of life. Nigerians have a life expectancy at birth of just fifty-three years (compared with seventy-eight to eighty-three years in advanced industrial countries). Nigeria demonstrates the ills of poverty, as do figures for India, which are also quite grim. But some poorer countries have coped more successfully than

others. Consider the difference between two formerly low-income nations: China and India. China's rapid economic development reached the level of Iran and nearly that of Brazil. China's health performance, always exceptional for a poor country, has improved further to an average life expectancy of seventy-nine years, and its infant mortality is thirteen per 1,000 live births. India's economy, although improving, has grown at a slower rate, and Indian life expectancy is sixty-five years and the infant mortality is forty-seven per 1,000. Fortunately, health conditions are improving in most of the poor countries, including India.

While the incidence of infant mortality and malnutrition is much lower in advanced economies, these problems are still serious among the poor in advanced industrial countries, such as the United States. The United States spends the largest proportion of its GDP on health care (approximately 15 percent, of which about half is from the public sector) of any country. At the same time, however, in 2011, the United States had a markedly higher infant death rate than Japan and Western Europe due to more widespread poverty, drug abuse, and unequal access to health care (which new policies are attempting to change). As Table 7.3 shows, Japan has an exceptional health record. It has the longest life expectancy and the lowest infant

TABLE 7.3
Health Outcomes
Government efforts can help combat the problems of low economic development for citizens' health.

Country	Physicians per 1,000 Citizens, 2011	Life Expectancy at Birth, 2011	Infant Mortality per 1,000 Live Births, 2011	Fertility Rate, 2012
Brazil	1.8	74	14	1.8
Britain	2.8	80	4	1.9
China	1.5	79	13	1.7
France	3.4	82	3	2.0
Germany	3.7	81	3	1.4
India	0.7	65	47	2.5
Iran	0.9	73	21	1.9
Japan	2.1	83	2	1.4
Mexico	2.0	75	13	2.2
Nigeria	0.4	53	78	6.0
Russia	4.3	69	10	1.5
United States	2.4	79	6	2.0

Source: World Health Organization (data downloaded June 9, 2013, from http://apps.who.int/gho/data).

mortality rate among all the study countries in this text. However, its low fertility rate means a declining population. (With no net migration, a fertility rate of approximately 2.1 is needed to produce a steady-state population.)

Education is another vital policy outcome, also stressed in the Millennium Development Goals. It provides individuals with skills and resources that enable people to engage in politics; these skills shape their life chances in establishing a career and improving their personal conditions. Education is also necessary for successful economic development and all that means for many other welfare outcomes. Table 7.4 provides a picture of educational and information attainment. In most industrial democracies, high school education is mandatory and college education is commonplace. At the high end in educational outcomes, France, Germany, Japan, and Britain have virtually all of their primary and secondary school–aged children in schools, and over half of the college-aged population is in some form of advanced education, as it is in Russia. In the United States, college education is even more common. Nigeria requires only children from ages six to twelve to attend school, and only 10 percent

of the appropriate age cohort is in tertiary education, by far the poorest record of these countries. The payoff of development and education is clearly reflected in literacy rates: About a quarter of adult men and half of adult women in Nigeria and India are unable to read or write. Yet China has less than 10 percent illiteracy.

Table 7.4 also highlights use of information technologies, especially the Internet. About 80 percent of the population have access to the Internet in wealthy and well-educated countries, such as Japan. Even in poorer countries, communication has become much easier. Television is widely available even in countries at modest development levels (e.g., Brazil and Mexico). Internet use is growing very rapidly. Over a third of the public in China and Mexico report having access to the Internet, as do almost half in Brazil. Even in desperately poor Nigeria, over a quarter of the population are Internet users. Despite the efforts of authoritarian governments in countries such as Russia, China, and Iran to control Internet use (see Chapters 12, 13, and 16, as well as the discussion of regulatory policies above), information potential is remarkable. In the developed countries, most adults and many children have cell phones, and even in India and

TABLE 7.4
Education, Equality, and Information
Education efforts, gender policies, and development shape information access and inequality.

Country	Gross Percentage of Relevant Age Group Enrolled, Tertiary, 2011	Percentage Fifteen Years and Above Illiterate, Male/Female, 2010	Ratio of Female to Male Earned Income, 2010	Income Share to Top 10%, Varied Years	Internet Users per 100 Inhabitants, 2011
Brazil	—	10/10	0.61	42	45
Britain	60	—	0.71	29	82
China	27	3/9	0.65	30	38
France	58	—	0.65	25	80
Germany	49	—	0.69	22	83
India	18	25/49	0.31	29	10
Iran	49	11/19	0.40	30	21
Japan	60	—	0.51	22	80
Mexico	29	6/8	0.44	38	36
Nigeria	10	28/50	0.41	38	28
Russia	76	—	0.65	32	49
United States	95	—	0.88	30	78

Source: World Bank, *World Development Indicators* (data downloaded July 9, 2013, from http://databank.worldbank.org/data); for female earned income inequality, Ricardo Hausmann et al., "Global Gender Gap Report 2011" (Geneva: World Economic Forum), app. D3 (data downloaded July 10, 2013, from www3.weforum.org/docs/wef).

Nigeria, there is already a cell phone for about every three people. The advent of cell phones makes it much easier to connect the rural population in developing countries where there are often very few landlines.

These statistics reveal the sobering difficulties of trying to change societies—even in an area such as literacy, where modern technologies are available. It is hard for a poor country to spend a high percentage of its GDP on education or health, because it must then make sacrifices elsewhere. Efforts will be further constrained if much of the country's productive effort has to go into feeding a rapidly growing population. Even if the government's efforts are substantial, they do not translate into much per child, because the resource base is small. And in many poorer countries, their best-educated young people often leave the country to take jobs in the big cities of the rich countries. Yet, despite these many difficulties and the huge gaps in personal well-being that remain across nations, much exciting progress is being made.

Fairness Outcomes

Fairness is one of the welfare outcomes discussed in the framework of Table 7.1. Concepts of fairness vary by culture and ideology. Despite these differences, promoting gender equality and empowering women appear on the Millennium Development Goals that were endorsed by so many nations (see again Box 7.1). The second column in Table 7.4 shows that women in developing countries often lag behind in literacy. Culture and policy also affect the male/female differences, as we see in comparing gender differences in Brazil and Iran, for example. The discrepancy between male and female literacy rates tells us something of the status of women and the achievement of fairness by gender. The third column provides additional insight by showing us the ratio of female to male earned incomes. Differences in the types of jobs in which they are employed and pay discrimination mean that women only earn about two-thirds of the income of men in many of the more equal countries—such as in China and in Britain, Germany, France, and Russia. In the United States, which reports great improvement in recent years, women earn less than 90 percent of the income of men. At the bottom of the scale, in Iran, India, and Nigeria, women earn only 40 percent of the income of men. Clearly, in many nations, achievement of gender fairness has far to go.

Faced with poverty, disease, and the absence of a social safety net, parents in poor countries traditionally want to have many children to ensure that some survive and can support them in old age. In large families, mothers usually have few opportunities to educate themselves or hold jobs outside the home (but see Boxes 7.3 and 7.4). Modernization generally improves

---

BOX **7.3**	Microcredit

One of the greatest obstacles to economic growth in many poor areas is the difficulty of obtaining credit. In advanced industrial countries, property owners (for example, farmers or homeowners) typically have a recognized title to their property. If they want to invest to expand their business or start a new one, they can borrow against this collateral. People in poor countries rarely have this opportunity, and it is especially difficult for poor farmers and women to obtain loans. As a result, they often cannot get the funds they need to tide them over during hard times or to take advantage of promising business opportunities.

Muhammad Yunus, a U.S.-educated professor of economics, noticed these problems in his native country of Bangladesh. In 1974, he began extending small loans to poor people to help them out of these circumstances. His first loan amounted to $27 from his own pocket, which he lent to forty-two people, including a woman who made bamboo furniture, which she sold to support herself and her family. In 1976, Yunus founded Grameen Bank to make loans to poor Bangladeshis. The bank has since given out more than $5 billion in loans. To secure its loans, the bank sets up a system of "solidarity groups," which meet on a weekly basis and support each other's efforts. As of May 2006, Grameen Bank had almost 7 million borrowers, 97 percent of whom were women. Their repayment rate is 98 percent. In 2006, Muhammad Yunus and the Grameen Bank received the Nobel Peace Prize for these efforts to help poor people improve their lives.

BOX 7.4   Women and the Informal Economy

Parmila is an Indian widow in her thirties with two young children. Although she comes from a wealthy family, her husband's death forced her to take various part-time jobs. She collects wood from local forests, dries it, and then, twice a week, walks five miles to sell it at a local market. In the winter (November to January), she works on farms dehusking rice. She gets to keep some of the rice she processes. Outside of the rainy season, she also works as a laborer on a construction site, where her boss pays her about half of the Indian minimum wage. Parmila's total income is very low by Western standards, but it is enough to allow her to send her two children to school. Parmila does not ask for sympathy or for financial support from her relatives. "Even in times of acute crisis, I held my nerves and did not give in to circumstances," she says. "My God has always stood with me."

Women make up an increasing share of the world's workers. In most non-Islamic countries, they now make up 40 percent or more of the labor force. But in many parts of the world, most women work in the informal economy, where their work is often poorly paid. It commonly also escapes taxation and regulation. In India and in many African countries, for example, more than four out of five women who work outside of agriculture are in the informal economy. Many women choose such jobs voluntarily. They may do childcare for others or produce arts and crafts, often for local consumption. These jobs may be attractive because they can be performed at home while the women also take care of their own children or relatives. But many women also work in the informal sector because they face discrimination elsewhere. And some are enticed or forced into exhausting, dangerous, or degrading work in sweatshops or in the sex industry. While the informal economy can offer job flexibility, it can also be a place where there is little protection against abusive working conditions.

Source: William Easterly, *The Elusive Quest for Growth: The Economists' Adventures and Misadventures in the Tropics* (Cambridge: Massachusetts Institute of Technology Press, 2001), 45.

the status of women and makes them better informed and more capable of making choices that lead to a stabler and healthier population. As women are educated and/or enter the labor force, they recognize the advantages of smaller families and become more aware of the importance of education and adequate health care. The important place of gender equality and empowering women in the Millennium Development Goals reflects these implications for other aspects of welfare as well as fairness itself.

Fairness in the treatment of minority ethnic, racial, and religious groups is also an issue in many countries. Although democracies are generally less abusive of minorities than are authoritarian systems, democratic majorities can often cruelly ignore their own standards of fairness in the treatment of minority groups. The Minorities at Risk project tracks the status of 282 minority groups using expert informants. The records of our twelve large nations showed that, in ten nations, at least one minority group was subject to "significant poverty and underrepresentation due to prevailing social practices by dominant groups" (www.cidcm.umd.edu/mar). Public policies either deliberately contributed to the problem or were inadequate to overcome discriminatory practices. Such minority groups included Afro-Brazilians in Brazil, Corsicans in France, scheduled tribes in India, Mayans in Mexico, Chechens in Russia, and Native Americans in the United States.

Often, unfair treatment of minorities is closely related to the problem of rural poverty. While there are many causes of the inequality between city and countryside in basic health facilities and income, government policy can contribute to the discrepancy. In many African states, for example, the rulers tend to favor the urban population because they want the country to modernize and industrialize. Sometimes, politicians also worry that a discontented urban population might riot and bring down the government. For these reasons, governments tend to keep food prices artificially low, which hurts farmers. Governments also tend to prefer targeted government agricultural programs (often subsidies), which help particular groups of farmers (often wealthy ones). Such targeted programs help governments gain political supporters but are often wasteful. Even in democratic countries where the majority of voters are poor farmers, government policies often do little for them. Many voters do not trust politicians who promise to deliver broad public goods (such as health care and education), but instead support candidates who promise targeted private goods (such as jobs and subsidies). These patterns sustain clientelistic party systems. Thus, even spending on schools becomes a way to create jobs rather than to educate children. In India, teachers' salaries account for 96 percent of recurrent expenditures in primary education. Even so, teacher absenteeism is rampant. When inspectors made unannounced visits to rural schools, about two-thirds of the teachers were absent.[9]

Of course, great income inequality of all kinds violates most standards of fairness. Indeed, the hope that new democratic governments would lead to greater equality has historically been one of the driving forces in democratization. Yet even in the wealthiest and most equal democracies today, the wealthiest 10 percent of the population earns about 20 percent of the income, as much as the poorest 40 percent. The fourth column of Table 7.4 shows the percent of income earned by the top 10 percent. In the United States and Russia, the gap between rich and poor is substantially larger, with the top group earning about a third of the income. One of the problems of economic development is that the middle stages of development are often associated with new concentrations of wealth and greater gaps between the newly prosperous, usually urban, middle class and those left behind. This gap between rich and poor continues to be a particular problem in middle-level countries like Brazil and Mexico, where the gap is much greater—the wealthiest earning three or four times the total income of the bottom 40 percent. Recent government policies in these countries have targeted these inequalities, which are sources of deep citizen dissatisfaction. (See Chapter 15 on Brazil.) Nigeria is also highly unequal. On the one hand, social and economic conditions, such as levels of literacy, occupational skills, and land holding, are derived from historic development experiences and continue to feed income inequality. On the other hand, government policies can play an important role through the progressiveness or regressiveness of revenue policies and the redistributiveness of welfare policies. There is a great deal of debate about this gap—how great an injustice it does to the poor, to what extent it is justified by the incentives it provides for individual efforts or by established property rights, and the degree to which it should be eased by the welfare state.

Liberty and Freedom Outcomes

One of the prime objectives of good government is to provide for the freedom and liberty of its citizens. Even if there is a popular myth that authoritarian governments help make societies more efficient, the goal of government is to empower its citizens so that they can control their own lives. We can measure individual liberty and freedom outcomes in several ways.

Table 7.5 shows political experts' ratings of the political rights and civil liberties scores for the countries included in this text. *Political rights* refers to citizen opportunities to participate in the choice of political leaders—voting rights, the right to run for office, and the like. *Civil liberties* refers to protections in such areas as freedom of speech, press, assembly, and religion, as well as to procedural rights, such as trial by a jury of peers and bans on arbitrary or cruel treatment. The levels of liberties reflect the outcomes of government policies, especially regulatory policies, but are also affected by social and economic conditions, such as prosperity,

TABLE 7.5
Political and Economic Rights and Liberties, 2013

Political rights, civil liberties, and economic freedom are strongly associated.

Country	Political Rights	Civil Liberties	Economic Freedom
Brazil	2	2	5.8
Britain	1	1	7.5
China	7	6	5.2
France	1	1	6.4
Germany	1	1	7.3
India	2	3	5.5
Iran	6	6	4.3
Japan	1	2	7.2
Mexico	3	3	6.7
Nigeria	4	4	5.5
Russia	6	5	5.1
United States	1	1	7.6

Note: Expert ratings of political rights and civil liberties for each country on 1 (highest) to 7 (lowest) scale. Economic freedom scored on summary scale from 0 (low) to 10 (high).

Source: From Freedom House web site, www.freedomhouse.org (data downloaded July 9, 2013); index of economic freedom, product of the Heritage Foundation and *The Wall Street Journal* (data downloaded July 9, 2013, from www.heritage.org).

inequality, and crime, in the societies. The affluent democratic countries all have positive ratings for both political and civil rights. India, Brazil, and Mexico, which have improved significantly in recent years, follow next. At the other extreme, China, Iran, and, most recently, Russia substantially suppress both political rights and civil liberties. China in particular has tried to control the media comprehensively (also see Figure 7.3) and sets few limits on government regulation vis-à-vis the individual. Nigeria is rated in the middle.

These rankings, of course, vary over time. Rights and liberties in the United States have improved since the civil rights movement of the 1960s. Nigeria's military governments of the 1990s were repressive and frequently brutal; political rights and civil liberties have improved there since power was turned over to an elected civilian president in 1999, but remain fragile. Nigeria was downgraded substantially after observers reported massive vote rigging and fraud in the (disputed) 2007 presidential and gubernatorial elections. The 2011 elections more successfully observed political rights, but civil liberties were downgraded in 2012 due to continuing massive corruption and various restrictions in response to terrorist attacks by an Islamist extremist group (see Chapter 18 on Nigeria).

There is a strong correlation between political and civil rights. No country that scores high on participatory rights also scores very low on civil liberties, and no country low on participatory rights is high on civil liberties. This suggests a strong relationship between popular participation and the rule of law and equitable procedure. Studies of governmental repression have also found that limitations on government abuses of physical integrity rights of citizens were best explained by the presence of democratic political institutions and conditions of peace and social order. Authoritarian states and those involved in internal or international war were the most frequent violators of personal integrity.

Table 7.5 also reports the level of economic freedom in each country. It is not always true that countries that are politically free also foster economic freedom, or vice versa. For example, Mexico shows substantially more economic freedom than Brazil or India, although its political freedom ratings are similar. And even though Britain and France score the same on political rights and liberties, Britain has a higher level of economic freedom. On the whole, though, political and economic freedoms tend to go together.

Domestic Security Outcomes

As Thomas Hobbes would have reminded us, maintaining domestic law and order and protecting persons and property are among the most basic government responsibilities. Without them, the conduct of personal, economic, and civic life is impossible.

High crime rates are primarily a problem of the larger urban areas where much of the population of modern countries resides. The causes of urban crime are complex. Rapidly increasing migration into the major cities, from the domestic countryside or from poorer foreign countries, increases diversity and often conflict. The pace of urbanization is particularly explosive in many developing countries, such as Brazil and Nigeria, where there are severe problems of poverty and infrastructure. The newly arrived city dwellers often find themselves uprooted from their cultures, unwelcome, without a job, and living in squalor far apart from their families and traditional communities. Also, inequality of income and wealth, unemployment, and drug abuse lie behind this general decline in public order and safety. Increased globalization of crime, especially in drugs and human trafficking, has also played its part.

Figure 7.4 presents figures on the number of homicides per 100,000 inhabitants for the nations in this text. Mexico, deeply troubled by battles with and between organized crime gangs as well as a traditionally high murder rate, has the most homicides per 100,000 inhabitants. Its murder rate is almost five times as high as that in the United States. Brazil's homicide rate is nearly as high as Mexico's. Nigeria and Russia also have considerably higher murder rates than the United States. In Russia, the crime rate doubled between 1985 and 1993 as the moral and legal order collapsed. Iran and India have rates about three-fifths that of the United States, while the other industrialized nations have rates that are a small fraction of that of the United States. Japan is the most crime-free among this set of nations. Yet crime rates have recently come down significantly in the United States and some other countries. The number of murders per 100,000 inhabitants in the United States peaked at 9.4 in 1994 and declined to 4.8 in 2010.

There are several reasons that crime rates might decrease. One is economic conditions, with crime rates decreasing when the economy is strong. A second reason is stricter law enforcement. This is partially

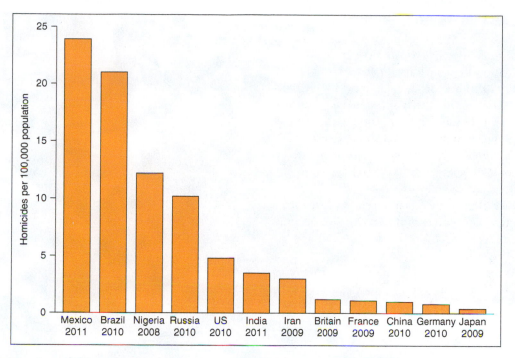

FIGURE 7.4

Homicides per 100,000 Population

Homicide rates vary greatly across countries.

Source: United Nations Office on Drugs and Crime (data downloaded July 10, 2013, from www.unodc.org/unodc).

reflected in the number of police officers relative to total population, which ranges from 1 police officer for every 350 persons in the United States to 1 per 820 in India and 1 per 1,140 in Nigeria. In the United States, both federal and state governments have also sought to reduce crime by increasing the length of imprisonment. A third cause of lower crime rates has been a decrease in the number of youths at the age at which most crimes are committed.

An even greater threat to personal security than private crime can be intense domestic political conflict culminating in civil war. In recent years, much of the world's media focus has been on conflicts in the Middle East, but conflicts in Africa have in fact been more frequent and devastating. Many African countries, newly independent from about 1960, but with borders arbitrarily drawn by colonial powers, have serious problems of national cohesion and have suffered from chronic civil war. Large-scale civil war in Nigeria (1967 to 1970) cost perhaps a million lives, and more sporadic conflict continues to the present time.

The Uppsala Conflict Data Project reports 141 armed conflicts worldwide (defined as involving at least twenty-five battle deaths) from 1989 through 2012. In 2012, there were thirty-two ongoing conflicts, of which six (in Syria, Afghanistan, Somalia, Pakistan, Yemen, and Sudan) involved more than 1,000 deaths. The total death toll in 2012 was estimated to be over 35,000 people.[10] All but one of these armed conflicts was a civil war occurring within state boundaries, although several were internationalized in that foreign powers were also involved. Such internationalized civil wars seem to be even more deadly and disruptive than purely domestic ones. In every year since the end of World War II in 1945, there have been more civil wars than interstate conflicts (wars between countries), and civil wars have also caused more casualties than interstate wars.

There are many reasons for the high incidence of civil war. Some are related to ethnic or religious conflicts, or separatist movements. But others seem mainly due to struggles between warlords over lootable resources, such as diamonds, gold, or oil. External actors—such as the UN, the United States, NATO, or strong regional powers—can sometimes help end civil wars, but in some cases (such as Angola), civil wars

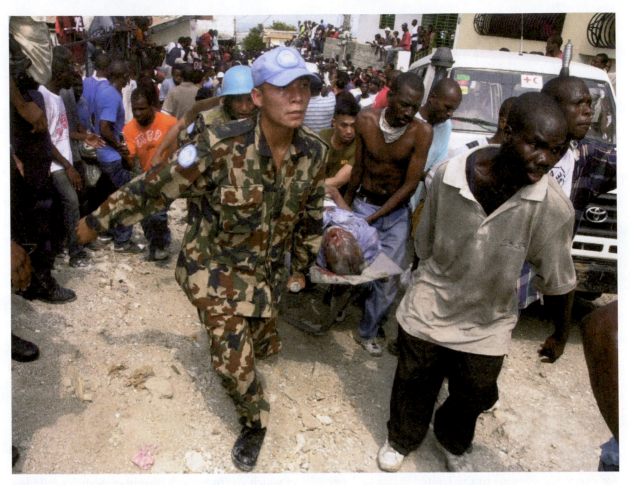

International Peacekeepers
Police and troops from a U.N. peacekeeping force carry a victim of a school collapse on November 7, 2008, in Pétionville, Haiti.

have been prolonged because foreign powers have been engaged on both sides of the conflict.

The UN in the post–Cold War world has intervened in some of these conflicts by providing peacekeeping missions when the parties to conflicts are ready to accept these mediations. As of July 2013, there were fifteen peacekeeping missions in various parts of the world. More rarely, the UN intervenes as a peacemaker, as in Bosnia and later in neighboring Kosovo in the 1990s, or when the peacekeeping mission in Sierra Leone (West Africa) was converted into a peacemaking effort. The UN's effectiveness in controlling domestic and international collective violence depends on consensus among the great powers.

Sometimes, governments undertake deadly attacks on ethnic or political groups in their own populations. These attacks can be designed to eliminate the groups and can emerge either as a part of civil war or as a pure expression of systematic government policy against unarmed civilians. When these attacks are designed to eliminate political adversaries identified by actions or ideology, they are called politicides. When they are designed to eliminate ethnic or religious groups, they are called genocides. These terrible policies are more frequently, although not exclusively, launched by nondemocratic regimes and in conditions of state disruption. Although reliable casualty figures are very hard to come by, there is no doubt that although these events are rare, costs are high. Barbara Harff identifies 37 such events in all parts of the world between 1955 and 2001.[11] Estimates for politicides or genocides in Cambodia, Pakistan, Indonesia, and Rwanda range up to 1 million deaths. In the last decade, scholars have begun to collect systematic data on these cases of deadly one-sided violence and to try to understand their causes.

International Outcomes

7.4 Discuss the international economic and security issues addressed by government policies and explain how they are affected by globalization.

Most states engage in a great variety of international activities. Economic, diplomatic, military, and informational activities may result in prosperity or depression, war or peace, secularization or the spread of particular beliefs.[12] The phenomenon known as *globalization* has increasingly demanded more economic, social, and political interaction by ever more states. National economies have become more dependent on international trade and capital flows, creating intense pressures from those advantaged by trade to ease restrictions and those hurt by international competition to increase barriers. These conflicting demands can be a major source of internal conflict.[13] Moreover, a major economic setback in one part of the world, such as the financial credit crisis in the developed nations in 2008–2009, ripples though many distant countries. Crippled industrialized economies import fewer goods, hitting the producing countries in turn. Increasingly, countries need coordinated political action to regulate capital flows and encourage trade. The very interdependence that globalization creates can threaten damage to all if key countries break off their involvement, as happened during the 1930s.

Environmental damage, too, flows beyond the boundaries of individual countries. For example, cumulative atmospheric emissions of greenhouse gases pose a threat to global climate stability. The social side of globalization has also expanded. Personal contacts and information flows, including television and Internet use, have increased, as has the presence of cultural (and economic) symbols such as McDonald's. These have brought pressures to respect international standards of personal integrity and gender equality (see Chapter 3). However, while individuals may benefit greatly from the opportunities that the Internet or McDonald's offer, these exposures may also threaten traditional values. Issues such as controlling immigration loom large in many countries.

Table 7.6 shows the KOF Index of Globalization, which tracks a variety of economic, social, and political measures. Countries with higher globalization scores have more trade and foreign direct investment relative to their GDP and lower import barriers. In social and political terms, they have more

TABLE 7.6
Change in the Index of Globalization, 1970–2010

Globalization has been increasing across the world, but government policies can affect the rate and level.

Country	1970	1980	1990	2000	2010
Brazil	37	43	44	58	59
Britain	57	67	73	82	85
China	15	20	35	54	59
France	58	65	75	86	84
Germany	47	58	61	84	81
India	24	25	29	44	52
Iran	25	27	22	35	40
Japan	35	43	48	61	64
Mexico	43	45	52	60	59
Nigeria	27	38	40	49	61
Russia	—	—	39	63	68
United States	60	65	71	78	75

Note: The KOF index of globalization, a 0-to-100 scale, is composed of economic, social, and political elements.

Source: Axel Dreher, "Does Globalization Affect Growth? Evidence from a New Index of Globalization," *Applied Economics* 38, no. 10 (2006):1091–110, (data downloaded March 13, 2013, from http://globalization.kof.ethz.ch/).

international telephone traffic and letters, more Internet users, and more memberships in international organizations. We see that globalization has increased in most countries during the last thirty-five years, especially since 1990. China, which was once at the lowest levels of globalization, expanded its global exposure—economic, social, and political—into the middle ranks, from 15 on a 100-point scale in 1970 to 59 in 2010. India and Brazil, too, have exploded onto the global stage, as has Russia since the breakup of the Soviet Union. At the same time, countries like France, Germany, Britain, and the United States, beginning from a much more globalized base, have further expanded their involvement in the global flows of trade, capital, and information. Of the countries in our set, by far the most resistant to globalization has been Iran, which, since the Islamic Revolution in 1979, has tried to maintain its general economic and social isolation. So, while globalization exerts powerful incentives for economic and social integration, government policies can powerfully promote or constrain it.

A different costly outcome of international interaction is warfare. Table 7.7 reports the numbers of deaths from international and internal collective violence for our twelve study countries for almost the entire twentieth century (1900 to 1995). The figures are mostly civilian and military deaths from interstate warfare. In some cases, they include government attacks on unarmed civilians, such as the slaughter of civilians in the efforts to implement communism in the Soviet Union and China, the holocaust of European Jews under the German Nazis (Hitler's National Socialist Party), many "ethnic cleansing" episodes in Europe and Africa, and civil wars in all parts of the world. They probably underestimate the true casualties, especially in the era before 1946. Moreover, the total indirect costs of war to civilians due to famine and disease are certainly far greater than estimated in these figures.[14] Although most of the deaths in this table are caused by World War I, World War II, and the Korean War, in the last decades of the twentieth century, more than three-quarters of the war deaths were civilian.[15]

Table 7.7 shows that the people of USSR/Russia, by a margin of more than two to one, were the most numerous victims of the tormented history of the twentieth century. The enormous Russian casualties during World War I destroyed the czarist regime. Its collapse was followed by the 1917 Bolshevik Revolution, the Civil War (1918 to 1921), and Stalin's Great Terror (particularly in the 1930s), each of which cost the lives of millions. Soviet suffering climaxed in World War II with a total of 17 million civilian and military dead. All told, the USSR/Russia suffered more than 24 million civilian and military deaths in the wars and political horrors of the twentieth century.

Germany suffered the second-largest number of deaths from twentieth-century collective violence. More than 3 million deaths, mostly military, occurred in World War I. In World War II, Germany suffered almost 5 million military and another 1.75 million civilian deaths. Other countries with huge losses include China, with 7 to 8 million deaths, and Japan, whose more than 2 million deaths include half a million civilians, notably many residents of Hiroshima and Nagasaki. French and British sufferings were of roughly similar magnitude.

After World War II, the most devastating conflicts have occurred in the Third World. The partition of formerly British India into India, Pakistan, and Bangladesh

---

TABLE 7.7
Deaths from Collective Civilian–Military Violence, 1900–1995

Citizens in some nations paid a terrible price for the international conflicts of the twentieth century.

Country	Civilian Deaths	Military Deaths	Unspecified Deaths	Total Deaths
Brazil	—	1,000	2,000	3,000
Britain	131,000	1,350,000	—	1,481,000
China	4,047,000	2,671,000	818,000	7,536,000
France	490,000	1,830,000	—	2,320,000
Germany	2,232,000	7,150,000	—	9,382,000
India	889,000	71,000	37,000	997,000
Iran	120,000	468,000	1,000	589,000
Japan	510,000	1,502,000	—	2,012,000
Mexico	125,000	125,000	10,000	260,000
Nigeria	1,005,000	1,000,000	6,000	2,011,000
USSR/Russia	12,028,000	11,901,000	96,000	24,025,000
United States	—	524,000	—	524,000
TOTALS	21,577,000	28,593,000	970,000	51,140,000

Source: Adapted from Ruth Leger Sivard, "Wars and War Related Deaths, 1900–1995," *World Military and Social Expenditures 1996* (Washington, DC: World Priorities, 1996), 18–19. U.S. deaths add Korean and Vietnam war totals, from U.S. Department of State figures, to Sivard report of World War I and II deaths.

produced numerous deadly conflicts within and among the three countries. Some 2 million lives, mostly civilian, were lost. The end of the Cold War around 1990 witnessed a wave of instability and conflict in Eastern Europe and Central Asia. The breakup of the Soviet Union and Yugoslavia resulted in bloody border wars and secession conflicts (for example, in Bosnia and Kosovo in the former Yugoslavia, and Chechnya in Russia). These conflicts brought another wave of ethnic slaughter, religious clashes, and struggles for power among different warlords.

Most recently, the number of wars and casualties has gradually declined. Although recent years have seen horrific acts of international terrorism, from New York, London, and Spain to Nairobi, its annual human toll has not changed much. Civil wars, as discussed above, continue to take a serious toll, especially in sub-Saharan Africa and the Middle East, but the costs are still less than those of the great international wars, and the trends are encouraging. Some students of international conflict see hope in what they call the "democratic peace," the fact that democratic countries hardly ever fight wars against one another. Nor are they as likely to commit genocide or politicide against their own citizens. As more countries become democratic, will the world also become more peaceful?[16] International warfare, which would be even more terrible if nuclear powers were involved, is potentially the greatest threat to human security.

The Complexity of Policy Choice

 7.5 Provide examples of the trade-offs that may be necessary between desired policy outcomes.

One of the hard facts about political goods is that we cannot always have them simultaneously. A political system often has to trade off one value to obtain another. Spending money on education is giving up the opportunity to spend it on welfare, or to leave it in the hands of the taxpayers. Politicians also have to decide how much to invest for the future rather than spend today (for example, when they determine future retirement benefits). Even more difficult are the trade-offs between security and liberty. Extreme liberty would give us a highly insecure world where the strong might bully the weak and where collective action would be difficult. Yet, without liberty, security may be little more than servitude or imprisonment. The trade-offs between political goods are not the same under all circumstances. Sometimes, increasing liberty will also increase security (for example, because riots against censorship will end). And, under some conditions, investment in education will be paid back many times in health and welfare, because trained citizens can better care for themselves and work more productively. These are positive trade-offs. But often you "cannot have your cake and eat it too." One of the important tasks of social science is to discover the conditions under which positive and negative trade-offs occur.

Political science has no way of converting units of liberty into units of safety or welfare. And we can never calculate the value of a political outcome gained at the cost of human life. Political decision makers often have to make such conversions, but as political scientists, we can only point to value judgments that they are willing to make. The weight given to various goods differs across cultures and contexts. A religious faith or a political ideology may tell us how one value should be traded against another and thus offer an orderly basis for choice. Such schemes may be invaluable for those pressed into action in the terrible circumstances of war, revolution, and famine. When people do not share these underlying values, there may be serious conflicts. Sadly, there is no ideology, just as there is no political science, that can solve all these problems objectively. However, governments should provide a means for the people to decide for themselves, because this may be the only acceptable resolution of complex policy choices.

REVIEW QUESTIONS

- What explains the growth of the welfare state?
- What are the advantages and disadvantages of different types of taxes?

- Why may a "windfall" of natural resources make it more difficult to introduce or sustain democracy?

- Do some governments tend to promote political rights while others promote civil rights, or do civil and political rights tend to go together?
- How is the welfare outcome for women changing in developing countries today?

- Why does globalization give rise to internal conflict within nations?
- What sorts of armed conflicts are most common in today's world, and what problems do they cause?

KEY TERMS

direct taxes
distribution
extraction
fairness

gross domestic product (GDP)
indirect taxes
policy goods

policy outcomes
political goods
public policy
policy outputs

regulation
rentier states
symbolic outputs

SUGGESTED READINGS

Bates, Robert H. *When Things Fell Apart: State Failure in Late-Century Africa.* New York: Cambridge University Press, 2008.

Boix, Carles. *Political Parties, Growth, and Equality: Conservative and Social Democratic Economic Strategies in the World Economy.* New York: Cambridge University Press, 1998.

Castles, Francis G., ed. *The Comparative History of Public Policy.* Cambridge: Polity Press, 1989.

Dahl, Robert. *Democracy and Its Critics.* New Haven, CT: Yale University Press, 1989.

Easterly, William. *The Elusive Quest for Growth: The Economists' Adventures and Misadventures in the Tropics.* Cambridge: Massachusetts Institute of Technology Press, 2001.

Flora, Peter, and Arnold Heidenheimer. *The Development of Welfare States in Europe and America.* New Brunswick, NJ: Transaction Books, 1981.

Franzese, Robert. *Macroeconomic Policies of Developed Democracies.* New York: Cambridge University Press, 2002.

Gourevitch, Peter. *Politics in Hard Times.* Ithaca, NY: Cornell University Press, 1986.

Halperin, Morton H., Joseph T. Siegle, and Michael M. Weinstein. *The Democracy Advantage: How Democracies Promote Prosperity and Peace.* New York: Routledge, 2010.

Lijphart, Arend. *Patterns of Democracy: Government Forms and Performance in Thirty-Six Countries.* New Haven, CT: Yale University Press, 2012.

Linos, Katerina. *The Democratic Foundations of Policy Diffusion: How Health, Family and Employment Laws Spread across Countries.* New York: Oxford University Press, 2013.

Persson, Torsten, and Guido Tabellini. *The Economic Effects of Constitutions.* Cambridge: Massachusetts Institute of Technology Press, 2003.

Putnam, Robert. *Making Democracy Work: Civic Traditions in Modern Italy.* Princeton, NJ: Princeton University Press, 1993.

Rogowski, Ronald. *Commerce and Coalitions: How Trade Affects Domestic Political Alignments.* Princeton, NJ: Princeton University Press, 1989.

Tsebelis, George. *Veto Players: An Introduction to Institutional Analysis.* Princeton, NJ: Princeton University Press, 2002.

Wilensky, Harold. Rich Democracies: Political Economy, Public Policy, and Performance. Berkeley: University of California Press, 2002.

ENDNOTES

1. This literature seems to have originated in studies of the Middle East. See the reviews in Michael L. Ross, "Does Oil Hinder Democracy?" *World Politics* 53 (2001): 325–61; and Thad Dunning, *Crude Democracy: Natural Resource Wealth and Political Regimes* (New York: Cambridge University Press, 2008). Also see Kiren A. Chaudhry, *The Price of Wealth: Economies and Institutions in the Middle East* (Ithaca, NY: Cornell University Press, 1997).

2. See especially Ross, "Does Oil Hinder Democracy?," who sketches multiple causal mechanisms proposed in the literature.

3. Samuel P. Huntington, *The Third Wave: Democratization in the Late Twentieth Century* (Norman: University of Oklahoma, 1991), 65.

4. Dunning, *Crude Democracy.*

5. See, for example, Carles Boix, *Political Parties, Growth, and Equality: Conservative and Social Democratic Economic Strategies in the World Economy* (New York: Cambridge University Press, 1998); Robert Franzese, *Macroeconomic Policies of Developed Democracies* (New York: Cambridge University Press, 2002); Shin-Goo Kang and G. Bingham Powell, Jr., "Representation and Policy Responsiveness," *Journal of Politics* 72 (October 2010): 1014–28; Michael D. McDonald and Ian Budge, *Elections, Parties, Democracy: Conferring the Median Mandate* (New York: Oxford University Press, 2005); and Harold Wilensky, *Rich Democracies: Political Economy, Public Policy, and Performance* (Berkeley: University of California Press, 2002).

6. Eric Kramon and Daniel N. Posner, "Who Benefits from Distributive Politics? How the Outcome One Studies Affects the Answer One Gets," *Perspectives on Politics* 11 (2013): 461–75.

7. Laurence J. Kotlikoff and Scott Burns, *The Coming Generational Storm: What You Need to Know about America's Economic Future* (Cambridge: Massachusetts Institute of Technology Press, 2004).

8. Steven C. Poe and C. Neal Tate, "Repression of Human Rights to Personal Integrity in the 1980s: A Global Analysis," *American Political Science Review* 88 (December 1994): 853–72; Steven C. Poe, C. Neal Tate, and Linda Camp Keith, "Repression of the Human Right to Personal Integrity Revisited," *International Studies Quarterly* 43 (1999): 291–313; also see Christian Davenport, *State Repression and the Democratic Peace* (Cambridge: Cambridge University Press, 2007).

9. Robert H. Bates, *Markets and States in Tropical Africa* (Berkeley: University of California Press, 1981); Philip Keefer and Stuti Khemani, "Why Do the Poor Receive Poor Services?" *Economic and Political Weekly* 28 (February 2004): 935–43; and World Bank, *World Development Report, 2002: Building Institutions for Markets* (Washington, DC: World Bank), 31–32.

10. See Lotta Themner and Peter Wallensteen, "Armed Conflict, 1946–2012," *Journal of Peace Research* 50 (2013): 509–21.

11. Barbara Harff, "No Lessons Learned from the Holocaust? Assessing Risks of Genocide and Political Mass Murder since 1955." *American Political Science Review* 97 (2003) 57–73. More recently, see "Deadly Assaults on Civilians," *Human Security Report 2012*, chap. 8, published online by Simon Fraser University (2013).

12. Peter Gourevitch, in his book *Politics in Hard Times* (Ithaca, NY: Cornell University Press, 1986), analyzes the policy responses of five Western industrial nations—Britain, France, Germany, Sweden, and the United States—to the three world depressions of 1870–1890, 1930–1940, and 1975–1985. Gourevitch shows how these crises affected business, labor, and agriculture differently in each country; consequences for political structure and policy varied greatly. Thus, the world depression of the 1930s resulted in a conservative reaction in Britain (the formation of a "National" government), a moderate left reaction in the United States (the "New Deal"), a polarization and paralysis of public policy in France ("Immobilisme"), a moderate social democratic reaction in Sweden, and a radical right-and-left polarization in Germany, leading to a breakdown of democracy and the emergence of National Socialism. While the causes of World War II were complex, the pacifism of Britain, the demoralization and defeatism in France, the isolationism of the United States, and the nihilism and aggression of Germany were all fed by the devastating worldwide economic depression of the 1930s.

13. See especially Ronald Rogowski, *Commerce and Coalitions: How Trade Affects Domestic Political Alignments* (Princeton, NJ: Princeton University Press, 1989).

14. Although there are some detailed studies of individual conflicts and politicides that try to estimate these costs by comparing death rates expected from prewar conditions to those reported in war time, these are difficult and have not been carried out systematically in many cases. For this reason, estimates vary wildly. Estimates of direct battle deaths are much more reliable, and have become more so, but even these are somewhat controversial. See the various *Human Security Reports* (published online by Simon Fraser University) and the many sources cited there, especially the International Peace Research Institute (PRIO) and the Uppsala Conflict Data Programme (UCDP).

15. Ruth Leger Sivard, *World Military and Social Indicators* (Washington, DC: World Priorities, 1993), 20.

16. Stephen Pinker, *The Better Angels of Our Nature: Why Violence Has Declined* (New York: Viking, 2011).

Country Bio

POPULATION
63.2 million

TERRITORY
94,525 square miles

YEAR OF INDEPENDENCE
From twelfth century

YEAR OF CURRENT CONSTITUTION
Unwritten; partly statutes, partly common law and practice

HEAD OF STATE
Queen Elizabeth II

HEAD OF GOVERNMENT
Prime Minister David Cameron

LANGUAGE
English; plus about 600,000 regularly speak Welsh and about 60,000 speak Gaelic; among immigrants, about 1,000,000 use an Indian language as their home language and 550,000 speak Polish

RELIGION
National census: Christian 37.2 million, of which the majority are nominally Church of England; Muslim 2.8 million; Hindu 900,000; Sikh 500,000; Jewish 300,000; other 300,000; no religion 16,000,000; no reply 5,000,000

CHAPTER 8

Politics in Britain

Richard Rose

LEARNING OBJECTIVES

8.1 Discuss the domestic and international challenges currently facing Britain, focusing on its coalition government and increased globalization.

8.2 Describe recent changes in British politics, from the development of the welfare state through left/right conflict over Thatcherism to less confrontational government under Tony Blair and David Cameron.

8.3 Identify the ways in which Britain is a "multinational state."

8.4 Explain the structure of British government and list the duties of Cabinet ministers and civil servants.

8.5 Summarize the collectivist and individualist theories of government, using examples from Britain.

8.6 List the five main influences on political socialization in Britain.

8.7 Contrast British citizens' participation in political versus nonpartisan activities.

8.8 Discuss the paths to elective office and high-ranking civil service jobs in Britain.

8.9 Describe the relationships, including privileged access, between various interest groups and Britain's governing parties.

8.10 Discuss the emergence of the multiparty system and how this is limited by the first-past-the-post electoral system.

8.11 Describe the "Whitehall obstacle race."

8.12 Discuss the roles of the central and local British governments and public and privatized institutions in delivering services.

8.13 Summarize the roles of laws, money, and personnel in Britain's public policies.

8.14 Identify the effects of global interdependence on Britain's economy and thus on its political capabilities.

In a world of new democracies, Britain is different because it is an old democracy. Its political system has been evolving for more than 800 years. In medieval times, the king of England claimed to rule France and Ireland too. While the claim to rule France was abandoned in the fifteenth century, sovereignty was gained over Wales and Scotland. The government of the **United Kingdom** was created in 1801 by merging England, Scotland, Wales, and Ireland under the authority of **Parliament** in London.

Unlike new democracies, Britain became a democracy by evolution rather than revolution. Democratization was a slow process. The rule of law was established in the seventeenth century, the accountability of the executive to Parliament was established by the eighteenth century, and national political parties organized in the nineteenth century. Even though competitive elections had been held for more than a century, the right of every adult man and woman to vote was not recognized until the twentieth century.

The influence of British government can be found in places as far-flung as India, Australia, Canada, and the United States. Just as Alexis de Tocqueville traveled to America in 1831 to seek the secrets of democracy, so we can examine Britain to learn more about causes of durable representative government. The limitations of the British model are shown by the inability of its institutions to be translated to countries gaining independence from the British Empire. Even more striking is the failure of institutions that have worked in England to bring political stability in Northern Ireland.

The evolution of democracy in Britain contrasts with a European history of countries switching between democratic and non-democratic forms of government. Whereas the oldest British people have lived in the same political system all their lives, the oldest Germans have lived under at least four constitutions, two democratic and two undemocratic.

At no point in history did representatives of the British people meet to decide a constitution setting out their form of government, as happened in America at the end of the eighteenth century, and as has happened many times in France. There is no agreement among political scientists about when England developed a modern system of government.[1] The most reasonable judgment is that this occurred during the very long reign of Queen Victoria from 1837 to 1901, when institutions were created or adapted to cope with the problems of a society that was increasingly urban, literate, industrial, and critical of unreformed traditional institutions. However, the creation of a modern system of government does not get rid of the problems of governing.

Current Policy Challenges

8.1 Discuss the domestic and international challenges currently facing Britain, focusing on its coalition government and increased globalization.

The outcome of the 2010 general election presented British party leaders with their biggest political challenge in more than half a century. Normally, the party with the most votes gains an absolute majority of seats in the House of Commons and automatically forms a government. However, in 2010, no party won the 326 seats needed to have a majority in the House of Commons. The **Conservative Party** under the leadership of David Cameron won 307 seats, Labour won 258 seats, and the **Liberal Democratic Party** came third with 57 seats. The result was a coalition government with the Conservative leader, David Cameron, the **prime minister**, and the Liberal Democratic leader, Nick Clegg, the deputy prime minister.

Since no member of parliament had ever served in a coalition government before, the biggest challenge the partners face is to keep the coalition together.

Two People, Two Party Leaders, One Coalition Government

An election outcome with no party winning a majority of seats has resulted in party leaders who campaigned against each other sharing power as prime minister (David Cameron, Conservative) and deputy prime minister (Nick Clegg, Liberal Democrat).

Doing so has been helped by the enactment of a law giving the House of Commons a fixed term of five years, instead of leaving the choice of an election date with the prime minister. This makes it hard for either coalition partner to break the coalition up for its electoral advantage. The two leaders have benefited by becoming nationally prominent, and many of their senior colleagues have also gained advantages that go with office. However, both parties are subject to internal tensions. Conservatives, especially those who are Thatcherite and see Liberal Democrats occupying government offices that they would like, complain that the coalition has kept the government from adopting more Thatcherite policies. Liberal Democrats cite this complaint as proof that they have had a positive effect on how Britain is governed. However, Clegg has come under fire from Liberals because the party broke an election pledge by accepting the introduction of high university tuition fees, and failed to secure an electoral reform that would benefit the party.

In addition, globalization raises a challenge to the doctrine of the sovereignty of Parliament, which British interpret to mean that the government can do whatever it wants as long as it has the backing of a majority in the House of Commons. However, the chief political and economic problems facing British government today cannot be dealt with by unilateral actions of British government. Many top ministers now spend as much as one day a week at meetings in other countries and are in almost daily contact with leaders of other countries whose actions influence Britain.

The British economy today imports food and raw materials and exports manufactured goods and sophisticated services in fields such as banking and education. The British pound sterling (£) is an international currency, but statements by the prime minister do not determine its international value. This is decided in foreign exchange markets in which currency speculators play a significant role. Since 1997, the value of the British pound in exchange for the dollar has ranged from above $2.50 to less than $1.25. At the beginning of 2014, the value of one pound fluctuated around $1.60 and it fluctuates with the ups and downs of the euro too.

In the decade before the global financial crisis of 2008, the British economy grew by two-fifths; this was higher than the average growth of European Union countries and similar to that of the United States. The 2008 global financial crisis has substantially affected Britain. The decline in demand from major trading partners has hurt exports, and the rise in the price of energy and food has driven up every household's cost of living. The Bank of England cut interest rates to below 1 percent and generated hundreds of billions of pounds of credit in hopes of stimulating economic growth with limited success. Banks threatened with bankruptcy have been taken into state ownership. Inflation has pushed up prices more than wages. Economic difficulties have reduced tax revenue, thus leading to an increase in the government's deficit.

Since the crisis hit Britain while a Labour government was in power, the Conservative-led coalition with Liberal Democrats that took office in 2010 could initially blame their problems on their predecessor. However, a change of the parties in power did not change the problems facing the new government. There are built-in pressures to increase public expenditure, because an aging population requires more health care, longer life increases the cost of pensions, and an educated population demands better education for their children. There are problems in boosting exports because other countries are under pressure to save more and spend less.

The first priority of the coalition government has been to cut the deficit in the belief that this will stimulate private sector investment and consumption and lead to economic growth regaining its precrisis level. In pursuit of this objective, it has cut public expenditure on a range of public services. This is congenial to Conservatives, who favor smaller government, but the effect has been limited since big-spending programs in health, education, and pensions are politically popular and are entitlements to which Britons have a right by law. Successive budgets have not resulted in the country's deficit falling, nor has growth been sufficient to restore the economy to the state it was in before the 2008 crisis. The government now blames the world recession as the cause of its difficulties, while the **Labour Party**, now in opposition, blames the coalition government.

Globalization also challenges the country's leaders to answer the question, "Where in the world does Britain belong?" Traditionally, the answer has been that Britain is a major world power having close ties with Commonwealth countries, the United States, and Europe. After World War II, the British Empire was transformed into the Commonwealth, a free association of fifty-three sovereign states with members on every continent. Its independence from London is shown by the absence of the word "British" from the name of the Commonwealth. Members range from Antigua and Australia to India, Pakistan, and Zambia. They differ from each other in wealth, culture, and commitment to democracy. The Commonwealth has no military or economic power, and its diplomatic influence is slight. When it sought to put pressure on the dictatorship of Robert Mugabe in Zimbabwe, Zimbabwe left the Commonwealth.

Every British prime minister claims a special relationship with the United States. Since the end of the Cold War, the emergence of the United States as a unique global force has made the relationship more attractive to Britain but less relevant to Washington. The reduction in British defense spending means that the chief contribution that Britain can make to an American-led military coalition is political, that is, to contribute some forces to American action that is being taken in pursuit of general values and not just the American national interest. An all-party House of Commons committee concluded that the idea of a special relationship should be abandoned as misleading. Britain should be "less deferential and more willing to say no to the U.S. on those issues where the two countries' interests and values diverge." A majority of the British public agrees.[2]

Since 1973, Britain has been a member of the European Union (EU). The Channel Tunnel makes the rail journey to Paris shorter than travel to the North of England or Scotland. Manufacturers such as the Ford Motor Company link their plants in Britain with factories across Western Europe, just as Ford links factories across American states. Collectively, EU countries are now Britain's major trading partner. Government ministers spend an increasing amount of their time negotiating about everything from the EU regulation of European banking to whether British beer should be served in metric units or by the traditional measure of a British pint.

Britain's governors have never shown the commitment to the EU of founder nations such as Germany and France. There is approval of EU measures to promote a single market but opposition to moving toward an ever closer union. The coalition government has sponsored an Act of Parliament requiring a national referendum to be held on any further changes in EU treaties. The Conservative Party is divided between those who are skeptical of the benefits the EU brings

and a hard core that would like Britain, like Norway, to have trade relations but not political ties to it. The Labour Party tends to view EU measures in terms of party advantage. The Liberal Democrats are very pro-EU but fewer in number. Most British voters do not regard EU membership as important.

Both Britain and the Brussels headquarters of the EU now face a challenge of conflict management. A majority of EU member states favor greater political integration in order to prevent the recurrence of the financial crisis in the eurozone. Since unanimous approval is required for the EU to gain new powers through a treaty, Brussels sees Britain as threatening a veto of the expansion of EU powers. Anti-EU pressure within the Conservative Party has been reenforced by the United Kingdom Independence Party (UKIP) drawing support from Conservative voters by its advocacy of withdrawal from the EU. Prime Minister David Cameron has pledged to seek renegotiation of the terms of British membership if reelected in 2015 and then call a referendum on whether or not Britain should remain in the EU. Other EU member states are unwilling to renegotiate what they regard as a British claim for special treatment. Hardcore eurosceptics favor British withdrawal from the European Union.

The Legacy of History

 Describe recent changes in British politics, from the development of the welfare state through left/right conflict over Thatcherism to less confrontational government under Tony Blair and David Cameron.

The legacy of the past limits current choices, and Britain has a very long past. The continuity of England's political institutions through the centuries is remarkable. Prince Charles, the heir to an ancient Crown, pilots jet airplanes, and a medieval-named chancellor of the Exchequer pilots the British economy through the deep waters of the international economy. Yet symbols of continuity often mask great changes in English life. Parliament was once an institution that aristocrats used to advance their interests against the reigning monarch. Today, it is a popularly elected institution deciding which party is in charge of government.

The 1940–1945 wartime coalition government led by Winston Churchill laid the foundations for the introduction of a welfare state. The Labour Party elected in 1945 introduced a comprehensive National Health

Service and state ownership of many major industries. Between 1951 and 1964, Conservative governments led by Winston Churchill, Anthony Eden, and Harold Macmillan maintained a consensus about the mixed economy welfare state. Economic growth, full employment, and low inflation brought consumer prosperity, and free university education began to expand. The Labour Party under Harold Wilson won the 1964 election campaigning with the vague activist slogan, "Let's go with Labour." New names were given to government department offices, but behind their doors, many officials went through the same routines as before. The economy did not grow as predicted. In 1967, the government was forced to devalue the pound and seek a loan from the International Monetary Fund. Labour lost the 1970 election.

The major achievement of Edward Heath's Conservative government that followed was to make Britain a member of the European Union. However, in trying to limit unprecedented inflation by controlling wages, Heath risked his authority in a confrontation with the left-wing National Union of Mineworkers,

which struck for higher wages. When Heath called the "Who Governs?" election in February 1974, the vote of both the Conservative and Labour parties fell. Labour formed a minority government with Harold Wilson as prime minister; he won a slight majority at a second election held in October. Inflation, rising unemployment, and a contraction in the economy undermined Labour's platform. James Callaghan succeeded Wilson as prime minister in 1976, and the economy deteriorated. A loan from the International Monetary Fund was followed by the Labour government adopting monetarist policies in an attempt to curb inflation.

When Margaret Thatcher won the 1979 election as leader of the Conservative Party, she became the first female prime minister of a major European country. Uniquely among modern British prime ministers, Margaret Thatcher gave her name to a political ideology; it stressed letting people make decisions in the market rather than relying on government to promote their well-being (see Box 8.1). While proclaiming the virtues of the market and attacking big government, Thatcher did not impose radical spending cuts on

---

BOX
8.1   **The Meaning of Thatcherism**

Margaret Thatcher succeeded against the odds of class and gender. She was the first member of her family to go to university and won a place at Oxford. She studied chemistry and then qualified as a lawyer, both heavily male professions. When elected to the House of Commons in 1959, she was one of 25 women MPs; there were 605 male MPs. When elected Conservative leader in 1975, she was the first female leader of a British political party, and in 1979, became the country's first female prime minister. She was also the first party leader in modern British history to win three successive general elections.

Among British prime ministers, Margaret Thatcher has also been unique in giving her name to a political ideology, **Thatcherism**. Her central conviction was that the market offered a cure for the country's economic difficulties. State-owned industries and municipally owned council houses were sold to private owners. What were described as "businesslike" methods were introduced into managing everything from hospitals to museums. She had more in common with the

market-oriented outlook of President Ronald Reagan than with the mixed-economy welfare state philosophy of her Conservative as well as Labour predecessors.

As long as she was in charge, Thatcher believed in strong government. She was prepared to "handbag" (that is, assert her personal authority) colleagues in Cabinet and civil servants. The autonomy of local government was curbed. In foreign policy, she was a formidable opponent of EU influence on what she saw as Britain's national interests. The 1982 Argentine invasion of the Falkland Islands, a remote British colony in the South Atlantic, led to a brief and victorious war there. Following her departure from office, Conservatives divided between Thatcherites, who sought to push market-oriented and anti-EU measures farther, and those who believed that the time had come to maintain the status quo. David Cameron gained office in 2010 by avoiding association with Thatcherism.

Sources: See Margaret Thatcher, *The Downing Street Years* (New York: Harper Collins, 1993); and Richard Vinen, *Thatcher's Britain* (London: Simon and Schuster, 2009).

popular social programs. Thatcher's ideology did not win favor with the electorate. On the tenth anniversary of Thatcher's tenure as prime minister, an opinion poll asked whether people approved of "the Thatcher revolution." Less than one-third said they did.[3]

Divisions among opponents enabled Thatcher to lead her party to three successive election victories. Militant left-wing activists seized control of the Labour Party, and in 1981, four former Labour **Cabinet** ministers formed a centrist Social Democratic Party (SDP) in an alliance with the Liberal Party. The Labour Party's 1983 election manifesto was described as the longest suicide note in history. After Thatcher's third successive election victory in 1987, the SDP leadership merged with the Liberals to form the Liberal Democratic Party.

During her third term of office, Thatcher became very unpopular in opinion polls. In autumn 1990, disgruntled Conservative Members of Parliament forced a ballot for the party leadership that caused her to resign. Conservative MPs elected a relatively unknown John Major as party leader, and he thereby became prime minister. In 1992, Major won an unprecedented fourth consecutive term for the Conservative government. However, a few months later, his economic policy, which was based on a strong British pound, crashed under pressure from foreign speculators. The Major government maintained such Thatcherite policies as the privatization of the coal mines and railways, but sniping from within the Conservative ranks and the rise of a reinvigorated Opposition undermined Major's authority.

After four successive election defeats, in 1994, the Labour Party elected Tony Blair as leader. He offered to replace the party's traditional socialist program with a vague Third Way philosophy modeled on that of President Bill Clinton. Blair pledged a pragmatic government that would do "what works" and appealed to the voters to "trust me." The strategy was electorally successful (see Box 8.2). Thanks to the unpopularity of the Conservative opposition, Blair led Labour to three successive election victories, even though the party's vote fell from 43 percent in 1997 to 35 percent by 2005.

The Blair government implemented Labour's long-standing program of constitutional reforms, including the **devolution** of powers to elected assemblies in Scotland and Wales and creation of a power-sharing government in Northern Ireland. Laws protecting individual human rights were adopted, but in the wake of terrorist attacks, the government sought to limit some rights in ways that drew protests from

---

BOX 8.2 The Electoral Success of Tony Blair

Tony Blair was elected Labour leader because he did not talk or look like an ordinary Labour Party member. Instead of being from a poor background, he was educated at boarding school, studied law at Oxford, and had parents who were Conservatives. Unlike his wife, Cherie Blair, Blair had shown no interest in party politics, let alone the Labour Party, until after he graduated from Oxford. After becoming a Labour MP in 1983, he took the side of those who wanted to reform the party. His unorthodox background helped him gain the party leadership against Gordon Brown, a traditional Labour man. Blair's goal was to win elections by appealing to middle-class voters and thereby become prime minister. He succeeded.

As prime minister, Blair sought to make his office the focus of attention. A high priority was given to media publicity, where a sound bite or a clever phrase is sufficient. Many media-oriented political advisors with little or no prior experience of government were brought into government. Political advisors used the prime minister's authority to push government ministers and civil servants to produce good headlines. Five years after becoming prime minister, Blair recognized the limits of a media-oriented strategy: "In opposition, announcement is the reality. For the first period in government, there was a tendency to believe this is the case. It isn't. The announcement is only the intention."

Sources: See Tony Blair, *Tony Blair: A Journey* (London: Hutchinson, 2010); Simon Jenkins, *Thatcher and Sons* (London: Allen Lane, 2006); and Peter Mandelson, *The Third Man* (New York: Harper Collins, 2010).

civil liberties groups. Blair welcomed such criticism as proof of his toughness. He also promoted changing the delivery of state-financed health and education services by introducing more market mechanisms. Many doctors, teachers, and public employees were demoralized or angered by these changes. In 2006, university teachers staged their first nationwide strike.

In international affairs, Blair succeeded in bonding with Republican President George W. Bush as well as with Bill Clinton. He borrowed arguments from Washington to quash opposition to British commitment to the Iraq War. Blair's popularity fell to the point at which he was more highly regarded in the United States than in Britain. When Labour's support fell in the opinion polls, he came under pressure to resign from within the Labour Party and did so in 2007.

The Labour Party unanimously elected as its leader Gordon Brown, who had been chancellor of the Exchequer for a decade. Brown boasted that the extent of economic growth, low inflation, and low unemployment while he was in charge of the British economy meant that he had ended the economic cycle of "boom and bust." The global economic crisis punctured this claim and left his government with difficult decisions about how to limit the resulting damage. Brown's hesitancy in making and explaining decisions, combined with a reserved personality, led to his approval rating in the polls falling as low as Blair at his worst. In May 2010, Brown led his party to defeat; Labour's 29 percent share of the popular vote was its second lowest since 1918.

After losing three successive elections, the Conservative leadership was desperate to gain office. For half a century, Liberal Democratic leaders claimed they wanted to be a party of government. A hung Parliament (that is, a House of Commons in which no party has an absolute majority) gave the Liberals an opportunity to gain office. The Conservative and Liberal Democratic parties formed the country's first coalition government since World War II (see Box 8.3). Conservative MPs head most government departments, with a Liberal Democrat as their deputy, but Liberal Democrats are in charge of major departments concerned with such issues as the environment and business. A thirty-six-page coalition pact required policy concessions by both parties.[4]

In opposition, the new leader of the Labour Party, Ed Miliband, has the task of explaining to Labour voters and would-be Labour voters where the party now stands.[5] This has required him to admit that previous Labour governments made some mistakes in fields such as immigration policy and the management of

---

BOX 8.3   Two Faces at the Top of Government

While a government can have only one head, the Conservative and Liberal Democratic coalition has two faces at the top: David Cameron, the Conservative prime minister, and Nick Clegg, the Liberal Democratic deputy prime minister. Both party leaders are youthful; each was forty-three years old on assuming the highest offices in government, and neither had held high office before. Both have been full-time politicians since leaving university.

Cameron started as a young assistant to a Conservative Cabinet minister and was then a lobbyist. He won the leadership on the grounds that he was not associated publicly with the electoral defeats of his predecessors and could present himself as a centrist, post-Thatcherite Conservative. In opposition, Cameron sought to make the party electable by moving it to the political center. He endorsed measures to improve the environment, accepted liberal policies on gay and minority rights, and endorsed such popular programs as the National Health Service. Cameron silenced Thatcherite critics by claiming that the alternative to changing the party was a fourth election defeat.

Clegg, a polylingual supporter of the EU, was an assistant to a Conservative in the European Commission in Brussels. Because of being pro-European, he joined the Liberal Democratic Party and served a term as a member of the European Parliament before becoming a British MP in 2005. Unlike some of his Liberal Democratic colleagues, he was never a member of the Labour Party, nor has he identified himself with the left of center, as have most of his predecessors as party leader.

Sources: See Peter Snowdon, *Back from the Brink* (London: Harper Press, 2010); and Robert Hazell and Ben Yong, eds., *The Politics of Coalition*. Oxford: Hart, 2012).

the economy. Left-wing critics respond to this diagnosis by arguing in favor of reaffirming traditional Labour policies; however, doing so is unlikely to gain the support of middle-of-the-road electors who are dissatisfied with the government's performance but uncertain whether Labour would be any better. A further complication is that even if Labour wins the most MPs at the next election, it might not have a majority, thus facing it with the alternatives of trying to govern with a minority of MPs or forming a coalition with the Liberal Democrats.

The Environment of Politics: One Crown but Five Nations

8.3   Identify the ways in which Britain is a "multinational state."

The Queen of England is the best-known monarch in the world, yet there is no such thing as an English state. In international law, the state is the United Kingdom of Great Britain and Northern Ireland. Great Britain is divided into England, **Scotland**, and **Wales**. The most distinctive feature of Wales is that one-quarter speak an old Celtic language, Welsh, as well as English. Scotland, once an independent kingdom, has been an integral part of Britain since 1707. However, the Scots have separate legal, religious, and educational institutions. The fourth part of the United Kingdom, **Northern Ireland**, consists of six of the nine counties of what was once the province of Ulster; the other three are part of the Republic of Ireland. Following a rebellion against the Crown in 1916, a separate Irish state was created in 1921.

The United Kingdom is a unitary state because there is a single source of authority, the British Parliament; however, the institutions of government are not uniform throughout the kingdom. In the minds of citizens, it is a multinational state, because people differ in how they describe themselves (see Table 8.1). In England, people often say they are English or British without considering the different meanings of these terms. This does not happen elsewhere in the United Kingdom. In Scotland, more than two-thirds see themselves as Scots. In Wales, a majority identify as Welsh. In Northern Ireland, people divide into three groups, some seeing themselves as British, some as Irish, and others as Ulster.

Historically, Scotland and Wales have been governed by British Cabinet ministers accountable to Parliament. An Act of Parliament gave responsibilities for some policies to elected assemblies in Scotland and in Wales, and they came into being in 1999. The revenue of both assemblies has been assigned as a share of UK tax revenue according to a complex and contested formula related to public expenditure on comparable policies in England.

The Scottish Parliament in Edinburgh has powers to legislate, to decide its own budget, and to initiate a variety of policies. Elections to the Parliament mix the traditional British **first-past-the-post electoral system** and proportional representation. After the 1999

TABLE 8.1
National Identities
Identities of people vary by nation.

	Nation of Residence			
	England	Scotland	Wales	Northern Ireland
British	43%	19%	34%	39%
English, Scots, Welsh, Northern Irish	42%	70%	54%	34%
Other, don't know	15%	11%	12%	27%*

*Identifies as Irish
Source: Data analysis by Centre for the Study of Public Policy, University of Strathclyde, Glasgow.

and 2003 Scottish elections, Labour formed a government in coalition with the Liberal Democrats. At the May 2007 Scottish Parliament election, the Scottish National Party (SNP) won one more seat than Labour and formed a minority Scottish government. In 2011, the SNP won an absolute majority, 69 of the Parliament's 129 seats. The remaining seats were divided between Labour (37), Conservatives (15), Liberal Democrats (5), and others (3).

Under the leadership of Alex Salmond as first minister, the SNP has demonstrated that it is capable of governing. It continues to promote independence, holding a referendum in September 2014 to vote on the question "Should Scotland be an independent country?" The SNP case for independence is that the country's 5 million people would be better governed by its own Parliament rather than by a British government that lacks majority support in Scotland. The parties forming the UK coalition government in 2010 won the vote of barely one-third of Scots, compared to almost two-thirds of English voters. The SNP argues that by European standards, Scotland has more people than nine member states of the European Union and a population equal to that of Denmark and Finland. The Better Together campaign for the rejection of independence emphasizes the costs and uncertainties of secession from the United Kingdom much more than the positive benefits of being subject to a Parliament in London. Public opinion polls consistently show that the median bloc of Scots want substantially more devolution from London than currently exists, while rejecting independence.

The Welsh Assembly in Cardiff has powers over a variety of local and regional services. It is bilingual, conducting its affairs in English and in Welsh. By comparison with Scotland, its powers of legislation are limited. The Assembly is elected by a mixed first-past-the-post and proportional representation ballot. Labour has consistently been the biggest party at each election, but has sometimes had to depend on Plaid Cymru for support in forming a government. This is possible because Plaid Cymru (the Welsh-language party) does not demand independence as the Scottish National Party does. After the 2011 Assembly election, Labour held thirty seats, the Conservatives fourteen, Plaid Cymru eleven, and the Liberal Democrats five; Labour took control on its own.

Northern Ireland is the most un-English part of the United Kingdom. Formally, it is a secular polity, but differences between Protestants and Catholics about national identity dominate its politics. Protestants, comprising more than half the population, want to remain part of the United Kingdom. Until 1972, the Protestant majority governed through a home rule Parliament at Stormont, a suburb of Belfast. Many in the Catholic minority did not support this regime, wanting instead to leave the United Kingdom and join the Republic of Ireland, which claims that Northern Ireland should be part of the Republic.

After Catholics launched protests against discrimination in 1968, demonstrations turned to violence in 1969. The illegal **Irish Republican Army (IRA)** was revived and, in 1971, began a military campaign to remove Northern Ireland from the United Kingdom. Protestants organized illegal armed forces in response. Political violence has killed more than 3,700 people since. After adjusting for population differences, this is equivalent to about 150,000 deaths in Britain or almost 750,000 political killings in the United States. In 1972, the British government abolished the Stormont Parliament, placing government in the hands of a Northern Ireland Office under a British Cabinet minister.

Intensive negotiations in which London and Dublin offered incentives to Irish Republicans and put pressure on Ulster Unionists to agree to a power-sharing form of government. Whatever the outcome of a Northern Ireland election, government offices must be shared between a majority of MPs representing the minority pro-Irish Catholics as well as a majority of pro-British Protestant MPs. This has been described as "a unique form of devolution-involuntary coalition."[6] A power-sharing government was initially formed in 2007 with Dr. Ian Paisley, an outspoken Unionist and Protestant, as first minister, and Martin McGuinness, a Sinn Fein politician associated with the IRA, as deputy first minister, plus representatives of the Ulster Unionist Party and the Social Democratic and Labour Party. Following the 2011 Assembly election, a five-party power-sharing executive was formed with Peter Robinson, the Democratic Unionist party leader, as first minister, and Martin McGuinness of Sinn Fein as deputy first minister.

While there is no agreement about national identity within the United Kingdom, there is no doubt about which nationality is the most numerous. England dominates the United Kingdom. It accounts for 84 percent of the UK population against 8 percent in Scotland, 5 percent in Wales, and 3 percent in Northern Ireland. In earlier editions, this chapter has been called "Politics in England" because, as Tony Blair once said, "Sovereignty rests with me, as an English MP, and that's the way it will stay."[7] However, changes in United Kingdom institutions have begun to affect politics in England. For example, in the 2005 British general election, the Conservative Party won the most votes in England but the Labour Party, thanks to its dominance in Scotland and Wales, won the most UK seats and formed a majority government. In 2010, the Conservative Party won an absolute majority of seats in England as well as having a big lead in votes there. However, because of its weak support in other parts of the United Kingdom, it fell short of an absolute majority.

A Multiracial Britain

For centuries, England has received a relatively small but noteworthy number of immigrants from other parts of Europe. The Queen is descended from a titled family that came from Hanover, Germany, to assume the English throne in 1714. Until the outbreak of anti-German sentiment in World War I, the surname of the royal family was Saxe-Coburg-Gotha. By royal proclamation, King George V changed the family name to Windsor in 1917.

The worldwide British Empire was multiracial, and so is the Commonwealth. Since the late 1950s, job seekers from the West Indies, Pakistan, India, Africa, and other parts of the Commonwealth have settled in Britain. The relatively prosperous British economy attracts workers from Eastern European parts of the EU. In addition, hundreds of thousands of people from Australia, Canada, the United States, and the EU flow in and out of Britain as students or as workers. Political

Younger Generation Is the Most Multiracial Generation
Schools and street scenes in big cities show that Britain is now a multiracial society.

disturbances around the world have resulted in immigrants who claim asylum as political refugees from troubled areas in the Balkans, the Middle East, and Africa. Some have valid credentials as refugees, whereas others have arrived with false papers or make claims to asylum that courts do not always uphold. In consequence, by the 2011 census, one in eight British residents was foreign-born and less than half the population of London are British-born and white and a substantial fraction have been born outside the United Kingdom.

Public opinion has opposed unlimited immigration, and both Labour and Conservative governments have passed laws trying to limit the number of immigrants. However, these laws contain many exceptions, and EU membership makes it difficult to restrict immigration from the continent of Europe. The government has tried to make deportation of illegal immigrants easier. Nonetheless, it admits that there are hundreds of thousands of illegal immigrants in Britain.

Official statistics define the minority population by the one characteristic that they have in common—they are not white. The population in this catchall category has risen from 74,000 in 1951 to approximately 8 million in the latest census. The Electoral Commission now issues information about how to vote in twelve different languages besides English, ranging from Arabic to Urdu.

Nonwhite immigrants are a heterogeneous category of people, divided by culture, race, language, and ethnicity. West Indians speak English as their native language and have a Christian tradition, but this is often not the case for black Africans. Ethnic minorities from India, Pakistan, and Bangladesh are divided between Hindus, Muslims, and Sikhs, and most speak English as a second language. Chinese from Hong Kong have a distinctive culture. In addition, there are gender differences. There is a tendency for immigrant women not to speak English as well as male immigrants, and this is particularly the case for immigrants from Pakistan and Bangladesh.

With the passage of time, the ethnic minority population is becoming increasingly British-born and British-educated. This raises an important issue: What is the position of Britishborn offspring of immigrants? Whatever their country of origin, they differ in how they see themselves: 64 percent of Caribbean origin identify themselves as British, as do more than three-fifths of Pakistanis, Indians, and Bangladeshis, and two-fifths of Chinese. However, some offspring of immigrants have rejected integration. A coordinated terrorist attack in London on July 7, 2005, killing more than fifty people, was organized by British-born offspring of Pakistani immigrants who had been converted to jihadism at British mosques. British-born jihadists received training in Pakistan and neighboring Afghanistan. The government has greatly increased police powers to use in pursuing alleged terrorists and has justified shoot-to-kill practices even when people wrongly suspected of being terrorists are the victims.

In response to terrorist attacks, the government has shifted from promoting multiculturalism to stressing the integration of immigrant families into the British way of life. The government seeks to foster a sense of Britishness by giving lessons about Britishness to immigrants wanting British passports. However, it has found it difficult to decide what being British means. For example, does it require a knowledge of British history, knowing how to claim welfare benefits and meet obligations such as paying taxes, or being able to write in English? British-born offspring of immigrants automatically gain citizenship. Whether they choose to adopt British ways is much influenced by family and ethnic background and by the character of their local community. Almost half live in areas where ethnic minorities are in the majority.

Many immigrants and their offspring are being integrated into electoral politics, since residential concentration makes their votes important in some parliamentary constituencies. A disproportionate number of minority ethnic people have voted Labour. There are now hundreds of elected minority ethnic councillors in local government, and both the Conservative and Labour parties are promoting the nomination of minority ethnic candidates. The twenty-seven minority ethnic MPs in the Commons today come from diverse backgrounds—India, Pakistan, the West Indies, Ghana, and Aden—and include three Muslim women.[8]

The Structure of Government

 8.4 Explain the structure of British government and list the duties of Cabinet ministers and civil servants.

The term *government* is used in many different senses in Britain. People may speak of the Queen's government to emphasize enduring and nonpartisan features; they may refer to a Conservative or Labour government to emphasize partisanship, or to David Cameron's government to stress a personal feature. The departments headed by Cabinet ministers advised by senior civil servants are referred to collectively as Whitehall, after the London street in which many major government departments are located. **Downing Street**, where the prime minister works, is a short street off Whitehall. Parliament—that is, the popularly elected House of Commons and the nonelected House of Lords—is at one end of Whitehall. The term *Parliament* is often used as another way of referring to the House of Commons. Together, all of these institutions are often referred to as **Westminster**, after the district in London in which the principal offices of British government are located. With devolution, separately elected executive institutions are found in Scotland, Wales, and Northern Ireland too (see Figure 8.1).

Descriptions of a government often start with its constitution. However, Britain has never had a written constitution. The **unwritten constitution** is a jumble of Acts of Parliament, judicial pronouncements, customs, and conventions that make up the rules of the political game. The vagueness of the constitution

makes it flexible, a point that political leaders such as Margaret Thatcher and Tony Blair have exploited to increase their own power. In the words of a constitutional lawyer, J. A. G. Griffith, "The Constitution is what happens."[9]

Comparing the written U.S. Constitution and the unwritten British constitution emphasizes how few are the constraints of an unwritten constitution (see Table 8.2). Whereas amendments to the U.S. Constitution must receive the endorsement of well over half the states and members of Congress, the unwritten British constitution can be changed by a majority vote in Parliament, where the government commands a majority. The government of the day can also change it by acting in an unprecedented manner and claiming that this is a new custom. Hence, the policy relevance of the American Constitution is much greater than that of the British constitution.

The U.S. Constitution gives the Supreme Court the final power to decide what the government may or may not do. By contrast, in Britain, the final authority is Parliament. Courts do not have the power to declare an Act of Parliament unconstitutional; judges simply ask whether the executive acts within its authorized powers.

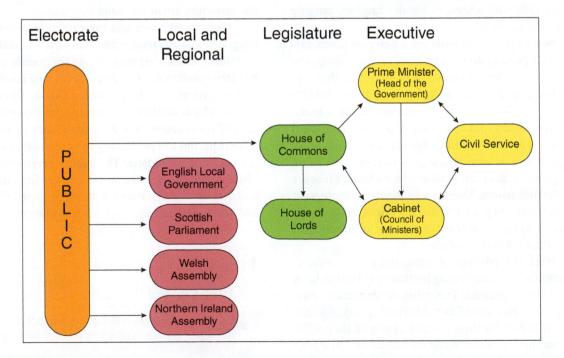

FIGURE 8.1
Popular influence must focus on Westminster
Structure of the British Government.

TABLE 8.2
British and American Constitutions
Comparing an unwritten and a written constitution.

	Britain (unwritten)	United States (written)
Origin	Medieval customs	1787 Constitutional Convention
Form	Unwritten, vague	Written, precise
Final constitutional authority	Majority in Parliament	Supreme Court
Bill of individual rights	Borrowed from Europe	Yes
Amendment	Ordinary vote in Parliament; unprecedented action by government	More than majority vote in Congress, states
Policy relevance	Low	High

Source: Adherents as defined in Encyclopedia Britannica 2009.

Many statutes delegate broad discretion to a Cabinet minister or to a public authority. Even if the courts rule that the government has improperly exercised its authority, the effect can be annulled by a subsequent Act of Parliament retroactively authorizing an action.

The Bill of Rights in the U.S. Constitution allows anyone to turn to the courts for the protection of their personal rights. Instead of giving written guarantees to citizens, the rights of British people are meant to be secured by trustworthy governors. An individual who believes his or her personal rights have been infringed must seek redress through the courts by invoking the European Convention on Human Rights and the 1998 British Human Rights Act, adopted to give the Convention the effect of law in Britain.

The **Crown** is the abstract concept that Britain uses in place of the continental European idea of the state. It combines dignified parts of the constitution, which sanctify authority by tradition and myth, with efficient parts, which carry out the work of government. Queen Elizabeth II is the ceremonial head of state; having been the monarch since 1952 makes her a symbol of tradition. The heir to the throne is her eldest son, Prince Charles. The Queen does not influence the actions of what is described as Her Majesty's Government; she is expected to respect the will of Parliament, as communicated to her by the leader of the majority in Parliament, the prime minister.

What the Prime Minister Says and Does

Leading a government is a political rather than a managerial task. The preeminence of the prime minister is ambiguous, and this is especially so in a coalition government. A politician at the apex of government is remote from what is happening on the ground. The more responsibilities attributed to the prime minister, the less time there is to devote to any one task. Like a president, a prime minister is the prisoner of the law of "first things first." The imperatives of the prime minister are as follows.

- *Winning elections:* A prime minister may be self-interested, but he or she is not self-employed. To become prime minister, a politician must first be elected leader of his or her party. Seven prime ministers since 1945—Winston Churchill, Anthony Eden, Harold Macmillan, Alec Douglas-Home, James Callaghan, John Major, and Gordon Brown—entered Downing Street during the middle of a Parliament rather than after a national election. In the eighteen elections since 1945, the prime minister of the day has ten times led the governing party to victory and eight times to defeat.

- *Campaigning through the media:* A prime minister does not need to attract publicity; it is thrust upon him or her by the curiosity of television and newspaper reporters. Media eminence is a double-edged sword, since bad news puts the prime minister in an unfavorable light. The personality of a prime minister remains relatively constant, but during a term of office, his or her popularity can fluctuate by more than 45 percentage points in public opinion polls.[10]

- *Patronage:* To remain prime minister, a politician must keep the confidence of a party, or in the case of coalition leader David Cameron, the confidence of two parties, the Liberal Democrats as well as Conservatives. The prime minister can silence potential critics by appointing them to posts as government ministers, who sit on front bench seats in the House of Commons. MPs not appointed to a post are backbenchers, some of whom ingratiate themselves with their party leader in hopes of becoming a government minister. In dispensing patronage, a prime minister can use any of four criteria: (1) personal loyalty (rewarding friends), (2) cooption (silencing critics by giving them an office so that they are committed to support the government), (3) representativeness (for example, appointing a woman or a minority ethnic MP), or (4) competence in giving direction to a government department.

- *Parliamentary performance:* The prime minister appears in the House of Commons weekly for half an hour of questions from MPs that involve the exchange of rapid-fire comments with a highly partisan audience. Unprotected by a speechwriter's script, the prime minister must show that he or she is a good advocate of government policy or suffer a reduction in confidence. Attending important debates in the Commons and occasionally mixing with MPs in its corridors and tea rooms helps the prime minister to judge the mood of the governing party.

- *Making and balancing policies:* As head of the British government, the prime minister deals with heads of other governments around the world; this makes foreign affairs a special responsibility of Downing Street. When there are conflicts between international and domestic policy priorities, the prime minister must strike a balance between pressures from the world "out there" and pressures from the domestic electorate. The prime minister also makes policy by striking a balance between ministers who want to spend more money to increase their popularity and Treasury ministers who want to cut taxes in order to boost their popularity.

While the formal powers of the office remain constant, individual prime ministers have differed in their electoral success, how they view their job, and their impact on government (see Figure 8.2). Clement Attlee, Labour prime minister from 1945 to 1951, was an unassertive spokesperson for the lowest common denominator of views within a Cabinet consisting of

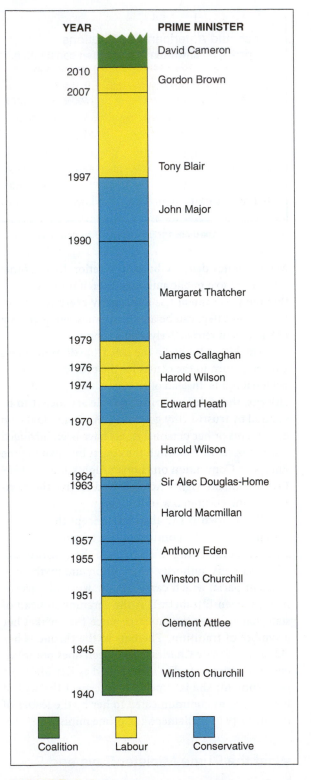

FIGURE 8.2

Long and short-term Tenures at Downing Street
Prime Ministers and Governments since 1940.

very experienced Labour politicians. When an aging Winston Churchill succeeded Attlee in 1951, he concentrated on foreign affairs and took little interest in domestic policy; the same was true of his successor, Anthony Eden. Harold Macmillan intervened strategically on a limited number of domestic and international issues while giving ministers great scope on everyday matters. Alec Douglas-Home was weak because he lacked knowledge of economic affairs, the chief problem during his short time in office. Both Harold Wilson and Edward Heath were initially committed to an activist definition of the prime minister's job. However, Wilson's major initiatives in economic policy were unsuccessful, and in 1974, the electorate rejected Heath's direction of the economy. Wilson won office again by promising to replace confrontation between management and unions with political conciliation. James Callaghan, who succeeded Wilson in 1976, also emphasized cooperation, but economic troubles and strikes continued.

Margaret Thatcher had strong views about many major policies; associates gave her the nickname "Tina" because of her motto: There Is No Alternative. Thatcher was prepared to push her views against the wishes of Cabinet colleagues and civil service advisors. In the end, her "bossiness" caused a revolt of Cabinet colleagues that helped bring about her downfall. Her former colleagues welcomed John Major as a consensus replacement. However, his conciliatory manner was often interpreted as a sign of weakness. Sniping from ministers led Major to refer to his Cabinet colleagues as "bastards."

Tony Blair won office by campaigning appealingly, and this was his priority in office too. Blair used his status as an election winner and control of ministerial patronage to silence potential critics in Cabinet. As the Treasury minister making decisions about departmental budgets, Gordon Brown used this power of the purse to build up support to secure his succession as prime minister. However, his personal style in that office lost him the support of Cabinet colleagues and of public opinion. Brown's critics were unwilling to mount an open challenge to his position, which is difficult to do under the party rules, and Brown led the government to electoral defeat.

The personalization of campaigning, encouraged by the media, has led to claims that Britain now has a presidential system of government. However, by comparison with a U.S. president, a British prime minister has less formal authority and less security of office (see Table 8.3). The president is directly elected for a fixed four-year term. A prime minister is chosen by his or her party for an indefinite term and is thus vulnerable to losing office if the party's confidence wanes. The president is the undoubted leader of the federal executive branch and can dismiss Cabinet appointees with little fear of the consequences. By contrast, senior colleagues of a prime minister are potential rivals for leadership and may be kept in Cabinet to prevent them from challenging him or her. A prime minister

TABLE 8.3
Prime Minister and President
Comparing the power of and processes for choosing a prime minister and a president.

	Britain (prime minister)	United States (president)
Media visibility	High	High
Route to top	Parliament	Governor, senator
Chosen by	Party vote	State primaries and caucuses
Elected by	Parliament	National election
Term of office	Flexible, insecure	Four years, secure
Constitution	Unitary	Federal
Domestic influence	High	So-so
International role	Semi-independent	Superpower
Checks	Informal	Congress, Supreme Court

Source: Adapted from Richard Rose, *The Prime Minister in a Shrinking World* (Boston: Polity Press, 2001), 242.

can be confident that a parliamentary majority will endorse the government's legislative proposals, whereas the president is without authority over Congress. Moreover, the prime minister is at the apex of a unitary government, with powers not limited by a federal structure or by the courts and a written constitution.[11]

In the coalition government created in 2010, the role of deputy prime minister, held by Nick Clegg, is far more important than that of an American vice president because the Conservative prime minister needs the support of Clegg's Liberal Democratic Party to have a parliamentary majority. When disagreements arise between the two parties on policy issues such as the European Union or curbing illegal or unethical media practices, David Cameron must consult with Clegg to agree on measures that both parties can support, or they must decide how to air their differences in public without breaking up the coalition government.

A coalition government gives new meaning to the doctrine of collective responsibility. Coalition leaders who have competed against each other at the previous election and expect to compete at the next election are expected to support each other in the Commons. Equally important, they are expected to persuade backbench Conservative and Liberal Democratic MPs to vote for compromises necessary to maintain the coalition, even if these compromises sometimes depart from previously endorsed party policies. However, political confrontation makes news, and journalists are always looking for signs of disagreement to publicize.

The compromises of coalition government tend to moderate the positions of both parties, and this has been congenial to the electoral strategy of David Cameron and Nick Clegg. The midterm review of their government was entitled "The Coalition: Working Together in the National Interest." However, this approach does not satisfy all their committed partisans. Since backbench Conservative and Liberal Democratic MPs are not bound by collective Cabinet responsibility, they may criticize a coalition policy when they dislike a compromise. Right-wing Conservatives complain that the government has not done enough to cut taxes and spending and to distance Britain from the European Union. Liberal Democrats who incline to the left favor boosting public spending in an effort to stimulate economic growth, and all in the party are disappointed that the coalition has not delivered electoral reform or created an elected House of Lords.

The Cabinet and Cabinet Ministers

The Cabinet consists of senior ministers appointed by the prime minister and, in the coalition government, by sharing offices among coalition partners. In Britain, ministers must be members either of the House of Commons or of the House of Lords. As MPs as well as ministers, they contribute to what Walter Bagehot described as "the close union, the nearly complete fusion of the executive and legislative powers."[12]

The Cabinet is the forum in which leading members of the governing party, many with competing departmental interests and personal ambitions, meet together to ensure agreement about major government policies. A half century ago, there were usually two Cabinet meetings a week, and when there were major disagreements among ministers, it took time to arrive at a political agreement. Tony Blair reduced the frequency of meetings to less than once a week and cut their average length to under an hour. Coalition government has revived the need for the Cabinet to meet in order to air different party views on major issues and arrive at an agreement.

Coalition policy building starts in government departments. In most departments, the minister in charge and a deputy are from different parties. Thus, before a departmental position can be established on issues where party differences are greater than department interests, the ministers must agree between themselves. If there is a disagreement between departments, it may be handled in the conventional way through Cabinet committees. However, if interdepartmental differences reflect partisan differences, competing claims of the coalition partners must be resolved by the Conservative and Liberal Democratic leaders in order to maintain the coalition's unity. The convention of Cabinet responsibility requires that all Cabinet ministers give public support to what the government does or refrain from public criticism even if they oppose a policy in private. However, ministers unwilling to share responsibility may leak their views to the press rather than resign.

Cabinet ministers are important as department heads, because most decisions of government are made within departments, and departments are responsible for overseeing all the services of government, most of which are delivered by public agencies subordinate to and distant from Whitehall (see the section on Centralized Authority and Decentralized Delivery of Policies: The members of the coalition Cabinet represent the following departments and positions:

- *External affairs:* Foreign and Commonwealth Affairs; Defense; International Development
- *Economic affairs:* Treasury; Business, Innovation and Skills; Energy and Climate Change; Transport
- *Legal and constitutional issues:* Lord Chancellor and Justice; Home Office
- *Social services:* Health; Education; Work and Pensions; Culture, Media and Sport
- *Territorial:* Environment, Food, and Rural Affairs; Communities and Local Government; Northern Ireland; Scotland; Wales
- *Managing government business:* Lord President of the Council and deputy prime minister; Leader of the House of Commons; Chief whip in the House of Commons; Paymaster General and Cabinet Office

Government departments vary greatly in their size and in the interests that they affect. The Department of Business, Innovation, and Skills has a larger staff than the Treasury. However, because of the importance of the Treasury's responsibility for taxation and public expenditure, it has more senior civil servants. The Business Department's staff has many concerns, including the competitiveness of industry, trade, employment, and university education. The Treasury concentrates on one big task: the management of the economy. The job of the chancellor of the Exchequer is more important politically, insofar as economic performance affects the governing party's electoral fate. But the head of the Department of Business, Vince Cable, is the Liberal Democratic Party's leading figure on economic affairs, and as a former Labour Party activist, his political background differs from that of the Conservative chancellor.

Cabinet ministers are willing to go along silently with their colleagues' proposals in exchange for endorsement of their own measures. However, ministers often have to compete for scarce resources, creating conflict between departments. Regardless of party, the Defense minister presses for increased spending, while Treasury ministers oppose this. Cabinet ministers resolve many differences in Cabinet committees or by informal talks between the ministers most concerned.

A minister has many roles: initiating policies, selecting among alternatives brought forward from within the department, and avoiding unpopular decisions. A minister is responsible for actions taken by thousands of civil servants nominally acting on the minister's behalf, including agencies to which Whitehall contracts responsibility for delivering public services. In addition, a minister is a department's ambassador to the world outside, including Downing Street, Parliament, the mass media, and interest groups. Not least, Cabinet ministers are individuals with ambitions to rise in politics. The typical minister is not an expert in a subject but an expert in politics. This skill has particular importance when MPs in two coalition parties must support what the minister is doing.

The Civil Service

Government could continue for months without new legislation, but it would collapse overnight if hundreds of thousands of civil servants stopped administering laws and delivering public services authorized by Acts of Parliament. The largest number of civil servants are clerical staff with little discretion; they carry out the routine activities of a large bureaucracy. Only if these duties are executed satisfactorily can ministers have the opportunity to make effective policies.

The most important group of civil servants is the smallest: the few hundred higher civil servants who advise ministers and oversee the work of their departments. Top British civil servants deny they are politicians because of the partisan connotations of the term. However, their work is political because they are involved in formulating and advising on policies. A publication seeking to recruit bright graduates for the higher civil service declares, "You will be involved from the outset in matters of major policy or resource allocation and, under the guidance of experienced administrators, encouraged to put forward your own constructive ideas and to take responsible decisions." In short, top civil servants are not apolitical; they are bipartisan, ready to work for whichever party wins an election. They are expected to be able to think like politicians in order to anticipate what their minister may want and how the opposition party and the media will react.

The relationship between ministers and higher civil servants is critical in giving direction to a government department. A busy politician does not have time to go into details; he or she wants a brief that can catch a headline or squash criticism. Ministers expect higher civil servants to be responsive to their political views and to give advice consistent with their outlook and that of the governing party or the coalition. Civil servants like working for a minister who has clear views on policy, but they dislike it when a minister grabs a headline by expressing views that will get the department into trouble later because they are impractical. In the words of a senior civil servant, "Just because ministers say to do something does not mean that we can ignore reality."[13]

The Thatcher government introduced a new phenomenon in Whitehall: a prime minister who believed civil servants were inferior to businesspeople because they did not have to "earn" their living, meaning that they did not have to make a profit. Management was made the buzzword in Whitehall. Businessmen were brought in to advise ministers and civil servants about how to get more value for money when administering policies. These changes have continued under subsequent Labour and coalition governments. Parts of government departments have been "hived off" to form separate public agencies, with their own accounts and performance targets.

When an agency's task is politically sensitive, such as the marking of national school examinations, the education minister cannot avoid blame if there are major errors in delivering examination grades to pupils. Moreover, independent agencies can show their independence by criticizing a government department. The Office of Budget Responsibility is expected to produce an independent forecast of the state of the economy before the government announces its annual budget, and its reports publicize when the Treasury is missing its targets for economic growth and cutting the deficit.

Government ministers of all parties want quick changes to satisfy their personal and partisan desire to be seen to be making an immediate impact. Tony Blair has called for civil servants to learn from companies that "reinvent themselves every year, almost month to month" and complained that "Rules of propriety are almost becoming an obstacle."[14] This clashes with the civil service view that their duty is to avoid cutting corners to justify a government policy, as Blair did in mobilizing support for the Iraq war. The politician's desire for instant impact, fed by pressures from around-the-clock media, also conflicts with the civil service awareness of how many years it can take to turn a pledge given to the media into an Act of Parliament that public officials can implement in order to have an impact on the ground. Politicians seek to resolve the conflict by bringing more outsiders into government in high-level positions, while civil servants have the option of quitting Whitehall to take jobs, often at a higher salary, in the private or not-for-profit sector.

The appointment of political advisors from outside Whitehall has caused difficulties with civil servants. The advisors are loyal to their minister and to the governing party. While experienced in dealing with personalities in the governing party and the media, they lack Whitehall experience. When departmental policies attract criticism, some ministers and even more advisors are now ready to blame civil servants rather than take responsibility themselves (Box 8.4).

Both ministers and senior civil servants have been prepared to mislead Parliament and the public. When accused in court in 1986 of telling a lie about the British government's efforts to suppress an embarrassing memoir by an ex-intelligence officer, the then-head of the civil service, Robert Armstrong, described the government's statements as a misleading impression, not a lie. It was being economical with the truth.

The Role of Parliament

In many parliaments, MPs sit in a half circle, symbolizing degrees of difference from left to right. By contrast, the House of Commons is an oblong chamber in which MPs supporting the government sit on one side and their adversaries sit opposite them on the other side. In the great majority of House of Commons divisions, MPs vote along party lines. The government's state of mind is summed up in the words of a Labour Cabinet minister who declared, "It's carrying democracy too far if you don't know the result of the vote before the meeting."[15] If a bill or a motion identified as a vote of confidence in the government is defeated, coalition government legislation provides for a 14-day period in which the vote may be reversed or a new government formed that does have the confidence of Parliament. The Opposition cannot expect to alter major government decisions because it lacks a majority of votes in the Commons. It accepts the

BOX 8.4   Friction in Whitehall

A newly elected government is full of ambitious ministers impatient to make a name for themselves and their government, and optimistic about changing the way Britain is governed. However, major changes can only occur with the assistance of civil servants in turning election pledges into legislation, organizing the administration of new policies, and training established staff in how new measures ought to be delivered.

The civil service claims to be a Rolls-Royce of government because of the intellectual quickness of its leaders, as demonstrated in the TV series *Yes, Minister*. Both Conservative and Labour ministers reject the comparison of the civil service with a smoothly running Rolls-Royce. Civil servants dislike being attacked in public and bullied in private by ministers who have far less experience of how government works than they do. One complaint is that politics has become too political; that is, ministers are happier looking to media experts for advice on policies that will win them positive headlines than to civil servants who can detail the faults and risks in notions that make good sound bites.

The friction between ministers of all parties and civil servants reflects long-term structural changes in what government can do. Civil servants lack the experience of managing costly and massive operations, such as installing computer systems in a department, or multibillion pound contracts for military equipment. Ministers whose lives are bound up in Westminster have little appreciation of the way in which their scope for choice is constrained by their predecessors' choices, a shortage of money, personnel and time, and the interdependence of what they do and what is done in the world beyond Westminster.

Sources: See Richard Rose, "Responsible Party Government in a World of Interdependence," *West European Politics*, in press, 2014; and Rachel Sylvester and Alice Thomson, "Whitehall at War," *The Times* (London), January 14–15, 2013.

frustrations that go with minority status because it hopes to win a majority at the next election.

Whitehall departments draft bills that are presented to Parliament, and few amendments to legislation are added without government approval. Laws are described as Acts of Parliament, but it would be more accurate if they were stamped "Made in Whitehall." In addition, the government rather than Parliament sets the budget for government programs. The weakness of Parliament is in marked contrast to the U.S. Congress, where each house controls its own proceedings independent of the White House. Furthermore, even though the U.S. president can ask Congress to legislate, the president cannot determine the language of a bill or the outcome of a vote there.

The first function of the Commons is to weigh political reputations. MPs continually assess their leader's ability to win or lose the next election. They also assess the performance of ministers, potential ministers, and coalition partners. MPs can force a minister to explain and defend what he or she is responsible for. If the minister's answers are unconvincing, the minister will lose political influence or even be dropped by the prime minister.

Second, backbench MPs can demand that the government do something about an issue. The party whip is expected to listen to the views of dissatisfied backbench MPs and to convey their concerns to ministers. In the corridors, dining rooms, and committees of the Commons, backbenchers can tell ministers what they think is wrong with government policy. If the government is unpopular and MPs feel threatened with losing their seats, they will be aggressive in demanding that something be done.

Publicizing issues is a third function of Parliament. MPs can use their position to call the media's attention to issues and to themselves. Television cameras are now in Parliament, and a quick-witted MP can provide the media with sound bites.

Fourth, MPs can examine how Whitehall departments administer public policies. An MP may write to a minister about a departmental responsibility affecting a constituent or interest group. MPs can request that the parliamentary commissioner for administration (also known as the ombudsman, after the Scandinavian original) investigate complaints about improper administration. Committees scrutinize policies by interviewing civil servants and

The Mother of Parliaments

Parliament has met in London by the River Thames for more than 800 years, and the clock tower of Big Ben is famous as a symbol of democracy in Canada and Australia as well as in Europe.

ministers and taking evidence from interested groups and experts. However, as a committee moves from discussing details of administration to issues of government policy, this raises a question of confidence in the government. A committee is then likely to divide along party lines, with MPs in the governing party in the majority.

A newly elected MP contemplating his or her role as one among 650 members of the House of Commons is faced with many choices.[16] An MP may decide to be a party loyalist, voting as the leadership decides without participating in deliberations about policy. The MP who wishes for more attention can make a mark by brilliance in debate, by acting as an acknowledged representative of an interest group, or in a nonpartisan way, for example, as a wit or by having a flamboyant appearance. An MP is expected to speak for constituency interests, but constituents accept that their MP will not vote against party policy if it is in conflict with local interests. The only role that an MP rarely undertakes is that of lawmaker.

To keep the published salary of MPs from rising, they have received generous expense allowances, including the upkeep of a second home, since many divide their time between London and their constituency outside London. Details of claims leaked to the press showed that MPs were claiming expenses for everything from cleaning the moat around their country house to remodeling a London flat that was quickly sold at a large profit. Hundreds of MPs paid back some expenses rather than defend their claims, and a few have been convicted for fraud in claiming expenses.

Backbench MPs perennially demand changes to make their jobs more interesting and to give themselves more influence. However, the power to make major changes rests with the government rather than the House of Commons. Whatever criticisms MPs make of Parliament while in opposition, once they are in government, party leaders have an interest in maintaining arrangements that greatly limit the power of Parliament to influence or stop what ministers do.

Among modern Parliaments, the House of Lords is unique because it was initially composed of hereditary peers. Today, hereditary peers elect ninety-two of their number to sit there; the remainder retain their title but do not have a seat in Parliament. More than five-sixths of the members of the Lords are life peers appointed for achievement in one or another public sphere. Recognition can be given because of previous service as a government minister, and a prime minister can "fast track" a few exceptional individuals into a ministerial post by making them life peers. Peers may be drawn from business, trade unions, or the not for profit sector, or may have been major financial donors to a political party. No party has a majority of seats in the House of Lords; less than one-third of peers are Conservative and one-third Labour. More than one-quarter of peers are cross-benchers who do not identify with any party.

The government often introduces relatively non-controversial legislation in the Lords, and it uses the Lords as a revising chamber to amend bills. Members of the Lords can raise party political issues or issues that cut across party lines, such as problems of disabled people or pornography. The Lords cannot veto legislation, but it can and does amend or delay the passage of some government bills. The transformation of the Lords into an assembly of people chosen by merit rather than heredity has given its members greater confidence in voting to send bills back to the House of Commons for reconsideration before they can become Acts of Parliament if the House of Commons overrides their opposition.

Although all parties accept the need for some kind of second chamber to revise legislation, there is no agreement about how it should be composed or what its powers should be. The Liberal Democrats made the popular election of the House of Lords a clause in the coalition agreement with the Conservatives. However, the party's proposals have not been adopted. The last thing the government of the day wants is a reform that gives an upper chamber that it does not control enough electoral legitimacy to challenge government legislation. Likewise, MPs do not want a second chamber to compete with their unique claim to be popularly elected.

In constitutional theory, Parliament can hold prime ministers accountable for abuses of power by the government. In practice, Parliament is an ineffective check on abuses of executive power, because the executive consists of the leaders of the majority in Parliament. When the government is under attack, MPs in the governing party tend to close ranks in its defense.

Whitehall's abuse of powers has been protected from parliamentary scrutiny by legislation on **official secrecy**. The Whitehall view is that "The need to know still dominates the right to know."[17] A Freedom of Information Act has reduced but has not ended the executive's power to keep secret the exchange of views within the Whitehall network. Information about policy deliberations in departments is often deemed to be not in the "public" interest to disclose, because it can make government appear uncertain or divided. The introduction of a coalition government is loosening these restrictions. The need to consult more widely and openly among ministers and MPs in two parties makes unauthorized leaks to the media more likely.

The Courts and Abuses of Power

There is tension between the principle that the elected government of the day should do what it thinks best and the judges' view that government should act in accord with the rule of law, whether it be an Act of Parliament or an obligation in a European treaty that the British government has endorsed. When judges hand down decisions that ministers do not like, ministers have publicly attacked them. Judges have replied by declaring that they should not be attacked for enforcing the law. If the government does not like it, judges say that it should pass a new Act of Parliament that changes the law.

The creation of a Supreme Court as the highest judicial authority in the United Kingdom in 2009 replaced the centuries-old practice of the highest court operating as a committee of the House of Lords. The Supreme Court consists of a president and eleven justices appointed by a panel of lawyers. It is the final court of appeal on points of law in cases initially heard by courts in England, Wales, and Northern Ireland. It also hears some cases from Scotland, which maintains a separate legal system with laws that are not in conflict with those elsewhere in the United Kingdom.

Although the new British Supreme Court has the same name as the highest court in the United States, its powers are much more limited. It can nullify government actions if they are deemed to exceed powers granted by an Act of Parliament, but it cannot declare an Act of Parliament unconstitutional. Parliament remains the supreme authority, deciding what government can and cannot do. Britain's membership in the EU offers judges additional criteria for deciding cases, since the United Kingdom is now bound to act in accord with EU laws and plaintiffs can challenge British government actions at the European Court of Justice. The 1998 Human Rights Act of the Westminster Parliament allows citizens to ask British courts to enforce rights conferred by the European Convention on Human Rights.

Terrorist activities challenge conventional norms about individual rights and the collective interests of the state. At times, British government forces have dealt with the violence of the Irish Republican Army and illegal armed Protestant groups by "bending" the law, including fabricating evidence to produce convictions that courts have much later overturned. However, the government is slow to admit it has erred. For example, it took thirty-eight years before it admitted that the British Army's killing of thirteen Irish demonstrators in Londonderry in 1972 was totally unjustified. In response to jihadist terrorist bombs in London in 2005, the police have been ready to use harsh measures against suspects, including shoot-to-kill responses when pursuing suspects.

Occasional abuses of executive power raise problems for civil servants who believe that their job is not only to serve the elected government of the day but also to maintain the integrity of government. This has led civil servants to leak official documents with the intention of preventing government from carrying out a policy that the leaker believes to be unethical or inadvisable. In one well-publicized case, a Ministry of Defense official leaked to the House of Commons evidence that questioned the accuracy of government statements about the conduct of the Falklands War. He was tried on the charge of violating the Official Secrets Act. The judge asked the jury to think about the issue this way: "Can it then be in the interests of the state to go against the policy of the government of the day?" The jury concluded that it could be; the official was acquitted.[18]

Government as a Network

The ship of state has only one tiller, but whenever a major policy decision comes up, many hands reach out to steer it. Policymaking involves a network of prime minister, Cabinet ministers, leading civil servants, and political advisors, all of whom share in what has been described as the "village life" of Whitehall.[19] However, the growth of government has increased specialization, so that policymakers see less and less of each other. For a given issue, a relatively small number of people are involved in the core executive group that makes a decision. However, the people in decision-making networks are a floating population; the core network is not the same for health or education as it is for agriculture or defense.

Within each Whitehall department, the permanent secretary, its highest-ranking civil servant, usually has much more knowledge of a department's problems than does a transitory Cabinet minister. Political advisors brought into a department to put the best spin on activities know less about the department's work than its career civil servants. However, they have the political advantage of knowing the minister better.

The prime minister is the single most important person in government. Since there is no written constitution, a determined prime minister can challenge the status quo and turn government to fresh ends, as Margaret Thatcher demonstrated. But to say that the prime minister makes the most important decisions invites the question, "What is an important decision?" Decisions on issues in which the prime minister is not involved, such as social security, are more numerous, require more money, and affect more lives than most decisions made in Downing Street. Scarcity of time is a major limitation on the influence of the prime minister. In the words of one Downing Street official, "It's like skating over an enormous globe of thin ice. You have to keep moving fast all the time."[20] Moreover, in a coalition government, major decisions cannot be made by a single politician because they require interparty agreement.

Political Culture and Legitimacy

8.5 Summarize the collectivist and individualist theories of government, using examples from Britain.

Political culture refers to values and beliefs about how the country ought to be governed (see Chapter 3). For example, there is a consensus that Britain ought to have a government accountable to a popularly elected parliament. This view is held not only by the major parties but also by the parties that demand independence, such as the Scottish National Party.

The values of the political culture impose limits on what government should and should not do. Regardless of party preference, the great majority of British people today believe that government ought to provide education, health services, and social security. Cultural norms about freedom of speech prevent censorship of criticism, and liberal laws about sexual relations and abortion allow freedom of choice in sexual matters. Today, the most significant limits on the scope of public policy are practical and political. For example, public expenditure on popular policies such as the health service is limited by the extent to which the economy grows and the reluctance of government to raise more money to spend on health care by increasing taxes or by imposing some charges for its use, as is done in continental European countries.

The **trusteeship theory of government** assumes that leaders ought to take the initiative in deciding what is collectively in the public interest. This theory is summarized in the epigram, "The government's job is to govern." The trusteeship doctrine is always popular with the party in government because it justifies doing whatever it wants to do. The opposition party rejects this theory while it is not in office.

The **collectivist theory of government** sees government as balancing the competing demands of sectors of society. From this perspective, parties advocating group or class interests are more authoritative than individual voters.[21] Traditional Conservatives emphasize harmony between different classes in society, each with its own responsibilities and rewards. For socialists, group politics has been about promoting trade union interests. With changes in British society, party leaders have distanced themselves from close identification with collective interests as they realize that votes are cast by individuals rather than by business firms or trade unions.

The **individualist theory of government** postulates that political parties should represent people rather than group interests. In the 1980s, Margaret Thatcher proclaimed that personal welfare should be the responsibility of each individual rather than of the state. She went so far as to declare, "There is no such thing as society." David Cameron has amended this view by emphasizing the importance of what he calls a big society, that is, institutions that are broader than the state. Liberal Democrats emphasize the freedom of individuals to live their own lifestyle free from government regulation of social behavior.

The legitimacy of government is shown by the readiness of the British people to conform to basic obligations such as paying taxes and cooperating with public officials. Dissatisfaction with government policies can stimulate popular protest, but the legitimacy of government means that protesters usually act within lawful bounds. The readiness of groups in Northern Ireland to use guns and bombs for political ends makes it the most "un-British" part of the United Kingdom.

British people make many specific criticisms of government. In reaction to changing standards of elite behavior, such as MPs making excessive claims for

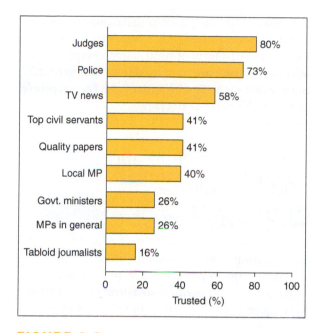

FIGURE 8.3
Most MPS Not Trusted
Source: Committee on Standards in Public Life Survey, 2010. Number of respondents: 1,900.

expenses and Cabinet ministers trashing the reputation of colleagues with whom they compete, citizens have become distrustful of many political institutions. Only one-quarter of Britons trusts MPs in general, and even fewer trust the tabloid press that claims to represent the voice of the people (Figure 8.3). The most trusted public institutions today are those that maintain order. This has been the case since the 2008 economic crisis too.[22]

The symbols of a common past, such as the monarchy, are sometimes cited as major determinants of legitimacy. However, surveys of public opinion show that the Queen has little political significance; her popularity derives from the fact that she is nonpolitical. The popularity of a monarch is a consequence, not a cause, of political legitimacy. In Northern Ireland, where the minority denies the legitimacy of British government, the Queen symbolizes divisions between British Unionists and Irish Republicans who reject the Crown. Habit and tradition appear to be the chief explanations for the persisting legitimacy of British government. A survey asking people why they support the government found that the most popular reason was "It's the best form of government we know."

Authority is not without defects. Winston Churchill made this point when he told the House of

Commons: "No one pretends that democracy is perfect or all wise. Indeed, it has been said that democracy is the worst form of government, except all those other forms that have been tried from time to time."[23] In the words of the English writer E. M. Forster, people give "two cheers for democracy."

Political Socialization and Participation

 8.6 List the five main influences on political socialization in Britain.

Socialization influences the political division between those who participate in politics and those who do not. Since political socialization is a lifetime learning process, the loyalties of voters are shaped by an accumulation of influences over many decades. Chronologically, the family's influence comes first; political attitudes learned within the family become intertwined with primary family loyalties. However, social change means that the views parents transmit to their children may not be relevant by the time their offspring have reached middle age. For example, a religious identification learned in childhood, such as Church of England or Catholic, no longer has relevance compared to distinctions between Christians and Muslims.

The electorate at any given point in time combines generations who were socialized in very different circumstances. Today, there are still some who remember World War II and were old enough to vote for or against Winston Churchill. The parents of the median voter by age were socialized when Britain effectively had a two-party system, while the median voter by age has always been offered an effective choice between three or more parties. At the next general election, the youngest voters will have been infants when Tony Blair became prime minister in 1997.

Family and Gender

A child may not know what the Labour, Conservative, or Liberal Democratic Party stands for, but if it is the party of Mom and Dad, this can be enough to create a youthful identification with a party. However, the influence of family on voting is limited, because more than one-third of adults do not know how one or both of their parents usually voted, or else their parents voted for different parties. Among those who report knowing which party both parents supported, just over half vote as their parents have. In the electorate as a whole, less than one-third know how both parents voted, and vote for the same party.[24]

As adults, men and women have the same legal right to vote and participate in politics and men and women tend to have similar political attitudes. For example, more than half of women and half of men favor capital punishment, and a substantial minority in each group oppose it. At each general election, the votes of women are divided in much the same way as the votes of men (see Table 8.5). However, socialization into gender roles leads to differences in political participation. Two-thirds of local government councillors are men; one-third are women. Women make up almost half the employees in the civil service but are concentrated in lower-level clerical jobs; women hold about one-third of the top appointments in the civil service. In 2010, a total of 143 women were elected to the House of Commons, but it remains more than three-quarters male. The initial coalition Cabinet had four women Cabinet ministers.

Education

The majority of the population was once considered fit for only a minimum level of education, but the minimum level has steadily risen. In today's electorate, the oldest voters left school at the age of fourteen and the median voter by the age of seventeen. Only a small percentage of young persons attend "public" schools, that is, fee-paying schools that are actually private. Whereas, half a century ago, Britain had few universities, today, more than two-fifths of young persons enter postsecondary institutions. However, many of the new institutions created in the past two decades lack the facilities of established research universities.

The stratification of English education used to imply that the more education a person had, the more likely a person was to be Conservative. This is no longer the case. People with a university degree or its equivalent now divide their votes between the Conservative, Labour, and Liberal Democratic parties (Table 8.5). Education is much more strongly related to active participation in politics: The more education a person has, the greater his or her chances of having a political career. More than one-third of MPs went to fee-paying private schools. University graduates make up three-quarters of the members of the House of Commons. The expansion of universities has broken the traditional dominance of Oxford and Cambridge; one-quarter of MPs went to these two institutions. The concentration of university graduates in top political jobs is a sign of a meritocracy, in which persons qualified by education have replaced an aristocracy based on birth and family.

Class

Class is relatively important in England because of the limited political salience of divisions in race, religion, or language found in the United States, Canada, or Northern Ireland. Historically, party competition has been interpreted in class terms, the Conservative Party being described as a middle-class party, and Labour as a working-class party.

Occupation has been the most commonly used indicator of class. Manual workers are usually described as the working class, and nonmanual workers as the middle class. Changes in the economy have led to a reduction in manual jobs and an increase in middle-class jobs. Today, many occupations, such as computer technician, have an indeterminate social status. When British people are asked about belonging to a class, more than half reject placing themselves in either the middle class or the working class.

The relationship between class and party has weakened. No party now wins as much as half the vote of middle-class or of skilled or unskilled manual workers (see Table 8.5). Due to the cross-class appeal of parties, less than two-fifths of voters now conform to the stereotypes of middle-class Conservatives or working-class Labour voters.

Most Britons have a mixture of middle-class and working-class attributes, and cultural values, ethnicity and tastes in consumption vary independently of occupation.[25] Thus, a host of social and economic characteristics can now influence voting. At each level of the class structure, people who belong to trade unions are more likely to vote Labour than Conservative. Housing also creates neighborhoods with political relevance. People who live in municipally built council houses occupied principally by the working class tend to vote Labour, while Conservatives do relatively well among homeowners, who are now a big majority of the electorate.

Media

The mass media's emphasis on what is happening today makes it an agency for resocializing people. Television is the primary source of political news. The law forbids selling advertising to politicians, parties, or political causes. Historically, radio and television were a monopoly of the British Broadcasting Corporation (BBC), which sought to educate its audience and was respectful of politicians. There are now many television channels and radio stations. The government of the day controls the renewal of the licenses of television companies and sets the annual fee that every viewer must pay for noncommercial BBC programs, currently about $220 a year. Broadcasters try to avoid favoring one party, because over time, control of government (and with it the power to make decisions that affect broadcasting revenue and licenses) is likely to shift between parties.

The British press is sharply divided into a few quality papers (such as *The Times, The Guardian, The Daily Telegraph, The Independent*, and *The Financial Times*), which carry news and comment at an intellectual level higher than American newspapers, and mass-circulation tabloids that concentrate on trivia and trash (such as *The Sun* and the *Daily Mirror*). *The Economist* is the best-known weekly periodical for politics and for economics; it circulates worldwide. Newspapers are now run as money-making activities rather than as the means of influencing public opinion. While most papers lean toward one party, if the party that they normally support becomes very unpopular, they tend to follow their readers and lean toward a party that is rising in popularity.

The Internet and use of new social media by a majority of Britons have opened up a wide variety of sources of information to the public. Government agencies, Parliament, and the Prime Minister's Office provide substantial details about their activities and policies. Political parties use Twitter and e-mail to communicate with targeted audiences, and MPs' hard drives overflow with communications from constituents and interest groups. Politicians are vulnerable to having opinions expressed in informal e-mails leaked to the press and embarrassing actions appear on YouTube.

In the aggressive pursuit of news and audiences, journalists are prepared to grab attention by making the government of the day look bad, and television interviewers seek celebrity by harassing MPs and ministers on the air. In pursuit of embarrassing stories, the popular press has engaged in illegal telephone tapping and has also paid bribes to the police for confidential information. These practices have led to the jailing of reporters and corrupt police and a major inquiry into their abuses chaired by Lord Leveson. His report recommended establishing a statutory body independent of the press to investigate complaints about media activities that violate privacy or harass innocent people in pursuit of headlines. The media has opposed regulation as a threat to freedom of the press.

Any party that is unpopular with the public is inclined to think it is the victim of media bias. A majority of MPs think that the media is to blame for popular cynicism about politicians and parties. However, opinion polls find that a majority of the electorate thinks that the conduct of politicians is just as much to blame for cynicism about politics as is the conduct of the media.

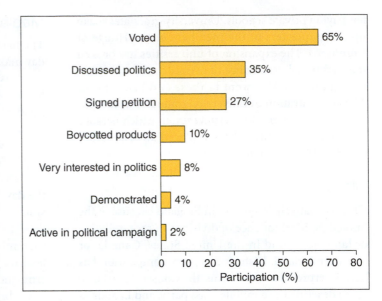

FIGURE 8.4

Participation in Politics

Most Britons are only voters.

Source: *Audit of Political Engagement 9: the 2012 Report*. London: Hansard Society, Part One. Sample survey of 1,163 respondents about their activities in the past two to three years.

Political Participation

 8.7   Contrast British citizens' participation in political versus nonpartisan activities.

An election is the one opportunity people have to influence government directly. Every citizen aged eighteen or over is eligible to vote. Local government officials register voters, and the list is revised annually, ensuring that nearly everyone eligible to vote is actually registered. Turnout at general elections has fallen from a high of 84 percent in the closely fought 1950 election to as low as 59 percent. In 2010, the closeness of the election increased turnout; it rose to 65 percent. However, only half of those who vote say they feel close to a political party.

Although there are many ways in which Britons could participate in politics, a majority of citizens are only voters and more than half say they have little or no interest in politics (Figure 8.4). Britons are much more inclined to participate in voluntary associations that they regard as nonpartisan, such as Oxfam, which is concerned with reducing world poverty. Even though questioned about activities over a time period that included a general election, barely one-third said that they had discussed politics in the past two or

three years. Just over one-quarter had signed a petition on a public issue, while one in ten reported boycotting a product because of objections to the conditions in which it was produced. The percentage describing themselves as very interested in politics was one in twelve Britons. Only 4 percent say they have participated in a demonstration in the past few years. The concentration of the media in central London means that a political demonstration there in which 10 thousand people participate will get national publicity.

Political Recruitment

 8.8   Discuss the paths to elective office and high-ranking civil service jobs in Britain.

We can view recruitment into politics deductively or inductively. The deductive approach defines the job to be done, and individuals are recruited with skills appropriate to the task; this practice is favored by management consultants. Alternatively, we can inductively examine the influences that lead people into politics and ask, "Given their skills and motives, what can such people do?" The constraints of history and institutions make the inductive approach more realistic.

The most important political roles in Britain are those of Cabinet minister, higher civil servant, partisan political advisor, and intermittent public persons analogous to Washington insiders. Each group has its own recruitment pattern. To become a Cabinet minister, an individual must first be elected to Parliament. Shortly after leaving university, ambitious politicians often become assistants to politicians and then "graduate" to lobbyist or journalist and then to parliamentary candidate for a constituency that their party normally wins. After leaving university, individuals enter the civil service by passing a highly competitive entrance examination; promotion is based on achievement and approval by seniors. Intermittently, other individuals gain access to ministers and civil servants because of the knowledge and position that they have gained by making a career outside party politics.

In all political roles, starting early on a political career is usually a precondition of success, because it takes time to build up the skills and contacts necessary to become a major political actor. Geography is a second major influence on recruitment. Ministers, higher civil servants, and other public persons spend their working lives in London. A change at Downing Street does not bring in policymakers from a different part of the country, as can happen in the White House when a president from Chicago succeeds a president from Texas. Since London is atypical of the cities and towns in which most British people live, there is a gap between the everyday lives of policymakers and the majority on whose behalf they act.

MPs and Cabinet Ministers

For a person ambitious to be a Cabinet minister, becoming an MP requires nomination as a parliamentary candidate, which is done by a constituency party committee. A candidate does not have to be resident in the constituency in which he or she is nominated. Hence, it is possible for a young person to go straight from university to a job working for an MP in the House of Commons or party headquarters, and then look around the country for nomination for a winnable seat. Unless he or she has a strong political sponsor, finding a safe seat usually takes years. Once selected for a constituency in which his or her party has a big majority, the MP can then expect to be reelected routinely for a decade or more. Population movement because of a change in constituency boundaries is a bigger threat to an MP than losing the support of voters.

Experience in the Commons does not prepare an individual for the work of a minister. An MP's chief concerns are dealing with people and talking about what government ought to do. A minister must also be able to handle paperwork, relate political generalities to specific technical problems facing his or her department, and make hard decisions when all the alternatives are unpopular.

The restriction of ministerial posts to MPs prevents a nationwide canvass for appointees. A prime minister or coalition leaders must distribute about a hundred jobs among approximately 200 MPs in the governing party who have not ruled themselves out of consideration on grounds of parliamentary inexperience, old age, political extremism, personal unreliability, or lack of interest in office. An MP has a better than even chance of a junior ministerial appointment if he or she serves three terms in Parliament. A few people who are not in Parliament but have special skills or the confidence of the prime minister can be given ministerial appointments along with a seat in the House of Lords.

A minister learns on the job. Usually, an MP is first given a junior post as a parliamentary under secretary and then promoted to minister of state before becoming a full member of the Cabinet. However, long periods of being in Opposition meant that in 2010, leading Cabinet ministers were starting at the top; they had not previously held even a junior post in government. Those inexperienced in government included David Cameron and Nick Clegg, and this was previously true too of Labour ministers such as Tony Blair and Gordon Brown. During the life of a Parliament, the average minister can expect to stay in a particular job for about two years before the prime minister undertakes a reshuffle of offices, dismissing some ministers and moving others to different departments to learn about a fresh set of issues and political interests.

The rate of ministerial turnover in Britain is one of the highest in Europe. The minister who gets a new job as the result of a reshuffle usually arrives at a department with no previous experience of its problems. Anthony Crosland, an able Labour minister, reckoned: "It takes you six months to get your head properly above water, a year to get the general drift of most of the field, and two years really to master the whole of a department."[26]

Higher Civil Servants

Whereas MPs come and go from ministerial office, civil servants can be in Whitehall for the whole of their working lives. Higher civil servants are recruited without specific professional qualifications or training. They are meant to be the "best and the brightest"—a requirement that has traditionally meant getting a prestigious degree in history, literature, or languages. The Civil Service Commission tests candidates for their ability to summarize lengthy prose papers, to fit specific facts to government regulations, to draw inferences from a simple table of social statistics, and to perform well in group discussions about problems of government.

Because bright civil service entrants lack specialized skills and need decades to reach the highest posts, socialization by senior civil servants is especially important. The process makes for continuity over half a century or more, since the head of the civil service usually started as a young official under a head who had himself entered the civil service many decades before.

In the course of a career, civil servants become specialists in the difficult task of managing ministers and government business. As the television series *Yes, Minister* shows, they are adept at saying "yes" to a Cabinet minister when they mean "perhaps" and saying "up to a point" when they really mean "no." Increasingly, ministers have tended to discourage civil servants from pointing out obstacles in the way of what government wants to do; they seek people offering "can do" advice from outside the civil service.

Political Advisors

Most advisors are partisans whose job is to mobilize political support for the Cabinet minister for whom they work. They are recruited on the basis of who they know in government. Because their background is in party politics and the media, such advisors bring to Whitehall skills that civil servants often lack and that ministers value. But because they have no prior experience of the civil service, they are often unaware of its conventions and legal obligations. Some tricks used by political appointees to put a desirable spin on what the government is doing can backfire, causing public controversy and even dismissal.

Experts in a given subject area, such as environmental pollution or education, can be appointed as political advisors on the basis of what they know. Even if inexperienced in the ways of Whitehall, they can contribute specialist knowledge that is often lacking in government departments, and they can be supporters of the governing party too.

Most heads of institutions such as universities, banks, churches, and trade unions do not think of themselves as politicians and have not stood for public office. They are principally concerned with their own field of work and profession. However, when government action impinges on their work, they become involved in politics, offering ministers advice and criticism of policies affecting them.

Selective Recruitment

Nothing could be more selective than an election that results in one person becoming prime minister of a country and less than two dozen people becoming ministers in charge of government departments. Yet nothing is more representative, because an election is the one occasion when every adult can participate in politics with equal effect.

Traditionally, political leaders had high social status and wealth before gaining political office. Because politics is today a full-time occupation, aristocrats, business people, or trade union leaders can no longer expect to translate their high standing in other fields into an important political position. As careers become more specialized, professional politicians become increasingly distant from other spheres of British life.

The greater the scope of activities defined as political, the greater the number of people actively involved in government. Government influence has forced company directors, television executives, and university heads to become involved in discussions of public policy. Leadership in organizations outside Whitehall gives such individuals freedom to act independently of government. However, the interdependence of public and private institutions is now so great that sooner or later they become intermittent public persons.

Organizing Group Interests

8.9 Describe the relationships, including privileged access, between various interest groups and Britain's governing parties.

Civil society institutions regularly discuss specific policies with public officials in expectation that this will put pressure on government to do what they argue is in the public interest as well as their own group's interest. Their scope varies enormously, from the narrow concerns of an association for the blind to the encompassing economic interests of business organizations and trade unions. Some groups have material objectives, whereas others advocate causes such as reducing violence on television.

The heads of Britain's biggest businesses usually have direct contacts with Whitehall and with ministers, whatever their party, because of the importance of their activities for the British economy and its place in the international economy. For example, the dividends of BP (British Petroleum) have been a major source of income for British investors; most of the oil it drills is outside the United Kingdom. And when things went wrong in the Gulf of Mexico in 2010, it created diplomatic problems. The City of London claims privileged access because of the substantial impact financial services have on the British economy, not all of which are positive, as the 2008 economic crisis demonstrated. The construction industry has access to government because home building is important for the national economy and Whitehall's tight control over land use influences where houses can be built. The Confederation of British Industries has members drawn from all sizes and kinds of businesses. The Institute of Directors represents individuals directing large and small businesses.

The members of the Trades Union Congress (TUC) are unions that represent many different types of workers, some white collar and some blue collar. Most member unions of the TUC are affiliated with the Labour Party, and some leading trade unionists have been Communists or Maoists. None is a supporter of the Conservative or Liberal Democratic parties. Changes in employment patterns have eroded union membership. Today, less than one-quarter of the labor force belongs to a trade union. Over the years, the membership of trade unions has shifted from manual workers in such industries as coal and railways to white-collar workers such as teachers and health service employees. Less than one in six private sector workers belongs to a trade union. By contrast, more than half of public sector workers are union members.

Britain has many voluntary and charitable associations, from clubs for supporters of a football team to the Automobile Association. It is also home to a number of internationally active nongovernmental organizations, such as Amnesty International, concerned with political prisoners worldwide. The latter organizations not only try to bring pressure on Westminster but also on organizations such as the World Bank and on repressive governments around the world.

Unlike political parties, interest groups do not seek influence by contesting elections; they want to influence policies regardless of which party controls government. Nonetheless, there are ties between interest groups and political parties. Trade unions have been institutionally part of the Labour Party since its foundation in 1900 and are the major source of party funds. Business is not formally linked to the Conservative Party, but the party's commitment to private enterprise is congenial to it, and businessmen are substantial donors. Notwithstanding common interests, both trade unions and business groups demonstrate their autonomy by criticizing their partisan ally if it acts against their interests.

Party politicians seek to distance themselves from interest groups. Conservatives know that they can only win an election by gaining the votes of ordinary citizens as well as prosperous businesspeople. Tony Blair saw the union link as an electoral handicap because union members are a minority of the public, and even though they tend to vote Labour, a significant minority do not. He sought to make the Labour government appear friendly to business and reaped large cash donations from very wealthy businessmen. However, this led union leaders to attack his government as unsympathetic, and a few small unions left the Labour Party.

To lobby successfully, interest groups must identify the officials most important in making public policy. When asked to rank the most influential offices and institutions, interest group officials named the prime minister first by a long distance; Cabinet ministers came second, the media third, and senior civil servants fourth. Less than 1 percent thought MPs outside the ministerial ranks were of primary importance.[27] However, interest groups do not expect to spend a great deal of time in Downing Street. Their contacts are usually with officials in government departments concerned with issues of little public or partisan concern but of immediate interest to the group.

What Interest Groups Want

Most interest groups pursue three major goals: the sympathetic administration of established policies, gaining information about possible changes in government policies, and influencing the making and implementation of policies. Whitehall departments are ready to consult with groups that can provide information about what is happening outside government, cooperate in implementing policies, and support government initiatives. As long as the needs of Whitehall and interest groups are complementary, they can bargain as professionals sharing common concerns and negotiate an agreement.

The more committed members are to an interest group's goals, the more confidently leaders can speak for a united membership. Changes in the economy, in class structure, and in the lifestyles of generations have resulted in a decline in the "dense" social capital networks of coal-mining villages and textile mill towns. Today's consumers are difficult to organize; for example, drivers of Ford cars are a category rather than a social group. Individuals have a multiplicity of identities that can be in conflict—for example, as workers desiring higher wages and as consumers wanting lower prices. The spread of mass consumption and decline in trade union membership has altered the balance between these priorities. As a trade union leader has recognized, "Our members are consumers too."[28]

Group members who care about an issue can disagree about what their leaders ought to do. Even if an interest group is internally united, its demands may be counteracted by opposing demands from other groups. In economic policy, ministers can play off producers against consumers or business against unions to increase their scope for choice and present their policies as "something for everybody" compromises.

The more a group's values are consistent with the cultural norms of society as a whole, the easier it is to equate its interest with the public interest. **Insider interest groups** representing children or mothers usually have values in harmony with every party. Insiders advance their case in quiet negotiations with Whitehall departments. Their demands tend to be restricted to what is politically possible in the short term, given the values and commitments of the government of the day.[29] Green interest groups face the dilemma of campaigning for fundamental environmental changes that are currently out of bounds politically, or they can become insiders working to achieve incremental policy changes. **Outsider interest groups** are unable to get far in Whitehall when their demands are inconsistent with the party in power. They often campaign through media-oriented activities. To television viewers, their

demonstrations appear as evidence of their importance; in fact, they are often signs of a lack of insider political influence.

Keeping Interest Groups at a Distance

Whitehall civil servants find it administratively convenient to deal with united interest groups that can implement agreements. For a generation after World War II, ministers endorsed the corporatist philosophy of bringing together representatives of business, trade unions, and government in tripartite institutions to discuss such controversial issues as inflation and unemployment. Corporatist bargaining assumed a consensus on political priorities and that each group's leaders could deliver the cooperation of those whom they claimed to represent. In practice, neither Labour nor Conservative governments found it easy to reach a consensus, and interest group leaders were often unable to deliver their nominal followers. By 1979, unemployment and inflation were both out of control.

The Thatcher administration demonstrated that a government firmly committed to distinctive values can ignore group demands and lay down its own pattern of policy. It did so by dealing at arm's length with both trade unions and business groups. Instead of consulting them, it practiced state distancing; the government kept out of such market activities as wage bargaining, price setting, and investment.

A state-distancing strategy emphasizes the use of legislation to achieve goals, since no interest group can defy an Act of Parliament. Laws have reduced the capacity of trade unions to frustrate government policies through industrial action by requiring a vote of members to authorize a strike as legal. The sale of state-owned industries has removed government from immediate responsibility for the operation of major industries. Labour Chancellor Gordon Brown gave the Bank of England responsibility for monetary policy. The 2008 economic crisis was met by the government taking ownership of very troubled banks, but its goal is to privatize them when they recover.

State distancing places less reliance on negotiations with interest groups and more on the authority of government. Business and labor are free to carry on as they like—but only within the pattern imposed by government legislation and policy. Most unions and some business leaders do not like being "outside the loop" when government makes decisions.

Education and health service interest groups like it even less, because they depend on public funds for their employment.

Party System and Electoral Choice

8.10 Discuss the emergence of the multiparty system and how this is limited by the first-past-the-post electoral system.

British government is party government. The candidates on the ballot in each parliamentary constituency are chosen by party members, and the party members also have a vote on the choice of party leader. The prime minister is not popularly elected but gains office by being the leader of the party with the most MPs. Nonentities who belong to major parties find it easier to get elected to Parliament than well-known people who choose to run as independents.

A Multiplicity of Choices

An election offers a voter a very simple choice between candidates competing to represent one of the 650 constituencies into which the House of Commons is divided. Within each constituency, the winner is the candidate who is **first past the post** with a plurality of votes, even if this is less than half the total vote. In the 2010 election, the winner in two-thirds of seats took less than half the vote and, in one English constituency, received only 29 percent of the vote. The winner nationally is the party gaining the most MPs. In 1951 and in February 1974, the party winning the most votes nationally did not win the most seats; the runner-up party in the popular vote formed the government.

Between 1945 and 1970, Britain had a two-party system; the Conservative and Labour parties together took an average of 91 percent of the popular vote and, in 1951, took 97 percent (see Figure 8.5). The Liberals had difficulty fielding candidates in a majority of constituencies and even more difficulty in winning votes and seats. A **multiparty system** emerged in the elections of 1974. The Liberals won nearly one-fifth of the vote, and Nationalists did well in Scotland, Wales, and Northern Ireland. The combined Conservative and Labour share of the vote dropped to 75 percent. The Liberal Democrats and Nationalist parties have maintained their strength. In recognition of this, the 2010 televised election debates gave equal attention to

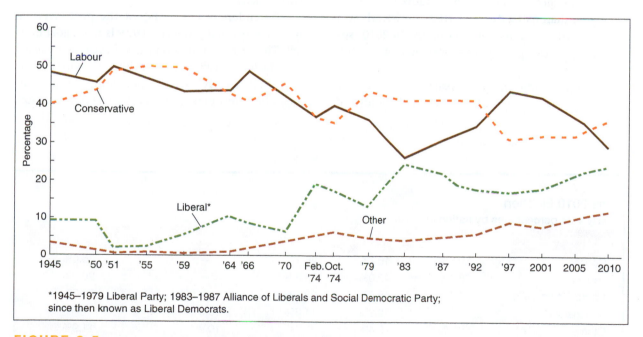

*1945–1979 Liberal Party; 1983–1987 Alliance of Liberals and Social Democratic Party; since then known as Liberal Democrats.

FIGURE 8.5

Ups and Downs of Electoral Fortunes of Parties
Votes Cast in General Elections since 1945.

Labour Prime Minister Gordon Brown, Conservative leader David Cameron, and Liberal Democratic leader Nicholas Clegg.

- The number of parties competing successfully for votes varies between the nations of the United Kingdom. In England, three parties—Labour, Conservatives, and Liberal Democrats—compete, and in 2010, the anti-EU United Kingdom Independence Party (UKIP) contested almost all seats too. In Scotland and Wales, there are normally four parties, including the Scottish National and Plaid Cymru (Welsh Nationalist) parties, respectively. In Northern Ireland, at least five parties contest seats, two representing Unionist and Protestant voters, two representing Irish Republican and Catholic voters, and the weakest a cross-religious Alliance of voters.

- The two largest parties do not monopolize votes. In the 2010 election, together they won only 65 percent of the popular vote (see Table 8.4). No party has won half the popular vote since 1935.

- The two largest parties in the House of Commons are often not the two largest parties at the constituency level. In more than one-quarter of constituencies, one or both of the two front-running parties were neither Labour nor Conservative in 2010.

- More than half a dozen parties consistently win seats in the House of Commons. In 2010, so-called "third" parties won more than one-eighth of the seats.

- Significant shifts in voting usually do not involve individuals moving between the Labour and Conservative parties but rather in and out of the ranks of abstainers or between the Liberal Democrats and the two largest parties. Nationalist parties in Scotland, Wales, and Northern Ireland win seats because they concentrate their candidates in one part of the United Kingdom.

The distribution of seats in the House of Commons is different from the distribution of the share of votes because of how votes are unevenly distributed across constituencies. In 2010, the Conservative Party won 47 percent of MPs with 36 percent of the vote, and the Labour Party won 40 percent of the seats with 29 percent of the popular vote (see Table 8.5 and Figure 8.6). The Liberal Democrats gained just under 9 percent of MPs with 23 percent of the popular vote.

British members of the European Parliament (MEPs) are elected by proportional representation, and this produces very different results. In 2009, the United Kingdom Independence Party came second in the vote to the front-running Conservatives; Labour came third; and the anti-immigrant British National Party and the Green Party also elected MEPs. However, when the choice in the following year was about who governs Britain, neither UKIP nor the British National Party won a single seat at Westminster.

Defenders of the first-past-the-post electoral system argue that proportionality is not a goal in itself. The current system is justified because it usually manufactures an absolute majority of seats for a single party, thus clearly fixing responsibility for government. In countries using proportional representation,

---

TABLE 8.4
The 2010 Election
Party vote percentages by nation in 2010.

	England	Scotland	Wales	Northern Ireland	United Kingdom
Conservative	39.5%	16.7%	26.1%	—	36.0%
Labour	28.1%	42.0%	36.3%	—	29.0%
Liberal Democratic	24.2%	18.9%	20.1%	—	23.0%
Nationalists*	—	19.9%	11.3%	89.3%	—
Others	8.2%	2.4%	6.2%	10.8%	11.9%

*Scottish National Party, Plaid Cymru (Wales), and in Northern Ireland the Alliance party, the Democratic Union and Ulster Unionist parties, and pro–Irish Republic Sinn Fein and the Social Democratic and Labour Party.

Source: General Election 2010: Preliminary Analysis. House of Commons Library Research Paper 10/36.

TABLE 8.5
Social Differences in Voting
In a multiparty system, no party has majority support in any social group.

	Conservative	Labour	Liberal Democrat	Other
Gender				
Women	38%	28%	22%	12%
Men	36%	31%	26%	8%
Age				
18–24	30%	31%	30%	9%
25–54	34%	30%	27%	9%
55–64	38%	28%	23%	12%
65 and over	44%	31%	16%	9%
Social Class				
Middle, professional	44%	23%	27%	7%
Lower middle	40%	28%	24%	9%
Skilled manual	37%	29%	22%	12%
Unskilled manual	31%	40%	17%	12%

Source: Ipsos MORI, *How Britain Voted in 2010* (**www.ipsos-mori.com/researchpublications/researcharchive/poll.aspx?oltemld=2613**); analysis of all who said they were absolutely certain to Vote or had already voted, interviewed March 5 to May 19, 2010 (*n* = 5,927).

coalition or minority governments are the norm. When a coalition is necessary, a party finishing third in the popular vote usually determines who governs by joining in a formal or informal coalition with one or the other of the two largest parties.

The strongest advocates of proportional representation are the Liberal Democrats, on the grounds that it is fair in matching a party's share of the popular vote to its share of MPs. In a proportional representation system, the Liberal Democrats would expect to win more than double the number of seats that they take in a first-past-the-post ballot. As the price of coalition, the Conservatives agreed to a referendum on a change to the alternative vote electoral system that asks voters to indicate their order of preference between candidates. If the front-running candidate lacks an absolute majority, the candidates finishing lowest in the constituency are progressively eliminated and the second preferences of their voters redistributed until one candidate gets a majority. A national referendum in 2011 rejected this change: 68 percent endorsed the first-past-the-post system and only 32 percent endorsed the alternative vote.

Elections that do not affect the composition of the Westminster Parliament make use of a variety of electoral systems.[30] The mayor of Greater London is elected by the alternative vote, and all members of the Northern Ireland Assembly are elected by proportional representation. The Scottish Parliament and Welsh Assembly use a mixed electoral system: Some representatives are elected by

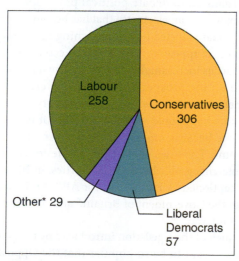

FIGURE 8.6
Seats in the House of Commons
The government moves to the right in 2010.

*Includes six Scottish Nationalists, three Welsh Plaid Cymru, eight Northern Ireland Democratic Unionists, five Sinn Fein, three Northern Ireland Social Democratic and Labour, one Green, and three others.

Source: Colin Rallings and Michael Thrasher, *British Electoral Facts 1832–2012* (London: Biteback Publishing, 2012), 60.

the first-past-the-post method and some by proportional representation.

Political parties are often referred to as "machines," but this description is very misleading, since parties cannot mechanically manufacture votes. Nor can a political party be commanded like an army. Parties are like universities; they are inherently decentralized, and people belong to them for a variety of motives. Party officials have to work hard to keep together three different parts of the party: those who vote for it, the minority of members active in its constituency associations, and the party in Parliament. If the party has a majority in Parliament, there is a fourth group: the party in government. Whether the party leader is the prime minister or the leader of the Opposition, he or she must maintain the confidence of all parts of the party or risk ejection as leader.[31]

Each party has an annual conference at which members debate policy and a headquarters that provides year-round services to party leaders and to constituency parties. Constituency parties are significant because each selects its own parliamentary candidate. Under Tony Blair, the Labour Party introduced more central direction in choosing candidates; doing so was justified on the grounds of securing more female MPs, and this has happened. Under David Cameron, the Conservatives have taken a similar initiative and increased the number of their women and minority ethnic MPs.

The Liberal Democrats have built up the party by winning council seats at local government elections and targeting House of Commons seats where the party is strong locally. This strategy has paid off; it has almost trebled its number of MPs from twenty in 1992 to fifty-seven in 2010, while its share of the popular vote has scarcely altered.

Party Appeals

The class-based terminology of "left" and "right" is common in ideological descriptions of parties, but it is rejected by the great majority of British voters. When asked to place themselves on a left/right scale, the median voter chooses the central position, and only a tenth place themselves on the far left or far right. Consequently, parties that veer toward either extreme risk losing votes. Tony Blair won elections for Labour because he avoided left-wing rhetoric and policies, and David Cameron led the Conservatives

to victory by moving the party toward the center of British politics.

When public opinion is examined across a variety of issues, such as inflation, protecting the environment, spending money on the health service, and trade union legislation, a majority of Conservative, Labour, and Liberal Democratic voters tend to agree. Big differences in contemporary British politics often cut across party lines.

The party preferences of the British electorate cannot be explained by social differences; all classes, age groups, and gender categories divide their support among four different parties (Table 8.5). While it is the case that the Conservatives come first among middle-class voters, in 2010 the party secured well under half the vote of this group. Labour came first among unskilled manual workers, but its poor performance in 2010 meant that the Conservatives secured more votes among skilled manual workers. There is a tendency for older Britons to favor the Conservative party, but it is not matched by younger voters favoring Labour. The under-25 age group divided almost equally between all three major parties at the 2010 election. Men and women voted much the same too.

Any attempt to impute a coherent ideology to a political party is doomed to failure, because they are not organized to debate political philosophy but to win votes from an electorate that has become skeptical of politicians. Instead of campaigning in ideological terms or by appealing to collectivist economic interests, parties increasingly stress consensual goals, such as promoting prosperity and fighting crime. They compete in terms of which party or party leader can best do what people want, or whether it is time for a change because one party has been in office for a long time. The titles of election manifestos are virtually interchangeable between the parties. In 2010, they were captioned "A Future Fair for All," "An Invitation to Join the Government of Britain," and "Change That Works for You."[32]

Much of the legislation introduced by the government is meant to be so popular that the Opposition dare not vote against the bill's principle. For every government bill that the Opposition votes against on principle in the House of Commons, up to three are adopted with interparty agreement.[33] MPs who rebel against their party whip are usually so extreme and insufficient in number that government bills are not threatened with defeat.

Centralized Authority and Decentralized Delivery of Policies

8.11 Describe the "Whitehall obstacle race."

8.12 Discuss the roles of the central and local British governments and public and privatized institutions in delivering services.

The United Kingdom is a unitary state with political authority centralized in Westminster. Decisions taken there are binding on all types of public agencies, including local government. The powers of elected bodies in Scotland, Wales, and Northern Ireland are those delegated by the authority of an Act of Parliament at Westminster, and it retains the power to alter them. In addition, Whitehall has centralized control of taxation and public expenditure to a degree unusual among other unitary states in Europe.

Centralization is justified as the best way to achieve **territorial justice**—that is, public services being at the same standard throughout the United Kingdom. For example, schools in inner cities and rural areas should have the same resources as schools in prosperous suburbs. This can be achieved only if tax revenues collected by central government are redistributed from better-off to poorer parts of the country. In addition, ministers emphasize that they are accountable to a national electorate of tens of millions of people, whereas local councillors are only accountable to those who vote in their ward. Instead of small being beautiful, a big, nationwide electorate is assumed to be better. The statement "Local councillors are not necessarily political animals; we could manage without them" was made by a left-wing law professor.[34]

There are many reasons why ministers do not want to be in charge of delivering the services that their department initially introduced. Ministers may wish to avoid charges of political interference, allow for flexibility in the market, lend an aura of impartiality to quasi-judicial activities, allow qualified professionals to regulate technical matters, or remove controversial activities from Whitehall. The prime minister prefers to focus upon the glamorous "high" politics of foreign affairs and economic management. However, since "low-level" services remain important to most voters' lives, ministers are under pressure to do something—or at least say something—in response to media demands for action, for example, when there is evidence of declining standards in schools or a flood following torrential rains.

For ordinary individuals, the actions of government are most evident when services are delivered locally: at a school, at a doctor's office, or rubbish collection at their doorstep. However, Whitehall departments usually do not deliver policies themselves. Most are delivered by agencies outside Whitehall, and five-sixths of public employees work for non-Whitehall agencies.[35] Making and delivering public policies thus involves intragovernmental politics.

Whitehall

A minister anxious to gain attention by introducing a popular bill in Parliament cannot do so on his or her own. Criticism by the opposition party is of less concern than attacks from MPs within the government's ranks. In a single-party government, approval of important measures may be needed from the prime minister, and from Cabinet colleagues on matters of lesser importance. The coalition government adds a new dimension: There are committees representing both the Conservative and Liberal Democrat leaders to check that legislation is acceptable to both parties in government.

Running the Whitehall obstacle race is the first step in intragovernmental politics. Most new policies must take into account their likely effects on existing policies that are likely to be administered by several different departments and affect non-Whitehall public agencies. Before a bill can be put to Parliament, the Cabinet minister sponsoring it must negotiate an agreement with ministers in other departments about how the principles of a new measure affect existing programs and party policy and how it will be implemented. Negotiations are time-consuming. Often a department will begin work on a new initiative under one minister and complete it under another or even under a different party in power. For example, the debate about whether to make London's biggest airport, Heathrow, bigger still or add runways at airports farther from populous suburbs has been running for more than two

Whitehall: A Long Street Full of Obstacles
Whitehall starts at Admiral Nelson's statute in Trafalgar Square and extends to the tower of Parliament's Big Ben, seen in the distance.

decades. It will take another decade to add a new runway, and longer still to build a new airport.

Because of Treasury control of public expenditure, before a bill can be put to Parliament, the Treasury must authorize the additional public money it requires. Even when the economy is booming, the Treasury seeks to guard against spending commitments that threaten to increase taxation, and when the economy is in trouble, more spending threatens an increased budget deficit. In the words of a veteran Treasury official, "the Treasury stands for reality."[36]

Devolution to Elected Officials

Local government councillors are elected, but within England, local government is subordinate to central government. Westminster has the power to write or rewrite the laws that determine what locally elected governments do and spend, and to abolish local authorities and create new units of government with different boundaries. Both Conservative and

Labour governments have used these powers to the full. Changes in local government boundaries reflect a never-ending search to find a balance between efficiency (assumed to correlate with fewer councils delivering services to more people spread over a wider geographical area) and responsiveness (assumed to require more councils, each with a smaller territory and fewer people). The government sponsoring the change is also well aware of the partisan effects of local government reorganization.

Local council elections are fought on party lines. In the days of the two-party system, many cities were solidly Labour for a generation or more, while leafy suburbs and agricultural counties were overwhelmingly Conservative. The Liberal Democrats now win many seats in local elections and, when no party has a majority, introduce coalition government into town halls. Most local councillors are part-time politicians, paid from a few thousand pounds to £20,000 a year for time spent on council business. London is exceptional in having a directly elected mayor; Conservative and

Labour mayors have used the office as a platform to promote London and their personal views. However, Whitehall refuses to give London the taxing and spending powers that American local government enjoys.[37]

Local government is usually divided into two tiers of county and district councils, each with responsibility for some local services. The proliferation of public–private initiatives and special purpose agencies has reduced the services for which local government is exclusively responsible. Today, there is a jumble of more or less local institutions delivering such public services as education, police protection, garbage collection, housing, and cemeteries. Collectively, local institutions account for about a fifth of total public expenditure.

Grants of money from central government are the largest source of local government revenue. There is no local income tax or sales tax, since the central government does not want to give local authorities the degree of fiscal independence that American local government has. There is a property tax on houses but not land; central government has set limits on its use. The Thatcher government introduced a poll tax on local residents in place of a property tax; it produced a political backlash, and the traditional property tax was reinstated.[38] The funding of local government services remains a contentious issue: Cabinet ministers do not want to be generous in funding local services for which councillors rather than they may claim visible credit.

Education illustrates the reluctance of central government to trust local government. It is authorized by an Act of Parliament, principally financed by central government, and two Cabinet ministers share overall responsibility for education. However, local government has managed schools. Dissatisfaction with local government has led Labour and Conservative governments to create city academies, secondary schools independent of local government but still dependent on Whitehall for funding. The Whitehall department responsible for schools employs only 1 percent of the people working in education. Success depends on actions taken by teachers in the classroom. Government policies designed to help specific groups of the population are even more fragmented (Box 8.5).

Nonelected Institutions

Executive agencies delivering many major public services are headed by appointed rather than elected officials. The biggest, the National Health Service (NHS), is not one organization but a multiplicity of separate institutions with separate budgets, such as hospitals and doctors' offices. Access to the National Health Service is free of charge to every citizen, but health care is not costless. Public money is allocated to hospitals and to doctors and dentists who must work within guidelines and targets established centrally. Because central

---

BOX 8.5 Young People must Integrate Policies that Institutions Divide

At election time, parties make special appeals to young people. But in government, the responsibility for providing public services for young people is divided among many departments. Schools are usually the responsibility of local government. Universities are independent of government; however, they are subject to central government financial pressures and regulations. Examination boards are separately organized. After-school sports and cultural activities are the responsibility of a different ministry.

On leaving school, a young person typically seeks a job, but economic conditions that are the responsibility of the Treasury influence whether jobs are available. Training youth in blue-collar or white-collar skills is affected by what employers are willing to provide.

Employers complain that too many young people lack a good basic and practical education, while government complains that employers are unwilling to spend enough money on training. International comparisons show British vocational education tends to be below continental European standards.

Government policies fail to reach one-sixth of British youths classified as NEETS, that is, Not in Education, Employment, or Training. For some youths, not immediately pursuing a career can be a temporary phenomenon before settling down. However, this group is also most at risk of engaging in behavior that leads to arrest, a police record, or even a jail sentence.

Source: See "NEETS Characteristics, Costs and Policy Responses in Europe" (Dublin: European Foundation, 2012).

government picks up the bill, the Treasury, as the monopoly purchaser, regularly seeks to squeeze the cost of providing increasingly expensive health care.

British government sponsors more than a thousand **quasi-autonomous nongovernmental organizations (quangos)**. All are created by an Act of Parliament or by an executive decision; their heads are appointed by a Cabinet minister, and public money can be appropriated to finance their activities. When things go wrong, ministers get the blame. For example, the UK Border Agency, responsible for processing hundreds of thousands of visa and immigration files, got so far behind in this work and made so many mistakes that in 2013, the Home Secretary decided it would be better to abolish it and return the work to the Home Office rather than have to answer for an agency that it did not directly control.

Advisory committees provide the expertise of individuals and organizations involved in programs for which Whitehall departments are responsible. Civil servants responsible for agricultural policies can turn to advisory committees for detailed information about farming practices of which they lack firsthand knowledge. Because advisory committees have no executive powers, they usually cost very little to run. Representatives of interest groups are glad to serve on such committees because this gives them privileged access to Whitehall and an opportunity to influence policies in which they are directly interested.

Administrative tribunals are quasi-judicial bodies that make expert judgments in such fields as medical negligence or handle a large number of small claims, such as disputes about whether the rent set for a rent-controlled flat is fair. Ministers may use tribunals to avoid involvement in politically controversial issues, such as decisions about deporting immigrants. Tribunals normally work much more quickly and cheaply than the courts. However, the quasi-judicial role of tribunals has created a demand for independent auditing of their procedures to ensure that they are fair to all sides. The task of supervising some seventy different types of tribunals is in the hands of a quango, the Council on Tribunals.

Turning to the Market

After winning the 1945 election, the socialist leaders of the Labour government acted on their belief that government planning and ownership was better for promoting economic growth and full employment than a market that had delivered depression in the 1930s. It nationalized many basic industries, such as electricity, gas, coal, the railways, and airlines. Some state-owned industries consistently made money, while others consistently lost money and required big state subsidies. Government ownership politicized wage negotiations and investment decisions, to the embarrassment of both Labour and Conservative governments.

The Thatcher government initiated the privatization of many government-owned industries and some administrative agencies. Selling council houses to tenants at prices well below their market value was popular with tenants. Thatcher sold off British Petroleum, British Airways, Jaguar, British Telecom, Rolls Royce, British Steel, Rover, and a host of other firms. Industries needing large public subsidies to maintain public services, such as the railways, have continued to receive subsidies after privatization.

Privatization has been justified on grounds of economic efficiency (the market is better than civil servants in determining investment, production, and prices); political ideology (the power of government is reduced); service (private enterprise is more consumer-oriented than civil servants); and short-term financial gain (the sale of public assets can provide billions in revenue for government). Although the Labour Party initially opposed privatization, it quickly realized that it would be electorally disastrous to take back privatized council houses and shares that people had bought at bargain prices.

Since many privatized industries affect the public interest, new regulatory agencies monitor telephones, gas, electricity, broadcasting, and water. Where there is a substantial element of monopoly in an industry, the government regulatory agency seeks to promote competition and has the power to fix price increases at a lower rate than inflation in order to encourage increased efficiency. Although the government no longer owns an industry, when things go wrong, ministers cannot ignore what has happened. An extreme example of government intervention occurred when several fatal accidents occurred on railway track maintained by a privatized transport company. It was taken back into public ownership.

The economic crisis of 2008 produced revelations of illegal activities and gross negligence in the financial sector involving hundreds of millions or billions of pounds. Most revelations result in cash fines of up to hundreds of millions of pounds on banks and investment companies, and in a few cases, criminal charges have led to malefactors going to jail. Some revelations have come from the United States, where federal agencies have fined British-owned companies for practices carried out on both sides of the Atlantic. The showing up of the weakness of existing regulatory agencies has led to demands for British government to act to restrain financial malpractice and fears that European Union restraints may preempt Britain's authority, to the detriment of financial interests in the City of London.

From Trust to Contract

Historically, the British civil service has relied on trust in delivering policies. British civil servants are much less rule-bound than their German counterparts and less threatened with being dragged into court than are American officials. Traditionally, intragovernmental relations between Whitehall departments and representatives of local authorities and other public agencies arrived at consensual understandings on the basis of trust. However, the Thatcher government preferred to contract out public services to new public agencies and private sector companies controlled by laws and the supply of finance. The Labour government intensified the use of targets to be met by agencies receiving public money. The coalition government endorses the idea too, in order to keep more spending off its own books.

Trust has been replaced by contracts with agencies delivering such everyday services as automobile licenses and patents. In addition, the government has sought to keep capital expenditure from visibly increasing public debt through private finance initiatives. Banks and other profit-making companies loan money to build facilities that will be leased by government agencies or even operated by profit-making companies. The theory is that government can obtain the greatest value for money by buying from the private sector services ranging from operating staff canteens in government offices to running prisons. However, the government's experience with cost overruns and failure to meet targets for expensive information technology services shows that either the market cannot supply what government needs, civil servants do not know how to deal with contracts for services costing hundreds of millions of pounds, or both.

Government by contract faces political limits, because a departmental minister must answer to Parliament when something goes wrong. The Prison Service is a textbook example. It was established as an executive agency separate from Whitehall in 1993 in order for private management to reduce unit costs in the face of rising "demand" for prisons due to changes in crime rates and sentencing policies. However, when prisoners escaped and other problems erupted, the responsible Cabinet minister blamed the business executive brought in to head the Prison Service. The Prison Service head replied by attacking the minister's refusal to live up to the terms of the contract agreed upon between them.

The proliferation of many agencies, each with a distinctive and narrow responsibility for a limited number of policies, tends to fragment government. For example, parents may have to deal with half a dozen different agencies to secure for their children all the public services to which they are entitled. Tony Blair promoted "joined up" government that would link the provision of related services so that they could be more easily accessed by individuals. To many public agencies, this looked like a device to increase Downing Street's power. In fact, it demonstrated the limited ability of a few people in Downing Street to determine the behavior of millions of employees of a multitude of public sector organizations.

The Contingency of Influence

The theory of British government is centralist; all roads lead to Downing Street, where the prime minister and the chancellor of the Exchequer have their homes and offices. The Foreign Office and the Treasury are only a few steps away. In practice, policymaking occurs in many buildings, some within Whitehall and others far from London. Institutions can be divided horizontally between ministries and executive agencies and vertically between central government, local authorities, and other nondepartmental bodies that deliver particular public services.

Influence is contingent; it varies with the problem at hand. Decisions about war and peace are made in Downing Street by the highest-ranking political and military officials. In the Iraq War, Tony Blair's media advisor was also heavily involved. By contrast, decisions about whether a particular piece of land should be used for housing are normally made by local authorities far from London.

The Conservative and Liberal Democratic coalition has sought to increase political consensus by having ministers from two parties vet policies. However, political decisions involving two or more government agencies still require discussion between government departments. The making of policy is constrained by disputes within government much more than by differences between the governing party and its opponents. Many tentacles of the octopus of government work against each other, as public agencies often differ in their definition of the public interest. For example, the Treasury wants to keep taxes down, while the Ministry of Defense wants more money to buy costly military equipment.

The influence of the government on the economy depends on how the private sector responds as well as on policies approved by Parliament. The incentives of the two groups often point in opposite directions. In response to economic crisis, the coalition government has encouraged private sector firms to invest more and consumers to spend more in order to boost economic growth. However, economic uncertainties encourage businesses and ordinary households to spend cautiously and reduce rather than increase their debts. Legislation about taxation is intended to generate revenue, but the complexities of taxation create many loopholes that allow businesses and the well-to-do to reduce the taxes they pay while respecting the law.

While the center of central government has been pressing harder on other public agencies, Whitehall itself has been losing influence, because of its European Union obligations. The Single Europe Act promotes British exports, but it also increases the scope for EU decisions to regulate the British economy. Whitehall has adopted a variety of strategies in its EU negotiations, including noncooperation and public dispute. Ironically, these are just the tactics that local government and other agencies use when they disagree with Whitehall.

Policy Performance

8.13 Summarize the roles of laws, money, and personnel in Britain's public policies.

In more than half a century, changes in public policies have gradually supported big changes in British society. Since 1951, infant mortality has declined by more than four-fifths. Life expectancy for men and for women has risen by twelve years. The postwar expansion of schools has significantly raised the percentage of youths completing secondary school, and more than two-fifths of British youths go on to universities, many of which did not exist half a century ago. Long-term economic growth has meant that many consumer goods that were once thought of as a luxury, such as owning a car or your home, are now mass consumption goods.

To produce the benefits of public policy, government relies on three major resources: laws, money, and personnel. Most policies involve a combination of all three resources, but not equally. Policies regulating individual behavior, such as marriage and divorce, are law intensive; measures that pay benefits to millions of people, such as social security, are money intensive; and public services such as education and health care are labor intensive as well as costing lots of money.

Laws are the unique resource of government, because private enterprises cannot enact binding laws, and contracts are only effective if they can be enforced by courts. Whitehall departments have the power to draft laws and regulations that are usually approved without substantial amendment by Parliament. Moreover, many laws give ministers significant discretion in administration. For example, an employer may be required to provide "reasonable" toilet facilities rather than having all features of lavatories specified in written regulations about the size and height of a toilet seat.

Public employees are needed to administer laws and deliver major services. The top civil servants who work in Whitehall are very few compared to millions of public employees. The number of public employees has been reduced by privatization. Nonetheless, more than a fifth of the entire British labor force directly depends on public spending for their jobs. The single biggest public employer is the National Health Service.

To meet the costs of public policy, British government collects almost two-fifths of the gross national product in taxation. Income tax accounts for 27 percent of tax revenue; the top rate of central government taxation is 45 percent on incomes over about $210,000 a year. Social security taxes are paid by deductions from wages and additional contributions of employers; these account for an additional 18 percent of revenue. Since there are no state or local income taxes, a well-to-do British person can pay taxes on income at a rate not much more than an American subject to federal, state, and local taxation in New York City.

Taxes on consumption are important too. There is a value-added tax of 20 percent on the sale of almost all goods and services. Gasoline, cigarettes, and alcohol are taxed very heavily. Taxes on consumption in total account for about one-quarter of all tax revenue. Since profits fluctuate from year to year, the government prefers businesses to make tax payments through Value Added Tax and the employer's contribution to social security. Taxes on the profits of corporations provide less than one-tenth of total tax revenue. Additional revenue comes from "stealth" taxes that ordinary citizens rarely notice and from taxes that do cause complaints, such as the council tax on houses. The government also raises money by taking a big cut from the National Lottery.

Social security programs are the most costly government measures; they account for 36 percent of public expenditure (see Figure 8.7). They are also the most popular, transferring money from government to more than 10 million older people receiving pensions, and to millions of the sick and invalids, the unemployed, women on maternity leave, poor people needing to supplement their limited incomes, and a very small fraction of people who abuse the system in order to claim benefits. Spending on the National Health Service claims almost one-fifth of the public budget, and education claims one-seventh. Together, these three social welfare programs account for two-thirds of total public expenditure. Next in total spending are the classic responsibilities of government—defense, economic activities such as transport, and payment of interest on the national debt.

Since there is no item in the public budget labeled as "waste," any government wanting to make a big cut in public spending must squeeze existing programs—and big savings can be made only by squeezing popular programs. When Margaret Thatcher entered office in 1979, the British Social Attitudes survey found that the public divided into three almost equal groups: those wanting to spend more and tax more, those in favor of cutting taxes even if it meant a reduction in public services, and a third in the middle wanting to leave things as they were. The Thatcher government's campaign against government spending produced a big backlash; by the end of her term of office, more than three-fifths favored higher spending financed by higher taxes.

During the Labour government that followed, the pendulum swung back; less than a third of the public favored higher taxes and spending. A year after the coalition government began introducing spending cuts to reduce the deficit, only 9 percent of the public favored cutting spending and taxes, while 36 percent favored more spending even if it meant higher taxes. The majority endorsed leaving things as they were. However, the government cannot readily do this because of population pressures to increase spending on health, education, social security, and debt interest, while an unfavorable economic climate reduces tax revenue but not tax rates.

Policy Challenges in a World of Interdependence

8.14 Identify the effects of global interdependence on Britain's economy and thus on its political capabilities.

A half century ago, an American secretary of state issued a big challenge to Britain's governors; he said the country had lost an empire but not yet found a role in the world. Britain's governors have responded by seeking to maintain a leadership role like that enjoyed in World War II. This strategy has been called "punching above our weight." While Britain's political, economic, and military assets have remained relatively constant, in the twenty-first century, other countries and continents have become collectively much weightier. Globalization has created policy interdependence; even countries weightier than Britain can no longer command followers.

Interdependence is most obvious in the economy: Britain is a trading nation in which its ability to pay for

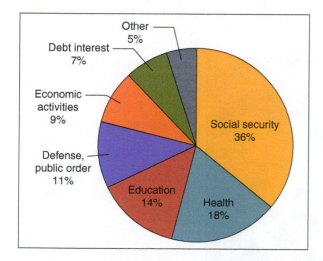

FIGURE 8.7

Slicing the Budget Pie

Public Expenditure by Program.

Source: Adapted from *Public Spending Statistics February 2013* (London: H.M. Treasury, 2013), table 8.

the food and goods it imports depends on the strength of its exports. Although commentators bemoan the country's economic decline relative to the United States and China, ordinary Britons do not compare their lives with those of people in other countries. The most important comparison is with their own past. Evaluating change across time shows great improvements in the material living conditions of most people compared with that of their parents or grandparents.

The City of London is no longer just the financial center of Britain; it is one of the world's most important financial centers. Institutions there are global leaders in exchanging currencies, whether pounds, dollars, euros, or yen; the London Stock Exchange is the biggest in Europe; hundreds of foreign banks have major offices in London; and British-based banks have a presence around the world. The 2008 economic crisis demonstrated that interdependence has a down side, since the collapse of Lehman Brothers in New York had a big impact in the City of London.

Britain's economy is not affected by the global financial crisis in the same way as the great majority of European countries because it is not a member of the EU's common currency area, the eurozone. Instead, the British government and the Bank of England can decide financial policies on their own. However, this has also meant that Britain cannot influence the steps that eurozone countries are taking to strengthen the political and economic unity of the EU in ways that the City of London fears may be to its disadvantage and cause a shift of financial activity to Frankfurt am Main in Germany.

A major challenge to Britain's governors today is to come to terms with the country's membership in the European Union. The Prime Minister, David Cameron, has pledged to renegotiate and loosen the terms of Britain's EU membership. However, it takes two to negotiate, and both EU officials and major countries such as France and Germany have no interest in reducing the unity of the EU by granting Britain special favors. Conservative MPs who favor withdrawal from the EU point to Norway as a prosperous non-EU member state. However, in order to maintain trade with EU countries, Norway is subject to many EU laws and regulations that it cannot influence. The Liberal Democrats are in the minority in wanting to increase Britain's engagement with Europe. The Labour Party has avoided taking sides, but if it heads the British government after the 2015 general election, it cannot avoid engagement with EU institutions and other member states. It will find that their leaders collectively have more weight than Britain.

Even though the Westminster Parliament remains the supreme legal authority of the United Kingdom, its authorization of elected assemblies has introduced interdependence in claims for political legitimacy. Scottish Nationalists argue that by winning a majority of seats in the Edinburgh Parliament, they have a better right to speak for Scots than the Westminster Parliament. Even if the SNP loses the 2014 referendum on independence, it will still seek the transfer of much greater powers from Westminster. If a Labour government was formed thanks to the big advantage Labour

A Stronghold of Global Capitalism Policy Challenges in a world of interdependence
The financial institutions of the city of London, such as the London Stock Exchange, pictured here, are a major source of earnings for the British economy when times are good and of losses when times are bad.

has in Scottish seats, while the Conservatives have the most seats in England, the latter could turn the SNP argument around to claim Labour had no right to govern England. In Wales, the nationalist party lacks the popular support to make such a claim. In Northern Ireland, Irish Republicans have never accepted that Westminster has a legitimate right to govern there and for more than three decades the IRA used violence to advance its claim. The compromise Northern Ireland executive maintains the formal claim of the authority of the Westminster Parliament, but informally it gives equal recognition to the legitimacy of the Republican movement and of Unionists who accept Westminster's authority.

As long as the economy is growing, interdependence can be a "positive sum game," since all may enjoy some benefits and the government enjoys a boost in tax revenue that can be spent to improve the economic circumstances of those who are less well off. However, the failure of the economy to grow since the economic crisis has meant that interdependence involves the distribution of costs. The Gini index that measures inequality had already been growing significantly in the 25 years previously under both Conservative and Labour governments. Although unemployment has not risen as much in Britain as in continental European countries, the crisis has meant that average incomes have risen slower than inflation. This hits low-income Britons more than the very visible London-based financial elite whose income from salaries and bonuses can be well over £1 million in a year.

The constraints on public expenditure arising from a growing deficit and political resistance to tax increases has given immediate political significance to the fact that the term *welfare state* is misleading. Total welfare in society is the sum of a "welfare mix," combining actions of government, the market, and the nonmonetized production of welfare in

the household. David Cameron sought to capitalize on this distinction by promoting a vision of the Big Society, in which people were themselves prepared to take initiatives to deal with problems in their community rather than turn to government. The idea has had little impact on the big problems that Cameron faces in government, because community groups cannot fund a modern hospital, build a new rail link or airport terminal, or decide about how to regulate banks in the City of London. Following Tony Blair's rejection of Socialism, the Labour Party has not argued for a big expansion of government policies, a tactic that would leave it vulnerable to awkward questions about how new policies would be financed.

Ironically, the one thing that politicians ought to be able to do something about—improving the system of government—appears to be beyond the reach of all parties. In 1973, when an opinion poll first asked Britons their views of the political system, 48 percent expressed general approval and 49 percent said it could be improved quite a lot or a great deal. Since then, popular satisfaction with the system of government has fluctuated around a downward trend. Shortly after the 2010 general election, 28 percent expressed themselves generally satisfied as against 69 percent dissatisfied.[39] This does not mean Britons are dissatisfied with democracy in principle, but it does show substantial reservations about how it works in practice and about the politicians who are meant to make it work.

Privately and sometimes publicly, British politicians share their views. After a few years in office, they are ready to cite the constraints of the system they have inherited and, increasingly, the constraints of the world of interdependence as explanations of why they have not succeeded as much as they had promised. As a former Conservative minister said of his Labour successors, "They inherited our problems and our remedies."[40]

REVIEW QUESTIONS

- How would you describe the unwritten constitution of Britain?
- What are the similarities and differences between being a president and being a prime minister?
- What are the nations of the United Kingdom, and how are they governed?
- What are the continents and countries with which Britain has the closest links?

- How would you describe the different parties that have seats in the House of Commons?
- What are the arguments for and against the use of the first-past-the-post electoral system in Britain?
- What policies claim the largest portion of public expenditures, and why?
- What are the main challenges facing the coalition government elected in the 2010 General Election?

INTERNET RESOURCES

Prime Minister's website: www.Number10.gov.uk.

House of Commons and House of Lords: www.parliament.uk.

Gateway to national statistics: www.statistics.gov.uk.

UK and global news: www.bbc.co.uk/news.

Commentaries on proposals to reform government: www.ucl.ac.uk/constitution-unit.

Public opinion polls: http://ukpollingreport.co.uk.

Political Studies Association, the professional body of British political scientists: www.psa.ac.uk.

KEY TERMS

Cabinet
centralization
class
collectivist theory of government
Conservative Party
Crown
devolution
Downing Street
first past the post

individualist theory of government
insider interest groups
Irish Republican Army (IRA)
Labour Party
Liberal Democratic Party
multiparty system

Northern Ireland
official secrecy
outsider interest groups
Parliament
prime minister
privatization
quasi-autonomous nongovernmental organization (quangos)

Scotland
territorial justice
Thatcherism
trusteeship theory of government
United Kingdom
unwritten constitution
Wales
Westminster

SUGGESTED READINGS

Allen, Nicholas, and John Bartle, eds. *Britain at the Polls 2010*. London: Sage Publications, 2010.

Bale, Tim. *The Conservative Party from Thatcher to Cameron*. Oxford: Polity Press. 2011.

Butler, David. E., and Gareth Butler. *British Political Facts*, 10th ed. Basingstoke, England: Palgrave Macmillan, 2011.

Campbell, Rosie. *Gender and Voting Behaviour in Britain*. Colchester, England: ECPR Press, 2006.

Flinders, Matthew. *Delegated Governance and the British State: Walking without Order*. Oxford: Oxford University Press, 2008.

Geddes, Andrew. *Britain and the European Union*. Basingstoke, England: Palgrave Macmillan, 2013.

Geddes, Andrew, and Jonathan Tonge, eds. *Britain Votes 2010*. Oxford: Oxford University Press, 2010.

Hazell, Robert, and Ben Yong, eds. *The Politics of Coalition: How the Conservative-Liberal Government Works*. Oxford: Hart, 2012.

Hood, Christopher. *The Blame Game: Spin, Bureaucracy and Self-Preservation in Government*. Princeton, NJ: Princeton University Press, 2011.

Jones, Bill. *Dictionary of British Politics*, 2nd rev. ed. Manchester, England: Manchester University Press, 2010.

Jordan, Grant, and William A. Maloney. *Democracy and Interest Groups*. Basingstoke, England: Palgrave Macmillan, 2007.

Jowell, Jeffrey, and Dawn Oliver, eds. *The Changing Constitution*, 7th ed. Oxford: Oxford University Press, 2011.

Keating, Michael. *The Government of Scotland*, 2nd ed. Edinburgh: Edinburgh University Press, 2010.

Page, Edward C., and Bill Jenkins. *Policy Bureaucracy: Government with a Cast of Thousands*. Oxford: Oxford University Press, 2005.

Park, Alison, ed. British *Social Attitudes Survey: The 28th Report*. Thousand Oaks, CA: Sage Publications, 2012.

Quinn, Thomas. *Electing and Ejecting Party Leaders in Britain*. Basingstoke, England: Palgrave Macmillan. 2012.

Rallings, Colin, and Michael Thrasher. *British Electoral Facts, 1832–2012*. London: Biteback Publishing, 2012.

Rhodes, R. A. W. *Everyday Life in British Government*. Oxford: Oxford University Press, 2011.

Rose, Richard. *The Prime Minister in a Shrinking World*. Boston: Polity Press, 2001.

———. *Representing Europeans: A Pragmatic Choice*. Oxford: Oxford University Press, 2013.

Rose, Richard, and Phillip L. Davies. *Inheritance in Public Policy: Change without Choice in Britain*. New Haven, CT: Yale University Press, 1994.

Social Trends. London: Stationery Office, annual.

Whitaker's Almanack. London: J. Whitaker, annual.

Whiteley, Paul. *Political Participation in Britain*. Basingstoke, England: Palgrave Macmillan, 2011.

Wilson, David, and Chris Game. *Local Government in the United Kingdom*, 5th ed. Basingstoke, England: Palgrave Macmillan, 2011.

ENDNOTES

1. See Richard Rose, "England: A Traditionally Modern Political Culture," in *Political Culture and Political Development*, ed. Lucian W. Pye and Sidney Verba (Princeton, NJ: Princeton University Press, 1965), 83–129.

2. House of Commons Foreign Affairs Committee, *Global Security: UKUS Relations* (London: Stationery Office, 2010), 77.

3. Cf. Andrew Dilnot and Paul Johnson, eds., *Election Briefing 1997*, IFS Commentary 60 (London: Institute for Fiscal Studies, 1997), 2.

4. *The Coalition: Our Programme for Government.* London: Cabinet Office, 2010; and David Laws, *22 Days in May* (London: Biteback, 2010).

5. See Richard Heffernan, "Labour's New Labour Legacy," *Political Studies Review* 9, no. 2 (2011): 163–77.

6. The opinion of Sir Nigel Hamilton, former head of the Northern Ireland Civil Service, quoted in *Public Service Magazine*, February–March 2009, 27.

7. John Kampfner and David Wighton, "Reeling in Scotland to Bring England in Step," *Financial Times*, April 5, 1997.

8. Maria Sobolewska, "Party Strategies and the Descriptive Representation of Ethnic Minorities," *West European Politics* 36, no. 3 (2013): 615–33.

9. Quoted in Peter Hennessy, "Raw Politics Decide Procedure in Whitehall," *New Statesman*, October 24, 1986, 10.

10. See Richard Rose, *The Prime Minister in a Shrinking World* (Boston: Polity Press, 2001), fig. 6.1.

11. For transatlantic comparisons of presidents and prime ministers, see Richard Rose, "Giving Direction to Government in Comparative Perspective," in *The Executive Branch*, ed. Joel Aberbach and Mark A. Peterson (New York: Oxford University Press, 2005), 72–99.

12. Walter Bagehot, *The English Constitution* (London: World's Classics, 1955), 9.

13. Quoted in David Leppard, "ID Cards Doomed, Say Officials," *Sunday Times* (London), July 9, 2006. See also an interview with Sir Robin Butler, "How Not to Run a Country," *The Spectator* (London), December 11, 2004.

14. George Parker, "Blair Calls on Companies to Boost Whitehall," *Financial Times*, June 29, 2010.

15. Eric Varley, quoted in A. Michie and S. Hoggart, *The Pact* (London: Quartet Books, 1978), 13.

16. Michael Rush and Philip Giddings, *Parliamentary Socialisation* (Basingstoke: Palgrave Macmillan, 2011).

17. Cf. Colin Bennett, "From the Dark to the Light: The Open Government Debate in Britain," *Journal of Public Policy* 5, no. 2 (1985): 209; italics in the original.

18. Graham Wilson and Anthony Barker, "Whitehall's Disobedient Servants?," *British Journal of Political Science* 27, no. 2 (1997): 223–46.

19. Hugh Heclo and Aaron Wildavsky, *The Private Government of Public Money* (London: Macmillan, 1974).

20. Bernard Ingham, press secretary to Margaret Thatcher, quoted in R. Rose, "British Government: The Job at the Top," in *Presidents and Prime Ministers*, ed. R. Rose and

E. Suleiman (Washington, DC: American Enterprise Institute, 1980), 43.

21. See Samuel H. Beer, *Modern British Politics*, 3rd ed. (London: Faber and Faber, 1982).

22. R. Eatwell and M. J. Goodwin, eds., *The New Extremism in 21st Century Britain* (London: Routledge, 2010).

23. House of Commons, *Hansard* (London: Stationery Office), November 11, 1947, col. 206.

24. See Richard Rose and Ian McAllister, *The Loyalties of Voters* (Newbury Park, CA: Sage, 1990), chap. 3.

25. Bennett, Tony, *Culture, Class, Distinction* (London: Routledge, 2008).

26. Quoted in Maurice Kogan, *The Politics of Education* (Harmondsworth, England: Penguin, 1971), 135.

27. Rob Baggott, "The Measurement of Change in Pressure Group Politics," *Talking Politics* 5, no. 1 (1992): 19.

28. Sir Ken Jackson, quoted by Krishna Guha, "Engineers and Electricians Turn Away from Moderate Traditions," *Financial Times*, July 19, 2002.

29. See W. A. Maloney, G. Jordan, and A. M. McLaughlin, "Interest Groups and Public Policy: The Insider/Outsider Model Revisited," *Journal of Public Policy* 14, no. 1 (1994): 17–38.

30. See Ministry of Justice, *The Governance of Britain: Review of Voting Systems* (London: Stationery Office, 2008), Cm 7304.

31. See the Symposium on Electing and Ejecting British Party Leaders, *Representation* 46, no. 1 (2010): 69–117.

32. The Labour Party used the first title, the Conservative Party the second, and the Liberal Democrats the third.

33. For details, see Denis Van Mechelen and Richard Rose, *Patterns of Parliamentary Legislation* (Aldershot, England: Gower, 1986), table 5.2; and more generally, Richard Rose, *Do Parties Make a Difference?* (Chatham, NJ: Chatham House, 1984).

34. J. A. G. Griffith, *Central Departments and Local Authorities* (London: George Allen and Unwin, 1966), 542; cf. Simon Jenkins, *Accountable to None: The Tory Nationalization of Britain* (Harmondsworth, England: Penguin, 1996).

35. See *Better Government Services: Executive Agencies in the 21st Century* (London: Office of Public Service Reforms and the Treasury, 2002).

36. Sir Leo Pliatzky, quoted in Peter Hennessy, "The Guilt of the Treasury 1000," *New Statesman*, January 23, 1987.

37. See Paul Peterson, "The American Mayor: Elections and Institutions," *Parliamentary Affairs* 53, no. 4 (2000): 667–79.

38. David Butler, Andrew Adonis, and Tony Travers, *Failure in British Government: The Politics of the Poll Tax* (Oxford: Oxford University Press, 1994).

39. Ruth Fox, *What's Trust Got to Do With It?* (London: Hansard Society, 2011), 12.

40. Reginald Maudling, quoted in David Butler and Michael Pinto-Duschinsky, *The British General Election of 1970* (London: Macmillan, 1971), 62.

North
Sea

English Channel

Lille •
NORD

Haute-
Normandie   PICARDIE

Basse-
Normandie   ★ Paris
             RÉGION
             PARISIENNE   CHAMPAGNE   LORRAINE   ALSACE   Rhine

BRETAGNE

PAYS DE'
LA LOIRE   Loire   CENTRE   BOURGOGNE   FRANCHE-
                                            COMTE

Nantes •

POITOU-
CHARENTE   Clermont-
            Ferrand •   LIMOUSIN   Lyon •   RHÔNE-
                                                ALPES   Grenoble •

Bay of Biscay

Bordeaux •   Garonne   AUVERGNE   Rhône

AQUITAINE   MIDIPYRÉNÉES   LANGUEDOC   PROVENCE-
                                          ALPES-CÔTE
                                          D' AZUR   Nice •
             Toulouse •   Marseille •   Toulon •   MONACO

F R A N C E   Mediterranean
               Sea

Corsica   CORSE

Sardinia

0   100   200   300 Miles
0   100   200   300 Kilometers

N

Country Bio

POPULATION
64.7 million

TERRITORY
211,208 square miles

YEAR OF INDEPENDENCE
486

YEAR OF CURRENT CONSTITUTION
1958

HEAD OF STATE
President François Hollande

HEAD OF GOVERNMENT
Prime Minister Jean-Marc Ayrault

LANGUAGES
French 100%, with rapidly declining regional dialects (Provença, Breton, Alsatian, Corsican, Catalan, Basque, Flemish)

RELIGION
Roman Catholic 89.5%, Muslim 7.5%, Protestant 2%, Jewish 1%

CHAPTER 9

Politics in France

Martin A. Schain

LEARNING OBJECTIVES

9.1 Identify five policy challenges currently faced by the French government.

9.2 Briefly recount the history of France's 3rd, 4th, and 5th republics.

9.3 Describe France's economy in comparison with those of other EU countries.

9.4 Discuss the governing principles of the French political system.

9.5 Describe the cultural characteristics that contribute to the French style of government.

9.6 Identify the agents of political socialization in France and describe the ways they have changed in recent years.

9.7 Discuss the makeup and recruitment of France's "political class."

9.8 List the three major types of interest groups in France and describe the ways they influence government.

9.9 Explain France's party system and the factors that have prevented emergence of a two-party system, with examples from recent French history.

9.10 Compare and contrast the French system of elections with that of the United States.

9.11 Which institutions in France have the capacity to check the actions of a government?

9.12 Discuss the decentralization of government that took place in France in the 1980s.

9.13 Identify the accomplishments and shortcomings of France as a welfare state.

9.14 Describe the effects of globalization on France, especially as an EU member.

Weary of the declining economy after 2009, as well as the sometime erratic behavior of President Nicolas Sarkozy, French voters rejected Sakozy's bid for a second term in May 2012, and elected a self-confessed "normal" Socialist, François Hollande, as president. A month later, Hollande's Socialist Party won a majority in the elections for the National Assembly. Hollande pledged to negotiate broad changes in the European austerity pact, changes that would build in instruments for growth. He also committed to preserve at least some of the key achievements of previous Socialist governments, in particular the 35-hour workweek, and to pass legislation that would legalize gay marriage.

Within its first year in office, the socialist government did indeed pass some important legislation that included labor market reforms and gay marriage, but failed to either reverse the austerity policies initiated under Sarkozy or the continuing rise of unemployment. Unemployment gradually rose to the highest levels of the Fifth Republic, the public debt continued to increase, economic growth continued to decline, and presidential popularity fell to the lowest level of any president under the Fifth Republic. Unlike Sarkozy's center-right government, which was able to gain political support among its core supporters for some aspects of austerity, Hollande's left coalition was under constant attack from its left wing for budget reductions and cutbacks.

Both presidents have been aware that the French electorate has been highly volatile, and critical of those who have governed them under the **Fifth Republic**. With the exception of 2007, in every legislative election between 1981 and 2012, voters have rejected the governing coalition. Nevertheless, although they have little confidence in those who govern them, French citizens now appear to have more confidence in the key institutions of the Republic than at any time in French history.

Current Policy Challenges

9.1   Identify five policy challenges currently faced by the French government.

At a time in U.S. history when the party system is highly polarized around fundamental socioeconomic issues, French politics—at least most of the time—seems almost tranquil by comparison. The French have lived with divided government (*cohabitation*) for most of the period since 1986 without impeding government effectiveness or undermining institutional legitimacy. At the same time, the French electorate is clearly concerned about some of the same issues that concern Americans.

In 2013, French citizens were most worried about the economic crisis, unemployment, and what they see as excessive pay and privileges for businessmen and large stockholders. More than the public in most other European countries (with the exception of the British), they are concerned with immigration and foreign goods coming through their frontiers. Compared with years past, the problems of the "suburbs"—the equivalent of the inner cities in the United States—poverty and violence, have faded from public concern. As the economic crisis has deepened, French voters have become increasingly pessimistic ("the European champions of pessimism," as one article noted). Although France has come through the economic crisis far better than Greece, Spain, or Italy, the French public tends to be more pessimistic than its less fortunate neighbors about its own economic future and that of its children. One major survey in 2013 noted that, far more than other countries in the **European Union (EU)**, French attitudes with regard to the EU were in "free fall." In one year, the percentage of respondents favorable to the EU fell 19 points, from 60 to 41 percent, the greatest drop of any country in the union.[1]

In 2013, the French were also concerned (perhaps obsessed) by an issue that they had ignored for many years. With revelations that the Socialist minister of the budget and economy had maintained tax-free bank accounts in Switzerland and Singapore for many years, it became clear that required declarations by public officials of wealth and income were far less demanding and transparent in France than in the United States, Germany, Italy, or the United Kingdom. To calm the growing storm, the president quickly altered these requirements for all government ministers, and pledged to change requirements for all other elected officials, in an attempt to "moralize" politics.

We should emphasize that many of the issues at the heart of contemporary American politics are of little concern to the French. French citizens are not much concerned about the size of the state. Recent governments have reduced the level of public spending, for which there is more support than in any other European country. Nevertheless, there is little support for massive cuts in the welfare state programs. Such welfare programs have always been more extensive in France than in the United States. In fact, surveys show that French voters are willing to sacrifice a great deal to maintain these programs, as well as state-subsidized social security and long vacations. Although the unemployment rate in France was about a third higher than that of the United States until the current economic crisis, that gap will certainly grow as the French unemployment rate continues to creep up. The French poverty rate, on the other hand, is among the lowest in the advanced industrial democracies and less than half that of the United States.

Unlike their American counterparts, French voters are deeply concerned about the environmental and health consequences of genetically modified organisms. Far more than Americans, French citizens are willing to pay for efforts to reduce pollution. Gas prices are more than double those in the United States, and state subsidies for a growing public transportation network are not challenged by public opinion.

Multiculturalism related to integrating a large and growing Muslim population (the largest in Europe) is another important policy challenge. In an effort to promote civic integration, the government passed legislation in 2004 prohibiting students in public schools from wearing conspicuous religious symbols, including Islamic head scarves worn by women. In 2011, a new law was passed that banned the burqa (a full-body covering worn by few Muslim women in France) in public places. On the other hand, government-promised reforms to address the special needs of immigrants have gone largely unimplemented.

Finally, although there was widespread sympathy for the United States just after the September 11, 2001, attacks on the World Trade Center and the Pentagon, there was a perceptible rise in anti-American sentiment and distrust of American policy in the wake of these events. This distrust generated a major transatlantic crisis when France took the lead in resisting the American-led military action against Iraq in the spring of 2003. A broad consensus of public opinion and political parties supported French opposition to the war. These tensions have moderated considerably as the Obama administration tilted policy toward greater multilateral collaboration in 2009 and 2010.

Nicolas Sarkozy was swept into office in June 2007 and gained considerable acclaim by appointing both minority women and Socialists to his Cabinet. During his first year in office, however, the government passed relatively little legislation to deal with the problems on which he focused during the presidential campaign. Although François Hollande's popularity declined rapidly, as the economic crisis deepened during his first year in office, he did succeed in enforcing parity between men and women in his government, and, despite pressure (mostly) from the right, passed legislation that legalized gay marriage and adoption for the first time.

A Historical Perspective

9.2 Briefly recount the history of France's 3rd, 4th, and 5th republics.

France is one of the oldest nation-states of Europe. The period of unstable revolutionary regimes that followed the storming of the Bastille in 1789 ended in the seizure of power by **Napoléon Bonaparte** a decade later. The French Revolution began with the establishment of a constitutional monarchy in 1791 (the First Republic), but the monarchy was overthrown the following year. Three more constitutions preceded

Napoléon's seizure of power on the eighteenth day of the revolutionary month of Brumaire (November 10, 1799) and the establishment of the First Empire three years later. The other European powers formed an alliance and forced Napoléon's surrender, as well as the restoration of the Bourbon monarchy. Another revolution in 1830 drove the last Bourbon from the French throne and replaced him with Louis Philippe of the House of Orléans.

Growing dissatisfaction among the rising bourgeoisie and the urban population produced still another Paris revolution in 1848. With it came the proclamation of the Second Republic (1848–1852) and universal male suffrage. Conflict between its middle-class and lower-class components, however, kept the republican government ineffective. Out of the disorder rose another Napoléon, Louis Napoléon, nephew of the first emperor. He was crowned Napoléon III in 1852 and brought stability to France for more than a decade. However, his last years were marked by ill-conceived foreign ventures. After his defeat and capture in the Franco-Prussian War (1870), France was occupied and forced into a humiliating armistice; radicals in Paris proclaimed the Paris Commune, which held out for two months in 1871, until it was crushed by the conservative government forces. In the commune's aftermath, the struggle between republicans and monarchists led to the establishment of a conservative Third Republic in 1871. The Third Republic was the longest regime in modern France, surviving World War I and lasting until France's defeat and occupation by Nazi Germany in 1940.

World War II deeply divided France. A defeated France was divided into a zone occupied by the Germans and a "free" Vichy zone in the southern half of France, where Marshall Pétain led a government sympathetic to the Germans. From July 1940 until August 1944, the government of France was a dictatorship. Slowly, a resistance movement emerged under the leadership of General **Charles de Gaulle**. It gained increased strength and support after the Allied invasion of North Africa and the German occupation of the Vichy zone at the end of 1942. When German forces were driven from occupied Paris in 1944, de Gaulle entered the city with the hope that sweeping reforms would give France the viable democracy it had long sought. After less than two years, he resigned as head of the Provisional Government, impatient with the country's return to traditional party politics.

In fact, the **Fourth Republic** (1946–1958) disappointed many hopes. Governments fell with disturbing regularity—twenty-four governments in twelve years. At the same time, because of the narrowness of government coalitions, the same parties and the same leaders tended to participate in most of these governments. Weak leaders had great difficulty coping with the tensions created first by the Cold War, then by the French war in Indochina, and finally by the anticolonialist uprising in Algeria.

When a threat of civil war arose over Algeria in 1958, a group of leaders invited de Gaulle to return to power and help the country establish stronger and stabler institutions. De Gaulle and his supporters formulated a new constitution for the Fifth Republic, which was enacted by a referendum in 1958. De Gaulle was the last prime minister of the Fourth Republic and then the first president of the newly established Fifth Republic.

Economy and Society

9.3 Describe France's economy in comparison with those of other EU countries.

Geographically, France is at once Atlantic, Continental, and Mediterranean; hence, it occupies a unique place in Europe. In 2010, a total of 64.7 million people, about one-fifth as many as the population of the United States, lived in an area one-fifteenth the size of the United States. More than 3.6 million foreigners (noncitizens) live in France, more than half of whom come from outside of Europe, mostly from North Africa and Africa. In addition, nearly 2 million French citizens are foreign born. Thus, almost 10 percent of the French population is foreign born, slightly less than the percentage of foreign-born people in the United States.

Urbanization has come slowly, but France is now highly urbanized. In 1936, only sixteen French cities had a population of more than 100,000; in 2013, there are thirty-nine. More than one-quarter of the urban population (and almost 20 percent of the total population) lives in the metropolitan region of Paris. This concentration of people creates staggering problems. In a country with centuries-old traditions of administrative, economic, and cultural centralization, it has produced a dramatic gap in human and material resources between Paris and the rest of the country.

The Paris region supports a per capita income almost 50 percent higher and unemployment substantially lower than the national average. The Paris region also has the highest concentration of foreigners in the country (twice the national percentage), and there are deep divisions between the wealthier and the poorer towns in the region.

Recent French economic development has compared reasonably well with that of other advanced industrial countries. In per capita GDP (2011), France ranks among the wealthiest nations of the world, behind the Scandinavian countries, the United States, Germany, and Britain; it is ahead of Japan, Italy, and the average for the EU (see Chapter 1). During the period from 1996 to 2006, the French economy grew at about the EU average, but with an inflation rate of a little more than half the European average. After 2008, however, the economy remained stagnant through the beginning of 2013, but avoided some of the worst predictions of decline. However, with the crisis of the euro that emerged in 2010, France's economic fate was tied to that of the rest of Europe, and it now faces its greatest economic crisis since the Great Depression.

Unemployment remains relatively high compared with the averages of the EU and the United States. In 2008, with an unemployment rate of 7.8 percent, France was already experiencing some of the same problems as some of the poorer countries of Europe: long-term youth unemployment, homelessness, and a drain on social services. All of these problems have grown worse since then, as unemployment moved rapidly higher to postwar record highs approaching 11 percent in 2013.

The labor force has changed drastically since the end of World War II, making France similar to other industrialized countries. During the 1990s, the labor force grew by more than 1.6 million, continuing a growth trend that was greater than in most European countries. Most of these new workers were young people, and an increasing proportion consisted of women. The size of the French workforce has grown slowly since 2000, but is projected to decline after 2013 as the population ages.

In 1954, women made up 35 percent of the labor force; today, they make up 47 percent (about two-thirds of French women of working age). For over a century, the proportion of employed women—mostly in agriculture, artisan shops, and factories—was higher in France than in most European countries.

Today, most women work in offices in the service sector of the economy. Overall, employment in the service sector has risen from 33 percent in 1938 to 77 percent today, above the average for the EU.

By comparison with other countries in the EU, the agricultural sector of France is more important economically. In spite of the sharp decline in the proportion of the population engaged in agriculture (it is now 2.6 percent), agricultural production increased massively during the past quarter century. France is the top farm producer and has more cultivated acreage than any other country in the EU. France is also the top recipient of subsidies from the EU Common Agriculture Policy (CAP).

Since 1945, there have been serious efforts to modernize agriculture, such as farm cooperatives, the consolidation of marginal farms, and improvements in technical education. Particularly after the development of the CAP in the European Community between 1962 and 1968, consolidation of farmland proceeded rapidly. By 2013, the average French farm was larger than that of any country in Europe except Britain, Denmark, and Luxembourg.

French business is both highly dispersed and highly concentrated. Even after three decades of structural reorganization of business, almost two-thirds of the 3.5 million industrial and commercial enterprises in France belong to individuals. As in other advanced industrial societies, this proportion has been slowly increasing. From the perspective of production, some of the most advanced French industries are highly concentrated. The few firms at the top account for most of the employment and business sales. Even in some of the older sectors (such as automobile manufacture, ship construction, and rubber), half or more of the employment and sales are concentrated in the top four firms.

The organization of industry and commerce has changed significantly since the 1990s. Privatization, initiated in the 1980s and mandated by the EU in the 1990s, has reduced the number of public enterprises by 75 percent and the number of those working in public enterprises by 67 percent. Despite a continuing process of privatization, relations between industry and the state remain close. In addition, more than 20 percent of the civilian labor force works in the civil service, which has grown about 10 percent during the past fifteen years, and more than a million people work for the Ministry of Education as of 2012, almost 80 percent of them as teachers.

The Constitutional Tradition

9.4   Discuss the governing principles of the French political system.

The **Constitution of 1958** is the sixteenth since the fall of the Bastille in 1789. Past republican regimes, known less for their achievements than for their instability, were parliamentary constitutional systems (see Chapter 6), based on the principle that Parliament could overturn a government that lacked a parliamentary majority. Such an arrangement works best when there are relatively few political parties, and when the institutional arrangements are not deeply challenged by important political parties and their leaders. These assumptions did not apply to the first four republics, and, at least in the early years, the Fifth Republic seemed to be destined to suffer a similar fate.

Nevertheless, direct popular election of the president has greatly augmented the legitimacy and political authority of the office. It has also had an impact on the party system, as the contest for the presidency has dominated party strategies. When **François Mitterrand** won the presidential election of 1981, as the leader of a coalition of the left that included the French Communist Party, and declared his acceptance of the institutional arrangements of the Fifth Republic, the fate of the Republic appeared to be secured (see Figure 9.1).

Beyond the Constitution itself, there are several principles that have become so widely accepted that they can be thought of as constitutional principles. The first of these is that France is a unitary state: a "one and indivisible" French Republic.[2] A second principle is that France is a secular republic, committed to equality, with no special recognition of any group before the law. These principles have special meaning for democracy in France, since they were regularly violated by the multitude of nondemocratic systems in France after 1789.

Since the First Republic in the eighteenth century, when the Jacobins controlled the revolutionary National Assembly, the French state has been characterized by a high degree of centralized political and administrative authority. Although there have always been forces that have advocated *decentralization* of political authority, as well as deconcentration of administrative authority, the French unitary state remained (formally) unitary. Essentially, this meant

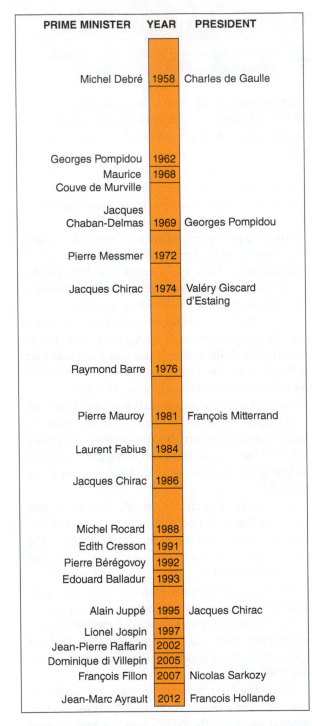

PRIME MINISTER	YEAR	PRESIDENT
Michel Debré	1958	Charles de Gaulle
Georges Pompidou	1962	
Maurice Couve de Murville	1968	
Jacques Chaban-Delmas	1969	Georges Pompidou
Pierre Messmer	1972	
Jacques Chirac	1974	Valéry Giscard d'Estaing
Raymond Barre	1976	
Pierre Mauroy	1981	François Mitterrand
Laurent Fabius	1984	
Jacques Chirac	1986	
Michel Rocard	1988	
Edith Cresson	1991	
Pierre Bérégovoy	1992	
Edouard Balladur	1993	
Alain Juppé	1995	Jacques Chirac
Lionel Jospin	1997	
Jean-Pierre Raffarin	2002	
Dominique di Villepin	2005	
François Fillon	2007	Nicolas Sarkozy
Jean-Marc Ayrault	2012	Francois Hollande

FIGURE 9.1

The French Executive

French presidents and prime ministers since 1958.

that subnational territorial units (communes, departments, and regions) had little formal decision-making autonomy. They were dominated by political

and administrative decisions made in Paris. Both state action and territorial organization in France depended on a well-structured administration, which kept the machinery of the state functioning during long periods of political instability and unrest. The reinforcement of departmental governments and the establishment of elected regional governments between 1982 and 1986 decentralized some decision-making power. Nevertheless, these governments do not have any substantial tax power, and have remained overwhelmingly dependent on centralized financing for almost all their projects.

Secularism is a separation of church and state that is quite different from that in the United States. It derives from the militant opposition to the established power of the Catholic Church both before the Revolution and in nondemocratic regimes. Thus, it has a militant and ideological aspect that derives from the deep historical conflicts of the last two centuries, which has not, however, prevented the granting of state subsidies to religious schools in exchange for state controls over many aspects of their curriculum.

Law and tradition in France are also biased against the recognition of special rights and benefits for religious, ethnic, and national groups. In theory, this means that there is no recognition of "minorities" or multicultural rights (as in Britain or the United States). However, in practice, programs favoring special school funding and "positive discrimination" for university entry for students from poorer geographic areas have existed for many years.

Political Culture

9.5   Describe the cultural characteristics that contribute to the French style of government.

Themes of Political Culture

There are three ways in which we can understand political culture in France: History links present values to those of the past, abstraction and symbolism identify a way of thinking about politics, and distrust of government represents a dominant value that crosses class and generational lines.

The Burden of History   Historical thinking can prove to be both a bond and—as the U.S. Civil War demonstrates—a hindrance to consensus. The French are so fascinated by their own history that feuds of the past are

The French National Assembly
The view from the left.

constantly superimposed on the conflicts of the present. This passionate use of historical memories—from the meaning of the French Revolution to the divisions between Vichy collaboration and the Resistance during the Second World War—complicates political decision making. In de Gaulle's words, France is "weighed down by history."

Abstraction and Symbolism In the Age of Enlightenment, the monarchy left the educated classes free to voice their views on many topics, provided the discussion remained general and abstract. The urge to discuss a wide range of problems, even trivial ones, in broad philosophical terms has hardly diminished. The exaltation of the abstract is reflected in the significance attributed to symbols and rituals. Rural communities that fought on opposite sides in the French Revolution still pay homage to different heroes two centuries later.[3] Street demonstrations of the left and the right take place at different historical corners in Paris—the left in the Place de la Bastille, the right at

the statue of Joan of Arc. This tradition helps explain why a nation united by almost universal admiration for a common historical experience holds to conflicting interpretations of its meaning.

Distrust of Government and Politics The French have long shared the widespread ambivalence of modern times that combines distrust of government with high expectations for it. The French citizens' simultaneous distrust of authority and craving for it feed on both individualism and a passion for equality. This attitude produces self-reliant individuals convinced that they are responsible to themselves, and perhaps to their families, for what they are and might become. The outside world—the "they" who operate beyond the circle of the family, the family firm, and the village—creates obstacles in life. Most of the time, however, "they" are identified with the government and the state.

Memories reaching back to the eighteenth century justify a state of mind that is potentially, if seldom overtly, insubordinate. A strong government is considered reactionary by nature, even if it "pretends" to be progressive. When citizens participate in public life, they most often hope to constrain government authority rather than encourage change, even when change is overdue. At times, this individualism is tainted with anarchism. Yet the French also accommodate themselves rather easily to bureaucratic rule. Since administrative rulings supposedly treat all situations with the same yardstick, they satisfy the sharp sense of equality possessed by a people who feel forever shortchanged by the government and by the privileges those in power bestow on others.

Although the Revolution of 1789 did not break with the past as completely as is commonly believed, it conditioned the general outlook on crisis and compromise, and on continuity and change. Sudden change, rather than gradual mutation, and dramatic conflicts that are couched in the language of mutually exclusive, radical ideologies are the experiences that excite the French at historical moments. The French are accustomed to thinking that no thorough change can ever occur except by a major upheaval (although this is not always true). Since the great Revolution, every French

adult has experienced occasions of political excitement followed by disappointment. This process has sometimes led to moral exhaustion and widespread skepticism about any possibility of change.

Whether they originated within the country or were brought about by international conflict, most of France's political crises have produced a constitutional crisis. Each time, the triumphant forces have codified their norms and philosophy, usually in a comprehensive document. This explains why constitutions have never played the role of fundamental charters. Prior to the Fifth Republic, their norms were satisfactory to only one segment of the polity and hotly contested by others.

The most important change since 1958 is the growing public acceptance of the Fifth Republic's constitutional institutions. And despite growing disillusionment with governments and politicians, this acceptance has grown stronger. Moreover, there is little significant variation in trust in institutions among voters by their party identity. French people invariably give the highest confidence ratings to institutions closest to them—that is, to local officials rather than to political parties or national representatives (see Figure 9.2). In recent years,

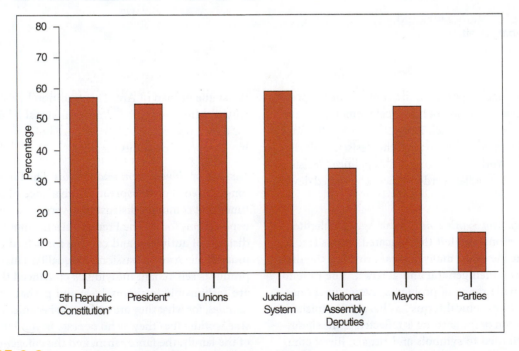

FIGURE 9.2
Feelings of Confidence in Various Political Institutions
People have more confidence in their local mayor than in their National Asssembly deputies or political parties.

Sources: *For the first two columns (5th Repubic Constitution and President) data are from Sofres, l'Etat de l'opinion 2001 (Paris: Edition du Seuil, 2001), p. 81; For the remaining five columns, the data are from Ronald Hatto, Anne Muxel and Odette Tomescu, Survey for the CEVPOF and the Institut de recherchede l'ecole militaire (Irsem), released on November 7, 2011.

distrust of government officials has been high, but expectations of government remain high as well.

Religious and Antireligious Traditions

France is at once a Catholic country—65 percent of the French population identified themselves as Catholic in 2012 (down from 87 percent in 1974)—and a country that the Church itself considers "de-Christianized." Only 5 percent of the population attended church regularly in 2012 (down from 21 percent in 1974), and 87 percent either never go to church or go only occasionally for ceremonies such as baptism or marriage.[4]

Until well into the twentieth century, the mutual hostility between the religious and the secular was one of the main features of the political culture. Since the Revolution, it has divided society and political life at all levels. Even now, there are important differences between the political behavior of practicing Catholics and that of nonbelievers.

French Catholics historically viewed the Revolution of 1789 as the work of satanic men. Conversely, enemies of the Church became militant in their opposition to Catholic forms and symbols. This division continued through the nineteenth century. Differences between the political subcultures of Catholicism and anticlericalism deepened further with the creation of the Third Republic, when militant anticlericalism took firm control of the Republic. Parliament rescinded the centuries-old compact with the Vatican, expelled most Catholic orders, and severed all ties between church and state so that (in a phrase often used at the time) "the moral unity of the country could be reestablished." The Pope matched the militancy of the Republic's regime by excommunicating every deputy (member of Parliament) who voted for the separation of church and state laws in 1905. As in other European Catholic countries, the difference between the political right and left was largely determined by attitudes toward the Catholic Church.

The gap between Catholics and agnostics narrowed somewhat during the interwar period and after they found themselves working side by side in the resistance movement during World War II. Religious practice has been declining in France and many other industrialized countries since the 1950s. Less than 5 percent of the population regularly attends church (once a week); farmers are the most observant group and blue-collar workers the least. In addition to secularization trends, important changes have occurred within the Catholic subculture. Today, the vast majority of self-identified Catholics reject some of the most important teachings of the Church, including its positions on abortion, premarital sex, and marriage of priests. Only 16 percent of identified Catholics perceive the role of the Church as important in political life, and Catholicism no longer functions as a well-integrated community with a common view of the world and common social values. During the two decades from 1990 to 2010, the number of parish priests declined by 50 percent, and even ceremonial events that are more frequently practiced (baptisms, confirmations, and church marriages) have continued to decline; there are now half as many Catholic marriages as in 1990. Nevertheless, among the smaller (and aging) group of practicing Catholics, there has been a tendency to move to the political, even radical, right since 2002. The opposition in the streets to gay marriage legislation passed in 2013 was dominated by groups of traditional Catholics.

Most private schools in France are nominally Catholic parochial schools, which the state subsidizes. The status of these schools (in a country in which state support for Catholic schools coexists with the separation of church and state) has never been fully settled. In 2012, 10 percent of primary schools and 31 percent of secondary schools were private, a decline compared with a decade earlier.

French Jews (numbering about 600,000, or less than 1 percent of the population) are generally well integrated into French society, and it is not possible to speak of a Jewish vote. One study demonstrates that, like other French voters, Jews tend to vote left or right according to degree of religious practice. Anti-Semitic attitudes and behavior are not widespread in France, although there has been an increase during the past decade. Attacks against Jews and Jewish institutions—mostly by young North African men in mixed areas of large cities—increased dramatically in parallel with the emergence of the second intifada in the Middle East (2000–2002), then declined, but have increased once again as the economy has grown worse. These incidents are also related to emerging patterns of urban ethnic conflict in France.

Protestants (1.7 percent of the population and growing) have lived somewhat apart. There are heavy concentrations in Alsace, Paris, and some regions of central and southeastern France. About two-thirds of Protestants belong to the upper bourgeoisie. Protestants hold a large proportion of high public positions.

Until recently, they usually voted more leftist than others in their socioeconomic position or region. Although many Protestants are prominent in the Socialist Party, their electoral behavior, like their activities in cultural and economic associations, is determined by factors other than religion.

Islam is now France's second religion. There are 4 million to 4.5 million people of Islamic origin in France, two-thirds of whom are immigrants or whose descendants are from Islamic countries. The emergence of Islamic institutions in France is part of a larger phenomenon of integrating **new immigrants**. In the last decade, the affirmation of religious identification coincided with (and to some extent was a part of) the social and political mobilization of immigrants from Islamic countries.

In 2002, the government created the French Council of the Muslim Religion (CFCM) to represent Islam with public authorities (similar institutions exist for Jews and Catholics). A survey in 2005 notes that regular attendance of services at mosques is just above 20 percent—somewhat higher than the average for the general population. More than 70 percent of those who identify as **Muslims** say that they attend services only occasionally.

The growth of Muslim interests has challenged the traditional French view of the separation of church and state. Unlike Catholics and Jews, who maintain their own schools, or Protestants, who have supported the principle of secular state schools, some Muslim groups insist on the right both to attend state schools and to follow practices that education authorities consider contrary to the French tradition of secularism. Small numbers of Muslims have challenged dress codes, school curriculums, and school requirements and have more generally questioned stronger notions of *laïcité* (antireligious atheism).

In response to this challenge, the French Parliament passed legislation in 2004 that banned the wearing of "ostentatious" religious symbols in primary and secondary schools. Although the language is neutral about religion, the law is widely seen as an attempt to prevent the wearing of Islamic head scarves. The new law was strongly supported by the French public, with surprisingly strong support among Muslims. In 2011, at the end of a long and confusing public debate about French identity in the context of a regional election campaign, the government passed a ban on public wearing of any garment that was "designed to hide the face," a reference to the burqa, worn by few Muslims in France.

In this context, it is important to point out that surveys indicate that French Muslims are better integrated than are those in other European countries (Britain and Germany, for example).[5] They identify most strongly as French, have the strongest commitment to "adopt national customs" rather than remaining distinct (78 percent), and have the most favorable view of their fellow citizens who are Christian or Jewish.

Class and Status

Feelings about class differences shape a society's authority pattern and the style in which authority is exercised. The French, like the English, are conscious of living in a society divided into classes. But since equality is valued more highly in France than in England, deference toward the upper classes is far less developed, and resentful antagonism is widespread.[6]

The number of citizens who are conscious of belonging to a social class is relatively high in France. About two-thirds of those surveyed in 2010 claimed to belong to a social class, higher than in 1966. However, specific class identity had changed. Most respondents in 1966 claimed working-class identity, while most in 2010 claimed to be middle class. Class identity is a poor predictor of political patterns in France. Among workers in 2010, 45 percent (far higher than any other group) identified with neither the left nor the right; young workers were the most likely to have moved away from identifying with the left.

Economic and social transformations have not eradicated industrial and social conflict. Indeed, periodic strike movements intensify class feelings and commitments to act. However, as the number of immigrant workers among the least qualified workers has grown, traditional class differences are crosscut by a growing sense of racial and ethnic differences.

Political Socialization

9.6 Identify the agents of political socialization in France and describe the ways they have changed in recent years.

French political attitudes have been shaped through experience with the political system as well as through some key institutions and agents. Some agents, such as political associations, act to socialize political values quite directly, while others, such as the family and the media, act in a more indirect manner.

Family

Particularly during the last forty years, the life of the French family, the role of its members, and its relationship to outsiders has undergone fundamental, and sometimes contradictory, changes. Very few people condemn the idea of couples living together without being married, and in 2013, France passed legislation that approved gay marriage. During the past generation, the French marriage rate has declined by more than 30 percent (to about half that of the United States), while the proportion of the population living in civil unions known as PACS has continued to grow, and is now close to that of married couples. Therefore, it is not surprising that in 2006, 59 percent of all first-born children were born outside of marriage (compared with 6 percent in 1968), including the children of the current French president, François Hollande, and the minister of justice in the previous conservative government. Very few of these children are in one-parent families, however, since, in virtually all cases, they are legally recognized by both parents before their first birthday. The number of divorces was 50 percent of the (very much reduced) number of marriages in 2012, and has more than doubled since 1976, when new and more flexible divorce legislation came into effect. A French Senate report indicates that dissolution of civil unions is far lower than the divorce rate.

Legislative changes have only gradually modified the legal restrictions on married women that existed in the Napoléonic legal codes. Not until 1970 did law proclaim the absolute equality of the two parents in the exercise of parental authority. The employment of more married women (80 percent of women between the ages of twenty-five and forty-nine are in the labor force) has affected the family's role as a vehicle of socialization. Working women differ from unemployed women with regard to religious practice, political interest, electoral participation, party preference, and so on. In their attitudinal orientations, employed women are far closer to the men of the same milieu, class, or age group to which they belong than to women who are not employed.[7]

Although family structure, values, and behavior have changed, the family remains an important structure through which political values broadly conceived are transmitted from generation to generation. Several studies demonstrate a significant influence of parents over the religious socialization and the left/right political choices made by their children. Moreover, in surveys, young people consistently indicate that they value their family in their lives.

The effectiveness of the family in socializing general religious and ideological orientations does not mean that succeeding generations do not have formative experiences of their own or that there are no significant political differences by age. Therefore, political socialization is a product not only of the family experiences but also of childhood experiences with peers, education, and the changing larger world. For instance, young people of Algerian origin, born in France, are far less likely than their counterparts born in Algeria to practice their faith.[8]

Associations and Socialization

The French bias against authority might have encouraged social groups and associations if the egalitarian thrust and the competition among individuals did not work in the opposite direction. The French ambivalence about participation in group life is not merely negativistic apathy but also reflects a lack of belief in the value of cooperation. On the one hand, this cultural ambivalence is reinforced by legal restrictions on associational life, as well as by a strong republican tradition hostile to groups serving as intermediaries between the people and the state. On the other hand, the state and local governments traditionally subsidize numerous associations (including trade unions). Some associations (not always the same ones that were subsidized) receive privileged access to decision-making power.

After World War II, *overall* membership in associations in France was comparable to that in other European countries, but lower than in the United States. However, in France, group membership was concentrated in politicized associations that reinforced existing political divisions. Membership in key professional organizations, especially trade unions, was much lower in France than in other European countries.

The number of associations has sharply increased over the past two decades, while the overall percentage of membership among the adult population has remained relatively constant. In a 2008 survey,

33 percent claimed to belong to one or more associations. This percentage has increased slowly during the last thirty years.[9]

The pattern of association membership, however, has changed considerably. The traditional advocacy and political groups, politicized unions, and professional associations suffered sharp declines in absolute (and proportional) membership. Sports associations, self-help groups, and newly established ethnic associations now attract larger numbers of people. Membership tends to increase with income, education, and age. As more middle-class people have joined associations, working-class people have dropped out. A higher percentage of workers now belong to sports associations than to unions.

To some extent, these changes reflect shifting attitudes about political commitment in France. Although associational life remains strong, the old kind of *militantisme* (voluntary work, with its implication of deep and abiding political commitment) has clearly diminished. Nevertheless, it is now clear that a newer kind of nonpolitical commitment is emerging. On average, about two-thirds of members of voluntary associations participate regularly, and more than half of members volunteer their services. New legislation has also produced changes. A 1981 law made it possible for immigrant groups to form their own organizations. This encouraged the emergence of thousands of ethnic associations. Decentralization legislation passed a few years later encouraged municipalities to support, with public funds, the creation of local associations, some to perform municipal services.

Education

One of the most important ways a community preserves and transmits its values is through education. Napoléon Bonaparte recognized the significance of education. Well into the second half of the twentieth century, the French educational system remained an imposing historical monument in the unmistakable style of the First Empire. The edifice Napoléon erected combined education at all levels, from primary school to postgraduate professional training, into one centralized corporation: the imperial university. Its job was to reinforce the national doctrine through uniform programs at various levels.

As the strict military discipline of the Napoléonic model was loosened by succeeding regimes, each discovered that the machinery created by Napoléon was a convenient and coherent instrument for transmitting the values—both changing and permanent—of French civilization. The centralized imperial university has therefore never been truly dismantled. The minister of education presides over a ministry that employs more than a million people and controls curriculums and teaching methods, the criteria for selection and advancement of pupils and teachers, and the content of examinations.

Making advancement at every step dependent upon passing an examination is not peculiar to France (it also occurs in Japan and other countries). What is distinctly French is an obsessive belief that everybody is equal before an examination. The idea that education is an effective weapon for emancipation and social betterment has had popular as well as official recognition. The **baccalauréat**—the certificate of completion of the academic secondary school, the *lycée*—remains almost the sole means of access to higher education. Such a system suits and profits best those self-motivated middle-class children for whom it was designed.

Nevertheless, during the Fifth Republic, the structure of the French educational system has undergone some significant changes, even while the basic features have remained in place. The secondary schools, which trained only 700,000 students as late as 1945, now provide instruction for 5.5 million. Between 1958 and 2012, the number of students in higher education rose from 170,000 to more than 2.3 million. The proportion of twenty- to twenty-four-year-olds in higher education (40 percent) is comparable to that in any other European country.

The introduction of a comprehensive middle school with a common core curriculum in 1963 altered the system of early academic selection. Other reforms eliminated rigid ability tracking. However, the implementation of reforms, whether passed by governments of the right or the left, has often faced difficult opposition from middle-class parents and from teachers unions of the left. Although 72 percent of the eligible student age cohort passed the baccalauréat in 2011 (more than triple the proportion of 1970), education reforms have altered only slightly the vast differences in the success of children from different social backgrounds. Blue- and white-collar workers comprise more than half the workforce, but their children comprise fewer than a third of the candidates for the baccalauréat.

Because of the principle of open admission, every holder of the baccalauréat can gain entrance to a university. As in some American state universities, however, there is a rather ruthless elimination at the end of the first year (particularly for students in such fields as medicine) and sometimes later. Students of lower-class backgrounds typically fare worse than the others. In addition, the number of students from such backgrounds is disproportionately large in fields in which diplomas have the lowest value in the professional market and in which unemployment is highest.

The most ambitious attempt to reform the university system came in the wake of the student rebellion of 1968, followed by other reforms in the 1970s and 1980s. They strove to encourage the autonomy of each university; the participation of teachers, students, and staff in the running of the university; and the collaboration among different disciplines. The government subsequently withdrew some of the reforms. Others failed to be implemented because of widespread resistance by those concerned. Administrative autonomy has remained fragmentary, as the ministry has held the financial purse strings as well as the right to grant degrees. After 2007, the autonomy question was once again on the agenda, this time with the objective of making French universities more competitive on the European and the global level. Perhaps the most important reform of the Sarkozy years was the increase of funding for universities (more than 20 percent), and the provision of incentives for private financing of university research. Nevertheless, the widely lamented crisis in the university system has hardly been alleviated, although the size of the student population appears to have stabilized.

Since 2003, the most important symbolic change in French higher education has been the introduction of affirmative action programs ("positive discrimination") for students in "priority education zones"—schools in poor areas, generally in or near larger cities. Some of the elite institutions of higher education (Sciences Po in Paris, for example) have created links to some of these schools and have established special conditions of admission for their best students. Although these programs involve only a handful of students, these experiments are important because they represent the first affirmative effort to integrate potential leaders from immigrant communities into the French system (which we will discuss later).

An additional characteristic of the French system of higher education is the parallel system of **grandes**

écoles, a sector of higher education that functions outside of the network of universities under rules that permit a high degree of selectivity. These schools include the most prestigious schools of higher education in France. While most are state institutions, some are private and fee paying. As university enrollment has multiplied, the more prestigious grandes écoles have only modestly increased the number of students admitted upon strict entrance examinations.[10] For more than a century, these schools have been the training ground of highly specialized elites. They prepare students for careers in science, engineering, business management, and the top ranks of the civil service, and, in contrast to university graduates, virtually all graduates of the grandes écoles find employment and often assume positions of great responsibility.

Socialization and Communication

The political effectiveness of the mass media is often determined by the way in which people appraise the media's integrity and whether they believe that the media serve or disturb the functioning of the political system. In the past, business firms, political parties, and governments (both French and foreign) often backed major newspapers. Today, most newspapers and magazines are owned by business enterprises, many of them conglomerates that extend into fields other than periodical publications. Nevertheless, every major newspaper and news magazine in France is subsidized by the state. During the Sarkozy years, subsidies doubled. A report in 2013 estimated that state subsidies between 2009 and 2011 were about 5 billion euros (or 6.6 billion dollars). Interestingly, the largest subsidies during this period, when the right was governing, went to the Communist newspaper, *l'Humanité*, and to several other publications of the left.

In spite of a growth in population, the number of daily newspapers and their circulation has declined since World War II. The decline in readership, a common phenomenon in most European democracies, is due to competition from other media, such as television, radio, and the Internet.

Television has replaced all other media as a primary source of political information in France and other Western democracies.[11] It is increasingly the primary mediator between political forces and individual citizens, and it has an impact on the organization and substance of politics. First, a personality that plays well on television is now an essential ingredient of politics. As in other countries, image and spectacle are important elements of politics. Second, television helps set the agenda of political issues by choosing among the great variety of themes, problems, and issues dealt with by political and social forces and magnifying them for the public. Finally, television now provides the arena for national electoral campaigns, largely displacing mass rallies and meetings.

Confidence in various sources of political information varies among different groups. Young people and shopkeepers are most confident in radio and television information, while managers are more confident in the written press than in television for political information.

Until 1982, all radio and television stations that originated programs on French territory were owned by the state and operated by personnel whom the state appointed and remunerated. Since then, the system of state monopoly has been dismantled. As a first and quite important step, the Socialist government authorized private radio stations. This move attempted to regularize and regulate more than a thousand existing pirate radio stations. Inevitably, this vast network of 1,600 stations was consolidated by private entrepreneurs who provide programming services and, in some instances, control a large number of local stations.

The 1982 legislation also reorganized the public television system. It granted new rights of reply to government communications and allotted free time to all political parties during electoral campaigns. During the following years, however, even greater changes were produced by a process of gradual privatization and globalization of television broadcasting. Today, more than 900 television channels from throughout the world are available to French viewers (depending on the system that they choose) compared with 3 in 1980 and 30 in 1990.

With stunning rapidity, the Internet has challenged all other media. France pioneered online communication in 1981 with telephone-linked computer service—the Minitel—that, by the late 1990s, provided over 25,000 video services to 20 percent of the households in France. The Internet rapidly overtook the Minitel after 2000, however. In 2000, about 14 percent of the French population used the Internet, compared with 41 percent four years later, and 69 percent in 2010, just below Norway, Denmark, Sweden, the United Kingdom, and Germany, but well above the European average. Although many French households still have their Minitels stored in the closet, they use the Internet on their computers for communication, information, and entertainment.

Recruitment and Style of Elites

9.7 Discuss the makeup and recruitment of France's "political class."

Together with members of Parliament, elected officials of municipalities, departments, and regions, some local party leaders, and a few journalists of national renown are counted among what is known in France as the **political class**. All together, they comprise not more than 15,000 or 20,000 people. From about 1879 on (the Third Republic), professionals (lawyers, doctors, and journalists) and farmers dominated the Chamber of Deputies, now the National Assembly. The vast majority were "local notables," trained in law and experienced in local administration, who benefited from the ability to hold local and parliamentary offices at the same time (see below).

A substantial change in political recruitment occurred during the Fourth Republic, when the percentage of professionals, self-employed, and farmers became a minority. Then, during the Fifth Republic, the number of blue- and white-collar workers declined due partially to the professionalization of parliamentary personnel, as well as to the decline of the Communist Party.

A large number of legislators now come from the public sector—about a quarter of the deputies in 2007 and 2012 were either civil servants or teachers. Although the majority of high civil servants usually lean toward parties of the right, more than 40 percent of those who sat in the National Assembly elected in 2012 were part of the Socialist group. In addition, the vast majority of teachers were Socialists. What is striking about the deputies in the last two National Assemblies is the growth of two categories, private managerial executives and retired people. The former are even more numerous in the 2012 assembly of the left than in the previous assembly of the right. The growth of retired people no doubt reflects the early age of official retirement in France.

Even more important than their number is the political weight that high civil servants carry in Parliament. Some of the civil servants who run for election to Parliament have previously held positions in the political executive, either as members of the ministerial staffs or as junior ministers. Not surprisingly, they are frequently candidates for a post in the Cabinet.

More than in any other Western democracy, the highest ranks of the civil service are the training and recruitment grounds for top positions in both politics and industry. Among the high civil servants, about 3,400 are members of the most important administrative agencies, the five **grands corps**, from which the vast majority of the roughly 500 administrators engaged in political decision making are drawn.[12] The recruitment base of the highest levels of the civil service remains extremely narrow. The knowledge and capability required to pass the various examinations give clear advantages to the children of senior civil servants. As a result, the ranking bureaucracy forms something approaching a hereditary class. Past attempts to develop a system of more open recruitment into the higher civil service have been only marginally successful.

The **École Nationale d'Administration (ENA)** and the **École Polytechnique**, together with the other grandes écoles, play an essential role in the recruitment of administrative, political, and business elites. Virtually all the members of the grands corps are recruited directly from the graduating classes of the ENA and the Polytechnique. What differentiates the members of the grands corps from other ranking administrators is their general competence and mobility. At any one time, as many as two-thirds of the members of these corps might be on leave or on special missions to other administrative agencies or special assignments to positions of influence.

They might also be engaged in politics as members of Parliament (thirty-four in the National Assembly elected in 2012), local government, or the executive. Twelve of the nineteen prime ministers who have served since 1959 were members of a grand corps and attended a grande école. The percentage of ministers in any given government who belong to the grands corps has varied between 10 and 64 percent— 64 percent of the ministers in 2009. Thus, the grandes écoles–grands corps group, though small in membership, produces a remarkable proportion of the country's political elite.

The same system is increasingly important in recruiting top-level business executives. Members of the grands corps can move from the public sector to the private sector because they can go on leave for years, while they retain their seniority, their pension rights, and the right to return to their job. (Few who leave do in fact return to serve as civil servants.)[13] In 2007, 75 percent of the members of the executive boards of the forty largest companies in France were graduates of a grande école. The relationship between the grandes écoles and the grands corps on the one hand and politics and business on the other hand provides structure for an influential elite and survives changes in the political orientation of governments. While this system is not politically monolithic, the narrowness of its recruitment contributes to a persistent similarity of style and operation and to the fairly stable—at times rigid—value system of its operators.

For outsiders, this tight network is difficult to penetrate. Even during the 1980s—the period when industrial restructuring and privatization of state-run enterprises encouraged a new breed of freewheeling businesspeople in the United States and in Britain—a similar process had a very limited impact on the recruitment of new elites in France.

The Importance of Gender

The representation of women among French political elites is almost the lowest in Western Europe. Women make up well over half the electorate, but made up 26 percent of the deputies in the National Assembly in 2012 and only 22 percent of Senate members in 2012. The percentage of women in politics is higher at the local level, where they made up 32 percent of the municipal councilors and almost 14 percent of the mayors in 2008, 40 percent more than seven years earlier.

Political parties structure access to political representation far more in France than in the United States. The left has generally made a greater effort to recruit women than has the right, although President Sarkozy made an effort to recruit women for cabinet posts. President Hollande has established a principle of parity for his cabinet appointments.

In contrast to the United States, political advancement in France generally requires a deep involvement in political parties, with a bias in favor of professional politicians and administrators. However, only recently have women begun to make this kind of long-term commitment to political life. One woman who has is **Ségolène Royal**. A graduate of the ENA and a member of the Council of State (one of the five grands corps), she has also been a Socialist government minister, a deputy (member) in the National Assembly, and president of one of the regions of France. She was the (unsuccessful) Socialist candidate for the presidential elections in 2007.

Periodically, governments and the political parties recognize this dearth of women in representative institutions, but little has been done about it. By the 1990s, leaders of all political parties favored amending the Constitution to permit positive discrimination to produce greater gender parity in representative institutions. Thus, with the support of both the **president of the Republic** and the prime minister, and without dissent, the National Assembly passed an amendment in December 1998 stipulating that "the law [and not the constitution] determines the conditions for the organization of equal access of men and women to electoral mandates and elective functions." Enforcement legislation requires greater gender parity, at least in the selection of candidates. More recently, President Sarkozy recruited record numbers of women for ministerial posts, and President Hollande has established a rule of parity for ministerial posts. This is a significant departure for the French political system, which has resisted the use of quotas in the name of equality.

Perhaps the most important change in the political behavior of French women is in the way they vote. During the Fourth Republic, a majority of women consistently voted for parties of the right. However, as church attendance among women declined, their political orientation moved from right to left. In every national election between 1986 and 1997, a clear majority of women voted for the left. By 2002, however, the pattern of voting among women changed once again. In 2002 and 2007, a majority of women supported the right in both presidential and legislative elections, even though Sarkozy's opponent in 2007 was a woman. In 2012, a majority of women supported the left, but in slightly lower proportions than men. To some extent, this is related to stronger support for the right among older women, as well as to an increase in the abstention rate among younger women (and men). It is also related to a decline in support for the left among the youngest age cohorts. On the other hand, women have given far less support than men to the extreme right.[14]

Interest Groups

9.8 List the three major types of interest groups in France and describe the ways they influence government.

The Expression of Interests

As in many other European countries, the organization of French political life is largely defined within the historical cleavages of class and religious traditions. Interest groups have therefore frequently shared ideological commitments with the political parties with which they have organizational connections.

Actual memberships in most economic associations have varied considerably over time by sector, but they are generally much smaller than comparable groups in other industrialized countries. In 2013, no more than 8 percent of workers belonged to trade unions (the largest decline in Western Europe over the past twenty-five years). About 50 percent of French farmers and 75 percent of large industrial enterprises belong to their respective organizations.[15] Historically, many of the important economic groups have experienced a surge of new members at dramatic moments in the country's social or political history. But memberships then decline as conditions normalize, leaving some associations with a membership too small to justify their claims of representativeness.

Many groups lack the resources to employ a competent staff, or they depend on direct and indirect forms of state support. The modern interest group official is a fairly recent phenomenon that is found only in certain sectors of the group system, such as business associations.

Interest groups are also weakened by ideological division. Separate groups defending the interests of workers, farmers, veterans, schoolchildren, and consumers are divided by ideological preferences. The ideological division of representation forces each organization to compete for the same clientele in order to establish its representativeness. Consequently, even established French interest groups exhibit a radicalism in action and goals that is rare in other Western democracies. For groups that lack the means of using the information media, such tactics also become a way to put their case before the public at large.

The Labor Movement

The French labor movement is divided into national confederations of differing political sympathies, although historical experiences have driven labor to

Pressure from Protest
Demonstration by medical interns in Paris in early 2003.

avoid direct organizational ties with political parties.[16] Union membership has declined steeply since 1975, although union membership is declining in almost every industrialized country (refer back to Figure 3.1). The youngest salaried workers virtually deserted the trade union movement in the 1990s. Although the decline in membership has slowed slightly in recent years, recruitment of young workers has lagged. In addition, after 1990, candidates supported by nonunion groups in various plant-level elections have attracted more votes than any of the established union organizations.[17] In fact, unions lost members and (electoral) support at the very time when the French trade union movement was becoming better institutionalized at the workplace and better protected by legislation.

Despite these clear weaknesses, workers still maintain considerable confidence in unions to defend their interests during periods of labor conflict. Support for collective action and confidence in unions and their leadership of strike movements remain strong. Indeed, during the massive strikes, public support for the strikers was far higher than confidence in the government against which the strikes were directed.[18]

Nevertheless, strike levels have declined over the past thirty years, and most strikes are limited to the public sector. Moreover, their impact has been limited by legal requirements to provide minimum service.

The decline in union membership has not encouraged consolidation. Unlike workers in the United States, French workers in the same plant or firm may be represented by several union federations. As a result, there is constant competition among unions at every level for membership and support. Even during periods when the national unions agree to act together, animosities at the plant level sometimes prevent cooperation.

Moreover, the weakness of union organization at the plant level—which is where most lengthy strikes are called—means that unions are difficult bargaining partners. Unions at this level maintain only weak control over the strike weapon. Union militants are quite adept at sensitizing workers, producing the preconditions for strike action, and channeling strike movements once they begin. However, the unions have considerable difficulty in effectively calling strikes and ending them. Thus, unions depend heavily on the general environment, what they call the "social climate," in order to support their positions at the bargaining table. Because their ability to mobilize workers at any given moment is an essential criterion of their representativeness, union ability to represent workers is frequently in question.

The left government passed legislation in 1982 and 1983 (the Auroux laws) to strengthen the unions' position at the plant level. By creating an "obligation to negotiate" for management and by protecting the right of expression for workers, the government hoped to stimulate collective negotiations. However, because of their increasing weakness, unions have not taken full advantage of the potential benefits of the legislation. This law refocused French industrial relations on the plant level, just where unions were weakest. In 2008, the Sarkozy government, in an attempt to weaken the influence of the smallest ("autonomous") unions, passed legislation that denied them the legal designation of "representative." This also deprived them of most state financial support and the ability to sign collective agreements.

The oldest and the largest of the union confederations is the **Confédération Générale du Travail (CGT)** (General Confederation of Labor). Since World War II, the CGT has been identified closely with the Communist Party, with which it maintains a considerable overlap of leadership. Yet by tradition and by its relative effectiveness as a labor organization, it enrolls many non-Communists among its members. Its domination diminished in the 1990s, however, mostly because the CGT lost more members and support than all other unions.

The second-largest labor organization in terms of membership is now the **Confédération Française Democratique du Travail (CFDT)** (French Democratic Confederation of Labor). An offshoot of the Catholic trade union movement, the CFDT's early calls for worker self-management (*autogestion*) was integrated into the Auroux laws. The leaders of the CFDT see the policy of the confederation as an alternative to the oppositional stance of the CGT. The CFDT now offers itself as a potential partner to modern capitalist management. In 2013, CFDT's support in social elections (26 percent) was on a level with that of the CGT.

This movement to the center created splits within several CFDT public service unions and resulted in the establishment of a national rival, the Solidaire Unitaire et Democratique (SUD) (Solidarity United and Democratic), in 1989. The SUD, in turn, was integrated into a larger group of twenty-seven militant autonomous civil service unions, **G-10** (*le Groupe des dix*), in 1998. SUD's best result in social elections was less than 4 percent.

The third major labor confederation, **Force Ouvrière (FO)** (Workers' Force), was formed in 1948 in reaction to the Communist domination of the CGT. Although its membership is barely half that of the two other major confederations, the FO made gains in membership in the 1990s and, with 16 percent in social elections, continues to have influence among civil servants.

One of the most important and influential of the "autonomous" unions was the **Fédération de l'Education Nationale (FEN)** (Federation of National Education)—the teachers union, now merged with other autonomous civil service unions in the Union Nationale des Syndicats Autonomes (UNSA) (National Union of Autonomous Unions). However, by 2013, support for UNSA in social elections had declined sufficiently that it no longer qualified as "representative" in legal terms.

In addition to the fragmentation that results from differences within existing organizations, there are challenges from the outside. In 1995, the **National Front (FN)** organized several new unions. When the government and the courts blocked these initiatives, the extreme-right party began to penetrate existing unions.

Thus, at a time when strong opposition to government action seems to give union organizations an opportunity to increase both their organizational strength and their support, the trade union movement is as fragmented as ever. As in the past, infrequent, massive strike movements have accentuated divisions and rivalries, rather than provoking unity.

Business Interests

Since the end of World War II, most trade associations and employers' organizations have kept within one dominant and exceptionally well-staffed confederation, renamed in 1998 the **Mouvement des Entreprises de France (MEDEF)** (Movement of French Business). However, divergent interests, differing economic concepts, and conflicting ideologies frequently prevent the national organization from acting forcefully. At times, this division hampers the confederation's representativeness in negotiations with government or trade unions. Nevertheless, the MEDEF weathered the difficult years of **nationalization** introduced by the Socialists, and the restructuring of social legislation and industrial relations, without lessening its status as an influential interest group.

Because the MEDEF is dominated primarily by big business, shopkeepers and the owners of many small firms feel that they are better defended by more movement-oriented groups.[19] As a result, a succession of small-business and shopkeeper movements have challenged the established organization and have evolved into organized associations in their own right.

Agricultural Interests

The defense of agricultural interests has a long record of internal strife. However, under the Fifth Republic, the **Fédération Nationale des Syndicats d'Exploitants Agricoles (FNSEA)** (National Federation of Agricultural Unions) is the dominant group among several farm organizations. The FNSEA has also served as an effective instrument for modernizing French agriculture.

The rural reform legislation of the 1960s provided for the "collaboration of the professional agricultural organizations," but from the outset, real collaboration was offered only to the FNSEA. From this privileged position, the federation gained both patronage and control over key institutions that were transforming agriculture. It used these instruments to organize a large proportion of French farmers. After establishing its domination over the farming sector with the support of the government, it then periodically demonstrated opposition to government policy with the support of the vast majority of a declining number of farmers.[20]

The principal challenges to the FNSEA in recent years are external—from Europe and the world market—rather than internal. The agricultural sector has suffered from the fruits of its own productive success. Under pressure from the EU, France agreed in 1992 to major reforms of CAP—the common EU policy that has governed the European agricultural market since the 1960s. The reforms of 1992 took substantial amounts of land out of production and replaced some price supports with direct payments to farmers. The enlargement of the EU toward the East has heightened pressures to reduce further the budget of CAP. The substantial opposition in France (and other parts of Europe) to the importation of genetically modified agricultural products has increased the tensions within the World Trade Organization (WTO).

Means of Access and Styles of Action

French organized interests are expressed through an impressive range of different kinds of organizations,

from the weak and fragmented trade union movement to the well-organized FNSEA. Overall, what seems to differentiate French groups from those of other industrial countries is their style of expression and their forms of activity.

In preceding regimes, organized interests saw Parliament as the most convenient means of access to political power. During the Third and Fourth Republics, the highly specialized and powerful parliamentary committees often seemed to be little more than institutional facades for interest groups that frequently substituted bills of their own design for those submitted by the government.

Among the reasons given in 1958 for reforming and rationalizing Parliament was the desire to reduce the role of organized interests in the legislative process. By and large, this has been accomplished. But interest groups have not lost all influence on rule making and policy formation. To be effective, groups now use the channels that the best-equipped groups have long found most rewarding, channels that give them direct access to the administration. The indispensable collaboration between organized private interests and the state is institutionalized in advisory committees that are attached to most administrative agencies. These committees are composed mainly of civil servants and group representatives.

It is not surprising that some interests have easier access to government bureaus than others. An affinity of views between group representatives and public administrators might be based on common outlook, common social origin, or education. High civil servants tend to distinguish between "professional organizations," which they consider serious enough to listen to, and "interest groups," which should be kept at a distance. The perspectives of interest representatives tend to reflect their own strength, as well as their experience in collaborating with different parts of the state and government. Trade union representatives acknowledge their reliance on the social climate (essentially the level of strike activity) to bargain effectively with the state. Representatives of business rely more on contacts with civil servants. Agricultural interests say that they rely more on contacts at the ministerial level.[21]

Tendencies toward privileged access, sometimes called **neocorporatism** (democratic corporatism—see below and Chapter 4), have, except in the areas of agriculture and big business, remained weak in France.

Central to the state interest group collaboration is the notion that the state plays a key role in both shaping and defining the legitimacy of the interest group universe. The state also establishes the rules by which the collaboration takes place. The French state, at various levels, strongly influences the relationship among groups and even their existence in key areas through official recognition and subsidies. Although representative organizations may exist with or without official recognition, this designation gives them access to consultative bodies, the right to sign collective agreements (especially important in the case of trade unions), and the right to obtain certain subsidies. Therefore, recognition is an important tool that both conservative and Socialist governments have used to influence the group universe.

The French state subsidizes interest groups, both indirectly and directly. By favoring some groups over others in these ways, the state seems to conform to neocorporatist criteria. However, in other ways, the neocorporatist model is less applicable in France than in other European countries. Neocorporatist policymaking presumes close collaboration between the state administration and a dominant interest group (or coalition of groups) in major socioeconomic sectors. Yet what stands out in the French case is the unevenness of this pattern of collaboration.[22]

If the neocorporatist pattern calls for interest group leaders to control organizational action and coordinate bargaining, the French interest groups' mass actions—such as street demonstrations, "wildcat" strikes, and attacks on government property—are often poorly controlled by group leadership. Indeed, it can be argued that group protest is more effective in France (at least negatively) than in other industrialized countries because it is part of a pattern of group–state relations. Protests are limited in scope and intensity, but the government recognizes them as a valid expression of interest (see Box 9.1).

BOX 9.1   Protest in France

During the long period of Gaullist governments, the most effective forms of opposition were massive protests in the streets, crowned by the "events" of May and June 1968 that destabilized the Fifth Republic. The Republic survived, but 1968 became a symbol of the power of the streets that endured into the period of Socialist governments of the 1980s. An increasing number of people—farmers, artisans, people in small businesses, truckers, doctors, medical students—took to the streets to protest impending legislation, often out of fear for their status. The demonstrations frequently led to violence and near-riots. The same scenario took place later under the conservative governments that followed. Demonstrations by college and high school students forced the withdrawal of a planned university reform in 1987. A planned imposition of a "youth" minimum wage in 1994, ostensibly to encourage more employment of young people, was dropped when high school students opposed it in the streets of Paris and other large cities. After a month of public service strikes and massive demonstrations in 1995, the new Chirac government abandoned a plan to reorganize the nationalized railway system and revised a plan to reorganize the civil service. A year later, striking truckers won major

concessions from a still-weakened government. In the autumn of 2000, a protest led by truckers and taxi drivers (that spread to England) against the rising price of oil and gasoline forced the government to lower consumer taxes on fuel. Finally, in 2006, the government passed legislation to establish a work contract (one among many) meant to encourage employers to hire young people under the age of twenty-five by making it easier to fire them during the first two years of their employment. After a three-month struggle of street demonstrations and school occupations by many of the same young people who were supposed to be the beneficiaries of the law (which was supported by all of the major trade unions and the major parties of the left—at least initially), the law was withdrawn. In 2013, when the new Socialist government of **François Hollande** proposed and then passed legislation that legalized gay marriage and adoption, groups from the right organized a succession of massive demonstrations against the law. This time, however, the government stood fast, and the law was promulgated within six weeks. One difference was that the political parties of the right (including the National Front) gave only lukewarm support to the demonstrations.

Political Parties

9.9 Explain France's party system and the factors that have prevented emergence of a two-party system, with examples from recent French history.

The Traditional Party System

Some analysts of elections see a seemingly unalterable division of the French into two large political families, usually classified as the "right" and the "left." As late as 1962, the left was strongest in departments where left traditions had maintained a solid foundation for more than a century. The alignments in the presidential contest of 1974 and the parliamentary elections of 1978 mirrored the same divisions. Soon thereafter, however, the left's inroads into formerly conservative strongholds changed the traditional geographic distribution of votes. Majorities changed at each legislative election between 1981 and 2002, and few departments now remain solid bastions for either the right or the left.

The electoral system of the Fifth Republic favors a simplification of political alignments. In most constituencies, runoff elections result in the confrontation of two candidates, each typically representing one of the two camps. A simple and stable division could have resulted long ago in a pattern of two parties or coalitions alternating in having power and being in opposition. Why has this not occurred?

Except for the Communists until the late 1970s, and more recently the Socialists and the **Union for a Popular Movement (UMP)**, French political parties have mostly remained weakly organized. French parties developed in a mainly preindustrial and preurban environment, catering at first to upper-middle-class and later to middle-class voters. Their foremost and sometimes only function was to provide a framework for selecting and electing candidates for local, departmental, and national offices. Even among the better-organized parties, organization has been both fragmentary at the national level and local in orientation, with only modest linkage between the two levels.

This form of representation and party organization survives largely because voters support it. An electorate that distrusts authority and wants protection against arbitrary government is likely to be suspicious of parties organized for political reform. For all their antagonism, the republican and antirepublican traditions have one thing in common: their aversion to well-established and strongly organized parties. As

late as the 1960s, no more than 2 percent of registered voters were party members. In Britain and Germany, for example, some parties have had more than a million members, a membership level never achieved by any French political party. Organizational weakness contributes to the endurance of a multiparty system.

In two- or three-party systems, major parties normally move toward the political center in order to gain stability and cohesion. But where extreme party plurality prevails, the center is weakened by the multitude of political choices. The lack of either a coherent left or right during the Third and Fourth Republics undermined the ability of parties to form stable governments.

Nevertheless, the Fifth Republic created a new political framework that has had a major, if gradual and mostly unforeseen, influence on all parties and on their relationships to each other. The emerging party system, in turn, influenced the way in which political institutions actually worked. The strengthening of parliamentary party discipline in the 1970s gave meaning to the strong executive leadership of president and prime minister and stabilized the political process. The main political parties also became the principal arenas within which alternative policies were debated and developed.

The main political parties dominate the organization of parliamentary work and the selection of candidates, but they have become far less important as mass membership organizations. In the 2012 legislative elections, the two main parties were supported by 82 percent of the electorate, with the FN and the Greens attracting an additional 8 percent. Thus, about 10 percent of the electorate supported an array of issue-based and personality-based parties, a sharp decline compared with previous elections. Nine parties are represented in the National Assembly in six parliamentary groups—four allied in the left majority (although the Socialist group alone has a majority) and two in the right opposition.

The Main Parties: The Right and Center

Union for a Popular Movement The UMP is the most recent direct lineal descendant of the Gaullist party. The original Gaullist party was hastily thrown together after de Gaulle's return to power in 1958. In several respects, the early Gaullist party differed from the traditional conservative parties of the right.

It appealed directly to a broad coalition of groups and classes, including a part of the working class. The party's leadership successfully built a membership that at one time reached several hundred thousand. Yet the membership's role was generally limited to appearing at mass meetings and assisting in propaganda efforts at election time. An important novelty was that the party's representatives in Parliament followed strict discipline in voting on policy. Electoral success increased with each contest until the landslide election—held after the massive strikes and student **demonstrations of May through June 1968**—enabled the Gaullists to hold a majority in the National Assembly. This achievement had never before been attained under a republican regime in France.

For sixteen years (from 1958 to 1974), both the presidency and the prime ministership were in Gaullist hands. In 1974, after the death of both Charles de Gaulle and Georges Pompidou, Valéry Giscard d'Estaing, a prominent conservative who was not a Gaullist, was elected president. After 1974, the Gaullist party's status deteriorated and electoral support declined.

For a time, Jacques Chirac reversed the party's decline by restructuring more as a mass party, and renaming it the **Rally for the Republic (RPR)**. In fact, the RPR was quite different from its Gaullist predecessors. Although Chirac frequently invoked Gaullism as his inspiration, he avoided the populist language that had served the movement at its beginnings. The RPR appealed to a restricted, well-defined constituency of the right, similar to the classic conservative clientele. Its electorate overrepresented older, wealthier voters, as well as farmers (now included as an important part of the UMP electorate in Table 9.1). Its voters were most likely to define themselves as being on the right, antileft, positive toward business and parochial schools, more likely to vote for personality than for ideas, and less supportive of a woman's right to abortion that had been passed by the Giscard government. After presiding over a government that dubbed itself neoliberal and that engaged in a round of privatization of previously nationalized industries between 1986 and 1988, Chirac set out to assure those who feared a challenge to the welfare state.

The party's electoral levels remained more or less stable in the 1980s, but at a relatively low level (see Table 9.2). Even in the massive electoral victory for the right in 1993, when the conservative coalition gained 80 percent of the parliamentary seats, the RPR just edged out its conservative rivals with less than 20 percent of the vote in the first round of the legislative elections. In 1997, its vote declined to 16.8 percent, less than 2 percentage points more than the FN. Nevertheless, with an estimated 100,000 members in 1997 (relatively low by European standards), the RPR was the largest party in France.

By 2002, the RPR was a long way from the party once dominated with a firm hand by Gaullist "barons" and defined by the organizing discourse of Gaullism. Jacques Chirac's victory in the 1995 presidential elections should have given him an opportunity to rebuild the RPR as a party of government. However, a seemingly unending series of political crises after the summer of 1995 and the disastrous losses in the June 1997 legislative elections only intensified the divisions within the party and with its partners. In 1999, Chirac (still president of the Republic) lost control over the party when his chosen candidate was defeated in an election for party president.

In the fall of 2000, Chirac's candidacy for reelection in 2002 seemed to be undermined by dramatic new evidence of massive corruption in the Paris party machine that directly implicated the president (and former mayor of Paris). However, the unexpected match against Jean-Marie Le Pen (leader of the FN—see section on the FN below) in the second round of the presidential race of 2002 gave both Chirac and the party a new lease on life.

Chirac's massive victory in the 2002 presidential election created the basis for the organization of the UMP, a new successor to the RPR. (The UMP was originally called the Union for a Presidential Majority in 2002.) The party included deputies from the RPR, some from the **Union for French Democracy (UDF)**, and some from other small parties of the right. With more than 60 percent of the new National Assembly, the UMP united the fragmented groups of the right behind the victorious president. By 2006, Chirac's detested rival within the party, **Nicolas Sarkozy**, had become party leader, minister of the interior, and virtually unchallenged party candidate for the presidency in 2007.

Like Chirac, Sarkozy had used his party base to win the presidency, and like Chirac, his control of the party began to wane soon after he became president. Sarkozy built his government on a broad partisan basis and included important personalities of the left in

TABLE 9.1

Voting Patterns in the 2012 Legislative Elections

Leftist parties disproportionately gain support from the young, as well as all professions except shopkeepers, businesspeople, and the unemployed, while the center-right draws comparatively more votes from older voters and those with higher incomes.

	PS/PC/Greens + Other Left (%)	UMP Center (%)	Extreme Right (%)
Sex			
Men	50	33	15
Women	47	40	12
Age			
18–24	50	31	17
25–34	48	34	17
35–44	53	30	15
45–59	49	32	17
60+	44	47	8
Profession			
Shopkeepers, craftsmen, and businesspeople	41	42	14
Executives, professionals, and intellectuals	57	34	7
Middle management	53	31	15
White collar	44	30	24
Workers	46	29	23
Unemployed	46	45	7
Level of Education			
No degree	46	31	20
Vocational degree	47	34	18
High school (academic)	41	40	18
Higher education	53	39	6
Family Income (Monthly in Euros)			
1200	48	32	18
1200–2000	50	33	16
2000–3000	47	38	14
3000–4500	48	38	12
4500+	49	43	7

Source: Ipsos/Logica Business Consulting, *Le Monde*, June 12, 2012, 12.

a number of important ministries. While, for a time, this projected an image of dynamism and renewal, it also weakened his influence among the parliamentary base, particularly after Sarkozy's popularity began to decline. In a close race in 2012, Sarkozy lost the presidency to Socialist leader François Hollande, and the UMP decisively lost to the Socialists in the legislative elections that followed. The loss left the party leaderless, or with at least two contending leaders,

and a weak opposition to an increasingly unpopular Socialist government in 2013.

Union for French Democracy Valéry Giscard d'Estaing's foremost concern was to prevent the center's exclusion from power in the Gaullist Republic. His small party, the Independent Republican Party (RI), was the typical party, or rather nonparty, of French conservatism. It came into existence in 1962,

TABLE 9.2
Parliamentary Elections in the Fifth Republic since 1997

Shifting party vote shares and parliamentary seats since 1997 are shown as percentage of votes cast, first ballot.

	1997		2002		2007		2012	
Registered voters (in millions)	39.2		41.0		43.9		46.1	
Abstentions (%)	32.0		35.6		39.6		42.8	
Party Seats	**%**	**Seats**	**%**	**Seats**	**%**	**Seats**	**%**	**Seats**
Communists (PCF)—Left Front in 2012	10.0	37	4.8	21	4.6	18	7.9	10
Socialists (PS)	23.7	245	25.3	141	27.7	201	29.2	302
Left Radicals	1.5	13	—c	8	—	7	1.7	13
UMP	—	—	33.3d	362d	45.5	335f	26.2	206
UDF (RI and other centrists)	14.8	109	4.9	22	7.7	4	2.4	25
Gaullists (RPR)	16.8	140	—	—	—	—	—	—
National Front	15.1	1	11.3	—	4.7	—	13.8	3
Others	18.7a	32b	16.3e	13	6.3	12e	16.4e	18e

aIncludes the Green party's vote of 6.3%, as well as votes for smaller movements of the right and the left.
bIncludes eight ecologists (Greens), seven dissident socialists, and other unaffiliated deputies.
cVotes for the left radicals in 2002 and 2007 are included with those of the socialists.
dUMP (Union of the Presidential Majority—new center-right party organized for the 2002 legislative election).
eIncludes ecologists (Greens) and dissidents of the right and the left (as well as one extreme right party [MNR] in 2002).
fIncludes affiliated independent deputies.
Source: Official Results from the Ministry of the Interior, www.assemblée-nationale.fr/elections.

when Giscard d'Estaing and a few other conservative deputies opposed de Gaulle's strictures against European unity and his referendum on direct elections for the presidency.

From that time on, the group provided a small complement for the conservative majority in Parliament. Giscard d'Estaing himself, a scion of families long prominent in business, banking, and public service, was finance minister under both de Gaulle and Pompidou before his election to the presidency in 1974. His party derived its political strength from its representatives in Parliament, many of whom held Cabinet posts, and from local leaders who occupied important posts in municipal and departmental councils.

To increase the weight of the party (the name was changed to the Parti Républicain [PR] in 1977), President Giscard d'Estaing chose the path that parties of the right and center have always found opportune: a heterogeneous alliance among groups and personalities organized to support the president in the 1978 legislative elections. The result was the UDF. It is estimated that all of the parties of the UDF combined had no more than 38,000 members in 2002, and its membership was declining.

After 1981, the UDF and the RPR generally cooperated in elections. As the radical right FN gained in electoral support after 1983, the UDF and the RPR presented more joint candidates in the first round of parliamentary elections to avoid being defeated by the FN. Nevertheless, even combined, they were incapable of increasing their vote beyond 45 percent. Still, they won majorities in Parliament in 1986, 1993, and 2002 (see Figure 9.3). The two governments organized after Chirac's election in 1995 under Prime Minister **Alain Juppé** were double coalitions: first, coalitions of factions within the RPR and the UDF and, second, coalitions between the RPR and the UDF. The government in 2002 was also a double coalition. Prime Minister Jean-Pierre Raffarin (who served until 2005) was a long-time member of the UDF. With the integration of most of the UDF deputies into the UMP, the UDF as a party lost most of its independent influence.

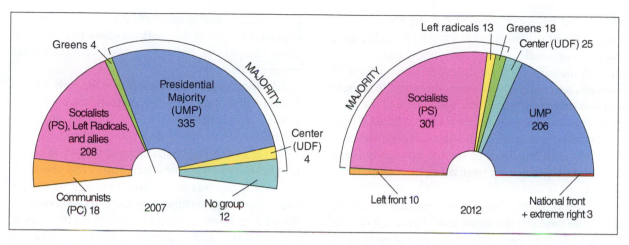

FIGURE 9.3

Distribution of Seats in the National Assembly

Political Representation in the National Assembly after the Elections of 2007 and 2012.

Nevertheless, under the leadership of François Bayrou, the UDF seemed poised to retain some influence as an anti-Chirac/anti-Sarkozy force among voters of the established right. With more than 18 percent of the vote in the first round of the presidential election of 2007, Bayrou attempted to maximize the negotiating position of the UDF in the legislative elections that would follow in June. Rechristened the Movement Démocrat (or MoDem), the party was denounced by former notables (including Giscard d'Estaing), and finally elected only three deputies. In local and regional elections in 2008 and 2010, the pattern of decline continued, and the party was reduced to insignificance in the presidential and legislative elections of 2012.

National Front Divisions within the right resulted, in part, from different reactions to the electoral rise of the FN. **Jean-Marie Le Pen** founded the FN in 1972, and, until the 1980s, it was a relatively obscure party of the far right. The FN did not attract more than 1 percent of the national vote in any of the elections before 1983. In the 1984 European Parliament elections, however, the FN built on support in local elections and attracted almost 10 percent of the vote.

Then, in the parliamentary elections of 1986, the FN won almost 10 percent of the vote (about 2.7 million votes—more votes than the Communists). This established it as a substantial political force. Two-thirds of the FN's votes came from voters who previously supported established parties of the right, but the remainder came from some former left voters

(mostly Socialists) or from new voters and former abstainers.

Profiting from the change to proportional representation elections in 1986, thirty-five FN deputies entered Parliament. In the 1993 legislative elections, FN candidates attracted almost 13 percent of the vote in the first round, but because the electoral system reverted to single-member districts, the party elected no deputies. With over 15 percent of the vote in the first round of the 1997 legislative elections, the FN sent a record number of candidates into the second round, but only one of these was elected. In fact, because of the electoral system, the FN never had more than two deputies in the National Assembly after 1988.

Nevertheless, the FN seemed well on its way to developing a network of local bases. In 1998, five UDF regional leaders formally accepted FN support to maintain their regional presidencies. In 1995, for the first time, the FN won municipal elections in three cities and gained some representation in almost half of the larger towns in France. The ability of Jean-Marie Le Pen to come in second—with 17 percent of the vote in the first round of the presidential elections of 2002—was a considerable shock to the political system. The FN results in the legislative elections two months later (11 percent) were far lower, but were a confirmation that the party—and not simply Le Pen—remained a political force.

The FN is often compared to the shopkeeper movement (the Poujadist movement), which attracted 2.5 million votes in the 1956 legislative elections and then faded from the scene.[23] But the FN draws its electoral and organizational support from big-city, rather than small-town, voters. Its supporters come more from transfers from the right than did those of Poujade, and FN has been more successful in attracting working-class voters (the social base of the left). In addition, the FN has been far more successful than the Poujadist movement in building an organizational network, with hundreds of elected officials at every level and deep influence over voters of other political parties.

Approval of the FN's issues increased dramatically among *all* voters in the 1980s and, after mid-1999, increased again. Moreover, the dynamics of party competition have forced other political parties to place FN issues high on their political agenda. Thus, Nicolas Sarkozy, in an attempt to attract FN supporters, used his position as minister of the interior to confront illegal immigration and deal with issues of law and order.

Although this strategy had been tried before, Sarkozy's efforts proved to be remarkably successful in the presidential elections of 2007. Jean-Marie Le Pen received 800,000 fewer votes than in 2002, and almost all of them went to Sarkozy. Nevertheless, with Sarkozy's influence waning in 2010, FN made an impressive comeback in regional elections, just as Jean-Marie Le Pen was ceding power to his politically astute daughter, Marine, who led the party into the elections of 2012. **Marine Le Pen** was spectacularly successful. With almost 18 percent of the vote in the first round of the presidential election, she exceeded her father's record in 2002, and with 14 percent of the vote in the first round of the legislative elections that followed, FN was firmly established as the third party in France; no other minor party came close to that level of support. Moreover, almost a quarter of blue- and white-collar workers voted FN. Similar to support for the Communist Party a generation ago, FN electoral support varied inversely with education and income. Thus, the FN is now, more than ever, a challenge to the French party system.

The Left

Socialist Party In comparison with the solid social democratic parties in other European countries, the French **Socialist Party (PS)** lacked muscle almost since its beginnings in 1905. Slow and uneven industrialization and reluctance to organize not only blocked the development of labor unions but also deprived the PS of the working-class strength that other European labor parties gained from their trade union affiliations.

Unlike the British Labour Party, the early PS also failed to absorb middle-class radicals, the equivalent of the Liberals in England. The Socialist program, formulated in terms of doctrinaire Marxism, prevented inroads into the electorate of the left-of-center middle-class parties for a long time. The pre–Fifth Republic party was never strong enough to assume control of the government by itself. Its weakness reduced it to being, at best, one of several partners in the unstable coalition governments of the Third and Fourth Republics.

Finally, the emergence of the French Communist Party in 1920 effectively deprived the Socialists of core working-class support. Most of the Socialists' working-class following was concentrated in a few regions of traditional strength, such as the industrial north and urban agglomeration in the center. However, the party had some strongholds elsewhere—among the winegrowers of the south, devotees of republican ideals of anticlericalism, and producers' cooperatives. The proportion of civil servants, especially teachers, and people living on fixed incomes has been far higher among Socialist voters than in the population at large.

The party encountered considerable difficulties under the changed conditions in the Fifth Republic. After several false starts, the old party dissolved, and a new Socialist Party emerged in 1969 under the leadership of François Mitterrand. The new party successfully attracted new members from the salaried middle classes, the professions, the civil service, and especially the teaching profession, and reversed its electoral decline.

As the Communist Party declined in influence after 1968, workers rallied to the PS in large numbers in the 1970s. In the 1970s, the PS did what other European Socialist parties were unable to do: It attracted leaders of some of the new social movements of the late 1960s, among them ecologists and regionalists, as well as leaders of small parties of the non-Communist left.[24]

François Mitterrand reaped the benefits of victory in the elections of 1981. With Mitterrand as president of the Republic and a Socialist majority in Parliament (but also supported by the Communists), the PS found itself in a situation it had never known—and for which it was ill prepared. The following years of undivided power affected the party's image and outlook. The years in office between 1981 and 1986 were an intense, and painful, learning experience for the PS at all levels. Under pressure from Mitterrand and a succession of Socialist governments, the classical socialist ideology of nationalization was partially dismantled, but the orientation of the party was a continuing subject of conflict and debate.

When reelected for a second seven-year term in 1988, Mitterrand carried seventy-seven of the ninety-six departments of metropolitan France. The Socialists made inroads in the traditionally conservative western and eastern areas of the country. However, this nationalization of Socialist electoral strength meant that the party's legislative majority depended on constituencies where voter support was far more conditional than it had been in the past. The decline of religious observance, urbanization, and the growth of the salaried middle classes (technicians, middle management, etc.) and the service sector of the economy, as well as the massive entry of women into the labor market, all weakened the groups that provided the right's stable strength. However, the corruption of power reduced electoral support for the Socialists among an electorate that was becoming far more volatile than it had been before.

Accusations, investigations, and convictions for corruption swept all parties beginning in the late 1980s. For the Socialists, however, this corruption undermined the party's image and contributed to the weakening of voter support. Also, rising unemployment rates, the growing sense among even Socialist voters that the party leadership was worn out, and the mobilization of large numbers of traditional Socialist voters against the government during the campaign for the Maastricht referendum all undermined Socialist support between 1992 and 1994. In the legislative elections of 1993, the PS lost a third of its electorate compared with 1988. If the Fifth Republic became normalized during the 1980s—in the sense that the left and the right alternated in government with each legislative election—the PS became like other governing parties in its dependence on governing power.

Under these circumstances, PS leader **Lionel Jospin** was a remarkably effective presidential candidate in 1995, winning the first round before being defeated in the second round by Jacques Chirac. The real test for Socialist leadership came when President

Chirac called surprise legislative elections in April 1997. Although Jospin and his colleagues were clearly unprepared for the short campaign, they benefited from Chirac's rapidly deteriorating popularity and the lack of efficacy of his majority, as well as from the electorate's tendency to vote against the majority in power. Jospin put together a thirty-one-seat majority (called the *plural left*), became prime minister, and formed the first cohabitation government of the left in June 1997.

The government passed a set of important but controversial reforms, including a thirty-five-hour workweek, domestic partnership legislation, and a constitutional amendment requiring parity for female candidacies for elective office. Finally, there were major structural reforms, and the presidential term was reduced to five years (with the agreement of the president).

Although the government's popularity had been declining, the elimination of Jospin in the first round of the 2002 presidential elections (by less than 1 percent) was entirely unexpected. It largely resulted from the defection of PS voters to marginal candidates of the left alliance, but left the candidate of the FN to challenge President Chirac in the second round. Jospin quickly resigned as party leader, and the left was defeated in the legislative elections that followed, as PS representation was cut in half.

Following a well-established rhythm, the Socialists—together with their allies on the left—rebounded two years later and swept the regional elections in 2004. They won control of all but one of the twenty-two regional governments in France, without clear leadership at the national level. Without strong leadership, however, the PS appeared to be engaged in a self-destructive struggle to choose a presidential candidate for the elections of 2007. In this environment, Ségolène Royal initiated a well-orchestrated and well-financed campaign for the nomination a full year and a half before the elections, directed toward the voters rather than toward the party members who vote for the nominee.

Royal, the first female candidate of a major political party, was a well-established political leader of the PS. A graduate of the ENA, she rose through the party ranks, first as a member of Parliament, then with various ministerial posts, and then as president of the Poitou-Charentes region. Her campaign substantially increased the membership of the PS to almost 200,000. Therefore, it was even more disappointing when Royal lost the election to Nicolas Sarkozy in May 2007.

Once again, in 2011, the PS appeared to be in deep trouble, even as it made strong advances in European, regional, and senatorial elections in the years after 2007. The clear favorite in the Socialist primary for presidential candidate, Dominique Straus Kahn, was eliminated from running, when he was arrested in New York on charges of rape (later dropped), prior to the primary. As a result, the field was left open, and the primary was finally won by François Hollande, former first secretary of the party, and former partner of Ségolène Royal (see Box 9.2). Projecting himself as an "ordinary man," he won a close race with President Sarkozy. The Socialists then won a decisive majority in the National Assembly elections that followed. Thus, quite unexpectedly, the Socialist Party now controlled all three national institutions, having won a small majority in the Senate in 2011.

After one year in power, however, the Socialist government suffered politically from the continuing and grinding economic crisis in Europe. The government was unable to halt either the decline in growth or the increase in unemployment, and the approval ratings of the president dropped to record lows. In addition, just in time for the first anniversary of its election, the government was challenged by a major scandal when it was revealed that the minister of the budget maintained secret bank accounts in Zurich and Singapore. Nevertheless, the government majority benefited from the stability of the institutions of the Fifth Republic, which gave them until 2016 to make things right. It also benefited from the disarray of the UMP, which was suffering from deep divisions and scandals of its own, including several investigations of former president Sarkozy.

French Communist Party Until the late 1970s, the **French Communist Party (PCF)** was a major force in French politics. It was the largest party on the left and had more members than any other political party in France, despite the fact that, except for a short interlude after World War II (1944–1947), it was rejected as a coalition partner in national government until 1981.

Over several decades, the party's very existence constantly impinged nationally, as well as locally, on the rules of the political game and thereby on the

---

BOX 9.2   President François Hollande, an "Ordinary Man"

While his predecessor was often referred to as "President Bling Bling" because of his show business style and his chaotic personal life, François Hollande liked to project himself as an ordinary man. He would bring dignity back to the office, he argued. He would be someone to whom ordinary French citizens could relate. To some extent, he reflected the ways that French society had evolved since 1968, in ways that would seem quite unusual in the United States. Although he had four grown children, whose mother was the previous Socialist candidate for president, like many of his contemporaries, Hollande had never been married. In other ways, he was a traditional French politician, with deep roots at the local level. Although he was the first secretary of the Socialist Party for eleven years (until 2008), his most important elected positions were in the provinces—mayor of Tulle and president of the general council of the Corrèze department in central France.

In other ways, he was a typical member of the political class. He graduated from the most prestigious institutions of higher education in the country, and then entered the Cour des Comptes, a stepping-stone into the French public and private elites. He began his political career, like much of his Socialist generation, as part of the group around François Mitterrand. He was always close to the center of power but, at least until now, was never a major figure in his own right.

However, his image as an ordinary man began to wear thin within the first year of his presidency, in part because this was by no means an ordinary political moment. Unemployment continued to increase to record levels, and France was on the edge of recession, with little hope of growth before 2014. In addition, his government was rocked by revelations that his minister of the budget possessed secret offshore accounts in Switzerland and Singapore. Although he continued to maintain a calm demeanor, he appeared to be surrounded by political storms over which he had little control. Before the end of his first year, Hollande held the distinction of having the lowest level of approval of any president of the Fifth Republic.

system itself. During the Fifth Republic, the party remained, until 1978, electorally dominant on the left, although it trailed the Gaullists on the right. In addition to its successes in national elections, the party commanded significant strength at the local level until the early 1980s.

The seemingly impressive edifice of the PCF and of its numerous organizations of sympathizers was badly shaken, first by the rejuvenation of the PS under Mitterrand's leadership in the 1970s and then by the collapse of international communism and the Soviet Union in the 1980s. The party's defeats in 1981 were only the beginning of a tailspin of electoral decline.[25] By 2007, its presidential candidate attracted a mere 2 percent of the vote and just 2 percent of the working-class vote. By 2012, the party was too weak to run its own candidate for president, and instead joined with a group of dissident socialists, who had left the PS in 2008 to form the Parti de Gauche (PG, the Left Party), in the Left Front. The Left Front then supported the PG leader, Jean-Luc Mélenchon, as its presidential candidate. Mélenchon did relatively well in the first round; he placed fourth, behind Marine Le Pen, with 11 percent of the vote.

Thus, to win elections, the Communists have grown increasingly dependent on alliances with other small groups of the left (Front de gauche), continued (and often difficult) cooperation with the Socialists, and the personal popularity of some of the party's long-established mayors. In 2010, disappointed by the evolution of the party, some 200 members of the "renewal" group within the party resigned en masse, which deprived the party of some of its most effective leaders, including numerous mayors and members of Parliament. In 2012, about half of the members of the Left Front parliamentary group were Communists, but the balance of power was clearly with the dissident Socialists.

The marginalization of the PCF has had an important impact on the French party system. It has healed the division that had enfeebled the left since the split of the Socialist Party in 1920, but a price has been paid—weakened political representation of the French working class. Although the fortunes of the PCF have fallen in inverse relation to the PS's electoral strength, the proportion of workers actually voting for both parties combined has declined by 30 percent since the 1970s, and more workers now vote for the right than for the left. Perhaps most important, it appears that many young workers, who previously would have been mobilized by Communist militants, are now being mobilized to vote for the FN.

Patterns of Voting

9.10 Compare and contrast the French system of elections with that of the United States.

Although France is a unitary state, elections are held with considerable frequency at every territorial level. Councilors are elected for each of the more than 36,000 **communes** in France, for each of the 101 departments (counties), and for each of the twenty-six regions. Deputies to the National Assembly are elected at least once every five years, and the president of the Republic is elected (or reelected) every five years (since 2002; every seven years before that). In addition, France elects representatives to the European Parliament every five years.

France was the first European country to enfranchise a mass electorate, and France was also the first European country to demonstrate that a mass electorate does not preclude the possibility of authoritarian government. The electoral law of 1848 enfranchised all male citizens over age twenty-one. However, within five years, this same mass electorate had ratified Louis Napoléon's *coup d'état* and his establishment of the Second Empire. Rather than restricting the electorate, Napoléon perfected modern techniques for manipulating it by gerrymandering districts, skillfully using public works as patronage for official candidates, and exerting pressure through the administrative hierarchy.

From the Second Empire to the end of World War II, the size of the electorate remained more or less stable. It suddenly more than doubled when women aged twenty-one and older were granted the vote in 1944. After the voting age was lowered to eighteen in 1974, 2.5 million voters were added to the rolls. By 2012, there were more than 46 million people over the age of 18 who were registered to vote in France.

Electoral Participation and Abstention

Voting participation in elections of the Fifth Republic has undergone a significant change and fluctuates far more than during previous republics. Abstention tends to be highest in referendums and European

Protest Politics
A demonstration in Paris.

elections and lowest in presidential contests, with other elections falling somewhere in between (see again Table 9.2). In the presidential election of 2007, a trend toward growing abstention was broken when 84 percent of registered voters voted in the first round, but the percentage voting declined once again in 2012 to 80 percent.[26] The elections for the European Parliament always attract relatively few voters; in 2009, more than 59 percent of the registered voters stayed home (slightly more than in 2004). For referendums, a new record was set in 2000: Almost 70 percent of the registered voters chose not to vote on a (successful) referendum to reduce the presidential term from seven to five years (after the elections of 2002).

In the two rounds of the legislative elections in 2012, more than 43 percent of registered voters abstained, a record for the Fifth Republic. Rising abstention seems linked to a larger phenomenon of change in the party system. Since the late 1970s, voters' confidence in all parties has declined, and the highest abstention rates are usually among those voters who express no preference between parties of the right and left. Nevertheless, in contrast with the United States, among the 90 percent of the electorate that is registered to vote, individual abstention appears to be cyclical and there are few permanent abstainers.[27] In this sense, it is possible to see abstention in an election as a political choice (42 percent of abstainers in 2002 said that they abstained because they had no confidence in politicians).[28] Nevertheless, as in other countries, the least educated, the lowest income groups, and the youngest and oldest groups vote less frequently.

Voting in Parliamentary Elections

France has experimented with a great number of electoral systems and devices without obtaining more satisfactory results in terms of government coherence. The stability of the Fifth Republic cannot be attributed to the method of electing National Assembly deputies, because the system is essentially the same one used during the most troubled years of the Third Republic.

As in the United States, electoral districts (577) are represented by a single member (deputy) who is selected through two rounds of elections. On the first election day, candidates who obtain a majority of all votes cast are elected to Parliament. This is a relatively rare occurrence (about 6 percent in 2012) because of the abundance of candidates. Candidates who obtain support of less than 12.5 percent of the registered voters are dropped from the "second round" a week later. Other candidates voluntarily withdraw in favor of a better-placed candidate close to their party on the political spectrum. For instance, pre-election agreements between Communists and Socialists (and, more recently, the Greens) usually lead to the withdrawal of the weaker candidate(s) after the first round. Similar arrangements have existed between the UMP and other parties of the center-right. As a result, generally three (or at most four) candidates face each other in the second round, in which a plurality of votes ensures election.

This means that the first round is similar to American primary elections except that, in the French case, the primary is among candidates of parties allied in coalitions of the left or center-right. There is considerable pressure on political parties to develop electoral alliances, since those that do not are at a strong disadvantage in terms of representation.

The FN has been more or less isolated from coalition arrangements with the parties of the center-right in national elections (though less so at the subnational level). Consequently, in 2012, with electoral support of 4 percent in the second round, two of the FN candidates were elected. In comparison, the Left Front benefited from an electoral agreement with the Socialists: With just over 1 percent of the vote, ten of their candidates were elected. Not surprisingly, the leading party (or coalition of parties) generally ends up with a considerably larger number of seats than is justified by its share in the popular vote.

Voting in Referendums

Between 1958 and 1969, the French electorate voted five times on **referendums** (see Table 9.3). In 1958, a vote against the new constitution might have involved the country in a civil war, which it had narrowly escaped a few months earlier. The two referendums that followed endorsed the peace settlement in the Algerian War. In 1962, hardly four years after he had enacted by referendum his "own" constitution, General de Gaulle asked the electorate to endorse a constitutional amendment of great significance: to elect the president of the Republic by direct popular suffrage. Favorable attitudes toward the referendum

and the popular election of the president, however, did not prevent the electorate from voting down another proposal submitted by de Gaulle in 1969, thereby provoking his resignation.

President Georges Pompidou called a referendum in 1972 for the admission of Britain to the Common Market. The first referendum during the Mitterrand period, in 1988, dealt with approval for an accord between warring parties on the future of New Caledonia; the referendum was a condition of the agreement. Sixty-three percent of the voters stayed home, but the accord was approved. The electorate was far more mobilized when the question of ratifying the **Maastricht Treaty** on the EU was submitted to referendum in 1992. The results were far more significant for the future of French political life. The 2000 referendum—on the reduction of the presidential term from seven to five years—was overwhelmingly approved (by 73 percent of those who voted), but the referendum was most notable for the record rate of abstention—almost 70 percent.

In contrast, the most recent referendum, in 2005 on a European constitutional treaty, attracted far more voter interest. As in a similar referendum in 1992 on the Maastricht Treaty, the campaign deeply divided both the right and the left (although the largest parties of both supported the "yes" vote), and abstention was relatively low. In contrast with 1992, however, the government decisively lost its gamble, and the majority voted no. When the Netherlands also rejected the document a few days later, the treaty was effectively killed.

Public opinion polls indicate that the electorate is positive toward the referendum as a form of public participation. It ranked just behind the popularly elected presidency and the Constitutional Council among the most highly approved institutional innovations of the Fifth Republic. In one of its first moves, the new government under President Jacques Chirac in 1995 passed a constitutional amendment that expanded the use of the referendum in the areas of social and economic policy.

Voting in Presidential Elections

Presidential elections rank as the most important elections for French voters. After the presidential elections of 1965, it was evident that French voters received great satisfaction from knowing that, unlike in past

TABLE 9.3
French Presidential Elections (Second Round) and Referendums

Date	Abstained (%)	Voted for: Winner (%)	Winning Candidate	Losing Candidate
Presidential Elections				
12/19/65	15.4	54.5	de Gaulle	Mitterrand
6/15/69	30.9	57.5	Pompidou	Poher
5/19/74	12.1	50.7	Giscard d'Estaing	Mitterrand
5/10/81	13.6	52.2	Mitterrand	Giscard d'Estaing
5/8/88	15.9	54.0	Mitterrand	Chirac
5/7/95	20.1	52.6	Chirac	Jospin
6/5/02	20.3	82.2	Chirac	Le Pen
5/10/07	16.0	53.1	Sarkozy	Royal
5/6/12	19.6	51.6	Hollande	Sarkozy

	Abstained (%)	% Voted Yes	Outcome
Referendums			
9/28/58	15.1	79.2	Constitution passed
1/8/61	23.5	75.3	Algeria settlement
4/8/62	24.4	90.7	Algeria settlement
10/28/62	22.7	61.7	Direct election of president
4/18/69	19.6	46.7	Defeat reform package
4/23/72	39.5	67.7	Britain joins Common Market
11/6/88	63.0	80.0	New Caledonia agreement
9/20/92	28.9	50.8	Maastricht Treaty
9/24/00	69.7	73.2	Reduction of presidential term
5/29/05	30.7	45.3	Defeat EU Constitution

Source: Official results from the Ministry of the Interior for each election and referendum, www.interieur.gouv.fr/misill/sections/a_votre_service/elections/resultats/accueil-resultats/view.

parliamentary elections, national and not parochial alignments were at stake and that they could use their vote to focus on national issues. The traditional attitude, that the only useful vote was against the government, no longer made sense when people knew that the task was to elect an executive endowed with strong powers. Accordingly, turnout in presidential elections, with one exception, has been the highest of all elections (80 percent in 2012).

The nomination procedures for presidential candidates make it very easy to put a candidate on the first ballot, far easier than in presidential primaries in the United States. So far, however, no presidential candidate, not even de Gaulle in 1965, has obtained the absolute majority needed to ensure election on the first ballot. In runoffs, held two weeks after the first ballot, only the two most successful candidates face each other. All serious candidates are backed by a party or a coalition of parties, but ten candidates were on the ballot in 2012.

Because the formal campaigns are short and concentrated, radio, television, and newspapers grant candidates and commentators considerable time and space. The televised duels between the presidential candidates in the last five elections—patterned after debates between presidential candidates in the United States, but longer and of far higher quality—were viewed by at least half of the population.

Informal campaigns, however, are long and arduous. The fixed term of the French presidency means that, unless the president dies or resigns, there are no snap elections for the chief executive. As a result, the informal campaign is quite intense years before the election. In many ways, the presidential campaign of 2012 began soon after the elections of 2007, intensified by a closely contested open primary in the Socialist Party in 2011. Although the 2007 presidential election deeply divided all of the major parties, the process of coalition building around presidential elections has probably been the key element in political party consolidation and in the development of party coalitions since 1968. The prize of the presidency is so significant that it has preoccupied the parties of both the right and the left. It influences their organization, their tactics, and their relations with one another.

Just as in the United States, coalitions that elect a president are different from those that secure a legislative majority for a government. This means that any candidate for the presidency who owes his nomination to his position as party leader must appeal to an audience broader than a single party. Once elected, the candidate seeks to establish political distance from his party origins. François Mitterrand was the first president in the history of the Fifth Republic to have been elected twice in popular elections. Jacques Chirac accomplished this same achievement, but served two years less because of the reduction in the length of the presidential term.

Policy Processes

9.11 Which institutions in France have the capacity to check the actions of a government?

The Executive

The French Constitution has a two-headed executive. As in other parliamentary regimes, the prime minister presides over the government. But unlike in other parliamentary regimes, the president is far from being a figurehead. A dominant role for the president was ensured by a constitutional amendment approved by referendum in 1962, which provided for the popular election of the president for a renewable term of seven years. In September 2000, the presidential term was reduced to five years—again by constitutional amendment—to coincide with the normal five-year legislative term. France is one of six countries in Western Europe to select its president by direct popular vote.

Under the Constitution, the president is given limited but important powers. He can appeal to the people in two ways. With the agreement of the government or Parliament, he can submit certain important legislation to the electorate as a referendum. In addition, after consulting with the prime minister and the parliamentary leaders, he can dissolve Parliament and call for new elections. In case of grave threat "to the institutions of the Republic," the president also has the option of invoking emergency powers. All of these powers have been used sparingly. Emergency powers have been used only once, for example, and dissolution was generally used by newly elected presidents, when the presidential and legislative terms were different. (Figure 9.4)

The exercise of presidential powers in all their fullness was made possible, however, not so much by the constitutional text as by a political fact: Between 1958 and 1981, the president and the prime minister derived their legitimacy from the same Gaullist majority in the electorate—the president by direct popular elections, the prime minister by the majority support in the National Assembly. In 1981, the electorate shifted its allegiance from the right to the left, yet for the ensuing five years, the president and Parliament were still on the same side of the political divide.

The long years of political affinity between the holders of the two offices solidified and amplified presidential powers and shaped constitutional practices in ways that appear to have a lasting impact. From the very beginning of the Fifth Republic, the president not only *formally appointed* to Parliament the prime minister proposed to him (as the presidents of the previous republics had done, and as the Queen of England does), but also *chose* the prime minister and the other **Cabinet** ministers. In some cases, the president also dismissed a prime minister who clearly enjoyed the confidence of a majority in Parliament.

Hence, the sometimes frequent reshuffling of Cabinet posts and personnel in the Fifth Republic is different from similar happenings in the Third and Fourth Republics. In those systems, the changes occurred in response to shifts in parliamentary support and, frequently, in order to forestall, at least for a short time, the government's fall from power. In the present system, the president or the prime minister—depending on the circumstances—may decide to appoint, move, or dismiss a Cabinet officer on the basis of his or her own appreciation of the member's worth (or lack of it). This does not mean that considerations of the executive are merely technical. They may be

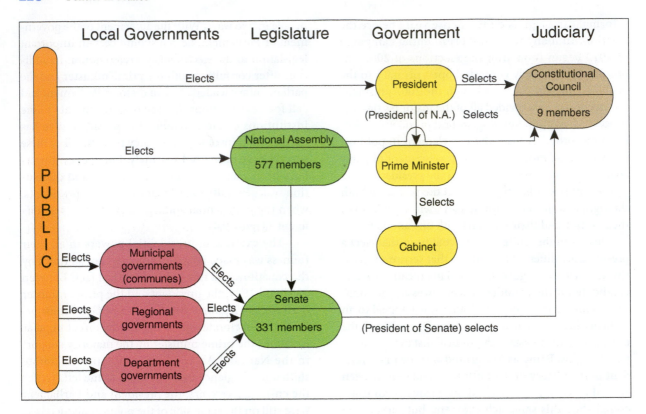

FIGURE 9.4
Structure of the French Government
The Process of Election and Selection.

highly political, but they are exclusively those of the executive.

Since all powers proceeded from the president, the government headed by the prime minister became essentially an administrative body, until 1986, despite constitutional stipulations to the contrary. The prime minister's chief function was to provide whatever direction or resources were needed to implement the policies conceived by the president. The primary task of the government was to develop legislative proposals and present an executive budget. In many respects, the government's position resembled that of the Cabinet in a presidential regime such as the United States, rather than that of a government in a parliamentary system such as Britain and the earlier French republics (see Figure 9.4).

Regardless of the political circumstances, weekly meetings of the Cabinet are chaired by the president and are officially called the **Council of Ministers**. They are not generally a forum for deliberation and confrontation. Although Cabinet decisions and decrees

officially emanate from the council, real decisions are in fact made elsewhere.

The **prime minister** is more than first among equals in relation to Cabinet colleagues (see again Figure 9.1). Among the prime minister's many functions is the harnessing of a parliamentary majority for presidential policies, since, according to the Constitution, the government must resign when a majority in Parliament adopts a motion of censure or rejects the government program. This provision distinguishes France from a truly presidential regime, such as the United States or Mexico.

The relationship between the president and the prime minister, however, has operated quite differently during the periods of so-called "cohabitation." From 1986 to 1988 and from 1993 to 1995, a conservative majority controlled Parliament, and the president was a Socialist. From 1997 to 2002, the left held a parliamentary majority, and the president was from a conservative party. Without claiming any domain exclusively as his own, the president (Mitterrand in the first two cases and Chirac from 1997 to 2002) continued to occupy the foreground in foreign and military affairs, in accordance with his interpretation of his mandate under the Constitution. The prime minister became the effective leader of the executive and pursued government objectives, but avoided interfering with presidential prerogatives.[29]

In part because of the experiences of cohabitation, the president's role is now less imposing than it was before 1986. Even during the interlude of Socialist government between 1988 and 1993, the Socialist prime minister was largely responsible for the main options for government action, with the president setting the limits and the tone. The relationship between President Sarkozy and his prime minister, **François Fillon**, indicated a reassertion of presidential prerogatives, however, and this pattern has continued under President Hollande and Prime Minister **Jean-Marc Ayrault**.

Thus, after the 1990s, the relationship between the president and the prime minister was more complicated than during the earlier period of the Fifth Republic and varied according to the political circumstances in which each had assumed office. The prime minister has a parallel network for developing and implementing policy decisions. The most important method is the so-called *interministerial meetings*, regular gatherings of high civil servants attached to various ministries. The frequency of these sessions, chaired by a member of the prime minister's personal staff, reflects the growing centralization of administrative and decision-making authority within the office of the prime minister and the growing importance of the prime minister's policy network in everyday policymaking within the executive.

Since the early days of the de Gaulle administration, the office of the chief of state has been organized to maximize the ability of the president to initiate, elaborate, and frequently execute policy. In terms of function, the staff at the Elysée Palace (the French White House), composed of a general secretariat and the presidential staff, is somewhat similar to the Executive Office staff of the U.S. president. Yet it is much smaller, comprising only forty to fifty people, with an additional support staff of several hundred people.

As the president's eyes and ears, his staff members are indispensable for the exercise of presidential powers. They are in constant contact not only with the prime minister's collaborators but also directly with individual ministries. Through these contacts, the president can initiate, impede, interfere, and attempt to assure himself that presidential policies are followed.

Parliament

Parliament is composed of two houses: the National Assembly and the Senate (see again Figure 9.4). The **National Assembly** of 577 members is elected directly for five years by all citizens over age eighteen. The government may dissolve the legislature at any time, though not twice within one year. Under the 1958 rules, the government, rather than the legislature, controls proceedings in both houses and can require priority for bills it wishes to promote. Parliament still enacts laws, but the domain of such laws is strictly defined. Many areas that in other democracies are regulated by laws debated and approved by Parliament are turned over to rulemaking by the executive in France.

The number of standing committees was reduced to six in 1958, and then increased to eight by reforms in 2008. The size of the committees, however, remains sufficiently large (well over 70) to prevent interaction among highly specialized deputies who could become effective rivals of the ministers. Each deputy is restricted to one committee, and party groups are represented in each committee in proportion to their size in the National Assembly. Several "special" committees have been created in recent years, and the National Assembly has asserted some independent power as well, by creating committees of enquiry. One novelty of the French system in recent years has been to give the opposition the chairs of a few committees.

Under the Constitution, more than one-half of the actual members of the National Assembly must formulate and pass an explicit motion of censure in order to dismiss a government. Even after a motion of censure is passed, the government may resist the pressure to resign; the president can dissolve the National Assembly and call for new elections. No government has been censured since 1962, and, since that time, every government has had a working (if not always friendly) majority in the National Assembly.

Despite restrictions on parliamentary activity, the legislative output of the Parliament in the Fifth Republic has been quite respectable. The average of about 100 laws per year enacted during the years of the Fifth Republic is double the British average for the same period. Although either the government or

Parliament may propose bills, almost all legislation is proposed by the government. The government effectively controls the proceedings in both houses and can require priority for those bills that it wishes to see adopted (see Figure 9.5). Article 44 of the Constitution empowers the government to force Parliament by the so-called **blocked vote** to accept a bill in its entirety with only the amendments agreed to by the government. In recent years, the government has used the blocked vote to maintain discipline within the majority, rather than to impose the will of the executive over a chaotic Parliament. Its use became an index of conflict within the governing party or coalition.[30]

Article 38 invites Parliament to abandon "for a limited time" its legislative function to the government if the government wishes to act as legislator "for the implementation of its program." Once Parliament votes a broad enabling law, the government enacts legislation by way of so-called **ordinances**. The government used this possibility of executive lawmaking twenty-two times between 1958 and 1986—often for important legislation and sometimes simply to expedite the legislative process. Decisions of the Constitutional Council have now limited the use of enabling laws, requiring that the enabling act spell out the limits of executive lawmaking with some precision.

Another constitutional provision gives the government a unique tool to ensure parliamentary support for any bill that it introduces. According to Article 49, Section 3, the prime minister may pledge

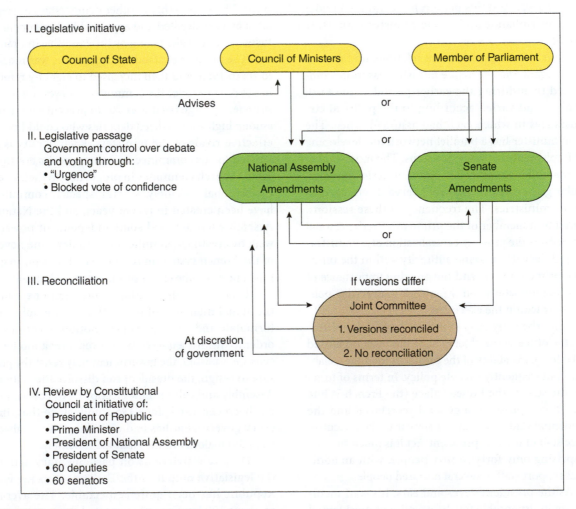

FIGURE 9.5

How a Bill Becomes a Law

The Legislative Process.

the "government's responsibility" on any finance bill or a bill (or section of a bill) dealing with social security legislation submitted to the National Assembly. In such a case, the bill is automatically "considered as adopted," without further vote, unless the deputies succeed in a **motion of censure** against the government according to the strict requirements discussed earlier (which in fact did not happen after 1962). The success of this motion would likely result in new elections. This section was of considerable importance for keeping majorities together, or speeding the legislative process along, before it was amended and limited to only a few instances in 2008, and when it applied to all legislation.

Other devices for enhancing the role of Parliament have become somewhat more effective over the years. In the 1970s, the National Assembly instituted a weekly question period that is similar to the British (and German) version, a process that was expanded by amendments in 2008. In 2012–2013, almost 20,000 written questions were presented to government ministers, and almost 12,000 evoked published results. The presence of television cameras in the chamber (since 1974) creates additional public interest and records the dialogue between the government representatives and the deputies.

By using its power to amend, Parliament has vastly expanded its role in the legislative process during the past decades. During the 1980s, proposed amendments averaged almost 5,000 a year. Since 1990, the number has increased to well over 20,000 a year (26,000 in 2012–2013), which coincides with the doubling of hours devoted to legislative debate each year. About two-thirds of the 10 percent of this total number of amendments that are eventually adopted are proposed by parliamentary committees working with the government. Thus, committees help shape legislation, and governments have all but abandoned their constitutionally guaranteed prerogative to declare amendments out of order. The long parliamentary session introduced in 1995 has enhanced the role of committee leaders in the legislative process. The amendments to the constitution passed in 2008 bring parliamentary committees directly into the legislative process by making the legislation reported out of committees the basis for parliamentary approval.

Finally, the role of Parliament is strengthened by the general support that French citizens give their elected deputies. Better-organized parties since the

1970s both add to the deputy's role as part of a group and somewhat diminish his or her role as an independent actor, capable of influencing the legislative process merely for narrow parochial interests. Nevertheless, individual deputies still command a considerable following within their constituencies. This pattern is enhanced because more than 80 percent of the deputies in the National Assembly in 2013 held local office, most of them municipal councilors or mayors. Large numbers were also on departmental or regional councils, and some were both municipal and departmental or regional councilors.

The National Assembly shares legislative functions with the **Senate**. The 331 members of the Senate (the "upper house") are elected indirectly from department constituencies for a term of six years (half are elected every three years—according to a new system adopted in 2003). They are selected by an electoral college of about 150,000, which includes municipal, departmental, and regional councilors. Rural constituencies are overrepresented. The Senate has the right to initiate legislation and must consider all bills adopted by the National Assembly. If the two houses disagree on pending legislation, the government can appoint a joint committee to resolve the differences. If the views of the two houses are not reconciled, the government may resubmit the bill (either in its original form or as amended by the Senate) to the National Assembly for a definitive vote (Article 45). Therefore, unlike the United States, the two houses are not equal in either power or influence (see again Figure 9.4).

In 2013, the Senate was controlled by a majority of the left, for the first time under the Fifth Republic. The Socialists are the second-largest group (just behind the UMP), a result of the PS's strong roots at the local level. The Communists continue to be well represented for the same reason. Together with the Ecologists and the Left Radicals, they now form a small majority since 2011. Although the Senate, prior to 2011, tended to be socially conservative, this was balanced by a forthright defense of traditional republican liberties and by a stand against demagogic appeals to latent antiparliamentary feelings.

The Senate, in the normal legislative process, is a weak institution that can do little more than delay legislation approved by the government and passed by the National Assembly. However, there are several situations in which the accord of the Senate is necessary. The most important is that any constitutional amendment needs the approval of either a simple or a three-fifths majority of senators (Article 89).

Some legislation of great importance—such as the nuclear strike force, the organization of military tribunals in cases involving high treason, and the change in the system of departmental representation—was enacted in spite of senatorial dissent. Nonetheless, until 1981, relations between the Senate and the National Assembly were relatively harmonious. The real clash with the Senate over legislation came during the years of Socialist government between 1981 and 1986, when many key bills were passed over the objections of the Senate. However, leftist government bills that dismantled some of the "law and order" measures enacted under de Gaulle, Pompidou, and Giscard d'Estaing were supported by the Senate. The upper house also played an active role when it modified the comprehensive decentralization statute passed by the Socialist majority in the Assembly. Most of the changes were accepted in joint committee. Of course, now, with a left majority in both houses of parliament, these conflicts can be avoided, at least for the moment.

Criticisms of the Senate as an unrepresentative body, and proposals for its reform, have come from Gaullists and Socialists alike. All of these proposals for reforming the Senate have failed, though some minor modifications in its composition and mode of election have been passed.

Checks and Balances

France has no tradition of judicial review. As in other countries with civil law systems, the sovereignty of Parliament has meant that the legislature has the last word. Until the Fifth Republic, France had no judicial check on the constitutionality of the actions of its political authorities. The **Constitutional Council** was originally conceived primarily as a safeguard against any legislative erosion of the constraints that the Constitution had placed on the prerogatives of Parliament.

The presidents of the National Assembly and Senate each choose three of the council's members, and the president of the Republic chooses another three for a (nonrenewable) nine-year term. Those who nominate the council's members were, until 1974, together with the prime minister, the only ones entitled to apply to the council for constitutional scrutiny. In 1974, an amendment to the Constitution made it possible for sixty deputies or sixty senators to submit cases to the Constitutional Council. Since then, appeals

to the council by the opposition, and at times by members of the majority, have become a regular feature of the French legislative process.

In a landmark decision rendered in 1971, the council declared unconstitutional a statute adopted by a large majority in Parliament that authorized the prefects to declare illegal any association that they thought might engage in illegal activities. According to the decision, to require any advance authorization violated the freedom of association, one of "the fundamental principles recognized by the laws of the Republic and solemnly reaffirmed in the preamble of the Constitution." The invocation of the preamble greatly expanded the scope of constitutional law, since the preamble incorporated in its wording broad "principles of national sovereignty," the "attachment to The Declaration of Rights of Man," and an extensive bill of rights from the Fourth Republic constitution. For introducing a broad view of judicial review into constitutional law, the decision was greeted as the French equivalent of the U.S. Supreme Court decision in *Marbury v. Madison* (see Box 9.3).

Whichever side is in opposition, conservative or left, routinely refers all major (and sometimes minor) pieces of legislation to the council. In a given year, as much as 28 percent of laws passed by Parliament have been submitted for review. A surprisingly high percentage of appeals lead to a declaration of unconstitutionality (70 percent in 2012). Few decisions declare entire statutes unconstitutional, and those that declare parts of legislation unconstitutional (sometimes trivial parts) effectively invite Parliament to rewrite the text in an acceptable way. The Constitutional Council's decisions have considerable impact and have sometimes modified short-term, and occasionally long-term, objectives of governments.[31]

The approval of the council's activities by a large sector of public opinion, as shown in Figure 9.2, has encouraged the council to enlarge its powers. These efforts were partially successful in 2008, as an amendment gave the council a role in the judicial system. Cases in which the defendant claims that a law violates "rights and liberties" guaranteed by the Constitution can now be appealed to the Constitutional Council, once the appeal is vetted by either the appeals court or the Conseil d'État (**Council of State**). The new provisions came into effect in March 2010, and were invoked in two cases within three months. There were twenty-nine such cases in 2012–2013.

Judicial Review in France and the United States

Judicial review has become part of the French legislative process, but in important ways, it is still quite different from judicial review in the United States. Direct access is limited, although citizens now have the right to bring appeals based on some constitutional issues before the constitutional council. The council, unlike the U.S. Supreme Court, considers legislation before it is promulgated. Since 1981, virtually all constitutional challenges have been initiated by legislative petition, a process that does not exist in the United States. A time element precludes the possibility of extensive deliberation: Rulings must be made within a month or, in emergency situations, within eight days. This is surely speedy justice, but the verdicts cannot be as explanatory as those rendered by constitutional courts in other countries. Dissenting opinions are never made public. Since 2008, there is a process in place for appealing court cases that involve a "priority constitutional question," as decided by either the Council of State or the Cour de Caussation, the highest court of appeal in France. This appeal process has been invoked with increased frequency since 2010.

Thus, the judicial appeal and the development of a judicial check on policymaking enhance the role of the much older Council of State, which in its present form dates back to 1799. The government now consults this council more extensively on all bills before they are submitted to Parliament and, as it has always done, on all government decrees and regulations before they are enacted. The council also gives advice on the interpretation of constitutional texts. While its advice is never binding, its prestige is so high that its recommendations are seldom ignored.

Unlike the Constitutional Council, the Council of State provides recourse to individual citizens and organized groups who have claims against the administration. The judicial section of the Council of State, acting either as a court of appeal or as the court of first instance, is the apex within a hierarchy of administrative courts. Whenever the council finds official acts to be devoid of a legal basis, whether those of a Cabinet minister or a village mayor, the council will annul them and grant damages to the aggrieved plaintiff.

The State and Territorial Relations

9.12 Discuss the decentralization of government that took place in France in the 1980s.

France is divided into 101 **departments** (including four overseas departments), each about the size of an American county. Each is under the administrative responsibility of a **prefect** and has a directly elected general council. Since 1955, departments have been grouped into twenty-two metropolitan **regions**, and now four additional overseas regions, each with its own appointed prefect (in addition to the departmental prefects). Since 1986, each region has an elected assembly and president as well as a prefect (see Figure 9.6). There are more than half a million elected municipal councilors in France, 4,000 departmental councilors, and 2,000 regional representatives. Legislation that was passed in 2010 will gradually reduce the number of departmental and regional representatives to a total of 3,000 beginning in 2014, by merging regional and departmental councilors, and will rename them "territorial councilors."

Centralization has always been more impressive in its formal and legal aspects than it has been in practice. The practical and political reality has always been more complex. Although France is renowned for its administratively centralized state, what is often ignored is that political localism dilutes centralized decision making (see Box 9.4).

The process of decentralization initiated by the government of the left between 1982 and 1986 was undoubtedly the most important and effective reform passed during that period. The reform built on the long-established system of interlocking relationships between central and local authorities, as well as on the previous patterns of change. The reform altered the formal roles of all the local actors, but the greatest change was that it formalized the previously informal power of these actors.

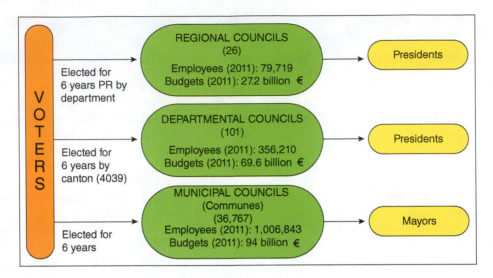

FIGURE 9.6
Subnational Governments in France
How They Are Elected.
Source: Ministère de l'Intérieur, DGCL, www.dgcl.interieur.gouv.fr/.

These powers are based on a system of mutual dependency between local political actors and the prefects, as well as field services of the national ministries. The administrators of the national ministries had the formal power to implement laws, rules, and regulations at the local level. However, they needed the cooperation of local elected officials, who had the confidence of their constituents, to facilitate the acceptance of the authority of the central state and to provide information to operate the administration effectively at the local level. Local officials, in turn, needed the resources and aid of the administration to help their constituents and keep their political promises. As in any relationship based on permanent interaction and on cross-functioning controls, it was not always clear who controlled whom. Both the autonomy and the relational power of municipalities were conditioned by the extent of the mayor's contacts within the political and administrative network, reinforced by the linkage to national decision making that mayors had established through **cumul des mandats**—the ability to hold several electoral offices at the same time (since 2000, deputies are prohibited from holding a local executive office, including mayor of a larger city).

The decentralization legislation transferred most of the formal powers of the departmental and regional prefects to the elected presidents of the departmental and regional councils. In March 1986, *regional councils* were elected for the first time (by a system of proportional representation). In one stroke, the remnants of

---

BOX
9.4   The Political Durability of Local Governments

One manifestation of the political importance of local government in France has been the ability of local units to endure. It is no accident that even after recent consolidations, there are still 36,551 communes (the basic area of local administration), each with a mayor and council, or about as many as in the original six Common Market countries and Britain together. Almost 33,000 French communes have fewer than 2,000 inhabitants, and of these, more than 22,000 have fewer than 500. What is most remarkable, however, is that since 1851, the number of communes in France has been reduced by only 400. Thus, unlike every other industrialized country, the consolidation of population in urban areas has resulted in almost no consolidation of towns and villages.

formal prefectural authorization of local government decisions were abandoned in favor of the decisions of local officials. The department presidents, elected by their department councils, are now the chief departmental executive officers, and they, rather than the prefects, control the department bureaucracy.

What, then, is left of the role of the central bureaucracy in controlling the periphery? The greatest loss of authority has probably been that of the prefects. Their role now seems limited to security (law and order) matters, to the promotion of the government's industrial policies, and to the coordination of the state bureaucracy at the departmental level.

In matters of financing, the principal mechanisms through which the state influences local government decisions (financial dependency and standards) have been weakened, but have not been abandoned. Particularly at the commune level, local taxes provide only 40 percent of the annual budget (collected by the state). The price for financial assistance from above is enforced compliance with standards set by the state. In areas in which the state retains decision-making power—police, education, a large area of welfare, and social security, as well as a great deal of construction—administrative discretion and central control remain important.

Decentralization in the 1980s, combined with the system of cumul des mandats, gave a new impetus to local officials to expand what they previously had done in a more limited way: to trade influence for private money, to direct kickbacks into party-funding operations, and to use their public office for private advantage. The pressures that led to corruption also led to more expensive political campaigns and an often poorly demarcated frontier between the public and private arenas in a country in which people frequently move easily between the two.

Performance and Prospects

9.13 Identify the accomplishments and shortcomings of France as a welfare state.

9.14 Describe the effects of globalization on France, especially as an EU member.

A Welfare State

The overall performance of democracies can be measured by their commitment and ability to distribute the benefits of economic growth. France has a mediocre record for spreading the benefits of the postwar boom and prosperity among all its citizens. In terms of income and wealth, discrepancies between the rich and the poor remain somewhat less in France than in other countries in Europe (refer back to Table 1.2). The income gap narrowed significantly between 1976 and 1981, and then even more during the first years of Socialist government. Yet subsequent austerity measures, especially the government's successful effort to hold down wages, have widened the gap again.

The emergence of long-term unemployment has increased the number of the new poor, who are concentrated among those who are poorly trained for a rapidly evolving employment market. As opposed to the past, the majority of the lowest-income group is no longer the elderly, the retired, and the heads of households with marginal jobs. Particularly since 1990, the unemployed are younger people, many of them long-term unemployed, especially younger single parents. Youth unemployment rates remain double the national average.

Since large incomes permit the accumulation of wealth, the concentration of wealth is even more conspicuous than the steepness of the income pyramid. In the 1970s, the richest 10 percent controlled between 35 and 50 percent of all wealth in France; the poorest 10 percent owned not more than 5 percent. In the 1990s, after a decade of socialist government, it was estimated that the richest 10 percent of the families in the country owned 50 percent of the wealth, while the richest 20 percent owned 67 percent. On the other hand, during the decade 2000–2010, income inequality declined marginally, and remained relatively low, compared to the United States and the United Kingdom.[32]

In spite of some assertions to the contrary, it is not true in 2013 (according to Eurostat) that the French economy is burdened with higher taxes than other countries of similar development in Europe. What is special about France is the distribution of its taxes. The share of indirect taxes—such as the value-added tax (VAT) and excise taxes—remains far higher in France than in other industrialized countries. Indirect taxes not only drive up prices but also weigh most heavily on the poor. The percentage of revenue collected through regressive indirect taxation was the same in 1986—after five years of Socialist government—as it had been in 1980, and remains about the same now (about 77 percent). In addition, above all, France is "the European champion" of taxes on corporations, more than 35 percent above the Eurozone average.

The French welfare state is most successful in meeting its goal in the area of social transfers. Spending on social programs is at about the same level as in Germany and Sweden but ahead of most other European democracies, and far ahead of the United States. A comprehensive health and social security system, established after World War II and extended since then, and a variety of programs assisting the aged, large families, persons with disabilities, and other such groups disburses substantial benefits (see Table 9.4). When unemployment benefits, the cost of job-training programs, and housing subsidies are added in, total costs are as high as the remainder of the public budget, with three-fourths of them borne by employers and employees.

The effectiveness of the French welfare state is most evident in the relatively low poverty rates—lower than in Germany, and far lower than in the United Kingdom and the United States. France has also maintained a high level of quality medical services and public services. High spending for welfare programs has also cushioned the worst impact of the economic crisis in 2008 and 2009. Much of the ad hoc stimulus

spending in the United States is already built into the way the welfare state functions in France.

In contrast with the other European countries (the United Kingdom, for example), there have been fewer cutbacks in welfare state programs in France in recent years—even after the cutbacks of pension benefits in 2003. Indeed, the population covered by health insurance has expanded, but financing for these programs has been at the heart of government concerns since 1995 (see Table 9.4). Although spending on social programs has remained stable as a percentage of the gross national product (GNP) since 1984, successive governments have cut public spending to reduce the budget deficit in what appears to be a successful effort to conform to criteria for the common European currency (by 2014). As France and Europe move into the next phase of the crisis, deficit reduction, it now seems clear that there will be some cutbacks in welfare state benefits, such as family allocations (see Figure 9.7).

In addition, some important gaps in benefits remain that are related to the impact of immigration. Studies of the French system indicate that there are important inequalities in France in access to services and in health outcomes. These disparities have grown since 1980, even as financial barriers to health care have diminished.[33] As immigrant

TABLE 9.4
Welfare State Spending
France ranks relatively high in government spending as a share of GDP and social service programs.

	General Government Expenditure as Percentage of GDP[a] 2011	Government Employment as Percentage of Total Employment[a] 2008	State Contributions to Social Programs as Percentage of GDP 2012	State Health Expenses as Percentage of GDP	
				1990	2010
Britain	47.5	17.4	24.1	4.9	8.2
France	52.7	21.9	32.1	6.4	9.2
Germany	43.8	9.6	27.8	6.3	8.9
Italy	48.7	14.3	27.8	6.1	7.2
Spain	41.1	12.3	26.0	5.1	6.9
Sweden	51.8	26.2	29.8	7.4	8.2
United States	38.8	14.6	19.2	4.8	8.3

[a]All levels of government.

Sources: OECD data: www.oecd.org/perm/publicemploymentkeyfigures, http://stats.oecd.org//index.aspx, and www.oecd.org/els/social/expenditure.

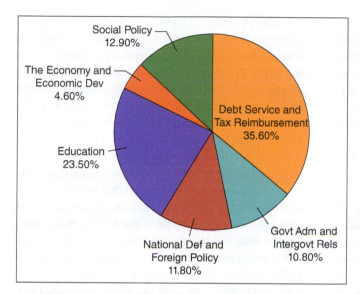

FIGURE 9.7

The French Budget, 2012

How public money is spent.

Source: Ministry of Finance, Projet de loi de finances, 2013, *Tableau de comparaison, à structure 2013, par mission et programme, des crédits proposés pour 2013 à ceux votés pour 2012.*

populations have become ethnic minorities, high levels of unemployment, social problems, and problems of homelessness create pressures to expand social programs, while diminishing the revenue base that finances them. As a result, when the Socialist government passed legislation instituting universal medical coverage in 1999, as part of the campaign to fight "social exclusion," this means-tested, tax-financed, and targeted health insurance program represented a departure from the tradition of social insurance in France.

In reaction to the riots of November 2005 in the suburbs of large French cities, the government vowed to increase social spending in these "immigrant" areas and to increase employment and educational opportunities for youth—a "Marshall Plan for the suburbs." These promises were placed on hold, however, until after the presidential and legislative elections of 2007, and still remain on hold, primarily because of the economic crisis. The "suburbs" of such large cities as Paris, Lyon, and Marseilles are old industrial and manufacturing centers that were developed outside of the city center more than a century ago. Now, as smokestack industry has almost disappeared, and as the native French working class has declined in numbers, these areas are populated by diverse groups of

relatively recent immigrants and their children. Thus, what the French call the suburbs is roughly the equivalent of what is called the "inner city" in the United States.

The Public Sector and Regulation

Government-operated business enterprises have long existed in France in fields that are under private ownership in other Western European countries. After several waves of nationalization in the 1930s and after the end of World War II, the government owned and operated all or part of the following: railroads, energy production (mining, electricity, nuclear energy), telecommunications (radio and television), air and maritime transport, the aeronautic industry, 85 percent of bank deposits, 40 percent of insurance premiums, one-third of the automobile industry, and one-third of the housing industry. All this was in addition to the old state monopolies of mail services, telephone, telegraph, tobacco, match manufacture, and various less important activities.

By the 1970s, public enterprises accounted for about 11 percent of the GNP. Fifteen percent of the total active population, or 27 percent of all salary and wage earners (excluding agricultural labor), were paid directly by the state as civil servants, either as salaried workers or on a contractual basis. Their total pay came close to one-third of the total sum of wages and salaries.

Legislation enacted during the first governments of the left in 1981 and 1982 completed the nationalization of the banking sector and expanded state ownership to thirteen of the twenty largest firms in France and controlling interest in many other firms. After 1982, however, the left government began to move toward partial privatization, in part as an effort to stem massive capital flight and raise money, and in part because of growing pressure from the European Union to conform to directives on competition.

The conservative government that held power in 1986 through 1988 substantially reduced the nationalized sector, accelerating a trend of partial privatization begun during the previous government of the left. Its ambitious plans for **privatization** were halted (40 percent completed) only a year after their implementation began, partially because of the stock market collapse in 1987.[34] Thus, some but not all of the companies that were nationalized by the Socialist government in 1982 were returned to private stockholders. The conservative government also privatized some companies that the state had long controlled. However, both the companies that were privatized and those that remained in the hands of the state were quite different from what they had been a few years before. Recapitalized, restructured, and modernized, for the most part, they were, in 1988, the leading edge of the French industrial machine.[35]

After the wave of privatization, the percentage of salary and wage earners receiving their checks directly or indirectly from the French state was reduced to about 22 percent in 1997, and has remained at about that level since. While this was high compared with the United States, it was not out of line with many other European countries. If one out of five French citizens depended on the state for his or her paychecks in 2005, so did about the same proportion of British and Italian citizens (see again Table 9.4). Moreover, under pressure from EU directives on competition and globalization trends, privatization is a continuing process. The state maintains only small minority interests in Air France and France Télécom, and discussions continue about selling off the few remaining state monopolies (notably the railroads and gas and electricity).

For the actual operation of French business, the move toward deregulation of the economy begun by the Socialists and continued by conservative governments was probably more important than privatization. The deregulation of the stock market, the banking system, telecommunications, and prices fundamentally changed the way business is conducted in both the private and public sectors. The combination of budgetary rigor, pressures from the EU, and state disengagement meant a real reduction of aid to industry, forcing sectors in difficulty to accelerate their rationalization plans and their cutbacks in workers.

As a result, the interventionist and regulatory weight of the state in industry is less important now than it was before the Socialists came to power in 1981. The old issue of nationalization and ownership has been bypassed and replaced by subtler issues of control and regulation in the context of global competition.

In other areas, the regulatory weight of the state has changed over the years. During the 1970s, France expanded individual rights by fully establishing the rights to divorce and abortion. Under the Socialist governments of the 1980s, capital punishment was abolished, the rights of those accused of crimes were strengthened, and detention without trial was checked by new procedures. After much wrangling, in 1994, the Parliament replaced the obsolete Criminal Code dating from the time of Napoléon. The new code is generally hailed as expressing a consensus across the political spectrum on questions of crime and punishment. Moreover, individual rights in France must now conform to the decisions of the European courts under the general umbrella of the EU. Finally, in conformity with the Maastricht Treaty, citizenship rights of EU residents in France have increased during the 1990s. In 2006, a right to the presumption of innocence in criminal cases was created under French law. Since 2010, individual rights have been enforceable by the Constitutional Council.

In still other areas, the regulatory weight of the state has increased. One of the most obvious is environmental controls. Beginning in the 1990s, the French state made its first significant efforts to regulate individual behavior that has an impact on the environment. The first limitations on smoking, for example, came into effect in the late 1980s and expanded after that. In February 2007, smoking was banned in most public spaces, and was extended to restaurants and bars in December 2007. Finally, in 2013, legislation was presented that would impose obligations on elected officials to reveal details of their wealth and income that until now had been considered private.

In an effort to deal with the politics of immigration, particularly after 1993, the state increased the regulation of all residents of foreign origin in ways that have diminished individual rights. In 2004, France moved to regulate clothing worn in schools (Islamic head scarves); in 2011, legislation was passed that would regulate clothing worn in all public places.[36]

Outlook: France, Europe, and Globalization

The main concerns that dominate French politics have changed dramatically from three decades ago. In the 1980s, a coalition of Socialists and Communists was promising a "rupture" with capitalism, and the ideological distance between left and right appeared to be enormous. Today, none of the major parties—including the FN—is proposing dramatic change in society or the political system. As in the United States, political parties are making their commitments as vague and as flexible as possible (with the exception of the FN). After an experiment with socialism, followed by a relatively mild conservative reaction, political parties appear to lack fresh ideas on how to deal with the ongoing economic crisis. The transition away from a smokestack economy has been difficult and painful, and the global economic crisis that began in 2008 has now hit Europe with considerable force. As in the United States, a trend toward deregulation has been reversed.

Political cleavages based on new conflicts are emerging, even if their outlines are still unclear. Indeed, the issues of this first decade of the twenty-first century may very well be more profound and untenable than those of the past. The political stakes have moved away from questioning the nature of the regime and are focused much more intensely on the nature of the political community. Between 1986 and the present, this has become evident in a variety of ways.

Immigration has given way to ethnic consciousness, particularly among the children of immigrants from North Africa. Unlike most of the immigrant communities in the past, those of today are more reluctant to assume all French cultural values as their own. This, in turn, leads to questioning the rules of naturalization for citizenship, integration into French society, and (in the end) what it means to be French. During the 1980s, the FN gave a political voice to growing ethnic tensions, which mobilized voters and solidified support based on racist appeals. In part because of the growing role of the FN, ethnic consciousness and diversity have grown in France and altered the context of French politics.

In the 1980s, the Cold War and the division of Europe were the basis for much of French foreign, defense, and, to some extent, domestic policy. The disintegration of the Soviet Communist experiment (and the Soviet Union) a generation ago has undermined the legitimacy of classic socialism and has thus removed from French (and European) politics many of the issues that have long separated left from right. Parties of the right have lost the anti-Communist glue that contributed to their cohesiveness, but parties of the left have lost much of their purpose.

Coincidentally, the disintegration of the Communist Bloc has occurred at the same time that the countries of the EU have reinvigorated the process of European enlargement and integration, with France in the lead. Membership in the EU shapes almost every aspect of policy and provides the context for the expansion and restructuring of the economy during the Fifth Republic.[37]

At the beginning of his presidency in the early 1980s, François Mitterrand expressed his satisfaction with the existing structures of the Common Market. Having experienced their weakness, however, he increasingly felt that some form of federalism—a federalist finality—was necessary to enable Western Europe to use its considerable resources more effectively. Thus, during the Mitterrand presidency, France supported a larger and a more tightly integrated Europe, including efforts to increase the powers of European institutions and the establishment of a European monetary and political union. French commitment to a common European currency generated plans to cut public spending, plans that many French citizens ferociously resisted. Nevertheless, in 1998, France met all key requirements for, and is now firmly part of, the European Monetary Union.

The opening of French borders, not only to the products of other countries but increasingly to their people and values (all citizens of the EU had the right to vote and run for office in most French local elections in 2001), feeds into the more general uneasiness about French national identity. Indeed, efforts to define and control international migration have slowly moved to the EU level, generally at the initiative of the minister of the Interior and then at that of President Sarkozy.

Europeanization and globalization have both strengthened France and complicated the policy process. The integration of French economic and social institutions with those of its neighbors and the world has progressively removed key decisions from the French government acting alone. The EU paid a large proportion of the bill for agricultural modernization. As a result, there are pressures to reduce CAP expenditures. With the enlargement of the EU in 2004 and the incorporation of more East European countries with large agricultural sectors, these pressures have increased. Since 1992, there has been a gradual movement of subsidies away from price supports (that encourage greater production) and toward direct support of farm income.

The orientation of French agriculture also means adjustment to the world economy. In 1992, the EU reached an agreement with the United States that the EU would reduce subsidized grain exports and cut back cultivation of oilseed products. France is the largest exporter of these products in the EU.

The more substantial issue is the continuing WTO negotiations that deal with the reduction of export subsidies for European and American agricultural products. Poorer countries have demanded the reduction of such subsidies for a long time. In 2007 and again in 2008, the Doha Round of trade negotiations broke down, in part over this issue. The negotiations are still stalled, despite a commitment by President Obama and other world leaders to conclude an agreement in 2010. The breakdown has been blamed on several factors, but specifically on the influence of agricultural groups in both France and the United States.

In a world where trade has become increasingly globalized, French companies have done well. The *Financial Times* reports that among the 500 largest industrial groups in the world in 2008, 31 were in France. France placed fifth in the number of firms on this list, behind the United States, Japan, the United Kingdom, and China, but ahead of all other European countries.

The rejection of the European Constitutional Treaty in 2005 reflected a deep questioning of two aspects of European development. First, the enlargement of Europe, particularly the candidacy of Turkey, has raised questions of both French and European identity, particularly among voters of the center-right. Second, the rapidly growing regulatory power of the EU and its liberal use of this power have deeply troubled voters of the left. French public opinion, at least until 2012, had been strongly supportive of the European Union. By 2013, however, public confidence in the institutions and policies of the EU had reached historic lows, lower than most other major EU countries, even those, such as Italy, that had suffered under EU-imposed requirements of austerity.

Nevertheless, this chapter presents the story of a strong, stable, and relatively open political system. The key to political stability remains, however, the party system, which has become increasingly volatile during the past decade. The forces destabilizing the party system are the major challenges now confronting all of the members of the EU: the problem of identity in an expanding EU and an independent world, an increasing skepticism of government and politicians by those who expect more from government, and, finally, governments that seem to lack the tools to control events in a more globalized world.

REVIEW QUESTIONS

- What are the most important institutions of the governmental system under the Fifth Republic?
- Compare the legislative process in France with that of Germany.
- How would you describe the relationship between the president and prime minister in the French system?

- Compare the role of the Constitutional Council in France with constitutional courts in other countries in Europe.
- How have issues of identity been important in French political life?
- Compare the welfare state in France and the United States.

KEY TERMS

Ayrault, Jean-Marc
baccalauréat
blocked vote
Bonaparte, Napoléon
Cabinet
communes

Confédération Française Democratique du Travail (CFDT)
Confédération Générale du Travail (CGT)
Constitution of 1958

Constitutional Council
Council of Ministers
Council of State
cumul des mandats (accumulation of electoral offices)

de Gaulle, Charles
demonstrations of May through June 1968
departments
École Nationale d'Administration (ENA)

École Polytechnique

European Union (EU)

Fédération de l'Education Nationale (FEN)

Fédération Nationale des Syndicats Agricoles (FNSEA)

Fifth Republic

Fillon, François

Force Ouvrière (FO)

Fourth Republic

French Communist Party (PCF)

G-10

grandes écoles

grands corps

Hollande, François

Jospin, Lionel

Juppé, Alain

Le Pen, Marine

Maastricht Treaty

Mitterrand, François

motion of censure

Mouvement des Entreprises de France (MEDEF)

Muslims

National Assembly

National Front (FN)

nationalization

neocorporatism

new immigrants

ordinances

political class

prefect

president of the Republic

prime minister

privatization

Rally for the Republic (RPR)

referendums

regions

Royal, Ségolène

Sarkozy, Nicolas

Senate

Socialist Party (PS)

Union for a Popular Movement (UMP)

Union for French Democracy (UDF)

SUGGESTED READINGS

Ambler, John, ed. *The Welfare State in France.* New York: New York University Press, 1991.

Bleich, Erik. *Race Politics in Britain and France: Ideas and Policymaking since the 1960s.* Cambridge: Cambridge University Press, 2003.

Bowen, John. *Why the French Don't Like Headscarves: Islam, the State and Public Space.* Princeton, NJ: Princeton University Press, 2007.

Chapman, Herrick, Mark Kesselman, and Martin Schain. *A Century of Organized Labor in France.* New York: St. Martin's Press, 1998.

Culpepper, Pepper D., Peter Hall, and Bruno Palier. *Changing France: The Politics That Markets Make.* Basingstoke, England: Palgrave, 2006.

Gordon, Philip, and Sophie Meunier. *The French Challenge.* Washington, DC: Brookings Institution Press, 2001.

Keeler, John T. S., and Martin A. Schain, eds. *Chirac's Challenge: Liberation, Europeanization, and Malaise in France.* New York: St. Martin's Press, 1996.

Lewis-Beck, Michael. *The French Voter: Before and after the 2002 Elections.* Basingstoke, England: Palgrave, 2004.

Perrineau, Pascal, and Luc Rouban. *Politics in France and Europe.* New York: Palgrave Macmillan, 2009.

Schain, Martin. *The Politics of Immigration in France, Britain and the United States: A Comparative Analysis*, 2nd ed. New York: Palgrave Macmillan, 2012.

Schmidt, Vivien A. *From State to Market: The Transformation of Business and Government.* New York: Cambridge University Press, 1996.

Stone, Alec. *The Birth of Judicial Politics in France: The Constitutional Council in Comparative Perspective.* New York: Oxford University Press, 1992.

INTERNET RESOURCES

Office of the President: www.elysee.fr/ang/index.shtm.

National Assembly: www.assemblee-nat.fr.

Senate: www.senat.fr.

Collection of websites for French institutions: www.assemblee-nationale.fr/liens.asp.

Embassy of France in the United States: www.info-france-usa.org.

ENDNOTES

1. Pew Research Center, *The New Sick Man of Europe: The European Union—French Dispirited; Attitudes Diverge Sharply from Germans* (Washington DC: Pew Research Center, May 13, 2013).

2. This description refers to the first article of the Constitution of 1793, which proclaims: "The French Republic is one and indivisible." The Constitution of the Fifth Republic repeats it.

3. Laurence Wylie, "Social Change at the Grass Roots," in *In Search of France*, ed. Stanley Hoffmann, Charles Kindleberger, Laurence Wylie, Jesse R. Pitts, Jean-Baptiste Duroselle, and François Goguel (Cambridge, MA: Harvard University Press, 1963), 230.

4. These figures are from Antoine Hérouard, *Guide 2013 de l'Église catholique en France* (Paris: Bayard, 2013).

5. See the Pew Global Attitudes Project, July 6, 2006, http://pewglobal.org/reports.

6. One important study found greater spontaneous class consciousness among French workers in the 1970s than among comparable groups of British workers. Duncan Gallie, *Social Inequality and Class Radicalism in France and Britain* (London: Cambridge University Press, 1983), 34. All of the figures in this section are taken from Guy Michelet and Michel Simon, « Le peuple, la crise et la politique, « *La Pensee*, numéro hos série, supplément au no. 368, Fondation Gabriel Péri, 2010.

7. See Janine Mossuz-Lavau, "Nicolas Sarkozy and Women," *Contemporary French and Francophone Studies* 16, no. 3 (2012): 347–56.

8. Ronald Inglehart, *Culture Shift* (Princeton, NJ: Princeton University Press, 1990), chaps. 1–3 and Table 2.4; Michele Tribalat, *Faire France* (Paris: La Découverte, 1995), 93–98; and Sylvain Brouard and Vincent Tiberj, *Français comme les autres?* (Paris: Presses de Sciences Po), 30–32.

9. Frédéric Luczak and Fela Nabli, "Vie Associative: 16 millions d'adhérents en 2008," Rep. 1327 (Paris: Institut National de la Statistique et des Études Économiques, 2010).

10. Which institutions qualify as grandes écoles is controversial. But among the 140 or so designated as such in some estimates, only fifteen or twenty, with an enrollment of 2,000 to 2,500, are considered important, prestigious schools. The number of private engineering and business schools that are generally considered to be grandes écoles has increased in recent years. Therefore, the total enrollment of all these schools has increased significantly to well over 100,000. (See below.)

11. These results are taken from Russell J. Dalton, *Citizen Politics in Western Democracies*, 5th ed. (Washington, DC: CQ Press, 2008), chap. 2.

12. There is no legal definition for a grande école, although it is widely alluded to by citizens, journalists, and scholars. On these issues, see J.-T. Bodiguel and J.-L. Quermonne, *La Haute fonction publique sous la Ve République* (Paris: PUF, 1983), 12–25, 83–94. The figures given here for grands corps (the elite administrative agencies) are approximations, based on a series of articles in *Les Echos,* June 20–22, 2006.

13. See *Le Figaro*, March 25, 2008.

14. Janine Mossuz-Levau, "Les Femmes," in *Presidentielle 2007: Atlas électoral,* ed. Pascal Perrineau (Paris: Presses de Sciences Po, 2007), 75–78.

15. These percentages are only approximations, since interest groups in France either refuse to publish membership figures or publish figures that are universally viewed as highly questionable. For this reason, relative trade union strength is usually estimated from percentages of support for their candidates in social elections for works committees and shop stewards published by the High Council for Social Dialogue.

16. Herrick Chapman, Mark Kesselman, and Martin Schain, *A Century of Organized Labor in France* (New York: St. Martin's Press, 1998).

17. Mark Kesselman, "Does the French Labor Movement Have a Future?" in *Chirac's Challenge*, ed. John Keeler and Martin Schain (New York: St. Martin's Press, 1996). The reports of the congresses of the two largest union confederations in 2006 confirm that less than 5 percent of their members are under age thirty. See *Le Monde,* June 12, 2006. For recent results, see Michel Noblecourt, "Les syndicats réformistes obtiennent la majorité," in *Le Monde*, March 30, 2013.

18. See Martin A. Schain, "French Unions: Myths and Realities," *Dissent* (Summer 2008): 11–15.

19. The most interesting recent study is Sylvie Guillaume, *Le Petit et moyen patronat dans la nation française, de Pinay a Rafferin, 1944–2004* (Pessac, France: Presses Universitaires de Bordeaux, 2004). An earlier study by Henry W. Ehrmann, *Organized Business in France* (Princeton, NJ: Princeton University Press, 1957), presents case studies about the contacts between the administration and the employers' organizations, but it is now dated.

20. John Keeler, *The Politics of Neocorporatism in France* (New York: Oxford University Press, 1987).

21. Frank Wilson, *Interest-Group Politics in France* (New York: Cambridge University Press, 1987), 151, 153, 162, and 164.

22. John T. S. Keeler, "Situating France on the Pluralism-Corporatism Continuum," *Comparative Politics* 17 (January 1985): 229–49. On subsidies, see "Patronat et organizations syndicales: un système a bout de soufflé," dossier special, *Le Monde*, October 30, 2007.

23. Stanley Hoffmann, *Le Mouvement Poujade* (Paris: A. Colin, 1956).

24. D. S. Bell and Byron Criddle, *The French Socialist Party: The Emergence of a Party of Government,* 2nd ed. (Oxford: Clarendon, 1988).

25. For an analysis of the decline of the Communist vote, see Martin Schain, "The French Communist Party: The Seeds of Its Own Decline," in *Comparative Theory and Political Experience*, ed. Peter Katzenstein, Theodore Lowi, and Sidney Tarrow (Ithaça, NY: Cornell University Press, 1990). Also see Jane Jenson and George Ross, *View from the Inside: A French Communist Cell in Crisis* (Berkeley: University of California Press, 1984), part 5.

26. It must be noted—and this is true for all figures on electoral participation throughout this chapter—that French statistics calculate electoral participation based on registered voters, while American statistics take as a basis the total number of people of voting age. About 9 percent of French citizens entitled to vote are not registered. This percentage must therefore be added to the published figures when one wishes to estimate the true rate of abstention and to compare it with the American record.

27. See Françoise Subileau and Marie-France Toinet, *Les chemins de l'abstention* (Paris: La Découverte, 1993); and Marie-France Toinet, "The Limits of Malaise in France," in *Chirac's Challenge,* 289–91.

28. *Le Monde,* June 15, 2002, 8.

29. John T. S. Keeler and Martin A. Schain, "Presidents, Premiers and Models of Democracy in France," in *Chirac's Challenge*, 23–52.

30. One of the very few analyses of the use of the blocked vote, as well as the use by the government of Article 49.3, is found in John Huber, "Restrictive Legislative Procedures in France and the United States," *American Political Science Review* 86, no. 3 (September 1992): 675–87. Huber also compares such tools with similar procedures in the U.S. Congress.

31. The best book in English on the Constitutional Council, though now dated, is Alec Stone, *The Birth of Judicial Politics in France* (New York: Oxford University Press, 1992).

32. See *Le Monde,* October 7, 1999, 6, and OECD income distribution and poverty database: www.oecd.org/els/social /inequality.

33. Victor Rodwin and contributors, *Universal Health Insurance in France: How Sustainable?* (Washington, DC: Embassy of France, 2006), 187.

34. As a result, the number of workers paid indirectly by the state declined. Nevertheless, the proportion of the workforce paid directly by the state (government employment) remained stable at about 23 percent, about a third higher than in the United States, Germany, and Italy, but lower than in the Scandinavian countries. See Vincent Wright, "Reshaping the State: The Implications for Public Administration," *West European Politics* 17, no. 3 (July 1994): 102–37.

35. They were also controlled by the same people as when they were nationalized. None of the newly privatized firms changed managing directors. See Michel Bauer, "The Politics of State-Directed Privatization: The Case of France 1986–1988," *West European Politics* 11, no. 4 (October 1988): 59.

36. Martin A. Schain, *The Politics of Immigration in France, Britain and the United States: A Comparative Study*, 2nd ed. (New York: Palgrave Macmillan, 2012).

37. See Pascal Perrineau and Luc Rouban, *Politics in France and Europe* (New York: Palgrave Macmillan, 2009).

GERMANY

POPULATION
81.1 million

TERRITORY
137,803 square miles

YEAR OF INDEPENDENCE
1871

YEAR OF CURRENT CONSTITUTION
1949

HEAD OF STATE
President Joachim Gauck

HEAD OF GOVERNMENT
Chancellor Angela Merkel

LANGUAGES
German

RELIGION
Protestant 34%, Roman Catholic 34%,
Muslim 4%, unaffiliated or other 28%

CHAPTER 10

Politics in Germany

Russell J. Dalton

LEARNING OBJECTIVES

10.1 Describe the economic and social challenges currently faced by Germany's government.

10.2 Discuss whether Germany's historical experiences contributed to the rise of the Third Reich.

10.3 Compare and contrast conditions in the two Germanies, both before and after reunification.

10.4 Describe five aspects of the social system in unified Germany.

10.5 Describe the structure of Germany's federal government.

10.6 Discuss the differences between the political culture in East and West following unification.

10.7 Identify the main sources of political socialization in Germany.

10.8 Contrast the past ways in which East and West Germans were encouraged to be politically active.

10.9 Describe how the long road to becoming a member of the German political elites affects their actions.

10.10 Discuss the composition and political influence of Germany's interest groups.

10.11 Explain the factors that strengthen the role of political parties in the German system.

10.12 List the benefits and limitations of having many parties represented in the Bundestag.

10.13 Describe the primary actors in the federal policymaking process.

10.14 Identify major policy outputs of government and the major sources of government funding.

10.15 Discuss three prominent policy challenges that Germany continues to address.

What if they held an election and no one won? To an extent, this is what happened in the 2013 German parliamentary elections. As the elections approached, Chancellor Angela Merkel argued that only she could find the right balance of policies to guide Germany through the difficult economic times produced by the 2008 recession. The rival Social Democratic party argued that Merkel's policies had hurt the German economy and its international competitiveness, and her economic austerity policies had harmed the citizenry during a time when government support was needed. Public opinion polls showed that most

Germans wanted Merkel to continue as chancellor. However, Germans do not vote directly for chancellor; they vote for parties instead. Merkel's Christian Democratic alliance had a strong showing at the polls, garnering 41.5 percent of the vote, but fell short of a parliamentary majority. Merkel's former coalition partner, the Free Democrats, failed to win any seats in parliament for the first time in the history of the Federal Republic. The leftist Green party and Linke party also lost votes from the previous election. A new anti-European Union party, the Alternative for Germany, barely failed to surmount the minimum needed to win parliamentary seats. The Social Democrats did increase their vote share, but they saw no way to assemble a center-left coalition.

This fragmented election result produced a months-long negotiation to create a new governing coalition. Eventually the Christian Democrats and Social Democrats agreed to share power in a new grand coalition. This will be an uncertain alliance, since the parties hold markedly different policy goals. Moreover, it leaves only a small minority in the parliament to serve as a loyal opposition debating and questioning government policy.

Germans pride themselves on the efficiency of the economy and the effectiveness of government. The outcome of the 2013 election reflects the uncertainty that has followed the 2008 recession. The German economy has performed better than most in Europe but has begun to slow, and the Merkel government vacillated in responding to the economic crises at home and throughout the European Union. The crisis over the euro and the worsening economic situation in Southern Europe have divided the public and the political parties over how to respond to these challenges. The new government has the votes to address Germany's policy challenges, but because of the divisions it is unclear whether it has the common will to act.

Current Policy Challenges

10.1 Describe the economic and social challenges currently faced by Germany's government.

What political problems do Germans typically read about when they open the daily newspaper or watch their favorite television newscast—and what political problems preoccupy policymakers in Berlin? Often, the answer is the same as in most other industrial democracies. When voters were asked to identify the most important problems at the time of the 2013 elections, the top five issues were unemployment, wages and the cost of living, the euro crisis, pensions, and social equality.

Economic issues are a recurring source of political debate. The economic challenges worsened with the worldwide recession that began in late 2008. When the recession decreased international trade and consumption within Europe, this created new economic strains. In 2009, Germany's GDP decreased by 5 percent and exports decreased by 14 percent. After a rebound in 2010, growth rates have slowly fallen. The recession ended plans for broad structural reforms of the economic system and social programs, and created major new challenges for the economy and policy system. The Federal Republic faces greater economic uncertainty than perhaps at any other time in its history. Joint European efforts to strengthen the banking and credit system, and ward off government defaults in Southern Europe, have created new economic costs and growing skepticism among the German public. The common euro currency is vital to Germany's export economy, but the public is divided on how far Germany should go to protect the euro. Since the depths of the recession, the German economy has grown more than its neighbors, but its future economic prospects are still very uncertain.

Germany still faces a series of economic and social problems that emerged from unification. Because the economic infrastructure of East Germany lagged far behind that of West Germany, the eastern economy has struggled to compete in the globalized economic system. Eastern plants lacked the technology and management of western firms, eastern workers lacked the training and experience of their western counterparts, and the economic infrastructure of the East was crumbling under the Communist regime. Consequently, government agencies and the European Union have invested more than 1,000 billion euros (€) in the East since unification—raising taxes for all Germans in the process. Still, the nightly news routinely chronicles the continuing economic difficulties in the East, which still affect the entire nation (see Box 10.1).

Social services are another area of policy debate. Pensions, health, and other social welfare costs have spiraled upward, but there is little agreement on how to manage these costs. As the German population ages, the demands being placed on the social welfare system are predictably increasing. Few economists believe that the present system of social benefits is sustainable in the future, especially as Germany competes in a global economic system and works to improve conditions in the East.

The process of becoming a multicultural nation creates another new source of political tension. Germany had a sizeable foreign-born population because of its foreign-worker programs of the 1960s and 1970s. During the 1990s, a large influx of refugees from the Balkan conflict, asylum seekers, and ethnic

BOX 10.1   The Curse of Unification?

The Federal Republic's efforts to rebuild its once-Communist East has required massive financial transfers from the West, extra taxes for the average citizen, and a drag on the nation's.

In 2004 a panel of experts, headed by former Hamburg mayor Klaus von Dohnanyi, examined the reconstruction of Germany's Eastern states. The panel concluded that the estimated €1.25 trillion ($1.54 trillion) in government aid has done little to help the economically depressed region. The experts also fear the €90 billion spent by the government each year was weakening the national economy. Now, a decade later, there is still a substantial gap in living standards between East and West; the government subsidies to the East are continuing, and the citizens still pay the solidarity tax to support these programs.

Source: *The Deutsche Welle Report*, April 4, 2004, 62.

Germans from East Europe expanded this population. Policy reforms restricted further immigration, and the government changed citizenship and immigration laws in the 2000s. However, the public is divided on the appropriate policies. Some people argue that "the boat is full" and new immigration should be limited, while others claim that immigration is essential for the nation's future. Germany struggles to address these issues, which are particularly difficult because of the legacy of Germany's past.

Finally, foreign policies are another source of public debate. The **European Union (EU)** is an increasingly visible part of political reporting, and everyday life is increasingly affected by EU decisions. The expansion of the EU to twenty-seven member states also reforms the terms of unification efforts. EU policies, such as protecting the euro and dealing with the budget problems of some EU states, are creating internal divisions over the nation's relationship to the EU. The public backlash to Merkel's efforts to protect the euro stimulated the challenge by the Alternative for Germany party (AfD) in the 2013 elections. Germany's allies ask it to contribute more to these efforts, while many German citizens think they have contributed enough.

In addition, Germany is trying to define its role in the post–Cold War world. For the first time since World War II, German troops took part in a military action outside of German territory—in Kosovo in 1999 and in Afghanistan in 2001. However, Germany actively opposed the U.S. invasion of Iraq in 2003, and public opposition to involvement in Afghanistan has grown. Nevertheless, Merkel has worked to strengthen Germany's ties to the United States through NATO military alliance and other foreign policy activities.

The Federal Republic is one of the most successful and vibrant democracies in the world today. It has made substantial progress in improving the quality of life of its citizens, strengthening democracy, and developing a secure nation, and it has become an important member of the international community. But the continuing burdens of German unification and the lack of consensus on future policy directions mean that recent governments have managed current policy challenges but have not taken decisive action to address them fully.

The Historical Legacy

10.2 Discuss whether Germany's historical experiences contributed to the rise of the Third Reich.

The German historical experience differs considerably from most other European democracies. The social and political forces that modernized the rest of Europe came much later in Germany and had a less certain effect. By the nineteenth century, when most nations had defined their borders, German territory was still divided among dozens of political units. Although most European states had developed a dominant national culture, Germany was split by sharp religious, regional, and economic divisions. Industrialization generally stimulated social modernization in Europe, but German industrialization came late and did not overturn the old feudal and aristocratic order. German history, even to the present, represents a difficult and protracted process of nation-building.

The Second German Empire

Through a combination of military and diplomatic victories, Otto von Bismarck, the Prussian chancellor, enlarged the territory of Prussia and established a unified Second German Empire in 1871.[1] The empire was an authoritarian state, with only the superficial trappings of a democracy. Political power flowed from the monarch—the **Kaiser**—and the government at times bitterly suppressed potential opposition groups, especially the Roman Catholic Church and the Social Democratic party. The government expected little of its citizens; they were to pay their taxes, serve in the army, and keep their mouths shut.

The central government encouraged national development during this period. Industrialization finally occurred, and German influence in international affairs grew steadily. The force of industrialization was not sufficient to modernize and liberalize society and the political system, however. Economic and political power remained concentrated in the hands of the traditional aristocratic elites and the bureaucracy. The authoritarian state was strong enough to resist the democratic demands of a weak middle class. The state was supreme; its needs took precedence over those of individuals and society.

Failures of government leadership, coupled with a blindly obedient public, led Germany into World War I (1914–1918). The war devastated the nation. Almost 3 million German soldiers and civilians lost their lives, the economy was strained beyond the breaking point, and the government of the empire collapsed under the weight of its own incapacity to govern. The war ended with Germany a defeated and exhausted nation.

The Weimar Republic

In 1919, a popularly elected constitutional assembly established the new democratic system of the **Weimar Republic**. The constitution granted all citizens, including women, the right to vote and guaranteed basic human rights. A directly elected parliament and president held political power, and political parties became legitimate political actors. Belatedly, the Germans had their first real experience with democracy.

From the outset, however, severe problems plagued the Weimar government. In the Versailles peace treaty ending World War I, Germany lost all its overseas colonies and a large amount of its European territory. The treaty further burdened Germany with the moral guilt for the war and the financial cost of postwar reparations to the victorious Allies. A series of radical uprisings threatened the political system. Wartime destruction and the reparations produced continuing economic problems that finally led to an economic catastrophe in 1923. In less than a year, the inflation rate was an unimaginable 26 *billion* percent! Ironically, the Kaiser's government, which had produced these problems, was not blamed for these developments. Instead, many people criticized the empire's democratic successor—the Weimar Republic.

The fatal blow came with the Great Depression in 1929. The Depression struck Germany harder than most other European nations or the United States. Almost a third of the labor force became unemployed, and people were frustrated by the government's inability to deal with the crisis. Political tensions increased, and parliamentary democracy began to fail. **Adolf Hitler** and his **National Socialist German Workers' Party (the Nazis)** were the major beneficiaries. Their vote share grew from a mere 2 percent in 1928 to 18 percent in 1930 and 33 percent in November 1932.

Increasingly, the machinery of the democratic system malfunctioned or was bypassed. In a final attempt to restore political order, President Paul von Hindenburg appointed Hitler chancellor of the Weimar Republic in January 1933. This was democracy's death knell.

Weimar's failure resulted from a mix of factors.[2] The lack of support from political elites and the public was a basic weakness of Weimar. Democracy depended on an administrative and military elite who often longed for the old authoritarian political system. Elite criticism of Weimar encouraged similar sentiments among the public. The fledgling state then faced a series of severe economic and political crises. These crises further eroded public support for Weimar and opened the door to Hitler's authoritarian and nationalistic appeals. The institutional weaknesses of the political system contributed to Weimar's political vulnerability. Finally, most Germans drastically underestimated Hitler's ambitions, intentions, and political abilities. This underestimation, perhaps, was Weimar's greatest failure.

The Third Reich

The Nazis' rise to power reflected a bizarre mixture of ruthless behavior and concern for legal procedures.

Hitler called for a new election in March 1933 and then suppressed the opposition parties. Although the Nazis failed to capture an absolute majority of the votes, they used their domination of the parliament to enact laws granting Hitler dictatorial powers. Democracy was replaced by the new authoritarian "leader state" of the **Third Reich**.

Once entrenched in power, Hitler followed extremist policies. Social and political groups that might challenge the government were destroyed, taken over by Nazi agents, or co-opted into accepting the Nazi regime. The powers of the police state grew and choked off opposition. Attacks on Jews and other minorities steadily became more violent. Massive public works projects lessened unemployment, but also built the infrastructure for a wartime economy. The government enlarged and rearmed the military in violation of the Versailles treaty. The Reich's expansionist foreign policy challenged the international peace.

Hitler's unrestrained political ambitions finally plunged Europe into World War II in 1939. After initial victories, a series of military defeats beginning in 1942 led to the total collapse of the Third Reich in May 1945. A total of 60 million lives were lost worldwide in the war, including 6 million European Jews who were murdered in a Nazi campaign of systematic genocide.[3] Germany lay in ruins; its industry and transportation systems were destroyed, its cities were rubble, millions were homeless, and food was scarce. Hitler's grand design for a new German Reich had instead destroyed the nation in a Wagnerian *Götterdämmerung*.

The Occupation Period

The political division of postwar Germany began as foreign troops advanced onto German soil. At the end of the war, the Western Allies—the United States, Britain, and France—controlled Germany's western zone, and the Soviet Union occupied the eastern zone. This was to be an interim division, but growing frictions between Western and Soviet leaders increased tensions between the regions.

In the western zone, the Allied military government began a denazification program to remove Nazi officials and sympathizers from positions of authority. The occupation authorities licensed new political parties, and democratic political institutions started to develop. The economic system was reorganized along capitalist lines. Currency and market economy reforms in 1948 revitalized the western zone, but also deepened divisions between the eastern and western zones.

Political change followed a much different course in the eastern zone. The new **Socialist Unity Party (SED)** was a tool for the Soviets to control the political process. Since the Soviets saw capitalism as responsible for the Third Reich, they tried to destroy the capitalist system and replace it with a new socialist order. By 1948, the eastern zone was essentially a copy of the Soviet political and economic systems.

As the political gap between occupation zones widened, the Western allies favored creation of a separate German state in the West. In Bonn, a small university town along the banks of the Rhine, Germans created a new democratic system. In 1948, a parliamentary council drafted an interim constitution that was to last until the entire nation was reunited. In May 1949, the state governments in the western zone agreed on the **Basic Law (Grundgesetz)** that created the **Federal Republic of Germany (FRG)**, or West Germany.

These developments greatly worried the Soviets. The Soviet blockade of Berlin in 1948, for example, partially sought to halt the formation of a separate West German state—though it actually strengthened Western resolve. Once it was apparent that West Germany would follow its own course, preparations began for a separate East German state. A week after the formation of the FRG, the People's Congress in the East approved a draft constitution. On October 7, 1949, the **German Democratic Republic (GDR)**, or East Germany, was formed. As in earlier periods of German history, a divided nation was following different paths (see Figure 10.1). It would be more than forty years before these paths converged.

Following Two Paths

10.3 Compare and contrast conditions in the two Germanies, both before and after reunification.

Although they had chosen different paths (or had these paths chosen for them), the two German states faced many of the same initial problems. The economic picture was bleak on both sides of the border. Unemployment remained high in West Germany, and average wages were minimal. In 1950, almost

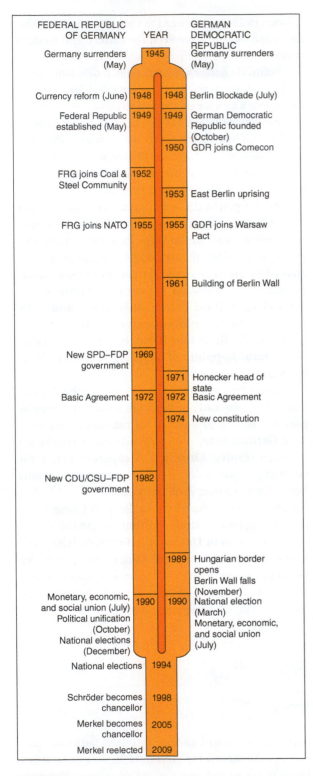

FEDERAL REPUBLIC OF GERMANY	YEAR	GERMAN DEMOCRATIC REPUBLIC
Germany surrenders (May)	1945	Germany surrenders (May)
Currency reform (June)	1948	1948 Berlin Blockade (July)
Federal Republic established (May)	1949	1949 German Democratic Republic founded (October)
	1950	GDR joins Comecon
FRG joins Coal & Steel Community	1952	
	1953	East Berlin uprising
FRG joins NATO	1955	1955 GDR joins Warsaw Pact
	1961	Building of Berlin Wall
New SPD–FDP government	1969	
	1971	Honecker head of state
Basic Agreement	1972	1972 Basic Agreement
	1974	New constitution
New CDU/CSU–FDP government	1982	
	1989	Hungarian border opens Berlin Wall falls (November)
Monetary, economic, and social union (July) Political unification (October) National elections (December)	1990	1990 National election (March) Monetary, economic, and social union (July)
National elections	1994	
Schröder becomes chancellor	1998	
Merkel becomes chancellor	2005	
Merkel reelected	2009	

FIGURE 10.1

The Two Paths of Postwar Germany

The history of the Federal Republic and the German Democratic Republic since 1949.

two-thirds of the West German public felt they had been better off before the war, and severe economic hardships were still common. The situation was even worse in East Germany.

West Germany was phenomenally successful in meeting this economic challenge.[4] Relying on a free enterprise system championed by the Christian Democratic Union (CDU), the country experienced sustained and unprecedented economic growth. By the early 1950s, incomes had reached the prewar level, and growth had just begun. Over the next two decades, per capita wealth nearly tripled, average hourly industrial wages increased nearly fivefold, and average incomes grew nearly sevenfold. By most economic indicators, the public in the West was several times more affluent than at any time in its entire history. This phenomenal economic growth is known as the **Economic Miracle (Wirtschaftswunder)**.

East Germany's postwar economic miracle was almost as impressive. Its economic system was based on collectivized agriculture, nationalized industry, and centralized planning.[5] From 1950 until 1970, industrial production and per capita national income increased nearly fivefold. Although still lagging behind its more affluent relatives in the West, the GDR was the model of prosperity among socialist states.

The problem of nation-building posed another challenge. The FRG initially was viewed as a provisional state until both Germanies could be reunited. The GDR struggled to develop its own identity in the shadow of the FRG, while expressing a commitment to eventual reunification. In addition, the occupation authorities retained the right to intervene in the two Germanies even after 1949. Thus, both states struggled to define their identity—as separate states or as parts of a larger Germany—and regain national sovereignty.

West Germany's first chancellor, **Konrad Adenauer**, followed a course of gaining national sovereignty by integrating the FRG into the Western alliance. The Western Allies would be more likely to grant greater autonomy to West Germany if it was exercised within the framework of an international body. For example, economic redevelopment was channeled through the European Coal and Steel Community and the European Economic Community. West Germany's military rearmament occurred within NATO.

The Communist regime in the GDR countered the FRG's integration into the Western alliance with calls for German unification, yet the GDR was simultaneously establishing itself as a separate German state. In 1952, the GDR transformed the East–West boundary into a fortified border, restricting Western access to the East and limiting Easterners' ability to go to the West. The GDR joined the Soviet economic bloc (the Council for Mutual Economic Assistance, COMECON), and it was a charter member of the Warsaw Pact military alliance. The Soviet Union recognized the sovereignty of the GDR in 1954. The practical and symbolic division of Germany became official with the GDR's construction of the Berlin Wall in August 1961. More than a physical barrier between East and West, it marked the formal existence of two separate German states.

Intra-German relations took a dramatically different course after the Social Democratic Party (SPD) won control of West Germany's government after the 1969 elections. The new SPD chancellor, Willy Brandt, followed a policy toward the East (**Ostpolitik**) that sought reconciliation with Eastern European nations, including the GDR. West Germany signed treaties with the Soviet Union and Poland to resolve disagreements dating back to the war and established new economic and political ties. In 1971, Brandt received the Nobel Peace Prize for his actions. The following year, the two Germanies adopted the Basic Agreement, which formalized their relationship as two states within one nation.

To the East German regime, *Ostpolitik* was a mixed blessing. On the one hand, it legitimized the GDR through its recognition by the FRG and the normalization of East–West relations. On the other hand, economic and social exchanges increased East Germans' exposure to western values and ideas, which many GDR politicians worried would undermine their closed system. The eventual revolution of 1989 seemingly confirmed their fears.

After reconciliation between the two German states, both spent most of the next two decades addressing their internal needs. SPD policy reforms in the West expanded social services and equalized access to the benefits of the Economic Miracle. Total social spending nearly doubled between 1969 and 1975. As global economic problems grew in the mid-1970s, Helmut Schmidt of the SPD became chancellor and slowed the pace of reform and government spending.

The problems of unrealized reforms and renewed economic difficulties continued into the 1980s.

In 1982, the CDU enticed the Free Democratic Party (FDP) to form a new government under the leadership of **Helmut Kohl**, head of the Christian Democratic Union. Kohl presided over a dramatic improvement in economic conditions. The public returned Kohl's coalition to office in the 1987 elections.

Worldwide economic recession also buffeted the GDR's economy starting in the late 1970s. The competitiveness of East German products declined in international markets, and trade deficits with the West grew steadily. Moreover, long-delayed investment in the country's infrastructure began to show in a deteriorating highway system, an aging housing stock, and an outdated communications system. Although East Germans heard frequent government reports about the nation's economic success, their living standards evidenced a widening gap between official pronouncements and reality.

In the late 1980s, East German government officials were concerned by the winds of change rising in the East. Soviet president Mikhail Gorbachev's reformist policies of *perestroika* and *glasnost* seemed to undermine the pillars supporting the East German system (see Chapter 12). At one point, an official GDR newspaper even censored news from the Soviet Union in order to downplay Gorbachev's reforms. Indeed, the stimulus for political change in East Germany came not from within but from the events sweeping across the rest of Eastern Europe.

In early 1989, the first cracks in the Communist monolith appeared. Poland's Communist government accepted a series of democratic reforms, and the Hungarian Communist Party endorsed democratic and market reforms. When Hungary opened its border with neutral Austria, a stream of East Germans vacationing in Hungary started leaving for the West. East Germans were voting with their feet. Almost 2 percent of the East German population emigrated to the FRG over the next six months. The exodus stimulated mass public demonstrations against the regime within East Germany.

Gorbachev played a crucial role in directing the flow of events in Germany. He encouraged the GDR leadership to undertake internal reforms with the cautious advice that "life itself punishes those who delay." Without Soviet military and ideological support, the end of the old GDR system was inevitable. Growing public protests increased the pressure on the government, and the continuing exodus to the West brought the East's economy to a near standstill. The government did not govern; it barely existed, struggling from crisis to crisis. In early November, the government and the SED Politburo resigned. On the evening of November 9, 1989, a GDR official announced the opening of the border between East and West Berlin. In the former no-man's-land of the Berlin Wall, Berliners from East and West joyously celebrated together.

Once the euphoria of the Berlin Wall's opening had passed, East Germany had to address the question of "What next?" The GDR government initially tried a strategy of damage control, appointing new leaders and attempting to court public support. However, the power of the state and the vitality of the economy had already suffered mortal wounds. Protesters who had chanted "We are the people" when opposing the Communist government in October took up the call for unification with a new refrain: "We are one people." The only apparent source of stability was unification with the FRG, and the rush toward German unity began.

In March 1990, the GDR had its first truly free elections since 1932. The Alliance for Germany, which included the eastern branch of the Christian Democrats, won control of the government. Helmut Kohl and Lothar de Maiziere, the new GDR leader, moved toward unification. On July 1, an intra-German treaty gave the two nations one currency and essentially one economy. On October 3, 1990, after more than four decades of separation, the two German paths again converged.

Unification largely occurred on western terms. Easterners sarcastically claim that the only trace of the old regime is one law kept from the GDR: Automobiles can turn right on a red light. Otherwise, the western political structures, western interest groups, western political parties, and western economic and social systems were exported to the East.

Unification was supposed to be the answer to a dream, but during the next few years, it must have occasionally seemed like a nightmare. The eastern economy collapsed with the end of the GDR; at times, unemployment rates in the East exceeded the worst years of the Great Depression. The burden of unification led to inflation and tax increases in the West and weakened the western economy. The social strains of unification stimulated violent attacks against foreigners in both halves of Germany. At the end of 1994, Kohl's coalition won a razor-thin majority in national elections.

Tremendous progress had been made by 1998, but the economy still struggled and necessary policy reforms went unaddressed. When the Germans went to the polls in 1998, they voted for a new government headed by **Gerhard Schröder** and the Social Democrats in alliance with the Greens (*Die Grünen*). The new government made some progress on addressing the nation's major policy challenges—such as a major reform of the tax system and continued investments in the East—but not enough progress. The coalition won the 2002 election, but with a reduced margin.

Mounting political pressures prompted Schröder to call for early elections in 2005, in which the SPD and the CDU/CSU gained the same share of the vote. Merkel eventually convinced a Schröder-less SPD to join the CDU/CSU in forming a Grand Coalition. The two parties struggled with their governing partnership for four years, but they did not enact significant new policy reforms, and then the recession struck in 2008. These events prompted the electorate's shift to the right in 2009, and the election of a new CDU/CSU-and-FDP governing coalition.

The uncertainty of the policy problems facing Germany following the 2008 recession produced the ambiguous results of the 2013 election. Without an effective governing majority on the Right or Left, Merkel eventually negotiated a new coalition agreement with the SPD. She would continue to serve as chancellor, and the SPD would share cabinet posts and the position of vice chancellor. This repeats the earlier experiment with a grand coalition in 2005-09, which struggled to respond decisively to the nation's needs. It is unclear whether the new grand coalition will be more effective.

Social Forces

10.4 Describe five aspects of the social system in unified Germany.

The new unified Germany is the largest state in the EU. It has about 81 million people, 68 million in the West and 13 million in the East, located in Europe's heartland. The total German economy is Europe's largest. The combined territory of the new Germany is also large by European standards, although it is small in comparison to the United States—a bit smaller than Montana.

The Wall Falls
Young people from East and West Berlin celebrate the opening of the Berlin Wall in November 1989.

The merger of two nations is more complex than the simple addition of two columns of numbers on a balance sheet. Unification created new strengths, but it also redefined and created potential strains on the social system that underlies German society and politics.

Economics

Postwar economic growth occurred at different rates in the West and East and followed different paths. In the FRG, the service and technology sectors grew substantially, and government employment more than doubled during the later twentieth century. In contrast, the GDR's economic expansion was concentrated in heavy industry and manufacturing.

By the mid-1980s, the FRG's standard of living ranked among the highest in the world. By comparison, the average East German's living standard was barely half that of a Westerner. Basic staples were inexpensively priced in the East, but most consumer goods were more expensive, and so-called luxury items (color televisions, washing machines, and automobiles) were beyond the reach of the average family. In 1985, about a third of the dwellings in East Germany lacked their own bathroom. GDR residents lived a comfortable life by East European standards, but fell far short of the West.

German unification meant the merger of these two different economies: the affluent Westerners and their poor cousins from the East, the sophisticated and technologically advanced industries of the FRG and the aging rust belt factories of the GDR. At least in the short run, unification worsened the economic problems of the East. By some accounts, eastern industrial production fell by two-thirds between 1989 and 1992—worse than the decline during the Great Depression. The government sold eastern firms, and the new owners often began by reducing the labor force. Even after twenty years, unemployment in the East is about double that in the West.

During the unification process, politicians claimed that the East would enjoy a new economic miracle in a few years. This claim was overly optimistic. The government assumed a major long-term role in rebuilding the East's economic infrastructure and encouraging investment in the East. Only massive social payments by the FRG initially maintained the living standards in the East. While economic conditions improved in the East, experts predict that true equality will require decades of further progress. The persisting economic gap between East and West creates a basis for social and political division in the new Germany.

The German economy has also struggled as a result of the recession that began in 2009. Germany has an export-oriented economy and has been a strong advocate of EU and global trade. A large share of the workforce depends on Germany's exports. Consequently, the global economic slowdown impacted Germany more than many of its neighbors. As banks, firms, and some EU member states have suffered financially, Germany has been called upon to provide assistance. This has created new pressures on the economic system and popular discontent about the state of the economy.

Religion

Catholics and Protestants traditionally were sharply divided in German politics. The postwar FRG experienced a moderation of these differences, partly because there were equal numbers of Catholics and Protestants and partly because elites made a conscious effort to avoid the religious conflicts of the past. Secularization also gradually reduced the public's religious involvement. And in the East, the Communist government sharply limited the political and social roles of the churches.

German unification shifted the religious balance in the new Federal Republic. Catholics make up two-fifths of Westerners but less than a tenth of Easterners. Even more dramatic, the majority of Easterners claim to be nonreligious. Thus, Protestants now slightly outnumber Catholics in unified Germany. There is also a small Muslim community that accounts for about 4 percent of the population. A more Protestant and secular German electorate will likely change the policy preferences of the public on religiously based issues such as abortion and may reshape electoral alliances.

Gender

Gender roles are another source of social differentiation. In the past, the three Ks—*Kinder* (children), *Kirche* (church), and *Küche* (kitchen)—defined women's role, while politics and work were male matters. Attempts to lessen these differences have met with mixed success. The FRG's Basic Law guarantees the equality of the sexes, but legislation to support this guarantee is underdeveloped. Cultural norms changed only slowly; cross-national surveys show that males in the West are more chauvinist than the average European and that women in the West feel less liberated than other European women.[6]

The GDR constitution also guaranteed the equality of the sexes, and the government aggressively protected this guarantee. After unification, eastern women lost some of the rights and benefits that they had held under East German law. For instance, in 1993, the FRG's Constitutional Court resolved conflicting versions of the FRG and GDR abortion laws and essentially ruled for the FRG's more restrictive standards. The GDR provided childcare benefits for working mothers that the FRG did not continue. The greater expectations of eastern women moved gender issues higher on the FRG's political agenda after unification. The government passed new legislation on job discrimination and women's rights in 1994.

Taking all things together, most eastern women feel they are better off today than under the old regime because they have made gains relative to life under the GDR. Merkel's selection as chancellor since 2005 has stimulated further changes in gender norms and policies.

Minorities

Germany's growing minority of foreigners creates another social cleavage.[7] When the FRG faced a severe labor shortage in the 1960s, it recruited millions of workers from Turkey, Yugoslavia, Italy, Spain, Greece, and other less developed countries. German politicians and the public considered this a temporary situation, and the foreigners were called **guest workers (Gastarbeiter)**. Most of these guest workers worked long enough to acquire skills and some personal savings, and then returned home.

A strange thing happened, however. Germany asked only for workers, but they got human beings. Cultural centers for foreign workers emerged in many cities. Some foreign workers chose to remain in the FRG, and they eventually brought their families to join them. Foreigners brought new ways of life, as well as new hands for factory assembly lines.

From the beginning, the foreign worker population faced several problems. They are concentrated on the low rung of the economic ladder. Foreigners—especially those from Turkey and other non-European nations—are culturally, socially, and linguistically isolated from mainstream society. The problems of social and cultural isolation are especially difficult for the children of foreigners. And there is opposition to further immigration.

The nation has struggled with the problem of becoming a multicultural society, but the solutions are still uncertain. The Federal Republic revised the Basic Law's asylum clause in 1993 (making it closer to U.S. policy), took more decisive action in combating antiforeigner violence, and mobilized the tolerant majority in society. The government changed citizenship laws in 2000 to better integrate foreign-born residents into German society. However, the gap between native Germans and Muslim immigrants seems to be widening. Attempts to liberalize naturalization of citizenship are linked to programs to educate new citizens about German language, culture, and political norms. Tensions rose in late 2010 when

Merkel declared that past policies of multiculturalism had been "a total failure." Addressing the issues associated with permanent racial/ethnic minorities (roughly 6 percent of the population) is a continuing concern.

Regionalism

Regionalism is a potential social and political division. Germany is divided into sixteen states (*Länder*), ten states in the West and six new states created in the East, including the city-state of Berlin. Many of the Länder have their own distinct historical traditions and social structure. The language and idioms of speech differentiate residents from the eastern and western halves of the nation.

Unification greatly increased the cultural, economic, and political variations among the states because of differences between West and East. It is common to hear of "a wall in the mind" that separates *Wessies* (Westerners) and *Ossies* (Easterners). Easterners still draw on their separate traditions and experiences when making political decisions, just as Westerners have their own traditions. Regional considerations thus are an important factor in society and politics.

The decentralized nature of society and the economy reinforces these regional differences. Economic and cultural centers are dispersed throughout the country, rather than being concentrated in a single national center. There are more than a dozen regional economic centers, such as Frankfurt, Cologne, Dresden, Düsseldorf, Munich, Leipzig, and Hamburg. The mass media are organized around regional markets, and there are even several competing "national" theaters.

These various social characteristics—economic, religious, gender, ethnicity, and regionalism—are politically relevant for many reasons. They define differing social interests, such as the economic needs of the working class versus those of the middle class, that are often expressed in policy debates. Social groups also are a source of political and social identity that links individuals to interest groups and political parties. Voting patterns, for instance, typically show group differences in party support. Thus, identifying the important group differences in German society provides a foundation for understanding the political process.

The Institutions and Structure of Government

10.5 Describe the structure of Germany's federal government.

When the Parliamentary Council met in Bonn in 1948 through 1949, its members faced a daunting task. They were supposed to design a political structure for a new democratic Germany that would avoid the problems that led to the collapse of the Weimar Republic.[8] If they failed, the consequences might be as dire as the last collapse of German democracy.

The Basic Law is an exceptional example of political engineering—the construction of a political system to achieve specific goals:

- Develop a stable and democratic political system.
- Maintain some historical continuity in political institutions (which, for Germany, meant a parliamentary system of government).
- Re-create a federal structure of government.
- Avoid the institutional weaknesses that contributed to the collapse of Weimar democracy.
- Establish institutional limits on extremist and antisystem forces.

The framers created a parliamentary democracy that involves the public, encourages elite political responsibility, disperses political power, and limits the influence of extremists.

The Basic Law was supposedly temporary until both halves of Germany were united. In actuality, the GDR's collapse in 1990 led to its incorporation into the constitutional and economic systems of the Federal Republic. In September 1990, the FRG and the GDR signed a treaty to unify their two nations, and the government amended the Basic Law to include the states in the East. Thus, the government of unified Germany functions according to the Basic Law. This section describes the key institutions and procedures of this democratic system.

A Federal System

One way to distribute political power and to build checks and balances into a political system is through a federal system of government. The Basic Law created one of the few federal political systems in Europe (see Figure 10.2). Germany is organized into sixteen states

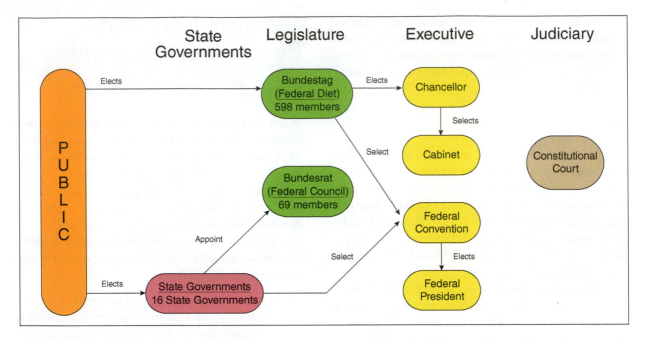

FIGURE 10.2
The Structure of Germany's Federal Government
Germany merges federalism with a parliamentary system and a Constitutional Court.

(Länder). Political power is divided between the federal government (*Bund*) and the state governments. The federal government has primary policy responsibility in most policy areas. The states, however, have jurisdiction in education, culture, law enforcement, and regional planning. In several other policy areas, the federal government and the states share responsibility, although federal law takes priority. Furthermore, the states can legislate in areas that the Basic Law does not explicitly assign to the federal government.

The state governments have a unicameral legislature, normally called a *Landtag*, that is directly elected by popular vote. The party or coalition that controls the legislature selects a minister president to head the state government. One significant feature of federalism is that party coalitions can vary widely across the states, including combinations that cut across the normal lines of national politics. This opens the door to experiments in party cooperation that sometimes have national implications.

The federal government is the major source of policy legislation. The states are primarily responsible for policy administration, enforcing most of the domestic legislation enacted by the federal government, as well as their own laws. The state governments

also oversee the operation of the local governments. Next to the federal chancellor, the minister presidents are among the most powerful political officials in the Federal Republic.

One house of the bicameral federal legislature, the Bundesrat, is composed solely of representatives appointed by the state governments. State government officials also participate in selecting the federal president and the justices of the major federal courts. This federal system thus decentralizes political power by balancing the power of the state governments against the power of the federal government.

Parliamentary Government

The federal government has a bicameral parliament: The popularly elected Bundestag is the primary legislative body; the Bundesrat represents the state governments at the federal level.

The Bundestag The **Bundestag (Federal Diet)** consists of at least 598 deputies who are the only national government officials directly elected by the German public.[9] Elections to select deputies normally occur every four years.

The Bundestag's major function is to enact legislation; all federal laws must receive its approval. Most legislation, however, is initially proposed by the executive branch. Like other modern parliaments, the Bundestag primarily evaluates and amends the government's legislative program. Another important function of the Bundestag is to elect the federal chancellor, who heads the executive branch.

The Bundestag is a forum for public debate in several different ways. Its plenary sessions discuss the legislation before the chamber. Debating time is given to all party groupings according to their size; both party leaders and backbenchers normally participate. The Bundestag televises its sessions, including broadcasts on the Internet, to expand the audience for its policy debates.[10]

The Bundestag also scrutinizes the actions of the government. The most common method of oversight is the "question hour" adopted from the British House of Commons. An individual deputy can submit a written question to a government minister; questions range from broad policy issues to the specific needs of one constituent. Government representatives answer the queries during the question hour, and deputies can raise follow-up questions at that time. Bundestag deputies posed more than 15,000 oral and written questions during the 2005–2009 term of the Bundestag. The opposition parties normally make greatest use of these oversight opportunities. Rank-and-file members of the governing parties also use these questions to make their own views known.

The Bundestag has a strong set of committees that strengthen its legislative and oversight roles. These committees have expertise to balance the policy knowledge of the federal agencies; the committees also conduct hearings in their area of specialization. Their oversight function is further strengthened because opposition parties chair a proportionate share of these committees, an unusual pattern for democratic legislatures.

Overall, the Bundestag has considerable oversight powers, especially for a legislature in a parliamentary system. Legislative committees can collect the information needed to understand and question government policymakers. Bundestag members can use the question hour and other methods to bring attention to political issues and challenge the government. And through its legislative process, the Bundestag often prompts the government to revise its proposals to gain passage.

The Bundesrat   The second chamber of the parliament, the **Bundesrat (Federal Council)**, reflects Germany's federal system. The state governments appoint its sixty-nine members to represent their interests. The states normally appoint members of the state cabinet to serve jointly in the Bundesrat; the chamber thus acts as a permanent conference of state officials. Each state receives seats in numbers roughly proportionate to the state's population, from three for the smallest states to six seats for the largest. Each state delegation casts its votes in a bloc, according to the instructions of the state government.

The Bundesrat's role is to represent state interests. It does this in evaluating legislation, debating government policy, and sharing information between federal and state governments. It must approve the subset of legislation that directly affects state interests. Thus, the Bundesrat is an essential part of the German federal system.

In comparison to other European parliamentary systems, the German parliament has more political influence than most. The Bundestag exercises more autonomy than the typical parliament. Especially if one includes the Bundesrat, the German parliament has considerable independence and opportunity to revise government proposals and to exercise oversight on the government. By strengthening the power of the parliament, the Basic Law sought to create a check on executive power. Experience shows that the political system has met this goal.

The Federal Chancellor and Cabinet

The Federal Republic has a dual executive, but the Basic Law gives substantially greater formal powers to the **federal chancellor (Bundeskanzler)** as the chief executive. Moreover, chancellors have dominated the political process and symbolized the federal government by their personalization of power. The chancellor plays such a central role in the political system that some observers describe the German system as a "chancellor democracy."

The Bundestag elects the chancellor, who directs the federal government. The chancellor thus represents a majority of the Bundestag and normally can count on their support for the government's legislative proposals. Chancellors usually have led their own party, directing party strategy and heading the party slate at elections. Each chancellor also brings a distinct personality to the office. Schröder was a doer who governed with a strong personality; Merkel prefers a more consultative and cooperative decision-making style, while still shaping the course of her government.

Another source of the chancellor's authority is control over the Cabinet. The federal government consists of fourteen departments, each headed by a minister. The Cabinet ministers are formally appointed, or dismissed, by the federal president on the recommendation of the chancellor (Bundestag approval is not necessary). The Basic Law grants the chancellor the power to decide the number of Cabinet ministers and their duties.

The federal government functions in terms of three principles described in the Basic Law. First, the *chancellor principle* says that the chancellor defines government policy. The chancellor's formal policy directives are legally binding on the Cabinet and the ministries. Thus, in contrast to the British system of shared Cabinet responsibility, the German Cabinet is subordinate to the chancellor in policymaking.

The second principle, *ministerial autonomy*, gives each minister the authority to direct the ministry's internal workings without Cabinet intervention as long as the policies conform to the government's guidelines. Ministers are responsible for supervising the activities of their departments, guiding their policy planning, and overseeing policy administration within their jurisdiction.

The *cabinet principle* holds that when conflicts arise between departments over jurisdictional or budgetary matters, the Cabinet will resolve them.

The actual working of the government is more fluid than the formal rules in the Basic Law. The allocation of ministries is a major issue in building a multiparty coalition after each election. Cabinet members also display great independence on policy despite the formal restrictions of the Basic Law. Ministers are appointed because of their expertise in a policy area. In practice, ministers often identify more with their role as department head than with their role as agent of the chancellor; their political success is judged by their representation of department interests.

The Cabinet thus serves as a clearinghouse for the business of the federal government. Specific ministers present policy proposals originating in their departments in the hope of gaining government endorsement. The chancellor defines a government program that reflects a consensus of the Cabinet and relies on negotiations and compromise within the Cabinet to maintain this consensus.

The Federal President

The Basic Law defines the office of **federal president (Bundespräsident)** as a mostly ceremonial post. The president's official duties involve greeting visiting heads of state, attending official government functions, visiting foreign nations, and similar tasks.[11] To insulate the office from electoral politics, the president is selected by a Federal Convention composed of all Bundestag deputies and an equal number of representatives chosen by the state legislatures. The president is supposed to remain above partisan politics once elected.

A New Nation
Chancellor Helmut Kohl addresses the first meeting of the all-German parliament (Bundestag) held in the Berlin Reichstag building in October 1990.

The president's limited political role does not mean that an incumbent is uninvolved in the policy process. The president appoints government and military officials, signs treaties and laws, and has the power of pardon. In these instances, however, the chancellor must countersign the actions. The president also nominates a chancellor to the Bundestag and can dissolve parliament if a government bill loses a no-confidence vote. In both instances, the Basic Law limits the president's ability to act independently.

Potentially more significant is the constitutional ambiguity over whether the president must honor certain government requests. The legal precedent is unclear on whether the president has the constitutional right to veto legislation, to refuse the chancellor's recommendation for Cabinet appointments, or even to reject a request to dissolve the Bundestag. Analysts see these ambiguities as a safety valve built into the Basic Law's elaborate system of checks and balances.

The office of the federal president has political importance that goes beyond the articles of the Basic Law. An active, dynamic president can influence the political climate through speeches and public activities. The president is the one political figure who can rightly claim to be above politics and who can work to extend the vision of the nation beyond its everyday concerns. Joachim Gauck was elected president in 2012 after a scandal prompted the former president to leave office. Gauck marks a break with the past; he is a former Lutheran pastor and was an outspoken critic of the GDR regime before its collapse. He is concerned with human rights issues and is willing to speak to the conscience of the nation.

The Judicial System

The ordinary courts, which hear criminal cases and most legal disputes, are integrated into a unitary system. The states administer the courts at the local and state levels. The highest ordinary court, the Federal Court of Justice, is at the national level. All courts apply the same national legal codes.

A second set of administrative courts hears cases in specialized areas. One court deals with administrative complaints against government agencies, one handles tax matters, another resolves claims involving social programs, and one deals with labor–management disputes. Like the rest of the judicial system, these specialized courts exist at both the state and the federal levels.

The Basic Law created a third element of the judiciary: the independent **Constitutional Court**. This court reviews the constitutionality of legislation, mediates disputes between levels of government, and protects the constitutional and democratic order.[12] This is an innovation for the German legal system because it places one law, the Basic Law, above all others. This also implies limits on the decision-making power of the parliament and the judicial interpretations of lower court judges. Because of the importance of the Constitutional Court, its sixteen members are selected for twelve-year terms in equal numbers by the Bundestag and Bundesrat. The Constitutional Court provides another check on the potential excesses of government and gives citizens additional protection for their rights. It is the third pillar of German democracy.

The Separation of Powers

One of the Basic Law's goals was to avoid a concentration of power in the hands of any one actor or institution. The framers wanted to disperse political power so that extremists or antidemocrats could not overturn the system; democracy would require a consensus-building process. Each institution of government has strong powers within its own domain but a limited ability to force its will on other institutions.

For instance, the chancellor lacks the authority to dissolve the legislature and call for new elections, something that normally exists in parliamentary systems. Equally important, the Basic Law limits the legislature's control over the chancellor. In a parliamentary system, the legislature typically can remove a chief executive from office by a simple majority vote. During the Weimar Republic, however, extremist parties wanted to destabilize the democratic system by opposing incumbent chancellors. To address situations where parliament might desire to remove the chancellor, the Basic Law created a **constructive no-confidence vote**.[13] In order for the Bundestag to remove a chancellor, it simultaneously must agree on a successor. This ensures continuity in government and an initial majority in support of a new chancellor. It also makes it more difficult to remove an incumbent. Opponents cannot simply disagree with the government; a majority must agree on an alternative.

The constructive no-confidence vote has been attempted only twice—and has succeeded only once. In 1982, a majority replaced Chancellor Schmidt with a new chancellor, Helmut Kohl.

The Constitutional Court is another check on government actions, and it has assumed an important role as the guarantor of citizen rights and the protector of the constitution. The distribution of power and policy responsibilities between the federal and state governments is another moderating force in the political process. Even the strong bicameral legislature ensures that multiple interests must agree before making public policy.

The federal system is another way to disperse power so that no one political institution can dominate the political process.

This complex structure complicates the governing process compared with a unified system, such as that in Britain, the Netherlands, or Sweden. However, democracy is often a complicated process. This system of shared powers and of checks and balances has enabled German democracy to grow and flourish.

Remaking Political Cultures

10.6 Discuss the differences between the political culture in East and West following unification.

Consider what the average German must have thought about politics as World War II was ending. Germany's history was hardly conducive to good democratic citizenship. Under the Kaiser, the government expected people to be subjects, not active participants in the political process; this style nurtured feelings of political intolerance. The interlude of the Weimar Republic did little to change these values. The polarization, fragmentation, and outright violence of the Weimar Republic taught people to avoid politics, not to be active participants. Moreover, democracy eventually failed, and national socialism arose in its place. The Third Reich then raised another generation under an intolerant, authoritarian system.

Because of this historical legacy, there were widespread fears that West Germany lacked a democratic political culture, thereby making it vulnerable to the same problems that undermined the Weimar Republic. Postwar opinion polls in the West presented a negative image of public opinion that was probably equally applicable to the East.[14] West Germans were politically detached, accepting of authority, and intolerant in their political views. A significant minority was unrepentant Nazis, sympathy for many elements of the Nazi ideology was widespread, and anti-Semitic feelings remained commonplace.

Perhaps even more amazing than the Economic Miracle was the transformation of West Germany's political culture in little more than a generation. The government undertook a massive political reeducation program. The schools, the media, and political organizations were mobilized behind the effort. The citizenry itself also was changing—older generations raised under authoritarian regimes were gradually being replaced by younger generations socialized during the postwar democratic era. The successes of a growing economy and a relatively smoothly functioning political system also changed the public's perceptions of politics. These efforts created a new political culture more consistent with the democratic institutions and processes of the Federal Republic.

With unification in 1990, Germany confronted another serious cultural question. The Communists had tried to create a rival culture in the GDR that would support their state and its socialist economic system. Indeed, the GDR's efforts at political education were intense and extensive; they aimed at creating a broad "socialist personality."[15] Young people were taught a collective identity with their peers, a love for the GDR and its socialist brethren, acceptance of the Socialist Unity Party, and a Marxist–Leninist understanding of history and society.

German unification meant the blending of these two different political cultures, and at first, the consequences of this mixture were uncertain. Without scientific social science research in the GDR, it was unclear if Easterners had internalized the government's propaganda. At the same time, the revolutionary political events leading to German unification may have reshaped even long-held political beliefs. What does a Communist think after attending communism's funeral?

Unification thus created a new question: Could the FRG assimilate 16 million new citizens with potentially different beliefs about how politics and society should function? The following sections discuss the key elements of German political culture and how they have changed over time.

Orientations toward the Political Community

A common history, culture, territory, and language created a sense of a single German community long before Germany was politically united. Germany was the land of Schiller, Goethe, Beethoven, and Wagner, even if Germans disagreed on political boundaries. The imagery of a single *Volk* binds Germans together despite their social and political differences.

Previous regimes had failed, however, to develop a common political identity to match the German social identity. Succeeding political systems were short-lived and did not develop a popular consensus on the nature and goals of German politics. Postwar West Germany faced a similar challenge: building a political community in a divided and defeated nation.

In the early 1950s, large sectors of the West German public identified with the symbols and personalities of previous regimes.[16] Most people felt that the Second Empire or Hitler's prewar Reich represented the best times in German history. Substantial minorities favored restoring the monarchy or creating a one-party state. Almost half the population believed that if it had not been for World War II, Hitler would have been one of Germany's greatest statesmen.

Over the next two decades, these ties to earlier regimes gradually weakened, and the bonds to the new institutions and leaders of the Federal Republic steadily grew stronger (see Figure 10.3). The number of citizens who believed that Bundestag deputies represented the public interest doubled between 1951 and 1964; public respect shifted from the personalities of prior regimes to the chancellors of the Federal Republic. By the 1970s, an overwhelming majority of the public felt that the present was the best time in German history—and the postwar Economic Miracle was continuing. West Germans became more politically tolerant, and feelings of anti-Semitism declined sharply. The public displayed a growing esteem for the new political system.[17]

Even while Westerners developed a new acceptance of the institutions and symbols of the Federal Republic, something was missing, something that touched the political spirit of the citizens. The FRG was a provisional entity, and "Germany" meant a unified nation. Were citizens of West Germany to think of themselves as Germans, West Germans, or some mix of both? In addition, the trauma of the Third Reich

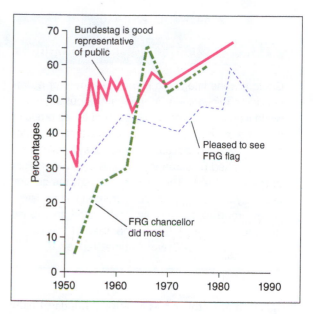

FIGURE 10.3

Support for the Democratic Regime

West Germans' support for the institutions and procedures of the Federal Republic grew substantially over time.

Source: Russell J. Dalton, *Politics in Germany*, 2nd ed. (New York: HarperCollins, 1993), 121.

burned a deep scar in the western psyche, making citizens hesitant to express pride in their nation or a sense of German national identity. Because of this political stigma, the FRG avoided many of the emotional national symbols that are common in other nations. There were few political holidays or memorials, one seldom heard the national anthem, and even the anniversary of the founding of the FRG received little public attention. This legacy means that even today, Germans are hesitant to openly express pride in the nation (see Box 10.2).

The quest for a national identity also occurred in the East. The GDR claimed to represent the "pure" elements of German history; it portrayed the FRG as the successor to the Third Reich. Most analysts believe that the GDR had created at least a sense of resigned loyalty to the regime because of its political and social accomplishments. Once socialism failed, however, the basis for a separate East German political identity also evaporated.

Unification began a process by which the German search for a national political identity could finally be resolved. The celebration of unification, and the

Could anyone imagine a French president or a British prime minister—or indeed just about any other world leader—refusing to say he or she was proud of his or her nationality? Yet this is a contentious statement in Germany, because expressions of nationalism are still linked by some to the excessive nationalism of the Third Reich. Thus, when, in 2001, the general secretary of the Christian Democratic Union declared, "I am proud to be German," he set off an intense national debate. A Green member of the Social Democratic Party–Green Cabinet replied that this statement demonstrated the mentality of a right-wing skinhead. President Rau tried to sidestep the issue by declaring that one could be "glad" or "grateful" for being German, but not "proud." Then Chancellor Schröder entered the fray: "I am proud of what people have achieved and our democratic culture. . . . In that sense, I am a German patriot who is proud of his country." It is difficult to imagine such exchanges occurring in Washington, D.C., or Paris.

Source: *Economist*, March 24, 2001, 62.

designation of October 3 as a national holiday, finally gave Germans a positive political experience to celebrate. Citizens in East and West remain somewhat hesitant to embrace an emotional attachment to the nation, and Easterners retain a lingering tie to their separate past. Yet the basic situation has changed. For the first time in over a century, nearly all Germans agree on where their borders begin and end. Germany is now a single nation—democratic, free, and looking toward the future.

Orientations toward the Democratic Process

A second important element of the political culture involves citizen attitudes toward the political process and system of government. In the early years of West Germany, the rules of democratic politics—majority rule, minority rights, individual liberties, and pluralistic debate—did not fit citizens' experiences. To break this pattern, political leaders constructed a system that formalized democratic procedures. Citizen participation was encouraged and expected, policymaking became open, and the public gradually learned democratic norms by continued exposure to the new political system. Political leadership provided a generally positive example of competition in a democratic setting. Consequently, a popular consensus slowly developed in support of the democratic political system. By the mid-1960s, there was nearly unanimous agreement that democracy was the best form of government. More important, the western public displayed a growing commitment to democratic procedures—a multiparty system, conflict management, minority rights, and representative government.[18]

Political events occasionally have tested popular commitment to democratic values in West Germany. For instance, during the 1970s, a small group of extremists attempted to topple the system through a terrorist campaign.[19] In the early 1980s, the Kohl government faced a series of violent actions by anarchic and radical ecology groups. In recent years, international terrorists and jihadist extremists have threatened the nation. In these instances, however, the basic conclusion was that the political system could face the onslaughts of political extremists and survive with its basic procedures intact—and without the public losing faith in the democratic process.

The propaganda of the East German government also stressed a democratic creed. In reality, however, the regime tried to create a political culture that was compatible with a communist state and a socialist economy. The culture drew on traditional Prussian values of obedience, duty, and loyalty; the government again told people that obedience was the responsibility of a good citizen and that support of the state (and the party) was an end in itself. Periodically, political events—the 1953 East Berlin uprising, the construction of the Berlin Wall, and the expulsions of political dissidents—reminded East Germans of the gap between the democratic rhetoric of the regime and reality.

One reason the popular revolt may have grown so rapidly in 1989 was that citizens no longer supported the principles of the regime, even if they might be hesitant to express such sentiments publicly under a *Stasi* police state. For instance, studies of young Easterners found that identification with Marxism–Leninism and belief in the inevitable victory of socialism dropped off dramatically during the mid-1980s.[20] At the least, the revolutionary changes that swept through East Germany as the Berlin Wall fell nurtured a belief in democracy as the road to political reform. A 1990 public opinion survey found nearly universal support for basic tenets of democracy among both West and East Germans.[21]

The true test of democracy, of course, occurs in the real world. Some studies suggest that Easterners' initial understanding of democracy was limited, or at least different from that of Westerners.[22] Yet Easterners in 1989 were markedly more supportive of democracy than were Germans in 1945. Rather than remaking this aspect of the East German culture, the greater need was to transform Easterners' support for democracy into a deeper and richer understanding of the workings of the process and its pragmatic strengths and weaknesses. And now, two decades after unification, with an Easterner as the chancellor, the principles of democracy are ingrained in the political culture—both West and East.

Social Values and the New Politics

Another area of cultural change in West Germany involves a shift in public values produced by the social and economic accomplishments of the nation. Once West Germany addressed traditional social and economic needs, the public broadened its concerns to include a new set of societal goals. New issues—such as the environment, women's rights, and increasing citizen participation—attracted public attention.

Ronald Inglehart explains these developments in terms of the changing value orientations of Westerners.[23] He maintains that a person's value priorities reflect the family and societal conditions that prevail early in life. Older generations, socialized before the post–World War II transformation, experienced uncertain economic and political conditions, which led them to emphasize economic security, law and order, religious values, and a strong national defense—despite the economic and political advances of the past half century. In contrast, because younger generations grew up in a democratic and affluent nation, they shifted their attention toward **New Politics** values. These new values emphasize self-expression, personal freedom, social equality, self-fulfillment, and quality of life.

Although only a minority hold these new values, they represent a "second culture" embedded within the dominant culture of FRG society. These values are less developed among Easterners. Still, the evidence of political change is apparent. Public interest in New Politics issues has gradually spread beyond its youthful supporters and developed a broader base.

Gas Hog
Greenpeace protests tax policies that benefit gas guzzlers.

Two Peoples in One Nation?

Citizens in the East and West share a common German heritage, but forty years of separation created cultural differences that now are blended into a single national culture.

Because of these different experiences, the broad similarities in many of the political beliefs of Westerners and Easterners are surprising. Citizens in both regions espouse support for the democratic system and its norms and institutions. There is also broad acceptance of the principles of Germany's social market economy. Thus, the Federal Republic's second transition to democracy features an agreement on basic political and economic values that is markedly different from the situation after World War II.

Yet other aspects of cultural norms do differ between regions.[24] For instance, although residents in both the West and the East endorse the tenets of democracy, it is harder to reach agreement on how these ideals translate into practical politics. The open, sometimes confrontational style of western politics is a major adjustment for citizens raised under the closed system of the GDR. In addition, Easterners endorse a broader role for government in providing social services and guiding social development than is found among Westerners.

There are also signs of a persisting gap in regional identities between East and West. The passage of time and harsh postunification adjustments created nostalgia for some aspects of the GDR among its former residents. Easterners do not want a return to communism or socialism, but many miss the slower and more predictable style of their former lives. Even while expressing support for western capitalism, many Easterners have difficulty adjusting to the idea of unemployment and to the competitive pressures of a market-based economy. There is a nostalgic yearning for symbols of these times, ranging from the Trabant automobile to consumer products bearing Eastern labels. The popularity of the 2003 movie *Goodbye Lenin!* is an indication of these sentiments—and a good film for students interested in this phase of German history. Moreover, even though Easterners favor democracy, only 39 percent in 2009 were satisfied with how it functions in the Federal Republic, compared with 61 percent among Westerners.[25] Easterners still feel that the political system overlooks their needs.

Germans share a common language, culture, and history—and a common set of ultimate political goals—although the strains of unification may magnify and politicize the differences. The nation's progress in blending these two cultures successfully will strongly affect the course of the new Germany.

Political Learning and Political Communication

10.7 Identify the main sources of political socialization in Germany.

If a congruent political culture helps a political system to endure, as many political experts maintain, one of the basic functions of the political process is to create and perpetuate these attitudes. This process is known as *political socialization*. Researchers normally view political socialization as a source of continuity in a political system, with one generation transmitting the prevailing political norms to the next. In Germany, however, the socialization challenges for the past half century have been to change the culture inherited from the Third Reich and then to change the culture inherited from the GDR.

Family Influences

During their early years, children have few sources of learning comparable to their parents—normally the major influence in forming basic values. Family discussions can be a rich source of political information and one of the many ways that children internalize their parents' attitudes. Basic values acquired during childhood often persist into adulthood.

In the early postwar years, family socialization did not function smoothly on either side of the German border. Many parents did not discuss politics with their children for fear that the child would ask, "What did you do under Hitler, Daddy?" The potential for parental socialization grew steadily as the political system of the FRG began to take root.[26] The frequency of political discussion increased in the West, and family conversations about politics became commonplace. Moreover, young new parents raised under the system of the FRG could pass on democratic norms held for a lifetime.

The family also played an important role in the socialization process of the GDR. Family ties were especially close in the East, and most young people claimed to share their parents' political opinions. The family was one of the few settings where people could openly discuss their beliefs, a private sphere where individuals could be free of the watchful eyes of others. Here one could express praise for—or doubt about—the state. But after unification, generations differ greatly in their political experiences, and presumably their expectations.

Despite the growing socialization role of the family, there is often a generation gap in political values in both West and East. Youth in the West are more liberal than their parents, more oriented toward noneconomic goals, more positive about their role in the political process, and more likely to challenge prevailing social norms.[27] Eastern youth are also a product of their times, now being raised under the new democratic and capitalist systems of the Federal Republic. Under the GDR, conformity was mandated; imagine what eastern parents think when their teenagers adopt hip-hop or punk lifestyles. The values and goals of many German youth are changing, often putting them in conflict with their elders.

Education

The educational system was a major factor in the creation of a democratic political culture in the FRG. As public support for the FRG's political system increased, this decreased the need for formal instruction in the principles of democracy and its institutions. Civics instruction changed to emphasize an understanding of the dynamics of the democratic process—interest representation, conflict resolution, minority rights, and the methods of citizen influence. The present system tries to prepare students for their adult roles as political participants.

The school system in the GDR also played an essential role in political education, although the content was very different. The schools tried to create a socialist personality that encompassed a devotion to communist principles, a love of the GDR, and participation in state-sponsored activities. Another cornerstone of the GDR's socialization efforts was a system of government-supervised youth groups. Nearly all primary school students enrolled in the Pioneers, a youth organization that combined normal social activities—similar to the Boy Scouts or Girl Scouts in the United States—with a heavy dose of political education. At age fourteen, most young people joined the Free German Youth (FDJ) group, which was a training and recruiting ground for future elite positions. Like other communist states, the GDR used mass sporting events as an opportunity for political indoctrination and used the Olympic medal count as a measure of the nation's international status. In short, from a school's selection of texts for first-grade readers to the speeches at a sports awards banquet, the values of the regime touched everyday life. Yet the rhetoric of the regime often conflicted with reality, so the GDR's education efforts remained incomplete. This changed, of course, with German unification, so that the schools now teach about common values across the nation.

Social Stratification   Another important aspect of education is its effect on social stratification. The secondary school system in the Federal Republic has three distinct tracks. One track provides a general education that normally leads to vocational training and working-class occupations. A second track mixes vocational and academic training. Most graduates from this program are employed in lower-middle-class occupations. A third track focuses on academic training at a gymnasium (an academic high school) in preparation for university education.

The selection of students for different educational tracks reinforces social status differences within society. The schools direct students into a track after only four to six years of primary schooling, based on their school record, parental preferences, and teacher evaluations. At this early age, family influences are still a major factor in the child's development. Thus, most children in the academic track come from middle-class families, and most students in the vocational track are from working-class families. Sharp distinctions separate the three tracks. Students attend different schools, so that social contact across tracks is minimized. The curriculums of the three tracks are so different that once a student is assigned, he or she would find it difficult to transfer. The gymnasia are more generously financed and recruit the best-qualified teachers. Every student who graduates from a gymnasium is guaranteed admission to a university, where tuition is free.

Reformers have made numerous attempts to lessen the class bias of the educational system. Some states have a single, comprehensive secondary school that all students may attend, but only about 10 percent of western secondary school students are enrolled in these schools. The GDR used a different educational system of comprehensive schools for all students, with less social stratification. There was some discussion that this might lead to reforms in the West. However, unification has generally led to the expansion of the West's tracked educational system to the East, rather than to reform of the western system to lessen social biases and grant greater opportunities to all.

Reformers have been more successful in expanding access to the universities. In the early 1950s, only 6 percent of college-aged youths pursued higher education; today, this figure is over 30 percent. The Federal Republic's educational system retains an elitist accent, though it is now less obvious.

Mass Media

The mass media have a long history in Germany; the world's first newspaper and first television service both appeared on German soil. The mass media of the Federal Republic were developed with the goal of avoiding the experience of Nazi propaganda and contributing to a new democratic political culture.[28] The FRG began with a new journalistic tradition, committed to democratic norms, objectivity, and political neutrality.

The press is highly regionalized. Instead of a few national newspapers as in Britain or France, each region or large city has one or more newspapers that circulate primarily within that locale. Of the several hundred daily newspapers, only a few—such as the *Frankfurter Allgemeine Zeitung*, *Welt*, *Süddeutsche Zeitung*, and *Frankfurter Rundschau*—have a national following.

The electronic media in the Federal Republic are also regionally decentralized. Public corporations at the state or regional levels manage the public television and radio networks. These public networks are still the major German television channels. To ensure independence from commercial pressures, the public media are financed mostly by taxes assessed on owners of radios and television sets. But the new technologies of cable and satellite television have undercut the government's media monopoly. Many analysts see these new media as expanding citizens' choices and the diversity of information, but others worry that the quality of German broadcasting has suffered as a result. Once, one could not even watch soccer matches on television because government planners considered it inappropriate. Now, cable subscribers can watch a previously unimaginable range of social, cultural, political, and sports programming.

The Internet is also a growing source of political information. A significant share of the public, especially among the young and better educated, use the Internet to read the news, visit party websites at election time, and share this information with friends on Facebook or its German equivalent, VZ-Gruppe. To catch this new media wave, Merkel introduced weekly podcasts on issues facing the government. In each election, the Internet is an increasingly important information source.

The mass media are a primary source of information for the public and a communications link between elites and the public. The higher-quality newspapers devote substantial attention to domestic and international reporting, although the largest circulation newspaper, *Bild Zeitung*, sells papers through sensationalist stories. The public television networks are also strongly committed to political programming; about one-third of their programs deal with social or political issues.

Public opinion surveys show that Germans have a voracious appetite for the political information provided by the mass media. A 2005 survey found that 52 percent of the public claimed to read news in the newspaper on a daily basis, 56 percent listened to news on the radio daily, and 70 percent said they watched television news programs daily.[29] These high levels of media usage indicate that Germans are attentive media users and well informed on the flow of political events.

Citizen Participation

10.8 Contrast the past ways in which East and West Germans were encouraged to be politically active.

In the 1950s, people in the FRG did not participate in the new political process; they acted like political spectators who were following a soccer match from the grandstand. German history certainly had not been conducive to widespread public involvement in politics. The final step in remaking the political culture was to involve citizens in the process—to have them come onto the field and participate.

From the start, both German states encouraged their citizens to be politically active, but with different expectations about what was appropriate. The democratic procedures of West Germany induced many people to at least vote in elections. Turnout reached up to 90 percent for some national elections. Westerners became well informed about the political system and developed an interest in political matters. After continued democratic experience, people began to internalize their role as participants. Most Westerners think their participation can influence the political process—people believe that democracy works.

The public's changing political norms led to a dramatic increase in involvement. In the 1950s, almost two-thirds of West Germans never discussed politics; today, about three-quarters claim they talk about politics regularly. Expanding citizen interest created a participatory revolution in the FRG as involvement in campaigns and political organizations increased. Perhaps the most dramatic example of rising participation levels was the growth of citizen action groups (*Bürgerinitiativen*). People interested in a specific issue form a group to express their demands and influence decision makers. Parents organize for school reform, taxpayers complain about the delivery of government services, and residents protest the environmental conditions in their locale. These groups expand citizen influence beyond campaigns and elections.

The GDR system also encouraged political involvement, but only in ways that reinforced allegiance to the state. For example, elections offered the Communist leadership an opportunity to educate the public politically. People were expected to participate in government-approved unions, social groups (such as the Free German Youth or the German Women's Union), and quasi-public bodies, such as parent–teacher organizations. However, participation was not a method for people to influence the government but for the government to influence its citizens.

Although they draw on very different experiences, Germans from both the East and the West have been socialized into a pattern of high political involvement (see Figure 10.4). Voting levels in national elections are among the highest of any European democracy. Almost 73 percent of Westerners and almost 68 percent of Easterners turned out at the polls in the 2013 Bundestag elections. This turnout level is very high by U.S. standards, but it has declined from nearly 90 percent in the FRG elections of the 1980s. High turnout partially reflects the belief that voting is part of a citizen's duty. In addition, the electoral system encourages turnout: Elections are held on Sunday when people are not working, voter registration lists are constantly updated by the government, and the ballot is always simple—there are at most two votes to cast.

Beyond the act of voting, many Germans participate in other ways. A survey conducted after the 2009 election illustrates the participation patterns of Easterners and Westerners (see again Figure 10.4). The majority in both regions say they are interested in politics, and this shows in their pattern of political activity. Half the public had followed the campaign in the newspapers, and significant numbers had visited a party's information table or attended a meeting or rally during the 2009 campaign. A slightly smaller number had been active in a citizens' initiative or participated

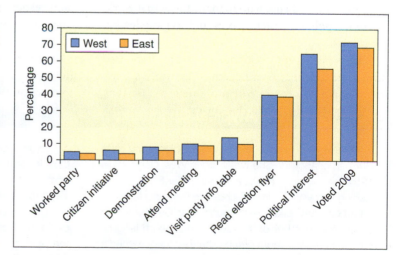

FIGURE 10.4

Participation Levels in Western and Eastern Germany

Westerners are generally more politically active than Easterners, although there are many ways people participate.

Source: 2009 German Longitudinal Election Study; voter turnout is from government statistics for the 2009 election.

in a demonstration during the past year, although this is larger than the number of those who worked for a political party. Other surveys show that Germans are active in contacting politicians, signing petitions, and other forms of participation.[30]

Across all of these political activities, Westerners participate more than residents in the East. Part of these differences reflects the greater political resources and experience of Westerners, who have grown up in the democratic system. In addition, many Easterners are somewhat dissatisfied with the Federal Republic's political process and feel they are second-class citizens—which distances them from political involvement.

In overall terms, however, Germans on both sides of the former border are now actively involved in politics. Moreover, participation extends beyond the traditional role of voting in elections to include a wide range of political activities. The spectators have become participants.

Politics at the Elite Level[31]

10.9   Describe how the long road to becoming a member of the German political elites affects their actions.

The Federal Republic is a representative democracy. This means that above the populace is a group of a few thousand political elite who manage the actual workings of the political system. Elites such as party leaders and parliamentary deputies are directly responsible to the public through elections. Civil servants and judges are appointed, and they are at least indirectly responsible to the citizenry. Leaders of interest groups and political associations participate as representatives of their specific clientele groups. Although the group of politically influential elites is readily identifiable, it is not a homogeneous power elite. Rather, elites in the Federal Republic represent the diverse interests in German society. Often, there is as much heterogeneity in policy preferences among the political elites as there is among the public.

One feature of elite recruitment that differs from American politics is the long apprenticeship period before one enters the top elite stratum. Candidates for national or even state political office normally have a long background of party work and office holding at the local level. Similarly, senior civil servants spend nearly all their adult lives working for the government. Chancellor Merkel's biography is an unusual example because she did not follow the typical model of a long career of party and political positions (see Box 10.3).

A long apprenticeship means that political elites have extensive experience before attaining a position of great power. National politicians know each other from working together at the state or local level; the paths of civil servants frequently cross during their long careers. These experiences create a sense of trust and responsibility among elites. For instance, members of a chancellor's Cabinet are normally drawn

---

BOX 10.3   The Atypical Chancellor

Angela Merkel has the most unlikely biography for a German chancellor. She was born in West Germany in 1954, and when she was a year old, her father, a left-leaning Protestant minister, chose to move his family to East Germany. Like many young East Germans, she became a member of the Communist youth league, the Free German Youth group. She eventually earned a Ph.D. in physics from the East Berlin Academy of Sciences in 1989. Merkel pursued a career as a research scientist until the GDR began to collapse in 1989. She first joined the Democratic Awakening and then the CDU and was elected to the Bundestag as a CDU deputy in 1990. She rose quickly through the ranks of CDU leaders, serving as minister for women and youth from 1991 to 1994 and as environment minister from 1994 to 1998. In 2000, Merkel became the national chair of the CDU. With her election in 2005, she became the first woman, and the first former citizen of the GDR, to head the German federal government. In 2013, *Forbes* magazine ranked Chancellor Merkel as number one on their list of the hundred most powerful women in the world. The German public agreed, and returned her to the chancellorship after the 2013 elections.

from party elites with extensive experience in state or federal government. Until Merkel was elected, chancellors since the 1960s had previously served as state minister president. Seldom can top business leaders or popular personalities use their outside success to attain a position of political power quickly. This also contributes to the cohesion of elite politics.

Because they represent different political constituencies, elites differ in many of their policy priorities. For instance, SPD elites and officials from labor unions are more likely to emphasize the need for greater social and economic equality, social security, and the integration of foreigners.[32] Church officials stress moral and religious principles, while CDU/CSU and business representatives typically have distinct economic positions. Green activists have their own alternative agenda. This method of representation gives citizens a voice in the decisions made by elites, and the clearer the link, the more direct the voice.

Interest Groups

10.10 Discuss the composition and political influence of Germany's interest groups.

Interest groups are an integral part of the German political process, even more so than in the United States. Specific interests may be different in their styles and effectiveness, but interest groups are generally welcomed as necessary participants in the political process.

Doctors, lawyers, and other self-employed professionals belong to professional associations that are established by law and receive government authorization of their activities, making them quasi-public bodies that set standards and enforce professional rules of conduct.

Interest groups also participate in various government commissions and bodies, such as that managing public radio and television. Some groups receive financial or administrative support from the government to assist them in carrying out policy-related activities, such as the administration of a hospital or the monitoring of environmental conditions. Federal administrative law requires that ministry officials contact the relevant interest groups when formulating new policies that may affect them. These consultations ensure that the government can benefit from the groups' expertise.

In some instances, the pattern of interest group activity approaches the act of governance. For example, when the government sought structural reform in the steel industry, it assembled interest group representatives from the affected sectors to discuss and negotiate a common plan. Group officials attempted to reach a consensus on the necessary changes and then implemented the agreements, sometimes with the official sanction of the government. Similar activities have occurred in other policy sectors.

This cooperation between government and interest groups is described as **neocorporatism**, a general pattern having the following characteristics (also see Chapter 4):[33]

- Social interests are organized into virtually compulsory organizations.
- A single association represents each social sector.
- Associations are hierarchically structured.
- Associations are accepted as formal representatives by the government.
- Associations may participate directly in the policy process.

Policy decisions are often reached in discussions and negotiations between the relevant association and the government; then, the agreements are implemented by government action.

This neocorporatist pattern solidifies the role of interest groups in the policy process. Governments feel that they are responding to public demands when they consult with these groups, and the members of these interest groups depend on the organization to have their views heard. Thus, representatives of the major interest groups are important actors in the policy process. Neocorporatist relations also lessen political conflict; for instance, strike levels and political strife tend to be lower in neocorporatist systems.

Another advantage of neocorporatism is that it makes for efficient government; the involved interest groups can negotiate on policy without the pressures of public debate and partisan conflict. However, efficient government is not necessarily the best government, especially in a democracy. Decisions are reached in conference groups or advisory commissions, outside of the representative institutions of government decision making. The "relevant" interest groups are involved, but this assumes that all relevant interests are organized and that only organized interests are relevant. Decisions affecting the entire public are often made through private negotiations, as democratically elected representative institutions—state governments and the Bundestag—are sidestepped and interest groups deal directly with government agencies. Consequently, interest groups play a less active role in electoral politics, as they concentrate their efforts on direct contact with government agencies.

Interest groups come in many shapes and sizes. This section describes the large associations that represent the major socioeconomic forces in society. These associations normally have a national organization, a so-called **peak association**, that speaks for its members.

Business

Two major organizations represent business and industrial interests. The **Federation of German Industry (BDI)** is the peak association for thirty-five separate industrial groupings. The BDI members represent nearly every major industrial firm, forming a united front that speaks with authority on matters affecting their interests.

The **Confederation of German Employers' Associations (BDA)** includes even more business organizations. Virtually every large or medium-sized employer in the nation is affiliated with one of its sixty-eight employer and professional associations.

The two organizations have overlapping membership, but they have different roles in the political process. The BDI represents business on national political matters. Its officials participate in government advisory committees and planning groups, presenting the view of business to government officials and members of parliament. In contrast, the BDA represents business on legislation dealing with social security, labor legislation, and social services. It also nominates business representatives for a variety of government committees, ranging from the media supervisory boards to social security committees. The individual employer associations in the BDA negotiate with the labor unions over employment contracts.

Business interests have a long history of close relations with the Christian Democrats and conservative politicians. Companies and their top management provide financial support for the Christian Democrats, and many Bundestag deputies have strong ties to business. Yet both the Social Democrats and the

Christian Democrats readily accept the legitimate role of business interests within the policy process.

Labor

The **German Federation of Trade Unions (DGB)** is the peak association that incorporates eight separate unions—ranging from the metalworking and building trades to the chemical industry and the postal system—into a single association.[34] The DGB represents more than 7 million workers. Union membership has declined, however, and today, less than a third of the labor force belongs to a union. The membership includes many industrial workers and an even larger percentage of government employees.

The DGB has close ties to the Social Democratic Party, although there is no formal institutional bond between the two. Most SPD deputies in the Bundestag are past or present members of a union, and about one-tenth are former labor union officials. The DGB represents the interests of labor in government conference groups and Bundestag committees. The large mass membership of the DGB also makes union campaign support and the union vote essential parts of the SPD's electoral base.

In spite of their differing interests, business and unions have shown an unusual ability to work together. The Economic Miracle was possible because labor and management agreed that the first priority was economic growth, from which both sides would prosper. Work time lost through strikes and work stoppages has been consistently lower in the Federal Republic than in most other Western European nations.

This cooperation is encouraged by joint participation of business and union representatives in government committees and planning groups. Cooperation also extends into industrial decision making through **codetermination (Mitbestimmung)**, a federal policy requiring that employees elect half of the board of directors in large companies. The system was first applied to the coal, iron, and steel industries in 1951, and in 1976, it was extended in a modified form to other large corporations. Initially, there were dire forecasts that codetermination would destroy German industry. However, the system generally has been successful in fostering better labor–management relations and thereby strengthening the economy. The Social Democrats also favor codetermination because it introduces democratic principles into the economic system.

Religious Interests

Religious groups are the third major organized interest. Rather than being separate from politics, as in the United States, church and state are closely related. Churches are subject to the rules of the state, and, in return, they receive formal representation and support from the government.

Churches are financed mainly through a church tax collected by the government. The government adds a surcharge (about 10 percent) to an employee's income tax, and the government transfers this amount to the employee's church. Officially, a taxpayer can decline to pay that tax, but social norms discourage this. Catholic primary schools in several states receive government funding, and the churches accept government subsidies to support their social programs and aid to the needy.

The churches are often directly involved in the policy process. Church appointees regularly sit on government planning committees that deal with education, social services, and family affairs. By law, the churches participate on the supervisory boards of the public radio and television networks. Members of the clergy occasionally serve in political offices, as Bundestag deputies or as state government officials.

Catholic and Protestant churches receive the same formal representation by the government, but the two churches differ in their political styles. The Catholic Church has close ties to the Christian Democrats and implicitly encourages its members to support this party and its conservative policies. The Catholic hierarchy is not hesitant to lobby the government on legislation dealing with social or moral issues, and often wields an influential role in policymaking.

The Protestant community is a loose association of mostly Lutheran churches spread across Germany. Church involvement in politics varies with the preferences of local pastors, bishops, and their respective congregations. In the West, the Protestant churches are not very involved in partisan politics, although they are seen as favoring the Social Democrats. Protestant groups also work through their formal representation on government committees or function as individual lobbying organizations.

Protestant churches played a significant political role in the GDR because they were one of the few organizations that were autonomous from the state. Churches were places where people could freely discuss the social and moral aspects of contemporary issues. As the East German revolution gathered force in 1989, many churches acted as rallying points for opposition to the regime. Religion was not the opiate of the people, as Marx had feared, but one of the forces that swept the Communists from power.

Church attendance in both West and East has decreased over time. About one-tenth of Westerners claim to be nonreligious, as are nearly half the residents in the East. The gradual secularization of German society suggests that the churches' popular base is eroding.

Germany's growing Muslim community represents a new aspect of religious interests. These communities have built mosques across Germany, often facing resistance from the local population. The mosques then receive tax support, just like the Catholic and Protestant churches. Some activists have demanded that schools teach the Koran and that they provide instruction in languages other than German. As more foreign residents become German citizens, this community is likely to become a more vocal participant in the political process.

New Politics Movement

During the late twentieth century, new citizen groups emerged as part of the New Politics movement. Challenging business, labor, religion, agriculture, and other established socioeconomic interests, these new organizations focus their efforts on the lifestyle and quality-of-life issues facing Germany.[35] Environmental groups are the most visible part of the movement. Following the flowering of environmental interests in the 1970s, antinuclear groups popped up like mushrooms around nuclear power facilities, local environmental action groups proliferated, and new national organizations formed. The women's movement is another part of the New Politics network. It developed a dual strategy for improving the status of women: changing the consciousness of women and reforming the laws. A variety of associations and self-help groups at the local level nurture the personal development of women, while other organizations focus on national policymaking.

Different New Politics groups have distinct issue interests and their own organizations, but they are also part of a common movement unified by their shared interest in the quality of the environment, the protection of human rights, and international peace. They draw their members from the same social base: young, better-educated, middle-class citizens. These groups also are more likely to use unconventional political tactics, such as protests and demonstrations.

New Politics groups do not wield the influence of established interest groups, although their combined membership now exceeds the formal membership in the political parties. These groups are important and contentious actors in the political process.

Party Government

10.11 Explain the factors that strengthen the role of political parties in the German system.

Political parties in Germany deserve special emphasis because they are such important actors in the political process, as much as or more than in other European democracies. Some observers describe the political system as government for the parties, by the parties, and of the parties.

The Basic Law is unusual because it specifically refers to political parties (the U.S. Constitution does not). Because the German Empire and the Third Reich suppressed political parties, the Basic Law guarantees their legitimacy and their right to exist if they accept the principles of democratic government. Parties are also designated as the primary institutions of representative democracy. They act as intermediaries between the public and the government and are a means for citizen policy input. The Basic Law further assigns an educational function to the parties, directing them to "take part in forming the political will of the people." In other words, the parties should take the lead and not just respond to public opinion.

The parties' centrality in the political process appears in several ways. There are no direct primaries that would allow the public to select party representatives in Bundestag elections. Instead, a small group of official party members or a committee appointed by the membership nominates the district candidates. State party conventions select the party-list candidates. Thus, the leadership can select list candidates and order them on the list. This power can be used to reward faithful party supporters and discipline party mavericks; placement near the top of a party list virtually ensures election, and low placement carries little chance of a Bundestag seat.

Political parties also dominate the election process. Most voters view the candidates merely as party representatives rather than as autonomous political figures. Even the district candidates are elected primarily because of their party ties. Bundestag, state, and European election campaigns are financed by the government; the parties receive public funds for each vote they get. The government provides free television time for a limited number of campaign advertisements, and these are allocated to the parties, not to the individual candidates. Government funding for the parties also continues between elections to help them perform their informational and educational functions as prescribed in the Basic Law.

Once an election is completed, the parties then shift to forming a government. Since no party has a majority, a group of parties with a majority of the votes must agree to form a coalition government. Often, such agreements are made before the election, but they sometimes wait until the votes are counted.

Within the Bundestag, the parties are also central actors. The Bundestag is organized around party groups (*Fraktionen*), rather than individual deputies. The important legislative posts and committee assignments are restricted to members of a party Fraktion. The size of a Fraktion determines its representation on legislative committees, its share of committee chairs, and its participation in the executive bodies of the legislature. Government funds for legislative and administrative support are distributed to the Fraktion, not to the deputies.

Because of these factors, the cohesion of parties within the Bundestag is exceptionally high. Parties caucus before major legislation to decide the party position, and most legislative votes follow strict party lines. This is partially a consequence of a parliamentary system and partially a sign of the parties' pervasive influence throughout the process.

As a result of these many factors, political parties play a large role in structuring the political process in Germany. Parties are more distinctive in their policy positions, more unified in their views, and more decisive in their actions. Representative democracy works largely through and by political parties as the means to connect voters to the decisions of government.

The Party System

10.12 List the benefits and limitations of having many parties represented in the Bundestag.

Following World War II, the Western Allies created a new democratic, competitive party system in the West. The Allies licensed a diverse set of parties that were free of Nazi ties and committed to democratic procedures. The Basic Law requires that parties support the constitutional order and democratic system of the FRG. Because of these provisions, the FRG developed a strong system of competitive party politics that is a mainstay of the democratic order. Early elections focused on the competition between the conservative Christian Democrats and the leftist Social Democrats, with the smaller parties typically holding the balance of power. From a two-and-a-half party system in the 1970s, the number of parties has grown as new political issues arose and unification reshaped the electoral landscape. Now Germany has a robust multiparty system competing for the voters' support.

The Political Parties

The creation of the **Christian Democratic Union (CDU)** in postwar West Germany signified a sharp break with the tradition of German political parties. The CDU was founded by a mixed group of Catholics and Protestants, businesspeople and trade unionists, conservatives and liberals. Rather than representing narrow special interests, the party wanted to appeal to a broad segment of society in order to gain government power. The party sought to reconstruct West Germany along Christian and humanitarian lines. Konrad Adenauer, the first party leader, developed the CDU into a conservative-oriented catchall party (*Volkspartei*)—a sharp contrast to the fragmented ideological parties of Weimar. This strategy succeeded; within a single decade, the CDU emerged as the largest party, capturing 40 to 50 percent of the popular vote and continues to be the major conservative party in Germany (see Figure 10.5).

The CDU operates in all states except Bavaria, where it allies itself with the Bavarian **Christian Social Union (CSU)**, whose political philosophy is somewhat

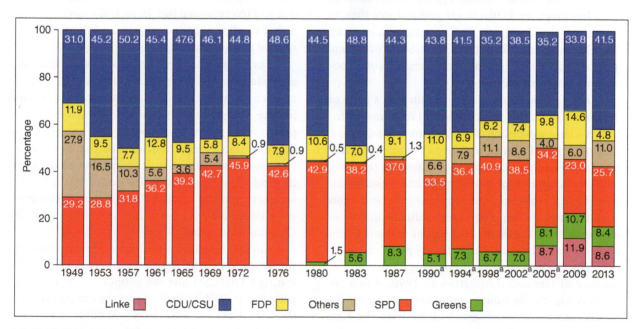

FIGURE 10.5

Shares of the Party Vote

The multiparty system has the CDU/CSU and SPD as the two largest parties, joined by a changing set of smaller parties.

[a]1990–2013 percentages combine results from Western and Eastern Germany.

more conservative. These two parties generally function as one (CDU/CSU) in national politics, forming a single parliamentary group in the Bundestag and campaigning together in national elections.

The postwar **Social Democratic Party (SPD)** in West Germany was constructed along the lines of the SPD in the Weimar Republic—a socialist party primarily representing the interests of unions and the working class. The SPD's initial image of the nation's future was radically different from that of the Christian Democrats. The Social Democrats initially espoused strict Marxist doctrine and consistently opposed Adenauer's western-oriented foreign policy. Over time the party moderated its position on both domestic and foreign policies. This new orientation allowed it to gain new voter support from moderates and the middle class—and eventually participate in the national government.

Among the many smaller parties at the formation of the German party system, the **Free Democratic Party (FDP)** was the most significant. The FDP was initially a strong advocate of private enterprise and drew its support from the Protestant middle class and farmers. It has often held enough Bundestag seats to have a pivotal role in forming a government coalition. This has given the FDP a larger political role than its small size would suggest. Its economic policies make the FDP a natural ally of the CDU/CSU in economic terms. Its liberal foreign and social programs often position it closer to the SPD.

The Greens (Die Grünen) are literally a party of a different color.[36] It was created in 1980, drawing together a loose association of local environmental groups. The party raised a broad set of New Politics issues that the established parties were not addressing: opposing nuclear energy, reshaping military policies, ensuring environmental protection, and supporting women's rights and multiculturalism. The Greens initially differed so markedly from the established parties that one Green leader described them as the "antiparty party."

The party system further changed as a consequence of German unification in 1990. When the GDR collapsed, the ruling communist party (Socialist Unity Party, SED) collapsed along with the East German regime. SED membership plummeted, and local party units abolished themselves. The omnipotent party suddenly seemed impotent. To save the party from complete dissolution and to compete in the upcoming democratic elections, the party changed its name to the **Party of Democratic Socialism (PDS)**.

The party became a representative for citizens in the East, especially those who suffered economically or socially as a consequence of unification. In 2005, the party joined forces with leftists in the West and, in 2007, rebranded itself as **Die Linke** (The Left).

Finally, in 2013, a new party appeared on the electoral stage. The **Alternative for Germany (AfD)** is critical of Germany's relationship with the European Union and many of the policies implemented by the EU. Its anti-EU rhetoric resonated among many voters, and it almost won the 5 percent of the vote that would have given it seats in parliament. Even without winning seats, its vote share probably cost the CDU/CSU-FDP government its reelection. If it endures, the AfD may provide a rallying point for those critical of the government and its European policies.

Electoral History

The CDU/CSU's voting strength in the 1950s allowed the party to control the government, first under the chancellorship of Adenauer and then under Ludwig Erhard, as shown in Table 10.1. The Federal Republic thus took shape under the policy direction of the Christian Democrats, who shaped its domestic policies and international ties. In each election, the number of smaller parties declined, and the CDU/CSU seemed to gain in strength.

The SPD's poor performance in early elections generated internal pressures for the party to broaden its electoral appeal. At the 1959 Godesberg party conference, the party renounced its Marxist economic policies and generally moved toward the center on domestic and foreign policies. The party continued to represent working-class interests, but by shedding its ideological banner, the SPD hoped to attract new support from the middle class. The SPD became a progressive catchall party that competed with the Christian Democrats.

An SPD breakthrough finally came in 1966 with the formation of the Grand Coalition when the governing CDU/CSU lost the support of its coalition partner, the FDP. By sharing government control with the CDU/CSU, the SPD decreased public uneasiness about the party's integrity and ability to govern. Political support for the party also grew as the SPD played an active part in resolving the nation's problems. Following the 1969 election, a new SPD–FDP government formed with Willy Brandt (SPD) as chancellor. After enacting an ambitious range of new policies,

TABLE 10.1
Composition of Coalition Governments
A listing of government parties and chancellors of the Federal Republic.

Date Formed	Source of Change	Coalition Partners[a]	Chancellor
September 1949	Election	CDU/CSU, FDP, DP	Adenauer (CDU)
October 1953	Election	CDU/CSU, FDP, DP, G	Adenauer (CDU)
October 1957	Election	CDU/CSU, DP	Adenauer (CDU)
November 1961	Election	CDU/CSU, FDP	Adenauer (CDU)
October 1963	Chancellor retirement	CDU/CSU, FDP	Erhard (CDU)
October 1965	Election	CDU/CSU, FDP	Erhard (CDU)
December 1966	Coalition change	CDU/CSU, SPD	Kiesinger (CDU)
October 1969	Election	SPD, FDP	Brandt (SPD)
December 1972	Election	SPD, FDP	Brandt (SPD)
May 1974	Chancellor retirement	SPD, FDP	Schmidt (SPD)
December 1976	Election	SPD, FDP	Schmidt (SPD)
November 1980	Election	SPD, FDP	Schmidt (SPD)
October 1982	Constructive no-confidence vote	CDU/CSU, FDP	Kohl (CDU)
March 1983	Election	CDU/CSU, FDP	Kohl (CDU)
January 1987	Election	CDU/CSU, FDP	Kohl (CDU)
December 1990	Election	CDU/CSU, FDP	Kohl (CDU)
October 1994	Election	CDU/CSU, FDP	Kohl (CDU)
September 1998	Election	SPD, Greens	Schröder (SPD)
September 2002	Election	SPD, Greens	Schröder (SPD)
September 2005	Election	CDU/CSU, SPD	Merkel (CDU/CSU)
September 2009	Election	CDU/CSU, FDP	Merkel (CDU/CSU)
September 2013	Election	CDU/CSU, SPD	Merkel (CDU/CSU)

[a]CDU: Christian Democratic Union; CSU: Christian Social Union; DP: German Party; FDP: Free Democratic Party; G: All-German Bloc Federation of Expellees and Displaced Persons; SPD: Social Democratic Party.

a period of economic recession led to Brandt's replacement by Helmut Schmidt in 1974. The SPD retained government control in the 1976 and 1980 elections, but these were trying times for the party.

The early 1980s were tough times for the SPD-level government because of a weakening economic situation. In 1982, the Christian Democrats and the Free Democrats formed a new conservative government through the first successful constructive no-confidence vote, which elected Helmut Kohl as chancellor. Public support for Kohl's policies returned the governing coalition to power following the 1983 and 1987 elections.

Once again in opposition, the SPD faced an identity crisis. It tried to appeal in one election to centrist voters and in the next election to leftist voters—but neither strategy succeeded. The party sensed the need to change and modernize, but it could not decide which direction of change was better. Moreover, a new party challenger entered the arena.

The Green Party won its first Bundestag seats in 1983, becoming the first new party to enter parliament since the 1950s. The Greens campaigned for an alternative view of politics, while adding a bit of color and spontaneity to the normally staid procedures of the political system. The typical dress for Green deputies was jeans and a sweater, rather than the traditional business attire of the established politicians. The party's loose and open internal structure stood in sharp contrast to the hierarchic and bureaucratized structure of the other parties. Despite initial concerns about the Greens' impact on the political system, most analysts now agree that the party brought necessary attention to political viewpoints that previously were overlooked.

The collapse of the GDR in 1989 provided a historic opportunity for the nation, and redirected attention away from the mounting shortfalls of the Kohl administration. While others looked on the events with wonder or uncertainty, Kohl embraced the idea of closer ties between the two Germanies. Thus, when the March 1990 GDR election became a referendum in support of German unification, the Christian Democrats were assured of victory because of their early commitment to unification. Kohl was victorious in the 1990 Bundestag elections.

Perhaps no one (except maybe the Communists) was more surprised than the SPD by the course of events in the GDR in 1989 and 1990. The SPD had been normalizing relations with the SED, only to see the SED ousted by the citizenry. The SPD and its chancellor candidate, Oscar Lafontaine, stood by quietly as Kohl spoke of a single German *Vaterland* to crowds of applauding East Germans. The SPD's poor performance in the 1990 elections reflected its inability either to lead or to follow the course of the unification. Similarly, to stress their opposition to western dominance of the East, the western Greens rejected an electoral alliance with the Eastern Greens in 1990. The eastern Greens won enough votes to enter the new Bundestag, but the western Greens failed to win any seats and dropped out of the Bundestag.

The Party of Democratic Socialism campaigned in these postunification elections as the representative of those who opposed the economic and social course of German unity. In the 1990 Bundestag elections, the PDS won 11 percent of the eastern vote but only 2 percent of the national vote. The PDS won Bundestag seats in the 1994 and 1998 elections, but failed to surmount the electoral threshold in 2002.

Meanwhile, Kohl's government struggled with the policy problems produced by unification. Germany made real gains in improving conditions in the East and building a stable new society. However, the reality fell far short of Kohl's optimistic election pronouncements. Taxes increased, social service budgets were drained, and the East improved slowly. The governing CDU/CSU–FDP coalition lost seats in the 1994 elections, but Kohl retained a slim majority in alliance with the Free Democrats.

By the 1998 elections, the accumulation of sixteen years of governing and the challenges of unification had taken their toll on the party and Helmut Kohl. The Social Democrats selected the moderate Gerhard Schröder as their chancellor candidate to challenge Kohl. The SPD vote share increased, and the party formed a coalition government with the Green Party. Kohl and the CDU/CSU fared poorly in the election, especially in the eastern Länder. The CDU/CSU loss was a rebuke to Kohl, and he resigned the party leadership.

Schröder's government pursued a middle course, balancing the centrist and leftist views existing within the coalition. For instance, the government allowed German troops to play an active role in Kosovo and Afghanistan, while mandating the phasing out of nuclear power. During the 2002 election, Schröder opposed U.S. policy toward Iraq to win support from leftist voters. The CDU/CSU chose Edmund Stoiber, the head of the CSU, as its chancellor candidate in 2002. The CDU/CSU gained the same vote share as the Social Democrats and nearly as many seats in the Bundestag (see Figure 10.6). However, an SPD-led coalition retained control of the government.

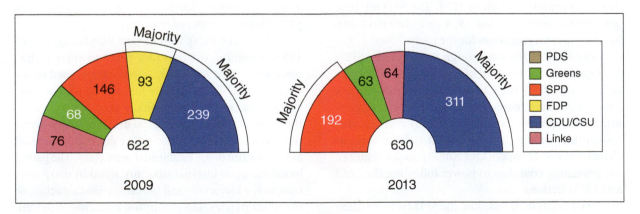

FIGURE 10.6

The Distribution of Bundestag Seats in 2009 and 2013

The 2013 election produced a stalemate between left and right, producing a new grand coalition.

In government, the Green Party struggled to balance its unconventional policies with the new responsibilities of governing—and steadily gave up its unconventional style. For instance, the party supported military intervention in Kosovo, despite its pacifist traditions, and it supported tax reform that lowered the highest rates in exchange for a new environmental tax.

In the mid-2000s, the economy was struggling under the SPD–Green administration, partly because of systemic problems and partly because of the accumulated costs of German unification. The government was criticized by some for doing too much to reform the economy and by others for not doing enough. As the economy stagnated and public dissatisfaction mounted, Schröder gambled and called for early elections in 2005. The CDU/CSU selected **Angela Merkel** as its chancellor candidate (see Box 10.3). The election ended as a dead heat between the CDU/CSU and the SPD.

After weeks of negotiation, the CDU/CSU agreed to form a Grand Coalition with its major rival, the Social Democrats (minus Gerhard Schröder). This was similar to the U.S. Democrats and Republicans sharing control of the government—a very odd set of political bedfellows. Government positions and Cabinet posts were split between the two parties. The differences in political philosophies between the two parties led to limited policy change.

The 2005 elections also produced a change in party alignments. Lafontaine, a former SPD chancellor candidate, orchestrated a coalition of leftist interests in the West and the PDS in the East. This new party drew the support of western leftists who were disenchanted by Schröder's government and PDS voters from the East. They nearly doubled the PDS vote over the previous election and gained more than fifty Bundestag seats. In 2007, the two parties formally merged under the label *Die Linke*.[37]

The 2008 recession strongly influenced voters' perceptions of the governing parties. Many leftists criticized the party for its economic reforms under Schröder and its collaboration with the CDU/CSU. In contrast, Merkel's skill as a political leader appeared when the global recession impacted Germany. She cautiously developed stimulus packages that stabilized the economy and protected jobs. She also successfully deflected much of the economic blame to international forces and her coalition partner, the SPD. The SPD lacked a clear message as to why voters should support it in the 2009 elections, and consequently experienced the lowest vote total in the history of the FRG. Many of these liberal votes went to Die Linke or the Greens. The conservative mood in 2009 propelled the FDP to its best showing in the history of the FRG and a share of the governing coalition with the CDU/CSU, and Merkel continued as chancellor for this new coalition.

The continuing economic challenges of Europe and an unstable international environment provided the context for the 2013 elections. The party's chancellor candidate, Peer Steinbrück, ran an ineffectual campaign that did not convince voters that the SPD offered a viable alternative to Merkel. By a two-to-one margin, the public wanted Merkel to continue as chancellor, but they were divided on which party to support to achieve this aim.

Merkel and the CDU/CSU emerged from the election as the largest party, with 41.5 percent of the vote and nearly half the seats in parliament. This was the second highest seat share in party history. However, when the FDP failed to win any Bundestag seats, this ended the incumbent governing coalition and created complex choices for an alternative coalition government. What followed was a protracted period of coalition negotiations under threats of a new election if the situation was not resolved. Eventually the CDU/CSU and SPD agreed to renew their earlier grand coalition. In a sense, the election did not decide Germany's future policy course because the two main rival parties are both part of the government. Merkel's challenge as the chancellor of the grand coalition will be to find common programs to address the nation's needs that both parties will accept, which will be even more difficult than the 2005-09 grand coalition because contemporary policy problems are greater.

The Role of Elections

When German parties compete in elections, they work within an unusual electoral system. The Federal Republic had two goals in mind when it designed the electoral system. One was to create a **proportional representation (PR)** system that allocates legislative seats based on a party's percentage of the popular vote. If a party receives 10 percent of the popular vote, it should receive 10 percent of the Bundestag seats. Another goal was to create a system of single-member districts as in Britain and the United States. It was thought that district elections would avoid the fragmentation of the Weimar party system and ensure some accountability between a district and its representative.

To satisfy both objectives, the FRG created a mixed electoral system. On one part of the ballot, citizens vote for a candidate to represent their district. The candidate with the most votes in each district is elected to parliament.

On a second part of the ballot, voters select a party. These second votes are added nationwide to determine each party's share of the popular vote, which determines its total representation in the Bundestag. Each party receives additional seats so that its percentage of the combined candidate and party seats equals its percentage of the second votes. These seats are distributed to candidates according to lists prepared by the state parties. Half of the Bundestag members are elected as district representatives and half as party representatives.[38]

An exception to this PR system is the 5 percent clause, which requires that a party win at least 5 percent of the national vote (or three district seats) to share in the distribution of party-list seats.[39] The law aims to withhold representation from the type of small extremist parties that plagued the Weimar Republic. In practice, however, the 5 percent clause restricts all minor parties and lessens the number of parties in the Bundestag.

This mixed system has several political consequences. The party-list system gives party leaders substantial influence on who will be elected to parliament by the placement of people on the list. The PR system also ensures fair representation for the smaller parties. The Greens, for example, won only one direct candidate mandate in 2013, yet it received sixty-two additional Bundestag seats based on its national share of the vote. In contrast, Britain's district-only system discriminates against small parties; in 2010, the British Liberal Democrats won 23 percent of the national vote but less than 9 percent of the parliamentary seats. The German two-vote system also affects campaign strategies. Although most voters cast both their ballots for the same party, the smaller parties encourage supporters of the larger parties to "lend" their second votes to the smaller party. Because of its mixed features, the German system is sometimes described as the ideal compromise in building an electoral system.[40]

The New Partners
Sigmar Gabriel (SPD), Angela Merkel (CDU), and Horst Seehofer (CSU) lead the governing parties in 2013.

The Electoral Connection

Democratic elections are about making policy choices regarding a future government, and Germans have a rich set of parties and policy programs from which to choose. Think of how the United States would be different if there were some communists and environmentalists as well as members of the two major parties elected to the House of Representatives. One of the essential functions of political parties in a democracy is interest representation, and this is especially clear in the case of German elections.

The voting patterns of social groups reflect the ideological and policy differences among parties. Although social differences in voting have gradually narrowed, voting patterns in 2013 reflect the traditional social divisions in German society and politics (see Table 10.2).[41]

TABLE 10.2
Electoral Coalitions in 2013

Voting patterns show the conservative social base of the CDU/CSU and the liberal base of the SPD, Greens, and Die Linke.

	CDU/CSU	SPD	Greens	Linke	FDP	AfD	Other
Election Result	41.5	25.7	8.4	8.6	4.8	4.7	6.1
Region							
West	42	27	9	6	5	4	6
East	39	17	5	23	3	6	7
Employment status							
Employed	40	26	10	8	5	5	7
Unemployed	22	25	10	21	2	7	13
Retired	48	29	5	9	4	4	1
Occupation							
Self-employed	48	15	10	7	10	6	4
Salaried employees	41	26	10	8	5	5	5
Civil servants	44	25	13	5	6	5	2
Blue-collar worker	38	30	5	11	3	5	8
Education							
Primary education	46	30	4	7	3	3	7
Secondary schooling	43	25	6	10	4	6	6
Abitur	39	24	12	8	5	5	7
University degree	37	23	15	9	7	5	4
Age							
Under 30	34	24	11	8	5	6	12
30–44 years	41	22	10	8	5	5	9
45–59 years	39	27	10	9	5	5	5
60 and older	49	28	5	8	5	4	1
Gender							
Men	39	27	8	8	4	6	7
Women	44	24	10	8	5	4	6

Note: Some percentages may not total 100 because of rounding.

Source: Regional data are from election statistics; social group information is from 2013 Bundestagswahl exit poll, Forschungsgruppe Wahlen.

The CDU/CSU primarily draw their voters from the conservative sectors of society, with greater support from older people, retirees, and the middle class, especially the self-employed. Other studies show that Catholics and those who attend church give disproportionate support to the party.

The SPD's voter base contrasts with that of the CDU/CSU: A disproportionate share of SPD votes comes from blue-collar workers, although middle-class citizens provide most of the party's voters. In some ways, the SPD has suffered because its traditional voter base—blue-collar workers—has declined in size and it has not established a new political identity that draws a distinct voter clientele.

The Greens' electorate is heavily drawn from groups that support New Politics movements: the middle class, the better educated, and urban voters. Despite the party turning thirty years old in 2010, it still appeals to the young, especially university-educated youth.

Die Linke also has a distinct voter base. This is first an East-oriented party, with a majority of its total vote in 2013 coming from the East. The party's leftist roots also appear in its appeal to the blue-collar workers and the unemployed. It is a party for those frustrated with the economic and political path Germany has followed since unification.

The FDP voters include a high percentage of the middle class, both white-collar employees and the self-employed. While the Greens attract liberal, educated youth, the FDP attracts a disproportionate share of young, better-educated conservatives. But squeezed on the left and right by other parties, the FDP's lack of a clear identity contributed to their failings in 2013.

The new contender in 2013 was the Alternative for Democracy (AfD). The party's criticism of the European Union's policies and the costs of Germany's contribution to the EU were the basis of its appeal to voters. This position resonated among retirees on fixed income, Easterners, and some youth. The AfD voter base suggests it drew support away from parties on both the left and right.

The social group differences between the larger parties have generally narrowed over time, as fewer voters make their decisions based on class, religious, or other cues. Instead, more voters are deciding based on their issue opinions or candidate evaluations. Yet the ideology and clientele networks of the parties still reflect these traditional group bases, so they have a persisting influence on the parties.

The Policymaking Process

10.13 Describe the primary actors in the federal policymaking process.

The policymaking process may begin with any part of society—an interest group, a political leader, an individual person, or a government official. These actors interact in creating public policy, making it difficult to trace the true origin of any policy idea. Moreover, once a new policy is proposed, other interest groups and political actors become active in amending, supporting, or opposing the policy.

The pattern of interaction among policy actors varies across policy issues. One set of groups is most active on labor issues, and these groups use the methods of influence that are most successful for their cause. A very different set of groups may try to affect defense policy and use far different methods of influence. This variety makes it difficult to describe policymaking as a single process, although the institutional framework for enacting policy is relatively uniform in all policy areas.

The growing importance of the EU also changes the policymaking process for its member states.[42] Now policies made in Brussels often take precedence over German legislation. Laws passed by the German government must conform to EU standards in many areas. The European Court of Justice has the power to overturn laws passed by the German government. Thus, policymaking is no longer a solely national process.

This section describes the various stages of the policy process and clarifies the balance of power among the institutions of the German government.

Policy Initiation

Most issues reach the policy agenda through the executive branch. One reason for this is that the Cabinet and the ministries manage the affairs of government. They are responsible for preparing the budget, formulating revenue proposals, administering existing policies, and conducting the other routine activities of government. The nature of a parliamentary democracy further strengthens the policymaking influence of the chancellor and the Cabinet. The chancellor is the primary policy spokesperson for the government and for a majority of the Bundestag deputies. In speeches, interviews, and formal policy declarations, the chancellor sets the policy agenda for the government.

It is the responsibility of the chancellor and Cabinet to propose new legislation to implement the government's policy promises. Interest groups realize the importance of the executive branch, and they generally work with the federal ministries—rather than Bundestag deputies—when they seek new legislation.

The executive branch's predominance means that the Cabinet proposes about two-thirds of the legislation considered by the Bundestag. Thirty members of the Bundestag may jointly introduce a bill, but only about 20 percent of legislative proposals begin in this manner. Most of the Bundestag's own proposals involve private-member bills or minor issues. State governments also can propose legislation in the Bundesrat, but they do so infrequently.

The Cabinet generally follows consensual decision making in setting the government's policy program. Ministers seldom propose legislation that is not expected to receive Cabinet support. The chancellor has a crucial role in ensuring this consensus. The chancellor's office coordinates the legislative proposals drafted by the various ministries. If the chancellor feels that a bill conflicts with the government's stated objectives, he or she may ask that the proposal be withdrawn or returned to the ministry for restudy and redrafting. If a conflict on policy arises between two ministries, the chancellor may mediate the dispute. Alternatively, interministerial negotiations may resolve the differences. Only in extreme cases is the chancellor unable to resolve such problems; when such stalemates occur, policy conflicts are referred to the full Cabinet.

The chancellor also plays a major role in Cabinet deliberations. The chancellor is a fulcrum, balancing conflicting interests to reach a compromise that the government as a whole can support. This leadership position gives the chancellor substantial influence in negotiations with Cabinet members. Very seldom does a majority of the Cabinet oppose the chancellor. When the chancellor and Cabinet agree on a legislative proposal, they have a dominant position in the legislative process. Because the Cabinet also represents the majority in the Bundestag, most of its initiatives are eventually enacted into law. In the fifteenth Bundestag (2002–2005), almost 90 percent of the government's proposals became law; in contrast, about 40 percent of the proposals introduced by Bundestag members became law. The government's legislative position is further strengthened by Basic Law's fiscal limit on the Bundestag's authority. The parliament can revise or amend most legislative proposals. However, it cannot alter the spending or taxation levels of legislation proposed by the Cabinet. Parliament cannot even reallocate expenditures in the budget without the approval of the finance minister and the Cabinet.

Legislating Policy

When the Cabinet approves a legislative proposal, it is sent to the Bundesrat for review (see Figure 10.7). After receiving the Bundesrat's comments, the Cabinet formally transmits the government's proposal to the Bundestag. The bill receives a first reading, which places it on the chamber's agenda and assigns it to the appropriate committee.

Much of the Bundestag's work takes place in these specialized committees. The list of committees generally follows the organization of the federal ministries, such as transportation, defense, labor, or agriculture. Committees have real potential for reviewing and amending their content. Committees evaluate proposals, consult with interest groups, and then submit a revised proposal to the full Bundestag. Research staffs are small, but committees also use investigative hearings. Government and interest group representatives testify on pending legislation, and committee members often have expertise in their designated policy area. Most committees hold their meetings behind closed doors. The committee system thus provides an opportunity for frank discussions of proposals and negotiations among the parties before legislation reaches the floor of the Bundestag.

When a committee reports a bill, the full Bundestag examines it and discusses any proposed revisions. At this point in the process, however, political positions already are well established. Leaders in the governing parties have taken part in developing the legislation. The parties have caucused to decide their official position. Major revisions during the second and third readings are infrequent; the government generally gets passage of its proposals as reported out of committee.

Bundestag debate on the merits of government proposals is thus mostly symbolic. The successful parties explain the merits of the new legislation and advertise their efforts to their supporters. The opposition parties place their objections in the public record. Although these debates seldom influence the outcome of a vote, they are still an important part of the Bundestag's information function.

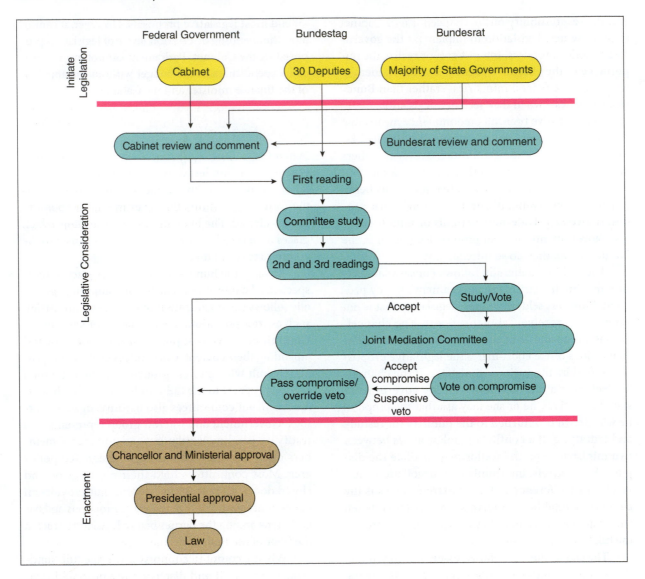

FIGURE 10.7
The Legislative Process
This figure describes the steps from the initiation to the passage of new laws.

A bill that passes the Bundestag is transmitted to the Bundesrat, which represents the state governments in the policy process. Much of the Bundesrat's work is also done in specialized committees where bills are scrutinized for both their policy content and their administrative implications for the states. The legislative authority of the Bundesrat equals that of the Bundestag in areas where the states share concurrent powers with the federal government or administer federal policies. In these areas, the Bundesrat's approval is necessary for a bill to become law. In the policy areas that do not involve the states directly, such as defense or foreign affairs, Bundesrat approval of legislation is not essential. Historically, about two-thirds of legislative proposals required Bundesrat approval, but a recent reform means only about 30 to 40 percent of legislation will now require Bundesrat approval.[43]

The Bundesrat's voting procedures give disproportionate weight to the smaller states; states representing only a third of the population control half the votes in the Bundesrat. Thus, the Bundesrat cannot claim the same popular legitimacy as the proportionally represented and directly elected Bundestag. The Bundesrat voting system also may encourage parochialism by the states. The states vote as a bloc; therefore, they view policy from the perspective of the state rather than the national interest or party positions. The different electoral bases of the Bundestag and Bundesrat make such tensions over policy an inevitable part of the legislative process.

Frequently, different party coalitions control the Bundestag and the Bundesrat. In one sense, this division strengthens the power of the legislature because the federal government has to negotiate with the opposition in the Bundesrat. However, divided government also prevents necessary new legislation in a variety of areas.

If the Bundesrat approves a bill, it transmits the measure to the chancellor to sign. If the Bundesrat objects to the Bundestag's bill, the representatives of both bodies meet in a joint mediation committee and attempt to resolve their differences.

The mediation committee submits its recommendation to both legislative bodies for their approval. If the proposal involves the state governments, the Bundesrat may cast an absolute veto and prevent the bill from becoming a law. In the remaining policy areas, the Bundesrat can cast only a suspensive veto. If the Bundestag approves of a measure, it may override a suspensive veto and forward the proposal to the chancellor. The final policy step is the promulgation of the law by the federal president.

There are several important characteristics of this process. On the one hand, the executive branch is omnipresent throughout the legislative process. After transmitting the government's proposal to the Bundestag, the federal ministers work in support of the bill. Ministry representatives testify before Bundestag and Bundesrat committees to present their position. Cabinet ministers lobby committee members and influential members of parliament. Ministers may propose amendments or negotiate policy compromises to resolve issues that arise during parliamentary deliberations. Government representatives may also attend meetings of the joint mediation committee between the Bundestag and Bundesrat; no other nonparliamentary participants are allowed. The importance of the executive branch is common to most parliamentary systems.

On the other hand, despite this large role played by the executive, the German parliament has greater autonomy than most parliamentary legislatures. By some accounts, it is one of the most powerful parliaments among contemporary democracies. The government frequently makes compromises and accepts amendments proposed in the legislature. The two houses of parliament often reflect different party coalitions and different political interests, so the government must take these into account.

The sharing of legislative power between the Bundestag and Bundesrat also has mixed consequences. State leaders can adapt legislation to local and regional needs through their influence on policymaking. This division of power also provides another check in the system of checks and balances. With strong state governments, it is less likely that one leader or group could control the political process by usurping the national government.

Thus, the process reflects the autonomy of both branches and the checks and balances that the framers sought in designing the Federal Republic's institutions. Compared to other parliamentary systems in Europe, the German system gives more voice to competing interests and is more likely to require compromise to enact new legislation.

Policy Administration

In another attempt to diffuse political power, the Basic Law assigns the administrative responsibility for most domestic policies to the state governments. As evidence of the states' administrative role, the states employ more civil servants than the federal and local governments combined.

Because of the delegation of administrative duties, federal legislation normally is fairly detailed to ensure that the actual application of a law matches the government's intent. Federal agencies may also supervise state agencies, and in cases of dispute, they may apply sanctions or seek judicial review.

Despite this oversight by the federal government, the states have some discretion in applying federal legislation. This is partially because the federal government lacks the resources to follow state actions closely. Federal control of the states also requires Bundesrat support, where claims for states' rights receive a sympathetic hearing. This decentralization of political authority provides additional flexibility for the political system.

Judicial Review

As in the United States, legislation in Germany is subject to judicial review. The Constitutional Court can evaluate the constitutionality of legislation and void laws that violate the Basic Law.[44]

Constitutional issues are brought before the court in one of three ways. First, individual citizens may appeal directly to the court when they feel that a government action violates their constitutional rights. More than 90 percent of the cases presented to the court arise from citizens' complaints. Moreover, people can file cases without paying court costs and without a lawyer. The court is thus like an ombudsman, assuring the average citizen that his or her fundamental rights are protected by the Basic Law and the court.

In addition, the Court hears cases based on "concrete" and "abstract" principles of judicial review. Concrete review involves an actual court case that raises constitutional issues and is referred by a lower court to the Constitutional Court. In an abstract review, the court rules on legislation as a legal principle, without reference to an actual case. The federal government, a state government, or one-third of the Bundestag deputies can request review of a law. Groups that fail to block a bill from becoming a law sometimes use this procedure. Over the last two decades, the court received an average of two or three such referrals a year.[45] Judicial review in the abstract expands the constitutional protection of the Basic Law. This directly involves the court in the policy process and may politicize the court as another agent of policymaking.

In recent years, the judicial review by the European Court of Justice (ECJ) has added a new dimension to policymaking in Germany and the other EU states.[46] Petitioners can challenge German legislation that they believe violates EU policies. Hundreds of German laws are reviewed each year, and anticipation of ECJ review influences the legislative process of the parliament.

Policy Performance

10.14 Identify major policy outputs of government and the major sources of government funding.

By most standards, both of the Germanies could boast of their positive records of government performance since their formation. The FRG's economic advances in the 1950s and early 1960s were truly phenomenal, and the progress in the GDR was nearly as remarkable. By the 1980s, the FRG had one of the strongest economies in the world, and other policies improved the education system, increased workers' participation in industrial management, extended social services, and improved environmental quality. The GDR had its own impressive record of policy accomplishments, even though it lagged behind the West. The GDR was the economic miracle of the Eastern Bloc, and it supported an extensive network of social programs.

The integration of two different social and political systems created strains that are still one of Germany's major policy challenges. In addition, the nation faces many of the same policy issues as other European democracies: dealing with the current recession and its political fallout, competing in a global economic system, addressing the issues of multiculturalism, and charting a foreign policy course in a changing world. This section describes Germany's present policy programs, and then we discuss the policy challenges currently facing the nation.

The Federal Republic's Policy Record

For Americans who hear politicians rail against "big government" in the United States, the size of the German government gives greater meaning to this term. Over the past half century, the scope of German government has increased both in total public spending and in new policy responsibilities. Today, government spending accounts for almost half of the total economy, and government regulations touch many areas of the economy and society. Germans are much more likely than Americans to consider the state responsible for addressing social needs and to support government policy activity. Total public expenditures—federal, state, local, and the social security system—have increased from less than €15 billion in 1950 to €269 billion in 1975 and over €1.182 trillion for a united Germany in 2012, which is over 40 percent of the total GDP. That is big government.

Public spending in Germany flows from many different sources. Social security programs are the largest part of public expenditures; however, they are managed in insurance programs that are separate from the government's normal budget.

In addition, the Basic Law distributes policy responsibilities among the three levels of government.

Local authorities provide utilities (electricity, gas, and water), operate the hospitals and public recreation facilities, and administer youth and social assistance programs. The states manage education, cultural policies, public security, and the administration of justice. The federal government's responsibilities include foreign policy and defense, transportation, and communications. Consequently, public expenditures are distributed fairly evenly over the three levels of government. In 2011, the federal budget's share was 31 percent, the state governments spent 27 percent, the local governments spent 16.6 percent, and 44 percent went to social insurance spending.

Figure 10.8 shows public spending by local, state, and federal governments, as well as social insurance expenditures. Public spending on social programs alone amounted to €615.6 billion in 2009, more than was spent on all other government programs combined. A compulsory social insurance system includes nationwide health care, accident insurance, unemployment compensation, and retirement benefits. Other programs provide financial assistance for the needy and individuals who cannot support themselves. Additional programs spread the benefits of the Economic Miracle regardless of need. For instance, the government provides financial assistance to all families with children and has special tax-free savings plans for the average wage earner. The unemployment program is a typical example of the range of benefits available (see Box 10.4). For much of the FRG's early history, politicians competed to expand the coverage and benefits of such programs. Since the 1980s, the government has tried to scale back social programs, but the basic structure of the welfare state has endured.

Unification put this system to an additional test. Unemployment, welfare, and health benefits provide

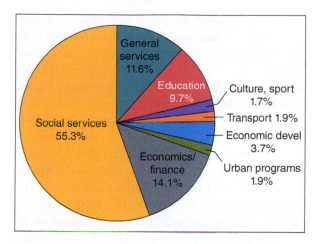

FIGURE 10.8

Total Public Expenditures, 2009

The largest share of public spending is for various social programs and then education.

Source: *Statistisches Jahrbuch für die Bundesrepublik Deutschland* (Berlin: Statistiches Bundesamt, 2012), 262. The figure presents 2009 spending in billions of euros.

for basic social needs in the East, and these needs have exceeded revenues. In addition, the 2008 recession further increased unemployment and other social needs. Germans generally agree that these programs need reform to make them more fiscally manageable, but they disagree on the exact reforms to enact.

The federal government is involved in a range of other policy activities. Education, for example, is an important concern of all three levels of government, accounting for about one-tenth of all public spending (see again Figure 10.8). The federal government is deeply involved in communications and transportation; it manages public television and radio, as well as owning the railway system.

BOX

10.4   **German Unemployment Benefits**

An unemployed worker receives insurance payments that provide up to 67 percent of normal pay (60 percent for unmarried workers and those without children) for up to two years. After that, unemployment assistance continues at a reduced rate for a period that depends on one's age. The government pays the social insurance contributions of individuals who are unemployed, and government labor offices help the unemployed worker find new employment or obtain retraining for a new job. If the worker locates a job in another city, the program partially reimburses travel and moving expenses. These benefits are much more generous than those typically found in the United States and may be a factor in the higher unemployment rate in Germany.

In recent years, the policy agenda has expanded to include new issues; environmental protection is the most visible example. Several indicators of air and water quality show real improvements in recent decades, and Germany has a very ambitious recycling program. The Green Dot system recycles about 80 percent of bottles used in commercial packaging, compared to about 20 percent in the United States. Government incentives have also made Germany a global leader in the development of photoelectric and wind energy.

Defense and foreign relations are another important government activity. The FRG's economy and security system were historically based on international interdependence. The Federal Republic's economy depends heavily on exports of goods and services. Exports now account for nearly half of the gross domestic product, a higher percentage than for most other industrial economies. Thus, the nation's membership in the EU has been a cornerstone of its economic policy. The FRG was an initial advocate of the EU and has benefited considerably from its membership. Free access to a large European market was essential to the success of the Economic Miracle, and it still benefits the FRG's export-oriented economy. Germany was one of the prime movers in the creation

of the euro in 2002, and now struggles with the consequences of this decision in the current euro crisis in Europe. Participation in EU decision making gives the Federal Republic an opportunity to influence the course of European politics on a transnational scale.

The Federal Republic is also integrated into the Western military alliance through its membership in NATO. Among the Europeans, the Federal Republic makes the largest personnel and financial contributions to NATO forces, and the German public supports the NATO alliance. In the post–Cold War world, however, Germany has reduced its defense spending to about €20 billion a year, or less than 3 percent of public spending.

Public expenditures show the policy efforts of the government, but the actual results of this spending are more difficult to assess. Most indicators of policy performance suggest that the Federal Republic is relatively successful in achieving its policy goals. Standards of living have improved dramatically, and health statistics show similar improvement. Even in new policy areas such as energy and the environment, the government has made real progress. The opinions of the public reflect these policy advances (see Figure 10.9). In 2011, most Westerners expressed relatively high

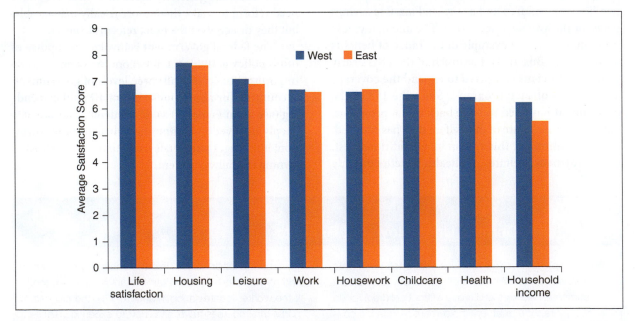

FIGURE 10.9

Satisfaction with Life Areas

Westerners are slightly more satisfied than Easterners with their life conditions.

Source: Statistisches Bundesamt, ed., *Datenreport 2011* (Berlin: Bundeszentrale für politische Bildung, 2011), 377.

satisfaction with most aspects of life that might be linked to government performance: housing, living standards, work, and income. Easterners' evaluations of their lives lag behind those of the West, but the gap has narrowed dramatically since the years immediately after unification.

Paying the Costs

Generous government programs are not, of course, due to government largesse. Funds from individuals and corporations support these programs. Therefore, large government outlays inevitably mean an equally large collection of revenues by the government. These revenues are the real source of government programs.

Three different types of revenue provide most of financing for public policy programs.[47] The health, unemployment, disability, retirement, and other social security funds are primarily self-financed by employer and employee contributions. Contributions to these programs are the largest single source of public revenues at over a third of all public finance (see Figure 10.10). Contributions to the pension plan amount to about 20 percent of a worker's gross monthly wages, health insurance is about 17 percent, and

unemployment is 3 percent. The various insurance payments are divided between contributions from the worker and from the employer.

Direct taxes that are assessed by and paid to the government are the next most important source of public revenues. A personal income tax shared by the federal, state, and local governments accounts for a large proportion. The rate of personal taxation rises with income level, from a base of 14 percent to a maximum of 45 percent for high-income taxpayers (plus a solidarity surcharge to benefit the East). Even after the recent reforms of the tax rates, the German rates are still significantly higher than those in the United States. Corporate profits are taxed at a lower rate than personal income to encourage businesses to reinvest their profits in further growth, although the share of public revenues coming from corporate taxes increased significantly in recent years.

Indirect taxes are the third major source of government revenues. Indirect taxes are based on the use of income, like sales and excise taxes, rather than on wages and profits. The most lucrative indirect tax is the **value-added tax (VAT)**—a charge that is added at every stage in the manufacturing process and that increases the value of a product. The standard VAT is 19 percent for most goods and 7 percent for basic commodities such as food. Other indirect taxes include customs duties and liquor taxes, tobacco taxes, and a green tax on the use of energy. Altogether, indirect taxes account for about two-fifths of all public revenues. Indirect taxes—one of the secrets to the dramatic growth of government revenues—are normally "hidden" in the price of an item, rather than explicitly listed as a tax. In this way, people are not reminded that they are paying taxes every time they purchase a product; it is also easier for policymakers to raise indirect taxes without evoking public opposition. Indirect taxes are regressive, however; they weigh more heavily on low-income families because a larger share of their income goes for consumer goods.

The average German obviously has deep pockets to fund the extensive variety of public policy programs; U.S. taxation levels look quite modest by comparison. A middle-class family pays about 45 percent of their income for taxes and social security contributions, compared with a rate of about 25 percent in the United States.

Even with these various revenue sources, public expenditures repeatedly exceed public revenues. To

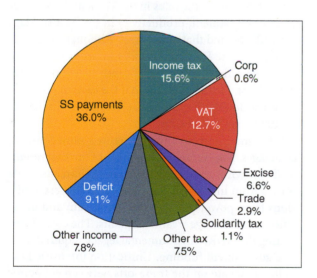

FIGURE 10.10

Sources of Public Revenues, 2009

Public spending is financed by a combination of direct taxes, indirect taxes, various fees, and deficit spending.

Source: *Statistisches Jahrbuch für die Bundesrepublik Deutschland* (Berlin: Statistiches Bundesamt, 2012), 261, 269. The figure presents 2009 government income in billions of euros.

finance this deficit, the government draws on another source of "revenue"—loans and public borrowing—to maintain the level of government services. The costs of unification increased the flow of red ink even to the present; then the Great Recession renewed budget problems. The public deficit was 4 billion euros in 2008, and then ballooned to 101 billion in 2009.

The German taxpayer seems to contribute an excessive amount to the public coffers, and Germans are no more eager than other nationalities to pay taxes. Still, the question is not how much citizens pay but how much value is returned for their payments. In addition to normal government activities, Germans are protected against sickness, unemployment, and disability; government pension plans furnish livable retirement incomes. Moreover, the majority of the public expects the government to take an active role in providing for the needs of society and its citizens.

Addressing the Policy Challenges

10.15 Discuss three prominent policy challenges that Germany continues to address.

The last decade has been a time of tremendous policy change and innovation for the Federal Republic as it has adjusted to its new domestic and foreign policy circumstances. While a government faces policy needs in many areas, we discuss three prominent issues. The first is to accommodate the remaining problems flowing from German unification. The second is to reform the German economic and social systems. And the third is to define a new international role for Germany.

The Problems of Unification

Some of the major policy challenges facing contemporary Germany flow from the unification of East and West. The first consequence of the November 1989 revolution was the collapse of the GDR's economic and social systems. During the first half of 1990, for instance, the GDP of the GDR decreased by nearly 5 percent, unemployment skyrocketed, and industrial production fell by nearly 60 percent.[48]

Unification was accompanied by the need to rebuild the economy of the East. The GDR's impressive growth statistics and production figures often papered over a decaying economic infrastructure and outdated manufacturing facilities. And as government-owned firms were privatized in 1990 through 1994, this created severe economic dislocations. One of the first actions of new owners was to reduce the bloated list of employees. Massive capital investments were necessary to bring eastern manufacturing up to the standards of the global economy. Disputes about property ownership further slowed the pace of development.

German unification had multiple economic byproducts. The high levels of unemployment strained the Federal Republic's social welfare programs. Unemployed eastern workers drew unemployment compensation, retraining benefits, and relocation allowances—without having made prior contributions to these social insurance systems. The FRG also took over the pensions and health insurance benefits of easterners. The government spent massive amounts, from rebuilding the highway and railway systems of the East, to upgrading the telephone system, to moving the capital from Bonn to Berlin. Even today, roughly 4 percent of the GDP is transferred to the East.

Economic progress is being made. Economic growth rates in the East often exceed those in the West by a comfortable margin. However, the East–West gap is still wide. Unemployment rates in the East are still more than double the rates in the West, and even after years of investment, productivity in the East still lags markedly behind that of the West. Although standards of living in the East have rapidly improved since the early 1990s, they remain significantly below standards in the West. Furthermore, even if the eastern economy grows at double the rate of the West, it will take decades to reach full equality.

German unification also created noneconomic challenges. For example, many areas of the East resembled an environmentalist's nightmare: Untreated toxic wastes from industry were dumped into rivers, emissions from power plants poisoned the air, and many cities lacked sewage treatment plants. The cost of correcting the GDR's environmental legacy required massive government funding. Unification intensified the political debate on the trade-offs between economic development and environmental protection.

Thus, despite the progress that has been made since 1990, a policy gap still exists between West and East. Germans still pay an extra "solidarity surcharge" on their income tax that funds part of the eastern reconstruction. Equalizing living conditions across regions remains a national goal, but it is a goal that will demand continuing resources and take decades to accomplish.

Reforming the Welfare State

The 1950s Wirtschaftswunder is a central part of the Federal Republic's modern history—but those miraculous times are now in the distant past. Contemporary Germany faces a series of new problems as its economy and social programs strain to adjust to a new global economic system.

For instance, the last decade has seen repeated government attempts to limit labor costs to ensure the competiveness of German products in the international market. The generous benefits from liberal social services programs require substantial employee and employer contributions. Other regulations impede the creation of new jobs or temporary employment. A recent report claimed that some German firms are mired in a spiderweb of government bureaucracy; they must provide 62 different data sets to government offices, file 78 reports for social insurance, supply another 60 forms for tax purposes, and complete no less than 111 more to comply with labor laws.

A related issue is the economic viability of Germany's social service programs. A rapidly aging population means that the demand for health care and pension benefits will steadily increase over time, but there are fewer employed workers to contribute to social insurance programs. For instance, in the 1950s, there were roughly four employees for every person receiving a pension; in 2010, there were about two employees for every pensioner. Similar demographic issues face Germany's other social programs. As the population ages, health care costs have also increased.

In the mid-2000s, the Schröder government implemented a reform program known as Agenda 2010 to address these issues. Some of the measures reformed the labor market by easing employment rules, reducing nonwage labor costs, and reforming the unemployment system. Other reforms reduced benefits in the pension and health care systems. Additional reforms restructured the tax system. Ironically, these efforts by the Schröder government created a backlash against the SPD among some leftist voters and groups that eventually hurt the party at the polls.

These reforms undoubtedly contributed to an improvement in the economy that started in 2005. But the global recession in 2008 reversed this trend. Unemployment again ticked upward, and the economy stagnated. The new CDU/CSU–FDP government had to grapple with these problems, first by a small stimulus program and then a shift toward government austerity. Furthermore, the debt crisis in the euro area created new economic challenges that required German contributions to a stabilization fund and further slowed economic recovery in Europe. Immediate economic priorities are taking precedence over longer-term economic reforms, partially because citizens and elites do not agree on what policies are most desirable. To protect the economy and encourage future economic growth, major welfare state reforms will eventually be required. The uncertainty of the grand coalition is that the CDU/CSU and SPD have sharply different basic policy positions on many of these issues. This raises the prospect that the current government is unlikely to enact significant new reforms.

A New World Role

The Federal Republic's role in international politics is linked to its participation in the NATO alliance and the EU. Both relationships have changed since 1989.

In mid-1990, Russia agreed to continued German membership in NATO in return for concessions on the reduction of combined German troop levels, the definition of the GDR territory as a nuclear-free zone, and Germany's continued abstention from the development or use of atomic, biological, and chemical weapons. With unification, Germany became a fully sovereign nation and now seeks its own role in international affairs.

Germany's military and strategic role is shaped by these agreements and the changing international context. Instead of a single focus on its NATO membership and the Western defense against the Soviet threat, Germany is becoming more active internationally. It wants to be an active advocate for peace within Europe, developing its role as a bridge between East and West. The nation is also assuming a larger responsibility in international disputes outside the NATO region, although the size of the German military is quite small. In 1993, the Constitutional Court interpreted the Basic Law to allow German troops to serve outside of Europe as part of international peacekeeping activities. In 1998, Schröder survived a no-confidence vote on sending German soldiers into former Yugoslavia, which changed the course of German foreign policy. In 2010, German troops served in twelve nations as part of international peacekeeping efforts, although many citizens remain skeptical of these actions. Gradually, the FRG is exercising a more independent foreign policy within a framework of partnership with its allies.

The Federal Republic's relationship to the EU is also changing.[49] Germany outweighs the other EU members in both its population and its GNP. Germany has been a strong advocate of the EU, but this has sometimes made other Western members uneasy. For instance, Germany had pushed for the eastward expansion of the EU and strongly supported the euro, while other nations favored a slower course. The 2007 Lisbon Treaty deepened the impact of the EU on Germany and other member states and increased the importance of decisions made in Brussels. But Germany is also likely to exert more independence in EU affairs, as seen in its cautious reaction to the 2010 debt crisis in Greece and debates on protecting the euro. At the least, it is clear that a united Germany will approach the process of European integration based on a different calculus than that which guided its actions for the previous forty years.

After the Revolution

Revolutions are unsettling, both to the participants and to the spectators. Such is the case with the German revolution of 1989. Easterners realized their hopes for freedom, but they also saw their everyday lives change before their eyes, sometimes in distressing ways. Westerners saw their hopes for German union and a new peace in Europe answered, but at a substantial political and economic cost to the nation. The Federal Republic is now forging a new social and political identity that will shape its domestic and international policies. Many Germans are hopeful about, but still uncertain of, what the future holds for their nation.

Unification and a changing international environment are presenting new social, political, and economic challenges for the nation. Unification created a new German state linked to western political values and social norms, and unity was achieved through a peaceful revolution (and the power of the DM), not blood and iron. However, the trials of the unification process are testing the public's commitment to these values. In addition, a turbulent international environment means Germany's future is more clearly tied to those of its neighbors, and not something it can control solely by itself.

REVIEW QUESTIONS

- In what ways were the democratic transitions in 1945 and 1989 similar, and in what ways were they different?
- What were the objectives of the framers of the Federal Republic's Basic Law, and what institutions and processes were created to reach these goals?

- Has full social and political unification of western and eastern Germany been achieved?
- Does Germany's proportional electoral system with many elected parties strengthen or weaken the democratic process?
- What are the benefits and problems that result from Germany's extensive social services programs?

KEY TERMS

Adenauer, Konrad
Alternative for Germany (AfD)
Basic Law (*Grundgesetz*)

Bundesrat (Federal Council)
Bundestag (Federal Diet)

Christian Democratic Union (CDU)
Christian Social Union (CSU)

codetermination (*Mitbestimmung*)
Confederation of German Employers' Associations (BDA)

Constitutional Court

constructive
   no-confidence vote

Die Linke

Economic Miracle
   (*Wirtschaftswunder*)

European Union (EU)

federal chancellor
   (*Bundeskanzler*)

federal president
   (*Bundespräsident*)

Federal Republic of
   Germany (FRG)

Federation of German
   Industry (BDI)

Free Democratic Party
   (FDP)

German Democratic
   Republic (GDR)

German Federation of
   Trade Unions
   (DGB)

guest workers
   (*Gastarbeiter*)

Hitler, Adolf

Kaiser

Kohl, Helmut

Merkel, Angela

National Socialist German
   Workers' Party (the
   Nazis)

neocorporatism

New Politics

Ostpolitik

Party of Democratic
   Socialism (PDS)

peak association

proportional
   representation (PR)

Schröder, Gerhard

Social Democratic Party
   (SPD)

Socialist Unity Party
   (SED)

The Greens (*Die Grünen*)

Third Reich

value-added tax (VAT)

Weimar Republic

SUGGESTED READINGS

Anderson, Jeffrey, and Eric Langenbacher, eds. *From the Bonn to the Berlin Republic: Germany at the Twentieth Anniversary.* New York: Berghahn Press, 2010.

Childers, Thomas, and Jane Caplan, eds. *Reevaluating the Third Reich.* New York: Holmes and Meier, 1993.

Crawford, Beverly. *Power and German Foreign Policy: Embedded Hegemony in Europe.* New York: Palgrave, 2007.

Fulbrook, Mary. *Anatomy of a Dictatorship: Inside the GDR, 1949–1989.* New York: Oxford University Press, 1995.

———. *History of Germany, 1918–2000.* Oxford: Blackwell, 2002.

Hough, Dan, and Emil Kirchner. "Germany at 60: Stability and Success, Problems and Challenges." special issue, *German Politics* 19, no. 1 (March 2010).

Green, Simon, and Willy Paterson, eds. *Governance in Contemporary Germany: The Semisovereign State Revisited.* Cambridge: Cambridge University Press, 2005.

Kershaw, Ian. *Hitler: A Biography.* New York: Norton, 2008.

Kolinsky, Eva. *Women in Contemporary Germany.* New York: Berg, 1993.

Kopstein, Jeffrey. *The Politics of Economic Decline in East Germany, 1945–1989.* Chapel Hill: University of North Carolina Press, 1997.

Krisch, Henry. *The German Democratic Republic: The Search for Identity.* Boulder, CO: Westview Press, 1985.

Less, Charles. *Party Politics in Germany: A Comparative Politics Approach.* London: Palgrave Macmillan, 2005.

Orlow, Dietrich. *A History of Modern Germany,* 5th ed. Englewood Cliffs, NJ: Prentice Hall, 2007.

Padgett, Stephen. *Organizing Democracy in Eastern Germany.* Cambridge: Cambridge University Press, 2000.

Padgett, Stephen, William Patterson, and Gordon Smith, eds. *Developments in German Politics 3.* London: Palgrave Macmillan, 2003.

Rohrschneider, Robert. *Learning Democracy: Democratic and Economic Values in Unified Germany.* New York: Oxford University Press, 1999.

Sinn, Gerlinde, and Hans-Werner Sinn. *Jumpstart: The Economic Unification of Germany.* Cambridge: Massachusetts Institute of Technology Press, 1992.

Sinn, Hans-Werner. *Can Germany Be Saved? The Malaise of the World's First Welfare State.* Cambridge: Massachusetts Institute of Technology Press, 2007.

Spielvogel, Jackson. *Hitler and Nazi Germany: A History,* 5th ed. Englewood Cliffs, NJ: Prentice Hall, 2005.

Streeck, Wolfgang. *Re-Forming Capitalism: Institutional Change in the German Political Economy.* Oxford: Oxford University Press, 2009.

Turner, Henry. *Germany from Partition to Unification.* New Haven, CT: Yale University Press, 1992.

Vanberg, Georg. *The Politics of Constitutional Review in Germany.* New York: Cambridge University Press, 2005.

INTERNET SOURCES

Bundestag: www.bundestag.de.

Federal government: www.bundesregierung.de.

German Information Center: www.germany.info.

German Politics and Society, University of California, Irvine: www.socsci.uci.edu/~rdalton/germany.html.

ENDNOTES

1. The First German Empire was formed in the ninth century through the partitioning of Charlemagne's empire.

2. Karl Dietrich Bracher, *The German Dictatorship* (New York: Praeger, 1970); and Martin Broszat, *Hitler and the Collapse of Weimar Germany* (New York: St. Martin's Press, 1987).

3. Raul Hilberg, *The Destruction of the European Jews,* 3rd ed. (New York: Holmes and Meier, 2003); and Deborah Dwork and Robert Jan van Pelt, *Holocaust: A History* (New York: Norton, 2002).

4. Karl Hardach, *The Political Economy of Germany in the Twentieth Century* (Berkeley: University of California Press, 1980); and Eric Owen Smith, *The German Economy* (London: Routledge, 1994).

5. Gregory Sandford, *From Hitler to Ulbricht: The Communist Reconstruction of East Germany, 1945–1946* (Princeton, NJ: Princeton University Press, 1983).

6. Eva Kolinsky, *Women in Contemporary Germany* (New York: Berg, 1993); Pippa Norris and Ronald Inglehart, *Rising Tide: Gender Equality and Cultural Change around the World* (New York: Cambridge University Press, 2003); and Russell Dalton, *Citizen Politics,* 6th ed. (Washington, DC: CQ Press, 2013), chap. 6.

7. Ruud Koopmans, Paul Statham, Marco Giugni, and Florence Passy, *Contested Citizenship: Immigration and Cultural Diversity in Europe* (Minneapolis: University of Minnesota Press, 2005); and Richard Alba, Peter Schmidt, and Martina Wasmer, eds., *Germans or Foreigners? Attitudes toward Ethnic Minorities in Post-reunification Germany* (New York: Palgrave Macmillan, 2003).

8. The Allied occupation authorities oversaw the drafting of the Basic Law and held veto power over the final document. See Peter Merkl, *The Origins of the West German Republic* (New York: Oxford University Press, 1965).

9. In 2002, the membership of the Bundestag was reduced from its previous size of 656. This resulted from redistricting to equalize the number of voters in each district.

10. Bundestag: www.bundestag.de.

11. Ludger Helms, "Keeping Weimar at Bay: The German Federal Presidency since 1949," *German Politics and Society* 16 (Summer 1998): 50–68.

12. Donald P. Kommers and Russell A. Miller, *The Constitutional Jurisprudence of the Federal Republic of Germany,* 3rd ed. (Durham, NC: Duke University Press 2012).

13. A second type of no-confidence vote allows the chancellor to attach a no-confidence provision to a government legislative proposal. If the Bundestag defeats the proposal, the chancellor may ask the federal president to call for new Bundestag elections. This tool was used by Kohl in 1983 and Schröder in 2005 to call for early elections.

14. Anna Merritt and Richard Merritt, *Public Opinion in Occupied Germany* (Urbana: University of Illinois Press, 1970); and Ralf Dahrendorf, *Society and Democracy in Germany* (New York: Doubleday, 1967).

15. Christiane Lemke, "Political Socialization and the 'Micromilieu,'" in *The Quality of Life in the German Democratic Republic,* ed. Marilyn Rueschemeyer and Christiane Lemke (New York: M. E. Scharpe, 1989).

16. Gabriel A. Almond and Sidney Verba, *The Civic Culture: Political Attitudes and Democracy in Five Nations* (Princeton, NJ: Princeton University Press, 1962); and David Conradt, "Changing German Political Culture," in *The Civic Culture Revisited,* ed. Gabriel Almond and Sidney Verba (Boston: Little Brown, 1980).

17. Conradt, "Changing German Political Culture," 229–31; and Kendall Baker, Russell Dalton, and Kai Hildebrandt, *Germany Transformed: Political Culture and the New Politics* (Cambridge, MA: Harvard University Press, 1981).

18. Conradt, "Changing German Political Culture."

19. Gerard Braunthal, *Political Loyalty and Public Service in West Germany* (Amherst: University of Massachusetts Press, 1990).

20. Walter Friedrich and Hartmut Griese, *Jugend und Jugend forschung in der DDR* (Opladen, Germany: Westdeutscher Verlag, 1990).

21. Russell Dalton, "Communists and Democrats: Democratic Attitudes in the Two Germanies," *British Journal of Political Science* 24 (1994): 469–93.

22. Richard Hofferbert and Hans-Dieter Klingemann, "Democracy and Its Discontents in Post-wall Germany," *International Political Science Review* 22 (2001): 363–78; and Robert Rohrschneider, *Learning Democracy: Democratic and Economic Values in Unified Germany* (New York: Oxford University Press, 1999).

23. Ronald Inglehart, *Modernization and Postmodernization* (Princeton, NJ: Princeton University Press, 1997); and Ronald Inglehart, *Culture Shift in Advanced Industrial Societies* (Princeton, NJ: Princeton University Press, 1990).

24. See Chapter 3; and Russell and Steven Weldon, "Germans Divided? Political Culture in a United Germany," *German Politics* 19 (March 2010): 9–23.

25. German Longitudinal Election Study 2009, study 1103 (http://www.gles.eu/index.en.htm).

26. Lemke, "Political Socialization and the 'Micromilieu.'"

27. Meredith Watts et al., *Contemporary German Youth and Their Elders* (New York: Greenwood, 1989); and Elizabeth Noelle-Neumann and Renate Köcher, *Die verletze Nation* (Stuttgart, Germany: Deutsche Verlag, 1987).

28. Peter Humphreys, *Media and Media Policy in Germany: The Press and Broadcasting since 1945,* rev. ed. (New York: Berg, 1994).

29. Commission of the European Union, *Eurobarometer 63.4.* (Brussels: Commission of the European Union, 2005).

30. Oscar Gabriel et al., *Political Participation in France and Germany*, ECPR Studies in European Political Science (Colchester, England: University of Essex, 2012).

31. Wilhelm Bürklin et al., *Eliten in Deutschland: Rekutierung und Integration* (Opladen, Germany: Leske and Budrich, 1997).

32. Rohrschneider, *Learning Democracy*; and Wilhelm Bürklin, "Einstellungen und Wertorientierungen ost-und westdeutscher Eliten 1995," in *Einstellungen und politisches Verhalten in Transformationsprozess,* ed. Oskar Gabriel (Opladen, Germany: Leske and Budrich, 1996), 235–61.

33. Volker Berghahn and Detlev Karsten, *Industrial Relations in West Germany* (New York: Berg, 1989); and Claus Offe,

"The Attribution of Political Status to Interest Groups," in *Organizing Interests in Western Europe*, ed. Suzanne Berger (New York: Cambridge University Press, 1981), 123–58.

34. Kathleen Thelen, *Union in Parts: Labor Politics in Postwar Germany* (Ithaca, NY: Cornell University Press, 1991).

35. Ruud Koopmans, *Democracy from Below: New Social Movements and the Political System in West Germany* (Boulder, CO: Westview Press, 1995).

36. Margit Mayer and John Ely, eds., *The German Greens: Paradox between Movement and Party* (Philadelphia: Temple University Press, 1998).

37. David Patton, *Out of the East: From PDS to Left Party in Unified Germany* (Albany: State University of New York Press, 2011).

38. If a party wins more district seats in a state than it should have based on its proportion of the second vote, the party keeps the additional seats and the size of the Bundestag is increased. After a constitutional challenge, this process was modified in 2011. In 2013, the actual Bundestag membership was 630.

39. A party that wins at least three district seats also shares in the PR distribution of seats. In 1994 and 1998, the PDS won four district seats in East Berlin, but in 2002, the PDS won only two district seats.

40. Matthew Shugart and Martin Wattenberg, eds., *Mixed-Member Electoral Systems: The Best of Both Worlds?* (Oxford: Oxford University Press, 2001). Also see Chapter 5.

41. For voting patterns in prior elections, see Russell Dalton and Willy Jou, "Is There a Single German Party System?" *German Politics and Society* 28 (2010): 34–52.

42. Vivien Schmitt, *The Futures of European Capitalism* (Oxford: Oxford University Press, 2002); and Alec Stone Sweet, Wayne Sandholtz, and Neil Fligstein, eds., *The Institutionalization of Europe* (Oxford: Oxford University Press, 2001).

43. A constitutional reform in 2006 changed the Bundesrat's legislative role. In exchange for greater state autonomy in several policy areas, the Bundesrat's approval is no longer required for the passage of various administrative proposals.

44. The European Court of Justice also has the power to evaluate German legislation against the standards of the EU agreements.

45. Kommers and Miller, *The Constitutional Jurisprudence.*

46. Karen Alter, *Establishing the Supremacy of European Law: The Making of an International Rule of Law in Europe* (Oxford: Oxford University Press, 2001).

47. Arnold Heidenheimer, Hugh Heclo, and Carolyn Adams, *Comparative Public Policy*, 3rd ed. (New York: St. Martin's Press, 1990), chap. 6.

48. Gerlinde Sinn and Hans-Werner Sinn, *Jumpstart: The Economic Unification of Germany* (Cambridge: Massachusetts Institute of Technology Press, 1992).

49. Maria Cowles, Thomas Risse, and James Caporaso, eds., *Transforming Europe* (Ithaca, NY: Cornell University Press, 2001).

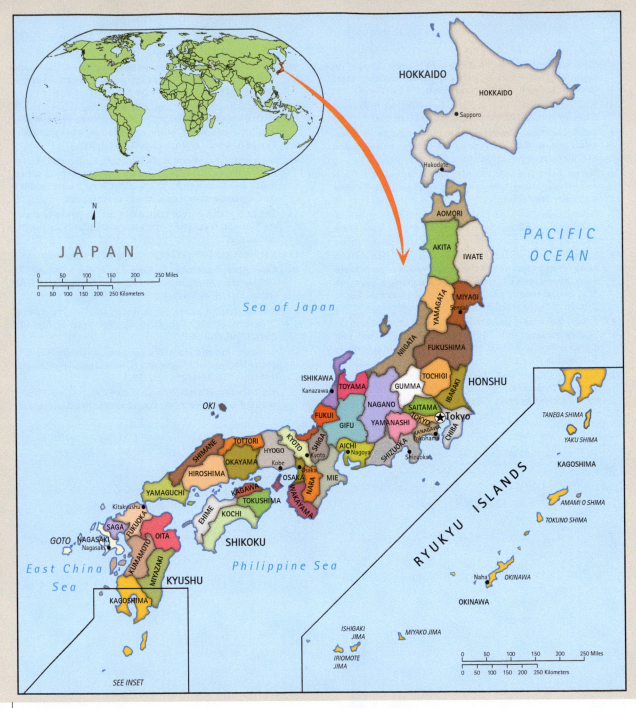

POPULATION
127.3 million

TERRITORY
145,882 square miles

YEAR OF INDEPENDENCE
660 BCE

YEAR OF CURRENT CONSTITUTION
1947

HEAD OF STATE
Emperor Akihito

HEAD OF GOVERNMENT
Prime Minister Shinzo Abe

LANGUAGE
Japanese

RELIGION
Observe both Shinto and Buddhism 84%;
other 16% (including Christian 2%)

CHAPTER 11

Politics in Japan

Frances Rosenbluth and Michael F. Thies

LEARNING OBJECTIVES

11.1 Identify four challenges currently faced by Japan's government.

11.2 Briefly discuss Japan's political history, focusing on the roles of warfare and the military.

11.3 Explain the "Peace Clause" and the post–World War II developments that set the stage for modern-day Japan.

11.4 Describe social conditions in Japan, focusing on population, gender equity, wealth, and safety.

11.5 Explain the structure of Japan's national and local governments.

11.6 Discuss Japanese culture's emphasis on conformity and hierarchy.

11.7 Identify the main sources of political socialization in Japan, along with recent changes in its political culture.

11.8 Describe Japanese voter engagement in terms of turnout, party alignment, and age demographics.

11.9 Explain Japan's two-tiered electoral system.

11.10 Discuss Japan's major parties and their election histories.

11.11 Identify the three major interest groups in Japan and describe their relationships with political parties.

11.12 Summarize the policymaking process in Japan's Diet.

11.13 Discuss Japan's recent domestic and foreign policies.

Japan has been a stable democracy since the promulgation of its post–World War II constitution in 1947. But for many observers, 2009 marked almost as profound a turning point in the country's political development. In August of that year, the **Liberal Democratic Party (LDP)**, which had controlled the government since 1955 (except for a few months in 1993 and 1994), was defeated in a general election by the **Democratic Party of Japan (DPJ)** and sent into opposition.

The advent of the DPJ government in 2009 raised hopes of policy responses to two decades of economic stagnation, worsening inequality, and an increasingly unpredictable foreign policy environment. Alas, the DPJ's first taste of government was brief and bitter.

Yukio Hatoyama, who led the party to victory, was out as prime minister after only nine months due to policy failures and a fundraising scandal. Two DPJ successors, **Naoto Kan** and then **Yoshihiko Noda**, survived only fifteen months and sixteen months, respectively.

During its brief tenure, the DPJ failed both to revive the Japanese economy and to stabilize relations with its East Asian neighbors. Perhaps most important, however, was the government's muddled and inadequate response to the March 11, 2011 "Triple Disaster." That day, a magnitude 9 earthquake, the largest ever recorded in Japan, struck off the northeast coast of Japan's main island of Honshu, about 230 miles north of Tokyo. The earthquake produced a tsunami that devastated cities and towns across the coast of the Tohoku region, killing at least 16,000 people (more than 2,000 officially remain unaccounted for two years later), and leaving millions without electricity or water. Initial efforts to search for survivors and provide emergency relief were hampered when it became clear that three reactors at the Fukushima Daiichi Nuclear Power facility were in meltdown. This led to the evacuation of hundreds of thousands, on top of those whose homes had been destroyed by the earthquake or tsunami.

Of course, the natural disaster could not be blamed on the government, and even any safety short-comings related to the nuclear plant could hardly be attributed to the DPJ. However, public dissatisfaction with the government's disaster response efforts caused public trust in the DPJ to plummet. Even after the plant was stabilized, tens of thousands remained homeless, and the ramifications for Japan's energy policies, its welfare state, and its macroeconomy were enough to persuade voters to throw the DPJ out. In December 2012, the DPJ was punished at the polls for perceived incompetence, and the LDP roared back into power. While careful study of the election results indicates that voters did not necessarily run back to the LDP, the LDP did benefit the most from the DPJ's travails, and its leader, Shinzo Abe, took over as prime minister.

Japan is the longest-lived democracy and wealthiest country in East Asia. For many years, the "Japanese development model" spawned admiration and imitation both in the region and beyond. While Japan's democracy has never seemed healthier, it is also more unpredictable, and its economy and social fabric are facing greater challenges than at any time since the end of the war. This chapter provides a survey of Japanese politics, both describing the rules of the game and the attitudes and resources of its players and assessing Japan's current policy challenges and prospects for the future.

Current Policy Challenges

 Identify four challenges currently faced by Japan's government.

After the devastation of World War II, the Japanese economy skyrocketed over the next two generations to become the second largest in the world and, by some measures, the world's wealthiest on a per capita basis. Remarkably, this rapid growth proceeded without much increase in inequality. Japan's so-called "economic miracle" ended in 1990, and since then, it has reeled from one recession to the next, from bad economic straits to worse. A banking crisis emerged from the bursting of the stock and property bubbles of the late 1980s, producing mountains of unrecoverable loans. Deflation, unemployment, and bankruptcies, all unheard of for decades, have mired the economy and shocked the national psyche. A series of Japanese governments have been ineffective in turning around a slumping economy. In the early 2000s, the economy showed signs of slow, albeit sustainable, recovery, only to be knocked backward again by the global financial crisis of 2008–2009. Since the LDP's return to power, the economy has resumed a pattern of slow growth, and there are indications that deflation might finally been tamed by the massive fiscal and monetary stimulus nicknamed "Abenomics." But the economy requires substantial structural reform, and the jury is still out on whether or not the government is willing and able to pursue such changes.

Japan's economic woes are exacerbated by a demographic time bomb—its rapidly aging population (see Figure 11.1). The share of the population over age sixty-five is already 22.5 percent, the highest in the world, and government estimates expect that number to rise to almost 33 percent by 2050.[1] This demographic change, due in part to extremely low birth rates, is reducing the relative size of the labor force, reducing government tax revenue, and increasing expenditures on pensions and health care dramatically.[2]

Over the last decade, the Japanese government has vacillated between efforts to deregulate its economy and concerns over compensation for groups who rely on government protection and who stand to lose if markets are liberalized. Domestic and foreign critics cite heavy-handed government intervention and cozy government-sponsored collusion in many economic sectors as causes of trade friction and economic slowdown. But dismantling these arrangements, cutting loose inefficient firms that the government has kept afloat, and allowing the expansion of competition are policy options that are more easily advocated than implemented. Even if deregulation might help the Japanese economy in the long run, it will cause massive economic disruption in the short run. Those who would be hurt have a strong incentive to flex their

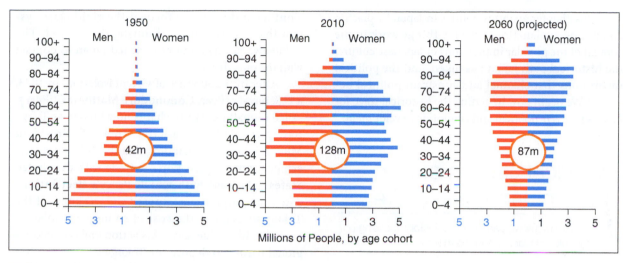

FIGURE 11.1

From Tree to Lantern to Urn

Japan's population is aging and shrinking, with enormous implications for the economy, politics, and policy.

Source: National Institute of Population and Social Security Research, http://www.ipss.go.jp/p-info/e/Population%20%20Statistics.asp, accessed May 16, 2015.

political muscles to forestall reforms. So the government has delayed and compromised, only to see the problems deepen and multiply. Most recently, Japan has decided to participate with 11 other Pacific Rim countries in the Trans-Pacific Partnership (TPP) negotiations—an effort to produce a comprehensive regional free trade agreement. But it is not clear how successful that effort will be, as Prime Minister Abe has promised to defend protections for Japan's agricultural sector—which would largely defeat the purpose of the TPP.

Along with deregulation of domestic economic markets, Japan also faces the need to modernize its immigration policies. One challenge of globalization for Japan, especially given its own internal demographic pressures, will be to accept the influx of unskilled workers from poorer parts of the world. For any country, immigration is disruptive, both economically and culturally. But for a country like Japan—literally closed to the world for over 250 years, and with high protectionist barriers ever since—a lack of experience with immigration is likely to create an even trickier policy minefield for the government to negotiate.Community building, never a difficult problem in a relatively homogeneous society such as Japan's, may become a policy challenge sooner rather than later.

Finally, the end of the Cold War has created new security policy challenges. Since its surrender in 1945, Japan has played the role of junior partner in the regional security policy scheme overseen by the United States. Now the U.S. government is less willing to spend money and manpower on Cold War–era concerns, and the possibility of a power vacuum in East Asia has forced Japan to face new choices. Before, simply providing bases for U.S. troops sufficed; now the issues include the extent to which Japan will participate in multilateral peacekeeping operations, fights against international terrorism, nonproliferation, and the like. North Korea has begun to appear more and more threatening. China also remains an unpredictable threat as its economy has grown at breakneck speed and surpassed Japan's in absolute size. China rattles its saber at Japan as well over the control of several long-disputed islands in the South China Sea. It seems clear that Japan's neighbors—for whom a militant Japanese foreign policy before and during World War II remains a bitter memory—are not anxious for it to assume a more active security posture in the region. While Japan's own national trauma over the memory of its failed past as a military power is not as acute as it was a generation ago, only a minority of Japanese citizens and leaders desire significant changes in foreign policy.

This chapter analyzes politics in Japan by placing competing explanations for how things work in the context of the popular impressions of Japanese culture, the historical path Japan has taken, and the political institutions that channel and constrain political behavior. We begin now by setting the historical stage for Japan's postwar political and economic development.

Historical Origins of the Modern Japanese State

11.2 Briefly discuss Japan's political history, focusing on the roles of warfare and the military.

The first inhabitants of Japan were most likely hunter-gatherers from the Asian mainland. The introduction of a new culture, known as *Jomon*, began in about 11,000 BCE. Artifacts suggest that from about 300 BCE., a rather abrupt shift from the Jomon culture occurred, possibly the result of invasions or waves of migration from the mainland through the Korean peninsula. The new culture, known as *Yayoi*, was characterized by the use of bronze and iron, including weaponry, and the development of wet-field rice agriculture. The Yayoi people spread from the southern island of Kyushu through Shikoku and much of the main island (Honshu) by the third century CE. During the Kofun period (300–710 CE), the most powerful clan, the Yamato, eventually asserted political control over much of the country. The Japanese court sponsored Buddhism, began to write histories using Chinese characters, wrote a constitution, and promulgated legal codes. In 794 CE, the capital was moved from Nara to Kyoto, which served as the home of the imperial court for the next thousand years. The court lacked an effective centralized military system, however, and warrior clans (later known as samurai) gradually began to assume more power. In the ensuing centuries, political control by the Imperial Court in Kyoto waned as power became decentralized under competing—and often warring—samurai families.

Japan's medieval period (roughly 1185–1600) was a time of continual tumult and frequent warfare. In 1600, the **Tokugawa clan** achieved preeminence and a considerable degree of national unity. The Tokugawa family ruled from Edo, present-day Tokyo, from 1600 to 1868. Under Tokugawa rule, the feudal structure of Japanese society took on a rigid, systematic form.

Confucian doctrine informed the rigid class system that was constructed during this period. The Tokugawa government also closed Japan to contact with the outside world.

After over 250 years of virtual isolation, in 1853, a U.S. naval officer, **Commodore Matthew C. Perry**, sailed a small fleet into what is now known as Tokyo Bay. Perry delivered a letter from U.S. President Millard Fillmore demanding that the Tokugawa government open Japan's ports to trade with the United States. The ease with which Perry's fleet intimidated the government exposed the weakness of the Tokugawa regime, the cost of so long an isolation from outside influences. This action emboldened regional barons to depose the Tokugawa clan and "restore" the emperor to power. The **Meiji Restoration** (1868), as this transition is called, was named for the young Emperor Meiji, who was nominally installed as the supreme political and religious leader. The new regime in fact gave the emperor little real power. The samurai who subverted the Tokugawa regime used the imperial institution as a symbol to unify the nation to further their own political ends. These ends entailed a centralization of political power beyond any previous experience in Japan. They established a national tax system based on land and eliminated the system of samurai stipends. The major goal of the Japanese government during the Meiji era was to catch up with the imperialist powers of the West by promoting industrial development and ridding itself of "unequal treaties" that had been forced upon Japan when its isolation was ended so abruptly.[3]

Although the new oligarchs had no intention of democratizing politics on any mass level, they did accede to the establishment of a constitution with an elected legislature. The government established the **Diet**, a bicameral legislative body, on the model of European parliamentary democracy. The Diet did not control the cabinet. Instead, the oligarchs managed to control cabinet decision making by choosing the prime minister and the ministers of the various government bureaucracies. Still, the 1889 constitution had given the Diet the ability to reject certain governmental actions (specifically the budget), so the cabinet had to bargain with nascent political parties on many issues. Parties became sufficiently obstreperous that they were able to increase their influence over time.

This creeping democratization reached its prewar apex from 1918 to 1932, which became known as the **Taisho Democracy**. (Emperor Taisho succeeded his father, Meiji, in 1912.) During this period, cabinets were dominated by the political parties that controlled the parliament. The remaining oligarchs felt it necessary to select prime ministers from among the party leaders in order to gain the Diet's cooperation. Throughout the 1920s, party-controlled cabinets became the norm.

By 1932, endemic political corruption and an ambitious military had eroded public support for the parties. After the assassination of Prime Minister Tsuyoshi Inukai by ultranationalists, the military took over the government with little visible public opposition. The end of civilian government brought a rapid increase in spending on munitions, especially after 1937, when the army began a full-scale war against China. When the U.S. government blockaded oil shipments to Japan in response to Japanese aggression in China, the Japanese navy responded by attacking sources of oil in Southeast Asia as well as U.S. warships and aircraft at Pearl Harbor.

American reluctance to enter the war evaporated at Pearl Harbor. The United States committed enormous resources in material and manpower against Japanese forces that controlled China, Korea, and much of South East Asia, as well as a scattering of islands from the Indian Ocean to the Pacific. The turning point in the Pacific War came in June 1942 in the battle for Midway, a physically insignificant but strategically located atoll in the mid-Pacific. Admiral Yamamoto's superior sea forces were destroyed by U.S. bombers, a defeat from which the Japanese navy never fully recovered. Japanese forces continued to fight, with dwindling chances of success. Fearing that the Japanese military would fight to the last man, President Truman made the controversial decision to use nuclear weapons to bomb the industrial cities of Hiroshima and Nagasaki in August of 1945; the bombings killed 150,000 and 75,000 civilians, respectively. The Pacific theater of World War II left 108,504 U.S. soldiers dead, and twice that number were recorded as missing. Japan lost 2 million soldiers in addition to the 3 million or so civilians who were killed in U.S. bombing raids, totalling about 3.5 percent of the 1939 population. Estimates of Chinese loss of human life in the war range from 10 to 20 million people, about 3–6 percent of the population. It was not until Japan's surrender in August 1945 that the military's role in politics was ended and civilian democracy was allowed to flourish.[4]

The Occupation

11.3 Explain the "Peace Clause" and the post–World War II developments that set the stage for modern-day Japan.

The **Allied Occupation of Japan** was administered by the **Supreme Commander for the Allied Powers (SCAP)**, under the direction of **General Douglas MacArthur** of the United States. Its initial objectives were to demilitarize and democratize Japan—to render Japan unable and unwilling to wage war ever again. It efficiently demobilized the army and navy and repatriated 3.3 million Japanese troops still left abroad at the end of the war. It also implemented wide-ranging measures to uproot the old elite and its basis of power. In the "Tokyo War Crimes Trials," twenty-five men were tried as "Class A" war criminals; seven were given death sentences, while the others received long prison terms. Another 200,000 were purged from politics, business, and the media for supposed complicity during the war. Holding companies, which owned and coordinated the wartime *zaibatsu* conglomerates, were outlawed, forcing the dissolution and decentralization of ownership control over much of the industrial economy.[5]

An even broader attempt at political reform involved the implementation of a new constitution. After rejecting the Japanese government's draft for retaining the sovereignty of Japan in the emperor and allowing the Diet to restrict individual freedoms,[6] SCAP produced its own draft, which added extensive guarantees for individual liberties, social equality, and gender equality.

Perhaps the best-known provision of the Japanese Constitution is **Article 9**, the "Peace Clause," in which Japan renounces the right to wage war or even to maintain a military capability (see Box 11.1). Conservative governments and courts have interpreted the provision flexibly (to say the least) to allow for a defensive capability. During the 1960s, public opinion tipped overwhelmingly against any amendment to the Constitution that would dismantle Article 9. That has begun to change, however, as the share of the population that remembers the war dwindles, and as Japan has emerged from its postwar geopolitical shell, participating in international peacekeeping operations and even sending troops to Iraq in early 2004.

Land reform represented the other major aim of the Occupation, and arguably was one of its greatest

BOX
11.1

BOX 11.1   Article 9 of the Constitution of Japan

ARTICLE 9. RENUNCIATION OF WAR

Aspiring sincerely to an international peace based on justice and order, the Japanese people forever renounce war as a sovereign right of the nation and the threat or use of force as means of settling international disputes.

2. In order to accomplish the aim of the preceding paragraph, land, sea, and air forces, as well as other war potential, will never be maintained. The right of belligerency of the state will not be recognized.

successes. At the time of the Japanese surrender, 70 percent of farmers were either full tenants or at least had to rent some land to supplement what they owned.[7] Many SCAP officials believed that poverty had been a significant factor in breeding right-wing radicalism and militarism in the 1930s. The creation of broad land ownership was intended to reduce these tendencies.

SCAP also created an independent trade union movement, protected from harassment by government and business. Article 28 of the new Constitution and the Trade Union Law of 1945 guaranteed the right to strike and bargain collectively and provided for labor relations boards at the national and prefectural levels.

The consolidation of Soviet influence in Eastern Europe and North Korea and the Communist takeover in China convinced the U.S. Department of State that Japan should become a "bulwark against Communism" and a vital link in the new U.S. policy of "containment."[8] Toward this end, SCAP worked with the Japanese government to crack down on labor unrest. A planned general strike was disallowed, business organizations were given the upper hand in dealing with unions, and antitrust measures were relaxed. Now looking at Japan as an ally in the Pacific, the United States switched its objectives to economic stabilization and growth.

In September 1951, Japan signed a general peace treaty in San Francisco with all Allied powers except the Soviet Union,[9] formally ending the Occupation and ceding Japan's postwar autonomy. At the same time, the **U.S.–Japan Mutual Security Treaty** was signed. This treaty allowed the United States to station troops in Japan and to continue to occupy Okinawa as a military base, a vital link in the U.S. anticommunist "containment strategy" during the Cold War. At the close of the Occupation—aided by the "Korean War Boom"—Japan's economy had recovered enough to match its prewar high, the political system was functioning smoothly, and Japan was once again a sovereign nation about to embark on a remarkable period of its history.

Social Conditions

11.4 Describe social conditions in Japan, focusing on population, gender equity, wealth, and safety.

Japan is the tenth most populous country in the world, with 127.3 million people, but that population is shrinking. Its crude death rate (per 1,000) people is 9.15, while its birth rate is 8.39. Immigration is far too low to make up the difference, so the population is shrinking by 0.77 percent per year. Japan's millions live in an archipelago roughly 90 percent of the size of California, and arable land constitutes only 12 percent of that area. Therefore, two-thirds of the population is crowded into urban areas, mostly in the corridor connecting Tokyo with the Kansai area that includes Osaka, Kyoto, and Kobe. At 36.5 million residents, metropolitan Tokyo is by far the largest city in the world, almost twice as large as Mexico City, and more than twice as large as Shanghai, China.[10]

Japan has very limited natural resources, so its postwar economic development has hinged on the import of raw materials and the export of manufactured goods. Japan today is among the wealthiest countries in the world, and its citizens enjoy a high quality of life. Literacy is universal, and poverty is rare. Japanese justifiably took pride in the egalitarian distribution of income during the postwar period, with more than 90 percent of Japanese considering themselves to be middle class. Over the last twenty years, however, per capita income has dropped to eighteenth in the world (adjusted by purchasing power parity), and inequality has increased. Among wealthy countries, Japan is now more unequal than all but Britain and the United States, in large part owing to its limited welfare state.

Japan has one of the world's most gender friendly constitutions: Article 14 states that "All of the people are equal under the law and there shall be no discrimination in political, economic, or social relations because of race, creed, sex, social status or family origin." Although this is an explicit statement of gender equality that American women sought and failed to get in the 1972 Equal Rights Amendment (ERA),[11] many Japanese women feel that gender equality lags in practice. The typical full-time female worker earns 33 percent less than a man, compared to the Organization for Economic Co-operation and Development (OECD) average gap of 17.6 percent (and a U.S. gap of 19 percent).[12] Over half of Japanese (more men than women, and more older people than young) believe that wives should stay at home, according to a 2012 *Yomiuri* newspaper poll. Such sentiments reflect enormous social pressure on women who have career ambitions after marriage and childbearing. Not surprisingly, a growing number of women have responded to this pressure by putting off marriage. The average age at which Japanese women marry today is 28.8 years, up from 24.2 in 1970. The percentage of women who had not married by age 50 had also increased, from 3 percent in 1975 to over 10 percent in 2010.

Although Japan may be gender-unequal, it lacks most of the other societal divisions present in many other countries around the world. The population is 99 percent ethnically Japanese, with few important religious, linguistic, or regional cleavages. The country is home to only 2 million "foreign" residents (including many whose families have lived in Japan for several generations, but who have not become citizens), a remarkably small number for such a large and wealthy economy.

Japan's extraordinarily high level of social order—manifested in neighborhood watchfulness and coordination—contributes to lower crime rates than in other countries with comparable levels of urbanization and development. Many Japanese oppose increased immigration in part because they believe—incorrectly—that foreigners are responsible for much of the crime that does occur, and they fear that social order would be threatened by greater diversity. We have no doubt that a greater influx of immigrants would influence

Japanese society—as it would any society—but there is no evidence that it would necessarily be for the worse. Indeed, a more liberal legal path to immigration might help to reduce the abuses that can occur when illegal immigration is driven by undeniable economic incentives but forced underground by political prohibitions.[13]

Political Institutions

11.5 Explain the structure of Japan's national and local governments.

The single most important event in postwar Japanese politics came right at the beginning, with the promulgation of the postwar Constitution in 1947. It vested sovereignty in the people for the first time, made the prime minister and Cabinet responsible to a democratically elected legislature, extended suffrage to women, and established a panoply of individual freedoms and rights.

The Bicameral National Diet

Japan's system of government is parliamentary, bicameral, and nonfederal (see Figure 11.2). Article 41 of the Constitution specifies that the parliament, the National Diet, "shall be the highest organ of state power, and shall be the sole law-making organ of the State." Thus, there is no separately elected executive with whom the Diet must share policymaking authority. The Diet consists of two legislative chambers: the **House of Representatives** (*Shuugiin*—the Lower House) and the **House of Councillors** (*Sangiin*—the Upper House). Both chambers must pass a bill in identical form for it to become law, with three important exceptions: the House of Representatives alone chooses the prime minister, passes the budget, and ratifies treaties. In these areas, the Upper House may offer an opinion or counterproposal, but it cannot compel the Lower House to pay any attention (as stipulated in Articles 59 and 60 of the Constitution). For all other legislation, however, the Lower House must accommodate the preferences of the Upper House, unless it can muster a two-thirds majority to override an Upper House veto. Thus, the Japanese Upper House is among the world's strongest.

Between 1956 and 1989, the LDP always held a majority of seats in both Houses of the Diet, so strong

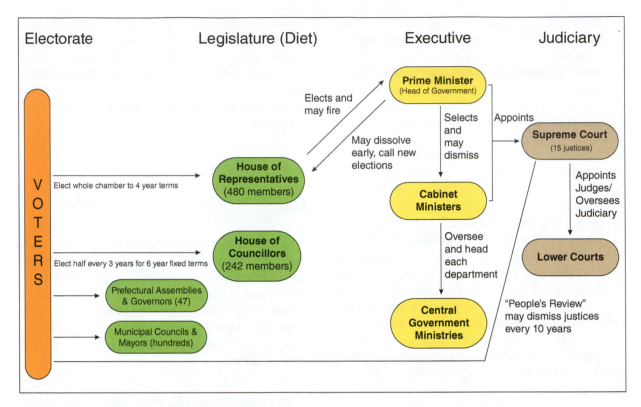

The Structure of Government in Japan
Japan has a bicameral, parliamentary, nonfederal system of government.

bicameralism "on paper" never really seemed to matter. Since 1989, no single party has controlled bicameral majorities, and multiparty coalitions have done so only about half the time. Since 2007, governing coalitions have not only fallen short of Upper House majorities but, most of the time, have had to contend with an Upper House controlled by a coherent opposition majority (sometimes neither the governing coalition nor the main opposition coalition can consistently control the Upper House). Japanese media call this state of affairs a "Twisted Diet" (*nejire kokkai*) and complained that too often, government proposals sail through the Lower House only to be vetoed by the Upper House, with policy gridlock the consequence. A recent study has shown that Japanese governments facing Twisted Diets do in fact see more of their bills amended or rejected, and so they propose fewer to begin with. Now that governments can no longer count on bicameral majorities, the true importance of bicameralism, always latent in the Constitution, has become all too apparent.[14]

As in all parliamentary systems, the first business of a new parliament (after an election) is to elect one of its members to serve as prime minister. The person elected is usually, but not always, the leader of the largest party in the Lower House. The Upper House may offer its own nominee, but Article 67 specifies that if the two chambers disagree, the choice of the Lower House prevails. The new prime minister then appoints a Cabinet, at least half of whose members must be legislators (Article 68). These appointees head up the Cabinet-level ministries and agencies that comprise the central government bureaucracy. From 1955 through 1993, and again from 1996 through 2009, the LDP leader won the prime ministership. There were three non-LDP prime ministers in the mid-1990s, and three DPJ prime ministers between 2009 and 2012 (see Figure 11.3).

Japanese prime ministers traditionally have played a "first among equals" role within the cabinet, managing competition between parties and factions, but only rarely stepping out front in a policymaking

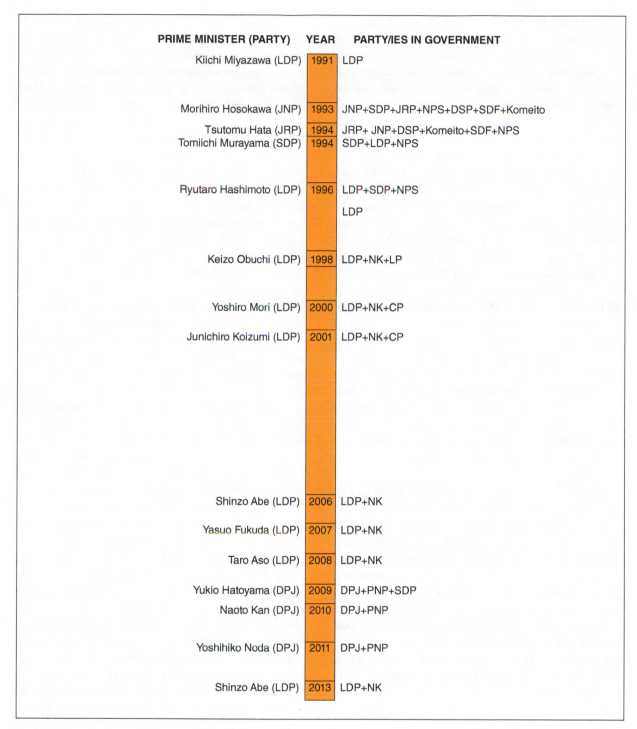

PRIME MINISTER (PARTY)	YEAR	PARTY/IES IN GOVERNMENT
Kiichi Miyazawa (LDP)	1991	LDP
Morihiro Hosokawa (JNP)	1993	JNP+SDP+JRP+NPS+DSP+SDF+Komeito
Tsutomu Hata (JRP)	1994	JRP+ JNP+DSP+Komeito+SDF+NPS
Tomiichi Murayama (SDP)	1994	SDP+LDP+NPS
Ryutaro Hashimoto (LDP)	1996	LDP+SDP+NPS
		LDP
Keizo Obuchi (LDP)	1998	LDP+NK+LP
Yoshiro Mori (LDP)	2000	LDP+NK+CP
Junichiro Koizumi (LDP)	2001	LDP+NK+CP
Shinzo Abe (LDP)	2006	LDP+NK
Yasuo Fukuda (LDP)	2007	LDP+NK
Taro Aso (LDP)	2008	LDP+NK
Yukio Hatoyama (DPJ)	2009	DPJ+PNP+SDP
Naoto Kan (DPJ)	2010	DPJ+PNP
Yoshihiko Noda (DPJ)	2011	DPJ+PNP
Shinzo Abe (LDP)	2013	LDP+NK

FIGURE 11.3

Japanese Governments since 1991

After nearly four decades of single-party (LDP) governments, shifting coalitions are now the norm in Japanese politics.

Party Abbreviations: Komeito or NK: Clean Government Party; CP: Conservative Party; DPJ: Democratic Party of Japan; DSP: Democratic Socialist Party; JNP: Japan New Party; JRP: Japan Renewal Party; LDP: Liberal Democratic Party; LP: Liberal Party; NPH: New Party Harbinger; PNP: People's New Party; SDF: Social Democratic Federation; SDP: Social Democratic Party.

role. During the LDP's long reign, the PM and the cabinet would essentially wait for policy initiatives to bubble up from "below." Specialist committees within the party would write draft bills in collaboration with relevant bureaucratic agencies, and pass them up the party and bureaucratic hierarchies until they reached the cabinet, which sits at the apex of both (the ministers being simultaneously senior LDP leaders and the heads of the various bureaucratic agencies). In the late 1990s, a new Cabinet Law increased the powers and resources of the prime minister's office to formulate policy proposals in a top-down manner. Jun'ichiro Koizumi (2001–2006) was the first to enjoy these expanded powers, and he used them forcefully. Of course, the bottom-up approach, while slow and deliberate, generally meant that any proposal that made it all the way to the cabinet was supported by all important stakeholders, and could then pass easily into law once formally proposed as a Cabinet bill. Nowadays, prime ministers have greater power to start the ball rolling and present policy initiatives to the Diet. However, the absence of prior consensus building also means that more proposals are likely to meet stiff opposition, even from within the governing parties, and be amended or rejected. Still, the new prime ministerial prerogatives make for a different style of leadership, and a more public, transparent policy deliberation process.[15]

Formally, Japanese prime ministers (as in all parliamentary systems) hold their positions by virtue of a vote by the (Lower House of the) Diet, but for all practical purposes, they serve at the pleasure of their own parties. The LDP's thirty-eight-year run as ruling party saw fifteen different prime ministers come and go. In the twenty years since the LDP first lost power in 1993, fourteen men (always men) have served as prime minister, capped by a remarkable seven in the most recent six years! Of these, only one was formally removed by the Diet (Kiichi Miyazawa in 1993, due to an LDP split)—all others have been obliged to resign by their own parties.

Local Government

Japan is divided administratively into forty-seven **prefectures**, each of which elects its own governor and legislature. The country's hundreds of municipalities elect their own mayors and city councils as well. Nevertheless, Japan is not a federal system. All local

government authority is delegated, and may be retracted or overruled, by the national government. Delegation to prefectural and municipal governments is extensive, and subnational governments account for about two-thirds of all government spending. However, it is interesting to note that they raise only about one-third of all tax revenues. Thus, on average, half of subnational government budgets are allocated to them at the discretion of the House of Representatives, which compiles the national budget annually.[16]

Recently, the Japanese government has undertaken to create larger local units via administrative mergers of neighboring municipalities. In an effort to adapt to an urbanizing electorate, the LDP appears to have decided that fewer, larger municipalities would be reflective of the Japanese population. Fewer municipalities would also mean fewer local politicians who act as lobbyists for policies favoring local areas.[17] In 1999, Japan had 3,232 cities, towns, and villages, with an average population of 36,387; by 2010, the number of municipalities had dropped to 1,730, and the average population had risen to 69,067. The number of towns with fewer than 10,000 people dropped during that period from 1,537 to only 457. The government plans to continue the mergers until the number of municipalities reaches 1,000. At the same time, some steps have been taken to delegate a little more fiscal and regulatory autonomy to local governments. As of 2013, decentralization is still very limited.

Still, local politics matters. Local frustration with national policy decisions often leads to the election of populist or progressive prefectural governors or mayors. These officials can be thorns in the side of the central government, loudly expressing their constituents' dissatisfaction. In some cases, this dissatisfaction signals to the party or coalition in control of the national government the political prudence of a change in policy. After all, the same voters who elect "protest candidates" to municipal or prefectural office might choose to vote similarly in the next round of national elections. So the national government is wise to keep abreast of trends in local politics. The most famous example of the importance of this mechanism came in 1970, when the LDP-dominated Diet undertook a drastic change in environmental policy by passing a slew of antipollution measures championed by progressive local governments that had used that issue to beat local LDP incumbents. Over the years, local governments have signaled their displeasure on all manner of national policies, from airport development to public works projects to waste disposal issues.[18] These protests do not *compel* the national government to change policy, but the national government is unwise to dismiss local complaints out of hand.

The Judiciary

The Japanese legal system ostensibly features the same degree of judicial independence that courts in the United States enjoy. Such independence is guaranteed in the Constitution (Articles 76–81). Nonetheless, independence does not appear to be the reality in Japan. Political domination and manipulation of the courts result from the government's ability to use appointment powers and bureaucratic mechanisms to avoid putting courts into positions where they might render decisions against the government's interests. The Cabinet directly appoints the fifteen members of the Supreme Court, and indirectly, through the administrative apparatus of the Supreme Court, helps to determine all lower court appointments as well. At the first General Election to be held after a judge ascends to the Supreme Court, voters have a chance to dismiss the new appointees. Judges are subject to further popular votes every ten years thereafter, but this is essentially irrelevant, since no judge ever serves that long—most are appointed within a few years of the mandatory retirement age of 70. In practice, no Supreme Court judge has ever been removed by the voters.

One important role for any judiciary is to check the impositions of the state on individual liberties and rights. A second is the adjudication of disputes among the other branches of government. Checks and balances—the sharing of political power by separately elected legislative and executive branches, or the conflicts between federal and state levels of government—lead to constitutional conflicts, and courts must step in as referees. This second role is much less important in a unitary parliamentary country, such as Japan, than in a federal, presidential system, such as the United States. Fewer checks and balances mean fewer conflicts for courts to mediate. When one institution—the Diet—holds all lawmaking power, there is much less need for a strong constitutional court.

Two examples show how different the judiciary's role is in Japan, as compared with the United States or Germany. First, the Supreme Court has consistently upheld the LDP's position that Article 9 of the Constitution allows the maintenance of armed forces for self-defense, as well as the government's definition of self-defense. Opponents contend—and judges in regional courts have ruled on several occasions—that Japan's **Self-Defense Forces (SDF)** are unconstitutional, as a Sapporo district court ruled in 1973. The Sapporo High Court reversed this decision the same year. The Supreme Court refused to hear an appeal in the case in 1982, effectively supporting the LDP's position. Not coincidentally, the district court judge who ruled against the government saw his career prospects take a turn for the worse.[19]

Second, district courts have frequently determined that the **malapportionment** in House of Representatives' elections had grown so large as to be unconstitutional. Since the LDP consistently wins a considerable proportion of its support from overrepresented rural areas, a forced reapportionment of Lower House seats would be detrimental to the party. The Supreme Court frequently threatens to intervene if malapportionment is not reduced, but it has not established a strict rule for reapportionment. Most important, it has never voided any election results. Before the December 2012 General Election, the Supreme Court again warned that absent a more thorough redistricting, the next election would be "in a state of unconstitutionality." The election went forward without any changes. Several district courts have declared specific election results to be invalid, but they have not demanded new elections. The LDP, now back in power, has again promised to consider redistricting carefully, but at present, no 2012 winner is in any danger of losing his or her seat.

Political Culture and Issue Cleavages

11.6 Discuss Japanese culture's emphasis on conformity and hierarchy.

Much of Japanese political behavior is attributed to Japan's culture. Some critics who characterize Japan as a second-rate democracy draw on the pre-Meiji-era history of feudalism and Confucianism to explain Japanese political behavior. They are quick to point out, moreover, that foreigners established Japan's postwar democratic institutions.

In discussions of Japanese political culture, the concepts of hierarchy, homogeneity, and conformity to group objectives take center stage.[20] Social hierarchy governs most Japanese relationships, and from an early age, Japanese have to "fit in" to be successful. Grade school and high school students are openly ranked in school so everyone knows how smart everyone else is (or is not) in any given subject, and what schools they can attend at the next stage depends on how well they do on exams. Transfers are extremely rare in high school or college. College entrance exams are notoriously hard, which is responsible for a flourishing after-school "cram school" industry. Which college one gets into determines to an extraordinary degree what kinds of jobs will be available upon graduation. That probably explains the otherwise puzzling phenomenon that so many University of Tokyo (Todai) students, presumably the smartest in the country, spend much of their four years in social and sports clubs having a good time. They have already passed the most important hurdle for getting a good job: signaling their competence merely by getting in to Todai. For many decades, most of Japan's government officials have been Todai graduates, followed by graduates of the University of Kyoto and a few other elite universities.

Once employed at a firm, it is very difficult to quit and take another job somewhere else. Japan's traditional "lifetime employment" system and seniority-based pay has meant that a worker has to get along with peers and satisfy superiors. Going out drinking with the boss after work is not just for fun, or maybe not even fun at all; it is a way of demonstrating loyalty and commitment. Not surprisingly, job satisfaction tends to be lower in Japan than in the United States and United Kingdom. Some share of these workers are stuck in ill-fitting jobs, holding on for dear life because it is hard to start over somewhere else. The Japanese term for these people, *madogiwazoku* (the guys by the windows) does not refer to the C-suite offices with windows. In Japan, being on the edges means being out of the loop.[21]

The emphasis on conformity cites the belief that individual goals should be sublimated to the objectives of the group.[22] Conformity to the good of the whole is sacrosanct; undermining the group by attention to one's own goals is not tolerated. This trait has been given much credit for Japan's postwar economic recovery and the vitality of Japanese firms, particularly manufacturers.[23]

Certainly, conformity and a respect for hierarchy have not stifled dissent or dissatisfaction with government in modern Japan. As might be expected in any country, public opinion surveys reveal widespread dissatisfaction, and not only due to the poor economic environment of the late 1990s. Figure 11.4 shows that citizens' trust in various institutions has fluctuated over time, but has been consistently low for politicians and even civil servants.

Clearly, Japanese culture affects the behavior of Japanese political actors, just as any culture constrains those operating within its sphere. By itself, reference to culture cannot explain many things that are interesting about Japanese politics. In the 1980s, the popular press invented a new term for the study of the uniqueness of Japanese culture: *Nihonjinron*, or "the theory of Japaneseness." The Japanese like to think of themselves as a people who value the group over the needs and wants of individuals. They value hard work, particularly when directed to the common cause, and are leery of people who seek to display extraordinary talent or native ability ("the nail that stands up is the one that is hammered down"). They view themselves as being hierarchically organized and status conscious. They believe they are unlike Westerners in seeking to avoid conflict whenever possible and in their preference for settling disputes through intermediaries rather than directly or adversarially through courts of law.

A quick review of Japan's colorful history, including literally hundreds of years of civil wars (1335–1600) and unending political upheavals, of vainglorious samurai warriors with shifting loyalties of convenience—even in the midst of a battle[24]—and of the often violent chafing of lower castes at the impositions of feudal hierarchy,[25] should be sufficient to dispel the most romantic versions of Japanese traditions and values. Nonetheless, a large part of political culture is the anthology of myths that societies build about themselves. While these might not always be historically accurate, they still inform political socialization and political behavior in modern times.

Women: At Home and in the Workplace

One manifestation of the emphasis on social hierarchy and order in Japan is the halting change in gender roles in the postwar period. Although women's opportunities are improving, prospects for women in

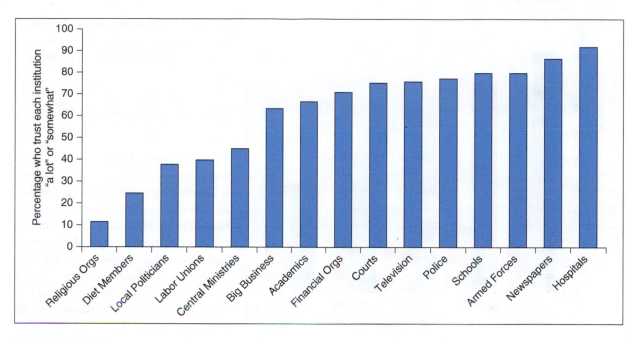

FIGURE 11.4

Feelings of Trust in Various Social Institutions

Japanese citizens have little faith in religious organizations or politicians, but greater trust in the police, the media, and the armed forces.

Source: Japan General Social Surveys, "Higashi-Nihon Daishinsai ga nihonjin no ishiki to koudou ni ataeta eikyo" ("The effect of the Great East Japan Earthquake on Japanese attitudes and behaviors") (2008), The JGSS Research Center, Osaka University of Commerce, http://jgss.daishodai .ac.jp/research/news/news_J12.pdf, last accessed May 5, 2013.

Japanese politics and in the workplace remain limited. The traditional role of "good wives and wise mothers" (*ryosai kenbo*) has been little altered by either evolving social values or legal prescription.[26]

Although the Constitution contains language guaranteeing equal rights for women, the judiciary has not actively enforced those rights. In June 2006, the Diet revised the **Equal Employment Opportunity Law** to bar discrimination in the workplace. The initial passage of the law did lead to an influx of women into the paid workforce. But prior to the 2006 revision, there was nothing to prevent discriminatory hiring practices based on such factors as physical appearance, and the "glass ceiling" was low and mostly impenetrable.

As a result, employment opportunities for women are inadequate in scope and duration. Women are commonly expected to find employment after completing school that serves only as a transition to marriage and childcare (see Figure 11.5). Few opportunities exist for secure employment, so, unsurprisingly, most women follow the established path. A large majority of women quit their jobs upon becoming

mothers;[27] less than a quarter of women find new jobs a year and a half after giving birth.[28]

Government has done little to assist the integration of women, either into the workplace or into politics. The Japanese welfare state is much less extensive than those in Europe. Consequently, it is very difficult to find appropriate childcare or elderly-care services that would help women to balance family and career. One unintended but understandable consequence of this is that Japanese women now marry later and bear fewer children than their counterparts in other advanced countries. This has exacerbated the rapid aging of the population, probably the most pressing problem that the Japanese government will face over the next few decades.

The representation of women in government is still the lowest among industrialized democracies—currently only 38 of 480 Lower House seats (7.9 percent) are held by women. This is down from 9 percent in 2005 and 11.3 percent in 2009. Women have fared somewhat better in the Upper House, with 43 of 236 seats (18.2 percent).

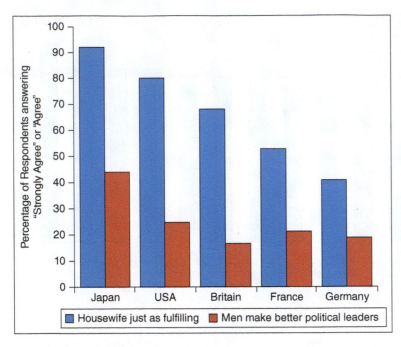

FIGURE 11.5

Persistence of Traditional Gender Roles in Japan

More Japanese than Westerners feel that "being a housewife is just as fulfilling as working for pay" and that "men make better political leaders than women do."

Source: *World Values Survey 2005–2008*, www.worldvaluessurvey.org, accessed 5 May, 2013.

Two trends may improve the status of women in Japanese society. The first is demographic. Despite the high longevity of Japanese citizens, birth rates have declined so far that the Japanese population has begun to shrink. The Japanese workforce is declining even more rapidly. The simplest way to stem the tide and forestall a decline in economic output would be to grant women a more equal role in the paid workforce. Doing this would require (and produce) changes in cultural attitudes and expectations, and would not be easy or unopposed.[29] The only alternative is to allow more immigration, likely a solution with even less support in Japan.

Second, the decline of lifetime employment in the Japanese economy means that there is less reason for Japanese employers to prefer hiring and promoting men over women. As long as firms expected to retain workers throughout their careers, the anticipated cost of investing in the human capital of women who might interrupt their careers for childrearing discouraged employers from giving women equal employment opportunities. As firms shorten their implicit contractual commitments to all workers, they will come to see men and women as more equal investment opportunities and risks.

Ethnic Homogeneity versus Immigration

Japanese political behavior and economic success have also been attributed, at least in part, to ethnic and cultural homogeneity. This homogeneity is credited with allowing Japan to focus in a unified manner on national goals—the foremost being economic growth. But Japan is not completely homogeneous, and the few minority groups that exist face significant discrimination. About 600,000 Koreans make up Japan's largest permanent ethnic minority. Brought to Japan as laborers during the war, Koreans are still treated poorly today. A few become naturalized Japanese citizens (citizenship does not come with birth in Japan) and manage to assimilate more or less fully. Those who do not may not vote or hold government jobs, and discrimination in the private sector workforce is widely recognized. Until 1992, those refusing the onerous demands of Japanese citizenship, including the taking of a Japanese name, were fingerprinted and required to carry alien registration identification.

The **Ainu** are another ethnic minority in Japan, an indigenous group who were pushed to the northern parts of the Japanese islands as the frontier was extended by the people now considered to be ethnic Japanese. Today, there are estimated to be fewer than 17,000 Ainu surviving, most living in the northernmost island, Hokkaido. Finally, **Burakumin**, though ethnically Japanese, are descendants of a feudal outcast class that performed jobs considered impure by the Buddhist elite. Although it is illegal, discrimination over employment and housing against members of this group continues. The Buraku Liberation League has fought resolutely for better treatment by the government and society. It estimates there are as many as 3 million Burakumin, mostly in western Japan, although official government estimates are much lower at less than 1 million.[30]

An understanding of why the Japanese feel confident that they are homogeneous may be found in the lack of strong issue cleavages. In many countries, there are a variety of societal cleavages over which politics is contested—language, religion, region, and race, to name the most prominent. But these sorts of issues rarely if ever arise in Japan.

This might not be the case for much longer, however. As Japan's economy becomes ever more integrated with those of its Asian neighbors and more distant trade partners, new immigrants—mostly from China, and South and Southeast Asia—are arriving in greater numbers, many illegally. These immigrants bring with them new demands on government services, as well as their own sets of cultural values and social practices, which are seen by many Japanese as incompatible with Japanese culture. Japan is in dire need of younger workers ready to take up the jobs that its own citizens are no longer willing to perform. Indeed, since Japanese society is aging even more quickly than most of its counterparts, and given that its native population is projected to shrink by nearly a sixth in the next few decades,[31] its need for immigration to keep the economy growing and to pay the pension and health care costs of so many retired citizens is that much more acute. But Japan is not accustomed to accepting immigrants, so the blending of Japanese society and culture with those of its new arrivals will likely create new and challenging problems for both its people and its government. Already, local governments and the national government have run into obstacles over health care benefits, access to housing and education, and even the relatively simple matter of producing administrative documents in languages other than Japanese, to say nothing of naturalization and citizenship rights such as voting. Clearly, the list of policy challenges at the start of this chapter will expand to include these sorts of issues in the very near future.

Political Socialization

 Identify the main sources of political socialization in Japan, along with recent changes in its political culture.

The Family

Political socialization begins at home, where values are transmitted from one generation to the next. Japanese families have traditionally lived in large, multigenerational households in which, as the older generation ages, the daughter-in-law cares for the oldest son's parents. As Japan has urbanized, younger generations have moved to big cities where they tend to live in nuclear families, whereas the elderly disproportionately still live in smaller towns, and villages are disproportionately populated by the elderly. In 2000, Japan passed new long-term care insurance in which the government has undertaken a larger role supporting the elderly in publicly subsidized nursing homes.[32] Not surprisingly, young women were strong proponents of this legislation.[33] Nevertheless, Japan's society has aged more quickly than public infrastructure can accommodate, and there is an acute shortage of nursing home places.

Values are changing in Japan one generation at a time, but even in the big cities, women typically work until their children are born, quit work until the youngest child is in kindergarten, and then return to the labor market in part-time jobs. This gives an "M" shape to Japanese women's labor market participation: the numbers go up through the early twenties, drop off upon marriage, and then pick up again after the children have gone to school. The second hump of the M, however, is usually part-time work that enables mothers to be home after children's school is over. Given the expectation that females will eschew or abandon their careers for childrearing, it is not surprising that families still socialize their daughters to prepare as much for the marriage market as for careers in the labor market.

Education

Japanese elementary and high school students consistently score toward the top of international league tables in math and science, far outpacing their American counterparts. Sixty percent of Japanese high school students also go to "cram schools" (*juku*) after school for supplemental lessons to get a leg up in the competition for getting into better schools.[34] What accounts for that level of exam anxiety is that top Japanese corporations hire workers disproportionately from the top colleges, and because many of those jobs in Japan are for life, which school one attends is of supreme importance.

The Japanese education system gets high marks for teaching basic skills, but the university system is in sorry shape. Entrance exams are extremely difficult, and students study obsessively in order to gain acceptance at the most prestigious schools. Once they have matriculated, however, it is the exception rather than the rule that a student learns much while a university student. During Japan's period of rapid growth, big businesses and even the vaunted central government ministries seemed to prefer things this way. The entrance exams would sort out the brightest and hardest working students, who would then be unspoiled by the liberal ideas of postsecondary education. After a four-year respite, they could move on to their new (and for the elite, permanent) employers, who would start by providing the necessary job-specific training that they would not have received in college anyway.

The economic stagnation since 1990 has meant fewer job openings than college graduates for the first time in generations, and the government, firms, and universities have begun to rethink the wisdom of this educational model. Increasingly, competition among universities is focusing more on the educational value for students, and less on the prestige of a high entrance exam score alone. In particular, the government has engaged in considerable soul searching as to whether the educational system produces students with enough creativity to succeed in the world's new high-tech economy. Another problem is that high levels of youth unemployment have discouraged many students from staying in school.[35]

From the standpoint of Japan's neighbors, a more pressing issue concerns the earlier stages of education, specifically the way that Japan's role in the Pacific War (1937–1945) is presented in the government-sanctioned textbooks. China's and Korea's governments continuously protest that the Japanese government and people remain insufficiently penitent for the depredations of the Japanese army in Asia, and Japanese textbooks remain a focal point in this debate. Insofar as it shapes Japanese attitudes toward foreign policy, this clearly is one area in which the effects of (arguably incomplete) education affect political socialization in important ways.

Mass Media

The Japanese media play a highly visible role in public life, comparable to that in the United States. Most Japanese get their news from traditional sources. A 2010 study showed that two-thirds of Japanese got their news mostly from TV, a number that was essentially unchanged from previous surveys in 2005 and 2000. After a late start, Internet penetration has increased rapidly in Japan, from 58 percent in 2002 to 78 percent in 2010.[36] The Internet has grown as a source of news from virtually nothing in 2000 to 8 percent in 2010, with a corresponding decline (from 24 percent in 2000 to 18 percent) in those who rely mainly on newspapers.[37]

Rare is the Japanese home without multiple televisions, and many homes have cable or satellite access to the same large number of channels as in the United States. Political commentary in Japan is a popular sport, particularly on weekends, when representatives of various parties face off on issues of the day, or face interviewers seeking a new angle. Despite the Japanese preference for television news, newspaper readership is easily the highest in the world, and the newspapers have national reach compared with the largely regional U.S. newspapers. The top three Japanese newspapers, *Yomiuri*, *Asahi*, and *Mainichi*, have a combined circulation of over 50 million readers, compared with less than 10 million for *The Wall Street Journal*, *The New York Times*, and *The Washington Post*. That is not to say that the Japanese are more likely to read *any* newspaper than Americans (and it takes no account of the Internet), but it does indicate that it is more likely they are reading the *same* paper regardless of where they live. The three main papers cover a range of political space, with the *Asahi* taking a center-left position against the *Mainichi*'s centrism and the *Yomiuri*'s more conservative stance.

Some observers have questioned the independence of the established press in Japan, because the "press club" system seems to entail a swap of inside information for docility. Government agencies and political parties each house a press club on their premises, in which reporters from various news media have desks, attend news briefings, and write their reports each day. Media reporters know that presenting unflattering information about the government or party officials whom they are covering could result in their being expelled from the press club, and they may self-censor as a result. However, media organizations almost always have separate reporters and news outlets that specialize in investigative reporting, leaving the regular press club reporters to gather routine information in peace. Once a scandal is made public by one of these investigative outlets, reporters at the press clubs are free to abandon their polite forbearance. The sensational and relentless coverage by the press of every political scandal since at least the Recruit case of the 1980s has been spearheaded by these weekly tabloids, and would be quite familiar to American veterans of post-Watergate investigative journalism, or British patrons of that country's aggressive fourth estate.

Transforming Political Culture

Japanese political culture today is in the process of dramatic transformation from relational to policy voting. Before the electoral reform of 1994, candidates' personal qualities and their ability to provide constituents with personal favors were of paramount value. More important now is the ability to present convincing arguments about policy issues, because these can reach a wider swath of the voting population more effectively.[38]

An example of how political culture can change quickly is the phenomenon of **Jun'ichiro Koizumi**, Japan's prime minister from 2001 through most of 2006. Koizumi was the most persistently popular prime minister in the postwar period, not despite but *because* of his public image as an iconoclast. He boldly asserted Japanese preferences in international dealings. He explicitly rejected the conformist politics of factional balancing and quiet deal making, frequently baiting his detractors into very public battles over policy. He railed against traditional political practices, and more often than not, he not only won these fights, but his popularity grew each time he poked a sacred cow. Koizumi embodied the "nail that stands up," and contrary to the theory of Japaneseness, he was applauded considerably more often than he was denigrated for his audacity.

Social expectations are sticky, and transformations of this kind occur slowly, but the recent visible shifts in electoral strategies and prime ministerial politics—and most recently in mass politics in the aftermath of the Tohoku earthquake, tsunami, and nuclear disaster—show how political culture can adapt to new circumstances.

Political Participation and Voting Behavior

11.8 Describe Japanese voter engagement in terms of turnout, party alignment, and age demographics.

By international standards, the political involvement of ordinary Japanese is low. Figure 11.6 shows that while nearly all eligible voters have voted at least once

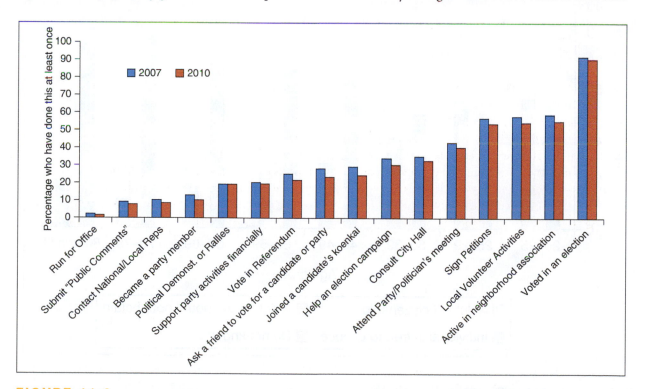

FIGURE 11.6

Forms of Political Participation in Japan

Japanese are much more likely to have participated in "citizen politics" activities than partisan activities.

Source: Waseda University/*Yomiuri Shimbun* Joint Survey, "Public Opinion Survey on Japanese Social Expectations and Elections," http://www.waseda-pse.jp/gse/jp/gcoe/wcasi/wcasi_waseda-casi2010_en.html, accessed 5 May, 2013.

in their lives, and nearly three out of five claim to have participated in a neighborhood or volunteer organization or signed a petition, other forms of participation are much less prevalent. In particular, party-related activities, especially membership, are rare. Most participation (voting aside) appears to be more at the local level.

Voter turnout at election time declined steadily on a nationwide basis from a peak of 77 percent in 1958 to a nadir of 59 percent in 1996 (Lower House). Party identification has declined as well, and self-proclaimed "independents" now make up the largest group in public opinion polls. Interestingly, in recent years, the two trends have gone in opposite directions—turnout has rebounded strongly, while dealignment continues. One manifestation of this odd confluence has been much larger vote swings between elections. The 2005 Lower House election coupled 67.5 percent turnout with a huge swing *for* the LDP, only to be followed in 2009 by 69.3 percent turnout and an even larger swing *away* from the LDP and to the DPJ. Then, in 2012, the

DPJ was hugely unpopular. Rather than swing back to the LDP, however, millions of 2009 voters abstained in 2012, and turnout plummeted to 59.3 percent. Still, the result of all of those 2009 DPJ voters staying home was another big win for the LDP, as we will discuss in the next section.[39]

The youngest Japanese citizens are the least interested in politics, and interest peaks in middle age. Figure 11.7 shows that twenty-somethings have the most cavalier attitude toward the simplest form of participation in politics, with fewer than one in five answering that voting is a duty of citizenship. Citizens in their sixties and seventies, those born before or during the war, feel the most duty-bound to vote. These snapshots cannot tell us is whether today's sixty-year-olds felt the same way forty years ago that today's twenty-year-olds do now. But there is good reason to believe that the relative complacency of today's youth is a reflection more of the times than of their youthfulness. The economic malaise of the last two decades and

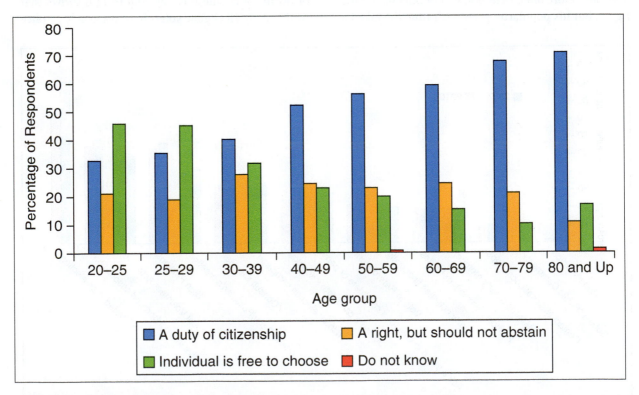

FIGURE 11.7
Is Voting a Duty or a Right?
Younger Japanese citizens feel the least duty-bound to vote.

Source: Akarui Senkyo Suishin Kyokai, "Dai 22 kai sangi-in tsujo-senkyo no jittai" ("The 22nd House of Councillors Election") (2011), http://www .akaruisenkyo.or.jp/wp/wp-content/uploads/2012/07/22sangaiyo.pdf, accessed 5 May, 2013.

Every so often, a country is buffeted by an event so cataclysmic that it shapes attitudes for an entire generation. World War II was such an event for the Japanese people, particularly those who were relatively young when the war ended. They turned their backs on their authoritarian leaders' xenophobia and wholeheartedly embraced democracy. Was the Triple Disaster of earthquake, tsunami, and nuclear meltdown that struck Japan on March 11, 2011, such an event for another generation of Japanese youth? Apparently not. On the one hand, young people volunteered in record numbers to help with relief efforts in the blighted regions or with resettling and provisioning refugees, and, according to a Cabinet Office survey in 2012, nearly 80 percent of respondents placed greater importance on community than before the earthquake. On the other hand, a poll conducted by a private think tank that same year found that 80 percent of Japanese youth said that they agreed or strongly agreed that they couldn't do anything to affect the government. This compared to 43 percent of American youth who felt that politically powerless. It will take more than the feel-good moments of postdisaster catharsis to cure Japanese youth of a political apathy born of years of economic malaise for which they blame their politicians. But if "3/11" did not wipe away political cynicism, it did link an unprecedented number of citizens through social networking and cyberspace. Web-based discussion and mobilization, as the domain of the younger generation, may yet redraw the lines of political activism in the future.

The percentage of college and graduate students involved in volunteer work increased from 0.7 percent in 2005 to 6 percent in 2011; the percentage of high school students who volunteered to help the disaster victims also jumped from 1.1 percent to 3 percent.

Sources: www.stat.go.jp/data/topics/topi670.htm; www8.cao.go.jp/survey/h23/h23-shakai/index.html; benesse.jp/berd/aboutus/katsudou/research_column/pt_02/23.html.

the uncertainty the young have about whether they missed out on the economic miracle creates angst and even resentment about the broken promises of their elders. It would be surprising if these feelings did not spill over into political attitudes (see Box 11.2).

Electoral Systems and Electoral Competition

11.9 Explain Japan's two-tiered electoral system.

Electoral rules structure the nature of competition among politicians for office. Such details as the size and location of electoral districts, the number of seats up for grabs, and the number and partisanship of competitors determine how politicians must behave in order to win. Also important, of course, are the particular configurations of voters' interests and the rules concerning what sorts of campaign activities are allowed and disallowed. Since voters care about what politicians do once they are elected, electoral rules also have had profound consequences for policy.

The two chambers of the National Diet use different electoral rules (see Table 11.1). Women were granted the right to vote in 1946, so now all citizens aged twenty or older may vote in both national and local elections. The electoral rules for the more powerful House of Representatives were changed in 1994, and six general elections have been held under the new rules. The electoral system for the House of Councillors also has been changed twice over the years, but not as dramatically.

The House of Representatives

Members of the House of Representatives are elected to four-year terms, but as in most parliamentary systems, terms usually end early, because the prime minister may dissolve the chamber and call elections at any time. In January 1994, several months after wresting power from the long-dominant LDP, a seven-party coalition government restructured the Lower House electoral rules.[40] Currently, the House of Representatives has 480 members, 300 of whom are elected by plurality rule on the basis of (supposedly) equal-sized

TABLE 11.1

Electoral Rules for the Two Houses of Japan's National Diet

Japanese Electoral Rules	House of Representatives (Lower House) 480 members, 4-yr terms		House of Councillors (Upper House) 242 members, 6-yr terms*	
	District Tier	List Tier	District Tier	List Tier
Election Rule	Plurality	Closed-list PR	SNTVᵠ	Open-List PR
Number of Seats	300	180	73/73*	48/48*
Number of Districts	300	11	47	1
Range of District Size	–	6 ~ 29	1 ~ 5	–
Avg District Size	1	16.4	1.55	48

ᵠSNTV: Single, nontransferable vote. Each voter casts one vote for a candidate, but in many districts, there would be more than one winner. For example, in a 3-seat district, the top three vote-getters all win seats.

*Half of the Upper House is elected every three years.

single-member districts (SMDs) and 180 of whom are elected from eleven regional districts by **proportional representation (PR)**. Each voter casts two votes: one for a candidate in the single-member district and one for a party in the PR region. A candidate may run in a district *and* appear on the corresponding party list in the larger region, so unsuccessful district candidates can be "saved" by the list. The Japanese press was quick to dub such politicians "zombies," inasmuch as they seemed to be revivified despite their district demise, and Japanese voters are not terribly fond of this aspect of the new rules.

This two-tiered electoral system seems to produce two different patterns of partisan competition. In each of the 300 SMDs, the race tends to come down to two viable candidates, and usually those two candidates are from the same two parties, nationwide. In the 2009 election, the DPJ and LDP combined to win 285 of the 300 SMDs (95 percent). That number declined a little in 2012, to 91 percent, mostly because a strong third party in the Kansai region won or finished second in several SMDs. On the whole, the SMD tier is bipartisan. By contrast, the PR component ensures that some small parties continue to survive, even if they have faded away in the single-member districts. Another important difference is that while PR ensures that vote swings are translated pretty proportionally into seat swings, we see much more volatility in the SMDs. Remember, plurality rule means that the candidate in a district with the most votes wins. It does

not matter if she has one vote more than the runner-up or 100,000 more. Therefore, if a party manages to convert many close losses into many close wins, then a small partisan swing across the country can be magnified into a huge seat swing. This "booster effect" is well known in Great Britain and Canada, and it happened in Japanese SMDs in 2005, 2009, and 2012. In the United States, by contrast, despite the use of SMDs and plurality rules, such exaggerated seat swings are unlikely because very few districts are close. Partisan gerrymanders are usually sufficient to insure most incumbents against negative partisan tides.

The House of Councillors

Japan's Upper House has 242 members, 146 elected from prefectural districts and 96 via a national PR system. Members serve fixed six-year terms, with half from each tier (so seventy-three and forty-eight, respectively) elected every three years. Each voter again has two votes: one cast in the prefectural district for an individual candidate and the second cast for a party in the national PR district. Unlike the Lower House system, Upper House candidates may not run in both tiers simultaneously.

Of the forty-seven prefectural districts, twenty-nine are SMDs, twelve elect two members, five elect three, and one (Tokyo) elects five members. So in at least forty-one of the forty-seven districts, voters will see only a single candidate from each party, and can base their choices on partisan affiliation. Similarly, in the now open-list PR tier, voters may choose individual candidates, but in a single national contest, they generally choose according to party loyalty. For example, in the 2010 election, 75 percent of voters eschewed the option of casting a preference vote for an individual within a party list, and instead simply voted for a party. Electoral rules have had a profound impact on the party system, political competition, and party organization. The next section describes the evolution of the Japanese party system over the postwar era, and especially since the 1994 Lower House electoral reform.

Campaigning and Electioneering

The rules that govern Japanese electoral campaigns are relatively restrictive by international standards. The campaign period for the Lower House is very short—only ten days. Candidates are restricted as to how much money they can raise and spend, and what expenses are allowed. TV and radio advertising are strictly curtailed. Candidates may distribute a limited number of posters and handbills, and door-to-door canvassing is forbidden. Each candidate is allowed one campaign car, and must pay for most staff independently. All of these restrictions are particularly troublesome for challengers. Incumbents presumably have natural advantages in terms of name recognition and message dissemination. Before a campaign begins, incumbents are able to communicate with constituents by virtue of their status as office holders. Challengers have to play catch-up, and that is difficult when most modes of campaigning are so tightly restricted.

When the electoral system was changed in 1994, most of these electioneering regulations remained. One important change, however, was the introduction of public financing. Every candidate now has a campaign budget. This is common in the democratic world, and is designed to reduce the temptation to engage in corruption in order to raise campaign funds. In April 2013, the Diet took another long-awaited step and relaxed the restriction on the use of campaign websites by candidates. Previously, politicians were allowed to have websites but could not change them during the campaign. It seems that the increasingly partisan (as opposed to personalistic) nature of Japanese elections over the last decade has rendered many of these restrictions anachronistic, so it is not surprising to see them beginning to be scrapped.[41]

The Japanese Party System

11.10 Discuss Japan's major parties and their election histories.

The history of the postwar Japanese party system can be divided into three distinct stages. The first lasted throughout the Occupation and a few years beyond; it was a rather volatile period in which no party or coalition stayed on top for very long. It was characterized by the appearance of new parties, the disappearance of existing ones, party splits, and party mergers. The second period began in 1955, with the formation (via mergers) of the LDP and its chief rival for the next four decades, the Japan Socialist Party (JSP). The tiny Japan Communist Party (JCP) rounded out the "1955 system." From 1955 until 1993, the LDP consistently won legislative majorities with about twice the strength of the JSP. This second period saw the formation of two important centrist parties, the **Democratic Socialist Party (DSP)**, which split off from the JSP in 1960, and the Buddhist-backed Clean Government Party (Komeito), which first won Lower House seats in 1967. The JCP and these new parties took some seats from both large parties over the ensuing decades, but never enough to deprive the LDP of its Diet majority.

The third period began with the split of the LDP in 1993, followed by the change in the electoral system that sent the rest of the party system into flux. This period has seen the halting emergence of a two-party system. Although some small parties survive because of the PR tier, the single-seat districts are dominated by the two large parties. In December 1994, the Komeito and DSP merged with several LDP splinter parties to form the **New Frontier Party (NFP)**. The NFP did well in the 1995 Upper House and 1996 Lower House elections, even outpolling the LDP in the PR tier of each election. But it collapsed in late 1997 over policy disagreements and leadership struggles. The DPJ emerged just before the 1996 election and took in much of the former NFP upon that party's demise a year later. The DJP established itself as a pillar of the new party system. See Figure 11.8 for a picture of support for the LDP over time, compared with that of its top rival in each election.

Throughout most of this third period, the LDP remained the largest party, but it governed in coalition first with the JSP and then with Komeito. In 2009, the

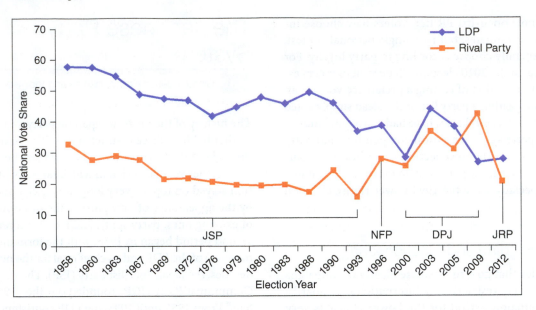

FIGURE 11.8

National Vote Share for LDP and Its Major Rival Party, 1958–2012

The LDP ceased to win the support of a majority of voters by the mid-1960s, but stayed in power because the opposition failed to coordinate until after 2000.

Note: Share of all votes going to a party's candidates, 1958–1993. Share of party vote in PR tier, 1996–2012.

DPJ won a large Lower House majority and took control of the government outright. It was the first time that any party had won more seats than the LDP. But the DPJ's first stint as a governing party lasted only three years. In December 2012, the LDP flipped the tables and resumed its place on top.

The Liberal Democratic Party

The LDP has always been a center-right, procapitalist, pro-Western party. But over the years, it expanded its support base to include not only big business interests but also organized interests in the inefficient, nontraded sectors of the economy, namely agriculture, construction, and retailing. It took in massive amounts of campaign finance from big firms and business federations in return for investment-friendly policies and a foreign policy that paved the way for the exports that drove economic growth. At the same time, the LDP paid for the votes of farmers and small business owners with profit-padding regulations and trade restrictions that protected these sectors from the full force of the free market. The champion of capitalism was also the source of protectionist regulation.

With tremendous economic growth came dramatic demographic change. Japan's rapid postwar urbanization and industrialization reduced the size of groups that were key parts of the LDP's support base, specifically agricultural workers and small retailers.[42] The rise of a new urban class and of the urban blights of industrialization (for example, pollution and overcrowding) fueled dissatisfaction with the LDP, and the party's legislative majorities decreased steadily. Nonetheless, the LDP maintained its majority of seats by virtue of electoral malapportionment, its more efficient nomination strategies, and its continued control over government purse strings. After its 2009 electoral humiliation, the LDP suffered defections. The party then bided its time, almost robotically opposing DPJ policies, especially after it took away the DPJ's Upper House majority in July 2010. As the DPJ stumbled and suffered its own internal splits, DPJ governments had to turn to the LDP for help passing legislation. In this way, the LDP recaptured its reputation with many voters as the natural party of government. It made that official with its 2012 Lower House win, and consolidated its hold on power by winning the 2013 Upper House elections as well.

The Democratic Party of Japan

The Democratic Party began its life as a spoiler. It was founded just weeks before the 1996 Lower House election—the first under the new electoral system—from a coalition of former LDP defectors, former JSP defectors, and some minor parties. The NFP had nearly bested the LDP in the 1995 Lower House election and hoped to come first in 1996. However, the unexpected presence of DPJ candidates in numerous constituencies split the anti-LDP vote and allowed the LDP to convert 39 percent of the district vote into 56 percent of the seats. When the NFP subsequently disbanded, the DPJ absorbed many of its refugees, and it increased its Lower House seat total from 52 in 1996 to 127 in 2000 and 177 in 2003. It suffered a setback in 2005, but after beating the LDP in the 2007 Upper House election, it won a staggering 308 (of 480) seats in the 2009 Lower House election, dwarfing the LDP's 119. Just three years later, however, it barely emerged from the 2012 election as the number two party.

The DPJ is still something of a cipher to most observers of Japanese politics. The party is more middle-of-the-road than the old JSP. It calls its philosophy "Democratic Centrism"—but that might be more because it is internally heterogeneous, given its origins in both the traditional left and the traditional right, rather than uniformly centrist. Its 2009 manifesto focused on providing more support for citizens whose economic fortunes had suffered as a result of the LDP's liberalization policies, as well as on reducing governmental power and decentralizing the Japanese state. Internal disagreements and public inconsistency over foreign policy, over tactics including how much to compete for traditional LDP support groups, and over whether to prioritize economic growth or expanded welfare provisions are reasons for the DPJ's declining popularity since it took office. This policy drift led to the resignation of the first DPJ prime minister, Yukio Hatoyama, after only nine months in office. The 2010 DPJ manifesto calls for "a strong economy, robust public finances, and a strong social security system," never mind the trade-offs between those goals that might be necessary. The next government, led by Naoto Kan, lasted for 15 months, but likely would have collapsed even earlier had it not been for the Tohoku earthquake, tsunami, and nuclear crisis that put politically wrangling temporarily on hold. Kan was succeeded by Yoshihiko Noda, who barely survived a major party split that almost cost the DPJ its Lower House majority. He adapted by reaching out to the LDP to help pass legislation through the Diet, including disaster relief bills and an unpopular consumption tax rise. The LDP's price for its cooperation was a new election, which spelled disaster for the DPJ.

The Clean Government Party (New Komeito)

The **Clean Government Party (Komeito)** formed as the political arm of a lay Buddhist organization called **Soka Gakkai**, which backed candidates in local elections starting in the 1950s. The Komeito appeared first in the Upper House in 1964, and then in the Lower House in 1965. Soka Gakkai, together with Komeito, grew in urban areas as postwar Japan underwent rapid urbanization. Local Soka Gakkai groups act as a neighborhood basis for party organization. They provide money, a volunteer labor force, and loyal, active voters. The Komeito's high degree of organization and concentration of supporters in urban areas allows it to maximize its seat shares. The Komeito's platform is based on "humanitarian socialism." It opposes revision of Article 9, but has come to support the U.S.–Japan alliance in recent years. However, the Komeito's connection to the Soka Gakkai prevented the party from extending its support base much beyond Soka Gakkai devotees. Unable to grow, the Komeito focused on coordinating with other centrist parties in many districts.

The Komeito got its first taste of government in 1993 as part of a seven-party coalition, and then, after a failed merger with the NFP, reemerged as "New Komeito." The party formed a partnership with the LDP that held power from 1998 to 2009. The two parties cooperate electorally, with the Komeito asking its (mostly urban) voters to support LDP district candidates in exchange for LDP support in the PR tier. The electoral cooperation survived that government's defeat in the 2009 election, and retook power in 2012. Over the course of their now fifteen-year alliance, New Komeito and the LDP have come to agree on most aspects of Japanese foreign policy and domestic economic policy. But one area of disagreement, evident in the two parties' 2012 electoral platforms, is over the question of constitutional reform. New LDP Prime Minister Shinzo Abe called for a revision to

Article 9 to explicitly endorse Japan's right to collective self-defense, whereas New Komeito staunchly opposed constitutional revision.

The "Third Force" Parties

The Japanese party system has developed along dual tracks since the 1994 electoral system reform: a two-party system in the single-member-district (SMD) tier and a multiparty system in the PR tier. This trend was interrupted in 2012, with the emergence of the so-called "Third Force" parties. These were a mixed bag. One, called the "Tomorrow Party of Japan" was formed just before the election, mostly by DPJ defectors who had left the party in protest of Noda's consumption tax hike. With sixty-one incumbents competing, the party performed terribly, winning only two SMDs and nine seats overall.

The second of the Third Force parties was "Your Party" (*Minna no To*), which formed from a splinter of the LDP after the 2009 election. Your Party won eight seats in 2009, and jumped to eighteen in 2012. It is a center-right party, close to the LDP on most economic matters and on foreign policy. It opposed the consumption tax hike in 2012, as well as the LDP's plan to restart nuclear reactors whose operations had been suspended after the March 11, 2011, disaster.

The most unexpected phenomenon of the 2012 election was the establishment and impressive showing of the Japan Restoration Party (*Nippon Ishin no Kai*). The JRP was founded only three months before the election by the young, charismatic mayor of Osaka, Toru Hashimoto. The day after the Diet was dissolved and the election scheduled, the JRP merged with another upstart party led by former Tokyo governor Shintaro Ishihara, long a nationalist gadfly and thorn in the LDP's side. Hashimoto is a populist who calls for a wide range of reforms, from eliminating the Upper House and halving the size of the Lower House to mandating the singing of the national anthem in schools, and from direct election of the prime minister to a quixotic campaign against public employees with tattoos. The JRP did extremely well in the districts around Osaka, winning twelve of its fourteen SMDs there, and displacing the DPJ as the number two party in several others. It ran candidates all over the country, and actually won more PR votes than the DPJ. While there is reason to believe that its Osaka area strength is sustainable, it is just as reasonable to suspect that its strong PR showing far from its home turf was a matter of being new and exciting at just the time that the DPJ was imploding, and that it will have a difficult time holding those seats in the next election.

The Old Left

From 1955 through 1993, the LDP's main rival was the **Japan Socialist Party (JSP)** (later renamed the Social Democratic Party). It was untainted by militarism and appealed to the strong pacifist sentiment in postwar Japan by defending Article 9 of the Constitution and vilifying conservatives who wished to remove the "Peace Clause." It called for a foreign policy characterized by "unarmed neutrality" and opposed Japan's Self-Defense Forces as unconstitutional. The JSP maintained complete opposition to the acquisition of nuclear weapons and even opposed the production of nuclear power. The Socialists found most of their support in the burgeoning postwar labor movement. Unions provided votes, campaign finance, and candidates for the party. In return, the party championed workers' rights and redistributive economic policies.

As manufacturing labor declined as Japan's economy grew, the JSP's support declined as well. The JSP peaked in the 1989 Upper House election, in which it bested the LDP for the biggest share of the seats up for grabs in that poll. But that victory turned out to be a last gasp. In the 1993 election, the JSP (by now the SDP) lost half of its Lower House seats (dropping from 136 to 70) as voters jumped at the chance to vote for LDP splinter parties. The party anchored the first anti-LDP coalition, but fell out with its partners over electoral reform and tax policy. It then somewhat surprisingly found itself in coalition with the LDP between 1994 and 1996. Party leader Tomiichi Murayama became the first socialist prime minister since 1947. Because the LDP condition for the job was that he renounce the JSP's long-standing foreign policy platform, the Social Democrats lost most of their remaining support in the 1996 election, plummeting from seventy seats down to only fifteen (and then to seven in 2009). They did join the first DPJ government in 2009 as a minor partner, but are all but defunct after winning only two seats in the 2012 election.

The far left end of the ideological spectrum is held by the **Japan Communist Party (JCP)**. The JCP formed in 1922, but was driven underground in the prewar era when many of its leaders were imprisoned for radicalism. SCAP legalized the party in 1945, but it garnered only small vote shares early on. The JCP's platform is antiemperor, anticapitalism, and antimilitary. For several years, it maintained close ties with the Communist Parties of the Soviet Union and China, but those relationships ended even before the Cold War did. Although the JCP has resolved to work within the democratic political system and has lately begun to look more like a traditional Eurocommunist party, it still ritualistically opposes nearly all government policies. Since the 1994 electoral reform introduced single-seat electoral districts, the JCP has never won a district seat, but it wins a handful of PR-tier seats each time (eight in 2012).

Patterns of Partisan Support

Table 11.2 shows the breakdown of party support for the four largest parties in Japan, as measured by a survey administered just after the 2007 Upper House

election. Other than the LDP's greater reliance on farmers and older voters, the differences between LDP and DPJ voters are small. Both parties do better with men than with women (the opposite is true for Komeito and the JCP), and both do better in small towns than in big cities. The LDP and Komeito rely more heavily on the least educated voters (with the JCP finding its supporters among the most educated). The table is also interesting for what it lacks—namely, any breakdown of party support by ethnic or regional cleavages. These are important determinants of the vote in many countries, but they are absent in Japan.

Until 2005, Japanese politics looked very different in urban areas than in rural areas. Elections in urban districts were very competitive, somewhat volatile, and, by the mid-1960s, involved several viable parties. By contrast, rural districts were generally uncompetitive. The LDP consistently won two-thirds of the rural seats, and the Socialists usually won the remainder.

TABLE 11.2
"Which party do you feel closest to?"

	DPJ	LDP	Komeito	JCP	Total
Occupation					
Worker	28.5	32.6	26.1	23.5	29.0
Self-employed	3.4	5.8	4.3	5.9	5.4
White-collar/government	67.0	54.1	69.6	70.6	61.9
Farmer	1.1	7.6	0.0	0.0	3.6
Education					
Incomplete Secondary	14.7	24.0	29.8	18.3	18.4
Completed Secondary	66.0	58.6	59.6	19.7	61.8
At least some college	19.4	17.4	10.6	62.0	19.3
Size of Town					
Less than 50,000	11.1	13.9	8.5	9.9	11.9
50,000–100,000	48.4	46.7	29.8	19.7	46.3
100,000–500,000	21.6	22.0	36.2	32.4	21.5
More than 500,000	19.0	17.4	25.5	38.0	20.2
Age					
Under 40	17.2	11.4	19.1	18.3	20.2
40–59	41.4	31.8	38.3	39.4	34.4
60 and over	41.4	56.8	42.6	42.3	45.4
Gender					
Male	51.9	55.2	38.3	45.1	47.3
Female	48.1	44.8	61.7	54.9	52.7

Source: Comparative Study of Electoral Systems Survey, Japan, Postelection July-August 2007, conducted by Central Research Service: Chuo Chosa Co (*n* = 2373). Some percentages may not sum to 100 because of rounding.

Because the LDP enjoyed this cushion of safe rural seats, and because malapportionment gave extra influence to rural voters, the LDP did not have to be particularly popular in Japan's burgeoning cities in order to secure its parliamentary majorities.[43]

This has begun to change in the last decade. The LDP's 2005 Lower House landslide was the result of an unprecedented huge positive swing in urban districts, but it also revealed the first cracks in the LDP's rural dominance—the party actually lost a few of its rural seats to opposition parties. In the 2007 Upper House and 2009 Lower House elections, the LDP fared even worse in rural districts, and even won fewer of the 100 most rural seats in 2009 than did the victorious DPJ. The LDP restored its rural supremacy in the 2010 Upper House and 2012 Lower House elections, but it seems clear that rural Japanese voters are now up for grabs in a way that urban voters have long been. No longer can the LDP take the rural vote for granted.

This is an important recent change in Japanese elections, and it is not difficult to explain. Former Prime Minister Jun'ichiro Koizumi (2001–2006) entered office determined to reconfigure the LDP's support base. He reasoned that as long as the LDP was beholden to backward, uncompetitive economic sectors and interest groups such as farmers, the party was doomed to a slow decline in a globalized world because it would be politically unable to push the sorts of economic reforms needed to restart a moribund economy. He therefore advocated policies, especially economic deregulation, that pleased urban consumers but angered rural producers. This made the LDP more competitive in the cities but broke the party's stranglehold on the countryside.[44] Elections since then have been more volatile in both rural and urban districts, and both the LDP and the DPJ struggle to find the optimal policy platform for a heterogeneous public.

The General Elections of 2005, 2009, and 2012

Japan's last three general elections have produced consecutive landslides, but in alternating directions (see Figure 11.9). In 2005, several of LDP Prime Minister Koizumi's reform bills were defeated due to defections by some LDP members. Koizumi responded to the defeat by calling a snap election, expelling the defectors, endorsing attractive young candidates to oppose them, and convincing the electorate that the election should be a referendum on "reform." It worked brilliantly. The LDP won 296 of 480 seats, and combined with the Komeito for an unprecedented supermajority of Lower House seats.

By 2009, the tables had turned. Now, the DPJ could criticize the post-Koizumi LDP for letting reform stall. They also empathized with the victims of the liberalization that had occurred and promised to provide a welfare safety net. Lose-lose had turned to win-win. The 2009 Lower House election produced a gain of 195 seats for the DPJ and a loss of 177 seats for the LDP (the LDP's coalition partner, Komeito, also lost 10 seats). The transition was big news. For the first time ever, a party other than the LDP controlled a single-party majority in the Lower House. The LDP lost every seat it had picked up in 2005 and saw many incumbents in rural and suburban districts toppled as well.

The DPJ's first stint in government, however, was unsuccessful. Its first prime minister, Yukio Hatoyama,

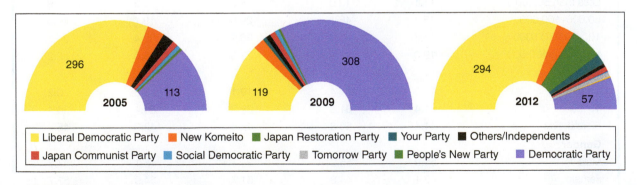

FIGURE 11.9

The Distribution of Lower House Seats in 2005, 2009, and 2012
Two LDP landslides separated by a DPJ landslide.

rashly promised to reduce the presence of U.S. troops in Okinawa, and when he was forced to renege by U.S. refusal to renegotiate, he resigned in disgrace. His successor, Naoto Kan, was unable to cope with internal discord fomented by Hatoyama and his ally, **Ichiro Ozawa**. The March 11 disaster gave Kan an opportunity to show strong leadership in a time of crisis, but instead, he faltered, due in no small part to Ozawa's machinations and the unwillingness of the LDP to cooperate until Kan promised to resign. Finally, Yoshihiko Noda faced the unenviable task of dealing with disaster recovery and the nuclear crisis, even while trying to balance the fiscal books. When he staked his political life on an increase in the national consumption tax, Ozawa led a rebellion that split the DPJ, and again the LDP provided the votes needed in the Upper House in exchange for a new election.

In the 2012 election, the DPJ was trounced. Having won 308 seats in 2009, it entered the 2012 election with 230 members, and won only 27 of 300 SMDs and 57 of 480 seats overall. It finished third in the PR tier, behind the JRP as well as the LDP. The LDP, by contrast, improved from 119 seats in 2009 to 294 in 2012. The LDP and its coalition partner New Komeito now hold a 325-seat supermajority in the Lower House. Interestingly, despite the LDP's 175-seat gain, its vote in the PR tier increased by only 1.6 percentage points! This means that it really was not any more popular in 2012 than it its disastrous election of 2009. How, then, did it gain 175 seats? The answer is twofold. First, voter turnout declined by 10 million in 2012, and for every ten extra abstentions, the DPJ lost nine votes. In other words, millions of unattached voters who swung to the LDP in 2005 and then to the DPJ in 2009 stayed home in 2012. Second, while millions of those who did vote in 2012 swung away from the DPJ, the emergence of the Third Force parties split the vote severely, and scores of LDP candidates in the SMDs snuck to victory with relatively modest vote totals. Whereas a candidate must win more than 50 percent of the SMD vote if there are only two candidates competing, she might be able to top a multicandidate field with less than 30 percent.

Thus, the LDP did not win a 2012 landslide because it was popular but almost by default, as the DPJ split the anti-LDP vote with a host of upstart parties.[45] The 2013 Upper House election followed a similar script. Amid record-low voter turnout, the LDP and its partner, Komeito, won a bare majority of the PR seats, but a dominant majority of the district seats (including 29 of the 31 single-seat districts) and they now control both Diet chambers comfortably.

Interest Groups

11.11 Identify the three major interest groups in Japan and describe their relationships with political parties.

In all democracies, well-organized groups that coordinate their actions with relative ease do well promoting their interests over those of less well organized groups.

In Japan, the most important of these interest groups are farmers, big business, and, sometimes, small retailers and small manufacturers. In contrast with other industrialized countries, however, labor unions are relatively weak and ineffective.[46] Least successful of all have been the diffuse interests, especially consumers, who have borne the burden of government support for the former groups. Big business, small manufacturers and retailers, and farmers all prospered under LDP rule, and for most of that time, their interests were not in direct conflict. This began to change in the mid-1980s as the Japanese economy globalized, and the fraying of the LDP's coalition of organized interests is a big part of the reason that the party finally fell from power.

Big Business

Japanese firms—thanks in part to the long-term dominance of a conservative, proproducer, progrowth party and the close relationship between business and government—have prospered in the postwar period. Firms such as Sony, Toyota, Mitsubishi, and Matsushita are dominant players in economic markets and household names throughout the world. The government has helped many of these firms through protection against foreign competition, the formation and maintenance of research cartels, and massive subsidies and tax incentives. Large firms are often linked to one another in industrial groupings known as *keiretsu*. The United States claims that the cross-shareholding and vertical integration among keiretsu member firms constitute informal trade barriers that should be prohibited under Japanese antitrust laws.

In the past, big business had little choice but to accept the LDP's attention to backward, inefficient sectors (such as farmers and small retailers), because the LDP was the only party clearly committed to business interests. Since the split in the LDP in 1993, however, the field has included new parties with similarly probusiness platforms, thus allowing business to hedge its bets for the first time since the 1950s. Big business prefers the center-right party (the LDP) to the center-left party (the DPJ). However, the majoritarian cast of Japan's new electoral politics creates a strong center of gravity in the middle that is not threatening to business. Big firms are happy to support any party that maintains a stable environment for investment and trade.

Small and Medium-Sized Businesses

From the outside, it may appear that large firms dominate the Japanese economy, but that is not completely correct. As of 2009, small and medium-sized enterprises employed 70 percent of Japan's labor force, and they have contributed more than half of the value added to the economy in every year since 1960.[47] In both manufacturing and retail sales, these well-organized firms have pursued their political objectives with great success. They gained considerable support from LDP policies over the postwar era. In return, these sectors were a good source of campaign funds (similar to big business) and, perhaps more important, offered a steady supply of votes for the LDP.

The benefits that have accrued to small and medium-sized businesses have varied across sectors. Small manufacturers enjoy a variety of tax breaks and direct subsidies. Furthermore, financial policies provide access to credit for small businesses even at the expense of big business. In the retail sector, small firms have been protected from competition with larger firms that would have threatened their existence. For example, the infamous Large Scale Retail Store Law protected "mom-and-pop" shops by limiting the entry of larger, more efficient retailers. Reduced competition allowed small retailers to remain profitable even as they became increasingly uncompetitive. Similar policies propped up small, inefficient banks.[48]

More recently, the government has rolled back many of these protective measures. The Large Scale Retail Store Law was weakened substantially, and the Ministry of Finance (MOF) allowed some insolvent banks to go under. This comes after decades of issuing subsidies and engineering profit-padding regulatory protections to ensure that this would never happen. While some of this liberalization preceded the electoral reform, it has accelerated since 1994, especially in the financial sector.[49] The "big bang" reforms in the financial system over the past fifteen years have reduced entry (and exit) barriers in that sector, forcing greater competition, lower prices, and better services for consumers.

Agriculture

Agricultural interests are very well organized politically, and they constitute a significant and geographically concentrated vote bloc for the LDP. Most farmers belong to local agricultural cooperatives whose national peak organization (Nogyo Kyodo Kumiai, or **Nokyo**) bargains with the government on their behalf.[50] Nokyo performs many quasi-governmental tasks, implementing programs that in other countries are controlled directly by government agencies. Local Nokyo offices function as monopoly providers of farming inputs (such as fertilizer, pesticides, and machinery), as monopsony purchasers of farm products (which they then resell), and as insurers and banks for farming communities. All of these roles are sanctioned by the government. This degree of autonomy speaks volumes for the effectiveness of agriculture's political lobbying efforts.

Farmers have been a significant source of votes for the LDP. Although the number of rural voters has declined precipitously in response to postwar urbanization, the malapportionment of the previous electoral system's districts benefited farmers. In return for their electoral support, farmers received price supports, minimal taxation, and tariff and quota protection from competing imported products Nonetheless, the LDP has learned that it cannot take the farm vote for granted. Many farmers perceive themselves as losers in Japan's new political economy, abandoning the LDP's increasing market orientation in favor of the DPJ's commitment to social security and economic redress. Thus, despite the LDP's landslide win in 2005, it actually lost seats in rural areas. The DPJ trounced the LDP in rural districts in the 2007 Upper House election and made further rural inroads in the 2009 Lower House poll.[51] The LDP won them back in 2012. However, it is now clear that the rural vote, long the core of LDP support, is up for grabs and cannot be taken for granted by any party.

Organized Labor

Because Japanese labor unions are organized on the basis of the workplace rather than by occupation, craft, or economic sector, they are called **enterprise unions**. Nonmanagerial employees of a firm are members of that firm's union. Ties between the workers of rival firms within a sector (say, for example, between Toyota workers and Nissan workers) are much weaker than in any other industrial democracy. Not surprisingly, this setup has reduced the tension between management and labor *within* firms (at the expense, many would argue, of worker welfare).[52] Cooperative management–labor relations have not led to similarly

cordial relations with the government. The major union federations traditionally have had adversarial relationships with the succession of LDP governments, but with little effect. Further, unionization levels have dropped over the past couple of decades in Japan, as has been true in Western Europe and North America. Never as numerous as in the highly unionized workforces of countries such as Germany and Britain, today, fewer than 20 percent of Japanese workers are union members.[53]

In the prereform party system, public-sector unions were tied closely to the Japan Socialist Party, while private-sector unions backed the Democratic Socialist Party. In 1989, seventeen public-sector unions and twenty-one private-sector unions together formed **Rengo**, the Japan Trade Union Confederation. As of 2010, Rengo claims 6.8 million members, 68 percent of all unionized workers.[54] It is now a major support base for the DPJ, although the centrist pressures of the new electoral rules keep the DPJ from championing its interests the way the JSP did in the past.

The Policymaking Process

11.12 Summarize the policymaking process in Japan's Diet.

Japan is a parliamentary democracy, with both houses of the National Diet directly elected, and with the prime minister and the Cabinet chosen by, and accountable to, the Lower House (see again Figure 11.2). In practice, the Diet, like all parliaments, tends to leave the proposal of legislation to the Cabinet, reserving the right to pass, reject, or amend those proposals as it sees fit. The Cabinet, in turn, delegates the task of drafting legislation—everything from regulation to the budget—to policy experts in the bureaucracy. The Cabinet ministers oversee this process in the broadest sense, but most of the expertise resides, and most of the action takes place, in the various bureaus and departments of the government ministries and agencies.

The Basics: How a Bill Becomes a Law

Members of either house of the Diet may submit legislation, and they do so quite often. But these "member bills" are almost always exercises in grandstanding for the sponsors' constituencies, where the proposal itself is the point. Such proposals rarely have any hope of passing into law. Therefore, the typical path for new legislation proceeds as follows. A ministry drafts legislation for some policy change in its jurisdiction and submits the bill to the Cabinet. The Cabinet may send the bill back, reject it, or amend it in any way it wishes. If and when the Cabinet is satisfied, it submits the bill to the Diet. The Diet may then do whatever it wants with the bill. Most bills are assigned to a particular committee, but committee powers are weak—bypassing or discharging a bill from a committee requires only a small number of signatures. Normal legislation must be passed in identical form by both houses, unless the Lower House can muster a two-thirds majority to override Upper House objections (this has happened only once). If the bill is the annual budget, or a treaty to be ratified, then only the Lower House need pass it; the Upper House may delay that passage for up to thirty days, but it cannot stop it. For all other draft legislation, if the two chambers disagree, they may work out their differences in a joint "conference" committee, but this is not required.

Any bill passed by the Diet becomes the law of the land. There is no separately elected president who may veto Diet actions, and Diet laws supersede any local laws that might conflict. The Supreme Court may declare a law unconstitutional, but as we explained earlier, this is exceedingly rare.

The final step in the process is policy implementation. The Diet can pass legislation, but it delegates the job of implementing and enforcing the new rules to the bureaucracy. Indeed, laws are often so vague that the bureaucrats must do considerably more than robotically carry out the Diet's orders. This is true in most countries. Legislators are not experts in every policy area, and they cannot foresee every circumstance under which the new law might apply. So bureaucrats are given resources and discretion with which to make the day-to-day decisions and rulings necessary to administer the laws passed by the Diet.

The circle is completed at the next election. Voters might have some idea of what goes on in the Diet, in the Cabinet, and in the halls of the government agencies, but their best view of policy is at the implementation stage. Do they approve of the policies they see

being administered? Do they believe themselves to be better off or worse off? Voters make these judgments and then reward or punish incumbent legislators and parties by voting either to retain or replace them at the next election.

Naturally, the actual policy process is more complex, given the rules that govern the Diet and bureaucracy. Even the internal decision-making process of the ruling party or coalition has an impact on policy outcomes. The following sections will demonstrate in greater detail some of this complexity.

The Diet: Rubber Stamp or Sovereign?

During the period of LDP dominance, comparative studies of the world's legislatures typically characterized the Japanese Diet as a weak, ineffectual institution. Observers pointed out that the Diet rarely rejected Cabinet-submitted bills, or even amended them. Debate was usually brief and pro forma. Bureaucrats were delegated a great deal more discretion than in the United States. While the bureaucrats seemed to have the skills to produce good policies for the country, the idea of bureaucratic government strikes many as somehow undemocratic. On the other hand, Article 41 of the Constitution declares that the Diet is all-powerful—the Cabinet is its appointee and the bureaucracy merely a staff of experts. How can we explain this paradox?

The key to the answer is that the continued control of the Diet and the Cabinet by the same political party allowed the *formal* legislative process to become routine and tranquil. This explains both the relative inactivity of the Diet and the extensive reliance on the bureaucracy.

The LDP internalized the policymaking process so that policy battles were fought "in-house," without the nuisance of opposition party tactics or public scrutiny. Once the party had come to a decision, it simply had its leaders (who controlled the Cabinet) submit those bills to the Diet, where the party could use its majority to approve its own proposals. In that sense, Japan was typical of parliamentary systems with single-party majority control. When a single party can work its will, there is no need to air internal discussions or squabbles publicly. The public portion of majoritarian politics *should* be boring and uneventful. A parliament that does not actively

A wave of people demand "Genpatsu Zero"
Demonstrations at Diet, prime minister's residence, and ministries two years after Fukushima disaster.

initiate or amend draft legislation, and rarely rejects government proposals, is not necessarily weak or ineffectual.

Thus, for most of the postwar era, the most interesting steps of the policy process were hidden within the policy apparatus of the LDP. Of course, if the LDP were to lose power, or have to share it with another political party, the policy process would become considerably less routine, and activity in the Diet would increase. The Diet would not become any more powerful, but the fact that its power would have to be shared by more than one party would cause it to become more active and interesting.

In fact, in 1989, the LDP did lose control of the Upper House. Its need to build coalitions with other parties in that chamber led to very public horse trading, most famously over the post–Gulf War decision to allow Japanese troops to participate in UN-sponsored peacekeeping operations. In 1993, the LDP finally

lost its Lower House majority as well. After a year in opposition, the LDP returned to govern, but always in coalition with other parties. In 2007, the DPJ won control of the Upper House, and used that perch to frustrate nearly all government attempts to pass laws. Lawmaking slowed significantly, not because the power of the Diet had changed but because partisan control of the Diet was divided. When the DPJ won its huge Lower House majority in 2009, it formed a coalition with two small parties in order to control the Upper House as well. These small partners have leveraged their Upper House importance to cause the DPJ a good deal of grief over policymaking. Indeed, the tiny Social Democratic Party pushed Prime Minister Hatoyama into a corner over the issue of relocating a U.S. military base in Okinawa, resulting in Hatoyama's resignation and the SDP's departure from the government. The DPJ failed to gain a single-party majority in the 2010 Upper House election, and so it found itself in the same predicament as the post-1989 LDP. In December 2012, even as the LDP enjoyed its landslide win in the Lower House, the next prime minister, Shinzo Abe, admitted that the LDP had to figure out a way to win the July 2013 Upper House election, lest its new government founder on the shoals of the Twisted Diet.

Policy Performance

11.13 Discuss Japan's recent domestic and foreign policies.

The LDP's long period of dominance was built on policy successes that produced social, economic, and geopolitical stability. Economic growth raised real incomes at a rapid pace, increasing the affluence of all levels of Japanese society. Beyond private financial gain, democracy instilled a variety of civil rights—including freedom of speech and of the press—that constrain the government's ability to interfere in the practice of individual liberties. The Japanese government has provided for high levels of law and order, boasting some of the lowest rates of crime in the industrialized world. Though sometimes criticized for emphasizing conformity over creativity, Japanese education policy produces one of the best-trained labor forces in the world.

It is not surprising, then, that the economic malaise that has gripped Japan since the early 1990s, and the variety of social problems that it has produced, coincides with a much more tumultuous political scene. A series of governments have failed to restart economic growth, and inequality has worsened as some bear a greater cost of the slump than others. The nearly simultaneous end of the Cold War has brought greater uncertainty to Northeast Asia. Japan's minimalist welfare state—never really a concern when the economy was expanding, employment was stable, and both childcare and elderly care could be provided within families—has proved inadequate for an aging and shrinking workforce in a stagnant economy.

Security and Foreign Policy

Since the end of World War II, Japan's security and foreign policy have centered on its close relationship with the United States. Bargaining from a position of weakness, Japan has been on the receiving end of most U.S. foreign policy decisions. With the end of the Cold War, Japanese voters have become more ambivalent about the alliance.

Over time, Japan has paid for an increasing share of the U.S. defense commitment to East Asia. Japan now pays fully 50 percent of all costs for the 40,000 U.S. troops on Japanese soil.[55] This is particularly controversial in the small southern prefecture of Okinawa, which hosts roughly two-thirds of those troops and must lease nearly 20 percent of its land for U.S. military installations. Some of this land is very close to population centers. Okinawans also bear the brunt of noise, pollution, and sometimes dangerous military accidents and violent crimes committed by American soldiers. In response to their protests, the United States and Japan agreed in 1996 to remove some troops to Guam, and to close the Futenma Marine Corps base and relocate its activities to another part of the prefecture. In 2009–2010, with the relocation plan still unrealized, newly elected DPJ Prime Minister Yukio Hatoyama promised to renegotiate this agreement to further reduce the U.S. military footprint, and to give greater voice to Okinawan citizens about the use of their land. When the United States refused to amend the deal, a humiliated Hatoyama was obliged to resign his office.

Just as the Cold War ended around 1989, Japan found itself the butt of international scorn for its refusal to send troops in support of the UN-sponsored Gulf War. It was accused of free-riding on the blood of others, although it did contribute 13 billion dollars to the effort, more than any country other than Saudi Arabia. In response, but not without enormous controversy, the Japanese government passed legislation to extend its military presence by agreeing to allow SDF personnel to participate in UN peacekeeping operations. After the terrorist attacks on the United States of September 11, 2001, Japanese Prime Minister Koizumi took another unprecedented step. Pledging solidarity with the United States, and support for the "global war on terror," Koizumi sent Japanese ships to the Indian Ocean to help the North Atlantic Treaty Organization (NATO) war effort in Afghanistan. He also deployed Japanese "boots on the ground" to assist the effort to stabilize Iraq.

Japan's own neighborhood in Northeast Asia has become more volatile over the past decade. Relations

Trouble in the East China Sea
The Japanese Coast Guard stops a vessel after Chinese activists land on one of the Senkaku Islands (Diaoyu to the Chinese).

with North Korea seemed to thaw somewhat when Koizumi became the first Japanese leader to visit Pyongyang in 2002. He extracted from North Korea an admission that its agents had kidnapped thirteen Japanese nationals (Japan says seventeen) between 1977 and 1983, presumably to train North Korean spies. In 2003, North Korea withdrew from the Nuclear Non-Proliferation Treaty and declared its intention to develop a nuclear capacity. Beginning in 2006, North Korea launched a series of (unarmed) missiles toward or past Japan. By 2009, North Korea had developed its first nuclear weapon. Since its leadership transition in 2012, North Korean saber rattling has escalated further, including threats to attack U.S. bases in Japan.

North Korea is not Japan's only concern in the region, however. Since 2010, its relationships with both China and South Korea have soured, as long-standing disputes over control of two different small island groups have flared up. While the quarrel over

Takeshima (Dokdo to Korea, which controls it) in the Sea of Japan has remained merely verbal and symbolic, China's aggressive moves concerning the Japanese-administered Senkaku Islands (Diaoyu to China) in the South China Sea are more worrisome. Although no shots have been fired as of this writing, the possibility of a mistake and subsequent escalation arises each time Chinese and Japanese naval vessels interact in the waters around the islands. The Japanese Coast Guard arrested a Chinese trawler captain who rammed one of its ships in 2010, only to meekly repatriate him after the Chinese government protested. China then retaliated by suspending the export of rare earths—vital metals for all manner of Japanese industrial products, for which China is the dominant worldwide supplier. Demonstrations by Chinese citizens against perceived Japanese slights have been allowed to get out of hand now and again, and include an attack on the Japanese embassy in Beijing in 2012.

One of the explanations for the DPJ's massive defeat in the 2012 general election was a perception that DPJ governments were dangerously incompetent in foreign policy. The LDP campaigned as the steady hand, and promised to shore up relations with the United States in the wake of the Futenma problem while also standing up to Chinese bullying. While Prime Minister Abe claimed to have mended fences on a visit to Washington, D.C., in February 2013, the tensions over the Senkakus do not seem to have diminished since, nor has North Korea seemed at all impressed by, the return of the LDP to government.

Welfare Policy: Health Care and Pensions

Health care in Japan is universally covered through a government-administered, single-payer program. That program requires all individuals to pay a health insurance premium based on income level. Standards of service are below what is commonly found in the U.S. private system, but the coverage ensures widespread access to basic health services. Despite many failings, the benefits of Japan's health care system are clear. Infant mortality, at 2.2 per 1,000 live births, is the lowest among industrialized nations, and life expectancy is the highest, now 87.4 years for women and 80.6 for men. The Japanese accomplish this even though total spending on health care constitutes a smaller percentage of gross national product in Japan (8.0 percent) than in the United States (15.7 percent), France (11.0 percent), Germany (10.4 percent), or Britain (8.4 percent).[56]

On pension policies, the Japanese government has been much less active. Public and private pensions are meager. In the early 1970s, as welfare became a prominent issue, the LDP set out on a program of building an advanced welfare state. However, the oil crisis of 1973 put the brakes on creating new welfare programs, extinguishing this political strategy. Nonetheless, overall welfare spending has grown steadily as Japanese society has aged. Figure 11.10 shows the shares of general account spending devoted to various categories in fiscal year 2013. Slowed economic growth expanded the government budget deficit (by reducing tax revenues) more than it actually impinged on continued welfare programs.

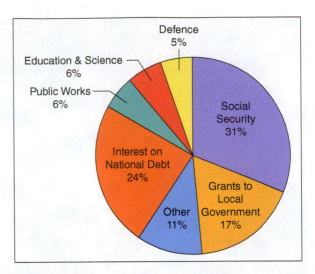

FIGURE 11.10

Japan's General Account Expenditures, Fiscal Year 2013

Central government transfers to individuals and to local governments together comprise half of the national budget, with interest payments on the national debt eating up half of the remainder.

An aging society in Japan is exacerbating the costs of welfare benefits and increasing the political desirability of expanding such programs. In 1950, only 4.9 percent of Japanese were over age sixty-five. In 2010, the figure is 22.5 percent, and population projections suggest that the figure will reach 32.3 percent in 2050. The Japanese government recently increased copayments on medical benefits in order to increase revenue and decrease overuse of the service. Such reductions of existing benefits may become more common as the government strives to keep up with the demographic changes that increase the number of people demanding assistance.

Energy Policy

As an archipelago nation heavily dependent on imported fossil fuels, securing reliable access to affordable energy is one of Japan's highest national security priorities. Particularly after the 1973 Organization of Petroleum Exporting Countries (OPEC) oil embargo that temporarily crippled the Japanese economy, a central prong of Japanese energy policy has been to nurture diplomatic ties to multiple oil-exporting countries around the world. Over 80 percent of Japan's

What Did I Do?
A small child is checked for radiation exposure in the aftermath of the "Triple Disaster" of March 11, 2011.

total energy consumption in 2010 was from imported fossil fuels: 40 percent oil, 22 percent coal, and 20 percent natural gas.

Just before the March 11 meltdown at the Fukushima nuclear power plant, Japan had over fifty operational nuclear power plants that supplied 11 percent of its total energy consumption and 25 percent of its electricity generation. The Japanese business community had pushed for increased development of nuclear power as a way to contain energy costs while reducing dependence on imports and controlling greenhouse emissions. The LDP's 2009 party manifesto reflected this enthusiasm, suggesting that Japan increase reliance on nuclear power to 40 percent of Japan's total energy consumption by 2030. Not that this was expected to be easy. Siting and building nuclear reactors in Japan has been a continuous challenge, in part because the horrors of Hiroshima and Nagasaki forged a large and enduring antinuclear coalition. The

Japanese government, in concert with regional power companies, situated power plants in economically depressed areas willing to accept the risks of nuclear power in an earthquake-prone country in exchange for jobs and sizable financial transfers.

The earthquake-tsunami disaster of March 11, 2011, that broke apart the reactors at the Fukushima nuclear plant also battered the fragile acceptance of nuclear power in Japan. The DPJ government shut down all of Japan's reactors for inspection, and promised to abolish nuclear power by the 2030s. The LDP in opposition was more equivocal, but also promised to "establish the social and economic structure that does not need to depend on nuclear energy," promising instead to focus on other forms of renewable energy such as wind, solar, and geothermal.[57] But that was brave talk. Now that the LDP is back in power, it does not have a viable plan for how to harness the forces of nature that endanger this string of islands sitting atop shifting tectonic plates, and has begun plans to reopen nuclear power plants. Japan has yet to solve its energy dilemma of balancing the risks of nuclear power against the geopolitical vulnerability and environmental degradation of fossil fuel dependency.[58]

Economic Liberalization

Ever since the bursting of its **asset price bubbles** (stocks and land) in 1990, the Japanese economy has been in the doldrums. Its world-beating banking sector was brought to its knees by mountains of nonperforming loans. Finance dried up, and with it, investment and the motor for future growth. Ever more desperate governmental efforts to stimulate the economy with public works spending only exacerbated the national debt (and covered the landscape in concrete and "bridges to nowhere"). Economists called for deregulation—the end to subsidies and the freeing up of markets so that inefficient firms could be allowed to fail and entrepreneurs could be allowed to innovate. The "big bang" financial reforms did just that—they removed artificial barriers between market sectors such as retail and investment banking, insurance, and securities. For the first time in decades, banks were allowed to fail if poorly run. The most well known advocate of reform was Jun'ichiro Koizumi, but in fact the deregulatory changes preceded his time in office. Most economists would agree that as lofty as Koizumi's rhetoric was, and as spectacular his political battles for change, much remained to be done when he left office in 2006. Koizumi's successors from both the LDP and the DPJ were largely hamstrung by the Twisted Diet—unable to pass bold reforms even when they were inclined to try. Among the biggest policy accomplishments since Koizumi's time is the consumption tax rise pushed through by Noda in 2012. However, that cost him his premiership in the end.

It is easy to understand Japan's failure to deregulate the economy for so long, given the LDP's electoral reliance on the protected economic sectors. Whenever a Japanese government has opened any of its markets, it has faced the wrath of stakeholders (e.g., farmers, small retailers, or postmasters) for doing so. Good policy does not always make for good politics. The DPJ beat the LDP in the 2007 and 2009 elections

by empathizing with the "victims" of deregulation and by calling for a more generous welfare state. Once in power, however, they ran up against the problem of paying for their programs and disappointed many voters and even suffered a major party split by pushing through a rise in the national consumption tax to reduce the government deficits. At 219 percent, Japan's debt-to-gross domestic product (GDP) ratio is among the highest in the world.

In the 2012 election campaign, when the doomed DPJ government announced its intention to join the TPP negotiations over a regional free trade agreement should it be reelected. The LDP campaigned against the TPP, essentially promising farmers that they would remain protected. Just two months later, new LDP Prime Minister Shinzo Abe announced his intention to join the TPP. He said that he would demand that some sectors (agriculture) be removed from the table, but the whole thrust of the TPP is for a comprehensive deal. The TPP negotiations will take months or years to complete. Interestingly, rural voters continued to support the party in the July 2013 Upper House election, but if the TPP deal ends up rolling back agricultural support programs, they may cast about for a better option, perhaps even by forcing a split in the LDP itself. (see Box 11.3).

Concluding Thoughts about Japanese Politics

After nearly four decades of one-party rule, Japanese politics appear to have become volatile. A landslide election for one party is followed by a landslide for the opposing party. The offset timing of elections for the Lower House and Upper House mean that a party or coalition can win control of one chamber, only to lose control of the other a few months later. Japan's "Twisted Diets" then make it very difficult for any prime minister and cabinet to actually govern. One consequence has been rapid turnover at the top: Japan saw a parade of seven prime ministers in the six years after Jun'ichiro Koizumi stepped down in late 2006. A greater consequence has been the Japanese government's inability to come to grips with the country's long-stagnant economy, now in its third decade without any significant growth. Nor has the government

BOX 11.3   The Education of Shinzo Abe and "Abenomics"

Shinzo Abe's first stint as prime minister seemed set up for success. He took over in September 2006 when Jun'ichiro Koizumi stepped down near the height of his popularity. Koizumi bequeathed the huge Lower House majority that he had engineered in the 2005 election by expelling the "dinosaurs" from the party and championing structural reform. But Abe squandered his inheritance almost immediately. He invited the dinosaurs to return to the party. Reform stalled while Abe tilted at nationalist windmills, calling for revision of Article 9 and for more patriotism in school textbooks, and seeming to backtrack on past governmental apologies for Japan's wartime depredations. Within one year, plunging popularity and poor health forced Abe from office, but not before he oversaw a 2007 Upper House electoral debacle. By any standard, he had been an abject failure as prime minister.

Fast-forward five years. The DPJ's shortcomings in their first chance at power made an LDP resurrection possible, but nobody expected an Abe comeback. He was the surprise winner of a party election, and ran as a man with a plan. He targeted deflation as the most pernicious economic problem and demanded that the (supposedly independent) central bank set a 2% inflation target immediately. He promised massive economic stimulus to create jobs and jumpstart consumption, and a renewed effort at structural reforms (i.e., deregulation) to stimulate entrepreneurship. Yes, Abe was still inclined to nod toward nationalist tropes, but the main focus of his speeches and of the popular reception of this "second act" has been all about "Abenomics." Abe delivered as large a Lower House majority in 2012 as Koizumi had in 2005, and he has since gone from strength to strength. His newly appointed central bank governors have initiated a massive monetary expansion. He announced ¥10.3 trillion in new spending, exacerbating Japan's world's worst debt-to-GDP ratio but causing the stock market to jump by 55% within six months. Exports (helped by a much weakened yen) are again driving growth. He defied the farm lobby by committing Japan to participate in the TPP free-trade talks. The LDP then took back the Upper House in July 2013, which underscores the extent to which Abe has been able to learn from his earlier failures and justify the party's decision to give him a second chance. Only time will tell if he can continue the momentum and is truly committed to difficult structural reforms, but, for now, Shinzo Abe finally appears to be following the script that Koizumi wrote for him nearly seven years ago.

taken sufficient measures to combat the unavoidable costs of a rapidly aging society. Japan desperately needs either to increase its labor force through both greater gender equality and more immigration or to somehow raise labor productivity dramatically, and it probably needs progress on all fronts. But these are difficult political decisions to make, and no Japanese government for many years has had the unity, control, or courage to address these issues seriously.

Now Shinzo Abe, in his second go-round as prime minister, has promised bold and refreshingly specific measures to tame deflation, jump-start the economy, and resume the structural reforms begun by Koizumi a decade ago but suspended beginning in Abe's first term. This platform was again successful in the 2013 Upper House election, and if the Abe government stays this course, then not only will the economy change, but party politics could change along with it.

If the LDP can wean itself off the organized support of protected economic sectors, especially farmers, it can position itself as a party of property and opportunity, a center-right, "liberal" force familiar in most advanced democracies but never really extant in Japanese politics. The DPJ, if it recovers from its 2012 and 2013 electoral humiliations, (or some new entrant if the DPJ cannot recover) could then advertise itself as a party of the center left, offering protection from unfettered market, and a welfare safety net for urban and rural voters alike. But in the short run, the increased sway of business cycles over parties' electoral fortunes introduces a countervailing force: A bad economy creates a safe haven for politicians who trumpet the interests of the downtrodden. The LDP defeated the DPJ by repackaging public works as a countercyclical policy benefiting everyone, while the DPJ government championed unpopular taxes to get enormous government deficits under control. The DPJ broke apart on the shoals of a bad economy; the LDP faces the same vulnerability in years ahead.

The good news for students of Japanese politics is that Japan is no longer a mysterious country with hidden rules and enigmatic patterns. The same tools for understanding politics anywhere work in the Japanese context: How do electoral rules incentivize politicians? How do voters choose between candidates and parties? We may have a hard time assigning political credit or blame; but this is because policy making is complicated, not because we are not Japanese.

REVIEW QUESTIONS

- Why, after nearly four decades of one-party rule, has Japanese electoral politics become so volatile of late, with a landslide by one party followed by a landslide by another party, and so on?
- Why has no Japanese prime minister since 2006 been able to stay in office for much more than a year?
- What was the political basis for Japan's postwar economic protectionism, and how has that changed?

- How is Japan's changing economic climate affecting the political culture?
- How can Japan "solve" its aging-society problem? What must it do to address the symptoms, and what can it do to address the causes? Finally, what will politics allow? What do you expect it will do?

KEY TERMS

Ainu
Allied Occupation of Japan
Article 9
asset price bubbles
Burakumin
Clean Government Party (Komeito)
Democratic Party of Japan (DPJ)
Democratic Socialist Party (DSP)
Diet
enterprise unions

Equal Employment Opportunity Law
Hatoyama, Yukio
House of Councillors (*Sangiin* —Upper House)
House of Representatives (*Shuugiin*— Lower House)
Japan Communist Party (JCP)
Japan Socialist Party (JSP)
Kan, Naoto
keiretsu

Koizumi, Jun'ichiro
Liberal Democratic Party (LDP)
MacArthur, General Douglas
malapportionment
Meiji Restoration
New Frontier Party (NFP)
Noda, Yoshihiko
Nokyo
Ozawa, Ichiro
Perry, Commodore Matthew C.
prefectures

proportional representation (PR)
Rengo
Self-Defense Forces
single-member districts (SMDs)
Soka Gakkai
Supreme Commander for the Allied Powers (SCAP)
Taisho Democracy
Tokugawa clan
U.S.–Japan Mutual Security Treaty

SUGGESTED READINGS

Campbell, John C. *How Policies Change: The Japanese Government and the Aging Society.* Princeton, NJ: Princeton University Press, 1992.

Doi, Takeo. *The Anatomy of Dependence*, trans. John Bester. Tokyo: Kodansha International, 1971.

Nakane, Chie. *Japanese Society.* Berkeley: University of California Press, 1970.

Ozawa, Ichiro. *Blueprint for a New Japan.* Tokyo: Kodansha International, 1994.

Pekkanen, Robert J., and Ellis S. Krauss. *The Rise and Fall of Japan's LDP: Political Party Organizations as Historical Institutions.* Ithaca, NY: Cornell University Press, 2011.

Pempel, T. J. *Regime Shift: Comparative Dynamics of the Japanese Political Economy.* Ithaca, NY: Cornell University Press, 1998.

Ramseyer, J. Mark, and Frances Rosenbluth. *Japan's Political Marketplace*. Cambridge, MA: Harvard University Press, 1993.

Rosenbluth, Frances McCall, and Michael F. Thies. *Japan Transformed: Political Change and Economic Restructuring*. Princeton, NJ: Princeton University Press, 2010.

Scheiner, Ethan. *Democracy without Competition in Japan: Opposition Failure in a One-Party Dominant State*. New York: Cambridge University Press, 2006.

Schoppa, Leonard. *Bargaining with Japan: What American Pressure Can and Cannot Do*. New York: Columbia University Press, 1997.

Schoppa, Leonard. *Race for the Exits: The Unraveling of Japan's System of Social Protection*. Ithaca, NY: Cornell University Press, 2008.

Souyri, Pierre. *The World Turned Upside Down: Medieval Japanese Society*. New York: Columbia University Press, 2003.

INTERNET RESOURCES

Harvard's Reischauer Institute maintains links to Japanese government, institutions, media, and myriad other sites: www.fas.harvard.edu/~rijs/resources/politics.html.

The Reischauer Institute has also spearheaded an "evolving, collaborative" digital archive of Japan's 2011 disasters: http://www.jdarchive.org/en/home.

Stanford University offers links to sites covering interest groups, the Supreme Court, and regional governments: http://jguide.stanford.edu/site/government_politics_16.html.

The UCLA library offers links to sites covering social sciences, humanities, and government sources of data: www.library.ucla.edu/libraries/eastasian/japanese-studies-online-resources.

Periodicals: *Asahi Shimbun*, www.asahi.com/english/english.html; *Japan Times*, www.japantimes.co.jp/; *Yomiuri Shimbun*, www.yomiuri.co.jp/index.htm; Japan Echo, www.japanecho.co.jp.

We are very grateful to Yui Margaret Komuro, Kota Matsui, and Evan Walker-Wells for their superb and enthusiastic assistance with both the research for and the editing of this chapter. We also acknowledge Professor Aiji Tanaka at Waseda University for the use of survey data from the Waseda University–Yomiuri Shinbun Joint Survey "Public Opinion Survey on Japanese Social Expectations and Elections."

ENDNOTES

1. Japan, Ministry of Health and Welfare, *Annual Report on Health and Welfare*, 1999, www.mhlw.go.jp/english/wp/wp-hw/vol1/p2c1s1.html.

2. Europe's population is aging rapidly as well. Among advanced industrial countries, the United States is an outlier for its continued (or more accurately, "renewed") youthfulness because of much greater immigration and higher fertility rates; see "Half a Billion Americans?" *The Economist*, August 24, 2002, 20–22.

3. Akira Iriye, *Pacific Estrangement* (Cambridge, MA: Harvard University Press, 1972).

4. For more thorough treatments of modern Japanese history, see Peter Duus, The Rise of Modern Japan (Boston: Houghton Mifflin, 1976); and Mikiso Hane, Modern Japan: A Historical Survey (Boulder, CO: Westview, 1986).

5. Kazuo Kawai, *Japan's American Interlude* (Chicago: University of Chicago Press, 1960), 22–24; Hans H. Baerwald, *The Purge of Japanese Leaders Under the Occupation* (Berkeley: University of California Press, 1959), 97; and T. A. Bisson, *Zaibatsu Dissolution in Japan* (Berkeley: University of California Press, 1954), 97–104.

6. Supreme Commander for the Allied Powers, Government Section, *Political Reorientation of Japan*, vol. 1 (Washington, DC: U.S. Government Printing Office, 1949), 98–109.

7. Hane, *Modern Japan*, 347–48.

8. John Lewis Gaddis, *Strategies of Containment: A Critical Appraisal of Postwar American National Security Policy* (Oxford: Oxford University Press, 1982), 75.

9. A dispute over the four small "Kuril" islands north of Hokkaido—which the Soviet Union annexed at the end of the war, and which post-Soviet Russia still controls—still holds up the formal normalization of relations between the two countries.

10. Data are 2010 estimates. *CIA World Factbook*, available at https://www.cia.gov/library/publications/the-world-factbook/geos/ja.html.

11. Article 14 of the Japanese Constitution provides that In 1972 the U.S. Congress passed a similarly worded Equal Rights Amendment to the U.S. Constitution, banning discrimination based on sex. The Amendment failed because only thirty-five states ratified the ERA, three short of the thirty-eight needed for constitutional amendment.

12. OECD tracks these data yearly for member states. The World Economic Forum's Gender Equality Project ranks Japan 101st out of 135 states for which gender-specific data on economic, political, and social equality are available. See http://222weforum.org/issues/global-gender-gap.

13. Lieba Faier, *Intimate Encounters: Filipina Women and the Remaking of Rural Japan* (Berkeley: University of California Press, 2009).

14. Michael F. Thies and Yuki Yanai, "Governance with a Twist: How Bicameralism Affects Japanese Lawmaking," in *Japan Decides 2012: The Japanese General Election*, ed. Robert Pekkanen, Steven R. Reed, and Ethan Scheiner (London: Palgrave, 2013), 225–44.

15. Margarita Estévez-Abe, Takako Hikotani, and Toshio Nagahisa, "Japan's New Executive Leadership: How Electoral Rules Make Japanese Security Policy," in *Japan and the World: Japan's Contemporary Geopolitical Challenges,* ed. Masaru Kohno and Frances Rosenbluth, CEAS Occasional Publications, vol. 2 (New Haven, CT: Yale University Council on East Asian Studies,, 2009), 251–88.

16. Home Affairs Ministry, *Chiho zaisei no shikumi to sono unei jitai* (Tokyo: Home Affairs Ministry, 1987); see also Hiromitsu Ishi, *The Japanese Tax System* (Oxford: Oxford University Press, 1989), 11.

17. Yusaku Horiuchi and Jun Saito, "Removing Boundaries to Lose Connections" (paper presented at the annual meeting of the Midwest Political Science Association, Chicago, Illinois, April 2–5, 2009).

18. "The Day of the Governors," *The Economist*, June 16, 2001, 41–42.

19. John Owen Haley, *Authority Without Power: Law and the Japanese Paradox* (New York: Oxford University Press, 1991), 189; and J. Mark Ramseyer and Frances Rosenbluth, *Japan's Political Marketplace* (Cambridge, MA: Harvard University Press, 1993), 162.

20. Thomas C. Smith, *The Agrarian Origins of Modern Japan* (Stanford, CA: Stanford University Press, 1959).

21. Michael Hechter and Satoshi Kanazawa, "Group Solidarity and Social Order in Japan," *Journal of Theoretical Politics* 5, no. 4 (1993): 455–93; and Toshio Yamagishi, "Trust as a Form of Social Intelligence," in *Trust in Society*, ed. Karen Cook (New York: Russell Sage, 2001), 121–47.

22. Bradley M. Richardson, *The Political Culture of Japan* (Berkeley: University of California Press, 1974), 3.

23. Ronald Dore, *British Factory–Japanese Factory: The Origins of National Diversity in Industrial Relations* (Berkeley: University of California Press, 1973).

24. Thomas Conlan, *State of War: The Violent Order of Fourteenth-Century Japan* (Ann Arbor, MI: Center for Japanese Studies, University of Michigan, 2004).

25. Pierre Souyri, *The World Turned Upside Down: Medieval Japanese Society* (New York: Columbia University Press, 2003).

26. Sharon Sievers, "Feminist Criticism in Japan Politics in the 1880s: The Experience of Kishida Toshiko," *Signs* 6, no. 4 (1981): 602–16.

27. Anna Cock, "Where Men Are Men and Still Born to Rule," *Sunday Telegraph*, March 26, 2006.

28. Mari Yamaguchi, "Japanese Government Report Urges Job Training and Business Money for Working Mothers," Associated Press Newswires, June 9, 2006.

29. American attitudes toward working mothers were also quite negative until the 1960s, and became more accepting only gradually beginning with the families and coworkers of working mothers themselves. See Ronald Rindfuss, Karin Brewster, and Andrea Kavee, "Women, Work, and Children: Behavioral and Attitudinal Change in the United States," *Population and Development Review* 9 (1996): 457–82.

30. Leslie D. Alldritt, "The Burakumin: The Complicity of Japanese Buddhism in Oppression and an Opportunity for Liberation," *Journal of Buddhist Ethics* 7 (July 2000).

31. Keizai Koho Center, *Japan 2005: An International Comparison* (Tokyo: Keizai Koho Center, 2004), 12.

32. Yumi Hashizume, "Releasing from the Oppression: Caregiving for the Elderly Parents of Japanese Working Women," *Qualitative Health Research* 20 (2010): 830–44.

33. Leonard Schoppa, *Race for the Exits: The Unraveling of Japan's System of Social Protection* (Ithaca: Cornell University Press, 2008).

34. Steve Bossy, "Academic Pressure and Impact on Japanese Students," *McGill Journal of Higher Education* 35, no. 1 (2000): 79–81; and Keiko Hirao, "Privatized Education Market and Maternal Employment in Japan," in *Political Economy of Low Fertility: Japan in Comparative Perspective*, ed. Frances Rosenbluth (Stanford, CA: Stanford University Press, 2007), 170–97.

35. Mary Brinton, "Trouble in Paradise: Institutions in the Japanese Economy and the Youth Labor Market," in *The Economic Sociology of Capitalism*, ed. Victor Nee and Richard Swedberg (Princeton, NJ: Princeton University Press, 2005), 419–44.

36. https://wiki.smu.edu.sg/digitalmediaasia/Digital_Media_in_Japan, accessed June 27, 2013.

37. Akihiro Hirata, Emi Morofuji, and Hiroshi Aramaki, "Television Viewing and Media Use Today: From 'The Japanese and Television 2010' Survey," *NHK Broadcasting Studies* 9 (2011), accessed June 27, 2013, https://www.nhk.or.jp/bunken/english/reports/pdf/11_no9_05.pdf.

38. Frances McCall Rosenbluth and Michael F. Thies, *Japan Transformed* (Princeton, NJ: Princeton University Press, 2010).

39. Steven R. Reed, Ethan Scheiner, Daniel M. Smith, and Michael F. Thies, "The 2012 Election Results: The LDP Wins Big by Default," in *Japan Decides 2012: The Japanese General Election*, ed. Robert Pekkanen, Steven R. Reed, and Ethan Scheiner (London: Palgrave, 2013), 34–47.

40. For more on why the electoral system was changed and how, see Steven R. Reed and Michael F. Thies, "The Causes of Electoral Reform in Japan," in *Mixed-Member Electoral Systems: The Best of Both Worlds?*, ed. Matthew Soberg Shugart and Martin P. Wattenberg (New York: Oxford University Press, 2001), 152–72.

41. Steven R. Reed, Ethan Scheiner, and Michael F. Thies, "The End of LDP Dominance and the Rise of Party-Oriented Politics in Japan," *Journal of Japanese Studies* 38, no. 2 (2012): 357–80.

42. Michael F. Thies, "When Will Pork Leave the Farm? Institutional Bias in Japan and the United States," *Legislative Studies Quarterly* 23, no. 4 (November 1998): 467–92.

43. Ethan Scheiner, *Democracy Without Competition in Japan: Opposition Failure in a One-Party Dominant State* (New York: Cambridge University Press, 2006).

44. Reed et al., "The End of LDP Dominance."

45. Reed et al., "The 2012 Election Results."

46. T. J. Pempel and Keiichi Tsunekawa, "Corporatism Without Labor? The Japanese Anomaly," in *Trends toward Corporatist Intermediation*, ed. Philippe C. Schmitter and Gerhard Lehmbruch (London: Sage, 1979), 231–70.

47. Japan Small Business Research Institute, "2009 White Paper on Small and Medium Enterprises in Japan," (Tokyo, 2012), available in English at www.chusho.meti.go.jp/pamflet/hakusyo/h21/h21_1/2009hakusho_eng.pdf.

48. Frances McCall Rosenbluth, *Financial Politics in Contemporary Japan* (Ithaca, NY: Cornell University Press, 1989).

49. Leonard J. Schoppa, *Bargaining with Japan: What American Pressure Can and Cannot Do* (New York: Columbia University Press, 1997); and Ross D. Schaap, *The Electoral Determinants of Regulatory Change: Explaining Japan's 'Big Bang' Financial Liberalization* (unpublished Ph.D. diss., University of California, Los Angeles, 2002).

50. Kent E. Calder, *Crisis and Compensation* (Princeton, NJ: Princeton University Press, 1988), chap. 5.

51. Reed et al., "The End of LDP Dominance," 357–80.

52. Dore, *British Factory–Japanese Factory*.

53. Keizai Koho Center, *Japan 2010: An International Comparison* (Tokyo: Keizai Koho Center, 2010).

54. Ministry of Health, Labour, and Welfare, *Basic Survey on Trade Unions*, 2009, www.jtuc-rengo.org/about/data/erng_pam_2010.pdf.

55. Joseph P. Kettl, Jr., *The Politics of Defense in Japan* (Armonk, NY: Sharpe, 1993), 173–205.

56. Source: World Health Organization National Health Account database (www.who.int/nha/en) supplemented by country data. Note: The latest updates on these data are accessible on WHO's National Health Accounts (NHA) website, www.who.int/nha/en/. For an in-depth look at medical as well as pension issues in Japan, see John C. Campbell, *How Policies Change* (Princeton, NJ: Princeton University Press, 1992).

57. 2012 LDP manifesto, http://special.jimin.jp/political_promise/.

58. Daniel P. Aldrich, "Post-Crisis Japanese Nuclear Policy: From Top-Down Directives to Bottom-Up Activism," AsiaPacific Issues vol. 103 (Honolulu, HI: East-West Center, 2012).

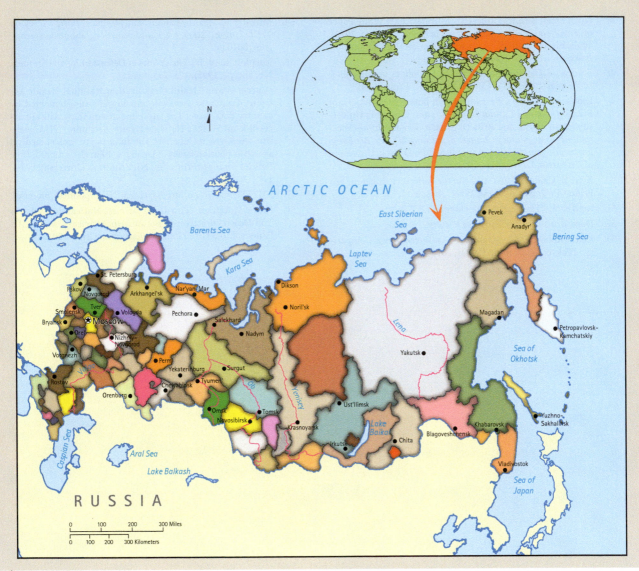

ARCTIC OCEAN

Barents Sea

Kara Sea

Laptev Sea

East Siberian Sea

Bering Sea

St. Petersburg
Pskov
Novgorod
Arkhangel'sk
Nar'yan-Mar
Smolensk
Tver'
Vologda
Bryansk
Moscow
Pechora
Orel
Nizhny-Novgorod
Voronezh
Perm'
Rostov
Yekaterinburg
Surgut
Orenburg
Chelyabinsk
Tyumen'
Omsk
Tomsk
Novosibirsk
Krasnoyarsk
Irkutsk
Lake Balkal
Ust'Ilimsk
Salekhard
Nadym
Dikson
Noril'sk
Yakutsk
Magadan
Pevek
Anadyr'
Petropavlovsk-Kamchatskiy
Sea of Okhotsk
Yuzhno-Sakhalinsk
Khabarovsk
Blagoveshchensk
Chita
Vladivostok
Sea of Japan

Volga
Ob'
Yenisey
Lena

Caspian Sea
Aral Sea
Lake Balkash

RUSSIA

0   100   200   300 Miles
0   100   200   300 Kilometers

Country Bio

POPULATION
143.3 million

TERRITORY
6,593,000 square miles

YEAR OF INDEPENDENCE
1991

YEAR OF CURRENT CONSTITUTION
1993

HEAD OF STATE
President Vladimir Vladimirovich Putin

HEAD OF GOVERNMENT
Premier Dmitrii Anatolievich Medvedev

LANGUAGE(S)
Russian, other languages of ethnic nationalities

RELIGION
Russian Orthodox heritage 74%; other Christian 2%; Muslim 7%; Buddhist 0.6%; Jewish 1%; other or nonreligious 15%

CHAPTER 12

Politics in Russia

Thomas F. Remington

LEARNING OBJECTIVES

12.1 Discuss the challenges of Russia's "resource curse" and of the country's changing demographics, along with the three main obstacles to their resolution.

12.2 Briefly describe Russia's political history, from its tsarist roots to the transitions of the twentieth century.

12.3 Describe the powers of the Russian president in relation to the other branches of government.

12.4 Discuss the contradictions within Russia's current political culture, focusing on the conflict between democratic and traditional Soviet values.

12.5 Explain the roles of propaganda, the educational system, the church, and the media in political socialization in Russia.

12.6 Describe avenues of direct and indirect participation in Russian politics.

12.7 Discuss the formation and activities of interest groups in post-Soviet Russia, with specific examples.

12.8 Examine the rise of the "party of power" in recent elections.

12.9 Describe the interplay between political and economic restructuring in contemporary Russia.

12.10 Briefly describe the route and obstacles to the rule of law in Russia.

12.11 Discuss Russia's conflicted international relations.

Ensuring Continuity of Leadership

On May 7, 2012, **Vladimir Vladimirovich Putin** took the oath of office as president of the Russian Federation. Putin had already served two terms as president from 2000 to 2008. (See Box 12.1: Vladimir Putin.) He had then stepped aside—formally complying with the constitutional prohibition against serving more than two terms in succession—to serve a four-year term as prime minister while **Dmitrii Anatol'evich Medvedev** occupied the presidency. The farcical nature of the proceedings was reinforced by the fact that upon taking the oath of office, he immediately named Medvedev as his prime minister. Cynical Russians recognized that Putin and Medvedev were simply trading offices (they called it a "castling move," as in chess). In the meantime, everyone understood that the real location of power had never changed—Putin had been the top leader the whole time. The country went through the formal motions of an election each time, but the election was closely controlled, and considerable fraud was used to guarantee the outcome.

Why would the Putin regime go to the trouble of pretending to hold a competitive election only to manipulate the outcome so visibly? The logic seems

BOX 12.1   Vladimir Putin

Vladimir Vladimirovich Putin was born on October 7, 1952, in Leningrad (called St. Petersburg since 1991). In 1970, he entered Leningrad State University and specialized in civil law. Upon graduation in 1975, Putin worked for the KGB and was first assigned to counterintelligence and then to the foreign intelligence division. Proficient in the German language, he was sent to East Germany in 1985. In 1990, after the Berlin Wall fell, Putin went back to Leningrad, working at the university but in the employ of the KGB. When a former professor of his, Anatolii Sobchak, became mayor of Leningrad in 1991, he went to work for Sobchak.

In 1996, Putin took a position in Yeltsin's presidential administration. He rose rapidly. In 1998, Yeltsin named Putin head of the FSB (the Federal Security Service—successor to the KGB) and, in March 1999, secretary of the Security Council. In August 1999, Yeltsin appointed him prime minister. Thanks to his decisive handling of the military operation in Chechnia, Putin's popularity ratings soared. On December 31, 1999, Yeltsin resigned, making Putin acting president. Putin ran for the presidency and, on March 26, 2000, won with an outright majority of the votes. He ran again in 2004 and won, stepped down from the presidency and served as prime minister with Dmitrii Medvedev as president from 2008 to 2012, and then returned to the presidency in 2012.

Putin cultivates the image of a tough, decisive, down-to-earth leader. Generally unemotional and mild-mannered, he occasionally allows himself to indulge in sarcastic or profane language to make a point. At other times, he projects an affable, relaxed demeanor. He is often shown in active, outdoors settings. Putin is self-possessed and guarded in dealing with others. Although he appears uncomfortable with the give and take of public politics, he is adept at handling live call-in programs where ordinary citizens can pose their questions and complaints. He is skillful at explaining complex issues in clear and plain language. Foreign business and political leaders who have met with him come away impressed at his mastery of policy detail.

puzzling to many outsiders. It is typical, however, of "competitive authoritarian regimes."[1] These are regimes where the rulers hold elections that allow opposition forces to run candidates but not to defeat the incumbents. From the standpoint of the Putin team, a controlled election serves several purposes: It lets the authorities keep an eye on the opposition, it gives the public some opportunity to vote for alternative parties, and it leaves the power of the ruling elite intact. An uncontrolled election creates the risk of an internal split within the political elite, as has happened in some other post-Soviet states.[2] Putin was intent on preserving political stability in the transfer of power in Russia while presenting the facade of a free election. Although Putin probably won an outright majority on the first ballot, considerable fraud was used to pad Putin's total. The Central Electoral Commission reported that Putin won with 63.6 percent of the vote; the true total was probably in the range of 50–55 percent.[3]

During the four-year interim period when Medvedev was president and Putin was prime minister, Putin remained in charge. Some expected some rivalry between the two, but none arose. Medvedev loyally played the part assigned to him, although he did attempt to launch policy initiatives of his own. That Putin was still superior to Medvedev in fact, while formally subordinate to him, vividly illustrates the gap between formal and informal power in Russia. Formally, the president has enormous power. In Medvedev's case, however, he could not exercise it because of the solid grip Putin retained over the informal centers of political power in the country—security and law enforcement agencies, major state business firms, regional governments, and the media. Medvedev might conceivably have tried to use his formal powers as president to build up an independent power base, but he chose not to try. Putin was justified in trusting that Medvedev would remain loyal. The regime remained stable, therefore, across the succession from Putin to Medvedev, and then from Medvedev to Putin. The tight control over leadership succession, however, deprived the regime of the benefits of leadership accountability and renewal that democratic systems enjoy. This deep preoccupation with stability therefore reinforces the tendencies toward rigidity and stagnation in the political system.

Current Policy Challenges

12.1 Discuss the challenges of Russia's "resource curse" and of the country's changing demographics, along with the three main obstacles to their resolution.

The greatest policy challenge for Russia is the need to reduce its dependence on natural resource exports. Even President Putin himself repeatedly makes this point. Russia's fortunes rise and fall with world oil prices. During the first two terms of Putin's presidency, Russia enjoyed high and steady economic growth rates. Part of this was due to greater confidence in Putin's leadership. A more important reason, however, was that world oil prices started increasing significantly and stayed high until 2008. As a major exporter of oil, gas, and other natural resources, Russia benefited from this trend: Real incomes tripled from 2000 to 2008. The decade of recovery in the 2000s followed a harsh decade of economic contraction and social dislocation in the 1990s following the painful transition from the socialist economic system to a market-oriented capitalist system. Russia benefited from opening its economy up to the world, as capital investment entered the country and raw materials exports brought in immense incomes.

Russia's dependence on revenues from natural resource exports had a steep downside, however, when the worldwide financial crash struck in 2008. Capital fled the country (the stock market lost two-thirds of its value in less than one year), and its highly indebted firms struggled to meet their obligations. As world oil and gas prices tumbled to one-third of their peak level, Russian budget revenues plummeted and the federal budget fell into a deep deficit. Consumer demand dropped, hurting Russia's manufacturers. Russia's economy contracted more than that of any other major power—its gross domestic product (GDP) fell almost 8 percent in 2009 alone and only began to recover slowly in 2010. Financial reserves that the government had set aside during the boom years of the 2000s spared the country many of the worst effects of the recession. The government pumped hundreds of billions of rubles into failing banks, industrial enterprises, unemployment benefits, and pensions. As a result, many Russians were shielded from poverty and the country was spared the massive financial instability that broke out in other heavily indebted states lacking Russia's deep reserves. However, since 2010, Russia's growth rate has been anemic. It currently runs at about 3 percent per year and is unlikely to grow much faster. A decline in world oil prices could again bring slower growth.

Russian leaders and experts are well aware of the dangers of the "resource curse" for Russia. This is the idea that in countries relying on windfall revenues from natural resources, the leaders avoid investing in the skills and knowledge of the population. As a result, such societies wind up with lower levels of economic and political development than in resource-poor countries. Oil-rich states in the Middle East are often cited as examples. Yet although President Putin and his government frequently call for more diversification and innovation in the economy, it is apparent that they lack effective policy instruments to bring it about. This illustrates a recurring dilemma in Russian history: Major reform requires an enormous and sustained exercise of power by the country's political leaders to overcome the resistance of administrative and social groups to change. To accomplish their goals, modernizing rulers have commonly resorted to centralizing power in their own hands, undermining the incentives for entrepreneurial initiatives outside the state that could drive sustained growth.

In a widely discussed article published in September 2009, then-President Medvedev denounced Russia's current economic structure as "primitive" for its dependence on natural resource production, its "chronic corruption, the outdated habit of relying on the state to solve our problems, on foreign countries, on some sort of 'all-powerful doctrine,' on anything and everything except on ourselves." He noted that "the energy efficiency and labor productivity of most of our enterprises are shamefully low" and added that the real tragedy was that most owners, managers, and state officials do not appear to be particularly worried about the situation.[4] As tough as his words were, though, Medvedev found himself powerless to do anything more than to deplore these problems.

Another serious policy challenge lies in the demographic crisis facing Russia. In most years since the end of the Soviet regime, deaths have outnumbered births. In-migration (especially from Central Asia) partly offsets natural population loss, but has brought other difficulties. Life expectancy at birth is very low, particularly for males, although it has risen in the last ten years (male life expectancy is sixty-four, about the same as in India or Pakistan). Regions in the Far North and Far East have seen a substantial outflow of population to regions with warmer climates, jeopardizing the sustainability of some of the remote cities built in Soviet times. High barriers to geographic mobility, such as large distances, high transportation costs, and an illiquid housing market, reinforce the enormous differences in living standards across regions. Some regions are thriving, while others are mired in deep poverty and stagnation.

But while Russian leaders have acknowledged the gravity of the problems facing the country, they have been unable to break through the obstacles standing in the way of solving them. Three in particular have proven to be stumbling blocks: the resistance by state officials to any reforms that weaken their power; the vast physical size of the country, which impedes efforts to control and coordinate bureaucratic activity; and the legacy of the Soviet development model, which concentrated resources in giant state-owned enterprises—often located in remote, harsh regions—that are nearly impossible to convert into competitive capitalist firms viable in a global marketplace. Taken together, these factors stack the deck against political and economic reform.

Historical Legacies

 Briefly describe Russia's political history, from its tsarist roots to the transitions of the twentieth century.

The Tsarist Regime

The Russian state traces its origins to the princely state that arose around Kiev (today the capital of independent Ukraine) in the ninth century. For nearly a thousand years, the Russian state was autocratic. That is, it was ruled by a hereditary monarch whose power was unlimited by any constitutional constraints. Only in the first decade of the twentieth century did the Russian tsar agree to grant a constitution calling for an elected legislature—and even then, the tsar soon dissolved the legislature and clawed back most of the constitutional concessions he had made.

In addition to autocracy, the historical legacy of Russian statehood includes lasting strains of absolutism, patrimonialism, and Orthodox Christianity. *Absolutism* means that the tsar aspired to wield absolute power over the subjects of the realm. *Patrimonialism* refers to the idea that the ruler treated his realm as property that

he owned, rather than as an autonomous community with its own legitimate rights and interests.[5] This concept of power continues to influence state rulers today. Finally, the tsarist state identified itself with the *Russian Orthodox Church*. In Russia, as in other countries where it is a dominant religious tradition, the Orthodox Church ties itself closely to the state, considering itself a national church. Traditionally, it has exhorted its adherents to show loyalty to the state in worldly matters, in return for which it has sought a monopoly of spiritual power. This legacy is still manifest in the present-day rulers' efforts to call upon the church to bless their rule and reinforce the social fabric, as well as in many Russians' impulse to identify their state with a higher spiritual mission.

Absolutism, patrimonialism, and orthodoxy have been recurring elements of Russian political culture, tending to reinforce deeply conservative and collectivist patterns of behavior in state and society. But alternative patterns have been influential as well. At particular points in Russian history, the country's rulers have sought to modernize its economy and society. Russia imported Western practices in technology, law, state organization, and education in order to make the state competitive with other great powers. Modernizing rulers—such as Peter the Great (who ruled from 1682 to 1725) and Catherine the Great (from 1762 to 1796)—had a powerful impact on Russian society, bringing it closer to West European models. The imperative of building Russia's military and economic potential was all the more pressing because of Russia's constant expansion through conquest and annexation of neighboring territories and its ever-present need to defend its borders. The state's role in controlling and mobilizing society rose with the need to govern a vast territory. By the end of the seventeenth century, Russia was territorially the largest state in the world. But for most of its history, Russia's imperial reach exceeded its actual grasp.

Compared with other major powers of Europe, Russia's economic institutions remained backward well into the twentieth century. However, the trajectory of its development, especially in the nineteenth century, was toward that of a modern industrial society. By the time the tsarist order fell in 1917, Russia had a large industrial sector, although it was concentrated in a few cities. The middle class was greatly outnumbered by the vast and impoverished peasantry and the radicalized industrial working class. As a result, the social basis for a peaceful democratic transition was too weak to prevent the Communists from seizing power in 1917.

The thousand-year tsarist era left a contradictory legacy. The tsars attempted to legitimate their absolute power by appealing to tradition, empire, and divine right. They treated law as an instrument of rule, rather than a source of authority. The doctrines that rulers should be accountable to the ruled and that sovereignty resides in the will of the people were alien to Russian state tradition. Throughout Russian history, state and society have been more distant from each other than in Western societies. Rulers and populace regarded one another with mistrust. This gap has been overcome at times of great national trials, such as the war against Napoleon and later World War II. Russia celebrated victory in those wars as a triumphant demonstration of the unity of state and people. But Russia's political traditions also include a yearning for equality, solidarity, and community, as well as for moral purity and sympathy for the downtrodden. And throughout the Russian heritage runs a deep strain of pride in the greatness of the country and the endurance of its people.

The Communist Revolution and the Soviet Order

The tsarist regime proved unable to cope with the overwhelming demands of national mobilization in World War I. Tsar Nicholas II abdicated in February 1917 (March 1917, by the Western calendar). He was replaced by a short-lived provisional government, which, in turn, fell when the Russian Communists—Bolsheviks, as they called themselves—took power in October 1917 (November, by the Western calendar). Their aim was to create a socialist society in Russia and, eventually, to spread revolutionary socialism throughout the world. Socialism, the Russian Communist Party believed, meant a society without private ownership of the means of production, one where the state owned and controlled all important economic assets and where political power was exercised in the name of the working people. **Vladimir Ilyich Lenin** was the leader of the Russian Communist Party and the first head of the Soviet Russian government. (Figure 12.1 lists the Soviet and post-Soviet leaders since 1917.)

Under Lenin's system of rule, the Communist Party controlled all levels of government. At each

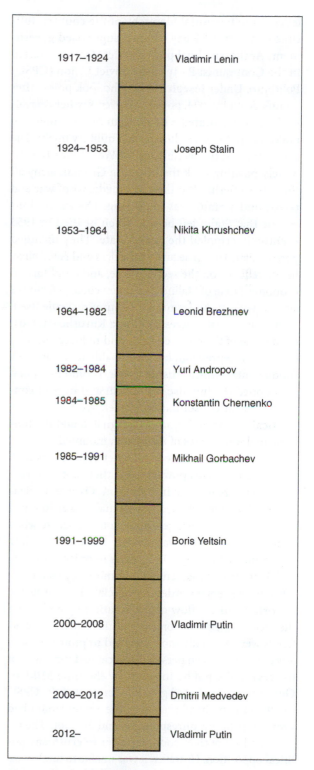

1917–1924	Vladimir Lenin
1924–1953	Joseph Stalin
1953–1964	Nikita Khrushchev
1964–1982	Leonid Brezhnev
1982–1984	Yuri Andropov
1984–1985	Konstantin Chernenko
1985–1991	Mikhail Gorbachev
1991–1999	Boris Yeltsin
2000–2008	Vladimir Putin
2008–2012	Dmitrii Medvedev
2012–	Vladimir Putin

FIGURE 12.1

Timeline of Russian Rulers Since 1917

Gorbachev was the last Soviet leader; Yeltsin was the first leader of post-Soviet Russia.

level of the territorial hierarchy of the country, full-time Communist Party officials supervised government. At the top, final power to decide policy rested in the Communist Party of the Soviet Union (CPSU) Politburo. Under **Joseph Stalin**, who took power after Lenin's death in 1924, power was even further centralized. Stalin instituted a totalitarian regime intent on building up Russia's industrial and military might. The state survived the terrible test of World War II, ultimately pushing back the invading German army all the way to Berlin. But the combined cost of war and terror under Stalin was staggering. The institutions of rule that Stalin left behind when he died in 1953 eventually crippled the Soviet state. They included personalistic rule, insecurity for rulers and ruled alike, heavy reliance on the secret police, and a militarized economy. None of Stalin's successors could reform the system without undermining Communist rule itself. Stalin's immediate successor, Nikita Khrushchev, loosened some of the harsh controls and reduced the level of political repression, but was unable to accomplish fundamental reform. His successor, Leonid Brezhnev, abandoned the impulse for reform and instead concentrated on consolidating power. As a result, the political system and economy stagnated and the fundamental weaknesses of the system mounted.

The problem of the late Soviet system was that, as vast as the state's powers were, their use was frustrated by bureaucratic immobilism. Overcentralization undermined the leaders' actual power to enact significant policy change—or even to recognize when serious policy change was needed. The center's ability to coordinate bureaucratic agencies in order to execute its initiatives was frequently undermined by tacit resistance to the center's orders by officials at lower levels, distortions in the flow of information up and down the hierarchy, and the force of inertia. Bureaucratic officials were generally more devoted to protecting and advancing their own personal and career interests than to serving the public interest. By the time **Mikhail Gorbachev** was elected general secretary of the CPSU in 1985, the political system of the Soviet Union had grown top-heavy, unresponsive, and corrupt. The regime had more than enough power to crush any political opposition. However, it was unable to modernize the economy or improve living standards for the population. By the early 1980s, the economy had stopped growing, and the country was unable to compete militarily or economically with the West.

After the deaths of three elderly leaders—Brezhnev, Andropov, and Chernenko—in quick succession in 1982, 1984, and 1985, respectively, the ruling party Politburo turned to a vigorous young (54-year-old) reformer named Mikhail Gorbachev to lead the country. Gorbachev quickly grasped the levers of power that the system granted the general secretary. He moved both to strengthen his own political base and to carry out a program of reform.[6] Emphasizing the need for greater openness—*glasnost'*—in society, Gorbachev stressed that the ultimate test of the party's effectiveness lay in improving the economic well-being of the country and its people. Gorbachev not only called for political democratization but also legalized private enterprise for individual and cooperative businesses and encouraged them to fill the many gaps in the economy left by the inefficiency of the state sector. He welcomed the explosion of new informal social and political associations. He made major concessions to the United States in the sphere of arms control, which resulted in a treaty that, for the first time in history, called for the destruction of entire classes of nuclear missiles.

Gorbachev railroaded his proposals for democratization through the legislature. In 1989 and 1990, Gorbachev's plan for free elections and a working parliament was realized as elections were held and new deputies were elected at the center and in every region and locality. When nearly half a million coal miners went on strike in the summer of 1989, Gorbachev declared himself sympathetic to their demands.

Gorbachev's radicalism received its most dramatic confirmation through the astonishing developments of 1989 in Eastern Europe. All the regimes making up the Communist bloc collapsed and gave way to multiparty parliamentary regimes in virtually bloodless popular revolutions. The Soviet Union stood by and supported the revolutions. The overnight dismantling of communism in Eastern Europe meant that the elaborate structure of party ties, police cooperation, economic trade, and military alliance that had developed with Eastern Europe after World War II vanished. Divided Germany was allowed to reunite.

In the Soviet Union itself, the Communist Party faced a critical loss of authority. The newly elected governments of the national republics making up the Soviet state one by one declared that they were sovereign. The three Baltic republics declared their intention to secede from the union. Between 1989 and 1990, throughout the Soviet Union and Eastern Europe, Communist Party rule crumbled.

Political Institutions of the Transition Period: Demise of the Soviet Union

Gorbachev's reforms had consequences he did not intend. The 1990 elections of deputies to the supreme soviets in all fifteen republics and to local soviets stimulated popular nationalist and democratic movements in most republics. In the core republic of Russia itself, Gorbachev's rival, Boris Yeltsin, was elected chairman of the Russian Supreme Soviet in June 1990. As chief of state in the Russian Republic, Yeltsin was well positioned to challenge Gorbachev for preeminence.

Yeltsin's rise forced Gorbachev to alter his strategy. Beginning in March 1991, Gorbachev sought terms for a new federal or confederal union that would be acceptable to Yeltsin and the Russian leadership, as well as to the leaders of the other republics. In April 1991, he reached an agreement on the outlines of a new treaty of union with nine of the fifteen republics, including Russia. A weak central government would manage basic coordinating functions. But the republics would gain the power to control the economies of their territories.

Gorbachev had underestimated the strength of his opposition. On August 19, 1991, a conspiracy of senior officials placed Gorbachev under house arrest and seized power. In response, thousands of citizens in Moscow and St. Petersburg rallied to protest the coup attempt. The coup collapsed on the third day, but Gorbachev's power had been fatally weakened. Neither the union nor the Russian power structures heeded his commands. Through the fall of 1991, the Russian government took over the union government, ministry by ministry. In November 1991, President Yeltsin issued a decree formally outlawing the CPSU. In December, Yeltsin and the leaders of Ukraine and Belarus formally declared the Union of Soviet Socialist Republics dissolved. On December 25, 1991, Gorbachev resigned as president and turned the powers of his office over to Boris Yeltsin. On New Year's Day, 1992, the Soviet flag was hauled down over the Kremlin and the white, blue, and red flag of independent Russia was raised in its place.

Political Institutions of the Transition Period: Russia 1990–1993

Boris Yeltsin was elected president of the Russian Federation in June 1991. Unlike Gorbachev, Yeltsin was elected in a direct, competitive election, which gave him a considerable advantage in mobilizing public support against Gorbachev and the central Soviet Union government (see Box 12.2).

Like Gorbachev before him, Yeltsin demanded extraordinary powers from parliament to cope with the country's economic problems. Following the August 1991 coup attempt, parliament granted him emergency decree powers to cope with the economic crisis. Yeltsin formed a government led by a group of young, Western-oriented reformers determined to carry out a decisive economic transformation. The new government's economic program took effect on January 2, 1992. Their first results were felt immediately, as prices skyrocketed. Quickly, many politicians began to distance themselves from the program: Even Yeltsin's vice president denounced the program as "economic genocide." Throughout 1992, opposition to the reforms grew stronger and more intransigent. Increasingly, the political confrontation between Yeltsin and the reformers on the one side and the opposition to radical economic reform on the other became centered in the two branches of government. President Yeltsin demanded broad powers to carry out the reforms, but parliament refused to go along. In March 1993, an opposition motion to remove the president through impeachment nearly passed in the parliament.

On September 21, 1993, Yeltsin decreed the parliament dissolved and called for elections for a new parliament. Yeltsin's enemies barricaded themselves inside the parliament building. After a ten-day standoff, the dissidents joined with some loosely organized paramilitary units outside the building and attacked the Moscow mayor's offices adjacent to the Russian White House. They even called on their followers to "seize the Kremlin." Finally, the army agreed to back Yeltsin and suppress the uprising by force, shelling the parliament building in the process.

The violence of October 1993 cast a long shadow over subsequent events. Yeltsin's decree meant that national elections were to be held for a legislature that, constitutionally speaking, did not exist, since the new constitution establishing these institutions was to be voted on in a referendum held in parallel with the

Boris Yeltsin: Russia's First President

Boris Yeltsin, born in 1931, graduated from the Urals Polytechnical Institute in 1955 with a diploma in civil engineering, and worked for a long time in construction. From 1976 to 1985, he served as first secretary of the Sverdlovsk *oblast* (provincial) Communist Party organization.

Early in 1986, Yeltsin became first secretary of the Moscow city party organization, but he was removed in November 1987 for speaking out against Mikhail Gorbachev. Positioning himself as a victim of the party establishment, Yeltsin made a remarkable political comeback. In the 1989 elections to the Congress of People's Deputies, he won a Moscow at-large seat, with almost 90 percent of the vote. The following year he was elected to the Russian republic's parliament, with over 80 percent of the vote. He was then elected its chairman in June 1990. In 1991, he was elected president of Russia, receiving 57 percent of the vote. Thus he won three major races in three successive years. He was reelected as president in 1996 in a dramatic, come-from-behind race against the leader of the Communist Party.

Yeltsin's last years in office were notable for his lengthy spells of illness and for the carousel of prime ministerial appointments. The entourage of family members and advisors around him seemed to exercise undue influence over him. Yet, infirm as he was, he judged that Russia's interests and his own would be safe in Vladimir Putin's hands. Yeltsin's resignation speech expressed contrition for his failure to bring a better life to Russians. After retiring, Yeltsin stayed out of the public eye. He died of heart failure on April 23, 2007, and was buried in Moscow with full honors.

Yeltsin's legacy is mixed. He was most effective when engaged in political battle, whether he was fighting for supremacy against Gorbachev or fighting against the Communists. He was gifted with exceptionally keen political intuition. He regarded economic reform as an instrument in his political war with the Communist opposition and used privatization to make it impossible for any future rulers to return to state socialism. Imperious and willful, he also regarded the adoption of the 1993 constitution as a major achievement and accepted the limits on his presidential power that it imposed.

parliamentary elections. Yet for all the turmoil, the constitution approved in the December 1993 referendum has remained in force ever since.[7]

The Contemporary Constitutional Order

 Describe the powers of the Russian president in relation to the other branches of government.

The Presidency

Yeltsin's constitution combined elements of presidentialism and parliamentarism. (See Figure 12.2 for a schematic overview of the Russian constitutional structure.) (Figure 12.2) Although it provided for the separation of the executive, legislative, and judicial branches and for a federal division of power between the central and regional levels of government, it made the presidency by far the strongest institution in the state. The president is directly elected for a six-year term and may not serve more than two consecutive terms. The president names the prime minister to head the government. The government must have the confidence of parliament to remain in power. Although the constitution does not call the president the head of the executive branch, he is so in fact, by virtue of his power to appoint the prime minister and the rest of the government and his right to issue **presidential decrees** with the force of law. (The decree power is somewhat limited in that decrees may not violate existing law and can be superseded by legislation.)

Over the years since the constitution was approved, some informal practices have come to govern the exercise of central power. For example, the president and government divide executive responsibility. The government, headed by the prime minister, is primarily responsible for economic and social policy. The president directly oversees the ministries and agencies concerned with the armed forces, law enforcement, and state security—the "force ministries." These include the Foreign Ministry, Defense Ministry,

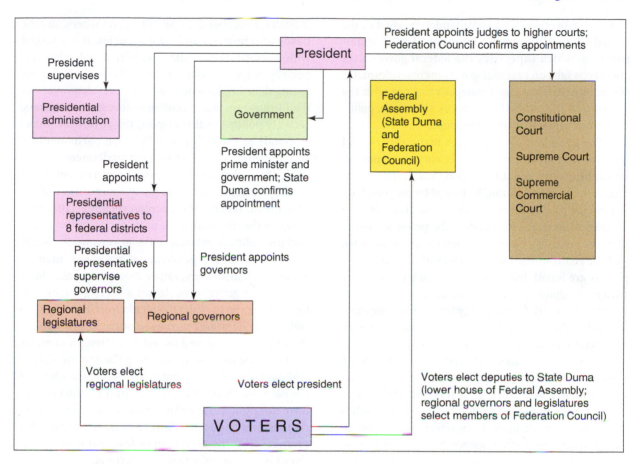

FIGURE 12.2
Structure of Russian Government
The three branches of government and the three tiers of the state.

Ministry of Internal Affairs (which controls the regular police and security troops), Federal Security Service (FSB—formerly the KGB), and several other security and intelligence agencies. The president and his staff set overall policy in the foreign and domestic domains, and the government develops the specific proposals and rules carrying out this policy. In practice, the government answers to the president, not parliament. The usual pattern is for the government's base of support to be the president, rather than a particular coalition of parties in parliament.

Despite the pronounced presidential tilt to the system, the parliament does have some potential for independent action. Its ability to exercise its rights, however, depends on the composition of political forces represented in parliament and the cohesiveness of the majority. Parliament's approval is required for any bill to become law. The State Duma (the lower

house of parliament) must confirm the president's nominee for prime minister. If, after three successive votes, the Duma refuses to confirm the nomination, the president must dissolve the Duma and call new elections. Likewise, the Duma may vote to deny confidence in the government. If a motion of no confidence carries twice, the president must either dissolve parliament or dismiss the government. During Yeltsin's tenure as president, the Duma was able to block some of Yeltsin's legislative initiatives. Since 2003, however, it has largely been a rubber stamp. The constitution allows for a variety of types of relationships among the president, government, and parliament, depending on the degree to which the president dominates the political system.

In addition to these powers, the president has a number of other formal and informal powers in his constitutional capacity as "head of state," "guarantor of the constitution," and commander-in-chief of the armed forces. He oversees a large presidential administration, which supervises the federal government and keeps tabs on regional governments. Informally, the administration also manages relations with the parliament, the courts, big business, the media, political parties, and major interest groups.

The president also oversees many official and quasi-official supervisory and advisory commissions, which he creates and directs using his decree power. One is the **Security Council**, chaired by the president. Besides the president, the Security Council consists of a permanent secretary, the heads of the power ministries and other security-related agencies, the prime minister, and the chairs of the two chambers of parliament. Its powers are broad, but shadowy. Putin has selectively used it to formulate policy proposals not only in matters of foreign and defense policy but also on issues having to do with the organization of the executive branch, and even to speak out on issues of public morality.[8]

Another prominent advisory body is the **State Council**, which comprises the heads of the regional governments and thus parallels the Federation Council. Still another is the **Public Chamber**, which is made up of 126 members from selected civic, professional, artistic, and other nongovernmental organizations (NGOs). Its purpose is to deliberate on matters of public policy, make recommendations to parliament and the government on pending policy issues, and link civil society with the state. Like the State Council, it is a quasi-parliamentary deliberative body that the president can consult at will. All three bodies duplicate some of the deliberative and representative functions of parliament—and therefore weaken parliament's role. They illustrate the tendency, under both Yeltsin and Putin, for the president to create and dissolve new structures answering directly to the president. These improvised structures can be politically useful for the president as counterweights to constitutionally mandated bodies (such as parliament), as well as providing policy advice and feedback. They help ensure that the president is always the dominant institution in the political system, but they undermine the authority of other constitutional structures such as parliament.

The Government

The *government* refers to the senior echelon of leadership in the executive branch and consists of the prime minister, a number of deputy prime ministers, and the heads of ministries and state agencies. It is charged with formulating the main lines of national policy (especially in the economic and social realms) and overseeing their implementation. (The president oversees the formulation and execution of foreign and national security policy.) In this respect, the government corresponds to the Cabinet in Western parliamentary systems. But in contrast to most parliamentary systems, the makeup of the Russian government is not directly determined by the party composition of the parliament. Indeed, there is scarcely any relationship between the distribution of party forces in the Duma and the political balance of the government. Nearly all members of the government are career managers and administrators, rather than party politicians. Overall, the government is not a party government, but reflects the president's calculations about how to weigh considerations such as personal loyalty, professional competence, and the relative strength of major bureaucratic factions in selecting Cabinet ministers. Although there is recurrent discussion of the idea that the party that forms the majority in the Duma should have the right to name the head of the government, no president has been willing to agree to institute this arrangement—no doubt out of fear that it would reduce his freedom of action in governing.

The Parliament

The parliament—called the Federal Assembly—is bicameral. The lower house is called the **State Duma**, and the upper house, the **Federation Council**. Legislation originates in the Duma. As Figure 12.3 shows, upon passage in the State Duma, a bill goes to the Federation Council for consideration. The Federation Council can only pass it, reject it, or propose the formation of an agreement commission (consisting of members of both houses) to iron out differences. If the Duma rejects the upper house's proposed changes, it can override the Federation Council by a two-thirds vote and send the bill directly to the president for his signature.

When the bill has cleared parliament, it goes to the president. If the president refuses to sign the bill, it returns to the Duma. The Duma may pass an amended version that incorporates the president's objections by a simple absolute majority. Alternatively, it may try to override the president's veto, for which

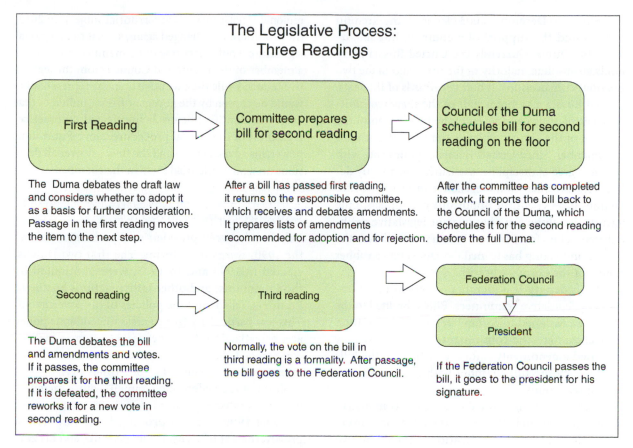

The Legislative Process: Three Readings

First Reading

The Duma debates the draft law and considers whether to adopt it as a basis for further consideration. Passage in the first reading moves the item to the next step.

Committee prepares bill for second reading

After a bill has passed first reading, it returns to the responsible committee, which receives and debates amendments. It prepares lists of amendments recommended for adoption and for rejection.

Council of the Duma schedules bill for second reading on the floor

After the committee has completed its work, it reports the bill back to the Council of the Duma, which schedules it for the second reading before the full Duma.

Second reading

The Duma debates the bill and amendments and votes. If it passes, the committee prepares it for the third reading. If it is defeated, the committee reworks it for a new vote in second reading.

Third reading

Normally, the vote on the bill in third reading is a formality. After passage, the bill goes to the Federation Council.

Federation Council

President

If the Federation Council passes the bill, it goes to the president for his signature.

FIGURE 12.3
The Legislative Process: How a Bill Becomes a Law

a two-thirds vote is required. The Federation Council must then also approve the bill by a simple majority if the president's amendments are accepted or by a two-thirds vote if it chooses to override the president. On rare occasions—and never since 2000—the Duma has overridden the president's veto; it has overridden the Federation Council more frequently. In other cases, the Duma has passed bills rejected by the president after accepting the president's proposed amendments. The president's control over the Duma has been so firm since 2003 that disagreements between president and parliament are rare and minor.

Until 2007, the Duma's 450 members were equally divided between deputies elected by plurality vote in 225 single-member districts and 225 deputies elected through proportional representation (PR) in a single national electoral district. A party receiving at least 5 percent of the vote on the party-list ballot was entitled to a share of the party-list seats in the Duma equal to its share of the party-list vote. As in other PR systems, votes cast for parties that fail to clear the barrier are redistributed to the winning parties. The 2007 and 2011 Duma elections were run under an all-PR system—all 450 deputies were elected proportionally from party lists in a single nationwide district, with the threshold for winning seats set at 7 percent.[9] In 2013, at Putin's urging, the Duma voted to return to the old half-and-half system. The frequent tinkering with the electoral law reflects the authorities' habit of manipulating institutions for short-term political gain.

The parties clearing the electoral threshold form their own factions in the Duma. According to Duma rules, deputies may not switch faction membership (those who are expelled from their faction lose their seats). Faction leaders are represented in the governing body of the Duma, the Council of the Duma. Factions are the main vehicle of political discussion in the Duma and give members a channel for proposing bills.

Since the December 2003 elections, the Kremlin has enjoyed the support of a commanding majority in the Duma. Currently the **United Russia** party holds an absolute majority of the seats, and in the two previous convocations, it had two-thirds of the seats. United Russia also holds half of the thirty committee chairmanships and seven of the twelve seats of the Council of the Duma, which is the steering body for the chamber. Since United Russia deputies vote with a high degree of discipline, the Duma consistently delivers the president solid legislative majorities. Other factions have very little opportunity to influence the agenda, let alone the outcomes of legislative deliberations. Therefore, United Russia's control over the agenda and voting has turned the Duma into a rubber stamp for the executive branch.

Each deputy is a member of one of the thirty standing legislative committees. Bills submitted to the Duma are assigned to committees according to their subject matter. The committees collect and review proposed amendments before reporting out the bills for votes by the full chamber with the committee's recommendations.

The Federation Council is designed as an instrument of federalism in that (as in the U.S. Senate) every constituent unit of the federation is served by two representatives. Thus, the populations of small ethnic-national territories are greatly overrepresented compared with more populous regions. The Federation Council has important formal powers. Besides acting on bills passed by the lower house, it approves presidential nominees for high courts, such as the Supreme Court and the Constitutional Court. It must approve presidential decrees declaring martial law or a state of emergency and any acts altering the boundaries of territorial units. It must consider any legislation dealing with taxes, budget, financial policy, treaties, customs, and declarations of war. The constitution also stipulates, however, that one of the two Federation Council members must represent the legislative branch, and the other must represent the executive branch. Finding a way to reconcile this requirement with the principle of electing representatives directly has proven difficult.

The procedure for choosing members of the Federation Council has been changed a number of times. President Putin pushed through a reform in the spring of 2000 under which the Federation Council's members were formally named by the governor and regional legislature of each territorial subject. In 2012, the procedure was changed again, so that each regional legislature would elect one of its members to serve as a member of the Federation Council from the legislative branch while the executive branch's representative would be chosen by the governor from candidates that he or she identified before being elected. In practice, regardless of the formal procedure, since Putin took power, his advisors have had the final say over all decisions on who would hold seats in the chamber.

Executive–Legislative Relations

Relations between president and parliament during the 1990s were often stormy. The first two Dumas, elected in 1993 and in 1995, were dominated by the Communist and other leftist factions hostile to President Yeltsin and the policies of his government. This was particularly true in areas of economic policy and privatization. On other issues, such as matters concerning federal relations, the Duma and president often reached agreement—sometimes over the opposition of the Federation Council, whose members fought to protect regional prerogatives.

The 1999 election produced a Duma with a progovernment majority. President Putin and his government built a reliable base of support in the Duma from a coalition of four centrist political factions. The 2003 election gave the president a still wider margin of support in the Duma and an overwhelming majority for the United Russia party—which meant that the president no longer had to expend much effort in bargaining with the Duma to win its support for his policies. Likewise, the Fifth Duma, elected in December 2007, and the Sixth, elected in December 2011, were also dominated by the United Russia party and gave loyal support to the Putin–Medvedev team.

Although the level of voting discipline within the majority party is similar to that in a Westminster-style parliament, as is the practice of reliably supporting the government's initiatives, the relationship between the Duma and the government is quite different. In a Westminster-type setting, parliament and government have mutually offsetting powers. If a government loses its majority in parliament, it must face the voters in a new election. Majority members of parliament would prefer to hold onto their seats as long as possible, and vote for the government's proposals so as to avoid a parliamentary dissolution and new election. By the same token, the government is usually unwilling to face a revolt on the floor of Parliament and the possible loss of its majority. Thus, the government and the majority party need each other. In Russia, the parliamentary deputies have almost no political resources outside the dominant party, United Russia, which is controlled by the presidential administration and government. The parliamentary deputies in the party cannot counterbalance the executive. A deputy who defies party discipline can be expelled (and lose his or her seat), and so has very few alternatives. If, in the future, a major shift in the alignment of political forces in society occurred, however, it could lead to a different relationship between executive and legislative power.

The Judiciary and Law Enforcement

The major institutional actors in the legal system are the **procuracy**, the courts (judiciary), and the bar. Each has undergone substantial change in the post-communist period.

The Procuracy Russia's legal system traditionally vested a great deal of power in the procuracy, which is considered to be the most prestigious branch of the legal system. The procuracy is comparable to the system of federal and state prosecuting attorneys in the United States, but has more wide-ranging responsibilities and is organized as a centralized hierarchy headed by the procurator-general. The procuracy is charged with fighting crime, corruption, and abuses of power in the bureaucracy. It seeks to ensure that all state officials and public organizations observe the law. It investigates criminal charges and prosecutes cases in court. The procuracy has traditionally been the principal check on abuses of power by state officials. But it is inadequately equipped to meet the sweeping responsibilities assigned to it, because of the difficulty of effectively supervising the vast state bureaucracy. Although the procuracy is nominally independent of the executive, the president names the procurator-general (subject to confirmation by the Federation Council) and informally supervises any politically significant cases.

The Judiciary In contrast to the influence that the procuracy has traditionally wielded in Russia, the bench has been relatively weak. Trial judges are usually the least experienced and lowest paid members of the legal profession—and the most vulnerable to external political and administrative pressure. In a few instances, judges have been murdered when they attempted to take on organized crime. Many judges have left their positions to take higher-paying jobs in other branches of the legal profession, and caseloads have risen substantially.

State officials pay lip service to the principle of judicial independence, but often violate it in practice by pressuring judges to render particular judgments in politically sensitive cases. At the same time, many reforms since the end of communism are intended to make the administration of justice more effective, and some increase the rights of defendants in criminal cases. For example, in the 1990s, trial by jury in major criminal cases was introduced in several regions on an experimental basis and since then has spread throughout the country in serious criminal cases. The goal of adopting the jury system was to make the judicial system more adversarial, so that the prosecution and the defense have equal status in the courtroom and the judge becomes a neutral arbiter between them.[10] In a number of high-profile cases, juries have acquitted defendants when they found the procuracy's case unconvincing.

The Russian judiciary is a unitary hierarchy. All courts of general jurisdiction are federal courts. There are also other specialized types of courts in addition to federal courts of general jurisdiction—among them, the commercial courts, the constitutional courts of the ethnic republics, the local municipal courts (equivalent to justices of the peace), and the military courts. Most criminal trials are held in district and city courts of general jurisdiction, which have original jurisdiction in most criminal proceedings. Higher-level courts, including regional and republic-level courts, hear appeals from lower courts and have original jurisdiction in certain cases. At the pinnacle of the hierarchy of courts of general jurisdiction is the Russian Supreme Court, which hears cases referred from lower courts and also issues instructions to lower courts on judicial matters. The Supreme Court does not have the power to challenge the constitutionality of laws and other official actions of legislative and executive bodies. The constitution assigns that power to the Constitutional Court. Under the constitution, the judges of the Supreme Court are nominated by the president and confirmed by the Federation Council.

There is a similar hierarchy of courts hearing cases arising from civil disputes between firms or between firms and the government called **commercial courts (*arbitrazhnye sudy*)**. Like the Supreme Court, the Supreme Commercial Court is both the highest appellate court for its system of courts and the source of instruction and direction to lower commercial courts. As with the Supreme Court, the judges of the Supreme Commercial Court are nominated by the president and confirmed by the Federation Council. In recent years, the Supreme Commercial Court has handed down a number of major decisions that clarify the rules of the market economy.

The Ministry of Justice oversees the court system and provides for its material and administrative needs. Its influence over the legal system is limited, however, because it lacks any direct authority over the procuracy.

The Bar Attorneys who represent individual citizens and organizations in both criminal and civil matters are called advocates (*advokaty*). They are comparable to barristers in Great Britain and litigating attorneys in the United States. Their role has expanded considerably with the spread of the market economy. They enjoy some autonomy through their self-governing associations, through which they elect officers and govern admission of new practitioners. In recent years, the stature and visibility of advocates have risen significantly. Private law firms are proliferating. The profession is attractive for the opportunities it provides to earn high incomes. A number of lawyers have become celebrities by taking on high-profile cases.

The Constitutional Court One of the most important reforms in postcommunist Russia's legal system is the establishment of a court for constitutional review of the official acts of government. The **Constitutional Court** has authority to interpret the constitution in a variety of areas. It has ruled on several ambiguous questions relating to parliamentary procedure. It has overturned some laws passed by national republics within Russia and has struck down several provisions of the Russian Criminal Code that limited individual rights. In 2013, it issued a significant ruling allowing individual voters to protest abuses of election law in their precincts (previously, the courts had held that only candidates and parties had the right to appeal in the case of alleged election fraud). Often, in disputes between individuals and state authorities, the court finds in favor of individuals, thus reaffirming the sphere of individual legal rights. It has consistently upheld the sovereignty of the federal constitution over regional governments.

However, in cases concerning the vast domain of presidential authority, the court usually defers to the president. One of its first and most important decisions in the 1990s concerned a challenge brought by a group of Communist parliamentarians to President Yeltsin's decrees launching the war in Chechnia. The court ruled that the president had the authority to wage the war through the use of his constitutional power to issue decrees with the force of law. In other, less highly charged issues, the court established legal limits to the president's authority. For instance, the court ruled that Yeltsin could not refuse to sign a law after parliament had overridden his veto. Since Putin took office in 2000, however, the court has taken care to avoid crossing the president. Nevertheless, even the possibility that it might exert a measure of independent political influence led Putin to move the seat of the court to St. Petersburg in 2008. This was probably intended as a means to marginalize it politically by removing it from the network of powerful elites in Moscow.

Central Government and the Regions

Following the breakup of the Soviet Union, many Russians feared that Russia would also dissolve into a patchwork of independent fiefdoms. Certainly, Russia's territorial integrity was subjected to serious strains. Under President Yeltsin, the central government granted wide autonomy to regional governments in return for political support. Yeltsin went so far as to sign a series of bilateral treaties with individual regions to codify the respective rights and responsibilities of the federal government and the given regional governments. Under Putin, however, the pendulum of federal policy swung back sharply toward centralization.

The demographic factor is one reason Russia did not break up. Eighty percent of Russia's population is ethnically Russian. None of its ethnic minorities accounts for more than 4 percent of the total (the Tatars form the largest of the ethnic minorities, constituting about 5.3 million of Russia's total population of 143 million). Rebuilding national community in post-Soviet Russia has been helped by Russia's thousand-year history of statehood. Yet, until 1991, Russia was never constituted as a nation-state: Under the tsars, it was a multinational empire, and under Soviet rule, it was nominally a federal union of socialist republics. State policy toward nationality has also varied over the centuries. In some periods, Russia recognized a variety of self-governing ethnic-national communities and tolerated cultural differences among them. In other periods, the state pressured non-Russian groups to assimilate to Russian culture.

Russia was formally established as a federal republic under the Soviet regime. In contrast to the Soviet Union, of which it was the largest component, only some of Russia's constituent units were ethnic-national territories formally recognizing and representing particular nationalities.[11] The rest were pure administrative subdivisions, populated mainly by Russians. The non-Russian ethnic-national territories were classified by size and status into autonomous republics, autonomous provinces, and national districts. In many of them, the indigenous ethnic group constituted a minority of the population. As of 2013, Russia comprises eighty-three constituent territorial units, officially termed "subjects of the federation." They represent six different types of units. Republics, autonomous districts (all but one of them located within other units), and the one autonomous *oblast* give formal political representation to ethnic minorities; *oblasts* (provinces), *krais* (territories), and two cities of federal status (Moscow and St. Petersburg) are treated as ordinary administrative subdivisions with no special constitutional status.

One of the centralizing measures President Putin pursued is the merger of smaller ethnic territories into larger surrounding units. In most of these cases, the smaller ethnic district was impoverished and hoped for better living standards by becoming part of a consolidated territory.[12] The mergers also reduced the patronage rights and political voice that came with an ethnic district's status as a constituent unit of the federation.[13] After the initial wave of mergers in the mid-2000s, however, no more have followed.

The ethnic republics jealously guard their special status. From 1990 to 1992, all the republics adopted declarations of sovereignty, and two made attempts to declare full or partial independence from Russia. Only one, however, **Chechnia (the Chechen Republic)**, resorted to arms to back up its claim. Chechnia is one of a belt of predominantly Muslim ethnic republics

Ramzan Kadyrov, President of the Chechen Republic
Kadyrov has established an autocratic, personalistic form of rule in Chechnia.

in the mountainous region of the North Caucasus, between the Black and Caspian seas. Chechnia's president declared independence from Russia in 1991, an act Russia refused to recognize but did not initially attempt to overturn by force. When negotiations failed, however, in December 1994, Russian forces attacked the republic directly, subjecting its capital city, Groznyi, to devastating bombardment. This forced tens of thousands of Chechen and Russian residents to flee and led to a protracted, destructive war. Fighting ceased in the summer of 1996, but resumed in 1999. Federal forces had established control over most parts of Chechnia by early 2000, but Chechen guerrillas have continued to carry out sporadic ambushes and suicide attacks against federal units.

In the mid-1990s, a radical fundamentalist form of Islam replaced national independence as the guiding ideology of the Chechen rebel movement. The guerrillas have resorted to terrorist attacks, including suicide terrorism, against civilian targets both in the North Caucasus region and in Moscow. One of the most shocking of these incidents was the seizure of a school in the town of Beslan, near Chechnia, in September 2004 (see Box 12.3). The brutal methods used by federal forces to suppress the uprising have fueled continuing hatred of the federal government on the part of many Chechens, which, in turn, facilitates recruitment by the terrorists. With time, order in Chechnia has been restored by the rule of its authoritarian president, Ramzan Kadyrov. Much of Groznyi has been rebuilt. Attacks and reprisals continue to occur occasionally, however, especially in ethnic republics neighboring Chechnia. And throughout the North Caucasus region, unemployment and social dislocation are severe, creating a favorable milieu for religiously inspired violence, which has sometimes spilled out beyond the borders of the North Caucasus and of Russia itself.[14]

Chechnia, fortunately, was an exceptional case. For the other twenty ethnic republics, Moscow reached an accommodation granting the republics a certain amount of autonomy in return for acceptance of Russia's sovereign power. All twenty-one ethnic republics have the constitutional right to determine their own form of state power so long as their decisions do not contradict federal law. Eight have presidencies, and another thirteen have an equivalent position called "head of republic." In many cases, the republic leaders have constructed personal power bases around appeals to ethnic solidarity and the cultural autonomy of the indigenous nationality. Often, they have used this power to establish personalistic dictatorships in their regions. Moscow tolerates such political machines so long as the leaders are loyal and maintain stability.

President Putin made clear his intention to reassert the federal government's authority over the regions. The reform of the Federation Council in 2000 was one step in this direction. Another was Putin's decree of May 13, 2000, which created seven new "federal districts." He appointed a special presidential representative to each district who monitors the actions of the regional governments within that district. This reform sought to strengthen central control over the

---

BOX 12.3   Beslan

September 1 is the first day of school each year throughout Russia. Children, accompanied by their parents, often come to school bringing flowers to their teachers. A group organized by the Chechen warlord Shamil Basaev chose September 1, 2004, to carry out a horrific attack. A group of heavily armed militants stormed a school in the town of Beslan, located in the republic of North Ossetia, next door to Chechnia. They took over 1,000 schoolchildren, parents, and teachers hostage. The terrorists crowded the captives into the school gymnasium, which they filled with explosives to prevent any rescue attempt. The terrorists refused to allow water and food to be brought into the school. Negotiations over the release of the hostages failed.

On the third day of the siege, something triggered the detonation of one of the bombs inside the school. In the chaos that followed, many of the children and adults rushed to escape. The terrorists fired at them. Federal forces stormed the school, trying to rescue the escaping hostages and kill the terrorists. Many of the bombs planted by the terrorists exploded. Ultimately, about 350 of the hostages died, along with most of the terrorists.

The media covered the events extensively. The Beslan tragedy had an impact on Russian national consciousness comparable to that of September 11 in the United States. While there had been a number of previous attacks tied to Chechen terrorists, none had cost so many innocent lives.

Putin claimed that the terrorists were part of an international terrorist movement aimed ultimately at the dismemberment of Russia itself and avoided linking the incident to Russian policy in Chechnia. In response to the crisis, Putin called for measures to reinforce national security. He also demanded increased centralization of executive power, including an end to the direct election of governors. Most observers assumed that Putin had wanted to make these changes anyway and that the Beslan tragedy simply gave him a political opening to enact them. Beslan was a tragic indication that the insurgency that began in Chechnia has spread throughout the North Caucasus region.

activity of federal bodies in the regions. Often, in the past, local branches of federal agencies had fallen under the influence of powerful governors.

Still another important centralizing measure was the abolition of direct popular election of governors, including the presidents of the ethnic republics. Before 2005, regional chief executives were chosen by direct popular election. Since 2005, however, the president has nominated a candidate, who must then be approved by the regional legislature (no legislature has dared to oppose a presidential appointment). Many Russians supported this change, believing that the institution of local elections had been discredited by corruption and fraud and that elections were more often determined by the influence of wealthy insiders than by public opinion. Critics of the reform accused Putin of creating a hypercentralized, authoritarian system of rule. Putin clearly hoped that appointed governors would be more accountable and effective, but the reform turned out to have disadvantages because the appointed governors often had less political authority in the region than elected ones. As a result, Putin has proposed returning to an elected model, but with features ensuring that the president can control the outcome. As is so often the case, constitutional arrangements are adjusted and readjusted by the leaders in order to solve short-term political problems.

Below the tier of regional governments are units that are supposed to enjoy the right of self-government—municipalities and other local government units. The right of local self-government has been given to a large set of units—such as urban and rural districts and small settlements—raising the total number of local self-governing units to 24,000. In principle, local self-government is supposed to permit substantial policymaking autonomy in the spheres of housing, utilities, and social services (and to reduce the federal government's burden in providing such services). However, the law provides no fixed, independent sources of revenue for these local entities. They thus depend for the great majority of their budget revenues on the regional governments. For their part, the regional governments resist allowing local governments to exercise any significant powers of their own. In many cases, the mayors of the capital cities of regions are political rivals of the governors of the regions. Moscow and St. Petersburg are exceptional cases because they have the status of federal territorial subjects like republics and regions. Elsewhere, city

governments must bargain with their superior regional governments for shares of power. Moreover, the centralizing trend of the 2000s has extended to local government as more and more localities have replaced elected mayors with appointed ones or city managers.

Russia's postcommunist constitutional arrangements allow considerable room for the arbitrary exercise of power. Both Yeltsin and Putin interpreted their presidential mandates broadly, and although President Putin repeatedly calls for adherence to the rule of law, he has also continued the practice of relying heavily on informal powers. Executives at lower levels, particularly in the regions, take similarly expansive views of their powers. But while Russia remains a long way from the ideal of the rule of law, the postcommunist regime has allowed far more open competition and consultation among organized social groups than did the communist regime. The limits of allowable debate and criticism are wider than in the Soviet era, and there is far more open articulation and aggregation of interests. At the same time, any organized political opposition to the regime is likely to meet with political repression. Moreover, since Putin returned to the presidency in 2012, repression of opposition groups has increased.

The actual operation of the constitutional arrangements originally established after the end of the communist regime depends on the balance of power in state and society. President Putin has eviscerated organized political opposition but tolerates a good deal of autonomous civic activity so long as it does not interfere with his power. Consistent with the pattern of "competitive authoritarianism," Putin's regime includes elements of democracy within a largely authoritarian framework. In this system, elections are held regularly, and a tame opposition is allowed a small, marginal role, while "extrasystemic" (i.e., uncontrolled) opposition is suppressed. The ruling authorities exercise substantial control over television and radio, although allowing much greater freedom to the print and Internet media. Business is given wide sway to pursue its economic interests but may not finance a political challenge to the authorities. Civil society organizations can offer policy proposals for debate. But elections are not a means for deciding who governs: The ruling authorities rarely allow elections to produce unplanned results. Moreover, corruption is rampant, and the state bureaucracy remains inefficient and poorly controlled. The centralization of power in the 2000s was more effective at pushing political opposition to the sidelines than at giving the authorities an effective way to control the bureaucracy.

Yeltsin and Putin used presidential power very differently without changing the formal rules of the constitution. Yeltsin ruled erratically and impulsively, but he respected certain limits on his power: He did not suppress media criticism, and he tolerated political opposition.[15] Faced with an opposition-led parliament, Yeltsin was willing to compromise with his opponents to enact legislation. However, Yeltsin grew dependent on a small group of favored **oligarchs** (business magnates with strong connections to government) for support and allowed them to accumulate massive fortunes and insider influence. Likewise, Yeltsin allowed regional bosses to flout federal authority with impunity because he found it less costly to accommodate them than to fight them. The loss of state capacity under Yeltsin illustrates one danger of an overcentralized political system. When the president does not effectively command the powers of the office, power drifts to other centers of power.

Putin's presidency illustrates the opposite danger. When Putin took over, he undertook to reverse the breakdown of political control and responsibility in the state. Although publicly he called for a system based on respect for the rule of law, he restored authoritarian methods of rule. And especially since his return to the presidency in 2012, he has cracked down harshly on political opposition. For example, in spring 2013, the procuracy and tax authorities conducted a sweeping inspection of NGOs. Some organizations receiving foreign funding—including human rights groups as well as respected public opinion research organizations—were accused of engaging in unauthorized political activity and required to reregister as "foreign agents" under the new and more repressive law on NGOs.

Russian Political Culture in the Post-Soviet Period

12.4 Discuss the contradictions within Russia's current political culture, focusing on the conflict between democratic and traditional Soviet values.

Russian political culture is the product of centuries of autocratic rule, war and terror in the 20th century, rapid but uneven improvement of educational and living standards, and exposure to Western standards of political life. The resulting contemporary political culture is a contradictory bundle of values: A sturdy core of belief in democratic values is accompanied by a firm belief in the importance of a strong state and a deep mistrust of most actual state institutions. Around three quarters of the population think that Russia should be a democratic country.[16] Majorities also say that party competition and elections are beneficial. At the same time, most accept that the state requires firm guidance by a capable president and give Putin credit for restoring order to the state. About as many people think Western-style democracy would be best for Russia as think that returning to a Soviet-style system would be best (28 percent vs. 27 percent).[17] Both short-term and long-term influences shape Russians' views about politics.

Generally, Russians judge political regimes according to their ability to provide stability, prosperity, and security. Many Russians cannot forgive Gorbachev and Yeltsin for pursuing policies that led to the breakup of the Soviet state, widespread poverty, the amassing of great wealth by a few individuals using unscrupulous methods, and the loss of status as a great world power. Some even believe that the ideals of democracy and the market economy represented misguided or malicious efforts to remold Russia along Western lines. The restoration of the state's power and prestige, therefore, is a criterion for judging the worth of democracy.

Democracy is also assessed by its ability to benefit individuals materially. Asked in a recent survey what freedoms were most important to them *personally*, over half the respondents named the "freedom to be protected by the state in case of illness, loss of work or poverty" and the "freedom to purchase what I want" as the most important; freedoms such as the right to vote for competing political parties or to participate in political demonstrations were named by only 13 percent and 10 percent, respectively.[18] Forty-six percent named the freedom to choose their job as being important to them personally, but only 30 percent named freedom of religion as personally important, while 38 percent named the freedom to acquire property such as real estate and a car as important.

This pragmatic view of democracy helps explain why many Russians praise Putin for strengthening democracy. Far from seeing "freedom" and "order" as necessary enemies, many recognize that freedom is only possible in an ordered society. But if forced to choose *between* freedom and order, Russians divide rather evenly. Based on extensive public opinion surveys, political scientist Henry Hale says that Russians support "delegative democracy." That is, they want a strong leader who has a great deal of power to deal with the country's problems, but who can be removed, is elected, and respects the rights of the opposition.[19] But as Hale points out, Russians do not have such a leader, because Putin has systematically eliminated constraints on his power.

We can understand these competing influences on Russian political culture when we consider the long-term forces shaping it, as well as the impact of recent history.

The reforms of the late 1980s and early 1990s raised expectations that Russia would enjoy a significant rise in living standards once it got rid of communism. The sharp fall in living standards that followed the collapse of the old regime dispelled any notion that changing that political and economic system could turn the country around overnight.

Another reason Russians take a conditional view of the value of democratic rights is the widespread view that political order is fragile, a view that the authorities have worked hard to keep alive. Russians have long been taught that a weakening of the internal cohesion of the state invites predation from outside powers, and many episodes of Russian history bear out this belief. The Putin leadership regards the wave of popular uprisings in the Arab world in 2011 not as broad movements for democracy but as further evidence that forcing dictators from office only invites disorder, violence, and even civil war—and more dictatorship. Many Russians agree. Asked what they consider the main internal threat facing Russia today, Russians expressed fear about political instability connected with political succession (16 percent), struggle among competing factions in power (12 percent), loss of control by the central government over the regions (9 percent), separatism in the North Caucasus (4 percent), and loss of control over the regions in the Far East located near China (4 percent).[20]

Surveys also show that citizens have little faith in most present-day political institutions, although, as Figure 12.4 shows, they have a good deal of confidence

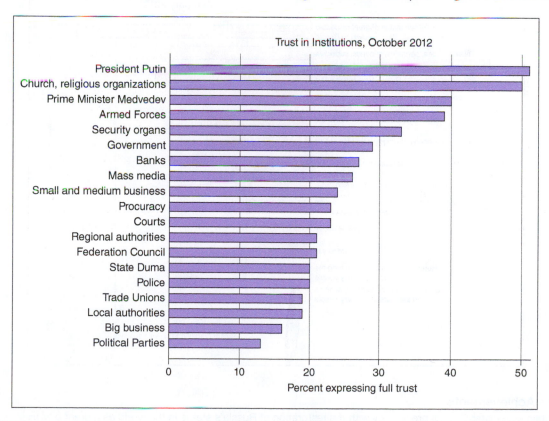

FIGURE 12.4

Political Trust

President Putin and the Church are the most highly-trusted institutions.

Source: Levada Center survey, October 2012. http://www.levada.ru/02-11-2012/doverie-institutam-vlasti Accessed May 6, 2013.

in the president and the Church. Confidence in elective bodies such as the parliament is low, and lowest of all in political parties. The great majority of Russians believe that they are not protected from arbitrary treatment by the state: Only a quarter of the population say that they feel any sense of protection from abuse at the hands of the police, courts, tax authorities, and other state structures.[21]

The concern with the strength of the state is also reflected in popular perceptions of Putin's achievements as president. Asked what Vladimir Putin has accomplished as president, the respondents gave highest marks to his efforts to restore the country's international stature and internal order (Figure 12.5).

The political culture thus combines contradictory elements. Russians do value democratic rights, but experience has taught them that under the banner of democracy, politicians can abuse their power to the detriment of the integrity of the state and the well-being of society. Russians also feel powerless to affect state policy. Little wonder that a leader such as Putin can command such widespread support despite the general mistrust Russians have for the post-Soviet political institutions. Russians see him as restoring order following a protracted period of social and political breakdown. As Richard Rose and his colleagues argue, the reason Russians generally approve of the Putin regime is not because they consider it to be ideal, but because it improved economic well-being, and, in any case, they see little prospect for changing it.[22]

Surveys also reveal considerable continuity with the past in support of the idea that the state should ensure society's prosperity and the citizens' material

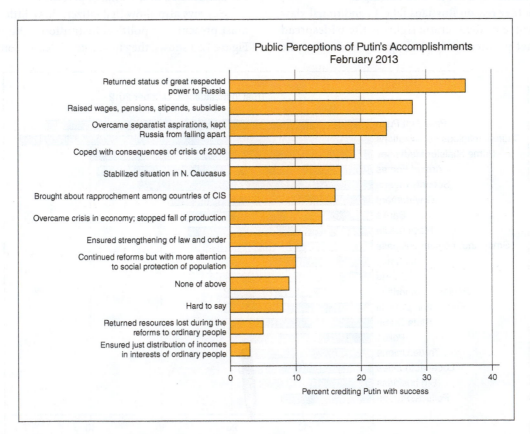

FIGURE 12.5

Putin's Achievements

The public associates Putin's presidency with the restoration of Russia's status in the world as a great power, improvements in living standards, and overcoming domestic crises.

Source: Levada Center, Survey February 2013 http://www.levada.ru/28-02-2013/god-so-dnya-prezidentskikh-vyborov-4-marta-2012-goda-otsenka-deyatelnosti-putina Accessed February 28, 2013.

security. About half the population would prefer an economy based on state planning and distribution, whereas only 36 percent would prefer one based on private property.[23] More so than citizens of Western Europe or the United States, Russians believe that the state is responsible for providing a just moral and social order, with justice being understood more as social equality than as equality before the law. This pattern reflects the lasting influence of traditional conceptions of state and society on Russian political culture. Still, few would support the reestablishment of Soviet rule or a reversion to a military dictatorship.

Political culture is also shaped by slower-acting but more lasting influences, including the succession of generations, rising educational levels, and urbanization. These changes are mutually reinforcing, as new generations of young people are exposed to fundamentally different influences than those to which their parents were exposed, while the older generations tend to have lower levels of education and less exposure to the more cosmopolitan way of life of cities.

Political Socialization

 12.5 Explain the roles of propaganda, the educational system, the church, and the media in political socialization in Russia.

The Soviet regime devoted enormous effort to political indoctrination and propaganda. The regime controlled the content of school curricula, mass media, popular culture, political education, and nearly every other channel by which values and attitudes were formed. The heart of Soviet doctrine was the Marxist belief that the way in which a society organizes economic production—feudalism, capitalism, socialism, and so forth—determines the structure of values and beliefs prevalent in the society. The idea was that the ruling class in each society determines the basic ideology of the society. Therefore, Soviet propaganda and indoctrination emphasized that Soviet citizens were part of a worldwide working-class movement to overthrow capitalism and replace it with socialism, in which there would be no private property. Needing to knit together a highly diverse multinational state, the Soviet regime downplayed national feeling and replaced it with a sense of patriotic loyalty to the Soviet state and to the working class's interests in the worldwide class struggle.

Today, the ideological content of Russian education has changed significantly, and there is much less overt political control over the formation of attitudes and values. In place of the idea of the class struggle and the international solidarity of the working class, textbooks stress love for the Russian national heritage and patriotic loyalty to the state. Historical figures who in the Communist era were honored as heroes of the struggle of ordinary people against feudal or capitalist masters are now held up as great representatives of Russia's national culture.[24] Patriotism and national pride are the key elements of the regime's effort to create a new sense of national community within the country's post-Soviet state boundaries.

The authorities are trying to impose a more consistent and uniform understanding of Russia's past in the schools. Putin has urged developing a single, agreed-upon history textbook for schools that would present a coherent conception of the tsarist, Soviet, and post-Soviet periods. It would emphasize the importance of the state in defending Russia from its enemies outside and inside and, rather than repudiating the Soviet past, build pride in the achievements of the Russian people in every era. Liberals object that the textbook would foster authoritarian values.

The authorities have also turned to the Orthodox Church as an aid in political socialization. They regard the Church as a valuable ally in building patriotism, national pride, and ethical values. The Church, in turn, seeks to protect its traditional status as Russia's state church, enabling it to block other Christian denominations from proselytizing in Russia. The Church would like a wider role, but the regime has been careful to acknowledge the rights of other religions that have had long-established followings in Russia (Muslims, Buddhists, and Jews) and not to turn the Orthodox Church into a state church. Recently, a new course was introduced into the fourth- and fifth-grade curriculums of schools, called "fundamentals of religious culture and ethics." Parents may choose among six different versions of the course, depending on which textbook is used: Orthodox Christian, Muslim, Buddhist, or Jewish, or one on world religions, or one on secular ethics. According to the Ministry of Education, by far the largest number of requests were for the secular ethics book, and only 20 percent of families requested the Orthodox Christian version.[25]

The Church's rising influence has prompted a backlash among many intellectuals, who criticize its hostility to liberal values (church leaders are deeply opposed to doctrines of individual freedom and of human rights). But many people, whether religious or not, also deplore the decay of morals in society and the relentless rise of consumerism and materialism as Russia opens itself to the global capitalist system. They see the Church, with its long history of partnership with the state, as a way of restoring traditional moral values in society.

In the 1990s, the regime generally respected media freedom. Under Putin, the authorities moved to set limits on the media (particularly television), but did not institute an elaborate political socialization system such as the Soviet state employed. Nevertheless, the authorities have used the media to build support for their foreign and domestic policies. The overall political line under Putin has been that Russia is rejecting both totalitarian communism and unbridled oligarchic capitalism, and is restoring the best traditions of Russia's political history. They praise democracy in general terms but insist that Russia must implement it in its own way.

Control over the media system is stratified. Television reaches almost everyone and is by far the most important source of news for the population. Accordingly, it is subjected to the tightest political control by the authorities, who give the editors of the main broadcast programs regular guidance on what to cover and what not to cover. Print media are allowed much more freedom, but they reach a far smaller audience, so they are of less immediate concern to the authorities. Nationally oriented business newspapers, such as *Kommersant* and *Vedomosti*, carry in-depth articles on public affairs, often publishing editorials quite critical of the government. For the most part, regional newspapers are closely controlled by the regional governments.

The Internet has remained relatively free of direct control, but, increasingly, the authorities are imposing restrictions on service providers.[26] Internet use has risen very rapidly, doubling in the last four years. Over half the adult population go online daily. Social media, including platforms that combine blogging with social networking, are extremely popular, especially among younger urbanites. (People who spend large numbers of hours online are often called "net hamsters.")[27] The social media have played a crucial role in enabling activists to mobilize large-scale demonstrations against election fraud in late 2011 and early 2012.

The impact of the social media can be seen in the sudden fame of particular bloggers. An example is a lawyer named Aleksei Naval'nyi, who has gained a large online following by blogging about corruption in government. When he called the dominant United Russia party "a party of thieves and swindlers," the phrase quickly caught on. Online searches for the phrase "party of thieves and swindlers" immediately returned United Russia's name. By April 2013, over half the respondents in a national survey agreed with the statement that United Russia was "a party of thieves and swindlers."[28] Needless to say, the authorities took umbrage and charged Naval'nyi with complicity in a scheme to embezzle funds from a timber company in 2009 (charges which had previously been investigated and dropped for lack of evidence). No one doubted that Naval'nyi was being prosecuted for daring to expose corruption among senior government officials.[29]

Although the authorities want to set limits on media freedom, they have not gone to the lengths of imposing a comprehensive system of political indoctrination, as the Soviet regime did. Aware of the stultifying effects of the old Soviet system of ideological control, the authorities' strategy is defensive, in that they want to limit access to the media by opposition forces.

Russian political socialization is therefore much less subject to direct state control than it was in the Soviet era. Of course, even then, awareness of the political and economic standards of the outside world filtered into the consciousness of the Soviet population. Today's authorities want to use schools and communications media to build loyalty to the state and its leaders, confidence in the future, and acceptance of a centralized regime, while at the same time spurring Russians to modernize the economy. At the same time, they want to prevent the media from being an arena of open political contestation.

Political Participation

12.6 Describe avenues of direct and indirect participation in Russian politics.

In a democracy, citizens take part in public life both through direct forms of political participation (such as voting, canvassing for a candidate, collecting signatures for a petition, demonstrating, and talking to officials) and through indirect forms of participation (such as holding membership in civic groups and in voluntary associations). Both kinds of participation influence the quality of government. By means of collective action, citizens signal to policymakers what they want government to do. Through these channels of participation, activists take on leadership roles. But, despite the legal equality of citizens in democracies, levels of participation in the population vary with differences across groups in resources, opportunities, and motivations. The better off and the better educated are disproportionately involved in political life everywhere, but the disproportion is much greater in some societies than others. And where deep inequality in the distribution of wealth and income reinforces differentials in political voice between rich and poor, democracy itself is at risk.

The Importance of Social Capital

A healthy fabric of voluntary associations has long been recognized as an important component of democracy. Participation in civic life builds social capital—reciprocal bonds of trust and obligation among citizens that facilitate collective action. Where social capital is abundant, people treat one another as equals, rather than as members of social hierarchies. They are more willing to cooperate in ways that benefit the society and improve the quality of government by sharing the burden of making government accountable and effective.[30] For example, where people feel less distance from and mistrust toward government, government and citizens can cooperate in improving the quality of governance. People are more willing to pay their taxes, so that government has more revenue to spend on public goods—and less ability and less incentive to divert it into politicians' pockets. The success of capitalism and democratic government rests on citizens' ability to cooperate for the common good.

In Russia, however, social capital has historically been sparse, compared with West European societies, and participation in civic activity has been extremely limited. Moreover, state and society have generally been separated by mutual mistrust and suspicion. State authorities have usually stood outside and above society, extracting what resources they needed from society but not cultivating ties of obligation to it. The Communist regime further depleted the stock of social capital by coopting

associations useful for the state and repressing those that threatened its interests. Therefore, social capital not only in Russia but also throughout the former Communist bloc is significantly lower than in other parts of the world.[31]

The weakness of intermediate associations linking political elites to ordinary citizens widens the felt distance between state and society. Thus, although Russians turn out to vote in elections in relatively high numbers, participation in organized forms of political activity is low. Opinion polls show that most people believe that their involvement in political activity is futile, and they have little confidence that they can influence government policy through their participation. Although there was an intense surge in political involvement in the late 1980s and early 1990s when controls over political expression and association were lifted, it ebbed substantially over the 1990s.

Membership in voluntary associations in contemporary Russia is extremely low. Only a small proportion of people—fewer than 8 percent—participate in voluntary organized public activity.[32] Many are purely nominal members of associations. For example, the great majority of Russian Orthodox believers are not members of a congregation, going to church only occasionally.[33] The same is true of trade union members. Most workers are enrolled in trade unions but tend to be inactive as members.[34]

One of the effects of the Putin era has been a demobilization of large sections of the population from public life. Although a sizable minority of the population—mainly educated urban groups—are actively interested in politics, most Russians report that they are "totally uninterested" in politics (20 percent) or "more uninterested than interested" (39 percent).[35] On the other hand, Russians do vote in high numbers in national elections—higher in fact than do their American counterparts.[36]

Moreover, Russians prize their right *not* to participate in politics. Today's low levels of political participation are a reflection of the low level of confidence in political institutions and the widespread view that ordinary people have little say in government. In the 2003 Duma elections, 4.7 percent of the voters expressed their dissatisfaction with the array of choices offered by checking the box marked "against all" on the party-list ballot.[37] But the authorities worried that this was too attractive a means of expressing disaffection and eliminated the option from later elections.

Elite Recruitment

Elite recruitment refers to the institutional processes in a society by which people gain access to positions of influence and responsibility. Elite recruitment is closely tied to political participation, because it is through participation in community activity that people take on leadership roles, learn civic skills (such as organization and persuasion), develop networks of friends and supporters, and become interested in pursuing political careers.

In the Soviet regime, the link between participation and elite recruitment was highly formalized. The Communist Party recruited the population into a variety of officially sponsored organizations—such as the Communist Party, youth leagues, trade unions, and women's associations. Through such organizations, the regime identified potential leaders and gave them experience in organizing group activity. The party reserved the right to approve appointments to any positions that carried high administrative responsibility or were likely to affect the formation of public attitudes. The system for recruiting, training, and appointing individuals for positions of leadership and responsibility in the regime was called the **nomenklatura** system. Those individuals who were approved for the positions on nomenklatura lists were informally called "the nomenklatura." Many citizens regarded them as the ruling class in Soviet society.

The democratizing reforms of the late 1980s and early 1990s made two important changes to the process of elite recruitment. First, the old nomenklatura system crumbled along with other Communist Party controls over society. Second, although most members of the old ruling elites adapted themselves to the new circumstances and stayed on in various official capacities, the wave of new informal organizations and popular elections brought many new people into elite positions. Today, the contemporary Russian political elite consists of a mixture of career types: those who worked their way up through the state bureaucracy and those who entered politics through other channels, such as elective politics or business.

Some of the old Soviet institutional mechanisms for recruitment are being restored. In the Communist regime, the party maintained schools to train political leaders, where rising officials received a combination of management education and political indoctrination. Today, most of those schools serve a similar function as academies for training civil servants and are overseen by the presidential administration. The authorities are working to systematize the selection and training of officials in order to ensure that a competent and politically reliable cadre is available for recruitment not only to state bureaucratic positions but even for management positions in major firms.[38]

There are two major differences between elite recruitment in the Communist regime and that in the present. The nomenklatura system of the Soviet regime ensured that in every walk of life, those who held positions of power and responsibility were approved by the party. They thus formed different sections of a single political elite and owed their positions to their political loyalty and usefulness. Today, however, there are multiple elites (political, business, professional, cultural, etc.), reflecting the greater degree of pluralism in post-Soviet society.

Second, there are multiple channels for recruitment to today's *political* elite. Many of its members come from positions in the federal and regional executive agencies. Putin relied heavily on the police (the regular police and the security services) and the military as sources of personnel for his senior-level appointments.[39] He also turned to colleagues he had worked with closely in St. Petersburg in the 1990s; an example is prime minister Dmitrii Medvedev. Medvedev has worked closely with Putin since 1990, when he became an advisor to Putin, who was serving as a deputy to the mayor. Medvedev then moved with Putin to Moscow in 1999, when Putin was made deputy head of the presidential administration under Yeltsin. Putin gave him ever broader responsibilities, first as head of the presidential administration and then as first deputy chairman of the government. This pattern of close patron–client relations, where a rising politician brings members of his "team" with him each time he moves up the career ladder, is a common feature of elite recruitment in Russia. One effect is to generate competition between rival groups of clients, sometimes called "clans." In Russia's case, there has been persistent behind-the-scenes rivalry between two such clans, both composed of associates of Putin. One is close to the security services, while the other, with a slightly more liberal cast, is made up of trained lawyers. When Putin chose Medvedev as his anointed successor, it was seen as a serious blow against the first group.

In the early years of the transition, many old-guard bureaucrats discovered ways to cash in on their political contacts and get rich quickly. Money from the Communist Party found its way into the establishment of many new business ventures, including several of the first commercial banks. Insiders took advantage of their contacts to obtain business licenses, office space, and exclusive contracts with little difficulty. Some bought (at bargain basement prices) controlling interests in state firms that were undergoing privatization and, a few years later, became millionaires.

Today's business elite still is closely tied to the state, both because state officials keep business on a short leash and because business provides material and political benefits to officials. In some cases, bureaucratic factions form around particular enterprises and industries such as the oil or gas industry. Businesses need licenses, permits, contracts, exemptions, and other benefits from government. Political officials, in turn, need financial contributions to their campaigns, political support, favorable media coverage, and other benefits that business can provide. The close and collusive relations between many businesses and government officials nurture widespread corruption. In the 1990s, a small group of ultrawealthy entrepreneurs—"oligarchs"—took advantage of their links to Yeltsin's administration to acquire control of some of Russia's most valuable companies. Their rapacity fueled a public backlash that made it politically viable for Putin to suppress some of them and destroy their business empires. In the meantime, under Putin, a different set of tycoons—sometimes known as "friends of Putin"—benefitted from their associations with Putin to acquire control of important state or commercial assets. Typically, they use their insider positions to accumulate wealth and power rather than to increase the productivity of their companies.

Interest Articulation: Statism, Corporatism and Pluralism

12.7 Discuss the formation and activities of interest groups in post-Soviet Russia, with specific examples.

The political and economic changes of the last two decades in Russia have had a powerful impact on the way social interests are organized. A diverse spectrum of interest associations has developed. The pattern of interest articulation, however, reflects the powerful impact of state control over society, as well as the sharp disparities in wealth and power that formed during the transition period. A few organizations have considerable influence in policymaking, while other groups have little. The system of interest groups in Russia reflects elements of all three of the major types of interest group systems—controlled, neocorporatist, and pluralist. However, under Putin, state control has become the dominant pattern in regime relations with social groups.

The Communist regime did not tolerate the open pursuit of any interests except those authorized by the state. Interest organizations—such as trade unions, youth groups, professional societies, and the like—were closely supervised by the Communist Party. Glasnost' upset this state-controlled model of interest articulation by setting off an explosion of free expression. This, in turn, prompted new groups to form and to make political demands. It is hard today to imagine how profound the impact of glasnost' was on Soviet society. Almost overnight, it opened the floodgates to a growing stream of startling facts, ideas, disclosures, reappraisals, scandals, and sensations. In loosening the party's controls over communication sufficiently to encourage people to speak and write freely and openly, the regime also relinquished the controls that would have enabled it to rein in political expression when it went too far.

As people voiced their deep-felt demands and grievances, others recognized that they shared the same beliefs and values and made common cause with them, sometimes forming new, unofficial organizations. Therefore, one result of glasnost' was a wave of participation in "informal"—that is, unlicensed and uncontrolled—public associations. When the authorities tried to limit or prohibit such groups, they generated still more frustration and protest. Associations of all sorts formed, including groups dedicated to remembering the victims of Stalin's terror, ultranationalists who wanted to restore tsarism, and nationalist movements in many republics. The explosion of the nuclear reactor at Chernobyl in 1986 had a tremendous impact in stimulating the formation of environmental protest, linked closely to nationalist sentiment in Belarus and Ukraine.[40] The late 1980s and early 1990s were the heyday of interest group pluralism, as Communist Party control over interest articulation crumbled.

The end of the state's monopoly on productive property resulted in the formation of new interests, among them, those with a stake in the market economy. Now groups can form to represent a diversity of interests, compete for access to influence and resources, and define their own agendas. Currently, there are over 300,000 NGOs on the books, although fewer than 40 percent of these are active.[41] However, the number of citizens who take part in the activity of NGOs is very small; those few who do typically are active in multiple organizations.

Some NGOs are the successors of recognized associations of the old regime, such as official trade unions. Often, these groups cling to their inherited organizational assets and continue to seek "insider" access to the state. Other groups sprang up during the glasnost' period or later, but must cooperate with local authorities in order to gain access to meeting places and media attention. All face an increasingly restrictive political climate under Putin.

Putin's approach to NGOs has been to combine repression and cooptation. That is, groups willing to accept political limits on their autonomy have been allowed to operate. Groups that seek to preserve their independence from the regime find it difficult to survive, especially if their activity involves defending human rights, free elections, and other causes that the regime considers to be political. New legislation requires that groups that accept foreign funding must register as "foreign agents," a term that is as pejorative in Russian as it is in English. Several groups that worked to defend human rights and to monitor elections, and had received foreign funding, have been threatened with prosecution for refusing to declare themselves to be "foreign agents." Even the reputable and independent Levada Center for public opinion research—the source of most of the survey figures cited in this chapter—has been told to reregister as a "foreign agent" because it has done survey research on contract to foreign companies.

On the other hand, the regime has also sought to reward those NGOs that are willing to play by its rules. The Public Chamber is a case in point. This is a state-run advisory body whose members are representatives of regime-friendly NGOs. The Public Chamber has been careful not to challenge the regime head-on, but does serve to some extent as a channel of communication between the public and the authorities. Similar chambers have been created in many regions.

Another clear illustration of cooptation is the use of government funds ($350 million in 2011) to give grants to NGOs through a nominally competitive application process. However, the selection process is not transparent, and the bulk of the funds wind up going to Moscow-based organizations that are close to the Kremlin.[42]

The system of interest group relations with the government is not fully corporatist and not fully controlled. Elements of pluralism remain. But under Putin, interest articulation has grown more controlled as the regime narrows the limits of autonomous activity.

Let us consider three examples of associational groups: the **Russian Union of Industrialists and Entrepreneurs (RUIE)**, the **League of Committees of Soldiers' Mothers**, and the **Federation of Independent Trade Unions of Russia (FITUR)**. They illustrate different strategies for organization and influence and different relationships to the state.

The Russian Union of Industrialists and Entrepreneurs

Most formerly state-owned industrial firms are now wholly or partly privately owned. Most industrial firms participate in a competitive market (and increasingly globalized) economic environment. Under the socialist regime, managers were told to fulfill the plan regardless of cost or quality. Profit was not a relevant consideration.[43] Now most managers seek to maximize profits and increase the value of their firms. Although many still demand subsidies and protection from the state, more and more want an environment where laws and contracts are enforced by the state, regulation is reasonable and honest, taxes are fair (and low), and barriers to foreign trade are minimized. These changes are visible in the political interests of the association that represents the interests of big business in Russia, the Russian Union of Industrialists and Entrepreneurs (RUIE). The RUIE is the single most powerful organized interest group in Russia. Its membership comprises both the old state industrial firms (now mostly private or quasi-private) and new private firms and conglomerates.

In the early 1990s, the RUIE's lobbying efforts were aimed at winning continued state support of industrial firms, but, with time, it has become the leading voice of big business in the market system. The RUIE helps broker agreements between business and labor and is a source of policy advice for government and parliament. All the major industrial firms belong to the RUIE and do much of their lobbying through it. Of course, on matters that concern individual firms, firms still seek to influence policy on their own.

Over time, the RUIE's role has changed according to the opportunities and limits set by the state authorities. It has expanded its in-house capacity for working with the government in drafting legislation. On a number of policy issues, such as tax law, pension policy, bankruptcy legislation, regulation of the securities market, and the terms of Russia's entry to the World Trade Organization, the RUIE has been active and influential. For the most part, it works behind the scenes to lobby for its interests, but, occasionally,

if it feels its voice has been ignored, it applies pressure more publicly.

Yet the limits of RUIE's power as the collective voice of big business are clear. When the Putin regime began its campaign to destroy the Yukos oil firm starting in July 2003 (see Box 12.4), the RUIE confined itself to mild expressions of concern. Its members, evidently fearful of crossing Putin, chose not to defend Yukos' head, Mikhail Khodorkovsky, or to protest the use of police methods to destroy one of Russia's largest oil companies. Instead, they promised to meet their tax obligations and to do more to help the country fight poverty. Perhaps if big business had taken a strong and united stand, they could have influenced state policy. But the desire of each individual firm to maintain friendly relations with the government and the fear of government reprisals undercut big business's capacity for collective action.

BOX 12.4 · Mikhail Khodorkovsky and the Yukos Affair

One of the most widely publicized episodes of the Putin era was the state takeover of the powerful private oil company, Yukos, and the criminal prosecution of its head, Mikhail Khodorkovsky. At the time of his arrest in October 2003, Khodorkovsky was the wealthiest of Russia's new postcommunist magnates. His career began in the late 1980s when he started a bank. Later, he acquired—at a bargain basement price—80 percent of the shares of the Yukos oil company when the government privatized it. At first, Khodorkovsky sought to squeeze maximum profit from the firm by stripping its assets. Soon his business strategy changed, and he began to invest in the firm's productive capacity. He made Yukos the most dynamic of Russia's oil companies. As he improved the efficiency and transparency of the firm, the share prices rose and, with them, Khodorkovsky's own net worth. At its peak in 2002, the company's assets were estimated at about $20 billion, of which Khodorkovsky owned nearly $8 billion.

Looking to improve his public image, Khodorkovsky created a foundation and launched several charitable initiatives. He recruited distinguished international figures to his foundation's board. He became active in Russian politics, helping to fund political parties and sponsoring the election campaigns of several Duma deputies.

Critics accused him of wanting to control parliament and even of wanting to change the constitution to turn it into a parliamentary system. There was talk that he intended to seek the presidency.

By spring 2003, the Putin administration decided that Khodorkovsky and Yukos had grown too independent. In a series of actions, Khodorkovsky and several of his associates were arrested and charged with fraud, embezzlement, and tax evasion. In December 2003, the government sued the company for billions of dollars in back taxes and froze the company's bank accounts. When Yukos failed to pay the full tax bill, the government seized its main assets and auctioned them off to a firm that, three days later, sold them to the state-owned oil company, *Rosneft'*. In May 2004, Khodorkovsky was sentenced to nine years' imprisonment and sent to a prison camp in Siberia. In 2006, the last remnants of the company were forced into bankruptcy. In 2010, his jail term was extended until 2017 after he was convicted on new charges.

On December 20, 2013, President Putin freed Khodorkovsky from prison as part of a broad amnesty to honor the twentieth anniversary of the Constitution. The case underscored the authorities' willingness to manipulate the law for political purposes.

Mikhail Khodorkovsky after His Release from Prison, December 2013
Immediately after his release, Khodorkovsky flew to Germany and held a press conference.

The Committee of Soldiers' Mothers

The Soviet regime sponsored several official women's organizations, but these mainly served propaganda purposes. During the glasnost' period, a number of unofficial women's organizations sprang up. One such group was the Committee of Soldiers' Mothers. It formed in the spring of 1989 when some 300 women in Moscow rallied to protest the end of student deferments from military conscription. Their protest came hard on the heels of Gorbachev's withdrawal of Soviet forces from the decade-long war in Afghanistan, where over 13,000 Soviet troops were killed in bitter and demoralizing fighting. In response to the Soldiers' Mothers' actions, Gorbachev agreed to restore student deferments. Since then, the Soldiers' Mothers' movement has grown, with local branches forming in hundreds of cities. Their focus has expanded somewhat but remains centered on the problems of military service. The league presses the military to end the brutal hazing of recruits, which results in the deaths (in many cases by suicide) of hundreds of soldiers each year. The league also advises young men on how to avoid being conscripted.[44]

The onset of large-scale hostilities in Chechnia in 1994–1996 and 1999–2000 stimulated a new burst of activity by the league. It helped families locate soldiers who were missing in action or captured by the Chechen rebel forces. It sent missions to Chechnia to negotiate for the release of prisoners and to provide proper burial for the dead. It collected information about the actual scale of the war and of its casualties. It also continued to lobby for decent treatment of recruits. Through the 1990s, it became one of the most sizeable and respected civic groups in Russia. It can call on a network of thousands of active volunteers for its work. These volunteers visit wounded soldiers in hospitals and help military authorities identify casualties. One of the movement's greatest assets is its members' moral authority as mothers defending the interests of their children. This stance makes it hard for their opponents to paint them as unpatriotic.

The Committee of Soldiers' Mothers plays both a public political role (for instance, it lobbied to liberalize the law on alternative civil service for conscientious objectors, and it fights for an end to the brutality in the treatment of servicemen[45]) and a role as service provider. Much of its effort is spent on helping soldiers and their families deal with their problems. It cooperates willingly with the Defense Ministry to help improve the lives of people serving in the armed forces.

It has been careful not to oppose military service or advocate pacifism.

Although the group enjoys a stable base of public support in Russia as well as widespread international recognition, it sometimes encounters hostility on the part of the authorities. Recently, for example, its St. Petersburg branch ran afoul of the authorities for receiving foreign funding.

The Federation of Independent Trade Unions of Russia

The Federation of Independent Trade Unions of Russia (FITUR) is the successor of the official trade union federation under the Soviet regime. Unlike the RUIE, however, it has poorly adapted itself to the postcommunist environment, even though it inherited substantial organizational resources from the old Soviet trade union organization. In the Soviet era, virtually every employed person belonged to a trade union. All branch and regional trade union organizations were part of a single labor federation, called the All-Union Central Council of Trade Unions. With the breakdown of the old regime, some of the member unions became independent, while other unions sprang up as independent bodies representing the interests of particular groups of workers. Nonetheless, the nucleus of the old official trade union organization survived in the form of the FITUR. It remains by far the largest trade union federation in Russia. Around 95 percent of all organized workers belong to unions that are, at least formally, members of the FITUR. The independent unions are much smaller. By comparison with big business, however, the labor movement is fragmented and poorly equipped to mobilize workers for collective action. The workers of as many as half of all enterprises do not belong to any union at all.[46]

The FITUR inherited valuable real estate assets from its Soviet-era predecessor organization, including thousands of office buildings, hotels, rest homes, hospitals, and children's camps. It also inherited the right to collect workers' contributions for the state social insurance fund. Control of this fund enabled the official trade unions to acquire enormous amounts of income-generating property over the years. These assets and income streams give leaders of the official unions considerable advantages in competing for members. But the FITUR no longer has centralized control over its regional and branch members. In the

1993 and 1995 parliamentary elections, for instance, member unions formed their own political alliances with parties. Thus, internal disunity is another major reason for the relative weakness of the FITUR as an organization. Much of its effort is expended in fighting independent unions to win a monopoly on representing workers in collective bargaining with employers, rather than in joining with other unions to defend the interests of workers generally.[47]

The ineffectiveness of the FITUR is also illustrated by the tepid response of organized labor to the severe deterioration in labor and social conditions in the 1990s. Unemployment rose to some 13 percent (very high given that it was essentially unknown under the communist regime), and even among employed workers, wage arrears were widespread. Surveys found that in any given year in the 1990s, three-quarters of all workers received their wages late at least once.[48] There were strikes—particularly among teachers—but far fewer than might have been expected given how dire the economic situation was. But, even when there were labor protests, in many cases, they were actually organized not by the unions but by governors seeking to pressure the central government for more money.[49]

Why are unions so weak? One reason is that many workers depend on the enterprises where they work for social benefits and guaranteed employment.[50] Another is the close relationship between the leadership of the FITUR and government authorities. As a result, it is very difficult for unions to mount protests. Workers generally feel unrepresented by their unions. While this situation would seem to favor the interests of business and the state, in fact, senior state leaders express some disquiet at how poorly organized the FITUR is; this means that neither business nor the state has a credible negotiating partner in dealing with issues concerning labor. As a result, the state fears the prospect that in a crisis, labor grievances could spread and become explosive, destabilizing the state.

New Sectors of Interest

Since the transition, many new associations have formed around the interests of new categories of actors. Bankers, political consultants, realtors, mayors of small cities, mayors of large cities, judges, attorneys, auditors, television broadcasters, political consultants, and numerous other professional and occupational groups have formed associations to seek favorable policies or set professional standards. Environmental groups, women's organizations, human rights activists, and many other cause-oriented groups have organized. Most of these operate in a particular locality, but a few have national scope. One of the most publicized movements is that of automobile owners, who have formed organizations in several cities to protest the abuse of privileges by VIPs (such as using flashing blue lights on top of their cars to cut through traffic jams).

The rise of the social media and the diversity of social interests have made it possible for many organizations to arise. Some have been able to mount protests, and many more have lobbied through the political process to defend their interests. As in other countries, interest organizations tend to favor the better educated and better connected. The Putin regime declares that it is in favor of a strong civil society. In fact, however, it has made it increasingly difficult for associations to operate freely.

The Dominant Party Regime

12.8 Examine the rise of the "party of power" in recent elections.

In most countries, political parties are the most important structure performing the vital task of interest aggregation—the process by which the infinite number of demands arising from society are pooled and sifted into a smaller number of policy choices. In a democracy, how well parties aggregate interests, define choices, and hold politicians accountable is of critical importance. In Russia, the party system has largely ceased to play the role of interest aggregation. Instead, it serves to mobilize support on the part of the public and the political elite for the incumbent rulers. As a result, the party system neither gives the voters meaningful choices over policy nor holds political officials accountable.

Although Russia's party system in the 1990s was fluid and fragmented, a clear structure emerged in the 2000s in which the United Russia party dominates and other parties are marginal. The reason that a dominant party regime arose is twofold. In the 1990s, parties were not anchored to defined social interests or associations, so that voters had little sense of attachment to

parties. Second, the Putin regime suppressed political competition and built up a single dominant party to represent its interests in elections and legislation.

Russians term a party that reflects the interests of the ruling elite and exercises a near-monopoly on power a "**party of power**." For politicians, the party is a vehicle for career advancement, while for the voters, it is the electoral face of the state. In the 1990s, there were several short-lived attempts to form parties of power, but in the 2000s, the United Russia party has become *the* unquestioned party of power. At the same time, the Kremlin also exercises influence over other parties in varying degrees, determining what political role each may play. Parties that refuse to play by the Kremlin's rules find it virtually impossible to operate. The Kremlin uses United Russia and other parties to secure its control over the State Duma and regional legislatures, to channel political competition into safe outlets, and to manage the careers of ambitious politicians—but not to subject itself to free elections.

Elections and Party Development

Table 12.1 indicates the official results of the party-list voting since 1993. The table groups parties into five categories that have characterized party identities since the early 1990s: *democratic* (those espousing liberal democratic principles), *leftist* (those advocating socialist and statist values), *centrist* (those mixing leftist and liberal democratic appeals), *nationalist* (those highlighting ethnic nationalism, patriotism, and imperialism), and *parties of power*.

Figure 12.6 shows how the election results translated into the distribution of seats in the Duma to various party factions following the 1999, 2003, 2007, and 2011 elections. Note how the spectrum of parliamentary parties has dwindled as United Russia has come to occupy a dominant position. It has been aided by some strategic engineering of the electoral system that has included tightening the rules for party registration, raising the threshold for representation from 5 percent to 7 percent, switching to an all-PR Duma, and prohibiting deputies from leaving their factions without losing their seats. Above all, the increasing use of electoral fraud to ensure overwhelming victories for United Russia has padded its margin. In the nearly twenty years since contested elections first were held, the party system has evolved from being one

TABLE 12.1
Party-List Vote in Duma Elections since 1993
Support for United Russia has grown at the expense of support for democratic, Communist, and nationalist parties.

Party	1993	1995	1999	2003	2007	2011
Democratic Parties						
Russia's Choice	15.5	3.9	—	—	—	—
Union of Rightist Forces (SPS)	—	—	8.5	4.0	0.9	—
Yabloko	7.8	6.8	5.9	4.3	1.5	3.43
Party of Russian Unity and Concord (PRES)	6.7	—	—	—	—	—
Democratic Party of Russia (DPR)	5.5	—	—	0.2	0.1	—
Right Cause	—	—	—	—	—	0.6
Centrist Parties						
Women of Russia	8.1	4.6	2.0	—	—	—
Civic Union[a]	1.9	1.6	—	—	—	—
Parties of Power						
Our Home Is Russia	—	10.1	1.2	—	—	—
Fatherland—All Russia (OVR)	—	—	13.3	—	—	—
Unity/United Russia[b]	—	—	23.3	38.2	64.3	49.3
A Just Russia	—	—	—	—	7.7	13.25
Nationalist Parties						
Liberal Democratic Party of Russia (LDPR)[c]	22.9	11.2	5.9	11.6	8.1	11.68
Congress of Russian Communities (KRO)[d]	—	4.3	0.6	—	—	—
Motherland (Rodina)	—	—	—	9.2	—	—
Patriots of Russia	—	—	—	—	—	.97
Leftist Parties						
Communist Party of the Russian Federation (CPRF)	12.4	22.3	24.2	12.8	11.5	19.2
Agrarian Party	7.9	3.8	—	3.6	2.3	—
Other parties failing to meet 5% threshold	10.9	26.8	12.5	11.1	2.1	—
Against all[e]	4.3	2.8	3.3	4.7	—	—

[a]In 1995 the same alliance renamed itself the Bloc of Trade Unionists and Industrialists.
[b]In 2003 Unity ran under the name United Russia, following a merger with the Fatherland party.
[c]In 1999 the LDPR party list was called the Zhirinovsky bloc.
[d]In 1999 this party was called Congress of Russian Communities and Yuri Boldyrev Movement.
[e]In 2007 and 2011 the "Against all" option was not available.

Source: Compiled by author from reports of Central Electoral Commission. See http://cikrf.ru.

with many weakly supported parties to an authoritarian dominant party system.[51]

From a Multiparty System to a Dominant Party Regime

A multiparty system began to develop with the elections, under Gorbachev, for the reformed Soviet and Russian Republic parliaments. Democratically oriented politicians coalesced to defeat Communist Party officials in the 1989 and 1990 elections and, once elected, formed legislative caucuses in parliament. There, they fought with Communist, nationalist, and agrarian groups. These parliamentary factions became the nuclei of political parties in the parliamentary election of December 1993.

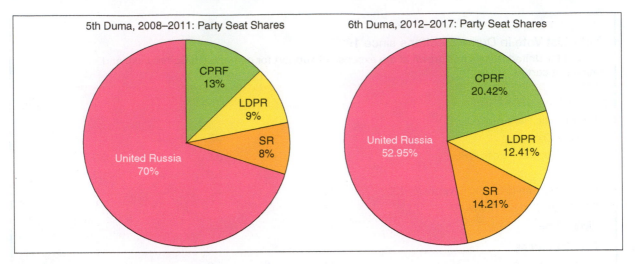

FIGURE 12.6

Duma Party Seat Shares

In the 6th Duma, United Russia's seat share fell back to a little over half.

Source: Compiled by author from reports of State Duma.

Polarization and the Party System Electoral contests in the late 1980s and early 1990s were aligned around two poles, one associated with Yeltsin and the forces pushing for democracy and a market economy, the other fighting to preserve the old system based on state ownership and control of the economy. Other parties positioned themselves in relation to these poles. For instance, Vladimir Zhirinovsky's nationalistic **Liberal Democratic Party of Russia (LDPR)** claimed to offer an alternative to both the democrats and the Communists, appealing to xenophobia, authoritarianism, and the nostalgia for empire. The party's unexpectedly strong showing in the 1993 election was a signal of widespread popular discontent with the Yeltsin economic reforms. Zhirinovsky has remained a durable figure in the political landscape ever since.

The main anchor of the left (statist and socialist) pole of the spectrum has been the Communists (**Communist Party of the Russian Federation [CPRF]**), who are the heirs of the old ruling CPSU and who espouse a mixture of communist and nationalist principles.

On the promarket and prodemocracy side of the spectrum have been several parties whose fortunes have fallen dramatically since the 1990s. One of these is *Yabloko*. Yabloko has consistently defended democratic principles and a social democratic policy in the economy and has opposed some of the policies pursued by Yeltsin and Putin that have sought to dismantle most of the old state supports and controls in the economy. It is no longer represented in the Duma because it has failed to attract enough votes to clear the 7 percent threshold.

Elections in the early to mid 1990s reflected the polarization between democrats and Communists, but also tended to produce a fragmented field of parties. In the 1993 and 1995 Duma elections, neither prodemocracy parties nor Communists won a clear majority, although democrats were in the minority, while Communists, nationalists, and their allies had a majority of seats. Except for a few parties (the CPRF, the LDPR, and Yabloko), most parties had shallow roots and tended to spring up shortly before elections. Many sought to avoid taking a clear programmatic stance, instead claiming to be "centrists" and pragmatists who would steer between the opposing poles of the democrats and Communists.

Presidential elections have not tended to stimulate party development as much as parliamentary elections have, because they have revolved more around the personalities of the candidates. When Boris Yeltsin ran for reelection in 1996, he started out with an approval rating in the single digits (at one point he even considered canceling the election), but ultimately he rallied his strength and succeeded in persuading voters that the election was about a choice between him and a return to communism. Yeltsin's displays of vigor during the campaign, his lavish promises to voters, and his domination of the media all contributed to a surge in popularity and a victory over Gennadii Ziuganov, his Communist rival.[52] The campaign took its toll on Yeltsin, however. Soon afterward he had major heart surgery, and for much of his second term, he was in poor health.

Building the Party of Power The 1999 election was dominated by the question of who would succeed Yeltsin as president. Many federal and regional officeholders wanted to rally around a new party of power in order to protect their jobs. A group of backroom Kremlin strategists formed a movement called Unity in the late summer of 1999. They wanted to create an electoral bloc that government officials throughout the country could rally around in the race for the Duma. They also intended it to serve as a political vehicle for Vladimir Putin, whom Yeltsin had just named prime minister and anointed as his successor. Conveniently for Putin, within days of Unity's formation and Putin's appointment, Chechen rebels launched raids into the neighboring region of Dagestan. Bombings of apartment buildings—officially blamed on Chechen terrorists—also occurred in Moscow and other cities. Putin's decisive handling of the military operations against the Chechen guerrillas gave him and the Unity movement a major boost in popularity. Unity, which had not even existed until late August, won 23 percent of the party-list vote in December.

The presidential election of 2000 occurred ahead of schedule, due to President Yeltsin's early resignation. Under the constitution, the prime minister automatically succeeds the president if the president leaves office early, but new elections must be held within three months. Accordingly, the presidential election was scheduled for March 26, 2000. The early election gave the front-runner and incumbent, Putin, an advantage, because he could capitalize on his popularity and the country's desire for continuity. Putin counted on the support of officeholders at all levels, a media campaign that presented a "presidential" image to the voters, and the voters' fear that change would only make life worse. His rivals, moreover, were weak. Several prominent politicians

prudently chose not to run against him. Putin's strategy worked brilliantly: He won an outright majority in the first round (Table 12.2 presents the results of the presidential elections from 2000 to 2012).

The 2003 and 2004 Elections Under Putin, the ideological divide between Communists and democrats that had marked the transition era nearly vanished. The political arena was dominated by the president and his supporters. The loyal pro-Putin party, Unity, was renamed United Russia after it absorbed a rival party, Fatherland. United Russia soon acquired a near monopoly in the party spectrum, squeezing other parties to the margins. A series of changes in the electoral law made it difficult for all but a few parties to compete in elections, while the Kremlin mounted a major effort to pressure regional governors and big business to back United Russia.

United Russia came to operate as a giant political machine, distributing political favors and material benefits to supporters, monopolizing decision making, and delivering reliable majorities in legislative assemblies. Nearly every regional legislature has a United Russia majority, and the vast majority of

---

TABLE 12.2
Russian Presidential Elections in the 2000s

Putin or Medvedev won in the first round by wide margins in each race.

	2000	2004	2008	2012
Vladimir Putin	52.9	71.3	—	63.6
Gennadii Ziuganov (CPRF)	29.2	—	17.7	17.8
Vladimir Zhirinovsky (LDPR)	2.7	—	9.3	6.2
Grigorii Yavlinskii (Yabloko)	5.8	—	—	—
Nikolai Kharitonov (CPRF)	—	13.7	—	—
Dmitrii Medvedev	—	—	70.2	—
Andrei Bogdanov (DPR)	—	—	1.3	—
Mikhail Prokhorov (independent)	—	—	—	7.89
Sergei Mironov (Just Russia)	—	—	—	3.85
Other	6.5	10.7	—	—
Against all candidates	1.8	3.4	—	—

CPRF: Communist Party of the Russian Federation; LDPR: Liberal Democratic Party of Russia; DPR: Democratic Party of Russia.

Note: The "Against all candidates" option was not available on the 2008 or 2012 ballot.

Vladimir Putin Inauguration, 2012
Vladimir Putin's inauguration as president for a third time was attended by many dignitaries, including the Patriarch of the Russian Orthodox Church.

governors belong to the party. Opposition parties control some seats in some regional and local assemblies and occasionally win a mayoral race. But, thanks to its close relationship to the presidential administration and seemingly unlimited access to media and organizational resources, United Russia occupies a place in the political system analogous to that of the Institutional Revolutionary Party (PRI) in Mexico during its long tenure in power, or that of other dominant parties in competitive authoritarian regimes.

The Kremlin's success in making United Russia the dominant party was demonstrated vividly in the 2003 parliamentary election. United Russia won 38 percent of the party-list vote and wound up with two-thirds of the seats in the Duma. The Communists lost almost half their vote share, and the democrats did even worse. For the first time, none of the democratic parties won seats on the party-list vote. The result underscored Putin's drive to eliminate any meaningful political opposition. Such an impressive showing for

United Russia assured Putin's reelection as president. The March 2004 race was a landslide. Putin won easily, with 71.3 percent of the vote, while his Communist rival received less than 14 percent of the vote. European observers commented that the elections were "well administered" but hardly constituted "a genuine democratic contest" in view of the president's overwhelming control of media coverage of the race and the absence of genuine competition.[53]

United Russia's dominance was confirmed in the 2007 Duma election. Shortly before the election, Putin declared that he would head the party's list (though he said he would not join the party and he did not intend to take his Duma seat).[54] This indicated that Putin intended to use the party as a basis for his power even after he left the presidency. Even though the Kremlin created a second party of power (called A Just Russia) as a mechanism to siphon off some votes on the left side of the spectrum and to offer an alternative outlet for some politicians who could not be accommodated in United Russia, United

Russia's overwhelming success was never in doubt, and it went on to win 64.3 percent of the vote. The authorities used a variety of methods to manipulate the election, ranging from grossly unequal access to the media for the parties to outright falsification of results in many regions (in some districts, the reported vote for United Russia was greater than 100 percent of the registered voters).[55]

Similarly, the authorities took no chances in the 2008 presidential election. They violated numerous election laws in order to guarantee the desired outcomes—for example, by disqualifying potentially serious opposition candidates, pouring money from the state budget into Medvedev's campaign, giving Medvedev disproportionate media coverage, and ignoring legal challenges over violations of the election law. Medvedev would probably have won in any case, but the large-scale manipulation of the election signaled that the authorities were in complete control of the succession. The authorities managed the outcome so successfully that Medvedev officially won over 70 percent of the vote—about 1 percentage point below Putin's reported margin in 2004.

The 2011–2012 Election Cycle The December 2011 parliamentary election saw the same four parties enter parliament. United Russia's official vote share fell somewhat, while that of the other parties rose somewhat. Overall, however, its dominant position— and that of the presidential team that controlled it— remained secure. And as in 2007–2008, widespread election fraud was used to produce the result the authorities desired.

In the 2012 presidential race the following March, Putin was back on the ballot, as were perennials Ziuganov (CPRF) and Zhirinovsky (LDPR). This time, the leader of the "A Just Russia" party, Sergei Mironov, also ran. There was also a newcomer, billionaire Mikhail Prokhorov (owner of, among other things, the New Jersey Nets). He offered a broadly probusiness platform but never directly criticized Putin, raising suspicions that the authorities were allowing him to run to draw off support from other candidates. In the end, he won almost 8 percent of the vote, according to the official results. Putin was declared to have won 63.6 percent.

In the 2011–2012 election cycle, the authorities again resorted to large-scale fraud to guarantee the outcome. This time, however, civic activists were prepared. They were able to document—sometimes even to record using smartphone cameras—numerous cases of election fraud. For example, in a technique called the "carousel," the authorities would drive a

Mikhail Prokhorov Campaigns for President, 2012
Billionaire Mikhail Prokhorov came in third, winning almost 8% of the vote.

busload of people around from one polling station to another to cast absentee ballots. (Independent election observers were often removed beforehand.) Another method was to set up special "temporary" polling stations that independent observers were not informed of beforehand. In some cases, someone would surreptitiously stuff large numbers of premarked ballots into a voting urn. Sometimes the fraud was even more direct: in tallying the numbers, election officials would systematically reduce vote totals for rival candidates and add them to United Russia or Putin's totals. And of course, as usual, media coverage and ballot access were highly skewed during the campaign. Independent estimates calculated that Putin's actual vote was probably 10 percent or more lower than the official total (but that he still probably won an outright majority in the first round), and that United Russia's actual total in December was closer to 34 percent nationally than to the officially reported 49 percent.[56]

The widespread procedural abuses prompted unprecedentedly large protests around the country after both the December 2011 Duma election and March 2012 presidential election. Three massive protests at the end of 2011 and early 2012 over election fraud revealed how widespread opposition was: The biggest demonstration in Moscow in early February 2012, in subzero temperatures, drew close to 100,000 participants. The protesters' demands focused on two main issues: fair elections and Putin's departure. Surprisingly, the authorities did not harass the demonstrators. Some observers spoke hopefully of a change to a freer and more open political system.

Since the first half of 2012, however, the protest movement has subsided. The authorities stepped up pressure on opposition forces, concocting criminal charges against leaders. Upon his return to power, Putin made it clear that he had no interest in dialogue with the opposition. The authorities also rallied conservative support for the regime by linking the opposition to foreign interests (a widely watched TV documentary accused opposition leaders of being paid agents of foreign security services) and by mobilizing popular resentment of urban intellectuals.[57]

In view of the lengths to which the authorities go to ensure victory for the United Russia party, it may seem surprising that members of the Putin team hold the party in low esteem. Some of them have been building up a kind of alternative movement, called the "All-Russian Popular Front," as a potential rival to United Russia. So far, they have treated the Popular Front as an organizational vehicle for various pro-regime social organizations, such as trade unions, rather than as a party. If Putin decides at some point to withdraw the Kremlin's life support from United Russia, he could well merge it into the Popular Front and create a new party of power. The constant tinkering with party organizations for short-term advantage underscores how weakly institutionalized Russia's party system is.

Nonetheless, the authorities appear wedded to the model of a dominant party regime, even if they are not committed to any particular dominant party. So long as United Russia remains the dominant party, the authorities' goal is to make it broadly appealing to all social strata rather than to a particular segment of society. As a result, social structure has become less and less significant as an influence on voting, while voters' attitudes toward the authorities in general and toward Putin in particular have become the most important predictor of voting preferences.

Although United Russia draws broadly from all parts of society, Table 12.3 shows that it does especially well among more conservative elements of the population—older people, less educated people, those with lower incomes, and women. Residents of Moscow and St. Petersburg are much less friendly to United Russia. Much of the party's support comes from its identification with Putin and the desire for stability. The party has relatively shallow roots in society. Putin and other Kremlin officials have warned the party that it cannot hope to rely on the Kremlin forever—though they are also unwilling to cut it loose.

Russia and the Resource Curse

12.9 Describe the interplay between political and economic restructuring in contemporary Russia.

The Transition from the Planned Economy

Russia's postcommunist transition was wrenching because the country had to remake both its *political*

TABLE 12.3
Social Support for Parties, Duma Election, December 2011

Voting behavior in Moscow and St. Petersburg differs significantly from the rest of the country—far fewer people report voting for United Russia. United Russia tends to draw disproportionately from among older people, women, and less educated people.

Party preference	United Russia	A Just Russia	LDPR	CPRF	Yabloko	Patriots	Right Cause	Did not vote or no answer	As share of sample
All:	40.2	5.8	4.1	9.6	1.4	0.2	0.2	38.5	100
Sex:									
Men	38.4	5.9	5.4	11.1	2.1	0	0.3	36.8	44.6
Women	44.7	5.7	3.1	8.4	0.9	0.4	0	36.8	55.4
Age group:									
18–29	26.3	4.1	5.3	5.2	1.8	0.4	0.2	56.7	24.8
30–39	41	3.6	5.4	2.6	1	0.1	0.3	46	17.9
40–49	45.2	3.4	3.9	10.6	1.1	0.2	0.3	35.3	16.7
50–59	46.1	9.5	4.3	10.2	1.2	0	0	28.7	18.2
60–	46.6	8.3	1.8	19	1.7	0.2	0.1	22.3	22.3
Education									
Elementary	49.4	2.4	0	8.4	0	0	0	39.8	2.2
Incomplete secondary	45.5	5.2	5.2	7.9	0	0	0	36.2	7.8
Secondary	40.6	4.9	4.6	7.3	1.4	2.6	0	38.6	21
Specialized secondary	38.3	6.5	3.2	10.2	1	0	1.5	39.3	36.5
Incomplete higher	29.4	3.2	3.2	8.9	2.4	1.2	0	51.7	6.7
Higher	43.2	6.5	5.4	11.6	2.5	0.2	0.5	30.1	24.9
Income level (rubles per month)									
<1000	41.7	4.2	2.1	10	0	0.4	0.4	41.2	6.5
10–20K	54.1	4.9	4.7	10.1	1.3	0.1	0	24.8	20.2
20–30K	43.7	6.7	2.9	0	1.8	0	0	44.9	18
30–40K	42.9	3.9	4.6	0.7	1.9	0.7	0.9	44.4	11.6
40–50K	32.2	4.4	3.7	0	1.5	0	0.7	57.5	7.3
> 50K	29.2	6.2	7	0	3.8	0	0	53.8	10.8
Metropolis residence/ not									
Rest of Russia	43.1	5.2	4	10.2	1	0.2	0	36.3	87.8
Moscow or St. Petersburg	21.2	9.8	4.7	5.7	4.5	0.4	0.8	52.9	13.2

(Note that figures should be read horizontally across the rows. For example, 44.7% of women voted for United Russia, but only 38.4% of men did so.)

Source: Data kindly provided by Henry Hale and Timothy J. Colton from the Russian Election Studies 2012. Survey conducted by the Moscow-based Demoscope survey firm. The survey is based on a multi-stage area probability sample designed to be nationally representative. N = April 1–May 18, 2012. Respondents were asked about their vote choices in the December 2011 Duma election.

and its *economic* institutions following the end of communism. The move to a market economy created opportunities for some and hardships for many more. Democratization opened the political system to the influence of groups that could organize to press for exclusive economic benefits for themselves. Many people who had modest but secure livelihoods under the Soviet regime were ruined by inflation and unemployment when the planned economy broke down. A smaller number took advantage of opportunities for entrepreneurship or exploited their connections with government to amass sizeable fortunes. One reason Vladimir Putin was so popular was that people gave him credit for restoring economic prosperity and cracking down on some of the tycoons who had amassed great fortunes by dubious means.

Stabilization   Russia pursued two major sets of economic reforms in the early 1990s: macroeconomic stabilization and privatization. Stabilization, which came to be called **shock therapy**, was intended to stop the country's financial meltdown. This required a painful dose of fiscal and monetary discipline by slashing government spending and squeezing the money supply. Such structural reform always lowers the standard of living in the short term for most of the population.

These reforms were not fully carried out. One reason was that those who benefited from the early steps to open the economy and privatize state assets exploited their privileged access to the authorities to lock in their own gains and to oppose any subsequent measures to expand competition. For example, officials who acquired ownership rights to monopoly enterprises then worked to shut out potential competitors from their markets. So did some state officials who benefited from collecting "fees" to issue licenses to importers and exporters or permits for doing business, and entrepreneurs whose firms dominated the market in their industry.[58] A fully competitive market system, with a level playing field for all, would have jeopardized their ability to profit from their privileged positions.

From Communism to Capitalism   Communist systems differed from other authoritarian regimes in ways that made their economic transitions more difficult. This was particularly true for the Soviet Union and its successor states. For one, the economic growth model followed by Stalin and his successors concentrated much production in large enterprises. This meant that many local governments were entirely dependent on the economic health of a single employer. The heavy commitment of resources to military production in the Soviet Union further complicated the task of reform in Russia, as did the

country's vast size. Rebuilding the decaying infrastructure of a country as large as Russia is staggeringly expensive.

The economic stabilization program began on January 2, 1992, when the government abolished most controls on prices, raised taxes, and cut government spending sharply. Almost immediately, opposition to the new program began to form. Economists and politicians took sides. The shock therapy program was an easy target for criticism, even though there was no consensus among critics about what the alternative should be. It became commonplace to say that the program was all shock and no therapy.

By cutting government spending, letting prices rise, and raising taxes, the stabilization program sought to create incentives for producers to increase output and find new niches in the marketplaces. But Russian producers did not initially respond by raising productivity. As a result, the population suffered from a sharp, sudden loss in purchasing power. People went hungry, bank savings vanished, and the economy fell into a protracted slump. Firms that were politically connected were able to survive by winning cheap credits and production orders from the government, which dampened any incentive for improving productivity. Desperate to raise operating revenues, the government borrowed heavily from the International Monetary Fund (IMF) and issued treasury bonds at ruinously high interest rates. IMF loans came with strings attached—the government pledged to cut spending further and step up tax collections as a condition of accepting IMF assistance, which fueled the depression further. Communists and nationalists got a rise out of audiences by depicting the government as the puppet of a malevolent, imperialist West.

Privatization   Stabilization was followed shortly afterward by the mass **privatization** of state firms. In contrast to the shock therapy program, privatization enjoyed considerable public support, at least at first. Privatization transfers legal title of state firms to private owners. Under the right conditions, private ownership of productive assets is efficient for society because, in a competitive environment, owners are motivated by an incentive to maximize their property's ability to produce a return. Under the privatization program, every Russian citizen received a voucher with a face value of 10,000 rubles (around $30 at the time). People were free to buy and sell vouchers, but they could be used only to acquire shares of stock in privatized enterprises or shares of mutual funds investing in privatized enterprises. The program sought to ensure that everyone became a property owner instantly. Politically, the program aimed to build support for the economic reforms by giving citizens a stake in the outcome of the market transition. Economically, the government hoped that privatization would eventually spur increases in productivity by creating meaningful property rights. Beginning in October 1992, the program distributed 148 million privatization vouchers to citizens. By June 30, 1994, when the program ended, some 40 million citizens had become, in theory, share owners. But these shares were often of no value, because they paid no dividends and shareholders exercised no voting rights in the companies.

The next phase of privatization auctioned off most remaining shares of state enterprises for cash. This phase was marked by a series of scandalous sweetheart deals in which banks owned by a small number of Russia's wealthiest tycoons wound up with title to some of Russia's most lucrative oil, gas, and metallurgy firms for bargain basement prices. The most notorious of these arrangements became known as the **loans for shares** scheme. It was devised in 1995 by a small group of business magnates with strong connections to government who persuaded Yeltsin to auction off management rights to controlling packages of shares in several major state-owned companies in return for loans to the government. If the government failed to repay the loans in a year's time, the shares would revert to the banks that made the loans. The government, as expected, defaulted on the loans, letting a small number of oligarchs acquire ownership of some of Russia's most valuable companies.[59]

Consequences of Privatization   On paper, privatization was a huge success. By 1996, privatized firms produced about 90 percent of industrial output, and about two-thirds of all large and medium-sized enterprises had been privatized.[60] In fact, however, the actual transfer of ownership rights was far less impressive than it appeared. For one thing, the dominant pattern was for managers to acquire large shareholdings of the firms they ran. As a result, management of many firms did not change. Moreover, many nominally private firms continued to be closely tied to state support, such as cheap state-subsidized loans and credits.[61]

The program allowed a great many unscrupulous wheeler-dealers to prey on the public through a variety of financial schemes. Many people lost all their savings by investing in investment funds that went bankrupt or turned out to be simple pyramid schemes. Privatization was carried out before the institutional framework of a market economy was in place. Markets for stocks, bonds, and commodities were small in scale and weakly regulated. The legal foundation for a market economy has gradually emerged, but only after much of the economy was already privatized. For much of the 1990s, the lack of liquidity in the economy meant that enterprises failed to pay their wages and taxes on time, trading with one another using barter.

The government fell into a debt trap. Unable to meet its obligations, it grew dependent on loans. As lenders saw that the government could not make good on its obligations, they demanded ever higher interest rates, deepening the trap. Ultimately, the bubble burst. In August 1998, the government declared a moratorium on its debts and let the ruble's value collapse against the dollar. Overnight, the ruble lost two-thirds of its value, and credit dried up.[62] The government bonds held by investors were almost worthless. The effects of the crash rippled through the economy. The sharp devaluation of the ruble made exports more competitive and gave an impetus to domestic producers, but also significantly lowered people's living standards.

As Table 12.4 shows, economic output in Russia fell for a decade before beginning to recover in 1999. The rise in the world prices for oil and gas in the 2000s brought a decade of steady growth from 1999 to 2008. As the economy revived, enterprises were able to pay off arrears in back wages and taxes. In turn, these taxes allowed government to meet its own obligations, thus allowing consumer demand for industry's products to rise, and so on. Living standards rose for all sections of the population and in most parts of the country.

The recovery was not due to a structural reform of the economy. There has been no substantial overhaul of the banking system, the structure of industry, or the institutional environment for entrepreneurship. The economy was vulnerable to the worldwide financial and economic crisis because of its dependence on exports of natural resources, which has only deepened under Putin: As of 2013, oil and gas generate about a quarter of Russia's GDP, half the central government's revenues and two-thirds of its exports.[63] President Putin has called for reducing the economy's reliance

TABLE 12.4
GDP and Inflation Growth in Russia, 1991–2012

Year	GDP	Inflation
1991	–5	160.4
1992	–14.5	2508.8
1993	–8.7	839.9
1994	–12.6	215.1
1995	–4.3	131.3
1996	–6	21.8
1997	0.4	11
1998	–11.6	84.4
1999	3.2	36.5
2000	7.6	20.2
2001	5	18.6
2002	4	15.1
2003	7.3	12
2004	7.1	11.7
2005	6.4	10.9
2006	7.4	9
2007	8.1	11.9
2008	5.6	13.3
2009	–7.9	8.8
2010	4	8.8
2011	4.3	6.1
2012	3.4	6.6

Note: GDP is measured in constant market prices. Inflation is measured as the percentage change in the consumer price index from December of one year to December of the next.

Source: Data drawn from Russian State Statistical Service (www.gks.ru).

on natural resource exports and increasing innovation. One means by which the leadership hopes to accomplish this is through a massive state-funded Russian version of "Silicon Valley" outside Moscow: a city devoted to high-tech research, education, and development of innovative start-up firms. Russia has attempted to interest Russian and international investors in the project. So far, there is little evidence that it has contributed to new commercially viable productive technologies. But the large-scale and poorly monitored flow of state funds has already produced a major corruption scandal. A senior official of the Skolkovo foundation has been charged with illegally paying a deputy in the Duma over 2 million rubles—some $750,000—for research and a series of lectures.[64]

Social Conditions Living standards fell sharply during the 1990s. A small minority became wealthy, and some households improved their lot modestly. Most people, however, suffered a net decline in living standards as a result of unemployment, lagging income, and nonpayment of wages and pensions.

Income inequality grew sharply both during the period of economic decline in the 1990s and during the period of economic recovery in the 2000s. This has been caused by many factors. In the 1990s, it was the result of the lag of wage increases behind price inflation, the sharp rise in unemployment, the deterioration of the pension and other social assistance systems, and the concentration of vast wealth in the hands of a small number of people. In the 2000s, poverty has decreased significantly, along with unemployment, and pension levels have risen. Yet inequality continues to rise as a result of large disparities in wage levels (two workers in the same occupation and in the same region might have widely different wages depending on the company), the extremely high earnings of managers in industries such as energy and finance, the different growth rates of different regions, the Putin regime's shift to a flat (13 percent) income tax, and abolition of estate taxes.

As a result of both government policy and current economic trends, therefore, economic prosperity is benefiting those at the upper end of income distribution much more than it is those at the lower end. This helps explain the sharp rise in the number of Russian billionaires (according to Forbes Magazine, Russia is second only to the United States in the number of billionaires, with China close behind).[65] Moreover, the actual level of income inequality is probably considerably greater than the official figure because of the large scale of unreported, "off-book" income.

The continuing rise in inequality and the absence of a growing middle class constitute a matter of some concern to Russian leaders. In his address to the State Council on February 8, 2008, President Putin declared that the current level of income inequality was "absolutely unacceptable" and should be reduced to more moderate levels; he called for measures that would bring about an expansion of the middle class. Its share of the population, he declared, should reach 60 or even 70 percent by 2020.[66]

An especially disturbing dimension of the social effects of transition has been the erosion of public health. Although public health had deteriorated in the late Communist period, the decline worsened after the regime changed. Mortality rates rose sharply after the transition, especially among males. Life expectancy for males in Russia is at a level comparable to that in poor and developing countries. Although male life expectancy has risen in recent years, the disparity between male and female mortality—enormous by world standards—reflects the higher rates of abuse of alcohol and tobacco among men. Other demographic indicators are equally grim. Rates of incidence of HIV and other infectious diseases, murders, suicides, drug addiction, and alcoholism are high.

Russia's leaders believe the demographic crisis poses a grave threat to the country's national security, both because of the growing shortage of labor in some regions (experts believe that there are 8–10 million illegal immigrants in Russia) and because of the army's inability to recruit enough healthy young men. Since 1991, Russia's population has fallen by 5 million people, over 3 percent of the population, due to an excess of deaths over births that is not offset by in-migration. Demographers estimate that Russia's population could fall by over one-third by 2050. President Putin has called for a series of measures to raise birth-rates, reduce mortality, and stimulate immigration. These have had a modest effect on raising birthrates.

Setting the country on a path of self-sustaining economic growth, where workers and investors are confident in their legal rights, requires a complete overhaul of the relationship of the state to the economy. The Soviet state used central planning to direct enterprises on what to produce and how to use resources. Much of the economy was geared to heavy industry and defense production, and government ministries directly administered each branch of the economy. The postcommunist state must have an entirely different relationship to the economy in order to stimulate growth. It must set clear rules for economic activity, regulate markets, enforce the law, supply public goods and services, and promote competition. Shifting

the structure of the state bureaucracy and the attitudes of state officials is a Herculean task.

We can get some idea of the legacy of the communist system, in the way the state was intertwined with the economy, by looking at the structure of the state budget. Figure 12.7 shows the breakdown of spending for the 2013 federal budget. Total spending was set at 11.6 trillion rubles, or about $374 billion. The share spent on national defense (at 9.4 percent) probably understates the actual amount, although it is rivaled by spending on national security and law enforcement. Over a third of the budget goes to social programs, with pensions taking up a huge and rising share of federal spending. Over 10 percent goes to support agriculture, transportation, manufacturing, and other economic interests.

The government recognizes that the revenues from oil and gas exports pose a serious danger of creating inflationary pressures in the economy. For this reason, like some other oil-rich states, Russia has created a "stabilization fund" that removes some of the revenues generated by high world energy prices from circulation when oil prices rise above a set threshold. This financial cushion allowed the government to cover its deficits as its revenues dropped and its social spending obligations rose when the 2008 financial crisis struck. The government drew down the fund heavily to subsidize big enterprises and banks.

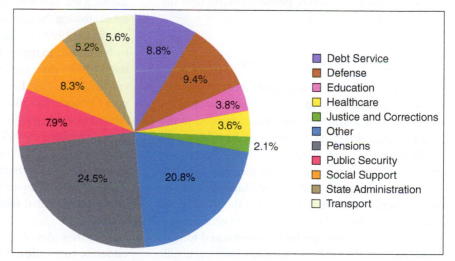

FIGURE 12.7

Russian State Budget Breakdown, 2013

Pensions take up a full quarter of the state budget, an expense that is likely to grow in coming years. It exceeds spending on education, health care, and assistance to the needy combined.

Source: Ministry of Finance website, www.minfin.ru

Toward the Rule of Law?

12.10 Briefly describe the route and obstacles to the rule of law in Russia.

The Law-Governed State

One of the most important goals of Gorbachev's reforms was to make the Soviet Union a **law-governed state (*pravovoe gosudarstvo*)**, rather than one in which state bodies and the Communist Party exercised power arbitrarily. Since 1991, Russian leaders have asserted that the state must respect the primacy of law over politics—even when they take actions grossly violating the constitution and infringing on the supposed independence of the judicial branch. The difficulty in placing law above politics testifies to the lingering legacy of the old regime's abuse of the legal system.

The struggle for the rule of law began well before Gorbachev. After Stalin died, his successors ended mass terror and took significant steps to reduce the use of law for political repression. Still, throughout the late Soviet era, the Communist Party and the KGB often used legal procedures to give the mantle of legal legitimacy to acts of political repression. The use of the legal system for political purposes by state authorities continues. Reforms in the 1990s took some steps toward making the judiciary independent of the authorities, but in the 2000s, political control over the legal system has increased.

Obstacles to the Rule of Law

In addition to the continuing abuse of the law for political purposes, corruption in the courts and law enforcement system, and the wide discretion granted to the security police, also stand in the way of the rule of law.

In the post-Soviet state, the security police continue to operate autonomously. In the Soviet period, the agency with principal responsibility for maintaining domestic security was called the KGB (State Security Committee). The KGB exercised wide powers, including responsibility for both domestic and foreign intelligence. Since 1991, its functions have been split up among several agencies. The main domestic security agency is called the Federal Security Service (FSB). Although the structure and mission of the security agencies have changed, they have never undergone a thorough purge of personnel. No member of or collaborator with the Soviet-era security services has been prosecuted for violating citizens' rights. In contrast to

Eastern Europe, there has been no review of officials' records for past collaboration with the secret police. This is one of several ways in which post-Soviet Russia has still not put its Communist past behind it.

The security police are regarded as one of the more professionally competent and uncorrupted state agencies. However, despite being assigned new tasks, such as fighting international narcotics trafficking and terrorism, they still demonstrate a Soviet-style preoccupation with policing the country's political life. For example, they have broad powers to shut down Internet providers and media outlets for publishing "extremist" content. Many Soviet-era police practices have been revived.

President Putin also resumed the Soviet-era practice of using the legal system to suppress potential political opposition. An example is the series of legal maneuvers taken against the owners of independent media in the early 2000s. These included police harassment and criminal prosecution, as well as civil actions such as bankruptcy proceedings. For example, the owners of two television companies were forced to divest themselves of their media holdings and transfer ownership to companies loyal to the administration. As a result, Russia's two relatively autonomous national television companies lost their political independence, one respected liberal newspaper was shut down, and the entire media establishment was sent a strong signal that it would be wise to avoid crossing the current administration.

In the 1990s, the bankruptcy laws were often used by businesses to drive rivals into bankruptcy in order to take them over; today, state companies use civil and criminal laws for the same purpose—to force a private company to sell out at a bargain price so that it can then be taken over and its assets stripped. For example, the state used charges of tax evasion and theft to force the Yukos oil firm into bankruptcy so that its most profitable elements could be sold at a low price to the state oil company, *Rosneft'*. These forced hostile takeovers are called *reiderstvo* (raiding).

Corruption Another obstacle to the rule of law is endemic corruption. Corruption increased substantially after the Soviet period. It is widespread both in everyday life and in dealings with the state. A survey in May 2010 found that 55 percent of respondents agreed with the statement that "everyone who deals with officials gives bribes," although 79 percent of the respondents had not paid a bribe themselves in the last 12 months.[67] Transparency International's

Corruption Perceptions Index in 2012 ranked Russia 133rd out of 174 countries in the pervasiveness of corruption. Experts estimate that the total volume of corrupt transactions in the economy exceeds the total value of the state budget.[68] Law enforcement (especially the traffic police), health care, education, and government registration offices are considered the worst offenders.

In an effort to reduce official corruption, the regime has passed legislation requiring officials to publish declarations of their income and property. So far, however, most observers believe that his drive has had little effect in reducing corruption. Around thirty members of the Duma filed for divorce, for example, at the time the declarations were due, in order to avoid reporting assets registered to their spouses.[69]

Corruption is hardly unique to Russia or to the former Communist world. However, it is especially widespread in Russia and the other former Soviet states. Corruption on this scale imposes a severe drag on economic development, both because it diverts resources away from public needs and because it undermines people's willingness to invest in productive activity.[70] Moreover, much corruption is tied to organized crime, which bribes government officials for protection and drives out legal businesses. The corruption of the police and courts ensures that many crimes go unpunished and forces legal businesses to compete in the market with illegal ones.

Corruption in Russia has deep roots, and many Russians assume that it is ineradicable. Comparative studies of corruption demonstrate, however, that a culture of corruption can be changed by changing the expectations of the public and the government.[71] The key is for the political leadership to make a serious effort to combat corruption and to back up this commitment with institutional reform and sustained attention to the problem.

Since the early 1990s, there have been a number of reforms, such as the adoption of trial by jury and the creation of the Constitutional Court, that have the potential to strengthen the judiciary's independence from both political pressure and corruption. However, the authorities' habitual use of the procuracy and the courts for political purposes and the powerfully corrosive effect of corruption continue to subvert the integrity of the legal system. In the long run, movement toward the rule of law will require that power be sufficiently dispersed among groups and organizations in the state and society so that neither private nor state interests are powerful enough to subordinate the law to their own purposes.

Russia and the International Community

12.11 Discuss Russia's conflicted international relations.

Russia's thousand-year history of expansion, war, and state domination of society has left behind a legacy of autocratic rule and a preoccupation with defending national borders. The collapse of the Soviet regime required Russia to rebuild its political institutions, economic system, national identity, and relations with the outside world. During the Soviet period, state propaganda used the image of an international struggle between capitalism and socialism to justify its repressive control over society and its enormous military establishment. Now the country's leaders recognize that only through strong ties with the world economy can Russia hope to prosper. Yet they also want to maintain strong controls over the political system in order to preserve stability and prevent threats to their power.

Gorbachev, Yeltsin, and Putin all asserted that the integration of Russia into the community of developed democracies is strategically important for Russia. Gorbachev was willing to allow Communist regimes to fall throughout Eastern Europe for the sake of improved relations with the West. Yeltsin accepted the admission of East European states into the North Atlantic Treaty Organization as a necessary condition for close relations with the United States and Europe. Putin repeatedly emphasized that he regarded Russia's admission to the World Trade Organization as critical for Russia's long-term economic success. Following the September 11, 2001, terrorist attacks on the United States, Putin immediately telephoned U.S. President George W. Bush to offer his support. Putin clearly saw an advantage for Russia in aligning itself with the United States against Islamic terrorism, which it identified as an immediate threat to its own security. Putin cited Russia's own war in Chechnia as part of the global struggle against Islamic terrorists.

At the same time, Russia has not accepted the constraints of international law. It has expanded its military presence in several former Soviet republics, pressuring them to become satellites of Russia. In August 2008, it launched a well-prepared military invasion of independent, pro-Western Georgia after Georgia attempted to use force to take back control of a Russia-backed break-away region, South Ossetia. The overwhelming Russian response was clearly intended to subjugate Georgia to Russia's interest in preserving a buffer of subordinate states in the territory of the former Soviet Union.

Likewise, in its brutal military campaigns in Chechnia from 1994 to 1996 and then again from 1999 to 2006, Russia refused to allow international human rights organizations to monitor Russian practices, which included mass bombardment of civilian areas. Putin has steadily increased spending on the military and has upgraded many weapons systems. As its economic and military power has revived, Russia has attempted to establish itself as a counterweight to American power and to rebuild Russian influence in the former Soviet region.

Russia's quasi-imperial behavior in parts of the former Soviet Union and its refusal to be bound by democratic principles have kept it from becoming fully integrated into the international community. Yet it is far more open than it was under Soviet rule, and its leaders recognize that they cannot retreat into isolation and autarky. They are also aware of the grave vulnerabilities Russia faces—its declining population, aging infrastructure, dependence on immigrant labor, and overreliance on natural resources for state revenues. Thus, while they seek to dominate the territory of the former Soviet Union, they also do not want to resurrect Russia's role as the United States' enemy in the bipolar world; they would prefer that Russia be one of several major powers in a multipolar world.

Russia's vast territory, weak government capacity, and tradition of state domination over society make it likely that the primary objective of its leaders for the foreseeable future will be to strengthen the state, in both its internal and its international dimensions. The end of the Communist regime and the dissolution of the Soviet Union damaged the state's capacity to enforce the laws, protect its citizens, and provide basic social services. Favorable economic conditions in the 2000s enabled the state to rebuild its power at home and abroad, but the crisis of 2008–2009 revealed Russia's susceptibility to trends in international financial and energy markets. In the long run, self-sustaining economic development will require the rule of law and effective institutions for articulating and aggregating social interests. The viability of Russia's postcommunist state will ultimately depend on how responsive and adaptive its institutions are to the demands of Russia's citizens in a globalized and interdependent world.

REVIEW QUESTIONS

- How did Yeltsin's "shock therapy" program contribute to the constitutional crisis of 1993?
- What effects did the constitutional struggles of 1992–1993 have on the features of the 1993 constitution?
- How did President Putin go about strengthening the power of the central government vis-à-vis regional governments? What were his reasons for shifting the balance of power in this way?

- What are the Putin regime's methods for dealing with civil society?
- Russians hold contradictory views of democracy. What explains these attitudes?
- What is a "party of power"?
- What are the main obstacles to the rule of law in Russia? What changes in the political system would be required to overcome them?

KEY TERMS

Chechnia (the Chechen Republic)
commercial courts (*arbitrazhnye sudy*)
Communist Party of the Russian Federation (CPRF)

Constitutional Court
Federation Council
Federation of Independent Trade Unions of Russia (FITUR)
glasnost'

Gorbachev, Mikhail
law-governed state (*pravovoe gosudarstro*)
League of Committees of Soldiers' Mothers
Lenin, Vladimir Ilyich

Liberal Democratic Party of Russia (LDPR)
loans for shares
Medvedev, Dmitrii Anatol'evich

nomenklatura

oligarchs

party of power

presidential decrees

privatization

procuracy

Public Chamber

Putin, Vladimir
   Vladimirovich

Russian Union of
   Industrialists and
   Entrepreneurs (RUIE)

Security Council

shock therapy

Stalin, Joseph

State Council

State Duma

United Russia

SUGGESTED READINGS

Aslund, Anders. *Russia's Capitalist Revolution: Why Market Reform Succeeded and Democracy Failed.* Washington, DC: Peterson Institute for International Economics, 2007.

Breslauer, George W. *Gorbachev and Yeltsin as Leaders.* Cambridge: Cambridge University Press, 2002.

Colton, Timothy J. *Yeltsin: A Life.* New York: Basic Books, 2008.

Fish, M. Stephen. *Democracy Derailed in Russia: The Failure of Open Politics.* Cambridge: Cambridge University Press, 2005.

Gustafson, Thane. *Wheel of Fortune: The Battle for Oil and Power in Russia.* Cambridge, MA: Belknap Press, 2012.

Hale, Henry. *Why Not Parties in Russia? Democracy, Federalism, and the State.* Cambridge: Cambridge University Press, 2006.

Hill, Fiona, and Clifford G. Gaddy. *Mr. Putin: Operative in the Kremlin.* Washington, DC: Brookings Institution Press, 2013.

McFaul, Michael. *Russia's Unfinished Revolution: Political Change from Gorbachev to Putin.* Ithaca, NY: Cornell University Press, 2001.

Sakwa, Richard. *The Crisis of Russian Democracy: The Dual State, Factionalism and the Medvedev Succession.* Cambridge: Cambridge University Press, 2011.

Treisman, Daniel. *The Return: Russia's Journey from Gorbachev to Medvedev.* New York: Free Press, 2011.

INTERNET RESOURCES

The official English-language version of the government website, with links to the websites of the president, the parliament, and the government and other bodies: http://gov.ru/index_en.html.

The University of Pittsburgh links to resources on Russia: www.ucis.pitt.edu/reesweb.

The *Moscow Times,* an English-language daily newspaper primarily for expatriates: www.themoscowtimes.com.

The Levada Center for Public Opinion Research is an independent, high-quality survey organization. Its English-language site: http://www.levada.ru/eng/.

ENDNOTES

1. Steven Levitsky and Lucan A. Way, *Competitive Authoritarianism: Hybrid Regimes After the Cold War* (Cambridge: Cambridge University Press, 2010).

2. Henry E. Hale, "Democracy or Autocracy on the March? The Colored Revolutions as Normal Dynamics of Patronal Presidentialism" *Communist and Post-Communist Studies* 39:3 (2006): 305–329.

3. Max de Haldevang, "Observer Group Questions Presidential Vote Result," *Moscow Times*, March 8, 2012.

4. President Dmitrii Medvedev, "Rossiia, vpered! [Go, Russia!]," as published on the presidential website http://kremlin.ru on September 10, 2009.

5. Richard Pipes, *Russia Under the Old Regime,* 2nd ed. (New York: Penguin Books, 1995).

6. Archie Brown, *The Gorbachev Factor* (New York: Oxford University Press, 1996).

7. In 2008, the constitution was amended at President Medvedev's request to extend the president's term of office from four years to six, and that of the Duma from four years to five. Both amendments took effect after the 2011–2012 election cycle. These are the only amendments to have been made so far to the constitution.

8. In April 2013, the director of the Security Council instructed his subordinates to develop proposals "to strengthen national security in the spiritual–ethical sphere." Representatives of the Security Council were unsure what he had in mind but thought it might have to do with fighting same-sex marriage. Taissiia Bekbulatova, Ivan Safronov, and Maksim Ivanov, "Na strazhe dukhovnoi bezopasnosti," *Kommersant*, April 25, 2013.

9. Many observers agreed that the point of the reform was to weaken the influence of local interests on Duma deputies, further centralizing power in the executive.

10. A vivid portrait of a jury trial in Moscow is presented by Peter Baker and Susan Glasser, *Kremlin Rising: Vladimir Putin's Russia and the End of Revolution* (New York: Scribner, 2005), 231–50.

11. On nationality policy in the Soviet Union, see Terry Martin, *The Affirmative Action Empire: Nations and Nationalism in the Soviet Union, 1923–1939* (Ithaca, NY: Cornell University Press, 2001).

12. Julia Kusznir, "Russian Territorial Reform: A Centralist Project That Could End Up Fostering Decentralization?" *Russian Analytical Digest* 43 (June 17, 2008): 8–10. Retrieved from www.res.ethz.ch/analysis/rad.

13. J. Paul Goode, "The Push for Regional Enlargement in Putin's Russia," *Post-Soviet Affairs* 20, no. 3 (July–September 2004): 219–57.

14. On the Chechen wars, see Daniel Treisman, *The Return: Russia's Journey from Gorbachev to Medvedev* (New York: Free Press, 2011).

15. Timothy J. Colton, *Yeltsin: A Life* (New York: Basic Books, 2008).

16. Henry E. Hale, "The Myth of Mass Russian Support for Autocracy: The Public Opinion Foundations of a Hybrid Regime," *Europe-Asia Studies* 63:8 (October 2011): 1364.

17. Viktor Khamraev, "Rossiiane vidiat vokrug demokratiiu," *Kommersant*, March 20, 2012.

18. Levada Center, May 26, 2010, http://www.levada.ru/ press/2010052618.html, accessed May 30, 2010.

19. Hale, "The Myth of Mass Russian Support," 1357–75.

20. Levada Center, February 8, 2008, www.levada.ru/ press/2008020800.html, accessed February 8, 2008.

21. Polit.ru, June 25, 2010. Interestingly, those most likely to report that they feel protected from arbitrary treatment are women, individuals with lower educational levels, and those with low incomes.

22. Richard Rose, William Mishler, and Neil Munro, *Popular Support for an Undemocratic Regime: The Changing Views of Russians* (Cambridge: Cambridge University Press, 2011).

23. Khamraev, "Rossiiane vidiat vokrug demokratiiu."

24. Elena Lisovskaya and Vyacheslav Karpov, "New Ideologies in Postcommunist Russian Textbooks," *Comparative Education Review* 43, no. 4 (1999): 522–32.

25. "Shkol'niki Rossii predpochli izuchat' svetskuiu etiku," *Vedomosti*, February 24, 2010; Polit.ru, March 26, 2010.

26. A law passed in 2012 requires Internet service providers to remove any sites that violate laws on illegal content. Although the law's sponsors argued that the law was needed to fight child pornography and other social harms, opponents warned that the language of the law was sufficiently broad that it could be used to block any politically objectionable sites. Human Rights Watch, "Laws of Attrition: Crackdown on Russia's Civil Society after Putin's Return to the Presidency" (New York: Human Rights Watch, 2013), available at http://www.hrw.org/sites/default/files/reports/russia0413_ForUpload_0.pdf, accessed May 7, 2013.

27. Facebook and Twitter are both available, but most Russians use equivalent Russian services, including a popular blogging host called "Live Journal." Prime Minister Medvedev uses Live Journal for his own blog (Putin does not use social media).

28. Levada Center, April 29, 2013, http://www.levada.ru /print/29-04-2013/svyshe-poloviny-strany-schitaet-er-partiei-zhulikov-i-vorov.

29. See, for example, Michael Weiss, "What the Alexei Navalny Case Says about Life in Putin's Russia," *The Atlantic*, April 22, 2013, available at http://www.theatlantic.com/international /archive/2013/04/what-the-aleksei-navalny-case-says-about-life-in-putins-russia/275175/.

30. Robert D. Putnam, *Making Democracy Work: Civic Traditions in Modern Italy* (Princeton, NJ: Princeton University Press, 1993).

31. Marc Morje Howard, *The Weakness of Civil Society in Post-Communist Europe* (Cambridge: Cambridge University Press, 2003).

32. I. Mersiianova, "Sotsial'naia baza rossiiskogo grazhdanskogo obshchestva," in *Grazhdanskoe obshchestvo sovremennoi Rossii. Sotsiologicheskie zarisovki s natury*, ed. E. S. Petrenko (Moscow, Institute Fonda Obshchestvennoe mnenie, 2008), 131.

33. Emil' Pain, "Ot vlasti avtoriteta k vlasti normy," *Nezavisimaia gazeta*, May 20, 2008.

34. Richard Rose, *Understanding Post-Communist Transformation: A Bottom Up Approach* (New York: Routledge, 2009): 62.

35. Maksim Ivanov, "Televidenie ostalos' v glavnoi roli," *Kommersant*, April 5, 2011.

36. Turnout for the 2012 presidential election was reportedly 64.5 percent, down slightly from 2008. In the United States, turnout of the eligible population for the 2012 presidential election was 58.2 percent.

37. A reform sponsored by President Putin and the United Russia Party has moved to eliminate the "against all" option from future elections. Although the goal is to force voters to support one of the given parties, many observers—including the chairman of the Central Election Commission—warn that this change will reduce electoral turnout.

38. Eugene Huskey, "Nomenklatura Lite? The Cadres Reserve (Kadrovyi reserv) in Russian Public Administration," NCEEER Working Paper (Washington, DC: National Council for Eurasian and East European Research, 2003).

39. Olga Kryshtanovskaya and Stephen White, "Putin's Militocracy," *Post-Soviet Affairs* 19, no. 4 (2003): 289–306.

40. Jane I. Dawson, *Eco-nationalism: Anti-nuclear Activism and National Identity in Russia, Lithuania, and Ukraine* (Durham, NC: Duke University Press, 1996).

41. Sergei Sergei Konovalov, "Grazhdan razlozhili na atomu," *Nezavisimaia gazeta*, December 21, 2011.

42. Nikolaus von Twickel, "Kremlin Earmarks $350M to Friendly NGOs," *Moscow Times*, March 9, 2011.

43. In a system where all prices were set by the state, there was no meaningful measure of profit in any case. Indeed, relative prices were profoundly distorted by the cumulative effect of decades of central planning. The absence of accurate measures of economic costs is one of the major reasons that Russia's economy continues to be so slow to restructure.

44. Article 59 of the constitution provides that young men of conscription age who are conscientious objectors to war may do alternative service rather than being called up to army service. Legislation specifying how this right may be exercised finally passed in 2002.

45. The chairwoman of Soldiers' Mothers estimated that some 3,500 servicemen lose their lives each year as a result of "various accidents and suicides," *RFE/RL Newsline,* February 14, 2008.

46. Polit.ru, June 18, 2009.

47. The FITUR reached a Faustian bargain with the government over the terms of a new labor relations code, which was adopted in 2001. Under the new legislation, employers no longer have to obtain the consent of the unions to lay off workers. But collective bargaining will be between the largest union at each enterprise and the management unless the workers have agreed on which union will represent them. Thus, the new labor code favors the FITUR at the expense of the smaller independent unions.

48. Richard Rose, "New Russia Barometer VI: After the Presidential Election," Studies in Public Policy no. 272 (Glasgow: Center for the Study of Public Policy, University of Strathclyde, 1996): 6; and Richard Rose, "Getting Things Done in an Anti-Modern Society: Social Capital Networks in Russia," Social Capital Initiative Working Paper no. 6 (Washington, DC: World Bank, 1998): 15.

49. Graeme B. Robertson, "Strikes and Labor Organizations in Hybrid Regimes," *American Political Science Review* 101, no. 4 (2007): 781–98.

50. In hard times, Russian enterprises tend not to lay off workers but instead put them on short hours and eliminate bonuses. Workers may still get a wage while looking for a job in the informal sector. Among other things, this preserves workers' pensions and medical benefits.

51. Ora John Reuter and Thomas F. Remington, "Dominant Party Regimes and the Commitment Problem: The Case of United Russia," *Comparative Political Studies* 42, no. 4 (2009): 501–26.

52. Stephen White, Richard Rose, and Ian McAllister, *How Russia Votes* (Chatham, NJ: Chatham House, 1997), 241–70.

53. Quoted from a press release of the election observer mission of the Organization for Security and Cooperation in Europe, posted to its website immediately following the election, as reported by *RFE/RL Newsline,* March 15, 2004.

54. In all, 108 candidates on the United Party list declined to take their seats in parliament. Such candidates were used as "locomotives"—they were used to attract votes, but had no intention of serving in the Duma once the party won.

55. On the scale of fraud in recent Russian elections, see Mikhail Myagkov, Peter C. Ordeshook, and Dmitri Shakin, *The Forensics of Election Fraud: Russia and Ukraine* (Cambridge: Cambridge University Press, 2009).

56. Arkady Lyubarev, "An Evaluation of the Results of the Duma Elections," *Russian Analytical Digest* 108 (Feb. 6, 2012): 2–5.

57. In a famous episode in February 2012, members of a female punk rock group called Pussy Riot entered the Cathedral of Christ the Savior in Moscow and tried to hold a "punk worship service" mocking Putin before being forcibly removed by police. They were charged with hooliganism and sentenced to two years' imprisonment. Although many thought the sentences excessive, most Russians were appalled by their actions.

58. Joel S. Hellman, "Winners Take All: The Politics of Partial Reform in Postcommunist Transitions," *World Politics* 50, no. 1 (1998): 203–34.

59. An excellent account of the "loans for shares" program, based on interviews with many of the participants, is Chrystia Freeland, *Sale of the Century: Russia's Wild Ride from Communism to Capitalism* (New York: Crown, 2000), 169–89.

60. Joseph R. Blasi, Maya Kroumova, and Douglas Kruse, *Kremlin Capitalism: Privatizing the Russian Economy* (Ithaca, NY: Cornell University Press, 1997), 50.

61. Blasi, Kroumova, and Kruse, *Kremlin Capitalism*; Michael McFaul, "State Power, Institutional Change, and the Politics of Privatization in Russia," *World Politics* 47 (1995): 210–43.

62. Thane Gustafson, *Capitalism Russian-Style* (Cambridge: Cambridge University Press, 1999), 2–3, 94–95.

63. World Bank, "Russian Economic Report: Recovery and Beyond," Russian Economic Report no. 29 (Moscow: World Bank, 2013): 25, available at http://www-wds.worldbank.org/external/default/WDSContentServer/WDSP/IB/2013/02/27/000356161_20130227124943/Rendered/PDF/755780NWP0RER200Box374338B00PUBLIC0.pdf, accessed May 8, 2013.

64. The episode provoked a heated exchange between Deputy Prime Minister Vladislav Surkov, who played a major role in developing Skolkovo, and a senior official in the Investigations Committee, which is in charge of the criminal investigation. After the Investigations Committee filed charges against the official, Surkov publicly objected and claimed that Skolkovo was "one of the cleanest projects in Russia." Evidently he overstepped the limits, because he was dismissed from office immediately after making that statement.

65. "Forbes, "The World's Billionaires," accessed May 8, 2013, http://www.forbes.com/billionaires/.

66. Quoted from Vladimir Putin's address to an expanded session of the State Council, February 8, 2008, "On the Strategy of Development of Russia to 2020," retrieved from president.kremlin.ru/text/appears/2008/02/159528.shtml.

67. Polit.ru, May 13, 2010.

68. Polit.ru, November 17, 2009.

69. Polit.ru, April 26, 2013.

70. Joel S. Hellman, Geraint Jones, and Daniel Kaufmann, "Seize the State, Seize the Day: State Capture, Corruption, and Influence in Transition," Policy Research Working Paper no. 2444 (Washington, DC: World Bank Institute, 2000).

71. Susan Rose-Ackerman, *Corruption and Government: Causes, Consequences and Reform* (Cambridge: Cambridge University Press, 1999), 159–74.

POPULATION
1,330 million

TERRITORY
3,705,386 square miles

YEAR OF PRC INAUGURATION
1949

YEAR OF CURRENT CONSTITUTION
1982 (amended in 1988, 1993, 1999, 2004)

HEAD OF PARTY AND STATE
Xi Jinping

HEAD OF GOVERNMENT
Li Keqiang

LANGUAGES
Standard Chinese or Mandarin (Putonghua, based on the Beijing dialect), Yue (Cantonese), Wu (Shanghaiese), Minbei (Fuzhou), Minnan (Hokkien-Taiwanese), Xiang, Gan, Hakka dialects, minority languages

RELIGION
Daoist (Taoist), Buddhist, Muslim 2–3%; Christian 1% (estimate); nation is officially atheist

CHAPTER 13

Politics in China

Melanie Manion

LEARNING OBJECTIVES

13.1 Discuss the challenges, rooted in its economy, currently faced by China.

13.2 Briefly distinguish the three main periods of China's political history, from 1949 through the present.

13.3 Describe China's social conditions, deriving from its size.

13.4 Describe the structures of the Chinese party-state, providing details on party makeup and elite recruitment.

13.5 Explain how the party dominates the party-state and exercises leadership in political structures.

13.6 Contrast China's "rule by law" with democratic "rule of law."

13.7 Describe the government's relationship to mass media and the education system as sources of political socialization.

13.8 Examine China's political culture in the light of its historical roots.

13.9 Discuss the "officially acceptable" and "unacceptable" forms of political participation at national and local levels in China.

13.10 Describe the evolution of interest aggregation in recent years in China.

13.11 List the three tiers and five stages of policymaking in China.

13.12 Discuss route and obstacles to policy implementation in China.

13.13 Explain the Chinese government's policy role in economic reform, environmental protection, and population control.

13.14 Describe China's relationship with Hong Kong.

13.15 Briefly discuss China's economic and political international role.

On October 1, 1949, **Mao Zedong**, the peasant revolutionary who had led the Chinese communists in war against the Japanese and in civil war, pronounced a basic communist victory, proclaimed a new regime, and promised a new era for China. From the centuries-old Gate of Heavenly Peace in Beijing, Mao formally inaugurated the People's Republic of China (PRC). For nearly three decades after, until his death in 1976, Mao was the chief architect and agitator for a comprehensive project of revolutionary transformation designed to lead a largely backward agrarian people to modernization, prosperity, and (ultimately) communist utopia. A few years after Mao's death, his successors officially and publicly rejected most of the premises, strategies, and outcomes of this revolutionary project, essentially declaring it a failure. They launched a new era of reform, ongoing today. Economic reform in post-Mao China is nearly as radical and dramatic as the revolutions that toppled most of the world's communist regimes in 1989 and 1990. The resulting transformation is awesome.

Without publicly abandoning the ultimate goal of communism, Mao's successors have defined their current quest mainly in pragmatic economic terms, rather than utopian ideological terms. They have identified economic growth as the nation's highest priority and the Communist Party's main assignment. To achieve this objective, the communist party-state has largely retreated from thirty years of direct administration of the economy. Openly acknowledging the superiority of the capitalist experience, Chinese reformers are promoting a "**socialist market economy**," with a place for foreign investors, private entrepreneurs, and stock markets. Indeed, at the November 2013 plenum of the Communist Party Central Committee, reformers newly proclaimed a "decisive role" for the market in China's economy. More than anything else, Chinese leaders have staked their legitimacy on the performance of this new economy.

While embracing economic markets, Chinese leaders have repeatedly rejected political pluralism. The communist party-state was in clear evidence in Beijing on June 4, 1989, when the People's Liberation Army employed its tanks and machine guns to clear the streets and main public square of thousands of protesters. The regime tolerates no organized challenge to the Communist Party's monopoly on political power.

For most of the 1.3 billion ordinary Chinese, political reform is mainly reflected in a new official acceptance of a private sphere and a new official tolerance of political apathy. Compared with the Maoist years, when a taste for the music of Beethoven signified dangerous "bourgeois decadence," much less in daily life today is considered political. Moreover, under the new regime, ordinary citizens need not necessarily demonstrate active support for official policies and the political system—so long as they do not engage in active opposition. Chinese leaders have not charted a road toward liberal democracy—at least not purposefully. Instead, the political system has become merely authoritarian in its limited reach, rather than pervasively totalitarian.

Yet post-Mao reform is more than the retreat of the state from the economy and the imposition of fewer demands on citizens politically. A project of institutionalization is underway in China to create an infrastructure promoting more transparency, stability, and responsiveness. In large part, this is to encourage investment and innovation, to support the goal of economic growth. At the same time, Mao's successors are also committed to political institutionalization for political reasons: to safeguard against the arbitrary dictatorship and disruptive politics of the Maoist past. The effort has included better-crafted laws and a new legality, more assertive representative assemblies, and popularly elected grassroots leaders.

Much of China's transformation in the past three decades is only partly a direct result of the various policies that constitute reform. It is at least as much a by-product of these policies. Reform has set in motion processes of economic, political, and social change that appear now largely beyond the control of leaders at the political center. Consider a few examples. Eased restrictions on population movement have created a "floating population" of some 140 million internal migrants from the countryside, seeking work outside their home counties, many of them unregistered urban squatters, all of them reflecting a new relationship between state authority, social welfare, and market opportunity. Local governments, empowered by a new fiscal federalism, pursue local economic growth with less and less heed to central guidelines. Growth in individual wealth and a telecommunications revolution have produced an astonishing 564 million Internet users in China, linking Chinese to one another and to the outside world in ways that are nearly impossible to control.

Current Policy Challenges

13.1 Discuss the challenges, rooted in its economy, currently faced by China.

China's current policy challenges arise very significantly from its economic successes in the past three decades. Beginning in 1978, Chinese leaders agreed to be judged mainly by their ability to foster economic growth and deliver a better material life for Chinese citizens. China's development has in fact been impressive. Its economy has grown at a rate of nearly 10 percent per year since 1980, faster and for a longer period of time than any other economy in history. In terms of purchasing power parity (PPP), China is now the world's second-largest economy (after the United States). In 2006, it overtook Japan as the world's biggest holder of foreign exchange reserves. Indeed, aided by massive government intervention, China emerged from the 2008 and 2009 global economic crisis more powerful than ever. This has fostered a new confidence: Chinese officials have criticized the United States for economic mismanagement, and senior Chinese bank officials questioned the reserve currency status of the U.S. dollar.

Economic success over the past 35 years has not been costless. It has provided more opportunities to pursue private gain, legally and also illegally through the abuse of public office. Despite decades of anticorruption efforts, year after year, ordinary citizens tell pollsters that corruption is one of China's most serious problems. In the cities, Chinese poke fun at the perceived insincerity of the anticorruption reforms: "not daring *not* to fight corruption, not daring to fight corruption seriously." In the countryside, villagers rise up to protest abuses of power by "local emperors" imposing illegal fees and excessive taxes.

In recent years, the requisition, rezoning, and sale of agricultural land by local governments has provoked rural riots, usually suppressed with great violence. Land is not privately owned, but rather is contracted for agricultural use by Chinese farmers. Local governments have seized on more lucrative opportunities for land use provided by real estate and industrial development. Farmers tend to be poorly compensated in these instances of eminent domain for local economic development (and local government profit). Top Chinese leaders have condemned these actions, not least of all because arable land is already scarce.

The growing wealth gap fuels the perceptions of official abuse. In the 1980s and 1990s, Chinese policymakers promoted a policy that "some get rich first." One result has been rapidly rising inequality. Urban household incomes are three times as high as rural incomes; within the cities, migrant workers without official resident status lack access to basic social welfare. Poorer Chinese deeply resent the newly conspicuous economic inequalities of the socialist market economy. As the wealth gap has exploded within a single generation, it has great potential to ignite social instability. More than 180,000 "public disturbances" erupted in 2010. Land takings, economic distress, environmental degradation, and political corruption provoked much of this unrest.

Chinese leaders have recently completed a major transition to a "fifth generation" of leaders. Xi Jinping and Li Keqiang, groomed for leadership for several years, took up positions as head of the Communist Party and head of government in 2012 and 2013, respectively. China is now ruled by the most educated and least technocratic generation of leaders ever. Most have college degrees, and even a graduate degree is not uncommon; many have majored in law or a social science rather than engineering.

China has thoroughly abandoned the strictures of communist ideology, has experienced an awesome economic revolution, and is taking its place as an important world power. Yet unlike most other communist regimes, which toppled in the face of popular uprisings, China has experienced no second political revolution. Today, it is still a communist party-state. Chinese policymakers have promoted limited liberalization, sometimes as an antidote to corruption at the grassroots. While they have opened up political processes to more diversified inputs, they have also firmly suppressed organized challenges to the Communist Party. A handful of leaders at the very top still monopolize the authority to choose what sorts of inputs from what sorts of groups are acceptable, and the decision rules are not always transparent.

Strikingly little remains of Mao's grand revolutionary schemes. Viewed from the perspective of the 1970s, the magnitude and pace of change in China in the past three decades is practically unimaginable. Chinese politics today is "post-Mao" politics in the sense that there is a new regime, not simply a change of leaders—and, given its dynamics, there appears to be no turning back. Of course, without a grasp of China's rich political history, it is not only impossible to appreciate what has (and has not) changed but also impossible to understand the crucial context of post-Mao reform: what has been rejected.

Historical Setting

13.2 Briefly distinguish the three main periods of China's political history, from 1949 through the present.

Chinese civilization emerged more than 6 thousand years ago. As a polity, imperial China was the longest-lived major system of governance in world history, enduring as a centralized state ruled with little change in political philosophy or bureaucratic organization for more than two millennia until the fall of the Qing, the last dynasty, in 1911.[1]

Traditional China was governed by an emperor and a unique bureaucracy of scholar-officials at the capital and in the localities, who gained their positions meritocratically through examinations that tested knowledge of the Confucian classics. Anyone was eligible to participate in the examinations, but successful performance required a classical education, usually through a private tutor, not available to most ordinary Chinese. **Confucianism** was basically a conservative philosophy. It conceived of society and the polity in terms of an ordered hierarchy of harmonious relationships. At the top of the hierarchy was the emperor, who maintained social order through his conduct as a moral exemplar. Confucianism blurred the distinction between state and society: It saw harmony (not conflict) as the natural social order, resulting from the virtuous emperor's example of correct conduct. Loyalty to the emperor was the highest principle in the hierarchy of relationships entailing mutual obligations throughout society.

Imperial Order to the Founding of the PRC

This remarkable imperial order began to crumble in the mid-nineteenth century, when Qing rulers proved unable to uphold their political authority and maintain territorial integrity in the presence of large-scale domestic rebellion and foreign economic and military encroachment. The republic founded in 1912 did not restore order or sovereignty to China but effectively collapsed within a few years, as dozens of Chinese regional warlords ruling with personal armies competed for control of territory.[2] Nearly four decades of political upheaval and continuous warfare ensued, as the Chinese sought solutions to the problems of governance that had brought down the Qing.

The dominant problems were the struggle for national sovereignty and the struggle for peasant livelihood. The former involved two sorts of claims: cession of Chinese territory in treaties imposed forcibly by Western powers beginning in the nineteenth century and outright military invasion and occupation by the Japanese in the 1930s. As for the Chinese peasantry, poverty in the countryside due to socioeconomic conditions of exorbitant taxes, high rents, and usurious credit was aggravated by frequent floods and droughts, which usually brought ruin.

These two struggles were played out in the context of a competition to unify the country. By the 1920s, the **Nationalist Party** and army had emerged as the most prominent political and military force in the country. The Nationalists had their strongest social base in the urban areas; in the countryside, they were mainly dependent on the support of the landlord class. This largely explains Nationalist reluctance to implement land and social reforms to resolve the problems of Chinese peasants. Peasant poverty was exacerbated by absentee landlordism and the replacement of ties of mutual obligation with economic ties enforced by managing agents. Land distribution was not part of the Nationalist agenda, nor were tax controls or provision of cheap credit effectively implemented.

Between 1924 and 1927, the Nationalists allied with the communists in a battle to eliminate regional warlords and to unify China. By the late 1920s, the Nationalists had practically realized this aim. In 1927, they broke their alliance with the communists in a violent massacre that reduced the Communist Party from nearly 58,000 to 10,000 members. The break inaugurated a new civil war that lasted a decade.

By contrast with the Nationalists, the intellectual revolutionaries who founded the **Chinese Communist Party** in 1921 were unlikely contenders for power. The rise and eventual victory of the communists owe much to historic opportunities in the 1930s and 1940s. These opportunities were available for other forces to exploit too, but the communists exploited them best.[3] Mao Zedong emerged as leader of the communists in the mid-1930s, consolidating his leadership in the early 1940s.[4]

After the Nationalist attack in 1927, many communists retreated to the countryside. Mao had already reported on the spontaneous impulse for radical social change among the peasantry and had proposed a revolutionary strategy different from that suggested by communist theory or Russian experience. Mao rejected the idea that the Chinese communists could win power through a revolution of the small urban working class in China. Instead, he argued, a communist victory could be achieved only by providing leadership for a nascent rural revolution and building a guerrilla Red Army to surround the cities from the countryside. From a base in southeastern China, Mao and other communists implemented a program of political education and social change, including land redistribution. In 1934, a major Nationalist offensive forced them into a strategic retreat, the historic Long March, that ended at the caves of Yan'an in China's northwest, where Mao and his communist forces, their numbers literally decimated, established their headquarters. From Yan'an, they built on the strategy of rural revolution to develop further support in the countryside.

The second indispensable component in communist victory was the 1937 Japanese invasion of central China, beyond territory in the northeast that the Japanese had occupied since 1931.[5] Mao seized the strategic initiative to call for a truce in the civil war so that Chinese could unite to resist Japanese aggression. Nationalist leaders were initially wary. This combination of Nationalist reluctance and strong anti-Japanese sentiment in the cities and countryside earned the communists enormous popularity as the true nationalist resistance to foreign aggression. From 1937 to 1945, the communists grew in force from 40,000 to more than a million. Japanese defeat in World War II ended the alliance between Nationalists and communists. A new civil war began.[6] In four years, the communists won victory, as peasant revolutionaries and Chinese nationalists, and the Nationalists were forced to retreat to the island of Taiwan in 1949. Once in power, they turned their energies to the construction of socialism.

History of the PRC

The history of the PRC can be divided into three major periods. In the first, between 1949 and 1957, the Chinese emulated the experience of the first and most powerful communist state, the Soviet Union. The second period began in 1958, when the Chinese introduced their own model of revolutionary development. Except for a few years at the beginning of the 1960s, this Maoist model prevailed until Mao's death in 1976. A short transitional period ensued, during which immediate problems of policy orientation and leadership succession were resolved with the arrest and trial of key radical leaders. In December 1978, the third period, a new era of reform, ongoing today, was inaugurated with a Central Committee declaration favoring learning from practical experience and rejecting the ideological constraints of Maoism—or any theory.[7] **Deng Xiaoping**, China's new "paramount leader," charted and presided over the reforms. In the same sense that Chinese politics in the two decades ending

in 1976 are appropriately characterized as the Maoist years, the last two decades of the twentieth century belong most to Deng—despite important differences in the power of these two leaders and how they wielded it.

Learning from the Soviet Union The Chinese communists had won power largely by ignoring Soviet advice. Once in power, however, they looked to the Soviet Union for a plan to build socialism. They concluded a treaty of friendship and alliance in 1950. Soviet financial aid to China in the 1950s was not large. Aid was mainly given in a massive technology transfer—over 12,000 Soviet engineers and technicians were sent to work in China, over 6,000 Chinese studied in Soviet universities, and tens of thousands more Chinese studied in Soviet factories on short-term training courses. With this Soviet assistance, the Chinese developed heavy industry, establishing a centralized bureaucracy of planning agencies and industrial ministries to manage the economy according to five-year plans. They nationalized private industry. In the early 1950s, they sent communists down to the grassroots to instigate and organize land reform, a violent "class struggle." Each peasant household was classified according to land holdings, and land seized from landlords was redistributed to poor peasants, the majority of the peasantry.[8] Agricultural collectivization followed. This process was also essentially coercive, especially in its later stages, but not as violent as land reform.

This period did feature some Maoist strategies, especially in political participation and socialization. The Chinese implemented many policies by mobilizing the masses in intensive campaigns, with essentially compulsory participation. For the Chinese communists, potential regime opponents—such as intellectuals and capitalists—were capable of being politically transformed through practices such as "thought reform." Communist leaders were sufficiently confident about the results of political education and regime accomplishments to invite nonparty intellectuals to voice criticism in the Hundred Flowers Campaign in 1957. When criticism was harsh, revealing weak support for the communist system, the leaders quickly reversed themselves. They launched an Anti-Rightist Campaign, which discovered more "poisonous weeds" than "blooming flowers." About a half-million people, many of them intellectuals, were persecuted as "rightists" in a campaign that effectively silenced political opposition for twenty years.[9] Mass campaigns, political education, and political labeling were all coercive measures that resulted in the persecution of millions. To some extent, this coercion had a characteristic Maoist (and Confucian) element: Fundamentally, it rejected the Stalinist version of political purge as physical liquidation, because it viewed the individual as malleable and ultimately educable. Yet "enemies of the people" were not spared; 1 to 3 million landlords and "counterrevolutionaries" were persecuted to death in the early 1950s alone.

Frictions in relations with the Soviet Union increased throughout the 1950s, resulting in the withdrawal of aid and advisors and a Sino–Soviet split that shocked the world in 1960. Major irritants included Soviet reluctance to support efforts to "liberate" Taiwan, Soviet unwillingness to aid China's nuclear development, and a relaxation of Soviet hostility toward the United States. At about the same time, Mao was reconsidering his view of the Soviet model of development and developing his own radical model of building communism.

Great Leap Forward The first five-year plan had invested in heavy industry, not agriculture. Following the Soviet model, central planners had not diverted resources from industry to promote agricultural growth. In 1958, Mao proposed a strategy of simultaneous development of industry and agriculture to be achieved in two ways: (1) the labor-intensive mass mobilization of peasants to increase agricultural output by building irrigation facilities, and (2) the organization of primitive production processes to give inputs to agriculture (such as small chemical fertilizer plants and primitive steel furnaces to make tools) without taking resources from industry. A crucial element of Mao's solution was an increase in the size of the collective farms. In order to build irrigation facilities, local communist officials needed to control a labor force of large numbers of peasants, larger than the current collectives that grouped together a few hundred households. By combining several collectives into one gigantic farm, Mao hoped to realize economies of scale. In 1958, with prodding from above, the people's communes were born, grouping together thousands of households in one unit of economic and political organization managed by Communist Party officials.

The Maoist model was not simply an economic development strategy. It was fundamentally a political campaign, a point exemplified in the main slogan of the **Great Leap Forward**: "politics in command."[10] The Great Leap Forward abandoned most material rewards for moral incentives. By 1958, in Mao's view, Chinese peasants had demonstrated tremendous enthusiasm and were ready to leap into communism, if properly mobilized by local leaders. In the politically charged climate, economic expertise was denigrated and caution criticized as lack of faith in the masses. Leaders in Beijing set output targets high, demanding that local leaders believe in the ability of the Chinese people to accomplish miracles. By implication, failure to achieve high targets could be due only to poor leadership. A dangerous vicious cycle was set in motion: Local leaders competed to demonstrate their political correctness; when communes failed to meet targets set in Beijing, local leaders calculated output imaginatively to report that targets had been met or exceeded; production results were increasingly exaggerated as reports went to higher and higher levels; the response from Beijing to the falsely reported leap in output was a further leap in targets.

In 1958, dislocation associated with forming the communes and peasant mobilization to help meet high steel output targets by making steel in primitive furnaces was so great that the autumn harvest was not all gathered. That year, too, a false belief in excess production led to reduction in areas sown in grain. Even with reduced acreage, peasant contributions to agricultural labor were decreasing due to physical exhaustion, weak material rewards, and the abolition of private plots (and, in some cases, private property, for complete communization). In 1959, when top Chinese leaders met to consider these problems, the minister of national defense criticized radicalism in policy implementation. In response, Mao accused the minister of factionalism, turned the meeting into a referendum on his leadership, and challenged others to dare to attack the Leap's radical principles.

The meeting was a terrible turning point. With political correctness reasserted, radicalism returned. Moreover, just as the 1957 Anti-Rightist Campaign had silenced opposition outside the party, Mao's 1959 accusations and threats effectively silenced opposition in the top echelons of party leadership.[11] That same year, large parts of China suffered from severe drought, and others from severe flooding, in one of the worst natural disasters experienced in decades.

Retreat from the Leap Over the next three years, the famine cost an estimated 27 million lives.[12] China retreated from Maoist radicalism. Mao retreated from day-to-day management of public affairs, but continued in his position as Communist Party chairman. In the early 1960s, the communes ceased to be relevant to agricultural production. Instead, peasant households contracted with the state for production, selling the surplus in newly established free markets. In industry, there was a renewed reliance on material incentives, technical expertise, and profitability as the standard to judge performance. The education system emphasized the creation of a knowledgeable and highly skilled corps of managers and leaders. Policy processes took into account advice by experts, rather than relying on mass miracles.

Cultural Revolution By the mid-1960s, Mao had further developed his radical critique of the Soviet model and extended it to the Chinese experience. In China, Mao saw a "new class" of economic managers and political officials, privileged by elitist policies that increased social antagonisms. In 1966, Mao argued that many communist leaders were corrupt "capitalist roaders" who opposed socialism and must be thrown out of power. He launched the Great Proletarian Cultural Revolution, yet another exercise in radical excess. The **Cultural Revolution** was simultaneously a power struggle, an ideological battle, and a mass campaign to transform culture. Compared with the Great Leap Forward, its impact on the Chinese economy was minor; its impact on society was devastating.

For Mao, the enemy of socialism was within the Communist Party. Unable to rely on the party to correct its mistakes, Mao instructed secondary school and university students to overturn "bourgeois culture" and "bombard the headquarters." The Communist Party became effectively powerless as an organization. For the first time since 1949, Chinese were free to organize politically. Unconstrained by the party, Chinese engaged in political action legitimated by their own interpretations of Mao Zedong Thought (the Chinese do not use the term "Maoism"). Students formed radical Red Guard groups to criticize and persecute victims, often chosen quite arbitrarily or for reasons more personal than political. In schools, factories, and government agencies, those in power were criticized and persecuted. Persecution

Cult of Mao in the Cultural Revolution
Defense Minister Lin Biao sits beside Chairman Mao Zedong and Premier Zhou Enlai during the Cultural Revolution. PLA soldiers wave the *Little Red Book* of quotations from Chairman Mao, a reflection of the cult of Mao that Lin helped to build.

was frequently physical. It was not uncommon for victims to be held in makeshift prisons, forced to do harsh manual labor, and subjected to violent public "struggle sessions" to force them to confess their crimes. Many were "struggled" to death, and many others committed suicide. Factional fighting was inevitable, as rival Red Guard groups fought for power, each faction claiming true representation of Mao Zedong Thought.[13]

In 1967, the country was near anarchy. The schools had been shut down; most party and government offices no longer functioned; transportation and communications were severely disrupted; and factional struggles were increasingly violent contests, some of them armed confrontations. Having unleashed social conflict, Mao had been able to manipulate it—but not to control it. Mao called on the army to restore order, a process that began in 1969.

The 1970s were years of more moderate conflict, mostly played out as a struggle at the apex of power rather than in society generally. Radical leaders (including Mao's wife) who had risen to power in the Cultural Revolution supported a continuation of radical policies. Other leaders, reinstated by Mao to balance the power of the radicals, supported policies of economic modernization. The conflict was ongoing at the time of Mao's death in 1976. Within two years, the economic modernizers had won. China embarked on a new course of reform, different from anything in the experience of any communist system.

Social Conditions

13.3 Describe China's social conditions, deriving from its size.

Chinese society has changed in various ways since the communists came to power. These changes include social structural transformations engineered by the regime, especially in the early decades. This section focuses on basic features that make up the social environment for Chinese politics that have not undergone fundamental transformation but have changed only in degree, if at all.

First among these is China's huge population. When the communists came to power in 1949, China's population was 540 million. Today, China remains the world's most populous country, with a population of 1.3 billion. As in the 1950s, most Chinese live in the countryside, but the proportion has shrunk dramatically with economic reform. Less than 20 percent of Chinese lived in cities when reform began in the late 1970s, but de facto relaxation of rural to urban migration restrictions liberated the underemployed farming population to seek work in cities. Rural industrialization and the growth of towns also changed the situation. By 2010, nearly as many Chinese lived in cities as in the countryside.

The second basic feature involves geography. Although China is the world's second-largest country in area, the population is concentrated in the eastern third of the land. This is largely because only about a quarter of China's land is arable. Population growth and reduction in cultivated area have greatly exacerbated the land shortage. Despite efforts to preserve arable land for farming, China's leaders have been unable to reverse the reduction in cultivated area. In part, this is a result of agricultural decollectivization and a return to household farming: Land is used for property borders, burial grounds, and bigger houses. In recent years, local government land requisitions for lucrative residential and industrial development have further reduced arable land and provoked much rural unrest.

The third feature is that China is a multiethnic state. About 92 percent of Chinese are ethnically Han, but there are fifty-five recognized **ethnic minorities**, ranging in number from a few thousand to more than 16 million. Although minorities make up a fairly small proportion of China's population, areas in which minorities live comprise more than 60 percent of China's territory, and much of this is in strategically important border regions.[14] This includes Tibet (bordering India) and Xinjiang (bordering three new post-Soviet states), which have experienced fairly continuous minority unrest over the decades. The Chinese have maintained large armed forces in these areas to quell secessionist efforts.

Finally, Han Chinese share the same Chinese written language, a unifying force in China for more than two millennia, practically defining what it is to be Chinese. The same written language is spoken in many different dialects, however, often making communication difficult. Mandarin, based on the dialect of the Beijing locality, is the official language promoted by the communist regime through the education system and mass media.

Structure of the Party-State

 13.4 Describe the structures of the Chinese party-state, providing details on party makeup and elite recruitment.

From top to bottom, Chinese politics has changed noticeably since the Maoist period. Yet the essential form of the Chinese political system retains an organizational design borrowed decades ago from the Soviet Union and developed nearly a century ago in Russia by Lenin—the design of the communist **party-state**.

Design Features

Lenin viewed political legitimacy in ways that justify a monopoly of power by a communist party elite that is not popularly elected. He believed that ordinary citizens do not understand their own real interests and that larger interests of society are not best advanced by aggregating interests that citizens articulate. According to Lenin, as ordinary citizens typically lack revolutionary consciousness and knowledge of communist theory, they are incapable of making the correct choices that will lead from capitalism to socialism and toward communism—a utopia characterized by a high level of economic prosperity, an absence of social conflict, and a minimal role for government. Lenin proposed a solution to this problem: a political party and political system built on the principles of guardianship and hierarchy.[15] To these two principles, Chinese leaders added the idea of the mass line, formulated by Mao in the 1940s. Guardianship and hierarchy define the communist party-state. The mass line adds another dimension, which moderates guardianship.

Guardianship describes the main relationship between the Communist Party and society. The party bases its claim to legitimate rule not on representation of the expressed preferences of a majority but on representation of the "historical best interests" of all the people. In theory, as most ordinary citizens do not know their best interests, society is best led by an elite vanguard party with a superior understanding of the historical laws of development. The Communist Party is therefore an exclusive organization—in China, membership is about 6 percent of the population—not a mass political party with membership open to all. The notion of Communist Party leadership is explicitly set forth in the constitution, as is some version of the notion of dictatorship. The constitution describes the political system as a socialist state under the "people's democratic dictatorship." As the Communist Party is the only organization with the politically correct knowledge to lead society, it is the authoritative arbiter of the interests of the people. In effect, dictatorship in the name of the people is Communist Party dictatorship. Party leaders today are more informed of public opinion than in the past, but there is no place in the Chinese political system (or in Leninist theory) for organized opposition to Communist Party leadership.

Chinese Communist Party guardianship is, in theory, informed by the practice of the mass line. The party leads, but its leadership is not isolated from the opinions and preferences of the mass public. The degree to which mass preferences actually find expression in public policy depends on their fit with larger goals determined by party leaders. Party leaders at all levels (but especially at the grassroots) are supposed to maintain a close relationship with ordinary citizens so that the party organization can transform the "scattered and unsystematic ideas" of the masses into "correct ideas" and propagate them "until the masses embrace them as their own." In this way, policy is supposed to flow "from the masses to the masses."[16]

Party Organization The Communist Party is organized around a hierarchy of party congresses and committees extending from the top of the system down to the grassroots. Lower party organizations are subordinate to higher party organizations, and individual party members are subordinate to the party as an organization. Inner-party rules for decision making are based on the Leninist principle of **democratic centralism**.

In democratic centralism, *democracy* refers mainly to consultation. It requires that party leaders provide opportunities for discussion, criticism, and proposals in party organizations (often including lower party organizations) as part of the normal process of deciding important issues or making policy.

Centralism requires unified discipline throughout the party: top-level official party decisions are binding on party organizations and members. Centralism is never sacrificed to democracy. Party members are allowed to hold personal views contrary to party decisions and to voice them through proper party channels, but they are not free to act in ways that promote these views. According to the Communist Party constitution, the formation of "factions" or any sort of "small group activity" within the party is a punishable violation of organizational discipline. Communist Party hierarchy and the requirement that party members observe party discipline are designed as organizational guarantees that the party, in exercising leadership over society, acts as a unified force, responsive to the leadership of the highest level of party organization.

Ideology is today both less prominent and less coherent in Chinese politics than it was in the past. The principles of guardianship, hierarchy, and the mass line are not inconsequential abstractions, however. They have concrete practical implications, evident throughout the Chinese political system. Change in the system is evident too, of course, both as a product and by-product of policies of reform in the past two decades. Yet while the political reforms of recent decades are not trivial, they do not add up to fundamental systemic change. For now, as in the past, the design of the communist party-state is a fair model of the organization of political power in China.

Two Hierarchies, with Party Leadership   The design of the communist party-state is perhaps most evident in the organization of power in two hierarchies of political structures, illustrated in Figure 13.1. Government structures are more or less duplicated at each level of the political system by Communist Party structures. In principle, there is a division of labor between party and government structures. In practice, the two often perform similar functions, with party structures and party officials exercising leadership over parallel government structures and government officials.

Both party and government structures have changed since 1949. The description in the following section focuses on the system that emerged in the reform era.

Government Structures

At the political center in Beijing, the key government structures are the **National People's Congress (NPC)**, which is China's legislature, and the **State Council**, which exercises executive functions. Under the State Council are government ministries and commissions, which have ranged in number from 32 to 100 since 1949. Below the political center, government structures extend downward in a four-tiered hierarchy

consisting of 31 provinces, 332 large cities, 2,853 counties and smaller cities, and 40,466 townships and towns. The provincial level includes four megacities (Beijing, Shanghai, Tianjin, and Chongqing). Local people's congresses, local governments, and government departments are found at all levels. As shown in Figure 13.1, Chinese voters elect delegates to township and county people's congresses only; municipal, provincial, and national congress delegates are elected by congresses one level down. At all levels, congress delegates elect their governments. Villages and urban neighborhoods elect self-governing grassroots organizations, not part of the formal government hierarchy.

National People's Congress   According to the constitution, the highest organization of state authority is the NPC.[17] The NPC and its permanent body, the NPC Standing Committee, exercise legislative functions. NPC delegates are elected for five-year terms by delegates in provincial-level congresses and the armed forces. Normally, NPC delegates assemble once annually for a plenary session of about two weeks. The number and composition of delegates are prescribed by law, but the NPC has always been huge. In 1986, the law set a ceiling of 3,000 delegates, which is about the number elected to each congress since 1983. Urban Chinese were overrepresented (by a ratio of eight to one, later changed to four to one) until a 2010 law gave rural residents equal representation in congresses at all levels.

Formally, the NPC has extensive powers, including amendment of the constitution, passage and amendment of legislation, approval of economic plans and government work reports, and appointment of top state and government leaders. For most of the year, when the NPC is not in session, its Standing Committee of about 150 members, who reside in Beijing and meet regularly throughout the year, serves as the working legislative assembly. The 1982 constitution considerably strengthened the role of the NPC Standing Committee. It now exercises all but the most formal powers of the NPC and prepares the agenda for the annual NPC plenary sessions, when the full NPC typically ratifies its interim legislative actions.

Is the NPC (and its Standing Committee) a "rubber-stamp" assembly? For the Maoist years, the answer is clearly yes. In recent decades, however, the NPC has become more assertive, and its Standing Committee has assumed a greater role in lawmaking.

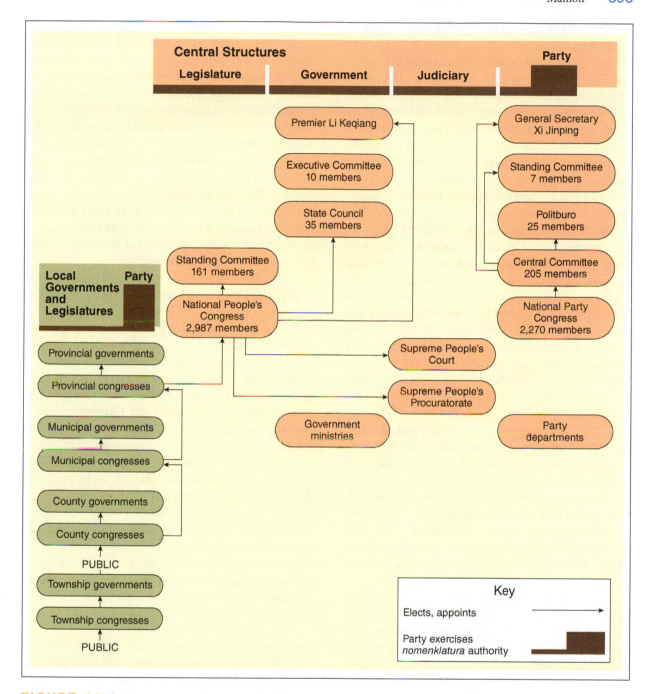

FIGURE 13.1
Chinese Political Structures
Parallel hierarchies of party and government structures exist, with party leadership at all levels.

This is part of the political reform undertaken in response to the extreme institutional nihilism of the Cultural Revolution. NPC assertiveness is evident in an increase in delegate motions (by an order of magnitude) and, more significantly, in dissenting votes. The practice of unanimous approval, once automatic, has ended, sometimes with embarrassing results.

The full NPC cannot be expected to function routinely as a credible legislature, because it is too large and meets too infrequently and briefly. More important is the lawmaking role of the less cumbersome NPC Standing Committee. In the early 1980s, many party and government elders retired from important positions in central and provincial administration to the NPC Standing Committee. Instead of retreating from political life, these elders used the Standing Committee as a channel for political influence. Their enhanced role was institutionalized with the establishment of a Legislative Affairs Committee (with significant staff) and nine permanent specialized legislative committees to consider draft legislation. With these changes, the NPC (and its Standing Committee) can no longer be dismissed as a rubber stamp. The legislature remains institutionally weak, however, for two main reasons (discussed later in this chapter): the practice of executive-led government (which does not distinguish the Chinese system from parliamentary systems in other countries) and the practice of Communist Party leadership (which is more fundamental).

State Council In lawmaking, the State Council is the center of government activity, although this role too is newly enhanced.[18] The State Council is composed of the premier, who is head of government, and his cabinet of vice-premiers, state councilors, ministers, auditor general, and secretary general (currently thirty-five members, all formally nominated by the premier and appointed by the NPC). In 2013, Li Keqiang became premier. The State Council has an Executive Committee, which meets twice weekly, with members reporting on work in their assigned portfolios. As in parliamentary systems, the bulk of legislation is drafted by specialized ministries and commissions under the direction of the cabinet. Also, however, as most Chinese laws are drafted in general and imprecise language, they require detailed "implementing regulations" to have any effect. These regulations are typically drafted by State Council ministries (under the direction of the newly reestablished State Council Legislation Bureau) and promulgated by the ministries or State Council without consideration by the NPC or its Standing Committee.

Communist Party Leadership The Communist Party exercises direct leadership over government and legislative functions in a variety of ways. Before the NPC assembles, party leaders convene a meeting of all delegates who are members of the Communist Party (about 70 percent of NPC delegates). At these meetings, leaders discuss the NPC agenda and offer "hopes" of the party leaders for the forthcoming session, including suggestions about the tone (how open or restrained NPC debate should be, for example). Also, NPC powers of appointment are effectively nullified by party control over candidate nomination and little to no electoral choice. For example, although the NPC formally appoints the president, vice president, premier, and cabinet members, there has never been more than one nominee for these positions, and candidate nomination is decided at the party meeting convened before the NPC assembles.

As to lawmaking, Communist Party leaders have veto power over all legislation of consequence. The system of party review of legislation that emerged in the early 1990s rejects party micromanagement of the State Council or NPC Standing Committee work. Nonetheless, all important laws, constitutional amendments, and political laws submitted to the NPC or its Standing Committee must have prior approval by the party center. In short, the Chinese system is executive-led government, but with an important difference: leadership by the Communist Party.

The president of the PRC is head of state. This is a purely ceremonial office, held by **Xi Jinping** (see Box 13.1). Xi is also head of the Communist Party organization and of the Central Military Commission, in which leadership of military forces is formally vested. The commission was established as a government structure only in 1982, but its Communist Party counterpart functioned long before then and remains in existence, with the same membership in party and government structures.

Judiciary Judicial authority rests with the Supreme People's Court at the center and with local people's courts below. Formally, the Supreme People's Court is responsible to the NPC. Courts at lower levels are responsible to the people's congresses at their respective levels and also take direction from courts above them.

The Supreme People's Procuratorate, restored in 1978 after decades of neglect, is the central prosecutorial agency. It sits at the top of a hierarchy of procuratorates extending down to the county level, each formally responsible to a local people's congress and each also under the direction of the procuratorate

BOX 13.1   Xi Jinping

China's current president, Communist Party chief, and head of the military is Xi Jinping. Born in 1953 to a high-ranking revolutionary veteran, Xi experienced a childhood of privilege but, like other "princelings," became the object of prejudice during the Cultural Revolution. Like other "fifth generation" leaders, he is highly educated but spent several Cultural Revolution years working in the countryside, where he joined the Communist Party. He graduated from Tsinghua University (China's MIT) in 1979, with a major in chemical engineering. After working several decades in various party and government posts, in Beijing and in the provinces, Xi was appointed to the Communist Party Politburo and groomed for five years in deputy positions to take up his current leadership offices in 2012–2013, in one of the most orderly leadership successions since the communists came to power.

above. The Supreme People's Procuratorate is responsible to the NPC.

Procuratorates act as a bridge between public security agencies and the courts. They supervise criminal investigations, approve arrests, and prosecute cases. Beginning in the mid-1980s, the most important role of the procuratorates has been investigation and prosecution of corruption. In each new congress session, the NPC appoints the chief justice of the Supreme People's Court and the chief procurator.

Party Structures

 Explain how the party dominates the party-state and exercises leadership in political structures.

At the political center in Beijing, the key party structures are the National Party Congress and its Central Committee, the Politburo, and the Politburo Standing Committee. In addition, party departments are organized under a secretariat. Below the center, down to the township level, are local party congresses and local party committees.

National Party Congress As in the government hierarchy, while the formal power of Communist Party structures is directly proportional to size, actual impact on policy is inversely proportional to size. The Communist Party constitution vests supreme authority in the **National Party Congress**, but this structure is too big and meets too infrequently to play a significant role in political decision making. The Central Committee determines the number of congress delegates and the procedures for their election. Since

1949, National Party Congresses have ranged in size from 1,000 to 2,000 delegates, with recent congresses at about 2,000 delegates. In the past, the congresses met irregularly, but party constitutions since 1969 have stipulated that congresses are normally convened at five-year intervals. This has been more or less the practice since 1969 and has been strictly observed in the post-Mao years, as shown in Table 13.1.

National Party Congress sessions are short, about a week or two at most. A main function is to ratify important changes in broad policy orientation already decided by more important smaller party structures. Although party congresses yield no surprises, these changes receive their highest formal endorsement at the party congresses. Therefore, the sessions have the public appearance of major historic events. A second function of the National Party Congress is to elect the **Central Committee**, which exercises the powers of the congress between sessions. Official candidates for Central Committee membership are determined by the Politburo before the congress meets. According to the 1982 party constitution, elections to the Central Committee are by secret ballot, and wide deliberation and discussion of candidates precedes them. Of course, centralism prevails; elections rarely offer choice (or much choice) among candidates.

Central Committee The Central Committee is the Chinese political elite, broadly defined; it is a collection of the most powerful several hundred political leaders in the country. All Central Committee members hold some major substantive position of leadership, as ministers in the central state bureaucracy or

TABLE 13.1

Chinese Communist Party Congresses and Growth of Party Membership, 1921–2012

Today, about 6 percent of Chinese are members of the elite CCP.

Congress	Year	Party Members
First	1921	More than 50
Second	1922	123
Third	1923	432
Fourth	1925	950
Fifth	1927	57,900[a]
Sixth	1928	40,000
Seventh	1945	1.2 million
Founding of the PRC, 1949		
Eighth	1956	11 million
Ninth	1969	22 million
Tenth	1973	28 million
Eleventh	1977	35 million
Twelfth	1982	40 million
Thirteenth	1987	46 million
Fourteenth	1992	51 million
Fifteenth	1997	60 million
Sixteenth	2002	66 million
Seventeenth	2007	74 million
Eighteenth	2012	83 million

[a]Communist Party membership dropped from 57,900 to 10,000 after April 1927, when the Nationalists broke the "united front" with the communists in a massacre that decimated communist forces and ignited civil war.

Source: *Beijing Review 41*, no. 8 (1998): 22; *China Today*, www .chinatoday.com/org/cpc/

provincial party leaders, for example. Membership on the Central Committee reflects this political power; it does not confer it. In this sense, the Central Committee is less important intrinsically as a political structure than extrinsically, for the different sorts of interests and constituencies represented by its members. The most recent party congress, which met in November 2012, elected a new "fifth generation" of political leaders to the Central Committee. Sixty-four percent of Central Committee members are new, highly educated leaders. Unlike previous cohorts of technocratic leaders, who mostly studied engineering, new Central Committee members majored in law, economics, or politics in college. Many hold graduate degrees. It is impossible to know how this educational experience

has prepared the new generation for power, but it is reasonable to speculate that these leaders will differ from previous cohorts.

Although the Central Committee does not initiate policy, changes in policy or leaders at the political center must be approved by it. This is done fairly routinely at plenary sessions now convened at least annually. Party leaders at the top rely on the bureaucratic and regional elites on the Central Committee to ensure that the "party line" is realized in practice. Central Committee membership brings these elites into the process as participants and, in effect, guarantors; in endorsing party policy, members also take on responsibility for its realization.

Politburo   The Central Committee elects the **Politburo**, the Politburo Standing Committee, and the party general secretary—all of whom are also Central Committee members. These leaders are at the very apex of the political system. The composition of these structures is determined by party leaders before the party congress, and elections are mainly ceremonial, featuring no candidate choice. The Politburo is the top political elite, usually no more than two dozen leaders, most of whom have responsibility for overseeing policymaking in some issue area. Its inner circle is the Politburo Standing Committee, typically no more than a half-dozen leaders, who meet about once weekly, in meetings convened and chaired by the party general secretary. Members of the Politburo and its Standing Committee are the core political decision makers in China, presiding over a process that concentrates great power at the top. The November 2012 leadership transition saw a major turnover of core decision makers too: fifteen of twenty-five Politburo members, including five of seven Politburo Standing Committee members, are new.

Top Leader and the Succession Problem   Since the abolition of the position of party chairman in 1982, the top party leader is the general secretary, a position held by Xi Jinping since 2012. The change in terminology reflects the effort to promote collective leadership, a reaction against norms of past years when Mao presided as nearly all-powerful chairman of the party until his death in 1976.

In communist systems, the death of the top leader has typically created a succession crisis; there is no formal or generally acknowledged position of second-in-command and no regularized mechanism to choose a new top leader. Mao's death ushered in a power struggle at the top, won by Deng and his fellow modernizers. Deng, already in his seventies at the time of Mao's death, chose to eschew top formal leadership of party or government in the interest of resolving the problem of succession.

In the late 1970s, Communist Party elders who had formerly held important positions of power were reinstated after years of forced retirement during the Cultural Revolution. Within a few years, however, many of them retired (or semiretired) to the "second line," to serve as advisors and involve themselves only in major policy issues or broad strategy.

At the very top, a half-dozen elders, all senior communist revolutionaries in their eighties or nineties, continued to play key roles in decision making and to occupy formal positions of leadership, although not the top party or government positions. The best example, of course, was "paramount leader" Deng himself. Deng never held the top formal position of leadership in party or government, although he was on the Politburo Standing Committee until 1987 and chaired the Central Military Commission until 1989. Just below this very small group at the top, elders retired to advisory positions on a Central Advisory Commission, set up in 1982. Other elders "retired" to formal positions on the NPC. Younger leaders were promoted to the top positions on the "first line" to allow them to develop their own bases of support and authority with the support of their elder patrons.

This arrangement did not provide a solution to the succession problem, however. In principle, elders on the second line used their prestige and informal power to support younger leaders in top executive positions. In practice, younger leaders on the first line, in the effort to establish their own authority, sometimes adopted positions at odds with the views of elder patrons. Friction with party elders resulted in two purges of top party executives in the 1980s: Hu Yaobang was dismissed as party general secretary in 1987, and his successor, Zhao Ziyang, was dismissed in 1989 (see Figure 13.2). The situation today is different; by the mid-1990s, most of the elders at the very top, including Deng, had "gone to see Marx," and the Central Advisory Commission had been dismantled, having served its purpose of easing leaders into retirement.

More recent successions have been remarkably orderly, observing several important formal and informal rules. For example, in 2012, as in the previous two successions, the established top party leader retired in favor of a younger leader who had been prepared to

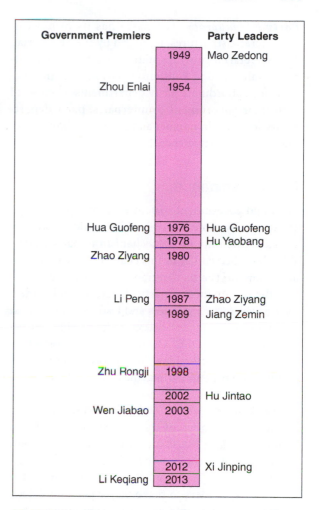

FIGURE 13.2

Top Party and Government Executives, 1949–present

Lifelong tenure is no longer the norm among Chinese leaders.

Note: Year refers to the year a leader assumed office.

succeed him, with an appointment five years earlier to a deputy party leadership office and a position on the Politburo Standing Committee. Politburo members who had reached age fifty-eight all retired, something the party newspaper affirms as a "rigorous rule." Institutional constituencies on the Politburo represent a balance across the communist party apparatus, the central government, and regional power holders; moreover, military representation is sharply limited. As in the past, the Politburo Standing Committee remains a "boy's club": The only "fourth generation" Politburo member not promoted to the Standing Committee in 2012 is a woman.

Party Bureaucracy The party has its own set of bureaucratic structures, managed by the Secretariat. The Secretariat provides staff support for the Politburo, transforming Politburo decisions into instructions for subordinate party departments. Compared with their government counterparts, party departments are fewer in number and have more broadly defined areas of competence.

Party Dominance

Party and government structures from top to bottom are staffed by more than 40 million officials on state salaries. One important mechanism of party leadership, described earlier in this chapter, is the structural arrangement: the duplication of political structures and the dominance of party structures and leaders over government structures and leaders. The Chinese Communist Party exercises leadership in political structures in other ways too. Among the most important are overlapping directorships, "party core groups," party membership penetration, and the *nomenklatura* system.

Nomenklatura System The **nomenklatura system** is the most important mechanism by which the Communist Party exerts control over officials. In some sense, it is the linchpin of the political system. Simply put, it is the party's personnel management system. It allows party leaders to make major personnel decisions (such as appointment, promotion, transfer, and removal from office) for all party and government positions of even moderate importance. From top to bottom, each party committee has authority over a list of positions one level down the hierarchy. The lists of positions are quite comprehensive: They include any party or government position of even moderate importance as well as managers of state enterprises and public institutions such as universities.[19] At the top of the system, the Politburo exercises direct management authority over all officials at the provincial level in the territorial hierarchy and at the ministerial level in the bureaucratic hierarchy—about 7,000 officials in all (including the entire NPC Standing Committee, for example).

The extension of management authority downward in a hierarchy of dyadic relationships that are known to officials has important implications. Party leaders have a means of ensuring that the real "boss" of every important official is the superior party committee—and ultimately the Central Committee and its Politburo. Party committees exercise personnel management through their organization departments, which vet incumbent and prospective officials regularly and provide information to party committees about performance. In looking ahead to career advancement, then, even officials who owe their positions formally to elections must look upward to "selectorates" of party committees rather than only (if at all) downward to electorates of congress delegates and ordinary citizens. Otherwise, they will not be promoted.

Party Membership Another means by which the Communist Party exercises leadership over officials is in party membership penetration in political structures. The vast majority of officials in political structures (including government structures and positions filled by elections) are Communist Party members. At their places of work, officials are members of party committees, general branches, or branches located in a hierarchy of basic-level party organizations. They meet regularly to participate in party "organizational life," which is quite apart from their professional work. They are obliged to observe the inner-party discipline of democratic centralism. The routine activities of party branches in government offices are supervised by departments specially assigned to ensure that the Communist Party remains an active force in government structures. Because the party monopolizes opportunities to get along and ahead in the Chinese political system, the organizational hierarchy and party discipline designed to guarantee unified party leadership over society also promote party leadership in political structures.

Party Core Groups Separate from the basic-level party organizations that bring party members in all workplaces under the Communist Party hierarchy are party core groups, formed in government structures only and composed of a handful of party members who hold the most senior positions.[20] The head of the party core group is normally also the head of the structure (for example, government ministers typically head party core groups of their respective ministries). Party core groups are appointed by the party committees one level up, and they answer to these party committees. While basic-level party organizations are mechanisms to promote unity and discipline under party leadership within political structures overall, party core groups are mechanisms to promote party leadership over leaders in their government host structures. Between 1987 and 1988, the system of party core groups was formally abolished (and many were actually dismantled) as part of a brief reform effort to separate party and government functions. Party core groups were quickly revived in 1989, however, after the purge of Zhao Ziyang, the leader most closely associated with the reform.

Overlapping Directorships Finally, the structural distinctions illustrated in Figure 13.1 mask some overlap of directorates in party and government structures. Xi Jinping is concurrently head of state, head of the party, and chairman of the Central Military Commission of both government and party. The practice of "wearing two hats" (party and government) has always been common. Premier Li Keqiang, as a member of the Politburo Standing Committee, is also at the apex of party power. Zhang Dejiang, who chairs the NPC Standing Committee, is also a member of the Politburo Standing Committee. Overlapping directorships were much more extensive in the past than they are now. Membership of local party committees and their parallel governments used to be indistinguishable. In the 1980s, overlapping directorships were retained at the political center but were practically eliminated at lower levels. There is some evidence that they are returning, partly to reduce local state expenditures.

Elite Recruitment Some key features of elite recruitment emerge from the discussion earlier in this chapter. First, membership in the Communist Party is a prerequisite for political elite status. Over the decades, the party has changed its focus of recruitment in society, reflecting larger changes in policy orientation. In the 1950s, for example, the party recruited most intensely among industrial workers to build a more traditional Communist Party from a largely peasant base. In the Cultural Revolution of the 1960s and 1970s, radical leftist standards dominated—and recruitment was directed toward those with less education and fewer connections. Since 1980, the party has focused its recruitment effort on intellectuals, professionals, and even private entrepreneurs—all social groups identified as important for China's development as a prosperous nation (see Box 13.2).

Second, the party not only controls accessibility to this fundamental prerequisite for elite status but also possesses a powerful organizational mechanism to recruit and promote elites: the nomenklatura system. Both appointed and elected leaders are vetted for office, level by level, so leaders are ultimately accountable to party committees at higher levels. Beijing has not relinquished this key power, despite significant economic decentralization in recent decades.

What determines who gets along and ahead in the current Chinese political system? That is, what criteria have leaders at higher levels viewed as most important

BOX 13.2 "Red Capitalists"

In the mid-1980s, many party and government officials plunged into the private sector economy, shedding their offices but not their Communist Party membership. With little fanfare, the party also began to recruit private entrepreneurs as new members—a practice that reflected the party's commitment to economic growth but met strong opposition from many as an abandonment of basic communist tenets. How could millionaire exploiters represent Chinese workers and peasants? When private entrepreneurs lent their support to protesters in 1989, leaders imposed a ban on their recruitment into the party. More than a decade later, in 2000, party leader Jiang Zemin introduced a convoluted new formula to justify welcoming

them back: the "three represents," added in 2004 to China's constitution. In this formula, the party does not simply represent workers and peasants but represents the developmental needs of the advanced social productive forces, the promotion of advanced culture, and the fundamental interests of the greatest majority of the people. In 2001, on the party's eightieth anniversary, Jiang proposed lifting the ban on recruitment of private entrepreneurs into the party. His proposal was soon implemented. Today, one-third of private entrepreneurs are party members. Even though "red capitalists" still account for only a very small proportion of party members, their inclusion reflects a highly significant policy.

for promotion? While much is made of the role of informal politics in China, economic performance is the most important determinant of elite promotion.[21] Leaders in localities with higher economic growth or revenue contributions to the center during their tenure are less likely to be demoted or retired from office. This is not surprising, as leaders in Beijing have staked their claim to legitimacy on delivering economic prosperity.

Rule by Law

13.6 Contrast China's "rule by law" with democratic "rule of law."

The principle of "**rule of law**" is traditionally associated with liberal democratic ideals. It implies a particular relationship between individuals and the state, the essence of which is protection of individual rights by limitations on arbitrary state power. Such limitations are enshrined in the law and in legal institutions. This notion makes no sense in traditional communist ideology; law is a weapon of the state to use in exercising dictatorship. In 1978, however, Chinese leaders began to revive and develop important ideas and institutions of legality that had flourished for a brief period in the 1950s. The new Chinese legality acknowledges **rule by law**.[22] Briefly, this means (1) there are laws and (2) all are equally subject to them. As the second principle is often violated, this may seem a trivial advance. It is not. The ongoing effort to establish rule by law in China has already changed in important ways how the Chinese act and think.

Socialist Legality The initial Chinese experiment with "socialist legality" began with the promulgation of the first constitution in 1954 and ended in 1957 with the Anti-Rightist Movement. Legalistic perspectives were rejected as examples of "bourgeois rightist" thinking. Legal scholars and legal professionals were criticized and labeled as "rightists." Work on development of criminal law stopped. Legal training and legal scholarship practically ceased. Defense lawyers disappeared from the legal process. Party committees took direct control of legal proceedings. The abandonment of law reached a peak during the Cultural Revolution, when violent "class struggle" and "mass justice" substituted for any regularized procedures to resolve social conflicts. This degree of radical lawlessness was not characteristic of the entire Maoist period, but a general official hostility to law prevailed from the late 1950s.

Legal Reform Legal reform began in 1978. The legal system, barely functioning at the time, required urgent action for a number of reasons. First, there was an immediate need to establish legitimacy by righting past wrongs; investigating and reversing verdicts of dubious legality issued during the Cultural Revolution were a high priority. Second, Deng Xiaoping and other leaders wanted not only to restore public order and stability after years of chaos and uncertainty but also to express their commitment to system building as a substitute for arbitrary political rule. Finally and not least of all, Chinese leaders hoped that the new legality would encourage economic investment and growth by promoting predictability—through transparent rules and impartial rule adjudication.

Rule by law requires laws. Nearly thirty years after the founding of the PRC, there was no criminal law. In 1978, Chinese leaders appointed committees of legal specialists to pick up work set aside for decades and to draft criminal codes for immediate promulgation. In 1979, the NPC passed the first criminal law and criminal procedure law. In the years that followed, as government agencies issued interim regulations that amended and clarified the hastily drafted laws, the NPC Legislative Affairs Committee worked on legal revisions. In 1996 and 1997, the NPC passed substantially amended and more precise versions of the laws. The 1997 amended criminal law takes into account changes in the Chinese economy that have created opportunities for economic crimes almost unimaginable in 1979 (such as insider securities trading). It abolishes the vaguely defined crimes of "counterrevolution." The 1996 amended criminal procedure law grants the accused the right to seek counsel (a right rejected in the 1950s) at an early stage of legal proceedings.

Rule by law implies equality before the law. This idea stands in sharp contrast to both the politicized view of law in communist ideology and routine practices in the Maoist years. In 1978, the NPC restored the procuratorates, which had been abolished in the 1960s. A new important role of procuratorates in the 1980s and 1990s became the investigation and prosecution of official crimes, for which procuratorates have full independent responsibility, according to law. Chinese leaders have regularly and prominently voiced a commitment to equality before the law, stating that officials who abuse public office and violate laws must be punished. Equality before the law, labeled "bourgeois" in the 1950s, is featured in the 1982 constitution—which also, for the first time, subjects the Communist Party (not only party members) to the authority of the law. At the same time, as described later in this chapter, there has been an explosion of corruption in recent years. In practice, the Communist Party, through its political–legal committees and its system of discipline inspection committees, routinely protects officials from equality before the law in cases involving abuses of power.

At the end of the 1970s, most Chinese were ignorant of laws and mistrustful of legal channels, a reasonable position when politics routinely superseded law. In the 1980s, the authorities launched a number of campaigns to educate ordinary citizens about the content of important laws and about certain ideas, such as equality before the law. Developing legal norms when legality has been actively denounced (not merely neglected) for decades has been difficult. Yet ordinary Chinese do use law to pursue their interests. One indicator of the effect of the legal education effort is the growth in lawsuits against government agencies and officials under the administrative litigation law. The number of such lawsuits processed in the legal system has increased steadily since passage of the law in 1989.

Criticism of Legal Practices Legal reform has provoked criticism of Chinese law and legal practices outside China.[23] Three examples illustrate this. First, Chinese criminal law stipulates the death penalty in "serious circumstances" of smuggling, rape, theft, bribery, trafficking in women and children, and corruption. In periodic intensive efforts to "strike hard" at crime, the authorities have resorted widely to capital punishment. Critics argue that capital punishment is excessively harsh for these crimes. Second, by design, criminal proceedings are inquisitorial (not adversarial), focused on determination of punishment (not guilt). As cases are prosecuted only after sufficient evidence has been collected to demonstrate guilt, most prosecutions result in guilty verdicts. The right to seek counsel at an early stage of proceedings is recognized in the law, but the requirement is only that a public defender be assigned no later than ten days before trial. By that time, the case has been prepared for prosecution and usually a confession (for which the law promises leniency) has already been obtained. This practice

of "verdict first, trial second" has been questioned and debated inside China and criticized outside China. Finally, despite abolition of specifically political crimes of counterrevolution, the Chinese authorities acknowledge "several thousand" political prisoners. While human rights groups estimate the number to be much larger, all critics view the situation as essentially inconsistent with the new law.

Nonetheless, the new legality has produced significant change. Today more than ever before, the Chinese state is more constrained by laws, while Chinese citizens are freer from political arbitrariness because of laws. Abuse of authority is acted on differently from before. Ordinary citizens use the law as a political weapon against perceived injustice because the regime has invested heavily in the new legality. The official effort to build rule by law, by making law salient, has produced a basis for "rightful resistance" to hold the regime accountable to its own proclaimed standards.

Political Socialization

13.7 Describe the government's relationship to mass media and the education system as sources of political socialization.

One result of the economic policy of opening up to the outside is that Chinese leaders today cannot control information as in the Maoist years.[24]

Mass Media

Ordinary Chinese are now routinely exposed to news and opinions about public affairs in their country through access to Hong Kong (which maintains relatively free and critical mass media) and the outside world in newspapers, books, radio and television broadcasts, and the Internet. Moreover, Chinese connect with one another to transmit information as never before through blogs, bulletin boards, e-mail, telephone, and text messages. China imported its first mobile phone facilities in 1987; today, 75 percent of the 564 million Internet users in China connect through their mobile phones. The Chinese authorities recognize the importance of the Internet for economic modernization, but also view it as a threat to their rule. The Communist Party Propaganda Department and State Council Information Office direct the world's most extensive system to control, censor, and monitor material considered politically subversive. Internet news is still mainly official news; news media are required to use the official Xinhua news agency as their news source. Despite great relaxation of media controls, certain topics remain taboo (multiparty competition, urban protests, and labor strikes, for example). In this way, the Internet allows the regime to spread its official message more effectively. The Chinese **Great Firewall** for Internet censorship blocks content by preventing Internet Protocol (IP) addresses from being routed through standard firewall and proxy servers at Internet gateways. As the government controls the domestic networks that connect service providers to international networks, it can block access to sites and delete Web pages considered subversive. Tens of thousands of "cyber cops" selectively block foreign news sites and terminate domestic sites that publicize politically sensitive information. For example, the authorities quickly blocked any use of the phrase "empty chair" when it appeared in numerous Chinese blogs as an expression of solidarity with 2010 Nobel Peace Prize winner Liu Xiaobo, imprisoned for political dissidence and represented at the ceremonies in Oslo by an empty chair. Of course, total control is counterproductive (see Box 13.3). Internet users circumvent official blockages through proxy servers based outside China and by slightly altering Chinese characters to refer to political events and activities.

Education System

The new content and style of political socialization are clearly evident in the education system. Mao's successors inherited an education system designed to build communist values—and fundamentally at odds with the priority of economic growth. During the Cultural Revolution, high school graduates were sent to factories or farms to acquire work experience and learn from the masses. University entrance examinations were replaced with recommendations by grassroots leaders, focusing on revolutionary political credentials. With the persecution of scholars and denigration of expert knowledge in the universities, the content of university education was redesigned to include more politics in every specialization. Graduates were more "red" than expert. An entire decade was lost. The generation that missed out on an education during this decade is known today as the "lost generation."

Today, with the return of the university entrance examinations and huge numbers of Chinese studying in foreign universities, the respect for expertise is thoroughly restored. Indeed, in fall 2006, on instructions from top party and government departments, colleges across the country reduced the seven compulsory courses on political ideology and party history to four, in the first major curricular change in twenty-five years.

BOX 13.3   Chinese Internet Censorship and Google

The Chinese government has issued dozens of documents regulating Internet content, but no official master list of taboo subjects has been made public. Instead, businesses interpret regulations and gauge the political environment as they censor and self-censor. Operating in this regulatory context, Google.cn, the Google search engine based in China until 2010, routinely filtered its content. Appearing at the bottom of each page of censored results on Google.cn was a notice informing readers that some information was hidden from them because of strictures from the Chinese authorities. In January 2010, Google announced it was no longer willing to filter its content; instead, it would attempt to negotiate a legal, unfiltered search engine. Failing that, it would close down its China operations. At the announcement, Chinese expressed their grief at the loss by laying flowers at the door of Google's Beijing offices; although the search engine's market share of 33 percent lagged far behind that of its Chinese competitor, Baidu, Google censored less than did Baidu; access to English-language periodicals was particularly valuable to Chinese researchers. In March 2010, with no Chinese flexibility on requirements to observe existing law, Google shut down its mainland offices to establish an unfiltered Google.cn in Hong Kong. Today, the Chinese Great Firewall regularly blocks searches of politically sensitive topics on Google.cn from within China.

Political Culture

13.8 Examine China's political culture in the light of its historical roots.

Older and middle-aged Chinese have experienced not only the radicalism of the Maoist years but also more than two decades of "reform and opening" to the outside world. Young Chinese have only the personal experience of the relatively open post-Mao years, including the decade of the 1990s that saw the "third wave" of democratization, with the triumph of democracy in nearly every communist country. Surely recent changes both inside and outside China have left their imprint on the way Chinese view their government and their relationship to political authorities.

Because Maoist-era leaders regarded social science with great suspicion, we have no good baseline of public opinion data by which to assess change over time in the beliefs of ordinary Chinese. We can say something about the Chinese political culture today, however, based on survey research in China, including surveys organized and conducted by political scientists based in the United States. What is the orientation toward politics of ordinary Chinese? In particular, to what extent do the beliefs of Chinese seem conducive to political change in the direction of further democratization?

Political Knowledge

An important building block for democracy is a citizenry knowledgeable about politics and interested in public affairs, able to monitor the performance of representatives and leaders. Most ordinary Chinese follow public affairs at least weekly, mainly through radio or television programs and somewhat less through newspapers, but politics is not something that is a regular topic of discussion in China. A majority say they *never* talk about politics with others, a stark reflection of lack of active interest.

Political knowledge and interest are not uniformly distributed in China, of course. A more active knowledge and interest are seen among men, the more highly educated, and Chinese with higher incomes, which is not so different from what we observe in other countries. Not surprisingly, Chinese in Beijing are much more interested in politics than Chinese overall; in fact, they discuss politics very frequently. Yet even if we consider the situation of Chinese overall, which includes the relatively less knowledgeable and less interested rural population, political knowledge in China today is higher than in Italy in the early 1960s, and political discourse is higher than in Italy or Mexico in the early 1960s.[25]

567 Million Chinese "Netizens"
Cyber cafés are popular with urban Chinese youth. Even with some 50,000 cyberpolice, it is impossible to monitor Internet activity fully.

Political Value

An interesting perspective on contemporary Chinese political culture is a comparative one that places mainland China in an Asian context. The 2002 Asian Barometer Surveys (ABS) asked representative samples of the population in eight East Asian polities (including Hong Kong and Taiwan) about their views on democracy.[26] Consider first the array of responses to two simple questions, presented in Figure 13.3. Overwhelmingly, East Asians support democracy. Surprisingly, support for democracy is comparatively high in mainland China, the only authoritarian regime among the eight: On a ten-point scale, mainland Chinese average 8.5 in their assessment of the suitability of democracy for their country; this is second only to Thailand, at 8.8. Even more surprising is the perceived existing amount of democracy in authoritarian China.

On this dimension, mainland China is also rather high: It ranks third, at an average 7.2, just behind Taiwan and somewhat farther behind Thailand. This is a puzzle, which cannot be simply dismissed as a product of fearful self-censored responses.

The explanation becomes only a little clearer when we consider the elasticity of the idea of democracy. On the one hand, for decades, ordinary Chinese have been indoctrinated in the notion of "socialist democracy," which rejects most liberal democratic institutions (such as multiparty elections) as tools of the bourgeois ruling class. On the other hand, Confucian cultural tradition associates good governance with paternalistic social welfare provided by rulers "specially qualified to govern by reason of their superior knowledge and virtue."[27] In this tradition, legitimacy derives not from procedural claims but from substantive

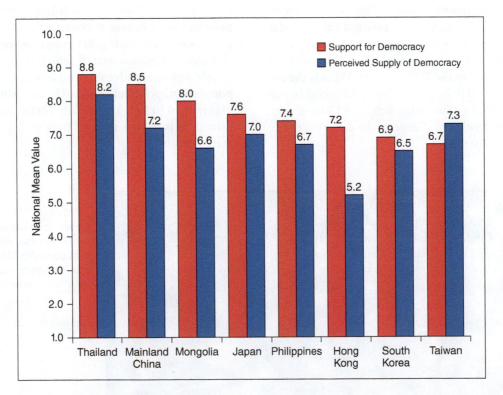

FIGURE 13.3

Support and Demand for Democracy in Comparative Perspective

A puzzle: authoritarian China compares favorably to other East Asian political systems in support and demand for democracy.

Note: Figures are from the 2002 Asian Barometer Surveys. For demand, interviewers asked: "If 1 indicates entirely unsuitable and 10 indicates entirely suitable, please tell us how suitable you think democracy is for your country." For supply, interviewers asked: "If 1 means entirely undemocratic and 10 means entirely democratic, please tell us how democratic you believe your country is under the current regime."

Source: Tianjian Shi and Jie Lu, "The Shadow of Confucianism," *Journal of Democracy*, vol. 21, no. 4 (2010): 124.

Big City Traffic, Big City Highways

China is no longer a bicycle nation. Chinese-designed and manufactured automobiles emit ten to twenty times more pollution than American or Japanese models.

policy outcomes, especially those involving the common welfare. When mainland Chinese see democracy in the workings of their political system, perhaps they are viewing it from a perspective different from that associated with liberal democracy—either a framework produced through socialist indoctrination or the reflection of a cultural outlook that equates legitimate rule with social welfare.

Fortunately, the 2002 ABS asked respondents "What does democracy mean to you?" Specific responses can be divided into four categories. The first is procedural democracy, which includes references to elections, checks and balances, and freedom of the press, for example. The second is populism and socialism, which encompasses both socialist democracy and Confucian benevolent dictatorship. It includes, for example, references to a government that brings tangible benefits to the people, that takes care of people's interests. Responses that refer to competitive political pluralism belong in the procedural democracy category, not this category. A third category comprises all other understandings of democracy, including democratic centralism, for example. The fourth category consists of nonresponses.

When mainland Chinese say they support democracy, this does not mean they necessarily can say what it means to them: Forty-two percent, by far the highest percentage among all eight East Asian polities,

fall into the fourth category; they cannot answer this question. Another 18 percent define democracy in populist or socialist terms only, 25 percent define it in procedural terms only, and 5 percent respond in ways that mix the two categories. Here then, is the answer to our puzzle: Twenty-three percent of mainland Chinese view democracy from a perspective at least partly colored by Confucian cultural tradition or socialist indoctrination or both. From this perspective, it is easier to understand the perception that the authoritarian regime in mainland China is also democratic. At the same time, 30 percent define democracy fully or partly in procedural terms—although support for multiparty elections, which is an essential component of most definitions of liberal democracy, is only about half this percentage. For these Chinese, the authoritarian regime surely falls short of the democratic ideal.

Political Participation

 13.9 Discuss the "officially acceptable" and "unacceptable" forms of political participation at national and local levels in China.

In the communist party-state, political participation, interest articulation, and interest aggregation differ from the processes normally found in liberal democratic systems. The source of difference is, of course, different conceptions of the relationship between leaders and citizens; the notion of guardianship is fundamentally incompatible with liberal democratic notions of representation. The Communist Party organization claims to represent the interests of all society. It rejects political parties other than itself as unnecessary and unacceptable. While there has been change in political processes in recent decades, the "officially acceptable" forms of political participation, interest articulation, and interest aggregation in the Chinese political system continue to reflect the relationship of guardianship between party and society. This section discusses political participation; the next section explores interest articulation and aggregation.

Changes in the Rules

An important aspect of political reform undertaken after Mao's death in 1976 has been the redefinition of what constitutes "officially acceptable" political participation in the Chinese system. Guidelines for the new political participation are evident in three categories of rule changes that have routinized participation and reduced its burden for ordinary Chinese. The changes reflect an official reaction against the disruption that characterized mass participation in the Maoist years (especially during the Cultural Revolution), an official assumption that economic growth is predicated on order and stability, and an official recognition that changes in economic relationships require adjustments in political relationships.

The first category of rule changes involves political participation, which has become essentially optional for ordinary Chinese since the early 1980s. In the first thirty years of communist rule, for a broad range of political activities, failure to participate was considered tantamount to opposition to the communist regime. Today, politics intrudes far less in the lives of ordinary Chinese. The scope and demands of politics have shrunk. The single most important measure signifying this change is the official removal, in 1979, of all class and political labels. After thirty years, the Chinese are no longer formally identified by class background or past "political mistakes." Not only does politics no longer dominate daily life, but, in the diminished sphere of political activities, political apathy is no longer risky for ordinary Chinese.

The second category is the assiduous avoidance by the regime of rousing the mass public to realize policy objectives. In the Maoist years, by contrast, the quintessential form of political participation was the **mass mobilization campaign**—intensive, large-scale, disruptive group action implemented by grassroots leaders. The Great Leap Forward launched in 1958 and the Cultural Revolution launched in 1966 were essentially mass campaigns, on a gargantuan scale. Typically in mass campaigns, grassroots party leaders, responding to signals from the political center, roused ordinary Chinese to achieve regime goals of various sorts, often aimed at identified categories of enemies—such as "counterrevolutionaries" in 1950 and 1951, the "landlord class" in 1950 through 1952, the "rightists" in 1957, and the "unclean cadres" in 1962 and 1963. Mass campaign methods were adopted for nonpolitical objectives too, such as the ill-conceived and ecologically harmful effort to eradicate "four pests" (sparrows, rats, flies, and mosquitoes) in 1956. Participation in campaigns was virtually compulsory. Only three years after Mao's death, Chinese leaders issued an official rejection of mass campaigns as a mode of political participation. Many leaders who emerged at the top echelons of power in the late 1970s had themselves been victims of persecution in the Cultural Revolution. The social disorder of campaigns was rejected as antithetical to the new priority of economic growth.

The third category is the rejection of mass mobilization as the dominant mode of political participation. Chinese leaders have instead encouraged ordinary citizens to express their opinions and participate in politics through a variety of regular official channels, some new, others newly revived: offices to receive complaints, centers and telephone hotlines to report abuses of power, and letters to newspaper editors, for example.[28] Not least of all, the authorities have introduced important reforms in elections. As a consequence, political participation in China is varied and extensive in scope. Figure 13.4 shows findings from a survey conducted in Beijing in the 1980s and 1990s. Beijing is surely the most highly politicized city in all of China, but the extent of citizen participation in a wide range of activities is nonetheless remarkable, not at all the picture of Maoist mobilization.

Elections and an electoral connection between citizens and leaders are integral to liberal democratic conceptions of representation. For this reason, governments and NGOs in liberal democracies have paid close attention to electoral reforms in China.

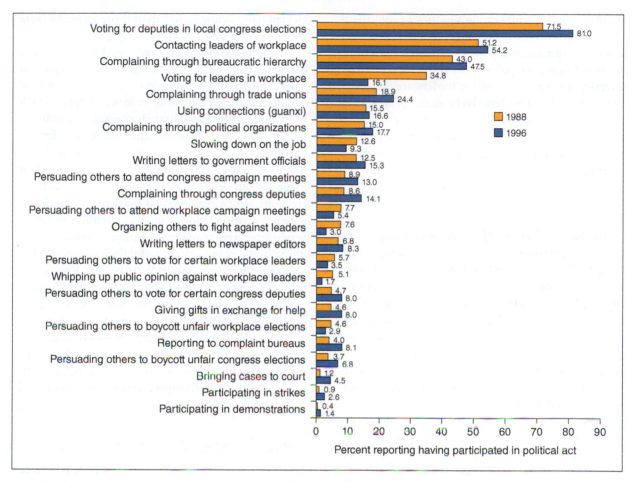

FIGURE 13.4

Political Participation in Beijing

Significant numbers of Chinese participate politically in officially acceptable ways.

Source: Based on Tianjian Shi, "Mass Political Behavior in Beijing," in *The Paradox of China's Post-Mao Reforms*, ed. Merle Goldman and Roderick MacFarquhar (Cambridge, MA: Harvard University Press, 1999), 155.

Local Congress Elections

Elections to local people's congresses in the Maoist years were political rituals, featuring no candidate choice and no secret ballot. Voters directly elected deputies to township-level congresses only; at higher levels, deputies were elected by congresses at the level immediately below. Such elections served as vehicles of regime legitimation, popular education, and political socialization, but they did not really allow ordinary citizens to choose representatives.

In 1979, a new election law introduced direct election of deputies to county-level congresses, mandated secret ballots rather than public displays of support, and required the number of candidates to

be one and a half times the number of deputies to be elected.

Although local Communist Party organizations continue to play a key leadership role in election committees, essentially vetting candidates, not all candidates can win under current rules. Some officially nominated candidates lose elections. Indeed, some candidates officially designated for government office lose elections. A growing number of candidates who are not Communist Party members have competed and won in elections. A smaller number of government executives nominated by deputies are not official candidates and win without official endorsement.[29] An electoral victory signifies some degree of popular support, while losing signifies a problematic relationship with the mass public. At a minimum, the new rules are a means for the Communist Party organization to gauge popular views about local officials, diversify the pool from which leaders are recruited, and monitor local leaders. To be sure, the new rules have not produced radical change. Nor can such an outcome be expected without further change in rules; no platform of opposition to the Communist Party is permissible.

Village Committees

China also now has nearly two decades of experience with rural grassroots democratization, formally approved in November 1987 when the NPC, after over a year of debate, passed a provisional version of the Organic Law on Village Committees. A final revised version was passed in November 1998. The law defines **village committees** as "autonomous mass organizations of self-government," popularly elected in elections featuring choice among candidates for three-year terms and accountable to a village council comprised of all adult villagers.

The introduction of popularly elected village committees in 1987 was designed to strengthen state capacity to govern in the aftermath of agricultural decollectivization. In the early 1980s, the people's communes had been dismantled and replaced with township governments. Land and other production inputs were divided among peasant households to manage on their own, free markets were opened, most obligatory sales to the state were abolished, and private entrepreneurship was promoted.[30] The results of these reforms were successful by most economic standards, but disastrous in their consequences for rural leadership. As villagers gained greater economic initiative and autonomy, the power of the Chinese party-state to exact compliance was enormously weakened. By the mid-1980s, village leadership had seriously atrophied. Leaders were enriching themselves at the expense of the community, and villagers were resisting their efforts to implement unpopular policies. Violent conflicts between villagers and village leaders had become common. The revitalization of village committees in 1987 was designed to make the countryside more governable by increasing accountability. Presumably, villagers would be more responsive to leaders

elected from below rather than those imposed from above as before.

In 1998, when the NPC affirmed the experience of village elections, most villages had undergone at least three rounds of elections, with enormous local variation in implementation. In many villages, the village Communist Party branch controlled candidate nomination, there was no candidate choice for the key position of village committee director, and voting irregularities were common. Even in villages that made serious progress—with genuinely competitive elections, widespread popular participation in candidate nomination, and scrupulous attention to voting procedure—real managerial authority often resided not with the popularly elected village committee but with the village Communist Party branch. Even today, too little is known to generalize about overall progress in village elections, its determinants, or its consequences.[31] Certainly, to the degree that the practices of grassroots democracy acquire the force of routine and expectations accumulate, however slowly, among nearly 625 million Chinese in more than 600,000 villages, political participation in the countryside will change profoundly.

"Unacceptable" Political Participation

More dramatic than the reforms that have redefined officially acceptable political participation has been the political action of ordinary Chinese in city streets and squares beginning in the late 1970s. With strikes, marches, posters, petitions, and occupation of public spaces, ordinary citizens have acted as if political reform comprehended or condoned mass political action and public disorder. The official record suggests the contrary, however.

In 1980, the right to post "big-character posters" (usually criticisms of leaders, written by individuals or groups and posted on walls), introduced during the Cultural Revolution, was removed from the Chinese constitution. In 1982, the constitutional right to strike was rescinded. As for mass protests, the official view was made clear in 1979 with the introduction of the "four fundamental principles" that political participation must uphold: (1) the socialist road, (2) Marxism–Leninism–Mao Zedong Thought, (3) the people's democratic dictatorship, and (4) the leadership of the Communist Party. Of these principles, only the last is necessary to restrict political participation effectively, as the content of the first three has become what party leaders make of it. Participants (especially organizers) face real risks of physical harm and criminal punishment. Why, then, did ordinary citizens engage in mass protests with increasing frequency in the 1970s and 1980s? Why did urban worker and peasant unrest increase in the 1980s and 1990s?

Different sorts of "officially unacceptable" political participation have different explanations, but none can be explained without reference to the post-Mao reforms. On the one hand, economic reforms have produced some socially unacceptable outcomes: more (and more visible) inflation, unemployment, crime, and corruption, for example. Rural unrest has typically been triggered by local corruption and exaction of excessive (often illegal) taxes and fees. Urban unrest—strikes, slowdowns, and demonstrations—has increased too, as state enterprises struggle to survive in the socialist market economy. A number of enterprises have been closed down; many have engaged in massive layoffs; others have been unable to pay bonuses and pensions. For the first time since 1949, many urban Chinese have been living on fixed incomes, no incomes, or unpredictable incomes as the cost of living increases.

Protesters and Reformers

In 1989, a different sort of urban unrest captured the attention of the world news media and, consequently, of the world. The demonstration that brought a million people to Tiananmen Square was the third major political protest movement since Mao's death. The first was in 1978 and 1979, the second in 1986 and 1987. All three were officially unacceptable, all were linked in some important way to official reforms and reformers, and all ended in failure for mass protesters (and resulted in setbacks to official reforms too).[32]

Despite links between protesters and official reformers, the post-Mao movements were not mass mobilization campaigns. As they were not explicitly initiated by the regime, once underway, they could not be easily stopped with an official pronouncement from the political center. Instead, the authorities turned to coercive force wielded by the police, the armed police, and ultimately the army to terminate the protests with violence.

Protests are officially unacceptable mainly because of their form of expression. The official consensus since December 1978 has been that the most important priority for China is economic growth, with social order and stability as prerequisites for growth. Mass protests are distinctly disorderly. Further, as a form of political participation, mass protests are a symptom of regime failure in two senses. By turning to the streets to articulate their demands, protesters demonstrate that official channels for expressing critical views are not working and that they do not believe the Communist Party's claim that it can correct its own mistakes. Further, protesters are clearly not alienated from politics. While they reject official channels of participation, they are not politically apathetic; indeed, they articulate explicitly political demands despite serious risks and the difficulty associated with organizing outside the system. In short, political protests signify that mass political participation can neither be contained within official channels nor deterred with a better material life.

For the most part, despite some radical elements, the protests have not been blatantly antisystem in their demands. This does not appear to be merely strategic. Rather, the protests are something of a rowdy mass counterpart to the official socialist reform movement, exerting more pressure for more reform, and (while officially unacceptable) often linked with elite reformers.

In the **Democracy Movement** of 1978 and 1979, Deng Xiaoping publicly approved many of the demands posted on Democracy Wall and published in unofficial journals, which called for a "reversal of verdicts" on individuals and political events. The demands were an integral part of the pressure for reform that surrounded the meetings of top leaders in late 1978, allowing elite reformers to argue for major changes in policy and political orientation. The poster campaign and unofficial journals were tolerated. To be sure, when a bold dissident named Wei Jingsheng demanded a "fifth modernization," by which he meant democracy of a sort never envisaged by the communists, the Chinese authorities promptly sentenced him to a fifteen-year prison term (ostensibly for revealing state secrets) and introduced the "four fundamental principles" to establish the parameters of acceptable debate[33] (see Box 13.4).

When the Communist Party congress convened in late 1987, party leader Zhao Ziyang acknowledged conflicts of interest in society at the current time. The years 1988 and 1989 were high points for political

In late 1978, in an atmosphere of great change that included official "reversals of verdicts" of the Cultural Revolution, many Chinese began to gather regularly at a large wall close to Beijing's Tiananmen Square to post, read, and discuss political posters. One of the boldest posters to appear on Democracy Wall was an essay by Wei Jingsheng. It argued that the ambitious new program to modernize agriculture, industry, national defense, and science and technology could not succeed without a "fifth modernization"—democracy. Wei wrote: "The hated old political system has not changed. Are not the people justified in seizing power from the overlords?" Wei published even more critical essays in his unofficial journal Explorations, one of more than fifty such journals circulating at the time. In March 1979, he posted an attack on Deng Xiaoping, asking "Do we want democracy or new dictatorship?" Wei was tried and convicted of "counterrevolutionary crimes" and "leaking state secrets" to foreigners. Some fifteen years later, Wei was released from prison, only to be rearrested for dissident activities. In 1997, after years of pressure from human rights groups and governments outside China, China's most famous political dissident was released and exiled to the United States, where he continues to criticize the Chinese authorities.

liberalization. The political criticism expressed in Tiananmen Square in 1989 largely echoed public views of elite reformers in the party and government. From the perspective of communist authorities, the real danger in 1989 was not the content of mass demands but the organizational challenge: Students and workers organized their own unions, independent of the party, to represent their interests.

The challenge was exacerbated by an open break in elite ranks when Zhao Ziyang voiced his support for the protesters and declared his opposition to martial law. Other party and government leaders and retired elders, including Deng Xiaoping—many of whom had been victims of power seizures by youths in the Cultural Revolution—viewed the problem as a basic struggle for the survival of the system and their own positions. The movement was violently and decisively crushed with tanks and machine guns in the **Tiananmen massacre** of June 4, 1989.[34]

All three protests ended in defeat for the participants: prison for the main protest organizers in 1979, expulsion from the Communist Party for intellectual leaders in 1987, and prison or violent death for hundreds in 1989. The defeats extended beyond the mass protest movement to encompass setbacks to the official reform movement too. When demands for reform moved to the city streets, more conservative leaders attributed the social disorder to an excessively rapid pace of reform. The result was a slower pace or postponement of reforms. Twice, the highest party leader was dismissed from office as a result of the mass protests (Hu Yaobang in 1987 and Zhao Ziyang in 1989) and the official reform movement lost its strongest proponent.

Interest Articulation and Aggregation

13.10 Describe the evolution of interest aggregation in recent years in China.

Most ordinary citizens engage in interest articulation without interest aggregation. This takes the form of personal contacts to articulate individual concerns about the effects of policies on their lives. Much of this interest articulation takes place at the workplace. For the most part, the function of interest aggregation is monopolized by the Communist Party, in a "controlled" interest group system. At the same time, the party's role in interest aggregation is being diluted, and the methods it employs have also evolved.

Organizations under Party Leadership

Under the formal leadership of the Communist Party are eight "satellite parties," a legacy of the communist pre-1949 strategy of provisional cooperation with

Facing Down the Tanks in June 1989
In 1989, ordinary Chinese participated in the largest spontaneous protest movement the communists had ever faced. A lone protester shows defiance of regime violence in his intransigent confrontation with a Chinese tank.

noncommunist democratic parties.[35] These parties have no real role in policymaking, but they are represented (with prominent nonparty individuals) in the Chinese People's Political Consultative Conference. In 1989, the Central Committee proposed greater cooperation with the noncommunist parties by regular consultation with their leaders on major policies—or at least a stronger effort to inform the parties of Communist Party policies. Of course, this proposal referred only to the eight officially tolerated parties. In 1998, the authorities arrested, tried, and imprisoned a veteran of the 1978–1979 Democracy Movement who attempted to register a fledgling China Democracy Party.

The other older formal organizations that aggregate like interests in the Chinese political system are the "mass organizations," extensions of the Communist Party into society, nationwide in scope and organized hierarchically. The All-China Federation of Trade Unions and the Women's Federation remain active and important mass organizations today. Mass organizations are led by Communist Party officials, who are specially assigned to these positions and who take direction from party committees. The main function of these organizations is not to aggregate and represent group interests for consideration in the policymaking process but to facilitate propagation of party policy to the relevant groups. Essentially, mass

organizations represent the interests of the Communist Party to the organized "interest groups" it dominates, not vice versa.

NGOs and GONGOs

A very different set of associations emerged in the late 1980s with official encouragement. These "social organizations," over 450,000 in number (and millions more unregistered), range widely in form and focus. In form, they include genuine NGOs and **government-organized nongovernmental organizations (GONGOs)**. Some GONGOs are essentially front organizations for government agencies, set up to take advantage of the interest of foreign governments and international NGOs in supporting the emergence of Chinese civil society. Other GONGOs have strong and mutually beneficial relationships with NGOs, acting as a bridge to government agencies. In focus, GONGOs and especially NGOs cover a wide range of interests and activities.

Among the most interesting GONGOs are the business associations set up to organize firms: the Self-Employed Laborers Association, the Private Enterprises Association, and the Federation of Industry and Commerce. The Federation of Industry and Commerce, which organizes the largest Chinese firms, has independent resources that have permitted it to create a separate organizational network (chambers of commerce), a national newspaper, and a financial institution to provide credit to members.

Among NGOs, the roughly 2,000 organizations that focus on environmental issues are at the vanguard of NGO activity.[36] The largest, best-funded, and best-organized environmental NGOs focus primarily on species and nature conservation and environmental education. With strong support from the media, these NGOs often work with central authorities to expose and counter local government failure to implement environmental laws and policies. One environmental NGO trains lawyers to engage in enforcement of laws, educates judges about the issues, and litigates environmental cases.

Individual environmental activists have also organized to influence political decisions. A good example is the independent publication of *Yangtze! Yangtze!*, a collection of papers by scientists and environmentalists critical of the world's biggest and most controversial hydroelectric project, the Three Gorges Dam. The study was released in early 1989 with the aim of influencing the widely publicized NPC vote to approve dam construction. Although it failed to halt approval, nearly a third of NPC delegates voted against the project or abstained—prompting the government to postpone dam construction until the mid-1990s.

Considering the "Leninist organizational predisposition" to thwart organizational plurality, the encouragement of NGO emergence and activity in the Chinese context seems puzzling.[37] It is explained by the closure of many state enterprises and the downsizing of government at all levels, in the 1980s and 1990s, creating a need for the growth of social organizations to take on some former government functions, especially social welfare functions. Essentially, this change shifts the burden from government to society. The 1998 plan to downsize the central government bureaucracy explicitly noted that many functions "appropriated by government" must be "given back" to society and managed by new social associations. This plan opened the political space for the emergence of NGOs. The authorities also recognize that NGOs can help the center monitor local government policy implementation; this is the role that environmental NGOs have played most prominently, for example.

For the most part, NGO activity is in fact well within the parameters of officially acceptable political participation. Most groups do not seek autonomy from the state, but rather seek "embeddedness" within the state. To be autonomous is to be outside the system and relatively powerless, unable to exercise influence. In sum, for the most part, the emerging Chinese civil society aggregates and articulates its interests without challenging the state.

To be sure, the authorities have taken measures to guarantee that NGOs work with (not against) them. An elaborate set of regulations requires social organizations to affiliate with a sponsor that is responsible for their activity, to register with the government, and to have sufficient funding and membership. The regulations also prohibit the coexistence of more than one organization with the same substantive focus at the national level or in any particular locality. This preserves the monopoly of the official mass organizations to represent the interests of women and workers, for example.

In practice, however, it is simply impossible really to control NGO activity; some NGOs register as businesses, others thrive as Internet-based virtual organizations, and government sponsors cannot monitor the organizations registered as their affiliates. For example, the All-China Women's Federation is responsible for more than 3,000 social organizations dealing with women's issues. In this context, Chinese NGOs can be expected to continue to grow.

It is important to note that one significant social group lacks a legitimate organizational channel (even a mass organization) that aggregates its interests: farmers. To the extent that Chinese farmers engage in collective action to articulate their interests, it is largely through petitions and protests.

Policymaking and Implementation

Today, it is inconceivable that a scheme such as the Great Leap Forward could be launched and implemented as it was in the 1950s. Controversial policies are no longer adopted at the whim of a single leader, experts play a significant role in policy formulation, experimentation in selected localities precedes widespread implementation, and local authorities no longer slavishly sacrifice local development goals to meet unrealistic campaign targets dictated by the center.

The single most important difference distinguishing policy processes of the 1950s from those of the 1990s and after, however, is the recent greater reliance on consultation and consensus building among a wider range of bureaucratic, local, and economic players. This change is partly due to economic reforms that provide increased opportunities and incentives for players to devote resources to projects outside the state plan rather than to state-mandated projects. In discussing policy processes, the Chinese often refer to the following expression: "The top has its policy measures; the bottom has its countermeasures." Having renounced campaigns and purges, policymakers at the top have instead worked to forge agreements with a variety of players at the political center and in the localities so that policies adopted are implemented, not ignored or radically reshaped in the course of implementation. At the apex of the system, consultation has become even more important, because no leader possesses either the experience or the personal prestige of a Mao Zedong or a Deng Xiaoping.

The political structures described at the beginning of this chapter are essential points of reference for the description of policymaking and policy implementation here. However, key features of policy processes are not well illustrated by consideration of these formal structures alone. As elaborated below, the formal distinction between party and government structures is less relevant than it appears; at least one key structure does not appear on formal organizational charts, and authority is more fragmented and less well bounded than formal structure suggests.

Policymaking

13.11 List the three tiers and five stages of policymaking in China.

Policymaking in China today is less concentrated and more institutionalized than ever before. It involves three sets of institutional players: the party, the government, and the legislature, shown in Figure 13.5. It is also useful to distinguish three tiers in the policymaking process. Different party, government, and legislative structures at different tiers interact at different stages of the process. Moreover, a number of individual players overlap, appearing in more than one set of institutions. This section traces the process by which

major policies emerge and are eventually formalized as laws. It is worth noting, however, that many important policy decisions do not go through the legislature at all. For example, the State Council has the power to issue administrative regulations, decisions, instructions, orders, and measures to local governments; central government ministries issue their own departmental regulations, clarifications, and responses to respective local government departments; and the Communist Party Politburo and individual party departments have their own separate systems of regulations, decisions, instructions, orders, and measures issued to counterparts in the localities and lower levels of the party bureaucracy.

Three Tiers in Policymaking At the very top tier are the leaders at the apex of the party—in the Politburo and its Standing Committee. The party generalists at this tier are each typically responsible for at least one broad policy area. As a group, they make all major policy decisions. Formally, the Politburo has the ultimate authority to determine major policies, but it probably meets in plenary session only about once monthly for a morning to ratify policies already approved by the Politburo Standing Committee. It is useful to recall here that the leaders at the top of the party hierarchy include not only party leaders but also the prime minister and the NPC chairman. Overlapping directorships help coordinate major decision making across the three sets of institutions.

The most thorough consideration of policy options and shaping of policy decisions occur at the second tier—within **leading small groups (LSGs)**, which are defined by broad policy areas.[38] LSGs are headed by leaders at the top tier of the party, although deputy heads are likely to be outside the top tier. LSGs have sweeping mandates to preside over policy research, formulation of policy proposals, sponsorship of policy experiments in the localities, and drafting of policy documents. LSGs bring together all the senior officials with responsibility for different aspects of a policy area.[39] They exercise leadership as policies emerge onto an initial agenda, and they make specific recommendations to the Politburo Standing Committee once policies are ready to move onto the legislative agenda. They are a crucial coordinating mechanism in the policymaking process, linking top decision makers to bureaucracies and bridging institutional systems.

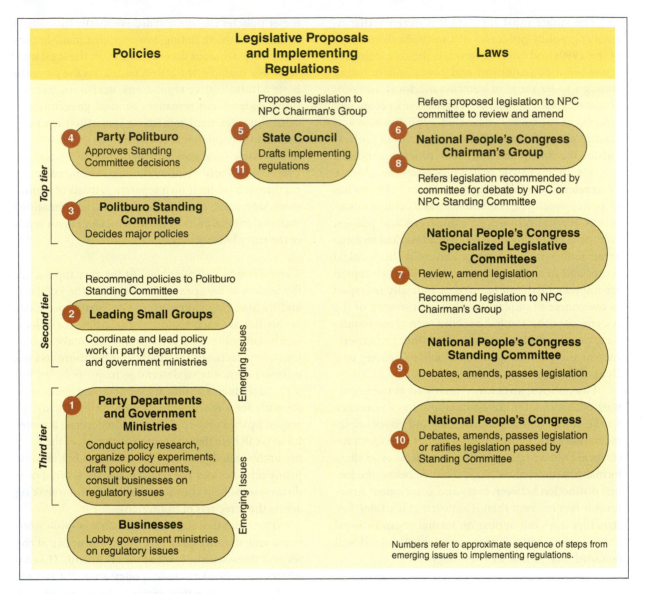

FIGURE 13.5

Chinese Policy Process

Policymaking is less concentrated and more institutionalized than ever before, involving more players.

Coordinating mechanisms are particularly important to policymaking in the Chinese system because authority is formally structured so as to require the cooperation of many bureaucratic units, nested in separate chains of authority. The fragmentation of formal authority and its resolution by formal and informal coordinating mechanisms at the top of the system have led some scholars to characterize the Chinese system as one of **fragmented authoritarianism**.[40]

In what ways is formal authority fragmented? The best example is the system of dual subordination. On the one hand, authority is organized in systems of vertical bureaucracies in hierarchies that extend from ministries at the center to lower-level departments in the localities. Each ministry under the State Council is at the top of a hierarchy of subordinate departments that exist at the provincial, county, and township levels of government. On the other hand, the central ministry and subordinate departments are all government departments and, as such, are subordinate to their respective governments too. The Chinese refer to the two structural arrangements as "lines" and "pieces." Authoritative communications are channeled from top to bottom (vertically, in lines) and also from governments to their departments (horizontally, in pieces). The two sorts of authority come together only at the center, at the level of the State Council. Simply put, then, all local government departments have two bosses in their formal authority relationships—not to mention their relationships with party departments in the same issue area and party committees with nomenklatura authority over them. In Chinese terminology, there are "too many mothers-in-law." This structure of formal authority routinely creates blockages in policy processes. Many policy issues cannot be resolved at lower levels but must be pushed up to a sufficiently high level, such as an LSG, that spans many authority structures and can overcome bureaucratic impasses below.

Below LSGs, at the third tier, are the relevant party departments and government ministries. As LSGs have little staff of their own, the research centers and staff in departments and ministries at the third tier do the actual work of gathering information and drafting policy documents. Increasingly, with a high proportion of policy related to economic matters, government ministries play a key role—but at this tier, it is the specific policy area that determines which bureaucratic players are most involved.

From Agenda Setting to Implementing Regulations

There are five main stages in policymaking and lawmaking: agenda setting; interagency review; Politburo approval; NPC review, debate, and passage; and the drafting of implementing regulations.[41] The two stages that have the most impact on substance are interagency review and drafting of implementing regulations. The State Council dominates both these stages.

LSGs provide leadership and coordination among party departments and government ministries, from which draft proposals emerge. Leaders of departments and ministries are continuously considering relevant policy issues and waiting for (or creating) opportunities to push proposals onto the agenda. A draft proposal is on the agenda when it is assigned to interagency review.

Interagency review is usually a very prolonged process, still at the third tier, initially involving only the most relevant ministries but gradually incorporating a wider group of departments, localities, and other players. At some point, either the State Council Legislation Bureau or the Legislative Affairs Work Committee approves a drafting group for the law. The last phase of interagency review is opinion solicitation. By then, most of the law's content has already been decided.

For policies that will involve passage of legislation, after interagency review, a draft proposal is included on the Legislation Bureau's or Legislative Affairs Work Committee's annual legislative plan. Politburo approval precedes NPC passage of any major piece of political, economic, or administrative legislation, although this practice is not formally required in any legal document.

Officially, legislation may be proposed by the State Council, its ministries, or groups of NPC delegates. Not surprisingly, in this quasi-parliamentary system, the overwhelming majority of legislation is proposed by the State Council and its ministries at the third tier. Although it is unusual for laws to pass through NPC review without amendment, a bill approved in principle by the Politburo is not normally opposed in the NPC.

The NPC review stage begins with referral (by the NPC Chairmen's Group) of the draft legislation to a specialized legislative NPC standing committee for review and amendment. The structure that links party and legislative institutions at this stage is the NPC Standing Committee party group. After draft legislation is recommended by an NPC legislative committee, the party group (acting officially through the NPC Chairmen's Group) decides whether the draft will be debated in the NPC Standing Committee or the full NPC. It is common for the NPC Standing Committee to debate and revise draft legislation many times before voting on passage. When draft legislation encounters significant opposition in the NPC, a vote is usually postponed to avoid a public show of opposition.

After a law is passed, implementing regulations are drawn up, usually by the State Council Legislation Bureau. Implementing regulations transform laws into language that can be applied by local governments and subordinate departments throughout the country. Through implementing regulations, the State Council regains design control over policy before releasing it for implementation.

Policy Implementation

13.12 Discuss route and obstacles to policy implementation in China.

Although the state has partially retreated from direct control over many aspects of the economy, politics, and society in recent decades, the proportion of decisions affecting all three spheres that is made at the political center in China remains higher than that in liberal democracies. Considering this scope, the fragmented structure of authority, and the size and regional diversity of the country, policymakers are seriously constrained in their efforts to elicit effective policy implementation, despite the recent trend toward greater consultation and consensus building to bring relevant departments and localities into the policy process at an earlier stage.

Despite problems and their consequences for unsuccessful policy implementation, the Chinese authorities have achieved impressive policy success in two areas designated as vitally important for the country's development: promoting economic growth and controlling population growth. They have been less successful in another policy area: environmental protection. These examples of policy performance are discussed at length later in this chapter. Here the focus is on general issues in policy implementation.

Monitoring The major issue of policy implementation is the monitoring problem, especially serious in China because of the constraints noted earlier.[42] How do China's policymakers ensure that central-level decisions are translated into actions at lower levels? Central authorities have a very limited capacity to monitor the many aspects of the economy, politics, and society affected by their policies. To cope, they adopt fairly simplistic performance indicators. Not only are these problematic as accurate measures of compliance, but they can also produce unanticipated results. Additionally, policymakers rely mainly on departments and localities, which have their own particular interests to pursue, for much of the information on which to base evaluations of performance. Leaders at the political center have attempted in recent years to develop channels of information independent of ministries and local governments. The National Bureau of Statistics has been given more resources and responsibilities to gather and compile information relevant to policymaking and assessment of policy performance. Research institutes and public opinion polls have also played a greater role in channeling different sorts of information to leaders at the political center. The State Auditing Administration and the Ministry of Supervision, both newly established in recent years, are designed to improve central capacity to measure and monitor implementation. Nonetheless, central authorities are unable to verify most reports independently. As a result, information is routinely distorted to make policy implementers appear compliant. Policymakers appear to take this bias into consideration when assessing implementation.

Policy Priorities As policymakers routinely communicate multiple (and conflicting) policy objectives downward through several channels, local authorities must arrive at a reasonable ordering of policy priorities. In deciding priorities, local objectives as well as the apparent priorities of the political center are considered. Local governments and parallel party committees are multitask agencies. Policy priorities communicated in documents channeled down from Beijing in the functionally specialized line hierarchies of government may not be treated as policy priorities by local governments. Policies appear more likely to be implemented in conformity with central directives when signals from the center indicate that top leaders have reached a consensus among themselves and are paying attention. This sort of signal is generally communicated through documents issued by executive organizations (not simply central ministries) of the Communist Party (not simply the government). Party executives may also signal their attention to the implementation of policy issues by speaking at work conferences convened to assess progress in particular areas or by establishing an ad hoc LSG to manage a particular policy problem.

Adapting Policy to Local Conditions Chinese politics presents no electoral incentives for top leaders to line up public policy with the expressed preferences of special interest groups or ordinary voters. To be sure, policymakers consult the players they view as relevant to policy outcomes. Yet, with restrictions on investigation or criticism by the mass media and the prohibition on organized opposition groups, policymakers face relatively little routine outside pressure in formulating policies. Despite increased consultation of players below the top tiers, the policymaking process is relatively closed compared with liberal democracies.

In a structural context that limits widespread input and provides no electoral connection to policymakers at the top, reshaping policy in the course of policy implementation is often the most effective way for officials to influence policy outcomes.

Corruption

Economic reform has produced unprecedented growth and prosperity but also the conditions for new forms of **corruption**. Since the early 1980s, the economy, no longer centrally planned but not fully marketized, has provided opportunities for officials to gain privately from abuse of their control over resources, contracts, and permissions. On the one hand, the new opportunities for corruption may have eased resistance by officials with the most to lose from economic reform. On the other, abuse of public office to pursue private gain has grown in scope, scale, volume, and severity to become one of the gravest challenges facing the regime, even threatening the Chinese armed forces.[43] In public opinion polls conducted over the years, Chinese citizens consistently view corruption as a serious social problem, often the most serious problem. The huge 1989 mass protests, as much about corruption as about democracy, reflected and aired this view.

Chinese leaders are alarmed about corruption, recognizing the threat to regime legitimacy and political stability. Since 1982, they have waged a nearly continuous corruption control effort. While corrupt officials have been prosecuted and punished, the battle against corruption suffers from a basic contradiction between Communist Party leadership and rule by law in China. In principle, as described earlier, equality before the law is a core component of the new legality. In practice, the Chinese legal system has not been used to full effect to control corruption. An important obstacle is a structural one, reflecting a more basic political obstacle. In 1978, party leaders reinstated discipline inspection committees, specialized departments subordinate to party committees at each level of the party hierarchy. Discipline inspection committees investigate misconduct and enforce ethical and political standards for party members. As the preponderance of officials are party members, discipline inspection committees investigate corruption. Regulations require the transfer of criminal cases to procuratorates, but party investigations and party punishments generally precede criminal investigations. Procuratorates routinely encounter obstacles in their efforts to prosecute such cases, not only because officials call up networks of cronies for support but also because successful prosecution is botched when officials have sufficient time to destroy evidence. In principle, the system holds Communist Party members to a higher standard of conduct than ordinary citizens. In practice, exemption from prosecution and substitution of disciplinary action for criminal punishment are very common for officials (but not for ordinary citizens). Public cynicism about corruption control is understandable. In the instances that high-ranking officials are removed from office and sentenced through the legal system, many interpret it as the outcome of a political power struggle.

The problem of corruption and corruption control reflects a basic contradiction between the principles of Communist Party leadership and rule by law. If law is supreme, the party is subordinate to law and under supervision by procuratorates and courts, not vice versa. So long as party leaders cannot commit to supervision by an impartial legal system, the building of a legal infrastructure will not amount to rule by law. Yet to commit to such supervision calls into question party leadership and the foundations of the communist party-state.

Policy Performance

 13.13 Explain the Chinese government's policy role in economic reform, environmental protection, and population control.

In late 1978, China's leaders defined economic growth as the most important policy priority for decades to come. Despite disagreement about the appropriate pace and scope of economic reform, there has been consensus on a broad strategy of retreat from direct state intervention. The Chinese state has been achieving more by directly controlling less. This strategy has applied not only to economic goals but also to most other policy goals in the reform era. This includes environmental protection, which is less well suited to such a strategy. The important exception has been population control, which Chinese leaders identified as a major policy priority in the late 1970s. The one-child family policy introduced in 1978 features the Chinese state in a more directly interventionist role in population control than ever before.

This section examines the performance of policies of economic reform, environmental protection, and compulsory family planning, focusing on the role of the state in achieving policy goals.

Economic Growth

Although the Chinese have moved only slowly on political reforms, they have been bold in economic reforms. Since 1978, Chinese leaders have staked their political legitimacy on economic growth, more than anything else. For the most part, the gamble has succeeded. Chinese economic growth, illustrated in Table 13.2, has averaged just under 10 percent per year since 1980, including a robust 9 percent in 2009, notwithstanding the financial crisis. Real GDP per capita has also grown, to more than $9,000 in PPP. China is still a developing country, but it is the world's second-largest economy in PPP terms.[44] Economic reform has been a remarkable success story. It has been achieved through three major strategies: opening up the economy to the world outside, marketizing the economy, and devolving authority downward to create incentives for local governments, enterprises, households, and individuals to pursue their own economic advancement.

TABLE 13.2
Reform-Era Economic Performance (in constant 2000 US$)

Chinese real economic growth has averaged about 10 percent per year in the reform era, a faster and longer growth than any other economy in history.

	GDP (billion $)	GDP per capita ($)
1980	183	186
1985	303	290
1990	443	392
1995	793	658
2000	1,199	949
2005	1,909	1,464
2010	3,246	2,427
2012 PPP estimate	US$12,380 billion	$9,100

Sources: 2012 Purchasing Power Parity estimates from Central Intelligence Agency, *World Factbook*, https://www.cia.gov/library /publications/the-world-factbook/; all other figures from World Bank, *World Development Indicators*, http://data.worldbank.org/.

In the late 1970s, Chinese leaders rejected the economic autarky of Maoist "self-reliance," instead opening up the country to foreign trade and investment. China has become a major trading economy. Its trade balance has allowed it to amass the world's largest foreign exchange reserves, including $895 billion in U.S. Treasury securities in 2010. It has also created friction with the United States and some other trading partners. Foreign-invested firms are responsible for much of China's exports, reflecting the country's appeal—through preferential policies, cheap labor, and a potentially huge market—as a destination for foreign direct investment (FDI).

Post-Mao leaders inherited a centrally planned economy, organized according to a Stalinist model borrowed from the Soviet Union in the 1950s. They did not initially set out with a stated goal or program to create a socialist market economy. Indeed, the goal to create a market system was not officially affirmed until 1993. Rather, economic reform proceeded incrementally, in a process often described as "crossing the river by groping for stones." Initially, some top party leaders envisaged only a small secondary role for the market economy, as a "bird in a cage" of the planned economy. By the mid-1990s, however, the Chinese economy had basically "grown out" of the plan.[45] In 1998, the Chinese approved a "shareholding system" that is essentially privatization, thinly disguised to maintain ideological orthodoxy.

A key economic reform strategy has been decentralization. Leaders in Beijing have devolved authority to empower local governments, enterprises, households, and individuals. Agricultural decollectivization in the early 1980s was the first such reform, replacing collective farming with household farming. Individual entrepreneurs emerged at about the same time, engaging in small-scale production or providing services (such as transportation of commodities to markets) long ignored under central planning. Existing rural enterprises were allowed to expand into practically any product line, rather than being restricted to "serving agriculture" as before. Most of these industries were organized as "collective enterprises," with formal ownership by the township or village community and with strong direct involvement of local government in management. These small-scale township and village enterprises (TVEs) proved themselves adaptable to the demands of the new market environment. They drove much of China's rapid growth in the 1980s and into the 1990s. Fiscal arrangements negotiated in the mid-1980s also favored local governments, at the expense of the center; in a renegotiation in the mid-1990s, the central government gained back some revenues, but without removing incentives for local economic initiative.

The reform of the state-owned enterprise (SOE) system began in the mid-1980s. Initial reforms created incentives to boost production by replacing government appropriation of all SOE profits with a system of taxing profits—allowing SOEs to retain a portion of profits. Of course, until prices reflected scarcity, the incentives remained weak. More important, SOEs employed (and employ) a very high proportion of urban workers. This effectively put SOEs on a "soft budget constraint": As local governments feared worker unrest, unprofitable SOEs did not fear bankruptcy; they could count on state banks to bail them out. In 1993, the Chinese authorities announced that one-third of SOEs were loss making and one-third were barely breaking even. In 1994, the Company Law was passed to provide a legal framework for corporatization. A strategy of "targeting the large, releasing the small" emerged: Beijing continued to nurture about 1,000 large SOEs, encouraging them to form giant conglomerates, assisting them with loans but imposing greater financial discipline; the smaller SOEs were left to confront market forces and reorganize themselves through mergers, takeovers, conversion into shareholding companies, or outright closure. After more than a decade of corporatization and reorganization, with increasing privatization through conversion to shareholding and greater political toleration of SOE closures and sales, including sales to foreign partners, SOEs account for a mere 3 percent of all enterprises (but more than 40 percent of enterprise assets) today.

The global financial crisis of 2008 and 2009 exposed the vulnerabilities of the Chinese economic model: excessive dependence on investment (which is less stable than consumption) and export demand (which is dependent on foreign consumption). At the same time, the decisive response of Chinese policymakers to the crisis revealed the advantages of concentrated political power: In November 2008, only weeks after statistics had revealed the severity of economic slowdown, Chinese leaders announced a $585 billion stimulus package focused on infrastructure investment. More important, credit from state-owned banks worked its way through to the real economy by the beginning of 2009, leading an economic recovery as early as March 2009. China's effective response stabilized the economy—and stabilized the global economy.

The Chinese response to the global financial crisis must be characterized as hugely successful. It was also pragmatic; considering the speed and severity of the economic decline, only an increase in investment could pump money into the economy quickly enough to offset crisis. Yet the stimulus is also costly in the longer term.[46] It has reversed the steady government retreat from economic intervention. It will also undoubtedly increase the number of nonperforming loans due to hasty investment decisions promoted by local governments eager to have projects approved. Most important of all, the investment boost of the stimulus did little to address the fundamental economic problem of low household consumption. Without the safety net of the socialist economy, Chinese households continue to anticipate future needs and save "too much."

Environmental Degradation

China's rapid economic growth has resulted in serious environmental damage. Environmental pollution and degradation have increased at a rate that outpaces the capacity of the Chinese state to protect the environment.[47] TVEs contribute more than half of pollutants of all kinds, dumping their untreated waste directly into rivers and streams and relying heavily on coal for energy. Use of coal, a major source of air pollution but a vital contributor to energy supply (see Box 13.5), has doubled since the economic reforms. Water scarcity poses a major challenge; prices do not reflect scarcity because most water is directed toward agriculture for irrigation, and local governments fear rural unrest will erupt with meaningful water price increases. Integration into the global economy has made China a global market for resource-intensive goods, such as paper and furniture—producing a massive drop in forest coverage with increases in logging by Chinese and multinational businesses. China has also become a destination of choice for some of the world's most environmentally damaging industries.

Environmental economists at the World Bank and other organizations estimate the cost to the

China depends on coal for more than 65 percent of its growing energy needs, but in 2005, the central government ordered more than 5,000 coal mines shut down. China's mines are the most dangerous in the world; in that year alone, nearly 6,000 Chinese coal miners died in mining accidents, almost 80 percent of the world's total mining fatalities. The mines ordered closed were both unsafe and illegal. Many were lucrative small-scale mines, managed as TVEs. Others were privately owned, often with local officials holding private (strictly illegal) shares. Mine managers routinely flout safety standards, taking local government acquiescence for granted. The miners generally resign themselves to the high risks, because mining pays better than alternative employment in agriculture. In such conditions, despite laws, orders, and rhetoric on industrial safety, dangerous mines will continue to operate. Undoubtedly, they include many mines shut down in 2005.

Chinese economy of environmental degradation and resource scarcity at 8 to 12 percent of GDP annually. This includes health and productivity losses associated with air pollution and water scarcity costs in lost industrial output. Even so, through the mid-1990s, leaders and the Chinese media continued to articulate the principle of "first development, then environment." The ideal of sustainable development, prominent in official rhetoric today, was incorporated into the economic planning process only in 1992.

Over the past decade, China has erected a legal and bureaucratic infrastructure of environmental protection. In 1984, the State Council established a central government department responsible for environmental matters; in 1989, the NPC adopted an environmental protection law; and in 1993, a specialized legislative environmental protection and natural resources committee was established in the NPC.

Nonetheless, in the policymaking process, the environmental bureaucracy is weak in negotiations with the many ministries with developmental priorities. The problem is even more serious at the local level. The laws that emerge tend to be too diluted and general to provide useful guidelines for enforcement.

The Chinese tally a great number of enforcement successes over the past decade: the resolution of more than 75,000 environmental law violation cases, the closure of more than 16,000 enterprises for illegal discharge of pollutants, and the issuance of more than 10,000 warnings to environmental polluters.[48] Yet the devolution of authority to local governments, a strategy that unlocked economic growth, constitutes a fundamental obstacle to enforcement.

Although local environmental protection bureaus (EPBs) are nominally accountable to both the State Environmental Protection Agency (SEPA) in Beijing and their local governments, they depend on local governments for their growth and survival—budgets, career advancement, staff size, and allocation of resources such as vehicles and office buildings. Local government developmental priorities practically always dominate efforts to enforce environmental standards, especially when enterprises are collective enterprises or firms with a large number of workers. Pollution discharge fees are routinely not collected (or not fully collected), and legal requirements to improve pollution control capacity are routinely waived. The 2006 policy decision to consider environmental protection performance, including energy use, in evaluating local governments may have some impact, but its importance is unlikely to trump economic growth in the near future.

Environmental protection is also underfunded. The five-year plan adopted in March 2006 budgeted 1.6 percent of GDP for environmental protection—an increase over past years but nonetheless an amount that Chinese scientists believe is well below what is needed to produce notable improvements.

Population Control

While reducing state intervention to promote economic growth, policymakers have increased their

Environmental Degradation
The policy of "first development, then environment" has taken a heavy toll. Pollution far outpaces the government's capacity for environmental protection.

intervention involving a new policy priority: population control. For most of the Maoist years, population planning was not actively promoted. In 1978, with the population close to a billion and amid rising concern about meeting economic goals and ensuring basic livelihood, employment opportunities, and social security support at the current rate of population growth, China's leaders declared population control a major policy priority. State-sponsored family planning was added to the constitution, and an ideal family size of one child was endorsed as national policy. According to this policy, most couples are required to stop childbearing after one or two births. Married couples in urban areas, with few exceptions, are restricted to one child. In rural areas, married couples are subject to rules that differ across provinces. In some provinces, two children are normally permitted; in others, only one child is permitted; in most provinces, a second child is permitted only if the first is a girl.

One-Child Family Policy The **one-child family policy** is inherently difficult to implement in China, particularly in the countryside, where nearly 50 percent of Chinese live.[49] There, the population is relatively poorly educated and has poor access to public health facilities—circumstances that do not facilitate an effective family planning program. Traditional views about the family prevail; as in most agrarian societies, big families and many sons are viewed as ideal. Moreover, in China, a married daughter joins the household of her husband, while a married son remains in the household to support aging parents. Decollectivization and the return to household farming in the early 1980s enhanced the value of sons compared to daughters, for their labor power. The dismantling of the commune system has also left the state less able to monitor compliance, just as the new economic independence of peasants has left the state less able to enforce compliance. Finally, population control involves the state as the dominant decision maker in choices that are traditionally viewed, in China as elsewhere, as private family matters.

Despite the inherent difficulties, the Chinese have curbed population growth dramatically, as is illustrated in Figure 13.6. A population structure normally resembles a pyramid; with relatively unchanged rates of births and deaths, the proportion of population from top to bottom is progressively bigger. The population pyramid in Figure 13.6 deviates from this form in a few places. The first, located at about the middle of the pyramid, reflects fewer births as well as differentially more deaths among the young in the disaster following the Great Leap Forward, in the cohort aged fifty to fifty-four in 2010. The second, evident beginning with the cohort aged thirty to thirty-four in 2010, reflects the impact of family planning policies introduced in the 1970s. Family planning policies do not apply to minority nationalities. Variation in policy emphasis by leaders at the political center is reflected in variation in number of births beginning in the mid-1970s. Implementation of the one-child family policy began in 1979. In 1983, responding to concerns at the political center, implementation became more coercive. From 1984 through the late 1980s, the policy was relaxed and implementation in the countryside faltered due to difficulties associated with decollectivization. Births rose immediately. Uniquely in the world, China has grown old before it has grown rich. In recent years, demographers have urged policymakers to end the one-child family policy because of the burden on the working-age population as the population ages. Previously, in cities, when both partners in married couples were only children, they were permitted to have two children; also, rural married couples were permitted to have a second child if their first is a girl, is disabled, or dies. In November 2013,

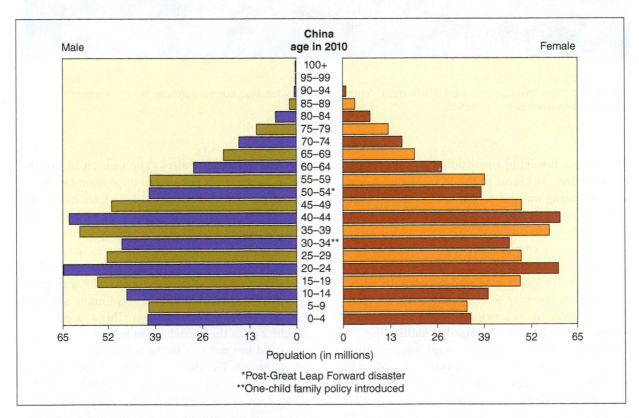

FIGURE 13.6

Population Structure, 2010 Midyear, by Age and Sex

Policies since the 1970s have reduced population growth in the world's most populous country.

Source: U.S. Census Bureau, International Data Base, www.census.gov/ipc/www/idb/country.php.

China's top leaders adopted a major policy shift: now, married couples are permitted to have two children even if only one partner is an only child.

Policy Implementation Policy implementation has taken a number of forms: a legal requirement of late marriage, a requirement of insertion of an intrauterine device after a first birth, and a requirement of sterilization of one partner after a second birth. There are incentives to sign a one-child family certificate after the first birth, including priority in entrance to schools and funding for health fees for the child. Fines are imposed on the family for policy violations. Birth planning workers at the grassroots are given birth quotas from higher levels, which they allocate on the basis of family circumstances. From the perspective of leaders at the political center, abortion is a sign of failure, not success, in policy implementation. At the grassroots, from the perspective of birth planning workers, however, the obvious fact is that abortions do not add above-plan births. Undeniably, birth planning workers have incentives to encourage abortions and face few disincentives for doing so.

Perverse Outcomes In recent years, policymakers have expressed concern about a perverse result of compulsory family planning: the shortage of young girls, compared with boys. Recent figures show an imbalance in the sex ratio, with the ratio of males to females at birth continually rising since the 1980s. The normal range worldwide is 103 to 107 males born for every 100 females; in China, that ratio was 120 males for every 100 females in 2010.

The shortage of girls reflects the traditional Chinese preference for male children in the context of compulsory family planning. Traditional practices of female infanticide as well as abandonment and severe neglect of girls beyond infancy have led to excess female infant mortality. Not least of all, missing girls are increasingly the result of sex-selective abortion, made possible with the widespread use of ultrasound technology in the early 1980s.

China's success in reducing population growth has strong supporters and detractors outside the country. The official Chinese response to criticism from human rights advocates has focused on "economic rights" that the government argues would be denied to all Chinese in the decades to come if population growth is not brought under control.

Hong Kong

13.14 Describe China's relationship with Hong Kong.

In 1842 and 1860, the island of **Hong Kong** and adjacent territory on the Chinese mainland were ceded by treaty to Britain in perpetuity. In 1898, more adjacent territory was ceded in a ninety-nine-year lease. These cessions were largely the outcome of British victory in wars fought to impose trade on China. For nearly a century, Hong Kong (including the adjacent territories) was a British colony, ruled by a governor appointed in London. Hong Kong flourished economically, with a disciplined labor force of Chinese immigrants, a free-market economy, and a government commitment to rule of law and civil liberties—but not an elected government.

In 1984, the Chinese communist authorities elaborated the principle of "**one country, two systems**," applicable to Hong Kong after 1997. China and Britain signed a joint declaration: Hong Kong would revert to Chinese sovereignty in 1997, but would continue to enjoy "a high degree of autonomy." The Chinese agreed that Hong Kong would enjoy economic, financial, and monetary autonomy, maintaining its capitalist system, legal system, and way of life for fifty years. At midnight on June 30, 1997, Hong Kong became a special administrative region of communist-ruled China.

The British had made little effort to democratize politics in Hong Kong through the 1980s. The governor had consulted business elites and other key constituencies on policy affairs, but there had been no elected legislature or government. Nor had political parties really developed in such an environment. All this changed in 1989.

The Tiananmen massacre galvanized Hong Kong Chinese and British expatriates into efforts to accelerate the pace of political democratization before 1997. In 1991, in the first direct elections to the Legislative Council, only a third of the legislative deputies were directly elected. In 1995, a controversial electoral reform bill introduced by Governor Christopher Patten guided elections: For the first time, ordinary Hong Kong citizens elected all deputies in the Legislative Council. Hong Kong's most liberal democratic parties won overwhelmingly in geographic voting districts. Openly pro-Beijing forces did poorly.

Communist authorities rejected the elections and the legislature as violations of the Basic Law, Hong Kong's miniconstitution passed in China's NPC in 1990. They supervised selection of a chief executive and provisional legislature in 1996. At the moment of the historic handover, this chief executive and provisional legislature officially replaced the governor and the legislature elected in 1995.

Since the handover, Beijing authorities have been less heavy-handed than feared. Hong Kong today enjoys most of the same civil liberties as under British rule. Human rights organizations and prodemocracy organizations that monitor and support progress in the PRC have bases in Hong Kong. Hong Kong newspapers provide information about politics in the PRC and are critical in ways not permitted on the mainland. Chinese communist authorities hope that success in implementing "one country, two systems" in Hong Kong will woo Taiwan back to the PRC too.

China and the World

13.15 Briefly discuss China's economic and political international role.

From 1949 through 1979, China's political status as a communist country formed the underpinning of its global role: as an ally of the Soviet Union until the Sino–Soviet split in the early 1960s, then as a nuclear power under the leadership of an unpredictable Mao. Relations with the United States were defined largely by declaration of an American interest in the security of **Taiwan (Republic of China)**, a mere hundred miles off the east coast of the Chinese mainland and governed by the Nationalists since 1945. In 1971, Taiwan lost its membership in the United Nations to China. In 1979, the United States recognized China diplomatically. With reform and opening in the 1980s, China's role in the global economy became more important than its political status. China's accession to the World Trade Organization in 2001 capped its emergence as a global economic player. In 2005, U.S. government officials welcomed China to an anticipated new role as a "responsible stakeholder" in the international system.

China has surely disappointed the United States and other Western powers as a global diplomatic player. China is the only country that could possibly influence an unpredictable nuclear North Korea, but it has done little more than set up the six-party talks in 2003. On the United Nations Security Council, it has voted for sanctions against North Korea and Iran for nuclear proliferation, but only after negotiating compromises so that sanctions are much weakened. China's need for raw materials (such as oil) certainly affects its diplomatic position on Iran; at the same time, Chinese leaders do not see Iran as a threat, do not believe sanctions are effective, and suspect a Western agenda of regime change underlies sanctions efforts.[50]

China today projects a more confident nationalism than ever before. This confidence reflects the country's high growth rates in the global economic recession and Chinese perceptions of the decline of the United States as a global superpower and its replacement by a multipolar global system in which China has more influence. Addressing international concerns about the bounds of its assertive new nationalism, Chinese leaders point out that they have used significant force outside their borders only twice since the communists came to power—in short wars against India in 1962 and Vietnam in 1979. They insist that China in its new role as a global player is merely defending its "core interests" and national dignity.[51]

China's Political Future

Two main themes have run through this study of Chinese politics today. First, despite very significant economic liberalization and a nascent political institutionalization, Chinese politics takes place within the boundaries of what is still essentially a communist party-state. Second, the dramatic changes sweeping the Chinese economy, polity, and society, many of which now seem beyond the control of political leaders, are as much a by-product of reform as a direct product of reform policies. The first theme cautions against liberal democratic optimism when considering China's political future. The second reminds us that the script of the political future will not be written by Chinese communist leaders alone.

In this new century, China must confront a number of key issues that will significantly determine its development. Can structures and processes that bolster and foster economic growth safeguard against the threat of more significant political liberalization and eventual democratization—which remain unacceptable to the Chinese authorities?

Around the world, political change in recent decades has created an age of democratization—the result, in many countries, of revolutions that toppled communist regimes older than the Chinese regime. Will the "third wave" of world democratization reach China early in the twenty-first century?

Chinese history provides no examples of democratic rule, and the Chinese cultural tradition expresses no concerns to protect individuals by checking state power. Past experience and cultural tradition, then, offer little encouragement to those looking for the seeds of democratization in China. Liberal democratic ideals and practices are alien to Chinese culture. At the same time, results from the 2002 ABS indicate that some basic procedural notions of democracy are supported by many Chinese.

Moreover, authoritarianism has not survived intact with economic modernization in many East Asian countries that have a similar lack of historical and cultural foundations for democracy. To be sure, even with continued economic growth, China will differ from these countries for many years to come. It will be bifurcated in its development: middle-class prosperity is emerging in the big cities and coastal regions, but Chinese in the countryside will remain relatively poor for some time.

With reform, for most ordinary Chinese, the party has demanded less and delivered more in recent decades. Unlike communist parties that gained (and held) power with the aid of Soviet troops and tanks, the Chinese Communist Party has indigenous and nationalist roots. Barring a major economic crisis, it is less likely to collapse in the face of the sort of mass discontent that toppled communist regimes in Eastern Europe. More likely, in the medium term at least, the party will continue to transform China in the years to come and to transform itself in order to continue to rule.

REVIEW QUESTIONS

- How does the Chinese Communist Party exercise leadership through governance structures?
- Legal reform is a key priority in political change in China since the 1980s. How successful has it been in meeting key challenges?
- How is political life for ordinary Chinese different today, compared to the Maoist era?
- What policy decisions account for Chinese economic growth in the past three decades?

- Why is population control especially difficult to achieve in China? How and how well has the government measured up to the challenge?
- China is better able than ever before to take up its responsibilities as a global player, but its performance has been mixed. Explain.

KEY TERMS

Central Committee
Chinese Communist Party
Confucianism
corruption
Cultural Revolution
Democracy Movement
democratic centralism
Deng Xiaoping
ethnic minorities

fragmented authoritarianism
government-organized nongovernmental organizations (GONGOs)
Great Firewall
Great Leap Forward
Hong Kong
leading small groups (LSGs)

Mao Zedong
mass mobilization campaign
National Party Congress
National People's Congress (NPC)
Nationalist Party
nomenklatura system
one-child family policy
one country, two systems

party-state
Politburo
rule by law
socialist market economy
State Council
Taiwan (Republic of China)
Tiananmen massacre
village committees

SUGGESTED READINGS

Bianco, Lucien. *Origins of the Chinese Revolution, 1915–1949.* Stanford, CA: Stanford University Press, 1971.

Chang, Jung. *Wild Swans: Three Daughters of China.* New York: Anchor, 1991.

Economy, Elizabeth C. *The River Runs Black: The Environmental Challenge to China's Future.* Ithaca, NY: Cornell University Press, 2004.

Gries, Peter Hays, and Stanley Rosen, eds. *Chinese Politics: State, Society and the Market.* London: Routledge, 2010.

Lieberthal, Kenneth. *Governing China: From Revolution through Reform,* 2nd ed. New York: Norton, 2004.

Nathan, Andrew J. *Chinese Democracy.* Berkeley: University of California Press, 1986.

Spence, Jonathan D. *The Search for Modern China.* New York: Norton, 1990.

Weston, Timothy B., and Lionel Jensen, eds. *China Beyond the Headlines.* Lanham, MD: Rowman & Littlefield, 2000.

Wong, Jan. *Red China Blues.* Sydney: Doubleday, 1996.

INTERNET RESOURCES

China Internet Information Center, State Council Information Office. Authorized Web site of Chinese government, link to National People's Congress. Access to government White Papers, news, statistical data: www.china.org.cn/english.

National Bureau of Statistics. Official monthly and yearly statistics, including downloadable Excel files: www.stats.gov.cn/english/.

China Daily. News from China directed toward external readership: www.chinadaily.com.cn.

People's Daily. Official newspaper of Communist Party of China: http://english.peopledaily.com.cn/.

South China Morning Post. News about Hong Kong and mainland China, from Hong Kong: www.scmp.com.

Contemporary China bibliography, Professor Lynn White, Princeton University: www.princeton.edu/~lynn/chinabib.pdf.

United States–China Business Council. Analysis and advocacy of policy issues of interest to U.S. corporations engaged in business relations with China: www.uschina.org.

ENDNOTES

1. For a good, very readable discussion of Chinese history beginning with the late Ming (seventeenth century) and extending into the 1980s, see Jonathan D. Spence, *The Search for Modern China* (New York: Norton, 1990). Other good historical overviews include Charles O. Hucker, *China's Imperial Past: An Introduction to Chinese History and Culture* (Stanford, CA: Stanford University Press, 1975); and Immanuel C. Y. Hsu, *The Rise of Modern China,* 5th ed. (New York: Oxford University Press, 1995).

2. See Hsi-sheng Chi, *Warlord Politics in China, 1916–1928* (Stanford, CA: Stanford University Press, 1976); and Edward A. McCord, *The Power of the Gun: The Emergence of Modern Chinese Warlordism* (Berkeley: University of California Press, 1993).

3. See especially Lucien Bianco, *Origins of the Chinese Revolution, 1915–1949* (Stanford, CA: Stanford University Press, 1971). See also Benjamin Schwartz, *Chinese Communism and the Rise of Mao* (Cambridge, MA: Harvard University Press, 1951).

4. The classic political biography of Mao is Edgar Snow, *Red Star over China* (New York: Grove Press, 1968). Of the many excellent studies by Stuart R. Schram, see especially *The Political Thought of Mao Tse-tung,* rev. ed. (New York: Praeger, 1969), *The Thought of Mao Tse-tung* (Cambridge: Cambridge University Press, 1989), and his biography of Mao, *Mao Tse-tung,* rev. ed. (Harmondsworth, England: Penguin, 1967). After Mao's death, scholars appraised Mao and his legacy from a variety of perspectives in Dick Wilson, ed., *Mao Tse-tung in the Scales of History: A Preliminary Assessment* (Cambridge: Cambridge University Press, 1977).

5. See Chalmers A. Johnson, *Peasant Nationalism and Communist Power: The Emergence of Revolutionary China* (Stanford, CA: Stanford University Press, 1962).

6. See Suzanne Pepper, *Civil War in China: The Political Struggle, 1945–1949* (Berkeley: University of California Press, 1978).

7. For a good selection of essays offering a comprehensive overview of PRC history, see Roderick MacFarquhar, ed., *The Politics of China: The Eras of Mao and Deng,* 2nd ed. (Cambridge: Cambridge University Press, 1997). Other good discussions of post-Mao history are found in Richard Baum, *Burying Mao: Chinese Politics in the Age of Deng Xiaoping* (Princeton, NJ: Princeton University Press, 1994); and Harry Harding, *China's Second Revolution: Reform after Mao* (Washington, DC: Brookings Institution, 1987). Good

discussions of particular topics of reform are found in Merle Goldman and Roderick MacFarquhar, eds., *The Paradox of China's Post-Mao Reforms* (Cambridge, MA: Harvard University Press, 1999).

8. The classic account is by William Hinton, who observed land reform before 1949 in *Fanshen: A Documentary of Revolution in a Chinese Village* (New York: Viking, 1966).

9. Roderick MacFarquhar, ed., *The Hundred Flowers Campaign and the Chinese Intellectuals* (New York: Praeger, 1960); and Fu-sheng Mu, *The Wilting of the Hundred Flowers Movement: Free Thought in China Today* (London: Heinemann, 1962).

10. See Dali L. Yang, *Calamity and Reform in China: State, Rural Society, and Institutional Change since the Great Leap Famine* (Stanford, CA: Stanford University Press, 1996).

11. See Frederick C. Teiwes, *Politics and Purges in China: Rectification and the Decline of Party Norms, 1950–1965* (Armonk, NY: M. E. Sharpe, 1979); and Frederick C. Teiwes, *Leadership, Legitimacy, and Conflict in China: From a Charismatic Mao to the Politics of Succession* (Armonk, NY: M. E. Sharpe, 1984).

12. See Jasper Becker, *Hungry Ghosts: Mao's Secret Famine* (New York: Free Press, 1996).

13. Some of the best accounts of the Cultural Revolution are biographical or autobiographical. See, for example, Gordon A. Bennett and Ronald N. Montaperto, *Red Guard: The Political Biography of Dai Hsiao-ai* (Garden City, NY: Doubleday, 1971); Jung Chang, *Wild Swans: Three Daughters of China* (New York: Anchor, 1991); Yuan Gao, *Born Red: Chronicle of the Cultural Revolution* (Stanford, CA: Stanford University Press, 1987); Liang Heng and Judith Shapiro, *Son of the Revolution* (New York: Knopf, 1983); Anne F. Thurston, *Enemies of the People: The Ordeal of the Intellectuals in China's Great Cultural Revolution* (Cambridge, MA: Harvard University Press, 1988); Daiyun Yue and Carolyn Wakeman, *To the Storm: The Odyssey of a Revolutionary Chinese Woman* (Berkeley: University of California Press, 1985); and Nien Cheng, *Life and Death in Shanghai* (New York: Grove Press, 1986).

14. See Dru C. Gladney, *Muslim Chinese: Ethnic Nationalism in the People's Republic* (Cambridge, MA: Council on East Asian Studies, Harvard University, 1991); and Stevan Harrell, ed., *Cultural Encounters on China's Ethnic Frontiers* (Seattle: University of Washington Press, 1995).

15. An excellent discussion of guardianship is found in Robert A. Dahl, *Democracy and Its Critics* (New Haven, CT: Yale University Press, 1989), chap. 4. On Leninism in general, see especially Alfred G. Meyer, *Leninism* (Cambridge, MA: Harvard University Press, 1957).

16. Mao Zedong, "Some Questions concerning Methods of Leadership," in *Selected Works of Mao Tse-tung*, vol. 3 (Peking: Foreign Languages Press, 1965), 117–22.

17. On the changing role of the NPC, see Murray Scot Tanner, *The Politics of Lawmaking in Post-Mao China: Institutions, Processes, and Democratic Prospects* (New York: Oxford University Press, 1999); and Murray Scott Tanner and Chen Ke, "Breaking the Vicious Cycles: The Emergence of China's National People's Congress," *Problems of Post-Communism* 45, no. 3 (1998): 29–47. For a historical perspective, see Kevin J. O'Brien, *Reform without Liberalization: China's National People's Congress and the Politics of Institutional Change* (Cambridge: Cambridge University Press, 1990).

18. See Murray Scot Tanner, "How a Bill Becomes a Law in China: Stages and Processes of Lawmaking," *China Quarterly* 141 (1995): 39–64.

19. See Melanie Manion, "The Cadre Management System, Post-Mao: The Appointment, Promotion, Transfer, and Removal of Party and State Leaders," *China Quarterly* 102 (1985): 203–33; John P. Burns, *The Chinese Communist Party's Nomenklatura System* (Armonk, NY: M. E. Sharpe, 1989); and Burns, "Strengthening Central CCP Control of Leadership Selection: The 1990 *Nomenklatura*," *China Quarterly* 138 (1994): 458–91.

20. See Hsiao Pen, "Separating the Party from the Government," in *Decision-Making in Deng's China: Perspectives from Insiders*, ed. Carol Lee Hamrin and Suisheng Zhao (Armonk, NY: M. E. Sharpe, 1995), 153–68.

21. See Zhiyue Bo, *Chinese Provincial Leaders: Economic Performance and Political Mobility since 1949* (Armonk, NY: M. E. Sharpe, 2002). For an earlier discussion of elite recruitment and mobility, based on case studies, see David M. Lampton, *Paths to Power: Elite Mobility in Contemporary China* (Ann Arbor: Center for Chinese Studies, University of Michigan, 1986).

22. For an overview of the change, see Richard Baum, "Modernization and Legal Reform in Post-Mao China: The Rebirth of Socialist Legality," *Studies in Comparative Communism* 19, no. 2 (1986): 69–103. For notions underlying the change, see Carlos W. H. Lo, "Deng Xiaoping's Ideas on Law: China on the Threshold of a Legal Order," *Asian Survey* 32, no. 7 (1992): 649–65. For a description of the law in practice in post-Mao China, see James V. Feinerman, "Economic and Legal Reform in China, 1978–91," *Problems of Communism* 40, no. 5 (1991): 62–75; Pitman B. Potter, ed., *Domestic Law Reforms in Post-Mao China* (Armonk, NY: M. E. Sharpe, 1994); Potter, "The Chinese Legal System: Continuing Commitment to the Primacy of State Power," *China Quarterly* 159 (1999): 673–83; and Stanley B. Lubman, *Bird in a Cage: Legal Reform in China after Mao* (Stanford, CA: Stanford University Press, 1999).

23. See, for example, Donald C. Clarke and James V. Feinerman, "Antagonistic Contradictions: Criminal Law and Human Rights in China," *China Quarterly* 141 (1995): 135–54.

24. See the account of "thought work" in Daniel Lynch, *After the Propaganda State: Media, Politics, and "Thought Work" in Reformed China* (Stanford, CA: Stanford University Press, 1999).

25. See Tianjian Shi, "Cultural Values and Democracy in the People's Republic of China," *China Quarterly* 162 (2000): 540–59; and Yang Zhong, Jie Chen, and John Scheb, "Mass Political Culture in Beijing: Findings from Two Public Opinion Surveys," *Asian Survey* 38, no. 8 (1998): 763–83. For a comparative perspective, see Gabriel A. Almond and Sidney Verba, *Civic Culture: Political Attitudes and Democracy in Five Nations* (Princeton, NJ: Princeton University Press, 1963).

26. See Tianjian Shi, "China: Democratic Values Supporting an Authoritarian State," in *How East Asians View Democracy*, Yun-han Chu, Larry Diamond, Andrew J. Nathan, and Doh Chull Shin, eds. (New York: Columbia University Press, 2008), 209–37; and Tianjian Shi and Jie Lu, "The Shadow of Confucianism," *Journal of Democracy* 21, no. 4 (2010): 123–30.

27. Dahl, *Democracy and Its Critics*, 52.

28. See the excellent discussion of forms of political participation in Tianjian Shi, *Political Participation in Beijing* (Cambridge, MA: Harvard University Press, 1997), chap. 2.

29. On the Maoist period, see James R. Townsend, *Political Participation in Communist China* (Berkeley: University of California Press, 1967). On post-Mao elections, see Andrew Nathan, *Chinese Democracy* (Berkeley: University of California Press, 1985); Robert E. Bedeski, "China's 1979 Election Law and Its Implementation," *Electoral Studies* 5, no. 2 (1986): 153–65; Barrett L. McCormick, *Political Reform in Post-Mao China* (Berkeley: University of California Press, 1990); J. Bruce Jacobs, "Elections in China," *Australian Journal of Chinese Affairs* 25 (1991): 171–200; and Melanie Manion, "Chinese Democratization in Perspective: Electorates and Selectorates at the Township Level. Report from the Field," *China Quarterly* 163 (2000): 133–51.

30. On rural decollectivization, see especially Daniel Kelliher, *Peasant Power in China: The Era of Rural Reform, 1979–1989* (New Haven, CT: Yale University Press, 1992); and Kate Xiao Zhou, *How the Farmers Changed China: Power of the People* (Boulder, CO: Westview Press, 1996).

31. See Melanie Manion, "The Electoral Connection in the Chinese Countryside," *American Political Science Review* 90, no. 4 (1996): 736–48; Tianjian Shi, "Economic Development and Village Elections in Rural China," *Journal of Contemporary China* 8, no. 22 (1999): 433–35; Anne F. Thurston, *Muddling toward Democracy: Political Change in Grassroots China* (Washington, DC: United States Institute of Peace, 1999); and Lianjiang Li, "Elections and Popular Resistance in Rural China," *China Information* 16, no. 1 (2002): 89–107.

32. On protest movements in the 1970s and 1980s, see especially Nathan, *Chinese Democracy*; Jeffrey N. Wasserstrom and Elizabeth J. Perry, eds., *Popular Protest and Political Culture in Modern China: Learning from 1989* (Boulder, CO: Westview, 1992); and Gregor Benton and Alan Hunter, *Wild Lily, Prairie Fire: China's Road to Democracy, 1942–1989* (Princeton, NJ: Princeton University Press, 1995).

33. James D. Seymour, ed., *The Fifth Modernization* (Stanfordville, NY: Human Rights Publishing Group, 1980).

34. On the 1989 protests, see Michel Oksenberg, Lawrence R. Sullivan, and Marc Lambert, eds., *Beijing Spring, 1989: Confrontation and Conflict, The Basic Documents* (Armonk, NY: M. E. Sharpe, 1990); Han Minzhu and Hua Sheng, eds., *Cries for Democracy: Writings and Speeches from the 1989 Chinese Democracy Movement* (Princeton, NJ: Princeton University Press, 1990); Tony Saich, ed., *The Chinese People's Movement: Perspectives on Spring 1989* (Armonk, NY: M. E. Sharpe, 1990); Jonathan Unger, ed., *The Pro-Democracy Protest in China: Reports from the Provinces* (Sydney: Allen & Unwin, 1991); and Craig Calhoun, *Neither Gods nor Emperors: Students and the Struggle for Democracy in China* (Berkeley: University of California Press, 1995).

35. See James D. Seymour, *China's Satellite Parties* (Armonk, NY: M. E. Sharpe, 1987).

36. See Fengshi Wu, *New Partners or Old Brothers? GONGOs in Transnational Environmental Advocacy in China*, China Environmental Series, no. 5 (Washington, DC: Woodrow Wilson Center Press, 2002); and Elizabeth C. Economy, *The River Runs Black: The Environmental Challenge to China's Future* (Ithaca, NY: Cornell University Press, 2004), 129–76.

37. For good discussions of NGOs and their relationship to the state, see especially Tony Saich, "Negotiating the State: The Development of Social Organizations in China," *China Quarterly* 161 (2000): 124–41; and Bruce Dickson, *Red Capitalists in China: The Party, Private Entrepreneurs, and Prospects for Political Change* (Cambridge: Cambridge University Press, 2003), 1–28.

38. The most thorough description and thoughtful analysis of leading small groups is by Carol Lee Hamrin, "The Party Leadership System," in *Bureaucracy, Politics, and Decision Making in Post-Mao China*, ed. Kenneth G. Lieberthal and David M. Lampton (Berkeley: University of California Press, 1992), 95–124. See also David M. Lampton, ed., *The Making of Chinese Foreign and Security Policy in the Era of Reform* (Stanford, CA: Stanford University Press, 2001), especially the contribution by Lu Ning, "The Central Leadership, Supraministry Coordinating Bodies, State Council Ministries, and Party Departments," 39–60.

39. These areas are defined in very comprehensive terms, such as party affairs, national security and military issues, foreign affairs, legal issues, personnel, finance, and the economy.

40. See Kenneth Lieberthal and Michel Oksenberg, *Policy Making in China: Leaders, Structures, and Processes* (Princeton, NJ: Princeton University Press, 1988).

41. See Tanner, "How a Bill Becomes a Law," 39–64; and Tanner, *The Politics of Lawmaking in Post-Mao China*.

42. See David M. Lampton, ed., *Policy Implementation in Post-Mao China* (Berkeley: University of California Press, 1987); and Yasheng Huang, "Administrative Monitoring in China," *China Quarterly* 143 (1995): 828–43.

43. See especially Ting Gong, "Forms and Characteristics of China's Corruption in the 1990s: Change with Continuity," *Communist and Post-Communist Studies* 30, no. 3 (1997): 277–88; Xiaobo Lu, "Booty Socialism, Bureau-preneurs, and the State in Transition," *Comparative Politics* 32, no. 3 (2000): 273–94; Yan Sun, "Reform, State, and Corruption: Is Corruption Less Destructive in China than in Russia?" *Comparative Politics* 32, no. 1 (1999): 1–20; and James Mulvenon, *Soldiers of Fortune: The Rise and Fall of the Chinese Military-Business Complex, 1978–1998* (Armonk, NY: M. E. Sharpe, 2001).

44. The bundle of goods a currency can purchase varies drastically from country to country, depending on availability of the goods, demand for the goods, and other factors. Purchasing power parity is an economic technique that solves this problem and permits more meaningful comparisons across countries. For example, the GDP per capita in the United States was about $50,000 in PPP in 2012, more than five times the comparable figure for China.

45. See Barry Naughton, *Growing Out of the Plan: Chinese Economic Reform, 1978–1993* (Cambridge: Cambridge University Press, 1996).

46. See especially Barry Naughton, "Understanding the Chinese Stimulus Package," *China Leadership Monitor* 28 (2009): 1–12; and Naughton, "China's Emergence from Economic Crisis," *China Leadership Monitor* 29 (2009): 1–10.

47. Two excellent recent sources on the environment are Elizabeth C. Economy, *The River Runs Black: The Environmental Challenge to China's Future* (Ithaca, NY: Cornell University Press, 2004); and Kristen A. Day, ed., *China's Environment and the Challenge of Sustainable Development* (Armonk, NY: M. E. Sharpe, 2005).

48. State Council Information Office, *Environmental Protection in China (1996–2005)*, White Paper on the Environment (Beijing: State Council Information Office, 2006).

49. See Susan Greenhalgh, Zhu Chuzhu, and Li Nan, "Restraining Population Growth in Three Chinese Villages, 1988–93," *Population and Development Review* 20, no. 2 (1994): 365–95.

50. Francois Godement, "A Global China Policy," *European Council on Foreign Relations Policy Brief* 22 (2010): 1–10.

51. See Michael D. Swaine, "Perceptions of an Assertive China," *China Leadership Monitor* 32 (2010): 1–18.

MEXICO

POPULATION
112.3 million (2010)

TERRITORY
761,602 square miles

YEAR OF INDEPENDENCE
1810

YEAR OF CURRENT CONSTITUTION
1917

HEAD OF STATE
President Enrique Peña Nieto

HEAD OF GOVERNMENT
President Enrique Peña Nieto

LANGUAGES
Spanish, Mayan, Nahuatl, Zapotec, and many other regional, indigenous languages

RELIGIONS
Roman Catholic 85%, religious non-Catholic 10%, nonreligious 5%

CHAPTER 14

Politics in Mexico

Wayne A. Cornelius and Jeffrey A. Weldon

LEARNING OBJECTIVES

14.1 List the most serious economic, social, and political challenges currently faced by Mexico.

14.2 Discuss Mexico's history, focusing on church–state relations and the social upheavals of the twentieth century.

14.3 Describe Mexicans' conflicted relationship with their political system.

14.4 Discuss the major sources of political socialization in Mexico and how they have changed.

14.5 Discuss the factors that have boosted participation in recent Mexican elections.

14.6 Describe the branches of Mexico's government and the changes they have undergone.

14.7 Discuss political recruitment in Mexico, focusing on the rise of the technocrats.

14.8 Explain the role of interest groups in Mexico, touching on corporatist and patron–client structures.

14.9 Discuss the ways that the reform of the Mexican electoral system since the 1990s has affected the political parties.

14.10 Describe the effects of Mexico's policies, focusing on economic development, the distribution of income, the rule of law, the environment, and international relations.

14.11 What recent developments bode well for political stability in Mexico?

On Monday morning, July 2, 2012, Mexicans woke up to a remarkable, new political reality. The day before, voters had put the **Institutional Revolutionary Party (PRI)** back in power, choosing a PRI president and pluralities of PRI members in both houses of Congress, twelve years after throwing the long-ruling party out of national power and just six years after the PRI presidential candidate had finished in a distant third place. The National Action Party (PAN), after two relatively successful presidencies, fell into third place. Unlike the previous two presidential elections, there were no serious challenges to the election results in 2012, but their significance was far from clear.

Tactically, the PRI succeeded in returning to power by offering a young, attractive candidate, **Enrique Peña Nieto**, who presented himself as the standard bearer of the "new PRI"—a modernized version supposedly shorn of its former authoritarian and corrupt trappings. But was this really the "new PRI," or a restoration of the old? Was the PRI's resurgence the end of a twelve-year experiment in democratic politics, or just a "normal" democratic turnover in government? Could the PRI rule effectively, retaining public support, in a political system that since 2000 had undergone drastic transformations in electoral rules and transparency in governance? In a country where the power of social media like YouTube and Twitter is ascendant, and public scrutiny of the behavior of politicians and bureaucrats is continuous?

Since the hotly contested but fraud-ridden presidential election of 1988, Mexico has experienced a remarkable passage from a political system in which systematic manipulation of elections by the ruling party was condoned by senior political leaders and cynically accepted by the general public to one in which government respect for voters' preferences is expected—indeed, demanded. This and other key elements of modern democratic politics have become routinized in Mexico.

Recurrent economic crises (1976–1977, 1982–1989, and 1994–1996) were among the most powerful catalysts for this revolution in citizen expectations. The vast majority of Mexicans suffered severe economic pain during these decades, directly attributable to government mismanagement of the national economy. Millions of jobs were lost, real wages were stagnant or declining in all but a few years of the period, savings and businesses were decimated by inflation and currency devaluations, and government benefits for the middle and lower classes were slashed in the austerity budgets necessitated by the economic crises.

These economic shocks set the stage for massive anti-PRI voting that eventually broke the party's seventy-one-year hold on national executive power in 2000. But by 2008, a severe global recession was dragging down Mexico's economy and testing the resilience of "opposition" rule. In 2012, the PRI criticized the weakness of economic growth under the two PAN administrations, even though Mexico actually had weathered the Great Recession better than the United States. By 2012, voters had decided to give the PRI another chance.

Current Policy Challenges

14.1 List the most serious economic, social, and political challenges currently faced by Mexico.

Mexico entered the twenty-first century with huge social and economic problems: an economy that produces too few jobs to accommodate the young people entering the labor market each year (even though the rate of labor force growth is now trending downward due to lower birth rates); an educational system sorely in need of modernization; a growing poverty population, with close

to half of all Mexicans still living below the official poverty line; a highly unequal distribution of income; a huge developmental gap between the affluent, urbanized, economically modern northern states and the poor, rural, heavily indigenous south; acute environmental problems that damage the health of both rural and urban dwellers; and a criminal justice system that barely functioned, routinely violating the human rights of citizens and heavily corrupted by drug trafficking. The PRI lost its grip on the Mexican political system in 2000 in large part because it had failed to deal effectively with these problems. The democratic "opposition," in power for twelve years, was able to manage them with only marginal success.

Several emerging economic policy challenges will be no less daunting. As a developing country, Mexico has to deal more directly with the global economic system; it must play catch-up with its international trade partners and competitors. The rise of China as a key competitor in global markets has had a particularly strong impact on Mexico. China has displaced Mexico as the second-largest exporter of manufactured goods to the **North American Free Trade Agreement (NAFTA)** market, and Chinese producers offer stiff competition to many Mexican firms within their domestic market. Mexico must modernize its agricultural sector to allow it to survive competition from the United States and Canada, where subsidies and more efficient methods make agricultural goods cheaper. This vulnerable sector was further challenged when trade barriers were eliminated completely under NAFTA in 2008.

Reforming the public education system, begun with constitutional changes enacted after Peña Nieto's election, remains an urgent priority. Constitutional amendments enacted in 2012, designed to break the power of the national teachers union and end the traditional practice of buying or inheriting teaching positions, must still be fully implemented. Government regulation of the telecommunications sector was strengthened by legislative reforms in 2012, but further steps are needed to increase competition and curb the power of monopolies in television and telephone service.

Mexico must renovate its energy sector—oil, electricity, and natural gas—either by increasing government spending or by allowing more private or foreign investment, which would require controversial constitutional amendments. Full privatization of the oil industry—nationalized in 1938—remains politically prohibitive, but something must be done to halt the steady decline in oil production. Oil production has plummeted from its peak in 2004, as the fields have been depleted. PEMEX, the government oil monopoly, has lacked both the capital and the technical expertise needed to reach harder-to-get, deep-water oil and on-shore deposits of shale oil and natural gas. Mexico, still ninth among the world's oil producers and the third-ranking source of foreign oil for the United States, has been forced to import ever-larger amounts of gasoline from U.S. refineries. The decline of the country's energy industry has huge implications for public finances, since the federal government gets one-third of its revenue from oil exports. Faced with this challenge, the new PRI government that took power in 2012 has proposed that foreign companies be allowed to partner with PEMEX in oil and gas exploration and share in the profits—a major historical departure.

An unfamiliar demographic profile is beginning to emerge—an aging population and a shrinking labor force. The growth of the over-sixty-five population means that Mexico must soon bolster the funding of private and government-sponsored pension plans. Mexico's fertility rate—the average number of children per woman—fell from 7.3 in 1960 to 2.4 in 2009, and this sharp decline is now being reflected in much smaller numbers of young people entering the work-force.[1] Within fifteen to twenty years, Mexico may have ceased exporting surplus labor to the United States, as it has done on a large scale since the 1880s. A shrinking labor force could push wages upward, benefiting many Mexicans, but it might constrain future economic growth and make it more difficult to finance pension plans.

Drug trafficking and the ancillary criminal activities that it has spawned remain a major challenge to the Mexican state. The government of PAN President **Felipe Calderón** waged all-out war against drug traffickers, which unleashed a torrent of violence that claimed the lives of more than 60,000 people, including traffickers and innocent citizen victims caught in the crossfire. The power of drug traffickers and other agents of organized crime in Mexico was not broken noticeably by Calderón's unprecedented effort to rein them in. While the number of drug war–related homicides declined 40 percent in the final year of President Calderón's term, there has been an increase in extortions, kidnapping, and human trafficking perpetrated by *narcos* (drug lords), who have discovered they can make more money from these activities than from transporting drugs to the United States. These types of crimes, far more than violence among the narcos, strike fear into average Mexicans and are more likely to impact them personally. PRI officials, including state governors, have long been suspected of collusion with the drug lords. The challenge to the new PRI government is to reformulate the country's antidrug strategy and implement it in a way that further reduces violence and cracks down effectively on related forms of organized crime.

On the political front, additional changes in electoral rules are needed to close loopholes concerning the financing of campaigns, to make it more difficult for elected officials to use government programs to promote their party's candidates. Another needed reform would reinstate the immediate reelection of legislators, which would make them more responsive and accountable to their constituents. Eliminating the *fuero*—constitutionally mandated immunity from criminal prosecution—for most elected officials would reduce corruption and improve accountability.

But in terms of consolidating a fully democratic system, these changes may be less important than the rapidly spreading belief that alternation in power among Mexico's main parties, at all levels of governance, is both desirable and achievable. After nearly two decades of generally democratic practices and ethos, dating back to the PRI's loss of majority control of the lower house of Congress in 1997, turning back the clock may be impossible, however much PRI traditionalists might want to. Public tolerance for abuses of authority, repression of demonstrators, wiretapping, and systematic official corruption clearly has diminished, as illustrated by the uproars provoked by several scandals involving PRI supporters that surfaced during the 2012 federal election campaigns.

Historical Perspectives

 Discuss Mexico's history, focusing on church-state relations and the social upheavals of the twentieth century.

Colonialism and Church–State Relations

Long before Hernán Cortés landed in 1519 and began the Spanish conquest of Mexico, its territory was inhabited by numerous indigenous civilizations. Of these, the Mayans on the Yucatán peninsula and the

Toltecs on the central plateau had developed the most complex political and economic organizations. Both of these civilizations had disintegrated, however, before the Spaniards arrived. Smaller indigenous societies were decimated by diseases introduced by the invaders or were vanquished by the sword. Subsequent grants of land and native labor by the Spanish Crown to the colonists further isolated the rural native population and deepened their exploitation.

The combined effects of attrition, intermarriage, and cultural penetration of native regions have drastically reduced the proportion of Mexico's population culturally identified as indigenous. According to 2005 census figures, 7.5 percent of the nation's population speak a native language.[2] The indigenous minority has been persistently marginal to the national economy and political system. Today, the indigenous population is heavily concentrated in rural communities that the government classifies as the country's most economically depressed and service-deprived, located primarily in the southeast and the center of the country. The indigenous population is an especially troubling reminder of the millions of people who have been left behind by uneven development in twentieth-century Mexico.

The importance of Spain's colonies in the New World lay in their ability to provide the Crown with vital resources to fuel the Spanish economy. Mexico's mines provided gold and silver in abundance until the wars of independence began in 1810. After independence, Mexico continued to export these ores, supplemented in subsequent eras by hemp, cotton, textiles, oil, and winter vegetables.

Since the Spanish conquest, the Roman Catholic Church has been an institution of enduring power in Mexico. Priests joined the Spanish invaders in an evangelical mission to convert the natives to Catholicism, and individual priests have continued to play important roles in national history. For example, Father Miguel Hidalgo y Costilla helped launch Mexico's War of Independence in 1810, and Father José María Morelos y Pavón replaced Hidalgo as spiritual and military leader of the independence movement when the Crown executed Hidalgo in 1811.

During Mexico's post-independence period, institutional antagonisms between the Church and the central government have occasionally flared into open confrontations on such issues as Church wealth, educational policy, the content of public school textbooks,

and political activism by the Church. The Constitutions of 1857 and 1917 formally established the separation of church and state and defined their respective domains. Constitutional provisions dramatically reduced the Church's power and wealth by nationalizing its property, including church buildings and large agricultural landholdings. Government efforts during the 1920s to enforce these constitutional provisions led to a civil insurrection that caused 100,000 combatant deaths, uncounted civilian casualties, and economic devastation in a large part of central Mexico.

The settlement of this "Cristero rebellion" established, once and for all, the Church's subordination to the state, in return for which the government relaxed its restrictions on Church activities in nonpolitical arenas. This accord inaugurated a long period of relative tranquility in church–state relations, during which the government and the Church ignored many of the anticlerical provisions of the 1917 Constitution (such as the prohibition on Church involvement in education).

In recent years, the central Catholic Church hierarchy—one of the most conservative in Latin America—has seethed at socially liberal policies (such as divorce, birth control, and gay marriage) even as it cooperated with the government on a variety of other issues, while posing no threat to state control. The main threats to the Church's continued influence among Mexicans are secularism and the rapid growth of charismatic, Protestant/evangelical churches, particularly in southern Mexico. The percentage of Mexicans self-identifying as Catholic has fallen from 98 percent in 1950 to about 85 percent today, of whom a large component are nonpracticing. Many young people find the evangelical congregations more accessible and welcoming, from their upbeat gospel music to their more visible commitment to meeting the needs of low-income people. Moreover, migrants returning from the United States are more likely to have been exposed to evangelical churches there.

Revolution and Its Aftermath

The nationwide civil conflict that erupted in Mexico in 1910 is often referred to as the first of the great "social revolutions" that shook the world early in the twentieth century. Mexico's upheaval, however, originated within the country's ruling class. The revolution did not begin as a spontaneous uprising of the common people against the entrenched dictator, Porfirio

Díaz, nor against the local bosses and landowners who exploited them. Even though hundreds of thousands of workers and peasants ultimately participated in the civil strife, most of the revolutionary leadership came from the younger generation of middle- and upper-class Mexicans who had become disenchanted with three-and-a-half decades of increasingly heavy-handed rule by the aging dictator and his clique. These disgruntled members of the elite saw their future opportunities for economic and political mobility blocked by the closed group surrounding Díaz.

Led by Francisco I. Madero, whose family had close ties with the ruling group, these liberal middle-class reformers were committed to opening up the political system and creating new opportunities for themselves within a capitalist economy, whose basic features they did not challenge. They did not seek to destroy the established order. Instead, they sought to make it work more in their own interest rather than that of the foreign capitalists who dominated key sectors of Mexico's economy during the Porfirian dictatorship.

Of course, some serious grievances had accumulated among workers and peasants. Once the rebellion against Díaz got underway, leaders who appealed to the disadvantaged masses pressed their claims against the central government. Emiliano Zapata led a movement of peasants in the state of Morelos; they were bent on regaining the land they had lost to the rural aristocracy by subterfuge during the Porfiriato. In the north, Pancho Villa led an army of jobless workers, small landowners, and cattle hands, whose main interest was steady employment. As various revolutionary leaders contended for control of the central government, the political order that had been created and enforced by Díaz disintegrated into warlordism—powerful regional gangs led by revolutionary *caudillos* (political-military strongmen) who aspired more to increasing their personal wealth and social status than to leading a genuine social revolution.

The first decade of the revolution produced a new, remarkably progressive constitution, replacing the Constitution of 1857. The Constitution of 1917 established the principle of state control over all natural resources, subordination of the Church to the state, the government's right to redistribute land, and rights for labor that had not yet been secured even by the labor movement in the United States. Even so, nearly two decades passed before most of these constitutional provisions began to be implemented.

During the 1920s, the central government set out to eliminate or undermine the most powerful and independent-minded regional caudillos by co-opting the local power brokers, known as *caciques*. These local political bosses became, in effect, appendages of the central government, supporting its policies and maintaining control over the population in their communities. By the end of this period, leaders with genuine popular followings (like Zapata and Villa) had been assassinated and control had been seized by a new postrevolutionary elite bent on demobilizing the masses and establishing the hegemony of the central government. The rural aristocracy of the Porfiriato had been weakened but not eliminated; its heirs still controlled large concentrations of property and other forms of wealth in many parts of the country.

The Cárdenas Upheaval

Elite control was maintained during the 1930s, but this was nevertheless an era of massive social and political upheaval in Mexico. During the presidency of **Lázaro Cárdenas** (1934–1940), peasants and urban workers succeeded for the first time in pressing their claims for land and higher wages; in fact, Cárdenas actively encouraged them to do so. The result was an unprecedented wave of strikes, protest demonstrations, and petitions for breaking up large rural estates.

Most disputes between labor and management during this period were settled, under government pressure, in favor of the workers. The Cárdenas administration also redistributed more than twice as much land as that expropriated by all of Cárdenas' predecessors since 1915, when Mexico's land reform program was formally initiated. By 1940, the country's land tenure system had been fundamentally altered, breaking the traditional domination of the large haciendas and creating a large sector of small peasant farmers (*ejidatarios*)—more than 1.5 million of them—who had received plots of land under the agrarian reform program. Even Mexico's foreign relations were disrupted in 1938 when the Cárdenas government nationalized oil companies that had been operating in Mexico under U.S. and British ownership.

Mexican intellectuals frequently refer to 1938 as the high-water mark of the Mexican revolution as measured by social progress; they characterize the period since then as a retrogression. Certainly, the distributive and especially the redistributive performance of the Mexican government declined sharply in the decades that followed, and the worker and peasant organizations formed during the Cárdenas era atrophied and became less and less likely to contest either the will of the government or the interests of Mexico's private economic elites. De facto reconcentration of landholdings and other forms of wealth occurred as the state provided increasingly generous support to the country's new commercial, industrial, and financial elites during a period of rapid industrialization.

The Cárdenas era fundamentally reshaped Mexico's political institutions. The presidency became the primary institution of the political system, with sweeping powers exercised during a constitutionally limited six-year term with no possibility of reelection; the military was removed from overt political competition and transformed into one of several institutional pillars of the regime; and an elaborate network of government-sponsored peasant and labor organizations provided a mass base for the official political party and performed a variety of political and economic control functions, using a multilayered system of patronage and clientelism.

By 1940, a much larger proportion of the Mexican population was nominally included in the national political system, mostly by their membership in peasant and labor organizations created by Cárdenas. No real democratization of the system resulted from this vast expansion of "political participation," however. Although working-class groups did have more control over their representatives in the government-sponsored organizations than over their former masters on the haciendas and in the factories, their influence over

public policy and government priorities after Cárdenas was minimal and highly indirect.

The Era of Hegemonic Party Rule

The political system shaped by Lázaro Cárdenas proved remarkably durable. From 1940 until the late 1980s, Mexico's official party–government apparatus was the most stable regime in Latin America (see Box 14.1). It had a well-earned reputation for resilience, adaptability to new circumstances, a high level of agreement within the ruling elite on basic rules of political competition, and a seemingly unlimited capacity to co-opt dissidents, both within and outside of the ruling party.

With the fall of the Communist Party of the Soviet Union in 1991, the PRI became the world's longest continuously ruling political party. Since 1929, when the "official" party was founded, both political assassination and armed rebellion had been rejected as routes to the presidency by all contenders for power. A handful of disappointed aspirants to the ruling party's presidential nomination mounted candidacies outside the party (in the elections of 1929, 1940, 1946, 1952, and 1988), but even the most broadly supported of these breakaway movements were successfully contained through government-engineered vote fraud and intimidation.

In the early 1970s, concerns had been raised about the stability of the system, after the bloody repression by President Gustavo Díaz Ordaz of a student protest movement in Mexico City on the eve of the 1968 Olympic Games. The student massacre marked

---

BOX 14.1 Mexican Presidents and Their Parties since 1940

1940–1946	Manuel Avila Camacho (PRI)	1982–1988	Miguel de la Madrid (PRI)
1946–1952	Miguel Alemán (PRI)	1988–1994	Carlos Salinas de Gortari (PRI)
1952–1958	Adolfo Ruiz Cortines (PRI)	1994–2000	Ernesto Zedillo (PRI)
1958–1964	Adolfo López Mateos (PRI)	2000–2006	Vicente Fox (PAN)
1964–1970	Gustavo Díaz Ordaz (PRI)	2006–2012	Felipe Calderón (PAN)
1970–1976	Luis Echeverría (PRI)	2012–2018	Enrique Peña Nieto (PRI)
1976–1982	José López Portillo (PRI)		

the opening of a "dirty war" in which the army and police forces are believed to have executed, without trial, more than 700 alleged enemies of the state. Many analysts at that time suggested that Mexico was entering a period of institutional crisis, requiring fundamental reforms in both political arrangements and economic development strategy.

The discovery of massive oil and natural gas resources during the late 1970s gave the incumbent regime a new lease on life. Continued support of the masses and the elites was purchased with an apparently limitless supply of petro-pesos, even without major structural reforms. The government's room to maneuver was abruptly erased by the collapse of the oil boom in August 1982, owing to a combination of adverse international economic circumstances (falling oil prices, rising interest rates, and recession in the United States) and fiscally irresponsible domestic policies. Real wages and living standards for the vast majority of Mexicans plummeted, and the government committed itself to a socially painful restructuring of the economy, including a drastic shrinkage of the sector owned and managed by the government itself.

The economic crisis of the 1980s placed enormous stress on Mexico's political system. In the July 1988 national elections, the PRI suffered unprecedented reverses in both the presidential and congressional races. The vote share officially attributed to the PRI's presidential candidate, **Carlos Salinas de Gortari**, was more than 20 percent below that of PRI presidential candidate Miguel de la Madrid in the 1982 election. Ex-PRIista Cuauhtémoc Cárdenas, son of the much-revered former President Lázaro Cárdenas, heading a hastily assembled coalition of minor leftist and nationalist parties, was officially credited with 31.1 percent of the presidential vote—far more than any previous opposition candidate but probably much less than he would actually have received if the vote count had been honest.[3] A diminished PRI delegation still controlled the Congress, but the president's party had lost the two-thirds majority needed to approve constitutional amendments.

A Harvard-educated technocrat, Carlos Salinas breathed new life into the creaking PRI apparatus. His brand of strong presidential leadership and his accomplishments—especially the toppling of corrupt labor union bosses, a sharp reduction in inflation, and the National Solidarity Program, a new-style antipoverty and public works program that increased

government responsiveness to lower-class needs—sufficed to rebuild electoral support for the PRI and to paper over the cracks within the ruling political elite. Salinas opened the Mexican economy to foreign trade and investment and privatized hundreds of inefficient state-owned companies. While political liberalization had proceeded slowly and unevenly under Salinas, far behind the pace of his sweeping free-market economic reforms, Mexico appeared to be coasting inexorably toward a transfer of power to yet another PRI national government in 1994.

The illusion of proximate economic modernity and political inevitability was shattered on New Year's Day 1994 by a "postmodern" peasant revolt in Chiapas, Mexico's most underdeveloped and politically backward state. An estimated 2,000 primitively armed but well-disciplined indigenous rebels seized control of four isolated municipalities and declared war on the central government—something that had not happened since 1938. The impoverished natives who took up arms against the state in Chiapas symbolized the many millions of Mexicans who had been left behind in the drive for economic modernity and internationalism.

Less than three months after the Chiapas rebellion erupted, President Salinas' handpicked successor, Luis Donaldo Colosio, was assassinated while campaigning in Tijuana. With a last great exertion of presidential will, Carlos Salinas imposed on the PRI another handpicked successor, economist-technocrat Ernesto Zedillo, to replace the slain Colosio. In August 1994, in a high-turnout election that was judged by most independent observers at the time to be the cleanest in Mexico's postrevolutionary history, the opposition parties were soundly defeated. Not only did the PRI retain control of the presidency (albeit with just a plurality of 48.8 percent of the total votes cast), it also maintained an ample majority in the federal Congress.[4]

The End of PRI Dominance

The appearance of restored stability created by the ruling party's impressive performance in the August 1994 elections was short-lived. In December 1994, a militarily insignificant renewal of the Zapatista rebels' activities in Chiapas, followed immediately by a sustained speculative attack on the overvalued peso by short-term foreign and domestic investors, opened a Pandora's box of economic and political troubles. What began as a currency and financial liquidity crisis quickly evolved into a massive capital flight and a deep recession.

By the late 1990s, the PRI once again appeared to be in a state of accelerated decomposition. Divisions within the party were deeper than at any time since the mid-1930s. The results of the 1997 elections for Congress were a stunning setback for the PRI, which lost 112 of 300 single-member districts. For the first time since 1929, the PRI had to surrender control of the Chamber of Deputies (the lower house of Congress) to a coalition of four opposition parties. The PRI also lost its two-thirds majority in the Senate, which is needed to approve constitutional amendments.

In the 2000 election, voters were furious at having been deceived twice by their government, first during the oil boom era of 1977–1981 and then during the Salinas presidency (1988–1994), periods when the government created an illusion of prosperity and

boundless future economic gains. For the first time in seventy-one years, the voters soundly rejected the presidential candidate of the PRI, turning to **Vicente Fox**, a maverick former-Coca-Cola-executive-turned-politician who ran under the banner of **Partido Acción Nacional (PAN)**.

The presidential election of 2006 featured three strong candidates and a deeply divided electorate. Roberto Madrazo, the PRI's president (2002–2005), won the party's 2006 presidential nomination. However, there was significant opposition within the party to his candidacy. Felipe Calderón, the president of the National Action Party in the mid-1990s, won the PAN's 2006 nomination through a series of three regional primaries. The **Partido de la Revolución Democrática (PRD)** chose **Andrés Manuel López Obrador**, the mayor of Mexico City from 2000 to 2005, as its 2006 presidential candidate.

After an extraordinarily negative campaign, Calderón and López Obrador were tied in all of the

Enrique Peña Nieto, Winner of Mexico's July 2012 Presidential Election
The youthful, photogenic candidate symbolized the "new PRI." His victory restored the party to executive power after twelve years of rule by two presidents from the National Action Party (PAN).

polls. On election day, July 2, 2006, the race was so close that both López Obrador and Calderón claimed victory. After the formal count, the Federal Electoral Institute (IFE) announced that Calderón had won by 0.58 percent, or about 244,000 votes out of the nearly 42 million cast. López Obrador immediately claimed that there had been electoral fraud, orchestrated by the PAN, the PRI, the Federal Electoral Institute, and the business community. To pressure the electoral tribunal to order a complete recount, the PRD launched a civil disobedience campaign in Mexico City. Thousands of protesters set up tents along the principal boulevard and the Zócalo (the central plaza), blocking all traffic in the heart of Mexico City. The partial recount and the subsequent nullification of some disputed precincts shifted only about 14,000 votes to López Obrador. Calderón's victory was certified by the electoral tribunal in early September. Nonetheless, López Obrador refused to recognize Calderón's victory.

The election results divided Mexico in two, with the PAN winning most of the northern states (except Zacatecas and Baja California Sur, both governed by the PRD). The PRD won every state to the south, except Yucatán (governed by the PAN) and Puebla (where the PRI governor was under the cloud of scandal). Calderón and López Obrador each won sixteen states. Madrazo, incredibly, won not a single state. More important, in terms of long-term consequences, the intense postelection conflict in 2006 set the stage for another round of electoral law reforms, enacted in 2007, designed to avoid another disputed presidential election.

The Return of the PRI

After its disastrous, third-place finish in the 2006 presidential election, and with its delegation in Congress reduced to about a fifth of the lower chamber, the PRI seemed to be retreating into its regional strongholds. However, in subsequent gubernatorial elections, the PRI recovered states that it had previously lost to the opposition (see Figure 14.1). By 2010, the PRI was well positioned to retake the presidency in 2012, fueled by a slow-growing economy and public disapproval of President Calderón's aggressive, violence-producing war against drug traffickers. In the federal elections of July 2010, PRI candidates won a majority of the state governorships being contested, but a PAN–PRD coalition won three states—Oaxaca, Puebla, and Sinaloa—previously held only by the PRI.

For the 2012 election, the PRD renominated López Obrador as its candidate for president. His only relevant opponent was Marcelo Ebrard, the progressive mayor of Mexico City. The elected PRDista mayor was well regarded on the left for having legalized abortion and gay marriage in the capital. López Obrador had spent much of the previous five years in a nationwide campaign to position himself for another presidential run. The PRD selected its candidate through opinion polling rather than a primary election. Two other parties on the left also endorsed López Obrador, reassembling the same coalition as in 2006. During the general election campaign, López Obrador presented himself as a more moderate and trustworthy alternative, quite different from his radical firebrand image of 2006.

The PAN chose Josefina Vázquez Mota, former Secretary of Education and Secretary of Social Development in the previous two PAN administrations, who was the first woman to be nominated as the presidential candidate of a major party. Her opponent in the party's national primary was Ernesto Cordero, former Secretary of Social Development and Secretary of the Treasury in the Calderón administration. PANistas viewed him as the favorite candidate of President Calderón, but, as in the 2006 election, the primary voters rejected the president's choice in favor of someone who they thought better represented the traditions of the party. Vázquez Mota's main campaign slogan in the general election was that she was "different," referencing in part her gender but also distancing herself somewhat from the previous two PAN presidencies, without discussing her differences in specific public policies.

The PRI selected, as a consensus candidate, Enrique Peña Nieto, former governor of the state of Mexico, which surrounds Mexico City and has the largest population of any state. He was also nominated by the Partido Verde Ecologista de México (PVEM), the Green party, which had also run as the PRI's coalition partner in 2006. As early as 2005, Peña Nieto was groomed as a presidential candidate by Televisa, Mexico's largest television network. Televisa's cameras and affiliated gossip magazines closely followed the recently widowed governor's romance and eventual marriage to one of the network's soap opera stars. In the general election, Peña Nieto ran on his accomplishments as

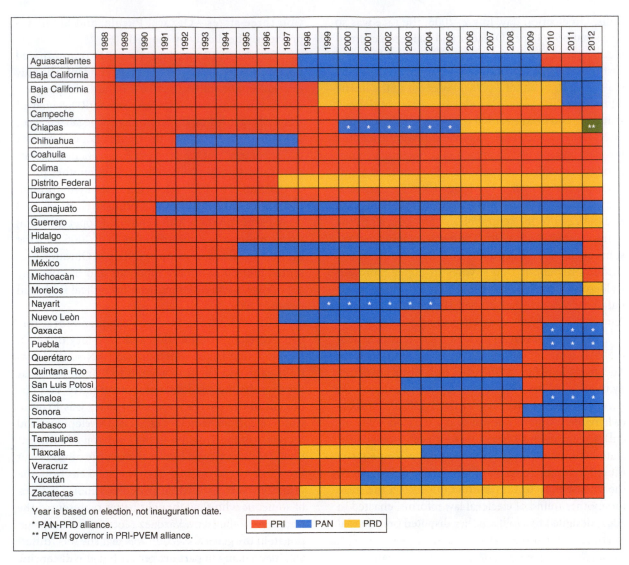

FIGURE 14.1

Party Control of Mexico's State Governments

Starting in the late 1990s, parties have alternated in power at the state level. Some states now have two-party (PRI–PAN or PRI–PRD) systems; others reflect the three-party system operating at the national level.

governor, a long list of promises he had made as governor that were checked off as the policy was implemented or the public work was built. He also asked voters to put their trust again in the PRI: a party with "experience," a party that "knew how to govern."

Peña Nieto held the lead in the polls throughout the campaign, but after the first of two televised debates of presidential candidates, when the PRD's López Obrador surpassed expectations, the most respected national opinion poll showed Peña Nieto leading López Obrador by only four points. But López Obrador failed

to sustain his momentum, and the race opened up somewhat through the remainder of the campaign.

On election day, July 1, 2012, Peña Nieto won by a surprisingly close 6.8 percentage points over López Obrador, with the PAN's Vázquez Mota winning just above a quarter of the vote (see Table 14.1). The PRI won 20 states—a remarkable recovery after losing every state in 2006. The PAN's performance was uneven. Vázquez Mota won two of its stronghold states (Guanajuato and Nuevo León) but lost another stronghold (Jalisco). She won in two traditional PRI strongholds

TABLE 14.1

2012 Presidential Election Results

The PRI recovered from a distant third-place finish six years before to win back the presidency in 2012, while the ruling PAN fell to third.

Candidate	Votes	% of Valid Votes
Enrique Peña Nieto (PRI-PVEM)	19,158,592	39.2
Andrés Manuel López Obrador (PRD-PT-MC)	15,848,827	32.4
Josefina Vázquez Mota (PAN)	12,732,630	26.0
Gabriel Quadri de la Torre (Nueva Alianza)	1,146,085	2.3
Nonregistered candidates	20,625	0.0
Invalid votes	1,236,857	
Total	50,143,616	100.0

Source: Instituto Federal Electoral (www.ife.org.mx).

(Veracruz and Tamaulipas) and finished close in other northeastern states. These states had suffered high levels of violence in the drug wars, and the PAN's strong showing there in 2012 was interpreted as an endorsement of President Calderón's national security policies. López Obrador won in the Federal District and in six states in the south and southeast where the PRD had performed well in previous elections.

Despite taking the presidency, the PRI–PVEM coalition failed to win majorities in either the Chamber of Deputies or the Senate. López Obrador asked the Electoral Tribunal to invalidate the election. He claimed that the television networks and most public opinion polls had been biased toward Peña Nieto. He also asserted that the PRI campaign had bought votes through the distribution of electronic cash cards. The Tribunal rejected his arguments and declared Peña Nieto the winner. Unlike 2006, there were no mass protests against the final result.

Thus began Mexico's second experience with PRI governance at the national level. While the PRI won pluralities of seats in both the Senate and the Chamber of Deputies, Peña Nieto's lack of majority control of Congress compelled him to negotiate all legislation with opposition party leaders. He entered office with the lowest public approval rating of any newly elected Mexican president since systematic polling began in the 1990s. It remained to be seen whether the PRI's election-year success in promoting nostalgia for an imagined past under the "official party" could be translated into a record of major new accomplishments that could lock in PRI hegemony for another generation.

Political Culture

14.3   Describe Mexicans' conflicted relationship with their political system.

Most of what we know empirically about Mexican political culture is based on research completed during the period of sustained economic growth and virtually unchallenged one-party rule in Mexico, from 1940 through the mid-1970s. The portrait of Mexican political culture that emerges from these studies can be summarized as follows: Mexicans are highly supportive of the political institutions that evolved from the Mexican Revolution, and they endorse the democratic principles embodied in the Constitution of 1917.

Nevertheless, Mexicans are critical of government performance, especially in creating jobs, reducing social and economic inequality, fighting crime, and delivering basic public services. Most government bureaucrats and politicians are viewed as distant, elitist, and self-serving, if not corrupt. Mexicans traditionally have been pessimistic about their ability to affect election outcomes, anticipating fraud and regarding attendance at campaign rallies and voting as ritualistic activities. The basic elements of this political culture remain in place, although Mexicans today are much more aware of their ability to determine election results and more demanding of electoral transparency.

On the surface, this combination of attitudes and beliefs seems contradictory. How could Mexicans support a political system that they see as unresponsive or capricious at best, in which they are mere "subjects" rather than true participants? Historically, popular support for the Mexican political system derived from three sources: the revolutionary origins of the regime, the government's role in promoting economic growth, and its performance in distributing concrete, material benefits to a substantial proportion of the Mexican population since the Cárdenas era. Each of these traditional sources of support has been undermined to some extent since 1976.

The official interpretation of the 1910 revolution stressed symbols (or myths), such as social justice, democracy, the need for national unity, and the popular origins of the current regime. The government's identification with these symbols was constantly reinforced by the mass media, public schools, and the mass organizations affiliated with the official party. Over the years, the party's electoral appeals were explicitly designed to link its candidates with agrarian reform and other revered ideals of the revolution, with national heroes like Emiliano Zapata and Lázaro Cárdenas, and with the national flag. (The PRI emblem conveniently has the same colors, in the same arrangement.) However, President Salinas broke decisively with so many tenets of "revolutionary ideology" (strict church–state separation, land reform, economic nationalism, etc.) that the PRI's claim to the revolutionary mantle became tenuous. Indeed, since the late 1980s, that mantle has been claimed by the PRD.

Relatively few Mexicans based their support for the system primarily on its revolutionary origins or symbolic outputs, however. For most sectors of the population, symbols were supplemented with particularistic material rewards: plots of land or titles to land that had been occupied illegally, schools, low-cost medical care, agricultural crop price supports, government-subsidized food and other consumer goods, and public sector jobs. For more than forty years, the personal receipt of some material "favor" from the official party–government apparatus, or the hope that such benefits might be received in the future, ensured fairly high levels of mass support for the system.

Even now, Mexicans' concept of democracy emphasizes economic and social outputs rather than procedural liberties, and the electoral strategies of all parties reflect this element of political culture.[5] For example, in the 2006 election, many voters were attracted to PRD candidate López Obrador by his performance as Mexico City mayor, delivering high-visibility public works and monthly payments to senior citizens. PAN candidate Felipe Calderón promised to reduce social inequality through a major

expansion of Oportunidades, a federal welfare program already benefiting 5 million low-income families. In the 2012 election, PAN candidate Vázquez Mota ran on her record of combating poverty as President Calderón's Secretary of Social Development. The PRI's Peña Nieto emphasized his accomplishments in creating public works projects as governor of the state of México, touting, for example, the number of basketball courts constructed by his administration.

While not on a par with traditional vote buying by the PRI—trading specific material payoffs like bags of cement and flour for tortilla making for votes at the individual level—such campaign strategies clearly resonate with an electorate whose concept of democracy is still largely distributive. In fact, under new electoral rules, the particularistic distribution of material benefits ("*despensas*") is arguably more important than ever in shaping Mexicans' voting behavior. In recent elections, polling data show that a very large segment of voters claimed to have experienced vote-buying attempts.

Private goods have become more important for **vote buying** than public goods (for example, public works), as governments affiliated with all three major parties have created antipoverty entitlement programs at the federal and local levels that can be manipulated for political gain. These programs provide such benefits as need-based scholarships for school children, access to preventive medical care, and hot breakfasts for senior citizens. Electoral reforms enacted in 2007 that drastically restrict candidates' access to the mass media while also controlling the content of their campaign advertisements have made it much more difficult for candidates to sway voters through persuasion. The incentive under the new electoral rules is to buy more votes more directly, for example, by promising to grant (or threatening to deny) benefits through entitlement programs.[6]

Despite their growing distrust of key political institutions (especially Congress and the political parties), a plurality of Mexicans have remained "system loyalists." Nevertheless, most Mexicans today do not hesitate to criticize the way in which local, state, and national governments function, and many more feel free to demonstrate their dissatisfaction through the use of social media and through the ballot box.

Historically, most Mexicans tolerated corruption in government as a price to be paid in order to extract benefits from the system or to deal with police harassment. But the unbridled corruption of the López Portillo and the Salinas administrations drastically reduced such tolerance, and an upsurge in drug-related corruption in the 1990s—reaching into the highest levels of the government bureaucracy and the national security apparatus—angered many Mexicans. They feared that their government had been taken over by *narco-políticos*—public officials in league with corrupt police and drug lords.

The slowness of the Fox and Calderón administrations to root out government and police corruption, despite their independence from the structure of corruption created under PRI rule, was a source of public anger after twelve years of PAN rule. When Mexicans were asked in 2011 what was most lacking in their country's democracy, a sizable majority (55 percent) specified reducing corruption, more than any other perceived deficiency (see Table 14.2). In its first year, the Peña Nieto government made some conspicuous efforts to punish corruption, jailing Elba Esther Gordillo, the long-time head of the national teachers union and the former PRIista governor of the state of Tabasco. But public outrage over official corruption remains high.

Despite much greater competition in the electoral system since the 1980s, the average Mexican remains relatively uninterested in politics. For example, at the beginning of the bitterly fought presidential election campaign of 2006, two-thirds of the interviewees in a national survey expressed little or no interest in politics, and 55 percent said they rarely or never discussed politics with other people.[7] In the last three national elections, however, Mexicans have shown themselves to be sensitive to short-term campaign stimuli, such as presidential candidates' debates, television ads, and news coverage.

In fact, Mexicans appear more susceptible to persuasive campaign appeals than voters in the United States and other established democracies. Most exposure to campaign stimuli is via the mass media, and media exposure has been a consistently strong predictor of voting participation in recent elections: More-informed Mexicans are more likely to vote than less-informed ones.[8]

In 2012, campaign effects were evident despite a new election code regulation prohibiting negative advertisements and a much shorter campaign than in previous presidential elections (exactly 90 days). The PRI's Peña Nieto lost two-thirds of his margin from the beginning to the end of the campaign. Relative to U.S. voters, more Mexicans change their party identification during the course of a campaign.[9] While such findings may indicate the absence of a core set of stable political beliefs, they reveal that Mexicans are paying close attention to the options provided by political competitors, at least during hard-fought national election campaigns.

TABLE 14.2

What Does Democracy in Your Country Lack Most?*

Mexicans see lack of progress in reducing official corruption as their democracy's greatest failing, cited by a higher percentage than in all but five other Latin American countries.

Country	Percentage Citing Corruption as Key Failing
Colombia	63
Argentina	61
Peru	59
Paraguay	59
Brazil	58
Mexico	**55**
Costa Rica	55
Venezuela	49
Chile	49
Bolivia	46
Dominican Republic	45
Guatemala	41
Ecuador	40
Honduras	39
Uruguay	39
Panama	38
Nicaragua	36
El Salvador	29

*The survey question was: "What do you think the democracy in your country lacks most?" Multiple responses were recorded. Percentages in this table reflect the total number of respondents who mentioned reducing corruption. A national probability sample was surveyed in each country.

Source: Corporación Latinobarómetro, *Informe 2011* (Santiago, Chile: Corporación Latinobarómetro, October 28, 2012), www.latinobarometro.org.

Mass Political Socialization

14.4 Discuss the major sources of political socialization in Mexico and how they have changed.

How do Mexicans form their attitudes toward the political system? In addition to the family, the schools and the Catholic Church are important sources of preadult political learning. All schools, including church-affiliated and secular private schools, must follow a government-approved curriculum and use the same set of free textbooks, written by the federal Ministry of Education. Although the private schools' compliance with the official curriculum is often nominal, control over the content of textbooks gives the government an instrument for socializing children to a uniform set of political values.

Under PRI rule, school-based political learning stressed the social and economic progress accomplished under postrevolutionary governments. The president was depicted as an omnipotent authority figure whose principal function is to maintain order in the country. Thus, despite the many egregious failures of presidential leadership that Mexicans have witnessed since the mid-1970s, many continue to express a preference for strong presidentialist government. However, mass public education has increased criticism of partisan politics and poor government performance. Higher levels of education are also associated with stronger support for the right to dissent and other democratic liberties.

The Catholic Church has been another key source of values affecting political behavior in Mexico. Church-run private schools have proliferated in recent decades. Along with secular private schools, they provide education for a large portion of children from middle- and upper-class families. Religious schools and priests have criticized anticlerical laws and policies, promoted individual initiative (as opposed to governmental action), and preached against abortion and gay marriage. They have also stressed the need for moral Christian behavior in public life.

As adults, Mexicans learn about politics from their personal encounters with government functionaries and the police. They also learn from participating in local community-based organizations and popular movements that seek collective benefits or redress of grievances from the government. There has been an impressive proliferation of popular movements in Mexico since 1968, when the student protest movement was violently repressed. The catalysts for this new wave of popular movements included gangsterism in government-affiliated labor unions, increasingly blatant PRI vote fraud in state and local elections during the 1980s, environmental disasters, and the implementation of neoliberal economic policies that adversely affected the low- and middle-class segments of society.

While most of these popular movements are quite localized in scope and concerns, a few have grown to embrace thousands of Mexicans in many different states. The Civic Alliance—a coalition of hundreds of nongovernmental organizations (NGOs), independent labor unions, and popular movements—has mobilized tens of thousands of Mexican citizens and hundreds of foreign observers to scrutinize the conduct of every national election since 1994 and publish reports on election irregularities. Nevertheless, NGOs remain heavily concentrated in the Mexico City metropolitan area, where nearly 30 percent of the country's NGOs are registered. By contrast, the state of Chiapas hosts only 0.3 percent.

For seven decades, the PRI government apparatus systematically used the mass media as an agent of political socialization. Although the government did not often directly censor the media, there were significant economic penalties for engaging in criticism or investigative reporting that seriously embarrassed the president. During the two PANista administrations, the mass media were more openly critical of government performance. Many newspapers and news magazines retained their PRI partisan bias and energetically criticized the president and other PANista officials. The independent media kept up their intense scrutiny of the executive branch and were also highly critical of what they saw as incompetence and inefficiency in Congress.

The print media reach only a minority of the Mexican population. Less than half of the adult population reads newspapers, and even the largest Mexico City newspapers have circulations under 100,000. Most Mexicans get their political information from television and talking with family and friends. Until recently, television was virtually monopolized by a huge private firm, Televisa, which had a notoriously close working relationship with the PRI government apparatus and invariably defended the incumbent president's performance. One consequence of the Salinas administration's privatization program was the breakup of Televisa's virtual monopoly. A formerly government-owned television channel in Mexico City has grown quickly into a rival network, TV Azteca, and Televisa itself adjusted to the competition by giving much more coverage to opposition voices.

One of the first reforms pushed through by the Peña Nieto administration further weakened the duopoly in television and attacked the dominant position of Telmex (owned by Mexico's richest man, Carlos Slim) in telephone communications. It created a new Federal Telecommunications Commission, with more teeth and greater autonomy than the previous regulatory agency. Both partisan politicians and industry insiders were barred from being commissioners until a certain number of years had passed. The law increases the sanctions on anticompetitive practices by the media giants. It prohibits the news broadcasts from presenting government propaganda under the disguise of news content. It also guaranteed broadband Internet access for all Mexicans through the federal public utility's fiber-optic network, run by public or private interests (but not the telecommunications industry) under government supervision. Furthermore, the Federal Competition Commission was strengthened and made more autonomous to eliminate anti-competitive practices and market concentration.

Social media are an increasingly important agent of political socialization, even though cell phone coverage in Mexico is the second lowest among Latin American countries (37 percent of Mexicans interviewed in a 2011 survey did not have a cell phone; only Nicaraguans were less likely to have a cell phone).[10] As discussed in Box 14.2, social media figured prominently in the 2012 presidential campaign, serving to mobilize student protesters in Mexico City against the PRI candidate and his perceived mass media allies.

BOX 14.2   Rising Power of Social Media: The #YoSoy132 Movement

On May 11, 2012, after a routine campaign speech to students at Mexico City's Universidad Iberoamericana, a private Jesuit university, PRI presidential candidate Enrique Peña Nieto found the exits from the university blocked from within by students. They were protesting the former state governor's authoritarian style and the perceived imposition of the candidate by Mexico's largest television network, Televisa, and other national media. News of the blockade spread in real time through social media, especially Twitter. Although the candidate was able to free himself shortly thereafter, the campaign's ham-handed response infuriated the students even more. Several persons who gave affidavits on social media supporting the PRI candidate and claiming to be Iberoamericana students were quickly identified as students of other universities who were likely working on the Peña Nieto campaign.

Thus was born the #YoSoy132 movement. Its name comes from a video of 131 students from the Iberoamericana who posted a video on YouTube, promoted by Twitter and Facebook, identifying themselves by name, student ID, and major, and claiming that they supported the protest. ("YoSoy132" means "I am the 132nd.") What made the movement unusual was that most of the organizers were from upper-middle-class families. Moreover, the focus was less on political parties than on the electoral process, particularly the role of the national electronic media.

Some observers thought that this protest movement could be the precursor of an "Arab Spring" in Mexico, but the students were not looking to overthrow the government and were not even especially interested in overturning what appeared to be an inevitable result (the

election of Peña Nieto). Some students were objecting to the selection of Peña Nieto as the PRI's candidate, but most were protesting what they believed to be media control over the presidential campaign. For example, the major networks refused to televise the first presidential debate. The electoral law did not require them to do so, and electoral authorities could not compel coverage. After a great deal of pressure, the networks did televise the second debate. The students organized a third debate, live-streamed on June 20. All major candidates except Peña Nieto participated.

A week after the initial #YoSoy132 protest, students from the Instituto Tecnológico Autónomo de México (ITAM) and the Instituto Tecnológico de Monterrey formed a human chain across the ITAM campus, over a freeway bridge, to the studios of Televisa. This protest was organized entirely via Facebook and Twitter. Within a couple of weeks, students from Mexico's largest public university, The National Autonomous University of Mexico, and other public universities joined the movement. This brought far greater numbers to the movement, but the public university students used their majorities to call for a laundry list of standard leftist demands associated with the PRD, which made it easier for the PRI to dismiss them as mere partisans. Although their voice became louder, the message was less penetrating.

After the elections, the students of the #YoSoy132 movement blockaded the downtown studios of Televisa and marched to the Federal Electoral Tribunal's headquarters, after it validated the election of Peña Nieto and dismissed charges of media manipulation. Televisa subsequently hired some of the #YoSoy132 protesters and gave them their own talk show.

University Students Protest Media Manipulation of the 2012 Presidential Election
Students communicating with each other through social media played a highly visible role in the 2012 electoral campaign, protesting what they viewed as biased coverage by Mexico's largest television network and organizing their own presidential candidates' debate, streamed online, which was boycotted by the PRI candidate.

Abuses of authority now come to light regularly via social media. For example, in 2012, when the daughter of the head of PROFECO, Mexico's consumer protection agency, asked her father's henchmen to close a restaurant that had refused her the table she wanted, the incident got out immediately via social media (Twitter), forcing the head of PROFECO to resign. In Veracruz, when federal government officials were tape-recorded discussing plans to manipulate funds from the Oportunidades federal antipoverty program to benefit PRI candidates in that state, the recordings were posted to YouTube and the miscreant officials were swiftly suspended. It has yet to be demonstrated that social media are influencing election outcomes or boosting voter participation in Mexico, but they clearly influence young people's perceptions of the political system.

Political Participation

14.5 Discuss the factors that have boosted participation in recent Mexican elections.

Traditionally, most political participation in Mexico has been of two broad types: (1) formal activities, such as voting or attending campaign rallies, and (2) petitioning or contacting of public officials to influence the allocation of some public good or service. By law, voting is obligatory in Mexico, though there are no civil penalties for not voting. Evidence of having voted in the most recent election has sometimes been required to receive public services. People participate in campaign rallies mostly because attending might have a specific material payoff (a free meal, a raffle ticket, a T-shirt), or because failure to do so could have personal economic costs. Some people, especially in rural areas, routinely sell their votes in return for handouts from local officials.

Since 1994, Mexico has experienced an explosion in political participation, evidenced not only by the virtually nonstop protests of citizens' movements of all types but also by a sharp rise in turnout in federal elections. The turnout of registered voters rose from 49 percent in the 1988 presidential election, to 61 percent in the midterm 1991 elections, to 78 percent in the 1994 presidential election. In the 2012 presidential election, over 50,000,000 Mexicans cast their votes, a turnout rate of 63 percent (see Figure 14.2). Unfortunately, valid comparisons with electoral participation rates in the pre-1988 period are impossible, since the 1988 presidential election was the first for which reasonably accurate turnout figures were made public. In all previous national elections, the government inflated turnout statistics in an effort to convince Mexicans and the outside world that it had succeeded in relegitimating itself in impressive fashion.

In 2012, the voters included 41,067 Mexicans living abroad, overwhelmingly in the United States, who were permitted to vote absentee in the presidential election for the second time. Although expatriate participation was up 24 percent from the 2006 election,

these voters represented just a tiny fraction of the more than 10.6 million voting-age Mexican immigrants in the United States.[11] Participation of migrants in Mexican elections is depressed by a cumbersome registration and voting process for expatriates (arguably designed by the political parties to discourage voting by a large, politically unpredictable group), and by the migrants' own increasing integration into U.S. society, which weakens their interest in home-country politics.

As long as electoral politics remain as competitive as in the period since 1988 and potential voters continue to believe in the security of the electoral system, we can expect further, gradual movement toward a genuinely participatory political culture in Mexico. In the 2010 national elections, voter turnout increased in all five states where the PAN and PRD ran coalition candidates to block PRI victories. While PAN–PRD coalitions were absent from the 2012 presidential contest, it is reasonable to expect that such left–right coalitions, by increasing competitiveness, will create stronger incentives to vote in future elections.

Rising educational attainment also will be crucial to boosting participation (research shows that actual

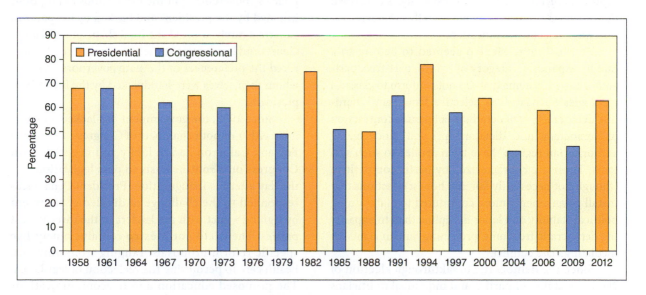

FIGURE 14.2
Turnout of Registered Voters in National Elections, 1958–2012*
Beginning in 1991, turnout rates reflect real increases in voter participation, not government padding.

*Beginning in 1970, the legal voting age was lowered from twenty-one to eighteen years.

Source: Data from Comisión Federal Electoral for 1958–1988; from Instituto Federal Electoral for 1991–2012.

voters in Mexico are generally more educated[12]), as will greater involvement in nonpolitical, community-level organizations. Participation in such organizations builds social capital—the social networks, norms, and trust that enable people to act together more effectively to pursue shared objectives. Research has shown that Mexicans who are active in their communities and thereby connected to their neighbors are far more likely to participate politically.[13]

Political Structure and Institutions

14.6 Describe the branches of Mexico's government and the changes they have undergone.

Mexican politics has long defied easy classification. In the 1950s and 1960s, some U.S. political scientists depicted the regime as a one-party democracy that was evolving toward "true" democracy (as practiced in the United States and Western Europe). They recognized certain imperfections, but in the view of these analysts, political development in Mexico was simply incomplete. After the government's massacre of student protesters in 1968 and 1971, most analysts described the system as authoritarian, but even this characterization was subject to qualification.

By the 1990s, Mexico seemed to belong to a rapidly expanding category of hybrid, part-free, part-authoritarian systems that did not conform to classical typologies. Such labels as "selective democracy," "hard-line democracy," *democradura* (a Spanish contraction of "democracy" and "dictatorship"), and "modernizing authoritarian regime" have been applied to such systems. These are characterized by partly competitive (though not necessarily fair and honest) elections that install governments more committed to maintaining political stability and labor discipline than to expanding democratic freedoms, protecting human rights, or mediating class conflict.

Since the democratic breakthrough election of 2000, the ability of parties and individual politicians to engage in undemocratic practices (for example, electoral fraud, selective repression of dissidents, and heavy-handed control of mass media) has declined. The functioning of all political institutions is scrutinized intensely, and officials are held to much higher standards than ever before. The political design issue is no longer regime transition but how to improve democratic institutions already in place, especially to eliminate the structure of corruption that still supports abuses of authority and the electoral process at the local level in some parts of the country.

On paper, the Mexican government is structured much like the U.S. government: a presidential system, three autonomous branches of government (legislative, executive, and judicial) with checks and balances, and federalism with considerable autonomy at the state and municipal level (see Figure 14.3). Until the late 1990s, however, Mexico's system of government was, in practice, far removed from the U.S. model. Decision making was highly centralized.

The president, operating with relatively few restraints on his authority, completely dominated the legislative and judicial branches. Supreme Court justices were presidentially appointed and confirmed by a simple majority of the PRI-dominated Senate. Each incoming president replaced most justices, which made the judges agents of the executive branch. Until 1997, the ruling PRI continuously controlled both houses of the federal legislature. Opposition party members could criticize the government and its policies vociferously, but their objections to proposals initiated by the president and backed by his party in Congress rarely affected the final shape of legislation. Courts and legislatures at the state level normally mirrored the preferences of the state governors, many of whom themselves were handpicked by the incumbent president.

Since 1997, the government has lacked a majority in either or both chambers of Congress. Presidents Fox and Calderón had to lobby and negotiate with Congress on a routine basis to pass legislation. On the day after his inauguration, President Peña Nieto responded to the challenge of divided government by signing a pact with the leaders of the three largest parties. The **Pacto por México** contains ninety-five specific reform proposals, ranging from universal health care to permitting the reelection of legislators. The proposed education and telecommunications reforms were implemented expeditiously under the guise of the Pacto, and a comprehensive banking reform was introduced in 2013, also under the terms of the interparty agreement. More reforms in electoral rules, the justice system, taxes, and energy were to follow.

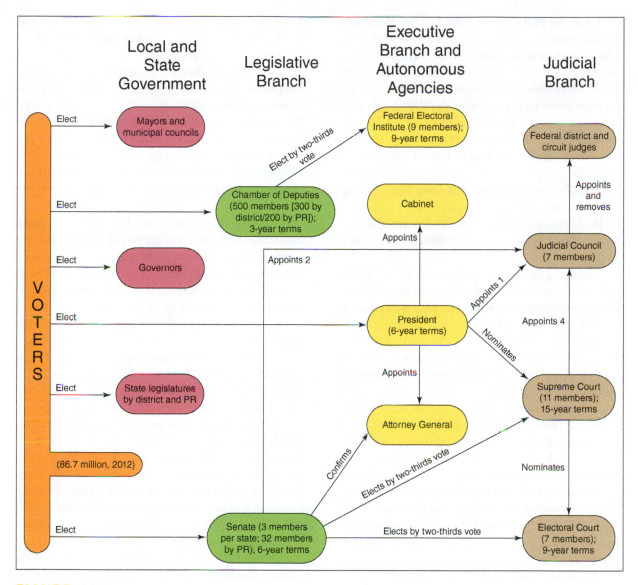

FIGURE 14.3
Structure of Mexico's Federal Government

The Pacto represents a significant innovation in Mexico's continuing experience with divided government. It appears to subordinate leaders in Congress, where no party commands a majority, to a supercommittee of political party leaders dealing directly with the president. The Pacto has no legal basis—only the political convenience of the key actors sustains it—and thus is potentially unstable. Indeed, by late 2013 it was widely expected that the PRD would withdraw because of its opposition to Peña Nieto's energy sector reform, perhaps making it too politically costly for the PAN to remain in the Pacto.

Federalism: A Double-Edged Sword

Despite the federalist structure of government that is enshrined in the 1917 Constitution and legal codes, with their emphasis on the *municipio libre* (the concept of the free municipality, able to control its own affairs), in practice, the Mexican political system has usually functioned in a manner best characterized as **political centralism**.

From the 1920s through the Salinas presidency, the concentration of decision-making power at the federal level in most policy areas was continuous. Control over the preparation, conduct, and validation of elections—placed entirely at the municipal and state levels by the initial postrevolutionary electoral code, enacted in 1918—also passed to agencies that were part of the federal government apparatus or state-level entities controlled by federal authorities. A high degree of political centralism has been considered one of the main factors underlying Mexico's long-term political stability, although research at the state and local levels has demonstrated that political control by the center has been far less complete than is commonly assumed.[14]

Mexico is divided into thirty-one states and the Federal District, each one divided into *municipios*—politico-administrative units roughly equivalent in size and governmental functions to county governments in the United States. Each of the country's 2,438 municipios is governed by an *ayuntamiento*, or council, headed by a *presidente municipal* (mayor). Municipal officials are elected every three years. Each successive layer of government in Mexico is significantly weaker, less autonomous, and more impoverished than the levels above it. In recent years, the federal government has raised well over 90 percent of total public revenues—one of the highest degrees of fiscal centralization in Latin America.[15] State governments now spend more than half of total revenues, but this is mainly because of federal revenue sharing that provides the states with much of their budget.

All of Mexico's seven most recent presidents entered office pledging to renew the "struggle against centralism," but serious efforts to decentralize have been made only since 1984. Under de la Madrid and Salinas, a limited form of revenue sharing was implemented, and the federal Constitution was amended to enhance the capacity of local governments to raise their own revenues. Partially successful efforts were also made to shift decision-making authority over public education and health care from the federal government to the states.[16] President Zedillo went so far as to sign an agreement with the country's state governors and mayors calling for constitutional amendments that would provide the legal framework for "a new Mexican federalism." Zedillo implemented a more equitable distribution of federal funds to the states and devolution of some functions that had been usurped by the federal government.

Under divided government, the states demanded and obtained from their federal legislators even greater revenue sharing. The state governors themselves represent a potential obstacle to the "new federalism." They retain control over all resources transferred from the federal government, and effective administrative decentralization down to the municipio level would require them to relinquish a major portion of their political power—something that they have successfully resisted.

It is clear that, even under a president strongly committed to redistributing resources and sharing power with subnational units of government, movement toward U.S.-style federalism in Mexico will meet with opposition from many different quarters, including federal government agencies and the states themselves. State-level elections have not democratized at the same pace as federal elections. Since the 1990s, governors of all parties have attempted to keep tight control over local candidate selection and the state's electoral apparatus, often using state government resources to assure victory for the ruling party.

Rejuvenated federalism can thus be a double-edged sword, with the potential to consolidate authoritarian enclaves at the state and local levels. Even in the federal government's war against narco-traffickers, decentralization has had unintended consequences. President Calderón's strategy of breaking the cartels into smaller components supposedly manageable by local authorities spawned greater competition among competing drug lords and, hence, more violence. Via revenue sharing with the state governments, municipal governments in Mexico today have access to far more resources than in previous eras. Electoral competition at the local level has increased greatly in recent decades, but divided government has negatively impacted the performance of city councils in many places. Thus, in Mexico, less central control does not necessarily translate into more electoral democracy, better governance, and greater public security.

The Legislative Branch

Mexico's political system has been commonly described as presidentialist or presidentially centered. Nonetheless, these characterizations were based on observed practices in a dominant-party regime, in which the institutional rules of the party had overwhelmed the formal constitutional rules. A careful examination of the Mexican Constitution reveals a president who is among the more constitutionally constrained in Latin America and a Congress with strong, sometimes dominant powers over the other branches of government. The difference between the informal and formal institutions is the history of the PRI government.

The federal Congress has two houses: a 128-member upper chamber, the Senate, and a 500-member lower house, the Chamber of Deputies. Both chambers employ a mixed-member system in which some of the members are elected by plurality vote in single-member districts while others are elected by a system of compensatory proportional representation on closed-party lists.[17] The current electoral rules for the Senate, dating to 1996, call for plurality elections in each of the thirty-two states whereby each party nominates a slate of two Senate candidates. The party that wins a plurality elects both candidates from the slate to the Senate. The party that places second sends the first candidate on the list to the Senate. Furthermore, thirty-two senators are elected by proportional representation on closed national lists, so that each party that wins at least 2 percent of the national vote elects its proportional share of the thirty-two list senators. The rules prevent any party from winning more than two-thirds of the seats in the Senate except under extraordinary circumstances (a party would have to place first in every state and win more than two-thirds of the national vote).

For the Chamber of Deputies, 300 members are elected by plurality in single-member districts, and an additional 200 deputies are elected by proportional representation in five regional closed lists. Each party that wins at least 2 percent of the national vote is entitled to its proportional share of the list deputies, with a few restrictions. First, no party can ever have more than 300 total seats, which restricts the largest party to less than the two-thirds majority required for constitutional reforms. Second, no party's share of the total number of seats can exceed by more than 8 percent its share of the national vote. This means that in order to win a majority in the lower chamber, a party must win more than 42 percent of the vote and a sufficient margin of victory over the second-place party (usually around 4 percentage points) to win enough plurality districts.

The mixed-member system directly affects the party system. Usually, plurality systems lead to two-party systems, as the voters find that it is better to coordinate their votes toward one of the two leading parties rather than waste them on third-party candidates. PR systems tend to create multiparty systems, because votes for the larger minority parties are not wasted. In Mexico, the mixed-member system has yielded a three-party system, in which most regions now have two-party systems (respecting the tendencies of the plurality system), but nationally, the vote is split into three main blocs. The three parties with significant representation in the Chamber of Deputies in the Sixty-Second Legislature (2012–2015) are the PRI (with 43 percent of the seats), the PAN (with 23 percent), and the PRD (with 20 percent). The low threshold allows small parties to attain representation in the Chamber of Deputies as well; four small parties won seats in the Sixty-Second Legislature (see Table 14.3).

The mixed-member system complicates creating majorities in either chamber. Since the 8 percent rule on maximum overrepresentation was established in the lower house, no party has been able to achieve a majority. The Senate rules went into effect fully for the first time in the 2000 elections. Now, when the race is close between the first- and second-place parties, it is also unlikely that a majority party will emerge in the Senate. This means that the party of the president will rarely have a majority in Congress, thus creating a situation of divided government.

Like the U.S. Constitution, the 1917 Mexican Constitution lists the legislative branch first. The Congress is primarily responsible for enacting nearly all public policy, with only a few exceptions. The president has constitutional decree powers only over questions of land reform (expropriation decrees) and tariffs and quotas in international trade (in which he can unilaterally adjust tariffs and quotas if the circumstances call for modifications). All regular legislation must be approved by both chambers in the same form and then submitted to the president for publication. The president must publish the bill within thirty days or return the bill to the chamber of origin (see Box 14.3).

A presidential veto can take two forms: One is a regular veto, in which the president expresses his rejection of a bill, and the second is a corrective veto, in which the president requests that Congress amend the

TABLE 14.3
Party Composition of the Congress*

	Seats Won by Plurality Vote	Seats Won by PR Vote	Total	Percentage
Chamber of Deputies				
Partido Revolucionario Institucional (PRI)[a]	164	49	213	42.6
Partido Acción Nacional (PAN)	52	62	114	22.8
Partido de la Revolución Democrática (PRD)[b]	58	42	100	20.0
Partido Verde Ecologista de México (PVEM)[a]	13	15	28	5.6
Movimiento Ciudadano[b]	8	12	20	4.0
Partido de Trabajo (PT)[b]	5	10	15	3.0
Nueva Alianza	0	10	10	2.0
Total	300	200	500	100.0
Senate				
Partido Revolucionario Institucional (PRI)	43	11	54	42.2
Partido Acción Nacional (PAN)	29	9	38	29.7
Partido de la Revolución Democrática (PRD)[b]	16	6	22	17.2
Partido Verde Ecologista de México (PVEM)[a]	5	2	7	5.5
Partido de Trabajo (PT)[b]	3	2	5	3.9
Movimiento Ciudadano[b]	0	1	1	0.8
Nueva Alianza	0	1	1	0.8
Total	96	32	128	100.0

*Data reflect party membership as of April 30, 2013.
[a]Alianza Compromiso por México.
[b]Alianza Movimiento Progresista.

bill, usually because of technical errors in the text. In either case, Congress can insist on the original text of the bill by a two-thirds vote, after which the president must publish the legislation. In the case of corrective vetoes, Congress often modifies the bill as requested and sends it back to the president for promulgation.

Each of the two chambers has exclusive powers and areas of specialization. The Chamber of Deputies specializes in fiscal legislation. All revenue bills must originate in the lower chamber. The Chamber of Deputies first approves the revenue and tax legislation, sending it to the upper chamber for Senate approval. However, only the Chamber of Deputies approves the appropriations legislation. This gives the Chamber of Deputies extraordinary influence over the federal public administration. Likewise, the lower chamber has exclusive powers over budgetary oversight and approves the public accounts.

The Senate has exclusive power to oversee foreign affairs. The upper chamber has the power to monitor foreign affairs, and it approves treaties submitted by the president by a majority vote. It approves presidential appointments of ambassadors and consuls, also by a majority vote. The Senate also has the power to remove state governors and depose state legislatures. The Constitution allows the Senate to topple state governments when it recognizes that the state can no longer provide for domestic security. This requires a vote of the upper chamber; afterward, the president proposes a list of three candidates from which the

BOX 14.3   How a Bill Becomes a Law in Mexico

- Bills can be introduced by federal deputies, senators, the president, or the state legislatures. All revenue bills, regardless of the sponsor, must be introduced in the Chamber of Deputies. Therefore, the president's annual economic package is sent to the Chamber of Deputies. However, senators can introduce revenue legislation directly in the Chamber of Deputies. All other legislation can begin in either the Chamber of Deputies or the Senate. The federal bureaucracy assists the president in preparing executive bills for introduction.

- All bills are sent to committees. There are fifty-six committees in the Chamber of Deputies and thirty in the Senate. Committees amend most legislation before reporting it to the floor (82 percent in the Chamber of Deputies, and 78 percent in the Senate). The federal bureaucracy often sends commentary on pending legislation to the relevant committees. The legislators are not required to heed these opinions.

- All legislation reported by committee is voted on the floor. The chamber can amend legislation from committees, but only 17 percent of the legislation is amended on the floor in the Chamber of Deputies, and only 21 percent on the floor of the Senate. If a bill is approved by the first chamber, it is sent to the other chamber for approval.

- In the second chamber, bills are sent to committee. Routine legislation is usually reported to the floor without amendment. Important bills are usually amended in committee. If the second chamber approves the bill on the floor without amendment, it is sent to the president; if the bill is amended, it is sent back to the first chamber for approval. Bills can be considered twice by each chamber before a final version is settled on.

- The president must sign or veto a bill within thirty days. If the president neither vetoes nor publishes the bill, the president of the chamber of Congress where the bill originated can order the bill to be published. The federal bureaucracy usually makes recommendations to the president on whether to sign or veto a bill. If the president vetoes a bill, it is sent to the first chamber for reconsideration. If the first chamber rejects the veto by a two-thirds vote, it is sent to the other chamber. If the second chamber also rejects the veto by a two-thirds vote, the president must publish the law. The president also has a corrective veto, in which he can return a bill to the first chamber, suggesting amendments. Each chamber may accept these amendments by a majority vote or reject the amendments by a two-thirds vote.

- The annual appropriations bill is considered by only the Chamber of Deputies. The president sends the appropriations bill to the chamber by September 8. The chamber must approve the bill, with or without amendments, by November 15, sending the bill back to the president. If the president vetoes the bill, the Chamber of Deputies can accept his suggestions by a majority vote or reject them by a two-thirds vote. The Senate never considers appropriations.

Note: Statistics pertain to the Sixty-First Legislature (2009–2012).

Senate elects the interim governor by a two-thirds vote. Prompted by PRI presidents, the Senate deposed many governors during the twentieth century, though usually for political reasons rather than for security motives. The Senate also regulates pacts between the federal and state governments concerning revenue sharing and program administration.

Federal deputies and senators have shown extraordinary levels of party discipline in recent years (see Table 14.4). For example, during the last two years of the Fifty-Seventh Legislature (1997–2000), on average, 99.6 percent of the PRIista deputies voted together on party bills. After 2003, PANista deputies voted together more than 98 percent of the time, nearly equaling the levels of PRI discipline when it held the presidency. When the PRI recovered the presidency in 2012, PRIsta discipline rose to pre-2000 levels (99.5 percent in the first year of the Sixty-Second Legislature). While these fluctuations in party discipline do not seem large, they have had major effects on public policy.

TABLE 14.4

Party Cohesion in Congress

Parties stick together in Congress on major party votes, and the party of the executive is the most cohesive.

Legislature	PRI	PAN	PRD
Fifty-Seventh (1997–2000)	**99.6**	92.0	93.5
Fifty-Eighth (2000–2003)	89.3	**93.6**	92.5
Fifty-Ninth (2003–2006)	90.5	**98.3**	95.8
Sixtieth (2006–2009)	94.4	**98.8**	95.2
Sixty-First (2009–2012)	94.7	**94.5**	87.6
Sixty-Second (2012–)*	**99.5**	96.6	90.1

Bold indicates the party of the president. Data for the Fifty-Seventh Legislature begin October 8, 1998; data for the Sixty-First Legislature end April 30, 2013. Major party votes are roll calls in which at least one of the three parties dissented from the rest. Party cohesion is the percentage of the party voting with the majority of that party.

Source: For the Fifty-Seventh Legislature, Jeffrey A. Weldon, "Institutional and Political Factors in Party Discipline in the Chamber of Deputies, 1998–2002," presented at the First Latin American Political Science Congress (Salamanca, Spain, July 2002). Data for the last five legislatures calculated from the *Diario de los Debates* and the *Gaceta Parlamentaria* of the Chamber of Deputies.

High party discipline in Mexico has two main sources.[18] First, consecutive reelection for deputies and senators is prohibited. This nearly eliminates accountability of the representatives to their constituents. Voters can neither reward their legislators for good performance nor punish them for bad representation. Since federal legislators are not required to seek cues from their electorate, they look elsewhere for guidance, and the party leadership is more than willing to provide it.

Second, nomination procedures in each of the parties are relatively closed, with party leadership usually selecting candidates directly. This further focuses the legislators on party leadership, because without the support of the party elite, their political futures would be dismal. Each party generally votes as a bloc in Congress, which creates incentives for the leaders of each of the parties to negotiate bills among themselves rather than allow the rank-and-file members to work out compromises in committee. Together, these institutions create a highly centralized legislative branch.

The Executive Branch

Despite the constitutionally limited powers of the executive branch, no one would dispute that the president was the dominant political actor in Mexico for the greater part of the twentieth century. In addition to his rather modest constitutional powers, the Mexican president possessed a broad range of unwritten but generally recognized "metaconstitutional" powers that traditionally ensured his dominance over all of the country's other political institutions. Mexicans use the term *presidencialismo* to connote this extraordinary concentration of powers, formal and informal, in the hands of the president, with the implication that incumbents frequently abuse these powers in pursuit of personal and political ends.

On any issue of national political significance, the federal judiciary would take its cue from the incumbent president. Until very recently, the Supreme Court never found presidential decisions or legislation enacted at the behest of the president to be unconstitutional, and Congress never challenged presidential appointments to the federal judiciary. The president had the informal power to seat and unseat state governors, mayors, and members of Congress. From 1929 through 1994, the president also functioned as the "supreme head" of the official party, choosing its leaders, dictating his legislative proposals to the PRI delegation in Congress, shaping the party's internal governance, imposing his personal choices for the PRI's gubernatorial and congressional candidates, and—most important—controlling the selection of the party's next presidential nominee.

The absence of a rigid, fully elaborated political ideology made it possible for a Mexican president to have a pragmatic, flexible program and style of governance. The so-called ideology of the Mexican Revolution was never more than a loosely connected set of goals or symbols. The only "revolutionary" ideology that has been scrupulously observed is the constitutionally mandated no-reelection principle for the presidency: The president is limited to a single six-year term.[19]

During the PRI's first seven decades of rule at the national level, three factors were required to create strong presidentialism. First, the president's party had to have a majority in both chambers of Congress. Under **divided government**, the opposition majorities in Congress are unlikely to follow the dictates of the president. Second, there must be high levels of discipline in the majority party of Congress. Third, the president must be the leader of his party. In the 1930s, the first two factors were in place, but the leader of the party, Plutarco Elías Calles, received all of the benefits of the disciplined party, not the president. After Cárdenas reorganized the official party along lines of authority that led directly to himself, strong presidencialismo was finally achieved.

Executive–Legislative Relations

The dynamics of executive–legislative relations in Mexico used to be determined by the metaconstitutional powers of the president. The operation of the three key factors outlined earlier—unified government, high party discipline in the ruling party, and the recognition of the president as the de facto head of the party—explained a compliant Congress. Today, the first and third factors no longer hold. Executive-legislative relations follow constitutional rather than partisan norms, and Mexico either enjoys or suffers from the everyday republican conflicts of separation of powers.

Comparing levels of productivity during specific Congressional periods allows us to evaluate the executive's influence over the legislative branch under varying applications of the metaconstitutional conditions listed earlier, as well as the relative strength of the president's party in the lower chamber (see Table 14.5).

During the Fifty-Fourth Legislature (1988–1991), the PRI held a small majority of 52 percent of the lower chamber. Despite the marginal majority, 98.6 percent of the executive's public bills were approved. Of the 110 bills approved during the Fifty-Fourth Legislature, nearly two-thirds originated in the executive branch. In the Fifty-Seventh Legislature (1997–2000), divided government prevailed for the first time since 1928. The PRI held just under 48 percent of the seats in the lower chamber, while the PAN and the PRD each had about a quarter of the seats. Thus, the first of the conditions for metaconstitutional power—unified government—was eliminated.

Under divided government, 90 percent of the president's bills were approved—a decline of nine percentage points from the previous legislature. Since 1928, a majority of the bills that the Chamber of Deputies approved had originated in the executive branch. In the Fifty-Seventh Legislature, this trend was abruptly reversed; only 31 percent of the bills approved in the term had been introduced by the executive, while nearly 60 percent had been sponsored by deputies.

By the time the Fifty-Eighth Legislature had convened in 2000, metaconstitutional presidentialism had ended. The first condition—unified

---

TABLE 14.5
Presidential Party Strength and Executive Bills
The president now initiates much less legislation than members of Congress, and fewer of his bills are approved.

Legislature	Party of the President	% of Deputies from President's Party	% Share of Total New Bills Introduced	% Share of Total Bills Approved	% of President's Bills Approved
Fifty-Fourth (1988–1991)	PRI	52	22.8	65.1	98.6
Fifty-Fifth (1991–1994)	PRI	63	42.4	62.6	98.5
Fifty-Sixth (1994–1997)	PRI	60	33.8	74.2	98.9
Fifty-Seventh (1997–2000)	PRI	48	10.1	31.0	90.0
Fifty-Eighth (2000–2003)	PAN	41	6.8	23.7	89.9
Fifty-Ninth (2003–2006)	PAN	30	2.8	8.6	73.2
Sixtieth (2006–2009)	PAN	41	2.2	10.4	70.4
Sixty-First (2009–2012)	PAN	29	1.5	6.6	77.0
Sixty-Second (2012–)[a]	PRI	43[b]	0.9	5.3	81.8

[a]Data for the Sixty-Second Legislature through April 30, 2013.
[b]Total is 48.2 percent with electoral ally, PVEM; 50.2 percent in legislative alliance with PVEM and Nueva Alianza.
Source: Data compiled from *Diario de los Debates* and the *Gaceta Parlamentaria* of the Chamber of Deputies.

government—remained unfulfilled. President Fox's PAN held only 41 percent of the seats in the lower chamber. Nor was Fox treated as the head of his party. Nearly 90 percent of Fox's bills were approved during the 2000–2003 term. However, nearly every bill that Fox sent to Congress had been extensively amended in at least one of the chambers. Never before had a higher percentage of executive bills been amended, either in committee or on the floor.

Mexico's first "opposition" president had difficult relations with a Congress in which the opposition parties—when united—had majority control. During the Fifty-Ninth Legislature (2003–2006), only 73.2 percent of the president's bills were approved, and a mere 8.6 percent of the bills approved by the Chamber of Deputies originated in the executive branch. In fall 2004, the opposition coalition in the Chamber of Deputies amended Fox's federal appropriations bill, decreasing or eliminating a number of federal programs and increasing pork barrel expenditures for PRI and PRD states. Fox vetoed the appropriations bill; this was the first budget veto cast by a president since 1933. The Chamber of Deputies disputed the veto by filing a suit in the Supreme Court, claiming that the president did not have the constitutional power to veto the budget (despite the fact that there had been forty-five vetoes of the budget between 1917 and 1933, none of which had been challenged on constitutional grounds by Congress). The Supreme Court suspended the expenditures to which the president had objected, and later ruled that the budget veto was indeed constitutional.

Felipe Calderón enjoyed a legislative plurality in the Sixtieth Legislature (2006–2009), with the PAN holding 41 percent of the seats and the PRI relegated to third place in the lower chamber. However, this was not enough to guarantee legislative success, as only 70.4 percent of his bills were approved in that term, representing only slightly more than a tenth of all of the bills approved. Nonetheless, the president has enjoyed legislative success despite divided government, accomplished by "logrolling" legislation with the PRI. For example, Calderón and the PAN won a major victory in tax reform through the creation of two new taxes.

Simultaneously, the PRI won an electoral reform to its liking. Party influence over the electoral authorities was increased, public and private campaign financing were reduced, and officeholders could no longer promote themselves while in office. Negative

campaign advertising (even if truthful) was banned. The law prohibits parties from buying television or radio time for their spots, instead using free media time allocated by the electoral authorities (this was opposed by the private television networks). However, no other person or organization can buy time to promote political ideas or candidates at any time. The president also won a series of major reforms in public security and judicial procedures.

Further, Calderón won a legislative victory yearned for by both Presidents Zedillo and Fox—a comprehensive energy reform. The president had asked for new interpretations of the laws prohibiting private investment in the oil industry, though he insisted that neither PEMEX nor any part of the process would be privatized. The committee report was a watered-down version of Calderón's bill, but the PAN and PRI, along with part of the PRD, passed the law. After suffering a defeat in the 2009 midterm elections, the PAN presence in the Chamber of Deputies was reduced to only 30 percent, and Calderón's legislative success rate remained relatively low, with only 77 percent of his bills approved; less than 7 percent of all of the approved bills had originated in the executive branch.

President Peña Nieto began his term with 43 percent of the seats in the lower chamber, but through a coalition with the PVEM and with Nueva Alianza, he could command 251 votes—the smallest possible working majority. This small majority has increased the approval rate of his executive bills to almost 82 percent in the first year of the legislature, but only 5.3 percent of the approved bills came from the presidency. The Pacto por México should increase the total productivity of the Congress, since the cooperation of the opposition parties is necessary to get bills through the Senate and to enact constitutional amendments in both chambers.

Recruiting the Political Elite

14.7 Discuss political recruitment in Mexico, focusing on the rise of the technocrats.

At least since the days of the Porfiriato, the Mexican political elite has been recruited predominantly from the middle class. The 1910 revolution did not open up the political elite to large numbers of people from peasant or urban laborer backgrounds. That opening occurred only in the 1930s, during the Cárdenas **sexenio (six-year term)**, and then mainly at the local and state levels rather than the national elite level.

In the last three PRI-dominated administrations (1982–2000), the national political elite was drawn heavily from the ranks of *capitalinos*—people born or raised in Mexico City. Postgraduate education, especially at elite foreign universities and in disciplines like economics and public administration, became much more important as a ticket of entry into the national political elite. Over half of the cabinet members appointed by Presidents de la Madrid, Salinas, and Zedillo had studied economics or public administration, and over half of those who received training in these subjects at the graduate level did so in the United States. The economic policy debacles presided over by technocrat presidents and cabinet ministers in the 1990s discredited this breed of Mexican officials in the eyes of the public as well as the party leadership. Significantly, a national PRI assembly in 1996 removed most technocrats from the line of presidential succession by requiring the party's future presidential nominees to have previously held elective office.

Relatively few card-carrying technocrats found their way into the cabinet of Vicente Fox, who favored people with nongovernmental experience, with a bachelor's or master's degree in business administration, educated in Mexico—like himself. Nearly half (45 percent) of Fox's top fifty-two appointees—many of them recruited through professional headhunting firms—had no previous public sector experience. The involvement of persons with private sector experience in the Fox administration (46 percent) was far greater than in any of the PRI governments since 1929. Fox also broke with his PRI predecessors in recruiting more top officials from outside of Mexico City (60 percent of his top officials were from the provinces), and more who had received their undergraduate education in private rather than public universities (54 percent). Most strikingly, 75 percent of Fox's original top fifty-two appointees had no known political party affiliation. Fewer than one-fifth were recruited from the PAN.[20] Only four members of Fox's original cabinet had a history of militancy in the PAN, and the dearth of card-carrying PANistas was even more conspicuous at the subcabinet level. Some ministries were nearly devoid of PANistas.

In terms of professional background, Felipe Calderón was something of a throwback to the late technocratic PRI presidents. Calderón clearly had the skill set of a *técnico*; he even had a master's degree from Harvard University. However, in contrast to the last five PRI presidents, Calderón also had extensive experience in party politics and elective office. His own economic cabinet was dominated by technocrats holding doctoral degrees from U.S. universities.

Peña Nieto's cabinet seems to combine the characteristics of cabinets before and after the rise of the technocrats. The median age of his cabinet secretaries is 10 years older than in the first Calderón cabinet, there are more than twice as many lawyers, and fewer hold international graduate degrees. However, his economic cabinet earned their doctoral degrees at the Massachusetts Institute of Technology, Yale, and the University of Pennsylvania. In fact, Calderón's technocratic finance minister moved to the foreign ministry under Peña Nieto.

Since the 1970s, kinship ties have become more important as a common denominator of those who attain top positions of political power. Increasingly, such people are born into politically prominent families that have already produced state governors, cabinet ministers, federal legislators, and even presidents. Family connections can give an aspiring political leader a powerful advantage over rivals. These political families are increasingly interconnected: At least one-third of the government officials and politicians interviewed by one researcher for several books on the pre-2000 Mexican political elite were related to other officials, not counting those related through marriage and the traditional rite of *compadrazgo* (becoming a godparent to a friend's child).[21] The importance of political families has not declined during Mexico's democratic era—indeed, their significance may be increasing. Regardless of their party affiliation, since 2000, at least one-third of politicians who have served as local legislators, mayors, members of Congress, Supreme Court justices, and assistant secretaries in the executive branch have been connected to political families.[22]

The growing importance of kinship ties and other indicators of increasing homogeneity in personal backgrounds causes some observers to worry that Mexico's political elite is becoming more closed and inbred. While its social base may indeed be narrowing, the modern Mexican political elite still shows considerable fluidity; the massive turnover of officeholders every six years is proof of that. This factor helps to explain why in Mexico—unlike other postrevolutionary countries, such as China and (until recently) the Soviet Union—the regime did not become a gerontocracy. In fact, the median age of cabinet members and presidential aspirants in Mexico has been dropping; in recent sexenios, most have been in their late thirties or early forties. Exemplifying this trend, Enrique Peña Nieto was forty-six years old when elected to the presidency.

Interest Representation and Political Control

14.8 Explain the role of interest groups in Mexico, touching on corporatist and patron–client structures.

In Mexico's presidentialist system, important public policies used to be initiated and shaped by the inner circle of presidential advisors before they were even presented for public discussion. Thus, most effective interest representation took place within the upper levels of the federal bureaucracy. The structures that aggregate and articulate interests in Western democracies (the ruling political party, labor unions, and so on) actually served other purposes in the Mexican system: limiting the scope of citizens' demands on the government, mobilizing electoral support for the regime, helping to legitimate it in the eyes of other countries, and distributing jobs and other material rewards to select individuals and groups. For example, the PRI typically had no independent influence on public policymaking—nor did the opposition parties, except where they controlled state or local governments.

From the late 1930s until the PRI's defeat in 2000, Mexico had a **corporatist** system of interest representation in which each citizen and societal segment was expected to relate to the state through a single structure "licensed" by the state to organize and represent that sector of society (peasants, urban unionized workers, businesspeople, teachers, and so on). The official party itself was divided into three **sectors**: (1) the Labor Sector, (2) the Peasant Sector, and (3) the Popular Sector, a catch-all category representing various segments of the middle class (government employees, other white-collar workers, small merchants, private rural landowners) and low-income urban dwellers.

Each sector in the PRI is dominated by one mass organization; other organizations are affiliated with each party sector, but their influence is dwarfed by that of the "peak" organization. Thus, the **Confederación de Trabajadores de México (CTM)** represents the Labor Sector, including most urban-dwelling labor union members. The **Confederación Nacional Campesina (CNC)** is the principal representative of the Peasant Sector, primarily ejidatarios—peasants who have received land through the agrarian reform program. The **Confederación Nacional de Organizaciones Populares (CNOP)** represents the Popular Sector, consisting of mostly urban-based service workers and small business owners. Under the PRI government that took power in 2012, the party's sectors have less power than ever before, with declining capacity to mobilize voters and with their influence over policymaking further diluted by the Pacto por México.

A number of powerful organized interest groups—entrepreneurs, the military, the Catholic Church—are not formally represented in the PRI. These groups traditionally dealt directly with the government elite, often at the presidential or cabinet level. They did not need the PRI to make their preferences known. They also had well-placed representatives within the executive branch who could be counted on to articulate their interests. In addition, the business community was organized into several government-chartered confederations. Since the Cárdenas administration, all but a small minority of the country's industrialists were required by law to join one of these employers' organizations, which channeled business interests into a few well-controlled outlets. These confederations still exist, but the Supreme Court ruled in 1999 that compulsory membership was an unconstitutional restriction on the freedom of association.

Because the ruling party and the national legislature did not effectively aggregate interests in the Mexican system, individuals and groups seeking something from the government often circumvented their nominal representatives in the PRI sectoral organizations and the Congress and sought satisfaction of their needs through personal contacts within the government bureaucracy. These **patron–client relationships** compartmentalized the society into discrete, noninteracting, vertical segments that served as pillars of the regime. Within the lower class, for example, unionized urban workers were separated from nonunion urban workers, ejidatarios from small private landholders and landless agricultural workers. The middle class was compartmentalized into government bureaucrats, educators, health care professionals, lawyers, economists, and so forth. Thus, competition among social classes was replaced by highly fragmented competition within classes.

The articulation of interests through patron-client networks assisted the PRI regime by fragmenting popular demands into small-scale, highly individualized, or localized requests that could be granted or denied case by case. Officials were rarely confronted with collective demands from broad social groupings. Rather than having to act on a request from a whole category of people (slum dwellers, ejidatarios, teachers), they had easier, less costly choices to make (as between competing petitions from several neighborhoods for a paved street or a piped water system).

The clientelistic structure thus provided a mechanism for distributing public services and other benefits in a highly selective, discretionary (if not always arbitrary) manner. This system put the onus on potential beneficiaries to identify and cultivate the "right" patrons within the government bureaucracy. The prohibition on consecutive reelection prevented local elected officials from taking on the role of patron. As they could be neither punished nor rewarded for their performance, elected politicians abdicated this responsibility, and it was only natural that the bureaucracy would replace them in the role of patron.

Unquestionably, the PRI's vaunted political control capabilities were weakened by the economic and political crises of recent sexenios. Nevertheless, the traditional instruments of control—patron–client relationships, *caciquismo* (local-level boss rule), the captive labor movement, and selective repression of dissidents by government security forces—remain effective in some PRI-controlled states. The PAN and PRD adopted milder clientelistic strategies in the states that they have governed.

In other places, however, the limited success of PAN administrations in solving high-salience public security and urban development problems has undermined attempts to build new, enduring state–society relationships. For example, in 2004, disillusioned voters in the key northern border city of Tijuana turned out the PAN after three terms, installing as mayor a traditional PRI politician with a reputation for corruption and authoritarianism. He quickly set about restoring the corporatist networks that his PANista predecessors had labored to dismantle.

Political Parties

14.9 Discuss the ways that the reform of the Mexican electoral system since the 1990s has affected the political parties.

The Partido Revolucionario Institucional

The PRI was founded in 1929 by President Plutarco Elías Calles to serve as a mechanism for reducing violent conflict among contenders for public office and for consolidating the power of the central government at the expense of the personalistic local and state-level political machines of the decade following the 1910–1920 revolution. Between 1920 and 1929, there had been four major rebellions against the national executive by these subnational political machines.

For more than half a century, the ruling party served with impressive efficiency as a mechanism for resolving conflicts, for co-opting newly emerging interest groups into the system, and for legitimating the regime through the electoral process. Potential defectors from the official party were deterred by the government's manipulation of electoral rules, which made it virtually impossible for any dissident faction to bolt from the party and win the election. Dissident movements did emerge occasionally, but before the neo-Cardenista coalition contested the 1988 election, no breakaway presidential candidacy had been able to garner more than 16 percent of the vote (by official count).

From the beginning, the official party was an appendage of the government itself, especially of the presidency. It was never a truly independent arena of political competition. A handful of nationally powerful party leaders, such as Fidel Velázquez, the patriarch of the PRI-affiliated labor movement until his death in 1997, occasionally constrained government actions, but the official party itself never determined the basic directions of government economic and social policies. Indeed, one of the key factors underlying the erosion of party unity and discipline since the late 1980s and the PRI's overwhelming defeats in state-level elections beginning in 1995, leading to its loss of the presidency in 2000, was the party's inability to distance itself from the unpopular austerity policies made by the technocrats in the federal government.

The PRI traditionally enjoyed virtually unlimited access to government funds to finance its campaigns. No one knew how much was actually being siphoned from government coffers to the PRI, because Mexico had no laws requiring the reporting of campaign income and expenditures. Reforms to the federal electoral code between 1993 and 1994 established minimal public reporting requirements for campaign income and expenditures, as well as Mexico's first-ever limits on individual and corporate contributions to electoral campaigns.

These reforms were strengthened by another round of electoral code reforms, passed by Congress in 1996, that limited total private contributions to any party to 10 percent of the total amount of regular public financing to all parties, and no individual could contribute more than 0.05 percent of the total regular public financing. The 2007 reforms further reduced private financing to 10 percent of the public financing given to each individual party. Also, the reforms greatly increased public funding for all parties. The law also added a new prohibition on "the use of public resources and programs to benefit any political party or electoral campaign."

Campaign finance abuses did not disappear, however. After the 2000 presidential election, the federal internal auditor discovered that the government-owned oil company, PEMEX, had made a $140 million loan to the oil workers' union, one of the two most important PRI-affiliated labor unions. These funds were subsequently donated to the campaign of PRI candidate Francisco Labastida.

Historically, the PRI's most potent advantage over the competition was its ability to commit electoral fraud with relative impunity. A wide variety of techniques were used: stuffing the ballot boxes; disqualifying opposition party poll watchers; relocating polling places at the last minute to sites known only to PRI supporters; manipulating voter registration lists, padding them with nonexistent or nonresident PRIistas, and/or *rasurando* (shaving off) those who are expected to vote for opposition parties; issuing multiple voting credentials to PRI supporters; buying, "renting," or confiscating opposition voters' credentials, often in return for material benefits; organizing *carruseles* (flying brigades) of PRI supporters transported by truck or van to vote at several different polling places; and so forth.

Moreover, until 1996, the PRI held majority representation in all of the state and federal government entities that controlled vote counting and certification. The PRI could count on these bodies to manipulate the tallies to favor its candidates or, in cases where the opposition vote got out of control, nullify the unfavorable election outcomes. Adding votes to the PRI

column, rather than taking them away from opposition parties, was the most common form of electoral fraud. In some predominantly rural districts, this practice led to election results in which the number of votes credited to the PRI candidate exceeded the total number of registered voters, or even the total number of adults estimated from the most recent population census. In a successful effort to build up domestic and international credibility for the 1994 national elections, the Salinas government introduced a number of important safeguards against fraud (see Box 14.4).

The share of the vote claimed by the PRI had been declining for three decades, but until the mid-1990s, the erosion was gradual and did not threaten the party's grasp on the presidency and state governorships (see Figure 14.4). In the 1980s and 1990s, however, Mexican elections became much more competitive. Over time, the "Soviet-style" precincts that regularly delivered 98 to 100 percent of their votes to PRI candidates have disappeared. In the four federal elections prior to 2006, the PRI did best among older voters, the less educated, and low-income people. It has also held the loyalty of a plurality of labor union members. However, the corporatist vote in general is no longer a dependable source of support for the PRI.

Another key factor accounting for the long-term decline in the PRI's effectiveness as a vote-getting machine is the massive shift of population from rural to urban areas that has occurred in Mexico. In 1950, 57 percent of the population lived in isolated rural communities of fewer than 2,500 inhabitants; by 2010, only 22 percent of Mexicans lived in such localities. The PRI is significantly weaker in cities with 100,000 or more inhabitants, where more than half of the Mexican population now lives. Mexico City has been a particular disaster area for the PRI in recent elections. The PRI lost the four mayoral races in Mexico City between 1997 and 2012 by large margins. Even in rural areas, the PRI's formerly safe vote continues to erode. While the PRI still gets a higher share of the vote in rural areas than any other party, the average vote for PRI candidates in rural precincts fell markedly from 1982 through 2012.[23]

After its defeat in the 2000 presidential election, the PRI had to adjust from being an official party—a political machine based on incumbency advantages—to being a party out of power. PRI legislators for the first time had to figure out how to vote without presidential leadership. The whole party had to define

BOX 14.4   Reforming Federal Elections

In 1994, Mexico's electoral law was amended to strengthen greatly and grant more autonomy to the IFE, which organizes and conducts federal elections. The PRI and its government representatives were denied a majority on the IFE's decision-making board. A new system of independent electoral tribunals was established to adjudicate election disputes, and a special prosecutor's office was established to investigate alleged violations of the electoral laws.

The new federal electoral law defined a broad range of electoral offenses not previously subject to prosecution as electoral crimes (though the special prosecutor was appointed by the president and reported to the federal attorney general, who was unlikely to bring charges against important PRI leaders or government officials). The role of independent, Mexican citizen observers in monitoring the casting and tallying of votes was formally recognized, and the presence of foreign electoral observers (euphemistically termed "international visitors") was legalized. Exit polls of voters and "quick counts" of the actual vote in sample precincts by the IFE as well as by private organizations were authorized and publicly announced on election night. New, high-tech, photo-identification voter credentials were issued to the entire electorate.

Taken together, these innovations, which cost the Mexican taxpayers more than $1 billion, represented a major advance toward improving the security, professionalism, and fairness of the Mexican electoral system. However, various types of irregularities—especially violations of ballot secrecy and efforts by local bosses to induce voters to support the PRI—were still widespread in the more isolated, rural areas. Subsequent state and local elections in various parts of the country have demonstrated that subnational PRI leaders continue to use direct threats and other forms of intimidation, particularly against peasant voters.

Another electoral reform, enacted in 1996, further increased the institutional autonomy of the IFE. The interior minister was removed as president of the IFE and replaced by a nonpartisan president and eight nonpartisan commissioners. These electoral commissioners are elected for a nine-year term by a two-thirds vote of the Chamber of Deputies. Since no party can control more than 60 percent of the seats in the lower chamber, the IFE commissioners are elected by consensus of all of the parties.

In 2007, reformers, pursuing greater equity in electoral competition, pushed through strong measures to control the content of campaign ads and limit access to the mass media for electoral purposes. Parties, their candidates, and organized interest groups can no longer purchase ads on radio and television. Instead, all political advertising time is now centrally allocated by the IFE, with spots being allotted to parties and election authorities according to rigid criteria. Negative advertisements are now prohibited, as well as government publicity about public programs, which in the past had boosted the ruling party's candidates. The IFE decides which spots "denigrate institutions and political parties or slander any person," and which do not. Campaigns were shortened to 90 days for presidential contests and 60 days in midterm elections.

In the national elections from 1997 through 2012, there was very little evidence of systematic fraud. Since the IFE controls most of the process in a nonpartisan manner (for example, all poll workers are chosen at random from voter registration lists, as jurors are selected in the United States), the key remaining source of electoral fraud is vote buying. The practice is illegal but difficult for electoral authorities to police.

---

its ideology as a political party, not as an instrument of power.

The PRI has steadily rebuilt its power since the 2006 debacle, when it found itself in third place in voter preference. By 2012, it had won back eight states from the opposition, plus Chiapas, which is now governed by the governor from the PVEM, the PRI's "green party" coalition partner. In the 2009 midterms, the PRI and the PVEM together won an absolute majority of seats (258 of 500) as they campaigned against the ineffectiveness of the Calderón government in dealing with the worldwide recession that began in 2008. In the 2010 gubernatorial elections, the PAN and PRD attempted to block the electoral recovery of the PRI. They formed left–right electoral alliances in five of the twelve states that were up for election,

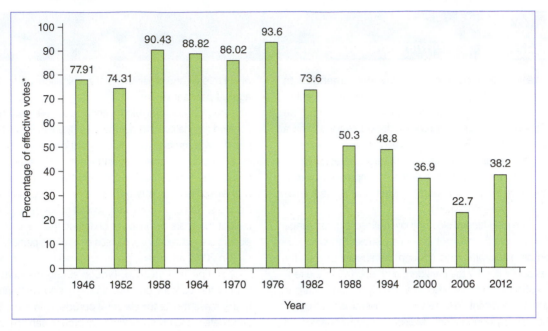

FIGURE 14.4

Support for PRI's Presidential Candidate, 1946–2012

Before rebounding in 2012, the PRI's vote share declined in tandem with more competitive elections and greater electoral transparency.

*Percentage base includes annulled votes and those cast for independent candidates.

Note: The 1976 PRI candidate, José López Portillo, ran virtually unopposed because the PAN failed to nominate a candidate. The only other significant candidate was Valentín Campa, representing the Communist Party, which was not legally registered to participate in the 1976 election. More than 5 percent of the votes were annulled.

Source: Data from Comisión Federal Electoral, 1946–1988; and Instituto Federal Electoral, 1994–2012.

winning in three of them. However, the PRI recovered two states from the PAN, and one from the PRD—all states without PAN–PRD alliances.

Now back in executive power, the PRI must abandon its strategy of opposing many fundamental reforms proposed by PAN presidents from 2000 through 2012 and propose its own. Since it lacks a majority in Congress, it must offer policies that are favored by at least one of the main opposition parties, or forge a consensus among the parties. Failing that, the "new PRI" could eventually face the kind of gridlock that the party was famous for creating over the previous twelve years.

The Partido Acción Nacional

The PAN was established in 1939, largely in reaction to the leftward drift of public policy under President Lázaro Cárdenas, particularly his policies in support

of socialist public education. Its founders included prominent Catholic intellectuals who espoused an early Christian democratic ideology, and the party has traditionally opposed government restrictions on church activities. The party attacked political centralism and advocated expanded states' rights long before it was fashionable to do so. The PAN's principal constituency has always been the urban middle class, but it has also attracted votes among socially conservative peasants and the urban working class.

Between 1964, when a primitive form of proportional representation increased opposition presence in the Chamber of Deputies, and the mid-1990s, when the PAN was governing many municipal and state governments, the focus of PANista representation was in the federal Congress, especially the lower chamber (the first PANista was not elected to the Senate until 1991). In these years, PAN deputies would typically begin their congressional terms fighting electoral fraud from the previous election in an attempt to increase the number of PANista deputies. Then they would settle in and begin to propose legislation. Until the Salinas years, these bills would almost always be ignored in the chamber at the time of introduction; but years later, most of the PAN's legislative proposals were adopted by the federal executive and reintroduced and approved by Congress.

Among the PANista ideas later embraced by PRI governments were increased proportional representation in both chambers of Congress, autonomous electoral courts and electoral agencies, the permanent voting credential, increased municipal autonomy, increased autonomy and authority for the Supreme Court, increased self-governance for the Federal District (Mexico City), federal revenue sharing with the states, liberalization of the social security systems, a national consumer protection agency, and profit sharing with employees.

The PAN's regional strongholds include the north and the west-central states, with increased influence in parts of the south and the Gulf states. Between 1989 and 2001, the PAN won gubernatorial elections in nine states. In 1995, the PAN retained control of the governorship of Baja California, thereby accomplishing something that no opposition party had previously done: the transfer of power from one elected opposition governor to another (the PAN has won two additional gubernatorial races in the state). During these years, the PAN governed nearly all of the twenty largest cities in Mexico, with the conspicuous exception of Mexico City, and it also governed most of the capital cities of the country.

While the classic "left–right" ideological distinction is less useful in Mexico than in many other countries,[24] the PAN could be classified as a center-right party, with strong elements of Christian socialism (which covers a wide range of policies, from center-left on labor issues to right-of-center on abortion), combined with traditional liberal attitudes on trade, municipal decentralization, and general democratization. The party is affiliated with international Christian Democratic organizations. The PAN's relative position on the ideological spectrum has depended mostly on the positioning of the PRI, whose pendulum has shifted to positions clearly to the left of the PAN (as in the 1970s) or to the right of the PAN (as was the case from 1988 to 2000).

Roll call votes in the Fifty-Seventh Legislature (1997–2000) placed the PAN at the center of the political spectrum, to the left of the PRI. Congressional debates suggest that the PAN held a similar position for most of the Salinas and Zedillo years. Despite the nationalist and populist background of their party, PRI deputies found themselves voting to the right of the PAN because they had to support the neoliberal economic policies and austerity measures of PRI presidents. However, since 2001, under a PANista president, PAN members generally voted to the right of the PRI. The PAN deputies had to support the austerity programs of their president, while PRI deputies were liberated to vote their conscience and constituencies rather than take cues from the president. Now that the PRI is back in power, the roll call votes of the first year of the Sixty-Second Legislature (2012–2015) demonstrate that the PRI is on the right, along with its legislative allies, the PVEM and Nueva Alianza, the party of the teachers union. The PAN has returned to the center.

The PAN has worked long and hard to develop a strong network of grassroots militants, though it has always had several major organizational weaknesses. Since the mid-1970s, it has been divided into moderate-progressive and militant-conservative factions, which have jockeyed for control of the party machinery and carried out purges of opposing faction members when they were in power.

Vicente Fox's ideology was closer to the moderate-progressives than to the neo-PANistas. This helped the PAN gain control of the presidency in 2000 by attracting an ideologically diverse group of voters, united mainly by their desire to remove the PRI from power.[25] During the Fox administration, the PAN continued its evolution toward a catch-all party, while still embracing with greater enthusiasm than its rivals the free-market, pro–foreign investment policies favored by the country's business community.[26] The Calderón administration was often perceived as less friendly toward business (for example, because of the new tax on business), and too focused on issues of national security. Furthermore, during his administration, many local PANista leaders and militants complained that Calderón had interfered too much in internal party affairs (through the imposition of national party leadership and several gubernatorial candidates), mimicking in some ways the old PRI traditions.

The Partido de la Revolución Democrática

Before 1988, the Mexican left had spawned political parties like the Partido Popular Socialista (PPS), which for decades served as a home for socialists and other left-of-center politicians willing to collaborate with the government and even to endorse the PRI's presidential candidates, in exchange for a seat in Congress. The more independent left—that is, those who did not cooperate openly with the ruling party—was traditionally represented by the Partido Comunista Mexicano (PCM). The Communists were allowed to compete legally in elections during the presidency of Lázaro Cárdenas, but their party was subsequently outlawed and did not regain legal representation until 1979, when its congressional candidates won 5 percent of the vote.

During most of the 1980s, even in the face of Mexico's gravest economic crisis since the 1910 Revolution, and despite a series of party mergers intended to reduce the fractionalization of the leftist vote, the parties on the left lost ground electorally. They were hampered by constant internal squabbling (motivated mostly by personalistic rivalries, and to a lesser extent by ideological cleavages) and an inability to do effective grassroots organizing.

The key to the left's rejuvenation in 1988 was a split within the PRI leadership—the most serious since the early 1950s. In August 1986, a number of nationally prominent PRI figures, all members of the party's center-left wing, formed a dissident movement within the PRI known as the Corriente Democrática (CD). The CD criticized the de la Madrid administration's economic restructuring program and sought a renewed commitment by the PRI to traditional principles of economic nationalism and social justice. Most urgently, CD adherents called for a top-to-bottom democratization of the PRI, beginning with the elimination of the *dedazo* (the unilateral selection by the outgoing president) as the mechanism for determining the party's presidential candidate. The CD's proposals were widely interpreted as a last-ditch attempt by the PRI's traditional politicos to recover leadership of the party by influencing the outcome of the 1987 and 1988 presidential succession. The CD's demands for reform were resoundingly rejected by the PRI hierarchy, and its leaders formally split from the party in October 1987.

Confronted with defeat within the PRI, Cárdenas accepted the presidential nomination of the Partido Auténtico de la Revolución Mexicana (PARM), a conservative, nationalist party established by another group of dissident PRIistas in 1954. Later, four other leftist parties joined with the PARM to form a coalition, the Frente Democrático Nacional (FDN), to contest the 1988 presidential election, with Cárdenas as their candidate. Soon after the 1988 elections, however, the left's long-standing ideological and personalistic cleavages reasserted themselves, and by 1991, when midterm elections were held, most of Cárdenas' 1988 coalition partners had gone their separate ways, leaving the newly constituted PRD as the principal standard-bearer of the left. Even within the PRD, serious disagreements emerged over such issues as the degree of democracy in internal party governance and strategies for dealing with the government (dialogue and collaboration on certain issues versus permanent confrontation).

The left's problems in the early 1990s were not all self-inflicted. Under Salinas, the government showed no inclination to negotiate seriously with the Cardenista left. Salinas showed much greater willingness to recognize electoral victories of the PAN than those claimed by the PRD. And when the PRD's victories (all at the municipal level) were recognized, the city governments under its control were punished and starved for resources by PRI state governors. Conflicts between PRD militants and local PRI caciques were bitter, with hundreds of PRD activists murdered during the first five years of the party's existence.

President Zedillo opened a new chapter in PRD–government relations, recognizing Cuauhtémoc Cárdenas' overwhelming victory in the 1997 mayoral race in Mexico City. During 1998–1999, the PRD won gubernatorial elections in the states of Zacatecas, Tlaxcala, and Baja California Sur. In 2000, it picked up the state of Chiapas and again won the Mexico City mayoralty. In 2001, the PRD finally won Cárdenas' home state of Michoacán, after nominating his son, Lázaro, for governor. In all of these early victories, except for Mexico City and Michoacán, the PRD candidates were defectors from the PRI who had been passed over for the party's gubernatorial nomination. In 2005, the PRD continued its success by winning the southern state of Guerrero.

These outcomes illustrate a key advantage for the PRD in Mexico's current three-party competition: In places where the PRI organization is fractured by internal rivalries, where the local factions are unable to reach consensus on a candidate, the PRD is usually the main beneficiary. For PRIistas whose political aspirations are thwarted by their own party, the PRD—the party run by ex-PRIistas—is a natural new home.

The PRD has continued to take policy positions to the left of the PRI on some issues (for example, arguing against the use of any taxpayer money to bail out bankers who made bad loans during President Salinas' term). Its differences with most recent government policies were matters of degree, pacing, and how much was being done to ameliorate the social costs of these policies, rather than their basic direction.

In the Fifty-Eighth Legislature (2000–2003), the PRD took a more radical stance on policy issues and was more intransigent in its relations with the other parties. In part, this was due to the diminished presence of the party in the Congress—about 60 percent smaller than the PRD delegation in the 1997–2000 period. It introduced bills that, taken together, amounted to a sweeping restructuring of the Mexican political system, designed to weaken the federal executive. One bill would have introduced a parliamentary system with an elected president, akin to the presidential/premier system in France. Once López Obrador became a viable candidate to win the presidency, the PRD backed off its proposals to weaken the executive branch.

In its early years, the PRD did a poor job of mobilizing previously uncommitted voters. It had retained many of the urban working-class voters who traditionally supported the parties of the independent left, but it was not very successful in establishing ties with the popular movements that had developed outside of the PRI-affiliated corporatist structures. However, its ties to the rural areas were underdeveloped, and the PRD had been dominated by Mexico City–based politicians and intellectuals for whom the provinces hardly existed. Central party leaders often shortchanged local organizers in their allocation of party funds. This trend was reversed in the 2006 and 2012 elections, when the PRD under López Obrador proved much more effective at mobilizing rural voters.

In the 2012 election, López Obrador deemphasized the leftist agenda, and focused more on criticizing corruption in the PANista federal government and in Peña Nieto's administration in the state of Mexico. But Mexico's political left remains divided between the

moderates who run the PRD bureaucracy and the militants in López Obrador's group. The moderates have generally supported the Pacto por México and have pushed for electoral alliances with the PAN. The faction supporting López Obrador is more intransigent, opposing most collaboration with the PRI on legislation or with the PAN for electoral coalitions.

López Obrador resigned from the PRD after the 2012 election and formed a new party, the Movimiento de Regeneración Nacional (National Regeneration Movement, MORENA). If MORENA becomes registered as a party for the 2015 midterm elections, the PRD will face a fierce battle to remain Mexico's principal party on the left.

The Shifting Social Bases of Mexico's Parties

The social bases of political support for the parties shifted significantly in the last three presidential elections. Before 2006, the PRI's most dependable base was the rural voter. It also did relatively well with women and older voters. In 2006, the PRD's López Obrador did best among rural voters, and Madrazo of the PRI finished third among such voters, even behind Calderón (PAN). As in 2000, the PAN did best among urban voters in 2006, but the PRD finished ahead of the PRI for the urban vote. In 2012, the PRI candidate won in both urban and rural areas, with the PAN and the PRD splitting the remainder of the rural vote almost evenly. The PRD once again outperformed the PAN among urban voters (see Table 14.6).

There was a sizable gender gap in the 2000 election, with the PAN doing particularly well among male voters and the PRI doing relatively better among women. In 2006, the PRD took the male vote by a small margin, but Calderón did much better among women. In both cases, women tended to support the candidate who appeared to pose less of a threat to economic stability. In 2012, the gender gap again was significant. The PRI and PRD candidates ran almost evenly among men, but the PRI's Peña Nieto rolled up a nearly two-to-one advantage among women, perhaps buoyed by the popularity of his soap opera star wife.

In all three of the most recent presidential elections, the PAN did best among voters under age thirty, while the PRI was preferred by older voters. This was probably because older Mexicans remembered the

TABLE 14.6
The Demography of Party Choice

In the 2012 presidential election, parties' supporters differed by where they live, gender, age, education, and ideology. The resurgent PRI did well in nearly all demographic groups.

	PAN (%)	PRI (%)	PRD (%)	Others (%)
Type of Locality				
Urban	26	37	34	3
Rural	26	44	29	1
Gender				
Male	25	37	36	2
Female	27	41	30	2
Age				
18–29	23	36	37	4
30–49	27	41	30	2
50+	28	40	30	2
Education				
None and primary	24	48	26	2
Secondary	28	33	37	2
University	29	29	39	3
Ideology				
Left	11	20	67	2
Center	23	40	32	5
Right	36	50	13	1

Source: Nationwide exit poll conducted by *Reforma* newspaper (Mexico City), July 1, 2012.

social benefits and economic growth achieved in the better years of PRI rule. In 2000, the PRI did better among voters with lower education, taking the vote among those with less than a secondary education. The PAN did best among better-educated voters. In 2006, education mattered less in determining the vote. Calderón attracted the most votes at all levels of education, and López Obrador placed second. López Obrador did relatively well among more highly educated voters because of the strong support that he received from public university students. In 2012, the PRI's candidate again won decisively among voters with only a primary education, while López Obrador was favored by voters with high school and college educations.

In 2006 and 2012, the PRD did best among the poor and the lower middle class. The PAN did much better among higher-income voters, who were attracted by its probusiness platform and frightened by the populism of López Obrador. In general, however, social class was not a strong predictor of voter choice in Mexico's most recent elections, despite explicit appeals to class interests by both the PAN and PRD candidates in 2006.

Left–right ideological distinctions map onto partisan choice in Mexico in complicated ways. When Mexican voters are asked to self-identify as "conservative" or "liberal," those identifying as conservative seem to be expressing a preference for authoritarian governance, and these voters disproportionately favor the PRI. In 2000 and 2006, for example, exit polls found that the majority of the "right-wing" electorate was PRIsta, while only a small minority of self-identified "leftist" voters supported the PRI. PRD and PAN partisanship increases as voters move from right to left on the ideological spectrum, and most independent voters place themselves in the center. On social issues like abortion and gay marriage, both PAN and PRI supporters are more conservative, while PRD partisans and independents tend to be more liberal.[27]

Government Performance

14.10 Describe the effects of Mexico's policies, focusing on economic development, the distribution of income, the rule of law, the environment, and international relations.

Promoting Economic Growth and Reducing Poverty

There is little debate about the importance of the state's contribution to the economic development of Mexico since 1940. Massive public investments in infrastructure (roads, dams, telecommunications, electrification) and generous, cheap credit provided to the private sector by Nacional Financiera and other government development banks made possible a higher rate of capital accumulation, stimulated higher levels of investment by domestic entrepreneurs and foreign corporations, and enabled Mexico to develop a diversified production capacity second only, within Latin America, to that of Brazil.

From 1940 until well into the 1970s, a strong elite consensus prevailed on the state's role in the economy. The state facilitated private capital accumulation and protected the capitalist system by limiting popular demands for consumption and redistribution of wealth, it established the rules for development, and it participated in the development process as the nation's largest single entrepreneur, employer, and source of investment capital. The state served as the "rector" (guiding force) of this mixed economy, setting broad priorities and channeling investment (both public and private) into strategic sectors. Acting through joint ventures between private firms and state-owned enterprises, the government provided resources for development projects so large that they would have been difficult or impossible to finance from internal (within-the-firm) sources or through borrowing from private banks.

The result, from the mid-1950s to the mid-1970s, was the much-touted "Mexican miracle" of sustained economic growth at annual rates of 6 to 7 percent, coupled with low inflation (5 percent per annum between 1955 and 1972). By 1980, the GNP had reached $2,130 per capita, placing Mexico toward the upper end of the World Bank's list of semi-industrialized or "middle-developed" countries. As sole proprietor of PEMEX, the state oil monopoly, the government was responsible for developing the crucial oil and natural gas sector of the economy. By the end of the oil boom (1978–1981), oil was generating more than $15 billion a year in export revenues and fueling economic growth of more than 8 percent per year—one of the world's highest growth rates.

It is the distributive consequences of this impressive performance in economic development and the manner in which it was financed by the PRI governments of the 1970s and 1980s that have been harshly criticized in retrospect. From Miguel Alemán (1946–1952) to the present, all but one or two of Mexico's presidents and their administrations reflected the private sector's contention that Mexico must first create wealth and then worry about redistributing it—the belief being that the state would quickly be overwhelmed by popular demands that it could not satisfy. By the early 1970s, however, there was convincing evidence that an excessively large portion of Mexico's population was being left behind in the drive to become a modern, industrialized nation.

This is not to say that some benefits of the development process did not trickle down to the poor. From 1950 to 1980, poverty in absolute terms declined. The middle class expanded to an estimated 29 percent of the population. From 1960 to 2010, illiteracy among adults dropped from 35 to 7 percent of the adult population, infant mortality was reduced from 78 to 12.8 per 1,000 live births, and average life expectancy rose from fifty-five to seventy-five years. Clearly, the quality of life for many Mexicans—even in isolated rural areas—did improve during this period, although several other Latin American countries (Chile, Colombia, Costa Rica, Cuba, Ecuador, El Salvador, and Venezuela) achieved higher rates of improvement on indicators of social well-being than did Mexico during the same period.

Poverty and socioeconomic inequality have remained stubbornly high, however. During the period of Mexico's "economic miracle," ownership of land and capital (stocks, bonds, and time deposits) became increasingly concentrated. Personal income inequality also increased, at a time when, given Mexico's middle level of development, the national income distribution should have been shifting toward greater equality, according to classical economic development theory. Indeed, Mexico apparently had a higher overall concentration of income in the mid-1970s than in 1910, before the outbreak of the revolution. By 2007, the poorest 40 percent of Mexican families received only 13 percent of household income, while the richest 20 percent of families received 53 percent of income. In one recent period, 2003 to 2006, income inequality did diminish, but only by an annual average of 0.5 percent—far less than in most other Latin American countries.[28]

Moreover, by every indicator of economic opportunity and social well-being, there are vast disparities among Mexico's regions and between rural and urban areas. Unemployment and underemployment are concentrated overwhelmingly in the rural sector, which contains at least 70 percent of the population classified as living in extreme poverty. The rate of infant mortality in rural areas is nearly 50 percent higher than the national average. In 2006, 91 percent of urban-dwelling Mexicans lived in houses with a sewerage system connection, but only 48 percent of the rural population had improved sanitary facilities.

Interregional disparities in social well-being are equally extreme. In 2000, the percentage of persons with incomes lower than two minimum salaries (a bare subsistence level) ranged from 22 percent in Baja California to 76 percent in Chiapas. A composite index of social well-being indicators shows the Federal District (Mexico City) and the northern border states as being the most privileged, and the southern states (especially Chiapas, Oaxaca, and Guerrero) as the most marginalized. This pattern of extreme regional inequalities has remained essentially unchanged for several decades.

The policies and investment preferences of Mexico's postrevolutionary governments contributed much to the country's highly inegalitarian development. At a minimum, the public policies pursued since 1940 failed to counteract the wealth-concentrating effects of private market forces. Evidence is strong that some government investments and policies actually reinforced these effects. For example, during most of the post-1940 period, government tax and credit policies worked primarily to the advantage of the country's wealthiest agribusiness and industrial entrepreneurs.

Government expenditures for social security, public health, and education remained relatively low by international standards. By the late 1970s, Mexico was still allocating a smaller share of its central government budget to social services than were some countries, such as Bolivia, Brazil, Chile, and Panama. The slowness with which basic social services were extended to the bulk of the population in Mexico was a direct consequence of the government's policy of keeping inflation low by concentrating public expenditures on subsidies and infrastructure for private industry, rather than on social programs and subsidies to consumers. Even during the period between 1970 and 1982, when populist policies were allegedly in vogue and government revenues were expanding rapidly because of the oil export boom, public spending for programs like health and social security remained roughly constant, in real per capita terms.

The economic crisis that erupted in 1982, after an unprecedented run-up in Mexico's domestic and externally held debt, made it impossible to maintain even that level of government commitment to social well-being. By 1986, debt service was consuming over half of the total federal government budget, necessitating deep cuts in spending for health, education, consumer subsidies, and job-creating public investments. Social welfare expenditures per capita fell to 1974 levels, and real wages fell by two-thirds between 1980 and 1989. The peso devaluation crisis of 1995–1996 caused most Mexicans to lose whatever ground they had gained during the Salinas years. By 2004, nearly half of Mexico's population (47 percent) was living at or below the World Bank's official poverty level, and one-fifth were living in extreme poverty. Family incomes were battered again by the international financial crisis that hit Mexico in 2008, falling 12.3 percent from 2008 to 2012.[29]

Under President Fox, macroeconomic stability was maintained through a combination of fiscal restraint and good fortune; government revenues were boosted by rising oil prices in global markets, and the U.S. market for Mexico's exports was strong after the U.S. economy recovered from the 2001 and 2002 recession. Government spending under Calderón remained under control (except for spending on the antidrug war, which mushroomed to $25 billion a year by the end of Calderón's presidency), and inflation was moderate (just 3.9 percent in 2010). Fiscal restraint under Calderón enabled Mexico to weather the Great Recession that began in 2008, averting a crisis in public finances like the ones that accompanied previous recessions dating back to the 1970s.

Under Mexico's four most recent presidents, the government has implemented a **neoliberal economic development model** stressing the need to give much freer rein to market forces. The primary objective of this "technocratic free-market revolution" has been to attract more private investment (especially foreign capital) and thereby push up Mexico's rate of economic growth. While drastically shrinking the public sector of the economy through a sweeping privatization program and opening up nearly all sectors of the economy to private investment (including those formerly reserved to the state), the technocrats were unwilling to completely surrender the government's traditional "rectorship" role in the economy.

This concern is reflected in the considerable spending by the last five administrations on social welfare initiatives, like Salinas' National Solidarity Program, Zedillo's PROGRESA program, and Fox's and Calderón's **Oportunidades program**—all efforts to construct a minimal safety net for the millions of low-income Mexicans who were the short-term "losers" from neoliberal economic policies and trade liberalization under NAFTA.

The "new PRI" government that took power in 2012 pledged to continue the Oportunidades program, and it initiated a "Crusade Against Hunger" using government agencies to distribute food to the poorest Mexicans. But these carefully targeted **entitlement programs** have not been sufficient to offset the structural impoverishment caused by falling or stagnant real wages, the elimination of millions of jobs, and the slashing of most consumer subsidies as consequences of neoliberal economic policies.

During the Fox administration, the government implemented a new health care program known as the **Seguro Popular** (Popular Health Insurance), designed to provide health services to people who were not covered by the Social Security Institute's health programs. Social security in Mexico provides health coverage for salaried persons, but the unemployed, the self-employed, and many rural workers are excluded from the system. The Seguro Popular program requires beneficiaries to enroll in the program and pay relatively affordable premiums. The poorest Mexicans (the bottom 20 percent) do not have to pay premiums. The goal of the Seguro Popular was to achieve universal health insurance coverage by 2013.

As a presidential candidate, Peña Nieto proposed creating universal health coverage, combining under one umbrella the formal Social Security health system, other public sector health organizations, the Seguro Popular, and state-level public health systems. This ambitious and expensive program is part of the Pacto por México, but as of mid-2012, no legislation to implement it had been introduced.

It is clear that the market-oriented development model of the past two decades has exacerbated—not alleviated—Mexico's poverty and inequality problems,

even when the model was apparently working well in macroeconomic terms (that is, from 1989 through 1992).[30] Moreover, Mexico's experience with rapid economic growth during the "miracle" years of the 1950s and 1960s and the oil boom of the late 1970s and early 1980s suggests that without strong, sustained government action to correct for market failures and improve human capital endowments through education and job training, income concentration and associated social problems will continue unabated.

With declining oil revenues, Mexico's tax base must be expanded to address these and other policy challenges. Tax evasion robs the state of huge resources and contributes powerfully to income inequality, since evasion rates are lowest (an estimated 15 percent) for blue- and white-collar wage earners, whose taxes are paid through payroll deductions, and highest (77–80 percent) among Mexicans who gain most of their income from owning property and businesses and professional activity.[31]

President Peña Nieto campaigned on the promise of a comprehensive tax reform, one that would raise significant new revenue by applying the value-added tax (VAT) of 16 percent to food and medicines, two major types of consumption that previously were exempt. Anticipating strong resistance from his own party, Peña Nieto did not include the VAT proposal in his tax reform package when it was introduced in Congress in September 2013. The final bill also eliminated two unpopular taxes that had been introduced early in the Calderón administration (an alternative minimum corporate tax and a tax on cash banking deposits). The government compensated for the potential revenue losses by increasing the income tax rate for middle-class people, introducing an excise tax on soft drinks and high-calorie processed foods ("junk food"), closing some major loopholes for business income taxes, and increasing the budget deficit.

Establishing the Rule of Law

The one area of performance in which the Mexican government has been failing most conspicuously, especially since the mid-1990s, is the rule of law and security. From the poorest urban workers to middle-class professionals to the richest business tycoons, Mexicans are appalled and incensed that the government seems totally incapable of dealing effectively with street crime—armed robberies, muggings, kidnappings, rapes, and homicides. Surveys in the late 1990s found that virtually every resident of Mexico City had either been a crime victim or had a close relative or friend who had suffered that fate in recent years. While Mexico faces a wide range of rule of law challenges—including a weak judiciary, widespread corruption, a lack of transparency and accountability, and human rights abuses—the proliferation of crime and violence has been among the top Mexican policy concerns over the last two decades.

Statistics on street crime (robberies, assaults, muggings) showed a steep increase in the mid-1990s. In Mexico City, for example, the total number of crimes reported to police doubled from 1993 to 1997. And official crime statistics understated the magnitude of the problem because of widespread underreporting. Three-quarters of crimes go unreported due to citizens' low expectation that the perpetrators will be caught and punished, and to fears of reprisals by either criminals or the police.[32]

President Zedillo began tackling the problems of the justice system by addressing the issue of the independence of the judiciary. In his first significant official act upon taking office in December 1994, he replaced all but two of the incumbent Supreme Court justices and reduced the size of the Supreme Court from twenty-four to eleven justices. He changed the terms of the justices from six-year periods, coinciding with the six-year presidential term, to fixed, fifteen-year terms. He also changed the requirement for confirmation of Supreme Court justices by the Senate, from a simple majority to two-thirds of the Senate. This means that the president's nominees must attract at least some votes from the opposition parties; they cannot be rubber-stamped by a PRI majority. Finally, Zedillo expanded the judicial review powers of the Supreme Court by explicitly granting the Court the ability to declare acts of Congress and other federal government actions unconstitutional.

The 1994 reforms made it possible for the opposition parties to bring various laws and government actions forward to the Supreme Court for constitutional review. However, several of these cases were dismissed on legal technicalities. In other cases, a six-to-five majority of the justices ruled against the federal government's position, but under the 1994 judicial reforms, it would have taken a *supermajority* of eight out of eleven justices to strike down a law or official action as unconstitutional, so the Court's decision had no practical impact in these cases.

A major limitation of Zedillo's 1994 judicial reforms is that they applied only to the top level of the federal judiciary; state-level courts continue to function as before, and the federal Supreme Court must still rely on state-level officials to implement its rulings. Until Court decisions based on abstract principles of law cannot be undermined by political actors whose interests could be damaged by those rulings, the goal of a "government of laws, not men" will remain elusive in Mexico.

Mexico's War against Drug Traffickers Continues
The aftermath of a drug-related shoot-out in an Acapulco neighborhood in May 2013.

To the average citizen, what matters most is being liberated from the constant preoccupation with matters of personal security: how to avoid becoming a victim of violent crime. In a 2011 survey of Latin American countries, a plurality of Mexicans cited crime as their country's most important problem, and a higher proportion of Mexicans held this view than in all but four other Latin American countries (Venezuela, Costa Rica, El Salvador, and Uruguay).[33]

The proliferation of organized crime, especially drug trafficking, has been a major contributor to rising public concern about security. In the 1990s, Mexico became an increasingly important conduit for illegal drugs destined for the U.S. market. In states where drug trafficking is concentrated (Baja California, Chihuahua, Sinaloa, Durango, Tamaulipas, Michoacán, and Guerrero), a high percentage of homicides and other violent crime are related to the operations of drug cartels and the federal government's war on narco-traffickers. As shown in Figure 14.5, such states account for a disproportionate share of drug-related killings, but what stands out is the pervasiveness of **narco-violence**; hardly any part of Mexico has been spared in recent years. Drug trafficking has also contributed mightily to the corruption of police, prosecutors, judges, and military personnel.

The Calderón government invested heavily to bring the narco-traffickers under control, but progress was halting. The government made numerous arrests of midlevel and major drug traffickers, particularly in the last two years of the Calderón administration, and by 2012, drug violence appeared to have leveled off or started to decline. However, overall levels of violence remained unacceptably high as the new

FIGURE 14.5

Drug-Related Killings in Mexico, January–December 2012

Most drug-related violence occurs in northern and west-central states, but no part of Mexico has escaped it entirely.

Source: Cory Molzahn, Octavio Rodríguez, and David A. Shirk, *Drug Violence in Mexico: Data and Analysis through 2012*, Justice in Mexico Project (San Diego: University of San Diego, February 2013), 23.

PRI government took power. President Peña Nieto declared that he would shift away from the targeted military operations and kingpin arrests used by the previous administration and focus on measures that would increase the security of ordinary citizens. While this raised concerns that the PRI would ignore the problem of organized crime, during his first year, Peña Nieto actually followed Calderón's example by sending troops to Michoacán and arresting the head of a major organized crime group known as the Zetas.

The police forces—federal, state, and local—themselves are a major source of Mexico's crime problem. Not only are they corruptible (because of low pay and low professionalization), they actually commit a sizable portion of crimes, especially in large cities. A remarkably large number of Mexican police officers are actually wanted for crimes, but the warrants for their arrest never get served because the offenders are protected by corrupt superior officers. Simply firing criminal elements in the police forces is not the solution, since they only return to the street as civilians, committing crimes with impunity. To address the institutional weaknesses of Mexican law enforcement, Peña Nieto restructured the federal police, proposing the creation of a gendarmerie—a military-style national guard—and seeking closer coordination between the state and federal governments to address crime.

Social and economic factors have also contributed powerfully to the recent epidemic of crime in Mexico. The rise in violent crime in the mid-1990s coincided with a sharp increase in the number of people living in poverty and the number of unemployed and severely underemployed people—all consequences of the deep economic crisis that erupted in 1994. In a quantitative analysis of homicide rates in a national sample of 1,750 municipios in Mexico, a general index of poverty was, by far, the single most important predictor of homicide rates at the local level. Other indicators of economic distress—the unemployment rate and the degree of income inequality in a municipio—were also significant predictors. So were certain demographic variables, like the percentage of single mothers.[34]

Finally, the inefficiency or malfunctioning of the criminal justice system is a major contributor to crime in Mexico. The actual probability of being caught and convicted and serving substantial prison time is far too low to serve as a significant deterrent to crime. For example, out of every hundred crimes committed in Mexico in 2001, only twenty-five were reported to police, only 1.2 went to trial, and only 0.4 cases resulted in a jail sentence of more than two years.[35]

Potential remedies for Mexico's dysfunctional criminal justice system include implementing tighter screening, testing, and monitoring of law enforcement personnel; increasing the pay and improving the training for police; making criminal proceedings more transparent and efficient by introducing oral argument; giving public prosecutors greater autonomy to prevent undue interference from politicians; standardizing sentencing guidelines nationwide; making the corrections system more humane and effective in rehabilitation; and funding more ambitious crime prevention programs aimed at young people. None of these possible remedies is a panacea, and most experts believe that real progress in reducing public insecurity will depend on addressing the root causes, including joblessness and extreme income inequality.

Nevertheless, significant reforms are being implemented. Oral trials before one or more judges, open to the public, where forensic evidence is presented and the accused has adequate legal representation, have been introduced in several states and will cover the entire country by 2016. For the first time, defendants will be presumed innocent until proved guilty, reversing the traditional assumption. Plea bargains and probation will be available to prosecutors and judges. Such changes are expected to speed court proceedings, increase public confidence in the criminal justice system, and reduce opportunities for organized crime to influence outcomes.

Environmental Challenges[36]

Mexico has made major strides in dealing with some of its environmental challenges through tighter government regulation. For example, air pollution in Mexico City—for decades one of the world's smoggiest metropolitan areas—has been drastically reduced. This was accomplished through a variety of measures aimed at curbing pollution from businesses, public transport, and individual motorists.

But heavy government subsidies for the use of electricity and fuel in agriculture, fisheries, and residential activities have strongly inhibited sustainable development in Mexico. These subsidies distort price signals, promote the overuse of resources, and discourage the adoption of efficient technologies. Energy subsidies also reward the rich over the poor.

For example, 80 percent of electricity subsidies for pumping water for agriculture benefit the richest 10 percent of Mexicans, and 89 percent of residential electricity subsidies go to them as well.[37]

Deforestation was a key environmental challenge in the 2000–2006 sexenio. President Fox made significant efforts to strengthen existing forestry policies, which reduced the rate of deforestation. However, livestock raising and agriculture remain prime causes of deforestation, and subsidies to support these economic activities encourage conversion of natural ecosystems into crop and pasture lands.

From 2007 through 2012, environmental sustainability became, for the first time, one of the five pillars of Mexico's National Development Plan. During these years, Mexico became a world leader in environmental issues by creating an institutional and policy framework to address climate change. This framework consisted of the National Strategy on Climate Change, adopted in 2007; a Special Program on Climate Change, promulgated in 2009; and a General Law on Climate Change, enacted in 2012.

During the Calderón sexenio, forests and biodiversity policies were strengthened through significant budget allocations and incorporating 2.8 million hectares of forested land into protection programs, 80 percent more than the previous administration. The Calderón administration also created new programs to promote energy efficiency in households, such as the Sustainable Light program, the National Program of Electric Domestic Equipment Replacement, and the Green Mortgage program.

Current environmental challenges include promoting urban sustainability, encouraging energy efficiency, and making the country more resilient to global climate change, the consequences of which the Mexican public is increasingly aware. Promoting environmental education is essential, as it creates the awareness and values needed to build a sustainable society.

A final challenge for the Peña Nieto administration is to promote a healthy marine environment by supporting sustainable fisheries. Twenty percent of Mexican fisheries have collapsed, and almost half are overexploited. Much-needed actions include adopting policies such as Territorial User Rights Fisheries (TURFs), establishing voluntary marine reserves, and cracking down on illegal fishing in Mexican waters. Sixty percent of all fishing activities in Mexico are conducted either without fishing permits, using illegal fishing technologies, or during prohibited months of the year.

International Environment

Since independence, Mexico's politics and public policies have always been influenced by proximity to the United States. Indeed, this proximity has made the United States a powerful presence in Mexico. A wide array of factors—the 2,000-mile land border between the two countries; Mexico's rich supplies of minerals, labor, and other resources needed by U.S. industry; and Mexico's attractiveness as a site for U.S. private investment—has made such influence inevitable.

Midway through the nineteenth century, Mexico's sovereignty as a nation was directly threatened when the U.S. push for territorial and economic expansion met little resistance in northern Mexico. Emerging from a war for independence from Spain and plagued by chronic political instability, Mexico was highly vulnerable to aggression from the north. By annexing Texas in 1845 and instigating the Mexican–American War of 1846 to 1848, the United States seized half of Mexico's national territory: disputed land in Texas; all of the land that is now California, Nevada, and Utah; most of New Mexico and Arizona; and part of Colorado and Wyoming.

This massive seizure of territory, along with several later military interventions and meddling in the politics of "revolutionary" Mexico that extended throughout the 1920s, left scars that have not healed. Even today, the average Mexican suspects that the United States has designs on Mexico's remaining territory, its oil, and its human resources, which is why opening the state-owned oil industry to foreign private investment is so controversial.

The lost territory includes the U.S. regions that have been the principal recipients of Mexican immigrant workers in this century. This labor migration, too, was instigated mainly by the United States. Beginning in the 1880s, U.S. farmers, railroads, and mining companies, with U.S. government encouragement, obtained many of the workers needed to expand the economy and transport systems of the Southwest and Midwest by sending labor recruiters into northern and central Mexico.

By the end of the 1920s, the economies of Mexico and the United States were sufficiently intertwined that the effects of the Great Depression were swiftly transmitted to Mexico, causing unemployment to rise and export earnings and GNP to plummet. As the depression moderated, Mexico tried to reduce its dependence on the United States as a market for silver and other exports. The effort failed. After 1940, Mexico relied even more heavily on U.S. private capital to help finance its drive for industrialization.

The United States experienced severe shortages of labor in World War II, and Mexico's dependence on the United States as a market for its surplus labor became institutionalized through the so-called *bracero* program of importing contract labor. Operating from 1942 to 1964, this program brought more than 4 million Mexicans to the United States to work in seasonal agriculture. After the demise of the bracero program, migration to the United States continued, with most new arrivals entering illegally (see Box 14.5).

By 2009, more than one out of ten people born in Mexico were estimated to be living abroad, 93 percent of them in the United States. This represents a seventeenfold increase in the Mexico-born population of the United States since 1970. Fifty-five percent of Mexican immigrants in the United States were there illegally.[38] Unauthorized migration has become the single most contentious issue in the U.S.–Mexico relationship, despite a preponderance of evidence that its net economic impact on the United States is positive.

The U.S. stake in Mexico's continued political stability and economic development has increased dramatically since World War II. In recent years, Mexico has been one of the three largest trading partners of the United States (with Canada and Japan). Employment for hundreds of thousands of people in both Mexico and the United States depends on this trade.

Despite the sharp fluctuations in its economy since the early 1980s, Mexico is one of the preferred sites for investments by U.S.-based multinational corporations, especially for investments in modern industries (such as petrochemicals, pharmaceuticals, food processing, machinery, transportation, and athletic footwear). In recent years, 55 percent of total foreign

---

BOX 14.5 — Dying to Get In
Mexicans Migrate Clandestinely to the United States

Each year, hundreds of thousands of Mexicans set out on a dangerous journey to the United States. They are drawn by jobs that do not exist in Mexico or do not pay enough to support their families, and by the desire to reunite with family members already living in the United States. Most migrants will pay $3,000 or more to a *coyote*—a professional people-smuggler—who will assist them in evading the U.S. Border Patrol. Most of this money is loaned by U.S.-based relatives—debts that take more than four months of work in the United States to repay.

Since 1994, the U.S. government has made it significantly costlier and riskier for Mexicans lacking legal entry papers to enter the country. Spending on border security and immigration enforcement activities in the U.S. interior reached $15 billion in Fiscal Year 2013. The Border Patrol has more than quadrupled in size. Almost 700 miles of new fencing has been built along the U.S.–Mexico border. Coyotes have raised their prices in tandem with U.S. border fortification and because they lead their clients through increasingly remote and life-threatening deserts and mountainous areas of the U.S. Southwest. More than 7,500 people have died in border-crossing attempts since 1995. They keep dying at a rate of five migrants every four days.

Since the Great Recession weakened U.S. demand for their labor, fewer Mexicans have been making this dangerous journey. But an estimated 400,000–660,000 unauthorized migrants did so in 2012, and most who try to enter the United States are not being kept out. They keep trying to get in until they succeed. Field research has found that more than nine out of ten who go to the border are able to enter eventually. Their tenacity is illustrated by the story of Briseida, a twenty-four-year-old undocumented migrant from the impoverished state of Oaxaca, who was caught by the Border Patrol six times in the month before she entered the United States successfully.

"The Border Patrol told me the first time, 'If we apprehend you a second time, we are going to put you in jail for two weeks. If we apprehend you a third time, it is going to be a month; the fourth time, three months. You could be in jail for up to a year.' I told them, 'Well, I just have to cross.' They asked me if I was sure. 'Maybe you should just go home,' they said. 'But I have to cross,' I told them. No matter what, the majority of us Mexicans are going to keep trying." (Interview by Mexican Migration Field Research and Training Program, University of California, San Diego, February 2008.)

Migrant Deaths Escalate as U.S. Fortifies the Border
In Mexico, a van load of migrants travel past a memorial to those who have died crossing into the United States. The memorial asks: "How many more have to die?"

direct investment in Mexico has come from the United States. Subsidiaries of U.S. companies produce half of the manufactured goods exported by Mexico. Firms in Mexico's own private sector have actively sought foreign capital to finance new joint ventures and expand plant facilities.

Mexico's external economic dependence is often cited by both critics and defenders of the Mexican system as an all-encompassing explanation for the country's problems. In fact, economic ties between Mexico and the United States usually explain only part of the picture. And these linkages do not necessarily predetermine the choices of policy and development priorities that are set by Mexico's rulers.

But Mexico's increasingly tight linkage to the U.S. economy limits the range of choices that can be made by Mexican officials, and economic fluctuations in the United States are a large source of uncertainty in Mexico's planning and policymaking. For example, the severe U.S. recession of 2007–2009 led to an even stronger economic contraction in Mexico, throwing millions of Mexicans out of work and sharply reducing the amount of money sent home by Mexicans working in the United States. But Mexico bounced back from the Great Recession faster than the United States, largely due to agile management of macroeconomic policy by the Calderón administration.

The international environment of Mexico's political system was transformed fundamentally by the signing of NAFTA in 1993. NAFTA made Mexico a much more attractive investment site for U.S. firms seeking low-cost labor and for Asian and European firms seeking privileged access to the U.S. market. The net macroeconomic impact of NAFTA has been positive for Mexico, as well as for the United States and Canada. However, NAFTA has not reduced the U.S.–Mexico income gap. GDP has risen in Mexico, but it has risen much more rapidly in the United States. Today, annual U.S. GDP per capita is more than six times that of Mexico.

If anything, NAFTA increased unauthorized migration to the United States and made Mexico's economy more dependent on money remitted by its citizens working in the United States, who continue to send home more money each year than Mexico earns from any other source except oil exports. NAFTA created jobs in Mexico's manufactured export sector, but competition from cheaper U.S. imports has put millions of small farmers out of work, and the nonagricultural jobs that have been created under NAFTA do not pay enough to lift most Mexican families out of poverty.

Mexico's Political Future

14.11 What recent developments bode well for political stability in Mexico?

Just since 2000, Mexico has had two pivotal national elections: one that ended seven decades of rule by a deeply entrenched "official party" and ushered in twelve years of governance by an opposition party, another that ended that experience with opposition rule and brought the PRI back to executive power.

The three-party system that began to emerge in the late 1980s has been largely consolidated. Mexican voters now seem quite comfortable with the idea of alternation in power, at all levels. Recent elections have demonstrated that voters are prepared to "throw the rascals out" for poor performance and corruption, regardless of party. Moreover, like voters elsewhere, Mexicans can get tired of an incumbent party, even if they have no serious disagreements with the government's policies. "Incumbent fatigue," after twelve years of PANista governance, helped to fuel the PRI's return to power in 2012.

Mexico's federal elections are now as democratic and transparent as in nearly any other Latin American country. Several waves of electoral law reforms have ended most forms of fraud that were typical in the past, except for vote buying. Extremely generous public financing of all parties' campaigns has leveled the playing field. Voters now have a clear choice among political parties that reflect a diverse set of policy options. Legislators still cannot be reelected, but the political parties have become more responsive to voters. The Federal Electoral Institute has achieved a strong record as a guardian of democracy.

Nevertheless, in the aftermath of every presidential election since 2000, Mexican intellectuals and members of the political elite have debated whether the country has successfully completed its transition to democracy, or whether deeper reforms in political structures and changes in political culture are necessary before their country can be considered a "consolidated" democracy.

But there is little doubt that Mexico can now be classified as a democracy in terms of electoral transparency and even personal freedoms. Despite all of the sound and fury between the executive and legislative branches under divided government, there is little doubt that Mexico now has one of the best-functioning democratic political systems in Latin America—closer to Chile and Costa Rica than to Brazil, Argentina, or Venezuela. Notwithstanding high levels of drug-related violence and violent events surrounding some local elections, Mexico is in little danger of becoming the "failed state" of which conservative U.S. critics have warned. There is little prospect of a wholesale breakdown of the rule of law or of everyday government functions. Organized crime remains a threat to ordinary citizens in many parts of the country, but it is not likely to destabilize the national political system.

The PRI government apparatus functioned for seventy-one years as a well-oiled political machine, maintaining absolute power in the executive branch and, for most of this period, in Congress as well. The advent of divided government arguably has concluded the heavy-handed, authoritarian era of Mexican politics. In 2012, a plurality of Mexicans voted for the PRI's presidential candidate but not for a PRI-majority Congress. The two- or three-party system now operating in most of the country makes it likely that divided government will continue, at least at the national level, for the foreseeable future.

But will Mexico, under the "new PRI," slip back into a machine politics model, in which certain traditional political practices like vote buying are condoned, corruption can flourish, and abuses of power once again can be committed with impunity? There is some basis for optimism that this will *not* be Mexico's political future. The public's access to information from government agencies is now assured by a well-functioning, U.S.-style "freedom-of-information" system, which can be used to attack petty corruption. Government secrecy has been greatly reduced, even on some security issues. Fights between party and Congressional leaders are now publicly visible: Mexicans see them on television! Social media are proving very useful in publicizing misdeeds and compelling the government to punish the responsible officials. All of this has changed how Mexicans see their government, giving them a sense of "citizen power."

The challenge for the "new PRI," and any ruling party that follows, is to function in this highly transparent, electorally competitive environment without resorting to the old ways, including self-enrichment of officials. The new alliances that PRI leaders are now building with private businesses, both domestic and foreign, could set the stage for a new burst of corruption. Moreover, the poverty alleviation entitlement programs (like Oportunidades) that both PRI and PAN governments have put into place in recent sexenios offer abundant opportunities for manipulation and vote buying. Low-income Mexicans who have come to depend on these programs can be kicked off the rolls at the discretion of low-level officials (frequently dominated by state governors) if their political loyalties are in doubt.

So Mexico's democratization process must receive an "Incomplete" grade. The possibility of a retrogression to the authoritarian past cannot be entirely dismissed. But that danger is mitigated by strong, transparent electoral institutions, Mexico's integration into the global economy, rising education levels, and new forces like social media that boost citizen's sense of political efficacy and raise their expectations for government performance.

REVIEW QUESTIONS

- What explains the shift in Mexicans' party preferences between 2000 and 2012? Which parties benefit and which lose out in this change in public preferences?

- Have the electoral reforms enacted since 1996 been successful in stemming electoral fraud and increasing electoral competitiveness? What further reforms could improve electoral transparency, competitiveness, and voter participation?

- What are the effects of the prohibition of immediate reelection of federal legislators? What are the effects of the absolute prohibition of reelection of the president?

- What are the benefits and costs of greater federalism in the Mexican political system? How can unintended consequences of decentralization be reduced?

- To what extent, and in what ways, do persistent poverty and socioeconomic inequality affect how democracy functions in Mexico today? What policies would be most effective in reducing such inequality?

- How does government performance in dealing with public security threats like drug trafficking affect political attitudes and behavior in Mexico? What strategies would be more effective in controlling drug trafficking and maintaining public support?

- What challenges do globalization and labor migration to the United States pose for Mexico's future development?

KEY TERMS

caciques
Calderón, Felipe
Cárdenas, Lázaro
Confederación de Trabajadores de México (CTM)
Confederación Nacional Campesina (CNC)
Confederación Nacional de Organizaciones Populares (CNOP)
corporatist
divided government
entitlement programs
Fox, Vicente
Institutional Revolutionary Party (PRI)
López Obrador, Andrés Manuel
municipios
narco-violence
neoliberal economic development model
North American Free Trade Agreement (NAFTA)
Oportunidades program
Pacto por México
Partido Acción Nacional (PAN)
Partido de la Revolución Democrática (PRD)
patron–client relationships
Peña Nieto, Enrique
political centralism
presidencialismo
Salinas de Gortari, Carlos
sectors (of the PRI)
Seguro Popular
sexenio (six-year term)
social media
técnico
vote buying

SUGGESTED READINGS

Bailey, John. *The Politics of Crime in Mexico: Democratic Governance in a Security Trap.* Boulder, CO: FirstForumPress, 2014.

Bruhn, Kathleen. *Taking on Goliath: Mexico's Party of the Democratic Revolution.* University Park: Pennsylvania State University Press, 1997.

Camp, Roderic A., ed. *The Oxford Handbook of Mexican Politics.* New York: Oxford University Press, 2012.

Centeno, Miguel Angel. *Democracy within Reason: Technocratic Revolution in Mexico*, 2nd ed. University Park: Pennsylvania State University Press, 1997.

Chand, Vikram K. *Mexico's Political Awakening.* Notre Dame, IN: University of Notre Dame Press, 2001.

Cleary, Matthew R., and Susan C. Stokes. *Democracy and the Culture of Skepticism: Political Trust in Argentina and Mexico.* New York: Russell Sage Foundation, 2006.

Cornelius, Wayne A., and David A. Shirk, eds. *Reforming the Administration of Justice in Mexico.* Notre Dame, IN: University of Notre Dame Press, 2007.

Cornelius, Wayne A., et al., eds. *Subnational Politics and Democratization in Mexico.* La Jolla: Center for U.S.–Mexican Studies, University of California, San Diego, 1999.

Cornelius, Wayne A., David Fitzgerald, Pedro Lewin-Fischer, and Leah Muse-Orlinoff, eds. *Mexican Migration and the U.S. Economic Crisis: A Transnational Perspective.* Boulder, CO and La Jolla, CA: Lynne Rienner, 2009.

Díaz-Cayeros, Alberto. *Federalism, Fiscal Authority, and Centralization in Latin America*. Cambridge: Cambridge University Press, 2006.

Domínguez, Jorge I., and Chappell Lawson, eds. *Mexico's Pivotal Democratic Election*. Stanford, CA: Stanford University Press, 2003.

Domínguez, Jorge I., and James A. McCann. *Democratizing Mexico: Public Opinion and Elections*. Baltimore: Johns Hopkins University Press, 1995.

Domínguez, Jorge I., Chappell Lawson, and Alejandro Moreno, eds. *Consolidating Mexico's Democracy: The 2006 Presidential Campaign in Comparative Perspective*. Baltimore: Johns Hopkins University Press, 2009.

Edmonds-Poli, Emily, and David A Shirk. *Contemporary Mexican Politics*. 2nd ed. Lanham, MD: Rowman & Littlefield, 2012.

Eisenstadt, Todd A. *Courting Democracy in Mexico: Party Strategies and Electoral Institutions*. Cambridge: Cambridge University Press, 2004.

Greene, Kenneth F. *Why Dominant Parties Lose: Mexico's Democratization in Comparative Perspective*. New York: Cambridge University Press, 2007.

Hamilton, Nora. *Mexico: Political, Social, and Economic Evolution*. New York: Oxford University Press, 2011.

Lawson, Chappell. *Building the Fourth Estate: Democratization and the Rise of a Free Press in Mexico*. Berkeley: University of California Press, 2002.

MacLeod, Dag. *Downsizing the State: Privatization and the Limits of Neoliberal Reform in Mexico*. University Park: Pennsylvania State University Press, 2004.

Magaloni, Beatriz. *Voting for Autocracy: Hegemonic Party Survival and Its Demise in Mexico*. Cambridge: Cambridge University Press, 2006.

Peschard-Sverdrup, Armand B., and Sara R. Rioff, eds. *Mexican Governance: From Single-Party Rule to Divided Government*. Washington, DC: Center for Strategic and International Studies, 2005.

Rubin, Jeffrey. *Decentering the Regime: Ethnicity, Radicalism, and Democracy in Juchitán, Mexico*. Durham, NC: Duke University Press, 1997.

Shirk, David A. *Mexico's New Politics: The PAN and Democratic Change*. Boulder, CO: Lynne Rienner, 2005.

Snyder, Richard. *Politics after Neoliberalism: Reregulation in Mexico*. Cambridge: Cambridge University Press, 2001.

Velasco, José Luis, *Insurgency, Authoritarianism, and Drug Trafficking in Mexico's Democratization*. New York: Routledge, 2005.

INTERNET RESOURCES

President's Office: www.presidencia.gob.mx.

Chamber of Deputies: www.diputados.gob.mx.

Senate: www.senado.gob.mx.

National Statistical Institute: www.inegi.org.mx.

National Population Council: www.conapo.gob.mx.

Federal Electoral Institute: www.ife.org.mx.

ENDNOTES

1. Jeffrey Passel, D'Vera Cohn, and Ana González-Barrera, "Net Migration from Mexico Falls to Zero—and Perhaps Less," (Washington, DC: Pew Research Hispanic Trends Project, Pew Research Center, April 23, 2012), http://www.pewhispanic.org/files/2012/04/Mexican-migrants-report_final.pdf.

2. This percentage represents an undercount, since the census identifies as Indians only people over age fifty. Indigenous peoples of all ages constitute an estimated 15 percent of the total population.

3. The actual extent of irregularities in the 1988 presidential vote will never be determined. Within a few hours after the polls closed, with early returns showing Cárdenas ahead by a significant margin, top authorities ordered the computerized count to be suspended. When results for a majority of the country's polling places were announced six days later, Salinas had won. There is no corroborating evidence from exit surveys of voters, because the government denied permission for such surveys in 1988. The PRI-controlled Congress later ordered the ballots stored in its basement to be burned, thereby eliminating any possibility of challenging the election outcome. Study of the partial, publicly released results and pre-election polling data has led most analysts to conclude that Salinas probably did win but that his margin of victory over Cárdenas was much smaller than the nineteen-point spread indicated by the official results.

4. According to statistics of the IFE, Zedillo won 50.18 percent of the valid votes (i.e., excluding "spoiled" ballots and write-in votes cast for unregistered candidates). However, if the calculation is based on total votes cast (including those annulled by electoral authorities), his share of the vote declines to 48.77 percent.

5. See Roderic A. Camp, *Citizen Views of Democracy in Latin America* (Pittsburgh, PA: University of Pittsburgh Press, 2001).

6. Eric Magar, "The Electoral Institutions," paper presented at the 2012 Mexican Public Opinion Panel Project Conference, Harvard University, Cambridge, Massachusetts, January 24–26, 2013.

7. James A. McCann and Chappell Lawson, "An Electorate Adrift?—Public Opinion and the Quality of Democracy in Mexico," *Latin American Research Review* 38, no. 3 (2003): 60–81; and Francisco Flores-Macías and Chappell Lawson, "Mexican Democracy and Its Discontents," *Review of Policy Research* 23, no. 2 (2006): 287–94.

8. Alejandro Moreno, "Who Is the Mexican Voter?," in Roderic A. Camp, ed., *The Oxford Handbook of Mexican Politics* (New York: Oxford University Press, 2012), 579.

9. McCann and Lawson, "An Electorate Adrift?"; and Jorge I. Domínguez and Chappell Lawson, eds., *Mexico's Pivotal Democratic Election* (Stanford, CA: Stanford University Press/ Center for U.S.—Mexican Studies, University of California, San Diego, 2003).

10. Corporación Latinobarómetro, *Informe 2011* (Santiago, Chile: Corporación Latinobarómetro, October 28, 2012), 70.

11. David Gutiérrez, Jeanne Batalova, and Aaron Terrazas, "The 2012 Mexican Presidential Election and Mexican Immigrants of Voting Age in the United States," *Migration Information Source,* April 26, 2012.

12. Moreno, "Who Is the Mexican Voter?," 579.

13. Joseph L. Klesner, "Who Participates?—Determinants of Political Action in Mexico," *Latin American Politics and Society* 51, no. 2 (2009): 59–90. As used here, the term "social capital" derives from the work of Robert D. Putnam. See Putnam, "Tuning In, Tuning Out: The Strange Disappearance of Social Capital in America," *PS: Political Science and Politics* 28, no. 4 (1995): 664–83.

14. See Alan Knight, "Historical Continuities in Social Movements," in *Popular Movements and Political Change in Mexico,* ed. Joe Foweraker and Ann L. Craig (Boulder, CO: Lynne Rienner, 1990), 78–102; Jeffrey W. Rubin, *Decentering the Regime: Ethnicity, Radicalism, and Democracy in Juchitán, Mexico* (Durham, NC: Duke University Press, 1997); and Wayne A. Cornelius, Todd Eisenstadt, and Jane Hindley, eds., *Subnational Politics and Democratization in Mexico* (La Jolla: Center for U.S.–Mexican Studies, University of California, San Diego, 1999).

15. Alberto Díaz-Cayeros, *Federalism, Fiscal Authority, and Centralization in Latin America* (Cambridge: Cambridge University Press, 2006), 8, 143–47.

16. See Victoria E. Rodríguez, *Decentralization in Mexico: From Reforma Municipal to Solidaridad to Nuevo Federalismo* (Boulder, CO: Westview, 1997); and Peter M. Ward and Victoria E. Rodríguez, *Bringing the States Back In: New Federalism and State Government in Mexico* (Austin: Lyndon Baines Johnson School of Public Affairs, University of Texas, Austin, 1999).

17. For a discussion of mixed-member electoral systems in general, and comparisons between Mexico's electoral regime with similar systems, see Matthew Soberg Shugart and Martin P. Wattenberg, eds., *Mixed-Member Electoral Systems: The Best of both Worlds?* (Oxford: Oxford University Press, 2001).

18. See Jeffrey A. Weldon, "Political Sources of *Presidencialismo* in Mexico," in *Presidentialism and Democracy in Latin America,* ed. Scott Mainwaring and Matthew Soberg Shugart (New York: Cambridge University Press, 1997), 225–58.

19. The purported rationale for this principle, applied to the president in the 1917 Constitution and extended to members of Congress in 1933, was to ensure freedom from self-perpetuating, dictatorial rule in the Porfirio Díaz style. However, the real reason for prohibiting the consecutive reelection of deputies and senators was probably to cut the ties between local political bosses and their federal legislators at a time when the ruling party was seeking greater centralization of authority.

20. David A. Shirk, *Mexico's New Politics: The PAN and Democratic Change* (Boulder, CO: Lynne Rienner Publishers, 2005), 191–94.

21. Unpublished data from Roderic A. Camp. See also Camp, "Family Relationships in Mexican Politics," *Journal of Politics* 44 (August 1982): 848–62; and Peter H. Smith, *Labyrinths of Power: Political Recruitment in Twentieth-Century Mexico* (Princeton, NJ: Princeton University Press, 1979), 307–10.

22. Roderic A. Camp, "Mexican Political Elites in a Democratic Setting," in Roderic A. Camp, ed., *The Oxford Handbook of Mexican Politics* (New York: Oxford University Press, 2012), 299–301.

23. Joseph L. Klesner, "Electoral Competition and the New Party System in Mexico," *Latin American Politics and Society* 47, no. 2 (2005): 103–42; and Klesner, "Social and Regional Factors in the 2006 Presidential Election," unpublished paper (Gambier, OH: Department of Political Science, Kenyon College, August 2006).

24. See, for example, Luis Estrada and Pablo Paras, "Ambidiestros y confundidos: Validez y contenido de la izquierda y la derecha en México," *Este País*, 180 (March 2006): 51–57.

25. Alejandro Moreno, *El Votante Mexicano* (Mexico City: Fondo de Cultura Económica, 2003).

26. As Joseph Klesner has shown, both the PAN and the PRD now exhibit catch-all characteristics, driven by the dealignment of the electorate from the PRI and the desire of its rivals to broaden their constituencies by capturing these "delinked" voters. Klesner, "Electoral Competition and the New Party System."

27. Moreno, "Who Is the Mexican Voter?," 588.

28. Nora Lustig, "Poverty, Inequality, and the New Left of Latin America," Woodrow Wilson International Center for Scholars, Latin American Program, *Democratic Governance and the New Left* series, no. 5, Washington, D.C., October 2009, p. 10.

29. "Encuesta Nacional de Ingresos y Gastos de los Hogares 2012" (Aguascalientes City, Aguascalientes: Instituto Nacional de Estadística y Geografía, July 2013).

30. A wealth of statistical data demonstrating these trends can be found in Enrique Dussel Peters, *Polarizing Development: The Impact of Liberalization Strategy* (Boulder, CO: Lynne Rienner, 2000).

31. John Bailey, *The Politics of Crime in Mexico: Democratic Governance in a Security Trap* (Boulder, CO: FirstForumPress, 2014), chap. 2.

32. Guillermo Zepeda Lecuona, "Criminal Investigation and the Subversion of the Principles of the Justice System in Mexico," in *Reforming the Administration of Justice in Mexico*, ed. Wayne A. Cornelius and David A. Shirk (Notre Dame, IN: University of Notre Dame Press, 1997).

33. Corporación Latinobarómetro, "Informe 2011," 65.

34. Andrés Villareal, "Structural Determinants of Homicide in Mexico," paper presented at the annual meeting of the American Sociological Association, Chicago, Illinois, January 5, 1999.

35. Zepeda Lecuona, "Criminal Investigation."

36. This section was prepared with the assistance of Jimena Ortega.

37. OECD Environmental Performance Reviews: Mexico 2013 (Paris: OECD Publishing, March 12, 2013).

38. Jeffrey S. Passel, "Mexican Immigrants in the United States, 2008: Fact Sheet" (Washington, DC: Pew Hispanic Center, April 2009); and Passel, Cohn, and González-Barrera, "Net Migration from Mexico."

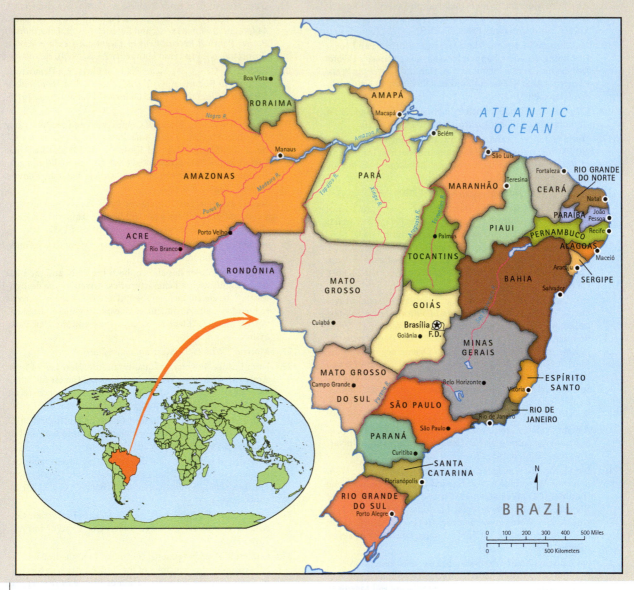

Country Bio

POPULATION
201 million

TERRITORY
3,287,612 square miles

YEAR OF INDEPENDENCE
1822

YEAR OF CURRENT CONSTITUTION
1988

HEAD OF STATE
Dilma Rousseff

HEAD OF GOVERNMENT
Dilma Rousseff

LANGUAGE
Portuguese

RELIGIONS
Roman Catholic 57%, Protestant 28%

CHAPTER 15

Politics in Brazil

Frances Hagopian and Timothy J. Power

LEARNING OBJECTIVES

15.1 Identify five challenges currently faced by Brazil's government.

15.2 Discuss the role of the military in Brazil's path to democracy.

15.3 Describe Brazil's economic fluctuations and the socioeconomic standings of its various population groups.

15.4 Describe the branches of government in Brazil and the checks and balances among them.

15.5 Discuss the role of religious, gender-based, and racial movements in relation to Brazil's political culture.

15.6 Identify the main sources of political socialization in Brazil.

15.7 Describe the ways in which individuals participate in Brazil's political process.

15.8 List five types of interest groups that influence politics in Brazil.

15.9 Discuss political party dynamics and Brazil's electoral system.

15.10 Describe the way laws are introduced and considered in Brazil's legislature.

15.11 List five recent public policy changes in Brazil and describe their effects.

15.12 Identify four ways in which Brazil has become prominent internationally.

In early June 2013, the municipal government of Brazil's largest city, São Paulo, the heart of the nation's most dynamic metropolitan area with more than 20 million inhabitants, raised bus fares by about nine cents to a little less than $1.50 per ride. The fare increase was met by some sporadic protests. Within a week, however, what began as the "Free Fare Movement" shocked the political establishment by mobilizing millions of Brazilians of all ages and social classes in major and small cities across Brazil in what was the most significant eruption of mass protest in thirty years.

What ignited the protests was not immediately clear to the puzzled authorities, whose misreading of the public mood undoubtedly fanned the flames of discontent. Indeed, the timing of the protests was hard to explain. A popular president and her iconic predecessor had presided over a decade of robust growth that had lifted nearly 40 million Brazilians out of poverty, reduced inequality, and left unemployment at its lowest level ever. It soon became apparent that the poor quality of transportation, health care, schools, and other public services, rampant crime, the government's massive investments in stadium construction for the 2014 World Cup, the apparent impunity for corrupt politicians, and creeping prices and a rising cost of living had led ordinary Brazilians to take to the streets. A new middle class of 95 million strong—representing nearly half of the population—which carried cell phones and often relied on public

The Protest Movement of Mid-2013
Residents of the city of São Paulo take to the streets on June 20, 2013. Although the protests were triggered by an increase in local bus fares, demonstrations quickly revealed many other sources of public dissatisfaction, especially corruption. The handmade signs refer to demands for improvements in health, education, public security, and political responsiveness. Political parties are invisible: people attempting to hoist party insignia were chased away by the crowds.

transportation, demonstrated its intolerance for poor government performance and for lavish spending on mega-events that only a few years earlier the popular President Lula had secured for Brazil in what appeared to be a stunning coup (Brazilian presidents are commonly but not always referred to by their first names).

The protests riveted the country and the world, drawing inevitable comparisons from the international press to protests occurring simultaneously in Turkey and Egypt. Bowing to the protesters' demands, bus fare increases were canceled and the Congress overwhelmingly rejected a proposed constitutional amendment to limit the power of federal prosecutors to investigate corruption and other criminal charges. It also voted to designate 75 percent of the royalties from new oil fields to education and 25 percent to health care. President Rousseff, proclaiming herself to be on the side of the protestors, promised to invest more than 23 billion dollars in public transportation, provide incentives to doctors and hospitals to better serve the poor, make corruption a felony, and initiate a debate on political reform. The protests ebbed, but not

before having set a powerful new agenda—for an honest government that works.

Current Policy Challenges

15.1 Identify five challenges currently faced by Brazil's government.

Brazilians share a common identity, allegiance to their government, and political community. There is no serious religious conflict or large linguistic minority, and the last armed confrontation between any region and the central government was in 1932. Yet, as the June 2013 protests showed, two other broad challenges—fostering development and strengthening democratic governance—are pressing. Moreover, an accumulated deficit of public policy challenges will be harder for government to meet in a slowing economy.

Recent Brazilian governments have been reasonably successful at generating growth. Under the administration of Luiz Inácio "Lula" da Silva (2003–2010), growth averaged 4.8 percent between 2003 and 2008. Inflation was controlled, the public debt was reduced, and Brazil repaid foreign loans ahead of schedule. Brazil recovered quickly from the global recession of 2009, rebounding impressively to grow by 7.5 percent in 2010, the country's best performance since 1986. Rich in energy, mineral, and agricultural resources, Brazil rode a worldwide commodity boom, overtaking Britain in 2012 to become the sixth largest economy in the world. Unlike in past growth spurts, the incomes of the poorest 10 percent of Brazilians rose nearly four times faster than the richest 10 percent from 1999 to 2009, substantially reducing poverty and inequality. President Dilma Rousseff has set her sights on eradicating extreme poverty in Brazil by 2015, ten years ahead of its Millennium Development Goal target.

Recently, however, growth has slowed, along with the Chinese economy that has become Brazil's biggest customer. In 2012, the economy expanded by an anemic 0.9 percent. Most worrisome is the fact that inflation, which had been under control for nearly twenty years, is again a threat. In the twelve months prior to the June 2013 protests, prices rose by more than 6.5 percent. This prompted the Central Bank to raise interest rates that are already the highest among twenty-six major world economies. High interest and tax rates threaten to choke private investment and constrain public sector investment, which is urgently needed to update the country's aging and crumbling infrastructure. Many economists believe that Brazil needs to lower tax rates (Brazil's tax-to-GDP ratio is twice as high as the rest of Latin America and equivalent to the EU average) and overhaul its tax structure.

Rising inflation and slowing growth also come at a bad time for a government that must now deal with a daunting social policy agenda. In the past two decades, successive governments have successfully expanded access to health and education. But now Brazilians are looking for better access to *and* higher-quality services. The public health care system on which the poor depend was long underfunded and inefficient, and Brazil's population is less literate and less well schooled than many of its neighbors. Given that poor schools are not merely unjust but also a constraint on economic development, a national consensus has elevated education as a national priority. The protests also shone a spotlight on inadequate public transportation systems in the nation's cities, which

cost too much and deliver too little, as well as the precariousness of the neighborhoods they serve.

Plaguing many communities are high rates of crime, violence, and drug trafficking. Brazil is the second-largest consumer of illegal drugs (after the United States). Although the Rio de Janeiro municipal government has taken dramatic steps to send in security forces to drive out drug traffickers and pacify some of the most dangerous slums in the city in advance of the 2016 Summer Olympic Games, the 2013 demonstrations underscored that residents of other cities are also acutely worried about corrupt police forces and the glaring lack of public security. The murder rate (over 40,000 homicides per year) is unacceptably high, violence against women and children is common, and the judicial system is overwhelmed. The police commonly torture poor criminal suspects in order to extract confessions and disguise extrajudicial killings as shootouts with dangerous criminals. Freedom House has charged Brazil's police as being among the world's most violent and corrupt, and has decried that "officers are rarely prosecuted for abuses and almost never convicted."[1]

Although income inequality has fallen over the past two decades, society remains stratified by region, race, and gender. In recent years, the movement of landless workers has dramatized the shortage of agricultural land for the tiller. Increasingly, Brazilians are also beginning to understand that their country faces the challenge of greater economic and social inclusion for Afrodescendants, who represent nearly half of the population but have historically faced racial discrimination and lacked educational and employment opportunities. The recent introduction of affirmative action policies for admission to federal universities is a step in that direction.

The environment and energy also require attention. Environmental protection is pressing, not merely because of the need to develop the Amazon region's natural resources in a sustainable way but also because many years of lax controls have compromised air and water quality. Brazil appeared to have become self-sufficient in energy, thanks to massive water resources and the world's largest hydroelectric plant, a world-leading biofuels industry, and the discovery of massive Atlantic oil fields in 2006 and 2008 by the state-owned oil behemoth Petrobras. But surging demand for fuel as more Brazilians bought cars, a lack of domestic refining capacity, a slower than anticipated pace of exploiting deep-sea oilfields, and a backlog of projects have recently forced Brazil to import foreign gasoline and even ethanol. Critics charge that the government's use of Petrobras to boost domestic industry and to fight inflation has saddled the energy giant with a nationalist mandate to buy ships, oil platforms, and other equipment from Brazilian companies, and has forced it to sell imported gasoline at below-market prices.

The 2013 protests also reignited demands for political reform. Government is widely perceived as handicapped by corruption and dysfunctional political institutions. At the time of the protests, none of the high-ranking public officials from the **Workers' Party (PT)** who had been convicted in the wake of a 2005 scandal (referred to as the *mensalão*, or "big monthly payment," a scheme in which the executive branch made illegal payments to legislators in turn for support on key Congressional votes) had yet been incarcerated, even more than six months after the Supreme Court had declared them guilty.[2] This stoked the widespread perception that corrupt politicians enjoy impunity. Trust in Congress, political parties, and politicians is at an all-time low. Brazilians have traditionally complained about their political parties, but the events of 2013 suggest an even more sweeping rejection of "politics as usual."

Now high on the agenda is a reform of the way in which electoral campaigns are financed, and a serious public debate has begun on the fractured relationship between representatives and constituents. The PT favors a system of closed-list proportional representation, which would enhance the accountability of politicians to their party leaders, while other actors endorse a system of single-member districts, which would strengthen the relationship between individual legislators and their constituents.

Unlike their counterparts in Turkey and Egypt, the Brazilians who took to the streets in 2013 were not protesting against their political *regime*; rather, they were decrying its *performance*. In fact, democracy is stronger than at any time in Brazil's history, but newfound social inclusion has led millions of Brazilians to question the quality of public policies. People are now openly asking whether the political system can sustain growth, eliminate poverty, improve the quality of public services, guarantee physical security, ameliorate past injustices, set the country on a course of sustainable development, and clean up government corruption. To understand Brazil's newly critical citizenry, we must first understand the economic, social, and political conditions that created the nation's current policy challenges.

Historical Perspectives

15.2 Discuss the role of the military in Brazil's path to democracy.

Brazil has a legacy of political order and several decades of competitive government, but genuine democracy is relatively recent. Brazil gained its independence from Portugal in 1822 not by insurrection, as in Spanish America, but by fiat of the Portuguese emperor's son. For seven decades, Brazil was governed as an "empire," and successive emperors exercised strong central authority. This type of rule prevented the fragmentation of territory and provided a unique degree of order and political stability in the New World.

Brazil became a republic in 1889, one year after slavery was finally abolished. The empire fell swiftly and suddenly when disgruntled military and agrarian elites separately withdrew their support. The military wanted to replace the empire with a strong central government committed to "order and progress"—a motto still emblazoned on the Brazilian flag. By 1891, however, civilian elites from the largest and economically strongest states had wrested control of the new republic from the military. They favored a decentralized federalism and framed a constitution that gave the states even wider latitude than did U.S. federalism, from which it drew its inspiration. The "Old Republic," as it was called, was dominated by the regional oligarchies of the strongest states. The overwhelming majority of Brazilians were without the effective legal rights, levels of literacy, or socioeconomic conditions of citizenship.

In 1930, a combination of labor unrest and protest from young army officers, the world depression, the crisis in Brazil's coffee economy, and regional rivalries brought down the Old Republic and spawned a "revolution" that brought a Southern politician, Getúlio Vargas, to the presidency. Vargas quickly strengthened the central government at the expense of the state and local governments, and enhanced bureaucratic autonomy. In 1937, impressed by the political and social organization of fascist Italy, he reneged on a promise to hold elections and instead exercised dictatorial powers in a regime he called the *Estado Nôvo* (New State).

Postwar Democracy

With the defeat of the Axis powers and the collapse of fascism in 1945, Vargas reluctantly restored democracy. The political system was opened to broader political participation and competition. Many new voters, especially from the urban areas of the South and Southeast, were incorporated into the political system through loose associations with populist leaders, parties, and institutions. Populist politicians claimed to represent the interests of the urban middle and working classes. In practice, however, the urban lower classes were well controlled, and urban informal sector workers lacked access to health care, old age pensions, and even many legal rights of citizenship. The rural poor were excluded from political life altogether. Their interests were not represented through any political party, they were not allowed to organize unions, and most rural workers (about 70 percent of the population), who were illiterate, could not vote.

In the next two decades, several political parties competed for power at the national level, although political bosses still exerted much local control. The country prospered, especially during the late 1950s, when physical infrastructure was laid. Foreign auto plants settled in São Paulo, and a new capital, Brasília, was built in the interior.

In the early 1960s, Brazil's political system began to strain. With thirteen political parties in the Chamber of Deputies and the share of seats won by small parties on the rise, the party system was so fragmented that Congress was ineffective and no president could count on a stable base of support. Elites became threatened by the mobilization of peasant leagues, the electoral advance of the populist **Brazilian Labor Party (PTB)**, and the leftist rhetoric of João Goulart, who assumed the presidency in 1961 (see Figure 15.1). In 1963 and early 1964, amid high inflation and a stagnating economy, Goulart advocated revolutionary change in the countryside and supported the mutiny of enlisted sailors against naval officers. Military officers, who had come to view movements of the left as threats to national security and economic stability as well as a breeding ground for subversive ideologies, seized power and an expanded role in government and in politics.

The Military Steps In

In April 1964, the Brazilian military deposed President Goulart and instituted direct military rule. In order to tackle inflation, attract foreign investment, and stimulate economic development, the military

Year	Nature of Government	President
1946	Civilian*	Eurico Dutra (PSD/PTB)
1951	Civilian	Getúlio Vargas (PTB/PSP)
1954	Civilian**	João Café Filho (PSP)
1956	Civilian	Juscelino Kubitchek (PSD/PTB)
1961	Civilian	Jânio Quadros (UDN/PDC/PL/PTN)
1961	Civilian**	João Goulart (PTB)
1964	Military	Humberto Castelo Branco
1967	Military	Artur Costa e Silva
1969	Military	Emilio Garrastazú Médici
1974	Military	Ernesto Geisel
1978	Military	João Figueiredo
1985	Civilian**	José Sarney (PFL/PMDB)
1990	Civilian	Fernando Collor de Mello (PRN)
1992	Civilian**	Itamar Franco
1995	Civilian	Fernando Henrique Cardoso (PSDB)
1999	Civilian	Fernando Henrique Cardoso (PSDB)
2003	Civilian	Luiz Inácio Lula da Silva (PT)
2007	Civilian	Luiz Inácio Lula da Silva (PT)
2011	Civilian	Dilma Rousseff (PT)

*Dutra, a general, was directly elected as a candidate of the PSD and headed a civilian government.
**Not directly elected.

FIGURE 15.1

Brazilian Administrations since 1945

For a quarter century, Brazil's governments have been headed by elected civilian presidents, who, since 1998, can be reelected.

centralized economic policymaking. It strengthened the executive branch by giving it exclusive powers over the budget and the authority to rule by decree. It also replaced politicians in top administrative positions with military officers and civilian economists, engineers, educators, and professional administrators. After one year in power, it abolished existing political parties and canceled future elections for state governors and mayors of state capitals and "national security" areas.

When "hard-line" military factions gained power in 1967, the regime turned harshly repressive, especially toward the labor and student movements. It suspended habeas corpus and imposed a state of siege. Like other Latin American militaries of this period, it subjected its enemies—real and imagined— to arbitrary detention, torture, exile, and even death. Nonetheless, on a per capita basis, deaths and disappearances were far lower in Brazil than under military dictatorships in Argentina, Chile, and Uruguay, and abuses were rare after 1974. Moreover, unlike other dictatorships, the Brazilian military did not eliminate elections and representative institutions altogether. It created a progovernment party—the National Renovating Alliance (ARENA)—and an official opposition known as the Brazilian Democratic Movement (MDB) to replace the parties it had abolished. It permitted these parties to contest elections for the national and state legislatures, mayors of most cities and towns, and local councils. The Congress remained in session throughout military rule for all but two brief periods. Of course, victories for ARENA were all but ensured by manipulation of electoral law, and legislators and other elected officials were divested of meaningful powers by the 1967 Constitution. Nonetheless, the veil of legality, a two-party system, and elections ultimately laid the conditions for Brazil's particular path to democratization in the 1980s.

Political liberalization began within the military itself. In early 1974, General Ernesto Geisel, the new, "soft-line" military president, signaled that he would "relax" military rule by easing up on press censorship, allowing a freer expression of ideas, and permitting slightly freer elections. Geisel hoped that more political freedom would check the power of military hard-liners, and that more competitive elections would increase voting turnout and enhance regime legitimacy. Despite the record-shattering growth rates

of the so-called "Brazilian Miracle" (the economic boom of 1968–1974), the opposition MDB won sixteen of the twenty-two open Senate seats in the 1974 elections. This stunning upset was largely due to an effective media campaign protesting rising social inequality despite double-digit growth rates, in addition to the demands of a growing urban middle class for greater freedom, access to the mass media, and higher education. Although the military regime subsequently limited party access to television and appointed one-third of the Senate in order to secure its advantage in Congress, the regular staging of elections allowed the regime's opponents to mobilize and pressure the government to stay the course of its *abertura política* (political opening).

The regime also faced an invigorated civil society in the 1970s. The political opening allowed the Catholic Church and several segments of elite opinion (including the press, bar association, and business community) to express grave reservations about military authoritarianism. As the political space opened, nonelite groups that had either been silenced (such as the labor movement) or previously unorganized (such as the women's movement) pressed for their specific interests as well as for greater political freedom.

Democracy Restored

The military regime finally came to an end in March 1985. Amid rising inflation and unemployment and popular disenchantment with the military, many of its civilian supporters abandoned it. Regime supporters and opponents together negotiated a series of political deals that paved the way for a smooth road to a democratic regime. A civilian opposition leader, Tancredo Neves, was elected president in an "electoral college" of elite officeholders. After his untimely death, vice president–elect José Sarney, the former president of the promilitary party, was sworn in as president. The franchise was extended to illiterate adults in 1985, and congressional elections followed in 1986.

A new constitution was passed in 1988 that swept away many authoritarian laws and guaranteed basic political and social rights. By 1989, when Brazilians went to the polls to vote for president for the first time since 1961, most observers considered Brazil to have established a democratic regime.

Economy and Society

15.3 Describe Brazil's economic fluctuations and the socioeconomic standings of its various population groups.

In the past seventy years, Brazil has undergone a socioeconomic transformation as profound as any country has ever experienced. It went from a nation that bore the obvious imprint of having been an agricultural colony and a slave society to one of the world's major industrial countries. In large part, the state orchestrated that transformation. In the 1990s, Brazil scaled back the scope of the state's economic intervention and allowed a greater role for market forces. Today, Brazil seeks to sustain economic growth while eradicating hunger, illiteracy, and other bitter vestiges of inequality.

Economy

Until 1930, plantation agriculture organized Brazil's economy and society. Large-scale sugar estates along the northeastern coast relied on slave labor well into the 1800s. In the early 1850s, more than a quarter of Brazil's population of 7.5 million were slaves. After the sugar economy declined, new fortunes were made farther south in the mid-nineteenth century in the cultivation of coffee, and coffee planters grew rich and politically powerful.

When the bottom fell out of the coffee economy with the stock market crash of October 1929, the Brazilian state, like many others in Latin America at the time, led an industrialization drive. It protected markets for nascent industries, subsidized energy, manipulated exchange rates to make imported industrial inputs cheaper, and controlled the labor force. This model, called "import-substituting industrialization," produced growth in the 1950s, but it became strained in the early 1960s when investment dropped and inflation rose.

Under military rule, the state promoted industrialization to an even greater degree. The military had long dreamed of developing the nation's vast mineral and agricultural resources and hydroelectric potential in order to make Brazil a great power. Swimming against the tide of radical free-market economic experiments pursued by its neighbors, the Brazilian military government increased the state's revenue base, controlled wages and prices, and ran hundreds of profitable public sector enterprises in the mining, petroleum, public utilities, and transportation sectors. It also attracted significant foreign investment in such sectors as automobiles and petrochemicals, which required large capital investments and sophisticated technologies. From 1968 to 1974, the model produced an "economic miracle." Gross national product doubled as the economy grew on average by 11 percent per year. But the fruits of growth did not trickle down to much of the population.

Growth rates finally slowed in 1974. Dependent for most of its energy needs on imported petroleum, Brazil was hit hard by soaring oil prices brought on by the Arab oil embargo and production cutbacks by the Organization of Petroleum Exporting Countries (OPEC). Military rulers borrowed from abroad to keep the economy growing and to pay the bills. This strategy backfired as oil prices continued to climb, interest rates rose, and a global recession closed the markets for Brazil's exports.

Brazil's indebtedness dramatically changed the country's economic prospects. Payments on the debt's interest and principal swallowed on average 43 percent of its export earnings from 1985 to 1989, and interest payments on the debt exceeded 4 percent of GNP in 1985. Servicing the debt plunged the nation into a deep recession for much of the 1980s. Inflation soared to four-digit annual rates.

By the early 1990s, then, the model of a heavily indebted producer state—which governed a protected and regulated market and generated high fiscal deficits and inflation—had become unsustainable. The government began to dismantle trade protection and deregulate prices and financial services, and it renegotiated the terms of its debt with its creditors in 1993. Brazil's stubborn inflation was finally tamed in 1994 by a currency reform known as the **Real Plan** (named for the new currency it introduced, the *real*). In the year immediately prior to the Real Plan, *monthly* inflation had averaged 39 percent; after the plan, *annual* rates fell to single digits. Seeing the plan as a first step, policymakers expected that foreign investment and privatization would accelerate new growth, and the victory over inflation would be secured through public sector reform.

Barriers to foreign direct investment were removed in 1995, and foreign direct investment poured into Brazil. From 1996 to 2000, Brazil attracted an annual average of $21 billion in investment. The only emerging market to receive more foreign investment in this period was China. Many of the largest state-owned enterprises were also privatized. One of the most significant accomplishments of reformist President Fernando Henrique Cardoso (1995–2002) was to control the deficit spending of the subnational governments. After years of hard negotiations, the federal government assumed the hefty debts of the state governments, which were given thirty years to repay them. In return, the state governments agreed to privatize their state banks and many state enterprises and limit their spending, especially on state payrolls.

However, reforms in other public sectors were slow in coming. Reform of the central administration enabled the federal government to reduce its payroll, and the government partially gained control of social security obligations. But the Cardoso administration failed to reform the tax code. All in all, stalled reform jeopardized the positive results that currency reform, foreign investment, and privatization had had on stability and growth. When the Asian financial crisis hit in 1997, the Brazilian government had to devalue the real.

Brazil's economic performance thereafter improved. Inflation averaged 5 percent annually in Lula's second term. Though it did not tackle tax reform, Lula's administration did reform the pension system for public sector workers, toughening the requirements for retirement and reducing benefits. In all, the government impressively produced a primary fiscal surplus of 4.25 percent of GDP, voluntarily exceeding the budget surplus target of 3.75 percent of GDP recommended by the International Monetary Fund (IMF). Its frugality allowed it to pay off its foreign public debt ahead of schedule.

In the past decade, Brazil reaped a windfall in exporting oil, soy, iron ore, and other commodities, mainly to a growing China. By 2013, China had surpassed the United States as Brazil's most important trading partner. The economy grew impressively by an average of 4.8 percent in the five-year period from 2004 through 2008, and by as much as 7.5 percent in 2010 and 2.7 percent in 2011, before slowing down in 2012 to 0.9 percent. In these years, real incomes grew, with the real value of the minimum wage nearly doubling between 2003 and 2013.

Brazil is now on its way to becoming an energy superpower. Its world-leading biofuels industry produces a successful alcohol fuel derived from sugarcane; light vehicles today run on either a blend of 25 percent ethanol or 100 percent ethanol. The Itaipu Dam alone provides 19 percent of the country's electricity. The state-owned oil giant Petrobras modernized and expanded operations in the 1990s when subjected to market forces. Using innovative drilling techniques, the company discovered massive deep-sea Atlantic oil fields in 2006 and 2008 that promise to greatly expand Brazil's petroleum production. By 2010, Petrobras was the second-largest energy company (after Exxon), and the seventh-largest firm by market value, in the world. But domestic exploitation of new oil finds has not met surging demand and has forced Brazil to import foreign gasoline and even ethanol to meet its energy needs. A backlog of ambitious projects has also depressed the value of the company.

Society

A Modern Society Brazil's rapid economic growth has fundamentally altered society. In 1940, when it was predominantly a rural, agrarian society, 68 percent of the population lived in rural areas. Today, only about 15 percent of Brazilians remain in the countryside, and there are eighteen metropolitan areas of more than a million residents. Greater São Paulo (with 20 million inhabitants) and greater Rio de Janeiro (with 12.6 million) have populations larger than those of many Latin American countries. About a sixth of the labor force works in agriculture and a third in industry and construction, with the rest employed in commerce and government and personal services. Agricultural workers are no longer primarily sharecroppers and renters; they are wage laborers on some of the most modern and productive farms in the world. In addition, women entered the labor force en masse over the past four decades. Between 1970 and 2011, women's participation in the labor force rose from 18 to 60 percent.[3]

Brazilians also have greater exposure to modern means of communication. In 2011, 97 percent of homes had at least one television set and 43 percent had a computer, 37 percent with direct Internet access (actual Internet penetration is far greater, since many people use public connections). Some 90 percent of homes had a telephone of some sort (fixed line or mobile) in 2011, compared to only 59 percent in 2001. Almost all of the growth was in cellular telephones, which have revolutionized daily life. By mid-2013, there were more than 265 active cell phone lines in Brazil, or approximately 1.3 phones per person.

The modernization of society, however real, is incomplete. Adult illiteracy stands at 10 percent of the population. Although Brazilians went to school on average for 7.3 years as of 2011, many repeated grades and did not complete primary school. Just under half of the workforce pays into the social security system. The quarter who work in the informal sector and the quarter who are self-employed do not have signed work cards and are not entitled to many of the worker protections enshrined in the 1988 constitution.

An Unequal Society Brazil has long been known as one of the countries with the most unequal distribution of wealth in the world. Despite a falling Gini coefficient, inequality persists among individuals, social classes, and geographic regions, which have developed unevenly across centuries. According to convention, Brazil has five regions: (1) Northeast, (2) North, (3) Southeast, (4) South, and (5) Center-West. In 2012, the nine states comprising the desperately poor and drought-plagued Northeast contained 28 percent of Brazil's population but generated only 14 percent of GDP in 2010 (see Figure 15.2). Poverty rates are poignantly illustrated by the fact that the Northeast has more than half of all *Bolsa Família* (federal cash transfer) beneficiaries, and nearly 20 percent of the population is illiterate, a rate more than three times higher than those of the more developed South and Southeast. The North, comprising Brazil's Amazon region, and the Center-West (Brazil's frontier) are relatively less populated and developed than the coastal regions. The Southeast (which includes São Paulo, Minas Gerais, and Rio de Janeiro), with 42 percent of the population and 54 percent of those who are college educated, generated 55 percent of national economic activity and wealth.

Society is stratified by color as well as by class and region. **Afrodescendants** comprise about half of the population, and there are also small populations of mixed white and indigenous blood, mixed black and indigenous blood, and fully indigenous groups. With 97 million Afrodescendants, Brazil is the country with the second-largest black population in the world, behind Nigeria. Afrodescendants make up 73 percent of the population of Brazil's North, 71 percent of the Northeast region, 57 percent of the Center-West, 43 percent of the Southeast, and about 21 percent of

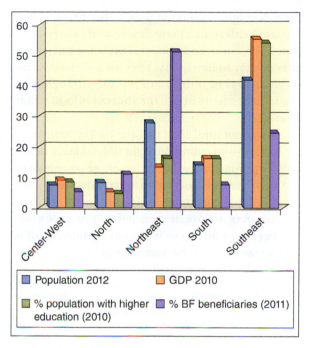

FIGURE 15.2
Regional Inequality
Overall inequality has been reduced in Brazil, but the Southeast remains wealthier and better educated than the Northeast, which has a quarter of the population but over half of Brazil's Bolsa Família recipients.
Source: Instituto Brasileiro de Geografia e Estatística.

the South. They are disproportionately poor, often suffer harsh treatment at the hands of the police, and typically find their promotions blocked in public and private life. They are twice as likely to be illiterate, and they earn considerably less than their white counterparts. In 2010, a fifth of whites but a third of Afrodescendants earned less than the minimum wage. At the other end of the pay scale, 2.8 percent of whites but only 0.6 percent of Afrodescendants earned more than ten times the minimum wage. Black Brazilians are also less educated than whites: Just one quarter (versus 35 percent of whites) reached secondary school and 7.8 percent (versus 16.8 percent for whites) attended institutions of higher learning. Racial discrimination, moreover, extends into the judicial system. In cases of violent crimes, defendants who are Afrodescendants are more likely than their white counterparts to be held in custody pending trial, to rely on public defenders, to be convicted, and to be severely punished.

Like the Afrodescendant population, Brazil's indigenous peoples have been seriously disadvantaged from Portuguese colonial days to the present. Portuguese settlers and their descendants coveted Indian labor, lands, and, more recently, the timber and minerals on Indian lands. They also threatened the very survival of indigenous culture through various schemes to integrate the Indians into Brazilian society.

It was not until 1988 that the collective rights of the Indians—including the right to hold lands necessary for production, preservation of the environment, and their physical and cultural reproduction—were constitutionally guaranteed. In contrast to the huge population of African descent, only a quarter of a million Brazilians belong to indigenous groups, most of which are located in the Amazon region.

Institutions and Structures of Government

15.4 Describe the branches of government in Brazil and the checks and balances among them.

Since the establishment of the republic in 1889, the Brazilian state has been federal and presidential, with three branches of government—executive, legislative, and judicial. However, the distribution of power, the limits on state and governmental authority, and how policy is framed and executed have changed substantially with each regime and constitution.

Nondemocratic governments centralized decision making and expanded state authority. Civilian elites have, as a reaction to authoritarianism, attempted to decentralize administration and limit central power. The framers of the 1988 Constitution targeted the unrestrained exercise of state power. In order to roll back the excessive centralization of the authoritarian period and executive branch domination of the state and of society, they strengthened the fiscal base of the subnational governments, the powers of the national Congress, and individual and collective civil and political rights.

Federalism: The Union, States, and Local Governments

Brazil is one of the most decentralized federations in the world. Its federal system has three tiers of autonomous governing bodies: (1) the central government called the *Union*; (2) the state governments; and (3) local governments called *municípios*, which are roughly equivalent to U.S. counties (see Figure 15.3).

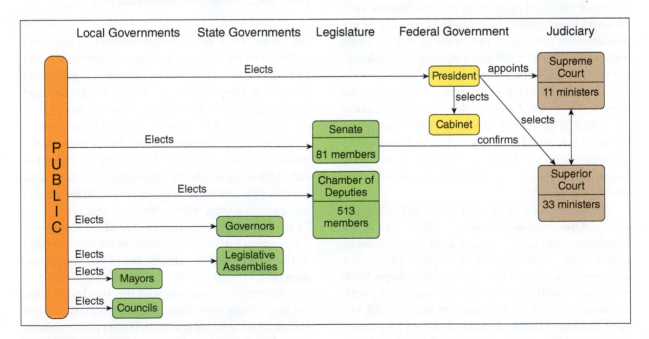

FIGURE 15.3
The Structure of the Brazilian Government
Brazil's federal, state, and local governments share revenues and responsibilities.

Each of Brazil's twenty-six states elects a governor, lieutenant governor, and representatives to a unicameral state legislature, known as the Legislative Assembly, who all serve four-year terms. The Federal District of Brasília (similar to Washington D.C.) also elects its governor and a District Assembly. Brazil's 5,570 *municípios* are governed by elected mayors, vice mayors, and local councils of from nine to twenty-one representatives (*municípios* with more than 1 million inhabitants have substantially larger councils).

Throughout its history as a republic, there has been a tension between the centralizing ambitions of the central government and the states' aspirations for greater autonomy. Under military rule, the central government restricted the use of federal revenue-sharing funds intended to supplement state and local taxes, and dictated the rates those state and local governments were allowed to levy.

With redemocratization, the Union restored substantial fiscal resources and autonomy to subnational governments. Regional politicians succeeded in writing a "new federalism" into the 1988 Constitution, which required that 21.5 percent of the income tax and the industrial products tax be returned to the states and 22.5 percent to the municipal governments, with no strings attached. These automatic transfers led to a massive increase in state and local government spending in the 1990s.

In May 2000, the Cardoso government passed the **Fiscal Responsibility Law**, which sets strict spending limits for all levels of government and prohibits the central government from refinancing subnational debt. It reinforced a provision of a 1995 law limiting all state government payrolls to 60 percent of total state revenues. After the Fiscal Responsibility Law went into effect, the share of total government expenditures accounted for by state and municipal levels of government declined.

The Executive Branch

The president is both the head of state and the head of government. The president and vice president are elected jointly for four-year terms (Figure 15.3). Since 1997, they can be immediately reelected once. The president has ample legislative powers, including the right to issue emergency decrees and to designate certain bills for priority consideration by Congress, forcing them directly to the top of the legislative agenda.

The Brazilian president has the exclusive right to initiate budgetary legislation. Also, unlike in the United States, the budget passed by Congress is merely a spending authorization. It is up to the president to decide which budget items will actually be disbursed. This discretionary authority gives the president enormous bargaining power in relation to Congress.

The Legislative Branch

The national Congress is made up of two houses that form a system of "balanced bicameralism" in that one house does not clearly dominate the other. Both can initiate legislation, and they share the power to review the national budget.

The upper house, the Senate, has three senators from each state and the Federal District, for a total of eighty-one. Senators serve staggered eight-year terms; elections are held every four years alternately for one-third and two-thirds of the Senate.

The lower house, the Chamber of Deputies, comprises 513 representatives from twenty-six states and the Federal District. Deputies serve four-year terms. Although deputies are supposed to be allocated to each state roughly in accordance to its population, the Constitution also establishes a minimum of eight and a maximum of seventy deputies for each state. This means that many small states are overrepresented, and the largest (São Paulo) has fewer representatives than it would with perfect proportional representation. While democracies often overrepresent underpopulated regions in *upper chambers* in order to safeguard the interests of all federal units (as in the U.S. Senate), the malapportionment of Brazil's *lower house* is unusual.

Even in a strong presidential system, Congress has important powers. It can initiate legislation, review the budget, approve or reject emergency laws, and override presidential vetoes. It conducts public hearings and can compel government ministers to appear before Congress to answer questions.

Moreover, with the approval of one-third of both the Chamber of Deputies and the Senate, Congress can set up **Parliamentary Commissions of Inquiry (CPIs)**. CPIs have inquired into the financial management of state enterprises and severe breaches of public ethics, including the 2005 scandal implicating the PT. In this case, the CPI concluded that aides to former President Lula had operated a scheme of payments to federal legislators timed around important votes in

Congress. Later referred to the Supreme Court, this investigation (the so-called *mensalão* or "big monthly payment" scandal) led to important convictions of PT leaders in 2012. Also in 2012, a congressional investigation was opened into violence against women. With their sweeping mandates, including the power to override bank secrecy or to compel testimony by high-profile witnesses, CPIs are one of the most visible forms of congressional action.

The Judiciary

The judicial branch is comprised of the Supreme Court, the Superior Court, five regional federal appeals courts, labor courts, electoral courts, military courts, and state courts. The Constitution stipulates criteria for entry into judicial service (by means of a competitive examination), promotion (by seniority and merit), and mandatory retirement at the age of seventy or after thirty years of service. Eleven justices, or "ministers," are named by the president to the Supreme (constitutional) Court—**Supremo Tribunal Federal (STF)**. These justices are approved by the Senate, as are thirty-three ministers to the Superior (civil) Court (see Figure 15.3).

The electoral courts constitute a subsystem of the federal judicial system. The Superior Electoral Court—**Tribunal Superior Eleitoral (TSE)**—came into being in 1932 to check the rampant electoral fraud in the Old Republic. Today, electoral courts at all levels rule on a variety of areas relating to party registration, the mandates of elected members of Congress, the admissibility of candidacies, procedures for counting ballots, and even the constitutionality of legislation governing these areas.

The labor courts were created in 1943. They were once the primary venue for settling grievances between labor and management. Superior and regional labor courts today arbitrate disputes between private sector workers and employers, and between public sector workers and governmental authorities when they cannot come to an agreement through collective bargaining.

The 1988 Constitution also retained a separate military justice system, but its reach has been scaled back since the dictatorship, when military courts had the jurisdiction to try civilians for crimes against national security. Today, federal and state military courts try military crimes. These include most crimes committed by military police, who are responsible for patrolling the streets (civilian police are investigators). Cases of intentional homicide by the military police against civilians are now tried before civilian judges and juries. Ordinary state courts enforce state constitutions and state laws.

The courts today are stronger than ever before. The 1988 Constitution notably expanded judicial power, broadened individual rights, and expanded access to the courts at all levels of the federal judiciary. It also enhanced judicial independence by guaranteeing judicial budget autonomy, establishing professional procedures of appointment, and maintaining stable terms for judges. As a result, judges enjoy a good deal of independence even from superiors.

While most of these reforms have had positive effects, there have also been drawbacks. Most notably, the federal courts' dockets are overloaded. Because lower courts' decisions are not binding or final, cases are appealed repeatedly until they finally reach the STF. Moreover, a legal instrument of abstract judicial review known as a **direct action of unconstitutionality (ADIN)** allows plaintiffs (the president, leaders of the Senate and Chamber, state governors, the organization of Brazilian lawyers, political parties in Congress, and national unions or class associations) to question the constitutionality of a policy directly at the STF level without going through the lower courts. These actors have used the federal court system strategically to stall or block policy.

Limitations on Governmental Authority

The opening paragraphs of Brazil's 1988 Constitution exalt the principles of sovereignty, citizenship, human dignity, social values, and political pluralism. Substantively, the Constitution extends the traditional guarantees of individual rights to social groups and prohibits discrimination against minorities. It also grants parties, unions, and civic associations legal recourse against the actions of other actors and permits them to challenge the constitutionality of legislation and administrative rulings. Individual rights are inviolable, and articles stipulating the federal form of the state, the direct, secret, universal, and regular periodic vote, and the separation of powers cannot be amended. Successful passage of constitutional amendments requires a three-fifths vote of both houses on two separate occasions.

Each tier of the court system has the power of judicial review. Traditionally, the courts had the power to review legislation only on a case-by-case basis. Today, courts may assume a more activist bent. The STF is charged to review the constitutionality of legislation, as well as to try the president and members of Congress for common crimes. A separate Supreme Electoral Court rules on the constitutionality of electoral laws.

The **Ministério Público (Public Prosecution)**, which became formally independent of the executive and judicial branches of government with the 1988 Constitution, constitutes another check on government. The Public Prosecution is responsible for defending the constitutional interests of citizens and society at large, safeguarding the environment, protecting consumers, guaranteeing minority rights, and monitoring public administration at both the federal and state levels. It can take to court any person or entity for any breaches of collective rights or the artistic and cultural autonomy of the nation, including mayors and members of Congress. The independence of its more than 300 federal and nearly 1,000 state-level members, who enter through a civil service exam, is safeguarded through life tenure.

Additionally, the **Tribunal de Contas**, a federal court of accounts, though formally part of the legislative branch (six of its nine members are appointed by Congress), acts more like an independent agency overseeing administration spending. It has broad oversight powers, and it can even investigate congressional accounts. Crucially, its members, like those of the Ministério Público, have job tenure.

Political Culture

15.5 Discuss the role of religious, gender-based, and racial movements in relation to Brazil's political culture.

Brazilian society is elite dominated, a consequence of a centuries-long pattern of socioeconomic inequality and the country's political inheritance. Although general laws exist for all citizens, they are not equally enforced. As one noted Brazilian anthropologist put it, social differentiation before the law means that the "somebodies" are above and beyond the reach of the law, but the masses are subject to and victims of the law. The "somebody" can say to "the people," "*Você sabe com quem está falando?*" ("Do you know with whom you are speaking?")[4]

Brazil also has a legacy of patrimonialism, a traditional system of domination of society by a strong state with a centralized bureaucracy. For most of the twentieth century, Brazilians from the left to the right of the political spectrum looked to the state for solutions. During the dictatorship, for the right, the state was too interventionist and impermeable to societal interests. For the left, the dream of an egalitarian state was turned into a nightmare of violence and repression. Many Brazilians thenceforth began to view their trust in the state as folly and looked instead to civil society to lead the way toward change, an impulse that was very much on display in the 2013 street protests.

Civil Society

During the military regime, ordinary citizens came together in independent organizations for social solidarity, to petition government for better services, and to oppose authoritarian rule. Civil society witnessed an unprecedented spate of associational activity among new social movements—of grassroots Catholics, women, Afrodescendants, ecologists, and neighborhood associations. These new social movements, some have contended, contributed to the democratization of political culture by socializing the religious workers, women, and slum dwellers who joined them into the norms of participatory democracy. Since the transition to democracy, membership in these organizations has grown, along with the participatory culture they have fostered.

Religion and Political Culture Brazil is a predominantly Catholic nation, and the country with the largest number of Catholics in the world. Nevertheless, religious observance has traditionally been low, and unlike many other Latin and Catholic countries, the Church did not exercise significant influence in the educational system. Religion was not an important factor in elections. Before 1964, the Church had a conservative orientation, and was generally supportive of the state and the dominant elites, but it did not attempt to impose a radically conservative order.

After 1964, the Brazilian Catholic Church earned the reputation of being one of the most progressive in the world. Much of the hierarchy shared with parish priests, nuns, and the laity, who helped to organize the labor movement, a vision of a "popular" church committed to the poor and to working for social justice. During the military regime, the Church became an important and effective opponent of authoritarian rule. It provided a safe haven for the victims of state repression of various faiths and their families. In the late 1970s, it sheltered striking workers. **Liberation theology**, which exhorted the faithful to embrace the poor as implied in the Gospels, gained widespread adherence in the 1970s. Even today, church groups continue to play an active role in helping to organize social movements in defense of the material as well as moral interests of their poor parishioners.

Perhaps the most important initiative of the popular church and the one with a direct bearing on the transformation of political culture in Brazil was the promotion of **ecclesial base communities (CEBs)**. These communities are small, relatively homogeneous, grassroots groups of ten to forty people who gather regularly to read the Bible and reflect on their daily lives in light of the Gospel. Brazil's bishops actively promoted the creation of CEBs in the spirit of the Vatican II reforms, which sought to energize the Church by making participation less ritualistic and more meaningful. CEBs were also a response to the shortage of priests. They handed the study of the Bible directly to the people, who had previously relied on priests to interpret the message of the Gospel for them, thereby transforming the attitudes of their members toward hierarchy and authority, within and outside the Church.

CEB members also gained from their participation in these local church groups the personal confidence and leadership skills that were necessary to broaden their participation in community affairs, neighborhood and women's movements, and eventually politics. In a 1993 survey, a remarkable 40 percent of women and 31 percent of men reported belonging to a CEB.[5] With the appointment of several conservative bishops and the constraints placed on liberation theologians by more conservative papal leadership, the message carried by CEBs has changed and the scope of their activities has narrowed. Nevertheless, there are still more than 100,000 of these communities across the country.

Competition from other religions has refocused Church leadership on evangelization and spirituality. As recently as the 1970s, some 90 percent of Brazilians still professed Catholicism (although many also

practiced religions of the African Diaspora). Today, only three in five Brazilians self-identify as Catholic. Pentecostal Protestantism has especially made inroads among those who are poorer, less literate, and seeking faith healing and personal redemption. In a 2013 survey, 28 percent described themselves as Evangelical and Pentecostal Christians. In the 2010 census, small numbers identified themselves as spiritists or as adherents to Afro-Brazilian and Eastern religions (8 percent claimed to be atheists).[6] Moreover, the prestige of the Catholic Church has declined. In the ten-year period from 2003 to 2013, the proportion of the São Paulo population that characterized the prestige of the Church as "high" had fallen from 58 to 35 percent.[7] The Pentecostal electoral and legislative presence is now significant.

Has participation in religious organizations changed Brazil's political culture? In Brazil as elsewhere, people who participate in church groups tend to join voluntary associations and participate more actively in politics. There are no appreciable differences in political participation rates, outlooks, and voting patterns among Catholics and Protestants. Catholic members of CEBs, however, are more likely to support the PT than are Catholics associated with conservative movements within the church, such as the Catholic Charismatic Renewal.[8]

Gender Relations   As a Latin American country, Brazil has not been immune to the cultural influences of *machismo*—which refers to an aggressive and virile form of masculinity. The feminine counterpart of *machismo* is *marianismo*, the cult of the Virgin Mary that views Latin American women as morally superior to men and as the force that holds together the family and brings up the children. Across Latin America, these traditional images and self-images of women contributed to their political conservatism. Brazilian women traditionally voted in larger numbers for candidates of the right than did men.

Under the military dictatorship, women's traditional orientations toward politics began to change. For the middle and upper classes, political opportunity followed educational and occupational opportunities. The percentage of girls graduating from secondary school soared from almost a tenth in 1950 to nearly half in 1980. By the time of the transition to democracy in the early 1980s, more women than men were enrolled in Brazil's universities.

Military rule, coincidentally, also exercised an important economic impact on poor women. With the drop in the value of the minimum wage and the lack of adequate social services and urban infrastructure, women found it increasingly more difficult to perform their ascribed feminine roles of securing the welfare of their families and communities. As wives and mothers, they assumed the lead in their communities' struggles for health care and sanitation, and even against the rising cost of living.

Women's movements formed with the political liberalization of the mid-1970s. The regime initially viewed women's movements as apolitical and allowed them greater political space than labor movements. Feminist organizations soon grew to as many as 400, and the Brazilian women's movement became one of Latin America's most powerful. Women's movements injected into the national political debate several issues that had previously been considered private: reproductive rights, violence against women, and childcare.

Several recent policy developments signal a change in public attitudes about gender and politics. Political parties have adopted many concerns of the women's movement in their party programs. The Constitution replaced the concept of *pater familiae*—which attributes greater authority to the man as the head of a married couple—with the concept of equal and shared authority. To combat violence against women, city governments have created police precincts staffed entirely by female police officers to process complaints of rape and domestic violence. In 1991, the law absolving men of the murder of their wives when in the "legitimate defense of their honor" was abrogated. Under pressure from feminists, more than a dozen public hospitals introduced legal abortion services (for victims of rape). In 2001, the Congress approved a new civil code granting men and women equality in marriage and rendering children equal in rights and obligations regardless of the circumstances of their birth. In 2013, the Senate debated a bill that would decriminalize abortion in the first trimester of pregnancy (abortion is permitted only in cases of anencephaly and rape and when the life of the mother is in danger). Sixty-seven percent of Brazilians support abortion when the mother's health is in danger, compared to 80 percent in the United States and 51 percent in Mexico.[9]

Shifts in attitudes among both women and men produced these changes. Exposure to secondary and higher education and the workplace made women more likely to be interested in politics, want to vote, watch an electoral campaign, and identify with a political party (particularly a party on the left).[10] Brazilians generally display favorable attitudes toward women holding office, and in 2010, two-thirds of the first-round presidential vote went to two women, Dilma Rousseff of the PT and Marina Silva of the small Green Party. In 2009, only about three in ten believed that men make better leaders than women.[11]

Changing perceptions of gender roles have also spilled over to a national debate about same-sex marriage. The Supreme Court ruled in 2011 that same-sex couples are legally entitled to the same rights enjoyed by co-habitating heterosexual couples, including adoption access, pension and health benefits, inheritance tax, and joint property ownership. But in what is perhaps a sign of the shifting terrain of public opinion, in May 2013, the Senate human rights committee took up a measure that would bring legislation about civil unions in line with court rulings. Marriage equality nonetheless faces strong opposition from religious groups, including the powerful Pentecostal caucus in Congress.

Race and Racial Politics   Until recently, few people acknowledged that Brazil had a "race problem." For decades, they believed the official myth that, compared with the United States, beset by bigotry and race-related violence, Brazil had a "racial democracy." Drawing from Gilberto Freyre's classic thesis that Portuguese masters viewed their African slaves more favorably and treated them less harshly than in North America,[12] the myth claimed that widespread miscegenation had blurred the boundaries of racial identification and prevented the development of conflict based on a polarized racial consciousness. Brazilians believed that the absence of state-sponsored segregation and the social recognition of intermediate racial categories made their country more racially and culturally accommodating than other multiracial societies. Following from this analysis, they also believed that disadvantage was based on class, not race.

The myth notwithstanding, racial prejudice in Brazil is pervasive and not as subtle as many people believe. Although the predominantly white upper middle class generally believes in equal opportunities for Afrodescendants, many white Brazilians perpetuate stereotypes about Afrodescendants (including that they are sexually promiscuous, averse to thrift and work, and untrustworthy) and would not marry one.

Cultural movements of Afrodescendants date back to the 1940s, but racial prejudice, disadvantage, and outright repression during the military regime sparked the formation of new movements during the political opening. The Unified Black Movement against Racial Discrimination—the Movimento Negro Unificado—formed in 1978 to call attention to racism and the poor quality of life of Afrodescendants. Although it initially lacked the political success of other movements, in part due to the disparate nature of the movement and even police repression, it did raise a new racial consciousness among Afrodescendants. Its campaign for affirmative action quotas took root (see Box 15.1), and it shone a spotlight on extrajudicial police killings of Afrodescended youth.

How Democratic Are Brazilians?

Have the expansion of civil society, the presence of new subcultures, and other factors added up to any palpable changes in the national political culture of Brazil? In particular, is there any evidence that Brazil is developing a more democratic political culture?

On the one hand, Brazilians are less tolerant of authoritarianism than ever before. In the early 1970s, the public generally accepted the military's role in politics. By the late 1980s, Brazilians expressed a clear preference for democracy over dictatorship. Support for democracy has solidified even more since then, with growing numbers espousing the belief that democracy is the best form of government and rejecting the notion that democracy can exist without political parties (see Figure 15.4). Brazilians also reject the plebiscitarian variant of democracy that has appeal elsewhere in Latin America: Clear majorities disagreed that the people should govern directly (and not through elected representatives), that the voice of opposition parties should be limited, and that those who do not agree with the majority represent a threat to the country. Moreover, they resoundingly support government checks and balances; eighty-five percent oppose the president

---

BOX 15.1   Brazil's Controversial Racial Quotas

At the World Conference on Racism in South Africa in 2001, with the facts of racial disadvantage no longer in dispute, Brazil's government report recommended the adoption of quotas to expand the access of students of African descent to public universities. Soon thereafter, the governments of Rio de Janeiro and Bahia announced they would reserve 40 percent of the places in their state universities for Afrodescendants. The Foreign Ministry (Itamaraty) also launched an affirmative action program to support Afrodescendants preparing for the public service entrance exam. In 2012, President Rousseff signed a sweeping Law of Social Quotas, which required federal public universities to reserve half of their admission spots for students coming from public secondary schools and those of African descent in proportion to the racial makeups of their states. The number of black and mixed-race students in the public universities was expected to rise from 8,700 to 56,000.

Even after the Supreme Court unanimously upheld its constitutionality, the quota system remains controversial. Quotas are popular among the poor, regardless of race, but not among the well off. Overall, two-thirds of Brazilians polled in 2010 agreed that it was fair for public universities to reserve spaces for Afrodescendants (45 percent "strongly" agreed). However, 18 percent strongly disagreed. Those who disagreed were better educated, wealthier, and more likely to be white.

Supporters of quotas, like former president Lula, argue that only a strong affirmative action program will lift Afrodescendants from poverty and compensate for a legacy of disadvantage. They cite the difficulty in finding a black doctor, dentist, or bank manager. Opponents charge that quotas exacerbate prejudice, lead to reverse discrimination, and insult Afrodescendants by presuming they cannot compete on their own merits. These critics also question how easy it is to identify just who is an Afrodescendant in Brazil. Antiracism activists counter wryly that if self-identification does not work, "a policeman always knows."

Sources: Amy Erica Smith, "Who Supports Affirmative Action in Brazil?," *Americas Barometer Insights: 2010*, No. 49 (Nashville, TN: Vanderbilt University), www.americasbarometer.org; and Simon Romero, "Brazil Enacts Affirmative Action Law for Universities," *New York Times,* August 31, 2012.

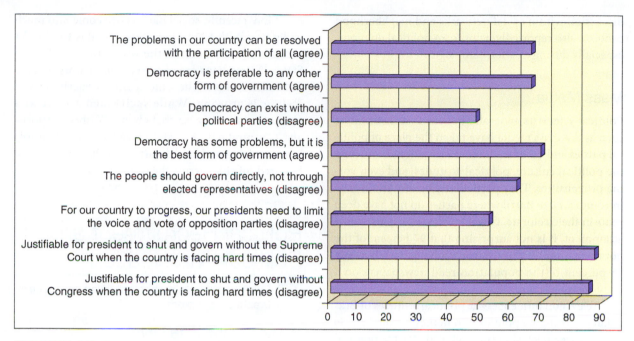

FIGURE 15.4

A Democratic Political Culture, 2012

Brazilians show strong support for representative and liberal democracy.

Source: Latin American Public Opinion Project (available at www.vanderbilt.edu/lapop).

shuttering Congress and the Supreme Court when the country is facing hard times.

On the other hand, if Brazilians are more committed to democracy today, they trust politicians, political parties, and democratic institutions less than ever. In a survey taken in São Paulo in June 2013, the percentage saying that the national Congress, political parties, and presidency had no prestige whatsoever was 42, 44, and 24 percent, respectively; this is up from 17, 22, and 9 percent a decade earlier.[13]

While such disenchantment with democratic institutions can be disturbing, the impatience of ordinary Brazilians appears to be less with the institutions than with the politicians occupying them. In particular, tolerance for corruption, already waning even before the 2005 *mensalão* vote-buying scandal involving the PT, has sunk even farther.[14] People are also demanding more responsive public policy. As such, an emerging culture of skepticism can be read as positive for strengthening the fabric of democracy.

In sum, there is little doubt that political culture in Brazil has changed in the past quarter century. People generally have grown more skeptical of hierarchy, less tolerant of corruption, and more supportive

of democracy. But this transformation is incomplete. Alongside the religious, feminist, and racial groups that have contributed to the democratization of civil society, other citizens who have not participated in these groups have been socialized in more traditional ways.

Political Learning

15.6 Identify the main sources of political socialization in Brazil.

In most countries, there is a consensus that a good deal of political learning takes place in such key social institutions as schools, the family, churches, and community groups. In Brazil, the first two of these institutions have traditionally been only weak agents of political socialization. The schools were poorly staffed and attended, and, until recently, much of the population did not stay in school past the third grade. In a context of extremely weak partisanship, moreover, families did not generally transmit political loyalties.

Religious, neighborhood, and workplace associations have been more significant sources of political socialization, especially in recent decades. Political discussion within social networks and neighborhood contexts also reportedly helps form political opinions, especially during election campaigns.[15]

Mass Media

Political scientists generally believe that institutions such as the mass media have taken the place of political parties and other traditional institutions in shaping the political culture, political attitudes, and even voting propensities. They particularly believe this is true in countries like Brazil where parties do not have deep roots in the electorate. Given low levels of educational attainment, it is not surprising that 97 percent of the population say they watch television regularly but only 25 percent of the population read newspapers on a daily basis.[16]

Television influences the political attitudes of Brazilians by bringing politics into homes via the *horário gratuito,* free television time set aside for the political parties to advertise their candidates and election messages. Moreover, free television time for candidates, televised debates, and television news shape voters' perceptions to a degree surpassed only by conversations with family and friends.[17]

The ownership of television and radio stations is extremely concentrated. The powerful Globo network, one of the largest networks in the world, commands the lion's share of the national audience, though the Brazilian Television System (SBT) and Record Network have been gaining ground in recent years. Most observers believe that the media, and particularly the Globo network, played a strong role in promoting the successful presidential candidacies of Fernando Collor de Mello in 1989 and Fernando Henrique Cardoso in 1994, both of whom defeated Lula in their respective elections. Globo was seen as hostile to the PT during this period, in part due to the strong antileftist views of its founder, Roberto Marinho. But with Marinho's death and Lula's accession to power (both in 2003), the network's coverage of the PT became more neutral.

State policy contributed to the politicization of the media. The Ministry of Communications notoriously awarded licenses for television and radio stations in return for political support. Politicians still use media empires in their home states to influence their coverage on local television and radio news and in major newspapers they own or control.

More recently, social media have come into much wider use. With 65 million users, Brazil is Facebook's second largest market in the world after the United States.[18] Brazilians are also frequent visitors to YouTube and Twitter. The time spent on Facebook and Twitter is growing. While social media serve as a venue for Brazilians to chat about TV shows, sports, and new products, they also played an important role in galvanizing and coordinating the 2013 protests in hundreds of cities across the country.

Political Recruitment and Political Participation

15.7 Describe the ways in which individuals participate in Brazil's political process.

Politics at the Elite Level

Elite Recruitment Traditionally, politics was elite dominated. Within the elite, recruitment took place within a small circle of political families. Typically, leading politicians were from landed families; schooled in law; served several terms of elective office as local councillor, state deputy, and eventually federal deputy; and built up their power base by joining the state Cabinet or becoming president of the state Legislative Assembly.

During the military regime, the structure of opportunity improved for the middle and upper middle classes. Technical credentials and competence became more broadly applied criteria for advancement, especially in the national Cabinet, federal and state bureaucracies, and public sector companies. The "technocrats" were by and large educated in engineering and economics in a few select universities.

With the political liberalization of the late authoritarian period and especially after the return to democracy, political recruitment patterns changed again. Technocratic expertise was still prized in the economic ministries, but politicians played a larger role in the political and social service ministries. Politics is now more open to representatives from diverse educational and class backgrounds, as evidenced by Lula's election in 2002. Although it is no longer necessary to belong to or be allied with an elite family to run for elective office, in some parts of Brazil and on some party labels, family connections can still be most helpful.

In running for reelection, incumbent deputies in Brazil have more of an advantage than in many Latin American countries but far less than in the United States. The turnover rate—that is, the percentage of deputies who did not occupy a seat in the previous Congress—was 45 percent in 2010. Although only about a quarter serve more than two consecutive terms, deputies are fairly adept at retaining their seats if they choose to run again. In 2010, 79 percent of the members of the lower house sought reelection; of these, 70 percent won back their seats.[19] The level and type of political experience of members of Congress also vary considerably along with their party label, reflecting their party's proximity to power.

How open is entry to the exclusive club of the Brazilian Congress? Women have gained many more seats than in earlier decades, when one or two at most were elected to the Congress. But progress has nonetheless been slow. In 1994, a breakthrough year, thirty-two women were elected as federal deputies and eighty-two as state deputies. That same year, five women were elected to the Senate. Although there have been flashes of success in the recruitment of women to high

office since then, overall progress in female representation in the corridors of political power has been slow. The presence of Brazilian women in elective office is also low compared with several other Latin American countries that have adopted effective quota laws and other affirmative action measures. In the 2011–2014 legislative session, for example, only 44 of the 513 federal deputies (8.6 percent) were women, despite a 1997 law that requires parties to award 30 percent of their candidacies to female aspirants to Congress. Parties typically fail to meet this legal requirement and have not been penalized for their inaction. Also, because the electoral system does not provide for an intraparty ranking of candidates (which virtually assures the election of the highest-ranked candidates on the slate), the increase in female candidates has not translated directly into a larger percentage of congresswomen. The overall result is that Brazil ranks 120th in the world, and second to last in Latin America, in terms of gender equity in the legislature.

The election of Brazil's first woman president notwithstanding (see Box 15.2), women are also underrepresented in top executive branch decision-making

---

BOX 15.2 Brazil's First Female President: Dilma Rousseff

Dilma Rousseff, the daughter of a Bulgarian immigrant, was born into an upper-middle-class family in 1947. Raised in a comfortable lifestyle, she attended traditional Catholic schools and had private French and piano lessons at home. As a high school student, she witnessed the military coup of 1964, an experience that awakened her politically. Like many other students from privileged backgrounds, Dilma joined a clandestine left-wing group fighting the dictatorship. Although she never participated in armed actions, members of her group robbed banks and fought the police. In 1970, Dilma was arrested and tortured by the military for twenty-one days. Sentenced to six years in prison, she was granted early release after three.

After finishing an economics degree, Dilma became a government bureaucrat in the Southern state of Rio Grande do Sul. During the democratic transition, she joined the PDT. Soon, Dilma was rising through the ranks of state and local government, holding positions such as

treasury secretary in the Porto Alegre city government and secretary of energy in the state government, and gaining a reputation as an excellent administrator. Dilma joined Lula's PT in 2000. After the PT captured the presidency in 2002, she became minister of Mines and Energy. Dilma's management skills won Lula's admiration; in 2005, he promoted her to presidential chief of staff and began grooming her as his successor. Despite never having run for office and only recently joining the PT, she effectively campaigned for and won the presidency in 2010.

Taking office in 2011, she soon began to step out of Lula's shadow. She broke with Lula's support of Iran, sacked ministers implicated in corruption scandals, and articulated a vision for national development that includes educating 100,000 scientists and engineers abroad. Although her approval ratings slid temporarily during the 2013 protests, her reelection chances will likely ride on the capacity of the Brazilian economy to rebound in 2014.

posts, the judicial system, and the diplomatic corps. During his entire presidency, Cardoso (1995–2002) appointed only two women to serve in Cabinet positions. In 2007, only 14 percent of Lula's Cabinet ministers were female, compared to the Latin American average of 24 percent. Today, 26 percent of ministers (including those heading Cabinet offices as well as secretariats and offices with ministerial status) are women, including the president's chief of staff, the highest-ranking member of the Cabinet. In 2000, a woman was appointed to the Supreme Court for the first time in history (today there are two), despite the fact that 29 percent of candidates who pass public examinations to become judges are women. In 2007, only 15 of Brazil's 166 diplomatic missions abroad (9 percent) were headed by women.

Consistent with the characterization of the UN Special Rapporteur on Racial Disadvantage of the "almost all-white corridors of political power," only forty-three deputies and two senators (less than 8 percent of the Congress) self-identified as Afrodescendants in 2013.[20] As part of a deliberate effort to open the process of elite political recruitment, Lula named four Afrodescendants to his Cabinet and appointed the country's first Afrodescended Supreme Court justice. The Supreme Court and the Ministry of Justice introduced racial quotas for staff employment.

Elite Orientations The Brazilian elite is generally not divided along economic, religious, or ethnic lines. It is more "moderate" than its counterparts elsewhere in Latin America. The business community supported the military coup of 1964 in an unstable economy. In the 1970s, facing an autocratic regime, many business leaders preferred a return to democracy. In the 1990s, most military and business leaders, public administrators, and members of the press identified themselves as "centrist" in their ideological orientation. They gave the democratic regime from 1985 to 1990 higher marks for establishing a viable political structure for the country, and they downgraded military governments for failing to raise the international prestige of the country, promote educational development, and reduce regional and social inequalities.[21]

Elites are predictably far less preoccupied with unemployment, health care, and drugs than respondents earning the minimum salary. They are, however, the *most* concerned about education and income concentration.

Politics at the Mass Level

Citizen Politics During the latter part of the military regime, Brazilians began to associate in civil society groups as they never had before. The combination of the easing of repression and the increased freedom of information, together with the continued authoritarian nature of decision making and the lack of genuine representation from formal political institutions and political parties, helped new social movements flourish. In addition to the women's movements and grassroots church groups discussed earlier, thousands of neighborhood associations emerged. These were the most explicitly political of all social movements in the waning years of the military dictatorship. They demanded, generally successfully, state regulation of real estate firms in their neighborhoods and state goods and services. In just the southern city of Porto Alegre, 540 neighborhood associations and 51 housing cooperatives emerged within a decade.[22]

In the early 1990s, only about one-third of Brazilians did *not* belong to a voluntary association; one-fifth belonged to three or more. Many were not formally political. In 2006, 13 percent of respondents to the National Election Study reported that they or someone in their household belonged to a labor union. Significant numbers were members of professional associations (8.6 percent) or social movements (8.7 percent), rates that were much higher than in other Latin American countries. A Latin American Public Opinion Project (LAPOP) survey in March–April 2012 (a year before the outbreak of mass protests in June 2013) found that 15.4 percent of the respondents had signed a petition and 10.8 percent had used social media such as Twitter or Facebook to circulate political information. The same survey found that 26 percent of Brazilians had participated in a neighborhood or community association in the past year, and that 63 percent had participated in a church or religious organization.[23]

Employing a variety of strategies—participating in government, enlisting international allies, and engaging in direct action—citizens have organized movements around various identities, single issues, and political and social rights. Indigenous organizations are but one example of citizen groups to emerge around the globe in the late twentieth century on the basis of identity—that is, organized around who people *are* rather than what they *produce*. After military development projects threatened the extinction of several of Brazil's indigenous tribes, these tribes organized nearly fifty citizen groups in the 1980s. Most were in the North, with twenty-three of them in the state of Amazonas.[24] Their efforts won constitutional protections for Indian lands and the collective rights of Indian nations, an impressive accomplishment given the small number of Indians in Brazil and their fragmentation into different tribes.

Citizen environmental groups have also been effective at enlisting international allies. Local and regional environmental organizations mobilized in the late 1980s to influence the new Constitution and the 1992 global summit on the environment held in Rio de Janeiro. Brazil's environmental movement has scored important achievements in the areas of controlling pesticides, nuclear waste and production, and the emission of chlorofluorocarbons. Somewhat paradoxically, environmental organizations have been slower to appear, less active, and less visible in the Amazon region than in the rest of Brazil. Rather, action on environmental issues of the Amazon region has been driven by indigenous groups and rubber tappers. Using tactics of direct confrontation, they effectively influenced international lenders, such as the World Bank, to establish environmental protection as a condition for aid.[25]

The tactics of direct confrontation are also used by the **Movement of Landless Rural Workers (MST)**, one of the most vibrant social movements in Latin America today. Adhering to the slogan "agrarian reform—by law or by disorder," landless families in the MST have effectively gained access to government-owned or unproductive private land that they have seized. The MST has also pressured the formal political system, including the courts (where it seeks legal title to land), and has staged disruptive and sometimes spectacular protests. Its members have occupied federal and state government buildings and roads in as many as twenty states. Brazilians are generally sympathetic to the occupation of land as a legitimate tactic to combat hunger and misery when it is carried out without violence. Of late, although people blame the government (more than landowners and the MST) for rural violence and favor shifting agrarian reform to the purview of the federal government, they generally believe that land invasions have a negative impact on agrarian reform negotiations and weaken democracy.[26]

Today, perhaps the most important avenues of citizen political participation are through nongovernmental organizations (NGOs). A worldwide phenomenon, NGOs are private groups, normally well funded and institutionalized, that often assume public functions. They may help implement health care, investigate ways to privatize national pension systems, press for civil rights for Afrodescendants, or monitor government compliance with environmental accords. Brazil's NGOs are part of a thriving nonprofit sector in the country. Of the 290,000 registered NGOs and philanthropic foundations, fully half were created in the past ten years. Nearly one-third of these organizations operate in the area of rights-based approaches to development.[27]

Mass Political Participation The sheer number of Brazilians participating in politics today is staggering, especially compared with earlier in the twentieth century, when less than 5 percent of adults voted in presidential elections. In 1960, only a third of the voting-age population turned out to vote for president. After the enfranchisement of illiterates in 1985 and the award of the franchise to sixteen-year-olds in 1988, four-fifths of adults voted in the 1989 presidential election. These high levels have continued to the present.

Today, Brazilians are among the most participatory citizens in Latin America—they turn out to vote and join civil organizations at higher rates, and participate in protests at a rate almost double the Latin American average. In 2010, some 82 percent of registered voters cast valid ballots (in the United States, just over 58 percent of the age-eligible population participated in the 2012 presidential election). Although voting in Brazil is mandatory and there are potential penalties for noncompliance, these are rarely enforced, and participation rates are still higher than in other countries with compulsory voting. Brazilians also show interest in politics, sign petitions, participate in community events and political campaigns, and attend party and neighborhood association meetings at comparatively high levels relative to advanced and emerging democracies around the world (see Figure 15.5). In 2012, just under 5 percent of Brazilians reported having participated in a demonstration. That was before millions took to the streets in the wave of 2013 protests. More respondents to a São Paulo survey (77 percent) supported the demonstrators than

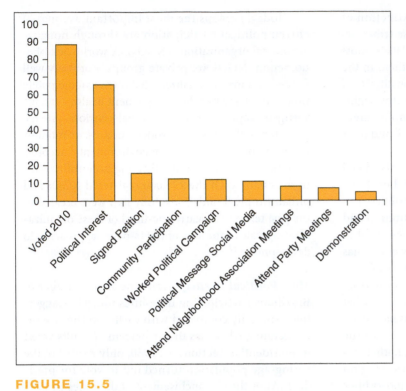

FIGURE 15.5

Political Participation in Brazil, 2012

Brazilians turn out to vote, attend community and party meetings, and protest at robust rates.

Source: Latin American Public Opinion Project (available at www.vanderbilt.edu/lapop).

favored direct elections in 1984 (71 percent) or advocated the impeachment of President Collor in 1992 (43 percent), the subjects of the two most important prior waves of protest in Brazil.

These spectacular instances of mass mobilization aside, since the 1990s, one of the most important forms of citizen political involvement has been through **participatory budgeting**. Participatory budgeting is a process in which hundreds or thousands of citizens meet in a series of open assemblies in order to establish spending priorities before the legislative budget cycle begins. Elected delegates negotiate the budget with state bureaucrats and monitor the previous year's spending and investment priorities. The idea is to allocate a share of public resources to reflect citizen priorities, not the political criteria of a notoriously clientelistic political system.

The results are very promising. In Porto Alegre, the percentage of the public budget available for investment rose almost immediately from 2 percent in 1989 to 20 percent in 1994. Running water and sewerage were quickly extended to 98 percent of all city residences. Participatory budgeting earned high marks from international agencies for enhancing the transparency of the budgeting process and for creating institutions of good governance. Students of democracy have also praised it for encouraging popular participation (particularly among the poor), strengthening civil society, and, ultimately, enhancing democracy in Brazil.

Participatory budgeting institutions are only one among a number of other councils, conferences, and venues for citizen participation. Health councils bring together representatives of the state, service providers, and representatives of the population with the legal mandate to formulate and implement health policies. By 2002, such councils were in place in 98 percent of Brazil's cities. Community organizations also have the right to veto city master plans.

These citizens' groups have increased the transparency of government and popular input into public policy. Have they contributed to more extensive and informed political participation than that channeled through long-established interest groups and political parties?

Interest Groups

15.8 List five types of interest groups that influence politics in Brazil.

Traditionally, political interests in Brazil have been organized and represented differently from those in liberal democracies, where plural and voluntary groups are the basic unit of interest group activity. In Brazil, interest groups came under state control during the Vargas era in a system known as **corporatism**.[28] Under corporatist law, modeled after the labor codes of fascist Italy, interest groups were defined in economic terms, recognized and funded by the state, and granted a legal representational monopoly in their area of activity. But in return, unions gave up their independence from the government.

The creation of new independent interest groups and the transformation of old ones from instruments of authoritarian social control to pressure groups in a democratic society are as important as any change in Brazilian politics of the last quarter century. Alongside labor unions and business and agrarian associations, single-issue interest groups have become effective lobbies for environmental and consumer protection.

Labor Unions

For labor unions, cooperation with state authorities during the corporatist era initially gained them recognition, institutions for setting wages and resolving disputes with employers, and benefits and social services for their members that they had been unable to secure by negotiating directly with firm owners. Under military rule, labor organizations were shackled, their elected leaders were removed and at times jailed, and strikes were brutally repressed for a decade.

Changes within Brazil's unions during the period of military rule began to break down corporatist structures. In the 1970s, a new generation of union leaders began to shun the old strategy of compromise with government representatives. Instead, these new activists adopted a more combative stance toward the state and, with the support of their own rank and file, toward their employers as well. The most famous of these leaders was Lula. As the head of the São Bernardo metalworkers union in the late 1970s, he led the highest-profile strikes in the modern era.

With the transition to democracy, labor staged general strikes in 1986, 1987, and 1989. It also successfully lobbied to have its interests represented in the Constitution. Article 8 grants freedom of union association. Public employees won the right to form unions, and workers were guaranteed the right to strike. Lifting the lid on union formation led to a proliferation of union organizations, especially among agricultural workers. The 2011 edition of the household survey conducted by the Brazilian Institute of Geography and Statistics (IBGE) estimated that 17.2 percent of the labor force was now unionized, down slightly from the record high of 18.6 percent in 2006.

Since the mid-1980s, labor unions have pressed the interests of their members through central organizations such as the **Central Única dos Trabalhadores (CUT)** that have eclipsed their corporatist predecessors. These central organizations advocate union independence from state authorities and are willing to forgo state financing and protection in exchange for the right to bargain collectively with their employers at the firm level and with employers' associations. The CUT draws much of its strength from the metalworkers unions (which include the autoworkers) and white-collar and public sector workers; geographically, it draws from the industrial heartland of the Southeast.

In the past twenty years, unions such as the Union of Metallurgical Workers and the Union of Bank Workers, both of the state of São Paulo, have grown more powerful than ever. The labor lobby, the **Departamento Intersindical de Assessoria Parlamentar (DIAP)**, is one of the most influential voices in Brasília. Labor unions had a "block" of sixty deputies in Congress in the late 2000s, which was larger than the delegations of a dozen political parties. Middle-class labor unions, especially those in the public sector, were key players in the battles over state reform.

Business Associations

Business associations were also formally organized into state federations of industry and commerce. Unlike labor, during the dictatorship, private sector elites enjoyed informal access to the president, to Cabinet heads, and to the heads of state-owned industries and banks. When entrepreneurs found that their access was closed, the business community became convinced that a reduction in state authority was necessary.

Since 1985, business leaders have engaged in several types of interest group activity—most notably election campaigns, lobbying, and collective bargaining—that they had abandoned during two decades of military rule. Like labor, industrialists attempted to influence the 1987–1988 National Constituent Assembly. However, business groups lost out to labor unions on many key issues in the constitutional convention. The 1988 Constitution severely restricted foreign investment and granted generous labor rights and privileges (although the restrictions on foreign investment were lifted in 1995). It also provided a 120-day paid maternity leave, a paternity leave, paid holidays, and the bonus known as the thirteenth-month salary. Even people who might applaud strengthening the rights of workers and working-class families agree that the Constitution imposed financial burdens on employers and the state that Brazil could not afford.

Business organizations may have only weakly represented business interests, especially relative to labor, because business was initially slower to reform its constraining corporatist structures. Since the 1990s, however, business has played catch-up, creating new organizations and turning its corporatist associations into interest groups to better promote and protect its economic interests. It has shifted its lobbying efforts from the executive to the legislative branch. The powerful National Confederation of Commerce (CNI), for instance, formed an advisory group for legislative affairs that circulates information about the legislative agenda in business outlets.[29] The most powerful business federations—especially the giant **Federation of Industries of the State of São Paulo (FIESP)**, which represents 100,000 firms employing 2 million workers[30]—have won favorable trade and pension policies, but have not been effective in securing lower corporate taxes.

Brazilian economic elites do not predominantly rely on one or two political parties of the right to defend their interests, as they do in some other countries. Rather, they hedge their bets and almost always support individual candidates rather than entire parties.[31] Even the PT, born of labor unrest and with strong Marxist tendencies in the 1980s, has received important private sector support since Lula captured the presidency in 2003.

Agrarian Elites

Traditionally, associations of landowners were the most powerful associations in Brazil. Rural societies all over the country are still independent of the state. Agricultural elites also have a network of sectoral federations—such as the Federation of Sugar Industries—that belong to the official system of interest representation. The representatives of these associations have served on the boards of state agencies charged with overseeing public policy, such as the Institute for Sugar and Alcohol, which helped to design Brazil's ambitious program to substitute sugarcane-derived alcohol for imported petroleum.

During the debates in the Constituent Assembly over land reform, the National Confederation of Agriculture and a new independent, radical right-wing group, the Ruralist Democratic Union (UDR), lobbied Congress. Large landowners organized public demonstrations to defeat an amendment to the Constitution that would have enacted a national program of agrarian reform. They mounted an antireform campaign in the press; attempted to influence members of the major

political parties, the president, and the military; and committed much violence in the countryside. The issue was thrown back to the state legislatures, where the power of agrarian elites appeared to have quietly killed the measure, at least until the Landless Movement forced it back onto the political agenda in the mid-1990s.

Since then, landowners have been effectively represented in the legislature by the "Rural Caucus" (Bancada Ruralista), known more formally as the **Frente Parlamentar da Agropecuária (FPA)** (Parliamentary Front for Agricultural and Livestock Production). In 2013, the size of this caucus reached a quarter of the Chamber of Deputies and a sixth of the Senate.[32] FPA members effectively protected the rights of large landowners in the new Forest Code promulgated in 2012. In 2013, FPA proposed a new constitutional amendment that would transfer from the presidency to the Congress the power to demarcate protected indigenous lands. In recent years, the Rural Caucus has ushered legislation through Congress that has slowed the review of occupied property (a prerequisite to expropriation), speeded compensation for expropriated lands, made more stringent the size and productivity thresholds for expropriation, and classified land occupation as a "heinous crime and act of terrorism."[33]

The Consumer Lobby

A web of civic organizations in various states has worked for consumer rights by raising public awareness of consumer issues and lobbying the government. The most prominent of these is the Brazilian **Institute for the Defense of the Consumer (IDEC)**. The IDEC has been active in a number of areas, including monitoring rate hikes in privatized public services and utilities, especially electric energy. Notably, it successfully pressed Brazil to become the first country in the world to prohibit the planting and marketing of genetically modified foods, most notably soybeans (Brazil is the world's second-largest producer of soy behind the United States, which permits the planting of genetically modified soy).

The Military

Paradoxically, the military is one of the most powerful but one of the least effective interest groups in Brazil today. Upon exiting from government in 1985, it retained more prerogatives—and conceded less civilian authority to supervise its expenditures, arms procurements, and control over its internal affairs—than most other militaries in the world. It also succeeded in preserving a controversial provision of the Constitution. Article 142 authorizes the armed forces to "guarantee the constitutional powers and, by initiative of any of these, law and order," which the military interprets as authorizing it to depose elected governments when law and order are threatened.

Despite its past capacity to frighten civilians, the military appears to be less and less capable of defending its interests. In the early 1990s, armed with a powerful mandate as Brazil's first elected president in nearly three decades and backed by emboldened legislators, Fernando Collor de Mello significantly trimmed military spending from its 1990 level (20.5 percent of the budget) to just over 14 percent.[34] Total defense outlays fell sharply from 2.7 percent of GDP in 1989 to only 1.5 percent in 1992.[35] Salaries fell, equipment aged, and morale sagged; many officers had to moonlight to get by. The situation has changed little over the past two decades. In 2012, despite much-improved government finances, Brazil still spent only 1.5 percent of GDP on the armed forces, compared to 2 percent in China, 2.5 percent in India, and 4.4 percent in Russia.

As military prestige and budgets have declined, the capacity of the armed forces to influence national policy on claims of national security also appears to have waned. For decades, military organization, training, and ideology were shaped by the Cold War and the perceived need to fight subversion within Brazil's own borders. With redemocratization, the military tried to reorient its mission toward external defense, particularly of the northern frontier and the Amazon's natural resources. Fearing the "internationalization of the Amazon," it built military airstrips, garrisons, and outposts as well as roads. The military also conducted agricultural and colonization projects along a vast stretch of the Amazon region as part of a project known as Calha Norte. For a while, the military resisted national and international pressure to reserve a continuous stretch of land along the Venezuelan border for the Yanomami Indians. It also resisted external assistance that required foreign monitoring of national compliance with "debt-for-nature" swaps. These swaps involve an international environmental group buying a portion of a country's debt in world financial markets, and then forgiving this debt in exchange for

setting aside matching funds for a particular environmental project. Eventually, the government reserved 94 million hectares for the Yanomami, left virtually unfunded the Calha Norte project, and reversed the country's opposition to debt-for-nature swaps. Although civilian interests prevailed in each case, much of the officer corps still clings to the view that the Amazon is Brazil's soft underbelly and that "foreign interests" have designs on the region.[36]

In recent years, the military also attempted to thwart various human rights initiatives by the Cardoso and Lula administrations, especially those revisiting torture and disappearances of political prisoners under the 1964–1985 military regime. An "Amnesty Law" passed in 1979 pardoned all crimes of a political nature committed after the coup of 1964, including both human rights abuses committed by military officers and violent acts by the left-wing guerrillas who took up arms against the dictatorship. Consequently, Brazil neither put military officers on trial (as did Argentina) nor established a "truth commission" (as did Peru and Chile) immediately after the transition to democracy. However, in 1995, the Cardoso administration formally recognized the responsibility of the Brazilian state for abuses after 1964. This made it legally possible for the state to pay reparations to former political prisoners and also to the survivors of the murdered and disappeared.

The Lula government went further, expanding the reparations program and awarding posthumous pardons to army officers who had left their posts to join the left-wing opposition in the 1960s. Meanwhile, human rights activists stepped up their efforts to revisit past abuses, filing repeated lawsuits claiming that the 1979 Amnesty Law did not protect torturers. In April 2010, the Supreme Court held in a 7-to-2 vote that the Amnesty Law was indeed a "two-way" amnesty that had been properly negotiated with the opposition during the dictatorship, and that torture was in fact a "political crime" covered by the statute. At the same time, however, the Court strongly recommended full disclosure of secret military files and a full airing of past crimes, along the lines of the Truth Commission proposals.

Within weeks of her presidential inauguration in 2011, Dilma Rousseff—who had been tortured by the security services as a 22-year-old and who had lost numerous friends to military repression—took up the issue of **transitional justice** as a personal cause. A Truth Commission with investigatory but not punitive powers was finally approved by Congress in November

The Truth Commission: Coming to Terms with the Authoritarian Past
All living presidents of Brazil meet at the Palácio do Planalto on May 16, 2012, for the swearing-in ceremony of the National Truth Commission. The commission was given two years to provide a full report on human rights abuses under the military dictatorship of 1964–1985. By standing shoulder to shoulder with her predecessors, President Rousseff aimed to show that transitional justice is not just the policy of a single administration but a long-term goal of the Brazilian state. Left to right: Presidents Collor, Sarney, Lula, Dilma, and Cardoso.

2011. The Commission was formally installed in May 2012 in an emotional ceremony in which Dilma was symbolically flanked by all four of her living predecessors (Sarney, Collor, Cardoso, and Lula) in an eye-opening depiction of the increasing political maturity of Brazilian democracy. The Commission was given two years to complete its work and will report publicly while Dilma is still president.

Conclusion

The proliferation of citizens' groups and the strengthening of interest groups that are autonomous from the state in Brazil diminished arbitrary state authority and the underlying foundations of authoritarianism. Yet the advance of civil society has also carried a danger and a trade-off. The danger is that citizen groups, NGOs, and organized interest groups may have outstripped the capacity of Brazil's political institutions to process their demands, or they may at least give that impression. The trade-off is that the gains of *participatory* democracy have been achieved at the price of a decline in *representative* democracy. In the sections that follow, we examine the institutions of representative democracy.

Political Parties and Elections

15.9 Discuss political party dynamics and Brazil's electoral system.

Traditionally, political parties in Brazil have been ephemeral, lacking in cohesion and discipline, and the party system has been highly fragmented. Until recently, traditional local bosses and the practice of clientelism dominated most parties. Few parties had ideologies or even programs of government. Politicians changed parties frequently and without penalty, eroding accountability. Not surprisingly, the parties did not lay deep roots in the electorate, and voters often cast ballots for different parties from one election to the next.

Many politicians and analysts claim that weak parties are at the core of many governance problems in Brazil today. But others contend that in the 1990s, the party system stabilized, party discipline rose, and parties developed distinctive ideological orientations and positions on a range of policy issues.[37] The one party that everyone agreed was different, the Workers' Party, was tarnished by the 2005 *mensalão* vote-buying scheme that led to major Supreme Court trials in 2012. The scandal made manifest just how high the hurdles were to creating truly responsible parties.

Historic Strains of Clientelism and Personalism

Brazil's parties were traditionally elite dominated and formed around personalities, not particular issues. In the early twentieth century, when elites in other Latin American countries were organizing competition within their own ranks, elites in each Brazilian state had their own Republican Party and intrastate monopolies on power. State oligarchies were supported by powerful local bosses, usually the largest landowners, who had their own militias, controlled local judicial officials, and shepherded their followers to the polls and told them which candidate to vote for. In exchange for delivering votes to the state elite, the local boss secured for his municipality roads, employment, and other resources. And for himself, he gained the power that came from the exclusive right to appoint all powerful posts in his jurisdiction. This system of traditional clientelism was known as **coronelismo** (for the *coroneis*, or colonels, whose forebears once held the rank of local commander in the National Guard).

The postwar party system divided along pro- and anti-Vargas lines. Vargas' supporters formed the elite Social Democratic Party (PSD) and the mass-based PTB. Vargas' opponents joined the National Democratic Union (UDN). The PTB espoused a vague platform of nationalism and populism. But, generally, parties lacked guiding ideologies. Party organizations represented loose agglomerations of patronage networks headed by state and local politicians. Local political bosses used the control of public appointments and urban-based political machines to hold onto power when people moved from the countryside to the cities. The growth of the electorate and the expansion of the state into new areas of regulation and distribution made clientelism as pervasive as ever.

In 1965, the military transformed the multiparty system into a two-party system. Most UDN and PSD politicians joined the progovernment ARENA; most PTB representatives joined the opposition MDB. The two-party system worked for a while. But voters began to identify more closely with the opposition beginning with the 1974 election. To hold onto votes, the military stepped up spending for agricultural credit, low-income housing, and basic sanitation programs.[38] In 1979, it also eased the restrictions on the formation of political parties in order to split the advancing MDB. ARENA leaders formed the Democratic Social Party (PDS), and MDB leaders formed the **Party of the Brazilian Democratic Movement (PMDB)**. Other, smaller parties were formed by competing currents within the opposition. After the transition to democracy, Brazil's communist parties were legalized and many more parties were formed.

Brazil's Contemporary Party System

The party system today is broadly representative of a wider range of ideological positions. Parties of the left, which won only 9 percent of the legislative seats in 1986, elected 37 percent of Congress in 2010. Members of the centrist and rightist parties won 27.1 and 35.9 percent of the seats, respectively (see Figure 15.6).

Brazil's party system remains one of the most fragmented in the world, despite the efforts of reformers to reduce the number of parties represented in Congress. A 1995 law stipulated that parties would have to receive 5 percent of the valid vote nationwide (and a minimum of 2 percent of the vote in at least nine states) in order to function as a congressional caucus, receive public financing of party activities, and have free television time during campaigns. The implementation of this "barrier clause" finally occurred after the 2006 elections. Small parties immediately protested to the Supreme Court, which struck the law down as unconstitutional. As a result, twenty parties entered parliament in 2007, rather than the seven that would have qualified under the rejected statute. There is currently no minimum percentage of the vote required for legislative representation.

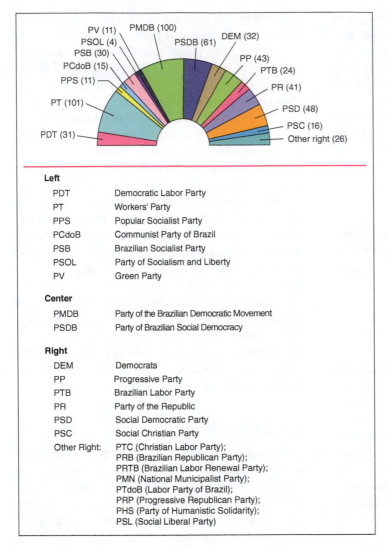

PV (11)   PMDB (100)
PSOL (4)   DEM (32)
PSB (30)   PSDB (61)
PCdoB (15)   PP (43)
PPS (11)   PTB (24)
                                            PR (41)
PT (101)   PSD (48)
                                          PSC (16)
PDT (31)   Other right (26)

Left

PDT	Democratic Labor Party
PT	Workers' Party
PPS	Popular Socialist Party
PCdoB	Communist Party of Brazil
PSB	Brazilian Socialist Party
PSOL	Party of Socialism and Liberty
PV	Green Party

Center

| PMDB | Party of the Brazilian Democratic Movement |
| PSDB | Party of Brazilian Social Democracy |

Right

DEM	Democrats
PP	Progressive Party
PTB	Brazilian Labor Party
PR	Party of the Republic
PSD	Social Democratic Party
PSC	Social Christian Party
Other Right:	PTC (Christian Labor Party); PRB (Brazilian Republican Party); PRTB (Brazilian Labor Renewal Party); PMN (National Municipalist Party); PTdoB (Labor Party of Brazil); PRP (Progressive Republican Party); PHS (Party of Humanistic Solidarity); PSL (Social Liberal Party)

FIGURE 15.6

Party Representation in the Brazilian Congress, July 2013

Brazil's ideologically diverse multiparty system is broadly representative of society, but makes forming governing coalitions in the Congress imperative.

Although many parties contest legislative elections, all five presidential elections since 1994 have been fought basically between the PT and the PSDB (see below for party profiles). Whereas the share of congressional seats jointly held by these two parties has hovered around 30 percent in the five elections from 1994 to 2010, the joint share of the first-round presidential vote given to the PT and PSDB candidates has ranged from 70 to 90 percent. To deal with a very fragmented Congress, PT and PSDB presidents have successfully built multiparty coalition cabinets

typically ranging in size from five to ten parties.

The Left

The most important leftist party is the PT. For two decades, the PT was perceived as a genuine labor party and a genuinely different party on the Brazilian political landscape. Its representatives voted the party line, did not switch to other parties, and did not promise to be brokers of clientelistic benefits. The party's congressional delegation was composed largely of intellectuals and workers. By 2002, however, the party had moved beyond its initial base, in the industrial unions of São Paulo, in the landless rural workers' movement, and among Catholic activists, toward the political center. This more moderate PT elected Lula president in 2002, along with three governors, ninety-one deputies, and fourteen senators. At least temporarily, the PT was the largest party in Congress.

About three in ten PT members consider themselves to be radicals. Some of these left-wing party activists and members of Congress became disgruntled with Lula's decisions in 2003 to invite parties of the center and right into his Cabinet, continue conservative monetary policies, and work to pass an unpopular social security reform. Several, like Senator Heloísa Helena, openly defied the president, for which they were promptly expelled from the party. The PT delegation shrank to eighty-one in 2005, when the cash-for-votes scandal came to light. The economic recovery in the mid-2000s, and Lula's remarkable personal popularity, allowed the party to rebound in the 2006 elections. In 2010, the PT won eighty-eight seats in the Chamber of Deputies and eleven of the fifty-four contested Senate seats, as well as five state governorships (see Table 15.1).

In 2005, Helena and other defectors formed the Socialism and Liberty Party (PSOL). The PSOL favors a sharp change in course, including slashing interest rates. It won only three seats in the lower house and two in the Senate in 2010. Other parties of the left

TABLE 15.1
Election Results, 2010
The four largest parties control half the seats in Congress and three-fourths of the state governorships.

Parties	Chamber of Deputies (seats)		Senate (seats)[a]		Congress[b]		Governors' Races
	#	Percent	#	Percent	Cumulative	Percent	#
PT Workers' Party	88	17.2	11	20.4	101	16.8	5
PMDB Party of the Brazilian Democratic Movement	79	15.4	16	29.6	98	16.7	5 —
PSDB Party of Brazilian Social Democracy	53	10.3	5	9.3	63	10.8	8 —
DEM Democrats	43	8.4	2	3.7	51	8.3	2 —
PP Progressive Party	41	8.0	4	7.4	46	7.7	—
PR Party of the Republic	42	8.2	3	5.6	46	7.7	—
PSB Brazilian Socialist Party	34	6.6	3	5.6	37	6.3	6 —
PDT Democratic Labor Party	28	5.5	2	3.7	32	5.4	—
PTB Brazilian Labor Party	21	4.1	1	1.9	27	4.5	—
PSC Christian Social Party	17	3.3	1	1.9	18	3.0	—
PCdoB Communist Party of Brazil	15	2.9	1	1.9	17	2.9	—
PV Green Party	15	2.9	—	—	15	2.5	—
PPS Popular Socialist Party	12	2.3	1	1.9	13	2.2	—
Minor parties[c]	25	4.9	4	7.4	30	5.1	1
Total	513	100	54	100	594	100	27

[a]Results only for the two-thirds of the Senate, or fifty-four seats, that were up for election in 2010.
[b]Total congressional delegation, comprising all eighty-one senators (including the twenty-seven seats that were filled in 2006 and were not up for reelection in 2010), plus all deputies elected. This excludes the new PSD, which was created only after the elections, and which is shown in Figure 15.6.
[c]PSOL (Socialism and Liberty Party), PTC (Christian Labor Party), PRB (Brazilian Republican Party), PRTB (Brazilian Labor Renewal Party), PTdoB (Labor Party of Brazil); PRP (Progressive Republican Party), PHS (Party of Humanistic Solidarity), and PSL (Social Liberal Party).
Source: Tribunal Superior Eleitoral (available at www.tse.gov.br).

include the **Brazilian Socialist Party (PSB)**, which won thirty-seven seats in Congress and six governorships in 2010, and the **Democratic Labor Party (PDT)**, which won thirty seats in the Chamber and Senate. Both parties refrained from nominating presidential candidates in 2010, preferring instead to support the PT candidate, Dilma Rousseff.

The Center

In the center of the political spectrum lies the PMDB. The PMDB is the largest party, with eighty deputies, twenty senators, and five governors. The party has no clear ideology and is organized as a loose federation of regional party branches run by political bosses. The **Party of Brazilian Social Democracy (PSDB)** broke off from the PMDB in 1988. Formed by several respected leaders of the PMDB, including Cardoso, the PSDB began as a center-left party. When the party was in government, however, it advanced an agenda of market reforms and moved to the right. In 1998, its best election, the PSDB elected the second-largest congressional delegation, the largest number of state governors, and the president. Today, it is the third-largest party in Congress, and eight states are led by PSDB governors. All of its presidential candidates since 1989 have been major political figures in the state of São Paulo, where the party has controlled the state government without interruption since 1994.

The Right

The most prominent party on the right of the Brazilian political spectrum is known simply as **Democrats (DEM)**. Called the Party of the Liberal Front (PFL) until 2007, it was formed in 1985 by defectors from the PDS—former supporters of the military regime. It held the vice presidency during the Cardoso government, and has been allied with the PSDB in almost all elections since 1994. In 2010, it elected only two state governors, but it had the fourth-largest delegation in Congress, with fifty-one members. In the Lula–Dilma years, the senior DEM leadership provided the most vociferous opposition to the PT. However, tensions caused by the party's long period in opposition led one faction of the DEM, organized by former São Paulo mayor Gilberto Kassab, to defect and form the new **Social Democratic Party (PSD)** in 2011. Despite the conservative origins of its founders, this new party maneuvered quietly to support President Dilma and formally entered her coalition in 2013.

Another significant conservative party is the **Progressive Party (PP)**, a probusiness, proeconomic reform party also with roots in the PDS. Other parties on the right include the PTB and the **Party of the Republic (PR)**. The PTB, which was re-formed in the wake of the 1979 party reform law, has seen its share of legislative seats shrink steadily over the years to less than 5 percent. It absorbed two minor parties after the 2006 election. The PR resulted from the merger of the Liberal Party (PL), once a probusiness party that later allied with the PT government and suffered from the corruption scandal that engulfed the government, and the rightist Party for the Reconstruction of National Order (PRONA). Several very small parties on the right remain, including some ultraconservative ones. Parties of the right have opposed agrarian reform and the liberalization of abortion laws, and tend to adopt a strong law-and-order stance. While the PFL/DEM party has been consistent in its ideology and in its long-time alliance with the PSDB, the smaller center-right parties such as the PP, PTB, and PR have been politically opportunistic, supporting both the Cardoso (PSDB) and Lula (PT) governments in recent years. Tellingly, most of the legislators involved in the 2005 *mensalão* scandal were members of these three parties. Whereas combined parties of the left increased their share of the vote from 20 percent in 1995 to 37 percent in 2010, parties of the right have seen their share decrease in the same period from nearly 45 percent to 36 percent.

Social Cleavages and Voting

For several years, the most important social cleavage in Brazil was territorial. Brazil had two electorates. One, which resided in the large, metropolitan areas of the Southeast and South, was more aware of the issues and more likely to vote for candidates on the basis of the issues. The other, located in the smaller, poorer, less industrialized, predominantly rural counties of the Northeast and Center-West, cast votes for strong personalities and in exchange for patronage. These poor and the poorly educated residents of remote areas generally voted for candidates of the right. Those who had higher levels of education and income favored the center-left PSDB and especially the leftist PT, as did younger voters.

This trend was still visible in the watershed 2002 election that initially brought Lula to power, but the election of 2006 displayed new voting patterns, which continued in the 2010 election. Dilma Rousseff drew votes equally from urban poor neighborhoods and nonmetropolitan counties (52 and 50 percent, respectively). Reversing the earlier trends, voters in the Northeast favored the PT standard-bearer by a two-to-one margin (see Table 15.2). Moreover, as the PT lost upper-middle-class votes over revelations of corruption, Rousseff cemented her support among those with only a primary school education as

TABLE 15.2

Social Bases of Presidential Voting in Brazil, 2010*

The PT cements its claim as the party of the poor.

	Dilma Rousseff (PT)	José Serra (PSDB)	Blank/Null/ None	Don't Know
Gender				
Male	55	39	4	2
Female	47	43	4	5
Age				
16–24	48	43	6	3
25–34	51	41	4	4
35–44	53	39	4	4
45–59	53	40	3	4
60 and over	49	45	2	4
Education				
Elementary	57	36	2	4
Secondary	48	43	6	3
College	40	51	6	3
Region				
North/Center-West	50	42	3	5
Northeast	63	30	3	4
Southeast	48	44	5	3
South	42	50	3	5
County Type				
Capitals and Metropolitan Regions	52	39	5	3
Interior	50	43	3	4
Household Income (in multiples of minimum wage)				
Up to 2	56	36	3	5
2–5	49	43	5	3
5–10	45	48	5	2
More than 10	39	54	6	1
Religion				
Catholic	53	40	3	4
Pentecostal Protestant	47	44	5	4
Mainline Protestant	45	45	4	6
No religion	53	37	8	3
All Voters	51	41	4	4

Source: DataFolha, October 29 and 30, 2010 (downloaded from http://datafolha.folha.uol.com.br/).
*Voting intentions for second-round presidential election revealed in nationwide sample of 6,554 adults in 257 municipalities. All figures in the table are percentages.

well as among those earning less than two times the minimum salary. In addition, a new religious cleavage emerged in 2010, with the PT standard-bearer polling better among Catholics and those who did not identify with any religion than among Pentecostal Protestants, for whom the abortion issue loomed large in the closing days of the campaign.

The Electoral System

Brazil employs three different electoral systems. The president, state governors, and mayors of cities with at least 200,000 voters are elected by majority vote. In the event that no candidate captures 50 percent of the vote in a first round, a runoff election is held between the top two vote getters. Senators and mayors of cities with less than 200,000 voters are elected by a second system called "first past the post." They need only win a plurality of the vote to gain office, and no runoff election takes place.

Federal and state deputies and local councillors are elected by yet a third system, **open-list proportional representation** with multimember districts. More than one representative is elected per district, which, in federal and state races, is the state itself. Deputies represent and draw votes from their entire states. Voters choose one candidate from any one of several party lists. Each party's list may contain up to one and a half times the number of candidates as the number of seats to be filled. The system works similarly for council elections, except that the municipality is the district, and each party may nominate up to three times the number of candidates as there are seats to be filled.

In a proportional representation system, the number of seats in a legislature or local council awarded to each party is based on the share of the total vote that the candidates for each party receive. In most electoral systems in which seats are awarded according to proportional representation, the list is "closed." Party leaders determine the rank order of the names on the party ballot. They can ensure the election of loyal deputies and those needed as Cabinet ministers by placing them high on the party list. They can just as easily punish those who were unfaithful in a key vote in Congress by placing them so low on the list that reelection is improbable. In Brazil's open-list proportional representation system, by contrast, voters determine which candidates on the party list will represent the party in the legislature.

Critics contend that electoral systems that empower the electorate at the expense of party leaders undermine political parties and encourage politicians to campaign against members of their own party more than against their opponents in other parties. Because party leaders have little control over who gets elected, party discipline in the legislature is expected to be weak. Open-list proportional representation rewards politicians who distribute favors to their constituents rather than adhere to the party platform. This makes it hard for governments to pass legislation and crucial policy reforms without awarding legislators substantial pork from state coffers for their constituents.

Electoral rules have obviously contributed to the fragmentation of Brazil's party system, the comparative lack of party cohesion in the legislature, and the lack of institutionalization of parties in the electorate. Yet the PT, the PSDB, and other parties are reasonably disciplined and programmatically oriented, and they have secured prominent places in Brazil's party system, which raises the question of whether Brazil's parties should still be considered weak.

Are Brazil's Parties Still Weak?

Brazil's political parties have traditionally been regarded as weak because they are unable to count on the loyalty of either their representatives in the legislature or the voters. Is this still the case? More specifically, do party legislative delegations lack cohesion and discipline? Is Brazil's party system still incoherent to voters? Do parties lack roots in the electorate?

Parties in Congress Traditionally, Brazilian parties were not cohesive; that is, representatives did not hold similar positions on key issues. Party discipline, or the ability of party leaders to enforce party-line voting in the legislature, was also weak. According to conventional wisdom, representatives of most parties in the legislature broke party ranks to vote to serve the interests of their states, a particular interest group, or even their own careers. Setting aside party programs in favor of securing patronage resources for their states and districts reinforced personalism, clientelism, and regionalism, and weakened party identities and accountability.

Today, Brazil's parties *are* still less disciplined than their counterparts elsewhere in Latin America. Nonetheless, party discipline is stronger than sometimes claimed. When party leaders in the Chamber of Deputies announce a position before a roll call vote, the vast majority of deputies follow their leader. In the 2003–2006 legislature, members of the seven largest parties voted with the official party position 88 percent of the time; the PT was the most disciplined party, with an average of 94 percent support of the party line.[39]

Brazilian politicians also change parties frequently, not because of philosophical differences with their party but to advance their personal electoral prospects by joining the party group they perceive will win the next election. Among legislators elected to the lower house in 2002, some 192 (37 percent of the Chamber) switched parties during the 2003–2007 legislative session.[40] Much of this was simple political bandwagoning; politicians abandoned opposition parties and joined the government coalition so as to have direct access to federal resources. However, in 2007, the Supreme Electoral Court ruled that congressional seats belonged to political parties and not to individual politicians. Party switching immediately slowed to a trickle, and parties losing a federal deputy to another party could replace the disloyal legislator with an alternate member. Party switchers have exploited legal loopholes to maintain their mobility; hundreds of cases are pending.[41]

Yet shallow party loyalty is an affliction of many but not all of Brazil's parties. Parties of the left evoke strong loyalty among their elite members, and their congressional delegations are more likely to remain faithful to their parties' positions than their counterparts on the right. Moreover, it appears that members of Congress value their parties' labels more today than a decade ago and are more willing to concede greater authority to party congressional leaders. In 1988, two-thirds of all respondents surveyed believed that a member of Congress who changed party affiliation should *not* lose her seat,[42] but in 2013, 67 percent believed that she *should* lose her seat for switching. Moreover, the share of legislators agreeing that "a political party should expel a Congressperson who votes against the orders of the party" increased from 51 percent in 2005 to 62 percent in 2013.[43]

Parties in the Electorate Brazilian parties are also considered weak because, with the exception of the PT, they lack deep roots in the electorate. In 2012, almost half of voters surveyed identified with any of the many political parties on offer. But almost half

of those voters identified with the PT (27 percent of all respondents). No other party really came close: The next most frequently mentioned parties were the PMDB (5 percent) and the PSDB (4 percent).[44] Were it not for the presence of the PT, party identification would be barely detectable among Brazilian voters.

Citizens, moreover, do not really actively participate in the parties of the center and right. Party "members," usually about twenty per municipality, actually belong to local governing directorates whose only say in state- and national-level party decisions is to elect delegates to nominating conventions. Ordinary citizens may be "affiliates" of local parties, a status that carries no rights or responsibilities. Because voters are sometimes attached to party labels only superficially, political scientists also measure partisanship by the (in)stability of party vote shares. By this measure, parties have grown somewhat stronger in the electorate. Electoral volatility (the turnover of votes from one party to its competitors from one election to the next) for the Chamber of Deputies, which averaged 43 percent in the first three elections after the transition to democracy, declined sharply beginning in 1994. By 2006, it had fallen to 27.6 percent,[45] matching the levels of some of the more institutionalized party systems in Latin America, including Mexico and Argentina.

Moreover, the relationship between parties and voters may be changing. Today, Brazilian politicians and political parties still control many public sector jobs and distribute public works projects and social services to reward politically loyal districts and individuals, but it is getting harder to do. New laws make state patronage jobs scarcer, limit earmarks that individual members of Congress can sponsor via amendments to the budget, and outlaw vote buying. Patronage politics has also been rendered less useful by government programs, such as Bolsa Família, that provide social assistance directly to the poor, without political interference. Public tolerance for clientelism and bossism is also clearly diminishing. The massive wave of protests in mid-2013 was a strongly antiparty movement: Demonstrators called loudly for parties to "clean up their acts," and party activists attempting to carry party banners into the crowds were sometimes attacked and driven away. Parties in the future will have to compete not merely on patronage but also on performance.

The Policymaking Process

15.10 Describe the way laws are introduced and considered in Brazil's legislature.

Policy in Brazil is framed and implemented through either the legislative process or in the Cabinet and bureaucracy. Although the legislature has gained in stature and strength since 1988, the executive branch still dominates the policymaking process in practice.

The Legislative Process

Laws may be initiated by any member of the Chamber of Deputies or Senate, the president, ministers of the Supreme Court, the attorney general, or citizens. Popular initiative requires 1 percent of the national electorate, representing no less than 0.3 percent of the electors in at least five states, to launch the legislative process. Debate on proposals initiated outside of Congress begins in the Chamber of Deputies. The first law to be passed in this fashion was the 1999 bill initiated by Catholic activists to make vote buying a crime punishable by loss of seat. In 2010, the Movement to Fight Electoral Corruption collected 1.6 million signatures and forced Congress to pass a bill known as *Ficha Limpa* (the Clean Record Law), which denies ballot access to any candidate who has been convicted of a crime.

A bill sponsored by a member of Congress can be introduced in either chamber (see Figure 15.7). If it is introduced in the Chamber of Deputies, it is first examined by the governing board of the house, the **Mesa Diretora** (made up of the chamber president, two vice presidents, and four secretaries), whose composition reflects party strength in Congress. The president, for instance, typically comes from the largest party. A second important leadership body is the **College of Leaders**. Its twenty-odd members comprise the official majority and minority leaders in the Chamber, leaders of legislative "blocks" (coalitions of two or more parties), and leaders of all parties that have more than five deputies. It organizes the legislative agenda on behalf of the *Mesa*. Committee chairs have much less freedom to set their agendas than their counterparts in the U.S. Congress.

Once a bill passes the leadership of the Chamber, it is directed to the appropriate legislative committees for review. Currently, there are twenty-one standing committees in the Chamber of Deputies and eleven

in the Senate, plus three joint committees drawing members from both houses (federal budget, climate change, and a committee comprising Brazil's delegation to the Mercosur Parliament). All proposed legislation is first reviewed by the judiciary committee for its constitutionality. If it passes this test, it is then sent to the committee or committees with jurisdiction in its area. An economic bill, for instance, would be reviewed by the economy committee and the finance committee.

If three committees approve a bill, it is sent directly to the Senate for consideration. If approved by two committees, or if it fails to secure the approval of a committee, it goes to the floor of the Chamber. Once approved in the Chamber, it must similarly be reviewed by the Senate judiciary and economic affairs committees. If approved by the full Senate, it is sent to the president, who may either sign it into law or veto it in whole or in part. An absolute majority of both houses is required to override a veto. A bill that originates in the Senate must also pass the Chamber of Deputies. Two of the most important types of executive-initiated bills—appropriations and emergency measures—are taken up by the legislature in joint session (see again Figure 15.7). Constitutional reform bills, which have the highest priority on the legislative agenda, must be passed by supermajorities—three-fifths of both chambers of Congress—on two separate occasions within the same legislature. Seventy-two amendments were added to the constitution between 1992 and 2013.

Presidential Legislative Powers

The Brazilian president dominates the legislative process through various prerogatives. According to the Constitution, only the president can initiate bills that determine the size of the armed forces, create public sector jobs, reorganize the Cabinet, or set pay levels for public employees. Crucially, only the president can introduce appropriations measures. Nearly nine in ten of the laws introduced by the president are passed by Congress within the year, compared to fewer than two in ten of proposals coming from members of Congress itself.[46]

The Brazilian president also can enact **provisional measures**, which take effect immediately upon issue. The provisional measures are a carryover from the infamous "decree laws" of the military period. The framers of the 1988 Constitution intended them

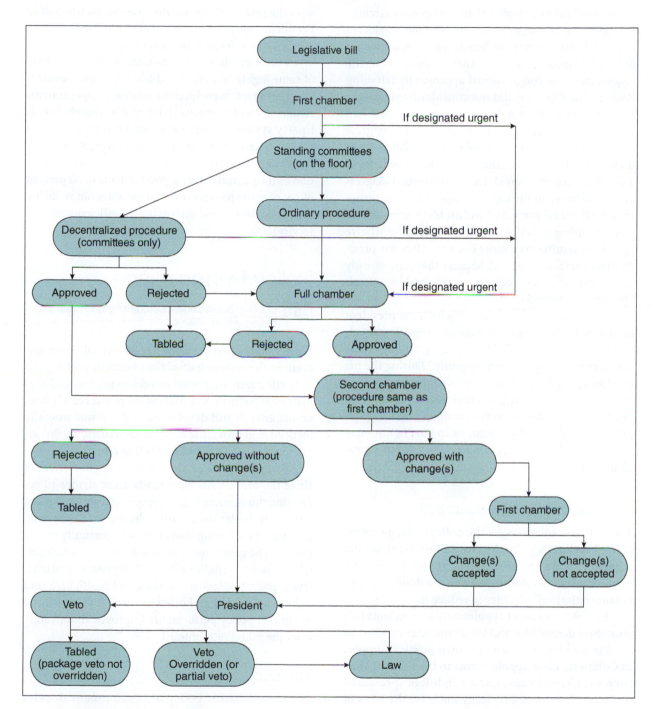

FIGURE 15.7
The Legislative Process in Brazil
Both the Congress and the president in Brazil can initiate legislation; the process of considering legislation is identical in both chambers.

Source: Paolo Ricci, "A produção legislativa de iniciativa parlamentar no Congresso: diferenças e similaridades entre a Câmara dos Deputados e o Senado Federal," in *O Senado Federal Brasileiro no Pós-Constituinte*, ed. Leany Lemos (Brasília: Unilegis, 2008), 271.

to be exercised in exceptional and temporary circumstances and with congressional consent, but presidents frequently relied on these "emergency" measures for dubious reasons. Moreover, they circumvented the requirement for congressional approval by reissuing decrees that Congress did not consider immediately. In a little more than a decade, four presidents had issued 619 decrees and reissued 5,491. The Congress sought to restrain presidential power in 2001, when it amended the Constitution to restrict presidents to a single reissue of a lapsed decree. However, Congress agreed to move to the top of its agenda any measure on which it had not acted within forty-five days of issue, enabling presidents to dominate the legislative agenda by issuing even more decrees. Also, few presidential decrees are rejected, because they have already taken effect and their policy impacts would be difficult for Congress to undo.

In addition to those areas in which the president has exclusive authority, she may also significantly alter the legislative agenda by requesting that Congress act on proposed legislation "urgently." During the life of a Congress, the president may designate more than a hundred pieces of legislation as urgent. Finally, the president has recourse to veto congressional legislation in whole (a *package* veto) or in part (a *line-item* veto), and only rarely has Congress overridden a presidential veto.

The Cabinet and Bureaucracy

The third essential rung of the policymaking process is the bureaucracy. By the late 1970s, the Brazilian regulatory state had grown so large that Brazil's last military president, João Figueiredo, established a "Debureaucratization" Ministry to reduce it.

In making Cabinet appointments, presidents balance their demand for technical competence with the need to build partisan and regional political support in Congress. Thus, appointments to the Foreign Ministry, the Central Bank, and a handful of specialized technical agencies are typically made on the basis of merit. But appointments to most ministries and federal agencies are frequently the object of horse trading among the parties in the ruling coalition. In President Dilma's administration, ten different political parties held Cabinet posts in 2013, and each made important partisan appointments to their respective ministries. The composition of the bureaucracy changes along

with the profile of the administration: Nearly half of President Lula's top 1200 bureaucratic appointments were, like him, former union activists.[47]

Therefore, despite the growth in professionalism of some highly dedicated and talented public servants in recent years, high-level bureaucratic appointments remain subject to the vagaries of a fragmented multiparty system, which naturally increases political pressures for expanding public employment. State administrative reform in the late 1990s and the restriction of the payrolls of state governments to 60 percent of net revenue has, however, made a dent in reducing the public payroll and improving the efficiency of state services.

Policy Performance

15.11 List five recent public policy changes in Brazil and describe their effects.

Brazil's policy performance has historically been uneven. In the second half of the twentieth century, the state effectively increased its own extractive and regulatory capacities and marshaled resources for economic growth and development. But it was woefully ineffective in providing basic social welfare, ameliorating racial inequality, and combating crime.

After decades of slow progress, governments since the mid-1990s have made great strides in reforming the economy, delivering social services more efficiently, better distributing the fruits of economic growth, and reducing inequality of opportunity and in the law. The government must still reform taxes, redistribute income, eradicate hunger, improve educational levels, provide adequate housing and health care, and fight drug-related and other crime. Yet there is little doubt that policy performance improved significantly from the mid-1990s onward.

The Economic Record

The most dramatic policy success for many decades was economic growth. With the state regulating economic activity, setting wages and prices, doling out agricultural credit, restricting imports, and controlling foreign-currency transactions, the economy grew by 7 percent per year for more than three decades across democratic and military regimes. Growth rates slowed after 1985, averaging less than 3 percent per year, due to a less favorable international climate. Relative to the 1960s and 1970s, foreign investment and trade opportunities lagged. During the 1980s, known across Latin America as the "lost decade," onerous service on the foreign debt contracted by military governments severely constrained the ability of governments to invest in economic growth and social services, and living standards declined.

The most dramatic economic failure of successive regimes was their inability to control inflation. Though the military immediately attacked inflation (which was running at 90 percent in 1964), after 1967, it accepted as livable annual inflation rates in the 20 percent range, and accorded all priority to growth. Rising world oil prices and interest rates undoubtedly contributed to driving Brazil's inflation rates to triple and then quadruple digits. But so did soaring government budget deficits (including those of the state governments) in the late 1980s and early 1990s. In the first decade of civilian rule, inflation *averaged* over 1,000 percent per year, and was more frequently measured in monthly, not annual, terms. Rising inflation dramatically eroded the purchasing power of the poor.

In the early 1990s, trade protection was dismantled and a handful of state-owned steel companies were sold. But otherwise, reform efforts stalled. Scholars contended that much-needed economic reform was slowed by too many "veto players"—the individual and collective actors (such as members of the executive branch, congressional leaders, governors, and political party leaders) who have to agree to any change in policy.

No administration seemed capable of stemming the tide until 1994, when Itamar Franco introduced the Real Plan. After that, the real value of the minimum wage began to recover. Brazil liberalized its economy more slowly than Chile, Peru, and Argentina. The pace of reform quickened with the Cardoso administration (1995–2002). In Cardoso's first year in office, Congress passed constitutional amendments to eliminate state monopolies in the gas, telecommunications, and petroleum industries, and to end constitutionally based discrimination against foreign investment. These legislative victories led swiftly to the privatization of many state-owned firms. Yet other reforms of the state sector deemed crucial for reducing the state's financial obligations were slower to pass. Administrative reform was important for streamlining

a public administration bloated by patronage in the preceding decade; without it, civil sector workers could not be dismissed on any grounds other than proven corruption. Pension reform was also key to economic stability because the social security system was strained by the ratio of workers to retirees (two to one), and the timing of retirement determined by years of service rather than age (public sector workers, in effect, could retire by age fifty). Eventually, administrative reform and a revision of the social security system for private sector workers were passed, but only after grave financial crises had weakened the currency and much time and political capital had been spent.

The Cardoso government was also successful in reforming the financial relationship between the subnational (state and municipal) and federal levels of government. Free-spending state and local governments had piled up staggering debts in the late 1980s and the 1990s. Much of this spending was directed to political patronage. After dragging their feet on reform and pressing Brasília to roll over state government debt for years, governors and congressional delegations finally agreed to privatize state banks, limit state payrolls, and repay the federal government.

In contrast to these successful reforms, Cardoso made less progress on deregulating financial and labor markets. Pension reform for public sector workers, as well as fiscal reform, was left to Lula. In 2003, the government pressed ahead with a pension reform bill that raised the retirement age for civil servants, required pensioners to contribute back into the system, and realigned benefits based on workers' ages and lengths of contribution, with caps for the highest earners.

The Brazilian state has as much extractive capacity as any Latin American state, and perhaps any developing country. The gross tax burden (tax revenue as a percentage of GDP) rose steadily from 22 percent in 1985 to 36.3 percent in 2012.[48] In recent years, the share of public sector revenue constituted by "contributions," which are levied on business activity and profits, financial transactions, and fuels, among others, has increased substantially (see Figure 15.8). Contributions are deposited into separate funds, which are then targeted for such specific purposes as social security, education, and roads. Notably, these revenues are not included in the revenue-sharing formula that benefits state and municipal governments. Personal and corporate income taxes, which are collected by

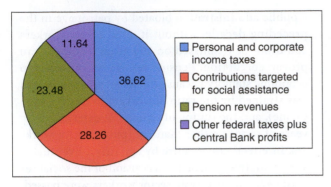

FIGURE 15.8

Sources of Federal Government Revenue, 2013

Brazil's taxes, the highest in Latin America, fall on corporate and individual income, property, consumption, and profits (figures are percentages).

Source: www.tesouro.fazenda.gov.br.

the federal government but shared with the states and municipalities, accounted for over a third of the federal tax take in 2013. Additional taxes levied by Brazil's 27 states (the **Tax on the Circulation of Goods and Services [ICMS]**) and 5570 municipalities (the urban property tax) amount to one-fifth of overall public sector revenue.

Social Welfare Performance

The record of successive Brazilian governments in the area of social policy was disappointing for many years. Much social policy was badly designed and inefficiently administered. In the mid-2000s, the federal government spent over $10 billion a year on public universities—the best in the country—which charge no tuition. While such a policy made free education theoretically accessible to all, in practice, it diverted funds away from primary education for the poorer segments of society. In 2010, the Ministry of Education spent $6.50 on universities and laboratories for every $1 directed to basic education. In effect, this policy subsidized the higher education of children of the upper middle and even upper classes, who could afford to pay. Brazilian social policy was also less effective than it might have been because appointments and spending decisions were made on the basis of political clientelism rather than merit. Clientelism was cited as the "single most effective impediment to redistributive reform in health care."[49]

In the past two decades, Brazil has made significant progress in social policy. Adult literacy rates increased from 82 to 91 percent, the infant mortality rate was slashed from 45 to 16 percent, and indigence rates fell sharply from 15 to 3.4 percent (see Table 15.3). This success is due at least in part to administrative decentralization and more efficiently targeted funding. It is also a result of the priority accorded to social policy by presidents Cardoso, Lula, and Dilma since 1995.

The Cardoso government reorganized and decentralized the delivery of crucial social services. It expanded access to school, and stepped up agrarian reform efforts. More than 600,000 landless peasant families were settled on homesteads during Cardoso's two terms, three times as many as in the preceding thirty years. But it left much to be done.

Lula placed early priority on eradicating hunger for the 15 percent of Brazil's population that goes hungry, in a social program known as "Zero Hunger." The symbolism of the program's launch by Brazil's first president to have experienced hunger first-hand as a child was enormous, but insufficient to make the program a success.

Learning from its early missteps, the Lula government consolidated several conditional cash transfer (CCT) and other social welfare programs into a single flagship social program known as **Bolsa Família**. Lula created the new Ministry of Social Development to oversee the program, which today reaches a quarter of the Brazilian population and is the world's largest CCT program (see Box 15.3). These reforms have produced tangible results in key areas of social policy.

Education The Cardoso government inherited a dismal educational system. Government spending on education had declined as a percentage of total expenditure from 1988 to 1993. The average number of years spent in school in Brazil was only 3.8. Sixty-five percent of children did not complete primary school, and of those who did, only 3 percent were able to do so in the normal eight years. Most failed and were forced to repeat several grades; it took students on average 11.2 years to complete primary school. Only 1 percent of the population reached university, the same percentage as in the 1960s.[50]

The Cardoso administration increased spending on education—to 5.2 percent of GDP in 1998.

TABLE 15.3
The Rising Performance of Brazilian Governments
Brazil registered economic gains, welfare improvements, and greater democracy under recent PSDB-led and PT-led governments.

	Collor-Franco 1990–1994	Cardoso 1995–2002	Lula 2003–2010	Dilma 2011–2012
Economy				
Growth[a]	1.24	2.31	4.06	1.80
Inflation[b]	1,321.28	9.24	5.79	6.17
Mean Real Minimum Wage[c]	324	338	496	635
Income Inequality—Gini coefficient[d]	0.600	0.598	0.558	0.522
Welfare				
Percentage Minimally Literate[e]	82.0	84.0	90.3	91.4
Percent Attending School[f]	83.5	94.6	98.0	—
Infant Mortality Rate[g]	45.1	30.1	25.1	15.6
Percent in Extreme Poverty[h]	15.0	10.0	6.0	3.4
Liberty[i]				
Political Freedom	2.20	2.63	2.00	2.00
Civil Liberties	3.40	3.63	2.38	2.00

[a]Average annual percent change in GDP.
[b]Average annual percent increase in consumer price index.
[c]Average monthly minimum wage under each administration, using a constant unit of reais of June 2013.
[d]Latest value available for each administration: 1993, 2002, 2010, and October 2012.
[e]Population aged fifteen and older, latest year available for each administration: 1993, 2002, 2009, and 2011.
[f]Population aged seven to fourteen, latest year available for each administration: 1993, 2002, and 2010.
[g]Figures are for 1991, 2000, 2006, and 2011.
[h]Latest year available for each administration: 1993, 2002, 2009, and 2011.
[i]As rated by Freedom House, averaged for each administration (1 = most free, 7 = not free).

Sources: Instituto de Pesquisa Econômica Aplicada (IPEA) (downloaded from www.ipeadata.gov.br); Instituto Brasileiro de Geografia e Estatística (IBGE) (downloaded from www.ibge.gov.br); and Freedom House, FH Country Ratings (available at www.freedomhouse.org).

Significantly, it redistributed educational resources to favor primary education and to reduce regional inequalities through a **Fund for the Maintenance and Development of Basic Education and Teaching (FUNDEF)**. The Fund specifically earmarked a percentage of federal funds for primary education, set a national minimum to be spent per student in grades one through eight, and required the federal government to make up the shortfall in districts too poor to meet the minimum. Between 1998 and 2000, annual spending per pupil grew by almost 50 percent nationwide but by 117.5 and 90 percent, respectively, in the poorer Northeast and North.[51] The law also encouraged a substantial increase in teachers' salaries. From 1994 to 2001, the number of students in primary school rose by 13.5 percent from 31.1 to 35.3 million. Secondary school enrollments rose even more dramatically, by 90 percent, from 4.4 to 8.4 million. In 2007, a successor program, FUNDEB, expanded the funding scheme to include high school education, with the increased expenditure to be partly covered by new co-payments from the states and municipalities. FUNDEB is intended to be a fourteen-year plan (2007–2020) to transform the educational system, increase human capital formation, and reduce regional inequalities.

Health   The delivery of public health constitutes a major challenge. The 1988 Constitution mandated a single, unified health system to replace the previous system that covered only formal sector workers. Although every citizen was entitled to medical treatment in public or contracted private facilities after 1988, in practice, access to the health care system was uneven and policy results were initially disappointing.

BOX
15.3

Out of Poverty? Bolsa Família

Social policy analysts have decried that many expensive social insurance programs in poor countries, including Brazil, disproportionately benefit the upper middle class. Brazil has innovated a new approach to poverty, known generically as conditional cash transfers. These CCTs target the poor with cash payments to meet specific policy objectives.

How does this work? Parents, ideally mothers (who are more apt than fathers to use the money for their children), are given 102 reais ($46) as a basic monthly benefit, with an additional 32 reais per child, up to a maximum of five children (the average family benefit in 2013 was 150 reais). In return, they must ensure that their children see a doctor regularly, receive their vaccinations, and stay in school. For very poor families, cash provides emergency assistance and allows them to forgo the earnings they would have received from their children's employment.

In terms of economic development, the program makes long-term investments in human capital, which ideally will help to break the cycle of poverty.

Few doubt that the program is achieving concrete results. School attendance and student retention have risen steadily, and one study showed that the program reduced infant mortality by 17 percent between 2004 and 2009. Approximately one quarter of the total reduction in income inequality over the past decade can be attributed to this one federal program. And the cost is modest. In 2013, Bolsa Família had a total expenditure of only 25 billion reais, less than one percent of the federal budget, and with this, it was able to cover 13.8 million families (approximately 50 million people, about a quarter of Brazil's population).

Sources: *O Globo*, May 5, 2013; and *Folha de São Paulo*, May 23, 2013.

In the mid-1990s, decentralizing the administration of health care to local governments and increasing federal spending raised the quality of health care. Access to primary care improved significantly in 1998 when Health Minister José Serra managed to triple federal transfers to the states and municipalities for this purpose. A 2001 constitutional amendment obliged all levels of government to increase their earmarks for health spending.[52]

These changes led to improved results. Life expectancy at birth rose from 67 years in 1991 to 73.4 in 2010. Brazil's infant mortality rate (the number of

A Brazilian Classroom
More children are in school today than ever before, thanks to more federal government financing and to a program that pays families a monthly stipend to keep their children in school.

deaths of babies of less than one year of age per 1,000 live births) dropped from forty-eight in 1990 to thirty-three in 2003 and again, sharply, to 15.6 in 2010. By reducing the rate of child mortality by 73 percent over the last two decades, Brazil surpassed the UN Millennium Development goal well ahead of the 2015 deadline. Moreover, Brazil has now distanced itself from other developing countries such as India and Nigeria (where the rates are forty-seven and seventy-eight, respectively), and it has closed the gap with China, Mexico, and Russia (thirteen, thirteen and ten respectively; see again Table 7.3). Moreover, the percentage of the population without access to sanitation also fell markedly, from 30 percent in 1990 to 21 percent in 2010 (see Table 7.2). The Brazilian government also gained international acclaim for its HIV/AIDS prevention strategies.

Racial Equality   The Cardoso administration promoted racial quotas in the higher education system as well as in several branches of government to enhance diversity. The use of quotas has been controversial (see again Box 15.1). Even with public support, however, it has not always been easy to fill the quotas set aside for Afrodescendants. In 2010, more than five years after the University of Brasília became the first federal university to establish a 20 percent quota for Afrodescendants, black and mixed-race applicants made up only 18.6 percent of the candidates taking the university's entrance exam.

Signaling a new priority, Lula created a Cabinet-level Special Secretariat for the Promotion of Racial Equality (SEPPIR) in 2003. In June 2010, after ten years of public debate, Congress finally passed a landmark **Racial Equality Statute**. The law provides legal definitions of racial inequality, racial discrimination, and "black population" (based on racial self-identification). Among many other measures, the Racial Equality Statute requires the teaching of Afro-Brazilian history and culture in schools, prohibits discrimination in hiring, directs the government to take measures to stop police violence against Afrodescendants, and creates an antiracism ombudsman's office within every government agency. However, all mandatory quotas—including proposed racial quotas in television broadcasting and in political party nominations—were left out of the final version of the statute due to Senate opposition (quotas can still be adopted voluntarily on a case-by-case basis). While activists lamented the dilution of the final bill, they nonetheless viewed the legislation as a major step toward recognizing racial inequality.

Crime, the Law, and Civil Liberties

Economic deprivation, an inadequate government response to the "social problem," and a surge in drug use have fueled an increase in crime. Drugs and crime

A Step toward Racial Equality
Lawmakers and activists celebrate on the Senate floor after the passage of the landmark Racial Equality Statute, Brasília, June 16, 2010.

are usually ranked by the public in polls as one of the country's three most pressing problems, typically just behind health and unemployment. Drug lords rule in many neighborhoods, perhaps nowhere as dramatically as in Rio de Janeiro, where there are estimated to be 10,000 heavily armed combatants. Police say that perhaps as much as 70–80 percent of violent crime in the country is related to the illegal drug trade. An estimated 200,000 people are employed in the narcotics business. In 2006, the city of São Paulo was paralyzed by a wave of violent actions directed by imprisoned gang leaders using cell phones. The murder rate has doubled since the mid-1980s; in 2003, it peaked at twenty-nine homicides per 100,000 people, approximately five times the rate in the United States. Over 45,000 people are murdered each year. According to the United Nations, Brazil has the highest rate of homicides caused by firearms for any country not at war—more than 70 percent. The wealthy have responded by resorting to private security. In 2010, there were 1.7 million private security guards in the country, more than twice the number of police. The poor often take the law into their own hands, with hundreds of reported lynchings and mob executions.

The failure of the Brazilian government to reduce crime is part of a broader failure to guarantee civil liberties and enforce the rule of law. Violence against peasants, rural workers, and their advocates is widespread and goes virtually unpunished. According to the Pastoral Land Commission of the Catholic Church, in 2012 alone, there were 1,364 land conflicts in Brazil, resulting in 295 death threats, 165 physical attacks, and 34 murders of peasants and rural workers.[53] Few of these will ever result in convictions, which is hardly surprising given that many areas with land conflicts, especially in the Northern and Northeastern states, have no judge or public prosecutor.[54] Most of the 5,000 agents of the federal police (which investigate crimes involving corruption, contraband, and human rights violations) are far away in Brasília. Clientelism has also undermined the efficient functioning of the law enforcement agencies. Many police commissioners are political appointees of the state governors who do not hold the law degree required by statute.[55]

Even more glaring is the state's failure to control the violence of its own military and police forces. Police officers themselves join death squads that murder street children and frequently torture

common criminals. The state civilian police (who are responsible for conducting investigations) justify their routine use of illegal methods of investigation and see the rule of law as an obstacle to social control. The state military police (who are in charge of patrolling and preventing crime) have been reported to commit blatant human rights violations, including summary executions of suspects. Military and police repression of prisoners is notorious in Brazil. The decrepit prison system, with 550,000 behind bars (nearly half in São Paulo), is overwhelmed: The incarceration rate (prisoners per 100,000) rose by 290 percent in twenty years, from 74 in 1992 to 288 in 2012, ten times more than the population did. Over the past decade, only the prison population in Cambodia and El Salvador grew faster than in Brazil. The police are systematically underpaid (at the lower ranks, officers earn only the minimum wage) and lack training.

In the 1990s, the Cardoso government created a Cabinet-rank secretariat charged with defending human rights, launched a national plan of action for human rights, and upgraded the crime of torture from a misdemeanor to a serious crime punishable by up to sixteen years in prison. It also made all rights violations federal crimes, in effect removing their investigation from the jurisdiction of state civil and military police forces. Lula created the National Coordination for the Protection of Human Rights Defenders, made up of government officials and civil society representatives, in 2003. In 2004, the government put into place a telephone hotline service that people can use to report rights abuses. The Lula administration also supported a blanket prohibition on the sale of firearms and ammunition, which eventually was defeated in a major national referendum held in October 2005 (only 36 percent of voters supported the proposed ban).

Yet policy reform in the areas of crime and public security is complicated by federalism. Control of the uniformed police has traditionally been in the hands of state governors, and presidents (who need the political support of these same governors) quietly respect this privilege. Proposals to rationalize public security through centralization—for example, by creating a Ministry of Public Security at the federal level—have therefore fallen on deaf ears. Clearly, there is much to be done before violence is curbed and justice established in Brazil.

International Relations

15.12 Identify four ways in which Brazil has become prominent internationally.

Brazil has long had a professional foreign service, but not until the Cardoso government did it begin to assume a position of respect on the world stage as a major player in international and regional affairs. Cardoso and, especially, Lula "presidentialized" Brazilian foreign policy, traveling tirelessly around the globe, engaging in summitry with world leaders, and generally raising the country's international profile. Brazil has cooperated with other countries on nuclear nonproliferation, environmental protection (especially implementing the Rio and Kyoto protocols), advancing human and women's rights, and reducing drug trafficking. In the Lula years (2003–2010), the focus of foreign policy was to reduce the gap between rich and poor nations, promote equality among peoples, and democratize the international system. Lula became a major voice on the world stage for developing nations, enthusiastically supporting deeper policy coordination among the emerging powers known as the BRICS

(a consultative mechanism launched in 2009 by Brazil, Russia, India, and China, and joined in 2011 by South Africa). While Brazil itself makes up only 2.8 percent of the gross world product, as a founder of the BRICS, it is now a leading voice in a bloc responsible for over 27 percent of global output. Lula was also personally instrumental in bringing the 2014 FIFA World Cup and the 2016 Summer Olympics to Brazil (Box 15.4).

The Lula government enjoyed a very positive reputation within international financial circles for honoring Brazil's external obligations and paying off a $15.5 billion IMF loan (contracted by the outgoing Cardoso administration in 2002) two years ahead of schedule. However, the PT-led administration also established warm relations with the rising number of left-wing governments in Latin America, including those headed by such controversial presidents as Hugo Chávez in Venezuela, Evo Morales in Bolivia, and Rafael Correa in Ecuador. The Lula government also maintained a cordial relationship with communist Cuba. Although sometimes criticized for failing to speak out against erosions of civil liberties in neighboring countries, Lula argued that dialogue was

---

BOX 15.4 Bringing the Sports World to Brazil: Is It Worth the Trouble?

From 2014 to 2016, Brazil will be in the global spotlight as the host of two athletic mega-events. The 20th FIFA World Cup of soccer will be held in twelve Brazilian cities in June–July 2014. Two years later, Rio de Janeiro will provide a telegenic backdrop to the XXXI Olympiad. The Lula government congratulated itself for winning these bids.

Given the well-known headaches associated with mega-events (most host countries suffer cost overruns while struggling to meet a difficult set of deadlines), why would a developing country commit the massive amount of resources necessary for such a short-lived initiative? President Lula clearly wanted to place Brazil on the global stage, and viewed the games as a way to enhance national visibility. His then chief of staff (and now president) Dilma Rousseff saw the mega-events as a way to fast-track huge investments in Brazil's aging and inadequate infrastructure, and Brazil's powerful construction companies were more than happy to back her. Governors and mayors, influenced by how

mega-events have transformed Barcelona and Sydney into global cities, were excited by the "legacy" planning that could spark increased tourism in the coming decades.

Predictably, problems emerged in the run-up to the games. An important "dress rehearsal," the FIFA Confederations Cup in mid-2013, was overshadowed by the wave of street protests against massive public investments in lavish stadiums (some in cities with no significant local sports teams) at a time of slowing growth. Dilma and FIFA president Joseph Blatter, who criticized Brazil for its sluggishness in preparations, were roundly booed in public appearances. Local activists in Rio complained that construction for the Olympics was displacing poor residents and placing new infrastructure where it was least needed. The international media criticized Brazil's airports, hotels, and local transportation. As the World Cup approached, many Brazilians wondered whether the benefits from the mega-events would be worth the increasingly steep price.

important to preserve Latin American unity, and that Brazil was simply upholding its tradition of noninterference in the internal affairs of other nations.

Foreign trade and opening export markets is one of the most important international issues. Brazil is a founding member of the South American regional trading bloc, **Mercosur**, the Common Market of the South. Mercosur was founded in 1991 by Brazil, Argentina, Uruguay, and Paraguay, with Brazil responsible for approximately 70 percent of the founding members' aggregate GDP. Mercosur eliminated tariffs on 95 percent of the goods traded among its member countries, created a market of 220 million people with a GDP of $1.3 trillion, and, in its first six years, expanded regional trade by more than 400 percent. Venezuela negotiated entry as a full member in 2006, although its accession was blocked by Paraguay until 2012; Bolivia and Ecuador, currently associate members, are expected to join soon. Over the years, Chile, Colombia, Guyana, Peru, and Suriname have become associate members as well. Total intrabloc trade grew by over 50 percent between 2007 and 2011, and about 13 percent of Brazil's exports (by value) are now traded within the Mercosur region. The Lula government also sought to build a broader political association of South American countries that would eventually supplant Mercosur and the older Andean Community of Nations (CAN). These efforts led to the founding of the **Union of South American Nations (UNASUR)** in 2008.

Emphasizing South American economic integration above all other priorities, Brazil deliberately dragged its feet in multilateral negotiations to create the **Free Trade Area of the Americas (FTAA)**. The FTAA was launched in 1994 with the goal of concluding an agreement by 2005. The United States, Mexico, and Chile all favored hastening the FTAA, while Venezuela and its left-wing allies opposed any further integration with the United States. During the negotiations, Brazil insisted it would make concessions on intellectual property rights, financial regulation, and market access and sign the agreement only when the United States provided fair access to its market for Brazil's agricultural exports. At issue were billions of dollars of agricultural subsidies that the United States pays its farmers, not to mention openly protectionist policies advocated by legislators from farm states (for example, until 2011, a tariff imposed on Brazilian sugarcane ethanol protected the less-efficient, corn-based

ethanol produced in the U.S. Midwest). With the impasse on the agricultural and intellectual property questions, and given the abandonment of the negotiations by several left-leaning governments, the FTAA process collapsed after a raucous summit in Argentina in 2005.

Since the demise of the FTAA, Brazil has continued to press for the rollback of U.S. farm subsidies by other means. It has worked for global trade reform through the World Trade Organization (WTO) and has joined forces with many smaller African nations in a movement to end the rich world's agricultural subsidies (the EU, too, pays out billions of dollars' worth of price supports to its farmers). In 2004, Brazil took the United States to WTO arbitration over subsidies to cotton farmers and won a ruling that ordered the United States to compensate Brazil.

As one of the world's largest countries in terms of territory, population, and economic activity, Brazil aspires to occupy a permanent seat on the United Nations Security Council (UNSC). Joining with Germany, Japan, and India in the so-called G-4, Brazil has proposed enlarging the UNSC to "reflect the twenty-first century's new balance of forces" by adding six non-veto-wielding permanent seats, to be allotted to these four countries plus two states from Africa. The proposal, though endorsed by Britain and France, has faltered due to divisions within the African Union, Chinese opposition to Japan's ascension, and U.S. opposition to enlarging the UNSC at this time. Brazil has been bolstering its case for UNSC membership via high-profile overseas actions, such as its leadership of MINUSTAH (the United Nations Stabilization Mission in Haiti) since 2004, and its efforts (jointly with Turkey) to broker a solution to the international crisis surrounding Iran's nuclear energy program in 2010.

Prospects for the Future

Although people took to the streets in 2013 to protest a wide range of policy issues, objectively speaking, Brazil's prospects remain relatively bright, and certainly far more promising than was the case two decades ago. The country by and large escaped the global recession of 2008 and 2009; it has emerged as an energy superpower; and both the coverage and quality of its health care, education, and programs assisting the poor have dramatically improved. These positive developments are only due in part to the good fortune of oil discoveries; mainly, they are the result of improved government performance. Unlike in other countries, no significant populist political leader or outsider has emerged in recent years. Presidents, executive branch staff, and members of Congress and the judiciary have steadily overcome many of the obstacles to smooth policymaking thrown up by the country's political institutions. Political parties, marked by increased cohesion and discipline, have begun to sink roots in the electorate by presenting voters with real policy choices and ideological alternatives.

Brazil's recent rise has been predicated on the willingness of presidents to build upon the successes of their predecessors, an aspect of its political maturity that has spared the country some of the wild policy swings of its neighbors. In the 1990s, Cardoso tamed inflation and began the reform of the state, leaving a legacy of

economic stability. In the 2000s, Lula preserved Cardoso's initiatives while expanding the social safety net, cementing his legacy of social inclusion. The sequencing could not have been otherwise—many of Lula's policies would not have been possible without the price stability and the state capacity that Cardoso secured—but these consensual goals gave Brazil a long 16-year cycle of economic reform and rising human development. For President Dilma, maintaining *both* economic stabilization and social inclusion has been a tall order, but a challenge she has embraced without equivocation.

Despite these advances, major challenges nonetheless remain. A sharp rise in consumption has led to new inflationary pressures and to a worrisome credit bubble. Sluggish growth could be aggravated even further by an expected downturn in growth in China, an important trading partner. Inequality has declined, but given just how unequal Brazil was in the

Brazil as an Emerging Power
President Dilma Rousseff poses with Indian Prime Minister Manmohan Singh, Chinese President Xi Jinping, South African President Jacob Zuma, and Russian President Vladimir Putin during the BRICS 2013 Summit in Durban, South Africa, on March 26, 2013. Together, these five leaders represent nearly 3 billion people.

early 1990s, it remains one of the twelve most unequal societies in the world. To maintain the momentum and avoid welfare dependency, it also needs to develop second-generation antipoverty programs. Persistent violence is the most visible manifestation of a crisis of public security. Moreover, massive new investments are needed to upgrade the country's physical infrastructure and secure future growth. Controlling corruption that erodes public confidence in government is another ongoing challenge. A larger role in world affairs and a permanent seat on the UN Security Council remain national goals.

Can Brazil rise to meet these challenges? Just as its recent successes have been the product of politics, so do its prospects for the future depend on the ability of its politicians to govern. An increasingly sophisticated electorate and mobilized citizenry are likely to demand that they do.

REVIEW QUESTIONS

- Brazil's military justified its twenty-one-year-long reign as necessary because civilian governments were too weak to stabilize Brazil's economy and jump-start growth. What have been the most notable economic achievements of democratic governments in the 1990s and 2000s? How were these brought about?
- Although the military left power nearly thirty years ago, scars of the dictatorship still remain. How is Brazil dealing with the legacy of the authoritarian past?
- Brazilians tend not to trust Congress and political parties, but they have high rates of political participation. What explains this paradox?
- How do Brazil's electoral institutions affect the ability of governments to enact policy?
- Brazilian presidents have by and large dominated the policy process. What partisan and constitutional tools have they used to do so?
- What explains the electoral and governing success of the PT, a party of the left with a history of radical political proposals?

- What are the arguments for and against racial quotas in Brazil? Are race relations in Brazil different from race relations in the United States, and if so, how?
- Historically, social policy in Brazil was inefficient and skewed away from the poor, but in recent years, policy outputs in areas such as health and education have appreciably improved. What new programs and financing schemes helped to make this possible?
- If the vast majority of Brazilians are better off economically than they were a decade earlier, why did they take to the streets in the protests of 2013?
- As one of the "BRICS," Brazil is assuming an important place in world politics, but it is doing so through actions in international economic markets and political institutions rather than through military might. What foreign policy actions has Brazil taken? Is it likely to achieve its goals?

KEY TERMS

Afrodescendants

Bolsa Família

Brazilian Labor Party (PTB)

Brazilian Socialist Party (PSB)

Central Única dos Trabalhadores (CUT)

College of Leaders

coronelismo

corporatism

Democratic Labor Party (PDT)

Democrats (DEM)

Departamento Intersindical de Assessoria Parlamentar (DIAP)

direct action of unconstitutionality (ADIN)

ecclesial base communities (CEBs)

Federation of Industries of the State of São Paulo (FIESP)

Fiscal Responsibility Law

Free Trade Area of the Americas (FTAA)

Frente Parlamentar da Agropecuária (FPA)

Fund for the Maintenance and Development of Basic Education and Teaching (FUNDEF)

Institute for the Defense of the Consumer (IDEC)

liberation theology

Mercosur

Mesa Diretora

Ministério Público (Public Prosecution)

Movement of Landless Rural Workers (MST)

open-list proportional representation

Parliamentary Commissions of Inquiry (CPIs)

participatory budgeting

Party of Brazilian Social Democracy (PSDB)

Party of the Brazilian Democratic Movement (PMDB)

Party of the Republic (PR)

Progressive Party (PP)

provisional measures

Racial Equality Statute

Real Plan

Social Democratic Party (PSD)

Supremo Tribunal Federal (STF)

Tax on the Circulation of Goods and Services (ICMS)

transitional justice

Tribunal de Contas

Tribunal Superior Eleitoral (TSE)

Union of South American Nations (UNASUR)

Workers' Party (PT)

SUGGESTED READINGS

Ames, Barry. *The Deadlock of Democracy in Brazil.* Ann Arbor: University of Michigan Press, 2001.

Avritzer, Leonardo. *Participatory Institutions in Democratic Brazil.* Washington, DC: Woodrow Wilson Center Press, 2009.

Baer, Werner. *The Brazilian Economy: Growth and Development*, 7th ed. Boulder: Lynne Rienner, 2013.

Bailey, Stanley R. *Legacies of Race: Identities, Attitudes, and Politics in Brazil.* Stanford, CA: Stanford University Press, 2009.

Bourne, Richard. *Lula of Brazil: The Story So Far.* Berkeley: University of California Press, 2008.

Brainard, Lael, and Leonardo Martínez-Díaz, eds. *Brazil as an Economic Superpower? Understanding Brazil's Role in a Changing Economy.* Washington, DC: Brookings Institution Press, 2009.

Burdick, John. *Legacies of Liberation: The Progressive Catholic Church in Brazil at the Start of a New Millennium.* Burlington, VT: Ashgate, 2004.

Cardoso, Fernando Henrique. *The Accidental President of Brazil: A Memoir.* New York: Perseus Books, 2007.

Cepaluni, Gabriel, and Tullo Vigevani. *Brazilian Foreign Policy in Changing Times: The Quest for Autonomy from Sarney to Lula.* New York: Lexington Books, 2012.

Gómez Bruera, Hernán F. *Lula, The Workers' Party and the Governability Dilemma in Brazil.* New York: Routledge, 2013.

Hochstetler, Kathryn, and Margaret E. Keck. *Greening Brazil: Environmental Activism in State and Society.* Durham, NC: Duke University Press, 2007.

Holston, James. *Insurgent Citizenship: Disjunctions of Democracy and Modernity in Brazil.* Princeton, NJ: Princeton University Press, 2009.

Hunter, Wendy. *The Transformation of the Workers' Party in Brazil, 1989–2009.* Cambridge: Cambridge University Press, 2010.

Kingstone, Peter R., and Timothy J. Power, eds. *Democratic Brazil Revisited.* Pittsburgh, PA: University of Pittsburgh Press, 2008.

Love, Joseph L., and Werner Baer, eds. *Brazil under Lula: Economy, Politics, and Society under the Worker-President.* New York: Palgrave Macmillan, 2009.

Luna, Francisco Vidal, and Herbert S. Klein. *Brazil since 1980 (The World since 1980).* Cambridge: Cambridge University Press, 2006.

Montero, Alfred. *Brazil: A Reversal of Fortune.* New York: Polity Press, 2014.

Power, Timothy J., and Matthew M. Taylor, eds. *Corruption and Democracy in Brazil: The Struggle for Accountability.* Notre Dame, IN: University of Notre Dame Press, 2011.

Roett, Riordan. *The New Brazil.* Washington, DC: Brookings Institution Press, 2010.

Samuels, David. *Ambition, Federalism, and Legislative Politics in Brazil.* Cambridge: Cambridge University Press, 2003.

Skidmore, Thomas E. *Brazil: Five Centuries of Change*, 2nd ed. New York: Oxford University Press, 2009.

Taylor, Matthew M. *Judging Policy: Courts and Policy Reform in Democratic Brazil.* Stanford, CA: Stanford University Press, 2008.

INTERNET RESOURCES

General informational website on Brazil: lanic.utexas.edu/la/brazil.

English-language news aggregator (Woodrow Wilson Center): brazilportal.wordpress.com.

Government website: www.brasil.gov.br.

Legislature websites: www.senado.gov.br; www.camara.gov.br.

Census Bureau website: www.ibge.gov.br.

Planning Ministry's research arm: www.ipea.gov.br.

Electoral tribunal website: www.tse.gov.br.

ENDNOTES

1. "Freedom in the World, Brazil (2010)" Freedom House, http://www.freedomhouse.org, accessed November 15, 2010.

2. In November 2013, several, including former Presidential Chief of Staff José Dirceu and former PT president José Genoino were taken into custody to begin serving prison sentences.

3. Instituto Brasileiro de Geografia e Estatística, "Anuário Estatístico do Brasil 1976" (Rio de Janeiro: Fundação IBGE), 62; and IBGE, "Pesquisa Nacional de Amostra por Domicílios 2008" (Rio de Janeiro: Fundação IBGE), www.ibge.gov.br.

4. Roberto Da Matta, *Carnavais, Malandros e Heróis: Para uma Sociologia do Dilema Brasileiro* (Rio de Janeiro: Zahar, 1978).

5. Peter McDonough, Doh C. Shin, and José Álvaro Moisés, "Democratization and Participation: Comparing Spain, Brazil, and Korea,"*Journal of Politics* 60 (November 1998): 925.

6. Instituto Brasileiro de Geografia e Estatística, "Censo Demográfico 2010," www.ibge.gov.br, accessed July 21, 2013.

7. Datafolha, "Protestos sobre Aumento na Tarifa dos Transportes II," Study PO813688 (São Paulo: Instituto de Pesquisas Datafolha, June 18, 2013), datafolha.folha.uol.com.br.

8. Antônio Flávio Pierucci and Reginaldo Prandi, "Religiões e Voto: A Eleição Presidencial de 1994," *Opinião Pública* 3, no. 1 (1994): 25.

9. Maria Fernanda Boidi and Margarita Corral, "Public Opinion and Abortion Rights in the Americas," AmericasBarometer: Topical Brief (Nashville, TN: Vanderbilt University, June 17, 2013), www.AmericasBarometer.org.

10. Lúcia Avelar, *O Segundo Eleitorado: Tendências do Voto Feminino no Brasil* (Campinas: Unicamp. 1989), 105–28.

11. *Informe Latinobarómetro 2009* (Santiago: Corporación Latinobarómetro, 2009), 50, www.latinobarometro.org.

12. Gilberto Freyre, *The Masters and the Slaves* (New York: Knopf, 1946).

13. Datafolha, "Protestos sobre Aumento na Tarifa dos Transportes II."

14. In 2002, 65 percent of respondents to the National Election Study disagreed with the assertion that "it doesn't matter if a politician robs, as long as he gets done things that the population needs," and 85 percent disagreed that a politician who delivers good government should be able to divert public money to finance his electoral campaign.

15. Andy Baker, Barry Ames, and Lucio R. Renno, "Social Context and Campaign Volatility in New Democracies: Networks and Neighborhoods in Brazil's 2002 Elections," *American Journal of Political Science* 50, no. 2 (April 2006): 382–99.

16. From market research conducted among 12,000 respondents in 639 municipalities between January and March 2010. See Secretaria de Comunicação da Presidência da República, "Hábitos de Informação e Formação de Opinião da População Brasileira" (Brasília: Governo Federal, 2010), www.secom.gov.br.

17. Respondents to a survey during the 1989 presidential campaign reported that their choice of candidate was much less frequently influenced by newspapers, radio news, neighborhood associations, the Catholic Church, union activists, and public opinion polls than by television. Joseph Straubhaar, Organ Olsen, and Maria Cavaliari Nunes, "The Brazilian Case: Influencing the Voter," in *Television, Politics, and the Transition to Democracy in Latin America*, ed. Thomas E. Skidmore (Baltimore: Johns Hopkins University Press, 1993), 123, 127–28, 133.

18. Loretta Chao, "Brazil: The Social Media Capital of the Universe," *The Wall Street Journal*, February 4, 2013.

19. Antônio Augusto de Queiroz, "Renovação tende a ser baixa na eleição no Congresso," February 6, 2010, http://congressoemfoco.uol.com.br.

20. "Participação de mulheres e minorias poderá ser tema da reforma política," Agência Senado, July 18, 2013, www.senado.gov.br.

21. Amaury de Souza and Bolívar Lamounier, *As Elites Brasileiras e a Modernização do Setor Público: Um Debate* (São Paulo: IDESP/Sumaré, 1992).

22. Gianpaolo Baiocchi, "Participation, Activism, and Politics: The Porto Alegre Experiment and Deliberative Democratic Theory,"*Politics and Society* 29 (March 2001): 55.

23. See http://www.vanderbilt.edu/lapop/brazil/Brazil_Tech_Info_2012_W_03.12.13.pdf.

24. Carlos Frederico Marés de Souza, Jr., "On Brazil and Its Indians," in *Indigenous Peoples and Democracy in Latin America*, ed. Donna Lee Van Cott (New York: Inter-American Dialogue/St. Martin's Press, 1994), 218–21, 230–31.

25. Kathryn Hochstetler and Margaret E. Keck, *Greening Brazil: Environmentalism in State and Society* (Durham, NC: Duke University Press, 2007), 165–66.

26. February 2006 poll, IBOPE Opinião (retrieved from www.ibope.com.br on August 7, 2006).

27. Instituto Brasileiro de Geografia e Estatistica, "Perfil das Fundações Privadas e Associações sem Fins Lucrativos em 2010," (Rio de Janeiro: Fundação IBGE), www.ibge.gov.br.

28. This is different from the democratic corporatist system described in Chapter 4 that presumes a democratic relationship between government and interest groups.

29. Eli Diniz, "Empresariado, Estado y Políticas Públicas en Brasil: Nuevas Tendencias en el Umbral del Nuevo Milenio," in *Política Brasileña Contemporánea: De Collor A Lula en Años de Transformación*, ed. Vicente Palermo (Buenos Aires: Instituto Di Tella/Siglo XXI, 2003), 462–63.

30. Peter R. Kingstone, *Crafting Coalitions for Reform: Business Preferences, Political Institutions, and Neoliberal Reform in Brazil* (University Park: Pennsylvania State University Press, 1999), 111–48.

31. Scott Mainwaring, Rachel Meneguello, and Timothy J. Power, "Conservative Parties, Democracy, and Economic Reform in Contemporary Brazil," in *Conservative Parties, the Right, and Democracy in Latin America*, ed. Kevin J. Middlebrook (Baltimore: Johns Hopkins University Press, 2000), 216–17.

32. "Bancada Ruralista é a mais atuante no Congresso," *Revista Panorama*, April 19, 2013, www.panorama.com.br.

33. Patricia M. Rodriguez, "The Participatory Effectiveness of Land-Related Movements in Brazil, Ecuador, and Chile: 1990–2004" (Ph.D. diss., University of Notre Dame, 2009), 116–19.

34. Wendy Hunter, *Eroding Military Influence in Brazil: Politicians Against Soldiers* (Chapel Hill: University of North Carolina Press, 1997), 112–13.

35. "The SIPRI Military Expenditure Database," Stockholm International Peace Research Institute, http://milexdata.sipri.org, accessed December 5, 2013.

36. Hunter, *Eroding Military Influence,* 123–24, 129–32.

37. See Timothy J. Power, "Optimism, Pessimism, and Coalitional Presidentialism: Debating the Institutional Design of Brazilian Democracy," *Bulletin of Latin American Research* 29, no. 1 (January 2010): 18–33.

38. Barry Ames, *Political Survival: Politicians and Public Policy in Latin America* (Berkeley: University of California Press, 1987), 204–06.

39. Fabiano Santos and Márcio Grijó Vilarouca, "From FHC to Lula: Changes and Continuity in Political Institutions and Impact upon the Political Reform Debate," in *Democratic Brazil Revisited,* ed. Peter R. Kingstone and Timothy J. Power (Pittsburgh, PA: University of Pittsburgh Press, 2008), 79.

40. Carlos Ranulfo Melo and Geralda Luiza de Miranda, "Migrações e partidos no governo Lula," paper presented to the Brazilian Political Science Association, Campinas, São Paulo, Brazil, July 26–29, 2006.

41. Party switchers claim either that their parties have changed their ideologies or that the party leadership has been persecuting them (both of which are acceptable legal reasons for abandoning a party). Only a few dozen of these cases are in Congress; most are in state and local legislatures.

42. Scott Mainwaring, "Politicians, Parties, and Electoral Systems: Brazil in Comparative Perspective," *Comparative Politics* 24, no. 1 (October 1991): 33, 36.

43. The data from 2005 and 2013 are from the Brazilian Legislative Surveys conducted by Timothy J. Power and Cesar Zucco Jr. (http://dvn.iq.harvard.edu/dvn/dv/zucco).

44. Survey data are from Instituto DataFolha, as cited in Oswaldo Amaral and Rachel Meneguello, "The PT in Power, 2003–2013," paper presented at the conference on Democratic Brazil Emergent, Oxford, February 21, 2013.

45. Denise Paiva and Simone R. Bohn, "Sistema partidário e volatilidade eleitoral no Brasil 1982–2006: Um estudo sobre a dinâmica inter-regional," paper presented at the ANPOCS conference, Caxambu, Minas Gerais, Brazil, October 22–26, 2007.

46. Argelina Cheibub Figueiredo and Fernando Limongi, *Executivo e Legislativo na nova ordem constitucional* (Rio de Janeiro: FGV, 1999), 105.

47. Maria Celina D'Araujo, "Elites burocráticas, dirigentes públicos e política no Poder Executivo do Brasil, 1995-2012," http://mariacelina.daraujo.net.

48. "Carga tributária bate recorde e atinge 36.27%," *O Globo,* March 4, 2013, g1.globo.com.

49. Kurt Weyland, *Democracy without Equity: Failures of Reform in Brazil* (Pittsburgh, PA: University of Pittsburgh Press, 1996), 182.

50. Pablo Guedes, "O future é a educação," *Exame,* October 8, 1997, 10.

51. Sônia M. Draibe, "Federal Leverage in a Decentralized System: Education Reform in Brazil," in *Crucial Needs, Weak Incentives: Social Sector Reform, Democratization, and Globalization in Latin America,* ed. Robert R. Kaufman and Joan M. Nelson (Washington, DC: Woodrow Wilson Center Press, 2004), 395–402.

52. Marta Arretche, "Toward a Unified and More Equitable System: Health Reform in Brazil," in Kaufman and Nelson, *Crucial Needs, Weak Incentives,* 178–79.

53. "Conflitos no Campo Brasil 2012," Comissão Pastoral da Terra, www.cptnacional.org.br.

54. Paulo Sérgio Pinheiro, "Popular Responses to State-Sponsored Violence," in *The New Politics of Inequality in Latin America,* ed. Douglas A. Chalmers et al. (New York: Oxford University Press, 1997), 271–72.

55. Pinheiro, "Popular Responses to State-Sponsored Violence," 272.

POPULATION
75.6 million

TERRITORY
636,296 square miles

YEAR OF INDEPENDENCE
550 BCE

YEAR OF CURRENT CONSTITUTION
1979, amended in 1989

HEAD OF STATE
Ali Khamenei

HEAD OF GOVERNMENT
Hassan Rouhani

LANGUAGES
Persian, Azeri, Kurdish, Arabic, and various regional languages

RELIGIONS
Twelver Shiite Muslim 90%, Sunni Muslim 10%, non-Muslims less than 1%

CHAPTER 16

Politics in Iran

H. E. Chehabi and Arang Keshavarzian

LEARNING OBJECTIVES

16.1 Identify five internal challenges currently facing Iran.

16.2 Discuss the interplay of political and religious leadership in Iran.

16.3 Describe and distinguish between appointed and elected offices in Iran.

16.4 Discuss political parties versus factions as they affect Iranian elections.

16.5 Identify five key features of Iran's political culture.

16.6 Describe how the mechanisms for creating national unity in Iran also contain elements of dissent.

16.7 Describe the sources of Iran's political elite.

16.8 Discuss the roles of clientelism and interest groups in Iranian politics.

16.9 Summarize the policymaking process, focusing on the groups that frequently work at cross-purposes.

16.10 Compare and contrast the results of Iran's recent policies relating to internal and international issues.

The Islamic Republic of Iran is the world's only **theocracy**, a form of government in which, ideally, all laws are grounded in religion and express the will of God, and a clergy exercises supreme power. While Islamic law has always been applied to varying degrees in Muslim states, it has routinely been complemented by some sort of nonreligious customary law. Moreover, various sultans, shahs, sheikhs, and, since the twentieth century, presidents or prime ministers have traditionally exercised political power in the Muslim world. Genuine theocracies have been rare. Although the **ulema**, as religious scholars are called in the Muslim world, have sometimes been critical of rulers who strayed from the path of Islam, they almost never aspired to exercise power directly as they do in Iran today. Therefore, far from being a manifestation of Islamic conservatism, Iran's current theocratic regime constitutes a break with Muslim tradition.

The Islamic Republic of Iran was established in 1979, a few months after a popular revolution uniting poor with middle class and religious with secular people overthrew **Mohammad-Reza Shah Pahlavi** (r. 1941–1979), the last ruler of the country's ancient monarchy. **Ruhollah Khomeini**, a charismatic clerical leader of Iran's majority Twelver Shiite community, who had authored a blueprint for theocratic government in the early 1970s, led the 1979 revolution. In this blueprint, Khomeini opposed democracy on religious grounds. Sovereignty, he argued, belongs to God alone. Divine law, known as the **shari'a**, as interpreted and applied by the ulema, takes precedence over laws made by human legislators. In spite of Khomeini's preference for clerical dictatorship, the regime that was established after the demise of the monarchy incorporated the ideals of a diverse revolutionary coalition including liberal nationalists, leftists, and lay

533

Islamists, who imagined religious rule with only symbolic authority bestowed on clerics. Thus, the constitution enshrined some republican principles and rights. Consequently, presidential, parliamentary, and local elections have offered citizens a choice of candidates advocating differing policies. The emergence of limited democratic practices and institutions under a regime founded on the negation of democracy is only one of many paradoxes found in Iran.

In the current millennium, this circumscribed political stage has led to the emergence and demise of a reformist movement seeking to use the ballot box to make the polity more pluralistic and accountable. In response, a populist countermovement emerged that champions redistribution, while enhancing the powers of the military and security apparatus. Finally, the June 2013 electoral victory of **Hassan Rouhani**, whose campaign slogans included "moderation," signals a desire for a shift to a more pragmatic and technocratic approach to domestic and foreign policy to address economic discontent, confrontational international relations, and a persistent call for greater state responsiveness. Making sense of these dynamics and struggles is one of the tasks of this chapter.

Current Policy Challenges

16.1 Identify five internal challenges currently facing Iran.

Americans are used to coming across Iran in newspapers and nightly news reports. In recent years, the vast majority of this discussion and analysis has focused on Iran's nuclear energy program that the U.S. government alleges is intended for military purposes. This has resulted in a decade-long confrontation between Iran and the United States involving negotiations via international organizations, public threats of war by both sides, and the implementation of one of the most comprehensive sanctions regimes ever imposed on any country. The drumbeat of war and the current diplomatic opening have masked an equally dynamic and high-stakes game of domestic politics.

Iran's rulers have faced a fundamental predicament: how to reconcile the demands of Khomeini and his confidants to establish a political, social, and economic order consistent with their understanding of Islam with the principles of republican government that ensure representation of and accountability to citizens.

It has not been easy to reconcile these principles. Not only may "God's sovereignty," popular sovereignty, and state interests conflict, but the successes and failures of the Islamic Republic's policies have also created new expectations and demands as well as new social and political actors with their own interpretations of Islam and good government.

During the first decade of the Islamic Republic, some redistribution of wealth took place as the government expropriated much of the property of the old prerevolutionary elite. The new leadership came mostly from humble or middle-class backgrounds and adopted populist policies that bettered the lot of the poorest. For instance, the new regime invested heavily in rural development, including health, women's education, and roads. However, the postrevolutionary reality is far from ideal, and poverty, inequality, and underemployment continue to be major public grievances. Possessing the world's second-largest oil and gas reserves, the people expect Iran's government to improve the lives of ordinary Iranians and establish the basis for long-term and sustainable development. However, transforming natural wealth into economic productivity and diversification has proven difficult.

The need to increase economic output to provide employment for a rapidly growing labor force is perhaps the greatest challenge facing the government. Iran's population grows by about 600,000 every year. Although the government has successfully brought down the birth rate, the effects of the lower population growth rate will not be felt for many years. Even under the best circumstances, it would be difficult to provide employment for the 800,000 men and women who enter the labor market every year. Moreover, the impact of international sanctions, various forms of economic mismanagement, and Iran's antientrepreneurial outlook make the situation even worse. Regional conflicts and the continuing tension between Iran and the United States discourage both foreign and domestic investment. At the same time, a vastly expanded educational system means that many of the young unemployed hold academic degrees, adding to their frustration and discontent. This discontent has produced massive migration. A 2006 IMF study of 90 countries ranked Iran as having the highest rate of brain drain, with more than 150,000 Iranians with university degrees leaving per year.[1] This trend has likely worsened as threat of war and imposition of sweeping sanctions by the United States and its allies have made the lives of ordinary Iranians even more difficult in recent years.

A new challenge concerns dissatisfaction with the status quo among some of Iran's ethnic minorities, especially those that are mostly Sunni, like the Kurds and Baluchis (see Figure 16.1).[2] Integrating these citizens into a national framework that is officially defined by its adherence to Twelver Shiism is increasingly difficult at a time when, fueled by complex geopolitical and regional rivalries, sectarian tensions are rising in surrounding countries.

Corruption makes inequality even less acceptable. It is a phenomenon debated by politicians in parliament and widely covered by journalists in the media. As many people struggle to find gainful employment and make ends meet, a new elite has made fortunes by exploiting personal connections to the officials who control access to hard currency, import and export licenses, state contracts, and privatization schemes.

For all these reasons, the promises of the Islamic revolutionaries to establish a more just and more moral society ring hollow with many Iranians, half of whom are too young to recall the corruption, political repression, and inequality under the Shah. As a result, the theocratic model of government has suffered

FIGURE 16.1
Map of Iran's Ethnic Minorities

www.lib.utexas.edu/maps/middle_east_and_asia/iran_ethnoreligious_distribution_2009.jpg

a massive loss of legitimacy. While many people may still be religious, the ulema no longer command their deference and respect. In addition, practicing Muslims and thinkers are developing Islam in new directions by questioning the right of the ulema to rule and exposing different interpretations of texts and opinions among the clergy.

While these social dynamics and tensions pose challenges to the regime, the political establishment also faces profound threats from within the ranks of the regime elite. Almost immediately after the establishment of the Islamic Republic, factions and fissures developed within the coalition of clerical and lay Islamists. During the 1980s, the war with Iraq, challenges from secular groups, and Khomeini's charisma and savvy politics helped unify the country's leadership. However, with the end of the war, Khomeini's death, and the massive challenges of normalizing revolutionary politics in the 1990s, disputes began to rage among the political elite. By the end of the regime's second decade, the political elite was divided into two broad camps—those who wanted to enhance republican institutions and popular participation and those who wanted to strengthen the pillars of Islamist rule and the office of the Leader.

In 2009, elite conflict and social discontent merged after the results of the June presidential elections were announced. Officially, **Mahmoud Ahmadinejad** received 62 percent of the vote, with **Mir-Hossein Mousavi** trailing with less than 34 percent of the vote. Turnout was a staggering 85 percent and was not challenged by any of the candidates or observers. As in 2005, Ahmadinejad had woven together support from core institutions of the Islamic republic, such as the office of the Leader (Ali Khamenei) and generals in the **Islamic Revolutionary Guard Corps (IRGC)**, as well as urban middle-class and lower-middle-class people who were mobilized by his populist message of redistribution, nationalism, and religious moralism. Yet Ahmadinejad's election victory was challenged by the reformist candidates and political leaders (including **AliAkbar Hashemi Rafsanjani** and **Mohammad Khatami**, both former presidents) and by a diverse array of Iranians drawn into what is known as the **Green Movement** (see Box 16.1). When the results were announced, Iran witnessed the largest and most protracted protests it had seen since 1979. The security apparatus used violence and intimidation against the leaders and supporters of the Green Movement to silence dissent. However, both social and elite tensions persist. By responding to the Green Movement with massive violence and intimidation, the Ahmadinejad government and pillars of the regime have alienated a social constituency responsible for managing and running society. Additionally, they angered key members of the Islamic Republic's political elite, including past presidents and ministers. Finally, when Ahmadinejad sought to carve out greater independence for himself and his allies, clashes between the president and Leader emerged and divisions within the conservatives multiplied. Despite regular media attention outside of Iran, during his second term in office, Ahmadinejad was largely disempowered by the Leader, conservatives in the parliament, and even defections from within his supporters.

These events set the stage for the most recent political struggle, the 2013 presidential election. A centrist candidate, Hassan Rouhani, vanquished a large field of more conservative candidates. While Rouhani benefited from the coordination between pragmatist regime insiders and the remnants of the Green Movement to generate mass support buttressed by elite resources, the divided conservatives fought among themselves, with the Leader seemingly uninterested and unable to unify his most loyal supporters. The most immediate challenge faced by the Iranian government is how to forge consensus among the elite and society in order to combat entrenched foreign pressure and revitalize the regime's legitimacy in disparate segments of society. At the time of publication, the Iranian political class has exhibited surprising unity and engaged in fruitful negotiations what is known as the P5+1, the permanent members of the UN Security Council plus Germany.

Historical Legacy

16.2   Discuss the interplay of political and religious leadership in Iran.

Iran, like China and Japan, is one of a handful of non-Western states that Europeans never formally colonized. Iran's borders were not drawn artificially by colonial powers but result from the historical balance of power between its shahs and their neighboring rulers. The Iranian state tradition is over twenty-five

BOX 16.1   The Green Movement

During the 2009 presidential election, former prime minister Mir-Hossein Mousavi's team adopted the color green as their symbol. The selection was a savvy one. Green is associated with Islam and, in particular, *seyyeds*, or people who claim descent from the Prophet Muhammad. Thus, Mousavi, who is a seyyed, reminded religious Iranians of his pious background. In addition, in Iranian culture and literature, the color green symbolizes spring, rebirth, and joy. Thus, green reminded secular Iranians of Mousavi's reformist platform and his departure from Ahmadinejad. Mousavi supporters publicly displayed their political allegiance by distributing green posters, bracelets, balloons, flags, and other campaign material. When the election results were announced on June 13, large numbers of Iranians questioned irregularities in the election procedures and challenged the results. Green became a unifying symbol for all those who challenged Ahmadinejad's reelection. In rallies and other forms of civil disobedience, Iranians asked, "Where is my vote?" and called for a reelection, challenging the authority of the president and even the Leader. Thus, Iran's "Green Movement" was born.

Who are Iran's so-called "Greens"? Given the harsh crackdown after the election, it is difficult to systematically analyze the social backgrounds of the movement's supporters. Having said that, most active supporters seem to be urban, educated, under the age of forty, and drawn from those who voted for Mousavi or the other reformist candidate, Mehdi Karroubi. The movement is sometimes referred to as a "middle-class movement." This is partially true, as members of the industrial working class (even union activists), the peasantry, and older Iranians did not join these protests in large numbers. However, it is important to recall that urban, literate, and professional men and women comprise a significant portion of contemporary Iranian society.

The Green Movement demands were associated with civil and political rights (e.g., right to assembly, greater government transparency, and freedom of the press). Although initially focused on the election and its immediate aftermath, the aspirations of the movement's participants have begun to diverge. Some "Greens," including Mousavi, Karroubi, and Khatami, call for strengthening the republican institutions and principles of the Islamic republic; others call for the eradication of the office of the Leader and the dismantling of the regime entirely. It is thus more precise to speak of different shades of green. While many of these critiques and aspirations are alive in Iran today, the regime's harsh crackdown on the Green leaders and organizations severely demobilized the movement.

Nonetheless, the 2013 presidential race saw some supporters of the Green Movement reemerge. Although the demands and expectations of the movement were tempered and some who participated in 2009 did not vote in 2013, many Greens voted for Hassan Rouhani (see Box 16.4). They retained their symbolic green wristbands and chanted Moussavi's name and slogans remembering political prisoners and those who lost their lives in the violent clashes during 2009–2010. Despite Rouhani's official slogan being "moderation" and his campaign selecting purple as its color, there was a distinct emerald hue to his rallies and eventual electoral victory.

Source: Kaveh Ehsani, Arang Keshavarzian, and Norma Claire Moruzzi, "Tehran, June 2009," *Middle East Report Online*, June 28, 2009; and Mohammad Ali Kadivar, "A New Oppositional Politics: The Campaign Participants in Iran's 2013 Presidential Election," *Jadaliyya*, June 22, 2013, http://www.jadaliyya.com/pages/index/12383/a-new-oppositional-politics_the-campaign-participa.

centuries old, but the current state was set up in the early sixteenth century by the Safavid dynasty. The dynasty's most lasting impact was the establishment of **Twelver Shiism** as the official state religion and the conversion of most Iranians who had been **Sunnis** to Shiism. Historically, the shrine cities of Iraq were the cradle of this branch of Islam, but with the establishment of a powerful Shiite state in Iran, Iran became the political center of the Shiite world.

Twelver Shiism

The split between Sunnis (who constitute about 90 percent of all Muslims) and Shiites came about after the death of the founder of Islam, the Prophet Muhammad. Muhammad was not only the founder of a new religion but also a political leader. Therefore, after he died in 628 CE, the nascent Muslim community had to find a leader to succeed him. A minority of believers, who later came to be known as *Shiites*, deemed the descendants of the Prophet to be his only rightful successors. Shiites call these hereditary successors to the Prophet *Imams*. Of particular importance is the Third Imam, Husayn, whose martyrdom in 680 CE symbolizes for Shiites the struggle of the just against the unjust. This event is still commemorated yearly in emotional processions that acquire a political dimension in times of political crisis.

While some Shiite sects believe in an unbroken line of Imams all the way to the present, the vast majority believe that the twelfth was the last of the Imams, hence their name. According to these Shiites, the Twelfth Imam disappeared from view as a child in 874 CE, but did not die. He is alive (rather like Elijah in the Jewish tradition) and will come forth and show himself to establish a just rule at the end of time. In other words, he is a messiah-like figure. From the moment the Twelfth Imam disappeared from public view, therefore, Twelver Shiite political thought faced a dilemma. The only figure who could exercise legitimate rule over the community of believers was not physically present, and no one knew when he would reveal himself. Most of the time, this dilemma did not matter in practice, because Shiites were a minority lacking political power, making their political theology inconsequential.

With the establishment of a Twelver Shiite state by the Safavid dynasty in the sixteenth century, the unavailability of the one truly legitimate ruler became an existential problem. In the absence of the Twelfth Imam, who had the right to rule in practice? Most ulema were willing to accord this right to the secular rulers, the shahs, so long as they ruled justly and in accordance with Islam. By the end of the seventeenth century, however, a minority of ulema argued that for the rule of a shah to be legitimate, he had to have the ulema's explicit endorsement. After the fall of the Safavids in 1722, Iran was in the grip of civil wars as various short-lived dynasties succeeded each other. The Qajar dynasty finally emerged victorious in 1796.

During the troubled eighteenth century, the ulema established themselves as an institution independent of the state. Since the state was in disarray much of the time, believers' tithes were increasingly paid to the ulema directly, assuring them of financial independence. Moreover, the center of Twelver Shiism, the city of Najaf, lay in Ottoman Iraq, outside the control of Iran's worldly authorities. Beginning in the nineteenth century, therefore, the ulema had greater social, political, and religious prominence in Iran than in the Sunni world. They had their own sources of income and were beyond the control of the state. Without this legacy, the establishment of a theocracy would not even have been conceivable in the 1970s.

In some ways, the role and function of the ulema resemble those of the clergy in Christian countries. However, while the Shiite ulema form a loose hierarchy, they are not organized in a pyramidal structure like the Roman Catholic Church. There is no equivalent of the pope, and no leader can define dogma in a way that is binding for everyone else. Consequently, the ulema has often disagreed among themselves on political and even minor religious matters, a state of affairs that, as we will see, has not ended with the creation of an Islamic state.

A Multiethnic Nation

The population of Iran comprises a number of different ethnic groups defined by language. Persian speakers are the largest group and constitute roughly half the total population, the most important others being Azeri Turks, Kurds, Lurs, Baluchis, Arabs, and Turkmens (see again Figure 16.1). Historically, this ethnic variety did not pose a political problem. There are three main reasons for this. First, Iran's largest non-Persian population, the Azeri Turks, share the same religion with the Persians and have always been prominent among the country's elites. Second, the cultural prestige of the Persian language was such that non-Persian speakers accepted its role as official language. Finally, the Iranian nation was defined territorially rather than ethnically, in the sense that "Iranian" meant coming from the land of Iran, which is the ancient name of the area between the Caspian Sea and the Persian Gulf.

Under the influence of ethnically defined European nationalism, the prerevolutionary elites of Iran defined Iran as a *Persian* country, ignoring its ethnic diversity. After the revolution, Twelver Shiism came to be the defining trait of the nation in the eyes of its leaders. This means that in recent Iranian history, two visions of what constitutes Iranian identity have contended with each other. One ignores the cultural specificity of non-Persian-speaking citizens, while the other marginalizes non-Twelver Shiites, of whom Sunnis are the largest community (approximately 10 percent). In addition, these linguistic and religious divisions are politicized by minorities lacking access to state resources and having fewer socioeconomic opportunities in the country's periphery where the majority of Kurds, Baluch, Arabs, and Turkmen live.

Constitutionalism

Iran's geographic location between the Russian empire in the north and the British Empire in the south allowed it to survive the heyday of European imperialism as an independent state. Both empires allowed it to remain a neutral buffer between their respective domains. Nevertheless, educated Iranians recognized the fragility of their country's sovereignty. As they became more familiar with Europe in the nineteenth century, they became more aware of their own backwardness. As long as Iran was less developed than Europe, it would forever remain vulnerable to imperialist encroachment. Consequently, "catching up with the West" became the major goal of Iran's intellectual and political elite. They believed that the rule of law was the secret of European superiority, whereas arbitrary rule prevailed in Iran. They concluded that constitutional government had to be introduced to strengthen the nation. Japan's victory over Russia in the war of 1905 confirmed Iranian constitutionalists in their view. For the first time, an Asian power had vanquished a European one, and Iranians argued that this reversal of fortunes occurred because Japan was the only constitutional power in Asia, while Russia was the only autocracy among the major European powers.

In 1905, widespread dissatisfaction with the way the country was governed led to a popular movement that wrested a constitution from the Shah in December 1906. Shiite ulema played a major role in the constitutionalist movement. Until a few years earlier, the state had been characterized by an implicit contract between worldly and spiritual authorities. The Shah upheld the official religion, and the ulema legitimated the Shah's rule. But by the early twentieth century, many politically active ulema, merchants, and Western-educated intellectuals shared the view that the powers of the monarchy needed to be curtailed. They believed that citizens had the right to elect a representative parliament. The Shah could name a prime minister only in agreement with parliament, and the parliament could hold the government accountable. These very European ideas were criticized by conservative ulema for being alien to Islam, but constitutionalist ulema found ways to justify them in Islamic terms. Most famously, Ayatollah Muhammad-Husayn Na'ini argued that a despotic shah violated the rights of the Twelfth Imam and those of the people, whereas rule by the people violated only the rights of the Twelfth Imam. He concluded that while neither form of government was ideal, the latter was the lesser evil and thus preferable to the former.[3] This argument implied the novel idea that as long as the Twelfth Imam chose to remain in hiding, the believers themselves were his deputies. This elegant formulation reconciled Shiism's core beliefs with modern notions of constitutionalism and is a legacy that the revolutionaries of 1979 could not ignore as they set out to create an Islamic state.

The Pahlavi Monarchy

The Constitution of 1906 did not bring the hoped-for progress, however. In a 1907 secret agreement, Britain and Russia divided Iran into two spheres of influence. During World War I, belligerents repeatedly violated Iran's neutrality and fought each other on Iranian territory, causing much hardship for the population. By the end of the war, local warlords were challenging the authority of the central government in peripheral regions.

In 1921, a *coup d'état* ended the rule of the old establishment. The commander of the troops, Reza Khan, lost no time in extending government control over rebellious provinces and began an ambitious modernization program to develop and centralize state authority. By 1925, he ousted the ruling Qajar dynasty and had parliament proclaim him the new ruler as Reza Shah Pahlavi. From his coronation in 1926 until his ouster by the British in the wake of the Allied occupation of Iran in 1941, he ruled as a dictator, although he left the Constitution formally in place. Reza Khan initially enjoyed the support of most of the clergy. But in the 1930s, his relations with the ulema deteriorated after he implemented reforms that reduced their social functions and aimed at westernizing the daily culture of Iranians, such as prohibiting women's veiling. With his departure into exile, politics opened up again. His twenty-one-year-old son and successor, Mohammad-Reza Shah Pahlavi, did not have the authority yet to continue his father's ways (see Figure 16.2).

Year	Head of State	President	Prime Minister
1941	Shah: Mohammad-Reza Pahlavi	—	Various cabinets
1951	—	—	Mohammad Mossadegh (51–53)
—	—	—	Various cabinets
1965	—	—	Amir-Abbas Hoveyda
1977	—	—	Jamshid Amuzegar
1979	Leader: Ruhollah Khomeini	—	Mehdi Bazargan
1980	—	Abolhasan Banisadr	—
1981	—	Ali Rajai, Ali Khamenei	Mir-Hosein Musavi
1989	Ali Khamenei	Ali-Akbar Hashemi Rafsanjani	*Position abolished*
1997	—	Mohammad Khatami	
2005	—	Mahmoud Ahmadinejad	
2013	—	Hassan Rouhani	

FIGURE 16.2

Iranian Regimes

Between 1941 and 1953, Iran's political system included three main camps. First, the pro-Western conservative establishment, including the Shah and the landlords, was supported tacitly by most of the ulema. Second was the pro-Soviet communist **Tudeh Party**. Third was the neutralist National Front, which aimed at establishing the full rule of law within the country and consolidating its standing among nations. As the National Front saw it, the nation's sovereignty was compromised by British control over Iran's oil resources through the British-owned Anglo-Iranian Oil Company (AIOC). The Iranian government had no say in the company, not even the right to see its books. From 1945 to 1950, the total net profits of the AIOC were £250 million after deducting high British taxes, royalties, and exaggerated depreciation figures; at the same time, royalties paid to Iran for its oil amounted to merely £90 million.[4]

The leader of the National Front, **Mohammad Mossadegh**, advocated nationalizing the Iranian oil industry. This occurred in March 1951, and, soon thereafter, Mossadegh was elected prime minister by parliament. Subsequent negotiations between the Iranian and British governments to resolve the oil dispute failed. Consequently, the British began plotting Mossadegh's overthrow, which was accomplished with the help of the U.S. Central Intelligence Agency (CIA) in August 1953.[5]

Iran's political system reverted to royal autocracy as the second ruler of the Pahlavi dynasty increasingly asserted himself and took full control over the emerging **rentier state** (see Chapter 7). With the help of a steady stream of oil revenue and U.S. support, the Shah launched the "White Revolution" reform program in 1963, which included land reform and granting suffrage to women. In the 1950s, the Shah had enjoyed the support of the clerical hierarchy, but by the early 1960s, his dictatorial methods and Westernizing policies elicited the anger of religious traditionalists. These traditionalists rioted in June 1963 in support of a new oppositional member of the ulema, Ruhollah Khomeini. The government suppressed the riots with bloodshed, and Khomeini was arrested and exiled. He finally settled in the Shiite shrine city of Najaf in Iraq. He remained there until October 1978, when he was expelled by Saddam Hussein and sought refuge in Paris until his triumphant return to Iran on February 1, 1979.

Until 1963, opposition to royal autocracy was carried out in the name of the Constitution of 1906, which the two Pahlavi shahs were criticized for not respecting. Free elections were the opposition's main demand. After 1963, however, opponents of the Shah, increasingly driven underground or abroad, despaired of ever attaining constitutional rule by peaceful means and became radicalized. Gradually, the Constitution itself suffered a loss of legitimacy. Opponents of the Shah demanded the abolition of the monarchy and its replacement by a new regime. Given the Shah's suppression of civil society and of the secular opposition, mosques and religious circles became the only places where one could speak one's mind. Thus, religion became a more prominent political force, despite the secularist policies of the state. By the 1970s, Shiite activists, many of them university students or followers of Khomeini, were arguing about the shape of the ideal Islamic state.

While the Shah's regime was increasingly contested at home, it received support from the West in general and the United States in particular. Since the Shah's rule had been made possible through the direct intervention of the CIA, his opponents thought of him as a U.S. puppet whose policies were designed to benefit the United States rather than Iran. Opposition to the Shah thus logically entailed opposition to the United States and Israel, with which the Shah had contracted a strategic alliance directed against radical Arab states, such as Egypt, Iraq, and Syria. More recent scholarship suggests that at the height of his power in the early 1970s, the Shah, far from being manipulated by the United States, was actually successful in manipulating U.S. policymakers to achieve his ends.[6]

Although Iran's first revolution failed to produce a constitutional state based on the rule of law, during the seven decades of its life, Iran acquired the trappings of a modern nation-state. The government acquired a monopoly on the use of force; introduced unified legal codes; developed a functioning civil service, including a territorial administration that extended the writ of the state into distant provinces; and secured the country's international borders. State-building having been accomplished, the Islamic state created in the aftermath of the revolution of 1979 became an Islamic republic.

The Islamic Revolution

In 1977, Jimmy Carter became U.S. president, and U.S. foreign policy began emphasizing respect for human rights by U.S. allies.[7] Unbeknownst to the public, the Shah had terminal cancer. To ensure a smooth transition to his heir at a time when U.S. support could no longer be taken for granted, he began liberalizing aspects of Iran's political system and removing longtime advisors and cronies. But various dissident and social groups with grievances took advantage of this liberalization to push for greater reforms. From late 1977 to early 1979, the calls for greater liberalization snowballed into a call for the abolition of the monarchy. This opposition coalition consisted of intellectuals,

university and high school students and teachers, bazaar merchants, politically active clerics and seminarians, industrial workers, and, in the final stage, state employees and white-collar workers.[8] The popular movement against the regime's despotism, corruption, and alliances with the United States and Israel united such diverse ideological factions as liberal adherents of the 1906 Constitution, Marxist-Leninist leftists, and **Islamists**. The latter comprised democrats whose reading of Islam was decidedly liberal and noncoercive, leftists who stressed the egalitarian aspects of Islam, and direct followers of Khomeini who championed an Islamic state supervised by clerics. These activists organized massive meetings, demonstrations, and strikes, and they distributed antiregime pamphlets in a largely peaceful manner.[9] The Shah vacillated between repressing the movement and making belated concessions. Consequently, the activists became ever more radicalized during 1978, finally driving him and his family into exile in January 1979.[10]

In the course of the revolutionary uprising and immediately after the departure of the Shah's family, Khomeini's followers were the best-organized and most united force. They rapidly sidelined the nonclerical currents in their coalition. The organizational power of Khomeini and his followers was enhanced by their access to independent sources of revenue, as traditionally observant Shiites pay their tithes directly to the ulema. In 1970, Khomeini had revived the strain in Twelver Shiite thought that called for clerical oversight of government and carried it to its logical conclusion. In a treatise titled "Islamic Government," he argued that God had revealed His laws to humankind, not so that they would be ignored until the moment the Twelfth Imam revealed himself, but in order to apply them here and now. Khomeini further observed that the people most suited to rule in accordance with divine law are those who know it best, namely, the ulema themselves. This principle came to be known as **velayat-e faqih**, which is best translated as "guardianship of the jurisprudent"[11] (see Box 16.2).

Given Khomeini's charismatic leadership of the revolution, his followers enshrined this principle in the new 1979 Iranian Constitution. However, in deference to the preexisting constitutional tradition and to placate the non-Islamists and moderate Islamists who had participated in the revolution, the Constitution maintained a parliament elected by universal suffrage. The Shah was replaced with an elected president.

Velayat-e faqih—the lynchpin of Iran's theocratic Constitution—is best translated as "guardianship of the jurisprudent." Ayatollah Ruhollah Khomeini described this while he was in exile in 1970 in Iraq. Khomeini argued that since God revealed the laws according to which Muslims should live and organize their community, Muslims should apply these laws in practice rather than just debating them theoretically. The most qualified people to supervise the application of these laws in the state, he wrote, are those who know them best (that is, the clerics who specialize in jurisprudence).

He concluded that such a cleric must therefore be the head of state. In 1979, this principle was enshrined in the Constitution of the Islamic Republic of Iran, and Khomeini himself became the ruling jurisprudent, referred to henceforth as "Leader." For the first time in Iranian history, religious and worldly authorities were fused. Velayat-e faqih is not strongly grounded in scripture, and most Twelver Shiite clerics disagree with the principle. They see the task of the Shiite clergy as that of guiding the believers and advising rulers, as can be seen in post-Saddam Iraq.

The Islamic Republic was thus born with a mixed political system that is informed by both a version of Twelver Shiite political doctrine and by Western notions of popular sovereignty and division of powers.[12]

From 1979 to June 1981, secular moderates, leftists, moderate Islamists, and radical Islamists inspired directly by Khomeini competed for power. As time went on, the confrontation between adherents of velayat-e faqih and their opponents became ever more implacable and violent. In fact, far more people were killed in confrontations among the revolutionaries than had died as a result of the Shah's efforts to suppress the revolutionary mass movement. By the summer of 1981, Khomeini's supporters gained the upper hand and began instituting Islamic law in all spheres of public life. Their suppression of all who opposed them was facilitated by the war that was now raging with neighboring Iraq.

Iran–Iraq War (1980–1988)

Soon after the revolution, Khomeini began calling for the overthrow of the Iraqi president, Saddam Hussein. This provoked Saddam Hussein to attack Iran in September 1980. The war that ensued lasted until 1988 and ended in a stalemate.

Officially termed the "imposed war" or the "sacred defense" in Iran, the war was a major watershed. Over 2 million Iranians were mobilized, with approximately a quarter of a million killed and more than double that number injured, many due to Iraq's use of chemical weapons. The war enabled the revolutionary regime to consolidate its hold on power by calling for national unity in the face of a foreign invasion. The war became a means to suppress dissent and public debate. The conflict created a "war generation" of young men who were shaped as much by their experiences at the front as by the revolution. Now many of these soldiers and officers are in their forties and fifties, and some are demanding a bigger say in national and local politics. Although this generation is symbolically powerful, they have not been unified behind any single politician or political current. For instance, some war veterans seem to have supported the reformist candidates in the last fifteen years, while others have supported Ahmadinejad.

Institutions of the Islamic Republic

16.3 Describe and distinguish between appointed and elected offices in Iran.

Two types of institutions coexist in the political system of the Islamic Republic of Iran: appointed and elected offices. This dualism reflects the attempted synthesis between divine and popular sovereignty enshrined in the Constitution. The institutional structure of Iran is further complicated by the existence of what is known as **multiple power centers**, institutions created by the revolutionaries to supplement the activities of the traditional state institutions, with which they share overlapping responsibilities (see Figure 16.3).

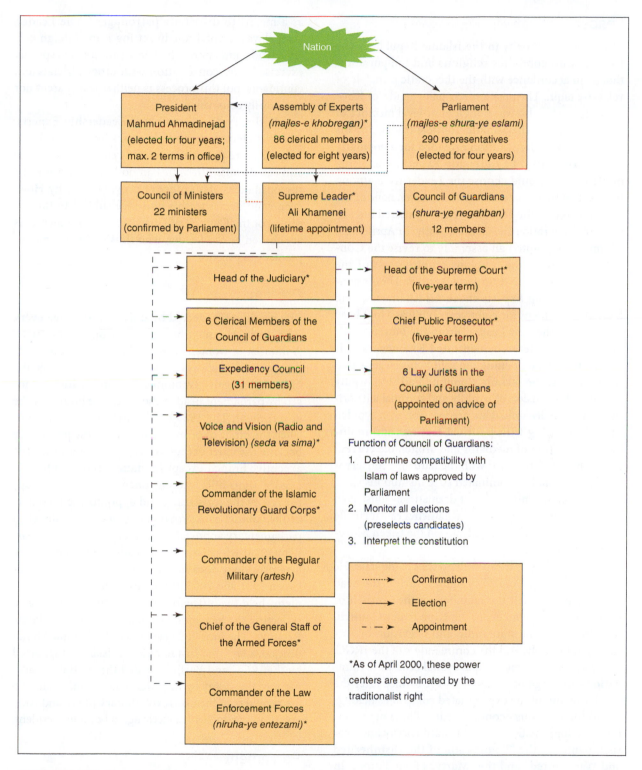

Constitutional Structure

Formal political power structure in Iran.

Source: Adapted from Wilfried Buchta, *Who Rules Iran? The Structure of Power in the Islamic Republic* (Washington, DC: Washington Institute for Near East Policy, 2000). © Wilfried Buchta, Rabat 2000.

Leader

The highest authority in the Islamic Republic is the **Leader**, who combines religious and temporal authority in accordance with the theocratic principle of velayat-e faqih. The position was tailor-made for Khomeini himself, who was both a high-level member of the ulema and a charismatic political leader. For his succession, the Constitution provided for a popularly elected **Assembly of Leadership Experts**, consisting of ulema who would choose the Leader from among the most learned ulema. By 1989, however, none of the ulema who had the requisite learning shared his notions of theocratic rule. Consequently, in April 1989, Khomeini appointed an assembly to revise the Constitution to relax the religious requirements of the office. Khomeini died on June 3, 1989. The Assembly of Leadership Experts chose **Ali Khamenei**, who had been president for eight years but was a low-level cleric, to be the new Leader. From the outset, much of the clerical hierarchy contested Khamenei's religious authority, reopening the split between state and "church" that the Islamic Republic had supposedly closed with its fusion of worldly and spiritual authorities. Additionally, unlike his predecessor, who avoided directly aligning with political factions and maintained a position of mediator and arbiter, the current Leader has publicly sided with the hard-line conservative faction that has dominated state institutions since the early 2000s. This was most dramatically illustrated after the 2009 election, when Khamenei categorically supported Ahmadinejad and labeled the Green Movement as treasonous.

The Leader sets the overall policies of the state. He also appoints some of its key figures, such as the head of the Judiciary, half the members of the **Council of Guardians**, the members of the **Expediency Council**, the director of the state radio and television broadcasting monopoly, and the commanders of the IRGC. He oversees the numerous **parastatal economic foundations** and organizations that were formed after the revolution out of the expropriated companies belonging to the previous economic elite. These organizations are supposedly oriented toward charity and bear such names as the "Foundation of the Disinherited and War Injured" and the "Martyr's Foundation." In fact, they are major holding companies that benefit from state resources and subsidies without being accountable to or regulated by the elected government. Khamenei has used these "nonprofit" organizations as a means to distribute patronage.[13] The Leader, also, plays a pivotal role in setting Iran's foreign policy agenda and approach. These powers are typically exercised after consultation with other officials and confidants, but this process is neither transparent nor necessarily consensual.

In theory, the Assembly of Leadership Experts, which is elected every eight years by universal suffrage, is more powerful than the Leader. It elects him and can dismiss him if he can no longer perform the responsibilities of his office or proves unworthy. However, candidacies to this body are subject to the approval of the Council of Guardians, whose members are chosen by the Leader, who thus maintains his supremacy in practice.

President

The president is elected by universal suffrage every four years. He must be a Twelver Shiite and male. A number of women have tried to become presidential candidates, always unsuccessfully. Until 1989, the office was largely ceremonial. A prime minister chosen by parliament headed the executive branch of the government. The 1989 constitutional revision abolished the office of prime minister, and the presidency became the chief executive. The president heads the executive branch except in matters reserved for the Leader, signs bills into law once they have been approved by the legislature, and appoints the members of the cabinet and provincial governors, subject to parliamentary approval. He can be impeached by parliament, at which point the Leader can dismiss him. The president does not have to be a cleric, but between 1981 and 2005, three different members of the ulema held the office for two consecutive terms each, reflecting the hegemony of that group in the Islamic Republic. The June 2005 election of Mahmoud Ahmadinejad, a lay (that is, a nonulema) Islamist supported by the IRGC and Basij, heralded the partial replacement of the clergy by the "war generation," men who are products of the postrevolutionary polity and society. However, in 2013, a cleric again became president.

Parliament

Iran's unicameral parliament, the **Majles**, has 290 members elected by universal suffrage for four-year terms. Members have to be Muslims, but the Constitution provides for five members of parliament (MPs) to represent Christians (three), Jews (one), and Zoroastrians (one).

The Majles has lawmaking powers, but its legislative output must not contravene the Constitution or Islam, as determined by the Council of Guardians (as we will discuss shortly). It has the right to investigate affairs of state, to approve or reject the president's cabinet appointments, and to call ministers to account and subject them to votes of no confidence. Interestingly, even the Seventh, Eighth, and Ninth Parliaments (2004 to present) that have been dominated by conservatives have often used these powers to challenge Ahmadinejad's cabinet choices and ministers. Rouhani has also seen some of his nominations for minister fail to garner votes, but significantly some of the critical posts such as minister of foreign affairs, minister of petroleum, and minister of culture and Islamic guidance.

In his treatise on Islamic government, Khomeini assigned little importance to parliament, arguing that Islam had already laid down laws for most matters. A legislative assembly's task was to draw up rules and regulations for minor issues not dealt with in Islamic jurisprudence. Since 1979, however, the Majles has shown remarkable initiative. For one, the traditional corpus of Islamic law proved woefully inadequate for governing a modern state, requiring parliament to fill some of the gaps. Furthermore, the legislative deputies have vigorously debated state business and held government officials accountable, the office of the Leader excepted.

In the First Parliament of the Islamic Republic, almost half of all deputies were clerics. Under the Shah, no free elections had taken place, so few people had enough name recognition to be elected to parliament. Consequently, in many places, voters chose the local cleric. The percentage of clerics in the Majles has declined over time, as seen in Table 16.1. Although the ulema had generally opposed female suffrage in 1963, the founders of the Islamic Republic maintained women's active and passive suffrage in spite of their patriarchal disposition. Since 1980, every legislature has included female deputies (see Table 16.1), although these figures have been quite low by international levels.

Nonetheless, two features of the political system seriously limit the Majles' legislative role. First, many policies, rules, and regulations are set by unelected specialized bodies. Second, all its bills are subject to the veto of the Council of Guardians. Under the Islamic Republic, the Majles is a forum where policies are discussed and proposals aired, and where some state officials are taken to account.[14]

Council of Guardians

In order to forestall any possibility of compromising the Islamic character of the state, the 1979 Constitution created a separate body to ensure the conformity of legislation with Islam: the Council of Guardians. The Council consists of six members of the ulema and six lay Muslim lawyers. The Leader appoints the ulema;

TABLE 16.1
Who Is in the Parliament?
The number of women is increasing, and the number of clerics is decreasing.

	Female MPs	Clerical MPs	Total MPs
First Majles (1980–1984)	4	131	263
Second Majles (1984–1988)	4	122	269
Third Majles (1988–1992)	4	77	267
Fourth Majles (1992–1996)	9	65	270
Fifth Majles (1996–2000)	10	53	274
Sixth Majles (2000–2004)	13	35	278
Seventh Majles (2004–2008)	12	42	281
Eighth Majles (2008–2012)	13	44	285
Ninth Majles (2012–)	9	27[a]	290

[a]This figure is drawn from www.tabnak.ir/fa/news/242818/نمودار (acccessed May 14, 2013).

the lawyers are nominated by the head of the Judiciary (who is himself appointed by the Leader) but approved by parliament. The compatibility of laws with Islam is determined by the six ulema members only; their compatibility with the Constitution is determined by the entire council. Through the years, the Council has rejected numerous bills because it interpreted them as violating the Constitution and/or Islamic law.

The Council of Guardians also supervises the elections to the Assembly of Leadership Experts, the presidency, and parliament. It has interpreted this provision of the Constitution to signify that it can vet candidacies. It uses this self-ascribed power to limit citizens' choice at elections by not allowing candidates of whose views it disapproves. When in 1991 the Majles passed a law stripping the council of these powers, the latter, unsurprisingly, declared the law to be contrary to the Constitution.

Expediency Council

Disagreement between the Majles and the Council of Guardians is endemic in the Islamic Republic, resulting in legislative gridlock. As long as Khomeini was alive, he was the ultimate arbiter when a protracted stalemate arose, and all involved deferred to him. In 1988, Khomeini established a new collective body to arbitrate such cases, and it was aptly called the "Council for the Determination of What Is in the Interest of the Regime," an unwitting admission that conformity to the teachings of Islam now took a backseat to political expedience. Indeed, official Iranian documents render the name of this body in English as the "Expediency Council." Its existence was anchored in the constitutional revision of 1989.

The Leader directly appoints over thirty members of this body, who are chosen mainly from among top government officials, key cabinet members and military leaders, the ulema members of the Council of Guardians, and ulema chosen for their personal prestige. In addition to arbitrating conflicts between the Majles and the Council of Guardians, the Expediency Council has the constitutional mandate of advising the Leader in formulating overall state policy.

An Honestly Undemocratic Constitution

As our discussion shows, the authority of the elective offices of the Islamic Republic, essentially the presidency and parliament, is systematically limited by unelected bodies. To be sure, the Leader is chosen by an elected body, the Assembly of Leadership Experts, but there is no limit on his term. This makes him, for all intents and purposes, an unremovable leader with vast powers. By appointing the head of the Judiciary and the commanders of the police, army, and IRGC, he controls the coercive apparatus of the state.

The limited authority of the president and parliament became startlingly blatant when liberalizing reformists won a string of elections in the late 1990s. They won control of the presidency in 1997 and 2001 with the election of Mohammad Khatami, and of parliament in 2000. However, Leader Ali Khamenei openly sided with antireformist conservatives, whom he chose as the head of the Judiciary and as the members of the Council of Guardians. When the lawyers proposed by the Judiciary to fill vacant seats on the Council of Guardians failed to gain the endorsement of the reformist parliament in 2001, the Leader simply refused to schedule the swearing-in ceremony of the reformist Khatami, who had just been reelected with 77.9 percent of the vote. In the end, the lawyers took their seats without gaining majority support in parliament, after which the Leader consented to swear in the president.

Although the reformists tried to bring about change by legal means, they were ultimately stymied by the Leader, the Council of Guardians, and the Judiciary, using powers granted to them by the Constitution. This shows that the Constitution is, if not liberal and democratic, at least honest; its provisions need not be violated to prevent democratic governance.

The same can be said for citizens' rights. Although freedom of speech and association, as well as the safety of the person, are guaranteed, these are usually qualified by the clause "within the criteria of Islam." This leaves the authorities considerable leeway to abridge these rights. The same is true for the equality of citizens. Christian, Jewish, and Zoroastrian Iranians are accorded some legal recognition and can practice their religion freely. However, Iran's largest non-Muslim minority, the adherents of the Baha'i Faith, are considered heretics and systematically discriminated against; to this day, they may not attend university, for instance. Even Sunni Muslims, representing about 10 percent of the total population, are systematically discriminated against in the civil service and are not allowed to maintain a mosque of their own in Tehran.

In the words of a prominent exiled Iranian human rights lawyer, in the Islamic Republic, "the rights of the clerics do not equal those of nonclerics, the rights of Twelver Shiites do not equal those of non-Twelver Shiites, the rights of Shiites do not equal those of Sunnis, the rights of Muslims do not equal those of non-Muslims, the rights of 'recognized religious minorities' do not equal those of other 'minorities,' and the rights of men do not equal the rights of women."[15] The explicit denial of legal equality to citizens found throughout Iran's constitution and legal system stands in sharp contrast to the universalist language of many other Third World regimes.

Multiple Power Centers

When the revolutionaries took over the state in 1979, they inherited an administrative bureaucracy whose commitment to the new ideology they did not trust. Not content with purging state institutions of individuals they deemed counterrevolutionary, they built new institutions whose competency overlapped with the old established ones. The idea was that the old institutions would more or less carry on with business as usual, while the new institutions would actively pursue the realization and defense of the new Islamic order (see again Figure 16.3). Examples include the Construction Jihad, which sent young people to rural areas to help develop them in parallel to the Ministry of Agriculture. The most important example is the IRGC. Its original function was to safeguard the revolution, but in time, it developed into a parallel army and even acquired an air force and a navy.[16]

As Khomeini and his followers consolidated their rule in the mid-1980s, they attempted to merge state and revolutionary organizations. However, these attempts were mostly unsuccessful, and the revolutionary organizations are still active. In the late 1990s, as some state institutions came under the control of the reformists, conservatives created new parallel institutions under the aegis of the office of the Leader. Thus, when the Ministry of Information, as the secret police is called, came to be staffed mainly by reformists, the Judiciary, whose head is named by the Leader, proceeded to set up a parallel secret police (which even maintains a prison system for political prisoners). These multiple power centers complicate policymaking considerably.

Elections and Parties

16.4 Discuss political parties versus factions as they affect Iranian elections.

The Prerevolutionary Legacy

With the brief exception of the 1940s, between 1906 and 1979, competitive elections were rarely held in Iran. In 1963, the Shah gave women active and passive suffrage. This action did not mean much in practice, because there were no free elections for the remainder of his reign, but it did establish standards that could not be undone. Although much of the ulema had vehemently opposed the extension of suffrage to women in 1963, the mobilization of women in the course of the revolution was so important that it was not possible to deprive them of the right to vote again.

Under the monarchy, political parties were mostly weak and ephemeral. After World War II, two groups succeeded in establishing a lasting societal presence: the Communist Tudeh party and the nationalist National Front of Mohammad Mossadegh. These two were revived in the course of the revolution of 1978. However, they were overshadowed by more radical leftist or Islamist groups that had emerged from the armed struggle against the Shah, such as the Marxist–Leninist Fada'iyan-e Khalq and the leftist Islamist Mojahedin-e Khalq. Initially, the Liberation Movement of Iran (LMI), a moderate Islamist offshoot of the National Front founded in 1961, fared somewhat better. Its leaders largely staffed the provisional government of Prime Minister Mehdi Bazargan that administered the country from February to November 1979, when they resigned in protest over radical students' seizure of U.S. diplomats as hostages. In 1981, the National Front, the Fada'iyan-e Khalq, and the Mojahedin-e Khalq were banned for advocating policies that contradicted the basic premise of the Islamic Republic. In 1983, the Tudeh party was disbanded and its leaders jailed for having spied for the Soviet Union. The LMI, for its part, has managed to maintain low-level activity within the country.

Postrevolutionary Parties

In early 1979, a group of Khomeini's loyal followers, including future president Rafsanjani and Leader Khamenei, founded a new party to work toward the realization of their version of an Islamic state: the Islamic

Republican Party (IRP). Soon, however, separate factions crystallized within the IRP around different economic, social, and foreign policy agendas. Factionalism having rendered the party dysfunctional, Rafsanjani and Khamenei announced the dissolution of the IRP in a letter to Khomeini in June 1987. They said that the party had achieved its goal, the establishment of velayat-e faqih, and had thus ceased to have a reason to exist.

But the underlying reasons for the factionalism did not go away. Some regime figures advocated more state intervention in the economy on the grounds that Islam is the religion of social justice, and therefore an Islamic government must look after the interests of the poor. Others argued that Islam protects the sanctity of private property, and therefore more laissez-faire policies were in order as long as everybody adhered to the rules that Islamic jurisprudence established for economic activities. As the leaders of the Islamic Republic grappled with the problem of translating Islam into a political ideology that provides guidance for the solution to all problems, it became clear that divergent policy options could be derived from Islamic principles. In 1987, Speaker of Parliament Rafsanjani admitted that there were "two powerful wings" within the Islamic Republic, adding that "basically they represent two unorganized parties. Indeed when they describe the positions they hold, they are two parties, not two wings."[17] The tensions came out into the open in 1988 when the Society of Militant Clergy, a pro-velayat-e faqih group, split in two as some less conservative members, including future president Mohammad Khatami, left to form the Association of Militant Clerics.

As long as Khomeini was alive, he acted as the ultimate arbiter among the factions. When government figures turned to him to break a factional deadlock over a policy, he would normally urge all to cooperate. But when pressed, Khomeini came out against the conservatives more often than not. After Khomeini's death in 1989, the fact that the leadership of the Islamic Republic included no high-ranking ulema combined with the rivalry of opinions among the ulema allowed many policy disagreements to remain unresolved. These disagreements were channeled into the political system and became the basis of electoral competition as different candidates espoused opposing views for which they sought people's votes. This factor has given Iranian elections a poignancy they lack in other nondemocratic states.

Ideological differences have become the basis of factional politics among three broad, and sometimes fractious, clusters in the political elite: conservatives, pragmatists, and reformers. The conservatives are clerics and lay politicians who favor stricter social rules (such as gender segregation in public places) and call for greater authority for the Leader at the expense of elected bodies, while simultaneously supporting freer, market-oriented economic policies.

Pragmatists, including Rafsanjani and many technocrats who staffed the ministries in the 1990s, are more accommodating on social issues and support economic liberalization and the privatization of state-owned and parastatal companies. Western media often describe these politicians as "moderates." Moreover, they toned down support for exporting the revolution and are somewhat more conciliatory regarding U.S.–Iranian relations. As their name suggests, depending on the issue, they align themselves with either the conservatives or reformists.

Finally, the reformers emerged in the 1990s. Many of the key members of this group were thought of as radicals, or the younger Islamist revolutionaries and clerics who were influenced by leftist and anti-imperialist politics. In the 1980s, they called for increased state control of the economy to ensure greater social justice and were active in supporting Islamist struggles in the Middle East. In the course of the 1990s, many of the radicals of the 1980s had a change of heart and moderated their views and came to be self-identified as "reformists." Their evolution had a number of reasons. For one, their exclusion from parliament in 1992 brought home the importance of fair elections and political pluralism. Furthermore, the collapse of communism in the Soviet Union and Eastern Europe delegitimized the state-centric approach to social and political organization. At the same time, a group of Muslim intellectuals, some of them ulema, challenged both the traditional jurisprudential approach to religion that led to the preeminence of the ulema and the survival of obsolete regulations and the ideologization of religion that led to the loss of spirituality and to totalitarian government. As such, the reformists explicitly challenge the conservative faction in Iran. This more liberal approach to religion created a tentative connection between Islamic reformists and social groups that had hitherto not participated in politics, boosting participation rates at elections in the late 1990s and subsequently helping to forge the "Green Movement" in 2009.

The rise of the reformists and the conservatives' seeming inability to win elections alarmed militants who felt that the Islamic Republic had betrayed its revolutionary ideals. They formed a new faction, calling themselves "principlists."[18] In 2005 and 2009, they were the most dedicated backers of Mahmoud Ahmadinejad.

In the 2013 campaign, the pragmatist Hassan Rouhani explicitly aligned himself with the reformist cause and against the conservatives and principlists. In a rare case, the pragmatists and reformists made an explicit alliance, with the reformist candidate stepping aside in favor of Rouhani only days before the ballot.

While a number of political parties have appeared in Iran, most are vehicles for one man's political ambitions and lack any grassroots organization. Additionally, the politics, alliances, and membership of these factions tend to be quite fluid, making it difficult to predict definitively or explain the actions and positions of politicians and political organizations. Since strong parties are absent, journals, newspapers, and, increasingly, websites play a key role as vehicles for discussing, formulating, and disseminating ideological alternatives.

مبارزه امروز ملت ایران
مبارزه سبزاندیشی با سیاه اندیشی است

ستاد مرکزی مردمی اقوام و اقشار استان تهران

A Poster from Mir Hossein Mousavi's 2009 Election Campaign
This poster depicts former reformist President Khatami bestowing a green scarf on Mir Hossein Mousavi as a symbol of their shared descent from the Prophet Muhammad. The slogan at the top reads: "The Iranian nation's struggle today is a struggle between green thinking and black thinking," where "green" refers to the reformist agenda of the Mousavi campaign and "black" to the Ahmadinejad camp and its policies.

Presidential Elections

In January 1980, Iran held its first-ever presidential election, resulting in the victory of a lay Islamist, Abolhasan Banisadr. But Banisadr was impeached by parliament and deposed by Khomeini in June 1981. His more pliant successor and the prime minister were killed two months later by a bomb attack. The next four elections had predictable results, as close companions of Khomeini—Ali Khamenei in 1981 and 1985 and Ali-Akbar Hashemi Rafsanjani in 1989 and 1993—easily won against minor challengers. Consequently, the voting participation rate went steadily down, as can be seen in Figure 16.4.

The pattern seemed to repeat itself in 1997. The speaker of parliament, conservative cleric Ali-Akbar Nateq Nuri, was endorsed by most of the government and the politically active ulema, including the Leader.

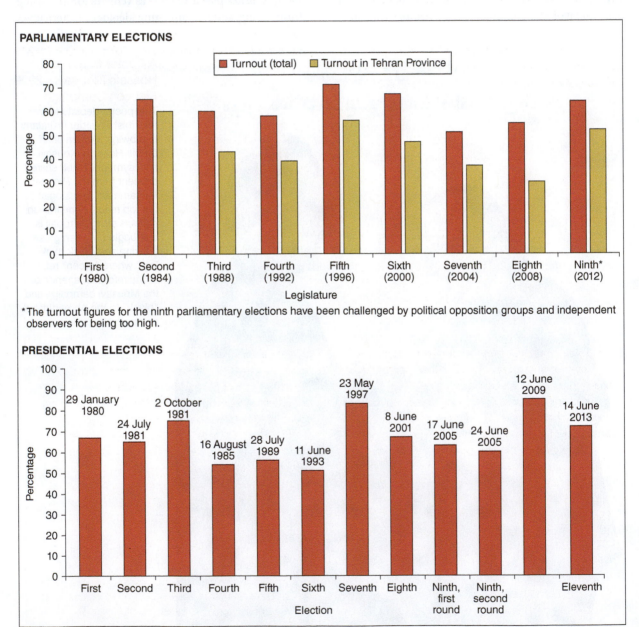

*The turnout figures for the ninth parliamentary elections have been challenged by political opposition groups and independent observers for being too high.

FIGURE 16.4

Electoral Participation

Turnout in Parliamentary and presidential elections fluctuates.

Source: Compiled by Arang Keshavarzian.

Most observers expected him to win. Instead, Moham-mad Khatami, a moderate cleric who had resigned as minister of culture in 1992 after conservatives gained control over parliament, ran a modern and effective campaign by reaching out to university students and active members of the nascent civil society, many of whom were the products of the regime's expansive edu-cational and social policies (see below). He won a land-slide victory. As an "outsider," Khatami appealed to all those who had been humiliated by the regime: educated people who felt that the state discriminated against them in favor of less educated but ideologically reliable Islamic activists, women who resented the legal restric-tions and discrimination to which they were subjected, and young people who were tired of daily harassment by the guardians of public morality. To all these groups, Khatami promised greater cultural openness, personal freedoms, and a more transparent and accountable government. Although his reforms were stymied by the conservatives after 1999, he was easily reelected in 2001.

For the first time since 1981, there was no official government candidate in the 2005 presidential elec-tions. Three allies of Khatami, four conservatives, and Rafsanjani ran for the highest elective office. Since no candidate gained a majority, there was a second-round runoff election pitting Rafsanjani against the populist mayor of Tehran, Mahmoud Ahmadinejad. At around 60 percent, voter participation in the two rounds was lower than in the previous two elections. Ahmadine-jad won an upset victory amidst allegations that IRGC and Basij commanders had illegally urged troops to vote for him, and perhaps even stuffed ballot boxes to increase his vote share in the first round. In any event, Ahmadinejad's message appealed to the poor whose concerns had not been addressed by the cultural liberalization of the Khatami years (see Box 16.3).

BOX 16.3 Biography of Two Presidents and Two Generations

Iran's previous two presidents—Mohammad Khatami (1997–2005) and Mahmoud Ahmadinejad (2005–2013)—illustrate the changing face of Iran's political elite, from an older generation formed by the struggle against the Shah and the revolution to a younger one shaped by the events of the postrevolutionary era. Moreover, the socioeconomic differences between Khatami and Ahmadinejad are telling.

Khatami was born in 1943 into a family of notable clerics and landowners. He is a cleric educated in the seminaries of Qom and holds a B.A. in philosophy from a secular university. He has authored several works on philosophy, is fluent in Arabic, and knows some German and English. After the revolution, he was minister of cul-ture and Islamic guidance (1982–1992), which regulates and censors all media and publications. There, he was known to support freedom of speech and the press. Khatami carved out some space for his cultural activi-ties, thanks to his close relationships with Khomeini and his son, as well as with journalists and students who later supported his presidency. Nonetheless, after grow-ing pressure from hard-line conservatives, Khatami was forced to resign in 1992 and became the director of the National Library until he successfully ran for president.

Ahmadinejad was born in 1956 to a blacksmith and moved to Tehran at a young age. He is a product of the prerevolutionary secular education system, and studied engineering. He participated in the Iran–Iraq war as a member of the IRGC. He later performed well during his three years as governor of the newly established Arda-bil Province (1993–1996). In 1997, Ahmadinejad earned a Ph.D. from a technical university and continued to teach there. In 2003, he was part of the new conserva-tive faction of younger politicians known as the "Alliance of Builders of Islamic Iran," which swept the Tehran city council elections, and he was elected as mayor.

What brings these disparate profiles and outlooks together is that both men were overwhelmingly elected president—against candidates favored by key elements of the establishment. Intriguingly, Hassan Rouhani, the current president, symbolizes a synthesis of his predeces-sors. Born in 1948, he is a cleric who studied at Tehran University before the revolution and in Scotland after 1979. He both speaks of rule of law and has risen through the ranks of the foreign policy and military–security apparatus of the state. While he forged an alliance with reformists during his campaign, he positioned himself as a centrist and was careful not to alienate any faction or institution.

Sources: Wilfried Buchta, *Who Rules Iran? The Structure of Power in the Islamic Republic* (Washington, DC: Washington Institute for Near East Policy, 2000), 30; www.bbc.co.uk/persian/iran/story/2005/08/050801_pm-mv-khatami-profile.shtml.

As mentioned earlier, the 2009 elections were highly contentious, but resulted in Ahmadinejad winning a second and last term in office. In 2013, however, the result of Hassan Rouhani's election was accepted by all (see Box 16.4).

Parliamentary Elections

Iran is divided into multimember constituencies for parliamentary elections, the largest being Tehran with thirty MPs. Each voter can write down the names of as many candidates as there are seats in a constituency. The top vote getters in each constituency are elected, provided they receive at least 25 percent of the total vote. If a constituency has more seats than candidates who passed the 25 percent barrier, a second round determines the remaining MPs from among the runners-up. In the second round, the number of candidates is twice that of the seats that remain to be filled. In the absence of organized political parties, candidates tend to be endorsed by a number of different political, religious, and cultural associations. This factor makes it difficult to deduce accurate figures about the relative popularity of different political groups from the election results.

In the first legislative elections of 1980, a few National Front, LMI, and regionalist candidates were elected to parliament. Since 1984, only candidates unequivocally committed to velayat-e faqih have been allowed to run. Radicals formed the majority in the Second (1984–1988) and Third (1988–1992) Parliaments. After Khomeini's death, the conservative-dominated Council of Guardians gave itself the right to vet candidates and invalidated the candidacies of most radicals. Consequently, conservatives dominated the Fourth (1992–1996) and Fifth (1996–2000) Parliaments, with pragmatist supporters of Rafsanjani

---

BOX 16.4   The 2013 Presidential Election

The 2013 presidential campaign began ominously. When the powerful past president Hashemi Rafsanjani and a close associate of Ahmadinejad registered to run for office, it seemed that the campaign would be a contest between two forces that were not only opposed to one another but also had the status to pose a challenge to the Leader's preeminent status. However, the Guardian Council used its power to disqualify these two candidates among many others and offer a list of lesser-known personalities drawn heavily from the most conservative voices within the establishment. Some pundits interpreted this as an indication that the Leader and his advisors were engineering an uneventful election with the winner being a pliant conservative beholden to Khamenei. As campaign rallies and televised debates took center stage, however, distinct differences on the nuclear negotiations, economic crisis management, and the political space for independent voices in the bureaucracy, universities, and media were aired. Meanwhile, the many conservative candidates not only did not unite behind a single candidate but openly criticized each other's past records. Conversely, the reformist candidate, who had gained the support of many within the Green Movement and of reformist figures such as former president Khatami, forged a pact with Hassan Rouhani and stepped aside and encouraged his supporters to vote for the former nuclear negotiator, member of the Supreme National Security Council, and associate of Hashemi Rafsanjani. What was equally critical for Rouhani, however, was that despite the contested nature of the 2009 election, large numbers of Iranians had to trust the election process enough to cast their ballots. Reformist-oriented candidates only do well when voter turnout surpasses 65 percent. The relative opening of the political sphere that accompanies all elections was seized by activists, previously associated with the Green Movement, who saw Rouhani's candidacy as an opportunity to roll back the militarized and monopolized polity that was forged by Ahmadinejad, the IRGC, and the Leader. This simultaneous coalition building of elites and energy and organization of campaigners resulted in the unexpected, but explainable, turnout of 72 percent, with 51 percent of the vote going to Hassan Rouhani. The second-place candidate, mayor of Tehran Baqer Qalibaf, won less than 16 percent. While it is unclear to what extent Rouhani wishes to adopt the more reformist agenda, his presidency creates new opportunities and challenges for all Iranians as well as foreign governments.

forming the minority. After Khatami's surprise victory in the presidential election of 1997, however, a record number of reformists became candidates. Since they were unknown to the Council of Guardians, they were allowed to run for office in 2000. They swept the elections, gaining around 70 percent of the vote.

For the 2004 parliamentary elections, the Council of Guardians disallowed about 2,000 reformist candidates, including about 80 sitting MPs. This was unprecedented, and many reformist personalities and groups called for an electoral boycott. Although participation diminished, 50 percent of the population still went to the polls. In many areas outside the main cities, voters do not judge candidates by their ideology but by what they can do (or have done) to further the interests of their constituents. Figure 16.4 shows that official turnout figures were again relatively high (55.3 percent) in 2008 despite the Guardian Council's vetting out a disproportionate number of reformist candidates.[19] Despite the conservatives and "principlists" winning the vast majority of seats in the Eighth Parliament, new divisions soon emerged among them; many "principlists" became outspoken critics of Ahmadinejad's economic policies and alleged disregard of the Leader's wishes. The parliamentary elections of 2012 were largely a contest between supporters of Ahmadinejad and supporters of Khamenei, with the latter winning a narrow majority.

Local Elections

Provisions of the 1979 Constitution calling for elected local government councils were first put into action in 1999, when Iranians elected city, town, and village councils. Reformists won control over most councils, including Tehran. With the conservatives stymieing the reformist camp, apathy overtook voters. Voting came to be seen by many as a futile exercise, since, ultimately, power rested with unelected bodies. In the second local elections in 2003, only 15 percent of the eligible voters in Tehran, mostly conservatives, bothered to vote, even though these were the freest elections in Iranian history. The Council of Guardians had not vetted candidates, and even avowed secularists were allowed to run. Consequently, the nation's capital, home to about 15 percent of its total population, got a uniformly conservative city council, which elected as mayor the man who, two years later, used

his position as a springboard for a successful bid for the presidency: Mahmoud Ahmadinejad. Elsewhere in the country, however, campaigns were more centered on concrete problems and participation was thus higher, testifying to a relatively high level of civic engagement of the citizenry.[20] Participation sharply increased in the third local elections of December 2006, and supporters of President Ahmadinejad won only a few seats. As if in rebuke for his incompetent management of the economy, his supporters won only three out of fifteen seats on Tehran's municipal council. In 2010, the parliament voted to postpone municipal elections until 2013, to coincide with the presidential elections. These elections have generated councils composed of members from diverse political affiliations and tendencies.

Political Culture

16.5   Identify five key features of Iran's political culture.

To a large extent, Iran's political culture results from its place in the international system. Iran survived the age of imperialism as a nominally sovereign state, but this independence did not prevent outside powers, mainly Great Britain and Russia, from meddling in Iran's domestic affairs and controlling its economy.[21] Having been a long-standing member of the international society of nations, Iranians have tended to compare themselves with the dominant countries of the West rather than with other Third World nations. Nevertheless, transforming their country's formal independence into genuine sovereignty has always been a key concern of politically conscious Iranians.

One result of foreign meddling in Iranian affairs is the Iranians' propensity to believe in conspiracies and to interpret politics in the light of conspiracy theories (that is, theories that purport to prove that politics is dominated by the ill-intentioned and conspiratorial machinations of small groups whose aims and values are profoundly opposed to those of the rest of society).[22] This was how the regime and some citizens reacted to events after the 2009 presidential election. In court cases, newspaper articles, Friday prayer sermons, and speeches by the Leader, the protests were dismissed. Demonstrators were described as pawns of U.S., European, and Israeli secret services, and the Green Movement was described as a foreign-inspired group modeled after the revolutions that brought down regimes in Eastern Europe and Central Asia. Belief in conspiracies as a force in history is common in the rest of the Middle East as well.[23] But in the Iranian case, the plausibility of such theories is enhanced by the fact that Iran *has* indeed been the victim of conspiracies, such as when the U.S. and British governments conspired with Iranian conservatives to reinstall the Shah in 1953. The main reason the seizure of the U.S. hostages in 1979 was so popular at the time was that it symbolically ended the era of foreign interference in Iranian affairs by allowing Iranians to occupy what most believed was the epicenter of all conspiracies: the U.S. embassy.

System Level

Iran is not a country whose borders and statehood are a bequest of European colonialism, which helps explain why the modern polity enjoys considerable historic legitimacy among Iranians. In spite of their ethnic diversity, Iranians with different mother tongues have lived with each other for centuries. The Iranian nationalism propagated by the Pahlavi shahs included pride in the glories of ancient Persia and in a continuous "national" history of 2,500 years. This history was interpreted as conferring upon Iranians an intrinsic nobility that neighboring peoples and states cannot match.

This intense national pride survived the revolution but changed garb. While the glories of pre-Islamic Iran are now much less emphasized than before, the new authorities and their supporters consider Iran to be the vanguard of the Islamic world's struggle against Western domination. This position fuses commitment to Islam with Iranian nationalism. In recent years, however, Pahlavi-type ethnic Persian nationalism has been making a comeback among Iranians who are disenchanted with theocratic rule, and in his contest with the religious leadership, Ahmadinejad has subtly used it.

By the same token, ethnic nationalism has become stronger among Iran's non-Persian populations. This is particularly noticeable among the predominantly Sunni Kurds, who resent the poverty of the Kurdish areas as well as discrimination on sectarian grounds. In the presidential election of 2005, for instance, a candidate who expressly addressed Sunni grievances carried the largely Sunni province of Sistan and Baluchestan. At the same time, an Azeri who emphasized his ethnicity carried the three largely Azeri-speaking provinces of northwestern Iran. In theory, there is no reason why this new ethnic assertiveness should not be compatible with a strong sense of Iranian civic nationalism, but that depends on how the central government manages it. Repressive measures are likely to erode the identification with the Iranian state in the ethnic periphery.

One time-honored way governments shore up their legitimacy is by appealing to feelings of patriotism. In Iran, the government has recently hoped to unite Iranians around the issue of developing nuclear technology. The Iranian leaders' insistence that Iran has a "right" to develop nuclear energy has struck a sympathetic chord among ordinary Iranians, even among many of those who oppose Islamist rule. If Americans, Europeans, Chinese, Israelis, and even Indians and Pakistanis have nuclear weapons, many people ask, why should Iranians not have them too?

Process Level

One indisputable result of the Islamic revolution was the dramatic increase in the number of citizens who participated in politics. The millions of Iranians who poured into the streets to demand the departure of the Shah throughout 1978 refused to become mere subjects of a theocratic state after the revolution was over. The same cannot be said for those who opposed either the revolution or the Islamic state to which it ultimately gave rise. Many emigrated, and those who remained behind tended to consider the "Association of Militant Clerics" and the "Society of Militant Clergy" little more than Tweedledum and Tweedledee. It was these passive subjects of the Islamic Republic that Khatami had in mind when he repeatedly asserted that he wanted to be the president of *all* Iranians. They participated for the first time since the inception of the new regime, carrying electoral participation rates to new heights. In the elections of 2004 and 2005, many of them boycotted the elections, feeling that their participation had not brought the country nearer to a more republican and less theocratic form of government. However, in 2009, Mousavi's savvy campaign team combined with strong feelings toward Ahmadinejad's policies

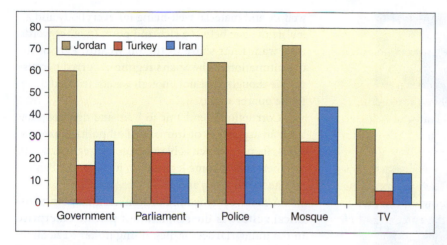

FIGURE 16.5

Citizen Trust

Iran compared to Jordan and Turkey.

Source: 2005–2006 *World Values Survey*.

encouraged 85 percent of Iranians to vote. After electoral irregularities and the extreme crackdown on protesters, many Iranians and Western experts expected that Iranians would not trust the electoral system enough to vote. However, the political space opened up by the election campaigns and cooperation between pragmatist and reformist organizations drew large numbers to the ballot box, even if some did boycott the elections and others voted with great skepticism. The 72 percent turnout is not as high as in 2009, but is still impressive in comparison to past elections and world averages. This participation has been cited by Rouhani's government to legitimate their position in negotiations over Iran's nuclear program.

Another key feature of Iran's political culture is extreme individualism and lack of trust. Most observers link this to the country's long history of despotism, which never developed a state of law that made life predictable and governed by rules rather than personal connections. The conspiracy belief mentioned earlier added to this absence of trust. Political opponents tend to accuse each other of being in league with foreign powers. This makes compromise (necessary for deliberative politics) very difficult, because one cannot compromise or negotiate with a "traitor." The fact that the revolutionary credentials of the leaders of the various factions are equally strong has led

to a certain mutual tolerance among those political leaders who remain faithful to velayat-e faqih. But even now, dissidents who question the system itself are invariably accused of doing the bidding of foreign (read: hostile) powers. The most consistent victims of this propensity to believe in conspiracies are religious minorities, especially Baha'is, who are widely presented as agents of "Zionism." This charge is motivated by the fact that the world center of the Baha'i faith is located in Israel, which is a historic accident.

Distrust not only permeates the political elite but is also evident among citizens. Results of the World Values Survey suggest that Iranians, like Turks, do not trust government (see Figure 16.5).[24] Since television channels are state run and much of the press is owned by the state or heavily monitored by it, the low levels of trust in these institutions also illustrate a lack of trust in government. Meanwhile, the relatively high level of trust in the "mosque" should be interpreted with caution. As we will soon see, "the mosque" is far from a homogeneous entity and does not necessarily reflect a particular political agenda or culture.

This individualism and lack of trust are underlying causes for the absence of true political parties and the constant splits that the few parties that did come into existence have undergone. While Iranians bemoan their inability to cooperate, it is this very inability that saved Iran from becoming a totalitarian state in the 1980s. If the ulema had the discipline and centralist organization of either the Roman Catholic Church or a Communist party, it is likely that their rule would be far more totalitarian and monolithic, and factionalism would never have been institutionalized.

A final consequence of the individualism and conspiracy belief prevalent in Iran's political culture is the periodic appearance of charismatic leaders. These leaders embody the yearning of the citizenry for overcoming the current order and the source of all problems—imperialists and autocrats. Mohammad Mossadegh, Ayatollah Khomeini, and even (to a much

هموطن ، من آمده ام ، تو هم بیا ...

۲۲ خرداد : به احمدی نژاد رأی می دهیم

حامیان دکتر محمود مردمی نژاد

www. mardominejad.ir

A Poster from Mahmoud Ahmadinejad's 2009 Election Campaign

This campaign poster shows how Ahmadinejad presents himself as the protector of the oppressed and downtrodden, represented by the young disabled boy and the crowd of people holding up the candidate's image. The caption reads: "Fellow citizens, I have come [to the fore], you come too . . . [On] the 22nd of Khordad [election day of June 12, 2009]; we will vote for Ahmadinejad. Support Doctor Mahmoud Mardomi-Nejad." Mardomi-Nejad, meaning "cut from the people's cloth," is a play on the president's name that reinforces his populism; the title "Doctor" reminds voters that he holds a Ph.D. in engineering.

lesser extent) Mohammad Khatami and Mahmoud Ahmadinejad exemplify this tendency. Some have argued that Twelver Shiism, with its expectation of the Twelfth Imam, predisposes Iranians to put their hopes in a charismatic savior figure.

Policy Level

Given the fact that the Iranian state derives most of its income from oil, Iranians expect the state to provide welfare and material well-being for everybody and alleviate the gap between rich and poor. In other words, they want their share of the oil wealth. Part of the delegitimation of the Shah's regime occurred because people thought that not enough wealth trickled down to the poorer strata.

Corruption is endemic in Iran, and fighting it has been an aspiration of Iranians of all political persuasions. Its persistence is blamed on the regime, which has thereby lost some legitimacy, just like the Pahlavi regime in the 1960s and 1970s.

A noteworthy feature of Iran's contemporary political culture is the suspicion of private enterprise in the industrial sector. Beginning under Reza Shah, the state took a leading role in the development of industry. Under Reza Shah's son, this statism was supplemented by an emerging class of capitalists who contributed considerably to Iran's industrialization in the 1960s and 1970s. But they were closely connected to the Shah and his relatives, they cooperated with foreign companies whose activities were suspicious for the mere reason that they were foreign, and some of them were members of religious minorities. Consequently, both the Islamists and leftists who carried the revolutionary movement opposed them and the mode of economic development they represented, calling them "exploiters." The legacy of this opposition is visible in Iran's Constitution, which puts heavy limits on foreign investment.

The populism propagated by the revolutionaries has intensified opposition to conspicuous consumption and privately owned large-scale economic activity. This has not affected rich bazaar merchants, who engage mostly in trade rather than production. Their activity is less immediately visible than that of an industrialist, as a merchant can deal in millions armed with nothing but a cell phone, sitting behind a desk in a small shop in the bazaar. In contrast, the factory and offices of an industrialist attract immediate attention.[25] This general distrust of industrialists means that citizens expect the state to be the main purveyor of development and increased living standards. Ahmadinejad mobilized this sentiment during his tenure in office, which highlighted his close affinity with "ordinary" Iranians and their needs and values.

While many Iranians thus expect the state to alleviate poverty and unemployment, others expect the state to provide an environment in which individual talent and creativity can flourish. Collectivism and individualism are both present in Iranian society, and the result is that Iran's political culture is highly conflictual. The citizenry is sharply divided over the very essence of the regime, with many, especially among the more educated, considering Islamic theocracy, if not the Islamic Republic, to be an anachronistic form of government.

Political Socialization

16.6 Describe how the mechanisms for creating national unity in Iran also contain elements of dissent.

The political socialization of citizens is a process simultaneously driven from above by state institutions and from below by social practices. In Iran, state-controlled institutions—such as the education system, television, and the military—transmit many of society's basic political norms and establish the framework for debating their meaning. Meanwhile, through their everyday practices as members of their family, neighborhood, or social group, Iranians negotiate, challenge, and even sometimes undermine these norms.

As in many postrevolutionary and postcolonial regimes, state-sanctioned political socialization in Iran has aimed at generating national unity and masking political, ethnic, and socioeconomic cleavages. The Pahlavi monarchy championed national unity in a mission to create a modern, industrial, and Western society. This vision presented the nation as secular, classless, and thoroughly Persian in identity. The schools, for instance, educated the entire Iranian population in the official language of Persian, a critical method to distance the significant numbers of Azeri, Kurdish, and Arabic speakers from their local and ethnic loyalties. The calls for greater economic equality, ethnic inclusion, and religious observance during the Islamic revolution dramatically questioned both the notion of national homogeneity and the perception that the Iranian nation accepted this image of itself. Under the Islamic Republic, the content of the official discourse and normative agenda has changed. However, the methods of socialization and the overwhelming elite desire to limit input from citizens and ignore the pluralistic nature of society remain quite similar to the prerevolutionary regime.

Education System

The school system is the principal agent of socialization for creating good Islamic citizens out of young Iranians. The school system was one of the first institutions to be Islamicized by the new regime. The government changed the school curricula to include a heavy dose of religious studies, yearly classes on the Islamic revolution, and more mandatory Arabic language courses. Meanwhile, rewritten textbooks present a state-sanctioned history of Iran, which highlights the role of the clergy in all "popular uprisings," erases or distorts any role played by nonreligious forces (such as liberal nationalists or leftist parties), and presents the Pahlavi monarchy (and all monarchs) as equally and continually oppressive and immoral.

Textbooks also depict the state's image of the family. Unlike the prerevolutionary textbooks that showed Iranian women as unveiled, families eating around a table, and children with non-Arabic and nonreligious names, the postrevolutionary textbooks depict all women as veiled (even inside the home), families sitting cross-legged around a simple spread on the floor, and children with Islamic names.[26] Schoolchildren also receive revolutionary doctrine by reciting chants and poems praising the greatness of Khomeini and the regime, while denouncing Israel and "the imperialists," most commonly the United States.

The authorities initially emphasized the role of primary and secondary schools for creating loyal and mobilized supporters. However, a group of Islamist activists and scholars also led a charge to "cleanse" the universities of "counterrevolutionary" elements by reviewing both the faculty and the curriculum. This "Cultural Revolution" was headed by what is now known as the Supreme Council for the Cultural Revolution. Because university campuses were the epicenter of antiregime activism, the Cultural Revolution closed all universities for three years (1980–1983) and worked to develop links between the universities and the religious seminaries. When the universities were reopened, strict entrance requirements were established, including religious examinations, to give greater opportunities to those the regime expected would be more supportive of its ambitions. In addition, war veterans and relatives of those killed in the revolution and the Iran–Iraq war were allotted special quotas in all universities.

The regime also established institutions to create a new set of technocrats and teachers to staff the ministries and the universities. Domestically producing engineers, scientists, economists, and other professionals was essential for ensuring the Islamic Republic's independence and withstanding the U.S. attempt to isolate Iran. For instance, Imam Sadeq University (ironically on the campus of a former business school affiliated with Harvard Business School) was fashioned to produce technocrats. Another new aspect of the university system was the establishment of the "Islamic Open University," with 400 separate campuses all over the country, including small towns. This university has offered higher education to Iranians living outside of the main population centers and provided opportunities for students who fail the highly competitive entrance examination for the elite national universities or whose families do not let them move to the larger cities.

The Islamic Republic transformed the content of higher education to promote and fund fields such as "Islamic Economics" and "Islamic Sciences" as ways to compete with what some viewed as the fundamentally distorted and anti-Islamic nature of Western academia. Over the years, the regime has also sponsored the establishment of proregime volunteer organizations (**Basij**) to monitor the political activities of students and faculty, and to mobilize students for proregime activities on the campuses.

The Islamic Republic's efforts to create obedient and loyal citizens out of the "children of the revolution" seem far from successful. Many of the investigative journalists who write about government abuses and incompetence, the staunchest supporters of reform, and the burgeoning civil society (such as arts organizations and women's nongovernmental organizations) are products of the school system and post-Cultural Revolution higher-education establishments. In fact, the universities that the state tried so hard to control in the wake of the revolution are again full of students publishing political journals and declarations, organizing talks challenging the regime, and flaunting and mocking the social mores and the state's policies regarding gender relations. The large student demonstrations of 1999, 2003, and 2009 are indicative of the inability of the regime to manage this politicized space fully or without coercion.

The Military and Veterans

Military conscription is another fundamental mechanism for creating national unity, at least for young men. The shared experience of basic training and interacting with the military bureaucracy was augmented by the experience of the long war with Iraq. With approximately 4–5 million Iranians serving in the armed forces during the eight-year war, it directly affected a very large percentage of Iranian families.[27] Various public commemorations and war murals, as well as stories in cinema and fiction, foster emotional bonds between the war generation and those who preceded and followed it.

Politically, however, the war has been divisive, with part of the ruling establishment questioning the continuation of the war even after the Iraqi army was driven off Iranian soil in 1982.[28] Moreover, Iran's military includes the IRGC and the Basij, which have become distinct institutions with growing political influence. These latter institutions are under the direct supervision of the Leader and were integrated into a single hierarchy in early 2009. In the parliamentary election of 2004, over a hundred former members of the Revolutionary Guards won seats. In 2005, Ahmadinejad, himself a former member of the IRGC, ushered the way for several members to enter his cabinet. The IRGC's political relevance reflects their significant and growing role in construction projects, manufacturing (including the oil sector), communications, trade, and banking since the 1990s and increasingly so since Ahmadinejad's presidency. This goes a long way in explaining the IRGC leaderships' overt support for the incumbent in 2009.

Religion and Religious Institutions

While most Iranians consider themselves religious and consider religious matters and practices as important aspects of their lives, results from the World Values Survey project suggest a more nuanced view.[29] Figure 16.6 shows that many Iranians believe religion is very important in life and participate in religious services, but at lower rates than in Jordan and Egypt. Moreover, while surveyed Iranians more often characterize themselves as "above all a Muslim" than as "above all a nationalist," about a third put nationalism first, far more than in either Egypt or Jordan.

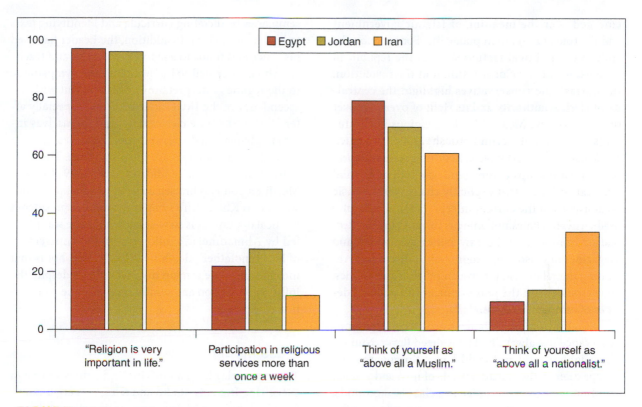

FIGURE 16.6

Religious Beliefs and Practice

Source: Mansoor Moaddel and Taghi Azadarmaki, "The Worldviews of Islamic Publics: The Case of Egypt, Iran, and Jordan," in *Human Values and Social Change: Findings from the Values Survey*, ed. Ronald Inglehart (Leiden: Brill, 2003), 75.

Notwithstanding these aggregate findings, under the Islamic Republic, religion and religious practice have played a more divisive than unifying role. On the surface, religion permeates daily life. Official speeches and pronouncements are peppered with religious expressions, the calendar is full of religious holidays, and religious observance is often public and conspicuous. Shiite Islam plays a central role both in official discourse and as a means to regulate who can gain high office in the state. Friday congregational prayers and commemorations of religious anniversaries are state-regulated events that bring together people from all walks of life at neighborhood public spaces. As if to underline the emasculation of Tehran University as the center of secular opposition to the Islamic regime, Tehran's official Friday congregational prayers are held on what used to be the campus' soccer field. On these occasions, government officials give sermons in which they passionately weave together religious and moral issues and the pressing political problems of the day.

In staging these public and mass religious meetings, the state consciously attempts to mobilize citizens in support of the regime and to transmit political messages. These events and state-owned radio and television are dominated by the well-versed and symbolic Shiite language of martyrdom and self-sacrifice, as exemplified by the Third Imam, in the name of justice and standing up to the great powers who usurp the rights of the innocent and faithful.

It is difficult, however, to monopolize the symbols, interpretations, and ephemeral beliefs that make up a religion. Over the years, the Islamic Republic has had difficulty controlling members of the political elite and clergy, let alone the hearts and minds of its citizens. Given the absence of a Shiite "pope," Iran's theocratic state has never fully imposed its politicized vision of Shiite Islam within Iran, let alone across the Shiite world. With the death of Khomeini and the appointment of the less religiously erudite and charismatic Khamenei, fundamental disagreements have emerged over the meaning of Islamic government and the role of religion in public life. For instance, the "reformist" political faction stresses the republican dimensions of the Constitution and the revolution. In contrast, the conservatives highlight the centrality of clerical authority and its right of oversight over the popular will. Meanwhile, lay religious intellectuals (such as Abdol-Karim Soroush) and clerics (such as Hasan Eshkevari) have called for a reformulation of the relationships among God, the individual, and political authority that explicitly challenges the basic assumptions of the current interpretation of velayat-e faqih. These debates not only percolate in the intellectual environments of the universities, seminaries, and magazines but also shape more public discussions regarding the relationship between religion and politics, and resonate with the philosophical and political debates of ordinary Iranians.[30]

Finally, in more organizational terms, religious observance has always had a localized flavor. Numerous neighborhood and guild-based Koranic reading groups cater to the spiritual needs of men and women of different regional, ethnic, and class backgrounds. These informal meetings act as grassroots and independent forums for religious practice, which escape the watchful eye of clerics affiliated with the regime. Sometimes escaping the attention of observers is the tension between the clerical state and the seminaries in the cities of Qom and Mashhad. With the vast majority of clergy historically shying away from politics and the seminary system historically maintaining financial independence, Khomeini's political innovation of cleric-led government has reconfigured "church"–state relations. For instance, job opportunities and income are available for clerics in the judicial system, in the ministries, and as Friday prayer leaders, the last being appointed by the office of the Leader. While the ulema have been prominent in the higher reaches of the regime, the actual running of the state has never been dominated by seminary graduates, and their presence has declined over the last quarter century. One indication is the decline in the number of clerics in parliament. In the very First Parliament, almost half of the MPs were clerics, but by the late 1990s, clerics constituted less than 20 percent of MPs.

For the vast majority of clerics—who remain in the seminaries to teach, study, and interpret religious texts—the regime has been intrusive. The authorities in Tehran have tried to monitor teaching in the seminaries by dictating curricula and identifying texts to be taught in Qom. In addition, the Leader has used his office and funds to support seminaries and teachers who are deemed to be "militant" and sympathetic to the regime's interpretations of Islam. But with the ascendancy of the IRGC after 2005 and especially after 2009, proregime clerics now find themselves increasingly marginalized, and their relationship with Ahmadinejad is an increasingly distant one. The most outspoken of his rival candidates in the 2009 elections, Mehdi Karroubi, is himself a cleric. Khomeini's grandson Hasan Khomeini's sympathy with the president's political opponents is so well known that he was heckled by Ahmadinejad's followers on the anniversary of his grandfather's death in 2010. The upshot is that mosque and state remain distinct entities despite the infusion of religion and seminarians into the constitution of the state.

Mass Media

The media play both a unifying and a divisive role in socializing Iranians. Radio and television are monopolized by the state and are one of the major means to transmit the official doctrine and to mobilize Iranians for elections and rallies across the country. Since the head of the Radio and Television Organization is directly appointed by the Leader, the organization has reflected the interests of the conservative wing of the regime. The strong bias of state television was clearly demonstrated during the presidency of Mohammad Khatami and the coverage of the 2009 presidential election and Green Movement, when news broadcasts either ignored or misrepresented many of the raging political debates.

In recent years, as satellite television has grown and the dishes have become less expensive, antiregime Persian language programming from abroad and foreign news outlets (CNN and BBC) have provided greater diversity for the viewing public. In response, the state has repeatedly tried to jam channels and outlaw private use of satellite dishes, although the law has not been applied consistently. The dishes can be seen on rooftops in major cities and even small towns.

The printed press has been the most diverse form of media in postrevolutionary Iran. In the first decade of the revolution, newspapers and journals became increasingly uniform in their coverage. But as the regime began to feel more consolidated and elite competition became more open after the death of Khomeini, a growing number of independent newspapers and magazines appeared on the scene. These publications reflected specific schools of thought and critical views from intellectuals on the right and left, as well as the more republican and the more authoritarian wings of the regime. A flourishing nonstate press and burgeoning investigative journalism were the backbone of Khatami's surprising election victory in 1997 and underpinned the enormous popularity of the reformist movement in his first term. The critics of the government (many of whom were part of the revolutionary establishment) and the many young journalists writing critical articles presented a new political language of accountability, civil society, and participation to the educated, urban, and young population of Iran. In doing so, these newspapers both reflected and produced deep cleavages among the ruling establishment.

During the authoritarian backlash against the reformist movement since 2000, the conservative-controlled Judiciary has clamped down on the most vibrant aspects of this press. Currently, journalists have turned to the Internet to publish their commentaries in online newspapers or in the mushrooming collection of blogs and Facebook pages. Today, Persian is one of the most widely used languages on the Internet and in the "blogosphere." Politicians, political dissidents, journalists, poets, students, and others inside and outside of Iran use blogging as a means to do everything from expressing opinions to documenting events and human rights violations. Today, journalists and newspaper editors, some of whom have been imprisoned or physically attacked, have become the new political heroes of many of the youth.

The Family and Social Groups

Political socialization takes place in the private sphere as well as in the public sphere. This is particularly the case in more authoritarian contexts. In Iran, under both the monarchy and the Islamic Republic, the home has been a relatively free place to discuss politics by recounting the unofficial history of the country or to debate current events with family members and friends. While patriarchy (and sometimes matriarchy) does prohibit unfettered debate in the family setting, the memory of key political episodes—such as the 1953 coup or the events leading up to the overthrow of the Shah in 1979—is transmitted in these settings. By

retelling stories from earlier eras or speculating about the conspiracies behind them, older family members indoctrinate the family's younger generation in a political memory and culture that are at variance with the official story, as contained in school textbooks and official rhetoric.

As more Iranians complete high school and attend universities, the family dynamic appears to have changed. Young men and women now have a certain authority, as they are the first generation in their families to graduate from high school and university. They interpret politics for their relatives by explaining differences between political factions and bringing campus politics into their homes. Such discussions take place while waiting for oven-fresh bread outside the local bakery, perusing headlines at the newspaper kiosk, or sharing a collective taxi with total strangers. These ritualistic acts of resistance prevent the state from fully dominating politics, but at the same time, they do not challenge regime power.

In short, political socialization under the Islamic Republic has shifted from being solely the domain of the state to one that is contested by counterelite and popular voices. The early revolutionary message of unity and mobilization in the name of revolutionary Islam once taught in school textbooks and recounted in Friday sermons and newspaper pages has given way to greater pluralism and contestation, intriguingly, by many of the same people who read those school texts and wrote those newspaper articles in the 1980s. The challenge today for the regime is either to accommodate and represent pluralistic discourse or to impose the single voice of unity. Their *decision and capacity* in this regard will determine whether Iran will move toward more democratic politics or authoritarianism.

Recruiting the Political Elite

16.7 Describe the sources of Iran's political elite.

What kinds of people govern Iran? Under the Shah, the small class of educated and secular Iranians who could demonstrate personal loyalty to the monarch held political offices. Many of the ministers came from landowning families and attended Western high schools and universities.[31] The Shah, however, made sure to prevent the rise of potential competitors with strong personalities or independent bases of support.

This policy produced a highly dependent inner circle whose members were unwilling to challenge the Shah and preferred to censor information and opinions in order not to offend His Imperial Majesty. This passive and dependent nature of the political elite prevented the Shah from acting in a timely and decisive manner as the revolts and political challenges of 1977 and 1978 snowballed into the revolution.[32]

Under the Islamic Republic, personalism also plays an important role, but in a broader sense. In the early years, political elites came from various backgrounds, but their most fundamental credentials were their revolutionary pedigrees. Those who could point to active participation in the Islamic revolution, and in particular the various groups associated with Khomeini and his students, leveraged this experience into positions in ministries, the parastatal economic foundations, the IRGC, and various other state-funded institutions. Thus, the new political elite that came to power immediately after the revolution were younger and less cosmopolitan; they were from more middle-class and lower-middle-class backgrounds, often hailing from the provinces rather than the capital.

In general, the state has expanded since the revolution. From 1976 to 1986, the number of employees in the public sector more than doubled, reaching more than 30 percent of all employed Iranians. In the 1980s, four-fifths of all new jobs were in the public sector.[33] This expansion was due to a number of reasons, including the requisites of the war effort, the state-led economic development program, and the revolutionary agenda to restructure and Islamicize society from above.

Initially, the clergy who were recruited into the state were trained in the seminaries in Najaf and Qom, where Khomeini and his students taught during the 1960s and 1970s. The Fayziyeh Seminary in Qom was the principal seminary producing these new judges and ministers. Over time, the Haqqani Seminary in Qom has grown in importance, partially because its alumni include staunch conservatives who have dominated the Judiciary, the Council of Guardians, and the security apparatus. The head of the seminary, Ayatollah Mohammad-Taqi Mesbah Yazdi, is the leading hard-line cleric of the Islamic Republic; he advocates abolishing its republican components. The graduates of this seminary, known as the Haqqani circle, include important figures in the conservative backlash against Khatami's attempts to institutionalize political reform. Since then, it has cooperated with hard-line elements

in the IRGC to support hard-line candidates in elections, including Ahmadinejad.

Nonclerical parliamentarians and ministers tend to emerge from educational and military institutions. Many attended the new Islamic universities. In the 1990s, think tanks and research centers were important in recruiting and producing political elites. Many of the reformists who dominated the Sixth Parliament and supported President Khatami were based in the Center for Strategic Studies. These younger members of the elite often are too young to have significant revolutionary credentials, but their studies in these universities and institutes give them technical know-how, intellectual credentials, and the social networks to gain access to various government and state institutions.

More recently, many of the new elite come from the ranks of the IRGC and the Basij. President Ahmadinejad, Mayor Mohammad-Baqer Qalibaf of Tehran, and many of the ministers were military figures from these corps or worked for the research institutes connected to the IRGC. It is worth noting that the regular army, navy, and air force do not have much influence in politics. This growing militarization of politics is a new phenomenon in modern Iran. Unlike neighboring Pakistan, Turkey, and Iraq, which have had numerous military coups and governments headed by generals, the Iranian political establishment was overwhelmingly civilian throughout the twentieth century.

Kinship ties are commonly used to gain political and economic power. Many of the sons and brothers, and, on some rare occasions, daughters and sisters, of government officials use their family ties to gain access to the state. Often, their contacts are used as means for rent-seeking (receiving subsidized hard currency or special import licenses, or securing subsidized loans) and personal enrichment. In addition, marriage is used as a powerful way to cement political alliances and create bonds between prominent families.

Interest Articulation and Aggregation

16.8 Discuss the roles of clientelism and interest groups in Iranian politics.

The mix of electoral politics and authoritarian powers generates multiple and competing forms of interest articulation and aggregation under the

Islamic Republic. The most institutionalized forms are regular presidential, parliamentary, and local elections. The least institutionalized, but probably the most prevalent and effective, is the use of personalistic ties and patron–client relations. As a consequence, representation under the Islamic Republic is highly fragmented, fluid, and contentious, although not fully pluralistic, competitive, and democratic.

Noninstitutional Forms of Interest Articulation and Aggregation

The principal means of interest aggregation is clientelism and the forging of relationships between political figures and citizens through patron–client networks. Given the state's access to external sources of revenue from the world oil market, Iranian political figures have exchanged political loyalty and support for access to such resources as subsidies, hard currency, subcontracts, and secure government jobs. This system of patronage can take a very direct form, where parliamentarians, ministers, or bureaucrats dole out these resources to kin, schoolmates, and people from the same city or province. Special access to powerful figures in the Leader's office, state-owned banks, and economic foundations benefit these clients, while ensuring their dependence, if not loyalty, to the political system. Since patron–client relations are based on the goods that the patron provides the client, if the patron loses power, so do his clients. This form of political aggregation undermines pretensions of institutional impartiality and meritocracy that are essential principles behind equal citizenship and participation.

In a less targeted manner, the government distributes large subsidies as a social welfare net and to ensure the loyalty and acquiescence of the population. Until 2010, food and medicine were subsidized at an annual rate of about $2 billion and, particularly, to benefit the urban poor. By contrast, the gasoline and electricity subsidy that kept the price of a gallon of gasoline to less than 40 cents was quite regressive because it benefited the middle and upper classes that own automobiles, homes, and electrical equipment. The subsidy reform in 2010 removed or lowered the subsidy of specific goods, such as gasoline, wheat, and water, but distributed cash payments to citizens to help them as prices increased.

Institutionalized Forms of Interest Articulation and Aggregation: Voting

Elections are regularized political events, but they do not provide complete pluralism nor necessarily entail a shift in power and policies, since the powers of the representative institutions are quite limited. Elections function more as an act and measurement of regime legitimacy, and only secondarily as a means for citizens to express their interests by selecting among candidates with specified policy positions. Thus, except for the most recent elections, there has been more discussion about election turnout than candidates. The turnout in the ten presidential and nine parliamentary elections averaged about 60 percent (see again Figure 16.4).

The 1997, 2005, and 2009 presidential elections, however, indicated that under certain conditions, elections can be moments of interest articulation and offer information regarding the preferences of citizens. In 1997, it was quite clear that the regime candidate was Ali-Akbar Nateq Nuri, the sitting speaker of the parliament and close confidant of the Leader. However, partially due to the burgeoning civil society and his low government profile, Mohammad Khatami, as the outsider and nonregime candidate, swept to victory with a surprising 70 percent of the vote. In somewhat similar fashion, although with a very different political agenda and significance, in 2005, Mahmoud Ahmadinejad surprised many pundits by defeating Ali-Akbar Hashemi Rafsanjani, who had been one of the cornerstones of the Islamic Republic since its establishment. These surprising outcomes indicate that in spite of the limited nature of elections, voters can express their views, and these preferences can matter even when they go against the wishes of the ruling establishment. The 2009 elections exposed the divisions with the political establishment, clerics, and society at large. Rather than processing these disputes through political forums and debates, the Leader and the conservatives turned the matter into a security issue and sought to silence the interests and views of a significant portion of society and even the regime's political establishment. In 2013, the regime simultaneously sought to "engineer" the election and demonstrated an understanding of the risks and costs associated with blatant rigging. The Guardian Council vetted candidates, but the ministries and security apparatus did not block the popular support for Rouhani or tamper with the results.

Given the weakness of party organizations, as mentioned earlier, political parties play no major role. The factions that contend for power and influence have not formed a clearly defined party system that would act as a mechanism for representing and aggregating the interests of constituents. Parties and political associations, such as the Society of Combatant Clergy or the Islamic Iran Participation Front, are groupings of the political elite that become active during elections. Yet, until now, they have been unable to maintain party discipline with direct and formalized links to the citizenry. The inchoate structure of the popular protests following the 2009 elections testifies to the weakness of political parties.

Institutional Groups and Professional Organizations

While political parties are less developed, groups based in state organizations have a more corporate identity and a greater ability to shape policy, in much the same manner as controlled interest group systems. The IRGC and the volunteer mobilization corps (Basij), consisting of approximately 120,000 and 90,000 men, respectively, are two of the most prominent arms of the state.[34] They directly represent the state's interests in various policymaking areas, although they were established to mobilize support for the regime. These ostensibly military and security forces also play a role in the economy through their business subsidiaries, which are involved in large-scale construction projects as well as allegedly importing consumer goods. Since the 2003 local council elections, the IRCG and Basij have taken a more visible role in politics. A number of their high-ranking figures have run for local offices, parliament, and the presidency. Finally, since they are in direct communication with the Leader, they have the ability to influence policy and coordinate actions beyond the oversight of the parliament.

There are a host of associations representing the interests of labor, business, professional groups, and industrial sectors. However, the House of Labor or the Iranian Chamber of Commerce, Industries, and Mines, and other such organizations, operate more as a means for state officials to manage these corporate entities rather than as vehicles to represent specific interests and shape policymaking. Only in very recent elections have professional organizations endorsed different candidates, which may signal the emergence of an independent role for these corporate groups in political competition.

In the course of the struggle against the Shah and in the years following his overthrow, neighborhood councils and guild associations sprang up all over the country as grassroots initiatives to address ordinary citizens' needs during the revolution and the war years. Over time, they have become integrated into the patron–client system, and today, they are either mere appendages of state officials or means for the state to penetrate society.[35] Hence, there is no clear separation between interest groups and government officials. Moreover, since the revolution, the government has encouraged workers, merchants, and students to establish Islamic associations in universities, factories, and guilds as the principal means of aggregating the interests of these groups.

In the 1990s and especially during the relatively less repressive administration of President Khatami, a large number of genuinely autonomous associations emerged to represent strata of society that had been largely sidelined by the revolutionary regime. For instance, various women's organizations of both secular and reformist Islamist persuasion formed and started initiatives seeking to change discriminatory laws, provide services, and raise general consciousness regarding women's issues. Most notable is the 2003 Nobel Peace Prize winner, **Shirin Ebadi**. She was the first woman to become a judge under the Shah, but she lost her job when women were barred from that position following the revolution. Ebadi was active in a host of legal organizations championing and defending the rights of women, children, and political dissidents. Simultaneously, students and secular intellectuals took advantage of these opportunities to form associations and publications that were independently minded and represented alternative visions of politics. These organizations are the backbone of the reformist movement as well as the target of repression by conservatives in the state apparatus. Today, many of their leaders have been sidelined by repression or are in exile.

Nonassociational Social Groups

Many social strata exist without independent associations aggregating and representing their interests. Among the historically and politically important social groups without corporate representation, it is worth mentioning the bazaari merchants.

Bazaari merchants based in the historic covered bazaars of Iran, ranging from retailers and brokers to wholesalers and even international traders, have played a central role in various political episodes, from the Constitutional Revolution (1905–1911), to the Oil Nationalization Movement (1951–1953), to the Islamic Revolution. Even though important differences exist among bazaaris in terms of socioeconomic status, political persuasion, and economic position, they have a sense of solidarity because of the well-defined and vibrant physical space of the bazaar, which ensures socially embedded and crosscutting relations. Their political significance is enhanced by both their economic power and their close relationship with the ulema. Since the revolution, bazaari economic interests have been threatened by the state's domination of the economy, while the homogeneity of bazaari interests has been undermined by key pro-Khomeini bazaari families being co-opted by the new regime.[36]

Veterans of the Iran–Iraq war, the families of those killed in the war (referred to as "martyrs"), and those disabled in the war are a large and politically important social group. They are ostensibly represented by various organizations, such as the Martyr's Foundation, the Foundation of the Disinherited, the Society of the Devotees of the Islamic Republic, and the Headquarters of the POWs. But these organizations have proved unable to address adequately the everyday demands of many of their constituents. They have shifted away from their original mandate of providing services to war veterans and their families. The state also supports this important constituency by setting up all kinds of affirmative action schemes (ranging from easier access to higher education to priority in flight reservations) and subsidizing consumer goods for veterans and relatives of both veterans and martyrs in order to enhance their socioeconomic standing. Yet these measures have not always worked adequately both to address the needs of this social group and to suppress challenges. Some prominent war veterans and former members of the IRGC have aligned themselves with the reformist faction, calling for greater political participation and freedoms. Others have accused the regime of turning its back on the wartime principles of self-sacrifice and justice. For much of the postwar era, there have been growing complaints by some war veterans that the memory of the war and respect for the sacrifices of the war generation have faded, while the veterans and relatives of the martyrs

have not been sufficiently provided for. This position was given voice by some ultraconservative newspapers, certain filmmakers engaged in producing war films, and outspoken figures of a group called Ansar-e Hezbollah (Partisans of the Party of God), who took it upon themselves to combat moral, political, and economic corruption.

Demonstrations and Public Protests

Given the closed nature of institutional interest representation and aggregation, many social and political groups have turned to civil disobedience to express their grievances. The relatively fresh memory of the demonstrations and strikes that constituted the revolution of 1978 and 1979 are a model for workers, students, activist women, and the urban poor to use public collective action to make their claims. For instance, throughout the 1990s, industrial workers protested against privatization policies, the selling of state-owned factories, and nonpayment of their wages. One high-profile tactic had workers blocking the main expressway connecting Tehran to the industrial satellite city of Karaj. On several occasions, protesters blocked the selling of state-owned factories to private business interests they suspected of planning to lay off workers. Teachers, bus drivers, sugarcane workers, and government pensioners have recently protested in front of parliament to draw attention to their inadequate income. Women's groups also increasingly organize protests against the male bias enshrined in the Constitution. Ethnic political groups, especially Kurdish and Arab activists on the Iran–Iraq border, have vocally called for greater distribution of wealth and local authority in their provinces.

The most dramatic protests, however, have been based in the universities and spearheaded by students. During the summers of 1999, 2003, and 2009, student organizations staged sit-ins and demonstrations to protest against authoritarian measures by the regime. They challenged the closure of a prominent reformist newspaper and the sentencing of an outspoken intellectual who had questioned clerical rule. These protests were originally based in Tehran University, but they spread to other cities and university campuses and persisted for several days. With little support or protection from reformist parties and other social groups, the volunteer forces (Basij) and police violently suppressed the demonstrators and prevented the movement from escalating. Yet in the aftermath of the 2009 elections, students and student organizations again were critical in coordinating actions and turning universities into sites of political dissent.

Although these and other events demonstrate that society is not completely passive in the face of government policies, the inability of these disparate groups to unite or coordinate their localized organizational capabilities is an indication of the overwhelming social atomization in contemporary Iran. Given the pervasive use of patron–client relations and lack of trust among Iranians, collective action and alliance building are particularly difficult. Moreover, these noninstitutional forms of politics reflect the lack of efficacy of institutional politics and the belief on the part of many people that their political voice cannot be heard unless it is in this form.

Policy Formulation

16.9 Summarize the policymaking process, focusing on the groups that frequently work at cross-purposes.

State policy is set by a number of bodies, some of them explicitly mentioned in the Constitution, some not. Given the mixed nature of the political system, overlaps, duplications, and even contradictions abound, and it is not rare for different policymaking bodies to work at cross-purposes.

State Institutions Mentioned in the Constitution

As befits a theocracy in which no state policy should contradict Islam, those who determine what does and does not contradict Islam have a preponderant voice in setting policy. First and foremost is the Leader. On numerous occasions, the first Leader, Ruhollah Khomeini, used his authority to determine state policy by issuing religious edicts (*fatwas*). On a few occasions, these edicts broke with established religious tradition, which is not astonishing given the charismatic nature of his leadership (see Box 16.5).

Khomeini's interventions in the state's policymaking were often necessary because of deadlocks between the Majles and the Council of Guardians. To avoid paralysis, in 1988, Khomeini amended his doctrine of velayat-e faqih (guardianship of the jurisprudent) by issuing an edict that gave the state, as embodied by its Leader, authority to override religious law when that is expedient. This "absolute dominion of the jurisprudent" (*velayat-e motlaqeh-ye faqih*), he stated, was the "most important of divine commandments and has priority over all derivative divine commandments . . . even over prayer, fasting, and the pilgrimage to Mecca."[37] The 1989 revised Constitution enshrines this reinterpretation of the theoretical principle.

Needless to say, most traditional Muslims and most members of the ulema were horrified by this subordination of religion to reason of state. The whole purpose of an Islamic state was the exact opposite. Moreover, no person other than Khomeini could conceivably get away with disregarding religion when it

---

<table>
<tr><td>BOX
16.5</td><td>Fatwas As a Tool of Governance</td></tr>
</table>

Leader Ruhollah Khomeini used fatwas to justify policies he wanted to pursue. One of the earliest examples was his ruling on caviar. According to Shiite (and Jewish) dietary laws, a fish can be eaten only if it has scales. The sturgeon, however, has no scales, and traditionally, its meat and, by extension, its roe (caviar) were not deemed permissible. But caviar is one of Iran's main exports, and so the matter was revisited. A specially appointed state commission concluded that the sturgeon does indeed have scales, but that they are of a peculiar shape. Taking note of this finding, in 1983, Khomeini issued a fatwa declaring that caviar could be eaten. In 1988, he broke with other time-honored legal traditions by authorizing the playing of chess, provided no bets were made on the outcome, betting and gambling being forbidden in Islam. He also liberalized the early republic's stifling cultural life by relaxing the rules pertaining to music and television programming.

Source: Asghar Schirazi, *The Constitution of Iran: Politics and the State in the Islamic Republic* (London: I. B. Tauris, 1998), 67–68.

was expedient for the state to do so. As a result, shortly before his death, Khomeini invested the newly established Expediency Council with the authority to advise the Leader on invoking the absolute authority. As president (1981–1989), Khamenei had been a member of the conservative faction, but as Leader, he initially tried to give the impression of remaining above the fray. However, with the onset of the Khatami presidency in 1997, he abandoned all pretense of neutrality and became the de facto leader of the conservatives who did their best to stymie the reformist zeal of the elected officials.

The Expediency Council is the institution that decides the most vital policies of the nation. The old establishment became apprehensive about President Ahmadinejad's populist policies that threatened not only the domestic status quo but also Iran's security.[38] In 2005, the chairman of the Expediency Council, none other than Ali-Akbar Hashemi Rafsanjani, extracted a letter from the Leader that granted the Expediency Council broad supervisory powers over all three branches of government. Despite the presidency's and parliament's being dominated by conservatives and "principlists" since 2005, the combination of institutional checks and balances and various intrafactional disputes limited the ability of Ahmadinejad and his supporters to make sweeping changes, although he used his executive powers to direct state funds to key supporters.

In the course of the 1988 revision of the Constitution, a body formed some years earlier was added to the official institutional structure: the National Security Council. Its members include the heads of the three branches of government, top military commanders, the foreign minister, the minister of information (that is, intelligence), and a few other figures named by the Leader. It is the nation's highest policymaking body in matters of foreign and security policy. In the case of the Islamic Republic, this includes the struggle against what is officially called "Western cultural aggression."

The Council of Guardians does not have a direct role in policymaking, but its six lay members are present in parliament and occasionally attempt to work with sympathetic MPs to introduce legislation. As for parliament itself, it has been largely emasculated as a policymaking body by the unelected bodies mentioned earlier. Legislative proposals come before it either from the cabinet or from a minimum of twenty-five MPs. While successive parliaments have tried to create frameworks for conducting economic policies and changing the penal and civil codes, the Council of Guardians has obstructed much of their activity.

The executive branch of government and parliament have influenced policies for setting the state budget, providing and regulating social and welfare services, and handling territorial administration, which includes redrawing provincial borders. Beginning in the mid-1980s, for instance, the MPs of the northwestern city of Ardabil campaigned for the creation of a new province around their city. Young men from Ardabil having died in disproportionate numbers in the Iran–Iraq war, the people of the city used the moral leverage that their sacrifices gave them to renew their demands with greater fervor after the war ended in 1988. All sorts of civic associations mobilized for the demand, which MPs expressed inside parliament. In the end, the administration of President Hashemi Rafsanjani introduced a bill in parliament providing for the new province. The bill was hotly debated, and it finally passed in a secret vote in early 1993.[39]

The extensive powers of the Leader and the existence of such unelected decision-making bodies as the Council of Guardians, the Expediency Council, and the National Security Council severely limit the policymaking role of the elected officials: the president, the individual cabinet members named by him and approved by parliament, and parliament itself. Popular sovereignty is thus severely undermined.

State Institutions Not Mentioned in the Constitution

The role of elected officials is further limited by councils that are not mentioned expressly in the Constitution and that were established to formulate state policy in a particular field. The most prominent example is the Supreme Council for the Cultural Revolution, which was set up by order of Khomeini in 1986 to perpetuate the policies unleashed during the 1980s Cultural Revolution that purged universities of leftists and secularists. Its tasks include determining state policies in the realms of culture, education, and research, as well as "the spread and reinforcement of the influence of Islamic culture in all areas of society." Its supremacy over parliament is seen from the fact that the Council of Guardians has at times vetoed legislation on the grounds that it contradicted policies determined by the Supreme Council for the Cultural Revolution, the latter having the approval of the Leader.

Power Centers and the Difficulty of Policy Coordination

Given the existence of multiple power centers, policies are often not coordinated, as some state institutions make and implement their own policies independently of the relevant ministries. This includes the Judiciary, which does not limit itself to implementing the law but takes it into its own hands. Similarly, the Revolutionary Guards wage their own struggle against dissent and pursue a foreign policy independent of that of the foreign ministry and even the National Security Council.

The impact of these inconsistencies became particularly apparent under President Khatami, when the dispute between reformists and conservatives added an ideological dimension to the diffuse, ill-defined, and overlapping competencies of many state bodies. A few examples will illustrate this.

Under Khatami, the Ministry of Culture, which controls censorship and issues licenses for newspapers and journals, adopted more liberal policies, inaugurating a period of press freedom and diversity. But the Judiciary, headed by a conservative ally of the Leader, used its powers to close down newspapers and indict and jail reformist journalists and editors who had incurred the displeasure of conservatives. For every newspaper that was closed down, the Ministry of Culture would issue a new license and the newspaper would appear under a new name.[40] But by 2000, the most critical voices had been silenced by the Judiciary and its allies in the armed forces.

Another example comes from the security apparatus. In late 1998, six months after the commander of the Revolutionary Guards had threatened violence against opponents of the regime, a number of opposition politicians, journalists, and writers were killed in what became known as the "chain murders." Khatami insisted on an investigation and persuaded Khamenei to give his consent. Soon, it became clear that members of the Ministry of Information had carried out the murders. This led to a purge in the ministry, which operates under the authority of the president and of parliament.[41] While the Ministry of Information

subsequently became more tolerant of dissent and respectful of the law, the Revolutionary Guards and the Judiciary set up their own parallel intelligence organizations, replete with prosecutors and prisons, to pursue the conservatives' agenda of suppressing dissent.[42] This is one of several legacies that the Rouhani government must confront if it is to make policymaking more coherent, effective, and just.

The result of the multiplicity of policymaking bodies is frequent incoherence and sometimes paralysis. On a positive note, this incoherence has prevented the system from becoming totalitarian, as the overlapping spheres of activity of various state institutions make centralized control of public life well-nigh impossible.

Economic Policymaking

One of the most contentious topics in the postrevolutionary era is economic policymaking. From the very outset, the founders of the Islamic Republic and the new elite in the ministries and parastatal organizations fundamentally differed on the best approach to foster economic development. Those who favored a more state-centered approach to development initially dominated policymaking through the Parliament, ministries, and institutions such as the Construction Jihad. In the 1980s, the state played a critical role in rationing hard currency, setting prices for consumer goods, and using the public banking system to distribute loans to key sectors of the economy. State control at the time occurred in large part due to the requirements of war, the necessity of redistributing the assets of the numerous industrialists who had been forced into exile, and the fact that international investment had come to a standstill.

A liberal approach to development that placed greater emphasis on the private sector and market mechanisms began to dominate policymaking circles in the late 1980s. This was encouraged by the conclusion of the Iran–Iraq war and the global rise of neoliberal development agendas in the wake of the Soviet Union's demise. The major impetus to redirect economic policies, however, was low oil prices, which caused budget shortfalls for the government, and the poor performance of the economy in terms of capital investment and economic growth (see discussion later in this chapter). Thus, both the Rafsanjani and Khatami administrations tried to restructure Iran's economy by selling state-owned assets, lifting trade restrictions, and encouraging private and foreign investment. These policies had mixed results. Iran liberalized its trade regime, with ministries and procurement boards now playing a less pronounced role. Furthermore, private banks and industries took advantage of incentives to export goods. Nonetheless, the deregulation of the economy also led to hardship and has therefore faced opposition. On the one hand, many state employees and those who rely on state subsidies have been hurt by economic insecurity and inflation. On the other hand, the government's attempt to reform the economy has challenged the economic powers and vested interests of the large economic foundations that control large portions of Iran's commercial, industrial, and agricultural sectors, and that are largely unaccountable to the Parliament, the central bank, and development policymaking bodies. Khatami's and the reformists' attempt to introduce greater transparency and competition into the economy was limited by the economic foundations' and parastatal organizations' autonomous and privileged access to resources and markets. Thus, any attempt to reform the economy, boost productivity, or direct investment toward exports must address the inequality and inconsistencies of the parallel economy controlled by these organizations.

Under Ahmadinejad and with the high oil prices of the 2000s, economic policymaking combined populist rhetoric of redistribution and various forms of highly publicized handouts with the simultaneous privatizing of state firms and functions.[43] While the language of social justice and attacking "the corrupt" aimed at shoring up a social base of support, privatization of manufacturing and the allocation of construction contracts aimed at rewarding Ahmadinejad's key allies. For instance, key contracts in the oil and gas sector and telecommunications were given to companies affiliated with the IRGC. While, for decades, there has been domestic debate and international pressure from lending agencies such as the IMF and World Bank for Iran to reduce its generous energy and consumer subsidies, ironically, it was Ahmadinejad who took the first concrete steps in 2010 to remove subsidies that act as a social welfare net. Thus, these IMF-lauded policies threaten to exacerbate inequalities

and create a new class of economic oligarchs, as was the case in Russia. The ability of the regime to both roll back sanctions and ensure that there is enough investment for domestic production and consumption has been severely hindered by international sanctions that have reduced Iran's oil earnings and access to world markets.

Policy Outcomes

16.10 Compare and contrast the results of Iran's recent policies relating to internal and international issues.

Spreading Progress and Prosperity

The chief complaint of the revolutionaries had been that the Shah's policies failed to benefit the majority of Iranians. While succeeding administrations in the Islamic Republic have been on the whole indifferent to the interests of the educated upper middle class, they have tried to adopt policies that will improve the lot of the poor.

The state educational system is astonishingly good, given the limitations imposed by the political system. Iranian students regularly win medals at international science Olympiads, and literacy rates have continued rising, reaching 89 percent for men, 81 percent for women, and 99 percent for those under the age of 24 by 2012.[44] Thus, analysis of Iran's nuclear program should consider the large pool of scientific talent and its vested interests in technological development.

After pronatalist policies in the 1980s, the government realized that birth rates had to be brought down and inaugurated multifaceted birth control policies. All forms of family planning advice and contraception are widely distributed and subsidized both in cities and in villages; clinics offer free sterilization to men and women. The state actively encourages couples to have "only two children, be they boys or girls." All over Iran, couples have fewer children than their parents' generation. The dramatic drop in fertility rates caused Khamenei to state in 2012 that Iran's population control policies had been "wrong," and many programs were discontinued. Whether this reversal will change the demographic behavior of Iranians or not is unclear. But the current growth rate of the Iranian population is approximately 1 percent, one of the lowest in the Middle East.

Health care is an area of considerable progress. Small clinics staffed by paramedics serve many villages, and there is no shortage of physicians. While the quality of medical care may not always be very high, it has emphasized prevention, and its public availability is respectable even when compared with rich Western countries. These rural social and economic development programs are successful partly because they are spearheaded by the local communities rather than by experts from distant urban areas, who typically are unaware of the local needs or social and cultural conditions.[45] Much effort has gone into improvements in the countryside. Paved roads now connect all towns and many villages, and many villages have clean water and electricity.

In spite of the state's efforts to create a welfare state financed by oil income, most Iranians struggle to make ends meet. To some extent, this is because the middle class has grown tremendously, and with it, popular expectations. People whose parents were illiterate, poor peasants now aspire to a middle-class lifestyle; they expect to eat meat every day, send their children to good schools, and have decent housing. Table 16.2 compares some basic human development indicators for Iran for 2012 with those of a few comparable countries.

The provision of basic services to the general public has been quite successful. Obviously, more than three decades of steady oil income have made a difference. In many ways, the indicators for Iran are closer to those of Turkey than to those of Egypt or Pakistan. However, many Iranians are unwilling to credit the government for this, and impute it to the natural development of a country with a large oil income. It is often argued that with better planning, more competent management, and an acceptance of Saddam Hussein's offer to end the Iran–Iraq war in 1982, the situation might have been much better still. Moreover, Iran's overall macroeconomic performance has fallen behind the newly developing countries in Latin America or East Asia. The per capita growth rates have not kept pace with the emerging economic powers of China and India.[46] In fact, Iran's growth indicators have been quite volatile, with a rather extended period of depression in the 1980s due to war, sanctions, high birth rates, and deficient industrial policies. Even with the gradual improvement in per capita GDP since the early 1990s, which

TABLE 16.2
Iran Compared to Other Developing Nations

Country	Population	Life Expectancy	Urban Population (%)	Adult Literacy Rate (% aged 15 and above)	Expected Years of Schooling (years)	Ratio of Males to Females in Percentage with At Least Secondary Education	Gross National Income per Capita in PPP Terms[a]
Iran	75,611,800	73.2	69.2	85.0	14.4	0.664	$10,695
Turkey	74,508,800	74.2	72.5	90.8	6.5	0.580	$13,710
Egypt	83,958,400	73.5	43.6	72.0	12.1	0.732	$5,401
Pakistan	179,951,100	65.7	36.5	54.9	7.3	0.502	$2,566
India	1,258,351,000	65.8	31.6	62.8	10.7	0.528	$3,285
China	1,353,600,700	73.7	51.9	94.3	11.7	0.778	$7,945
Mexico	116,146, 800	77.1	78.4	93.1	13.7	0.901	$12,947
Nigeria	166,629,400	52.3	50.3	61.3	9.0	n.a.	$2,102

[a]PPP, purchasing power parity in constant 2005 international dollars.
Source: UNDP, *Human Development Report* (New York: United Nations Development Programme, 2013).

was largely due to the rise in oil prices, unemployment remains the number one worry for young people, and the growth rate of the economy is not nearly enough to absorb the growing population.[47] The current sanctions imposed on Iran by the United States and its allies have deteriorated these economic conditions by limiting Iran's ability to export oil, attract foreign investment, and import critical foreign technology. Iranians have witnessed a rapid decline in the value of the rial and their ability to purchase imported food and medicine or finance travel and education abroad.

Islamicization of Society

Another of the government's policy motivations is the desire to roll back secularism and spread Islamic moral values among the population. Since the early 1980s, alcohol consumption has been banned except for the non-Muslim minorities, veiling is enforced in public spaces, the state is in theory committed to minimizing contact between unrelated men and women, the religious content of education is vastly expanded, and gruesome physical punishments chastise adulterers, homosexuals, and other offenders of religious morality.[48] Divine law, as interpreted by the state, also allows capital punishment. In 2012, the number of death penalties carried out in Iran (314) was second only to China (many thousands), and more than in Iraq (129), Saudi Arabia (79), and the United States (43), which were the next three highest practitioners of the death penalty.[49] Media reports in 2013 suggest that there may be an increase in executions against people that are often described as "smugglers," but may be victims of factional conflicts between the conservative-dominated judiciary and the new government.

Outwardly, the Islamicization of society has been a success. Women cover their hair in public, people are more familiar with religious doctrine than before the revolution, the country has more mosques, Friday congregational prayers are routine in towns and cities, and all flights of Iran Air (the national airline) begin with a prayer. Even the best hotels serve no alcohol, even to foreign guests. Underneath the surface, however, the situation is more complicated. Prostitution is rife, driven by poverty. Over 2 million Iranians are drug addicts. Bootlegging flourishes, often with the connivance of the forces of order, which get a cut. As

education continues longer and the marriage age has gone up, young people are much more likely to have premarital sex than were their parents' generation, at least in Tehran. Corruption operates at almost all levels, from the petty official who will do his job only if he is paid a bribe to the relatives of the top leaders who have enriched themselves by controlling economic life.

All of this should not be construed to mean that Iranians have become irreligious. But religious practice has become more private, as the influence of clerics over religious life has declined. One study, comparing data gathered in 1975 and in 2001, demonstrates that while levels of personal religiosity (such as frequency of prayer) have remained relatively constant, participation in organized religion (such as attendance of congregational Friday prayers) has declined, reflecting a growing ambivalence toward state-sponsored public religious practices.[50]

Iranian Islam has always contained an anticlerical strain, as believers have always criticized clerics for their greed and hypocrisy. The ulema's assumption of power in the Islamic Republic has given a new fillip to this tendency. Taxi drivers are known not to stop for clerics, many of whom have taken to wearing civilian clothes in public. Foreign observers are often astonished by how few turbaned clerics they see in the streets of Tehran.

The rise of anticlericalism has led some of the more thoughtful members of the Shiite clergy to revisit the relations between church and state and to call for a separation of the two. They do so not because they advocate secularism but out of concern for the collective reputation of the ulema. In the Muslim world, advocates of the separation of church and state had always been secularists. In Iran, for the first time, *religious* arguments are being made for that separation on the grounds that coercively imposed religion harms spirituality.[51] One may even wonder whether some of the pious people who voted for Mahmoud Ahmadinejad in the 2005 and 2009 presidential election did so in order to rebuke the ulema, many of whom—such as the 2005 losing candidate, Hashemi Rafsanjani—have joined the country's ruling class and are seen to have been corrupted by power. Moreover, during his tenure in office, Ahmadinejad has often confronted staunch criticism from the traditional clerical establishment for his sometimes unorthodox and messianic understanding of Shiism. This relationship reached an all-time low in the aftermath of the 2009 elections, when only one of the top clerics congratulated him on his "victory."

Gender Relations

One of the key reproaches that Islamists addressed to the Shah's regime before the revolution was that its promotion of Western lifestyles turned women into sex objects and was generally conducive to moral corruption and sexual depravity—hence the effort to re-order gender relations and place them on an authentic Islamic footing.

From a secular perspective, the legal status of women improved under the Pahlavi monarchy. However, the majority of society remained more conservative than the laws governing it. After the revolution, much of the legislation that reduced the gender gap was repealed. According to the Islamic penal code introduced in 1981, the value of a woman's life is half that of a man's, in the sense that the law of the talion ("an eye for an eye") instituted by that code explicitly states that the blood money of a woman is half that of a man.[52] In practice, this means that if a man kills another man, the relatives of the victim can either ask for the execution of the murderer or accept a legally fixed amount of blood money. But if a man kills a woman, her relatives can ask for the murderer's execution only if they pay half a man's blood money. By the same token, in courts of law, the testimony of one man is worth that of two women. In some cases (such as adultery or murder), a woman's testimony does not count at all. A man can easily divorce his wife, whereas, in principle, a woman can initiate divorce proceedings only under exceptional circumstances; polygamy is recognized under the law. To travel abroad, a wife needs the formal permission of her husband, but the latter can leave the country as he pleases. The foreign wife of an Iranian man can easily acquire Iranian citizenship, whereas an Iranian woman cannot obtain Iranian citizenship for her foreign husband and her children from that husband.[53]

In addition to these legal restrictions on women's rights, the Islamic Republic has instituted all sorts of ad hoc discriminations. In the early years of the Islamic Republic, many fields of study, such as agronomy and mining engineering, were closed to female students at the universities on the assumption that they were too rough for women. Women's sports were severely restricted because the attire worn by female athletes is incompatible with veiling. This differential treatment of men and women is in stark violation of the International Convention on Civil and Political Rights, an international treaty that prohibits discrimination on religious and gender grounds. Iran acceded to the Convention in 1975 and remained a party after its regime changed. But from the point of view of theocracy, divine law obviously supersedes obligations incurred under international law.

Despite *and* because of these legal restrictions, Iranian women have continuously increased their participation in public life and their presence in the public sphere since strict Islamic law began to be enforced.[54] At the same time, they have challenged the logic of patriarchy. There are a number of reasons for this seemingly paradoxical development. The widespread participation of women in the mass anti-Shah demonstrations of 1978 made it unlikely that their interest in public affairs would end once the revolution was over. During the Iran–Iraq war, millions of men were serving at the front, and this forced many women to do jobs hitherto performed by men. Many women became their families' main breadwinners. Furthermore, the aspiration to a middle-class existence awakened by the revolution, coupled with the slow growth of the economy, has meant that women increasingly supplement their husbands' incomes by working. Given the strictly enforced rules on veiling and gender interaction in the public sphere, more-traditional women feel more at ease entering the public sphere. In addition, more-traditional men are less reluctant to let their wives, daughters, or sisters work outside the house. Restrictions that are offensive and limiting to nontraditional women have thus had a liberating effect on religiously observant women—and these constitute, after all, a majority of the female population.

The antitraditional attitude toward women's roles in society is reflected in the comparative results of the World Values Survey. For instance, while only 4 percent of Egyptians and 12 percent of Jordanians disagree with the statement that "marriage has become an outdated institution," 17 percent of surveyed

Iranians agree.[55] A plurality of surveyed Iranians disagree with the statement that "women need to have children in order to feel satisfied," whereas only 12 percent of Egyptians and 9 percent of Jordanians disagree with it.[56] Finally, 40 percent of Iranians agreed with the statement that "a working mother can develop intimate relationships with her children just like a nonworking mother," a rate that is double that of surveyed Egyptians and Jordanians.[57] Thus, despite the regime's initial attempts to inculcate a traditional image and role for women in the family and society, Iranian men and women seem to hold a less narrow view of women.

The visitor to today's Iran encounters women everywhere; they staff government agencies, work in offices, sell goods in shops, and own and run businesses. Most dramatically, women now constitute over 60 percent of the student body at the universities. Restrictions on what they can study were gradually lifted throughout the 1990s to the point where none remain. In Persian literature, the traditional emphasis on poetry has given way to a boom in the writing of novels—and most novelists are women. In sports, a daughter of then-President Hashemi Rafsanjani took a personal interest in women's sports in the early 1990s. Using her father's clout, she instituted a system whereby women compete under international rules and in normal athletic gear but at locations to which no men are admitted. This change led to many more women becoming coaches, referees, paramedics, and state sports officials.[58] Even veiling is now enforced less strictly, and the partial covering of the head that hard-liners call "mal-veiling" has spread. None other than Khomeini's granddaughter complained in an interview with a U.S. journalist about the state's intrusiveness in this regard.[59]

The widening gap between women's growing participation in public life and the legal system governing their society, and the many-voiced debates about this discrepancy, have had repercussions for Islam itself in Iran. Given the impossibility of criticizing any state of affairs from a secular perspective, feminists couch their arguments in Islamic terms. This has led to the emergence of "Islamic feminism," which is espoused both by truly observant Muslim women and by secular women who have no other way of articulating their demands. Given the continued religiosity of Iranians in general, Islamic feminism has been arguably more effective in raising the gender consciousness of the average woman than secular feminism would have been. These Islamic feminists are discreetly supported by a few sympathetic clerics who have helped them contest discriminatory policies or laws by proposing ways to circumvent them or even suggesting alternative readings of the relevant scriptural passages and legal principles. Small gains have thus been made. Take the issue of divorce: According to Islamic law, marriage is a contract whose clauses have to be agreed on freely by both husband and wife. A woman has always had the right to ask that her marriage contract include a clause giving her the right to initiate divorce proceedings, but this clause had to be added on to the standard contract issued by the state. Very few bridegrooms consented to it. Since the early 1980s, however, the standard contract includes the clause, meaning that for the woman not to have the right to divorce, bride and bridegroom have to ask for its removal—to which, nowadays, few educated women consent.

The greater success of women in higher education and the fact that the vast majority of Iranian drug addicts are men, coupled with the continued existence of domestic violence against women, have led Shirin Ebadi, who personifies women's struggles and occasional successes, to quip that Iran has not a "women's question" but a "men's question."

Foreign Policy

Like the French, Russian, Chinese, and Cuban revolutionaries before them, Iran's Islamic revolutionaries saw themselves as the vanguard of a vast revolutionary wave that would also encompass other countries. According to the preamble of the Constitution of 1979, the role of the army and the IRGC is not limited to "securing the borders" of the country but includes "struggling to spread the rule of divine law in the world." Managing the inherent tension between an ideological commitment to help overthrow or weaken other governments, on the one hand, and dealing with these governments on a daily basis, on the other, poses a tremendous challenge.

Beginning in the early 1990s, "national interest" rather than "export of the revolution" dominated the foreign policy agenda. The best example is the discreet support Iran gave to Christian Armenia in its conflict with Muslim (and predominantly Shiite) Azerbaijan in the war that followed the breakup of the Soviet Union.

But, as elsewhere in the world, there is little consensus as to what constitutes a nation's national interest. Many Iranians argue that national interest demands the solidification of its ties with the rest of the Islamic world.

Ultimately, the foreign policy of the Islamic Republic is driven by a "Third Worldist" desire to escape the hegemony of the Western world. In the parlance of Iran's leaders, Western hegemony is referred to as "world arrogance." In its struggle against "world arrogance," Iran has sought alliances, and these can be conceptualized in terms of three concentric circles. The outermost circle consists of Third World nations, the middle circle is made up of Muslim countries and movements, and the innermost one is constituted by the Shiites in West and South Asia (Lebanon, Iraq, Bahrain, Afghanistan, and Pakistan).

Iran's regional foreign policy enjoys an economic dimension related to the movement of people and goods. Iran now trades a greater share of goods and services with countries in the Middle East and the rest of Asia than it previously did. Some of this is driven by the economic growth of East Asian economies, and it reflects the desire of Iranian leaders to participate in the world economy without being dependent on Western economies, as was the case under the Pahlavi monarchy. Additionally, Iran has forged commercial relations with Dubai's entrepôt economy and the war economies of Iraq and Afghanistan. Alongside this trade, weapons, drugs, and humans are trafficked to, from, and through Iran. Conflicts in neighboring countries also resulted in Iran's becoming home to one of the largest refugee populations in the world. Finally, ordinary Iranian citizens have turned to new destinations for tourism and pilgrimage. Given tight visa restrictions for travel to Western Europe and North America, Dubai, Turkey, China, Malaysia, and Indonesia are now places where vacationers and pilgrims increasingly head, only to encounter Iranian businessmen and politicians on their voyages. Contemporary Iran's economy and society, hence, are far more integrated and engaged with regional dynamics than was the case during the Pahlavi era.

Many Third World countries greeted the revolution of 1979 with sympathy. However, the subsequent triumph of hard-line Islamists put a damper on pro-Iranian sympathies in non-Muslim nations. In recent years, President Ahmadinejad's defiance of the United States, which is perceived as an arrogant "bully" by many people in the Third World, has made Iran popular in a number of countries, especially in Latin American states with strong populist movements. Consequently, political cooperation and trade links with countries such as Venezuela, Ecuador, Bolivia, and even Brazil have grown substantially.

Sunni Islamists, for their part, were divided over support for revolutionary Iran. As the *Shiite* nature of the *Islamic* Republic became ever more apparent, and as Khomeini refused to accept Saddam Hussein's offer to end the Iran–Iraq war, most Sunni Islamists turned away from Iran. Saudi Arabia encouraged this estrangement because its Wahhabi version of Sunni Islam is hostile to Shiism. With U.S. connivance, Saudi money helped create a Sunni *cordon sanitaire* around Iran to contain the spread of revolutionary Shiism in such countries as Afghanistan and Pakistan; the Taliban operating in these two countries have been an unanticipated consequence of that policy.

This leaves Twelver Shiites as the only group among which Iranian efforts to spread the revolution have been somewhat successful. The founding of Lebanon's Hezbollah in the early 1980s was facilitated by Iran, and Iran continues to support the party and its social welfare activities financially. Iran also sponsored formation in Iran of the Supreme Council for the Islamic Revolution of Iraq (SCIRI). The party, ironically, played a major role in Iraq after the ouster of the Saddam Hussein regime in the wake of the U.S. intervention of 2003, which resulted in Twelver Shiites becoming the politically dominant community in Iraq, marginalizing the Sunnis. The ascendancy of Shiites in Iraq and the civil war in Syria, in which a regime closely allied with Iran fights a largely Sunni insurgency supported by pan-Sunni Islamist governments (e.g., Saudi Arabia) and organizations, have exacerbated sectarian tensions throughout the Muslim world. The Iranian state has unequivocally backed both the Iraqi and the Syrian regimes, providing advice, weapons, and manpower. This has put the Islamic Republic at odds with most Muslim countries, and, today, Iran maintains only a few client movements among Sunnis, most notably the Palestinian Islamic Jihad.

While increasing Iran's influence in the Middle East, Saddam Hussein's ouster also affected Iran's domestic politics. The consolidation of a semi-independent Kurdish state in northern Iraq has emboldened the Kurds of Iran, some of whom now regard it as an alternative to Iran that they would like to emulate or join. Likewise, the Arabs in Iran's Khuzistan province, until now loyal to the Iranian state because they are mostly Shiites, may become less certain of their national affiliation now that their kith and kin rule in Iraq. All of Iran's ethnic minorities straddle the country's borders with neighboring states (see again Figure 16.1). Until the 1990s, this did not matter much, since they constituted minorities on the other side as well. But the events in Iraq and the breakup of the Soviet Union, which created an independent Azerbaijan that attracts Azeris in Iran, has changed the situation. Iran's relations with its neighbors are now inextricably intertwined with its domestic ethnic politics.

In its relations with the West and the Soviet Bloc, the early Islamic Republic had as its motto "Neither East nor West." Iran was a U.S. ally under the Shah, but after the revolution, it joined the nonaligned movement. In practice, however, Iran's foreign policy in the first decade of the Islamic Republic, like that of many other Third World "nonaligned" countries, was far more anti-Western than anti-Soviet. In the case of the Islamic Republic, this stance reflected the revolutionaries' mistrust of a West that had supported the hated Shah, and the geographic proximity of the Soviet Union, whose occupation of neighboring Afghanistan in December 1979 was a constant reminder of the need for caution. Today, the Islamic Republic maintains cordial relations with Russia, but Iran has not had diplomatic relations with the United States since the United States severed them in response to the seizure of U.S. diplomats as hostages in 1979. Iranians have paid a heavy price for their government's hostility to the West. In the last stages of the war against Iraq, most Western powers discreetly assisted the Iraqi side. The United States maintains an economic embargo on Iran. For instance, Iranian airlines have difficulty purchasing a sufficient number of modern passenger aircraft and adequate spare parts for the old ones. As a result, "Iran's civil aviation sector suffers from one of the world's highest rates of accidents and incidents."[60]

After Khomeini's death, Presidents Hashemi Rafsanjani and Khatami tried to lessen Iran's diplomatic isolation. Relations with Arab countries, most of which had supported Iraq in the war, improved, and Iran made an effort to mend its ties with Europe and Japan. In the 1990s, the EU embarked on a policy of "critical dialogue" with Iran, which offered Iran concessions in exchange for improvement in the field of human rights. During the Khatami years, the policies of the government did indeed become less repressive, but given the overall control of unelected bodies, none of these liberalizing measures could be institutionalized.

In the aftermath of September 11, 2001, Iran found itself surrounded by U.S.-installed governments in Afghanistan and Iraq, and by U.S. troops and military bases in the countries to the north and south. This partially explains the anti-Western belligerence of the Ahmadinejad administration and its attempts to forge alliances with such countries as Russia and China.

The main issue confronting current Iranian diplomacy in its relations with the West is Iran's nuclear program. Since the days of the Shah, successive Iranian governments have declared that they are not interested in developing nuclear weapons. The official line of the government is that all weapons of mass destruction are contrary to Islamic ethics. Iran is a signatory of the Nuclear Nonproliferation Treaty, whose Article IV grants its signatories the "inalienable right" to "research, develop, produce, and utilize" nuclear technology for peaceful purposes. On that basis, the government embarked on a vast program to develop a self-sufficient nuclear industry by mastering the fuel cycle in which uranium is enriched to produce the fuel needed to power reactors. Western countries worry that this knowledge will allow Iran to produce highly enriched uranium or plutonium that could be used for nuclear weapons. What lends this worry a certain plausibility is Iran's development of long-distance missiles to which nuclear warheads could be fitted, and the fact that some nuclear facilities and experiments were kept secret. To allay Western fears, the Khatami administration agreed to negotiate with France, Germany, and the United Kingdom, while temporarily suspending the enrichment program and allowing international inspectors greater access to Iran's nuclear facilities. When these negotiations failed, Iran resumed the enrichment program in 2004. Given President Ahmadinejad's virulent verbal attacks on the West and on Israel, not to mention his questioning of the veracity of the Holocaust, the Iranian government's claim that its nuclear program is of an entirely peaceful nature has met with widespread skepticism in the West. Inspectors of the **International Atomic Energy Agency** have regularly visited Iranian installations and have found no evidence that Iran has diverted its nuclear know-how for military ends, but the government's cooperation has not been deemed satisfactory either by the agency or by Western governments. While the threat of military attack on Iran by the United States and/or Israel has loomed large, logistical impediments and global diplomatic critique have directed the U.S. government's energies toward fashioning a policy of ever-tightening sanctions against Iran, both unilaterally and internationally. In June 2010, the Security Council imposed a wide-reaching set of financial and commercial sanctions on Iran aimed at making its policymakers change its nuclear and foreign policy. In November 2013, a breakthrough was made when Iran and the P5+1 agreed to an interim agreement in which for six months Iran would scale back its nuclear program and the western powers would consent to some limited sanctions relief. Meanwhile, the parties plan to iron out a final agreement in 2014.

Evidence to date suggests that not only have the sanctions not resulted in Iran foregoing its nuclear program, but they have led to a more confrontational relationship between Iran and its international opponents.[61] Instead, the sanctions imposed on Iran have hurt Iran's private sector and made life more difficult for ordinary Iranians, who have more limited access to imported goods ranging from machinery to medicine and face greater impediments in exporting goods and traveling abroad. Ordinary Iranians, meanwhile, have suffered from a rapid decline in the value of the rial, which has fueled already high inflation rates and difficulties associated with the lifting of subsidies during Ahmadinejad's second term. However, the relative high price of oil has enabled the government to withstand the pressure and enabled the IRGC and regime insiders, who have access to hard currency and other critical resources, to create monopolies. Nonetheless, Iran's ability to both produce and export oil has dramatically declined since the imposition of the international sanctions, and, as a result, Iran has had

to develop costly ways to work around the restrictions. Foreign trade has been largely redirected to Asian countries, especially China, which, in 2008, surpassed Germany as Iran's largest trade partner. Western sanctions against Iran have thus had the paradoxical result of globalizing Iran's foreign policy ambitions by inducing it to find alternative trading partners as well as strengthening the very hard-line forces within the regime that U.S. policymakers claim to want to weaken.[62]

Conclusion

Iranian politics in the twentieth century were tumultuous. The century started with a constitutionalist movement seeking to make a monarchy more accountable and ended with a reformist movement striving to make a theocracy more republican. Between these two bookends, nationalist, religious, secular, and Marxist ideologies competed for followers, while social relations were restructured by processes associated with modernization. The Pahlavi monarchy promised to usher Iran into the modern industrial age, and because of both its successes and failures in doing so, the Shah was overthrown by a revolution that established a republic that incorporated the clergy.

To manage the many objectives of the revolutionaries, the Islamic Republic has created a bewildering set of institutions and organizations, many of which compete with one another and occasionally work at cross-purposes. The regime has been in continuous conflict with the United States and some regional powers, such as Israel. It has provided social welfare to many of its citizens, which unintentionally resulted in challenges to the establishment from the increasingly educated, urban, and individualist society. By the admission of many of its own leaders, "the economy is sick" and "social pathologies" tarnish all layers of society. Contestation is pervasive and sometimes public, even among state officials. The Islamic republic is an authoritarian regime that circumscribes participation and contestation but, because it was born out of a mass revolution, has sustained a norm of public participation and engagement.

How has a regime that faces so many challenges and contradictions survived for over three decades, and what are the prospects for significant change? The irony is that the same institutions that have created conflicting interests and allowed a degree of pluralism in Iran have also contributed to the regime's survival and ability to withstand opposition.[63] The fragmented nature of the state enables differences to emerge and persist, but it is this very fragmentation that prevents the aggregation of interests and demands of a dynamic society. Thus, even though many of the founders of the Islamic Republic have called for quite fundamental changes to it or have even defected from it, they have not had the leverage to restructure the regime. Indeed, the regime continues to enjoy a robust coercive apparatus, is financially solvent due to oil revenue, and enjoys the sympathies of some citizens, who either agree with its Islamist ideology or are repulsed by international efforts to weaken Iran. Elite politics in Iran today is factional politics, not party politics encompassing debates over specific policies and specified platforms and visions of the future.

Meanwhile, a myriad of patron–client networks, in conjunction with a coercive apparatus and an individualist political culture, creates a fragmented state with divisions at all levels of society. Corporate and associational interests are ill defined and undermined by personalism, and even ideologically similar groups often battle one another over access to assets. State–society relations as they are constituted now hinder coordination and trust between citizens and rulers as well as ultimately preventing the emergence of public deliberation and consensus building. This pattern has confused and frustrated some foreign diplomats and journalists, who expect Iranian politics to be narrowly defined and managed by the Leader. However, the lack of absolute political monopoly by Khamenei and the elite's unwillingness to devise institutions such as a free press and fair elections for powerful elected bodies have prevented the ability to formulate a unified and acceptable position on such matters as the negotiations over Iran's nuclear program or its position in regional affairs.

The problems faced by the Islamic Republic have reopened the debate on the proper relation between religion and politics in Iran. Going farther than revisiting Islamic law, some reformist Muslims are questioning whether religious law is as central to Islam as, say, ethics or personal experience of transcendence. These reformers impute the current preoccupation with Islamic law in Muslim governance to the prominence of the ulema in Muslim society, pointing out that the ulema are, after all, merely legal scholars.

As we said at the beginning of this chapter, Iran was the first state in which Islamists were able to exercise political power. The problems they have faced, the forces they have unleashed, and the responses they have elicited from society could have profound implications for political Islam in the rest of the world. In practice, however, Iran's experience remains of limited relevance to Islamists elsewhere. The experience of both the rulers and the ruled in the Islamic Republic is shaped more by Iran's historical trajectory, socioeconomic conditions, cultural configurations, and geopolitical context than by a static religious doctrine and uniform model of political Islam.

REVIEW QUESTIONS

- How do the republican components of Iran's institutional structure interact with the Islamic ones? Has their relative importance changed over time?
- How does Iran's prerevolutionary legacy of constitutionalism affect its current politics?
- *Theocracy* literally means "government by God." Since God does not rule directly, how is the idea of divine government implemented in practice in Iran?
- What is meant by elite politics being factional politics? What are these factions, what issues divide the elite, and how are their rivalries managed?
- Which social groups participated in the revolution of 1978 and 1979, and why? What factors led to the overthrow of the Pahlavi monarchy and support for Ayatollah Khomeini?
- The founders of the Islamic republic sought to create an Islamic society composed of Islamist citizens. How did they seek to do this, and how successful were they?

KEY TERMS

Ahmadinejad, Mahmoud

Assembly of Leadership Experts

Basij

Council of Guardians

Ebadi, Shirin

Expediency Council

Green Movement

Hashemi Rafsanjani, Ali-Akbar

International Atomic Energy Agency

Islamic Revolutionary Guard Corps (IRGC)

Islamists

Khamenei, Ali

Khatami, Mohammad

Khomeini, Ruhollah

Leader

Majles

Mossadegh, Mohammad

Mousavi, Mir-Hossein

multiple power centers

Pahlavi, Mohammad-Reza Shah

parastatal economic foundations

rentier state

Rouhani, Hassan

shari'a

Sunnis

theocracy

Tudeh Party

Twelver Shiism

ulema

velayat-e faqih

SUGGESTED READINGS

Abrahamian, Ervand. *A History of Modern Iran*. Cambridge: Cambridge University Press, 2008.

Adelkhah, Fariba. *Being Modern in Iran*. New York: Columbia University Press, 2000.

Amir Arjomand, Saïd. *After Khomeini: Iran under His Successors*. New York: Oxford University Press, 2009.

Asadi, Houshang. *Letters to My Torturer: Love, Revolution, and Imprisonment in Iran*. Oxford: Oneworld, 2010.

Atabaki, Touraj. *Azerbaijan: Ethnicity and Autonomy in Twentieth-Century Iran*. London: British Academic Press, 1993.

Azimi, Fakhreddin. *Iran: The Crisis of Democracy, 1941–1953*. New York: St. Martin's, 1989.

Bayat, Assef. *Making Islam Democratic: Social Movements and the Post-Islamist Turn*. Stanford: Stanford University Press, 2007.

Chehabi, H. E. "Religion and Politics in Iran: How Theocratic Is the Islamic Republic?," *Daedalus* 120 (Summer 1991): 69–91.

Gasiorowski, Mark. *U.S. Foreign Policy and the Shah: Building a Client State in Iran*. Ithaca, NY: Cornell University Press, 1991.

Gheissari, Ali, ed. *Contemporary Iran: Economy, Society, Politics*. New York: Oxford University Press, 2009.

Keshavarzian, Arang. *Bazaar and State in Iran: The Politics of the Tehran Marketplace*. Cambridge: Cambridge University Press, 2007.

Kurzman, Charles. *The Unthinkable Revolution in Iran*. Cambridge, MA: Harvard University Press, 2004.

Martin, Vanessa. *Islam and Modernism: The Persian Revolution of 1906*. London: I. B. Tauris, 1988.

Moin, Baqer. *Khomeini: Life of the Ayatollah*. London: I. B. Tauris, 1999.

Moslem, Mehdi. *Factional Politics in Post-Revolutionary Iran*. Syracuse, NY: Syracuse University Press, 2002.

Mottahedeh, Roy. *The Mantle of the Prophet: Religion and Politics in Iran*. Oxford: Oneworld, 2000.

Paidar, Parvin. *Women and the Political Process in Twentieth-Century Iran*. Cambridge: Cambridge University Press, 1995.

Sanasarian, Eliz. *Religious Minorities in Iran*. Cambridge: Cambridge University Press, 2000.

Tajbakhsh, Kian. "Political Decentralization and the Creation of Local Government in Iran: Consolidation or Transformation of the Theocratic State?" *Social Research* 67 (2000): 377–404.

Vahdat, Farzin. *God and Juggernaut: Iran's Intellectual Encounter with Modernity*. Syracuse, NY: Syracuse University Press, 2002.

INTERNET RESOURCES

Ministry of Foreign Affairs, Islamic Republic of Iran: www.mfa.gov.ir.

Payvand (news and information portal): www.payvand.com.

Encyclopaedia Iranica: www.iranica.com/.

Iranian Studies Group at Massachusetts Institute of Technology: www.isg-mit.org.

Iran Data Portal: http://www.princeton.edu/irandataportal/index.xml.

The Middle East Research and Information Project: www.merip.org.

ENDNOTES

1. Frances Harrison, "Huge Cost of Iranian Brain Drain," BBC News, January 8, 2007, http://news.bbc.co.uk/2/hi/middle_east/6240287.stm. From the Washington Institute (accessed at http://washingtoninstitute.org/templateC05.php?CID=1556).

2. Sonia Ghaffari, "Baluchestan's Rising Militancy," *Middle East Report* 250 (Spring 2009): 40–43.

3. Abdul-Hadi Hairi, *Shiism and Constitutionalism in Iran* (Leiden: Brill, 1977).

4. Nikki R. Keddie, *Modern Iran: Roots and Results of Revolution* (New Haven, CT: Yale University Press, 2003), 123.

5. Mark Gasiorowski, "The 1953 *Coup d'État* in Iran," *International Journal of Middle East Studies* 19 (1987): 261–86.

6. See Roham Alvandi, "Nixon, Kissinger, and the Shah: The Origins of Iranian Primacy in the Persian Gulf," *Diplomatic History* 36 (2012): 337–72.

7. Richard W. Cottam, *Iran and the United States: A Cold War Case Study* (Pittsburgh, PA: University of Pittsburgh Press, 1988), 156–69.

8. Ahmad Ashraf and Ali Banuazizi, "The State, Classes, and Modes of Mobilization in the Iranian Revolution," *State, Culture, and Society* 1 (1985): 3–39.

9. Misagh Parsa, *Social Origins of the Iranian Revolution* (New Brunswick, NJ: Rutgers University Press, 1989).

10. Ironically, even the Shah himself believed in the omnipotence of the United States and Britain; after his ouster, he blamed these countries for having engineered his demise.

11. Ruhollah Khomeini, "Islamic Government," in *Islam and Revolution: Writings and Declarations of Imam Khomeini*, trans. and annotated Hamid Algar (Berkeley, CA: Mizan, 1981).

12. See H. E. Chehabi, "The Political Regime of the Islamic Republic of Iran in Comparative Perspective," *Government and Opposition* 36 (2001): 48–70.

13. See Suzanne Maloney, "Agents or Obstacles? Parastatal Foundations and Challenges for Iranian Development," in *The Economy of Iran: Dilemmas of an Islamic State*, ed. Parvin Alizadeh (London: I. B. Tauris, 2000), 145–76; and Ali Saeidi, "The Accountability of Para-Governmental Organizations (*Bonyads*): The Case of Iranian Foundations," *Iranian Studies* 37 (2004): 479–98.

14. Bahman Baktiari, *Parliamentary Politics in Revolutionary Iran: The Institutionalization of Factional Politics* (Gainesville: Florida University Press, 1996).

15. Abdol-Karim Lahiji, "Moruri bar vaz'-e hoquqi-ye Iranian-e gheyr-e mosalman," *Iran Nameh* 19 (2001): 1379–80. On the legal discrimination of women, see section on gender relations in this chapter.

16. Mehran Kamrava and Houchang Hassan-Yari, "Suspended Equilibrium in Iran's Political System," *Muslim World* 94 (October 2004): 495–524.

17. Asghar Schirazi, *The Constitution of Iran: Politics and the State in the Islamic Republic* (London: I. B. Tauris, 1998), 134.

18. Walter Posch, "The End of a Beautiful Friendship? Mahmoud Ahmadinejad and the Principalists," in *Iran and the Challenges of the 21st Century: Essays in Honour of Mohammad-Reza Djalili*, eds. H. E. Chehabi, Farhad Khosrokhavar, and Clément Therme (Costa Mesa, CA: Mazda, 2013), 50–78.

19. See Farideh Farhi, "Iran's 2008 Majlis Elections: The Game of Elite Competition," Middle East Brief no. 29 (Waltham, MA: Crown Center for Middle East Studies, Brandeis University, May 2008), www.brandeis.edu/crown/publications/meb/MEB29.pdf.

20. Kian Tajbakhsh, "Political Decentralization and the Creation of Local Government in Iran: Consolidation or Transformation of the Theocratic State?" *Social Research* 67 (2000): 377–404.

21. Before World War I, Westerners considered Iran and other non-Western but nominally sovereign countries, such as China and Thailand, to be "semicivilized" nations, which had some but not all of the attributes of a full-fledged member of the international community. See Gerrit Gong, *The Standard of "Civilization" in International Society* (Cambridge: Cambridge University Press, 1984).

22. Houchang E. Chehabi, "The Paranoid Style in Iranian Historiography," in Touraj Atabaki, ed., *Iran in the 20th Century: Historiography and Political Culture* (London: I. B. Tauris, 2009), 155–76, 294–303.

23. See L. Carl Brown, *International Politics and the Middle East* (Princeton, NJ: Princeton University Press, 1984), 233–52.

24. Mansoor Moaddel and Taghi Azadarmaki, "The Worldviews of Islamic Publics: The Case of Egypt, Iran, and Jordan," in *Human Values and Social Change: Findings from the Values Survey*, ed. Ronald Inglehart (Leiden: Brill, 2003), 81.

25. This line of reasoning is based on Azadeh Kian-Thiébaut, "Entrepreneurs privés: entre développement statocentrique et démocratisation politique," *Les Cahiers de l'Orient* 60 (2000): 65–92.

26. Peter Chelkowski and Hamid Dabashi, *Staging a Revolution: The Art of Persuasion in the Islamic Republic of Iran* (New York: New York University Press, 1999), 130–31.

27. Kaveh Ehsani, "Islam, Modernity, and National Identity," *Middle East Insight* 11 (1995), 51.

28. Farideh Farhi, "The Antinomies of Iran's War Generation," in *Iran, Iraq, and the Legacies of War*, ed. Lawrence C. Potter and Gary G. Sick (New York: Palgrave Macmillan, 2004), 101–20.

29. Moaddel and Azadarmaki, "The Worldviews of Islamic Publics."

30. Ahmad Sadri, "The Varieties of Religious Reform: Public Intelligentsia in Iran," in *Iran: Between Tradition and Modernity*, ed. Ramin Jahanbegloo (Lanham, MD: Lexington Books, 2004), 117–28.

31. Marvin Zonis, *The Political Elite of Iran* (Princeton, NJ: Princeton University Press, 1971).

32. Khosrow Fatemi, "Leadership by Distrust: The Shah's *Modus Operandi*," *Middle East Journal* 36 (1982): 48–61.

33. Mehran Kamrava, *The Modern Middle East: A Political History since the First World War* (Berkeley: University of California Press, 2005), 261.

34. Figures are from Wilfried Buchta, *Who Rules Iran? The Structure of Power in the Islamic Republic* (Washington, DC: Washington Institute for Near East Policy, 2000), 68.

35. Assef Bayat, *Street Politics: Poor People's Movements in Iran* (New York: Columbia University Press, 1997).

36. Arang Keshavarzian, "Regime Loyalty and *Bazari* Representation under the Islamic Republic of Iran: Dilemmas of the Society of Islamic Coalition," *International Journal of Middle East Studies* 41 (May 2009): 224–46.

37. Quoted in Saïd Amir Arjomand, *The Turban for the Crown: The Islamic Revolution in Iran* (New York: Oxford University Press, 1988), 182.

38. In fact, Ahmadinejad belongs to a current of thought that considers the return of the Twelfth Imam imminent. This messianic expectation sets him apart from most other leaders of the Islamic Republic and may yet be the source of friction.

39. For details, see H. E. Chehabi, "Ardabil Becomes a Province: Center-Periphery Relations in the Islamic Republic of Iran," *International Journal of Middle East Studies* 29 (May 1997): 235–53.

40. For an inside account, see Elaine Sciolino, *Persian Mirrors: The Elusive Face of Iran* (New York: Free Press, 2000), 248–60.

41. For details, see Buchta, *Who Rules Iran?* 156–70.

42. How this multiplicity of power centers affects individuals is seen in the story of Dariush Zahedi, an Iranian-American political scientist who had met with dissidents while visiting Iran one recent summer for his research. He was arrested by the Ministry of Information and held prisoner for two months before being told that, as far as the Ministry was concerned, he was innocent—except that upon leaving the prison, he was immediately rearrested by the intelligence agency of the Revolutionary Guards, who held him for another two months in solitary confinement and subjected him to similar interrogations as his preceding jailers, only in a less respectful tone. He was finally released and returned to the United States through the intervention of a number of Iranian diplomats after academics in the United States publicized his plight.

43. Kaveh Ehsani, "Survival through Dispossession: Privatization of Public Goods in the Islamic Republic," *Middle East Report* 250 (Spring 2009): 26–33.

44. United Nations Statistics Division.

45. Ervand Abrahamian, "Why the Islamic Republic Has Survived," *Middle East Report* 250 (Spring 2009): 10–16; Homa Hoodfar, "Activism under the Radar: Volunteer Women Health Workers in Iran," *Middle East Report* 250 (Spring 2009): 56–60; and Eric Hooglund, "Thirty Years of Islamic Revolution in Rural Iran," *Middle East Report* 250 (Spring 2009): 34–39.

46. Massoud Karshenas and Hassan Hakimian, "Oil, Economic Diversification, and the Democratic Process in Iran," *Iranian Studies* 38, no. 1 (March 2005): 67–90.

47. Djavad Salehi-Isfahani, "Iranian Youth in Times of Economic Crisis" Working Paper no. 3 (Dubai Initiative, Dubai School of Government and Belfer Center for Science and International Affairs, Harvard Kennedy School, September 2010).

48. Mehrangis Kar, "*Shari'a* Law in Iran," in *Radical Islam's Rules: The Worldwide Spread of Extreme Shari'a Law*, ed. Paul Marshall (Lanham, MD: Rowman & Littlefield, 2005), 41–64.

49. The numbers are from Amnesty International.

50. Abdolmohammad Kazemipur and Ali Rezaei, "Religious Life under Theocracy: The Case of Iran," *Journal for the Scientific Study of Religion* 42, no. 3 (2003): 347–61.

51. See Mahmoud Sadri, "Sacral Defense of Secularism: Dissident Political Theology in Iran," in *Intellectual Trends in Twentieth-Century Iran*, ed. Negin Nabavi (Gainesville: University Press of Florida, 2003), 180–92.

52. Mahmud Abbasi, *Qanun-e Mojazat-e Eslami* [Islamic Penal Code] (Tehran: Hoquqi, 2002), 108.

53. Following the victory of the Mujahidin in Afghanistan, as the Iranian government became keen on repatriating Afghan refugees to Afghanistan, tens of thousands of Iranian women who had married Afghan refugee men in Iran were told by the authorities that they faced the choice of either seeking a divorce from their husbands or following them to their country.

54. Mehrangiz Kar, "Women's Political Rights after the Islamic Revolution," in *Religion and Politics in Modern Iran: A Reader*, ed. Lloyd Ridgeon (London: I. B. Tauris, 2005), 253–78.

55. Moaddel and Azadarmaki, "The Worldviews of Islamic Publics," 77.

56. Moaddel and Azadarmaki, "The Worldviews of Islamic Publics," 78. Forty-five percent of Iranians agree with this statement, while 88 and 89 percent of Egyptians and Jordanians, respectively, agree.

57. Moaddel and Azadarmaki, "The Worldviews of Islamic Publics," 79.

58. For details, see *The International Encyclopedia of Women and Sport* (New York: Macmillan, 2001), "Iran," 586–87. For an eyewitness account by a Western journalist, see Geraldine Brooks, "Muslim Women's Games," in *Nine Parts of Desire: The Hidden World of Islamic Women* (New York: Anchor Books, 1995), 201–11.

59. Asked whether she would ever "want to throw off the head scarf in public," she answered: "Do you want to issue me my death sentence?," *International Herald Tribune*, April 3, 2003, 2.

60. Najmedin Meshkati, "Iran's Nuclear Brinkmanship, the U.S. Unilateralism, and a Mounting International Crisis: Can Civil Aviation Industry Provide a Breakthrough?," *Iran News*, July 26, 2004, 14.

61. Bijan Khajehpour, Reza Marashi, and Trita Parsi, "'Never Give In and Never Give Up': The Impact of Sanctions on Tehran's Nuclear Calculations" (Washington, DC: National Iranian American Council, March 2013).

62. Thierry Kellner, "Iran's Asian Strategy: The Importance of Economic Ties," in *Iran and the Challenges of the 21st Century: Essays in Honour of Mohammad-Reza Djalili*, eds. H. E. Chehabi, Farhad Khosrokhavar and Clément Therme, (Costa Mesa, CA: Mazda, 2013), 245–65.

63. Arang Keshavarzian, "Contestation without Democracy: Elite Fragmentation in Iran," in *Authoritarianism in the Middle East: Regimes and Resistance*, ed. Marsha Pripstein Posusney and Michelle Penner Angrist (Boulder, CO: Lynne Rienner, 2005), 63–88.

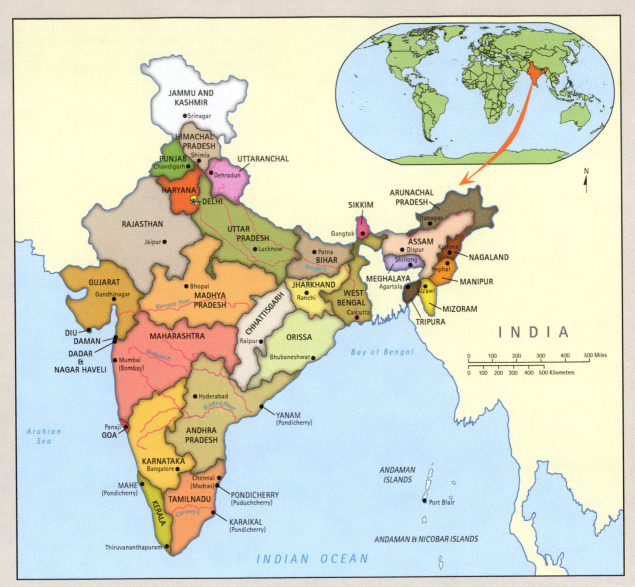

INDIA

Country Bio

POPULATION
1.241,000 billion (2011)

TERRITORY
1,269,338 square miles

GDP PER CAPITA,
1489 US dollars. (2012)

YEAR OF INDEPENDENCE
1947

YEAR OF CURRENT CONSTITUTION
1950

HEAD OF STATE
President Mr. Pranab Mukherjee

HEAD OF GOVERNMENT
Prime Minister Mr Manmohan Singh

OFFICIAL LANGUAGES
English, Hindi (primary tongue of 41% of the people), Bengali, Telugu, Marathi, Tamil, Urdu, Gujarati, Malayalam, Kannada, Oriya, Punjabi, Assamese, Kashmiri, Sindhi, Sanskrit (note: there are 24 languages, each of which is spoken by a million or more people)

RELIGION
Hindu 80.5%, Muslim 13.4%, Christian 2.3%, Sikh 1.9%, Buddhist 0.8%, Jain 0.4%, other 0.6%

SCHEDULED CASTES
16.2% of population

SCHEDULED TRIBES
8.2% of population

CHAPTER 17

Politics in India

Subrata K. Mitra

LEARNING OBJECTIVES

17.1 Discuss India's increased international profile and the challenges posed by its emergence.

17.2 Describe the creation of modern India and contrast its evolution with that of other countries of South Asia.

17.3 Identify the components of Indian social identity and discuss the ways they have fragmented national identity.

17.4 Compare and contrast the Indian political system with those of the United States and Britain.

17.5 Differentiate between powers held by the Union and the States in India.

17.6 Describe the types of organizations that represent special interests in India and their methods of engagement.

17.7 Discuss the makeup and influence of India's national and regional political parties.

17.8 List Morris-Jones' three idioms of Indian politics, and discuss their interplay in the political culture.

17.9 Discuss the increase in voter turnout in India's national and regional elections and the alternative political actions engaged in by citizens.

17.10 How well are the various social groups of India represented in the political institutions?

17.11 Summarize the fluctuations in India's economy, the government's responses, and the outcomes.

India was seen as the epitome of backwardness and economic stagnation by specialists and travelers to that country barely a few decades ago. Though numerous symbols of poverty and underdevelopment still persist, many developments that have taken place since the liberalization of the economy in 1991, and the nuclear tests of 1998, have added a new aura to India's international profile, promoting the country to the rank of an emerging economy. The ubiquitous mobile phones, new highways, overpasses in capital cities, foreign firms, and shopping malls selling brand-name consumer goods speak for India's rapid integration into the global market economy. Leaders of business and industry and politicians from abroad are regular visitors to the centers of power and high finance in

India such as Bangalore, Hyderabad, and Chennai—directly connected to international hubs of business with their new, international airports—in addition to the obligatory visits to New Delhi, the national capital, and Mumbai, which continues to be the finance capital of the country.

Are these symbols of high-tech prowess merely the latest addition to the multilayered diversity of India, or do they signify a takeoff to sustainable growth? Are the new symbols of prosperity and economic growth spreading across society and the different regions of India, or are they confined to the privileged strata, creating discontent, lessening the sense of citizens' efficacy and the legitimacy of modern, democratic institutions? Do the state and the democratic political process have the capacity to defeat leftist and secessionist movements, or, for that matter, ethnic conflict, terrorism, or violence aimed at disrupting public order?

This chapter answers these questions by analyzing the interaction of the modern state and traditional society in contemporary India. It analyzes the dilemmas arising out of India's complex and diverse political process, the political tradition steeped in a culture of hierarchy, and its steady transformation under the impact of the democratic process and a fast-changing economy. As is the case in all changing societies, the institutionalization of these achievements is one of the key problems in India. The interplay of federalism, elections, informal and institutionalized forms of power sharing and party competition, the active and socially engaged judiciary, growing markets and globalization, and the watchful eye of Indian and international media and human right movements have combined to produce a political environment that has helped to sustain democracy and development.

The resilience of India's democracy poses a theoretical puzzle from a comparative point of view. Why has India's democracy survived, in contrast to its demise in the majority of post-colonial states? The fortuitous availability of leaders like Gandhi, Nehru, and Patel during the crucial years of transition from colonial rule has certainly played a crucial role in guiding India toward electoral democracy. Trained in law, these leaders honed their skills at parliamentary politics through long years of struggle against colonial rule. They adapted the imported institutions of parliamentary democracy to Indian context and culture. But that is not the full story. The hybridization of modern and traditional political norms and values, and the innovation of new institutions, besides the stretching of imported modern institutions to suit the needs of state formation and nation-building, have been an asset for India's economic development and democratic transition.[1] Beyond explaining the anomaly of India's resilient democracy, the chapter provides an insight into the richness and complexity that India embodies, based on Almond's comparative framework, and tempered by rational choice neoinstitutionalism.

In addition to being an interesting story in its own right, the Indian case holds great interest for cross-cultural comparisons of the transition to democracy and development in a postcolonial context. India—with its democratic political system, secular

constitution, liberalized but still **mixed economy**, mass poverty, and complex ethnic composition—is a favorite example for general theories of development and modernization of both capitalist and socialist persuasions. Both of these perspectives see some limitation on political participation as a necessary price to pay for the transformation of underdeveloped societies into liberal democracies.[2] India, with its dual commitment to democratic rights and development, has been seen as something of an anomaly. As things stand now, India has not radically changed its basically liberal Constitution adopted in 1950, nor its institutional arrangements, or democratic practice. Yet rapid economic growth has been achieved over the past two decades. The chapter looks at the apparent contradiction between conventional theories of political transition and the Indian case by analyzing India's history, society, economy, institutions, and policy process.

Current Policy Challenges

17.1 Discuss India's increased international profile and the challenges posed by its emergence.

India's emergence as a fast-growing economy, its growing nuclear arsenal, major purchases of military hardware, the growing presence of Indian farms in the global market, and spectacular terrorist attacks have created a new, worldwide focus of interest on contemporary India. The country's growing market, joint ventures between Indian and foreign firms, and the availability of skilled, low-cost, young, English-educated technical people adept at information technologies (IT) present new opportunities for global business, industry, and political leadership. The new international environment poses a sharp challenge to India's traditional policy of **nonalignment**—known in India as **panchasheela**—which was typical of India's postwar foreign policy under Prime Minister Jawaharlal Nehru, causing India's leadership to reconsider international diplomatic alignments.

Under the impact of the new contextual and indigenous developments, India is re-examining its approach to international and regional organizations and increasingly looking in the direction of global and regional linkages. Nehru was a great supporter of international peacekeeping, mediation initiatives, a staunch advocate of Asian regional co-operation and non-alignment. Contemporary India, which often claims that the sources of her insecurity lie in the territories of her neighbors, has so far refused to have the issues discussed as a common problem of South Asia, preferring, instead, to take things up at the bilateral level. It can be argued that a regional body like the South Asian Association for Regional Cooperation (SAARC) could perhaps facilitate India's room to maneuver. However, regional co-operation can work only when one of two conditions exists. The first is the presence of a dominant regional power that can regulate regional behavior, or the existence of a set of regional players with roughly similar resource endowments, or similar threat perceptions by members of the region from outside the area. The leading role of the United States in the western hemisphere and the successful regional organizations in Europe and South East Asia are examples of these conditions. Neither condition obtains in South Asia. A successful solution to the issue of joint management of security threats at the regional level could possibly reduce India's security burden and increase her support from regional powers at the international arena, but India might not find it easy to move in that direction because of the country's long standing conflict with neighboring Pakistan on the issue of Kashmir. In the multipolar world of today, and with the emergence of the **BRICS**–an informal association consisting of Brazil, Russia, India, China and South Africa–and a thaw in India–China relations (China is currently India's largest trading partner)–India's foreign policy finds itself in a radically altered context compared to the situation that prevailed during the Cold War.

The international visibility of India's successful IT sector, the outsourcing of routine, clerical functions by many of the world's major companies to India to take advantage of lower wages, and fast economic growth have shifted global attention from India's mass poverty toward new opportunities that the emerging economy presents. Measured in terms of "openness"— the sum of exports and imports divided by GDP— India's international status has steadily gone up during recent times, starting from the liberalization of the economy in 1991 (see Figure 17.1). The consequences can be seen in the increase of the relative share of the service industry in the economy going up from 32 percent in 1980–1981 to 44 percent in 2004–2005. The share of agriculture in the GDP has consequently gone down from 35 percent to 18 percent in the same period.

In terms of mass literacy, India still lags behind the industrial nations, as well as China and most of the "tiger" economies of East Asia. The intellectual backup for India's prowess in IT, biotechnology, and medical research is provided by a few elite institutions—such as the famous IIT (Indian Institute of Technology), IIM (Indian Institute of Management), and the major metropolitan universities. Beyond these institutions, which cater to the educational needs of a small portion of the population, the infrastructure for mass literacy and for the kind of technical training that a growing economy demands is sorely lacking. Under the federal division of powers, education is the responsibility of India's regional governments, which makes coordination for mass education difficult to achieve at the national level.

India's infrastructure, particularly road transport and shipping facilities, are inadequate to meet the needs of a rapidly growing economy. The current project to build a system of expressways that would link India's major cities indicates the importance that the government attaches to this issue. The problem has a historical background. India's transport network, particularly the railway, was originally put in place by British colonial rulers. The main objective was to safeguard the need to move troops rapidly from one corner of the vast subcontinent to another. As such, the rail network that independent India inherited was vast in terms of mileage, but the connectivity of ports with hinterlands and mines was lacking. The acceleration of the pace of economic growth and the challenge of global competition have added saliency to the issue of infrastructure. (See Figure 17.1)

The entanglement of politics and religion continues to be a source of anxiety for India's secular state. An earlier generation of Indian political specialists thought that religious beliefs impeded the functioning of modern politics and economy, and were a major obstacle to the transformation of the social hierarchy sanctioned by traditional religions into a democratic, egalitarian social order. By an extension of the same argument, they believed that with modernization, religion would decline in importance.[3] In contrast, recent political developments have shown that religious networks can also become a political vehicle for social movements. Religion, many defenders of modernity have noticed to their dismay, can impart a sense of identity to social groups feeling discriminated against or threatened by other groups. This confluence

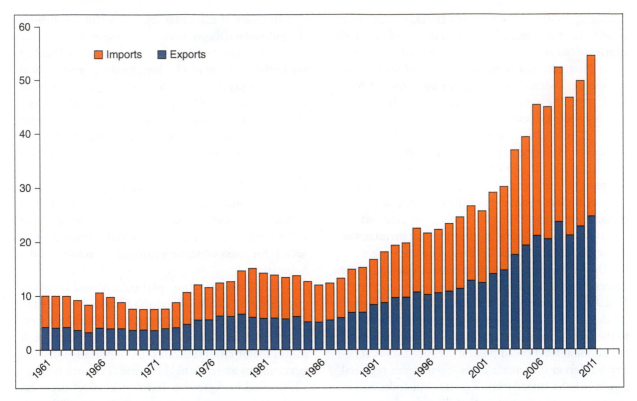

FIGURE 17.1

Openness of India's Economy

Indian exports and imports increased rapidly in the last decade.

Source: World Bank, Database, Imports of goods and services (% of GDP) (http://data.worldbank.org/indicator/NE.IMP.GNFS.ZS) and Exports of goods and services (% of GDP) (http://data.worldbank.org/indicator/NE.EXP.GNFS.ZS), last accessed on February 11, 2013.

between the search for identity and political competition is frequently present in the public sphere.[4] When adherents of a religion are regionally concentrated, such as Sikhs in Punjab and Muslims in Kashmir, there is a convergence between religion, regional identity, and political majorities. This convergence generates a corresponding demand that the regional government incorporate the sacred beliefs of the religion. This severely stretches the limit of India's secular state that constitutionally bars religion from playing any role in public institutions.[5]

Hindu nationalist movements, acting on the basis of the fact that over 80 percent of Indians are Hindus, extend this logic by demanding the embodiment of Hindu cultural ideals and historical symbols within the structure of the modern state. Religion—particularly the exclusive right to places of worship and the right to make religious processions in religiously mixed neighborhoods—is one of the main

causes of conflict in India today. North India is dotted with mosques that stand next to Hindu temples or are built on spots where Hindu temples are believed to have stood. Many of these Islamic structures are now at the center of the religious storm that continues to incite sacred fervor and political passion.

Indo–Pakistani rivalry, with its potential for nuclear war, remains a source of great anxiety. The conflict between the two neighbors over Kashmir dates back to 1947. Kashmir, with its Muslim majority, is claimed by Pakistan on the basis of the **two-nation theory**. India justifies its claim to Kashmir on the grounds of its legal accession to India after independence, and holds the continuation of this Muslim majority region as an integral part of the Indian federation, indispensable to the credibility of India's status as a secular state. The conflict over Kashmir led to war between India and Pakistan in 1947–1948, 1965, and 1999. The international community geared up

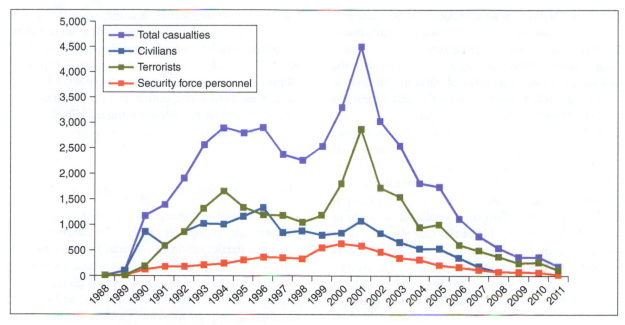

FIGURE 17.2
Chronology of Casualties: Kashmir (1988–2011)
Source: www.satp.org.

for an arms race and the intensification of conflict in South Asia following the **nuclear tests** of 1998. But contrary to such apprehensions, soon after the tests, India and Pakistan started a series of negotiations and confidence-building measures (CBMs). The **composite dialogue** between India and Pakistan[6] that started in 2004, and set up a wide range of issues, including the status of Kashmir, as the basis of negotiation between the two countries, appears to have held sway over the occasional flare-up of conflict. The Kashmir conflict, however, remains a live issue, in both India's domestic politics and international politics. In many ways, Kashmir has become the Achilles' heel of Indian diplomacy, a critical determinant of India's relation with Pakistan, and beyond it, of India's international profile.

Current developments, particularly the sharp decline in militancy in Kashmir, thanks to the effective use of democracy-enhancing measures and effective antiterrorist operations combined with material incentives (see Figure 17.2), point toward cautious optimism. Indian opinion in favor of a negotiated outcome to the Kashmir conflict has gone up from 33.5 percent to 59.3 percent between 1996 and 2004, and support for a military solution has come down from 11.1 percent to 8.8 percent during the same period.[7] The initiative taken by the **Bharatiya Janata Party**

(BJP) leading the **National Democratic Alliance (NDA)** coalition to negotiate with Pakistan has been followed by the current Congress Party–led **United Progressive Alliance (UPA)**, in power since 2004. The decline in militancy and a tacit consensus on the global war on terror have enhanced the capacity of the Indian state to take a bold stand on national security and territorial integrity.[8] (See figure 17.2)

History in the Making of Contemporary Politics

17.2 Describe the creation of modern India and contrast its evolution with that of other countries of South Asia.

India's history, both colonial and premodern, affects current politics in a different manner from that of Western liberal democracies. India has not experienced an industrial revolution that caused a great rupture with tradition, as in the case of European democracies, nor a violent Marxist revolution, which caused a similar break with tradition in Russia and China. Nor is the Indian state the outcome of wholesale colonization of an entire territory, such as that of the United States, Canada, or Australia by white settlers. In contrast, India is an ancient civilization, transformed by successive waves of immigrants who have been accommodated, adding their cultures, rituals, and social networks as integral parts of this diverse civilization. It is a country where the past appears to flow seamlessly into the present, where historical incidents like the destruction of Hindu temples by Islamic invaders can reappear as issues of great emotional significance in current politics. Great popular interest in Indian epics such as the *Mahabharata*, telecast as prime-time serials, signify this tendency. However, while the existence of organized political authority in premodern times, capable of city planning, sophisticated methods of governance, and tax collection, is suggested by texts like the *Arthasastra*—written four centuries BCE—the institutional form and social basis of the early state, capable of acting as a blue print for the modern state, is the subject of considerable historical controversy. Burton Stein, in his seminal work, questions the conventional notion of the highly organized feudal state with one paramount ruler and an omnipotent bureaucracy.[9] Instead, he suggests that the early state was "segmentary," where political authority and control were localized, and formed part of loosely organized empires, drawing on many different factors, such as agrarian systems, kinship, and religious networks.[10]

The British Raj

There is a vast literature dealing with why and how India slipped into British colonial rule. There was a combination of factors such as Britain's superior arms, centralized political organization, and effective military intelligence, and internal strife among Indian rulers, typical of the segmentary state, of which the British traders and adventurers took full advantage. These factors explain the inexorable expansion of the British Empire, reaching its peak in 1858, once the Sepoy Mutiny was quelled. Having established their rule, the British succeeded in bringing various local and regional units under a central government, which nevertheless drew heavily on indirect rule through quasi-autonomous intermediaries, such as native princes, tribal leaders, and *zamindars* (Hindi for landlords).[11]

While, on the whole, British rule was marked by economic stagnation and deindustrialization of India,

both of which, according to some, were the direct consequences of colonial exploitation, it nevertheless left behind a rich legacy of social change through legislation, rule of law, incremental devolution of power, administrative unity of a specific territory, a welfare state, a modern army, police and professional bureaucracy, and an English-speaking middle class well versed in the skills of representation, governance, and communication.

The Independence Movement

The anticolonial movement based its struggle on a platform that strategically combined agitation for self-rule with participation in colonial institutions and administration. The movement as a whole was constitutionalist and liberal in nature. Although it had elements of nativism, religious intolerance, and radical, socialist rhetoric, the movement was mostly under the control of leaders who had been educated in the West. These leaders believed in social progress, political accommodation, and a leadership based on consensus, and committed to transition to democracy. They generally stood against the use of race or religion to generate political support. During the last phase, the national movement split between the Indian National Congress and the Muslim League, with the latter advocating the creation of Pakistan as a separate state for the Muslims of India. The Congress Party initially resisted the idea of the Partition of India on the basis of religion, but reluctantly agreed to the idea during the final stage of negotiation with the British for Independence and the Transfer of Power. The **partition** was marked by terrific violence, with millions of immigrants crossing over the new border separating the two neighbors, in both directions, and the bitter legacy of enduring conflict over Kashmir.

The Congress Party opposed partition of British India on the basis of religion, and believed, instead, in the creation of a united, secular, modern India after independence from British colonial rule. British rule ended in 1947, with independence and partition. In the case of India, it meant the transfer of power to the Indian National Congress, which was at the forefront of the independence struggle during the last phase of British rule. The Indian National Congress was the main political party in the Constituent Assembly that produced the Indian Constitution and subsequently formed the government, having won the first general election.

Gandhi: The Story of Independence

Mohandas Karamchand Gandhi, popularly known as Mahatma—The Great Soul—was born in 1869 in Porbandar, a small seaport in the western State of Gujarat. He was trained as a barrister in England. After his return to India, he went to South Africa to take a position as a lawyer. There, he initiated a protest movement against the discrimination experienced by the Indian community and became well known for his method of nonviolent resistance. Back in India in 1915, he immediately joined the Freedom Movement led by the Congress Party. Drawing on his South African experience, he developed the concept of satyagraha as a principle and technique of nonviolence and civil disobedience to fight injustice and to revolt against British colonial rule. In 1920, he became the undisputed leader of the Congress Party and turned it into a mass movement, uniting all the different and sometimes even mutually hostile strands of Indian society. Under Gandhi's leadership, the Congress Party steadily broadened its reach, in terms of both social class and geography. To mobilize mass support, Gandhi introduced indigenous political practices, such as fasting and general strikes or *hartal* (a form of boycott accompanied by a work stoppage). Gandhi was against the partition of British India on the basis of religion and tried to reconcile the growing antagonism between Hindus and Muslims. In 1948, only one year after his vision of an independent India had been reached, he was assassinated by Nathuram Godse, a young Hindu extremist, who accused him of appeasement of Pakistan.

Mahatma Gandhi, the best-known leader of India's struggle for independence and a continued source of moral inspiration, developed the method of *satyagraha*—nonviolent resistance, combining institutional participation and strategic protest—while he was in South Africa working for an Indian law firm. The South African experience also taught Gandhi the importance of cross-community coalitions, a strategy that he subsequently transformed into Hindu–Muslim unity. This factor became a salient feature of Gandhi's politics upon his return to India from South Africa in 1915. Under his leadership, the Indian National Congress became increasingly sensitive to the gap between the predominantly urban middle-class Congress Party and the Indian masses, and shifted its attention to the Indian peasantry (see Box 17.1).

The British responded to increasingly vocal demands for political participation with the Government of India Act of 1935. This act is a landmark in India's constitutional development and subsequently became an important blueprint for the Constitution of independent India. Even though the 1945 Act continued the voting franchise based on a property qualification, the electorate expanded from 6 million to 30 million. Provincial elections held under this act gave the Congress Party a valuable experience in electoral campaigns and governance. Both became crucial assets for the establishment of an orderly political process after India's independence.

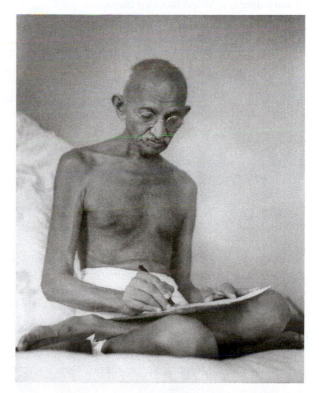

Gandhi: Apostle of Nonviolence and Leader of the Freedom Movement

Gandhi had a keen understanding of the nature of Indian politics and of the difficulties inherent in uniting a population easily divided by race, religion, and caste. His resistance to the salt tax provided a "common denominator" for mobilizing the Indian population to "nonviolent resistance."

India became independent on August 15, 1947, though full republican status came only in 1950. **Jawaharlal Nehru,** India's first prime minister, was a leading figure in the anticolonial campaign and a proponent of nonalignment for India. Unlike the postrevolutionary elites of China and the Soviet Union, Nehru and his associates formed a national leadership through consensus building, by including rather than eliminating challengers, and accommodating a broad political spectrum. The character of the new political system was shaped by the legacies of Indian history and social diversity, but most of all by the nature of the local and regional resistance to colonial rule. In contrast to China and the former Soviet Union—which made self-conscious attempts to cut themselves off from their prerevolutionary history—no general anti-British campaign with racial overtones occurred in India either before or after its independence. The complex legacies of colonial rule and the resistance to it have deeply affected modern India.

Recent Political History

The Republic of India started its political career in 1950 (see Figure 17.3). It was the first major Third World democracy to emerge out of colonial rule and the first major state to stay away from military alliances with either of the blocs led by the United States and the Soviet Union. Instead, under the leadership of Prime Minister Jawaharlal Nehru, India decided to follow a nonaligned foreign policy. At home, India sought to avoid the extremes of socialism and capitalism, opting instead for a "mixed economy" that combined state regulation in investment, planning, and distribution with room for free enterprise in industry, agriculture, services, and trade.

India's democracy, despite a short stint of authoritarian rule in the form of the "emergency regime" of **Indira Gandhi** (1975–1977), has acquired breadth, depth, and resilience through electoral mobilization, legislative and constitutional amendment, and empowerment of women, former untouchables, and

1947	Independence Day (August 15), partition, and the transfer of power. Accession of Kashmir to India; the first Indo-Pakistan war in Kashmir.
1950	Inauguration of the Republic of India (January 26).
1951–1952	First general election of federal and provincial assemblies.
1962	Sino–Indian War.
1964	Nehru dies following a stroke (May 26).
1965	Indo–Pakistan War.
1971	Indo–Pakistan War. Pakistan splits—establishment of Bangladesh.
1974	First nuclear test.
1975–1977	National emergency.
1984	Indian Army attacks the Golden Temple of Amritsar to dislodge Sikh terrorists (June). Assassination of Indira Gandhi (October 31).
1991	Liberalization of the Indian economy begins.
1992	Babri mosque destroyed.
1993	Seventy-third Amendment of the Constitution makes village councils autonomous units and makes a quota of at least 33% of seats for women mandatory.
1998	Nuclear tests by India and Pakistan.
1999	Kargil War between India and Pakistan.
2004	Surprise defeat of the BJP-led NDA coalition in the national polls.
2005	Mahatma Gandhi National Rural Employment Guarantee Act passed by Parliament.
2008	Indo–US Civilian Nuclear Agreement signed into law.
2009	UPA, led by Sonia Gandhi, wins the national polls.
2010	Women's Reservation Bill (providing a quota of 33% of all Lok Sabha and state assemblies' seats for women) is pending after having passed Rajya Sabha (in March).

FIGURE 17.3

A Chronology of Major Events Since Independence

BOX 17.2 — Jawaharlal Nehru to Sonia Gandhi: Democracy and Dynastic Rule

Born in 1889 in Allahabad as the eldest son of Motilal Nehru, a prominent nationalist leader and close friend of Mohandas K. Gandhi, Jawaharlal Nehru—like Gandhi—was educated in England before he returned to his hometown as a barrister. He entered national politics in the 1920s and began a long and close association with Gandhi. Inclined to socialist ideas and to the vision of a rapid process of modernization, it is Nehru who in many ways was the architect of independent India. He announced the birth of the Indian state in his famous "Freedom at Midnight" speech, where he caught the spirit of the historical moment. Soon afterward, Nehru became the first prime minister of India, a position he occupied until his death in 1964. But the Nehru "dynasty" continued to dominate Indian politics in the person of his daughter Indira Gandhi, who became prime minister in 1966, and subsequently his grandson Rajiv Gandhi, who was prime minister from 1984 until 1989. Following Rajiv's death in an explosion carried out by a Tamil suicide bomber from Sri Lanka, his Italian-born widow, Sonia Gandhi, was gradually inducted into national politics. Following the victory of the UPA coalition under her leadership in 2004, Sonia was invited to become the prime minister. She declined, preferring instead to provide leadership from outside the government as the president of the Congress Party. She has continued in this role after the victory of the UPA coalition in the elections of 2009.

other disadvantaged social groups. (see box 17.2) Many of the other salient features of the Indian state, however, have been sorely tested over the last six decades. Several wars—against Pakistan on the issue of Kashmir, and a border war with China in 1962 on the northwestern and northeastern frontiers, in the high Himalayas—threatened India's territorial integrity and challenged its resolve to follow a foreign policy based on nonalignment and peaceful resolution of conflicts. The support of the Soviet Union, which helped India meet the growing mutual support of its two hostile neighbors, Pakistan and China, was no longer available once the Cold War ended and the Soviet Union unraveled. India has met this challenge by developing its own military and nuclear capability. The Indo–US Civilian Nuclear Agreement, which was signed into law in 2008, has given India much-needed access to nuclear fuel and technology.

The resolution of the Government of India to "liberalize" the economy in 1991 started with dismantling the apparatus of the planned economy. India's rapid integration with the international market economy had some salutary effects on its growth rate. Finally, despite the wars against the Islamic Republic of Pakistan and the rise, in the 1980s, of militant Hinduism, and the periodic outbreak of violent intercommunity conflict, the state as a whole has managed to safeguard its status as a secular state that seeks to provide a level playing field to all religions, castes, races, and ethnic groups.

The "Givens" of Indian Society

 17.3 Identify the components of Indian social identity and discuss the ways they have fragmented national identity.

The key to many of the issues arising out of India's politics is found in the interaction of India's traditional institutions, social diversity, and the modern democratic political process. This interaction explains why, despite a culture traditionally based on the concept of "homo hierarchicus" where higher social orders dominate the lower, with large groups of people still steeped in mass poverty and illiteracy six decades after independence, India has nevertheless succeeded in establishing a resilient democratic and egalitarian political order.

Religious Diversity and Political Conflict

India is a multicultural, multidenominational, and secular state. India's decennial census shows the country to be a Hindu "majority" country, with 80.5 percent of the population classified as Hindus. But Hindus themselves are divided into many sects and denominations and can hardly be considered to be a "community" in the political sense. However, the rapid rise of the Hindu nationalist Bharatiya Janata Party is a reminder of the political appeal of pan-Indian Hinduism as an ideology. The idea of a politically mobilized Hindu majority, threatening the plural and democratic character of the political process, is a source of some anxiety among the minorities. Opinions on the issue of the city of **Ayodhya** (see Box 17.3) illustrate this polarization. India's political process appears to be robust enough to inject a degree of moderation into extreme sectional demands. Cultural plurality is an integral part of Hinduism. Its many sects and their separate traditions influence one another, leading to the growth of new forms.[12] Many Hindus believe in the concept of "unity in diversity." Each cultural–linguistic area has its own "little" tradition and local gods, and it is within the local sects that most Hindus live their religious life. The classical ideals of Hinduism and local traditions have freely interacted with each other in the past, leading to the growth of regional traditions, hybrid forms of ritual and belief, and cross-regional movements.[13]

Other major religions of the world are also present in India. Muslims constitute 13.4 percent of the population, and are a majority in the State of Jammu and Kashmir. A good number of India's Muslims are converts from Hinduism. Despite the change of religion, many have retained their languages, food habits, occupations, and stations in the local social hierarchy. As such, Muslims as a whole reflect the diversity of Hindus—a fact that the Muslim leadership under British rule, and indeed political Islam today, has sought to overcome in favor of a more homogeneous Islamic community.

The demand for a separate homeland for Muslims by the Muslim League during British colonial rule led to the partition of British India and the creation of Pakistan in 1947, a new state with the explicit purpose of becoming the homeland of South Asia's Muslims. About two-thirds of Indian Muslims and the bulk of the leaders of the Muslim League subsequently left India for Pakistan following the partition. Over the past decades, the Muslim community in India has developed a new leadership, identity, and political assertiveness. Muslim representation in legislative bodies and in public life has grown since India's independence, and political competition has enhanced the sense of group assertion and increased the number, intensity, and geographic spread of communal conflicts.[14]

Sikhism—born about 400 years ago as a resistance movement against Islamic invaders—took on many of the theological and organizational features of both Hinduism and Islam. Some Sikhs feel that their identity is threatened by modernization and assimilation with Hinduism. Many of them had envisioned the creation of a sovereign Khalistan state as an exclusive homeland for Sikhs. The Sikh majority in the northern Indian State of Punjab has been reduced through emigration to other parts of India and abroad. Some Sikhs fear the further loss of the Sikh majority because of the influx of non-Sikhs from poorer parts of India, attracted to Punjab by better wages. These anxieties fueled a political movement that took an increasingly violent turn, leading to the army's siege of the Golden Temple in the holy city of Amritsar and, in revenge, the assassination of Prime

---

BOX 17.3   Ayodhya (1992) and Its Aftermath, Godhra (2002)

The city of Ayodhya in the northern State of Uttar Pradesh came to international prominence on December 6, 1992. A long-standing point of contention between Hindus and Muslims was a mosque, built in 1528 by the first Moghul emperor Babur that, Hindus claim, stood where a temple once marked the birthplace of Rama. The Hindu nationalist BJP launched a *rathyatra* (holy procession of a chariot) to Ayodhya in order to build a Hindu temple on the birth place of Rama spot. The mosque was demolished by the *karsevaks* (activists) of two front organizations of Hindu nationalism, followed by communal riots in many parts of India. On the eve of the tenth anniversary of the Babri mosque's destruction in February 2002, a Muslim mob attacked a train at the Godhra station filled with Hindu activists returning from a pilgrimage to Ayodhya. This incident triggered a pogrom against the Muslims in Gujarat, causing a violent intercommunity conflict. The opposition accused the BJP-led Gujarat State government of complicity with anti-Muslim mobs; the government defended itself with statistics showing that about a third of the casualties were caused by police shooting under orders, mostly against Hindu mobs.

Minister Indira Gandhi by two of her Sikh body-guards on October 31, 1984.[15] However, a combination of repression of dissidents and accommodation of some of their demands and the induction of some of their leaders into the government has seen law and order return to Punjab.

Hindu nationalist movements demand the embodiment of Hindu cultural ideals within the structure of the modern state at the national level. Political parties and movements that draw their strength from religious beliefs and aspirations are also quite strong in political and cultural self-assertion.[16] Still, religion—particularly the exclusive right to places of worship and the right to make religious processions in religiously mixed neighborhoods—is one of the main causes of conflict in India today. North India is dotted with mosques that stand next to Hindu temples or are built on spots where Hindu temples are believed to have stood. This is an integral part of the collective memory of the Islamic conquest of India from the eighth century onward. Many of these Islamic structures are now at the center of the political storm that continues to incite religious fervor and political passion.

Caste and Politics

Local **castes** referred to as *jatis* are the basic social units that still govern marriages, social networks, food taboos, and rituals in India. In the past, caste regulated the choice of occupation as well, which was typically caste-specific and hereditary. This has changed rapidly because of modernization, legislation, and urbanization. In addition, the government quota system has opened up top jobs to former untouchables and tribals that once were the prerogative of the upper castes. Though the caste system is considered to be an essential part of Hindu society, there are caste like structures among other religions such as Islam and Christianity as well.

There are more than 2,000 jatis in India, traditionally divided into four hierarchically ranked broad categories called *varnas*:

1. The Brahmins, who originally performed the traditional function of priests.
2. The Kshatriyas, who were the rulers and the warriors.
3. The Vaisyas, who were the mercantile classes.
4. The Sudras, who were the service groups, agriculturists, and artisans.

Originally, the caste system presupposed the interdependent relationship of occupational groups, referred to as the *jajmani* system.[17] Jatis were linked to one another through ties of reciprocal economic, social, and political obligations. In the center of this scheme of reciprocity stood social groups with controlling interests in land, whom other castes provided with services, and from whom they received a share of the harvest. The relationship of the lower castes to the high-caste landowners was hierarchic, but their dependent status also carried some traditional rights, such as disaster relief at times of natural calamities. All behavior within the system, however, emphasized social hierarchy and inequalities of power, wealth, and status. Control over land was the critical lever of social status and power. These institutions and traditions derived their legitimacy from the unifying concept of *dharma*, which signified the natural order of things. Though specific to Hinduism, dharma dominated local society, tradition, and belief systems. The oppressive aspects of the caste system have been increasingly contested by those at the bottom of the pyramid, particularly the former "untouchables" and the lower castes, mentioned in the Constitution's Scheduled Castes (SC), Scheduled Tribes (ST), and Other Backward Classes (OBC).

The former untouchables are excluded from social interaction with the four varnas, because of the "polluting" nature of their traditional occupation as scavengers. They make up about a sixth of India's population. Attempts to elevate them into full membership in society through legislation, affirmative action, and competitive politics have accelerated since independence. Politically conscious and increasingly assertive former untouchables now refer to themselves as *dalits*, which in Hindi means "the suppressed groups." Many Indians see the caste system as the cause of India's social fragmentation and economic backwardness. But castes are also the only basis of identity and social interaction for vast numbers of people. Democracy and economic change have thus sometimes worked at cross-purposes, creating conflict, fragmenting large castes into new social groups, and fusing several existing groups into caste associations. As new opportunities for enterprise and political linkage open up, castes are increasingly the basis of community formation. The new "political caste" is an instrument for the promotion of collective interest by social groups that come together for that purpose. The instrumental role that caste plays in raising consciousness and electoral mobilization actually undermines the ideological basis of social hierarchy and helps question the more odious aspects of caste domination.[18] The politics of northern India has been recently dominated by coalitions of dalits and the "Backward Classes," who usually belong to the lowest social strata.

The situation of India's aborigines, known as **tribals**, who represent 8.2 percent of the population, parallels that of the former untouchables. The colonial practice declared the areas largely inhabited by them as reserved or "scheduled areas," where tribal lands could not be easily acquired by non-tribals. This policy continued after India's independence. Although tribals exist all over India, and some tribal groups living in nontribal areas have caste-like status, the majority are concentrated in three main regions: the northeast (primarily in Nagaland, Meghalaya, and Arunachal Pradesh), the hill areas of central India, and western India. Overall, these regions are socially and economically backward, but the spirit of political competition pervades them as well. Movements for the creation of autonomous regions are indicative of this tribal self-assertion.

Language

Along with caste and religion, language is one of the key components of Indian identity. Language is also one of the main social cleavages in other South Asian nations, such as Pakistan and Sri Lanka. India's major languages, each having evolved over many centuries, are concentrated in different regions. As such, the mother tongue has become the focus of regional identity. Although Hindi is common in northern India, the different regions (and subregions) have their distinct dialects. Many are very highly developed, with their own distinguished literary traditions. In the 1920s, subnational loyalties based on language developed simultaneously with the nationalist movement. The Indian National Congress demanded that Britain redraw the map of India along linguistic lines. Congress itself was organized on the basis of regional languages as early as 1920. In 1956, the government redrew the administrative map of India, and since then, the Indian States have been organized on the basis of the mother tongue. The elevation of the main vernacular to the status of official language of a region has reinforced the multinational character of the Indian political system.

Indian languages can be divided into two main groups: the Indo–Aryan languages of the north (such as Punjabi, Hindi, Kashmiri, and Bengali) and the Dravidian languages of the south (such as Telugu, Tamil, Kannada, and Malayalam). The largest single language in India is Hindi, which, along with English, is recognized as an official language of India. A complex three-language formula gives Hindi the status of the national language while equalizing the chances of non-Hindi speakers in India for government jobs by conceding to English the status of a link language. Regional languages are the main medium for official purposes within regions. Additionally, the adoption of regional languages as administrative languages brings government closer to the people. Linguistic movements in India have thus contributed to the greater differentiation of the political system as well as to the overall legitimacy of the state, without, at the same time, damaging the basis of national integration.

Social Class

Unlike in China and Vietnam, despite the presence of both mass poverty and radical politics, India did not develop a revolutionary peasant movement that could cut across the barriers of caste, region, language and ethnicity. When peasant uprisings inspired by Marxism appeared in southern India shortly after India's independence and in West Bengal in the 1960s, they did not spread to other parts of India. The nature of colonial rule and Indian resistance to it—particularly the role of Gandhi, the Indian class structure, and the country's social fragmentation—are responsible for the muted nature of class conflict in India. The slow pace of industrialization and urbanization and castes, tribes, and ethnic groups that cut across class lines led to a highly uneven pattern of class formation. This pattern has severely inhibited the development of class identities and political mobilization based on class appeals.

As a group, India's industrial working class is quite small, and only a minority is unionized. Protected by strong labor legislation and surrounded by workers in insecure jobs, unionized labor constitutes something of a labor aristocracy. The rural class system is complex. The land reforms of the 1950s eliminated some landlords (zamindars). In their place, there emerged a powerful new rural force composed of a mixed-status group of middle-peasant cultivators called "bullock capitalists." They are a powerful political force in rural India, and have challenged urban interests, upper-caste-dominated parties, and the formally dominant position of the older social notables. However, with the political mobilization of the former untouchables, who constitute the social layer just below, their superior position is also gradually being challenged.

The landless and small landowners (those holding fewer than 2.5 acres of land), divided by caste as well as by class lines, do not share a common interest. The small landowners also do not identify with the needs and aspirations of the rural landless population. Under the pressure of mechanization, which requires a larger unit of production, the pressure on land has increased, leading to enhanced landlessness. The dominant social groups are being challenged in some parts of India through the independent political organization of the former untouchables, who are frequently landless agricultural workers. Such movements constitute an important challenge to the dominance of the upper social strata.

In summary, from a comparative perspective, India is a highly pluralistic and segmented society where the twin processes of modernization and democratization have transformed a hierarchical society into groups that see themselves as legitimate political actors. But the cultural basis lacks uniformity at the national level because social networks are often confined to region and locality. Regions have increasingly acquired their own distinct identities in terms of economic and political status, and cross-regional coalitions deeply influence the course of national politics.

Political Institutions and the Policy Process

17.4 Compare and contrast the Indian political system with those of the United States and Britain.

Following independence, India, like many former British colonies, adopted the model of British parliamentary democracy, based on the accountability of the executive to the legislature, a professional and politically neutral military and career civil service, and the rule of law. Some salient features of the political system of the United States—such as federalism, the separation of powers, and fundamental rights of individuals protected by a Supreme Court—were also introduced.

Compared to many other postcolonial states, India started with several advantages that eventually facilitated the growth of a parliamentary democracy.

The transition from colonial rule was marked by a continuity of leadership to which power was transferred. A professional bureaucracy and security apparatus, already manned mostly by Indians, was immediately available. Above all, the development of the Congress Party into a nationwide electoral organization made for an effective exercise of power by democratically elected leaders. The partition of India, by removing the Muslim League, which had been the main political challenger to the Congress Party, from India's political arena, produced a smaller but more cohesive state. The leaders of the Indian successor state quickly adapted themselves to the new, competitive political environment, based not so much on nationalist ideals as on the pragmatic politics of social and economic reform and the acquisition of power. This led to the creation of a political system that institutionalized representation, competition, and accountability, besides making enormous patronage available to the ruling Congress Party. Finally, Nehru's adoption of nonalignment as the cornerstone of India's foreign policy created a generation of political leaders focused on domestic politics. They saw fair and regular elections and the growth of a self-reliant economy as the main basis of legitimacy.

This basic institutional structure has survived the challenges of the past six decades, a period that includes the demise of the generation of leaders who were in charge at the time of India's independence, the upward mobility of lower social strata, left- and right-wing radicalism, famine, mass poverty and large-scale changes in the economy, a major border war against China in 1962, and four wars against Pakistan.

One legacy of the Indian resistance to British rule was a deep distrust of authority and a determination to secure the maximum possible freedom for citizens. The members of the Constituent Assembly, which met from 1947 to 1950, gave shape to these aspirations in the institutions they devised. In some cases, they drew on India's cultural and political legacies, but in others, they borrowed widely from the major constitutions of the Western world. The result was the separation of power among the executive, the legislature, and the judiciary at the national level. An equally robust division of power between the federal government and the regions was also established.

In its solicitude for the decentralization of power, the Constituent Assembly did not stop there. There were strong hopes for the devolution of power below the level of the regional governments, to be exercised directly by the representatives of the people. This hope took a concrete shape in 1957 when the Balwantrai Mehta Committee recommended the creation of a *panchayati raj* (literally, the rule of the five) to set up representative bodies at the district, subdistrict, and village levels. They were endowed with a measure of administrative autonomy, charged with developmental functions, and given financial means for that purpose. The implementation of panchayati raj has been far from uniform, but thanks to the Seventy-third Amendment to the Constitution in 1993, all of India's half-million villages are covered by directly elected village councils in which representation of women, Scheduled Castes, and Scheduled Tribes is mandatory.

The structure resulting from India's countervailing powers has tremendous potential for political fragmentation. But India's "state-dominated pluralism" provided the right balance between central direction and respect for regional and local autonomy.[19] To cope with extraordinary situations where rapid action was imperative, the Constitution gave a series of emergency powers to the national executive to meet the challenge of grave political crises. Although the Constitution formally vested authority in the president, everyday exercise of executive power and legislative initiative were intended to be in the hands of the prime minister.

The President

The role of the President as the head of state was designed with the British monarch in mind. In practice, however, the office combines the ceremonial roles of head of state with some substantive powers. Under the Indian Constitution, executive power is formally vested in the president, elected by a special electoral college consisting of members of the legislative assemblies of the States and of the national Parliament. The total voting strength of both groups of electors carry equal weight, in order to induce a balance between the Union and the States. The president is expected to exercise these powers on the advice of the Council of Ministers, with the prime minister at its head. The real lines of control, as shown in Figure 17.4, (see Figure 17.4 below) nevertheless indicate otherwise.

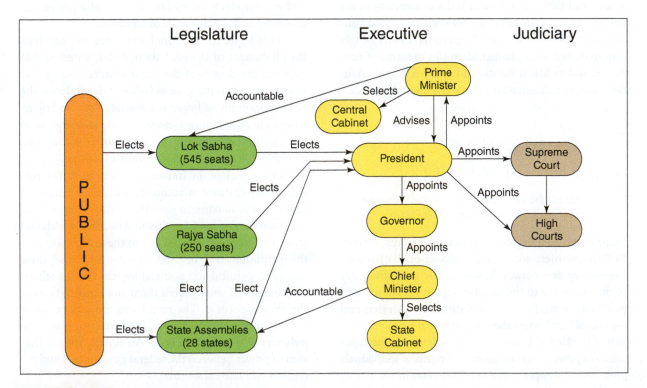

FIGURE 17.4
India's Institutional Arrangement
India's political institutions are vertically and horizontally linked.

The president appoints the prime minister and has the authority to dismiss him. But, by convention, these powers are severely limited. The President invites the leader of the majority party or coalition in the Lok Sabha (the Lower House of the Indian Parliament) to form the government. The Indian President exercises his authority as advised by the prime minister. But that does not mean that the president is merely a rubber stamp. The president might identify a potential leader when there is no clear parliamentary majority emerging from an election. Early presidents, like Rajendra Prasad and S. Radhakrishnan, were eminent statesmen who were not seen as politicians even though they were elected. That is not the case anymore. The president's five-year term can be renewed. The president can be removed through impeachment by the Parliament. The Constitution confers an impressive range of powers on the president. It provides the president with the authority to suspend fundamental rights and to declare a state of national **emergency** under Article 352, with the authority to impose the "President's Rule" in a region, under which the State is ruled directly by the Union executive (Article 356), and with a provision for financial emergency under Article 360. But in true republican fashion, even while leaving the decision to the president and the prime minister, the Constitution requires the presidential proclamations to be laid before Parliament for approval within two months, failing which, they will lapse.

The appointment of the highest elected executive of India (see Figure 17.5) appears democratic in contrast with many developing countries where replacement of the chief executive often occurs by nondemocratic means. However, during most of the time since its independence, India was ruled by members of the Nehru family, indicating a form of dynastic rule.[20] The continuity of Indian democracy was briefly breached through the imposition of a national emergency in 1975.[21] The national emergency, which lasted from 1975 to 1977, was declared by the president of India under Article 352 of the Constitution, at the advice of Prime Minister Indira Gandhi. During this period, the fundamental rights guaranteed under the Constitution were suspended and the general election to the Lok Sabha was postponed by one year; 150,000 people, including several members of Parliament who stood up against the draconian measures taken by the government, were incarcerated. This was the

PRIME MINISTER (RELIGION)	YEAR	PRESIDENT (RELIGION)
Jawaharlal Nehru (H)	1947	
	1950	Rajendra Prasad (H)
	1962	Sarvepalli Radhakrishnan (H)
Gulzarilal Nanda (H)	1964	
Lal Bahadur Shastri (H)		
Gulzarilal Nanda (H)	1966	
Indira Gandhi (H)		
	1967	Zakir Hussain (M)
	1969	Varahagiri Venkata Giri (H)
		Muhammad Hidayatullah (M)
		Varahagiri Venkata Giri (H)
	1974	Fakhruddin Ali Ahmed (M)
Morarji Desai (H)	1977	Basappa Danappa Jatti (H)
		Neelam Sanjiva Reddy (H)
Choudhary Charan Singh (H)	1979	
Indira Gandhi (H)	1980	
	1982	Giani Zail Singh (S)
Rajiv Gandhi (H)	1984	
	1987	Ramaswamy Venkataraman (H)
Vishwanath Pratap Singh (H)	1989	
Chandra Shekhar (H)	1990	
P. V. Narashima Rao (H)	1991	
	1992	Shankar Dayal Sharma (H)
Atal Behari Vajpayee (H)	1996	
Inder Kumar Gujral (H)	1997	Kocheril Raman Narayanan (H)
Atal Behari Vajpayee (H)	1998	
	2002	Abdul Kalam (M)
Manmohan Singh (S)	2004	
	2007	Pratibha Devisingh Patil (H)
	2012	Pranab Mukherjee (H)

FIGURE 17.5
Prime Ministers and Presidents of India
Succession to India's highest political offices reflects increasing diversity in gender, religion, and political affiliations.

H, Hindu; M, Muslim; S, Sikh.

The Importance of Being Sonia: Lineage and Power in India
Sonia Gandhi and her son Rahul Gandhi, respectively President and Vice-President of the Indian National Congress.

first major test of strength for the democratic political system. While the emergency was presented as a measure against an imminent threat to the stability of the state, many thought the motives had more to do with the political survival of Indira Gandhi. Both the partisan motivation behind the declaration of emergency and the relative ease with which it could be imposed exposed the vulnerability of the Indian political system to authoritarian rule. But the electoral defeat of Indira Gandhi at the polls in 1977 following the withdrawal of the emergency produced an important political precedent against future attempts at derailing Indian democracy.

Dismissing elected governments at the regional level and applying direct rule from Delhi became more frequent during the prime ministership of Indira Gandhi. However, President K. R. Narayanan, the first dalit (former untouchable) to have achieved this high office, set an important precedent in 1998 by turning down a Cabinet recommendation to impose the President's Rule on the State of Bihar.[22] Today, a declaration of emergency is seen as a self-corrective procedure written into India's Constitution rather than as an authoritarian exercise of power.[23]

The Prime Minister

The connecting link between the Cabinet and the president as well as between executive and Parliament, the Prime Minister continues to be, as Nehru used to describe it, "the linchpin of Government" (see again Figure 17.4). In contemporary India, when the prime minister leads a multiparty coalition, the job of consensus building within the ruling majority is a daunting task, requiring much patient negotiation. This sometimes leads to the open articulation of defiance against the authority of the prime minister, a situation that would have been unthinkable during the days of Nehru. Together with the ministers, the prime minister controls and coordinates the departments of government and determines policy through the submission of a program for parliamentary action. If the prime minister is defeated on any major issue, or on a no-confidence motion, by convention, the government must resign. This has happened several times.

Other practices of Cabinet government have become institutionalized in India as well. The Cabinet provides the necessary backing to the prime minister. This model was sorely tested during the tenure of Indira Gandhi, whose authoritarian tendencies and distrust of colleagues reduced the Cabinet's role as a source of policy and administrative leadership, in sharp contrast to previous practice. The phenomenon was described as "deinstitutionalization."[24] Subsequent governments have restored the conventions of parliamentary government and the principle of collective responsibility.

The steady rise in the stature of Prime Minister Narasimha Rao in the 1990s was a testimony to the institutionalization of the office. Starting as a temporary replacement for Rajiv Gandhi and then as a compromise leader, Rao, with the help of his finance minister Manmohan Singh, initiated the liberalization of India's economy, even without a solid legislative majority. His leadership skills were immensely valuable in ensuring a smooth transition after the assassination of Rajiv Gandhi and during the post-Ayodhya period.

As Prime Ministers, Rao's successors, first Deve Gowda and then Inder Kumar Gujral, followed very much in the mold of consensus and accommodation. The real test came only in 1998, when Prime Minister Atal Bihari Vajpayee, leading the first Hindu nationalist government of India, inducted many individuals who lacked previous ministerial experience into the central government. However, the BJP government continued to rule through consensus within the coalition, thus maintaining continuity in the areas of reform and security policy. The dexterity with which Manmohan Singh has continued the tradition of prime ministerial leadership despite the multiple pressures of coalition politics, and in effective coordination with Sonia Gandhi, the president of the Congress Party, is further testimony to the resilience of the practice of consultation and cohesion at the highest echelon of government in India.

The office of the Prime Minister is the pinnacle of the career of politicians in India. However, despite the fact that the office is quintessentially political and therefore partisan, over the years, the occupants of this office "have often achieved a kind of transcendence" and "provide moral leadership to the country, which is rather surprising for leaders who are partisan figures."[25] The explanation of this remarkable evolution, which finds the Indian prime minister combining elements of the British and U.S. heads of state and of the chief executive, derives from the key roles of coordination, initiative, and leadership that are germane to it. The Prime Minister provides cohesion, unity, and purpose to a system that would be fragmented otherwise. In recognition of this functional importance of the role of the prime minister to the smooth functioning of governance in India, a new organ of the government—the Prime Minister Office (PMO)—has gained considerable salience over the past years.

The Parliament

Even while they campaigned against British rule in India, the leaders of India's Freedom Movement aspired to a parliamentary democracy modeled on British institutions. For many of them, schooled in the British tradition, independence brought the opportunity to design India's Constitution in the image of British parliamentary democracy. The Parliament of India consists of two houses, the **Lok Sabha (House of Commons)**, the lower house, and the **Rajya Sabha, (the Council of States)** the upper house (see again Figure 17.4). The Lok Sabha (House of the People) consists of 545 members: 543 are directly elected and 2 are nominated by the president of India as representatives of the Anglo–Indian community. Elections of the members of the Lok Sabha are run on the basis of a simple majority, from single-member constituencies. The term of the Lok Sabha is five years unless it is extended because of emergency conditions. The Lok Sabha can be dissolved before the end of its five-year mandate, or extended beyond five years, by the President on the advice of the Prime Minister. The principle of hereditary membership of landed aristocrats in the House of Lords has no equivalence in India. Besides, unlike Britain, India is a federation. As such, the upper house—the Rajya Sabha (the Council of States)—has some features of the U.S. Senate. Reflecting India's commitment to social justice through positive discrimination, the Parliament provides guaranteed representation of the former untouchables and tribals through a quota system of "reserved seats."

The Parliament is primarily an instrument of democratic accountability. The Constitution specifies that the Lok Sabha must meet at least twice a year, with no more than six months between sessions. The business of Parliament, avidly reported in the press, is transacted primarily in English or Hindi, but there are provisions for the use of other Indian languages as well. Keeping to the British practice, a number of parliamentary committees impart a sense of continuity and specialization to the functioning of the Parliament. Some are primarily concerned with organization and parliamentary procedure. Others, notably the three finance committees, act as watchdogs over the executive. Specific committees scrutinize the budget and governmental economy, appropriations and expenditures, the exercise of delegated power, and the implementation of ministerial assurances and promises.

The first hour of the parliamentary day (known as the "zero hour") is devoted to questions that bring the ministers to public scrutiny. The question hour extends the principle of parliamentary and public accountability. Written questions are submitted in advance. Supplementary questions, which test the minister's ability to master the technical details of governance, can be asked during the question hour.

The Lok Sabha's ultimate control over the executive lies in the motion of no confidence that can bring down the government. After the long years of hibernation during the era of uninterrupted rule by the Congress Party with its huge majorities, the Parliament now exercises its right to hold the government responsible, during the recent phase of coalition politics and unstable majorities. However, this has not created the kind of paralysis that occurred in the Fourth Republic of postwar France. The high number of leaders with ministerial experience both in the government and in the opposition ensures that the Parliament is both the scene of continuous challenges to the government, while at the same time, providing an opportunity to collaborate in the interest of governance.

The total strength of membership of the Lok Sabha being 545, a political party or coalition needs to have at least 273 members in order to form government. However, the UPA coalition fell short of this magic figure in 2004 and 2009. On both occasions, the UPA secured a working majority through support by the Left Front. It did not join the UPA coalition formally but supported it from outside, which gave it influence without responsibility, and the political clout to obstruct policies crucial to the UPA such as the pace of liberalization and the Indo–U.S. nuclear deal. This arrangement came to an end when the Left Front withdrew its support on a confidence vote in the Lok Sabha in 2012. The UPA survived the trial of strength by securing the support of the Samajwadi Party and a few independent members of Parliament. (see Figure 17.6).

The Rajya Sabha consists of a maximum of 250 members, of whom. 12 are nominated by the President for their "special knowledge or practical experience" in literature, science, art, or social service. Reflecting the federal principle, the allocation of the remaining seats corresponds with the size of the respective populations of the regions, except that small states have a larger share than their actual population proportion would imply. The members of the state legislative assembly elect members of the Rajya Sabha for a term of six years. The terms are staggered, so that elections are held for one-third of the seats every two years.

The Rajya Sabha was seen merely as a "talking shop" during the earlier periods of Congress Party hegemony when the party dominated both houses

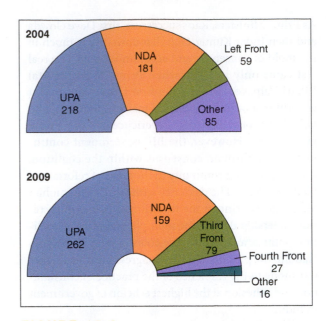

FIGURE 17.6
Lok Sabha Elections 2004 and 2009 Results

of Parliament. Because most of the real power of accountability and finance inhere in the lower house, the center of political gravity naturally lies beyond the reach of the smaller, and constitutionally less powerful, upper house. Still, the increasingly competitive character of the Indian political process has increased the importance of the Rajya Sabha, too.

The role of Parliament is normally confined to the scrutiny of legislation for its technical aspects because, reflecting the conventions of parliamentary democracy, most of the initiative for legislation lies with the Cabinet. The legislators do not have the finances or personnel that the political system of the United States bestows on members of Congress. Indian committee hearings are not public occasions and therefore do not have the power of U.S. House or Senate committee hearings. As such, they provide only a forum for wide political consultation.[26]

The Legislative Process

The legislative process generally follows the British practice. Laws are initiated in the form of government bills or private members' bills. The latter are more an opportunity to air grievances and to draw attention, because few if any ever become laws. The initiation of most legislation clearly lies with the government. All bills except money bills—with implications for spending, revenue, borrowing, or India's financial reserves—can be introduced in either house. The Ministry of Law and the Attorney General of India are consulted on legal and constitutional aspects. Ordinary bills go through three readings in each house. The second reading is the most vital, because at this stage, the bill receives the most detailed and minute examination and may be referred to a Select Committee or a Joint Committee of both houses of Parliament. These committees do not have the same standing or resources as the committees in the U.S. House or Senate. They are neither called on to investigate the affairs of the government in public hearings nor asked to approve executive appointments. Their power derives from the tradition of bipartisanship, which, as in the United Kingdom, gives them a sense of legitimacy and trust (see Figure 17.7).

Once both houses pass a bill, it requires the president's assent to become a law. This assent is not a mere formality. The president sometimes asks for technical details and expert advice in order to examine the constitutional implications of a bill before giving his or her assent. Potentially, this is a formidable threat in view of the fragility of coalitional politics where a

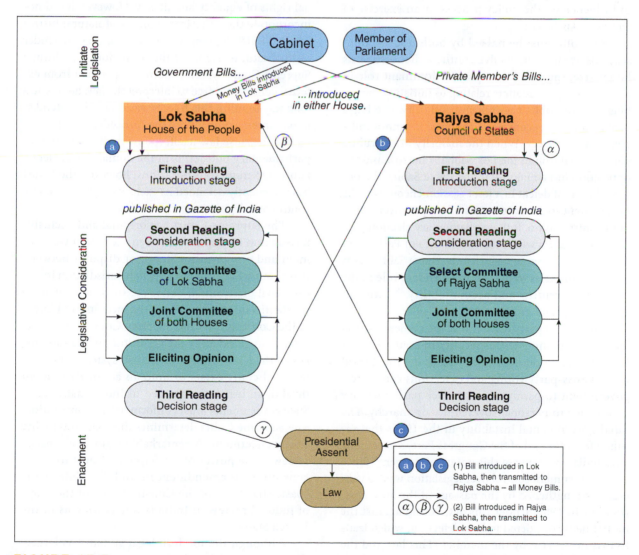

FIGURE 17.7

India's Legislative Process

The passage of a bill through both chambers of the Parliament shows the bicameral system at work.

united stand by the Cabinet against an adversary is relatively difficult to sustain. A president determined to delay or obstruct legislation can do so through the simple expedient of not returning a bill, with or without assent, before the end of the current parliamentary session. In effect, this means that the government will need to repeat the entire legislative process for the bill in the next session. If the president withholds his assent and the Parliament passes the bill again, he would be obliged to give it presidential assent. But these are exceptional situations. Unlike in the United States, the president is not expected to take legislative initiative, and there is no practice of presidential veto as a source of influence on the policy process or an exercise of checks and balances.[27]

As a bill must be passed by both houses, joint sessions are used to resolve conflicts. Because of its larger size, the Lok Sabha plays a dominant role in such meetings. In matters relating to initiating money bills, the Lok Sabha has exclusive authority. The Rajya Sabha can only recommend changes; it cannot initiate, delay, or reject. When the majority of the ruling party or coalition in the Lok Sabha is narrow and the opposition has a majority in the Rajya Sabha, the potential peril of defeat in a joint session encourages the government to think in terms of cooperation rather than confrontation. If the parliamentary election produces a situation where the two houses of Parliament do not have the same majority, the Rajya Sabha gains in power and tries to play an independent role in the matters of scrutiny and accountability.[28] This has already happened in 1996, 1998, and 2004.

The lack of party discipline is the nemesis of parliamentary democracy, especially in countries like India, where modern institutions lack deep historical roots. Cross-party voting and defections can drive a government to paralysis and reduce parliamentary democracy to personal sovereignty or anarchy. The rapid governmental instability in the 1960s that resulted from the end of the Congress Party's hegemony gave India a warning of this potential danger.[29] Since then, government control over legislation was considerably strengthened by the passage of the antidefection law in 1985. Under this act, voting against the party line is considered to be a defection, which leads to loss of the seat by the member. This law and the electorate's disapproval of political opportunism have induced some stability at the level of the central and state governments.

Occasionally, an urgent need for legislation when Parliament is not in session can be met by an ordinance, issued by the president. Ordinances carry the force of law but must be passed by the Parliament once it convenes, during the span of six weeks, failing which, it lapses. Ordinance making contributes to the efficiency and flexibility of the legislative process in the era of globalization, when rapid action is very important.[30]

The Judiciary

The Constitution of India committed itself to individual rights of equality and liberty. However, it did not incorporate the American concept of natural justice where the U.S. Supreme Court is the ultimate defender of the "natural" rights of the individual. The Indian Supreme Court, which is both independent from external control and free to interpret the law, has come a long way to fulfill this role. It was originally intended to be supreme only within the "procedure established by law," because law itself, following the tradition of parliamentary politics, is in the domain of the legislature. On numerous occasions, however, the Court has vehemently defended its exclusive right to exercise control over legislation.

The Supreme Court has original and exclusive jurisdiction in disputes between the Union Government and one or more States, or disputes between two or more States. It has appellate jurisdiction in any case, civil or criminal, that is certified as involving a substantial question of law in the meaning and intent of the Constitution. The Supreme Court is the interpreter and guardian of the Constitution, the supreme law of the land. Unlike the British system, where no national court exists to hold an act of Parliament invalid, all legislation passed in India's national or State governments must conform to the Constitution. The Supreme Court determines the constitutionality of any enactment. A remarkable feature of judicial review is the power of the Supreme Court to rule a constitutional amendment invalid if it violates the "basic structure" of the Constitution, but the scope of judicial review in India is not as wide as in the United States.

Although the modern legal system has largely displaced traditional customary law, traditional groups use the modern system for their own ends. The Supreme Court has dealt with such contentious issues as the Ayodhya case, which kept the dispute within the political system rather than let it slip out of the process of adjudication altogether (see again Box 17.3). The Court's landmark decisions—for example, its 1995 ruling that *hindutva*, the core of the ideology of the BJP, was part of Indian culture and not necessarily of a religion—have deeply influenced the nature of political discourse in India. Recent survey findings rate the Indian Supreme Court along with the Election Commission as the most trustworthy of institutions.[31]

Since the core judicial doctrine of the Constitution of India is based on the "procedure established by law," the Supreme Court was initially accorded a status below the Parliament but above the national executive in terms of authoritative interpretation of the law. But the Supreme Court has gradually asserted its supremacy in such matters as well. This evolution was facilitated by the steady erosion of the massive legislative majorities of the government since the early decades after India's independence, the rise of media influence, and the mobilization of interest groups at the national level. The emergency rule of Indira Gandhi (1975–1977) dented the Court's authority and autonomy. Since then, its authority has bounced back.[32] The Court has earned a high level of esteem and trust in the eyes of the Indian public by drawing on the initiatives taken and innovations made in judicial practice and procedure. The Court exercises wide judicial review on subjects ranging from the highly abstract and technical, such as personal law and industrial jurisprudence, to topical and controversial issues. The Court has also appointed itself as the guardian of vulnerable social groups and neglected areas of public life, such as the environment. Known as Public Interest Litigation (PIL), this is one of the most celebrated and contentious innovations of India's Supreme Court.

Today, the Supreme Court of India is seen as an important institutional protector of liberty, secularism, and social justice. Its power and legitimacy are the consequence of the long evolution of judicial culture under colonial rule and the important role played by lawyers in India's freedom struggle.

The Bureaucracy

The administrative backup for the Indian political system comes from a bureaucratic apparatus that is both professionally organized and politically accountable. The Indian bureaucracy is an enormously complex system that combines national or all-India services with regional and local services, as well as technical and managerial staff responsible for administering public sector undertakings. Recruitment by merit, based on competitive examinations (a quota is set aside for candidates from Scheduled Castes and Scheduled Tribes), is the general rule, with political appointments such as those in the United States being the rare exception. The bureaucracy's reputation for probity, high under colonial rule, has suffered on account of allegations of corruption, often involving members of the political class as well, during the past years.[33] As a measure to promote transparency in public transactions and to combat corruption, the government has passed the **Right to Information Act 2005 (RTI)**. The act applies to all States and Union territories of India except the State of Jammu and Kashmir. Jammu and Kashmir has its own act called Jammu & Kashmir Right to Information Act, 2009. Under the provisions of the act, any citizen may request information from a "public authority," which is required to reply expeditiously or within thirty days. The act also requires every public authority to computerize their records for wide dissemination.

The main services—like the Indian Administrative Service (IAS) and the Indian Police Service (IPS)—retain some of the features of their pre-independence structures. But like the rest of the top services of India, they have been reorganized to create a federal balance in recruitment. Recruitment is supervised by the Union Public Service Commission—an independent advisory body appointed by the president—and extensive new facilities exist for training new recruits. Although candidates are recruited centrally, the IAS is composed of separate cadres for each federal State. This composition strengthens federal links, because regional loyalties are balanced by the provision that at least half of the members of the IAS cadre come from outside the region. This practice creates language problems for officers who originate from outside, but it also encourages India's top administrators to learn the local language, contributing to the process of nation-building and cross-regional linkages. Members of district administrations seek to combine rule of law, efficient management and coordination, and, increasingly, local democracy.

The Federal Structure

17.5 Differentiate between powers held by the Union and the States in India.

In contrast with many postcolonial states, particularly neighboring Pakistan, the unity of the Indian Union has stood the test of time. The successful accommodation of regional identity within the federal structure has increased the number of federal States to twenty-eight, besides seven Union Territories. Subnational movements, demanding recognition as a separate political unit within the Indian state, are now seen as a democratic articulation of legitimate interests compared to the early years after independence when such agitations evoked the fear of "Balkanization." The "cooperative" federalism of India is the result of the conciliation of the contradictory needs for central coordination, as befits a political system that was committed to centrally planned development and, simultaneously, recognition of regional identity.

Numerous special features of the Indian Constitution give it its highly centralized form. Of these, the two most important are the division of powers between the central government and the States, with a bias in favor of the center, and the financial provisions affecting the distribution of revenues, weighted in favor of the central government. In India, unlike in the United States, the federal States do not have their own separate constitutions. The State of Jammu and Kashmir is an exception, because it has a special status under Article 370 of the Indian Constitution.[34]

The Constitution of India, in the tradition of written agreements between the central government and the states, defines the division of powers between both sides in its seventh schedule. The Union List gives the center exclusive authority to act in matters of national importance; this list includes ninety-seven items, such as defense, foreign affairs, currency, banking, and income tax. The State List, which allocates exclusive rights of legislation to the States, includes sixty-six items of local and regional importance, such as public order and police, welfare, health, education, local government, industry, agriculture, and land revenue. The Concurrent List contains forty-seven items in which the center and the States share legislative authority. In case of a conflict, the central law prevails. Civil and criminal law and social and economic planning are the important items in this list, as these subjects are crucial to issues of identity and economic development.

The residual power lies with the Union. Unlike the classic model of federalism, in India, the central government, acting through the Parliament, can create new States, alter the boundaries of existing ones, and even abolish a State by ordinary legislative procedure without recourse to constitutional amendment.

Not only does the central government have a wide range of powers under the Union List, but these powers are enhanced because the central government has a variety of powers that enable it, under certain circumstances, to extend its authority to the domain of the states. These special powers take three forms: (1) the emergency powers under Articles 352, 356, and 360; (2) the use of Union executive powers under Articles 256, 257, and 360; and (3) special legislative powers granted under Article 249.

The emergency powers in the Indian Constitution can enable the Union executive to transform the federation temporarily into a unitary state when the president makes a declaration to that effect. Under these emergency provisions, the central executive and legislature can simply substitute the corresponding organs of the regional governments. Even under nonemergency conditions, the central government may assume executive powers over regional governments in the "national" interest. These powers, used by the president at the advice of the prime minister, are closely monitored by the Parliament, the media, and the judiciary. In this context, the Rajya Sabha acts as the custodian of the States' interests.

The center's right to influence the federal division of powers is reinforced by the Constitution's financial provisions. The central government has vast powers over the collection and distribution of revenue, which makes the States depend heavily on the central government for financial support. Financial assistance flows from the central government to the states in several ways. Most of the lucrative taxes, like income tax, corporate tax, and import and export duties, are collected by the central government. The center and the States share these funds under a formula devised by the Finance Commission, which is appointed by the president but is guaranteed independence from interference by the center and States. The center alone has the power over currency, banking, and international borrowings. The States also have their own sources of income. But these taxes, such as land revenue or irrigation taxes, for example, have not been particularly lucrative. Agricultural income is notoriously difficult to ascertain, and taxes on such income are difficult to collect.

As a result of the financial provisions in the Constitution and their evolution over time, the States are routinely short of funds. These shortfalls are met through central assistance in the form of loans, grants-in-aid, and overdraft facilities—provisions that compromise the autonomy of the states. This situation has been further reinforced by the centralizing tendencies of the national five-year plans and the powers exercised by the Congress Party on state governments, ruling both at the center and in the States virtually uninterrupted for two decades following India's independence.

Despite these centralizing tendencies, however, the Indian political system has a distinct pattern of cooperation between the center and the States. This cooperation was helped by rapid economic growth in some cases and the assertion of cultural identity and autonomy in others. Freed from the tutelage of central dominance because of the decline of the "one-dominant-party system" and liberalization of the economy since 1991, Indian federalism has become more robust in recent years.

The Articulation of Interests

17.6 Describe the types of organizations that represent special interests in India and their methods of engagement.

The aggressive pursuit of interests by a politically mobilized citizenry can strain the limited capacity of political institutions in rapidly changing societies. This section examines how interest and pressure groups, and an assortment of protest movements, engage in political transaction at the national, regional, and local levels.

The formal representation of interest in India reflects three key features. First is the vast range of modes of representation, stretching from efficiently arranged, modern organizations of employers, businessmen, industrialists, and labor on the one end to traditional forms, involving caste, tribe, and ethnic groups, on the other. In addition, there are unconventional political forms like satyagraha, *dharna,* boycott, and *rasta roko*—stopping traffic as a method of collective protest—to name just a few of the many indigenous and hybrid forms of direct political participation

inspired by Gandhi. There are also radical organizations that resort to collective violence and suicide. The second feature is that there is no practice of "closed shop," where specific organizations have monopoly control over the representation of particular interests. However, more can be less! Fierce competition among organizations to recruit members from within the same occupation or trade fragments the cohesive articulation of collective interests. This situation has stymied the growth of interest articulation as an independent and powerful phenomenon in its own right, which is usually the case in industrial liberal democracies. Third, people with a cause or a grievance combine effectively in various forms of action and organizations, such as parties, interest and pressure groups, movements, and spectacular forms of political protest. Consequently, India's level of interest articulation and aggregation is comparable to that found in long-established and more prosperous Western democratic states even in the absence of formal organizations of interest representation at the same scale.

Trade Unions and Employers' Associations

Under India's labor law, any seven workers can formally set up a trade union. State-appointed labor inspectors provide counsel and inquire into the conditions of work. Trade unionism in India today is built on the historical legacy of some leading trade unions and employers' organizations that date back to British colonial rule. For example, the All India Trade Union Congress (AITUC), one of the largest central trade union organizations in the country, was established in 1920 and is the oldest Indian trade union. The AITUC was founded by the Indian National Congress as a mainstream labor organization during India's independence movement, in which it played a significant role. A second example is the All India Railwaymen's Federation (AIRF), founded in 1925, which today has a membership of more than a million railway workers.

Similar to that of workers, several well-organized interest representations of employers can be found in India. One famous example is the Confederation of Indian Industries (CII), founded in 1895 as the Engineering and Iron Trades Association. CII is now the most visible business association in India, with over 8,100 member companies, nine overseas offices, and institutional partnerships with 223 organizations in ninety countries. Similarly, the Federation of Indian Chambers of Commerce and Industry (FICCI) together with the Associated Chambers of Commerce and Industry (ASSOCHAM) function as the apex for trade associations and industry in India. Both groups are key actors in policy formulation and the socioeconomic transformation of the country. They also have a significant role in the making of government economic policy.

Unlike in liberal democracies where interest groups concentrate on the conditions of work that they seek to improve through collective bargaining, India's unions are closely affiliated with political parties and thus become especially active at election time. The culture of effective collective bargaining is not deeply entrenched. Rather than organized strikes and protest movements (see the photo "a trade union rally" below) as the ultimate weapon, India's unions often resort to illegal stoppage of work (referred to as "wildcat strikes") and rely on state intervention on their behalf to win better conditions. Additionally, they are highly fragmented, with an increasing number of unions competing for a limited pool of workers. Intraunion feuds also reduce the effectiveness of the union movement as a whole.[35]

Trade unionism has gone through several broad phases since India's independence, corresponding to structural changes in the economy. The period 1980–1991 was characterized by uneven economic development, so decentralized bargaining and independent trade unionism gained ground. Interregional variations in the labor–management regimes grew wider, with unions gaining strength in the more prosperous economic sectors. A new phase started with the economic reforms of the early 1990s. It is characterized by demands for greater labor market flexibility, especially

A Trade Union Rally
Protesters asking for (in Hindi) 'Education for all, work for all.'

in employment and industrial dispute management. Reforms are considered vital to stimulate India's manufacturing sector, but they are resisted particularly by political parties of the left.

Local Politics: Democracy at the Grassroots Level

The emergency of 1975–1977 brought together a wide range of political forces for the defense of civil liberties. These forces—consisting of lawyers, journalists, academics, social workers, and political activists—became an important pressure group starting in the 1980s. Their presence and intervention have publicized the struggles of vulnerable social groups and exposed acts of administrative injustice and, in more extreme cases, state repression.

This development led to the emergence of a new social class of mediators in the political process, generally called the "social activists." These are often upper- and middle-class citizens who identify themselves with the lower orders of society, a whole variety of social strata ranging from the untouchable castes to the destitute among the tribes and ethnic minorities. One speaks today of political movements as a generic form of political action. There is a new genre of "movements" that have an economic content but are multidimensional and cover a large terrain in practice. This new genre includes the high-profile environmental movements, the women's movement, the civil liberties movement, movements for regional self-determination and autonomy, and the peasants' movement. Other groups focus on peace, disarmament, and denuclearization. In India, civil society activism comprising conventional and unconventional political actions has embraced the wider spectrum of social movements. This development of civil society activism has strengthened the process of democratic consolidation in India. The recent Jan Lokpal Bill Movement under the general leadership of Anna Hazare, building on the legacy of a similar broad-based popular movement under the leadership of Jai Prakash Narayan against the authoritarian rule of Indira Gandhi in 1975, shows the power of India's civil society as a foundation stone of this postcolonial democracy.

The coalition that brought the Janata Party to power in 1977 in many ways benefited from the civil rights movement during the emergency of 1975–1977. These movements have helped bring many anti-system forces into the mainstream, turning rebels into stakeholders. However, as continuing insurgency in parts of the country shows, the process is far from being complete.

At a larger, systemic level, the rise of this new consciousness of civil rights provides a balancing factor to the growth of authoritarian tendencies and the advocacy of a muscular, developmental state, committed to rational management and modern technology. These grassroots movements also signify a new understanding of the democratic process, which has moved from an almost exclusive preoccupation with parties and elections to new issues, such as women's rights, minorities, and the dignity of migrant workers and internally displaced people, that the political system has not addressed. The process of democratic transition and consolidation has been reinforced by the rise of new actors on the scene, new forms of political expression, and new definitions of the content of politics.[36] The growth of local protest movements as a method for articulating interests and demanding administrative redress was facilitated by the wide acceptance of lobbying and contacting decision makers, and other techniques of direct action, such as forcing public officials to negotiate by **dharna**—a form of sit-in strike—or to bear on them by physically surrounding them (*gherao*).[37]

Security and Law and Order

The military and paramilitary forces of India, numbering over a million men and women, deserve special attention. Although the number of armed military has increased significantly, the civilian government of India remains firmly in control. In contrast to many developing countries, especially in Africa, the Indian middle classes opted for civil service and professional jobs under colonial rule, and have continued to prefer political careers after independence. In India, this situation contributed to the professional and apolitical character of the army. Consequently, the officer corps of India, traditionally accustomed to civilian control and indoctrinated with the appropriate disposition in the course of their training, has remained nonpartisan even during political turmoil.

Under India's federal division of powers, law and order is a state subject. As such, the Indian police are recruited, trained, and deployed by the regional governments. However, the central government also exercises considerable power over law-and-order management through different methods. In the first place, the central government recruits and trains some special police forces. In principle, central forces can be sent to trouble spots in the regions at the request of the State governments, and, once deployed, they are under the orders of State officials. The district magistrate and the superintendent of police normally belong to the Indian Administrative Service and the Indian Police Service, respectively, both of which are central services. These officials thus typically have some accountability to the central government in their professional judgments; they are, nevertheless, also accountable to regional governments, run by regional politicians. As such, the administration of law and order also becomes the subject of negotiation between the nation and region, helping in the articulation and aggregation of dormant issues and social forces.

In extreme cases, the Constitution provides for a direct rule by the center under Article 356 (the President's Rule, which we discussed earlier). Central intervention in Punjab and Kashmir in the 1980s occurred under similar conditions where the regional government proved either unwilling or unable to take effective measures. Effective law–and-order management certainly contributed to the restoration of the political process in Punjab. The regions of India and the state itself continuously share with each other knowledge of law-and-order management, which results in the creation of new administrative forces or major changes in equipment, training, and service conditions of the police and paramilitary forces.

The Party System

17.7 Discuss the makeup and influence of India's national and regional political parties.

The party system of contemporary India is built on the foundation of six decades of growth under British rule prior to India's independence. It is a complex system characterized by the continuous presence of the Congress Party in the national political arena during the early decades after Independce, the emergence of a powerful Hindu nationalist movement, a strong communist movement that has held power in various regions of India for a considerable period, and the growth of strong regional movements that have become well-entrenched regional political parties. The

picture becomes much clearer if we divide the post-independence period into the "one-dominant-party system" period (1952–1977) and its subsequent transformation into a multiparty system.[38]

Universal adult franchise was introduced in 1952. All political parties present at that time, including the Communist Party of India and the Jan Sangh, a Hindu right-wing party, were authorized to participate in the election. Thanks to the extension of suffrage, the electorate expanded and brought into the political arena a large number of voters with no previous electoral experience. Such a sudden influx of new voters could have been a recipe for disaster for democracy and political order, particularly in conjunction with the violence that accompanied the partition of India. But the subsequent course of parliamentary democracy—thanks to the continuity of the institutions of state and the structures of leader–constituent relations—saw parties and elections becoming an essential part of the political culture of postindependence India.

The Indian National Congress

Pre-independence The Congress Party, as an office-seeking and anticolonial movement, became the instigator and beneficiary of reform. The Morley–Minto Reforms of 1909 had conceded limited Indian representation and provided for separate electorates to give minorities additional weight. The reforms of 1919 provided for a relatively large measure of responsibility at the local and provincial levels in areas such as education, health, and public works that were not "reserved" or deemed crucial for colonial control. The Congress Party took advantage of these reforms to participate in the local and municipal elections, which greatly enhanced the potential for democratic government after India's independence. By making common cause with middle-class aspirations, it earned the trust and loyalty of the middle class and the upper social strata while challenging the authority and legitimacy of British rule. These same social groups were among its more important social bases of support. In addition, the Congress Party developed the ability to aggregate interests, a talent for sustained and coordinated political action, and skills of administration through vigorous participation in elections, particularly those to the provincial legislature under the 1935 Government of India Act. The leaders of the Congress Party also gained what few anticolonial movements had—namely, a taste of genuine political competition and the experience of patronage as a tool of political transactions and means to power.

For over half a century, following its formation in 1885 and the final coming of independence in 1947, the Congress Party remained the focus of the national struggle against British rule. It followed a strategy that combined political objectives with those of social reform and nation-building. This complex repertoire of competition and collaboration with the foreign rulers became the hallmark of the Congress Party. It steadily expanded the political agenda to include virtually all aspects of national life, becoming a catchall movement that inducted peasants, workers, women, minorities, and students into the mainstream of the anticolonial movement under its banner, exerting pressure on the British to concede more power to Indian hands. It used the power and resources thus gained to strengthen its mass organization and political network with the social elites, leaders of Indian business and industry, and anticolonial movements at the international level.

Post-independence   The first two decades following independence in 1947, roughly corresponding to Nehru's stewardship of Indian politics, were crucial to the transition from a colonial state to a democratic government. The years between 1950 and 1967 were the period of solid dominance of the Congress Party, which ruled at the center as well as in the states by drawing on its legacy as the party of Gandhi, Nehru, and the Freedom Movement.

The Congress Party established its dominance essentially by a process of progressive expansion of its social base, so that ever-new layers of recruitment and support were available to it, making it able to tilt a majority in its favor in most regions and to continue in its position of dominance.[39] This expansion occurred in several ways. Soon after India's independence, the Congress Party co-opted landed gentry, businessmen, peasant proprietors, new industrialists, and the rural middle peasants into its organization. Building on the aura of Gandhi's identification with the village and Nehru's penchant for modernity, socialism, a modern scientific outlook, and secularism, the Congress developed the profile of a quintessentially catchall party. In addition, the Congress Party developed an elaborate network of patronage, which made it possible to bargain with a wide spectrum of social groups for political support in return for economic

and social benefits.[40] The Congress Party's solid dominance of Indian politics during the first two decades after independence can thus be explained in terms of its leadership, who carried the aura of their preindependence prominence, their administrative and political acumen, and the resources at the command of the government. Most of all, the linkage between the Congress Party and the rural "vote banks" enhanced the party's electoral fortunes.

However, the steady mobilization of the lower social orders who found upward mobility within the party hierarchy blocked by higher castes led the new social elites to move over to the opposition parties. The opposition to Congress dominance took the form of a large anti-Congress coalition, which brought the competitors of the Congress to coordinate their electoral strategies. The consequence of this became clear at the national level in the election to the Lok Sabha in 1967, where the number of seats won by the Congress Party fell from 361 in 1962 to 283. It still had the requisite majority in the Lok Sabha to form the government, but the political consequences of the electoral debacle were serious for the intraparty politics of the Congress Party.

The party split in 1969, with the party's organization and the parliamentary wing going in different directions. The parliamentary wing, which constituted itself as the Congress (Requisitionist), won a landslide victory under the leadership of Indira Gandhi in 1971 and formed the government at the center. However, the emergency rule of 1975–1977 led to the victory of the Janata Party—a coalition of socialists, the Hindu nationalist Bharatiya Jana Sangh Party, and the Swatantra Party, based on economic liberalism—in 1977. The internal contradictions of the coalition soon surfaced, and the short-lived first non-Congress government of India fell in 1980, leading to new elections. The Congress (R), which had split again in 1978, came back triumphant under a new party label—Congress (Indira), in 1980, exposing in the process the scope for 'popular authoritarianism' in Indian politics. Following Indira's assassination by her Sikh bodyguards in 1984—in revenge for the military action against Sikh terrorists based in the Golden Temple of Amritsar, the holiest shrine of the Sikhs—her son Rajiv Gandhi was inducted as the national leader of Congress (I). In the election to the Lok Sabha that followed, buoyed by the sympathy factor, the party came back with its best-ever electoral performance, with 415 seats and 48 percent of votes in 1984.

The Congress Party went through an electoral decline during the decade that followed but has bounced back, at the head of the United Progressive Alliance coalition. The party reached its electoral nadir in 1999 when it managed to win only 114 out of 543 total seats in the Lok Sabha election. However, like the phoenix, the Congress appears to be rising from its ashes; its 206 seats in the 2009 election and the effective joint leadership style that Prime Minister Manmohan Singh and the Congress President Sonia Gandhi have developed, have transformed the currently ruling UPA coalition very much into a virtual Congress government. Its policies are closely identified with such hallowed Congress principles as secularism and the conflation of a capitalist economy with socialist rhetoric.

The resurgence of the Congress Party is caused partly by the disarray within the BJP leadership but mostly because of its coming to terms with the logic of coalition politics, which has a very significant implication for the party. As a national party, the Congress is always at a disadvantage against regional parties when it comes to the championship of local and regional demands as against the interest of the country as a whole. As such, once the regional arenas emerged as the most important sites of political competition in India, all national parties started seeking partnership with regional parties. The Congress used to prefer to go it alone in elections, but has worked out an elaborate coalition strategy with regional partners. Stooping to conquer, as one can see in its spectacular and unexpected victory in 2004 and reelection in 2009—a rare feat in India's contentious politics—is a testimony to its new political savvy. Compared to the low tide of 1999, during subsequent elections, substantial sections of many important social groups, such as Muslims and the educated middle-class voters who had earlier left the party, have come back into its fold. With the return of the Congress Party to power, some claim that India might be getting back to the days of "dynastic" rule, because of the meteoric rise of Rahul Gandhi, the son of Rajiv and Sonia Gandhi—who was "elected" vice president of the Congress in 2013 as part of the party's grand strategy for the general elections scheduled for 2014.

The Bharatiya Janata Party

The BJP traces its origin to the Hindu right-wing Bharatiya Jana Sangh (BJS) Party that was formed shortly after independence. Despite its coherent ideology and well-knit organization, the Bharatiya Jana Sangh had not managed to win office during the first two decades of independence. The opportunity came when it joined the other opposition parties to form the Janata Party, which defeated the Congress Party in the Lok Sabha election of 1977 and formed the government. However, the deep ideological and personal differences among the constituents of the Janata Party made its government unfeasible, leading to its fall. In the Lok Sabha election of 1980, the bulk of the members of the erstwhile BJS walked out of the Janata Party and founded the BJP. Its first electoral performance was lackluster, but it gradually worked its way toward a much more prominent political position, riding on the agenda of assertive Hindu nationalism.

In the course of its rapid rise to power, the party drew on the desire of many Hindus to see a more prominent role for Hindu culture within the institutions of the secular state and to deny special treatment to minorities, such as special status for the Muslim majority State of Jammu and Kashmir. The BJP came to power riding the crest of Hindu nationalism and promising to build a temple for **Rama** in the city of Ayodhya where the Babri mosque stood. In the 1991 election, the BJP confirmed its position as the main challenger to the Indian National Congress by winning 120 seats and over 20 percent of the popular vote. When the mosque was demolished by a mob of Hindu zealots, the State government of Uttar Pradesh (where Ayodhya is located), led by the BJP, accepted responsibility for its failure to uphold law and order, and resigned. Subsequently, the imperatives of India's coalitional politics have caused the party to moderate its stand on cultural and religious issues. During the short-lived tenure of Vajpayee as prime minister (1998–1999), the party spoke more of good governance and less of Hindu nationalism. Back in office in 1999 and with a clear majority for the NDA, of which the BJP was the largest partner in the Lok Sabha, with 182 seats, Prime Minister Vajpayee announced the commitment of his government to follow the same moderate policies that he had launched during his previous tenure.

The general election of 2004 to the Lok Sabha took place about six months before the end of the five-year term of the National Democratic Alliance government led by the BJP. When the government called for early elections, nearly all opinion polls predicted a comfortable victory on the strength of its record in office as well as the personal popularity of Prime Minister Vajpayee. Thus, the upset victory by the Congress Party–led UPA took everyone by surprise. In retrospect, the NDA's campaign slogan, "India Shining," which celebrated its achievements in the unprecedented rate of growth of the economy, seems to have backfired. Those who had not gained from the liberalization of the economy, those who stood to lose from the removal of subsidies, the population in rural areas of India, and some religious minorities appear to have voted against the coalition. For the first time, the Congress Party made pre-election alliances with regional parties opposed to the Hindu nationalist BJP on a "secular" platform. The Congress Party used the votes cast in favor of the UPA efficiently, greatly enhancing the number of its own seats in the Lok Sabha. The BJP, which leads the NDA coalition, lost the election again to the UPA coalition in 2009.

Communist Party

Founded in 1927, the Communist Party of India is one of the oldest in the world. It was proscribed for most of the time under British rule, except toward the end, when the party came out openly in support of the war effort once the Soviet Union came under attack from Nazi Germany. The party went through factional struggle and several splits on ideological grounds following India's independence. The Telengana uprising of 1946 and 1947, modeled after the Chinese revolution, was rapidly put down by the Indian army. This discredited the leftist faction. Under the leadership of the pro-parliamentary group ('right faction'), the party took part in the first general election, emerging as the second largest party after the Congress Party, though it was far behind it in terms of actual number of seats. Subsequently, the Communist Party won the regional election in the southern State of Kerala in 1957, the first victory for communism in a democratic election. Following the resolution of the Soviet Communist Party to support "peaceful transition to democracy," the Communist Party of India looked poised for a bigger role in Indian politics. However, that was not to be. The dismissal of the Communist government of Kerala after two years in office by the Congress Party in the center under Article 356 of the Constitution showed the limits of "bourgeois democracy," exactly as the left faction of the party had argued. More

bad news was to follow. Differences with China on the boundary led to a border conflict in 1962, which caused members of the left faction to come out in favor of China, leading to their incarceration. The split was formalized in 1964 with the founding of the Communist Party of India (Marxist) (CPM), which followed a radical, pro-Chinese line compared with the Communist Party of India (CPI), which stuck with a more moderate, pro-Congress and pro-Soviet line. The CPM itself split five years later when its own left wing emerged as a new party—the Communist Party of India (Marxist–Leninist).

Two main trends have emerged since these turbulent times. The CPM, which came to power in West Bengal in the late 1970s, became one of the longest-serving, democratically elected communist governments anywhere in the world. Nationally, communist parties generally receive less than 10 percent of the vote in parliamentary elections (see Figure 17.8). However, the urge for revolution, powerfully articulated by the "Naxalites"—this is how the Indian Maoists named themselves—lives on under different names in different parts of India. Their violent activities continue to be a source of anxiety for the Indian government.

The Social Bases of the Parties

Public opinion surveys provide basic information about the distribution of support to the main political parties across social formations (see Table 17.1). The social base of the Congress Party cuts across all social groups and cleavages of India, making it India's quintessential catchall party. Nevertheless, the Congress Party has relatively greater support in the lower social order and among religious minorities.

The social profile of the Hindu nationalist BJP presents a sharp contrast. It is very much a party of the "Hindu-Hindi belt," which normally indicates the northern Indian Gangetic plains. The BJP continues to be very much a party of the upper social order and Hindu upper caste but has nevertheless already succeeded in extending its reach to the former untouchables and tribals, and even to a small section of Muslim voters and politicians.

By the standards of its national support base, the left, consisting of both communist parties (CPM and CPI), attracts proportionally more support from the lower social classes as well as support from the more

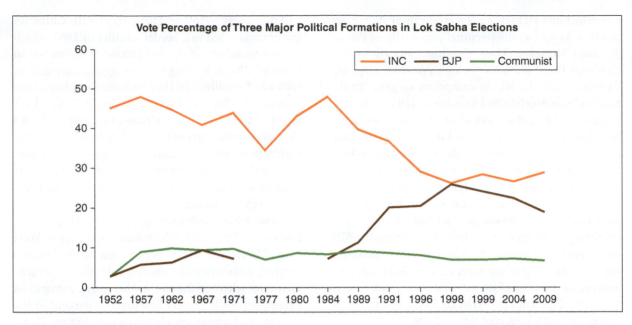

FIGURE 17.8

The Big Three: The INC, The BJS/BJP, and Communists

The relative vote share of the main political parties shows the decline of the congress.

Note: The label INC includes: Indian National Congress (1967), Congress (Requisionist) (1971), and Congress (Indira) (1980). BJP (Bharatiya Janata Party) was, until 1976, named BJS (Bharatiya Jana Sangh). The BJS did not participate in the elections of 1977 and 1980 under its own name because it formed part of the Janata Party coalition. The label CPI includes the CPI (Communist Party of India) and the CPI (M) (Communist Party of India [Marxist]).

educated voters. The rise of India's regional parties is a comparatively recent phenomenon. Like the Congress Party, in the regional context, these parties cut across all social groups and compete with the Congress Party for the same social base, except for the OBC, a social group sandwiched between the Hindu upper classes and the former untouchables. The leaders of many of India's regional parties are drawn from the OBC, which in consequence tends to provide proportionally more support to the regional parties.

At India's independence, the introduction of universal adult franchise empowered underprivileged social groups with a new political resource. The right to vote by secret ballot—exercised at a polling booth conveniently located at a public place where one could vote freely—created an environment that was helpful for political participation. The right to vote in secrecy and without coercion allowed the newly mobilized lower castes and religious minorities, who felt empowered thanks to the value of the vote, to directly challenge social dominance.

Social mobilization and its political containment appear to have taken place in India as two independent but ultimately convergent processes. The pace of social change has accelerated through social reform legislation, recruitment of new social elites into the political arena, and political mobilization through electoral participation. Their overall impact on the stability of the political system has been moderated by intermediary functions and parties at the regional and local levels. Lloyd and Susanne Rudolph have described the process as *vertical, horizontal* and *differential* mobilization.[41] Typically, as the marginal social groups discovered the negotiable value of the vote during the early years after independence, they became avid players in the political arena at the local and regional levels. Established **jajmani systems**—reciprocal social bonds based on the exchange of service and occupational specialization—broke down to create new groupings. Finally, caste associations, based on shared social and economic interests, emerged as links between parties and the society.[42]

TABLE 17.1
Election 2009
Social Basis of Political Parties and Coalitions.

		UPA Congress+	NDA BJP+	Left	BSP	Fourth Front SP+	Share in 2009 Survey
Area	Rural	35	24	8	7	6	71.9
	Urban	41	24	6	5	2	28.1
Gender	Male	36	25	7	7	5	54.1
	Female	37	23	8	6	5	45.9
Caste/Community	Upper caste	33	42	10	3	2	14.0
	Peasant proprietors	38	23	3	2	4	7.3
	Upper OBC	31	26	3	3	10	22.8
	Lower OBC	31	29	9	4	4	12.6
	Dalit	34	15	11	20	4	16.2
	Adivasi	46	26	7	1	1	7.8
	Muslim	47	6	11	6	9	12.6
	Sikh	45	46	1	3	<1	1.9
Education	Nonliterate	37	21	7	8	7	31.4
	Up to primary	38	22	11	5	4	22.5
	Up to matric	35	25	8	6	4	25.3
	College and above	35	30	6	5	5	20.7
Economic Class	Rich	37	30	3	5	6	14.2
	Middle	37	26	5	5	4	27.2
	Lower	36	23	7	6	5	29.7
	Poor	36	20	12	8	6	18.0
	Very poor	36	22	14	9	7	10.8

Note: The table displays the percentage of support from each social group for each party.
Source: A 2009 post-poll party vote by social background, from the Centre for the Study of Developing Societies (CSDS) 2010.

These developments created useful 'room to maneuver' for the national, regional, and local elites.[43]

Political Culture

17.8 List Morris-Jones' three idioms of Indian politics, and discuss their interplay in the political culture.

India's per capita GNP in terms of purchasing power parity is about 6 percent that of U.S. GNP, and its literacy rate is 74 percent, according to the 2011 Census. Despite pockets of mass poverty and illiteracy, India has sustained the democratic form of government it adopted at independence. The coexistence of mass poverty and illiteracy on the one hand, and the resilience of democracy on the other, is puzzling. To explain this phenomenon, it is necessary to analyze the political attitudes that underpin political behavior in Indian society and how people came to acquire them (see Box 17.4).

The Interaction of Tradition and Modernity

Those unfamiliar with Indian politics might be amazed at the entanglement of modern institutions and

BOX
17.4

The Right to Vote: Power of the Powerless

A report in *India Today*, India's most widely circulated newsmagazine, gives an interesting insight into the strong support given by the backward classes to the government of the Janata Dal in the 1995 elections. A fifty-five-year-old dalit woman, "pointing to the stain of indelible ink on her finger," says, "I voted for Laloo." The reporters "point to the gaping cracks in her roof, her grandchildren who have nothing to wear, the medicine she does not have, the two meals she cannot afford, and ask, 'Why?'" She replies, "All that has been there for thousands of years." Saying this, she remembers the day the chief minister's helicopter landed on the nearby paddy field. "Laloo came to visit us," she announces. "Since I was born, not even a crow has flown over our village."

The second report is equally revealing. A forty-five-year-old landless laborer, when asked about Laloo, breaks into what looks like a strange dance. He falls on his knees, and with hands stretched in front, presses his forehead flat against the ground and begins to crawl backward. "Now I don't do this when my landlord walks by," he shouts, "because Laloo said so."

Source: Raj Kamal Jha and Farzand Ahmed, "Laloo's Magic," *India Today*, April 30, 1995.

pre-modern practices, beliefs, and symbols within the framework of the modern state. In his introduction to India's political culture, W. H. Morris-Jones explains this phenomenon in terms of three idioms: the modern, the traditional, and the saintly.[44] The modern idiom understands politics as a competitive process of articulation and aggregation of interests. This modern idiom of Indian politics consists of the Constitution and the courts, parliamentary debate, the higher administration, the upper levels of all the main political parties, and the entire English-language press and much of the Indian-language press. The main debates of Indian politics—on issues of federalism, economic development, planning, or defense expenditure, for example—take place in the modern language of politics and, as such, are accessible to Western students of Indian politics.[45] However, there is rarely an occasion when Indian politicians do not take recourse to some traditional concepts, like jati or dalits, or some that are deeply embedded in Indian religions and values, like *shaheed* (martyrs) or *ahimsa* (nonviolence). The saintly idiom mobilized with insuperable skill by Gandhi's satyagraha reflects on the core values of society that cut across both modern and traditional cleavages and does not necessarily refer to the spiritual or the otherworldly. Messages from leaders like Gandhi expressed in this mode can reach the whole society and "stir the imagination of the advanced radical and the conservative traditionalist alike."[46]

Although these three political idioms are conceptually distinct, they are entwined in reality. In fact, the same individual may embody all three: a University of California–trained computer engineer based in Bangalore might have daily transactions with his business partner in California's Silicon Valley. He might have an arranged marriage within his jati and linguistic region and punctiliously follow the food taboos and social rituals of his caste. He might also belong to an Internet network, avidly exchanging messages with the worldwide network of the VHP, the World Council of Hindus.

Depending on the region, locality, length and depth of colonial rule, and the individual's class, gender, and age, one idiom may be more clearly pronounced than another. Political actors manipulate all those idioms in terms of their perception of particular cases and contexts. Consequently, the three appear functionally related to one another in the competitive political marketplace of India. The tribe, or jati network—operating as a caste association—can very well carry the modern message of individual rights, entitlement, and electoral preferences to people who are first-generation voters. Simultaneously, modern satellite television, broadcasting the *Ramayana* and *Mahabharata* (Hindu religious classics), can spread the message of an indigenous Indian identity that claims to be unique, authentic, and exclusive. Since India's independence, such interactions have created new political forms and processes as well as the emergence of two new themes of Indian political culture: the instrumentality of politics and the politics of identity. The simultaneous use of participation and protest drawing on modern institutions and traditional symbols and networks has caused the three idioms of politics to conflate. Consequently, the political process in India acts as a mechanism to weave separate identities together into a national, collective identity. This search for identity expresses itself not only in terms of national movements like those associated with Hindu nationalism but also in the assertion of Sikh identity in Punjab and the tribal Jharkhand identity in southern Bihar. Similar aspirations for welfare and identity also underpin politics in Kashmir and India's northeast, violently clashing with one another and the Indian state in their determination to assert their own vision of the state and nation. Once in power, however, cultural nationalist parties have downplayed separatist themes, like a Tamil homeland or an exclusive homeland for the sons of the soil, and they have gradually accommodated themselves within the Indian Union and the thriving Indian market.

The data on political efficacy and legitimacy present two interesting facets of the political culture in India. Efficacy, which measures individuals' self-perception with regard to the powers-that-be, shows a steady rise over the recent past, going up from 48.5 percent of the national population in 1971 to 67.5 percent in 2004. Legitimacy of the political system has also climbed, from 43.4 percent in 1971 to 72.2 percent in 2004.

A question designed to measure legitimacy asked, "Suppose there were no parties or assemblies and elections were not held—do you think that the government in this country can be run better?" The question was deliberately phrased in the negative, requiring the interviewees to show their commitment to democracy by formulating the answer in the negative—not a simple thing to do, considering the radical difference in the status of the interviewer and interviewee with the backdrop of a traditional society where social deference and a tendency to agree with those who represent superior power point in the same direction. The percentages of those who consider India's current institutional arrangement to be consistent with their own value preferences have steadily gone up, from 43.4 to 70.5 percent.[47]

These data show that ordinary people feel empowered enough to "kick the rascals out." When the vital foundations of democracy are threatened by political adventurers, support for them ebbs and democratic institutions reemerge. Once again, as we can see from the example of the national emergency of 1975–1977, the Indian political system has experienced situations where this potential is transformed into the breakdown of democracy and the rise of 'popular authoritarianism,' but democracy eventually bounces back.

Elections and Participation

17.9 Discuss the increase in voter turnout in India's national and regional elections and the alternative political actions engaged in by citizens.

After independence, political transactions and election campaigns became the chief instrument of political socialization in India. In a daring move, India's leaders put everything on the auction block of electoral politics right at the outset, in the first general election of 1951 and 1952. Even the very definition of the nation, its physical boundaries, and the basic principles of its economic organization were not considered above politics. Since then, every election (and there have been a great many—Parliament, State assembly, district and local councils and municipalities, and a myriad of school committees and other groups) became an occasion for individuals to recognize the value of their votes. The result was that the great school of democracy quickly multiplied the numbers of its enthusiastic pupils and continued to produce both knowledge and skill, even when the first teachers left the scene.

Since regular and frequent political consultation was the most effective instrument of political socialization, we need to examine indicators of political participation. Revealing statistics can be found from participation in the general elections to the Lok Sabha, the lower house of the federal legislature and the highest repository of legislative authority and governmental accountability in the country. These are illustrative of India's success at organizing an electoral process at a continental scale. Large-scale poverty and illiteracy notwithstanding, India, under the supervision of the independent Election Commission, has organized elections involving very large electorates who, by law, have to be provided with polling booths within easy walking distance. The campaigns themselves are strictly monitored. It is not unusual for polling to be stopped and re-polling ordered in the event of electoral fraud or violence.[48]

The level of participation, spread over all social classes, went up steadily, from 45.7 percent in the first general election to the Lok Sabha held in 1952 to 58 percent in the third general election held in 1962. It has remained stable at almost 60 percent between 1962 and the fifteenth elections in 2009 (Figure 17.9). Men tend to turn out in greater numbers than women, but the participation of women has grown over the years. An equally interesting phenomenon is the participation of the former untouchable castes, which, both for men and women, keeps pace with the population as a whole, a significant achievement considering their oppressive exclusion by the upper social strata in the past.

At the height of the Freedom Movement, India's leaders, many of whom were lawyers by training, had learned how to combine institutional participation with strategic protest. The strategy was finely crafted by Mahatma Gandhi, who had successfully used such political weapons as satyagraha to mobilize support among peasants, workers, the middle classes, and the lower reaches of the caste system. This two-track strategy forced the state institutions of colonial rule to be more inclusive with regard to the domain of modern political institutions. Combining conventional and nonconventional forms of politics introduced many social institutions and ritual practices into the realm of politics. This practice of combining elections, pressure groups, and lobbying with unconventional methods of direct action has enriched the range of political tools in post-independence politics. The results are twofold. On the one hand, this gives legitimacy to the democratic political process in a society where elections do not have the same long history as in Western democracies. On the other hand,

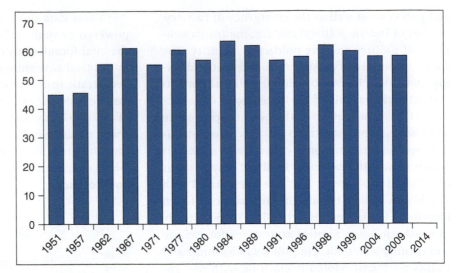

FIGURE 17.9
Turning Out to Vote
The majority of the public votes in most Lok Sabha elections.

Source: Election Commission of India, General Elections 1951–2004 (http://eci.nic.in/eci_main/miscellaneous_statistics/Graphs_Voteage_NoofContestants.pdf) and General Elections 2009 (http://eci.nic.in/eci_main/archiveofge2009/Stats/VOLI/08_VotersInformation.pdf), last accessed February 11, 2013.

the availability of nonelectoral means of politics gives an impetus to a whole host of actors—those who have failed to make their mark on the electoral arena, and ambitious politicians who are trying to launch their careers—to resort to direct political action without first exhausting the electoral option. This has turned India, as the Nobel Prize–winning Indian author V. S. Naipaul has famously put it, into a country of a "Million Mutinies."[49]

Political Recruitment

17.10 How well are the various social groups of India represented in the political institutions?

If political participation is a minimum criterion of democratic rule, a persuasive case can be made that India has caught up with the West. To facilitate the growth of political socialization, high levels of participation are necessary but not sufficient. We therefore call on two further sources of evidence: political recruitment to the highest legislature of the country and the social composition of the local elite.

Political recruitment is important because once people have knowledge of the normative structure of the system and the skill with which to engage in political transactions, they tend to elect representatives who reflect the main cleavages of society. Of course, the representative character of the elected elite is unlikely to become mathematically accurate, because very small groups are often penalized because of the "first-past-the-post" system of voting. However, by looking at the data over time and across different regions, one can draw some general conclusions.

The percentage of politicians of rural origin in the Lok Sabha has grown over the years and, correspondingly, the weight of "agriculturists" as well. The percentage of women has doubled but is still far below their share of the population.[50] The percentage of Brahmins has dropped significantly.[51] The former untouchables and tribals, who continue to occupy a little over a fifth of the membership, reflect their weight in the population of the country. This results from a system of "reservation," which sets a quota for these underprivileged groups. Quite interestingly, although there is no quota system for the election of Muslims to the Parliament (and the electoral rules do not provide for proportional representation), their total number is not far below their proportion in the Indian population.

Policy Outputs: Economics, Welfare, and Poverty

17.11 Summarize the fluctuations in India's economy, the government's responses, and the outcomes.

According to recent statistics, India's economy grew at an estimated annual rate of over 9 percent from 2007 until 2009 (see Figure 17.10).[52] This caps a sevenfold increase in total GNP over the past forty years. Measured in terms of PPP, India has reached $3,100 per capita. Within the region, only the Chinese economy shows higher growth rates.

In terms of absolute poverty, denoted by the number of people who live on less than $1.25 a day, India reduced the share from 66 percent in 1978 to 49 percent in 1994 and, further, to 33 percent in 2010. But the absolute number of people living on less than

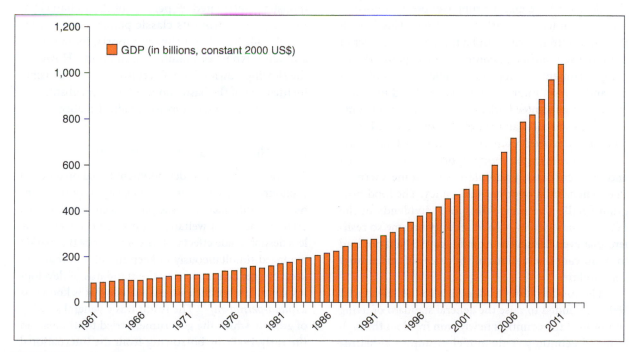

FIGURE 17.10

India's Economic Growth

Gross Domestic Product (GDP) has grown more than sixfold from 1980 until today.

Source: World Bank, Database, GDP (constant 2,000 US$) (http://data.worldbank.org/indicator/NY.GDP.MKTP.KD), last accessed on February 11, 2013.

$1.25 a day rose from 436 million in 1990 to 456 million in 2005 due to the growing population.[53]

Although the picture is slightly better in terms of relative poverty, measured by the percentage share of the income of the lowest 20 percent as compared with the United States, China, or Brazil (refer back to Table 1.4), the poor performance on the indicators of welfare (such as access to sanitation, safe water, or infant mortality) reinforces the picture of mass poverty in India.

Politics of Incremental Growth and Redistribution

India's economic growth during the early decades after independence, though unspectacular, was nevertheless strong enough, compared to the stagnation of the long years of colonial rule, to impart a sense of strength, purpose, and legitimacy to India's political institutions. The first gains came in the 1950s through an expansion of the area under cultivation and irrigation works. The 1960s accelerated agrarian production through a series of technical innovations, like seeds of the high-yielding variety, new pesticides, chemical fertilizer, and the supply of precise information on weather and market conditions. This "Green Revolution" transformed India from a net importer of food to a self-sufficient country. Through the 1970s, the government developed a complex system of storage and market interventions called "Food Procurement" that guaranteed prices to maintain a steady flow of food production and supply to consumers. India's food policy evolved in reaction to chronic food shortages that necessitated food imports at huge financial and political costs, particularly during the Vietnam War, when India opposed U.S. policy. The food program finally started yielding rich dividends in the 1980s. India's system of food security became so resilient that even the severe droughts of 1987 did not lead to significant fluctuations in the prices of agricultural commodities.[54]

The modernizing leadership around Jawaharlal Nehru intended to raise the general standard of living and protect the country's newly won freedom through a mixed economy. This model of import substitution, planned economic growth, and a policy of self-reliance did not leave much room for integration into the international market. In part, this situation reflected a certain Gandhian nostalgia for **swadeshi**—the consumption of only homemade goods—but also a basic distrust of the West. During the first half of the twentieth century, from 1900 to 1946, Indian national income under colonial rule had risen by 0.7 percent annually, while its population grew at the rate of 0.8 percent. The lesson was not lost on the generation of Nehru. Thanks to the developmental initiatives from 1950–1951 to 1990–1991, India more than doubled the size of its economy. While its growth rate was well above preindependence levels, it fell far below expectations. India was considerably below the 8 to 10 percent rate of the fastest-growing countries in Asia—Japan, South Korea, Taiwan, Hong Kong, and Singapore—and lagged substantially behind China.

In spite of its poor performance relative to worldwide economic growth, India did achieve some significant results. Despite the low level of industrialization, by the mid-1980s, India was one of the twenty most industrialized nations in terms of total industrial production. India was self-sufficient in consumer goods and in basic commodities, like steel and cement. It also produced a range of intermediate-level manufactured goods, ships, locomotives, trucks, machine tools, and sophisticated electronic equipment. By the late 1980s, industry contributed 29 percent of the Indian GNP. In a departure from its classic patterns of international trade based on primary exports, India started a modest export of manufactured goods. However, the slowing down of India's economy and the visible inefficiency of the basic model of import substitution became compelling factors for a radical change.

Liberalization of the Economy

The model of planned development based on a mixed economy—where the *commanding heights* of the economy were dominated by the public sector—achieved a certain amount of welfare, but it also produced some less desirable side effects. State control over the market managed simultaneously to keep inflation low and to keep budget deficits low by the standards of developing countries, but the system created what is known as a *quota-permit-raj*.[55] The result was a general slowing of growth, which the government tried to stimulate in the early 1980s by borrowing from the international market. However, this was done without any radical changes in the structure of management of the economy. The result was a serious financial crisis by the end of the 1980s. Most alarmingly for India's policymakers and the international financial establishment, India's debt-to-GDP ratio went up by 100 percent in the span of a decade. In 1991, Manmohan Singh, then finance minister, and Prime Minister Narasimha Rao introduced the first structural reform of the economy, which came to be known as "**liberalization**" (see Box 17.5).

The first policies introduced by Manmohan Singh sought a drastic reduction of state control over the market, whether open or disguised. The government reduced subsidies on several items and relaxed strict import and export controls. The system of licensing new industries and closing those that were no longer profitable but could not be closed off because of labor-protection legislation was amended to bring a new flexibility to the market. Areas of production that the government had brought under its control during the heyday of nationalization in the 1970s under the concept of "essential commodities" were gradually returned to the market. Important areas of production—such as electricity generation, parts of the oil industry, domestic air transport, roads, and some telecommunications—were opened up for private initiative and enterprise. The government welcomed foreign investment and participation in the process of production through "joint ventures." India attempted to make its economy attractive for foreign investors by lowering tariffs in a significant departure from the previous policy of import substitution and autarchy. There was an easing up of imports, and Singh encouraged export through the devaluation of the rupee by 24 percent in 1991. The rupee was also made partly convertible into foreign currencies. The government gradually reduced the heavy taxes on entrepreneurs, as well as the direct tax on income. The top rate of income tax came down from 56 percent to 40 percent, and the top rate of corporate tax came down from 57.5 percent to 46 percent.[56]

These measures were reinforced with a communication revolution that saw a deregulation of broadcasting. This development gave Indian consumers easy access to foreign-made televisions and radios, and to a hitherto unavailable choice of programs through satellite and cable channels. State broadcasting took on the challenge and introduced a modest degree of variety through internal competition.

In some ways, the fiscal policies of 1991 to liberalize the economy and implement a policy of privatization of public sector undertakings went against the grain of Indian politics. As far as ancient Indian tradition goes, the *Arthasastra* had allocated a number of key sectors of the economy to the exclusive authority of the king. This tradition of state monopoly was continued by practically all the rulers of India, coming to a peak under British colonial rule. Indian commercial and industrial entrepreneurs had chafed under the British monopoly and colonial obstacles to the expansion of their activities, and they had enthusiastically supported the swadeshi program of Mahatma Gandhi. They were content after independence to find a secure niche within the structure of the mixed economy. Each obstacle to free enterprise was also the visible tip of a powerful vested interest. As such, it comes as no surprise that attempts to roll back the state have

---

BOX

17.5   Manmohan Singh

The current Indian prime minister, Manmohan Singh, is the first Sikh to occupy the most important political office in the country. He is an economist by training, with a distinguished academic record and prestigious appointments with the Reserve Bank of India and the World Bank. When India faced a severe fiscal crisis in 1991, as India's finance minister, he initiated the structural reform of India's economy. Following the victory of the UPA coalition in the 2004 parliamentary elections, Manmohan Singh was drafted in as the leader of the UPA parliamentary coalition. Consequently, the president of India invited him to form the central Cabinet. Sonia Gandhi, leader of the Congress Party, has institutionalized the process of regular consultation between her and the prime minister, creating, in the process, the scope for two centers of power within the coalition. However, the coordination between Sonia Gandhi and Manmohan Singh appears to have worked quite effectively, facilitating better coordination among the constituent parties of the ruling coalition and also a sense of cohesion within the government.

produced a powerful backlash from a formidable co-alition: socialists who want to protect the poor and underprivileged from the ravages of capitalism, rich farmers who fear the loss of government subsidies, the swadeshi lobby that is apprehensive about the loss of Indian political autonomy and cultural identity, and regional leaders who fear the growing gap between rich and poor parts of India without the presence of a powerful, redistributive center.

Liberalization thus sparked a heated debate among India's political parties. India's communist parties predictably expressed staunch opposition to the liberalization of trade regulations. They saw these reforms as an attempt by international financial establishments like the IMF and the World Bank to dictate terms to India. They demanded that the entry of foreign capital be governed by the technological "needs"

of India, which are presumably to be determined by India's planners. For the Left, the public sector as a whole, and especially public sector employment, needed to be defended against attempts at privatization that could lead to job losses. The Congress Party, which had introduced the liberalization measures in the first place, was muted in the defense of liberalization, having sensed its lack of electoral appeal. The Bharatiya Janata Party, which had traditionally drawn support from the trading communities and the better-educated and urban populations, took a complex position on this whole issue. The party manifesto called for "full liberalization and calibrated globalization"; it argued in favor of initiative and enterprise but wanted to retain the role of the state in protecting national industry and trade against "unfair" international competition. The BJP also intended to exclude foreign

Sweet and Sour: Growing Trade Relations between India and China, Despite Continuing Political Differences
Dr. Manmohan Singh (right), a career economist and India's first Sikh prime minister, shaking hands with President Hu Jin-Tao of China, indicating the growing relations between the two neighbors.

intrusion from areas crucial to India's security interests, and foreign competition from consumer goods industries, with catchy slogans like "computer chips yes, potato chips no."

In a context where coalitional politics is inordinately sensitive to popular mood swings, the uncertain feelings of the electorate are also reflected in the radical fluctuations of public policy. It was therefore remarkable that the BJP-led NDA government continued the policy of liberalization started by its predecessor in spite of the opposition within its ranks.

India and the Financial Crisis

Going by the record of the past few years, Prime Minister Manmohan Singh, the architect of the first major reform, has become quite adept at balancing the multiple pressures on the economy. India has coped with the world's biggest financial crisis since the Great Depression better than most other countries. What began in the United States as a subprime banking crisis in 2007 eventually turned into a global financial crisis, causing an economic slump in growth and stock markets worldwide. India was among the few countries in the world to grow, despite the crisis.

Nevertheless, there was substantial impact on the Indian economy in terms of a slowdown in GDP growth rates as well as contractions in trade and stock market performance. The real growth in GDP declined from a more than 9 percent growth rate between the years 2005 and 2007 to around 6 percent at the end of 2008, but recovered to a rate of growth of over 8 percent for the first quarter of 2010.[57] It should be noted that growth rates were already declining *before* the crisis hit, partly the effect of deliberate policies to forestall fears of an overheated economy as well as the result of delayed structural reforms that stunted further growth.[58]

Export and import growth rates turned negative in the last quarter of 2008 and in 2009, but recovered ground to increase in the first quarter of 2010.[59] Worst affected was the export-oriented manufacturing sector (for example, engineering goods and auto parts). The most important Indian stock market index, the Sensex 30 (which lists the thirty largest Indian companies on the Bombay Stock Exchange), registered a massive shock when it declined by two-thirds between January and March 2008.[60] Apart from the effects of the international crisis, analysts have argued that this slump also reflects a readjustment to more representative market levels. After this significant downswing, the Sensex 30 subsequently recovered more than half its losses by mid-2010.[61]

In response to the decline, the government initiated three stimulus packages beginning in December 2008. These measures mainly gravitated around cuts in excise duty and service tax, infrastructure spending, and bank capitalization. Estimates of the size of India's fiscal stimuli vary from 0.5 percent of the GDP (IMF estimate) to 3.5 percent (Indian Finance Minister). According to some analysts, the fiscal stimuli did not have the intended effect, causing the government to emphasize social protection policies as well as infrastructure investment programs as articulated in its 2009 and 2010 budget.[62] These social policy measures, in combination with substantial loan waivers for indebted farmers as well as the stimulus packages, further increased the already high budget deficit. A major concern has been the increase in inflation, especially relating to food prices. But overall, it was widely noted that the Reserve Bank of India (the Central Bank of India) acted resolutely and promptly in smoothing the credit supply.

Analysts have proposed a number of reasons for India's relative resilience in the face of the financial crisis. The most prominent argument has been that, despite a much higher integration into the world economy within the last two decades, India's financial sector remains largely regulated, and more than two-thirds of total assets in the banking sector are owned by public sector banks. In general, India's banking sector is regarded to be sound in terms of both capitalization and regulation. Furthermore, there was limited exposure to financially unsound assets from the U.S. financial markets. Other reasons include India's gradualist reforms, especially in the area of privatization, and hence the still-dominant public sector. Additionally, in contrast to China, India's trade volume with OECD countries decreased over recent years in favor of "south–south trade," especially with the Middle East and China.

There are still problems aplenty: poor infrastructure, political wrangling over educational quotas, deep pockets of poverty and illiteracy, and tragic farmers' suicides as a form of protest against the side effects of globalization. But over and above it all, there is also a sense of optimism about growth, and pride in India's growing global profile. This sense of buoyancy is borne out by recent public opinion data.[63]

Conclusion: Conflation of Democracy and Development

Barely a decade after India began its journey as a multiparty democracy, Selig Harrison, voicing the pessimism of many Western observers, warned: "Odds are almost wholly against the survival of freedom [...] the issue is, in fact, whether any Indian state can survive at all."[64] These opinions echoed misgivings expressed about self-rule leading to chaos.[65] After six decades of democratic rule and fifteen national elections, the issue of India's survival as a democracy could probably be taken off the agenda.

The key question that now confronts India is what kind of Indian democracy will emerge over the next decades. Will it be a liberal democratic, affluent, and secure India, able to sustain the pace of reform and the current rate of growth? Or will India remain a majoritarian political democracy, reforming but still poor, armed with nuclear teeth (see Box 17.6), threatening its neighbors and scuttling the chances of nuclear nonproliferation, wishing nevertheless to enjoy the benefits of trade and scientific exchange with the rest of the world?

Drawing on the development of institutions and the policy process in India during the past six decades, this chapter has argued that the likelihood of the collapse of the Indian state and its democratic political system is slim.[66] The sense of optimism is reflected in public opinion. The national elite, evolved over the years, understands the benefits of cooperation and compromise with all sections of the population. India's leaders of all political shades increasingly voice their concerns about national security and prosperity.

When political demands overtake the capacity of the system to satisfy them, as American political scientist Samuel Huntington warned in the 1960s, the gap can enhance political disorder.[67] But when political participation occurs in the context of a state that combines accommodation with the repression of antisystem forces, the combined effort can lead to the resilience of a democratic political process. In this context, India's record on the management of law and order, which has successfully brought down the number of riots per million inhabitants from its peak in the mid-1980s (see Figure 17.11), deserves special attention, particularly because of the critical attention that India has recently received about human rights violations from human rights groups within the country and abroad.

The Indian case demonstrates how transactional politics within firm boundaries laid down and defended with overwhelming force by the state have helped in the functioning of representative political

---

BOX 17.6   A Nuclear Surprise

The 1998 nuclear test by India, followed within weeks by Pakistan, set alarm bells ringing in the major capitals of the world. India and Pakistan are not signatories of the Nuclear Nonproliferation Treaty (NPT). Therefore, although the tests were not violating a treaty agreement as such, it was feared that they would jeopardize the cause of nonproliferation, and thus increase the likelihood of nuclear conflict. Thanks to the CBMs that India and Pakistan have since put in place, South Asia appears to have entered a period of moderate stability.

India's nuclear program actually started in 1946. Subsequently, the Atomic Energy Commission (AEC) was established in 1948, and the first two civilian nuclear reactors opened in 1956 and 1960. Simultaneously with the developing of nuclear energy for peaceful purposes, India advocated general global disarmament, including nuclear weapons in particular. However, with the Chinese testing of the nuclear bomb (1964) and the feeling among India's leaders that the world powers were unlikely to jettison their nuclear stockpiles, India attempted to enter the nuclear club with a "peaceful nuclear device" in 1974. For the next three decades, other nations placed heavy sanctions on India, cutting off the supply of nuclear know-how, technology, and sufficient fuel supply. Following the 1998 test, India's leaders strongly justified their claim to membership in the exclusive nuclear club. Besides the military and political reputation, nuclear power is also crucially important for India's continued economic growth in view of its chronic dependence on imported petroleum. With the tests of 1998, India finally entered the exclusive nuclear league. The U. S.–India Nuclear Cooperation Approval and Nonproliferation Enhancement Act, initiated in 2005 and signed into law on October 8, 2008, helped integrate India's nuclear program with the international market and the control regimes in fissile material in which the United States plays a key role.

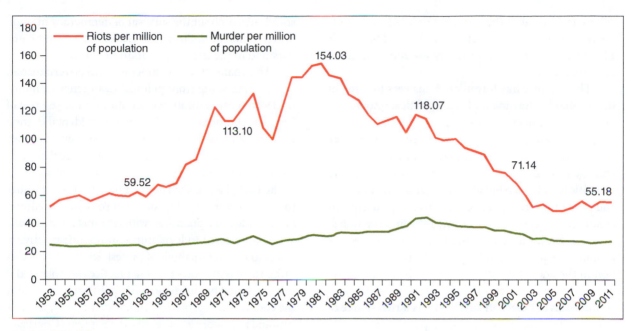

FIGURE 17.11

Violence

Riots and murders, after declining in past decades, appear to have gone up slightly.

Sources: Data on riots and murders: Government of India—Ministry of Home Affairs—National Crime Records Bureau (various years), *Crime in India*; data for 1954–2006 retrieved from Integrated Network for Societal Conflict Research (INSCR): http://www.systemicpeace.org/inscr/inscr.htm; 2007: http://ncrb.nic.in/cii2007/cii-2007/FIGURES_2007.pdf; 2008: http://ncrb.nic.in/cii2008/cii-2008/figure%20at%20a%20glance.pdf; 2009: http://ncrb.nic.in/CII-2009-NEW/cii-2009/figure%20at%20a%20glance.pdf; 2010: http://ncrb.nic.in/CII2010/cii-2010/figure%20at%20a%20glance.pdf; and 2011: http://ncrb.nic.in/CD-CII2011/cii-2011/figure%20at%20a%20glance.pdf. Data on Indian total population 1953–2010: United Nations—Department of Economic and Social Affairs—Population Division (2011), *World Population Prospects—The 2010 Revision*, http://esa.un.org/unpd/wpp/Excel-Data/population.htm. Data on Indian total population 2011: World Bank, Database, http://data.worldbank.org/indicator/SP.POP.TOTL/countries/1W?display=default. All data last accessed February 12, 2012.

institutions. They provided the channels of political recruitment to aspiring social elites as well as the means for upward mobility to the lower social strata. One consequence is the absence of significant social groups that feel sufficiently discriminated against to undertake collective rebellion. However, the recent spate of suicides by indebted and impecunious farmers shows the limitation of this strategy of accommodation.

India's experience contrasts with that of other countries of the subcontinent, which share some of India's cultural, political, and historical legacies. The difficulties faced by the democratic process in these countries confirm the postulates of conventional social theory: that successful political democracy requires the preconditions of literacy and economic development,[68] institutionalization of political power prior to the introduction of popular participation,[69] or a victorious bourgeoisie acting as the social base for democratic institutions.[70] The Indian "counter example" thus raises a main question: Why has India—despite a culture based on social hierarchy and

authoritarianism, mass poverty, and high illiteracy—been able to establish a successful democratic political order?[71]

Unlike the majority of postcolonial countries, India retains the territory, constitution, and political system that marked its emergence as an independent country in 1947. In spite of external conflicts and internal insurgencies, elections have been held regularly and with rates of participation from almost 50 percent in the early elections to about 60 percent since the 1960s. India has achieved a minimum of welfare and food security, and inflation and explosive population growth have been tamed; now, with the liberalization of India's economy, international business confidence in India remains high. Despite these achievements, some dark spots continue to blight the democratic credentials of India—mass poverty and illiteracy persist.

Just as the imperative of governance forced Hindu nationalists in power to moderate their stance, so has the political temptation to garner the advocates of hindutva—believers in the rightful claim that Hindu values are central to the Indian state—led to the outbreak of pogroms between Hindus and Muslims.[72] The puzzles of India's democracy are rooted in these contradictions.[73]

This chapter has formulated answers to some of these issues by drawing on India's political resources—its trusted and respected modern political institutions that bridge social and cultural diversity and produce a political community, its experience of colonial rule and the resistance to it, the efforts of a modernizing and visionary leadership at nation- and state-building, and the policy process aimed at strategic, citizenship-enhancing, social and economic reform since India's independence. These were the main components that facilitated democratic rule, and orderly state contraction in the era of liberalization. With its political parties, movements, elections, multiple conflicts, and conflict-solving mechanisms, India is a rich source of data for students of comparative politics, especially with regard to an illustration of the main theoretical concepts of the discipline—from interest articulation, aggregation, and adjudication to the interaction of politics, policy, and economic development. This resilience of India's democratic political system appears even more astounding because India's main political institutions—the legislature, executive, and judiciary, and individual rights—have not evolved entirely from within its society and culture. On the contrary, many of these are colonial transplants. Yet their legitimacy is not questioned by India's main political parties, including those that draw their strength from mobilization along the lines of religious cleavages or class conflict.

In attempting to address these topics, this chapter has pointed not in the direction of Indian culture but to its institutions, process, and the political economy that has evolved from the conflict and conflation of tradition and modernity. It has pointed toward cross-culturally comparable factors that account for the Indian success at sustaining a stable political system that combines both democracy and development. In India, norms of democracy are widely shared by all major political parties—including the Communist Party and right-wing Hindu-nationalist parties like the Shiv Sena and the Bharatiya Janata Party—although they differ radically in their ideological positions. Even in the lowest political arenas, the right to democratic participation is no longer considered an exotic idea. This Indian achievement—puzzling in view of the negative implications of conventional

social theory about the survival of democracy in poor, postcolonial, preindustrial societies—needs to be understood in the larger comparative context.

The challenges to democracy and governance in India—emanating from political insurgency, communal riots, "criminalization of politics,"[74] and the rise of "popular authoritarianism"—are not accidental or incidental features of India's political system. Ironically, they sometimes originate from the same process that gives rise to, and sustains, representative political institutions in the first place. India's democratic process continues to be open and inclusive, so much so that, sometimes, locally influential politicians with criminal records manage to get elected to legislatures and political activists resort to forceful methods of protest, leading to the disturbance of public order. These practices are tolerated if not condoned by the democratic political process. But the countervailing forces of India's democracy, federalism, and regulatory agencies like the Supreme Court and the Election Commission ensure that they do not spread beyond a point that would choke the vitality of the democratic process and the rule of law altogether.

One sometimes comes across the criticism that the political process of India accepts democracy only at the level of interest aggregation and accommodation and not at the level of liberal values, such as respect for the freedom and dignity of individuals. A further extension of this argument is that vote counting is neither necessary nor sufficient as a guarantee for the long-term survival of a democracy. Scholarly concerns about the rise of popular authoritarianism in the wake of competitive and aggressive populism are based on such misgivings. These criticisms reinforce the apprehensions of a possible collapse or a surreptitious gnawing away at democratic institutions until the system is reduced to an empty shell.[75] The existence of the danger of a collapse of democracy cannot be ruled out altogether, but survey data regarding legitimacy, efficacy, the recruitment of new local elites, and the empowerment of former untouchables, religious minorities, and women show the strength and the potential for a further unfolding of "prodemocracy" forces in India. This is further supported by statistical data on governance, political order, participation, and legitimacy. The results of national surveys are supplemented with evidence of the upward social mobility of underprivileged social groups and the complementarities of institutional as well as radical modes of participation at the local level. The marketplace of politics continues to operate as an arbiter of the contradictory values of the dignity of the individual and the identity of the group and, more recently, of the imperative of integration with the international political economy. At the same time, the need to maintain India's cultural distinctiveness, as well as the interests of the least privileged, remains.

In the final analysis, the universal significance of the Indian experiment lies in showing the democratic potential of politics from below. When it is combined with representative political institutions and tied to political competition and social reform, it can produce unexpected results that support and promote democratic transition and consolidation. This process occurs notwithstanding the absence of material affluence or cultural roots of individual rights. At the same time, it must also be remembered that the process is unlikely to be fully consensual. Empowerment of the marginal social groups, while crucial to the functioning of the Indian system, is, in India as everywhere in the world, contested by entrenched and privileged social groups. But the commitment of India's key institutions—such as the judiciary, the Parliament, the media, the army, the bureaucracy, and the national and regional leaders—to democracy and secularism remains steadfast. The Indian case shows how modern institutions and a democratic political process, ensconced in the context of a responsive state and accountable elites well versed in the art and science of governance, can pave the way for transition to liberal democracy and its consolidation despite predictions to the contrary.[76]

REVIEW QUESTIONS

- How has the Indian political system succeeded in holding together a country of continental dimensions, marked by extreme diversity of language, religion, class, and levels of development?
- Why has India, unlike the majority of postcolonial states, been successful in sustaining a democratic form of government *and* economic development? Explain with reference to the structure of the political system and state–society relations in India.
- What consequences have liberalization of India's economy and globalization had on economic growth and social justice?
- What changes have taken place in Indo–U.S. relations during the last decades compared to earlier periods, and why?
- Compare the room to maneuver of the Indian executive vis-à-vis the legislative and judicial wings of the government with that in the United States and the United Kingdom.
- What are the special features of the Indian federation compared to that of the United States?
- What are the main threats to orderly and democratic governance in India today, and how capable is the government of meeting these challenges?

KEY TERMS

Ayodhya
Bharatiya Janata Party (BJP)
BRICS
castes
composite dialogue
dalits
dharma
dharna
emergency
Gandhi, Indira
Gandhi, Mahatma
gherao
hindutva
jajmani
jatis
liberalization
Lok Sabha (House of the People)
mixed economy
National Democratic Alliance (NDA)
Nehru, Jawaharlal
nonalignment
nuclear test
panchasheela
panchayati raj
partition
Rajya Sabha (the Council of States)
Rama
Right to Information Act 2005 (RTI)
satyagraha
swadeshi
tribals
two-nation theory
United Progressive Alliance (UPA)
varnas
zamindars

SUGGESTED READINGS

Bardhan, Pranab. *The Political Economy of Development in India.* Oxford: Basil Blackwell, 1984.

Brass, Paul R. *Language, Religion, and Politics in North India.* London: Cambridge University Press, 1974.

Brown, Judith. *India: The Origin of an Asian Democracy.* Delhi: Oxford University Press, 1985.

Embree, Ainslie, ed. *From the Beginning to 1800.* Vol. 1 of *Sources of Indian Tradition.* New Delhi: Penguin, 1991.

Forster, E. M. *A Passage to India.* Harmondsworth, England: Penguin, 1985; first published 1924.

Haq, Mahbub ul, and Khadija Haq. *Human Development in South Asia, 1998.* Karachi: Oxford University Press, 1998.

Hay, Stephen, ed. *Modern India and Pakistan.* Vol. 2 of *Sources of Indian Tradition.* New Delhi: Penguin, 1991.

Indira Gandhi Institute of Development Research. *India Development Report, 2008.* Delhi: Oxford University Press, 2008.

Jaffrelot, Christophe, and Sanjay Kumar, eds. *Rise of the Plebeians?: The Changing Face of the Indian Legislative Assemblies.* London: Routledge, 2008.

Jenkins, R. *Democratic Politics and Economic Reform in India.* Cambridge: Cambridge University Press, 2000.

Kashyap, Subhas. *Our Parliament.* New Delhi: National Book Trust of India, 1989.

Kohli, Atul. *The Success of India's Democracy.* Cambridge: Cambridge University Press, 2001.

Kothari, Rajni. *Politics in India.* Boston: Little Brown, 1970.

Manor, James. *From Nehru to Nineties: The Changing Office of the Prime Minister in India.* London: Hurst, 1994.

Mitra, Subrata K., ed. *The Post-colonial State in Asia: The Dialectics of Politics and Culture.* Hemel Hempstead, England: Wheatsheaf, 1990.

———. *Power, Protest, and Participation: Local Elites and the Politics of Development in India.* London: Routledge, 1992.

———. *Culture and Rationality.* New Delhi: Sage, 1999.

———. *The Puzzle of India's Governance.* London: Routledge, 2005.

———, ed. *Politics of Modern South Asia.* 5 vol. London: Routledge, 2008.

———. *Politics in India: Structure, Process, Policy.* London: Routledge, 2011.

———, ed. *Citizenship in the Era of Globalization: Structure, Agency, Power, and the Flow of Ideas.* New Delhi: Samskriti, 2012.

Mitra, Subrata K., and V. B. Singh. *When Rebels become Stakeholders: Democracy, Agency and Social Change in India.* New Delhi: Sage, 2009.

Mitra, Subrata K., Siegfried Wolf, and Jivanta Schoettli. *A Political and Economic Dictionary of India.* London: Europa, 2006.

Moore, Barrington. *Social Origins of Dictatorship and Democracy: Lord and Peasant in the Making of the Modern World.* Boston: Beacon Press, 1966.

Morris-Jones, W. H. *The Government and Politics of India.* Wistow, England: Eothen Press, 1987.

Nandy, Ashis. *The Intimate Enemy: Loss and Recovery of Self under Colonialism.* Delhi: Oxford University Press, 1983.

Panagariya, Arvind. *India: The Emerging Giant.* New York: Oxford University Press, 2008.

Rudolph, Lloyd, and Susanne Rudolph. *In Pursuit of Lakshmi: The Political Economy of the Indian State.* Chicago: University of Chicago Press, 1987.

Sen, Kunal. *Trade Policy, Inequality and Performance in Indian Manufacturing.* New York: Routledge, 2009.

Sontheimer, Guenter D., and Hermann Kulke, eds. *Hinduism Reconsidered.* New Delhi: Manohar, 1989.

World Bank. *World Development Report, 2009. Development and Climate Change.* Washington, DC: World Bank Publications, 2009.

INTERNET RESOURCES

Government of India: Directory of official websites: www.goidirectory.nic.in.

Indian Parliament: www.parliamentofindia.nic.in.

Prime Minister's Office: www.pmindia.nic.in.

Constitution of India: www.indiacode.nic.in.

Indian National Congress: www.congress.org.in.

Bharatiya Janata Party: www.bjp.org.

Newspaper *The Hindu*: www.thehindu.com.

Fortnightly magazine *Frontline*: www.frontlineonnet.com.

Journal *The Economic and Political Weekly*: http://epw.in.

ENDNOTES

1. See Subrata K. Mitra, *The Puzzle of India's Governance* (London: Routledge, 2005), *Politics in India: Structure, Process, Policy* (London: Routledge, 2011), and *Citizenship in the Era of Globalization: Structure, Agency, Power, and the Flow of Ideas* (New Delhi: Samskriti, 2012), and Mitra and V. B. Singh, *When Rebels become Stakeholders: Democracy, Agency and Social Change in India* (New Delhi: Sage, 2009), for elaborations on this argument.

2. See Barrington Moore, *Social Origins of Dictatorship and Democracy: Lord and Peasant in the Making of the Modern*

World (Boston: Beacon Press, 1966), for an analysis of the capitalist, socialist, and fascist models of development and his characterization of India as an anomalous case.

3. "There is a good chance that 20 years from now, many of India's constitutional anomalies regarding the secular state will have disappeared. It is reasonable to expect that by that time there will be a uniform civil code and that Hindu and Muslim law, as such, will have ceased to exist. Legislation having already dealt with the most serious abuses in Hindu religion there will be little need for further interference by the state." D. E. Smith, *India as a Secular State* (Princeton, NJ: Princeton University Press, 1963), 134.

4. Subrata Mitra, "The NDA and the Politics of 'Minorities' in India," in *Coalition Politics and Hindu Nationalism*, Katherine Adeney and Lawrence Sáez, eds. (London: Routledge, 2005), 77–96.

5. Subrata Mitra, "Desecularizing the State: Religion and Politics in India after Independence," *Comparative Studies in Society and History* 33 (October 1991): 755–77.

6. See Sajad Padder, "The Composite Dialogue between India and Pakistan: Structure, Process and Agency," in *Heidelberg Papers in South Asian and Comparative Politics*, 65 (February 2012), http://www.ub.uni-heidelberg.de/archiv/1.

7. See Mitra, *The Puzzle of India's Governance*, 128, for a detailed analysis of these figures, cross-tabulated by party support.

8. In a bold assertion of state capacity (but, perhaps, also with a fine eye to the general elections due in 2014), the Government of India executed Ajmal Kasab, the only survivor among the terrorists who attacked Mumbai in 2009, in late 2012, and Mohammad Afzal Guru, the main accused in the case of the terrorist attack on Parliament in 2001, in February 2013. See Smita Gupta, "The Role of Pranab Mukherjee in Afzal Guru's Hanging," *Hindu*, February 10, 2013, http://www.thehindu.com.

9. Burton Stein, *Peasant, State, and Society in Medieval South India* (New Delhi: Oxford University Press, 1980).

10. See Hermann Kulke, ed., *The State in India, 1000–1700* (New Delhi: Oxford University Press, 1985), for an excellent introduction to the diversity of historical scholarship on the political form and social base of the early state in India.

11. Judith Brown, *Modern India: The Origins of an Asian Democracy* (New Delhi: Oxford University Press, 1985).

12. For excellent sources on the origin of political institutions and attitudes in India, see *Sources of Indian Tradition*, vol. 1, *From the Beginning to 1800*, Ainslie Embree, ed. (London: Penguin, 1991), and vol. 2, *Modern India and Pakistan*, Stephen Hay, ed. (London: Penguin, 1991).

13. The Jagannath cult of Orissa is an example of this form of syncretism. See Subrata K. Mitra, "Religion, Region, and Identity: Sacred Beliefs and Secular Power in a Regional State Tradition of India," in *Aspects of India: Essays on Indian Politics and Culture*, ed. Noel O. Sullivan (Hull, England: University of Hull, 1994), 46–68.

14. Brass, Paul R. *Language, Religion, and Politics in North India.* London: Cambridge University Press, 1974); and Christophe Jaffrelot, *Rise of the Plebeians? The Changing Face of the Indian Legislative Assemblies* (London: Routledge, 2008).

15. Gurharpal Singh, "Ethnic Conflict in India: A Case-study of Punjab," in *The Politics of Ethnic Conflict Regulation*, ed. John McGarry and Brendan O'Leary (London: Routledge, 1993), 84–105.

16. See Subrata Mitra, "Desecularising the State: Religion and Politics in India after Independence," *Comparative Studies in Society and History* 33, no. 4 (October 1991): 755–77.

17. Alan Beals, *Gopalpur: A South Indian Village* (New York: Holt, Rinehart & Winston, 1963), 41.

18. Caste consciousness transforms caste from an ascriptive status to a politically convenient self-classification. For a discussion of the efforts to improve the material conditions of the former untouchables through the policy of reservation and the upper-caste backlash against it, see Subrata Mitra, "The Perils of Promoting Equality," *Journal of Commonwealth and Comparative Politics* 25 (1987): 292–312.

19. Lloyd Rudolph and Susanne Rudolph, *In Pursuit of Lakshmi* (Chicago: University of Chicago Press, 1987), 247, 255–58.

20. With the nomination of Rahul Gandhi, the son of Rajiv and Sonia Gandhi, as vice-president of the Congress Party in 2013 and presumably the Congress prime ministerial candidate in the general elections of 2014, India can look forward to five generations of Nehrus at the helm of the Indian politics.

21. The legal basis of the emergency rule of 1975–1977 has been the subject of an intense controversy. Most observers see this period as a breakdown in the democratic political system in India. See W. H. Morris-Jones, "Creeping but Uneasy Authoritarianism in India," *Government and Opposition* 12 (1977): 39–47.

22. President's Rule, under which a region is ruled directly by the center for a specific period, is indicative of a failure of representative government. It happened relatively infrequently during the first two decades of independence, with the imposition of the President's Rule eight times during the prime ministerial tenures of Nehru and Shastri (1950–1966). The most celebrated case was the dismissal of the elected Communist government of Kerala in 1959. It became more common during the governmental instability of the mid-1960s, with the imposition of the President's Rule eight times during the prime ministerial tenures of Nehru and Shastri (1950–1966). However, during the two periods of tenure of Mrs. Gandhi, the President's Rule was imposed forty-two times.

23. If the president of India is satisfied that a grave emergency exists whereby the security of the nation or of any part of the territory thereof is threatened, whether by war, external aggression, or internal disturbance, he or she may make a declaration to that effect (Article 352). While a proclamation of emergency is in operation, nothing in Article 19 "shall restrict the power of the state to make any law or to take any executive action" (Article 358). Article 356 makes similar provisions for the suspension of democratic government in a region. It should be pointed out that emergencies are conceived of as temporary, and the scope for legislative accountability is not altogether absent.

24. James Manor, who had earlier talked about the "deinstitutionalization" of India, has subsequently talked about the "regeneration" of institutions. See James Manor, *From Nehru to Nineties: The Changing Office of the Prime Minister in India* (London: Hurst, 1994).

25. Manor, *From Nehru to Nineties*, 13.

26. For a more detailed discussion, see Subhas Kashyap, "The Legislative Process: How Laws Are Made," in *Our Parliament* (New Delhi: National Book Trust of India, 1989), 121–56.

27. For a brief period during the last years of the presidency of Zail Singh, presidential assent became an effective instrument to delay legislation. But commentators on Indian politics have attributed this more to the personal pique of Singh against Prime Minister Rajiv Gandhi than to any explicit policy difference between them.

28. Such situations are not unknown in parliamentary democracies. But the French solution of "cohabitation" of a president and a legislative majority belonging to different parties or the

German "grand coalition" are not yet available, though they cannot be excluded in the future.

29. See Subrata Mitra, *Governmental Instability in Indian States* (New Delhi: Ajanta, 1978), for an analysis of the rapid rise and fall of governments in Indian States during the 1960s.

30. The Government of India ended a complex power struggle between two regulatory agencies, the Insurance Regulatory and Development Authority (IRDA) and the Securities and Exchange Board of India (SEBI), with regard to the right to regulate hybrid products that combine features of insurance and investment. The ordinance, promulgated in June 2010 by President Pratibha Patil, amended the Reserve Bank of India (RBI) Act, the Insurance Act, the SEBI Act, and the Securities Contracts Regulation Act to bring about clarity on regulation of Unit Linked Insurance Products (ULIPs). "ULIPs are a hybrid instrument that combines both insurance and investment. While the Securities and Exchange Board of India saw ULIPs as investment products and hence asserted its right to regulate those products, the IRDA treats them as insurance instruments." See "IRDA Will Regulate ULIP Scheme: Ordinance Promulgated to Make Necessary Changes in Law," *Hindu*, June 20, 2010, http://www.thehindu.com/stories /2010/06/20/st/2010060261022100.htm.

31. The survey was conducted through face-to-face interviews during May and June 1996, in the aftermath of the eleventh parliamentary elections. A representative sample of about 10,000 adults was interviewed under the guidance of the Center for the Study of Developing Societies (CSDS), Delhi.

32. S. K. Verma and Kusum, eds., *Fifty Years of the Supreme Court of India: Its Grasp and Reach* (Delhi: Oxford University Press, 2000), narrates this success story.

33. Commenting on a recent corruption scandal, *The Hindu*, India's highly respected mass circulation newspaper, comments, "Defence deals, done under the thick, dark cover of national security, are notorious for their lack of transparency. . . . Bofors is India's most famous defence scandal, with deep political and diplomatic ramifications, but it was neither the first nor the last in a long line of defence purchases that have become keywords associated with the stink of corruption in the public mind. Reports of bribery by the Italian defence firm Finmeccanica in the supply of 12 Agusta Westland helicopters for VVIP transport have thus come as no surprise. . . . Evidently, all manufacturers feel compelled to pay bribes disguised as commissions on a percentage basis to middlemen and lobbyists for obtaining supply orders from the Indian government." "Editorial," *Hindu*, February 16, 2013. See *Public Office, Private Interest: Bureaucracy and Corruption in India* (Delhi: Oxford University Press, 2001) by S. K. Das, a former civil servant, for a succinct analysis of bureaucratic corruption in India.

34. The central government is referred to as the *Union Government* and the Indian federation is referred to as a *Union of States* in Article 1 of the Indian Constitution.

35. Rudolph and Rudolph refer to the two phenomena respectively as "state dominated pluralism" and "involuted pluralism." See Rudolph and Rudolph, *In Pursuit of Lakshmi*, 259–89.

36. For a discussion on new social movements in India, see Gail Omvedt, *Reinventing Revolution: New Social Movements and the Socialist Tradition in India* (London: East Gate, 1993).

37. Subrata Mitra, *Power, Protest, and Participation: Local Elites and the Politics of Development in India* (London: Routledge, 1992).

38. See Subrata K. Mitra, Mike Enskat, and Clemens Spiess, eds., *Political Parties in South Asia* (Westport, CT: Praeger, 2004).

39. See Myron Weiner, *Party Building in a New Nation: The Indian National Congress* (Chicago: University of Chicago Press, 1968).

40. See Subrata Mitra, "Party Organization and Policy Making in a Changing Environment: The Indian National Congress," in *How Political Parties Work: Perspectives from Within*, ed. Kay Lawson (Westport, CT: Praeger, 1994), 153–77.

41. *Vertical mobilization* refers to political linkages that draw on and reinforce social and economic dominance. *Horizontal mobilization* takes place when people situated at the same social and economic levels get together to use their combined political strength to improve their situation. *Differential mobilization* refers to coalitions that cut across social strata. Lloyd Rudolph and Susanne Rudolph, *The Modernity of Tradition: Political Development in India* (Chicago: University of Chicago Press, 1967).

42. For the formulation of these ideas in terms of an analytical framework on elections and social change in India based on a model of electoral norms and organizational structures corresponding to them, see Subrata Mitra, "Caste, Democracy and the Politics of Community Formation in India," in *Contextualising Caste,* ed. Mary Searle-Chatterjee and Ursula Sharma (London: Blackwell, 1994), 49–72.

43. For an application of this concept as a framework for the discussion of political participation in India, see Subrata Mitra, "Room to Maneuver in the Middle: Local Elites, Political Action and the State in India." *World Politics* 43, no. 3 (April 1991): 390–413.

44. W. H. Morris-Jones, *The Government and Politics of India* (Wistow, England: Eothen Press, 1987), 58.

45. This theme has been developed further by Jyotirindra Dasgupta, "India: Democratic Becoming and Combined Development," in *Democracy in Developing Countries,* ed. Larry Diamond, Juan Linz, and Seymour Martin Lipset (Boulder, CO: Lynne Rienner, 1989), 62.

46. Morris-Jones, *The Government and Politics of India,* 61. The statement, first made in 1962, turned out to be prophetic, because J. P. Narayan became a rallying point for opposition to the emergency in 1975.

47. See Mitra, *Politics in India: Structure, Process and Policy* (2011), pp. 60–61, for a detailed discussion of the questions asked to measure efficacy and legitimacy, and the cross-tabulation of these with subpopulations. It is interesting to notice that minorities and former untouchables do not lag behind the sample averages.

48. Following allegations of irregularity in the northern Indian constituency of Amethi where Prime Minister Rajiv Gandhi was a candidate, the Election Commission, an independent body that supervises the conduct of polling, ordered new voting to take place. Thus, one can notice both the political will and institutional capacity at the systemic level to minimize the cases of electoral tampering.

49. V. S. Naipaul, *India: A Million Mutinies Now* (London: Heinemann, 1990). Examples of "wildcat strikes" in industries, protest action by individuals, and collective social movements are plentiful, and not restricted to any particular region or social class. The regularity of the use of these techniques and the attempt by the state to combine accommodation with repression in dealing with them have given these methods an almost institutional status. A recent report in the media is revealing. "India's government resolved to send paramilitary troops to break the blockade of Manipur, a State in the remote northeast. The rebellious Naga tribesmen, who had enforced the blockade, lifted it the next day. Sixty-five days without imported food or medicine had brought Manipur to the verge of collapse. The Nagas are agitating to change the State's boundaries." *Economist*, June 19, 2010, 8.

50. The percentage of women representatives in India's highest legislature is low in terms of absolute numbers but does not compare

too unfavorably to those in developed European democracies. Only 6 percent of the members of the then House of Commons of Britain were women in 1995. "United Nations Economic Commission for Europe," *Economist,* March 18–24, 1995, 33.

51. See Jaffrelot, *Rise of the Plebeians.*

52. Data from CIA World Factbook, https://www.cia.gov/library/publications/the-world-factbook/index.html, last accessed February 13, 2014.

53. World Bank, Database 2013, http://data.worldbank.org/indicator/SI.POV.DDAY, last accessed February 15, 2013. When using the $2 a day poverty line, the reduction in poverty looks less impressive, with 89 percent in 1978, 82 percent in 1994, and 69 percent of the population living in poverty in 2010 (World Bank, Database 2013, http://data.worldbank.org/indicator/SI.POV.2DAY, last accessed February 15, 2013).

54. See John Wall, "Foodgrain Management: Pricing, Procurement, Distribution, Import, and Storage Policy in India," World Bank Staff Working Paper no. 279 (Washington, DC: World Bank, 1978), 88–89.

55. The term usually implies the proclivity of the Congress Party regime to practice patronage politics. Liberalization has attempted to put an end to these practices by removing these areas of enterprise from the government control.

56. *Economist,* January 21–26, 1995, 7.

57. See Economist Intelligence Unit, "Country Report India, December 2009" (Kiel, Germany: Leibniz Information Centre for Economists), 19; and Economist Intelligence Unit, Views-Wire, "India Economy: GDP Growth Picks Up" (London: Economist Intelligence Unit, June 1, 2010).

58. Ajay Chhibber and Thangavel Palanivel, "India Manages Global Crisis but Needs Serious Reforms for Sustained Inclusive Growth," paper presented at the Tenth Annual Conference on Indian Economic Policy Reform, Stanford, California, October 22–23, 2009.

59. See Economist Intelligence Unit, "Country Report India, June 2010" (Kiel, Germany: Leibniz Information Centre for Economists), 17; and The Hindu Business Line, "India's Q4 Export Growth Highest among Top Economies," *Hindu,* June 5, 2010, http://www.thehindubusinessline.com/2010/06/05/stories/2010060552980400.htm.

60. See Historical Stock Prices of Sensex 30, e.g., at Yahoo Finance BSE Sensex 30, http://finance.yahoo.com/q/hp?s=^BSESN+Historical+Prices, last accessed February 13, 2014.

61. Ibid.

62. Chhibber and Palanivel, "India Manages Global Crisis," 33.

63. When asked in a national opinion survey in 2004 about the financial prospects they expected, 49.2 percent of the national sample thought their financial conditions would improve, 6.2 percent thought they would worsen, 19.4 percent thought they would remain the same, and about 25 percent were not sure. In the same survey, 67.5 percent thought their vote had an effect on how things are run in the country, compared with 17.5 percent who thought the opposite; see Center for the Study of Developing Societies, "National Election Survey" (Delhi: Center for the Study of Developing Societies, 2004).

64. Selig Harrison, *India: The Most Dangerous Decades* (Delhi: Oxford University Press, 1960), 338.

65. Conservative opinion in Britain was generally opposed to Indian independence before an acceptable solution to the communal problem between Hindus and Muslims was found. This cautious approach was criticized by some who cited the successful functioning of elected governments in eight out of eleven provinces after the 1937 elections held under the Government of India Act of 1935; see Henry Noel Brailsford, *Democracy for India* (London: Fabian Society, 1942).

66. These arguments are stated in detail by Subrata Mitra, *Culture and Rationality* (Delhi: Sage, 1999); and Subrata Mitra and V. B. Singh, *When Rebels become Stakeholders.*

67. Samuel Huntington, *Political Order in Changing Societies* (New Haven, CT: Yale University Press, 1968).

68. Seymour M. Lipset, "Some Social Requisites of Democracy: Economic Development and Political Legitimacy," *American Political Science Review* 53 (1959): 69–105. Lipset suggests that in order to succeed as a democracy, a society has to attain certain levels of social and economic development.

69. Huntington, *Political Order in Changing Societies,* 55.

70. The puzzle has a direct bearing on the pessimistic prognosis of Moore, *Social Origins.*

71. India's experience stands in sharp contrast to its South Asian neighbors. Universal adult franchise was introduced in Ceylon in the early 1930s, even before limited franchise was available in some Indian provinces. The Muslim League—which, under the leadership of Jinnah, championed the cause of Pakistan—became the ruling party in the new state after independence. Neither of the two states has been as successful as India in sustaining democracy. See Mick Moore, "Sri Lanka: The Contradictions of the Social Democratic State," and Hamza Alavi, "Authoritarianism and the Legitimation of State Power in Pakistan," in *The Post-colonial State in Asia: The Dialectics of Politics and Culture,* ed. Subrata Mitra (Hemel Hempstead, England: Wheatsheaf, 1990), 155–92 and 19–71.

72. There is considerable controversy among scholars regarding the causes and probability of Hindu–Muslim conflict. See Ashutosh Varshney, *Ethnic Conflict and Civic Life: Hindus and Muslims in India* (New Haven: Yale University Press, 2002), and Paul Brass, *The Production of Hindu-Muslim Violence in Contemporary India* (Seattle: University of Washington Press, 2003), for contrary views. Christophe Jaffrelot gives a graphic account of Hindu–Muslim riots in Gujarat in "Communal Riots in Gujarat: The State at Risk?" *Heidelberg Papers in South Asian and Comparative Politics,* 17 (2003), http://www.sai.uni-heidelberg.de/SAPOL/HPSACP.htm. Steven Wilkinson suggests a link between electoral competition and ethnic riots in India in *Votes and Violence: Electoral Competition and Ethnic Riots in India* (Cambridge: Cambridge University Press, 2004).

73. "Nothing in India is identifiable, the mere asking of a question causes it to disappear or to merge into something else." E. M. Forster, *A Passage to India* (Harmondsworth, England: Penguin, 1985; first published in 1924), 92.

74. The rise of lawlessness and the criminalization of politics have been observed by several scholars. See the epilogue in Morris-Jones, *The Government and Politics of India,* 259–72. The mass-circulation *India Today* talks about "the elevation of violence, defiant indiscipline, and lawlessness to a cult" everywhere in the country, "not just [among] the armed militants of the Jammu and Kashmir Liberation Front or the Khalistan Commando Force, but ordinary people, lawyers, policemen, shopkeepers, civil servants, students, trade unionists" as well. "Cult of Anarchy," *India Today,* August 31, 1990.

75. The emergency of 1975–1977, which is seen as an aberration of the political process in India, is a major landmark in the country's political development. For further information, see "Images of the Emergency," the theme of a symposium on the subject in *Seminar* 212 (March 1977); and P. B. Mayer, "Congress (I), Emergency (I): Interpreting Indira Gandhi's India," *Journal of Commonwealth and Comparative Politics* 22 (1984): 128–50.

76. See Mitra, *Politics in India* for a detailed analysis of this argument.

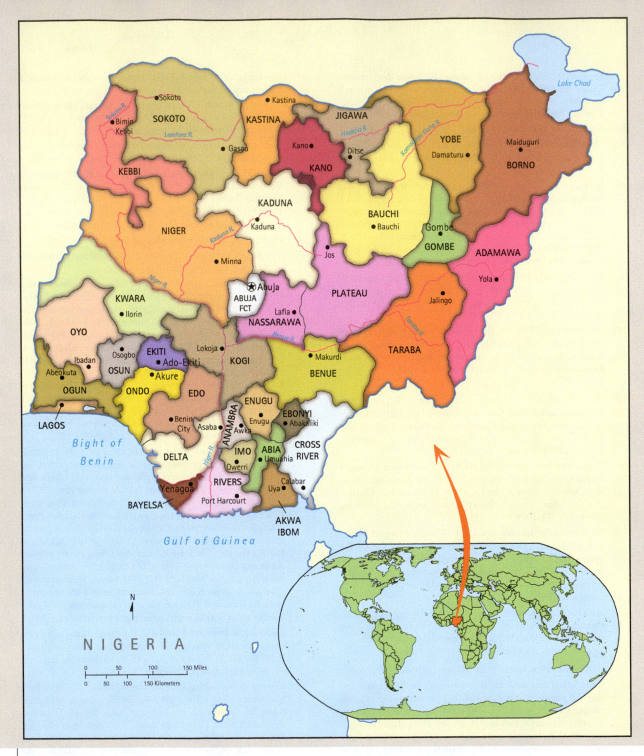

NIGERIA

0   50   100   150 Miles

0   50   100   150 Kilometers

Country Bio

POPULATION
166 million

TERRITORY
356,668 square miles

YEAR OF INDEPENDENCE
1960

YEAR OF CURRENT CONSTITUTION
1999 Constitution, based on the 1979 Constitution (including revisions drafted in 1995)

HEAD OF STATE
President Goodluck Jonathan

HEAD OF GOVERNMENT
President Goodluck Jonathan

LANGUAGES
English (official), Hausa, Yoruba, Igbo, and 250 other ethnic groups

RELIGIONS
Muslim 50%, Christian 40%, indigenous beliefs 10%

CHAPTER 18

Politics in Nigeria

A. Carl LeVan and Oladimeji Aborisade

LEARNING OBJECTIVES

18.1 Discuss the challenges faced by Nigeria as a new democracy.

18.2 Describe the fragmentary nature of Nigeria's political structure in precolonial and colonial times.

18.3 Discuss the contribution of colonial, environmental, and global factors to current conditions in Nigeria.

18.4 List the types of subcultures that exist in Nigeria, and discuss how they affect the political culture.

18.5 List four agents of political socialization.

18.6 Describe and compare the military and educational routes to political positions in Nigeria.

18.7 Explain the evolution of Nigeria's political structure and discuss national versus federal powers.

18.8 List five forms of interest articulation and contrast their strength in the north and south of Nigeria.

18.9 Describe the major parties and their bases of support, and discuss the checkered history of elections.

18.10 Discuss how factors such as oil and ethnic diversity impact economic performance

18.11 Describe the source and forms of Nigeria's influence in the region and the world.

In the African context, Nigeria is a megastate. Even on a world scale, Nigeria is a major country. Larger than France or Britain, it claims over one-fifth of the people in Africa and has the world's largest black population. Its petroleum and its substantial standing military force guarantee its prominence in international relations, and with 129 universities, Nigeria contains a large proportion of Africa's centers of learning and research.

For these reasons alone, one should know about Nigeria. But learning about Nigeria is also an efficient approach to learning about Africa, because Nigeria embodies much of the variety of African political experience within its borders. Its traditions include the large-scale emirates of the North and the small kingdoms and village-level republics of the South. Although both were administered by Britain, the

North and South of Nigeria experienced different versions of colonial rule. The problems and prospects of many African countries are found in Nigeria, but at a more daunting scale and level of complexity. Since independence in 1960, it has struggled with coups, civil conflict, and economic setbacks. Its dictatorships and democratic governments alike have struggled with ethnic politics and religious differences between Christians and Muslims.

Each country in Africa is clearly unique, but familiarity with the Nigerian experience is a good way to understand some common themes in the study of African politics. The colonial origins of the state meant that nationalists in the 1950s had to articulate a new narrative of nationhood, and even today, this shapes peoples' attitudes about the government. Independence in 1960 ushered in an era of unbridled, and perhaps unrealistic, optimism that soon faded. As in many countries in the 1970s and 1980s, a series of dictators promised that a strong leader could unite the country and overcome developmental failures. An economy dependent on a single export made the country vulnerable to changing commodity prices, and this led to massive foreign borrowing and unpopular economic reforms in the 1980s. Political liberalization and democratization in the 1990s brought down a brutal dictator and helped steer the country away from these troubles. But democracy remains highly imperfect, with recurring electoral fraud, political violence, and poor service delivery. Its economic growth in recent years has been significant but has not trickled down to the vast majority of the population.

This chapter explores economic, social, and political transformations in Nigeria, situating recent progress and ongoing challenges within broader historical and international contexts. For Nigeria and many African countries, whether new political structures, leaders, or policies can overcome historical legacies remains a central question of inquiry.

Current Policy Challenges

18.1   Discuss the challenges faced by Nigeria as a new democracy.

Nigeria is now enjoying the longest period of civilian rule in its history, but it faces failures of governance and ongoing challenges to constitutional authority that keep democracy in a precarious state. The country's ethnic, regional, and religious divisions have intensified in recent years. Leading political elites and some violent groups argue for breaking up the country into a weak federation or even completely independent states if political power and economic resources are not distributed more justly. Electoral violence, persistent inequalities, recent rebellions, and failures of government performance all contribute to popular skepticism about democracy.

The transition to democracy in 1999 began hopefully with the election of **Olusegun Obasanjo** as president and then a new democratic legislature a few weeks later. In 2003, President Obasanjo was reelected in a landslide, and his party also captured most other important political offices. A new president, **Umar Musa Yar'Adua**, was elected in 2007, but only after a failed attempt by Obasanjo's supporters to change the constitution to extend his stay in office another term. The constitution faced a fresh test when President Yar'Adua disappeared from public view after falling seriously ill in November 2009. After months of inaction, the National Assembly voted to appoint the vice president as acting president—even though it lacked explicit constitutional authority to do so. When Yar'Adua passed away in April 2010, Nigeria seemed to survive another test when Vice President **Goodluck Jonathan** was officially sworn in as president. The succession was also controversial because it transferred power from a northern Muslim to a southern Christian. When Jonathan won nationwide elections in 2011, a thousand people died in a sudden wave of violence, and many northerners were angry that the ruling party did not insist on keeping the presidency with the north.

Beyond these political tests, Nigerians remain frustrated with the failure of democracy to harness

Political Violence Reaches Abuja
Until recently, political and religious violence generally took place outside the capital. This changed in 2010, when MEND blew up the cars pictured here during a celebration on the anniversary of Nigeria's independence.

their country's wealth to provide basic human needs, education, potable water, reliable transportation, and communications. Power generation has actually declined since 1999, creating an expensive and difficult climate for private investment into the expanding economy. Income levels per capita are barely a tenth of the income in the United States or Western Europe; in 2013, the UN ranked Nigeria 153rd among the 187 nations in its Human Development Index. This is a slight improvement over recent years, moving the country into the bottom of the "medium human development" group. The failure to prosecute rampant corruption impairs economic development, and the country's ranking in the Corruption Perceptions Index, developed by Transparency International, declined in 2012. Nigeria now ranks 139th out of 176 countries due to inaction on dozens of major cases.

The current regime has thus far avoided the fate of previous attempts at democracy. But with poor government performance, persistent sectarian tensions along ethnic, regional, and religious lines, and struggling democratic institutions, the allure of authoritarianism has not entirely faded. In the discussion that follows, the reader should consider the historic and structural roots of the country's challenges as well as the evolving social values that inform political behavior. Whether the country consolidates democracy or reverts back to familiar and destructive political patterns depends upon some combination of principled leadership, civic activism, and sound institutions that inspire the confidence of citizens and investors.

The Effects of History

 18.2 Describe the fragmentary nature of Nigeria's political structure in precolonial and colonial times.

The concept of Nigeria dates to 1914, and since the name and the boundaries were imposed by colonial fiat, some dissident voices today refer to "the mistake of 1914" as a way of expressing frustration with regional differences.[1] Before we can explore the country's contemporary politics, and how it has survived despite bewildering diversity, this section considers the ancient roots of its many rich cultures. In a sense, then, there are many Nigerias. In what follows, we consider the political origins of distinct political cultures, and the varied colonial experiences of peoples from the north, east, and west of what is today Nigeria.

The Enduring Effects of Precolonial Events

Our images of precolonial Africa have been plagued by misunderstandings, sometimes in the form of simple ignorance but often as the result of prejudice. Many in the industrial world still view traditional Africa as "primitive," composed of a series of "tribes."[2] As we shall see from the case of Nigeria, even early civilizations organized at the village level developed complex systems of political limitations on their rulers. All these peoples interacted in trade, cultural diffusion, and war for many centuries before the creation of today's nation-states, and their belief systems were as complex and nuanced as any in the world. To reiterate, there was no single Nigeria a century ago. The **Hausa** people began forming city-states in northern Nigeria between 1000 and 1200 CE, and came under the influence of Islam no later than the fifteenth century. By the next century, mosques and Koranic schools were flourishing, and Hausa princes were international rivals of Morocco and the Ottoman Empire. The fortunes of these systems waxed and waned through the centuries, but they were decisively changed when non-Hausa court officials rose against them early in the nineteenth century. These officials were **Fulani**, a people with their origins in western Sudan who had entered the Hausa lands as herders and, more important, as teachers, traders, and eventually court advisors. A Fulani scholar and preacher, Usman dan Fodio, inspired a religious and political revolt against the Hausa kings. A Fulani-dominated caliphate was established in Sokoto, now northern Nigeria. This Fulani Empire controlled most of the North until the British defeated it in 1903. Sokoto retains its role as the Muslim religious capital of Nigeria to this day. The Hausa and Fulani cultures have become so intertwined, with extensive intermarriage and with Hausa the primary language of both, that the dominant culture of the North is usually referred to as **Hausa-Fulani**. The descendants of the rulers of the Hausa-Fulani kingdoms, identified by the Islamic title *emir*, continue to hold court in the major cities of northern Nigeria.

In the forest region of the southwest, the **Yoruba** and Bini peoples began forming kingdoms between the twelfth and fifteenth centuries at Oyo, Ife, and Benin. In the seventeenth and eighteenth centuries, the kingdom of Oyo subdued its rivals and extended its control over the entire southwestern part of Nigeria. These political systems developed intricate methods of limiting the powers of their rulers. For example, the ruler of Oyo, the alafin, was chosen by a council of chiefs. Historians believe that if the council felt the alafin had exceeded his powers, they could compel him to commit suicide. To ensure that the council did not abuse this authority, one of their members had to die with the alafin.[3] Other peoples inhabiting the land that now constitutes Nigeria organized themselves without kingdoms or states. For example, the **Igbo** communities in the southeast governed at the village or extended family level. "The political system is conciliar and competitive," explains one anthropological study. "Leadership is democratic in character, and the village government gives much latitude to the youth. It is *ability* rather than *age* that qualifies for leadership."[4] The Yoruba and the Igbo examples illustrate how accountability and limited government come in a variety of forms.

Because Nigeria was defined through the colonial experience, we must ask how and why the eventual British domination occurred. The immediate cause for British interest in West Africa was trade, and the first such international trade of any importance was in slaves. Coastal groups began exchanging captives for goods with European trading ships as early as the sixteenth century. Wars among the various kingdoms ensured a plentiful supply of captives, particularly in southwestern Nigeria. For the next 300 years, this trade was sustained: Benin, Lagos, Bonny, and Calabar thrived as slave trade centers, exporting upward of 20,000 persons per year to the Americas.

In 1807, the British Parliament outlawed the slave trade. In a remarkable turnabout, the British navy replaced British slave ships and began patrolling the West African coast to cut off the trade, which was not completely eliminated until about 1850. The established slave-trading patterns were gradually converted to other goods. British consuls established themselves on the coast and began to intervene in local politics, favoring those candidates for ruling positions who would give them commercial advantages over other European traders. The British succeeded in obtaining treaties of British protection and trade along the coast. These were treaties between unequals, increasingly favorable to the British as they established first commercial and then political control.

The Colonial Interlude (1900–1960)

In order to avoid war resulting from the competition for colonies, the great European powers met at the Conference of Berlin in 1884 and 1885 and divided Africa into spheres of influence. In effect, the European powers decided to seize control of the continent rather than merely trading with its rulers and merchants. In a wave of negotiations, imperialist wars, and conquests, their efforts were successful, and by the beginning of World War I in 1914, maps of Africa showed clearly drawn lines with areas color-coded according to the European power claiming control. Thus, in 1886, the Royal Niger Company was granted a royal charter to control Nigerian trade. That charter was replaced in 1900 by the creation of the Colony of Lagos and the Protectorates of Northern and Southern Nigeria. Like most Africans, Nigerians remain sensitive to this history of external interference. Indeed, the name "Nigeria" itself was coined by an Englishwoman who later married Sir Frederick Lugard, the architect of colonial Nigeria.

There was an unfortunate interaction between the colonial penetration and West Africa's natural environment: Cultures tend to be affected by climate and ecology, as people adapt differently to life in the rainforest, grasslands, or desert. In West Africa, the prevailing climate and ecological zones run east and west (see Figure 18.1). However, the colonial thrust was from the coast of the Gulf of Guinea inland, and colonial boundaries were established on the coast and then extended northward, intersecting the climate zones. This virtually guaranteed that the colonies thus established would be composed of peoples coming from vastly different cultures.

Nigeria first became an entity in 1914, when the Northern and Southern Protectorates and Lagos were brought under a single colonial administration. This unifying action was largely symbolic, however, as its two parts continued to be governed separately. The Northern and Southern Provinces replaced the Protectorates, each under a lieutenant governor. Northern Nigeria remained apart as such political structures as a legislative council evolved in the South. Northerners did not sit on the Nigerian Legislative Council until 1947. Indeed, the North proved to be the perfect setting for the "indirect rule" elaborated by the governor, Lord Lugard: The British administration would not intervene directly in everyday life in its colonies but would support the rule of traditional leaders,

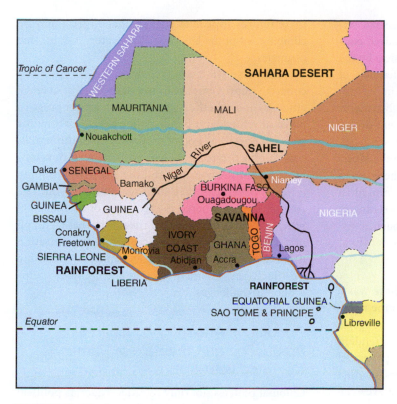

FIGURE 18.1

Political Boundaries in Tropical West Africa

The unification of Northern and Southern Protectorates into what is today Nigeria brought together peoples from vastly different climates, cultures, and histories.

such as the Fulani emirs. This, Lugard argued, was the most efficient means of controlling the colonies. As part of the understanding, the British also prohibited Christian missionaries from proselytizing in the North, a largely Muslim region. In southern Nigeria, Western-educated elites challenged the authority of the traditional rulers where they existed (as among the Yoruba); this complicated the strategy of indirect rule. In southeastern Nigeria, among the Igbo and other peoples, there really were no traditional kings or chiefs. Attempts to create village chiefs where the concept was unknown produced results that were sometimes comical and often tragic. As a result of these different traditions, the applicability of indirect rule served to distinguish further the political experiences of the regions.

The British colonial administration also faced the problem of incompatible objectives. In order to make the colony self-sustaining, Britain needed an export economy. However, the conversion of peasant societies from subsistence to a market orientation eroded the foundations of traditional rule. Except in the North, chiefs and kings had no traditional right to collect taxes, yet this became a central duty in the colonial system. Also, the development of a modern system of transportation and communication, necessary to stimulate commerce, encouraged the movement of people from the countryside to cities and from one part of the country to another, all under the protection of the colonial authorities. Urbanized populations and immigrants from other cultures could scarcely be expected to show deference to traditional rulers, nor did they see any good reason for paying taxes.

Along with commerce and administration, the British brought missionaries and education. Missionaries of many denominations—Anglicans, Presbyterians, Catholics, Baptists, Adventists, and others—brought the Gospels to Nigeria, although only to the South; the Northern emirates had an understanding with the British that Christian proselytizing would not be permitted in their domains. Christianity spread especially rapidly in the southeast and somewhat less so in the southwest; with it went formal schooling. As Nigerian children learned the English language and customs, they acquired the tools with which to challenge colonial rule on the rulers' own terms. However, the Western-educated elite that emerged came largely from the South. Thus, the culture is divided north and south along religious lines, but the difference has to do with much more than religion.

Modern constitutional development began within a few years of the creation of Nigeria as a single colony, with elective office first provided in 1922. An early nationalist leader, Herbert Macaulay, established a political party soon thereafter. As a Nigerian-centered political life grew up among the formally educated, other organizations arose, and the British colonial administration was pressed with demands for participation.

From then on, constitutions promulgated by various governors (and named after them) were always somewhat behind the expectations of Nigerian political activists. What southern politicians judged conservative, however, was usually seen as radical by the conservative elites in the North. These differences of opinion among Nigerians resulted in 1954 in the creation of a federal system of three regions: Northern, Eastern, and Western. A single ethnic group dominated each region: the Hausa-Fulani in the Northern, the Igbo in the Eastern, and the Yoruba in the Western. Under pressure from their leaders, the Eastern and Western Regions received self-government in 1957; the Northern Region became self-governing in 1959, a few months before national independence.

Nigerian Independence

As Nigeria approached independence, there was a general consensus that the nation should come to independence as a single country. Independent Nigeria was born on October 1, 1960. Nigeria's independent governments at the federal and state levels experienced a very short "honeymoon." Within two years, conflict had torn apart the ruling coalition in the Western Region. The next year, suspicions about the national census (as we will see later) destroyed what little trust there was among the regions. Finally, in 1965, law and order broke down in the Western Region over election-related fraud and violence, and the military ended the First Republic in a January 1966 coup.

Environmental Potential and Limitations

18.3 Discuss the contribution of colonial, environmental, and global factors to current conditions in Nigeria.

Nigeria has made great economic progress in recent years, pointing to a new wellspring of optimism. In terms of purchasing power parity (PPP), which controls for relative differences in the value of currencies across countries, Nigeria's per capita GDP was $2,533 in 2011, up from $1,130 in 2000. Its GDP grew on average 6.6 percent per year between 2001 and 2011. (We will discuss Nigeria's GDP later in this chapter; see Table 18.4 and accompanying text.) This constitutes a vast improvement over an earlier era, when per capita GNP actually declined by 1.7 percent annually between 1980 and 1991. At the aggregate level,

these figures appear to suggest that Nigeria may be climbing out of the UN classification for "low-income countries."

Yet these statistics translate into very limited concrete improvements in the daily lives of average citizens, and whether we can attribute progress to political reform and better policy decisions remains an open question. Policy options remain limited, in part due to the colonial legacy of uneven development within the country, and the Nigerian economy is highly dependent on a single commodity—oil. The country thus weathered the recession of 2008 to 2009 reasonably well, partly out of sheer luck that world oil prices remained so high. The economic diversification necessary to stabilize these gains requires overcoming a difficult physical environment and complex socio-economic challenges.

Conditions Affecting Agricultural Production and the Sale of Primary Commodities

Colonial policies not only retarded Nigeria's political development but also had profound, if mixed, effects on its economy. Since early in the colonial period, southern Nigerians have been producing cocoa, palm oil, timber, and rubber. The timber, sold mostly as tropical hardwoods for use in furniture and construction, came from the now-dwindling rainforests in the south. In the north, the principal market products were cattle, hides and skins, cotton, and peanuts.

The growth of trade in these commodities was not entirely spontaneous. The British interest in Nigeria was primarily commercial, with its origins in the United Africa Company (UAC). When the UAC was granted a charter as the Royal Niger Company in 1886, it was given police and judicial power, and it was authorized to collect taxes and to oversee commerce. Not surprisingly, its policies aimed at developing the Nigerian economy to be compatible with British needs. Also, public sentiment in Britain never solidly favored creating a colonial empire, and powerful voices in Parliament favored keeping the costs of the empire to a minimum. Colonial administrations were under heavy pressure to be self-sufficient—to develop local sources of revenue to cover their costs of administration. As a result, colonial administrators pressured peasant farmers away from subsistence agriculture and into commercial farming, particularly of export crops. Furthermore, cost-efficient marketing meant emphasis on just a few of the most needed products; in Nigeria (and elsewhere in West Africa), these turned out to be palm oil, cocoa, peanuts, and cotton. Thus, British demand for raw materials and the need to finance a self-sufficient colonial administration distorted the economy: Nigeria became dependent on the export of a small number of agricultural commodities, rather than creating finished goods profitable for domestic industry.

The combination of population growth and the commercialization of agriculture strained relationships between agricultural techniques and the ecology that had been in place for centuries. Colonial officials sometimes assumed that productivity could be greatly increased in tropical regions with the introduction of "modern" methods, without recognizing the different ecological conditions of production in a tropical setting. Lush tropical rainforest could not simply be replaced by plantations. Rainfall, temperature, and soil conditions meant that farming techniques effective in England or North America would be unsuccessful or even disastrous in Nigeria. Only gradually, and much later, were the efforts of agronomists applied to maximizing agricultural production in the tropics, especially to food production for local consumption.

Nigeria broke with some colonial economic development policies, especially the need to diversify production, because it offered a large, ecologically diverse environment. But the need for foreign exchange meant that agriculture continued to emphasize exportable commodities, even as investment capital was largely directed toward industrialization. Economists in both the industrial and Third World countries associated industry with prosperity, and agriculture was seen as the "cash cow" from which to extract savings for investment in other areas. Also, Nigerian government officials, trained in the need to balance budgets, balanced appropriations bills with overly optimistic estimations of "expected revenue." When these fell short, the difference was made up from cash reserves accumulated by the Central Produce Marketing Board, a government agency that purchased all the goods from farmers. However, "since those reserves were derived from the price differential between what was paid to the farmer and what the Board earned in export earnings . . . for close to a decade, Nigeria existed only through the exploitation of her farmers."[5]

In addition to keeping agricultural prices low to provide such reserves, Nigerian governments also tried to satisfy urban demands for cheap food by holding down the price paid to farmers in the domestic market. This action contributed to the unattractiveness of agricultural work and enhanced the lure of the cities.

Disease

Physical illness is a part of the human condition, and the higher disease rates of poorer nations are largely explained by the lack of resources to acquire medicines, medical facilities, and personnel. But environment contributes as well; some of the most common human diseases, including malaria, can survive only in tropical climates. In tropical Africa, virtually every long-term resident carries the malaria virus, and large proportions of the population are affected by it. It is usually not fatal, but it is extremely debilitating, and it has a documented effect on labor productivity. Various river-borne diseases also account for long-term illness and fatalities, contributing especially to the high mortality rate among children. As with agricultural problems, research can attack these diseases, yet a vastly disproportionate share of the world's resources applied to health problems is focused on ailments more common to the industrialized world. In recent times, AIDS has topped the list of the most dreadful diseases in Africa. The World Bank reported in 2013 that 3.7 percent of all Nigerians between the ages of fifteen and forty-nine were infected. This reverses a period of improvement in the mid-2000s, when the Obasanjo administration's commitments to fight HIV brought the rate down to barely 3 percent. In many African countries, the AIDS epidemic slows down national productivity and especially agricultural productivity because it requires so much labor effort.

Population Growth

Nothing is more striking to a visitor to Nigeria than the youth of the population. About 43 percent of the Nigerian population is less than sixteen years of age.[6] Children are considered a valuable resource in labor-intensive agricultural societies, and in a country with high infant mortality rates and no social security system, parents would be imprudent not to have enough children so that some would grow up to provide for them in their old age. This behavior becomes dysfunctional

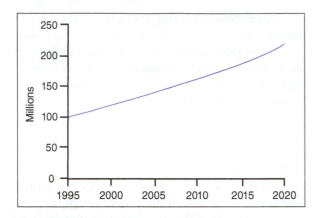

FIGURE 18.2

Nigeria's Projected Population Growth, 1995–2020

Nigeria has one of the most rapidly growing populations in the world, creating major development challenges.

Source: Based on Richard Sklar and C. S. Whitaker, Jr., "Nigeria," in Political Parties and National Integration in Tropical Africa, ed. James S. Coleman and Carl Rosberg (Berkeley: University of California Press, 1964).

at the societal level, of course, as increasing populations struggle to survive. Nigeria's life expectancy—estimated at 52 years in 2012—bears this out, since it is even lower than some of its poorer neighbors such as Benin.

Figure 18.2 illustrates the projected population growth through 2020. Between 1975 and 2000, the population of Nigeria grew an average of 2.9 percent annually. Even with a high economic growth rate of 6.6 percent since 2000, rapid population growth brings the figure down to only 4 percent in per capita terms. In this environment of rapid population growth and urbanization, children become economic liabilities. Thus, the "dependency ratio" (the proportion of nonworking population to working population) has steadily risen since the early 1960s, placing a great strain on the country's underdeveloped facilities for social welfare and education.[7]

Counting the population in Nigeria has always been controversial because of its implications for the distribution of resources and political districting. Protests and some violence followed the most recent official census in 2006, and there actually has not been a widely accepted census since 1963.

Urbanization

Nigeria shares a pattern of urbanization common in Africa: Although the country is still primarily rural,

it is urbanizing rapidly. Between 1970 and 1995, the share of Nigeria's urban population increased from 20 to 39 percent. The United Nations Development Program predicts that by 2015 an amazing 56 percent of the population will live in urban areas.

A number of factors are driving internal migration to the cities. For example, millions of people have flocked to **Abuja**, the federal capital. More than 60 percent of all government activity takes place there, and this means civil service jobs as well as large growth in the service sector. Abuja is also alluring because public services tend to be better in the capital; smaller cities typically offer inferior services. Migration is also caused through internal displacement. The National Commission for Refugees estimates that 3.2 million people were displaced by militant violence in the Niger Delta between 2004 and 2008, and floods in 2011 displaced another 480,000 people in several other states. More recently, Christians have been fleeing religious violence in the north. In an effort to discourage additional migration, big city governments often implement harsh policies, including the destruction of informal housing. Nearly 200,000 people were made homeless in 2010 in order to make way for the construction of a shopping mall in the southern city of Port Harcourt.[8]

Nigeria's largest city is **Lagos**, within the state by the same name. Lagos State recently reversed years of economic decline after increasing tax enforcement, attracting new foreign investment, and investing in infrastructure. Since it is one of the few states run by a governor belonging to the country's opposition party, many people are watching to see if good governance will have a spillover effect into other states.[9]

The population shift means that a smaller proportion of the labor force is available for agricultural work. That is a normal pattern of modernization, of course, but unless the productivity of agricultural workers increases, it means a drop in food production per capita. Urbanization also has political consequences, since dense living arrangements are conducive to organizing; this was in fact one reason for the military's decision to create Abuja as a new capital in an area with low population density.

Petroleum

Like the countries discussed in Chapter 7, Nigeria is a rentier state. The magnitude of Nigeria's petroleum reserves became apparent in the 1950s, with the first shipload of crude exported in 1958.

At independence, the federal government was collecting modest royalties from private Western oil companies. In 1971, within a few years of the Biafran civil war, Nigeria joined the **Organization of Petroleum Exporting Countries (OPEC)** and also formed a government entity to directly participate in oil production, the Nigerian National Oil Corporation (NNOC). Within a few years, the government had acquired a majority interest in all oil production activities. The NNOC was merged with the Ministry of Petroleum Resources to form the Nigerian National Petroleum Corporation. Over this same period (the mid-1970s), petroleum prices had risen dramatically, from $3.30 per barrel in 1972 to $21.60 in 1979. Thus, the sale of crude oil directly by the Nigerian federal government to multinational oil companies came to provide the greater part of federal government revenues and, through the federal system, of state and local revenues as well.

Nigeria was engulfed in a bloody civil war from 1967 to 1970, which brought a halt to oil exports. At war's end, however, Nigerian petroleum production began to boom, and it grew at a dramatic rate through the 1970s. Although such a valuable mineral resource is an asset to any country, its effects on Nigeria were not all beneficial. The country's economy became distorted by the great disparity of value between petroleum and the traditional agricultural products; soon, young workers were abandoning their farms and villages and flocking to the cities and the oil fields. Figure 18.3 shows that the source of Nigeria's hard currency shifted dramatically from agricultural products to petroleum in the early 1970s.

Oil revenues hit a peak in 1979. World demand for oil decreased each year from 1979 to 1983. At the same time, oil production in countries that were not part of OPEC, especially Mexico, Norway, and the United Kingdom, grew substantially. Nigeria's planners were slow to realize the implications of rising supply and stagnant demand. The glory days of seemingly limitless oil revenues ended abruptly in April 1982, when production of crude oil in Nigeria dropped from 2.1 million to 0.9 million barrels per day; oil export revenues fell correspondingly, from $1.35 billion to $0.7 billion per month. In the preceding decade, Nigeria had become dependent on oil revenues for imports

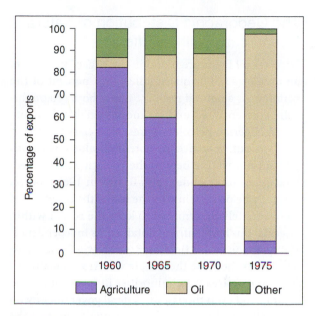

FIGURE 18.3

Composition of Nigerian Exports
With the decline of agriculture and the rise of oil exports, Nigeria's economy has become less diversified and in some ways more vulnerable.

Source: Peter O. Olayivola, *Petroleum and Structural Change in a Developing Country* (New York: Praeger, 1987).

and large-scale development projects. As was commonly the case in the Third World, Nigeria fell behind in its debt payments, which forced the government to impose unpleasant austerity measures. A further fall in oil prices in 1986 pushed the country into a severe recession.

Today, petroleum accounts for about 85 percent of export earnings. After world oil prices increased due to the Iraq War that started in 2003, Nigeria again began earning huge revenues. It applied some of this windfall constructively, for example, by paying down most of its foreign debt in 2006. This helped insulate the country from the effects of the global recession in 2008–2009. Some of the oil windfall has also stimulated economic diversification and new investment. Most notably, the service sector rose from 25 percent of the GDP in 2000 to 37 percent in 2011; wholesale and retail trade constitute half of this sector's growth, and communications (including the spread of cell phones) has also grown. Such encouraging trends have inspired the African Development Bank and some private investors to wonder if Nigerians are starting to cure the "curse" of oil.

The Geographic Distribution of Natural Resources: Political Effects

Nigeria's oil fields are found in the Niger Delta basin, an area of 43,500 square miles, or 8 percent of the country. As a natural resource that is both geographically concentrated and far more valuable than any other, Nigerian petroleum presents a classic problem for distributive justice. Its potential value was an important motivation behind the Eastern Region's declaration of independence as **Biafra** in 1967, and oil certainly helps explain why the rest of the country was so obstinately determined to keep the region within Nigeria. But had Biafra maintained its independence, the question of oil field ownership would not have gone away, because the people who traditionally inhabited that area were minorities in Igbo-dominated Biafra. And even though the federal government won the civil war, local peoples continue to protest the spread of oil wealth over the whole country while their land pays the price of environmental degradation from the oil operations.

As a result, bitter and violent combat has broken out among various youth organizations in the Delta. Protests organized by groups such as the Movement for the Actualization of the Sovereign State of Biafra (MASSOB) are testing Nigeria's commitment to democratic freedoms by resurrecting memories of the civil war. If these groups feel impeded from expressing themselves, though, they may become more militant. This seems to be the case with the **Movement for the Emancipation of the Niger Delta (MEND)**, which took dozens of foreigners hostage in protest over conditions in the oil-producing areas. Militant groups and numerous criminal gangs seeking profit engage in oil theft known as "bunkering," which cost the government at least $100 billion between 2003 and 2008. At the rebellion's peak in 2008–2009, as many as 300,000 barrels a day were lost to "blood oil" being used either to finance the rebels or to line the pockets of complicit government officials.[10] Since then, the rebellion has subsided, largely due to a government-sponsored "amnesty" that demobilized 25,000 young men, who turned in their guns in exchange for payments and job training. However, grievances remain, especially as many former rebels feel like elites benefited more from the amnesty than they did.

The six core oil-producing states of the "south south" geopolitical zone, however, are not the only part of the country where petroleum wealth has generated resentment. Just months after the amnesty took place, a new, even more violent rebellion took root in the northeast (see Box 18.1). The democratic regime has struggled to accommodate these various grievances through peaceful channels, and has increasingly resorted to violence to deter rebellion.

The International Environment

Nigeria, like most African countries, has been profoundly affected by its birth at the height of the Cold War, and by the sudden end of the bipolar war with the dissolution of the Soviet Union. During the Cold War, new nations were pressured to choose sides. The West and East granted foreign aid to developing nations as a reward for loyalty. Nigeria at independence was considered to be conservative and "pro-Western."

Many Nigerian intellectuals equated the West's capitalism with colonialism, however, which they contended continued after independence through **neocolonial** economic ties. Political discourse through the first thirty years of Nigerian independence was often based on the ideological poles of capitalism and socialism, and relationships with the major powers involved staking a position between the two camps. In the civil war that resulted from the Eastern Region's declaration of independence as Biafra in 1967, the Soviet Union sided with the Nigerian federal government, while the U.S. government attempted to maintain a neutral position, even though the Biafran cause was widely supported by Americans. Economics finally dictated Nigeria's international position: The West was best equipped to prospect for Nigeria's oil fields, and only the West had the technology to extract and market this natural resource. Thus, a close relationship developed between the Nigerian federal government and some of the world's major oil companies.

The end of the Cold War brought a new era to the relations between Nigeria (and other poorer nations) and the industrial world. The West's fear of the spread of communism had caused it to pay some attention to many poor, small countries, and it often led to the support of pro-Western dictatorships in countries such as Zaire (now the Democratic Republic of the Congo), the Ivory Coast, and Nigeria. By the 1990s, supporting tyrants didn't seem worthwhile in Third World countries that lacked significant resources or strategic value. This contributed to a common perception

BOX 18.1   Radical Islam's Challenge to Democracy

Nigeria is facing a new wave of violent attacks by Islamic extremists who have targeted churches, police stations, and even schools. They call themselves Jama'atu Ahlus-Sunnah Lidda'Awati Wal Jihad ("People Committed to the Propagation of the Prophet's Teachings and Jihad"), but they have become popularly known as **Boko Haram**, a phrase in the Hausa language that roughly translates to "Western education is sinful." According to data compiled by the Council on Foreign Relations, at least 3,000 people have been killed in the violence since 2009—with about half of those deaths caused by the heavy-handed use of force by police and the military. Most of the attacks have taken place in the northeast, but bombings killed dozens of people at the United Nations office in Abuja in 2011 and killed 200 people in the north central city of Kano in January 2012.

Boko Haram's ideology, goals, and tactics have evolved. It began as a devout, and relatively obscure, Muslim sect based in Maiduguri, Borno State, under the leadership of a charismatic Imam (religious scholar), Mohammed Yusuf, in 2002. A series of altercations with the authorities over the years, often over minor issues like traffic stops and funeral processions, escalated. A final showdown in July 2009 culminated with the capture of Yusuf by the military, and his immediate, public execution by the police. Human rights organizations have documented that about 800 people died in a sprawling conflict over several days. Since then, the violence has followed painful cycles of attack and retribution, leading some scholars and analysts to blame

that incident for the group's radicalization. In April 2013, the government attacked another village in Borno, and hundreds more people were killed in what has become known as the "Baga Massacre." Human Rights Watch caused a sensation when it broadcast before and after satellite photos of hundreds of burnt homes.

Boko Haram highlights several important phenomena about Nigeria: Even though its tactics are rejected by virtually all Nigerians, its support for Islamic law and its underlying critique of northern underdevelopment are actually within the mainstream political discourse. Many Nigerians see shari'a as an attractive alternative to a criminal justice system that has failed to reduce crime and is composed of laws disconnected from cultural traditions. But some interpretations of shari'a are harsh, such as cutting off the hands of thieves or punishing people for moral transgressions such as adultery. Christians, including an apparently growing number in the north, see shari'a as a threat to their faith and a violation of the secular compromises at the core of Nigerian constitutionalism. Boko Haram thus illustrates the complex relationship between north and south—two very different regions brought together by imperial fiat a hundred years ago, which sometimes struggle to find common cause. The sect's stronghold near the northeastern borders, and concerns about its possible links with global terrorist organizations such as Al Qaeda, also highlight how extremist ideologies (and weapons) can spread in a globalized world.

---

that Africa was being marginalized. The situation appears to be changing, as growing economies in Brazil, India, and China are seeking out African resources and investing in the continent. Trade increasingly accompanies aid, as well. For example, under President George W. Bush, between 2001 and 2008, overall trade between the United States and Africa tripled, and the United States committed billions of dollars of new foreign aid.

Nigeria shared in a common Third World experience following the oil crisis of 1973 as it accumulated massive international debts. A sudden boom in oil prices resulted in huge new deposits in the world's banks, which made credit plentiful. The military

governments of the decade failed to invest sustainably in infrastructure, and an overvalued currency led to inflation as elites bought imports that were now inexpensive. Borrowing to spend seemed to make sense to all sides until commodity prices collapsed. Third World debt mushroomed in the 1980s, and several governments defaulted. Nigeria's indebtedness grew from $8.9 billion in 1980 to $34.5 billion in 1991; by 1995, it represented 274.5 percent of the annual value of the country's exports and 140.5 percent of GNP. After the transition to democracy in 1999, President Obasanjo made debt reduction a high priority for his administration. By 2006, thanks in large part to earnings from the high price of oil, Nigeria became the first African country to pay off its Paris Club debt (from multilateral lending institutions), reducing its total debt by $30 billion. Economists are worried that borrowing is coming back: The Central Bank of Nigeria reported a 24 percent increase in debt between 2010 and 2011 alone. Like many developing countries, the temptation to borrow from anticipated economic growth is often too great to resist.

A final aspect of Nigeria's international environment is its regional context—West Africa. As an accident of colonial rule, Nigeria is entirely surrounded by former French colonies: Benin (formerly Dahomey), Niger, and Cameroon. Nigeria is increasingly a regional leader, participating in peacekeeping operations on the continent and exercising its influence in regional organizations such as the African Union.

An increasingly important feature of Nigeria's regional identity concerns the rise of radical Islamic groups. The rise of a group known as **Boko Haram** in the northeast since 2009 (see Box 18.1) has raised concerns about the spread of violent extremism across the Sahel—a vast region stretching to northern Africa. After the fall of the Libyan dictator Muammar Gaddafi in 2011, weapons found their way across the porous borders of this region, and some of them ended up in the hands of the Islamic radicals who took over northern Mali in 2012. In early 2013, the United States began building military bases in Niger, just over Nigeria's northern border. The Nigerian government shares Western concerns about terrorism, though the security services' heavy-handed tactics are controversial with human rights activists and those concerned about civilian control of the military.

Political Culture and Subcultures

18.4 List the types of subcultures that exist in Nigeria, and discuss how they affect the political culture.

The political culture of Nigeria is extremely heterogeneous and complex. Analysis of it must take into account a Western value system overlaid on those of its various precolonial traditions; it must assess the impact of a variety of religious beliefs and of the continuing effects of Christian and Muslim proselytizing efforts. Since the colonial experience have come new divisions based on social class and on the different experiences of urban and rural dwellers. The whole range of modern political ideologies is found among the belief systems of the politically active population. Here we will give greatest attention to the political implications of ethnic identity, religious beliefs, social and economic status, contact with urban life, and civil society.

Public Education to Encourage Farming
As the oil boom drained the rural workforce, signs urged Nigerians to return to agriculture.

Ethnic Identity

Because of the geographic separation of ethnic groups, Nigerians can be easily identified based on language and cultural traits. These groups vary tremendously in size, and only three of them—the Hausa, Igbo, and Yoruba—are particularly numerous and influential in the country's politics. The influence of these three major groups is a cause of great concern to the remaining minority groups. Because there has been a high degree of geographical separation of ethnic groups in Nigeria (a result of the country's policies during and since the colonial period), Nigerians can easily identify the origins of their fellow citizens by observing their dialect (or accent in English), their manner of dress (if it is traditional), and, in some cases, "tribal marks," patterned facial scars that formerly were created as part of rites of passage to indicate ethnic identity. There are also differences in wealth and political awareness.

In the absence of a widely accepted census, the size of Nigerian ethnic groups can only be estimated. Approximately one-half of the country's population is in the north, and about one-fourth each in the southeast and southwest. The Hausa represent about two-thirds of the north's total population, the Igbo about two-thirds in the east, and the Yoruba about two-thirds in the west. Thus, other groups represent about one-third in each region and one-third overall. Here we will briefly consider the three largest groups.

Hausa-Fulani The Hausa-Fulani people live mostly in the northern half of the country. As noted earlier, this hyphenated identity came from the imposition of Fulani rule over the Hausa population in the nineteenth century. The two cultures became intricately intertwined, although they have never become completely homogenized. Thus, the term "Hausa" is often used as a short form of "Hausa-Fulani." "Hausaland" actually straddles the border to the north between Nigeria and Niger , a former French colony, and the people in these two countries maintain many cultural and commercial ties. A greater proportion of Hausas engage in subsistence agriculture and live in rural villages than is true of southern Nigerians. There are sizable Hausa communities in cities all over Nigeria, where they carry on trade and commercial activities while maintaining kin and client relationships with their home region. The vast majority of Hausas are Muslim. The Hausa heartland is itself still organized as a series of emirates: Each of the major cities in northern Nigeria is the seat of an emir, one of the kings through whom the British applied their indirect rule. There is no official role for the emirs in modern Nigeria, and their unofficial role is hotly disputed, even in the north. Yet they retain great influence in their localities and, through Hausa prominence in national politics, in the rest of the country as well.

Igbo The Igbo (also spelled *Ibo*) occupy the southeastern part of the country, from the banks of the Niger River east. Most of the region is developed for market agriculture, with Igbo farmers growing palm products,

rice, and yams. The Igbo people lived in politically independent, socially endogamous villages, usually no larger than 8,000 people, and did not have a sense of common Igbo identity until the colonial period.

The Igbo are known for the fervor with which they adopted Western culture. Although the encounter with British colonialism was a wrenching shock forcefully described in Chinua Achebe's novel *Things Fall Apart*, the Igbo responded enthusiastically to Western education and the missionaries who brought it. They used new skills and knowledge to seek advancement in modern commerce and civil service. Igbo people also emigrated widely throughout the country and seem less concerned than other groups with maintaining separate communities where they are "strangers." (In Nigeria, the term "stranger" refers specifically to a person living outside his or her "home" community.) They are employed on the basis of their education and modern skills in all parts of the country, including the north.

Igbo officers led the first military coup in 1966, and thousands of Igbos living in northern cities were attacked and killed in reaction to that coup. The Igbos retreated to their home region. The next year, they followed the call of one of their own, Lieutenant Colonel Odumegwu Ojukwu, in the secession from Nigeria of Igbo-dominated Biafra. The three-year civil war that ended in the defeat of Biafra in 1970 caused great hardship, but within a few years, Igbos were again active in commerce across the land (they were by then generally barred from government work in other localities). Nevertheless, the Biafran experience and the civil war left long-term mistrust between the Igbos and other Nigerians.

Yoruba The Yoruba live mostly in the southwestern part of Nigeria, including the sprawling metropolitan area of Lagos, the former federal capital. Traditionally subsistence farmers, rural Yoruba people began growing cocoa and palm products for export in the colonial period. Although they share a common language, traditional religion, and myths of origin, the precolonial Yoruba were divided into a number of independent and warring kingdoms that give them separate identities today. The Yoruba have a long tradition of commerce, and both men and women are prominent in trade networks and markets throughout West Africa.

The Yoruba kingdoms were marked by complicated institutions that balanced power between an *oba* (king) and lineage chiefs. In their effort to impose indirect rule, the British upset these structures by supporting the obas against all challengers. In the process, the obas frequently became autocratic and lost much of their legitimacy with their own people; their influence in contemporary politics varies greatly but is generally much less than that of the northern emirs.

Because the Yoruba had, on the one hand, a highly stratified society complete with kings but were, on the other hand, quite receptive to missionaries and their schools, they are often seen as being in an intermediate position between the stratified and change-resistant Hausa and the egalitarian and innovative Igbo. In their sometimes strident assertion of their identity and interests, they also have provoked their share of mistrust among other Nigerians.

Given the ethnic-based strife so common in the world today, it should not come as a surprise that group identities are deeply rooted and emotionally charged in Nigeria as well. Ethnic rivalries often have their roots in precolonial warfare and are frequently refreshed by economic rivalries. While nationalism may serve as a cement where the feeling is shared by a country's entire population, the same feeling at a subnational level can destroy a political system.

Because the major ethnic groups are regionally based, political issues affecting such groups are often defined geographically, and Nigeria has preserved a sense of permanent attachment between a people and its "traditional" homeland to the degree that it is more difficult to become a "citizen" of another state in Nigeria than it would be for a Nigerian to acquire citizenship in many foreign countries. Discrimination against "non-indigenes," referring to people who may have migrated into a given state decades ago, has been regularly linked to tensions and sometimes serious violence, even during the current democratic regime.[11]

Multiple ethnic identities even at the local level have had a fragmenting effect on political structure. Particularly since 1976, there have been numerous disputes over the site of local government headquarters, with the "loser" often petitioning the state and federal governments for a division of the local government area. The conflict between the Ife and Modakeke in Oranmiyan local government is but one of many examples that could be cited. Local ethnic conflict affects policy outputs as well, where local governments

build health centers or markets that are not used by some ethnic groups, thus throwing off planners' projections.

Religion

Each of the groups identified in the previous section had traditional religious institutions and beliefs in place long before the arrival of Christianity and Islam. In some cases, these earlier beliefs have maintained their vigor, especially among many Yoruba. However, the missionaries brought their religion with formal education in the southern regions; most major Christian churches are well established in the south, and indigenous Christian sects have split off from them in a myriad of denominations. Not surprisingly, the Christian denominations themselves tend to be geographically and ethnically concentrated, with a higher proportion of Roman Catholics among the Igbo, a Baptist concentration among the Yoruba of Ogbomoso, the Evangelical Church of West Africa predominant in Igbomina and Kwara State, and so on. A significant proportion of Yoruba—perhaps half—are Muslim. Under the agreement between the colonial administration and the northern emirates, Christian proselytizing was barred from the north; except for the "strangers" living there, almost the entire population is at least nominally Muslim, and the Hausa bring their religion with them when they move south. This movement is offset by the establishment of churches in northern cities by immigrants, mostly from the south.

Missionaries built and staffed the great majority of schools during the colonial period. Thus, the north–south education gap, with its effect on political awareness, attitudes toward civil rights, and the like, itself derives from the prohibition of missionaries in the north. There is, then, an overlay of religion on ethnicity that intensifies the north–south cultural split, and the case can be made that the most sensitive issues now involve religion rather than ethnicity. These overlapping cleavages are more dangerous because they accentuate regional differences. Because some fundamentalists among Christians as well as Muslims have found it unacceptable to live in a pluralist society, those seeking a basis for political stability in Nigeria must be sensitive to finding a balance between the two major faith groups, which each constitute about half of the population. Religious harmony has been elusive, though, when additional factors accent these cleavages. In the 1980s, the Maitatsine Islamic movement, composed largely of young men marginalized by the socioeconomic changes, rioted against the Christian presence in northern Nigeria (as well as against police repression), with loss of life estimated in the thousands. Not long after, southerners vociferously protested when President **Ibrahim Babangida** proposed in 1986 that Nigeria join the Organization of the Islamic Conference (OIC), a group of more than fifty predominantly Muslim countries. Shortly after the 1999 transition, Nigeria experienced a new wave of ethnic and religious tension. Riots between Christian Igbos and local Muslims in the northern city of Kaduna left hundreds dead in brutal violence. The sensitivity over Islam in Nigeria was highlighted again in 2002, when the Miss World beauty pageant took place in Abuja. A newspaper suggested that the contestants were so beautiful that the religion's founding prophet would have chosen one of them. Over two hundred people died when tensions between Christians and Muslims flared up.[12] Overall, it was reported in 2010 by the Human Rights Watch that at least 13,000 people had been killed since 1999.

The return of democracy has possibly contributed to the heightened religious and regional identities. Surveys in 2008 reported that nearly three-fourths of Nigerians say they belong to religious associations, and half of Nigerians describe themselves as active members. Support for Islamic law is widespread, especially in the predominantly Muslim north—although there is tremendous variation regarding its meaning, and how to implement it. Sometimes this has contributed to fundamentalism, as with the Maitatsine movement or with the Izala movement (an abbreviation for the Society for the Removal of Heresy and Reinstatement of Tradition). Christians have also mobilized against the implementation of Islamic criminal law in the north. Organizations such as the Christian Association of Nigeria have opposed these changes as violations of Nigeria's constitution. A core challenge for democratic consolidation is thus balancing these regional identities with a sense of Nigerian nationhood, and also resolving ongoing questions about the state's relationship to religion.

The Evolution of Nigerian Nationalism

All of our preoccupation with Nigerian subcultures should not obscure the fact that the British colonial administration was responding to Nigerian nationalist forces when it granted independence in 1960. There were three major sources of nationalist sentiment. The first was a small number of freed slaves from North America and others of African descent from the Caribbean who settled on the West African coast and developed a culture unrelated to any of those indigenous to the country. Second, nationalist fervor grew out of the experience of Nigerians who fought for the British in World War II and felt frustration at the lack of recognition of their service. A third category of nationalists consisted of those Nigerians who studied in England and especially in the United States, including one of the most prominent among them, **Nnamdi Azikiwe** (see Box 18.2). Although they came from a variety of ethnic backgrounds, in their quest for independence, these activists developed a sense of

| BOX 18.2 | The Story of Nnamdi Azikiwe |

Although an Igbo, Nnamdi Azikiwe was born in Zungeru in northern Nigeria in 1904. He received his basic education in Nigeria and then went to the United States, where he studied at Lincoln University in Pennsylvania, Stores College in West Virginia, and the University of Pennsylvania. He also worked in the United States as a coal miner, laborer, and dishwasher. Upon his return home, he joined the Nigerian Youth Movement. His interest in self-rule led to his presence at the founding of the National Council of Nigeria and the Cameroons (NCNC) and to his founding of a pro-self-rule newspaper, the *West African Pilot*. He then moved to the Gold Coast (now Ghana), where he published an article, "Has the African a God," which resulted in a sedition charge. He won his case on appeal and went on to serve as the premier of the Eastern Region and, from 1963 to 1966, as president of Nigeria. He died in 1996 at the age of ninety-two.

Nigerian nationalism and succeeded in forming cross-ethnic alliances.

Civil war also stimulated Nigerian nationalism. The two military coups before the Biafran war were clearly ethnic in their origins. However, the Biafran conflict brought together a military force that was cross-ethnic (excluding, of course, Igbos, who were at the heart of the Biafran succession).

A study of Nigerian political culture must focus on orientations toward national (federal) political institutions. Nigerians oriented toward public political activities can be identified by (1) exposure to formal education and (2) involvement in the modern economy. As concerns interest in public policy, many Nigerians, particularly in rural areas and in the north, may be less engaged in issues of general political concern. Yet they still have to deal with local government officials on issues affecting themselves and their families. In Nigeria, as elsewhere in Africa and the Third World, such concerns are likely to be handled through personal-interest contacting. In most cases, such contacting is part of a *clientelist* arrangement: Citizens go to an individual who is politically influential for help and expect to "pay" for help through a long-term arrangement that may include payment in kind (as in bribes), or by turning out to vote when asked to do so, even while remaining uninterested in politics. Political activity is widespread and virtually all-embracing; interest in public affairs is strongly conditioned by education and employment.

Democratic Norms and Values

In order to assess Nigeria's chances for achieving political democracy, we must first consider the distribution of norms that might support democratic institutions. The legitimacy of opposition, manifested as tolerance for criticism, opposition, and competition for control, is an obvious prerequisite for stable democracy.[13] The history of political activism in Nigeria since 1960 suggests problems, even under democratic civilian regimes. As single parties gained control in each region, opponents were treated very roughly, with armed thugs hired to disrupt their meetings and attack their leaders. Harassment of political opposition by the government still occurs, and incumbents often use their positions to gain unfair advantages.

Since the military's exit in 1999, the number of Nigerians who describe the country as democratic

(42 percent) has declined. Yet strong norms in favor of democratic governance have emerged. In 2008, for example, 72 percent of Nigerians agreed with the statement "democracy is preferable to any other form of government." Such information suggests a wide gap between demand for and supply of democracy, and implies a good deal of disillusionment about current government performance.[14]

The Political Role of Women

Because of Nigeria's ethnic diversity, the position of women varies considerably. In Igbo, Yoruba, and other southern Nigerian traditions, women had considerable control over their own affairs in what anthropologists label "dual-sex" systems. That is, there were parallel systems of political and social organization for men and women. Scholars of colonial history contend that women lost most of their autonomy under colonialism, because British custom at the time gave women less control of their own affairs than did the African societies they controlled.

In the north, Islamic custom greatly restricts women's roles in society. Although Hausa women have considerably more freedom than their counterparts in the Middle East, including significant roles in local production and trade, they generally were not allowed an active political role at the time of independence. Northern women voted for the first time in 1979.

The contemporary involvement of women in political leadership is similar to that of many countries; in most parts of the country, Nigerian women vote in equal numbers with men but are generally underrepresented in politics. The modest gains that women initially made in the initial years after the transition have had some setbacks. The 2007 elections brought twenty-six women to the 360-seat House of Representatives and nine women to the Senate (out of 109 seats). After the 2011 elections, these figures declined to only twelve in the House and seven in the Senate. Men still hold a vast majority (perhaps as much as 90 percent) of the elected and appointed positions. Women are even more poorly represented in state governments, and there are sharp regional disparities. For example, not a single woman was elected to the state houses of assembly in any of the six states in northwest Nigeria.[15]

Political Corruption

Pervasive corruption has been a problem ever since the late colonial era, and it manifests itself on all rungs of the social ladder. Police frequently ask for small bribes at checkpoints along the road, and civil servants sometimes demand "expedition" fees. The huge sums of money that passed through officials' hands as a result of the oil boom greatly aggravated the problem; unprecedented forms of flagrant corruption appeared when oil revenues began to fill the federal treasury of General Yakubu Gowon in the early 1970s. His military governors spent large sums on openly lavish lifestyles, thus tarnishing the image of the military, which had supposedly come to power in reaction to the corruption of the First Republic. The coup against Gowon in 1975 was a direct result, as was the assassination of his successor, General Murtala Muhammed, in 1976.[16] **Sani Abacha** and his family in the 1990s channeled enormous sums of money from petroleum revenue accounts into their private accounts. As part of its campaign to promote transparency in government and fight corruption, the Obasanjo administration successfully recovered $2 billion from the Abacha family.

Since the return of democracy in 1999, the National Assembly has removed several leaders, including a Speaker of the House who directed public funds to remodel her houses. In 2002, the National Assembly passed the **Economic and Financial Crimes Commission (EFCC)** Establishment Act. Its purpose is to "prevent, investigate, prosecute, and penalize economic and financial crimes." Crimes within its jurisdiction include money laundering, Internet fraud, bank fraud, bribery, and misuse of public funds. The EFCC was often accused of selective prosecution of the president's political enemies. For example, it launched an investigation of Vice President Atiku Abubakar in 2006, when he was running for president. The Commission's critics suspected that the charges were brought because Abubakar had opposed President Obasanjo's efforts to amend the Constitution so as to make him eligible for a third term in office.[17]

During President Yar'Adua's brief tenure, EFCC prosecutions virtually ground to a halt, and the United States suspended some of its technical assistance out of concern for the EFCC's integrity. Anticorruption investigations have produced very few high-level convictions, with the notable exception of former governor James Ibori—though he was successfully prosecuted in Britain after he mysteriously escaped from custody in Nigeria. The blame for corruption needs to be shared, too: In 2010, the American oil contractor Halliburton paid $35 million in a settlement with the U.S. Department of Justice regarding improper payments to Nigerian officials.[18]

The EFCC commissioner during Obasanjo's administration claimed credit for recovering over $5 billion and successfully prosecuting eighty-two people. This record gave him some grassroots appeal, and, in 2011, he ran for president. Though he received a small share of the vote, his campaign got noticed for energizing young people fed up with corruption. New political constituencies demanding integrity, and experienced civil society activists, may be gaining traction.

Political Socialization

18.5 List four agents of political socialization.

Nigerians develop their political beliefs and attitudes through the influence of socialization "agents," such as the family, religious organizations, primary and secondary groups, formal education, the media, and government-sponsored activities.[19] A caveat is necessary, however, when comparing the political socialization process in Nigeria with the established liberal democracies. Political socialization in the developed world occurs through fairly stable institutions. We treat the fluidity of party alignments in France or events such as the Vietnam War in the United States as exceptional, whereas in Nigeria, people have grown up under political arrangements that shift constantly, even to their very core. Add to this the upheaval of urbanization and the sudden and dramatic impact of petroleum on the culture and the economy, and the need for a different perspective on socialization is apparent. Nevertheless, there is a universal quality to the importance of the agents of socialization we have identified, even as the nature of those institutions and the objects of political attitudes and values they shape may differ greatly from those in Europe or North America.

The Family

The family, whether nuclear or extended, remains the core unit of political activity in Nigeria. In many Nigerian traditions, families are identified with a particular trade or role in society. Thus, among the

Yoruba, a family of warriors is called *Jagunjagun*, farmers are *Agbe*, and traders are *Onisowo*. To traditionally minded Nigerians, such identification remains important to the determination of one's appropriate role in modern politics.

Many Nigerians have grown up in polygamous families.[20] There is no law preventing a man from taking more than one wife, although Muslims are theoretically limited to a maximum of four and Christians of mainstream denominations to one. All indigenous traditions in Nigeria accept polygamy, and little stigma is attached to the practice. Some Christian denominations in Nigeria enforce monogamy only on those men who hold office in the church.

The large family units that result from polygamous households and the broader definition of family give kinship special political importance. A politician may be able to count on the support of literally hundreds of actual kin, and even larger numbers if one considers clan affiliations based on a sense of kinship even where exact genealogical ties cannot be demonstrated. Kinship provides the most powerful sense of identity and loyalty to many in Nigeria and elsewhere in Africa, and it is the model (and often the real-world basis) for clientelist relationships.

Schools

In most contemporary nations, schools play a central role in developing a sense of community. This is clearly an important mission in Nigerian schools, and balancing various loyalties is a delicate task for Nigerian educators. Also, formal education is one of the principal benefits Nigerians expect from government. The school certificate is highly regarded throughout the developing world as a means to economic and social advancement, and this is especially true in Nigeria.

As Nigeria approached independence in the 1950s, the two southern regions invested massively in expansion of their educational systems, especially at the primary level. There is a broad consensus that primary education should be free and universal. Beyond that basic agreement, however, Nigeria has struggled with how to shape the curriculum and how to make it available.

There was only one university in 1948 and five in 1962. The oil boom of the 1970s stimulated a massive wave of secondary and postsecondary school expansion, even though, amid this prosperity, there was a lack of properly trained instructors at all levels. Today, there are 129 universities, including 41 new private universities created since the 1999 transition; the higher-education system also includes 75 polytechnics and colleges of technology and of education. Corruption has touched the higher education system too: in 2013, an EFCC investigation helped shut down 41 universities operating illegally.[21]

Enrollment rates in Nigerian universities doubled every four to five years in the 1960s, 1970s, and 1980s. They slowed somewhat in the 1990s but increased after the 1999 transition to democracy. Between 2005 and 2010, the primary enrollment rate declined from 67 to 57 percent, while the secondary school enrollment rate increased from 34 to 44 percent. However, equal access has remained illusory for years, and the problem becomes more acute as one moves from the primary to the secondary and then postsecondary level. The bias is, on the one hand, socioeconomic—children of the elite occupy a disproportionate share of the enrollments—and, on the other hand, reflects gender. Between 2005 and 2010, enrollment of girls unfortunately declined at the primary level, from 62 percent to 54 percent, but it increased at the secondary level from 31 to 41 percent of all students.

Another important disparity exists between the north and south.[22] There have been indirect political effects of the education gap across regions. As the number of secondary graduates increased in the south, many of them sought jobs in the north and were embittered by rejection. At the same time, northerners grew alarmed at the prospect of being inundated by educated southerners. Differences in educational achievement thus contributed to the resentments that exploded in violence in 1966. Today, northern political dominance in the face of higher-educational achievement in the south continues to aggravate interregional political conflict. Since 2009, the radical Islamic group Boko Haram (see Box 18.1) has said they wanted to cleanse northern Nigeria, which is "polluted by Western education."[23]

Language is an aspect of community building that is often taken for granted, but language usage in school can have a major impact on political attitudes. As noted previously, English is the official language of Nigeria and remains the vehicle of instruction in Nigeria from primary school through the university. Furthermore, English is the language of government and, for the most part, of the mass media. Because

English is a second language in most Nigerian homes, school plays an especially critical role in enabling access to the political system.

As a nation-building effort, the three major indigenous languages—Hausa, Igbo, and Yoruba—are also taught through secondary school and are topics in the Senior School Certificate Examinations. Proficiency in English is required for admission to a university, where the local languages are used only in programs where they might specifically be required. The connection between English usage and government activities gives added weight to the usual relationship between education and political efficacy.

Whatever the effect of intentional socialization in the schools, studies of political culture invariably affirm the effect of education on political participation. This is particularly true in less-developed countries, where the cultural gap between those with and without formal education is especially great.

The Mass Media

The presence of a lively and politically independent press goes back at least to Azikiwe's *West African Pilot*. By the time of independence, a considerable number of competing newspapers existed in Nigeria. The political effect of the press is naturally limited in a country where one-third of the adults are illiterate. A 2008 survey found that only 25 percent of Nigerians get their news from newspapers at least a few times a week. But that same survey reported that 57 percent of Nigerians are somewhat or very interested in public affairs.

Most Nigerians still get their news from radio, and 58 percent of Nigerians list television as a source of news at least once a week. For decades, radio and television were state-controlled media and were therefore faithful purveyors of the government's perspective on political events. After 1999, citizens enjoyed a variety of new choices through exposure to independent stations, satellite news, and dozens of new privately owned newspapers. While few Nigerians can afford computers, Internet cafés are common and inexpensive in cities, thus increasing access to other independent news sources.

The authoritarian regimes imposed a substantial number of restrictions on the media. According to the Center for Free Speech, a Nigerian watchdog organization, the military issued twenty-one decrees between 1966 and 1995 limiting press freedoms or even proscribing particular publications outright. There was a high level of tension between military governments and the press, and the life of a journalist was not easy. Many journalists were arrested, and,

Graduation at the University of Ibadan
At the time of independence, the University of Ibadan boasted modern structures and a 100,000-book library. After years of decay, the government is trying restore the university to its previous elite status.

in 1986, a prominent critic of the government was killed by a letter bomb.

The 1999 Constitution reversed many media restrictions instituted under the previous military rulers. Although it guarantees broad freedom for the media, journalists can still face criminal punishment for defamation of public officials, and a 1999 decree requires them to be accredited by a government-run media council. In addition to occasional government harassment, journalists also face great risks. Three journalists were killed while covering riots in 2010, and Boko Haram killed one reporter in Maiduguri in 2011, claiming he was a spy. Even though press freedom corresponds with formal democracy, some journalists and bloggers have had to flee the country for their safety.[24]

The State

Nigerian political attitudes are far more likely to be affected by everyday contact with the state than by the state's direct, intentional efforts to shape attitudes. In Nigeria's federal system, direct contact comes largely through local officials. Rural residents without English language proficiency find that, even at the local level, officials are much more educated than they and generally expect and get deference. Government is remote and must be approached through some form of informal mediation. For those with formal education, contact with local government is relatively simple; furthermore, because Nigerian policy is to hire civil servants from their home areas, there is neither a social nor a cultural difference between the educated citizen and the public servant. Nigerians expect to pay for expeditious service, and while they are aware of norms of honesty and ethics that are higher than the behavior they perceive, they are not scandalized by the difference. Perceptions of policymakers are not usually the result of direct contact.

Nigerians generally express great cynicism about the motivations of policymakers at all levels, civilian or military, but for the most part, this results from media accounts of venality and corruption. Whether through direct contact or media portrayal, they most often get what they expect from governmental officials.

One would expect that the unhappy experience with military rulers would leave Nigerians cynical and disillusioned. There certainly have been such effects, but there is a remarkably abiding faith in the

importance of politics, especially among the educated. There is an impact here of the oil economy. Profits from the sale of petroleum have flowed through the central government, so that the stake in access to those in government, especially at the top, is high. For many intellectuals, however, the knowledge that important resources will be distributed through the government is offset by the uncertainty of the outcome of any attempt to become involved. They tend, thus, to leave the political field to a collection of seasoned politicians, those who have assembled a voter base every time a regime has offered the prospect of new elections.

Political Recruitment

 Describe and compare the military and educational routes to political positions in Nigeria.

All the chief executives of Nigeria since independence are identified in Table 18.1. Several features of Nigeria's political leadership stand out. The population of the north and south is roughly equal, and this has promoted a general expectation that neither region should rule the country for too long. But the composition of government has not always reflected such balance. During the decolonization era, northerners were underrepresented in the civil service but dominated the military's officer corps. In the early years of independence, a military career lacked prestige, especially among more-educated southerners. In an effort to speed the replacement of remaining British officers, the Balewa government actively recruited university graduates into the officer ranks. One result was the introduction of large numbers of educated Igbos into officer ranks; another was the politicization of the army.

The first coup leaders in 1966 professed great regret at the necessity to intervene and promised that their stay would be temporary. They were removed and killed in the second 1966 coup before their sincerity could be tested. General Gowon's regime prosecuted the civil war and then went on to lay a constitutional framework for civilian rule. When Gowon seemed inclined to settle in for the long term, he was overthrown, and General Obasanjo set and abided by his 1979 deadline. Thus, through the first period of military rule, although there was serious profit taking on the part of many military leaders, none of them expected to have long-term political careers.

TABLE 18.1
Nigerian Chief Executives, 1960–2013

Dates	Name	Title	Ethnicity	Cause of Departure
1960 to Jan. 1966	Tafawa Balewa	Prime Minister	Hausa-Fulani (north)	Coup (killed)
1963 to Jan. 1966	Nnamdi Azikiwe	President [appointed]	Igbo (east)	Coup (removed)
Jan.–July 1966	Agusi Ironsi	Military Head of State	Igbo (east)	Coup (killed)
July 1966–1975	Yakubu Gowon	Military Head of State	Tiv ("Middle Belt")	Coup (removed)
1975–1976	Murtala Muhammed	Military Head of State	Hausa-Fulani (north)	Coup (killed)
1976–1979	Olusegun Obasanjo	Military Head of State	Yoruba (southwest)	Handed power to civilian government
1979–1983	Shehu Shagari	President	Hausa-Fulani (north)	Coup (removed)
1983–1985	Muhammed Buhari	Military Head of State	Hausa-Fulani (north)	Coup (removed)
1985–1993	Ibrahim Babangida	Military Head of State	Gwari (north)	Forced out of office
Aug.–Nov. 1993	Ernest Shonekan	Interim Head of State [appointed]	Yoruba (southwest)	Forced out of office
Nov. 1993 to June 1998	Sani Abacha	Head, Provisional Ruling Council	Kanuri (north)	Died in office
May 1998 to May 1999	Abdulsalami Abubakar	Head, Provisional Ruling Council	Gwari (north)	Handed power to civilian government
May 1999 to May 2007	Olusegun Obasanjo	President	Yoruba (southwest)	Civilian-to-civilian transfer
May 2007 to April 2010	Umar Musa Yar'Adua	President	Hausa-Fulani (north)	Died in office
May 2010 to present	Goodluck Jonathan	President	Ijaw (south south)	—

Source: NCNC: National Council of Nigeria and the Cameroons; AG: Action Group; NPC: Northern People's Congress.

When the military controlled the country again between 1983 and 1999, an officer's commission came to be seen as the most regular path to political power. This second round of military power produced a gradual change in the perspectives of at least some military officers. Many observers have wondered about the military leadership's annulment of the 1993 presidential election results and the abolition of state and local elective offices already filled. Most feel that if the presumed winner, Moshood Abiola, had been allowed to assume power, he would have been unable to deal effectively with the country's problems, would quickly have lost an already dubious legitimacy, and would thus have prepared the way for a return of the military with acceptance by the population. As it was, the Abacha regime faced massive resistance and was able to rule only on the basis of force, at least in much of the south. Many observers assume that Abacha's actions, while certainly supported by elements in the north that could not stomach a Yoruba president, also reflected the strong desire of a new generation of

military officers to enjoy the fruits of power that come from oil revenues and from the potential profits that flow from the corruption of public office. The country witnessed open jockeying for positions as state governors or "chairmen" of local governments, which were allocated according to military rank. National-level offices were usually filled by generals, brigadiers, or colonels; state governors were mostly colonels; and local chairmen were lieutenant colonels and majors, often retired from active service. Politics in Nigeria is still largely a game of money; therefore, the retired military, business groups, and some retired civil servants dominate the elective positions, while a few academics have political appointments, like minister, commissioner, or in the foreign service.

Today, there are more routes to professional advancement than simply joining the military, and education has arguably become more important. Nigerian universities produce large numbers of trained public administrators, and they follow long-term careers in federal, state, or local administration that usually are not affected by changes at the top. By the time of the 1979 transition, 89 percent of the bureaucrats at the assistant secretary or permanent secretary level held university degrees.[25] An appropriate educational level had come to be expected in the civil service. This is not to say that the civil service offered a stable career; an estimated 11,000 administrators were removed when Murtala Muhammed came to power in 1975 and took vigorous action against corruption. But to the degree that the administrative system continues to function through the many regime changes, it does so because of the permanence of the civil service.

Recruitment into political positions at the local and state levels generally excludes "strangers," even though they may be long-time residents of a community and, of course, Nigerian citizens. There are some exceptions: Where "strangers" are sufficiently numerous, they can run and win. In most places, however, regulations have expressly limited candidacy to indigenous candidates. In addition to simple democratic fairness, the advantage of creating a multiethnic council is that it stimulates identity and participation in the community on the part of populations that are otherwise excluded. An important characteristic of recruitment into political or administrative office, however, is the effort to "reflect the **federal character** of Nigeria" faithfully. In practice, this has become Nigeria's own version of affirmative action, which fills government positions with regard to identity. This reduces fears of political exclusion by attempting to ensure that government is an ethnic microcosm of the locality or state it controls.

Appointments of military personnel to government posts to reflect federal character seemed to make sense in the past, as Nigeria strove for national integration in the postindependence years. Ethnic politics still very much dominate the politics of Nigeria. But the virtue of appointing people based on identity rather than strictly merit remains controversial. Shortly before he passed away in 2013, the novelist Achebe called federal character "morally bankrupt and deeply corrupt."[26]

Political parties, the National Assembly, and other federal institutions also make appointments based on Nigeria's six geopolitical zones. After all, it is easier to distribute appointments on the basis of six units rather than thirty-six states. Some politicians even want to rotate the presidency on the basis of a "zoning" arrangement, which would require the office to rotate automatically among the zones, so that every major group could have a turn. Like federal character, though, this has also been challenged since the democratic transition, because qualified and experienced people eventually have to be rotated out in order to fill the position with someone from another zone. The National Assembly proposed similar constitutional reforms in 2001, and again in 2012, but this customary practice has yet to be formally enshrined.

Political Structure

18.7 Explain the evolution of Nigeria's political structure and discuss national versus federal powers.

Before we can assess—or perhaps appreciate—Nigeria's political structure, it is critical to understand the instability that preceded the current "dispensation," as Nigerians frequently refer to regimes. After a tumultuous postindependence history with five successful coups, three civilian constitutions, and Babangida's annulment of the 1993 elections, the country seemed to heave a sigh of relief when Obasanjo was sworn in as president in 1999. It is thus important to evaluate the mixed democratic progress since then, bearing in mind the 2003 elections and the country's first peaceful transfer of civilian authority in 2007. After decades of constitutional fragility and failures of previous constitutional arrangements discussed in this section, the shortcomings of the Obasanjo, Yar'Adua, and Jonathan administrations may start to sound like small setbacks outweighed by the relative stability experienced by the political system under their stewardship.

The first political institution in which Nigerians participated as Nigerians was the legislative council mandated by the Clifford Constitution of 1922, which provided for elected representatives from Lagos. Elections were introduced in this way and stimulated political activity. Through successive constitutional changes in the 1940s and 1950s, elective office was extended to local and regional governments, and the first provisions for a federal structure were introduced.

Because of the numerous military interludes after independence, constitution drafting and large-scale reform efforts almost seem like a regular part of politics. Nigeria adopted new constitutions in 1963, 1979, and 1989, and a prolonged debate in 1995 took place during Sani Abacha's dictatorship. The 1995 draft was widely discussed as the basis for election procedures in 1997 and 1998—yet the document was only officially promulgated by a transition government in May 1999, following the mysterious death of Abacha.

The Development of the Constitution of 1999

From 1983 to 1999, politics in Nigeria took the form of a succession of military regimes that constantly planned a return to democracy. The current constitution is the culmination of a successful transition that enshrined various political bargains. Many believed that Moshood Abiola, a Yoruba from the southwest, won the 1993 presidential election, a view buttressed by preliminary results released by the electoral commission and then by the Campaign for Democracy (CD). Babangida annulled the election and postponed the return to democracy, and the country erupted in protest. A short-lived interim government took over in August, but the country remained volatile. General Sani Abacha staged a coup in November 1993, and, like his predecessors, promised a return to civilian government. When Abiola declared himself president in June 1994, with the support of many civil society groups, he was arrested and charged with treason.

Abiola died in prison in August 1998, only three months after Abacha died, which many Nigerians see as an entirely improbable set of events. With the democratic heir apparent gone, and the military in disrepair after Abacha's brutal regime, political elites moved quickly to draft a constitution based on the 1979 version. The public played virtually no role in this process, and this has encouraged marginalized groups to question the Constitution's legitimacy. After all, it was decreed, unlike most transitions since the 1990s, which approve new constitutions by popular referenda. Groups such as MOSSAB and MEND often talk about the need for a "sovereign national conference" that would draft a new constitution from the grassroots. However, the Constitution has also lasted longer than any other, and this durability does generate some loyalty to it. The overall structure of the current Constitution is outlined in Figure 18.4.

Federalism

In a country as vast and complex as Nigeria, many political decisions are not made at the national level. A federal system was established in 1954 as Nigeria prepared for independence. Each constitution since then has embraced federalism in principle as a means of reassuring the nation's many ethnic and regional interests. In the face of formal federalism, however, stands a fiscal condition that calls the federal concept into question: All levels of government derive the largest portion of their revenues from oil, distributed through the national government. Beyond this fiscal fact of life, the military has governed Nigeria for a majority of the time since independence: twenty-nine years since 1960. It is difficult to define federalism under a military chain of command. As political activists in the south have become convinced that northerners are bent on dominating any central government in Nigeria, they have argued for greater state or regional autonomy. Moreover, with the emergence of militant groups, such as MEND and Boko Haram, the federal government has had to confront visible and violent movements that want greater local control.

State-level politics has often been dominated by local ethnic rivalries, as states are called upon to settle local government boundary disputes and to decide on the competence of various traditional institutions. Pressures analogous to those at the local level have led to an expansion of the number of states. The three colonial regions, which became the states of federal Nigeria, quickly became four. With the outbreak of civil war in 1967, the country was divided into twelve states, a number that was increased to nineteen in 1976, to thirty in 1991, and to thirty-six in 1996 (plus the Federal Capital Territory; see Figure 18.5). The number of local government areas within the states has progressively increased, too, with different ethnic or subethnic groups vying for representation.

Federal character is one tool for dealing with these tensions at the national and local levels, since it guarantees various ethnic groups a proportionate share of civil service positions. This is an application of the consociational model, a common solution where countries are deeply divided by religion or ethnicity.[27] If appointments were made on competence alone, the educational advantage of the southernmost populations would result in their having a disproportionate share of civil service jobs. Federal character is thus widely accepted as a means of integrating the government and building confidence among disparate groups.

The constitution establishes a three-level federalism. In such other large federations as the United

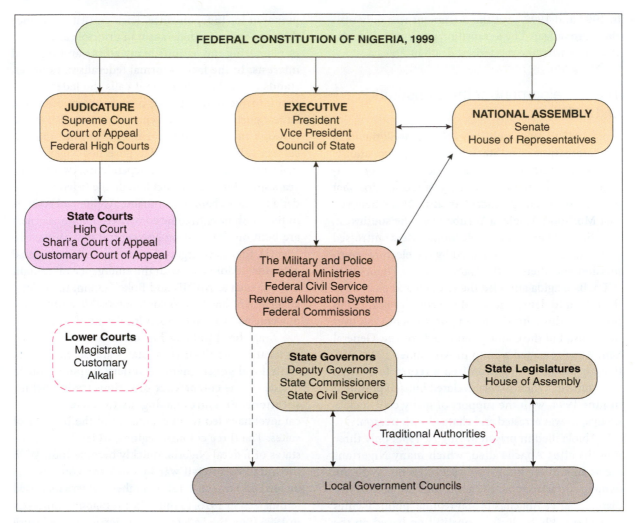

FIGURE 18.4
The Structure of Government under the 1999 Constitution
Nigeria has a presidential system with a bicameral legislature.
Source: Based on United Nations Development Program, Human Development Report 2009.

States, Canada, and Australia, the constitution focuses on the federal–state relationship, with local government principally in the domain of the state or province. The fact that Nigerian constitutions have specified a uniform structure and common functions for local government is rather unusual. While there are no doubt advantages to this uniformity of structure and function, it does not allow for local governments to reflect the diversity of local cultures present in the country, nor is experimentation possible of the sort that has produced the manager and commission systems at the local level in the United States. Since colonial times, however, local government has really been little more than local administration of federal policy, a situation unlikely to change until local governments acquire independent sources of revenue. Clearly, in an oil-centralized system, the demand for local governments cannot be explained by the control of decision making. Rather, ever more local government is attractive because of the formula-driven allocation of funds that supports local activities. In 1981, the Second Republic's National Assembly decided to allocate 10 percent of federal revenues and 10 percent of state revenues to the localities. However, not only were state governments unwilling to abide by this mandate, they also frequently tapped for their own

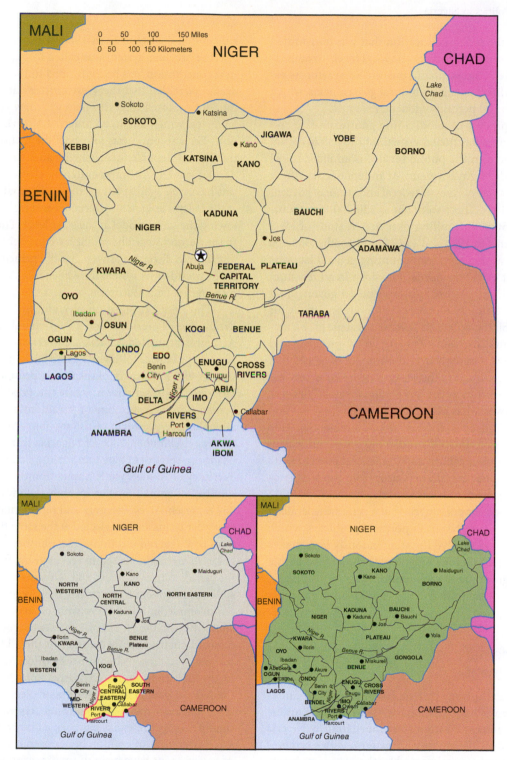

FIGURE 18.5

The Creation of States, 1960–1996

Factors driving the creation of new states have been demands from minority groups seeking distinct representation and the revenue allocation system of federal grants.

Note: Lower left: Dark border (lower left map) shows original three regions, increased to four by the creation of the Midwestern Region, and to twelve in 1967. Lower right: Nineteen states, 1976–1991. Above: Thirty states, 1991–1996. (Current thirty-six states are shown at the beginning of the chapter.)

purposes the federal allocation that was transmitted to them for distribution at the local level. To address this problem, subsequent constitutional reforms established direct payments to local governments, which now receive 20 percent of federal revenues.

The process of subdividing administrative and political units has fueled growth of the public sector. Employment in the public service is an indicator of the growth of government. At independence, there were 71,693 employees of federal and regional government; by 1974, there were about 630,000, not counting the 250,000 in military service. A study of local governments in 1978 and 1979 found another 386,600 positions at that level, not counting general laborers or district or village heads. The drop in oil revenues in the mid-1980s brought an end to government growth.[28] Since 1999, competition among states for the distribution of federal revenues is acute in two arenas: first in disagreements between the president and the National Assembly over the amount of money that should be returned to the oil-producing areas, or what Nigerians refer to as the "derivation formula." Second, the controversy has played out between the states and the federal government in a series of major Supreme Court decisions in 2002 concerning states' entitlement to offshore oil revenues and the federal government's right to exempt certain expenses from funds distributed under the derivation formula.

Some observers suggest that a genuine federalism would help cure Nigeria's political problems, which almost always involve the tremendously large stakes in the oil-rich nation's federal government. Perhaps a national government with limited resources would result in a federation that is not viewed as a high-stakes zero-sum game.

Parliamentary versus Presidential Government

Without exception, British colonies came to independence with a parliamentary system based on the mother country's Westminster model. Initially, Nigeria followed the Commonwealth pattern, with a ceremonial governor-general named by the British monarch. In 1963, the formal structure was redesignated a republic, with Nnamdi Azikiwe as president with mostly ceremonial powers; the parliamentary system was maintained, with a prime minister as head of government. Because Nigeria's first experience with civilian

rule ended disastrously in 1966, it is not surprising that the previous system was called into question as a new constitution was being framed in the 1970s. The drafters decided that the Westminster parliamentary model promoted majority rule with few checks and balances, which alienated much of Nigeria's population. Their solution was to model the Constitution of the Second Republic unabashedly after the U.S. presidential model: An independently elected president was balanced against a two-house National Assembly at the federal level, with governors and legislatures following the same model at the state level. The disorder in the Second Republic might have brought presidentialism into disrepute as well, but the principal aspects of the presidential system have been maintained in the more recent constitutions.

The 1999 Constitution provides for an independently elected president and a dual-chamber National Assembly at the federal level. Governors and single-house legislatures follow the same basic model at the state level. The Speaker of the House presides over the House of Representatives, while the president of the Senate, who is in the line of presidential succession after the vice president of the republic, presides over the upper chamber. Each of Nigeria's thirty-six states has three senators (plus one for the Federal Capital Territory of Abuja), while population determines the number of constituencies in each state for a total of 360 representatives. Senators and representatives serve four-year terms and are elected at the same time, rather than in staggered elections. The number of standing committees has increased in recent years, fragmenting the jurisdiction over issues and often making it impossible for members to carry out their responsibilities. For example, in 2010, there were eighty-six standing committees in the House of Representatives! Members demand chairmanships because of the additional resources, benefits, and power they offer. As permitted by the Constitution, the Executive Branch introduces the federal budget and other major pieces of legislation, and how much the National Assembly can or should modify these bills has been a hotly contested issue. Differences of opinion between the two branches of government have been dramatic, even though the president's party has consistently enjoyed a majority in both legislative chambers since 1999.

Nigeria's problems with achieving stable constitutional rule have made it an important case study in arguments over the relative advantages of presidentialism compared to parliamentarism in conditions of cultural pluralism. On the face of it, the fault may seem to lie with defects in the various constitutional frameworks, but the problem may actually be the intractable nature of Nigerian pluralism. A constitutional document by itself cannot promote trust among the country's subcultures.

The Judiciary

Nigeria came to independence with a well-established legal system that included a court system and a thriving legal profession in the British tradition. The federal and state courts are integrated into a single system of trial and appeal courts. Thus, the 1999 Constitution provides a Supreme Court, a Court of Appeal, and state and federal High Courts with original and appellate jurisdictions. Traditional authorities maintain their greatest influence in their judicial powers, as states are explicitly allowed to constitute customary and *shari'a* (Muslim Koranic law) courts, both original and appellate. A dozen northern states maintain shari'a courts, a point of contention between Muslim authorities and those who see such official recognition as divisive.

Successive military regimes undermined the judiciary as the country's dictators ruled by decree, often whimsically. Abacha seemed to deliver the final blow to judicial independence because his government had little inclination to respect the legal system. It reacted to court orders by changing the rules and establishing special military tribunals, even for common crimes such as robbery.

Interest Articulation

18.8 List five forms of interest articulation and contrast their strength in the north and south of Nigeria.

There are at least two aspects of political influence in Nigeria. First is the effect of organized interest groups, such as unions and trade associations and religious bodies. The second involves the more informal channels of participation through individual relationships often described by the term "clientelism."

The activities of formal associations and institutions often offer the most vigorous expression of societal independence from a government. Characteristically, voluntary associations were either brought under control or abolished in the authoritarian regimes

that took hold in Africa soon after independence. This was not, however, the case in Nigeria, where even during military regimes, organizations such as the Nigerian Women's Union have maintained an independent existence, even as their political influence was reduced.

Ethnic and Religious Associations

Many of the first formal associations in Nigeria had an ethnic base. For example, the Igbo Federal Union later became the Igbo State Union, formed by eastern intellectuals.[29] The Egbe Omo Oduduwa was organized among young, urban, Yoruba professionals. Minority groups especially found comfort in formal associations such as the Ibibio State Union, the Edo National Union, the Urhobo Renascent Convention, and others. These associations often formed the organizational base for parties and contributed to the latter associations' ethnic orientations. In the north, where individual clientelist ties are relatively stronger, associations even of the ethnic type have played less of a role.

An ethnic association of contemporary significance is the Movement for the Survival of the Ogoni People (MOSOP), founded by **Ken Saro-Wiwa**. MOSOP claims to speak for the 500,000 Ogoni people whose land is now occupied by Shell Oil drilling rigs. In the 1990s, the Ogoni complained that they bore the brunt of the inconvenience of Nigeria's oil industry and received little in return. Tensions reached a peak when four Ogoni chiefs were murdered by young militants. Saro-Wiwa and fourteen other Ogonis were arrested and charged with murder for inciting the youths. In a blatant frame-up and an example of how Abacha's government undermined the courts, he and eight codefendants were summarily convicted in 1995. This shocked world leaders and highlighted the deplorable state of human rights in Nigeria. The South African leader Nelson Mandela, himself recently released from prison, said at the time, "General Sani Abacha is sitting on a volcano, and I am going to make sure that it blows up under him."[30] In November, the Ogonis were hanged, despite pleas of clemency from around the world. Saro-Wiwa's legacy remained sensitive, and it was not until 2002 that the federal government allowed the families to exhume the bodies of Ken Saro-Wiwa and the others for a proper burial.

As in many other countries, religious institutions and associations play an important part in Nigerian politics. These groups are especially durable and resilient because when political activity is repressed, they remain organized around denominational objectives, and, where an ethnic association might have to play a less obvious role, neither Christian nor Muslim religious groups and leaders find it necessary to camouflage their identities. As in other countries, religious-based interest groups take several forms: the formal institutions (churches, Koranic schools); leadership roles such as bishops, pastors, and *mallams* (Muslim teachers and learned men); and voluntary denominational associations. The effectiveness of religious institutions in articulating concerns to government has been reduced by intergroup conflicts, most frequently between Christians and Muslims, which put the government in the role of mediator.

Not surprisingly, associational life is most active in the south. With migration to the cities, community self-help organizations with membership based on ethnicity have grown, since they offer tools to help new arrivals adjust to urban life. However, the north is home to an Islamic "mystic brotherhood," the Tijaniyya, which is particularly influential among lower-class Hausa Muslims and is looked on with suspicion by the representatives of orthodox Islam (another brotherhood, the Khadiriyya, is identified with the traditional elite of the north). The existence of such groups blurs the distinction between "modern" associations and "traditional" institutions. A new breed of ethnic organizations has emerged under democracy, with groups such as the Arewa People's Congress, which declares its mission as "defending northern interests," and the Odua People's Congress, militating for its version of Yoruba interests in the southwest.

Associational Groups

Voluntary associations in Nigeria take a variety of forms. Much of their early history is intertwined with the nationalist movements, while their modern history is closely related to a social movement for democracy in the 1990s. Professional organizations—such as the Nigerian Bar Association, the Nigerian Medical Association, and the Nigerian Union of Journalists—were often harassed during the era of military rule, and this contributed to their politicization and rising demands for democracy.

Trade unions have played a role in Nigerian politics since the colonial period. University students and faculty were some of the earliest critics of military

rule. Strikes by staff and students remain common today; it is not unusual for a student's undergraduate education to take six or seven years! Certain sectors of the workforce tend to have a disproportionate impact on politics when they undertake a labor action. In particular, unions representing the petroleum workers hold great sway because oil is so important to the national economy. Strikes by the National Union of Petroleum and Gas Workers (NUPENG) and the Petroleum and Natural Gas Senior Staff Association (PENGASSAN) were instrumental in pressuring the military government in 1994. Other labor actions are organized collectively through the **Nigeria Labour Congress (NLC)** and its affiliated unions. Since 1999, the NLC has led protests for better wages and working conditions, and it has been a persistent critic of recurring government attempts to eliminate a subsidy that keeps the price of fuel artificially low. If the economy continues to grow and diversify, Nigeria will likely see a proliferation of new unions and professional associations. When the "Occupy" movement camped out on Wall Street in the United States in 2011–2012, sister organizations with ties to labor popped up in Nigeria and other African countries.

Civil society groups such as the National Democratic Coalition (NADECO) and the CD were at the forefront of the struggle for democracy. After Abacha died in 1998, a new coalition, the Transition Monitoring Group (TMG), emerged as an advocate for electoral form and a watchdog against electoral fraud. During each of the recent elections, it trained thousands of election monitors who fanned out across polling stations to report on the quality of the elections. They sometimes prepare reports critiquing the president's governance record or offering recommendations for policy reform.

Nonassociational Groups

A clear Nigerian example of the nonassociational interest group, but shadowy in its definition, is the famous "**Kaduna Mafia**." Hardly any informal conversation on Nigerian politics fails to mention this network of powerful northern leaders, who are said to maintain strong influence over the military and Nigerian politics. Richard Joseph offers this description:

> In a general sense [Kaduna Mafia] refers to members of the Northern intelligentsia who assumed positions of political and social influence during the decade of

military rule after the civil war. These individuals are, on the whole, better educated than their predecessors in the emirate North who held similar positions in the first decade after independence. [They also] were less dependent on the patronage of the traditional rulers to advance in their careers.[31]

This group was highly influential in the Babangida years, but Sani Abacha distanced himself from it. General Shehu Musa Yar'Adua, a political reformer and a leading figure in the Kaduna Mafia who served in military administrations in the 1970s, died in prison in 1997. When his brother, Umar Musa Yar'Adua, was elected president in 2007, some saw this as a return of the Kaduna Mafia's influence.

Given that most of Nigeria's labor force is involved in agriculture, one expects to find strong associational activity among farmers. However, the ethnic divisions in the country have prevented the formation of any national-level farm organizations. Those groups that do exist are usually engaged in local cooperative activities and are not active beyond the regional level. More commonly, the interest articulation activities of farmers are relatively spontaneous and unorganized, or take the form of clientelism (as we will discuss later).

Finally, one institution is far more than an interest group: the military itself. We will address its political role later. The Nigerian military is not a cohesive interest, as was demonstrated in the transition from Abacha to Abubakar. The enlisted personnel and lower-ranking officers have not seen any direct benefit from military rule, and many of them supported efforts to return to civilian rule. Also, the country's ethnic divisions are reflected in the military as well, although they compete there with a well-ingrained military professionalism. The military rank and file were originally drawn mostly from northern non-Hausa minorities. Later recruitment drew from all over the country, but the minorities, especially from the "Middle Belt," remain disproportionately numerous. The early preponderance of Igbo officers ended with the second coup and the Biafran civil war, which resulted in the northern dominance in the officer corps that is present today. However, there is wide ethnic diversity among the officers, and ethnicity is only one factor in the complex disputes within the military. There is a constant possibility that new factions will emerge to challenge the current leadership, to forestall or delay the return to civilian control.

Patron–Client Networks

An alternative structure for interest representation is found in the **patron–client network**. Powerful Nigerian political figures are able to mobilize support through personal "connections" with subordinates, who may themselves serve in a corresponding role of "patron" for a yet-lower set of "clients." **Clientelism** was an integral aspect of political life in the larger-scale precolonial systems of the Hausa, the Yoruba, and others. Those who are not represented by formal associations may be able to take advantage of their connections to achieve political ends, particularly at the local level and where traditional rulers and their political systems maintain some influence. Furthermore, the pattern of personal contacts is ingrained in the culture and thus remains important as an approach to powerful modern figures independent of any local traditional context.

Resting on these patron–client networks in Nigeria is a patronage system in which a ruler or an official gives a public office to an individual client in return for his loyalty in delivering political support at some lower level. The prevalence of such a system in Nigeria is not dependent on particular regimes, civilian or military.[32] Their durability makes the "restructuring" of Nigerian administration difficult when regimes are under pressure to develop an "austerity" budget.

Political Participation

Given the lack of either good census data or reliable voter registration figures, it is difficult to be precise about voter turnout figures, but estimates are in the range of 40 to 60 percent in some earlier elections, an impressive level for a majority poor and illiterate populace. Part of the explanation is found in the prevalence of patron–client systems, the "machine politics" that connects ordinary voters to the electoral process through personalistic ties with political activists.

Interest in elections declined during Nigeria's long stretch of authoritarianism prior to 1999 as citizens felt betrayed as each promise of a transition was broken. But return to civilian rule has engendered a renewed interest in electoral participation. In the presidential election of February 1999, turnout was estimated at 52 percent. Voter turnout for the 2003 election was an estimated 69 percent. Reflecting the underlying problems with the 2007 election, official estimates of turnout are unavailable, but unofficial estimates are around 57 percent. Reliable estimates report 54 percent turnout for the presidential election but only 29 percent for the legislative. Turnout was again 54 percent in the 2011 presidential election.

Violence also is employed frequently, from the use of "thugs" by political parties in both republics to the confrontations with police in Lagos and the southwest during the last days of the Babangida regime and in the challenges to Abacha's seizure of power. Violence by the state, although less common than in many authoritarian regimes, has played a major role in Nigerian politics: Upward of fifty people were executed for participating in the failed coups of 1986 and 1990; death sentences against those accused in 1995 were not carried out, but only because members of the Provisional Ruling Council (PRC) could not agree among themselves on whether to do so. The greatest example of political violence was, of course, the Biafran civil war from 1967 to 1970. Nigeria experienced over 2 million deaths in wars from 1960 to 1992, the vast majority of them during the civil war. Though on a lesser scale, the government remains complicit in human rights violations following the 1999 transition. Violence often takes the form of reprisal attacks—often on a large scale—by security forces after one of their own is killed. Extrajudicial killings by police are not unusual, and have increased since the Boko Haram insurgency erupted in 2009.[33]

Nigeria has been a highly politicized country ever since independence. If democracy offers better representation, rule of law, and improved government performance, one hopes that this will reduce the sense of alienation and frustration that inspires much of this violence.

Parties and Elections

18.9 Describe the major parties and their bases of support, and discuss the checkered history of elections.

Nigeria's early political parties were influenced by the divisive effects of colonialism, which strengthened regional attachments. The National Council of Nigeria and the Cameroons (NCNC) emerged as a diverse nationalist movement in 1944 under the leadership of Nnamdi Azikiwe.[34] The Action Group (AG), an opposition party with its stronghold in the west, emerged under the leadership of a young Yoruba lawyer, Obafemi Awolowo. From the beginning, there were forces within parties arguing for multicultural,

TABLE 18.2
Ethnic Distribution of Party Leaders, 1958

Party[a]	Igbo	Yoruba	Hausa-Fulani
NCNC	49.3	26.7	2.8
AG	4.5	68.2	3.0
NPC	—	6.8	51.3

[a]NCNC: National Council of Nigeria and the Cameroons; AG: Action Group; NPC: Northern People's Congress.
Source: Richard Sklar and C. S. Whitaker, Jr., "Nigeria," in *Political Parties and National Integration in Tropical Africa,* ed. James S. Coleman and Carl Rosberg (Berkeley: University of California Press, 1964).

issue-based, cross-regional coalition building. But strong regional governments and electoral reforms in the 1950s created incentives for the parties to appeal to their ethnic, regional bases (see Table 18.2).

Unlike the NCNC and AG, the major northern political parties never really tried to obtain political support outside their own region. Britain's successful application of indirect rule in the north had resulted in an alliance between the colonial administration and the traditional emirs that impeded the formation of modern political movements. Reformist political organizations such as the Northern Elements' Progressive Union (NEPU) had more limited appeal. A more conservative movement, the Northern Peoples' Congress (NPC), was taken over by the Sardauna (a traditional title) of Sokoto and a Hausa commoner, Abubakar Tafawa Balewa. The NPC, the traditional emirates, and the pre-independence administrative structure were intertwined such that young administrators could run successfully for public office, but only if they had the support of their administrative superiors and of the local traditional elite. This political structure grew up among a population that was not as educated (less than 15 percent were literate) as in the south and that was much more loyal to their traditional authorities. The NPC did not emphasize national independence in its campaigns, which often made appeals based on religion.

When General J. T. U. Aguiyi Ironsi assumed power following the breakdown of political order in the Western Region and the first coup, one of his first moves was to abolish all parties and a large number of political associations. It was a move imitated by later dictators, who sought either to eliminate political competition to consolidate power or to limit it as part of a managed transition to democracy. The country operated without political parties during General Yakubu Gowon's tenure from 1966 to 1975. When Murtala Muhammed then took over, he set in motion a process to return to civilian rule, including drafting a new constitution and establishing strict rules for political parties, which he thought should be "genuine and truly national political parties."[35] The constitution drafters in response specified that to be elected president, a candidate would have to poll at least 25 percent of the votes cast in each of at least two-thirds of the states. Parties were required to register with an electoral commission, and their governing boards had to reflect the country's "federal character"—specifically, coming from at least two-thirds of the states.

The elections of 1979 and 1983 are difficult to analyze because five parties competed for president, Senate and House seats, and state assemblies with varying degrees of success. Looking at the Senate, House, and state assemblies overall, most states were controlled by a single party. Following the military coup in 1983, Nigeria went nearly ten years before it held national elections again, and political parties were repeatedly banned, unbanned, and manipulated.

In 1998, the transition government under Abubakar allowed new parties to form, and he created the **Independent National Election Commission (INEC)** to organize and certify elections. In order to participate in the elections of 1998 and 1999, parties were required to demonstrate a nationwide organization. On the basis of the cases they submitted, nine parties were qualified to compete in the local elections of December 1998. The three parties that received the highest number of votes in the 774 local governments were then allowed to compete in the state and national elections of 1999. The **People's Democratic Party (PDP)** won in 389 local governments, the All People's Party (APP) in 182, and the Alliance for Democracy (AD) in 100, with other parties winning in the remaining 103. The APP and the AD formed an alliance, presenting a single candidate. There were ultimately just two candidates in the 1999 presidential election: Olusegun Obasanjo, representing the PDP, and Olu Falae, leading the APP/AD. The election results certified by INEC declared Obasanjo the winner with 62.8 percent compared with Falae's 37.2 percent.

In 2003, Obasanjo won reelection by a landslide, winning almost twice as many votes as his opponent; former military ruler Muhammed Buhari ran with the APP, renamed the All Nigeria People's Party (ANPP). The PDP increased its majority in both houses of Congress and won twenty-eight out of thirty-six governorships. Obasanjo was reelected by a landslide, winning almost twice as many votes as Buhari. He and the PDP particularly improved their position in the southwest, where they captured five governorships from the AD. The AD has reinvented itself as the Action Congress Nigeria (ACN), a name that invokes Awolowo's history with the AG.

The 2007 election season began with a campaign by President Obasanjo's supporters to change the constitution in order to allow him a third term in office. Because his vice president, Atiku Abubakar, wanted to run, this led to an acrimonious battle within the PDP that carried regional dimensions too, since Abubakar is from the north. Abubakar failed to win the nomination in highly suspect primaries, and the dispute has left a lasting scar on the party. After the third-term bid failed, Umar Musa Yar'Adua won the nomination and went on to be elected president in 2007. Following Yar'Adua's death in office in 2010, Jonathan won election in 2011 with nearly 59 percent of the vote (see Table 18.3). At every level, the PDP remained strong. It secured a large majority in the Senate, but some of its support in the House eroded; it again won most of the governorships. International and domestic observers widely condemned the elections as fraudulent, and the courts threw out at least eleven gubernatorial and nine senatorial elections. In fact, the 2007 election of President Yar'Adua was not upheld by the Supreme Court until December 2008.

TABLE 18.3
Results of 2011 National Elections

	PDP	CPC	ACN	ANPP	AGPA	Others
Share of vote in presidential election (%)	58.89	31.98	5.41	2.40	—	1.32
Seats in House of Representatives	205	37	38	28	7	22
Senate Seats	71	7	18	7	1	5
Governorships	23	1	6	3	2	1

Note: PDP: People's Democratic Party; Congress for Progressive Change; ACN: Action Congress Nigeria; ANPP: All Nigeria People's Party; AGPA: All Progressive Grand Alliance.
Source: The Independent National Electoral Commission and the National Democratic Institute for International Affairs.

Nigeria loomed on the edge of constitutional crisis again in November 2009, when Yar'Adua disappeared from public as his heart-related ailments increased. The cabinet (loyal to the chief executive in a presidential system) declined to assess his condition, as called for by the constitution. Under pressure from global leaders and new civil society organizations such as the Save Nigeria Group, the National Assembly swore in Vice President Goodluck Jonathan as "acting president." When Yar'Adua died in April 2010, Jonathan was formally sworn in as president, ending an awkward—and potentially explosive—impasse. Jonathan's administration has an ambitious reform agenda; he began by refusing to reappoint the top INEC official who oversaw the troubled elections of 2003 and 2007. Jonathan won with 59 percent of the vote in the 2011 presidential election, while Buhari, running under the banner of a new party, the Congress for Progressive Change (CPC), received 32 percent. According to Human Rights Watch, about 800 people were killed in postelection violence, mostly in the north, where Buhari's base is strongest.

Since the PDP has continued to hold the presidency, most governorships, and comfortable majorities in the National Assembly, many consider it a dominant party. Buhari has been defeated in three elections now: 2003, 2007, and 2011. But there are signs that electoral democracy is becoming more vigorous. To start from a clean electoral slate for 2011, INEC successfully registered over 73 million voters in barely three weeks, and eliminated 870,000 duplicate voters from the rolls, following a public display. International observers hailed the election as possibly the freest and fairest ever organized by a civilian government in Nigeria. Moreover, the CPC garnered widespread support even though it only formed in 2009. In 2013, it began negotiating a merger with other major opposition parties, including the ANPP and the ACN.[36]

Ethnic Solidarity and Party Loyalty

Arguably, ethnicity still drives much of the political organizing in the country, and political leaders undermine truly national parties through ethnic appeals. The PDP today is so large that it seems to transcend such differences, but, in other ways, it merely operates as a coalition of ethnic and regional elites. Figure 18.6 shows the formation of Nigerian political

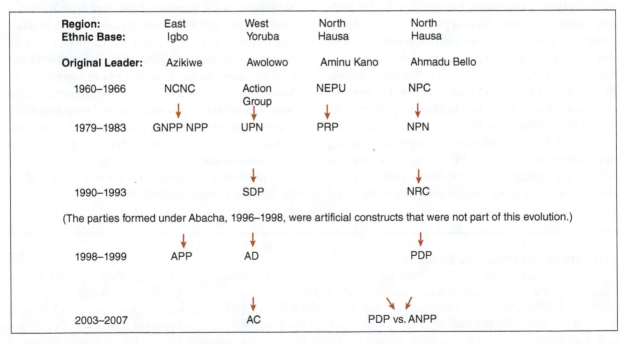

Region:	East	West	North	North
Ethnic Base:	Igbo	Yoruba	Hausa	Hausa
Original Leader:	Azikiwe	Awolowo	Aminu Kano	Ahmadu Bello
1960–1966	NCNC	Action Group	NEPU	NPC
1979–1983	GNPP NPP	UPN	PRP	NPN
1990–1993		SDP		NRC

(The parties formed under Abacha, 1996–1998, were artificial constructs that were not part of this evolution.)

1998–1999	APP	AD		PDP
2003–2007		AC		PDP vs. ANPP

FIGURE 18.6

The Evolution of Political Parties in Nigeria
Although the PDP offers the promise of overcoming the historically regional nature of Nigeria's major parties, its dominance over political competition has been criticized.

Source: Federal Republic of Nigeria. www.nigeria.gov.ng

parties, notably their reemergence with the same regional ethnic bases they had in the 1960s, even before the military regimes. Ethnicity and regionalism complicate the role of political parties as instruments of interest aggregation and articulation. Until the election of Obasanjo in 1999, Hausas captured the top office in national elections. The annulment of the 1993 elections denied the south an apparent victory, which compounded the frustration for a region that had lost the presidency in 1979 and 1983. The annulled elections also created a "political debt" of sorts to the Yorubas, which heavily factored into the political party formations during the 1999 transition.

In 1979, the Hausa-dominated NPN won the ultimate prize, the presidency, essentially on the basis of a combination of northern voters and minority voters in the southern regions. The most significant difference for parties between the First and Second Republics turned out to be the carving up of the original three regions into nineteen states. Ethnic groups other than the "big three" were dominant in a number of these states and had thus broken free of regional ethnic dominance. Party strategists henceforth combined a strong base in one of the main ethnic group areas with a successful appeal for support among minorities and potentially among dissident groups in the home bases of the other two major groups.

The same five parties remained in existence through the four years of the Second Republic and contested again in 1983 for the presidency, seats in the Senate and House, and state-level positions. However, the smallest parties, the PRP and the GNPP, had been weakened by their lack of access to resources. And, as is normal in a presidential system where the ultimate prize, the presidency, is a winner-take-all election, there were pressures on the two major opposition parties to combine against the incumbent. Such cooperation proved impossible, however, when neither Azikiwe nor Awolowo would defer to the other as presidential candidate. In a campaign marked with violence and vote rigging, the NPN won a solid victory, recording gains against the opposing parties in their home areas. The NPN victory was short-lived, though. Three months into its second term, it met an early demise at the hands of Nigeria's fourth military coup. This time, the military's abolition of political parties had some political support because the parties were seen as so corrupt.

The two-year reign of Muhammed Buhari (1983–1985) presented no timetable for a return to democracy, but electoral politics were not entirely absent from his successors' regimes. Babangida created a new electoral commission and organized local elections in 1987. His military government favored a two-party system, and it eventually overruled the electoral commission and created two by fiat: one for a party "a little to the left," the other to fit a party "a little to the right" on the political spectrum. Even the parties' names were assigned by the government: The party on the left would be the Social Democratic Party, and that on the right would be the National Republican Council (NRC).

Nigerians reacted to these developments with a mixture of cynicism and hope. This transition process suffered its first setback in 1992, when the regime nullified the results of the parties' efforts to produce presidential candidates. Nigerians were ever more skeptical as to whether the military really intended to leave. Babangida scheduled a new election for June 1993, ordered the parties to produce new candidates, and set August 27, 1993, as the date for turning over power to the civilian government. Under more careful control, the parties reconvened their national conventions and nominated new candidates. The NRC selected a relatively unknown figure, Bashir Tofa (a Kanuri from the northeast), while the SDP nominated Moshood Abiola, then a wealthy businessman from the southwest. The election finally took place on **June 12, 1993**. Nigerian and international observers reported that it was a generally fair election, and the NRC did not announce any plans to contest the outcome. Abiola, from the south, appeared to have won a majority of the votes in nine northern states, including his opponent's home state of Kano. The results seemed to suggest that under a two-party system, factionalism in each region and state could be exploited to prevent a strictly regional outcome.

However, the 1993 results were never officially announced, and the transition's second setback came two weeks later, when Babangida annulled the election. "June 12" became a term forever etched into Nigerian memory, particularly for political activists in the southwest who claimed the Yoruba had been denied the presidency for the second time. Party politics, even the contrived variety invented by the Babangida regime, had once again proved to be an exercise unacceptable to the military leadership and their allies. The Abacha regime announced guidelines for the creation of new parties in June 1996, but NADECO and other opposition groups denounced the exercise as a sham. The five parties certified for local elections in March 1997 all nominated Abacha for the presidency.

Following Abacha's death in 1998, the transition government dissolved all five parties, nullified the local and state elections, and began a new start toward democracy with freely formed parties and a promise to hand over power to an elected president on May 29, 1999. Of the nine parties originally certified by INEC in October 1998, the three that survived the local elections represented some degree of continuity with earlier party formations—each with a base among one of the three major ethnic groups. However, because of the requirement to have a national base and for other strategic considerations, the candidates of each party were not necessarily of the ethnic group presumably dominant in it. Most importantly, even though the PDP was said to have its base in the north, its leaders threw their support for the presidential nomination to General Obasanjo, who had only recently been released from Abacha's prison. As both a southerner (both he and his principal opponent, Olu Falae, were Yoruba) and a former military ruler, Obasanjo was seen by many as the individual most likely to provide effective leadership in the postmilitary state. Overcoming the doubts of southerners skeptical of the PDP's northern support, and civil society activists who questioned Obasanjo's commitment to democracy, the military stayed in the barracks and Obasanjo was sworn in as president on May 29, 1999.

The 2003 elections in Nigeria were the first civilian-conducted elections in twenty years. This development represents one big step toward establishing an enduring democracy in Nigeria. The election of Umar Musa Yar'Adua, the governor of Katsina State, in the 2007 presidential contest, constituted another big step. It marked the first civilian-to-civilian transfer of power in the country's history, and the peaceful transfer of power from a southerner to a northerner. Such alternation is enshrined by an informal agreement within the PDP, known as "**power shift**." Yar'Adua

Goodluck Jonathan Launches His Campaign
Goodluck Jonathan's political intentions were unclear during his term as "Acting President" and even after he was sworn in as president. He formally declared his candidacy in September 2010 at this rally.

received nearly 70 percent of the votes, meaning that the PDP still dominated politics, and the party that took second place received less than 13 percent. International observers and domestic monitors criticized election preparations and the conduct of voting even more harshly than in 2003. The major national civil society coalition, the Transition Monitoring Group, called for the results to be canceled outright. The EU's Observation Mission said that the "State and Federal elections have fallen far short of basic international and regional standards for democratic elections." A report issued immediately after the elections noted "significant evidence of fraud" and concluded that the elections "cannot be considered to have been credible." The defeated vice president, Atiku Abubakar, and other candidates challenged the 2007 election results, which the courts did not formally resolve for over a year. Election tribunals sifted through hundreds of other results, overturning several key governorships, further confirming the fundamental problems with the voting process. When Yar'Adua passed away in 2010, many northerners argued that allowing then vice president Goodluck Jonathan to succeed to the presidency would violate power shift (even though it was consistent with the constitution), since he is from the south. The resolution of this tension amounted to a third step toward deepening democracy. But it also underscores the central importance of political balancing between the northern and southern regions—a tradition that dates back to the colonial era. The distribution of electoral support illustrated in Figure 18.7 shows that Jonathan failed to secure a plurality in a single northern state in the 2011 presidential election. Like many African countries, ethnicity and cultural loyalties clearly still play a significant role in politics.

FIGURE 18.7

Geographical Distribution of Support for the Major Parties in the 2011 Presidential Election

Source: Adapted from Nigeria Elections Coalition, nigeriaelections.org

Policy Formation and Implementation

18.10 Discuss how factors such as oil and ethnic diversity impact economic performance

In comparing Nigeria's various civilian and military regimes, the ultimate question must always be their *performance*. This is certainly the "bottom line" for Nigerians, whose support of these various regimes is based on the quality of life they experience under them. This section thus focuses on the *decisions* governments have made, particularly in raising revenues, dispersing funds, and implementing programs. It will also discuss some background issues, such as planning and conducting the federal census, the results of which underlie all policy. Finally, it presents the constraints imposed on Nigerian decision making by the outside world, particularly in the World Bank–supported **Structural Adjustment Program (SAP)**. Dealing with "SAP," as the economic restructuring program is commonly called, leads us back to the discussion of environment with which we began. Policy relating to Nigeria's international economic situation has responded to initiatives from other African countries, world powers, international organizations, and multinational firms. Here we consider the critical constraints that the world economy puts on the choices available to a Third World country, even one as large and resource-rich as Nigeria.

Extractive Performance

Nigeria inherited a fiscal system in 1960 that depended mainly on taxes on international trade. Indirect taxes provided 64 percent of total revenues, direct taxes only 16.5 percent, and other revenues 19 percent. The colonial administration had developed a revenue system that operated through agricultural marketing boards. Ostensibly created to provide price stability to farmers, marketing boards accumulated surplus funds in good years that tempted government officials with development projects in mind. Peasant farmers also paid direct taxes, of which they were much more aware. Widespread tax riots broke out in the Western Region in 1968 and 1969, a period during which tax collection was halted, eventually to be replaced by a lower, much simpler flat tax.

In the First Republic and under the Gowon administration, the state governments collected the personal income, sales, and poll taxes. Tax collections generally declined as new states were created, without fiscal institutions in place and with smaller tax bases than the old regions. At the same time, rising oil revenues strengthened the fiscal position of the federal government (and those states with oil fields).

In a pattern typical of Third World oil-exporting countries, Nigeria today depends almost entirely on the revenues from this single industry. Since there is no indication that the world's appetite for oil will diminish in the near future, it is a reliable revenue source that substitutes for the various forms of taxes on private income. This enables its authoritarian military regimes to pay for social programs without risking the wrath of taxpayers, and to construct patron–client networks. Though the states do little to internally generate revenue through taxation, since they know they will receive oil revenues from the federal government, there are signs that this is changing. Lagos State, which has a large share of the country's private sector, has imposed new taxes on its citizens in recent years—and services have visibly improved. Even some poor northern states like Sokoto appear to be trying new means of internally generating revenue, rather than relying on grants from the central government.

Vast petroleum reserves have also meant that Nigerian governments have not actively sought large amounts of direct foreign aid, unlike many African countries. They have, however, used the country's oil reserves as the collateral for massive borrowing from foreign and international banks in the 1970s and 1980s. The funds supported massive capital expenditures and gave Nigeria an enormous external debt, which rose from 10 percent of GNP to 140.5 percent between 1980 and 1995. Oil wealth did not bring the country financial independence; to the contrary, the debt gave international lenders a predominant voice in Nigeria's allocation of public funding. The debt payoffs in 2006 arguably insulated Nigeria from such outside influences, but the return of extensive borrowing since 2010 might bring back foreign lenders' leverage.

Distributive Performance

As a producer of high-grade petroleum, Nigeria has an unusually great potential to move out of the ranks of the less-developed into the middle-income nations.

In the 1970s, impressive projects, such as road development and irrigation projects, as well as the launching of Abuja as the nation's capital, were signs that potential might become reality.

Unfortunately, political corruption grew apace and probably began consuming a higher proportion of national wealth than in the pre-oil period. When oil revenues suddenly began their decline in 1980, "corruption and mismanagement prevented any kind of disciplined adjustment," and "the economy was plunged into depression and mounting international indebtedness. . . . Sucked dry of revenue by the corruption, mismanagement, and recession, state governments became unable to pay teachers and civil servants or to purchase drugs for hospitals, and many services (including schools) were shut down by strikes."[37]

In spite of the country's raw material advantage, Nigerians have not seen their lives improve in recent years. The UN Development Program publishes the Human Development Index based on three factors: life expectancy at birth, adult literacy, and per capita GDP (see Table 18.4). Nigeria has a rank of 153 out of 187 countries on the HDI and a rank of 127 on per capita GDP alone. It is not surprising to find the less-developed countries low on these listings. However, per capita GDP is a good measure of distributive potential. Thus, the comparison of per capita GDP and the HDI ratings can be an indicator of how well a country has done for its people compared with other countries with similar capacity. Because Nigeria's per capita GDP ranking is much higher than its HDI ranking, this suggests that the Nigerian advantage in oil revenue has had little noticeable impact on the overall quality of life.

Budgetary priorities are important in analyzing distributive performance. In the case of a country ruled by the military for most of the last decade, one might expect that military expenditures would loom especially large. In Nigeria, the military budget increased from $234 million to nearly $1.5 billion between 2000 and 2009. However, there are believed to be significant additional military expenditures that are not publicly reported. Extremely modest in size at independence, Nigeria's armed forces grew to 250,000 at the height of the Biafran civil war. Then the Gowon regime began a program of gradual attrition that reduced the force to about 100,000 in the mid-1980s. After the 1999 transition, it shrank to about 85,000. This still constitutes a major military force, and, as we will discuss later, Nigerian leaders have used this military strength to maintain a high profile in West Africa. Increases in the military's size since 2010, to about 100,000 soldiers, along with human rights violations in the northeast and beyond, have raised new concerns about civilian control of the military—especially as abuses routinely go unpunished.

Nigerians have a great enthusiasm for education, and parties and regimes have promised universal access to it. Some progress can be noted. In 1964, Nigeria ranked twenty-ninth among African nations in enrollments, with 5 percent of the school-aged population in primary school; it was nineteenth in secondary

TABLE 18.4
Nigeria's Ranking on GDP per Capita and Human Development Index (HDI)

Country	Life Expectancy at Birth, in 2012	Adult Literacy Rate 2012 (%)	GDP per Capita PPP in 2011	HDI Rank in 2013
United States	78.7	—[a]	42,486	3
Japan	83.6	—[a]	30,660	10
United Kingdom	80.3	—[a]	32,474	26
Mexico	77.1	93.1	12,776	61
Botswana	53.0	84.5	12,939	119
Indonesia	69.8	92.6	4,094	121
China	73.7	94.3	7,418	101
Nigeria	52.3	61.3	2,221	153
Benin	56.5	42.4	1,428	166

[a]No data reported to UNDP.

Source: United Nations Development Program, *Human Development Report 2013* (New York: UNDP 2013).

enrollments, with 5 percent of the appropriate age group in school. Ten years later, 24 percent of the school-age population was in school, and Nigeria was fifteenth in Africa on this measure. Primary enrollments stood at about 57 percent in 2010; youth literacy was 72 percent in 2010, up from 65 percent in 1985.

The Nigerian government's performance in the area of health has been mediocre overall. Nigeria's infant mortality rate has dropped from 185 (per 1,000 live births) in 1960 to 139 in 1970, 114 in 1980, and 78 in 2013. However, nearly one-fifth of all children die before reaching the age of five. These statistics reflect an unfortunate and perhaps surprising trend, mirrored in old age: In 2013, life expectancy was only fifty-two years, showing surprisingly little improvement over earlier data. The government has recently poured more resources into the health sector, but spending remains low in per capita terms—again reflecting the challenges of a population growing so rapidly.

With petroleum firmly established as the major source of foreign exchange in Nigeria, and with that industry under government control, the distribution of wealth is heavily influenced by policy decisions. Private consumption surged as oil revenues multiplied

in the 1970s, about 8 percent per year. This average figure conceals tremendous increases in wealth at the top; the lower 40 percent of the population benefited very little. Government expenditure grew at an even greater rate than private consumption, both in absolute terms and as a proportion of GDP.[38] This aspect of expenditure, of course, includes sums lost in corrupt payments to individuals. Nigeria should have reaped another windfall during the Gulf War, as petroleum prices temporarily shot up, but increased revenues never showed up in national accounts. In 1994, economist Pius Okigbo examined the books of the Central Bank of Nigeria; he reported (as he left the country) that $12.6 billion was not accounted for. The skimming of oil profits had indeed reached astronomical proportions.

Income distribution is also affected by inflation, which followed from the rapid increase in the money supply during the 1970s oil boom and continued apace later on, as governments followed a time-honored approach to balancing budgets when revenues decline: They printed money. The result was continuous inflation, a problem that became especially serious in the 1990s, as shown in Figure 18.8. A case study

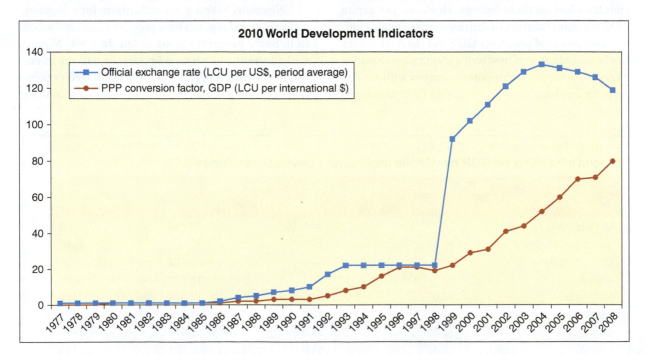

FIGURE 18.8

Naira Exchange Rate

Whereas a powerful naira once made foreign imports cheap for Nigerians, its value has declined in recent decades.

Source: Nigeria Exchange Rates to Dollar History www.nairaland.com

BOX 18.3 The Effects of Inflation: A Case Study

A young graduate with a new doctoral degree won a position as an instructor at a Nigerian university in 1977. His salary and benefits totaled 6,000 naira per year. At that time, one naira equaled $1.50, so his salary was the equivalent of $9,000—modest by industrial world standards but very comfortable in Nigeria. Twenty years later, this same man achieved the rank of full professor, at a salary of 51,000 naira per year, with fringe benefits raising his total annual compensation to 90,000 naira. However, at the parallel market exchange rate of 80 naira to the dollar, his salary was the equivalent of $1,125 per year, a figure not taking into account the effect of inflation on the purchasing power of the dollar since 1977. In 1998, a national review of faculty salaries increased the professor's salary to the equivalent of $5,000 per year.

This discussion implies that salaries are regularly paid. However, in early 1999, the Abubakar government was in such financial straits that it failed to provide salary payments at all. In 2000, President Obasanjo improved the workers' pay generally and moved university teachers' pay to 130,000 naira per month, the equivalent of $1,000 per month. He did this to discourage brain drain in Nigeria and to promote high-level productivity in all sectors.

(see Box 18.3) shows the effect of this inflation on individual income. Consumer inflation peaked at 75 percent in 1995. Since the return of democracy, it has fluctuated but has hovered in the low teens since 2007. This is still a great financial burden for most people in a poor country.

Governments have attempted to deal with inflation by enforcing an official exchange rate for the **naira**, Nigeria's national currency. The result was a huge divergence in official and market exchange rates, causing chaos in the financial system. That chaos dried up investments and stimulated corruption, since anyone with access to foreign exchange at the official rate can then sell the foreign currency "on the street" for a large profit. Since 1999, the government has reduced its role in stabilizing the currency, allowing the value of the naira to be largely determined by forces of supply and demand.

As a policy issue, distribution in a large country such as Nigeria is also seen as a geographic question, not just one of policy priorities. Nigerians have a fondness for referring to the national budget as the "national cake," and they see state and local governments as the major recipients of "slices." The federal government now spends between two-thirds and three-fourths of public monies and also has great control over how the money distributed to state and local governments will be spent. On the contentious question of how to distribute resources as the number of states and local governments expanded, governments settled on relatively straightforward formulas, a combination of equality (across-the-board distributions to all states) and population. States other than Lagos now depend on the federal Revenue Allocation System (RAS) for 70 to 90 percent of their recurrent revenues. In order to fund local governments, the RAS was extended to cover them directly in 1981. Beginning in 1982, federal revenues were shared according to set percentages among the three levels of government. Given the set formulas in the RAS, it is not surprising that regions and localities strive for statehood and local autonomy and that population counts loom large as a political issue.

Dealing with Debt and Structural Adjustment

Nigeria's debt repayments and rescheduling in 2006–2007 solved a problem that began with fiscal indiscipline during the 1970s oil boom, when high levels of public spending hurt productivity and monetary policies contributed to inflation. Like many African governments in the 1980s, Nigeria turned to heavy borrowing from international financial institutions, principally the IMF and the World Bank. By 1991, Nigeria's debt represented 257 percent of the annual value of the country's exports and 109 percent of GNP. The annual cost of servicing the debt consumed 25 percent of the value of exports (up from 4 percent in 1980); the weight of this burden made repayment almost impossible, and debt repayments probably diverted spending from the social sector.

When Ibrahim Babangida seized power in 1985, he opened a "national debate" on the issue. He claimed to fashion a Nigerian version of structural adjustment (while at the same time negotiating with the IMF). As the program's austerity measures began to be felt, the SAP became extremely unpopular. Babangida forbade candidates to criticize the program, but at the same time, he eased off on the necessary austerity measures. The net result was that SAP neither reduced debt nor reformed the troubled financial system.

Rather than allow the naira to float as urged by the IMF, the Abacha regime fixed an official exchange rate. In 1995, the exchange rate was partially opened to market forces, but this neither stabilized the economy nor satisfied the international sector. The total external debt reached almost $8 billion, and the Nigerian National Petroleum Corporation owed over $1 billion to its foreign partners. In responding to gasoline shortages, however, the government lowered the subsidy on petroleum products.

Each attempt by the government to eliminate the subsidy and raise the price at the pump has been met with widespread protests and long lines at filling stations. Ordinary citizens fear the impact such reforms would have on not only the cost of public transportation but also food and other daily essentials. For this reason, one recent study noted: "Virtually every fuel price hike that was announced by the government has been massively unpopular and has in almost all cases been resisted by most Nigerians."[39] This was validated again when a nationwide strike, organized by the NLC and other unions, virtually shut down the country in January 2012 after the minister of finance suddenly announced the elimination of the subsidy. There could hardly be a more dramatic demonstration of policy failure: a country rich in petroleum incapable of providing its citizens with fuel except through a corrupt, heavily subsidized fuel distribution system. Under President Jonathan's administration, debt started rising again as the government and the states borrowed out of a sense of confidence generated by the high oil prices on the world market.

Regulative Performance

At independence in 1960, the Nigeria Police Force was essentially regionalized. Because the police were frequently mobilized for political purposes during the rough-and-tumble politics of the 1960s, the military regime decided to consolidate the police function at the national level. It is this national police force that now enforces traffic laws and other government legislation. In rural communities, traditional leaders still often play a role in adjudicating disputes, maintaining law and order, and taking responsibility for "strangers" who arrive in the area. With the increase in terrorist violence since 2009, though, the military's role in law enforcement has become significant.

Nigeria's judicial system remains vigorous, and until the advent of Abacha's period in office, it had been surprisingly diligent at following a rule of law through the various informally constituted regimes. Still, military regimes intruded on that rule of law. The regime imposed the State Security (Detention of Persons) Decree in 1984, which allows detention without trial of those "suspected of posing a threat to national security." State officials seemed to intervene with increasing frequency in the judicial system where political questions are involved. Though Nigeria's democratic regime appears committed to ending such arbitrary exercises of authority, detention without trial remains a serious problem due to inefficiencies, inadequate resources, and few public defenders. Amnesty International reported in 2011 that 38,000 out of Nigeria's 49,000 prisoners were being held without trial—often in the most miserable prison conditions.

The Census Issue   One policy issue, the census, has overshadowed all the others since independence, because the outcome often determines how political goods will be distributed. A minor policy issue in some countries, in Nigeria, the population counts have been fraught with conflict. In a country where federal subsidies make up the lion's share of budgetary allocations at all levels, the distribution of population directly affects the distribution of resources.

After almost two additional decades of continued reliance on the 1963 figures, the Babangida government commissioned a new census to be conducted by a National Population Commission. Following methodical pretesting and sampling, a census in November 1991 put the country's total population at 88.5 million, a substantial downward revision from estimates that had exceeded 100 million. According to this census, the highest population concentrations were in the states of Bauchi, Kaduna, Kano, Katsina, and Sokoto in the north and Lagos, Oyo, and Rivers in the south. The census caused new consternation in the south, where feelings ran high that the figures had again been "cooked" to favor the north. As mentioned earlier, the 2006 census effort fared only slightly better. "Political acceptability, rather than statistical accuracy or demographic reliability, clearly remains the most important determinant of the fate of the census in Nigeria," writes one expert on population counts. "As such, it is a sad commentary on the continuing ethnopoliticization of basic demographic information in the country."[40]

Conclusions on Performance

As with many African countries over the last decade, we need to judge Nigeria's performance with nuance and fair treatment of its complexity. On the one hand, its political culture has cultivated the idea that public policy is merely a means of dividing up the "national cake"—an analogy suggesting that the government's resources should merely be distributed in proportion to the political influence of various constituencies. When constituencies are defined in ethnic terms, politics becomes a competition among ethnic groups for larger slices of cake. This mentality has inspired recurring ethnic conflict, fueled corruption at all levels of society, and undermined democratic consolidation. On the other hand, citizens and civil society groups are increasingly demonstrating their ability to hold politicians accountable. Battles over the federal budget between the National Assembly and the presidency often resemble brinkmanship, but they have also increased the transparency of federal spending, and have stimulated public dialogues about how to best spend the people's money. Improving government performance may require not only political institutions that generate responsive leaders but also civic education

and a change in Nigeria's political culture. The norms of community participation and public articulation of goals, rooted in Nigeria's ancient cultures, may have to be rediscovered.

Nigeria in Africa and in the World

18.11 Describe the source and forms of Nigeria's influence in the region and the world.

Nigeria has the population and resource base to be a regional power, and it has stimulated hopes and fears among its neighbors concerning that potential. Under the First Republic (1960–1966), Nigeria generally focused inward and played a rather minor role in the continent's turbulent politics. But then came the civil war over Biafra in 1966; Nigeria's army grew from 10,000 to 250,000, the country's oil potential became known, and, as we have seen earlier, world powers took an interest in the war's outcome.

Some West African governments offered clear support to Biafra, a support Nigerians suspected grew from a desire to see their country divided up and thus reduced in influence. This was thought especially to be the case with Cote d'Ivoire (the Ivory Coast) under President Houphouet-Boigny, who favored Biafra with French support. When the war ended, relations among these countries were, as might be expected, strained.

Subsequently, Nigeria under General Gowon took a leading role in establishing, in 1975, the **Economic Community of West African States (ECOWAS)**, hoping to bring Nigeria closer to other West African countries while at the same time countering French influence in the region. The Ivoirian government had taken the lead in forming the Economic Community of West Africa, an exclusively French-speaking organization, and was wary of the predominant position that Nigeria might play in a wider regional organization. But Nigeria was successful in first approaching Togo, Benin, and Niger, the French-speaking countries with which it already had close ties, offering attractive economic inducements that included special petroleum prices. With this group in hand, Nigerian diplomats cast their net wider, and the representatives of sixteen West African governments signed the Treaty of Lagos. The ECOWAS treaty specified a two-year phase during which intracommunity tariffs would be frozen, followed by an eight-year period that would end with the removal of duties on trade among members. Finally, a common external tariff wall would be created.

Thus, West Africa under Nigerian leadership is partaking in the worldwide movement toward free trade zones. As elsewhere, however, progress has been difficult. Ten years after its creation, ECOWAS reported that it had not made "tangible progress in practical terms," and by 1989, the member governments were $80 million in arrears in their contributions to the organization. The proportion of intracommunity trade in the member countries' total international trade has not changed since 1980. At the same time, ECOWAS has had better success as a regional political organization, especially in mediating disputes among member states, and in 1990, a Nigerian proposal was approved that created a standing mediation committee.[41]

Because of its prominence on the continent, Nigeria's international financial problems have been especially embarrassing. Forced, along with other African nations, to accept stringent structural adjustment planning from the World Bank and IMF, Nigeria has reacted with frustration and anger. It has led the region's governments in their critique of international lenders' policies, hosting the meeting that led to the Lagos Plan of Action as a response to international debt-structuring proposals. When the Obasanjo administration renegotiated and paid off most of the country's debts, this move was seen as liberating the country from foreign pressures, allowing Nigeria to assume its rightful place as a giant on the continent. Sub-Saharan Africa's great powers—Nigeria, Kenya, and South Africa—increasingly believe that Africa deserves permanent representation on the UN Security Council.

Of all the world powers, France plays the most prominent role in West Africa. Although the French interest focuses on its own former colonies, in recent years the French have come to believe that Nigeria's size and potential wealth should not be overlooked, and France actively promotes closer economic ties with Nigeria, a move that upsets Nigeria's French-speaking neighbors. The Western powers, especially Britain and the United States, were openly critical

of Nigeria's military rulers and supported the country's return to civilian rule, especially during the Babangida regime and once again with Abdulsalami Abubakar. The United States and Britain condemned Babangida's 1993 election annulment, and they suspended aid as a result. However, this relationship was not important enough to Nigeria's rulers to modify their behavior. Presumably, an embargo on purchases of Nigerian oil would have had that effect, but the industrial nations' governments did not have the will to take such a drastic step. Most observers saw the Abacha regime's treatment of dissenters as a calculation of how far it could silence opposition without provoking more severe international sanctions. In contrast, many Nigerians were critical of what they saw as the West's premature zeal over actions that until then were only *promised* by Abubakar in 1998. Western support returned with enthusiasm upon Obasanjo's inauguration.

Nigeria has played a prominent role in the region through commitment of its substantial military capacity, notably in supplying the leadership and the majority of troops for the Economic Community of West African States Monitoring Group (ECOMOG), the ECOWAS-sponsored peacekeeping force in Liberia. That operation was viewed as a success, with armed conflict halted and elections held. Nigerian troops have also been stationed in Sierra Leone to protect that country's borders from incursions of Liberian rebels, and have confronted a Sierra Leonean military junta that overthrew an elected civilian government, an action more than a bit ironic given the origins of the Abacha regime. Nigeria has participated in wider-ranging UN operations in Lebanon, Rwanda, the former Yugoslavia, and Somalia.

Nigeria moved beyond peacekeeping during the Obasanjo and Yar'Adua administrations, demonstrating regional leadership on a variety of other foreign-policy issues. The Chief of Defense Staff affirmed the military's respect for civilian authority in 2010 and then went on to note that the military needs to be "more proactive and responsive to nonmilitary stimuli and developments."[42] This is reflected in issues such as drug and human trafficking, which led the government to establish new agencies to confront these growing transnational criminal networks. Nigeria recognizes that some of these security problems originate within its borders, too, for example, as international ties of some militant groups have been exposed. The United States is very concerned about both the incubation of Islamic extremism in the north and threats to the flow of oil in the Niger Delta. Nigeria often prefers to treat such challenges as domestic problems first, although ECOWAS is becoming increasingly important to its foreign policy and as a lens for formulating a regional understanding of terrorism and other security threats.[43]

Prospects for Development

Nigeria's political and economic setbacks do not equal the tragedies of Rwanda, Sudan, or Somalia, but the frustrations are nonetheless deep and enduring. Billions of desperately needed naira have been wasted, a few people have grown rich at the expense of the poor, and accountability in government has proved highly elusive. Poet Tanure Ojaide captured this frustration in "No Longer Our Own Country," written in 1986:

> We have lost it,
> the country we were born into.
> We can now sing dirges
> of that commonwealth of yesterday—
> we live in a country
> that is no longer our own.[44]

In much of the world, the attraction of democracy has been its association with prosperity. Like other people, Nigerians are more interested in the outcome of the political process than in the process itself. Calls for better leadership and the welcome initially extended to some military regimes suggest that Nigerians' highest priorities are economic security and the rule of law. If these could be provided by generals, the country would probably accept an authoritarian system. However, at least since Plato, we have known that benevolent authoritarianism is an elusive concept. Western democracies have developed on the premise that democracy is a necessary, if not sufficient, condition for accountable leadership. And Nigerians have had enough opportunities to compare the results of military rule with their expectations that a majority of them are ready for another try at elective civilian rule. Perhaps another constitutional correction will be enough to usher in the long-term political stability for which they have hoped.

This discussion highlighted so many problems (alongside a few hopeful solutions) that the reader might feel overwhelmed by the sheer complexity of the Nigerian case. There are a handful of enduring questions, though, that characterize Nigeria's past, present, and future challenges. First is the relationship between the state and the economy. "Stable democracy is associated with an autonomous, indigenous bourgeoisie, and inversely associated with extensive state control over the economy," writes Larry Diamond. "In Nigeria, and throughout much of Africa, the swollen state has turned politics into a zero-sum game in which everything of value is at stake in an election, and hence candidates, communities, and parties feel compelled to win at any cost."[45]

Oil wealth exacerbates the problem because so much money accrues to the central government, giving federal politicians vast resources for patronage. Part of the answer appears to be the emergence of a vigorous private sector capable of counterbalancing political power emanating from the capital. Nigerians have a reputation for entrepreneurship around the world, and the recent economic development of Lagos gives us some idea of what such a political counterweight might look like—especially since it is one of the few states controlled by a governor from the opposition party. Another part of the answer lies in creating an environment conducive to such investment, where rule of law protects the political rights of citizens and entrepreneurs do not have to spend huge portions of capital on generating power or surviving poor roads.

A second and related problem stems from the exploitative and destructive nature of oil itself. The vast environmental destruction throughout the Niger Delta gave rise to the Ogoni movement and, later, more militant groups such as MEND. Unlike the Biafran secession movement, their rallying cry has often been "resource control," rather than demands for political independence. Even though Goodluck Jonathan is the first president to come from the Niger Delta region, he must reassure the area that his policy promises are more credible than the years of betrayal and neglect these communities have suffered. The broad amnesty plan has brought thousands of militants out of the swamps and into a rehabilitation and reintegration process since 2009, but such progress has largely fallen by the wayside absent sustained political commitment and massive public investment in the region. As a technical committee convened by the federal government in 2008 concluded, the region does not necessarily need new ideas or government agencies; it merely needs the government to implement the critical recommendations of seventeen previous committees on the Niger Delta.

Finally, representation remains a central debate within the political structure and across society. Born of an awkward amalgamation of two distinct colonies a century ago, Nigeria's two regions may not always exist in harmony, but they do create a political equilibrium that has helped the country survive. After eight years of a southern president, there was a broad national consensus in 2007 that there must be a "power shift" to the north. After Yar'Adua passed away in office, tensions resumed over succession to Jonathan, a southerner, in 2010 and his election in 2011. Whether Nigerians will continue to insist on federal character, power shift in the presidency, and other efforts to balance ethnoregional identities remains a pressing question. Beyond those fundamental distinctions between north and south, the country's system of zones, states, and local governments adds progressively complex layers of representation, often at the core of civil tensions. Nigerians have a wealth of ideas, abundant resources, and a rich history on which to draw in formulating solutions for Africa's twenty-first-century giant.

REVIEW QUESTIONS

- What factors—cultural, historical, or otherwise—explain Nigeria's ongoing underdevelopment despite its tremendous oil wealth?
- After so many failed democratic transitions, why did the one in 1999 succeed?
- How have Nigeria's constitutional structures and political traditions attempted to deal with the country's tremendous ethnic and religious diversity?

- What were some of the lasting influences of colonialism on politics after independence?
- What are some examples of the informal nature of politics in Nigeria, where political recruitment and interest aggregation often take place?
- Given the range of factors creating a sense of divisiveness in Nigeria, how has it endured as a country?

KEY TERMS

Abacha, Sani

Abuja

Azikiwe, Nnamdi

Babangida, Ibrahim

Biafra

Boko Haram

clientelism

Economic and Financial Crimes Commission (EFCC)

Economic Community of West African States (ECOWAS)

federal character

Fulani

Hausa

Hausa-Fulani

Igbo

Independent National Election Commission (INEC)

Jonathan, Goodluck

June 12, 1993

Kaduna Mafia

Lagos

Movement for the Emancipation of the Niger Delta (MEND)

naira

neocolonial

Nigeria Labour Congress (NLC)

Obasanjo, Olusegun

Organization of Petroleum Exporting Countries (OPEC)

patron–client network

People's Democratic Party (PDP)

power shift

Saro-Wiwa, Ken

Structural Adjustment Program (SAP)

Yar'Adua, Umar Musa

Yoruba

SUGGESTED READINGS

Achebe, Chinua. *A Man of the People.* New York: Doubleday-Anchor, 1967.

———. *There Was a Country: A Personal History of Biafra.* New York: Penguin, 2012.

Adichie, Chimamanda Ngozi. *Half of a Yellow Sun.* New York: Random House, 2006.

Balogun, M. J. *The Route to Power in Nigeria.* New York: Palgrave Macmillan, 2009.

Beckett, Paul, and Crawford Young, eds. *Dilemmas of Democracy in Nigeria.* Rochester, NY: University of Rochester Press, 1997.

Campbell, John. *Nigeria: Dancing on the Brink.* Lanham, MD: Rowman and Littlefield, 2nd ed., 2013.

Coleman, James S. *Nigeria: Background to Nationalism.* Berkeley: University of California Press, 1958.

Collier, Paul, Catherine Soludo, and Charles Pattillo, eds. *Economic Policy Options for a Prosperous Nigeria.* New York: Palgrave Macmillan, 2008.

Cunliffe-Jones, Peter. *My Nigeria: Five Decades of Independence.* New York: Palgrave Macmillan, 2010.

Diamond, Larry. *Class, Ethnicity, and Democracy in Nigeria: The Failure of the First Republic.* Syracuse, NY: Syracuse University Press, 1988.

Diamond, Larry, Anthony Kirk-Greene, and O. Oyediran, eds. *Transition without End: Nigerian Politics and Civil Society under Babangida.* Boulder, CO: Lynne Rienner, 1997.

Falola, Toyin, and Matthew Heaton. *A History of Nigeria.* Cambridge: Cambridge University Press, 2008.

Hill, J. N. C. *Nigeria since Independence: Forever Fragile?* New York: Palgrave Macmillan, 2012.

Ikein, Augustine, D. S. P. Alamieyeseigha, and Steve Azaiki, eds. *Oil, Democracy, and the Promise of Federalism in Nigeria.* Boulder, CO: University Press of America, 2008.

Joseph, Richard A. *Democracy and Prebendal Politics in Nigeria: The Rise and Fall of the Second Republic.* Cambridge: Cambridge University Press, 1987.

Koehn, Peter H. *Public Policy and Administration in Africa: Lessons from Nigeria.* Boulder, CO: Westview, 1990.

Lewis, Peter M., Pearl T. Robinson, and Barnett R. Rubin. *Stabilizing Nigeria: Sanctions, Incentives, and Support for Civil Society.* Washington, DC: Brookings Institution Press, 1998.

Nafziger, E. Wayne. *The Economics of Political Instability: The Nigeria-Biafran War.* Boulder, CO: Westview, 1983.

Obadare, Ebenezer, and Wale Adebanwi, eds. *Encountering the Nigerian State.* New York: Palgrave Macmillan, 2010.

Oyediran, Oye, ed. *Nigerian Government and Politics under Military Rule 1968–79.* London: Macmillan, 1979.

Paden, John. *Muslim Civic Cultures and Conflict Resolution.* Washington, DC: Brookings Institution Press, 2005.

Smith, Daniel Jordan. *A Culture of Corruption: Everyday Deception and Popular Discontent in Nigeria.* Princeton, NJ: Princeton University Press, 2007.

Soyinka, Wole. *You Must Set Forth at Dawn.* New York: Random House, 2006.

Suberu, Rotimi T. *Federalism and Ethnic Conflict in Nigeria.* Washington, D.C.: U.S. Institute of Peace, 2001.

INTERNET RESOURCES

Federal government of Nigeria: www.nigeria.gov.ng.

Most of the major daily papers can be obtained through: www.AllAfrica.com.

Most civil society organizations mentioned in this chapter also maintain a Facebook page.

Pambazuka News: www.pambazuka.org/en/.

Vanguard newspaper: www.vanguardngr.com.

The Punch newspaper: www.punchng.com.

Centre for Democracy and Development: www.cddwestafrica.org.

Stakeholder Democracy Network: www.stakeholderdemocracy.org.

Nigeria Elections Coalition: www.nigeriaelections.org.

Transition Monitoring Group: www.tmgnigeria.wordpress.com.

Federation of Muslim Women's Associations in Nigeria: www.fomwan.org.

Twitter feeds:

The Guardian Nigeria@NGRGUARDIANNEWS

Punch Newspapers@MobilePunch

The Nation @TheNationNews

DailyTrust@daily_trust

Vanguard Newspapers@vanguardngrnews

Independent National Electoral Commission@inecnigeria

ENDNOTES

1. Editorial, "Don't Celebrate 1914 Amalgamation," *Punch*, August 19, 2012.

2. The term "tribe" has been applied indiscriminately to small groups of villages or whole empires, and often in conjunction with the adjective "primitive." Thus, "tribe" has lost any specific meaning and imparts prejudicial notions.

3. Michael Crowder, *The Story of Nigeria* (London: Faber and Faber, 1978).

4. Victor Chikezie Uchendu, *The Igbo of Southeast Nigeria* (Fort Worth, TX: Harcourt Brace Jovanovich College Publishers, 1965), 103.

5. Billy Dudley, *An Introduction to Nigerian Government and Politics* (Bloomington: University of Indiana Press, 1982), 230.

6. World Bank, "World Development Indicators," in *World Development Report, 2012* (Washington, DC: World Bank, 2012).

7. Patrick Smith, "Economy," in *Africa South of the Sahara 1994* (London: Europa, 1994), 660.

8. Amnesty International, "Forced Evictions," accessed May 15, 2013, http://www.amnesty.org.uk/issues/Forced-evictions.

9. Kaye Whiteman, "At Last, Something Is Happening in Lagos," *New African* 479 (2008): 50–52; and "Nigeria: Strategy for Reversing Development Crisis," *This Day*, August 12, 2009.

10. Judith Burdin Asuni, "Blood Oil in the Niger Delta," Special Report 229 (Washington, DC: U.S. Institute of Peace, August 2009).

11. A. Carl LeVan and Patrick Ukata, "Nigeria," in *Countries at the Crossroads* (New York: Freedom House, 2010).

12. Associated Press, "Hundreds Flee Nigerian City Swept by Riots," November 25, 2002.

13. Robert A. Dahl, *After the Revolution* (New Haven, CT: Yale University Press, 1971); see also the discussion in Dudley, *An Introduction to Nigerian Government*, 80–83.

14. Afrobarometer "Neither Consolidating nor Fully Democratic: The Evolution of African Political Regimes, 1999–2008" Briefing Paper no. 67 (Legon-Accra, Ghana: Afrobarometer, May 2009).

15. Mustapha Muhammad, "In the Shadows of Men: Women's Political Marginalisation," *InterPress Service*, March 12, 2010; and Ghaji Badawi, "Libraries and Women's Participation in Nigerian Politics," *IFLA Journal* 33 (2007): 168–75.

16. See the discussion in Dudley, *An Introduction to Nigerian Government*, 80–83.

17. BBC News, "Nigerian Leaders 'Stole' $380 Billion," October 20, 2006; BBC News, "Nigeria Governors in Graft Probe," September 28, 2006; and BBC News, "Obasanjo Accuses Deputy of Fraud," September 7, 2006.

18. "Halliburton to Pay Nigeria $35 Million to Settle Bribery Case," *Wall Street Journal,* December 22, 2010.

19. The discussion that follows draws on Crawford Young's treatment of socialization in his chapter on "Politics in Africa"*in earlier editions of this book.*

20. In anthropological usage, *polygamy* is a general term for marriage to more than one spouse. *Polygamy* is preferred to describe the marriage of one man to more than one woman (and *polyandry* for the reverse). However, *polygamy* is the term in general use in Nigeria and elsewhere in English-speaking Africa.

21. Bode Gbadebo, "NUC Shuts Down 41 Illegal Universities," *Leadership*, May 16, 2013.

22. *A Handbook of Information on Basic Education 2003* (Abuja: Federal Ministry of Education, 2003).

23. David Smith, "Nigerian 'Taliban' Offensive Leaves 150 Dead," *Guardian* (UK), July 27, 2009; and Segun Awofadeji, "150 Killed in Bauchi Religious Crisis," *This Day*, July 27, 2009.

24. Committee to Protect Journalists, "Attacks on the Press 2012: Nigeria," accessed February 15, 2013, http://www.cpj.org/2013/02/attacks-on-the-press-in-2012-nigeria.php.

25. Peter H. Koehn, *Public Policy and Administration in Africa: Lessons from Nigeria* (Boulder, CO: Westview, 1990), 16.

26. Chinua Achebe, *There Was a Country: A Personal History of Biafra* (New York: Penguin Press, 2012).

27. As noted in Chapter 5, the concept of consociational arrangement comes from Arend Lijphart, *Democracy in Plural Societies* (New Haven, CT: Yale University Press, 1977).

28. Koehn, *Public Policy and Administration in Africa*, 17–18, cites various sources for these totals.

29. Richard Sklar and C. S. Whitaker, Jr., "Nigeria," in *Political Parties and National Integration in Tropical Africa*, ed. James S. Coleman and Carl G. Rosberg, Jr. (Berkeley: University of California Press, 1964), 636.

30. Wole Soyinka, *You Must Set Forth at Dawn* (New York: Random House, 2006), 421.

31. Richard A. Joseph, *Democracy and Prebendal Politics in Nigeria* (Cambridge: Cambridge University Press, 1987), 133–34.

32. Joseph, *Democracy and Prebendal Policy in Nigeria*. Joseph calls the Nigerian version of patronage *prebendalism*: "patterns of political behavior which rest on the justifying principle that such offices should be competed for and then utilized for the personal benefit of officeholders as well as for their reference or support group. The official public purpose of the office often becomes a secondary concern, however much that purpose may have been originally cited in its creation or during the periodic competition to fill it" (8).

33. Human Rights Watch, *Spiraling Violence: Boko Haram Attacks and Security Force Abuses in Nigeria* (New York: Human Rights Watch, 2012).

34. "Cameroons" here refers to the English-speaking portion of the contemporary country of Cameroon (French Cameroun) on Nigeria's eastern border. The former German colony of that name was divided into League of Nations Trust Territories after World War I under British and French control. The NCNC was meant to include members from the British trust territory as well as from Nigeria, but in a preindependence plebiscite, the English-speaking Cameroonians opted for incorporation into Cameroon. The NCNC then was renamed the National Convention of Nigerian Citizens.

35. Address of Brigadier Murtala Muhammed, reprinted as the preface to the *Report of the Constitution Drafting Committee* (Lagos: Ministry of Information, 1976), quoted in Dudley, *Introduction to Nigerian Government,* 127.

36. Muideen Olaniyi, "How Party Mergers Will Shape 2015 Elections," *Daily Trust,* January 13, 2013.

37. *Class, Ethnicity, and Democracy in Nigeria: The Failure of the First Republic* (Syracuse, NY: Syracuse University Press, 1988), 53.

38. I. William Zartman and Sayre Schatz, "Introduction," in *The Political Economy of Nigeria*, ed. I. William Zartman (New York: Praeger, 1983), 13. The military figures cited here come from Ruth Sivard, *World Military and Social Expenditures 1996* (Leesburg, VA: WMSE Publications, 1996), and Sivard, *The Military Balance 2001–2002* (London: Oxford University Press, 2001).

39. Obiora Chinedu Okafor, "Between Elite Interests and Pro-Poor Resistance: The Nigerian Courts and Labour-Led Anti-Fuel Hike Struggles (1999–2007)," *Journal of African Law* 54 (2010), 95–118.

40. Rotimi T. Suberu, *Federalism and Ethnic Conflict in Nigeria* (Washington, DC: US Institute of Peace, 2001), 169.

41. The preceding treatment of the formation of ECOWAS is drawn from Carol Lancaster, "The Lagos Three: Economic Regionalism in Sub-Saharan Africa," in *Africa in World Politics*, ed. John W. Harbeson and Donald Rothchild (Boulder, CO: Westview Press, 1991), 249–67.

42. Air Chief Marshal Paul Dike, "Preface," in *Winning Hearts and Minds: A Community Relations Approach for the Nigerian Military*, ed. Ebere Onwudiwe and Eghosa Osaghae (Ibadan, Nigeria: John Archers, 2010).

43. Cyril Obi, "Nigeria's Foreign Policy and Transnational Security Challenges in West Africa," *Journal of Contemporary African Studies* 46 (April 2008), 183–96.

44. Tanure Ojaide, *The Blood of Peace and Other Poems* (London: Heinemann, 1991), 9.

45. Diamond, "Nigeria," 69.

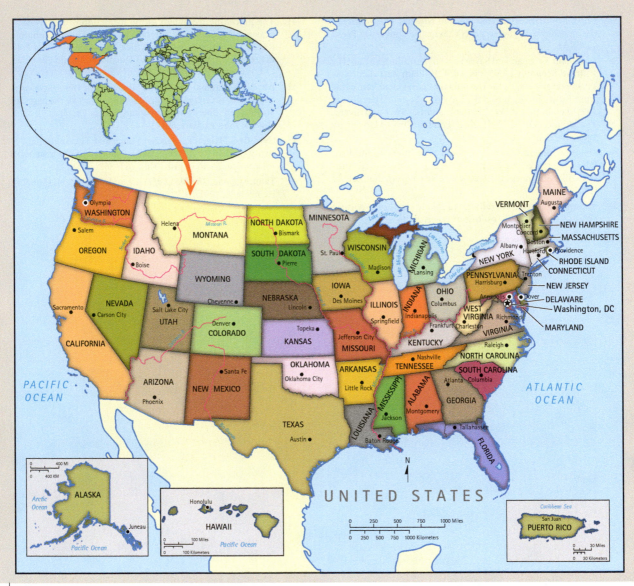

Country Bio

POPULATION
316 million

TERRITORY
3,475,031 square miles

YEAR OF INDEPENDENCE
1776

YEAR OF CURRENT CONSTITUTION
September 17, 1787, effective March 4, 1789

HEAD OF STATE
President Barack Obama

HEAD OF GOVERNMENT
President Barack Obama

LANGUAGES
English, Spanish (spoken by a sizeable minority)

RELIGIONS
Protestant 50 percent, Roman Catholic 25 percent, Muslim 1 percent, Mormon 1 percent, Jewish 1 percent, none or not stated 20 percent

CHAPTER 19

Politics in the United States

Thad Kousser and Austin Ranney

LEARNING OBJECTIVES

19.1 Describe the domestic and foreign challenges facing the United States, focusing on the interparty conflicts over these issues.

19.2 Identify three divisive areas in U.S. political history and discuss their current status.

19.3 State the size of the United States in terms of geography, population, and economy.

19.4 List the three distinctive features of the U.S. constitutional system and describe the interrelated nature of their powers.

19.5 Identify and discuss the two theories of cultural blending in the United States.

19.6 Discuss the role of mass communications media in U.S. politics, along with the government's ability to regulate the media.

19.7 Compare and contrast U.S. nominating and voting processes and turnout with those in other countries, and describe alternative forms of political participation.

19.8 Describe PACs and interest groups and contrast their methods in the United States with those of similar groups in other countries.

19.9 Discuss the level of polarization between the major U.S. political parties and its impact upon policymaking.

19.10 Explain the U.S. policymaking process, as it generally occurs through Congress and as it occasionally occurs via the president.

19.11 Compare U.S. tax levels and types to those of other countries.

19.12 Discuss three problem areas regulated by the U.S. government.

And what should they know of England
  Who only England know?
  Rudyard Kipling[1]

Why a chapter on the United States in a book on comparative politics? One reason is that most of its readers are Americans, and politics in the United States affects our lives far more than politics in any other country. Moreover, however feeble we may feel that our personal power is to influence the actions of our government, it is certainly greater than our personal power to influence the actions of other nations' governments.

The question Rudyard Kipling asked about the English in the quotation above can be asked with equal relevance about Americans. There are, of course, many excellent textbooks on the American political system written by American authors and intended for American students. But most of them make few references to, let alone systematic comparisons with, other political systems. Thus, viewing American politics with a special focus on how it resembles, and differs from, politics in other nations will help us better meet our version of Kipling's challenge. It may even give us some insight into how the distinctive ways of American politics are likely to affect our country's ability to meet the enormous challenges it will face in the years ahead.

Current Policy Challenges

19.1 Describe the domestic and foreign challenges facing the United States, focusing on the interparty conflicts over these issues.

After a decade dominated by international conflict—from the terrorist attacks of September 11, 2001, through the Iraq War and the ongoing war in Afghanistan—as well as the effects of a worldwide recession, America's primary policy challenges are now domestic in scope but no less daunting. Will the **Affordable Care Act**, the health insurance law that represents the most massive expansion of the social safety net in a generation, achieve its goals of broadening coverage, controlling costs, and satisfying patients as it is widely implemented in 2014? Will the nation's political leaders reach a compromise over immigration that satisfies the clashing constituencies calling for, on one side, a tightened border and, on the other, a path to citizenship for the nation's 11 million illegal immigrants? Can America's ever-growing **public debt** be reduced, and will future generations be able to pay the cost of retiree pensions and health care? As public opinion swiftly changes on issues such as gay marriage and marijuana legalization, how will political leaders and institutions negotiate the nation's contentious social divides?

All of these domestic debates will play out in an economy still plagued by high unemployment and a world that is sure to deliver unexpected foreign policy crises. The resolution of these disputes will come through a democratic system that, while polarized along partisan lines and often gridlocked in Washington, D.C., has proven to be remarkably adaptive to societal changes and resilient in the face of the constant governing challenges it has faced.

As in any democracy, our political system serves as the battleground of ideas for confronting these challenges. American democracy not only allows but also encourages internal conflict, bringing the competition between diametrically opposed approaches to policy challenges into the open during electoral campaigns and legislative debates. This sort of democracy can often appear loud, bitter, and messy. Indeed, politics in the United States today features the most expensive campaigns in history, while the level of partisan polarization—the magnitude of the ideological gulf between Republican and Democratic elected officials—has grown unabated for a generation. A quick glance at cable television news or any political blog shows evidence of the decline in civility.

These trends pose political challenges, but not insuperable ones. By making the fight between divergent approaches toward the nation's policy challenges transparent to voters, today's rancorous American democracy presents the electorate with clear choices. Through a series of nail-biting, momentous elections over the past decade, voters placed control of government fully in the hands of Republicans in 2000, then shifted power completely back to Democrats by 2008, and finally split control between a Democratic chief executive and a Republican House of Representatives in 2010. The reelection of Barack Obama in the same 2012 election that solidified Republican control of the House promises more political conflict in the years to come. The two parties, led by a relatively liberal President Barack Obama and by staunchly conservative Republican leaders in Congress, seek to move policy in dramatically different directions.

Does America's political system, then, promise only conflict and stalemate in response to the nation's pressing policy challenges? A look back at recent history shows that even with polarized parties fighting over the control of governing branches that the constitution keeps separate, America's combative politics can deliver sweeping changes in both international and domestic policy.

Though he was elected by the narrowest of margins in 2000, George W. Bush quickly moved beyond the controversies of butterfly ballots and hanging chads in Florida to make his imprint on the nation's policy direction. President Bush pushed for and won a major tax cut in his first year in office. The policy challenges facing the United States radically shifted from domestic to international with the events of 9/11, the most lethal terrorist attacks committed against the United States on American soil. Planned and executed by members of Al Qaeda, an international terrorist organization led by Osama bin Laden, the attacks were met by a U.S.-led "war on terror" that has been fought not only against Al Qaeda but also against any organization or nation-state that has sheltered terrorists, financed them, or supported them in any way.

The tactics used to fight this war—surveillance both on the ground in dozens of other countries and in the air through interception of wireless communications, some originating in America—are new and often controversial. Through legal cases and debates in Congress, the nation has had an open, ongoing discussion on the proper balance between tightening security and loosening liberties. Although President Obama campaigned on a promise to close the Guantanamo detention camp, the challenge of shutting down this site for the indefinite detainment of accused terrorists without introducing security risks left Obama's promise unfulfilled five years into his administration. The Boston Marathon bombing of 2013 reminded the nation that terrorism, whether committed by international or domestic actors, remains a threat.

The 9/11 attacks also spurred American involvement in two conventional wars, one in Afghanistan and one in Iraq. Because Al Qaeda planned its attack on New York City from remote bases in Afghanistan, under the tacit protection of the ruling Taliban regime, the U.S.-led invasion of this isolated nation was swift and uncontroversial in domestic and international political circles. Many other nations lent troops and support to the war, which appeared to be immediately successful. It began less than a month after 9/11, and by December of that year, the Taliban had been toppled from power and Al Qaeda driven into hiding. Hamid Karzai became Afghanistan's first elected president in 2004, but by the time he was reelected in a contest marred by fraud in 2009, his administration was tainted by allegations of corruption and struggled to control outlying areas such as the Kandahar province. Persistent violence has kept U.S. troops in the country. Though U.S. casualties in Afghanistan have been relatively low, at 2,220 troops killed in action by 2013, this conflict has overtaken Vietnam as America's longest-running war.

The second war that followed in the wake of 9/11 was much more controversial, both in America and across the globe. While only a single member of Congress voted against the invasion of Afghanistan in 2001, the resolution to authorize an attack on Iraq—which was not directly involved in the terrorist attacks—was opposed by 133 U.S. representatives and 23 senators. President Bush's decision in March 2003 to invade Iraq despite the U.S. failure to win endorsement from the UN Security Council also met with international opposition from traditional allies such as France and Germany (though the United Kingdom, Australia, and Poland lent support and troops to the effort). The war was quick, with Saddam Hussein's regime in Baghdad falling within weeks. Yet winning the peace proved much more difficult than winning the war, as it became clear that the United States committed too few troops and was too optimistic in its hopes to be welcomed as a liberator. Ongoing conflict with insurgents claimed the lives of 4,486 American troops, though the intensity of this war subsided after reaching its highest levels in 2007. Barack Obama, a critic of the war since its inception, campaigned openly against the Bush administration's policies during the presidential contest and began a troop drawdown shortly after he was inaugurated, completing the withdrawal of U.S. military personnel by December 2011. Even in the face of much domestic political controversy, both presidents were able to move foreign policy in the divergent directions that they, their advisors, and their supporters favored.

American policymakers exerted less control over the global economic crisis that peaked in 2008–2009 but caused persistent unemployment in that nation for years afterward. U.S. stocks crashed sharply in September 2008 as home foreclosures and a credit crunch sent America, and then much of the world, into a spiraling recession. The economy of nearly every developed nation abruptly contracted, consumer spending plummeted, and unemployment reached sustained levels not seen in America since the Great Depression of the 1930s. Eager for change, the American electorate responded to this crash by brining a new party into the White House, electing Democrat Barack Obama by a wide margin in November 2008 largely on the basis of dissatisfaction with the economy's performance under Republicans.

With his party controlling both houses of Congress, Obama moved quickly to reverse the nation's economic and policy direction. In February 2009, the president and his allies passed a $787 billion economic stimulus plan—a mixture of tax cuts and spending increases—without a single Republican vote in the House. With lagging popularity but loyal majorities in Congress, President Obama pressed to pass two more pieces of legislation that, combined with the stimulus bill, amount to perhaps the sharpest policy shifts since Franklin Delano Roosevelt's "New Deal." Succeeding where Presidents Truman, Nixon, and Clinton had failed before him, Obama championed a **health care**

reform package that set the country on a path toward universal medical coverage through publicly subsidized private insurance. After nearly a year of debate on this controversial overhaul, Congress passed the bill by a razor-thin margin in March 2010, and the Supreme Court narrowly upheld it in June 2012. Another enormous bill passed by miniscule majorities was the financial reform bill that enacted a strong set of consumer protections and banking regulations in July 2010.

In reaction both to these sharp leftward policy swings and to the slow pace of economic recovery, voters put the House of Representatives back into Republican hands in the 2010 midterm election (see Box 19.3). While the president's party nearly always loses seats in midterm elections, the sixty-three seats that then-Speaker Nancy Pelosi's Democrats lost signified a major electoral swing and ensured that President Obama would be forced into conflict with incoming Speaker John Boehner's Republican majority in Congress. Over the next two years, as the 2012 presidential contest approached, neither side proved willing to compromise over what has become the defining issue of the day: how to reduce the nation's debt, which grew as America fought two expensive wars and paid for a stimulus package at the same time that the recession shrank tax revenues. After Obama won reelection (see Box 19.4), he was able to reach a tax policy deal with Republican leaders that prevented the nation from falling over a "fiscal cliff" of severe tax hikes and spending cuts on New Year's Day 2013, but the two sides continued to negotiate over a permanent budget balancing deal that spring. At the same time, a bipartisan coalition of senators, dubbed the "Gang of Eight," pushed for an overhaul of immigration laws, a lightning rod of contention in recent American politics. Adding to the controversies playing out in Washington, D.C., many states have allowed same-sex marriage and legalized the medical or recreational use of marijuana, embarking on passionate and divisive debates while demonstrating the exceptional—compared to nearly all other nations—autonomy of American state governments.

The events of the twenty-first century's turbulent first decade have demonstrated both America's vulnerability and power on the world stage as well as the responsiveness of its political system. The nation moved sharply over the course of the decade: from economic boom to bust, from unified Republican control of government to unified Democratic control to divided government, from a series of tax cuts to major enlargements of government services, and from unchallenged superpower to an embattled yet still potent world player. The American political system has not always delivered such sharp partisan swings or reacted so nimbly to policy challenges, but its basic features, described in this chapter, have remained unchanged.

History

19.2 Identify three divisive areas in U.S. political history and discuss their current status.

Founding of the Nation

Ever since its founding as the world's first modern democracy, America has been dramatically expanding its place in the world. Americans have been renegotiating exactly who will be included within our democracy. The nation has grown more and more prominent in the global community throughout its history, transforming itself from a loose confederation of thirteen states surrounded by the colonial holdings of European powers into a continental power, then a hemispheric player, and, finally, taking its current position as a world superpower. The path of American democracy has been less straightforward and linear than the route of America's global influence. Under the founders, America was a democracy constituted of white males who owned property. The electorate expanded slowly, with the nation at times reversing its course to take away voting rights from those who once possessed them. Today, men and women of any race or ethnicity can vote, though differences in turnout rates across these categories persist. There are many parts to tell in the story of American history, so this brief retelling focuses on changes in our nation's place in the world as well as on how inclusive its democracy has been.

The revolution by a disparate set of colonies against the English throne was a long shot from the start that remained a risky proposition through the nation's early history. Putting their lives and their considerable fortunes at risk, the signers of the Declaration of Independence began a guerilla war against the British, the world's leading imperial power at the time. George Washington and his fellow colonists took advantage of the military training that they had received by fighting for the British in the French and Indian War, as well as the more steadfast commitment of their troops, to win a shocking victory. The first government they crafted, organized under the Articles of Confederation, was largely a failure, too weak to provide a common defense against threatening foreign powers or to bring the new states together in the pursuit of unified goals. The truly exceptional step that marked America's historical path as unique and magnificent came next, when the weak confederation was replaced not by a strong dictator but by a muscular democracy. The other major revolutions in world history—in France and in Russia—eventually led to tyranny, but America's revolution of 1776 led to the crafting of the Constitution in 1787. This successful system produced the stablest democracy that the world has seen and has influenced the design of governmental systems the world over. Its essential characteristics—separation of powers, presidentialism, judicial independence, and, in its first ten amendments, a Bill of Rights that limits the government's powers—have appeared in whole or in part in constitutions from the Philippines to Latin America to modern Russia.

Still, at the edge of a continent controlled by rival European powers, the Americans remained in peril. The War of 1812, in which the British burned the new capital city of Washington, served as a reminder of the young nation's vulnerability. Yet with a strong constitution keeping the agriculture-based, slave-reliant colonies of the South in a strained but workable alliance with the industrial, antislavery colonies of the North, America prospered and used some of its wealth to purchase land from France (in the 1803 Louisiana Purchase) and Russia (acquiring Alaska in 1867). Assembling a military that became the preeminent power in the Western Hemisphere, America also expanded its borders to the Pacific Ocean after the Mexican–American War ended in 1848.

Also growing during the nineteenth century was the size of the electorate eligible to vote in America. After the revolution, states imposed various requirements that white men had to own property or hold wealth to vote, every state barred women from taking part in most elections, and only a few northern states granted the franchise to African Americans. By 1792, France had surpassed the United States in the scope of its democracy when the new republic there granted universal male suffrage (though this expansion of rights ended as the republic became Napoleon's Empire). American states gradually caught up in the early 1800s, reducing property-holding requirements so that white men of every class could vote. The Democratic-Republican Party, led by the charisma of war hero Andrew Jackson and the organizational genius of professional politician Martin Van Buren, helped to turn this legal right into electoral reality when its grassroots party groups ushered in an era of high turnout among white men. The energetic advocates of women's voting rights won partial victories—and put America near the forefront of the women's suffrage movement—when twenty states allowed women to vote in referendums to prohibit alcohol sales, and when Wyoming became the first state to allow female suffrage in 1869. Still, the final victory for this movement did not come until the ratification of the Nineteenth Amendment, giving all American women the right to vote in 1920. Much more discouraging was the fight for African American voting rights, which were won and then lost in the south after the Civil War.

Civil War

The Civil War (1861–1865) is the United States' great historical watershed. Before 1861, it was a much-disputed question as to whether the United States was merely a convenient alliance made among independent sovereign states—states that had every right to secede whenever they wished—or an indissoluble sovereign nation whose people chose to divide power between the national government and the state governments. In the terminology introduced in Chapter 6 of this book, the United States was a "confederation" during this period. After 1865, in both law and fact, it was established that the United States was, as every American schoolchild is drilled to know, "one nation, indivisible," and not a federation of sovereign states.

Before 1861, many Americans, especially those in the eleven southern states that seceded to form the Confederacy, felt that they were first and foremost citizens of their states and thus derived their American citizenship from the membership of their states in the union. (The most famous example was Robert E. Lee; he strongly opposed both slavery and secession, and yet when Virginia seceded, he refused command of the Union Army and cast his lot with Virginia because he felt he owed his primary loyalty to his state, not his nation.) The Fourteenth Amendment to the Constitution, ratified in 1868, removed all doubt by declaring, "All persons born or naturalized in the United States, and subject to the jurisdiction thereof, are citizens of the

United States and of the State wherein they reside." In short, all Americans are now primarily citizens of the United States, and derivatively become citizens of the state in which they reside. (Interested readers can see the broader discussion of federalism in Chapter 6.)

By cementing the union of American states, the Civil War also solidified American power abroad. The vast military might assembled to fight this internal war left the nation able to challenge even European powers, as it did successfully in the Spanish–American War of 1898. More difficult was the fight to transform America into a nation that uniformly accepted civil rights. Passed in the Civil War's wake, the Fifteenth Amendment guaranteed voting rights to American citizens regardless of "race, color, or previous condition of servitude." Still, it took the might of the north's military occupation of the south to keep polls open to former slaves. When the troops left the south in 1876, massive political violence made African American voting dangerous, and a series of state laws began to make it nearly impossible. By 1900, these laws—including poll taxes that imposed fees on all voters, literacy tests that could be administered in a discriminatory fashion, and blunter instruments like the "white primary"—reversed the voting rights gains won in the Civil War and left black voter turnout below 10 percent in the south.

Twentieth Century

After experiencing staggering, if uneven, industrial growth in the late 1800s, America was ready to take its place as an economic and military leader on the world stage by the turn of the century. Theodore Roosevelt's mediation of the Russo–Japanese War (1905) and America's belated entry (1917) into World War I (1914–1918) signaled the nation's willingness to engage in world affairs beyond its own hemisphere. Ever since America emerged from World War II (1939–1945) as a clear military victor and the strongest remaining economy, it has been a leading player on the world stage. Of course, superpower status has come with immense dangers and costs. From 1948 to 1989, world politics was dominated by the "Cold War" between the two great superpowers and their allies: the United States, leading an alliance of Western capitalist/democratic nations, and the Soviet Union, leading an alliance of Eastern communist/authoritarian nations. The Cold War came to an end in the early 1990s when the Soviet Union was formally dissolved (see Chapter 12) and Eastern European nations established their independence.

The defining internal struggle in American politics during the century was again the fight for African American political rights. During World War II, many blacks fought valiantly abroad, while others migrated from the south to cities across the country to work in factories. These geographic and economic migrations brought social change and a well-organized push for civil rights in the south and across the country. Galvanized by the Supreme Court's 1954 *Brown v. Board of Education of Topeka* decision, the push to integrate schools and other public institutions moved from Kansas to Little Rock to the University of Alabama. When some southern leaders reacted with explicitly racist rhetoric and police officers met the Reverend Martin Luther King's peaceful protests with violence, popular opinion across the nation turned toward the side of African American rights. Congress passed important Civil Rights Acts in 1957 and 1964, but it was the Voting Rights Act of 1965 that finally enfranchised black Americans in practice by giving the federal courts and the U.S. Department of Justice the power to enforce voting rights. The political and social transformation that followed in the south and in other areas of the country have served as an example to civil rights advocates around the world, demonstrating the potential for translating legal changes into vast societal shifts.

America Today

With an expanded electorate, America now has a much more diverse set of elected leaders. In 2013, 101 of the 535 U.S. representatives and senators were women, 43 were African American, 32 were Hispanic, 30 were Asian American or Pacific Islander, and 4 were Arab American. Comparing this representation of women with other democracies, America ranks ahead of Russia, Iran, Ireland, Japan, and South Korea, but behind the United Kingdom, Mexico, and France, and far behind Germany, the Netherlands, and Argentina. The election of President Barack Obama is an obvious watershed event in the representation of racial and ethnic minorities, but it should be viewed as the culmination of a series of advances rather than a singular event. George W. Bush's administration featured two African American secretaries of state in Colin Powell and Condoleezza Rice. Although the nation has never elected a female president, Hillary Clinton is an early favorite for the Democratic nomination in 2016, Sarah Palin played a very prominent role as the vice-presidential nominee on the Republican ticket in 2008, and the Democratic Party made Geraldine Ferraro its nominee for vice president as early as 1984.

Of course, political rights and equality also do not guarantee economic equality. Women earn less than men, on average, in America, and the problem of the economic and social status of African Americans remains high on the agenda. While African Americans today are in many respects better off than they were a generation ago, they still lag behind whites in many areas, including family incomes, crime and imprisonment rates, formal education, housing quality, family stability, vulnerability to such diseases as AIDS, and life expectancy. The nation's attention was focused on many of these inequalities after Hurricane Katrina flooded and destroyed many areas of New Orleans, a heavily African American city, in August 2005. The lack of planning for this frequently predicted emergency and the agonizingly slow response to it by all levels of government led many, both black and white, to question whether the race and poverty of New Orleans residents put them especially at risk.

Immigration into America has increased its social diversity at the same time that it has moved the politics of diversity beyond black-and-white divides. In the new millennium, our nation of immigrants will once again debate immigration policy and the nature of U.S. citizenship. The acceleration in recent decades in the ethnic and linguistic diversity of nearly every state, along with a rise in the number of illegal immigrants, has led to demands for a more inclusive citizenship policy as well as calls for increased border security. Immigrant rights activists demonstrated their organizational muscle when millions of people in cities from Chicago to Dallas to Los Angeles participated in marches held on May 1, 2006, to protest Congressional legislation that would have classified illegal immigrants and anyone who aided them as felons. That bill eventually died, but voters concerned with illegal immigration won a victory in April 2010 when Arizona passed a law mandating a crackdown on illegal immigrants in that border state. Immigration became a contentious issue in the 2012 presidential contest, with many observers noting that the Republican Party's tough stance cost it votes in an increasingly diverse electorate made up of many newly naturalized citizens. In response, in 2013, a handful of Republican senators allied with Democrats to form a "Gang of Eight" pushing for an immigration overhaul delivering a path to citizenship for illegal immigrants. Whether or not their policy proposal proves successful, the debate over immigration and the incorporation of new groups is likely to continue.

Social Conditions

19.3 State the size of the United States in terms of geography, population, and economy.

Geography

The United States has jurisdiction over a territory totaling 3,475,031 square miles. This makes it geographically the fourth-largest nation in the world, smaller only than Russia (6,592,800 square miles), Canada (3,849,674 square miles), and the People's Republic of China (3,696,100 square miles).[2] The United States is bounded by the Atlantic Ocean on the east, the Pacific Ocean on the west, Canada on the north, and Mexico on the south. This secure location—great oceans on two sides, militarily weak nations on the other two sides—made feasible the foreign policy of isolation from alliances and wars with foreign countries that the United States pursued until the end of the nineteenth century. In these days of intercontinental ballistic missiles, orbiting spy satellites, and international terrorism, however, no nation, including the United States, can count on its geographical location to keep it isolated from world politics.

Population

The U.S. Bureau of the Census estimated that the total population in the United States approached 316 million in 2013. This makes it the third most populous nation in the world, behind China with 1.3 billion and India with 1.2 billion.[3] The U.S. rate of population increase has been impressive. The first census in 1790 reported a total population of 3.9 million, so the 2013 figure represents a staggering increase of 8,102 percent in 220 years. Over 50 million people have moved from other parts of the world to the United States—a phenomenon characterized by British analyst H. G. Nicholas as "the greatest movement of population in Western history."[4] Accordingly, one of the most important facts to recognize about the United States is that, more than any other nation in history, it is a nation of immigrants. The census classifies only 1.2 percent of the population as being of Native American, Alaskan native, or Hawaiian ancestry;[5] the rest are immigrants or descendants of immigrants from all over the world.

Most immigrants came in one or the other of three historic waves: first, 1840 to 1860, mainly from Western Europe, Britain, and Ireland; second, 1870 to 1920, mainly from Asia, Eastern Europe, Italy, and Scandinavia; and third, 1965 until the present, mainly from Latin America and Asia. In the 1920s, Congress imposed a ceiling on the number of immigrants allowed, and the immigration rate dropped sharply. It rebounded after the Immigration and Nationality Act was amended in 1965 to eliminate caps on the number of people who could migrate from each country. Today, about 700,000 to 1 million *legal* immigrants continue to arrive in America every year. In addition, an estimated 11 million *illegal* immigrants—those who are foreign-born and enter the country without inspection or violate the terms of a visa—reside in the United States.[6] Figure 19.1 divides up America's foreign-born population (including both legal and illegal immigrants) according to places of birth.

Thus, from its beginnings, the United States has received far more immigrants than any other nation in history, and it has the most ethnically and culturally diverse population that the world has ever seen (only India comes close). Later, we will consider some of the consequences for American politics.

Economy

Even after the "dot.com" bust of 2000 to 2003 and the global financial crisis of 2008 and 2009, America remains the world's largest economy. In 2009, its gross national income (GNI), or the total value of all the goods and services it produced plus income from foreign sources, was calculated at $14.2 trillion, compared with Japan's $4.9 trillion, China's $4.9 trillion, and Germany's $3.5 trillion.[7] The American dollar continues to be the world's basic monetary unit; the value of most nations' currencies is customarily measured by how many euros, pounds, rubles, yen, and other units it takes to exchange for part or all of a dollar.

Some economists believe that American economic dominance has ended. The United States, which for many years was the world's greatest creditor nation, has become the world's greatest debtor nation, in part because Americans continue to buy billions of dollars more of foreign goods than foreigners buy of American goods, and in part because of the long-standing enormous deficits in the federal government's budget. From 1980 through 1997, the federal government spent a total of $3.1 trillion more than it took in, then ran modest surpluses from 1998 to 2001, but has returned to record-setting deficits since then. By 2011, the accumulated gross national debt was an estimated $15.5 trillion.[8]

America has long been regarded as the citadel of capitalist economic ideas and institutions and the main antagonist of people and nations who believe in socialism. Yet American economic institutions and practices have never come close to meeting the standards for completely free enterprise laid down by such *laissez-faire* economists as Adam Smith in the eighteenth century and Milton Friedman in the twentieth. These economists advocated the barest minimum of government interference in economic affairs, including no government regulation of the operations, profits, and wages paid by successful businesses, and no

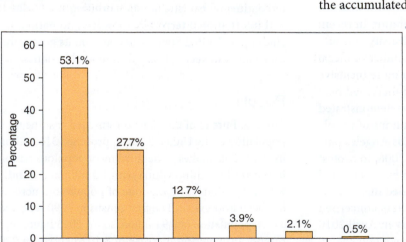

FIGURE 19.1

Birthplaces of Foreign-Born Population, 2009

Source: *Statistical Abstract of the United States: 2012* (Washington, DC: Bureau of the Census, 2012), Table 42.

government subsidies or "bailouts" for unsuccessful businesses.

Yet even aside from Congress authorizing a $700 billion bailout of financial institutions and other large corporations in the fall of 2008, American governments subsidize American businesses in many ways. They conduct research that businesses can use to develop new products and pay to market American products in other countries. State, local, and federal governments work together to provide public goods, such as education and a transportation infrastructure. Congress imposes tariffs and import quotas on certain foreign manufactured goods to prevent them from undercutting American manufacturers. Federal laws guarantee that all workers will be paid a certain minimum wage regardless of what they would get in a truly free market, and this wage has been raised repeatedly in recent decades. Quasi-public enterprises like Fannie Mae and Freddie Mac, put under full federal conservatorship in 2008, make it easier for homebuyers to obtain loans. Federal tax law subsidizes the pensions and health plans that businesses offer to their employees, creating a hybrid public–private safety net that works something like a European welfare state, though only for those who get jobs with good benefits.[9] As the effects of the health care reform bill passed in 2010 begin to phase in, America will look even more like a European nation by mandating and subsidizing universal coverage. Most of these policies have come from political pressure by business associations, labor unions, and other pressure groups. Thus, it seems fair to say that, while most Americans say they believe in free enterprise, they prefer to practice safe enterprise. The recent economic disaster and the massive bailout of private enterprise that it spurred serve as reminders that free market ideologies can yield quickly in a time of crisis and that the public treasury assumes the risks of private corporations deemed "too big to fail."

The Constitutional System

19.4 List the three distinctive features of the U.S. constitutional system and describe the interrelated nature of their powers.

As in most modern nations (Great Britain and Israel are two notable exceptions), the basic structure of the American system of government is set forth in a written constitution—the Constitution of the United States, a document drawn up in 1787, ratified in 1788, and inaugurated in 1789. It is the world's oldest written constitution still in force.

Of course, the Constitution of today differs from that of 1789 in a number of important ways. It has been formally amended twenty-seven times, the most recent being the 1992 amendment that provided that no law changing the compensation for members of Congress shall take effect until an election of members of the House has been held.[10] The first ten amendments, known collectively as the **Bill of Rights**, list the rights of individuals that the national government is forbidden to abridge (see Box 19.1).

| BOX 19.1 | The U.S. Bill of Rights |

1. Freedom of religion, speech, press.
2. Right to bear arms.
3. Freedom from quartering soldiers without owner's consent.
4. No unreasonable searches and seizures.
5. Trial of civilians only after indictment by a grand jury; no double jeopardy; prohibition against compelled self-incrimination; no deprivation of life, liberty, or property without due process of law; no taking of private property for public use without just compensation.
6. In criminal prosecutions, right to speedy and public trial by an impartial jury; defendant must be informed of the nature and cause of accusations; defendant has power to compel testimony by witnesses in his or her favor; right to assistance of counsel.
7. Guarantee of trial by jury where the amount in controversy is over twenty dollars.
8. No excessive bail, no excessive fines, no cruel and unusual punishments.
9. Enumeration of certain rights in the Constitution shall not be construed to deny or diminish others retained by the people.
10. Powers not delegated to the national government nor prohibited to the states are reserved to the states or to the people.

One of the most important amendments is the Fourteenth Amendment, ratified just after the Civil War. It makes national citizenship legally superior to state citizenship, and prohibits the states from violating the "privileges and immunities" of U.S. citizens—which, by judicial interpretation, has come to mean nearly all the rights guaranteed against the national government by the first ten amendments. Other major amendments have outlawed slavery (the Thirteenth), guaranteed the right to vote to former slaves (the Fifteenth) and women (the Nineteenth), limited presidents to two elective terms (the Twenty-Second), and spelled out the conditions under which an incapacitated president can be replaced (the Twenty-Fifth). Even with these amendments, most of the basic elements of the 1789 Constitution have remained in force, whereas the written constitutions in many other countries and in most of the American states have been replaced altogether several times. Thus, if durability is a mark of constitutional strength, the Constitution of the United States is one of the strongest in history.

Yet the words in the Constitution do not tell all there is to be told about the basic structure of the American constitutional system. A number of customs, usages, and judicial decisions have significantly altered our way of governing without changing a word in the Constitution. Examples are the addition of judicial review, the development of political parties, and the conversion of the presidential selection process from a closed process by small cliques of insiders to popular elections open to all citizens.

Taken together, the provisions of the written Constitution of the United States and their associated customs and usages add up to a constitutional system that has three distinctive features: federalism, separation of powers, and judicial review.

Federalism

Federalism is a system in which governmental power is divided between a national government and several subnational governments, each of which is legally supreme in its assigned sphere. This system has some ancient precursors, notably the Achaean League of Greek city-states in the third century BCE and the Swiss Confederation founded in the sixteenth century CE. But the men who wrote the American Constitution established the first modern form of federalism. They

did so because they had to. The 1787 convention in Philadelphia was called because its members felt that the new nation needed a much stronger national government than the Articles of Confederation provided, but the representatives from the small states refused to join any national government that did not preserve most of their established powers. The framers broke the resulting stalemate by dividing power between the national and the state governments and gave each state equal representation in the national Senate. Only thus could the large and small states agree on a new constitution.

Even so, some of the framers regarded federalism as more than a political expedient. James Madison, for example, believed that the greatest threat to human rights in a popular government is the tyranny of popular majorities that results when one faction seizes control of the entire power of government and uses it to advance its own special interests at the expense of all other interests. He saw a division of power between the national and state governments, combined with separation of powers, as the best way to prevent such a disaster.

Federalism has been widely praised as one of the greatest American contributions to the art of government. A number of nations have adopted it as a way of enabling different regions with sharply different cultures and interests to join together as one nation. The clearest examples of such nations today are Australia, Canada, Germany, Nigeria, Russia, and Switzerland, but significant elements of federalism are also found in systems as disparate as those of Brazil, India, and Mexico.

The American federal system divides government power in the following principal ways:

- Powers specifically assigned to the federal government, such as the power to declare war, make treaties with foreign nations, coin money, and regulate commerce between the states.
- Powers reserved to the states by the Tenth Amendment. The main powers in this category are those over education, marriage and divorce, intrastate commerce, and regulation of motor vehicles. However, the federal government often grants money to the states to help them build and operate schools, construct and repair highways, make welfare payments to the poor and the sick, and so on. The states do not have to accept the

money, but if they do, they also have to accept federal standards governing how the money is to be spent and federal monitoring to make sure it is spent that way.

- Powers that can be exercised by both the federal government and the states, such as imposing taxes and defining and punishing crimes.
- Powers forbidden to the federal government, mainly those in the first eight amendments, such as abridging freedom of speech, press, and religion, and various guarantees of fair trials for persons accused of crimes.
- Powers forbidden to the state governments. Some of these are in the body of the Constitution, but the main ones are the Fourteenth Amendment's requirements that no state shall "abridge the privileges or immunities of citizens of the United States; nor shall any State deprive any person of life, liberty, or property without due process of law; nor Deny to any person within its jurisdiction the equal protection of the laws." A number of U.S. Supreme Court decisions have interpreted these phrases to mean that almost all the specific liberties guaranteed against the federal government in the first eight amendments are also guaranteed against the state governments by the Fourteenth Amendment.

When all is said and done, however, perhaps the most important single point to note about the nature of American federalism is made in Article VI of the Constitution:

> This Constitution, and the laws of the United States which shall be made in Pursuance thereof; and all Treaties made, or which shall be made, under the Authority of the United States, shall be the supreme Law of the Land; and the Judges in every State shall be bound thereby, any Thing in the Constitution or Laws of any State to the Contrary notwithstanding.

In short, while the federal government cannot constitutionally interfere with the powers assigned exclusively to the states, whenever a state constitution or law is inconsistent with a law or treaty the federal government has adopted in accordance with its proper powers, the conflicting state constitution and law must yield. Moreover, it is the Supreme Court of the United States, an organ of the federal government and not of the state governments, that decides which acts of the federal government and the state governments are within their respective powers. Thus, to the extent that the American federal system is a competition between the national government and the states, the chief umpire is a member of one of the two competing teams.

Separation of Powers

Since most analysts of the American system maintain that separation of powers is the most important single difference between the U.S. system (which is called a **presidential democracy**) and most other democratic systems (which are called **parliamentary democracies**), let us be clear on the institution's main features.

Separation of powers denotes the constitutional division of government power among separate legislative, executive, and judicial branches (see Figure 19.2). The Constitution of the United States specifically vests the legislative power in Congress (Article I), the executive power in the president (Article II), and the judicial power in the federal courts, headed by the Supreme Court (Article III). The constitutions of many other nations, including most of Latin America's democracies, are presidential systems modeled after America's system of separated powers.

The three branches are separated in several ways, the most important of which is the requirement in Article I, Section 6: "No Person holding any Office under the United States, shall be a Member of either House during his Continuance in Office." This provision means that each branch is operated by persons entirely distinct from those operating the other two branches. Thus, for example, when Senator John Kerry was appointed secretary of state in 2013, he had to resign his seat in the Senate before he could take up his new post. This, of course, is the direct opposite of the fusion-of-powers rule in many parliamentary democracies, such as Great Britain, which require the head of the executive branch to be a member of Parliament.

The persons heading each branch of the U.S. government are selected by different procedures for different terms. Members of the House of Representatives are elected directly by the voters for two-year terms, with no limit on the number of terms they can serve. Members of the Senate are elected directly by the voters for six-year terms, without term limits, and their terms are staggered so that one-third of the Senate comes up for election or reelection every two years.[11]

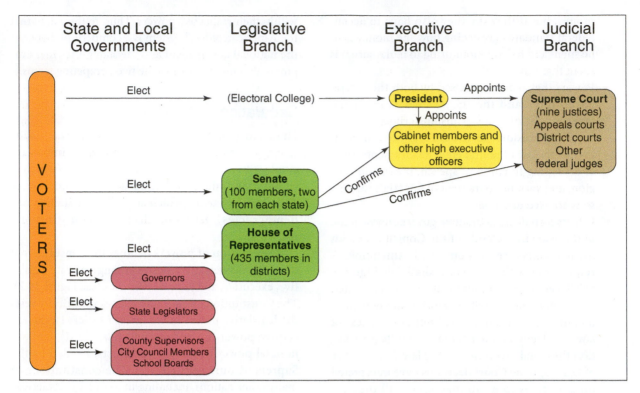

FIGURE 19.2

The Government of the United States

Source: *The United States Government Manual 2005/2006* (Washington, DC: U.S. Government Printing Office, 2005), 21.

The president is elected indirectly by the **electoral college** (which is selected by direct popular election) for a four-year term and is limited to two full elected terms. All federal judges, including the members of the Supreme Court, are appointed by the president with the approval of a majority of the Senate, and they hold office until death, resignation, or removal by Congress.

The other main devices ensuring the separation of powers are the **checks and balances** by which each branch can keep the other two branches from invading its constitutional powers. For example, the Senate can disapprove top-level presidential appointments and refuse to ratify treaties. The two chambers of Congress acting together can impeach, convict, and remove the president or federal judges from office. They can (and often do) deny the president the legislation, appropriations, and taxes he requests. The president, in turn, can veto any act of Congress, and the Constitution requires a two-thirds vote of both chambers to override the veto. The president also makes the initial

appointments of all federal judges. Presidents have normally nominated judges who are likely to agree with their political philosophies and policy preferences, but once appointed and confirmed, judges rule without political supervision.

Some scholars believe that the American system is more accurately described as a system of "separated branches exercising shared powers," since getting government action usually requires some kind of joint action by Congress and the president, with the acquiescence of the Supreme Court. *Separation of powers* is what most political scientists have called this feature of the system since the time of the *Federalist Papers*. Whatever it is called, this constitutional feature, more than any other, makes the American system different from most other democratic systems.[12]

Judicial Review

Judicial review can be defined as the power of a court to render a legislative or executive act null and void on the ground of unconstitutionality. All American courts, including the lower federal courts and all levels of the state courts, exercise this power on occasion. But the final word on all issues involving an interpretation of the national Constitution (which, as we have seen, is "the supreme law of the land") belongs to the U.S. Supreme Court. The Supreme Court can declare any act of the president or Congress null and void on the ground that it violates the Constitution. Such a decision can be overturned only by a constitutional amendment or by the Court, usually with new members, changing its mind.

Although every democracy has to determine who has the final word on what its constitution allows and prohibits, the United States is one of the few democracies in which that power is given to the top appellate court of the regular court system. Some countries, such as Italy, give the final word to special tribunals rather than to bodies in their regular court systems, while in others (such as Mexico and Switzerland), the power includes only the "federal umpire" power, and not the power to override decisions of the national executive and legislature. Thus, judicial review is a prominent but not exclusive feature of the American constitutional system.

Because of the important authorities granted to the Supreme Court by the American Constitution, the Court plays an active role in shaping policies that affect the everyday lives of Americans. Abortion rights are an issue of utmost importance both to right-to-life and to pro-choice activists, and ever since the Court's 1973 *Roe v. Wade* decision created federal protections for basic abortion rights, the drive to overturn or uphold this decision has motivated much political participation. The landmark decision applied a constitutional right to privacy to abortion rights, while those advocating a right to life have won some restrictions through Congress and the Supreme Court on late-term abortion practices. This has not been the only major debate decided by the Supreme Court in recent years. In the 2010 session alone, the Court issued landmark opinions granting corporations the right to spend unlimited amounts of money on elections, broadening Second Amendment protections by casting the constitutionality of state and local gun control laws into doubt, and narrowing the rights of criminal defendants. It was only by a narrow majority that the Supreme Court in 2012 upheld the Affordable Care

Act (President Obama's universal health care law), and the decision that upheld it also set great constraints on the power of Congress and presidents to regulate interstate commerce in the future. With the Court's impact looming so large, and with presidents able to reshape the Court when they nominate new members to replace departing justices, the direction of the judicial branch becomes an important part of presidential elections in America.

Political Culture and Socialization

19.5 Identify and discuss the two theories of cultural blending in the United States.

19.6 Discuss the role of mass communications media in U.S. politics, along with the government's ability to regulate the media.

The American constitutional system, though important to how Americans make political decisions, is not the whole story. To a considerable degree, the American political system functions as it does because it is operated by Americans rather than by Britons, Italians, Mexicans, or Iraqis, and it does what it does because Americans have a distinctive **political culture** that underlies, animates, and shapes all of the formal institutions we have reviewed.

Chapter 3 of this book discusses political culture and socialization in a comparative perspective, and America's unique political culture deserves close attention here.

Melting Pot or Patchwork Quilt?

Most Americans are immigrants or descendants of immigrants who came from many different cultures in Africa, Asia, Western and Eastern Europe, and Latin America. In this sense, globalization has always played a role in shaping America. Throughout most of its history, the United States has had to deal with how best to fit the immigrants and their different cultures into American economic, social, and political life.

Throughout our history, two visions of how immigrants should become incorporated into society have clashed in intellectual discourse, policy debates, and actual practice. One vision is of a "**melting pot**" that blends all the different cultures of immigrants into one uniquely American culture, which is expressed and passed on in one language, the American version of English. Some room is left for such special ethnic folkways as Polish weddings, Irish wakes, and Mexican food, but the paramount task given to the educational system is to turn everyone into English-speaking Americans imbued with the main values and attitudes of the nation's political culture. Embodied in this vision is a normative commitment to civic patriotism: The central identity of any citizen should be as an American, with the nation's political heritage and its Constitution superseding ethnic or religious identities for everyone and these shared principles binding the nation together.

A contrasting vision sees America as a true cultural "**patchwork quilt**" (the phrase is civil rights leader Jesse Jackson's)—an array of the languages, history, customs, and values of each of the nation's major ethnic groups, each receiving the same attention, respect, and importance as every other, with none dominant. This view rejects the melting-pot idea that the ancient and distinct cultures of immigrant groups should be homogenized into one prevailing national culture—a culture that, they say, is not truly a blend of all cultures but rather is the culture of Western Europe, especially Great Britain. While the patchwork quilt metaphor was recently coined and is today associated with some leaders among the African American, Latino, and Asian communities, members of various immigrant groups have sought to cling to their cultural identities and native languages for over a century. Italian, Irish, and especially German immigrants often resisted melting into America's customs and language, and reshaped the mainstream culture and even the English language.

Among the policies advocated by adherents to the patchwork quilt vision are bilingual education (educating minority group children in their native languages rather than forcing them to learn English as their primary language), printing ballots and other official documents in languages other than English, and broadening school curricula so as to give full and fair attention to the contributions of African, Asian, and Latin cultures as well as of British and Western European cultures.

Some opposition has set in against this movement. One manifestation is the laws adopted by several states and the May 2006 vote by the U.S. Senate declaring English to be the official language. Political scientist Sam Huntington's book, *Who Are We? The Challenges to America's National Identity*, offered a controversial defense of the Anglo-Protestant culture against a threatened erosion by today's wave of immigration from Latin America. The clash between the competing melting-pot and patchwork quilt visions of immigrant assimilation will likely continue throughout the twenty-first century.

Main Elements of the Traditional American Political Culture

The first dimension of political culture that political scientists usually consider is the level of trust in government that a nation's residents exhibit. In 1958, when the National Election Study first asked Americans whether they trusted their government to

Democratic Diversity in America
The voting coalition that put Barack Obama, a candidate with a multiracial heritage, into office and supported his party's congressional candidates in 2010 was made up of voters from many racial and ethnic groups. The demographic diversity of America constantly shapes its politics.

do what is right, 73 percent replied that they trusted government just about always or most of the time. In the decades since then, trust in government has eroded, with a sharp decrease occurring during the Vietnam War and after the Watergate scandal, followed by fluctuations that reflect the path of the nation's economy. For the last thirty years, Americans have trusted their government in boom times yet looked more skeptically at Washington during bust years. After the global financial crisis of 2008 and 2009, unemployment levels rose to historic highs, while trust in government plummeted to historic lows. By the year 2010, only 22 percent of Americans trusted their government to do the right thing all or most of the time, though this figure rebounded to 26 percent as the economy recovered in 2013.

Yet the Americans who do not always trust their government remain deeply proud of their nation and willing to sacrifice for it. Comparing Americans with Western Europeans on these dimensions is instructive. Studies have shown that more Americans say they are very proud of their country (80 percent) and are willing to fight for it (71 percent) than the citizens of Great Britain, Spain, Italy, France, and Germany in relation to their countries (where the proportions range from 55 and 62 percent in Great Britain to 21 and 35 percent in Germany).[13] Thus, while Americans may trust their governments to do what is right less than some Western Europeans do, they are nevertheless more patriotic than many Western Europeans. How can we explain this paradox?

The answer may lie in the fact that throughout history, most Americans have strongly held two ideas that may be logically (but not emotionally) inconsistent. One is the idea that ordinary Americans are good, solid, reliable folks with plenty of common sense, and that America is a wonderful country. Conversely, they feel that the *government*, which is not the same thing as the country, is, as president Ronald Reagan put it, "the problem, not the solution," and they feel that the professional politicians who fill its offices, lead its parties, and conduct its business are self-seeking lightweights more interested in winning votes and getting reelected than in making courageous and forward-looking policies to solve the nation's problems. Thus, many Americans love their country but distrust the politicians who run its governments.

Another dimension of political culture is the degree to which ordinary people believe that their preferences significantly influence public officials. One of the findings of the first major comparative study of political cultures was that Americans score higher on this dimension than people in Great Britain, Germany, Italy, and Mexico, and that in all five countries, better-educated people score higher than less-educated people.[14] Subsequent studies have confirmed that Americans generally feel more "politically efficacious" in this sense than do the citizens of most other nations.

Another exceptional feature of our nation is the depth of the conviction among most Americans—black and white, women and men, young and old—that they have certain basic rights and that the best way to make sure they get their rights is often not to wait for executives, legislatures, and bureaucrats to do the right thing but to file lawsuits to force public officials—and other private individuals—to honor their rights. The **litigiousness** of Americans—that is, their tendency to file lawsuits against government officials and other private citizens for violating their rights—gives the courts a central role in America. American legal scholar Robert Kagan argues that litigation in the United States accomplishes (at a much higher cost) the same things that European nations accomplish through regulation.[15] America has pursued this different path most likely because of the notion, espoused by populists like President Andrew Jackson, that the common man has enough wisdom to supervise everything, even his government.

Political Socialization

Political socialization is the process by which children are introduced to the values and attitudes of their society, shaping their notions of what the political world is like and which people, policies, and institutions are good and bad. That process in America is much the same as in every other modern, populous, industrialized democracy. The main agencies shaping Americans' political socialization are their families (especially their parents), schoolteachers, friends, schoolmates, work associates, and the mass communications media. While parents have historically had the most powerful impact on socialization, the influence of the mass communications media in the past few decades, and especially of social networking websites in the past few years, has begun to reshape the process of political socialization.

The term **mass communications media** includes all the devices used to transmit information, thought, or feeling to a mass audience that does not see the communicator face-to-face. They fall into two categories: the print media (newspapers, magazines, books, and pamphlets) and the electronic media (the Internet, broadcast television, cable and satellite television, and radio).

The United States, like most other industrialized democracies, has a mixture of publicly owned and privately owned television and radio stations and networks. The privately owned media are much more important than the publicly owned in America; there are three times as many private as public broadcasting stations, and the public stations usually have only about 10 percent of the viewers. Additionally, nearly all high-circulation newspapers, magazines, and websites are privately owned and supported by advertising revenues and subscribers.

The political content produced by print media outlets is almost entirely unregulated by government because of the First Amendment's protection of freedom of the press (see again Box 19.1). About the only restrictions on what is printed are libel and slander laws, but in the landmark case of *New York Times v. Sullivan* (1964), the U.S. Supreme Court held that public officials and public figures cannot collect damages for remarks made about them in the print media unless those comments are (1) knowingly false or made with a "reckless disregard" for their truth and (2) made with proved "malice" as a deliberate attempt to damage the victim's public reputation and standing—a charge that is very difficult to prove.[16]

By contrast, radio and television stations are much more closely regulated than the print media. They can broadcast only if they are granted a license by the Federal Communications Commission (FCC). That license requires that the political content of programs meet certain standards. For example, the stations must make available to all candidates for a particular political office an equal opportunity to make their appeals; they do not have to *give* any of them free time, but if they do give time to one candidate, they must give it to all. If they sell time to one candidate, they must sell it to all at the same rates and offer comparably desirable times. They cannot charge political advertisers higher rates than they charge commercial advertisers.

The U.S. Supreme Court has consistently upheld the government's power to impose such restrictions on the electronic media while denying government any comparable power over the print media. The reasons have to do with what is generally called the **scarcity doctrine**: The Court has found that there is no limit, other than economic, on the number of newspapers, books, magazines, or pamphlets that can be printed and circulated. But there is a physical limit on the number of television or radio stations that can operate in a given portion of the broadcast spectrum. Accordingly, said the Court, broadcasting is a public resource, much like the national parks or navigable rivers; this gives the government the right not only to allocate frequencies but also to set standards to ensure that their use will promote "the public convenience, interest, or necessity."[17]

Much less regulated are the websites, Facebook pages, and Twitter feeds that today play an ever more prominent role in transmitting political fact and opinion and breaking scandals, real or manufactured. Independent Internet sites, which are not subject to licensing requirements, do not have to stay in the good graces of a large range of advertising clients and have little reputation to lose if they publish news reports that become discredited. Blogs, by activists from every part of the ideological spectrum, play an increasingly important (and often criticized) role in campaigns, with their ability to spread fact, rumor, and baseless accusation across cyberspace with unchecked speed. Yet even in the brave new world in which smartphones give us a constant connection to social media and other Internet sources, many traditional sources of news have adapted and thrived. According to a study by the Pew Research Center, half of cell phone users and more than half of tablet owners use their devices to access the news and often go to established sites such as CNN and the New York Times that they trust (though, of course, members of the two parties are now deeply polarized about which news sources they trust, with 67 percent of Republicans trusting Fox News but only 37 percent of Democrats trusting it, and with figures for the New York Times almost the mirror image of that). Mobile connectivity has led many people to spend more time on these sites, deepening their connection to politics, than they did in the early days when computers were only desktops and laptops.

Political Participation and Recruitment

19.7 Compare and contrast U.S. nominating and voting processes and turnout with those in other countries, and describe alternative forms of political participation.

Participation by Voting

Since voting in elections is the main way in which ordinary citizens in all democracies actually participate in their nations' governing processes, most political scientists believe that **voting turnout**—the percentage of all the people eligible to vote who actually do so—is one of the most important indicators of any democratic system's health. Studies of voting turnout in the world's democracies, like that in Figure 19.3, usually find that the turnout is lower in the United States than in most other democracies.

Many commentators in America have also pointed to figures suggesting that U.S. voter turnout has declined dramatically over the past few decades as a sign

of a deep sickness in U.S. politics. They have claimed, variously, that it is a symptom of too much negative campaigning, too few good candidates, the rising role of money in campaigns, the diminishing role of parties in grassroots politics, and many other ills. However, recent research shows that these are false diagnoses of what turns out to be a healthy patient; turnout has remained fairly stable in America over the past thirty years.

The conventional wisdom that turnout had dropped was wrong because it relied on a misleading approximation of turnout, which calculated the percentage of those old enough to vote who actually did so. The problem with this measure is that many people who are old enough to vote in the United States are not eligible to cast a ballot, some because they are not citizens and some because they are convicted felons living in states that bar them from voting. As the percentage of Americans who are noncitizens (including both legal and illegal immigrants) or felons has grown in recent decades, a smaller portion of the voting-aged population has been eligible to vote. Scholars who counted up these groups and correctly calculated the percentage of eligible voters who participate found that turnout in presidential elections has remained steady at 55 to 60 percent since 1972 (after the Twenty-Sixth Amendment gave eighteen-year-olds the right to vote, and turnout in fact dropped).[18]

Further scrutinizing what goes into these turnout figures makes America look better compared to the rest of the world and points out a key obstacle to voter participation. When voting turnout is counted in exactly the same way in the United States as it is in other democracies—as a percentage of registered voters—the American record looks much better. In America, as in most of the world's other democracies, citizens' names must appear on voting registers before they can legally vote. But the United States differs from other nations in one important respect: In most other countries, getting on the register requires no effort by the voter. Public authorities take the initiative to get all eligible citizens enrolled, a job often made easier in countries that have a national list of residents. As a result, almost every citizen of voting age is registered to vote.

In the United States, by contrast, there is no list of residents, and each state regulates **voting registration**. In most states, would-be voters must make an effort to get on the register; no public official will do it for them. Moreover, in most democratic countries, when voters move from one part of the country to another, they are automatically struck off the register in the

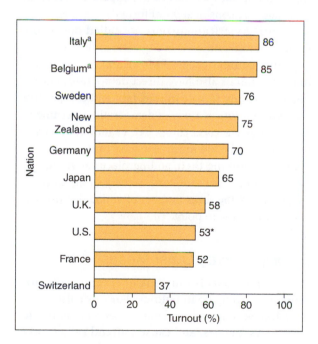

FIGURE 19.3
Levels of Turnout, 2000s*

*Presidential election turnout in the United States, parliamentary elections in other countries
aCompulsory voting law

Source: Based on Russell J. Dalton, *Citizen Politics in Western Democracies,* 5th ed. (Washington, DC: CQ Press, 2008), 37.

place they leave and are added to the register in the place to which they move, all with no effort on their part. In contrast, when people move from one U.S. state to another, they are not automatically added to the register in their new state.[19] One study that compared turnout of registered voters in the United States, which averages 86.8 percent, with turnout of registered voters in twenty-four other democracies found that the United States ranks eleventh-highest on this measure.[20]

This ranking is still lower than many might expect from the world's self-described citadel of democracy. Another explanation for America's low voting turnout arises from the fact that American voters are called on to cast far more votes than the citizens of any other country (only Switzerland comes close). In the parliamentary democracies, the only national elections are those for the national parliament, in which voters normally vote for one candidate or for one party. They also vote periodically for a candidate or a party in the elections for the city or rural district in which they live. In the federal systems, they also vote for a member of their state or provincial parliament. Hence, in most democracies other than the United States and Switzerland, the typical voter makes a total of only four or five voting decisions over a period of four or five years.[21] In some, such as Sweden, the typical voter would make only one voting decision over a four-year period, since all national and local elections take place at the same time.

In the United States, the combination of separation of powers, federalism, the direct primary, and, at the state and local levels, the initiative and referendum means that citizens may be faced with several *hundred* electoral decisions in a period of four years. At the national level, voters are called on to vote in the presidential primaries of their parties, and in the general election to decide (mostly) between the Democratic and Republican candidates. They are also expected to vote in primary elections and general elections every two years for members of the House of Representatives and twice in every six years for members of the Senate. At the state and local levels, not only are the leading executive officials (governors and mayors) and members of the legislatures nominated in primary elections and elected in general elections, but in most states and localities, a considerable number of other offices that are appointed positions in most other democracies—for example, state secretaries of state, attorneys general, treasurers, superintendents of education, judges, school superintendents, and members of local school boards, sanitary commissions, park commissions, and so on—are selected by much the same primary-plus-general-election procedures.

Direct democracy processes, such as the **direct initiative** (a proposal for a new law that goes before voters if enough of them sign a petition) and the **popular referendum** (a vote on whether to keep an existing law), give many Americans even more choices to make at the ballot box. Although the U.S. federal government has never held a direct democracy election, twenty-four states and many local governments make the initiative process available, meaning that about 70 percent of Americans live in a city or state with the initiative.[22] This sometimes adds as many as thirty complex policy choices to a ballot. Voters in states with recall provisions face more elections still, as sitting lawmakers must fight for their political lives in special contests called when enough voters sign petitions for their ouster, as happened recently in Colorado, Wisconsin, and California.

Thus, American citizens are called on to vote far more often and on more questions than those of any other country except Switzerland (where voters in many cantons also have direct democracy). Surely the opportunity to vote in free, fair, and competitive elections is a *sine qua non* of democratic government, and therefore a good thing. Yet a familiar saying is that there can be too much of a good thing, and many Americans leaving their polling places after casting their ninetieth (or more) vote of the year are likely to conclude that the sheer number of voting decisions in America is a case in point.[23]

Participation by Other Means

Voting, of course, is only one of several ways citizens can participate in politics. They can also serve in office; work in political parties; donate money to candidates, parties, and causes; attend rallies; take part in street demonstrations; send letters, telegrams, faxes, and e-mail messages to their elected representatives; write letters and op-ed pieces to newspapers; call radio and television talk shows; try to persuade families and friends; file lawsuits against public officials; and so on. These other forms of participation have not been studied as extensively

TABLE 19.1
Nonvoting Forms of Political Participation in Four Democracies (in percentages)

Activity	United States	Great Britain	France	Germany
Campaign Activity				
Attempted to convince others how to vote	44	44	28	29
Participated in campaign	30	25	7	7
Contacted by party/candidate	47	26	13	7
Communal Activity				
Worked with others in community in the past five years	35	23	20	26
Protest Activity				
Signed a petition in past year	35	34	21	35
Boycotted a product in past year	24	23	29	34
Attended protest in past five years	6	12	24	12

Sources: All figures are from Russell J. Dalton, *Citizen Politics in Western Democracies,* 5th ed. (Washington, DC: CQ Press, 2008). Campaign activity figures are taken from pp. 44–46, communal activity from p. 49 and p. 68, and protest activity from p. 68.

as voting, but Russell Dalton has collected some interesting comparative data on conventional and unconventional forms of participation in the United States and some Western European countries (see Table 19.1).

The responses in Table 19.1 show that citizens of France are more likely than citizens of the United States, Great Britain, or Germany to participate in demonstrations and political strikes, whereas Americans are more likely to persuade other people how to vote, attend a campaign meeting and/or rally, work with citizen groups, sign a petition, and/or join in a boycott.

Several other studies have found that the form of participation most frequently claimed by Americans is voting in elections (53 percent), followed by stating their political opinions to others (32 percent), contributing money to campaigns (12 percent), displaying political bumper stickers and signs (9 percent), and attending political meetings or rallies (8 percent). Only 4 percent report belonging to a political club or working for a political party.[24]

In short, Americans participate in politics in ways other than voting in elections as much, or more, than the citizens of the other Western democracies for whom we have reliable information. These data certainly do not support the conclusion that Americans are in any way more alienated or lazier than the citizens of other democracies.

Recruitment of Leaders

Recruitment is the process whereby, out of the millions of a nation's citizens, a few hundred or thousand emerge who hold elective and appointive public office, play leading roles in parties and pressure groups, decide how the mass communications media will portray politics, and, within the limits permitted by the general public, make public policy.

Many scholars have studied leadership recruitment in many countries and have found certain general tendencies that are also evident in American politics. For instance, American leaders, like leaders in other countries, are drawn disproportionately from the middle and upper ranges of wealth and status. The reason lies not in the existence of any conspiracy to oppress the lower classes but rather in the kinds of knowledge and skills a person must have to win the support needed for selection as a leader. These skills are more likely to be acquired and developed by well-educated rather than poorly educated people. For example, people's chances to climb in a political party or a pressure group, to be selected for public office, or to be appointed to higher administrative offices are considerably enhanced if they have the ability to speak well in public, and, for elected officials increasingly, to look and sound good on television.

The federal and state governments choose most of their administrative employees by procedures and standards other than the unabashed political patronage that prevailed until the late nineteenth century. In today's system, initial selection is made according to the applicants' abilities to score well on standardized examinations or possession of other abilities and experience desired by their employers, and salary increases and promotions depend on job performance rather than on party connections. Since the merit system was established in 1883, an increasing number of federal positions have been placed under it or under the "general schedule" category, and today, only about 1 percent are available for purely political appointments.

Accordingly, in most respects, elite recruitment in the United States differs very little from its counterparts in other advanced industrialized democracies. But in one aspect of that process—the nomination of candidates for elective office—the United States is unlike any other nation in the world.

The Unique Direct Primary

We can divide the process of electing public officials into three parts: (1) *candidate selection*, the process by which political parties decide which people to name as their standard-bearers and campaign for; (2) *nomination*, the process by which public authorities decide which people's names will be printed on the official ballots; and (3) *election*, the process by which the voters register their choices among the nominees.

Many political scientists believe that candidate selection is the most important of the three processes. After all, the recruitment of public officials is essentially one of narrowing the choices from many to one. For example, in 2010, about 176 million Americans satisfied all the constitutional requirements for being elected president. Theoretically, all 176 million names could have been printed on the ballot, and each voter could have had an absolutely free choice among them. But, of course, no voter can possibly make a meaningful choice among 176 million alternatives, and so a practical democratic election requires that the choices be narrowed down to a manageable number. The same is true for elections to office in all democratic countries.

In the United States, as in every other democracy, the narrowing process is accomplished mainly by the political parties. Each party chooses its candidates and gives their names to the election authorities, and those names appear on the ballot.[25] Accordingly,

in 2012, the Republicans chose Mitt Romney to be their presidential candidate over Ron Paul, Newt Gingrich, Rick Santorum, Buddy Roemer, Rick Perry, Jon Huntsman, Jr., Michelle Bachmann, Gary Johnson, Herman Cain, Thaddeus McCotter, and Tim Pawlenty, while President Obama went unchallenged in his party's primary. By narrowing the field from thirteen candidates to two, these nominations made it relatively easy for the voters to make the final choice between Romney and Obama.

Given the crucial role of candidate selection in democratic elections, it is important to recognize that the United States is the only nation in the world that makes most of its nominations by direct primaries. In nearly all the parliamentary democracies, the parties' candidates for parliament are chosen by the parties' leaders or by small groups of card-carrying, dues-paying party members. A few countries, such as Germany and Finland, require the parties to choose their candidates by secret votes of local party members in procedures that resemble, but strictly speaking are not, direct primaries. Consequently, in every nation except the United States, the candidates are selected by only a few hundred, or at most a few thousand, party insiders.[26]

In the United States, nominations for almost all major elective public offices are made by **direct primaries**, in which candidates are selected directly by the voters in government-conducted elections rather than indirectly by party leaders in caucuses and conventions. Direct primaries make candidate selection in the United States by far the most open and participatory in the world. Moreover—and this is the key difference between America's direct primaries and the primary-like procedures in other countries mentioned earlier—public laws, not party rules, determine who is qualified to vote in a particular party's primary. In 2012, twenty-one states held **closed primaries** for both parties' presidential contests, in which only persons preregistered as members of a particular party could vote in that party's primary. Seventeen states held **open primaries**, in which there is no party registration of any kind, and voters can vote in whichever party primary they choose (they can, however, vote in only one party's primary in any particular election) with no public disclosure of their choice. The remaining states either used different systems for each party or held some form of crossover primaries, which are the same as closed primaries except that voters do not have to make a public choice of the party primary in which they will vote until Election Day. In its 2000 *California Democratic Party v. Jones* decision, the U.S. Supreme Court prohibited California's **blanket primary** (which allowed voters to switch back and forth between the parties in voting for nominees for particular offices) on the grounds that it violated a party's First Amendment right to free association. This decision, which also caused Alaska and Washington to alter their primary systems, makes clear the extent to which nomination procedures are formal, regulated by the government, and structured by the Constitution.

Direct primaries make candidate selection in the United States by far the most open and participatory in the world. As noted earlier, in all other countries, only a few thousand dues-paying party members at most participate in choosing candidates; in the United States, they are chosen by any registered voter who wants to participate, and millions do in every election cycle. To give just one example, although American presidential candidates are formally selected by national nominating conventions, a great majority of the delegates to both conventions are chosen by direct primaries. In 2008, a grand total of 58,140,064 votes were cast in the Democratic and Republican presidential primaries.[27]

The American system for choosing its presidents may be wiser or more foolish than the ways other democracies select their top political leaders, but it is far more participatory.

Gang of Eight

In 2013, a bipartisan group of senators came together to negotiate a compromise immigration policy. Here, New York Democrat Chuck Schumer is joined by Arizona Republican John McCain and other members of the group.

Interest Articulation: PACs and Pressure Groups

 19.8 Describe PACs and interest groups and contrast their methods in the United States with those of similar groups in other countries.

As we have seen throughout this book, every society has a number of different and conflicting political interests, and the more advanced the economy and the more heterogeneous the society, the more individuals and groups there are with interests that to some degree conflict with other interests. The inevitable clash of these interests generates the political process, which consists of two main parts: (1) interest articulation, by which the persons and groups make known their desires for government action or inaction, and (2) interest aggregation, by which various demands are mobilized and combined to press for favorable government policies.

In most democracies, interests are articulated mainly by pressure groups and political parties, and the governing parties also aggregate interests in formulating and implementing their programs. In the United States, however, the political parties are much weaker and less cohesive than those in most other democratic systems. Consequently, pressure groups play a major role in both interest articulation and aggregation in the United States.

Many foreign observers of America's peculiar politics have been especially struck by the great variety and power of our organized political groups.[28] Today, they are even more numerous and important than in the past. They take two main forms, each of which specializes in a particular technique for influencing government: (1) political action committees and campaign contributions and (2) pressure groups and lobbying.

PACs and Campaign Contributions

Strictly speaking, a **political action committee (PAC)** is any organization that is not formally affiliated with a particular party or candidate and spends money to influence the outcome of elections. PACs differ from political parties in two main respects. First, unlike parties, they do not nominate candidates and put them on ballots with PAC labels; rather, they support or oppose candidates nominated by the parties. Second, PACs are interested mainly in the policies that public officials make, not in the party labels those officials bear. Hence, a PAC will often support candidates of both major parties who are sympathetic to the PAC's particular policy preferences.

Such organizations have operated in American politics at least since the Civil War, and some of them have had considerable success. For example, the Anti-Saloon League, which was founded in 1893 to support both Democratic and Republican candidates for Congress, pledged to support a constitutional amendment outlawing the manufacture and sale of alcoholic beverages. Most historians believe that it deserves much of the credit (or blame) for the adoption of the Eighteenth Amendment (Prohibition) in 1919. One of the most powerful organizations in the second half of the twentieth century was the Committee on Political Education (COPE) of the American Federation of Labor and Congress of Industrial Organizations (AFL-CIO), which has supplied millions of dollars and thousands of election workers for candidates (mostly but not entirely Democrats) sympathetic to organized labor.

The greatest increase in the number and activity of PACs in American history has come since 1974, as an unanticipated (and, by many, unwanted) consequence of that year's amendments to the Federal Election Campaign Act. The amendments set low limits on the amount of money individuals could contribute to a candidate or a party but considerably higher limits on what organizations could contribute. They also stipulated that although labor unions and business corporations could not directly contribute money to election campaigns, they could sponsor PACs, and their PACs could make campaign contributions as long as the funds came from voluntary contributions by sympathetic individuals rather than by direct levies on union and corporate funds.

In ruling on the constitutionality of these amendments, the Supreme Court upheld the limits on direct contributions, but said that limiting the amounts of money that an individual or an organization can spend on behalf of a candidate (that is, by broadcasting or publishing ads *not* controlled by candidates or parties) was a violation of the First Amendment's guarantee of free speech.[29]

These changes in the substance and interpretation of the campaign finance laws led most politically active interests to conclude that forming a PAC was the best way to influence election outcomes, and that is just what they have done. In 1974, only 608 PACs operated in national elections; by 2009, the number had exploded to 4,611 (see Box 19.2 for a list of some of the biggest PACs operating today).

At present, each PAC must register with the Federal Election Commission and periodically report its receipts (who contributed and how much) and its expenditures (to what candidates it gave contributions and how much, and how much it spent on its own independent campaigning). A PAC can contribute $5,000 to a particular candidate in a primary election and another $5,000 in the general election. Yet there is no limit on the total amount it can contribute to all candidates and party committees. There is also no limit on the amount it can spend on behalf of a particular candidate or party as long as its beneficiaries have no say in how the money is spent. The enactment in 2002 of the McCain-Feingold bill prohibited all "soft money" contributions—formerly unlimited contributions that were made to federal, state, and local political parties. However, a perceived loophole in this law has allowed "527 Committees" (a name that comes from their categorization in the tax code) to play the role that parties formerly played by collecting the same sorts of unlimited contributions and spending them independently to influence campaigns.

Although many PACs take some part in presidential election campaigns, the federal government finances most of the costs of those campaigns. Thus, most PACs make most of their contributions to House and Senate campaigns. It is estimated that they now contribute about 34 percent of all the funds for those campaigns.[30]

The most important PACs can be classified in one of three main categories:

1. **Narrow material interest PACs.** These are PACs concerned mainly with backing candidates who will support legislation that favors a particular

BOX 19.2 — Top Ten PACs in Overall Spending, 2013

Rank	PAC Name	Overall Spending
1	Emily's List	$8,678,355
2	SEIU COPE (Service Employees International Union Committee on Political Education)	$6,133,599
3	D.R.I.V.E.—Democrat, Republican, Independent Voter Education (The PAC of the International Brotherhood of Teamsters)	$3,491,883
4	International Longshoremen's Association AFL-CIO Committee on Political Education ILA-Cope	$2,551,768
5	American Federation of State County & Municipal Employees People	$2,434,131
6	Voice of Teachers for EDUC/CMTE on POL EDUC of NY State UNTD Teachers (Vote/Cope) of NYSUT	$2,247,751
7	Our Country Deserves Better PAC—Teapartyexpress.org	$2,153,559
8	International Brotherhood of Electrical Workers Political Action Committee	$2,135,759
9	International Union of Painters and Allied Trades Political Action Together Political Comm	$1,993,210
10	Honeywell International Political Action Committee	$1,902,535

Source: Federal Elections Commission, "Top 50 PACs by Disbursements, January 1, 2013–June 30, 2013," accessed at http://www.fec.gov /press/summaries/2014/ElectionCycle/6m_PAC.shtml, January 16, 2014.

business or type of business (for example, Chrysler, Coca Cola, General Electric, General Motors, Texaco), and many corporations have their own PACs, as do many labor unions, including the Air Line Pilots Association, the American Federation of State, County, and Municipal Employees, and the American Federation of Teachers. In addition, a number of PACs represent the interests of whole industries, such as the Dallas Energy Political Action Committee (oil), the Edison Electric Institute (electric power), and the National Association of Broadcasters (radio and television).

2. **Single, nonmaterial interest PACs.** These PACs promote candidates who favor their positions on a particular nonmaterial issue. For example, the National Abortion Rights Action League (prochoice) and the National Right to Life Committee (antiabortion) are concerned with the abortion issue, and the National Rifle Association (anti–gun control) and Handgun Control, Inc. (pro–gun control) focus on the gun control issue.

3. **Ideological PACs.** Finally, a number of PACs support candidates committed to strong liberal or conservative ideologies and issues. Liberal PACs include MoveOn, the National Committee for an Effective Congress, and the Hollywood Women's Political Committee. Conservative PACs include the Republican Issues Campaign and the Conservative Victory Committee.

Pressure Groups and Lobbying

Another tactic that PACs use to advance their interests is **lobbying** through their Washington representatives. This stratagem concentrates on inducing public officials already in office to support government actions (including administrative and judicial rulings as well as legislative acts) the groups favor and to block those the groups oppose.

In the "bad old days," pressure groups often used straight bribes in the form of cash payments or guarantees of well-paid jobs after retirement. Sadly, bribes are still occasionally offered and accepted, but the laws against them are strict, and the mass media's investigative reporters love to expose bribe taking. In a recent example, the San Diego *Union-Tribune*'s

2005 investigation of Congressman Randall "Duke" Cunningham for accepting over $2 million in bribes in exchange for influencing defense contracts led to an eight-year prison term for Cunningham, as well as a Pulitzer Prize for the newspaper. Congress reacted to the Cunningham scandal and the investigations that forced the resignation of House Majority Leader Tom DeLay and sent lobbyist Jack Abramoff to jail by considering new ethics legislation. These scandals played a major role in the Democratic surge in the 2006 congressional elections. Ethics investigations of prominent Democratic Representatives Charlie Rangel and Maxine Waters, though less serious than Cunningham's, hurt their party on the eve of the 2010 congressional contests (see Box 19.3). Calls for reform are likely to fade, though, as the scandals pass. Such was the case with the "Teapot Dome" influence-peddling scandal of the 1920s, which caused huge outrage at the time but is now a quaint historical footnote. Bribery is quite rare in everyday American politics, since most interest groups and public officials have decided that giving or taking bribes is either too immoral, too risky, or both.

The main tactic of lobbyists is now *persuasion*—convincing members of Congress (and their staffs, who play key roles in making most members' decisions) that the legislation the lobbyist seeks is in the best interests of the nation and of the member's particular district or state. After all, almost all members of Congress feel that their job is to do the best they can for the interests of their particular constituents. Since it is those constituents rather than the rest of the nation who determine whether the members will be reelected, their likely reactions must be the members' first concern.

Accordingly, lobbyists for all interests use the most persuasive evidence and arguments they can to convince a particular member that the actions their groups want will be in everyone's best interest—the voters in the particular district or state, the member's,

---

BOX 19.3   The Congressional Elections of 2010

For the second time in a short four-year period, voters shifted control of the House of Representatives during the 2010 midterm elections. Democrats led by Nancy Pelosi had capitalized on voter dissatisfaction with President George W. Bush's handling of the Iraq War and with the Republican congressional leaders' handling of a multitude of scandals to pick up thirty-one seats and claim control of the House in the 2006 elections. Four years later, the political pendulum swung sharply back. With voters in the political middle unhappy with President Barack Obama's handling of the economy and with the leftward turn that Congress had taken in policy areas such as health care and deficit spending, Republicans led by John Boehner captured sixty-three seats to gain a comfortable 242–192 majority in the House.

Democrats also lost six seats in the Senate but, after the election, still clung to a 53–47 edge in the upper house. One factor that may have prevented the Republicans from gaining total victory in both houses was the role played by the "Tea Party," a loosely organized faction of Republican voters and activists who were focused primarily on fiscal conservatism (but who gave voice to many other strands of political conservatism in areas such as social issues, immigration, and race relations). Tea Party activists worked within the Republican Party to nominate House and Senate candidates with staunchly conservative views and often little electoral experience. In some cases, these candidates energized the Republican base and drove home the party's anti-incumbent message. Florida's Marco Rubio and Kentucky's Rand Paul were Senate candidates strongly linked to the Tea Party who won convincing victories in competitive states and rocketed to national prominence. In several key Senate races, however, nominating conservatives appeared to cost Republicans the opportunity to gain seats. Christine O'Donnell, lampooned on *The Daily Show* for her views on sex education and for dabbling in witchcraft, lost badly in Delaware, and her fellow Tea Party favorite Sharron Angle lost a winnable race in Nevada. Although the 2010 elections brought a clear landslide victory for the Republican Party, political observers debated whether the Tea Party movement helped or hindered the cause. Regardless, the movement remained strong in 2012, an election in which Republicans maintained strong control in the House even during a decisive Obama victory.

and the nation's. Lobbyists who work for interest groups that also have PACs may sometimes hint that the PAC will be contributing to the campaigns of legislators who see the light on their issues. Surprisingly, however, most lobbyists and PACs work quite independently of one another, and a great volume of studies by political scientists have failed to provide any clear evidence that campaign contributions influence the votes cast by legislators. Contributions may ensure access to politicians, scholars have found, but they do not buy votes.

Although American interest groups most frequently employ electioneering and lobbying, they sometimes use tactics that are more widely used in other countries, such as mass political propaganda, demonstrations, strikes and boycotts, nonviolent civil disobedience, and sometimes even violence. There is one tactic, however, in which the United States leads the world: the use of **litigation** for political purposes. In their book, *Politics by Other Means: The Declining Importance of Elections in America*, political scientists Benjamin Ginsberg and Martin Shefter note that from 1955 to 1985, the number of civil cases brought in federal district courts increased from 50,000 a year to over 250,000 a year. One of several reasons for that enormous increase, they say, is the fact that a growing number of interest groups that have done poorly in both elections and lobbying have filed suits in the courts to reverse their losses in other arenas:

> Civil rights groups, through federal court suits, launched successful assaults on Southern school systems, state and local governments, and legislative districting schemes. . . . Environmental groups used the courts to block the construction of highways, dams, and other public projects that not only threatened to damage the environment but also provided money and other resources to their political rivals. Women's groups were able to overturn state laws restricting abortion as well as statutes discriminating against women in the labor market.

Conservative groups have countered by trying to ensure that **conservatives** rather than liberals or feminists are appointed to the Supreme Court and other federal judgeships. Liberal groups have also organized campaigns to influence appointments and confirmation battles in order to populate the judicial branch with those who are sympathetic to their goals. Ever since Democrats in the Senate failed to confirm President Ronald Reagan's nomination of Robert Bork to the U.S. Supreme Court in 1987, nearly every appointment to the nation's highest court has been fought with intense lobbying, with public pressure, and even with avalanches of television ads. The fact that interest groups are involved in judicial battles far more in America than in any other democracy should not surprise us, because the popularity of pursuing one's individual rights through litigation is one way in which the political culture of America differs significantly from the political cultures of most other countries.

The most important special trait of interest articulation and aggregation in the United States, however, is the very different party environment in which they take place. In most of the democracies discussed in this book, most interests operate closely within political parties. (Indeed, in several instances, particular interest groups are formally associated with particular parties, such as the trade unions with the British Labour Party.) Their main tactic is to persuade the parties with which they are associated to give their demands prominent places in the parties' programs and actions in government.

In contrast, American political parties are so much weaker and so much less important in the policymaking process that the interest groups operate largely outside the parties and are little concerned about whether they are helping or hurting the parties. In 1980, for example, the National Organization for Women (NOW) fought for a rule in the Democratic Party to prevent the party from helping to elect any Democratic candidate who opposed the Equal Rights Amendment. In 1984, NOW said that it would refuse to support the party's national ticket unless a woman was nominated for the vice presidency (and, indeed, Geraldine Ferraro was nominated). In the 2009–2010 election cycle, Emily's List, a PAC supporting women candidates, spent almost $23 million to help female campaigns, the fourth-largest amount spent by any PAC.[31]

The same observation applies to the Republican Party. For some time before 1994, many business PACs contributed much more campaign money to incumbent Democrats than to their Republican challengers, even though the Republican political philosophy is much closer to that of business. The national leaders of the Republican Party complained bitterly about what they regarded as treason to the party and to conservatism, but Doug Thompson, the leader of the National Association of Realtors, rejected the

Republicans' complaints and has spelled out his PAC's political priorities:

> We are a special interest group. Our interest is real estate and housing issues; it is not Contra aid, it is not abortion, it is not the minimum wage. . . . Our members are demanding a lot more accountability. Gone are our free-spending days when we poured money into a black hole called "challenger candidates." Our marching orders on PAC contributions are very clear: Stop wasting money on losers.[32]

In short, interest articulation and aggregation are in many respects different in the United States because its political parties are in most respects very different from those in any other democracy.

The Special Characteristics of American Political Parties

19.9 Discuss the level of polarization between the major U.S. political parties and its impact upon policymaking.

A Two-Party System

The American party system is usually a nearly pure two-party system—that is, one in which two major parties are highly competitive with one another and, taken together, win almost all the votes and offices in elections.[33] The most notable exception since the 1930s came in 1992, as Figure 19.4 shows, when independent H. Ross Perot won 19 percent of the popular vote for president (Democrat Bill Clinton won 43 percent and Republican incumbent George H. W. Bush won 38 percent). After the election, Perot founded the Reform Party and ran as its presidential candidate in 1996, but, as the figure shows, his vote share fell to 8.6 percent. He did not run in 2000, but his party's presidential candidate, Pat Buchanan, received less than 1 percent of the vote.[34]

In 2012, in addition to Republican Mitt Romney and Democrat Barack Obama (see Box 19.4), there were presidential candidates from nine other parties (including the Socialist, Socialist Workers, Socialist Equality, Prohibition, and NSA Did 9/11 parties) on the ballot in at least one state. However, all these other parties polled a combined 1.7 percent of the popular vote. In addition, nearly all the members of the House and Senate for the past several decades have been affiliated with one of the two major parties. Although the 2010 elections were marked by the emergence of the "Tea Party," this group was in fact not a party but a faction of energetic voters and organizers who worked almost exclusively within the Republican

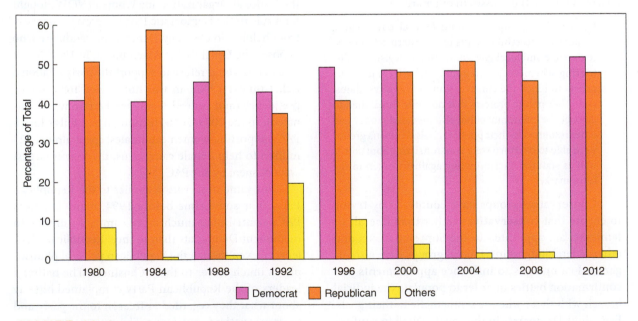

FIGURE 19.4

Party Shares of Presidential Votes, 1980–2012

Sources: *Statistical Abstract of the United States: 2010* (Washington, DC: Bureau of the Census, 2010), Table 385; and Federal Elections Commission for 2012.

The Presidential Election of 2012

After the groundbreaking presidential election of 2008 led to the election of the nation's first African American president and a shift from eight years of Republican control of the White House, the 2012 campaign marked a return to the more prosaic and conventional themes of American politics. Voters in the two major parties were polarized in their views of incumbent Barack Obama, further cementing the divide between blue states and red states. Vast sums of money poured into both President Obama's campaign and the coffers of his challenger, former Massachusetts governor Mitt Romney. Much of the record-setting spending in this campaign went into attack ads aired in the nine battleground states whose electoral college votes would decide the contest. By defending his policy achievements and convincing voters that the shrinking economy he had inherited at the beginning of his administration was turning around, Obama won reelection by a margin that was convincing, though much closer than his 2008 triumph.

As the sitting president, Obama went unchallenged in his party's primary. The Republican primary field, by contrast, was crowded with candidates eager to unseat a president whose approval ratings dipped below 40 percent in 2011. Romney, a businessman whose much-lauded management of the 2002 Winter Olympics in Salt Lake City had catapulted him to the governorship of Massachusetts later that year, was the GOP's presumptive frontrunner from the start. But as a relatively moderate Republican who had failed to inspire much passion from the party's base in his failed 2008 candidacy, Romney had to overcome a series of challenges by more conservative rivals. These candidates drew support from the "Tea Party" activists who had galvanized the 2010 congressional elections, while sometimes shifting the party too far to the right to find electoral success (see Box 19.3). Texas Governor Rick Perry, former Godfather's Pizza CEO Herman Cain, former House Speaker Newt Gingrich, and former senator Rick

Santorum each took a turn pulling ahead of Romney before their campaigns faded. As each proved too conservative or too inexperienced to serve as credible challengers to the president, GOP primary voters returned to the solid, if unexciting, Romney. After a bruising series of primaries, Romney secured his party's nomination in the spring just as the economy—and, as a result, President Obama's approval ratings—began to recover.

The general election campaign was fought over issues such as the national debt (which grew at an accelerated pace over the course of the Obama administration), health care (with Romney's critique of Obama's national insurance mandate made more difficult by the fact that it was modeled after a plan Romney had championed as governor), and jobs (with both candidates arguing over who was to blame for the recession and the nation's sluggish recovery from it). Debates had a major impact on the ebb and flow of polling, with the president stumbling badly in the first clash but performing better in later debates. The overall price tag of the campaign season set a record by surpassing $2 billion in spending by the candidates and by outside groups. Heading into Election Day, polls showed that Republican voters were more enthusiastic than Democrats, but the Obama campaign countered this deficit by investing in a massive and cutting-edge grassroots mobilization effort. His campaign turned out enough voters to win a convincing reelection, even if his victory was not accompanied by the optimism and exultation his supporters had felt in 2008.

Candidate	Popular Votes	Electoral Votes
Barack Obama, Democrat	65,899,660 (51.1%)	332
Mitt Romney, Republican	60,932,152 (47.2%)	206
Others	2,236,079 (1.7%)	0

Party to nominate and support fiscally conservative Republican candidates. The United States is one of the most distinctive two-party systems in the world.

The "Americanization" of Electioneering

Electioneering—what parties and candidates do in campaigns to maximize their votes in elections—has

changed considerably in most democratic nations since the 1950s, and the United States is generally credited with (or blamed for) leading the way. Before the 1950s, electioneering in democracies was conducted mainly by party leaders and workers. The party workers made direct contacts with their candidates' known and potential supporters and used the mass media mainly to publish newspaper advertisements and to print pamphlets and flyers for the party workers to distribute.

Since the 1950s, American parties and candidates have replaced the old techniques with new, more sophisticated tactics. They now depend mainly on paid television advertisements and broadcasters' interviews and talk shows to showcase their candidates and policies to the voters. They employ experts to conduct frequent polls of the voters to test how well their strategies are working. They store and analyze information about the demographics, past electoral behavior, and vast amounts of consumer behavior of individuals in computerized "microtargeting" databases. They also have transferred control of electioneering from party politicians to paid professional campaign consultants trained in advertising agencies rather than party organizations. They have made televised debates among the candidates the most important events in campaigns.

Party leaders and candidates in other democracies have watched U.S. electioneering. Many have deplored it, and some have vowed never to "Americanize" (their term) their own campaigns. Nevertheless, campaigners in most democracies have adapted some or all of the high-tech American methods for their own uses. For example, the United States held its first nationally televised debates between presidential candidates in 1960. Similar debates among leading parties and candidates are now regularly held in Brazil, Chile, Denmark, France, Germany, Mexico, Norway, Sweden, and Venezuela. Most parties in most democracies now hire professional campaign consultants, some of them American or trained in America, to plan their campaigns. They use private polls to assess the effectiveness of their campaigns, and they use the mass media, especially television, as their main device for soliciting voters' support. They have followed America's lead by increasingly using negative advertising to sharpen the contrasts between candidates or to ruin an opponent's reputation. In short, while the "Americanization" of electioneering may or may not

be a healthy development, it has happened to some degree in all democracies and to a considerable degree in many.[35]

Differences between the Major Parties

Throughout the 1950s and 1960s, foreign observers (and many Americans) saw few differences between the Democratic and Republican parties. Today, however, the split between the two major parties is sharp and meaningful, and there is a vast gap between the views of Democratic and Republican voters on issues like health care reform, abortion rights, and foreign policy. In Congress, the Democratic caucus has moved further and further to the left since 1970, just as Republicans have become increasingly conservative.[36] Thus, the level of mass and elite **partisan polarization** in America is now quite high, as it is in most European nations.

This does not mean that there is no one left in the middle of the American political spectrum; indeed, most Americans see themselves as moderates who lean only slightly in the liberal or conservative direction. Instead, the increase in partisan polarization reflects the fact that Americans today have sorted themselves into the party that most accurately reflects their ideology.[37] No longer are there many conservative

Presidential Debate in 2012
During the first debate of the 2012 general election campaign, at the University of Denver, Republican challenger Mitt Romney (R) was widely credited with defeating Barack Obama, vaulting Romney into the lead in many polls.

Democrats in the south or liberal Republicans in New England or the Midwest. This sorting has taken place among elected officials, party activists, and ordinary voters alike. Because of it, the parties now differ significantly in both the social composition of the voters who identify with them and the policy positions taken by their elected leaders.

As is shown in Figure 19.5, by 2008, Americans were more likely to identify themselves as Democrats (51 percent) than as Republicans (38 percent) or independents (11 percent). (It should be noted also that most of these independents lean toward one party and vote for its nominees quite loyally.)[38] Democrats have greater support among women than men, among blacks than whites, and among people with lower incomes and educations than upper-status people. Other research shows that the link between income and party affiliation has grown in recent decades: "The relatively poor are increasingly Democratic and the rich Republican."[39] There are, of course, many, many rich Democrats, but the overall trend is that Americans with higher incomes are more likely to be Republicans. Thus, as income inequality has increased in America, the gap between the two parties has widened. Finally, the parties now differ more than ever in how religious their members are, with Republican presidential candidates doing better among regular churchgoers than Democrats.[40]

These rising differences in each party's social base help to explain why Democratic and Republican members of Congress increasingly take different policy positions. Table 19.2 explores these divisions by looking at roll call votes on some significant

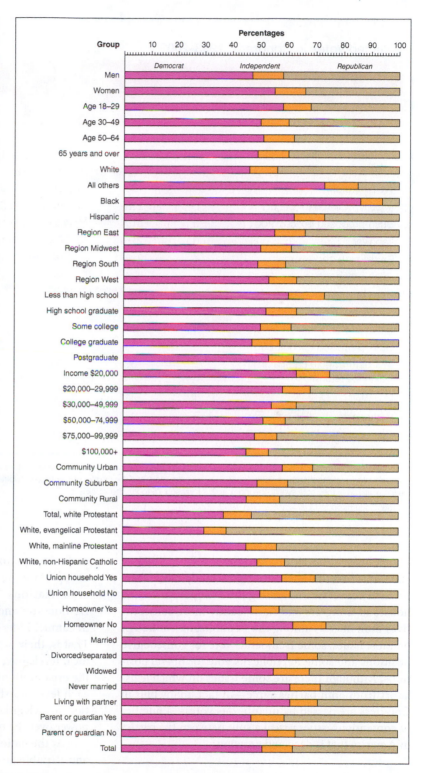

FIGURE 19.5

Social Composition of Major Party Identifiers, 2008

Source: Harold W. Stanley and Richard G. Niemi, *Vital Statistics on American Politics, 2009–2010* (Washington, DC: CQ Press, 2010), Table 3-2, 119.

TABLE 19.2
Selected Votes in Congress, 1993–2003

	Republicans			Democrats		
	Liberal	Conservative	Cohesion Index[a]	Liberal	Conservative	Cohesion Index[a]
House						
Lift ban, leave gays-in-military issue to Clinton	101	157	22	163	11	88
Welfare reform	30	165	70	226	4	96
Impeach Clinton for perjury	5	223	98	200	5	98
Bush-proposed tax cut, 2001	0	219	100	197	10	91
Iraq War	6	215	95	126	81	22
Partial-birth abortion ban	4	218	96	137	63	37
Bush-proposed tax cut, 2003	1	224	99	198	7	93
Senate						
"Brady bill" for handgun control	8	47	70	28	16	28
Welfare reform	1	51	96	23	23	0
Bush-proposed tax cut, 2001	0	50	100	38	12	52
McCain-Feingold campaign finance reform	12	38	52	47	3	88
Iraq War	1	48	96	21	29	16
Partial-birth abortion ban	3	47	88	30	17	28
Bush-proposed tax cut, 2003	3	48	88	46	2	92

[a]The cohesion index is a measure of the extent to which members of a particular party in a legislature vote alike on a matter of public policy. The percentages of the members voting each way are calculated, and the smaller percentage is subtracted from the larger. If they all vote alike, the index is 100. If they split evenly, the index is 0. If they split 75 to 25, the index is 50.

Source: *Congressional Quarterly Reports, 1993–2003.*

issues before the House and Senate from 1993 to 2003. It shows that there are significantly more liberals than conservatives among the Democrats in both houses of Congress and significantly more conservatives than liberals among the Republicans—although on most issues, some Democrats vote for conservative positions and some Republicans vote for liberal positions. Although there are some issues on which legislators from both parties agree—in fact, many bills in Congress are passed by unanimous votes—a number of contentious issues reveal a split between the parties in America that is deep and growing.

Decentralized Organization

Most political parties in most democracies are organized as hierarchies, with a national leader and national organization at the top holding the power to supervise the activities of local and regional party organizations. In sharp contrast, the American Democratic and Republican parties are organized, in Samuel Eldersveld's apt phrase, as "stratarchies."[41] That is, their organizations at the national, state, and local levels have little power, legal or extralegal, over the organizations at the other levels. Moreover, within each level, most parties have an executive organization and a legislative organization, and neither has any power over the other.

At the national level, for example, the Democrats and Republicans each have a **presidential party** and a **congressional party**. For the party that holds the presidency, the presidential party consists of the president, the national committee, the national chairman, and the national nominating conventions. The party that does not hold the presidency has no single person as its universally acknowledged leader.

Each party in each house of Congress has a caucus consisting of all the party's members in the particular chamber (and thus equivalent to what in most democracies is called the *parliamentary party*). A floor leader is selected by the caucus to serve as the main coordinator of the party's legislative strategy and tactics. A policy committee, chosen by the caucus, advises the floor leader and the caucus on matters of substantive policy and legislative tactics. The whips are chosen by the caucus to serve as channels of communication between the leaders and the ordinary members. The campaign committees are chosen by the caucus to raise money and distribute it among the campaigns of selected candidates for the particular chamber.

We should emphasize, however, that the presidential party has little formal connection with the congressional party, and that any effort by the president (to say nothing of the national committee or the national chairman) to intervene in the congressional party's selection of its leaders or the determination of its policies or strategy is resented and rejected as "outside interference." In many other nations, this would be viewed as the normal course of party politics.

At the state level, both parties usually have a gubernatorial party and a legislative party. The gubernatorial party consists of the governor (the other party has no single, acknowledged leader), the state central committee, the state chair, and the state conventions. The legislative parties, like the congressional parties, usually have caucuses, elected floor leaders, policy committees, and whips. But each state's gubernatorial and legislative parties have no power over one another, and the national parties have no power over any part of the state parties. The national and state parties are simply different strata, not higher and lower levels in a chain of command headed by the national agencies.

At the various local levels, there are congressional district committees, county committees, city committees, ward and precinct committees, and others too numerous to list here. In most states, the local party committees and conventions are, both in law and in fact, independent of the state and the national party agencies. Hence, they constitute a third stratum, which is just as independent from the state agencies as the state agencies are from the national agencies.

Far more than almost any major party in any other modern democratic nation, then, American party organizations are agglomerations of hundreds of different leaders and committees distributed among various organizational strata, each of which has little or no power to command or obligation to obey any other agency in its own stratum, let alone any agency in any other stratum. Former Georgia governor and senator Zell Miller's speaking career exemplifies this. A moderate Democrat from a state with many such voters, he delivered the keynote address to the Democratic National Convention in 1992. After growing disenchanted with national Democrats and supportive of President Bush, Miller gave the keynote at the Republican National Convention in 2004, but remains a Democrat. Even more tellingly, Connecticut senator Joe Lieberman went from being Al Gore's vice-presidential running mate in 2000 to losing the Democratic primary for the Senate in 2006 to running (and winning) that year as a third-party candidate on the "Connecticut for Lieberman" party label. In America, candidates can use parties when they are helpful in campaigns and abandon parties when they are an electoral hindrance, the opposite of the candidate–party relationship in most nations.

Low Cohesion

The parliamentary parties in most modern democratic nations have high **party cohesion**, a term that denotes the degree to which the members of a legislative party vote together on issues of public policy. Abstentions and even votes against the party leaders' wishes are not unknown in those parties, and in some countries, their frequency has increased, though very slowly, in recent years. But these are, at most, minor deviations from the norm, which is that all the members of parliamentary parties in other countries vote solidly together in most parliamentary votes.

By sharp contrast, the only matters in either chamber of Congress on which all Democrats regularly vote one way and all Republicans vote the other way relate to "organizing" the chamber—that is, selecting the Speaker of the House, the president pro tem of the Senate, and the chairs of the leading standing committees. On all other issues, the parties rarely vote unanimously, though most usually vote together.

On the issues shown in Table 19.2, party cohesion was generally higher among House Democrats than among Senate Democrats, and even higher among House and Senate Republicans. On some issues, one party or the other approached the cohesion levels of most major parties in other democracies. For example, the House Democrats' opposition to President Clinton's impeachment was very high, while House Republicans had perfect cohesion for President George W. Bush's tax cut proposal in 2001. On the other hand, House Democrats split more evenly on gays in the military and Bush's tax cut.

Consequently, the congressional parties have some party cohesion. It is especially high on such issues as higher spending for social welfare measures and greater regulation of business—with the Democrats usually voting predominantly (but not unanimously) in favor and the Republicans usually voting predominantly (but not unanimously) against. On the other hand, on issues that cut sharply across party lines—especially moral issues such as abortion, capital punishment, and the regulation of pornography—both parties regularly split relatively evenly. Thus, in comparison with the major parliamentary parties in most other democratic nations, the American congressional Democrats and Republicans have low cohesion on most issues.

This situation has important consequences for the role of American parties in the policymaking process, which we will consider later. It also has several causes, the most important of which is the fact that, compared with most other democratic parties, the leaders of the Democrats and the Republicans have very weak disciplinary powers.

Weak Discipline

The leaders of most major parties in the world's democracies have a number of tools to ensure that the legislators bearing their parties' labels support the parties' policies in the national legislatures. For one, they can make sure that no unusually visible or persistent rebel against the party's positions is given a ministerial position or preferment of any kind. If that fails to bring the fractious member into line, they can expel him or her from the parliamentary party altogether. Many parties in many countries give their leaders the ultimate weapon: the power to deny the rebel reselection as an official party candidate at the next election.

In sharp contrast, in the United States, any person who wins a party's primary for the House or Senate in any congressional district or state automatically becomes the party's legal candidate for that office, and no national party agency has the power to veto the nomination. On one notable occasion, called by historians "the purge of 1938," Franklin D. Roosevelt, an unusually popular and powerful national party leader, tried to intervene in the primary elections of several states to prevent the renomination of Democratic senators who had opposed his New Deal policies. He failed in twelve of thirteen attempts, and most people have since concluded that any effort by a national party leader to interfere in candidate selection at the state and local levels is bound to fail.

To be sure, presidents and their parties' leaders in Congress can, and often do, plead with their fellow partisans to support the president's policies for the sake of party loyalty, or to increase the party's chances at the next election, or to keep the party from looking foolish. If persuasion does not work, leaders can (but rarely do) promise to provide future campaign funding to a reluctant member or grant a hearing to a stalled bill authored by that member. Unless they have some strong reason to do otherwise, most members of Congress go along. However, unlike the leaders of most parties in most other countries, neither the president nor his party's congressional leaders have any effective disciplinary power to compel their members in Congress to vote in ways contrary to their consciences—or to what they perceive to be the interests and wishes of their constituents.

A Special Consequence: Divided Party Control of Government

In a pure parliamentary democracy, one party cannot control the legislature while another party controls the executive. If the parliament refuses a cabinet request, either the cabinet resigns and a new cabinet acceptable to the parliament takes over or the parliament is dissolved, new elections are held, and a new cabinet is formed that has the support of the new parliamentary majority. There can never be more than a short interim period in which the parliamentary majority and cabinet disagree on any major question of public policy.

In the United States, in contrast, separation of powers and the separate terms and constituencies for the president, the members of the House, and the members of the Senate make it possible for one party to win control of the presidency and the other party to win control of one or both houses of Congress.

How often does it actually happen? From the election of 1832 (when most historians say the modern electoral and party systems began) through the election of 2008, there have been a total of eighty-nine presidential and midterm elections. Each of these elections could have resulted in either divided party control or unified party control. In fact, fifty-six (63 percent) produced unified control, and thirty-three (37 percent) produced divided control.

Even more noteworthy is the fact that since the death of Franklin D. Roosevelt in 1945, **divided party control** has occurred so frequently that many observers feel it has become normal, not exceptional. In the period from 1946 through 2008, there have been thirty-two elections. Only thirteen (40 percent) have produced unified control (ten with a Democratic president and Congress, and three with a Republican president and Congress), and nineteen (60 percent) have produced divided control (see Figure 19.6).

The election of 2000 initially produced unified Republican control, with President George W. Bush joining the Republican-controlled Congress. But it did not last long; in 2001, Senator James Jeffords of Vermont announced that he was leaving the Republican Party to become an independent, and that he would vote with the Democrats. That gave the Democrats only a 50-to-49 margin, but with Jeffords' support, they regained control of the Senate and once again became part of a divided government. In 2002, the voters restored control of both houses to the Republicans, but then delivered both the Senate and the House of Representatives to Democrats in 2006 and the presidency to Democrats in 2008. In the 2010 midterm elections, voters once again switched control of the House to the Republican Party, and left Democrats clinging to a narrow majority in the Senate. This dynamic continued in 2012 (see Figure 19.6).

The most obvious cause for this situation (which is both unknown and impossible in parliamentary democracies) is the fact that the chief executive and the members of both houses of Congress are, as we have seen, elected separately by overlapping constituencies and with different terms. The constitutional structure thus makes it possible for American voters to do something that voters in most parliamentary democracies cannot do, namely, "split their tickets"—that is, vote for a member of one party for president and for a member of the other party for Congress.

Year	Congress	President
1946	Republicans	
1948	Democrats	Harry S Truman, Democrat
1950	Democrats	
1952	Republicans	Dwight D. Eisenhower, Republican
1954	Democrats	
1956	Democrats	
1958	Democrats	
1960	Democrats	John F. Kennedy, Democrat
1962	Democrats	
1963	Democrats	Lyndon B. Johnson, Democrat
1964	Democrats	
1966	Democrats	
1968	Democrats	Richard M. Nixon, Republican
1970	Democrats	
1972	Democrats	
1973	Democrats	Gerald R. Ford, Republican
1974	Democrats	
1976	Democrats	James E. Carter, Democrat
1978	Democrats	
1980	S–R, H–D	Ronald W. Reagan, Republican
1982	S–R, H–D	
1984	S–R, H–D	
1986	Democrats	
1988	Democrats	George H. W. Bush, Republican
1990	Democrats	
1992	Democrats	William J. Clinton, Democrat
1994	Republicans	
1996	Republicans	
1998	Republicans	
2000	S–D, H–R	George W. Bush, Republican
2002	Republicans	
2004	Republicans	
2006	Democrats	
2008	Democrats	Barack Obama, Democrat
2010	S–D, H–R	
2012	S–D, H–R	

FIGURE 19.6

United/Split Party Control of the Presidency and Congress, 1946–2012

Ticket splitting explains the increasing frequency of divided party control. Figure 19.7 shows the changing percentages of respondents in the National Election Studies of all presidential elections from 1952 through 2008 who reported voting for the presidential candidate of one party and a candidate of another party for the House of Representatives. This figure shows that split-ticket voting rose steadily from 1952 until 1980. It has fallen since then, as partisan polarization in the electorate has increased, but in 2008, it was still higher than it was in 1952. In 2012, split-ticket voting fell even further, to only 9 percent of voters, yet party control of Congress and the presidency remained divided.

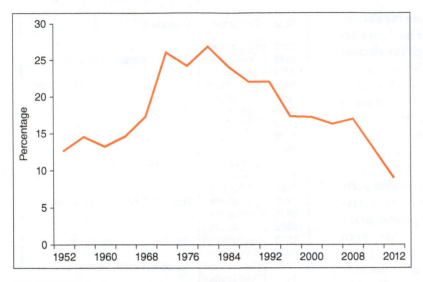

FIGURE 19.7

Trend in Split-Ticket Voting, 1952–2012

Source: American National Election Studies, Inter-University Consortium for Political and Social Research, University of Michigan, compiled by Gary Jacobson. Data points are the percentage reporting a different vote for the presidential and House of Representatives elections; third-party candidates are excluded from the calculations.

However, divided government apparently does not significantly weaken (or strengthen) the federal government's ability to make public policies. David Mayhew's careful study of the most important pieces of legislation passed from 1946 to 1990 shows that the rate of production was about the same in periods of divided party control as in periods of unified control.[42]

The Policymaking Process in America

19.10 Explain the U.S. policymaking process, as it generally occurs through Congress and as it occasionally occurs via the president.

When we consider the policymaking process in the United States, we must first understand that the constitutional framework within which the process operates was carefully designed to keep government from doing bad things, not to make it easier for it to do good things. To be sure, in writing the Constitution, the men of Philadelphia hoped to achieve a more effective national government than that provided by the Articles of Confederation. But making and implementing effective, coherent, and forceful national policies was not their prime goal.

They believed that government should never be regarded as some kind of benevolent mother, doing whatever is necessary to keep all her children well fed and feeling good. We should never forget, they warned, that government is a powerful and dangerous institution created by fallible human beings. Its prime objective—indeed, its only legitimate reason for existing and being obeyed—is to secure every person's right to life, liberty, and property. Anything that government does beyond that, they believed, is not only less important but not even acceptable if it in any way abridges those basic rights.

The best way to make a government strong enough to secure the rights of its citizens without becoming so powerful that it overrides them, they believed, is to disperse its power among many different agencies—among the federal and state governments by federalism, and within the federal government by separation of powers. The power should be divided, they held, so that no single faction would likely ever get control of the whole power of government and promote its interests at the expense of all the others.[43]

Accordingly, they did not think that policy deadlocks, in which the government cannot act because one of its parts blocks action by other parts, are some kind of terrible failure that should be avoided wherever possible and unblocked as soon as possible. Rather, they regarded such deadlocks as highly preferable to any government action that rides roughshod over the interests and objections of any significant part of the community. Consequently, whenever a deadlock blocks today's government from making effective policies to deal with budget deficits, mounting national debt, crime, health care, campaign finance, the war on terror, or any other public problem, we can at least say that the policymaking process is operating as the framers intended.

The governmental apparatus they assembled to slow down policy movement to a deliberative pace is depicted in Figure 19.8. This rough schematic of

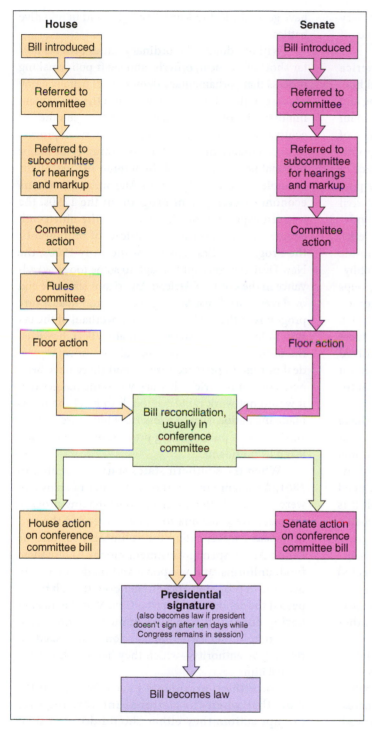

FIGURE 19.8
How a Bill Becomes a Law in America

both the House (where each of the 435 representatives vote on behalf of districts containing roughly 650,000 residents) and the Senate (where pairs of senators represent states that range in population from 520,000 in Wyoming to 38 million in California). In each body, legislation is assigned to a committee, making it vulnerable to the will of the committee's chair and its members, and then must pass on the floor. This is an especially difficult hurdle in the Senate, where sixty votes out of one hundred are needed to end a potential filibuster on any bill other than the annual budget resolution and the policy changes necessary to reconcile law with the new budget. (This "reconciliation" process opens the door to passing major legislation with a fiscal effect, such as President Obama's health care reform bill, with only fifty-one rather than sixty votes, but such a step is rarely taken.) Even after both houses act in tandem, they must agree on a final bill that sorts out any differences between the Senate and House versions, and pass it. Then the bill moves on to the president's desk, where the leader of the executive branch can always veto the measure and ask for legislative changes. Compared to the parliamentary systems that fuse their legislative and executive branches and often privilege one house above the other, the American system of policymaking puts in place many roadblocks where a bill can be stopped.

Traditional Ways of Avoiding Deadlocks

From the opening of the First Congress in 1789 to the twenty-first century, Americans have found that, however dangerous to human rights it may be, the government of the United States has to make and implement at least *some* policies. It has to regulate interstate and foreign commerce, increase or decrease the supply of money, conduct relations with foreign nations, levy taxes, make appropriations, and so on. Americans have developed ways of getting policies made despite the constitutional system's many roadblocks and general tendency toward inertia. One

how a bill becomes a law illustrates the parallel paths that legislation must take through the two houses of Congress that represent very different constituencies. To become law, versions of a bill must first pass set of ways has been traditionally used in ordinary times, and the other set has been called on in times of great crisis.

In ordinary times, public policies in America have been made mainly by putting together ad hoc, issue-specific coalitions of interests by bargaining and cutting deals among their representatives. The main coalition builders have included public officials of all kinds, including presidents and their chief political aides in the Cabinet and the Executive Office of the President; members of Congress and their professional staffs; political heads and permanent civil servants in the executive departments and the independent agencies; and federal judges and their clerks. At least as active and often as powerful as these inside players are the outside players, especially the lobbyists representing the major organized interest groups that feel they have large stakes in the policy outcomes. The usual result is that, while each contest over each policy produces winners and losers, it never produces total victory or total defeat for any highly involved interest. Each contestant gets something of what it wants but never all, and each manages to stave off total disaster.

Many commentators, past and present, have been highly critical of this process. They claim that it usually takes far too long to get anything done, and that what is done is usually messy, full of inconsistencies, self-defeating, and in constant need of repair. They are also struck by how difficult it is to get closure on any major policy. Typically, when a coalition loses in the presidency, it tries in Congress; when it loses in Congress, it tries in the bureaucracy; when it fails to persuade incumbent elected and appointed officials, it tries to replace them; and when it loses everywhere else, it turns to the courts to upset or water down policies made by the other agencies.

In recent years, for example, environmentalists have increasingly focused their efforts on lobbying the federal agencies that implement natural resources legislation rather than only the members of Congress who pass it. As another example, when civil rights advocates in the 1950s failed to get Congress to abolish racial segregation in the schools, they turned to the U.S. Supreme Court and won their victory in the landmark decision of *Brown v. Board of Education* (1954). Those who today advocate same-sex marriage rights have found success in several court cases, while they have generally lost in legislative fights and in initiative battles.

Without doubt, the ordinary-times process falls far short of the neat, orderly, and swift policymaking process that parliamentary democracies usually enjoy because of their fusion of powers and the consequent impossibility of prolonged deadlock between the executive and the legislature. Yet the American process has undeniably produced a large number of major national policies, many of them quite successful: for example, the establishment of Alexander Hamilton's economic development program in the 1790s, the western expansion of the country in the nineteenth century, the absorption of millions of immigrants, the Progressive Era reforms of the early 1900s, the New Deal, the constant (though to some too slow) advance in the status of African Americans since the end of slavery, the Great Society welfare and health care programs of the 1960s, the drastic overhaul of the tax system in 1986, and so on. Even at its best, however, the ordinary-times process has always taken a great deal of time to produce results, and there have been occasions in American history when the danger that it would not work rapidly enough to meet the needs made the nation turn to a less rigid but more controversial type of policymaking process: unilateral action taken by presidents.

When the southern states started seceding in 1861, Abraham Lincoln took a number of steps that were far outside the ordinary policymaking process. By executive proclamations, he suspended the writ of *habeas corpus*; called for volunteers to join the Union Army; spent government money to buy them food, uniforms, and weapons; and made the fateful decision to provision Fort Sumter even though he expected the action would start a Civil War. Then, after having done all this, he summoned Congress into session, told them what he had done, and asked for retroactive authority—which they had no choice but to give him.

Since then, presidents have often taken the view that when the national interest requires prompt action, they either should do it on their own, as Lincoln did, or persuade Congress to rush through their radical reform measures, as Franklin D. Roosevelt did in the 1930s when it seemed clear that in the absence of extraordinary measures, the economy would collapse under the stress of the Great Depression.

Presidents usually exert these extraordinary powers in foreign rather than domestic crises, as when Truman ordered American troops into Korea in 1950; Kennedy and Johnson followed suit in Vietnam in the 1960s; George H. W. Bush ordered troops to Panama, the Persian Gulf, and Somalia in the 1980s and early 1990s; Clinton sent troops to Haiti in 1994 and to Bosnia in 1995; and George W. Bush, in 2001 and 2002, sent American soldiers and airmen to Afghanistan to overthrow the terrorist-sheltering Taliban government and, in 2003, sent the armed forces to invade Iraq and depose Saddam Hussein. The War Powers Act of 1974 was designed to limit the president's power to take this kind of action without congressional approval, but in fact it has restrained presidents very little. No one doubts that in any future crisis, especially in foreign affairs, presidents will again bypass the ordinary policymaking process and do what they feel needs to be done.

Recent experience, however, makes it clear that the presidential dictatorship escape valve does not stay open indefinitely. When a military action drags on for months and years with huge expense, many casualties, and little hope of a clean-cut final victory—Korea and Vietnam are so far the leading examples, and Iraq and Afghanistan may take their places on the list—the president eventually loses popular and then congressional support, and the nation returns to the ordinary process. In any case, a leader who is held to account for his actions in free elections every four years is no dictator.

He can also be checked by the courts and by the press, which happened to President George W. Bush with increasing frequency. The *New York Times* revealed in December 2005 that the National Security Agency, at the president's request, was conducting surveillance on domestic and international telephone calls without obtaining court warrants as proscribed by the Foreign Intelligence Surveillance Act (FISA). The Bush administration argued that the presidency's inherent powers justify bypassing this congressional act during a time of war, but the president faced tough questioning on this issue from reporters and from some members of Congress. In June 2006, the U.S. Supreme Court ruled that detainees held at Guantanamo Bay could not be put on trial before secretive military commissions, in part because the commissions were created without congressional authority. This landmark case points out the limits of executive power, even in wartime.

Policy Performance

19.11 Compare U.S. tax levels and types to those of other countries.

19.12 Discuss three problem areas regulated by the U.S. government.

Tax Policies

When considering policy performance in the United States, it is important to remember that we are dealing with the outputs of many governments, not just the one in Washington, D.C.[44] In 2007, there were over 89,000 governmental units in America, including the federal government, 50 states, 3,033 counties, 19,492 municipalities, 16,519 towns and townships, 13,051 local school districts, and 37,381 special districts—each of which had some constitutional or statutory power to make policies.[45]

Of these 89,527 authorities, the federal government extracts the greatest share of revenues; it collects 57 percent of revenues from all sources. Its share is, of course, smaller than the shares taken by the national governments of unitary nations—such as Great Britain, Japan, and Sweden—but it is larger than those taken by the national governments in any of the federal systems except Austria.[46]

Table 19.3 displays the main types of taxes as percentages of total revenue in the United States and six other industrialized nations in 2008. This table shows that the United States relies more on personal income taxes than any other nation. Social Security taxes paid by employees in America are higher than average. The United States relies less on sales and other taxes on consumption than any other country. Part of the reason is that, unlike most European governments, the U.S. national government has never levied a sales tax or a value-added tax, although most American states levy sales taxes as well as income taxes. Accordingly, the tax structure in the American federal system as a whole is more progressive (in the sense of placing the heaviest burden on people with the greatest ability to pay) than that in most but not all other nations.

Americans frequently complain about the heavy tax burden they bear, and Republican presidents

TABLE 19.3

Tax Sources as Percentages of Total Revenue, 2008

	Personal Income	Corporate Income	Employees' Social Security	Employers' Social Security	Sales and Consumption	Specific Goods
Great Britain	29.9	9.9	7.9	10.8	17.8	9.8
Canada	37.3	10.7	5.8	8.3	13.2	8.5
France	17.4	6.8	9.2	25.3	16.8	6.9
Germany	26.8	5.2	15.9	17.2	19.4	8.5
Italy	26.8	8.6	5.5	21.2	13.7	8.3
Japan	32.6	22.8	Not available	Not available	14.5	11.2
United States	37.9	8.9	10.8	12.4	7.8	6.2

Source: *Statistical Abstract of the United States: 2012* (Washington, DC: Bureau of the Census, 2012), Table 1361. These figures combine federal, state, and local taxes.

Ronald Reagan, George H. W. Bush, and George W. Bush all made cutting taxes the cornerstones of their economic programs. Just how great is the tax burden of Americans compared with that borne by the residents of other industrialized democracies?

The answer depends on what measure is used. Expressed as a percentage of GDP, American taxes take a total of 25.6 percent, the lowest figure among the major industrialized nations (Sweden, at 50.6 percent, is the highest). Moreover, the take from GDP has increased at a slower rate than in any other industrialized democracy since 1980 (again, Sweden leads with the highest rate of increase).[47] In summary, compared with the tax systems of most other industrialized countries, the American system is one of the more progressive in its structure but takes a smaller proportion of the GDP than any of the others.

Another way to evaluate a tax system is by whether a government raises enough money to pay for the spending commitments that it makes. Because Congress and the president are not constrained to pass a balanced budget—and face no external pressures to exert fiscal discipline in the way that European Union nations often do—the nation has often committed more in spending than it has raised in taxes. The Congressional Budget Office projected a federal deficit in 2013 of $845 billion, or 5.3 percent of the nation's gross domestic product. The combination of a recession and the stimulus spending and tax cuts implemented to fight it has pushed the national debt higher than it has been, relative to the nation's economy, since the early 1950s. While the deficit is expected to be cut in half by 2015, both political parties will doubtless tout their plans to reduce the debt over the long run. Doing so, however, will require raising taxes, cutting spending, or both, and it remains to be seen whether Washington, D.C.'s polarized parties will be able to reach an agreement on how much of each painful policy to enact.

Distributive Performance

Figure 19.9 gives an overview of how the federal government allocated its budget in 2010. This figure shows that the federal government spent 62 percent of its budget on domestic welfare and education functions, 18 percent on defense-related functions, 5 percent for interest on the national debt, and 15 percent in other areas. State and local governments in America also spent $3.2 trillion on their own, with the bulk of this spending going toward education, health care, and welfare.

Among the world's other democratic governments, only Israel spends as high a proportion of its budget on defense as the United States. (Some developing countries, such as North Korea, Oman, and Saudi Arabia, spend even higher proportions.) Some Americans argue that defense spending is far too high, especially now that the Cold War has ended. Others counter that the events of 9/11 demonstrate that the world is still a dangerous place, and America needs to spend whatever it takes to win the **war on terror**. Whatever the merits of these positions, the trend up to 2001 was toward lower proportions of

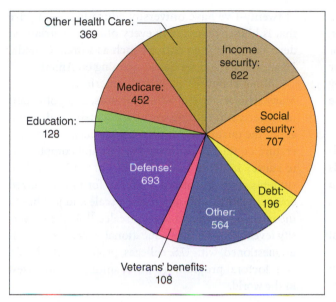

FIGURE 19.9

Federal Spending by Function, 2010 (in billions of dollars)

Source: *Statistical Abstract of the United States: 2012* (Washington, DC: Bureau of the Census, 2012), Table 473.

federal spending on defense, but defense spending then climbed from 2002 through 2010.

Other international comparisons show that U.S. per capita expenditures on health care are by far the highest in the world, followed at some distance by Switzerland and Germany.[48] And in proportion of the GDP spent on education, the United States (with 7.3 percent) ranks second behind South Korea (8.2 percent) and ahead of Denmark (7.1 percent), Iceland (6.7 percent), and Sweden (6.5 percent).[49]

Regulatory Performance

Like all modern industrialized democracies, the United States is a welfare state in the sense that many of its policies proceed from the conviction that government has an obligation to guarantee certain minimum levels of life's basics to all its citizens, especially to those who cannot provide them for themselves. However, nations differ markedly in both the particular items of basic needs that government should provide and the levels at which they should be provided. In this section, we briefly review the major policies adopted by American governments in three main problem areas.

Social Insurance The United States was among the last of the modern industrialized nations to embrace the goals of the welfare state, and today, the proportion of the nation's GDP spent on public welfare programs is lower than that in most industrialized nations. Even so, the federal, state, and local governments together have a wide range of policies intended to put a floor beneath the income and living conditions of the poor. For that purpose, they use two main instruments: social insurance and welfare as well as public assistance.

1. *Social insurance and welfare.* This category includes programs to protect citizens against the risk of loss of income due to old age, retirement, sickness, industrial accidents, and unemployment. The basic federal legislation is the Social Security Act of 1935, which established a fund from mandatory contributions by employees and employers from which all wage earners are entitled to receive cash payments at retirement or on reaching a certain age. Since the benefits are available to all who contribute, most Americans regard its benefits as entitlements, not handouts. No stigma attaches to receiving Social Security checks, and most Americans of all income levels approve of the program.

2. *Public assistance.* This category includes both direct cash and in-kind payments to poor people, such as cash aid to families with dependent children, food stamps, free milk for young children, and day care for children of working mothers with low incomes. Unlike Social Security, these programs are noncontributory and thus constitute obvious income transfers from upper-income to lower-income people. As a result, some social stigma does attach to receiving public assistance benefits, and these welfare programs are much more controversial than the social insurance programs.

For years, there were many complaints that the welfare system, especially Aid for Families with Dependent Children (AFDC), was removing recipients' incentives to work and making them into life-long dependents on government handouts. Then, in 1996, the Republican Congress passed, and President Clinton signed, a bill for **welfare reform**. The new law ended the federal guarantee of direct AFDC payments to all eligible families. Instead, the federal government gave $16.4 billion in block grants to the states to develop and fund their own new welfare programs, *provided* that the states impose work requirements for welfare recipients, develop job-training programs for them, and put time limits on welfare benefits (thereby replacing welfare with "workfare," according to the new law's advocates).[50]

Education In the United States, as in other industrialized nations, education is provided mainly by schools financed and operated by the government, although there are more privately owned and operated schools, especially universities, in America than in most other countries (they are also important in Japan and Great Britain).

What sets the American school system apart from systems in other countries is its high degree of decentralization. Most schools, from kindergartens through universities, are financed and regulated by state and local governments, although the federal government provides considerable subsidies for many special programs, each of which carries restrictions on how the money is to be spent. For example, in awarding federally funded scholarships and other forms of financial aid for students, schools may not discriminate against applicants because of their race or gender. The local financing and regulation of schools has many consequences, not the least of which is the fact that schools in poor states and poor districts generally spend considerably less money per pupil than schools in richer states and districts.

Whatever the consequences of these differences, the United States still has a higher proportion of its population with college degrees than any other nation. A number of industrialized nations operate on the theory that higher education should be reserved for only the most talented and accomplished students. They therefore require that only those students who do well in demanding, nationally administered tests after finishing one level may advance to a school at the next higher level. The United States, in contrast, operates on the theory that as many people as possible should be given a chance at a college education. Consequently, it is much easier for American eighteen-year-olds to enter some kind of postsecondary education—a four-year college or university or a two-year community college—than for their peers in any other country, and many more do so. According to the Census Bureau, 28 percent of Americans over the age of twenty-five have university educations—a figure that is higher than nearly every other industrialized democracy (though nations such as Korea, Canada, Japan, and Ireland are quickly gaining on America).

What about the *quality* of American education? Many scholars, school administrators, and politicians in America have long and inconclusively debated about the quality of our primary schools, and the literature on the subject is far too vast and complicated to survey in detail here. We will note only that U.S. students score just above the mean for industrialized countries on a combined reading scale and just below the mean on math and science scales.[51] At the university level, the American educational system's quality is unquestioned, with U.S. colleges, professional schools, and doctoral programs ranking among the strongest in the world.

Environmental Protection Of the policy areas considered here, environmental protection is the most recent to take center stage, not only in the United States but most other industrialized nations as well. From the beginning of the Industrial Revolution in the late eighteenth century until well after World War II, one of the highest goals of every nation was economic growth—constantly increasing the nation's production of goods and services, both for home consumption and for sale abroad.

For many purposes, that goal remains highly desirable today, since economic growth allows governments to reach a diverse set of policy goals, including boosting their military strength and diplomatic clout; providing more food, shelter, and medical care for the poor; and increasing the coverage and improving the quality of health care and education. In recent years, however, policymakers in many nations, including the United States, have come to realize that economic growth, especially unrestrained and rapid growth, has great costs. Nowhere is this cost greater than in the area of toxic emissions and solid wastes that have been the by-products of large-scale industrialization.

As a result, policymakers in the United States and elsewhere have become increasingly aware that they must grapple with environmental problems. Some nations, especially Japan and Great Britain, have approached these problems less by relying on government regulations than by encouraging corporations and labor unions to work together to develop their own plans for dealing with pollution. Early in the era of environmental policy, the United States took a quite different approach. It enacted a series of stringent laws, beginning with the Clean Air Act of 1970. These laws require manufacturers to sharply reduce their emissions that pollute the air and water by installing expensive devices (such as smoke scrubbers and water purifiers) to recycle solid wastes, and to clean up, mostly at their own (and/or their insurance companies') expense, the toxic waste dumps they had created. The federal government established a special agency, the Environmental Protection Agency (EPA), to make sure these laws are strictly enforced.

More recently, U.S. policymakers have moved away from stringent regulations and toward incentives, voluntary industry goals, and tradable permits that seek to reduce pollution in the most cost-effective way possible. Perhaps the clearest indication that the United States has moved away from the forefront of environmental regulation is the federal government's refusal to ratify the Kyoto Protocol, an international agreement designed to stave off global warming by reducing emissions of "greenhouse gases," such as carbon dioxide. Opponents have argued that abiding by the protocol's targets would slow down economic growth in the United States, and that it places too much of a burden on industrialized nations while putting much looser limits on developing countries. During his campaign, Barack Obama argued against this position, promising swift action to limit greenhouse gas emissions and more energetic American leadership in the fight against global warming. Yet, because of Congressional opposition, President Obama has not been able win any landmark victories on global climate change since he took office.

American Exceptionalism: Myth or Reality?

The Idea in History

During much of its history, many of the United States' leaders and citizens—and some foreign commentators and many of the millions of immigrants who left their native countries to become Americans—have regarded the United States as not just another polity in a world of many polities, but as significantly different from other political systems. Some have viewed it as a great social experiment from which all political systems can and should learn lessons relevant to founding and reforming their own systems.

In his first inaugural address, George Washington said, "The preservation of the sacred fire of liberty, and the destiny of the republican model of government, are justly considered as deeply, perhaps as finally staked, on the experiment entrusted to the hands of the American people."[52]

In December 1862, when the very existence of the American system was at stake in the Civil War, Abraham Lincoln said to Congress, "We of this Congress and this administration, will be remembered in spite of ourselves. . . . The fiery trial through which we pass, will light us down, in honor or dishonor, to the latest generation. . . . We shall nobly save, or meanly lose, the last, best hope of earth."[53]

How True Is It?

It seems altogether fitting and proper that we should end this chapter by asking not whether the idea of **American exceptionalism** is noble or vainglorious, but rather how true it is. That is, in what respect and to what degree does the American system resemble and differ from the world's other political systems? Our conclusions are summarized in Table 19.4.

How the American System Closely Resembles Other Systems It is a government that has jurisdiction over a certain territory and peoples. It makes laws governing their behavior and enforces them with means up to and including capital punishment.

American society is composed of many different groups with different interests, and its political process is essentially a contest among them to advance their interests. Few if any policies benefit all groups and interests equally, and most political decisions have, relatively speaking, some winners and some losers.

In addition, this book's basic theoretical scheme for comparing governments is as applicable to the United States as to any other nation.

How the American System Resembles a Few Nations but Differs from Most As Table 19.4 notes, the United States is a democracy along with other democracies. It is based on the principle of constitutionalism. Its society is diverse in the ethnic and religious makeup of its residents.

TABLE 19.4
The United States Compared with Other Nations: A Summary

Characteristic	How the U.S. Is Like Other Nations	How the U.S. Resembles a Few Nations but Differs from Many	How the U.S. Is Unique, or Nearly So
Society	Consists of many different groups with different interests	Large population of immigrants and descendants of immigrants High religious diversity	
Political System	Has a government, which makes and enforces laws	Is a democracy	Central place of the Constitution in framing and resolving political and policy disputes
Structure of Government		Based on principles of constitutionalism Federal system	Extensiveness of system of checks and balances
Executive Branch	Has a chief executive	Presidential system rather than parliamentary system Chief of state and head of government roles performed by same person President is directly elected through an electoral college	
Legislative Branch	Has a national legislature	Both houses of the legislature are directly elected	Legislative committees play a critical role
Judicial Branch	Courts settle civil and criminal disputes	All national judges appointed; some state and local judges elected Most courts have power of judicial review	Many political issues settled by courts rather than by parties or legislatures
Parties and Elections	Has regular elections	Has a two-party system Elections use single-member districts and plurality decisions Elections held on fixed dates; no power of dissolution Parties closely regulated by law Executive and legislative branches can be and often are controlled by different parties	Candidates selected by direct primaries Voter registration is decentralized and responsibility of voter Voters have many elections and many choices at each Party leaders have no power to admit or expel party members Parties are decentralized and largely undisciplined and uncohesive

The United States is a presidential democracy rather than a parliamentary democracy, based on the separation of powers rather than on their fusion. The head of government is elected rather than hereditary. Furthermore, the roles of chief of state and head of government are performed by the same official.

The United States is also unusual because it is a federal system rather than a unitary system. State governments and the local governments that they create exert a strong, independent influence over the lives of Americans, bringing meaningful representation to voters on a much smaller and more accessible scale.

The legislative system displays differences from other systems. The presiding officers of its legislative chambers are partisan rather than neutral. Its legislative committees play a critical role in the legislative process. And American legislators are largely free of party discipline and control their own votes.

The U.S. legal system is based on English common law rather than on continental European civil law. This means that our legal precedents are derived from the prior decisions of judges rather than from an extensive codification of principles constructed by legislative or executive branch officials. Also, our highest court has the power to declare acts of other government officials and agencies unconstitutional and thereby render them null and void.

U.S. elections use the single-member, plurality system rather than proportional representation. Because of this, they are almost always contested by only two major parties. Not only can different parties control different branches of government at the same time, but they often do. American elections are held on fixed dates, and there is no power of dissolution. The practice is well established by law and custom that members of the national legislature must live in the states and districts they represent. Particularly in some states and localities, though not at the national level, there is extensive use of popular initiatives and referendums.

How the United States Is Unique, or Nearly So
Finally, Table 19.4 highlights many of the unique aspects of the American political system. For instance, the nation's brief, brilliant Constitution looms larger in America's daily political life than nearly any other country's governing plan. Its grants of rights guarantee the free flow of information through the press and check the actions of government officials in areas that range from criminal arrests to the regulation of private property. Americans appeal to the Constitution in political debates over issues such as gun control and gay marriage. In laying out the broad contours of how American government should operate, our founding document has functioned with very few amendments from 1787 to today.

America is also distinct in many of the key details of how its democracy operates. Committees within Congress are more powerful and autonomous than committees in nearly every other national legislature. American political parties choose most of their nominees for office by direct primaries conducted and regulated by public law, not by party rules. Many

Implementing the Affordable Care Act
The most controversial policy of the Obama administration, the universal healthcare law, has also been the most challenging to implement. Flaws in this website earned the administration much criticism in 2013 and 2014.

The Republican House Leadership

Just four years after Democrats won control of the U.S. House of Representatives and elected Speaker Nancy Pelosi after the 2006 elections, Republicans regained control of the House with a landslide victory in November 2010. Controlling a majority of House seats set them up to elect Ohio congressman John Boehner, shown here as the next speaker.

of its executive officers, particularly at the state and local levels, are directly elected and nominated by direct primaries; consequently, the U.S. voter faces more frequent elections and more decisions to make at each election than voters in any other democratic nation except Switzerland. In addition, America's systems for registering voters are largely decentralized and put most of the burden on the voters.

Political parties are closely regulated by law. But political parties do not control who can become and remain their members, and the parties are, compared with those in other democratic systems, uncohesive, undisciplined, and decentralized.

Because candidates run as individuals rather than as local representatives of national party teams, and because no publicly financed free media time is given to parties or candidates, the raising and spending of large amounts of money are more important in American elections than in most other democracies.

The court system is also unusual. A higher proportion of political issues are settled in the courts than in any other democracy. Consequently, lawyers play a more important role in the American political system than in any other.

Conclusion

It seems fitting to end this chapter comparing the American political system to the world's other systems with a quotation from one of its greatest foreign observers, the English scholar and statesman, Lord Bryce:

> All governments are faulty; and an equally minute analysis of the constitutions of England, or France, or Germany would disclose mischiefs as serious . . . as those we have noted in the American system. To any one familiar with the practical working of free governments it is a standing wonder that they work at all. . . . What keeps a free government going is the good sense and patriotism of the people . . . and the United States, more than any other country, are governed by public opinion, that is to say, by the general sentiment of the mass of the nation, which all the organs of the national government and of the State governments look to and obey.[54]

REVIEW QUESTIONS

- Why is voter turnout lower in the United States than it is in most democracies?

- How has immigration policy changed over the past century? What effect has this had on American political culture?

- What impact has the direct primary had on the power of political parties in the United States? Why?

- How has America's traditional approach to environmental issues differed from the strategies pursued in Europe? In what ways has our approach changed recently?

- On which areas of government does the United States spend more than the rest of the world does?

KEY TERMS

Affordable Care Act

American exceptionalism

Bill of Rights

blanket primary

checks and balances

closed primaries

congressional party

conservatives

direct initiative

direct primaries

divided party control

electoral college

federalism

health care reform

judicial review

litigation

litigiousness

lobbying

mass communications media

melting pot

open primaries

parliamentary democracies

partisan polarization

party cohesion

patchwork quilt

political action committee (PAC)

political culture

popular referendum

presidential democracy

presidential party

public debt

scarcity doctrine

separation of powers

ticket splitting

voting registration

voting turnout

war on terror

welfare reform

SUGGESTED READINGS

Bryce, James. *The American Commonwealth*, 2nd ed. London: Macmillan, 1889.

Davidson, Roger H., and Walter J. Oleszek. *Congress and Its Members*, 7th ed. Washington, DC: CQ Press, 2000.

Fiorina, Morris P. *Culture War? The Myth of a Polarized America*. New York: Pearson-Longman, 2005.

Ginsberg, Benjamin, and Martin Shefter. *Politics by Other Means: The Declining Importance of Elections in America*, rev. ed. New York: Basic Books, 1999.

Hamilton, Alexander, James Madison, and John Jay. *The Federalist Papers*, ed. Clinton Rossiter. New York: New American Library, 1961.

Issenberg, Sasha. *The Victory Lab: The Secret Science of Winning Campaigns*. New York: Crown Publishers, 2012.

Jacobson, Gary C. *A Divider, Not a Uniter: George W. Bush and the American People*. New York: Pearson-Longman, 2007.

King, Anthony S. *Running Scared: Why American Politicians Campaign Too Much and Govern Too Little*. New York: Martin Kessler Books, 1997.

Mayhew, David R. *Divided We Govern: Party Control, Lawmaking, and Investigations, 1946–1988*. New Haven, CT: Yale University Press, 1991.

McCarty, Nolan, Keith T. Poole, and Howard Rosenthal. *Polarized America: The Dance of Ideology and Unequal Riches*. Cambridge: MIT Press, 2006.

Neustadt, Richard E. *Presidential Power and the Modern Presidents: The Politics of Leadership from Roosevelt to Reagan*. New York: Free Press, 1990.

Sides, John, and Lynn Vavrek. *The Gamble: Choice and Chance in the 2012 Presidential Election*. Princeton, NJ: Princeton University Press, 2013.

Tocqueville, Alexis de. *Democracy in America: The Henry Reeve Text*, 2 vols. Revised by Francis Bowen, ed. Phillips Bradley. New York: Alfred A. Knopf, 1945.

INTERNET RESOURCES

White House: www._whitehouse._gov.

U.S. Senate: www._senate._gov.

U.S. House of Representatives: www._house._gov.

U.S. Courts: www._uscourts._gov.

Library of Congress: lcweb._loc._gov.

National Political Index: politicalindex._com.

ENDNOTES

1. "The English Flag," in *Barrack-Room Ballads and Other Verses* (London: Methuen, 1892), stanza 1.

2. *The World Almanac and Book of Facts 2002* (New York: World Almanac Books, 2002), 782, 804.

3. *Statistical Abstract of the United States: 2010* (Washington, DC: U.S. Census Bureau, 2010), Table 1296.

4. H. G. Nicholas, *The Nature of American Politics*, 2nd ed. (New York: Oxford University Press, 1986), 4.

5. *Statistical Abstract of the United States: 2010*, Table 11.

6. See *Statistical Abstract of the United States: 2010*, Table 4, for figures on legal immigration, and Table 47, for estimates and definition of illegal (or unauthorized) immigration.

7. *Statistical Abstract of the United States: 2012* (Washington, DC: U.S. Census Bureau, 2012), Table 1348.

8. *Statistical Abstract of the United States: 2012*, Table 470.

9. See Jacob Hacker, *The Divided Welfare State: The Battle Over Public and Private Benefits in the United States* (New York: Cambridge University Press, 2002).

10. The Twenty-First Amendment repeals the Eighteenth (prohibition) Amendment, so there are, in effect, only twenty-five amendments. The resistance to amending the Constitution even with quite popular provisions was demonstrated in June 2006, when an amendment that would have given Congress the power to ban flag burning fell one vote short of gaining the required two-thirds majority in the U.S. Senate. See Johanna Neuman and Faye Fiore, "Flag Measure Fails By 1 Vote," *Los Angeles Times*, June 28, 2006.

11. Fifteen states have term limits for members of their legislatures. A number have also tried to impose similar limits on their members of Congress, but the U.S. Supreme Court ruled in 1995 (*U.S. Term Limits, Inc. v. Thornton*) that the states have no constitutional power to limit the terms of national legislators.

12. In recent years, an old dispute has been revived by a number of political analysts who argue that presidential democracy is inherently inferior to parliamentary democracy and that the United States should convert to a system of parliamentary democracy similar to Great Britain's. Other analysts reply that, judging by the results—effective policies, loyal citizens, and stability—the American system has done at least as well as the parliamentary systems. See Chapter 6 for a discussion of the issues and arguments in the dispute's current version.

13. James Q. Wilson and John J. DiIulio, *American Government*, 6th ed. (Lexington, MA: D.C. Heath, 1995), 81, Table 4.3.

14. Gabriel A. Almond and Sidney Verba, *The Civic Culture: Political Attitudes and Democracy in Five Nations* (Princeton, NJ: Princeton University Press, 1962), 186.

15. Robert A. Kagan, *Adversarial Legalism: The American Way of Law* (Cambridge, MA: Harvard University Press, 2003).

16. *New York Times v. Sullivan*, 376 U.S. 254 (1964).

17. The two key cases are *National Broadcasting Co. v. United States*, 319 U.S. 190 (1943), and *Red Lion Broadcasting Co. v. Federal Communications Commission*, 395 U.S. 367 (1969).

18. See Michael P. McDonald and Samuel Popkin, "The Myth of the Vanishing Voter," *American Political Science Review* 95, no. 4 (December 2001), 963–74.

19. In 1993, Congress passed the "Motor Voter" act, which was intended to make registration much easier and thereby increase voting turnout. The legislation requires the states to allow citizens to register when applying for a driver's license, to permit registrations by mail, and to provide registration forms at public assistance agencies, such as those distributing unemployment compensation and welfare checks. While most political scientists applaud the new law, its effectiveness is not yet clear. Turnout of eligible voters, which stood at 61 percent in the 1992 presidential election, *dropped* to 53 percent in 1996. It rose to 56 percent in 2000, and then to 61 percent in 2004.

20. David Glass, Peverill Squire, and Raymond E. Wolfinger, "Voter Turnout: An International Comparison," *Public Opinion* 6 (December 1983/January 1984), 49–55.

21. Russell J. Dalton, *Citizen Politics*, 2nd ed. (Chatham, NJ: Chatham House, 1996), 45–47.

22. See John G. Matsusaka, *For the Many or the Few: The Initiative, Public Policy, and American Democracy* (Chicago: University of Chicago Press, 2004).

23. One distinguished foreign observer of American politics argues persuasively that American public officials, such as members of the House of Representatives, face elections far more frequently than do their counterparts in other democracies. Consequently, he says, they have to spend large parts of their time in office raising money, touring their districts, appearing on television, and otherwise preparing for the next election. These necessities leave them less time than is needed for the careful study of public issues and the formulation of good public policy. See Anthony S. King, *Running Scared: Why America's Politicians Campaign Too Much and Govern Too Little* (New York: Martin Kessler Books, 1997).

24. Robert S. Erikson, Norman R. Luttbeg, and Kent L. Tedin, *American Public Opinion*, 4th ed. (New York: Macmillan, 1991), 5, Table 1.2.

25. In the United States, as in many democratic countries, voters can write names other than the parties' nominees on their ballots, but few voters do so, and write-in candidates almost never get more than a handful of votes. An exception came in

the 2004 mayor's race in San Diego, when write-in candidate Donna Frye came within a few hundred votes (and a disputed vote tabulation procedure) of getting elected mayor of the nation's seventh-largest city.

26. See Reuven Y. Hazan, "Candidate Selection," in *Comparing Democracies 2: New Challenges in the Study of Elections and Voting*, edited by Lawrence LeDuc, Richard Niemi, and Pippa Norris (Thousand Oaks, CA: Sage Publications, 2002).

27. Federal Election Commission, *Election Results for the U.S. President, the U.S. Senate and the U.S. House of Representatives* (Washington, DC: Federal Election Commission, 2008).

28. See, for example, Alexis de Tocqueville, *Democracy in America: The Henry Reeve Text*, vol. 1, revised by Francis Bowen, ed. Phillips Bradley (New York: Alfred A. Knopf, 1945), 191–93; and Michel Crozier, *The Trouble with America*, trans. Peter Heinegg (Berkeley: University of California Press, 1984), 81.

29. *Buckley v. Valeo*, 424 U.S. 1 (1976).

30. Harold W. Stanley and Richard G. Niemi, *Vital Statistics on American Politics 2009–2010* (Washington, DC: CQ Press, 2010), Table 2-10.

31. Stanley and Niemi, *Vital Statistics on American Politics 2009–2010*, Table 2-13.

32. *New York Times*, November 21, 1988.

33. Arend Lijphart puts the United States at the top of his list of democratic nations with the smallest number of effective legislative parties, closely followed by New Zealand, the United Kingdom, and Austria: *Democracies: Patterns of Majoritarian and Consensus Governments in Twenty-One Countries* (New Haven, CT: Yale University Press, 1984), Table 7.3, 122. Austin Ranney's ranking of "two-partyness," based on the somewhat different measure of "party fractionalization," which includes both the number of effective parties and the closeness of electoral competition between them, ranks the U.S. parties second behind New Zealand (although in 1995, New Zealand adopted proportional representation, and since then it has had a multiparty system): *Governing: An Introduction to Political Science*, 8th ed. (Englewood Cliffs, NJ: Prentice Hall, 2001), Table 8.6, 181.

34. Richard Scammon, Alice McGillivray, and Rhodes Cook, *America Votes* (Washington, DC: CQ Press, 2001), 8.

35. For a recent survey of changes in electioneering in the United States and other democratic nations, see David Butler and Austin Ranney, eds., *Electioneering: A Comparative Study of Continuity and Change* (New York: Oxford University Press, 1992).

36. Gary C. Jacobson, *A Divider, Not a Uniter: George W. Bush and the American People* (New York: Pearson-Longman, 2007), chaps. 1 and 2.

37. Morris P. Fiorina, *Culture War? The Myth of a Polarized America* (New York: Pearson-Longman, 2005), 18, 5.

38. Bruce E. Keith et al., *The Myth of the Independent Voter* (Berkeley: University of California Press, 1992).

39. Nolan McCarty, Keith T. Poole, and Howard Rosenthal, *Polarized America: The Dance of Ideology and Unequal Riches* (Cambridge: MIT Press, 2006), 12. But note that the very rich often vote for and contribute to Democrats, making the 90210 postal code in Beverly Hills a top fundraising area for the Democratic Party.

40. Fiorina, *Culture War?*, 70.

41. Samuel J. Eldersveld, *Political Parties in American Society* (New York: Basic Books, 1982), 133–36.

42. David Mayhew, *Divided We Govern* (New Haven, CT: Yale University Press, 1991).

43. The fullest exposition of this philosophy is, of course, *The Federalist Papers*, especially the tenth paper, by James Madison. See Alexander Hamilton, James Madison, and John Jay, *The Federalist Papers*, ed. Clinton Rossiter (New York: New American Library, 1961).

44. Hundreds of books have been written comparing American public policies with their counterparts in other nations. We have drawn heavily on two: Arnold J. Heidenheimer, Hugh Heclo, and Carolyn Teich Adams, *Comparative Public Policy*, 3rd ed. (New York: St. Martin's Press, 1990); and Harold Wilensky and Lowell Turner, *Democratic Corporatism and Policy Linkages* (Berkeley: Institute of International Studies, University of California, 1987).

45. *Statistical Abstract of the United States: 2010*, Tables 416, 418, and 457.

46. Heidenheimer, Heclo, and Adams, *Comparative Public Policy*, 198, Table 6.5.

47. OECD, *Revenue Statistics 1965–2004* (Washington, DC: OECD, 2005), Table 3, 68.

48. *Statistical Abstract of the United States: 2006*, Table 1323, 871 (Washington, DC: Government Printing Office, 2006).

49. OECD, *OECD in Figures, OECD Observer 2005/Supplement 1* (Washington, DC: OECD, 2005), 66–67.

50. For the law's details, see *Congressional Quarterly Almanac, 1996* (Washington, DC: CQ Press, 1997), 6-13–6-24.

51. *Statistical Abstract of the United States: 2010*, Table 1333.

52. *The Addresses and Messages of Presidents of the United States*, vol. 1, compiled by Edwin Williams (New York: Edward Walker, 1846), 32.

53. Address to Congress, December 1, 1862, in *The Collected Works of Abraham Lincoln*, vol. 5, ed. Roy P. Basler (New Brunswick, NJ: Rutgers University Press, 1953), 537.

54. James Bryce, *The American Commonwealth*, vol. 1, 2nd ed. (London: Macmillan, 1889), 300–301.

Credits

Photo Credits

p. 5: Holger Hill/Getty Images; **p. 7:** Wolf Kern/VISUM/The Image Works; **p. 10:** Sucheta Das/Reuters/Landov; **p. 11:** Peter Endig/dpa/Landov; **p. 31:** Elizabeth Dalziel/AP Images; **p. 36:** Les Stone/Sygma/Corbis; **p. 45:** Jose Goitia/AP Images; **p. 50:** Lemouton Stephane/ABACA/Newscom; **p. 63:** Ilyas Dean/The Image Works; **p. 64:** Sebastien Feval/AFP/GettyImages; **p. 69:** Eduardo Verdugo/AP Images; **p. 76:** Jean-Philippe Ksiazek/AFP/Getty Images; **p. 93:** Rebecca Blackwell/AP Images; **p. 111:** AP Photo/Virginia Mayo; **p. 113:** Jonas Esktrmer/Scanpix Sweden/Sipa Press; **p. 115:** AP Photo/Manish Swarup, pool; **p. 126:** Benoit Tessier/Reuters/Landov; **p. 131:** Mahesh Kumar A/AP Images; **p. 142:** Thony Belizaire/AFP/Getty Images; **p. 150:** David Bebber/AFP/Getty Images/Newscom; **p. 158:** Diverse Images/Universal Images Group/Getty Images; **p. 168:** Maksym Gorpenyuk/Shutterstock; **p. 184:** James Emmerson/Robert Harding Picture Library Ltd/Alamy; **p. 190:** Simon Dawson/Bloomberg/Getty Images; **p. 201:** Thomas Coex/AFP/Getty Images; **p. 211:** Pascal Le Segretain/Getty Images; **p. 224:** Philepe Hugen/Getty Images; **p. 253:** AP Photo/Lionel Cironneau; **p. 258:** Martin Athenstadt/picture-alliance/dpa/Newscom; **p. 263:** Torsten Leukert/vario images GmbH & Co.KG/Alamy; **p. 278:** Reynaldo Paganelli/NurPhoto/Sipa/Newscom; **p. 321:** Keizo Mori/UPI/Newscom; **p. 325:** Christpher Jue/EPA/Corbis; **p. 327:** Christpher Jue/EPA/Corbis; **p. 329:** Kim Kyung Hoon/Reuters; **p. 351:** Vasily Deryugin/ZUMA Press/Newscom; **p. 364:** Ole Spata/picture-alliance/dpa/AP Images; **p. 370:** Vladimir Rodionov/Ria Novosti/Kremlin Pool/EPA/Newscom; **p. 371:** SIPA France/Jiang Kehong/Xinhua/Sipa Press/Newscom; **p. 391:** SZ Photo/The Image Works; **p. 407:** xPacifica/The Image Works; **p. 413:** Jeff Widener/AP Images; **p. 423:** Fang xinwu/Color China Photo/AP Images; **p. 440:** AP Photo/Eduardo Verdugo; **p. 448:** AP Photo/Marco Ugarte; **p. 472:** Pedro PARDO/AFP/Getty Images; **p. 484:** Agência Brasil; **p. 508:** Agência Brasil; **p. 522:** John Maier, Jr./The Image Works; **p. 523:** Jose Cruz, Agência Brasil; **p. 527:** Sabelo Mngoma, Agência Brasil; **p. 549:** Arang Keshavarzian; **p. 556:** Arang Keshavarzian; **p. 589:** India Images/Dinodia Photos/Alamy; **p. 598:** Hindustan Times/Newscom; **p. 606:** Subir Halder/India Today Group/Getty Images; **p. 620:** Gurinder Osan/AP Images; **p. 632:** AP Images; **p. 642:** Bruno Barbey/Magnum Photos; **p. 649:** George Esiri/Reuters/Landov; **p. 664:** Afolabi Sotunde/Reuters/Landov; **p. 692:** Jim Watson/AFP/Getty Images; **p. 699:** Bill Clark/CQ Roll Call/Newscom; **p. 706:** AP Photo/Eric Gay; **p. 721:** AP Photo/Jon Elswick; **p. 722:** Roger L. Wollenberg/UPI/Newscom.

Text Credits

Chapter 1

p. 4: Max Weber, *Economy and Society*, ed. Guenther Roth and Claus Wittich (Berkeley: University of California Press, 1978), 389; **p. 7:** Based on United Nations Development Program, Human Development Report 2013 (New York: United Nations, 2013); **p. 9:** Based on World Bank Indicators for 2011. Gross National Income is per capita based on purchasing power parity; years of schooling is for the population over age 15. Figure is based on 150 largest nations by population for which data are available; **p. 10:** Hania Zlotnik, "Statement to the Thirty-Eighth Session of the Commission on Population and Development," April 4, 2005 (www.un.org/esa/population/cpd/Statement_HZ_open.pdf); **p. 10:** Amartya Sen, "Population: Delusion and Reality," *New York Review of Books*, 22 September 1994, pp. 62ff; **p. 12:** Based on Freedom House, Freedom in the World 2013 (www.freedomhouse.org). The figure displays the percentages for all states; **p. 13:** Based on World Bank Indicators for 2011. Gross National Income is per capita based on purchasing power parity; based on 150 largest nations by population for which data are available; **p. 14:** Courtesy of United Nations Publications. UN News Center, February 27, 2006; **p. 15:** Paul Light, Government's Greatest Achievements of the Past Half-Century (Washington, D.C.: Brookings Institution, 2000) (www.brookings.edu/comm/reformwatch/rw02.pdf); **p. 19:** "U.S. Embassy Criticizes Pardons in Nigerian Corruption Cases," from *The New York Times* (March 15, 2013).

Chapter 2

p. 22: Alexis de Tocqueville to Louis de Kergolay, 18 October 1847, in Alexis de Tocqueville: *Selected Letters on Politics and Society*, ed. Roger Boesche (Berkeley: University of California Press, 1985), 191; **p. 23:** Ernest Barker, ed., *The Politics of Aristotle* (London: Oxford University Press, 1977), 386; **p. 24:** Andrew Bennett and Alexander George, "An Alliance of Statistical and Case Study Methods: Research on the Interdemocratic Peace," APSA-CP: Newsletter of the APSA Organized Section in Comparative Politics 9 no. 1 (1998): 6; **p. 28:** For Contemporary Members, Information Office, United Nations. Data to 1945 from Charles Taylor an Michael Hudson, World Handbook of Political and Social Indicators (New Haven, CT: Yale University Press, 1972).

Chapter 3

p. 41: Selected nations from the 2005–2008 World Values Survey and the 2000–2002 World Values Survey for Nigeria. Figure entries are the percentage "proud" and "very proud"; missing data are excluded from the calculation of percentages; **p. 42:** 2000–2002 World Values Survey and 2005–2008 World Values Survey. Respondents were asked their support for either democracy or authoritarian system (either a nondemocratic leader or military regime); the ambiguous category is those who express equal approval for both; **p. 43:** A Ugandan government official cited in Bruce Gilley, *The Right to Rule: How States Win and Lose Legitimacy* (New York: Columbia University Press, 2009), 78; **p. 44:** Selected nations from the 2005–2008 World Values Survey; missing data are excluded from the calculation of percentages; **p. 46:** Produced by the authors; emancipative values are measured using questions on support for freedom of expression and equality of opportunities asked in the 1999–2004 and 2005–2008 World Values Survey (www.worldvaluessurvey.com); the voice and equality index 2011 is from the World Bank Indicators database.

Chapter 4
p. 59: Based on Election turnout data is percent of voting age public for most recent national legislative election from the International Institute for Electoral Assistance and Democracy, from www.idea.int August 21, 2013; 2005–2008 World Values Survey for other statistics. Some of the participation questions were not asked in each survey, and these missing items are noted by a dash in the table. China has no national elections; **p. 65:** Based on International Labour Organization, International Statistical Inquiry into Trade Union Density and Collective Bargaining Coverage 2008-2009 (www.ilo.org). The figure plots union membership as a percentage of employed population. For China, Iran and Russia ILO data are missing and the figure is the percentage of respondents who mentioned being a member of a labor union in the 2005-2008 World Values Surveys; **p. 68:** Contains Parliamentary information licensed under the Open Parliament License v1.0. www.publications.parliament.uk/pa/cm/cmallparty/register/beer.htm.

Chapter 5
p. 81: Based on Robert Michels, *Political Parties* (New York: Free Press, 1962); **p. 85:** Based on Arend Lijphart, *Patterns of Democracy: Government Forms and Performance in Thirty-Six Countries* (New Haven, CT: Yale University Press, 1999); www.ElectionGuide.org; www.Wikipedia.org; **p. 89:** Larry Diamond, "Thinking about Hybrid Regimes," *Journal of Democracy* 13 (2002): 26.

Chapter 6
p. 105: Anibal Perez-Linan, *Presidential Impeachment and the New Political Instability in Latin America* (New York: Cambridge University Press, 2007). Reprinted with the permission of Cambridge University Press; **p. 108:** Senator Roman Hruska quoted in *Time Magazine*, March 30, 1970; **p. 118:** Based on Corruption Index: http://www.transparency.org/cpi2012/results#myAnchor1; Corruption perceptions index 2012, GNI, PPP:http://data.worldbank.org/indicator/NY.GNP.PCAP.CD, GDP: http://data.worldbank.org/indicator/NY.GDP.MKTP.CD.

Chapter 7
p. 124: Adapted from http://mdgs.un.org/unsd/mdg/; **p. 125:** Patrick Henry, Speech at St. John's Church, Richmond, VA. March 23, 1775; **p. 127:** Samuel P. Huntington, *The Third Wave: Democratization in the Late Twentieth Century* (Norman: University of Oklahoma, 1991), 65; **p. 128:** Based on International Monetary Fund, downloaded from www2.imfstatistics.org/GFS on June 4, 2010; **p. 130:** Based on World Bank, World Development Indicators, data downloaded from http://databank.worldbank.org/data on July 10, 2013; **p. 132:** Based on World Bank, World Development Report 2005, Chapter 5; William Easterly, *The Elusive Quest for Growth: The Economists'Adventures and Misadventures in the Tropics* (Cambridge: Massachusetts Institute of Technology Press, 2001), 233; **p. 133:** Based on www.worldbank.org/governance/wgi/) on a 0-to-100 scale where 100 is most regulated. Press freedom rating also on a 0-to-100 scale, where 100 is most controlled, data downloaded from www.freedomhouse.org on July 9, 2013; **p. 134:** Based on World Bank, World Development Indicators (data downloaded July 9, 2013, from http://databank.worldbank.org/data); **p. 135:** Based on World Health Organization, data downloaded June 9,

2013, from apps.who.int/gho/data; **p. 136:** Based on World Bank, World Development Indicators (data downloaded July 9, 2013, from http://databank.worldbank.org/data); for female earned income inequality, Ricardo Hausmann, et al., Global Gender Gap Report 2011, Appendix D3, Geneva: World Economic Forum (data downloaded July 10, 2013, from www3.weforum.org/docs/wef); **p. 138:** Easterly, William R., *The Elusive Quest for Growth: Economists' Adventures and Misadventures in the Tropics*, p. 45, © 2001 Massachusetts Institute of Technology, by permission of The MIT Press; **p. 138:** www.cidcm.umd.edu/mar; **p. 139:** Based on Freedom House web site, www.freedomhouse.org (data downloaded July 9, 2013); index of economic freedom, product of the Heritage Foundation and the *Wall Street Journal*, data from www.heritage.org (downloaded July 9, 2013); **p. 141:** Based on United Nations Office on Drugs and Crime, data downloaded from www.unodc.org/unodc on July 10 2013; **p. 143:** Based on Axel Dreher, "Does Globalization Affect Growth? Evidence from a New Index of Globalization," *Applied Economics* 38, no. 10 (2006):1091–110, data downloaded March 13, 2013, from http://globalization.kof.ethz.ch/; **p. 144:** Adapted from Ruth Leger Sivard, "Wars and War Related Deaths, 1900–1995," *World Military and Social Expenditures 1996* (Washington, D.C.: World Priorities, 1996), 1 8–1 9. U. S. deaths add Korean and Vietnam war totals, from U. S. Department of State figures, to Sivard report of World War I and II deaths

Chapter 8
p. 152: House of Commons Foreign Affairs Committee, Global Security: UK US Relations, Chatham House, British Attitudes towards the UK's International Priorities (London: Royal Institute of International Affairs, 2010), 77; **p. 153:** Based on Margaret Thatcher, *The Downing Street Years* (New York: Harper Collins, 1993); Richard Vinen, *Thatcher's Britain* (London: Simon and Schuster, 2009); **p. 154:** Based on Tony Blair, *Tony Blair: a Journey* (London: Hutchinson, 2010). Simon Jenkins, Thatcher and Sons (London: Allen Lane, 2006); Peter Mandelson, *The Third Man* (New York: Harper Collins, 2010); **p. 155:** Based on Peter Snowdon, *Back from the Brink* (London: Harper Press, 2010). Robert Hazell and Ben Yong, eds., *The Politics of Coalition*. (Oxford: Hart, 2012); **p. 156:** Calculated from the 2011 British Social Attitudes Survey, June – November 2011 (n=3,311); Professor Richard Rose FBA Director, Centre for the Study of Public Policy University of Strathclyde, Glasgow, www.cspp.strath.ac.uk; **p. 156:** Margaret Thatcher, 1987; **p. 157:** The opinion of Sir Nigel Hamilton, former head of the Northern Ireland Civil Service, quoted in Public Service Magazine, February March 2009, 27; **p. 158:** John Kampfner and David Wighton, "Reeling in Scotland to Bring England in Step," *Financial Times*, April 5, 1997; **p. 160:** Quoted in Peter Hennessy, "Raw Politics Decide Procedure in Whitehall," New Statesman (London), October 24, 1986, 10; **p. 163:** Adapted from Richard Rose, *The Prime Minister in a Shrinking World* (Boston: Polity Press, 2001), 242; **p. 164:** Walter Bagehot, *The English Constitution* (London: World's Classics, 1955), 9; **p. 166:** Quoted in David Leppard, "ID Cards Doomed, Say Officials," *Sunday Times* (London), July 9, 2006. See also an interview with Sir Robin Butler, "How Not to Run a Country," *The Spectator* (London), December 11, 2004; **p. 166:** Sir Robert Armstrong, Baron Armstrong of Ilminster; **p. 166:** Eric Varley, quoted in A. Michie and S. Hoggart, *The Pact* (London: Quartet Books, 1978), 13; **p. 167:** Based on Richard Rose, *A Responsible Party Government in a World of Interdependence@*, West European Politics, in press, 2014 and Rachel Sylvester and Alice Thomson "Whitehall at War," *The Times* (London), January 14–15, 2013; **p. 169:** Cf. Colin Bennett, "From

the Dark to the Light: The Open Government Debate in Britain," *Journal of Public Policy* 5, no. 2 (1985): 209; italics in the original; **p. 170:** Graham Wilson and Anthony Barker, "Whitehall's Disobedient Servants?," *British Journal of Political Science*, 27, no. 2 (1997): 223-46; **p. 170:** Bernard Ingham, press secretary to Margaret Thatcher, quoted in R. Rose, "British Government: The Job at the Top," in *Presidents and Prime Ministers*, ed. R. Rose and E. Suleiman (Washington, D.C.: American Enterprise Institute, 1980), 43; **p. 171:** Committee on Standards in Public Life Survey, 2010. http://www.nationalarchives.gov.uk/doc/open-government-licence/version/2/; **p. 174:** Based on Audit of Political Engagement 9: the 2012 Report. London : Hansard Society, Part One. Sample survey of 1,163 respondents about their activities in the past two to three years; **p. 175:** Quoted in Maurice Kogan, *The Politics of Education* (Harmondsworth, England: Penguin, 1971), 135; **p. 181:** Colin Rallings and Michael Thrasher, *British Electoral Facts 1832–2012* (London: Biteback Publishing, 2012) **p. 60; p. 181:** Ipsos MORI, How Britain Voted in 2010 (www.ipsosmori.com/researchpublications/researcharchive/poll.aspx?oltemld=2613); analysis of all who said they were absolutely certain to vote or had already voted, interviewed March 5-May 19, 2010 (n=5,927); **p. 183:** J. A. G. Griffith, Central Departments and Local Authorities (London: George Allen and Unwin, 1966), 542. Cf. Simon Jenkins,*Accountable to None: The Tory Nationalization of Britain* (Harmondsworth, England: Penguin, 1996); **p. 185:** Based on NEETS Characteristics, Costs and Policy Responses in Europe. Dublin: European Foundation, 2012; **p. 189:** Adapted from Public Spending Statistics February 2013 Table 8. (London: H.M Treasury, 2013); **p. 191:** Reginald Maudling, quoted in David Butler and Michael Pinto-Duschinsky, *The British General Election of 1970* (London: Macmillan, 1971), 62.

Chapter 9

p. 202: Based on Sofres, L'Etat de l'Opinion 2001 (Paris: Edition du Seuil, 2001), 81; Ronald Hatto, Anne Muxel and Odette Tomescu, survey for the CEVPOF and the Institut de recherchede l'ecole militaire (Irsem), released on November 7, 2011; *Le Monde*, November 8, 2011; **p. 217:** Based on Ipsos/Logica Business Consulting, *Le Monde*, June 12, 2012, p.12; Presidoscopie (2012) 'Electoral study undertaken by Ipsos-Logica Business Consulting for Le Monde Cevipof, Fondapol and the Jean Jaures Foundation, accessed at http://www.cevipof.com/fr/2012/recherche/panel/presidoscopievague10/; **p. 218:** Based on Official Results from the Ministry of the Interior, www.assemblée-nationale.fr/élections; **p. 226:** Based on Official results from the Ministry of the Interior for each election and referendum, www.interieur.gouv.fr/misill/sections/a_votre_service/elections/resultats/accueil-resultats/view; **p. 234:** Based on data from Ministère de l'Intérieur, DGCL, www.dgcl.interieur.gouv.fr/; **p. 236:** Sources: Based on OECD data: www.oecd.org/perm/publicemploymentkeyfigures; http://stats.oecd.org//index.aspx; www.oecd.org/els/social/expenditure.

Chapter 10

p. 247: Based on The Deutsche Welle Report, April 4, 2004, 62; **p. 261:** Russell J. Dalton, *Politics in Germany*, 2nd ed. (New York: HarperCollins, 1993), p. 121; **p. 262:***The Economist*, March 24, 2001, 62. © The Economist Newspaper Limited, London (2001); **p. 267:** Based on 2009 German Longitudinal Election Study; voter turnout is from government statistics for the 2009 election; **p. 279:** Based on Regional data from election statistics; social group information is from 2013 Bundestagswahl exit poll, Forschungsgruppe Wahlen; **p. 285:** Based on Statistisches Jahrbuch für die Bundesrepublik Deutschland (Berlin: Statistiches Bundesamt, 2012), 262. The figure presents

2009 spending in billions of euros; **p. 286:** Based on Statistisches Bundesamt, ed., Datenreport 2011 (Berlin: Bundeszentrale für politische Bildung, 2011), 377; **p. 287:** Based on Statistisches Jahrbuch für die Bundesrepublik Deutschland (Berlin: Statistiches Bundesamt, 2012), 261, 269. The figure presents 2009 government income in billions of euros.

Chapter 11

p. 297: Based on National Institute of Population and Social Security Research. http://www.ipss.go.jp/p-info/e/Population%20%20Statistics.asp, accessed May 16, 2015; **p. 301:** Article 14, The Constitution of Japan; **p. 301:** Article 41, The Constitution of Japan; **p. 307:** Based on Japan General Social Surveys, 2008. "Higashi-Nihon Daishinsai ga nihonjin no ishiki to koudou ni ataeta eikyo (The effect of the Great East Japan Earthquake on Japanese attitudes and behaviors." The JGSS Research Center, Osaka University of Commerce. http://jgss.daishodai.ac.jp/research/news/news_J12.pdf (last accessed 5 May 2013); **p. 308:** World Values Survey 2005–2008 (www.worldvaluessurvey.org). Accessed 5 May 2013; **p. 311:** Based on Waseda University/Yomiuri Shimbun Joint Survey. "Public Opinion Survey on Japanese Social Expectations and Elections." http://www.globalcoe-glope2.jp/wcasi/wC10POST_codebook_Ver1.pdf, (Accessed on 5 May 2013); **p. 312:** Based on Akarui Senkyo Suishin Kyokai, 2011. "Dai 22 kai sangi-in tsujo-senkyo no jittai. [The 22nd House of Councillors Election] http://www.akaruisenkyo.or.jp/wp/wp-content/uploads/2012/07/22sangaiyo.pdf. (Accessed on 5 May 2013.); **p. 313:** Based on www.stat.go.jp.data/topics/topi670.htm; www8.cao.go/jp/survey/h23/h23-shakai/index.html; benesse.jp/berd/aboutus/katsudou/research_column/pt_02/23.html; **p. 319:** Based on Comparative Study of Electoral Systems Survey, Japan, Postelection July-August 2007 conducted by Central Research Service: Chuo Chosa Co (N= 2373). Some percentages may not sum to 100 because of rounding.

Chapter 12

p. 338: Steven Levitsky and Lucan A. Way, Competitive Authoritarianism: Hybrid Regimes After the Cold War. (Cambridge: Cambridge University Press, 2010); **p. 367:** Compiled by author from reports of Central Electoral Commission. See http://cikrf.ru; **p. 368:** Compiled by author from reports of State Duma; **p. 376:** Based on data drawn from Russian State Statistical Service (www.gks.ru).

Chapter 13

p. 398: Based on Beijing Review 41, no. 8 (1998): 22; *China Today*, www.chinatoday.com/org/cpc/; **p. 409:** Based on Tianjian Shi, "Mass Political Behavior in Beijing," in T*he Paradox of China's Post-Mao Reforms*, ed. Merle Goldman and Roderick MacFarquhar (Cambridge, MA: Harvard University Press, 1999), 155; **p. 420:** Based on 2012 Purchasing Power Parity estimates from Central Intelligence Agency, World Factbook, https://www.cia.gov/library/publications/the-world-factbook/; all other figures from World Bank, World Development Indicators, http://data.worldbank.org/; **p. 424:** U.S. Census Bureau, International Data Base, www.census.gov/ipc/www/idb/country.php.

Chapter 14

p. 443: Based on data from Instituto Federal Electoral (www.ife.org.mx); **p. 445:** Based on Corporación Latinobarómetro, Informe 2011 (Santiago, Chile, October 28, 2012, www.latinbarómetro.org); **p. 449:** Based on data from Comisión Federal Electoral for 1958–1991; from Instituto Federal Electoral for 1994–2006; **p. 456:** Based on For the Fifty-Seventh Legislature, Jeffrey A. Weldon, "Institutional and Political

Factors in Party Discipline in the Chamber of Deputies, 1998–2002," presented at the First Latin American Political Science Congress, Salamanca, Spain, July 2002. Data for the last five legislatures calculated from the Diario de los Debates and the Gaceta Parlamentaria of the Chamber of Deputies; **p. 457:** Based on data compiled from Diario de los Debates and the Gaceta Parlamentaria of the Chamber of Deputies; **p. 464:** Based on data from Comisión Federal Electoral, 1946–1988; and Instituto Federal Electoral, 1994–2012; **p. 468:** Based on Nationwide exit poll conducted by Reforma newspaper (Mexico City), July 1, 2012; **p. 473:** Cory Molzahn, Octavio Rodríguez, and David A. Shirk, *Drug Violence in Mexico: Data and Analysis Through 2012, Justice in Mexico Project*, San Diego: University of San Diego, February 2013, p. 23; **p. 476:** Interview by Mexican Migration Field Research and Training Program, Center for Comparative Immigration Studies: University of California, San Diego, February 2008.

Chapter 15

p. 485: Freedom House, "Freedom in the World, Brazil (2010)," www.freedomhouse.org; **p. 491:** Instituto Brasileiro de Geografia e Estatística; **p. 498:** Based on Amy Erica Smith, "Who Support Affirmative Action in Brazil?" *Americas Barometer Insights: 2010*, No. 49, www.americasbarometer.org; *New York Times*, "Brazil Enacts Affirmative Action Law for Universities," August 31, 2012; **p. 499:** Latin American Public Opinion Project available at www.vanderbilt.edu/lapop; **p. 504:** Latin American Public Opinion Project available at www.vanderbilt.edu/lapop; **p. 507:** Article 142, Constitution of Brazil; **p. 511:** Based on data from Tribunal Superior Eleitoral (available at www.tse.gov.br); **p. 513:** Based on DataFolha, October 29 and 30, 2010 (downloaded from http://datafolha.folha.uol.com.br/); **p. 517:** Based on Paolo Ricci, "A produção legislativa de iniciativa parlamentar no Congress: diferenças e similaridades entre a Câmara dos Deputados e o Senado Federal," in O Senado Federal Brasileiro no Pós-Constituinte, ed. Leany Lemos (Brasília: Unilegis, 2008), 271; **p. 520:** www.tesouro.fazenda.gov.br; **p. 520:** Kurt Weyland, *Democracy without Equity: Failures of Reform in Brazil* (Pittsburgh, PA: University of Pittsburgh Press, 1996), 182; **p. 521:** Based on Instituto de Pesquisa Econômica Aplicada (IPEA) (downloaded from www.ipeadata.gov.br); Instituto Brasileiro de Geografia e Estatística (IBGE) (downloaded from www.ibge.gov.br); Freedom House, FH Country Ratings (available at www.freedomhouse.org); **p. 522:** Based on *O Globo*, May 5, 2013; Folha de Sao Paulo, May 23, 2013.

Chapter 16

p. 535: Courtesy of the University of Texas Libraries, The University of Texas at Austin: www.lib.utexas.edu/maps/middle_east_and_asia/iran_ethnoreligious_distribution_2009.jpg; **p. 537:** Based on Kaveh Ehsani, Arang Keshavarzian, and Norma Claire Moruzzi, "Tehran, June 2009," *Middle East Report Online*, June 28, 2009 and Mohammad Ali Kadivar, "A New Oppositional Politics: The Campaign Participants in Iran's 2013 Presidential Election," *Jadaliyya*, June 22, 2013 http://www.jadaliyya.com/pages/index/12383/a-new-oppositional-politics_the-campaign-participa; **p. 543:** Adapted from Wilfried Buchta, *Who Rules Iran? The Structure of Power in the Islamic Republic* (Washington, D.C.: Washington Institute for Near East Policy and the Konrad Adenauer Stiftung, 2000); **p. 547:** Abdol-Karim Lahiji, "Moruri bar vaz'-e hoquqi-ye Iranian-e gheyr-e mosalman," *Iran Nameh* 19 (1379–80/2001): 19. Foundation for Iranian Studies; **p. 548:** Asghar Schirazi, *The Constitution of Iran: Politics and the State in the Islamic Republic* (London: I. B. Tauris, 1998); **p. 550:** Compiled by Arang Keshavarzian, New York University; **p. 551:** Adapted from Wilfried

Buchta, *Who Rules Iran? The Structure of Power in the Islamic Republic* (Washington, D.C.: Washington Institute for Near East Policy and the Konrad Adenauer Stiftung 2000), www.bbc.co.uk/persian/iran/story/2005/08/050801_pm-mv-khatami-profile.shtml; www.mardomyar.com/aspx2/aboutme.aspx; **p. 555:** 2005–2006 World Values Survey; **p. 559:** Mansoor Moaddel and Taghi Azadarmaki, "The Worldviews of Islamic Publics: The Case of Egypt, Iran, and Jordan," in *Human Values and Social Change: Findings from the Values Survey*, ed. Ronald Inglehart (Leiden, The Netherlands: Brill, 2003): 75; **p. 566:** Asghar Schirazi, *The Constitution of Iran: Politics and the State in the Islamic Republic* (London: I. B. Tauris, 1998); **p. 566:** Quoted in Saïd Amir Arjomand, *The Turban for the Crown: The Islamic Revolution in Iran* (New York: Oxford University Press, 1988), 182; **p. 570:** Based on UNDP Human Development Report, 2013; **p. 575:** Najmedin Meshkati, "Iran's Nuclear Brinkmanship, the U.S. Unilateralism, and a Mounting International Crisis: Can Civil Aviation Industry Provide a Breakthrough?" *Iran News*, July 26, 2004, 14.

Chapter 17

p. 586: The World Bank: Imports of goods and services (% of GDP) http://data.worldbank.org/indicator/NE.IMP.GNFS.ZS, Exports of goods and services (% of GDP) http://data.worldbank.org/indicator/NE.EXP.GNFS.ZS; **p. 587:** Based on data from www.satp.org; **p. 598:** James Manor, *From Nehru to Nineties: The Changing Office of the Prime Minister in India* (London: Hurst, 1994), p. 13; **p. 613:** 2009 Post-Poll Party vote by Social Background, Centre for the Study of Developing Societies (CSDS) 2010. Reprinted with permission; **p. 614:** Raj Kamal Jha and Farzand Ahmed, "Laloo's Magic," *India Today*, April 30, 1 995; **p. 614:** W. H. Morris-Jones, *The Government and Politics of India* (Wistow, England: Eothen Press, 1987); **p. 616:** Based on Election Commission of India, General Elections 1951–2004 http://eci.nic.in/eci_main/miscellaneous_statistics/Graphs_Voteage_NoofContestants.pdf, General Elections 2009 http://eci.nic.in/eci_main/archiveofge2009/Stats/VOLI/08_VotersInformation.pdf, last accessed 11th February 2013; **p. 617:** World Bank, GDP (constant 2000 US$) http://data.worldbank.org/indicator/NY.GDP.MKTP.KD; **p. 622:** Selig Harrison, *India: The Most Dangerous Decades* (Delhi: Oxford University Press, 1960), 338; **p. 623:** Based on data on Riots and Murders: Government of India – Ministry of Home Affairs – National Crime Records Bureau (various years) Crime in India; data for 1954–2006 retrieved from: Integrated Network for Societal Conflict Research (INSCR), http://www.systemicpeace.org/inscr/inscr.htm.2007: http://ncrb.nic.in/cii2007/cii-2007/FIGURES_2007.pdf, 2008: http://ncrb.nic.in/cii2008/cii-2008/figure%20at%20a%20glance.pdf, 2009: http://ncrb.nic.in/CII-2009-NEW/cii-2009/figure%20at%20a%20glance.pdf, 2010: http://ncrb.nic.in/CII2010/cii-2010/figure%20at%20a%20glance.pdf, 2011: http://ncrb.nic.in/CD-CII2011/cii-2011/figure%20at%20a%20glance.pdf. Data on Indian Total Population 1953 - 2010: United Nations – Department of Economic and Social Affairs – Population Devision (2011) World Population Prospects - the 2010 Revision, http://esa.un.org/unpd/wpp/Excel-Data/population.htm; Data on Indian Total Population 2011: World Bank, Database, http://data.worldbank.org/indicator/SP.POP.TOTL/countries/1W?display=default.

Chapter 18

p. 634: Victor Chikezie Uchendu, *The Igbo of Southeast Nigeria* (Fort Worth, TX: Harcourt Brace Jovanovich College Publishers, 1965), 103; **p. 637:** Billy Dudley, *An Introduction to Nigerian Government and Politics* (Bloomington: University of Indiana Press, 1982), 230; **p. 639:** Peter O. Olayivola, *Petroleum and Structural Change in a Developing Country* (New York: Praeger, 1987); **p. 647:** Economic and Financial

Crimes Commission (EFCC) Establishment Act; **p. 657:** Wole Soyinka, *You Must Set Forth at Dawn* (New York: Random House, 2006), 421; **p. 659:** Richard A. Joseph, *Democracy and Prebendal Politics in Nigeria* (Cambridge: Cambridge University Press, 1987), 133–34; **p. 660:** Based on Richard Sklar and C. S. Whitaker, Jr., "Nigeria," in *Political Parties and National Integration in Tropical Africa*, ed. James S. Coleman and Carl Rosberg (Berkeley: University of California Press, 1964); **p. 661:** Based on The Independent National Electoral Commission, results, www.inecnigeria.org; **p. 667:** Diamond, Larry. *Class, Ethnicity, and Democracy in Nigeria: The Failure of the First Republic*. Syracuse, NY: Syracuse University Press, 1988. 53; **p. 667:** Based on United Nations Development Program, Human Development Report 2009; Diamond, Larry. *Class, Ethnicity, and Democracy in Nigeria: The Failure of the First Republic*. Syracuse, NY: Syracuse University Press, 1988. 69; **p. 670:** Obiora Chinedu Okafor, "Between Elite Interests and Pro-Poor Resistance: The Nigerian Courts and Labour-Led Anti-Fuel Hike Struggles (1999–2007)," *Journal of African Law* 54 (2010), 95–118; **p. 672:** Air Chief Marshal Paul Dike, *Preface to Winning Hearts and Minds: A Community Relations Approach for the Nigerian Military*, ed. Ebere Onwudiwe and Eghosa Osaghae (Ibadan, Nigeria: John Archers, 2010); **p. 673:** *The Blood of Peace and Other Poems,* Tanure Ojaide, Pearson Education Limited (London: Heinemann, 1991).

Chapter 19
p. 679: Rudyard Kipling "The English Flag," in *Barrack-Room Ballads and Other Verses* (London: Methuen, 1892), stanza 1; **p. 683:** 14th Amendment, Constitution of the United States of America; **p. 685:** H. G. Nicholas, *The Nature of American Politics,* 2nd ed. (New York: Oxford University Press, 1986), 4; **p. 686:** Statistical Abstract of the United States: 2012 (Washington, D.C.: Bureau of the Census, 2012), Table 42; **p. 689:** 14th Amendment, Constitution of the United States of America; **p. 689:** Article VI, Constitution of the United States of America; **p. 689:** Article I, Constitution of the United States of America; **p. 690:** The United States Government Manual 2005/2006 (Washington, D.C.: U.S. Government Printing Office, 2005), 21; **p. 695:** Russell J. Dalton, *Citizen Politics in Western Democracies*, 5th ed. (Washington, D.C.: C.Q. Press, 2008), 37; **p. 697:** Based on figures from Russell J. Dalton, *Citizen Politics in Western Democracies*, 5th ed. (Washington, D.C.: C.Q. Press, 2008). Campaign activity figures are taken from pp. 44–46, communal activity from p. 49 and p. 68, and protest activity from p. 68; **p. 701:** Federal Elections Commission, "Top 50 PACs by Disbursements, January 1, 2013–June 30, 2013," accessed at http://www.fec.gov/press/summaries/2014/ElectionCycle/6m_PAC.shtml, January 16, 2014; **p. 703:** Benjamin Ginsberg and Martin Shefter. *Politics by Other Means: The Declining Importance of Elections in America; p. 704:* PAC's Hear, and Make, Calls for Their Abolition from *The New York Times* November 21, 1988; **p. 704:** Statistical Abstract of the United States: 2010 (Washington, D.C.: Bureau of the Census, 2010), Table 385, and Federal Elections Commission for 2012; **p. 707:** Based on Harold W. Stanley and Richard G. Niemi, *Vital Statistics on American Politics, 2009–2010* (Washington, DC: CQ Press, 2010), Table 3-2, 119; **p. 707:** Nolan McCarty, Keith T. Poole, and Howard Rosenthal, *Polarized America: The Dance of Ideology and Unequal Riches* (Cambridge: Massachusetts Institute of Technology Press, 2006), 12; **p. 708:** Based on Congressional Quarterly Reports, 1993–2003; **p. 712:** American National Election Studies, Inter-University Consortium for Political and Social Research, University of Michigan, compiled by Gary Jacobson. Data points are the percentage reporting a different vote for the presidential and House of Representatives elections; third-party candidates are excluded from the calculations; **p. 716:** Statistical Abstract of the United States: 2012 (Washington, D.C.: Bureau of the Census, 2012), Table 1361. These figures combine federal, state, and local taxes; **p. 717:** Statistical Abstract of the United States: 2012 (Washington, D.C.: Bureau of the Census, 2012), Table 473; **p. 719:** *The Addresses and Messages of Presidents of the United States, vol. 1*, compiled by Edwin Williams (New York: Edward Walker, 1846), 32; **p. 719:** Address to Congress, December 1, 1862, in Roy P. Basler, ed., *The Collected Works of Abraham Lincoln, vol. 5*, (New Brunswick, NJ: Rutgers University Press, 1953), 537; **p. 722:** James Bryce, *The American Commonwealth, vol. 1*, 2nd ed. (London: Macmillan, 1889), 300–301.

Index